SC 203155

Aganist a background
throwing tank rides t
The smoke rises from
one of the largest ir
Ninth Army troops th
was made.   3/3

RESTRICTED--Signal Corps Photo #ETO-HQ-45-24553
(T/5 V.E. Ecklund) Orig. neg. rec'd from OCSigO
Hdqrs., SOS, European Theatre of Operations, USA,
April 1945. Released by Overseas Field Press Censor,
SHAEF, 4/2/45
4x5 orig neg   Lot 11023

THE DEFEAT OF GERMANY
THEN AND NOW

You will enter the Continent of Europe and, in conjunction with the other United Nations, undertake operations aimed at the heart of Germany and the destruction of her Armed Forces.

DIRECTIVE TO THE SUPREME COMMANDER
ALLIED EXPEDITIONARY FORCE,
FEBRUARY 12, 1944

THE DEFEAT OF GERMANY THEN AND NOW

Edited by Winston Ramsey

Credits

ISBN: 9 781870 067843
© After the Battle 2015
Editor-in-Chief: Winston G. Ramsey.
Designed by Jean Paul Pallud and Winston Ramsey.

PUBLISHERS
Battle of Britain International Ltd
The Mews, Hobbs Cross House
Hobbs Cross, Old Harlow, Essex CM17 0NN

PRINTERS
Printed and bound in China by 1010 Printing International Limited.

FRONT COVER
Men of the 45th Division, US Seventh Army, wave the Stars and Stripes from the very dais from which Hitler addressed the huge audiences drawn up in the Luitpold Arena in Nuremberg, constructed for the pre-war Nazi Party rallies.

REAR COVER
Knocked out in a tank battle on March 6 by an M26 Pershing of the 3rd Armored Division, this Panther (often described in wartime captioning as a Tiger) lying in front of the cathedral in Cologne became a focal point for many photographers. This particular picture was taken by T/4 Charles R. Pearson on June 27, 1945 and released for publication by the SHAEF Press Censor on June 30.

 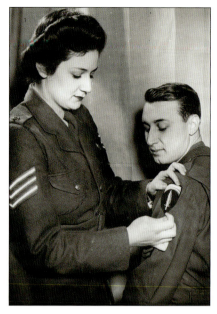

The emblem of the Supreme Headquarters Allied Expeditionary Force (SHAEF). It was designed by Colonel Norman Lack, assisted by an ATS girl, Corporal Doreen Goodall, incorporating a flaming sword based on the one on the US 2nd Division Memorial in Washington. By March 1944 it was in general use, its correct heraldic interpretation being descriptive of SHAEF's mission: 'Upon a field of heraldic sable [black], representing the darkness of Nazi oppression, is shown the sword of liberation in the form of a crusader's sword, the flames arising from the hilt and leaping up the blade. This represents avenging justice by which the enemy power will be broken in Nazi dominated Europe. Above the sword is a rainbow, emblematic of hope, containing all the colours of which the National Flags of the Allies are composed. The heraldic chief of azure above the rainbow is emblematic of a state of peace and tranquility, the restoration of which to the enslaved people is the objective of the United Nations.'

Editorial Note

This book tells the story of the defeat of Germany as seen through the eyes of the Supreme Headquarters of the Allied Expeditionary Force. SHAEF issued regular daily communiqués on the progress of the offensive — over 400 by May 1945 — and these have been reproduced unedited without any omissions.

Although one normally would be consistent, I have left ranks as printed in the original and retained the spelling of words like armor/armour and center/centre, as well as numerals, as they appear in the original communiqué for it is apparent that they were compiled by both American and British press officers. Although it may look typographically clumsy, I have retained the military style of the documents which use capitals for all town names. Also their teleprinters could not accent characters but these have been added in the index.

Although these communiqués were issued by SHAEF headquarters, which moved ten times before it was dissolved on July 6, 1945 (see *After the Battle* No. 84), censorship in the field was the responsibility of army group commanders. Censors were guided by a 200-page 'bible' containing the censorship policy of the British, Canadian and US forces in the European theatre. In censoring news, they were guided by the principle that 'the minimum of information would be withheld from the public consistent with security'. In general, information was not to be released that might prove helpful to the enemy, neither were unauthenticated, inaccurate or false reports, or reports likely to injure the morale of the Allied forces — see SHAEF and the Press, page 510.

Eisenhower had instructed that nationalities were not to be mentioned in favour of the broad term 'Allies' so it is interesting to see this rule broken in Communiqué No. 139 on page 142.

This policy extended to photographs that had to be submitted to SHAEF Field Press Censors before release into the 'war pool'. The late Roger Bell, my friend and European Theater of Operations advisor for 40 years, amassed a huge collection of original wartime press photos, and it is these that have been used throughout this volume. In many cases, if one had to rely on the censored caption as published without the location being given, it would be useless as a guide to be able to take a comparison in our 'then and now' theme, but on Roger's original prints one can usually read the blocked-out name of the town depicted.

The operation for the defeat of Germany was called 'Overlord' although this has been often been misunderstood as just referring to the landings in Normandy in June 1944 which we covered in our two-volume *D-Day Then and Now*.

Now, 70 years later, we continue the story up until the day when General Eisenhower was able to signal: 'The mission of this Allied Force was fulfilled at 0241, local time, May 7th, 1945'.

WINSTON RAMSEY, EDITOR-IN-CHIEF,
FEBRUARY 2015

Contents

6	Introduction by the Supreme Commander
8	Prologue
14	JUNE 1944 Invasion
68	JULY 1944 Stalemate
108	AUGUST 1944 Break-out
154	SEPTEMBER 1944 Over the Frontiers
194	OCTOBER 1944 Problems of Supply
230	NOVEMBER 1944 The Battle Bogs Down
262	DECEMBER 1944 Counter-Attack
304	JANUARY 1945 The Tide Turns
340	FEBRUARY 1945 The Final Offensive Begins
372	MARCH 1945 Over the Rhine
424	APRIL 1945 Over-running Germany
484	MAY 1945 Surrender
510	SHAEF and the Press
518	Casualties
520	Credits
522	Index

Introduction by the Supreme Commander

The broad strategy behind our main effort against the German war machine included as a highly desirable preliminary the successful conclusion of operations in North Africa and their extension across Sicily to the Italian mainland. With these accomplished, with the Mediterranean 'flank' freed for Allied shipping, and with the necessary special equipment built or in sight, we were at last in a position to prepare for the final cross-Channel assault which had been agreed upon since April 1942 as our main operation against Germany. It was correctly believed that only on the historic battlefields of France and the Low Countries could Germany's armies in the west be decisively engaged and defeated.

America and England — the Western Allies — could not be sufficiently strong to undertake the assault against France until June 1944, but the broad tactical plans for the operation were completed and approved by the Combined Chiefs-of-Staff in August 1943, prior to my assumption of command of the European Theater in February 1944.

As part of our basic strategy, and in accordance with the task given to the Strategic Air Force under the Casablanca Directive in January 1943, the bombing of Germany, begun early in the war by the British Bomber Command, was intensified in May 1943 and continued with mounting strength to the end of the campaign. Neither the contemplated invasion of Europe nor the direct attack on the German industrial and economic system would be feasible until we had achieved supremacy over the German Air Force. This struggle for air supremacy, which had been going on throughout the war, was given added impetus by a new directive (known as 'Pointblank') in January 1943 which aimed at subjugating the enemy air force by the spring of 1944. In the event, German air might was thoroughly dominated by D-Day and we were free to apply the immense strength of the Allied air forces in the manner we wished and to launch the invasion confident that our plans could not be seriously upset by the German air force. In addition, air bombardment had disrupted the German communications system, immeasurably aiding our ground forces by impeding enemy movements.

Our main strategy in the conduct of the ground campaign was to land amphibious and airborne forces on the Normandy coast between Le Havre and the Cotentin peninsula and, with the successful establishment of a beach-head with adequate ports, to drive along the lines of the Loire and the Seine rivers into the heart of France, destroying the German strength and freeing France. We anticipated that the enemy would resist strongly on the line of the Seine and later on the Somme, but once our forces had broken through the relatively static lines of the beachhead at St-Lô and inflicted on him the heavy casualties in the Falaise pocket, his ability to resist in France was negligible. Thereafter our armies swept east and north in an unimpeded advance which brought them to the German frontier and the defenses of the Siegfried Line.

Here enemy resistance stiffened, due primarily to the fact that he had fallen back on long-prepared defenses. At the same time our own offensive capabilities were lessened because our forces had, in their extremely rapid advance, outdistanced supply lines which had been maintained only by herculean efforts. By mid-September our armies in the north and center were committed to relatively static warfare and faced the threat of stabilization. This was true also on our southern flank, where forces landed from the Mediterranean against the south of France in mid-August had swept north through the Rhône Valley to link with the Central Group of Armies and close the Belfort Gap.

At this time we planned to attack quickly on the northern front in an effort to establish a bridgehead over the lower Rhine while the German armies were still reeling from our blows, but the airborne operation launched at Arnhem was not altogether successful in this respect, although considerable ground was gained and our positions in this area improved. Coincidentally with approving the Arnhem operation, it was directed that operations be undertaken to clear Antwerp as a supply port on the north, essential to our continued offensive action. This was accomplished in November.

While our forces moved slowly in attacks launched at selected points on the front to close to the Rhine, the enemy on 16 December launched a desperate and last counter-attack designed to throw our campaign into disorder and to delay our planned advance deep into Germany. The attack was not without its immediate effect upon us, but the sturdy defense by our forces followed by our rapid and continuous counter-attacks brought home clearly to Germany's military leaders that this last effort had failed completely and that the Nazi war machine faced inevitable disaster.

My plan was to destroy the German forces west of the Rhine along the entire length of the front in a series of heavy blows beginning in the north, and it was my expectation that the enemy would, as he had done in Normandy, stand without giving ground in a futile attempt to 'fight it out' west of the Rhine. Moreover, the air forces were used intensively to destroy his mobility. By March, when our forces crossed the river north of the Ruhr, at Remagen, and at various points to the south, resistance on the eastern bank was again reduced to resemble that in France following the breakthrough, particularly because the enemy, mistaking our intentions, crowded a great part of his remaining forces into the Ruhr area.

Our attack to isolate the Ruhr had been planned so that the main effort would take place on the front of the Northern Group of Armies with a secondary effort on the Central Group of Armies' front. This secondary effort was to be exploited to the full if success seemed imminent. Clearing the left bank of the Rhine throughout its length released the means required to strengthen this secondary effort. With the capture of the Remagen bridgehead and the destruction of enemy forces west of the Rhine, the anticipated opportunity became almost a certainty.

Our forces were now able to bridge the Rhine in all sectors and they fanned out in great mobile spearheads through Western Germany, disrupting communications, isolating one unit from another, and in the area of the Ruhr completing perhaps the largest double envelopment in history, rendering that great industrial area useless to support what was left of the Nazi armies.

As our forces moved rapidly eastward with the main effort in the center, to establish contact with the advancing Russian armies at the Elbe, and in turn to swing swiftly north and south to cut off any remaining refuge, the German High Command reluctantly recognized defeat and belatedly initiated negotiations which terminated with unconditional surrender on 7 May 1945.

In these campaigns the United States of America and Great Britain worked as one nation, pooling their resources of men and material. To the Combined Chiefs-of-Staff, through whom the directives of the two governments were expressed, we constantly accorded our admiration for their well-devised system of command by which they applied the concerted national efforts. Their political leaders, the President of the United States and the Prime Minister, also contributed immeasurably to the success of our armies in the field; once they had committed themselves to a course of action they never failed to give us unstinted support.

GENERAL DWIGHT D. EISENHOWER,
SUPREME COMMANDER,
ALLIED EXPEDITIONARY FORCE,
REPORT TO THE COMBINED CHIEFS-OF-STAFF,
JULY 13, 1945

Today the statue of General Eisenhower in London faces his office on the first floor of No. 20 Grosvenor Square. He first used this building as his headquarters when he arrived in Britain in June 1942 to take up the post of American Commander, European Theater of Operations. Ike's statue by Robert Dean of Oklahoma was unveiled by the Prime Minister, the Rt. Hon. Margaret Thatcher, and the US Ambassador, Charles Price, on January 23, 1989 — not quite the exact 45th anniversary of Eisenhower returning to the same office in January 1944.

'While my appointment as Supreme Commander did not become official until the receipt of a directive from the Combined Chiefs-of-Staff on February 14, and while the status of my Headquarters — to be known as SHAEF — was not recognised until the following day, the basic work of planning continued during this transitional period. The staff brought into being as COSSAC (Chief-of-Staff to the Supreme Allied Commander) came under my control and was greatly expanded as the pressure of time and the vast scope of our work required.'

Prologue

In November 1943, two top-level conferences were held to map out the future course of the war. In Cairo, the 'Sextant' conference was attended by President Franklin D. Roosevelt and Prime Minister Winston Churchill and their staffs from November 23-26. No firm decisions were made, although the Allied Commander-in-Chief in the Mediterranean, General Dwight D. Eisenhower, pressed emphatically for continuing support for the Italian campaign and he stressed the 'vital importance of continuing the maximum possible operations in an established theatre since much time was invariably lost when the scene of action was changed, necessitating as it did the arduous task of building up a fresh base'.

General Dwight D. Eisenhower, 53 years old when appointed Supreme Commander for Operation 'Overlord', graduated from West Point in 1915, his first assignment being with the 19th Infantry Regiment. After the war, he commanded tank corps troops at Fort Dix, New Jersey, and at Fort Benning, Georgia. From 1919 to 1922, he served in various tank battalions until he moved to the Panama Canal Zone where he served as executive officer at Camp Gaillard. In 1925, he attended the Command and General Staff School at Fort Leavenworth, graduating as an honour student in June 1926. A brief tour with the 24th Division followed. In 1927, and again in 1928, he was on duty with the American Battle Monuments Commission in Washington and France. From November 1929 to February 1933, he was with the Assistant Secretary of War, and from then until September 1935 he worked in the office of the Chief-of-Staff (General Douglas MacArthur). He served as assistant to the military adviser of the Philippine Islands from September 1935 to 1940 when he was assigned to the 15th Infantry Regiment. In November that year, he became Chief-of-Staff of the 3rd Division; in March 1941 Chief-of-Staff of the IX Corps, and in June 1941 Chief-of-Staff of the Third Army. He joined the War Plans Division of the War Department in December 1941 and became chief of the division in the following February. On June 25, 1942, he was named Commanding General of the European Theater of Operations (ETO) and in November 1942 he commanded the Allied landings in North Africa (Operation 'Torch') and in the same month became Commander-in-Chief Allied Forces in North Africa. As commander of Allied Forces in the Mediterranean, he directed operations in Tunisia, Sicily, and Italy until December 1943. His appointment as chief of Supreme Headquarters, Allied Expeditionary Force, was announced on Sunday, January 16, and he was introduced to the press the following Tuesday.

Sicily, December 1943. Eisenhower has just been informed by President Franklin Delano Roosevelt that he is to be the Supreme Commander for Operation 'Overlord'.

The focus then shifted to Teheran in Persia where the Big Three Conference opened on November 28. Churchill and Roosevelt were meeting Marshal Josef Stalin for the first time, and the Soviet leader stated that the Red Army was depending upon the opening of the 'Second Front' in 1944. He was told that 'Overlord' (the liberation of north-west Europe) was scheduled for 'some time in May', the final official communiqué announcing that 'our military staffs have joined in our round table discussions, and have concerted our plans for the destruction of the German forces. We have reached complete agreement as to the scope and timing of the operations which will be undertaken from the east, west and south.'

DIRECTIVE TO SUPREME COMMANDER, ALLIED EXPEDITIONARY FORCE

1. You are hereby designated as Supreme Allied Commander of the forces placed under your orders for operations for the liberation of Europe from the Germans. Your title will be Supreme Commander, Allied Expeditionary Force.

2. *Task.* You will enter the Continent of Europe and, in conjunction with the other United Nations, undertake operations aimed at the heart of Germany and the destruction of her armed forces. The date for entering the Continent is the month of May, 1944. After adequate Channel ports have been secured, exploitation will be directed towards securing an area that will facilitate both ground and air operations against the enemy.

3. Notwithstanding the target date above, you will be prepared at any time to take immediate advantage of favorable circumstances, such as withdrawal by the enemy on your front, to effect a re-entry into the Continent with such forces as you have available at the time; a general plan for this operation when approved will be furnished for your assistance.

4. *Command.* You are responsible to the Combined Chiefs-of-Staff and will exercise command generally in accordance with the diagram at Appendix A. Direct communication with the United States and British Chiefs-of-Staff is authorized in the interest of facilitating your operations and for arranging necessary logistic support.

5. *Logistics.* In the United Kingdom the responsibility for logistics organization, concentration, movement and supply of forces to meet the requirements of your plan will rest with British Service Ministries so far as British Forces are concerned. So far as United States Forces are concerned, this responsibility will rest with the United States War and Navy Departments. You will be responsible for the co-ordination of logistical arrangements on the Continent. You will also be responsible for co-ordinating the requirements of British and United States Forces under your command.

6. *Co-ordination of operations of other Forces and Agencies.* In preparation for your assault on enemy-occupied Europe, Sea and Air Forces, agencies of sabotage, subversion, and propaganda, acting under a variety of authorities, are now in action. You may recommend any variation in these activities which may seem to you desirable.

7. *Relationship to United Nations Forces in other areas.* Responsibility will rest with the Combined Chiefs-of-Staff for supplying information relating to operations of the forces of the USSR for your guidance in timing your operations. It is understood that the Soviet forces will launch an offensive at about the same time as OVERLORD with the object of preventing the German forces from transferring from the Eastern to the Western front. The Allied Commander-in-Chief, Mediterranean Theater, will conduct operations designed to assist your operation, including the launching of an attack against the south of France at about the same time as OVERLORD. The scope and timing of his operations will be decided by the Combined Chief-of-Staff. You will establish contact with him and submit to the Combined Chiefs-of-Staff your views and recommendations regarding operations from the Mediterranean in support of your attack from the United Kingdom. A copy of his directive is furnished for your guidance. The Combined Chiefs-of-Staff will place under your command the forces operating in Southern France as soon as you are in a position to assume such command. You will submit timely recommendations compatible with this regard.

8. *Relationship with Allied Governments — the re-establishment of Civil Governments and Liberated Allied Territories and the administration of enemy territories.* Further instructions will be issued to you on these subjects at a later date.

February 12, 1944

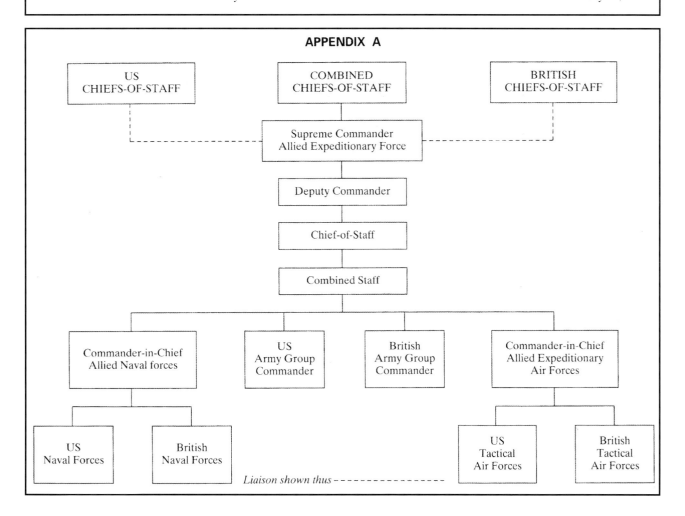

On January 31, invitiations were extended to the Press for a photo session with 'certain members of the Supreme Command'. The location of the photoshoot was not given as it 'must be regarded as secret'. The journalists were just told to rendezvous at 9 a.m. on Tuesday, February 1, at the Public Relations Office of ETOUSA (United States Army European Theater of Operations). After their credentials had been checked, the SHAEF invitation stated that 'all photographic and newsreel correspondents will then be conducted on buses to the location which must be regarded as "SECRET".' It was of course a very short journey from the Public Relations Office at 28 Grosvenor Square to St James's Square, less than a quarter of a mile.

L-R: Lieutenant General Omar N. Bradley, senior commander of US Army ground forces with the Allied Expeditionary Force (AEF); Admiral Sir Bertram H. Ramsay, Commander-in-Chief of the AEF's naval forces; Air Chief Marshal Sir Arthur William Tedder, Deputy Commander-in-Chief; General Dwight D. Eisenhower, Commander in Chief of the AEF and of US forces in the European Theater of Operations; General Sir Bernard L. Montgomery, commander of the British ground forces; Air Marshal Sir Trafford Leigh-Mallory, Commander-in-Chief of the AEF's air forces, and Lieutenant General Walter B. Smith, Chief-of-Staff of the AEF and of the US forces in the European Theater of Operations.

Top: Before the war, Norfolk House was the headquarters of the British Aluminium Company, and it was in the former boardroom — blacked out on the sixth floor — that the 'Overlord' commanders met the Press. *Right:* In 1977-78, Norfolk House was totally gutted behind its listed exterior and a new central lift shaft installed to completely modernise the interior, unfortunately losing the boardroom with its wood panelling. But this is exactly the same corner and when we took this photograph it was the accounts section of Lamco Paper Sales Ltd.

Air Chief Marshal Sir Arthur W. Tedder, 53, joined the Royal Flying Corps in January 1916 when he obtained his 'wings'. He served as British air commander in the Middle East in 1942, and from February 1943 until the end of the year as Commander-in-Chief, Mediterranean Allied Air Forces, which included RAF Middle East, RAF Malta Air Command, and the North-West African Air Forces. In January 1944, he was appointed Deputy Supreme Commander, SHAEF.

Lieutenant General Walter Bedell Smith, 48, became Secretary, General Staff, in September 1941, and in February 1942 was named US secretary of the Combined Chiefs-of-Staff. General Eisenhower chose him in September 1942 to be Chief-of-Staff of the European Theater of Operations and later he became Chief-of-Staff of the Allied forces in North Africa and of the Mediterranean theatre. At the end of the 1943, he was appointed Chief-of-Staff of SHAEF.

Air Chief Marshal Sir Trafford Leigh-Mallory, 51, was Allied Air Commander-in-Chief. He had served in the Royal Flying Corps and had been awarded the Distinguished Service Order in 1919. In 1937, he became Air Officer Commanding-in-Chief, No. 12 Group, and from November 1942 to December 1943 he served as AOC Fighter Command. As Allied Air C-in-C, he was to command the tactical air forces in support of the Allied Expeditionary Force. He was killed in a plane crash in November 1944.

General Sir Bernard Law Montgomery, 56, commanded the British 3rd Division in France in 1939-40. He was given temporary command of II Corps at Dunkirk and later V Corps and, in 1941, the XII Corps. In 1942, he became head of South-East Command and that summer was selected to command the Eighth Army. He won the battle of El Alamein, and pursued Rommel's forces to their defeat in Tunisia. Later, he led the Eighth Army to Sicily and Italy. His appointment as Commander-in-Chief, 21st Army Group, was announced in December 1943. He commanded the Allied land forces in Normandy, serving in that capacity until September 1, 1944, when General Eisenhower assumed control of field operations.

Admiral Bertram H. Ramsay had retired in 1938 after 42 years' service with the Royal Navy. He saw action in the First World War as commander of the destroyer *Broke*, and ended his service with three years as Chief-of-Staff, Home Fleet. He was recalled to duty in 1939 as Flag Officer Commanding, Dover, and in that post organised the naval forces for the evacuation of Dunkirk. Later, he helped plan the 'Torch' operation; commanded a task force in the Sicilian invasion, and became British naval commander in the Mediterranean. He was selected to be the Allied Naval Commander-in-Chief, Expeditionary Force (ANCXF) in October 1943, aged 60, and served in that post until his death in a plane crash on January 2, 1945.

Lieutenant General Omar N. Bradley, 50, was an assistant secretary of the General Staff in the US War Department in 1940 and in February 1941 was given command of the Infantry School at Fort Benning. Later, he commanded the 82nd Division, followed by the 28th Division. In February 1943, he went to North Africa to act as an observer for General Eisenhower, becoming Deputy Commander of II Corps under General Patton, and then commander when Patton was given the task of planning the Sicilian campaign. He fought with the corps in Tunisia and Sicily. In September 1943, he was selected to head the US First Army in the invasion of north-west Europe as well as a US army group headquarters — the 1st (later 12th) Army Group.

Left: Lieutenant-General Sir Frederick E. Morgan, 49, served in France in 1940 with the 1st Armoured Division. In May 1942, he was appointed to command the I Corps District, which included Lincolnshire and the East Riding of Yorkshire. In October that year, he was made commander of I Corps and placed under General Eisenhower. He was given the task of preparing a subsidiary landing in the western Mediterranean either to reinforce the initial landings or to deal with a German thrust through Spain. When neither operation proved necessary, he was directed to plan the invasion of Sardinia. When this was abandoned, he began planning the invasion of Sicily although this project was later given to the armies in North Africa. In the spring of 1943, he became Chief-of-Staff to the Supreme Allied Commander (COSSAC) and as such directed planning for the invasion of north-west Europe at Allied Forces Headquarters (AFHQ) in Norfolk House located in the south-eastern corner of St James's Square *(right).* When the Supreme Commander was appointed and Eisenhower chose General Smith to be the SHAEF Chief-of-Staff, General Morgan agreed to serve as Smith's deputy.

At Teheran, Stalin had pressed the question as to the identity of the Allied commander for 'Overlord', but the answer was side-stepped by Roosevelt saying that he and Churchill would make the final decision when they returned for further talks in Cairo. It had already been agreed at the Quebec conference the previous August that the final choice would be the President's responsibility, the two contenders being either General George C. Marshall, his Chief-of-Staff in Washington, aged 63, or General Eisenhower, ten years his junior. The former deserved command of 'Overlord' as he had already been closely concerned with its planning, but Eisenhower, on the other hand, had already proved himself with a string of victories in the Mediterranean, confirming that a unified Allied command was not only possible but eminently successful in battle. Roosevelt deliberated for several days, finally reaching his decision on the evening of December 6, telling Marshall, who was travelling with the President: 'I don't think I could sleep at night with you out of the country'.

Meanwhile, Lieutenant-General Sir Frederick E. Morgan, who had served in France in 1940 with the 1st Armoured Division, had been appointed in May 1942 to command the I Corps District which included Lincolnshire and the East Riding of Yorkshire. In October that year he was made commander of I Corps and placed under General Eisenhower, being given the task of preparing a subsidiary landing in the western Mediterranean either to reinforce the initial landings or to deal with a German thrust through Spain. When neither operation proved necessary, he was directed to plan the invasion of Sardinia. When this, in turn, was abandoned, he began planning the invasion of Sicily although this project was later given to the armies in North Africa.

In the spring of 1943, he became Chief-of-Staff to the Supreme Allied Commander (COSSAC) — although the actual commander had not yet been appointed — and as such directed planning for the invasion of north-west Europe at Allied Forces Headquarters (AFHQ) located at Norfolk House in St James's Square, London. When General Eisenhower was given the job of Supreme Commander, he chose General Walter Bedell Smith to be the SHAEF Chief-of-Staff. General Morgan agreed to serve as Smith's deputy.

The first full meeting of Eisenhower with his commanders was held in Norfolk House on Friday, January 21, 1944. General Bernard Montgomery, the 21st Army Group commander, had already spent three weeks examining the plans for 'Overlord' and strongly recommended that the planned assault by three divisions (all that Morgan had been allowed) be increased to five with a two-division follow-up, the 'minimum to make a proper success of the operation'.

By the end of the day-long conference, important fundamental issues had been agreed, firstly that the assault must be widened with five divisions landing simultaneously; that port facilities were essential on 'the far shore', and that the tactical advantage must be seized as early as possible after the landing.

A cable setting out the criteria for the revised plan, which would require an additional 47 large tank-carrying ships (LSTs), 144 tank landing craft (LCTs), 72 large infantry craft (LCI(L)s), five cruisers and 24 destroyers, was despatched to the Combined Chiefs-of-Staff in Washington on January 23. A reply was received by Eisenhower on January 31 authorising the enlarged assault, although it failed to specify which other operations planned in the Mediterranean and Pacific would have to be robbed to provide the additional ships required.

As yet, Eisenhower had not received a formal 'directive' from the Combined Chiefs confirming his appointment and defining his precise task and the extent of his powers. This finally arrived on February 14 after more than five weeks of haggling behind the scenes in an effort to reconcile British and American points of view. Like all political communiqués, words are carefully chosen to please all parties, the initial British draft specifying that Eisenhower obtain a lodgement

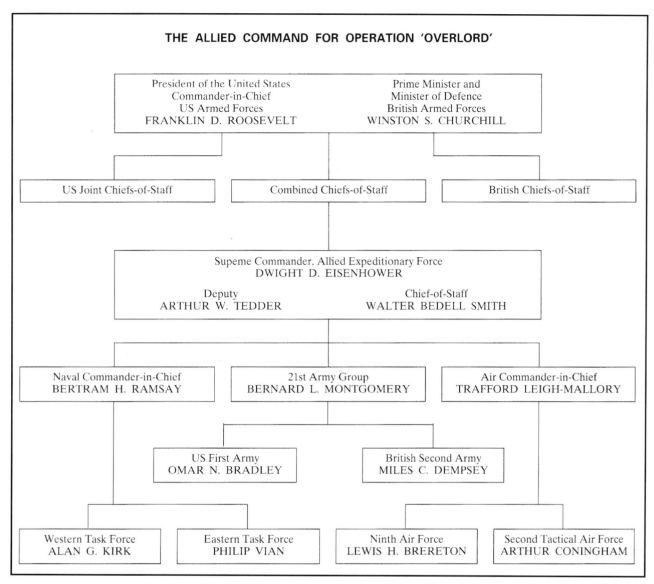

THE ALLIED COMMAND FOR OPERATION 'OVERLORD'

- President of the United States / Commander-in-Chief / US Armed Forces — **FRANKLIN D. ROOSEVELT**
- Prime Minister and Minister of Defence / British Armed Forces — **WINSTON S. CHURCHILL**
- US Joint Chiefs-of-Staff
- Combined Chiefs-of-Staff
- British Chiefs-of-Staff
- Supreme Commander, Allied Expeditionary Force — **DWIGHT D. EISENHOWER**
  - Deputy — **ARTHUR W. TEDDER**
  - Chief-of-Staff — **WALTER BEDELL SMITH**
- Naval Commander-in-Chief — **BERTRAM H. RAMSAY**
- 21st Army Group — **BERNARD L. MONTGOMERY**
- Air Commander-in-Chief — **TRAFFORD LEIGH-MALLORY**
- US First Army — **OMAR N. BRADLEY**
- British Second Army — **MILES C. DEMPSEY**
- Western Task Force — **ALAN G. KIRK**
- Eastern Task Force — **PHILIP VIAN**
- Ninth Air Force — **LEWIS H. BRERETON**
- Second Tactical Air Force — **ARTHUR CONINGHAM**

area in France from which 'further offensive action can be aimed at the heart of Germany'. This the Americans rejected, rephrasing the sentence; 'striking at the heart of Germany'. In the end, the final version (reproduced on page 9) was less specific which as far as Eisenhower was concerned, was all to the good as it allowed him more leeway. On the other hand, it failed to give him overall authority over the strategic air forces (RAF Bomber Command and the US Eighth Army Air Force) which was to cause much argument in the future.

Nevertheless, his orders were simple: . . . 'to undertake operations aimed at the heart of Germany and the destruction of her armed forces'.

Left: **Eisenhower leaves Norfolk House on Friday, January 21, after the first full meeting with his commanders. General Montgomery had already spent three weeks examining the plans for 'Overlord' and strongly recommended that the planned assault by three divisions (all that Morgan had been allowed) be increased to five with a two-division follow-up, the 'minimum . . . to make a proper success of the operation'.**
Right: **From the outside, Norfolk House presents the same face today as it did in 1944, save for the repaired windows and the addition of two commemorative plaques.**

JUNE 1944
INVASION

SC 320901
American assault troops in a landing craft huddle behind the protective front of the craft as it nears a beachhead, on the Northern Coast of France. Smoke in the background is Naval gunfire supporting the landing.
6 June 1944

ETO-HQ-44-4754-19 (R-400-4754-19)
Released by Field Press Censor, 7 June 1944
Lot 8744   mk/ms

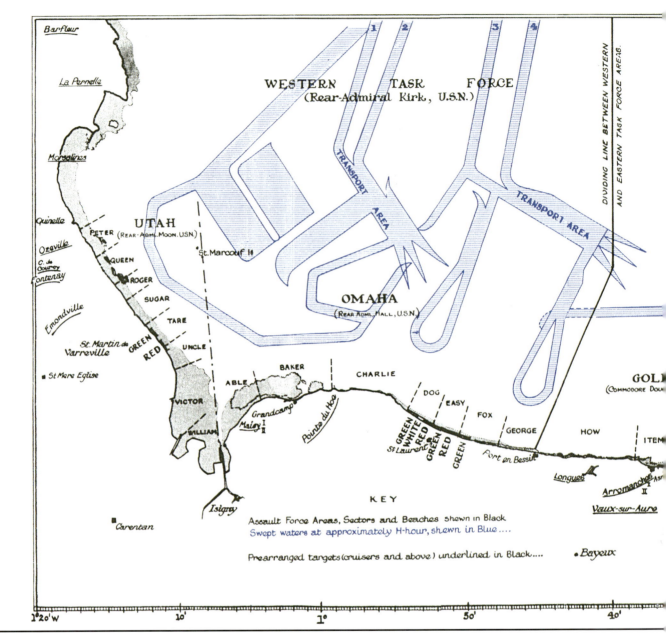

The assault area for Operation 'Neptune' was defined as being bounded on the north by the parallel of 49°40′N, and on the west, south and east by the shores of the Bay of the Seine. This area was divided into two Task Force areas, the boundary between them running from the root of the Port-en-Bessin western breakwater in an 025° direction to the meridian of 0°40′W and thence along this meridian to 49°40′N. The Western Task Force area of which Rear Admiral Alan G. Kirk *(left)* was the Naval Commander, was divided into two assault force areas: Utah covering the east coast of the Cotentin peninsula to the River Vire, and Omaha from there to the British area. Two Naval assault forces, Force 'U' and Force 'O' respectively, were responsible for all naval operations in these areas. The Eastern Task Force area, commanded by Rear-Admiral Sir Philip Vian *(right)*, was divided into three: Gold area from Port-en-Bessin to Ver; Juno area from there to a point west of Langrune; and Sword area eastwards to Ouistreham — served by Naval Assault Forces 'G', 'J' and 'S' respectively.

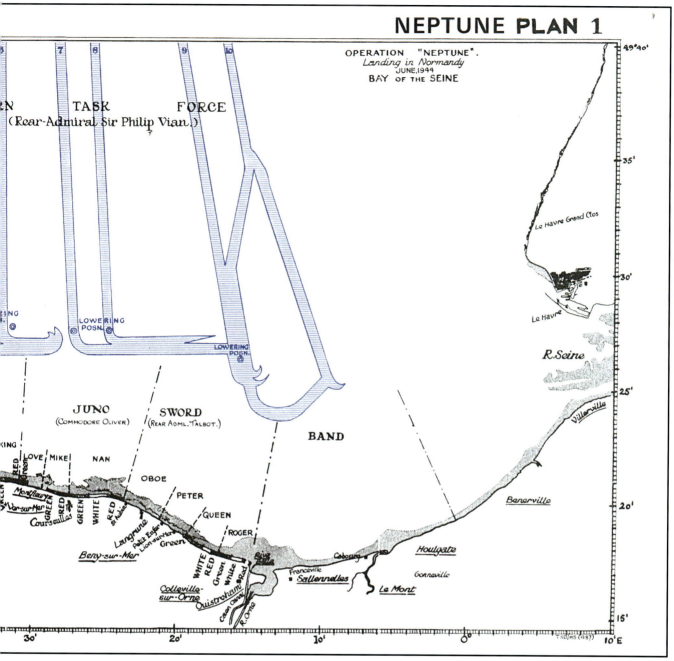

The mineclearing plan adopted fell into four phases, viz: clearing and marking two channels for each assault force; finding or making clear areas for the bombarding forces and anchorages close inshore; widening the approach channels and clearance of mines from neighbouring areas in order to give sea room; and the clearance of mines laid after the assault. On arrival in the assault area, bombarding ships formed part of the assault forces to which they were allocated. Flag and senior officers commanding British bombarding forces were therefore requested to implement the intentions of task or assault force commanders. Rear-Admiral W. R. Paterson was the Senior Officer of Force 'D', the Bombardment Force covering Force 'S'. His battleship was HMS *Ramillies*, fitted with eight 15-inch guns which could lob a shell of 1,938lbs some 32,000 yards — over 18 miles. She carried 110 rounds per gun. In addition, she had twelve 6-inch guns, each with 130 112lb shells. (HMS *Rodney* was the most powerful ship off Normandy, armed with nine 16-inch guns which could fire a shell weighing a ton over 20 miles.)

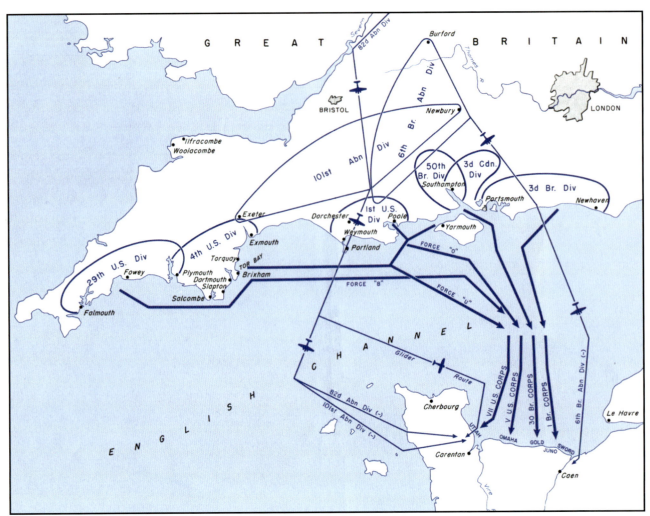

The assault beaches were to be protected on either flank by airborne troops landing by glider or by parachute. The British 6th Airborne Division under Major-General Richard Gale was to deal with the eastern flank on six landing zones, the main task being to seize the bridges across the River Orne and Caen Canal (which was later named 'Pegasus Bridge'). The American airborne operation was shared between the 82nd Airborne Division under Major General Matthew B. Ridgway and the 101st commanded by Major General Maxwell D. Taylor and it was to his men that General Eisenhower paid a farewell visit on the evening of June 5. At Greenham Common, he was pictured walking through the paratroopers and, in particular, speaking with Lieutenant Wallace C. Strobel of Company E of the 502nd Parachute Infantry.

Left: At the Caen Canal Bridge, three men from the first glider (91) piloted by Staff Sergeant Jim Wallwork, carrying No. 1 Platoon under Lieutenant Herbert 'Den' Brotheridge, were detailed to rush a pillbox and put it out of action with grenades. Meanwhile, the remainder of the platoon, led by Brotheridge, was to dash across the bridge. Lieutenant David Wood's platoon in the second glider (92), flown by Staff Sergeant Oliver Boland, was to attack the trenches, machine gun and the anti-tank gun along the eastern bank, while No. 3 Platoon under Lieutenant 'Sandy' Smith in the third glider (93) piloted by Staff Sergeant Geoffrey Barkway, was to reinforce the bridge party. Just after midnight, the three gliders of the coup de main party crash landed close to Pegasus Bridge in what was described by Air Chief Marshal Leigh-Mallory as the finest piece of airmanship in the entire war. *Right:* The original lifting bridge across the canal was removed just prior to the 50th anniversary of D-Day in 1994 but it has been preserved within the museum located nearby.

The attacking force — a company of the 52nd Foot (the Oxfordshire & Buckinghamshire Light Infantry) — were the first Allied soldiers to set foot in France, but one of the gliders (No. 93) broke apart landing on the flooded ground and Lance Corporal Fred Greenhalgh was drowned. He was the first man to die in Normandy and was buried with three commandos beside the road. Later these graves were moved to Row C of Plot V (Graves 2-5) in La Délivrande War Cemetery although the inscription on Greenhalgh's headstone stated incorrectly that he died on June 7. In 1995, *After the Battle* contacted the Commonwealth War Graves Commission with the evidence of what had occurred and the date was later changed.

COMMUNIQUE No. 2   June 6

Shortly before midnight on 5 June, 1944, Allied light bombers opened the assault. Their attacks in very great strength continued until dawn.

Between 0630 and 0730 hours this morning, two Naval Task Forces, commanded by Rear-Admiral Sir Philip Vian, flying his flag in HMS *Scylla* (Captain T. M. Brownrigg, RN), and Rear-Admiral Alan Goodrich Kirk, USN, in USS *Augusta* (Captain E. H. Jones, USN), launched their assault forces at enemy beaches. The naval forces, which had previously assembled under the overall command of Admiral Sir Bertram Ramsay, made their departure in fresh weather and were joined during the night by bombarding forces which had previously left northern waters.

```
                Communique Number 1

                                    6 June 1944

UNDER THE COMMAND OF GENERAL EISENHOWER, ALLIED NAVAL
FORCES, SUPPORTED BY STRONG AIR FORCES, BEGAN LANDING
ALLIED ARMIES THIS MORNING ON THE NORTHERN COAST OF
FRANCE.
```

The invasion beaches in Normandy were split into five areas: Utah, Omaha, Gold, Juno and Sword, and each was further sub-divided into sectors and then into Red, White and Green Beaches. This Ninth Air Force Maurader overflies Red and White Beaches in Queen Sector of Sword assigned to the British 3rd Infantry Division.

One of the first newsmen ashore with the British Army Film and Photographic Unit (AFPU) was Sergeant George Laws who was shooting cine: 'I took several shots of the other assault craft on the way in, and as we neared the beach everybody was ordered to crouch below the top edge of the craft for the final run in. The din of covering gun-fire and the screech of the rocket-launching ships, and the oncoming return fire, was terrific. About 30 yards from touch-down, with mortar bombs dropping around us, there was an almighty explosion which caused the LCA to lurch sideways, throwing everybody into a heap.'

Channels had to be swept through the large enemy minefields. This operation was completed shortly before dawn and, while minesweeping flotillas continued to sweep towards the enemy coast, the entire naval force followed down swept channels behind them towards their objectives.

Shortly before the assault, three enemy torpedo boats with armed trawlers in company attempted to interfere with the operation and were promptly driven off. One enemy trawler was sunk and another severely damaged.

The assault forces moved towards the beaches under cover of heavy bombardment from destroyers and other support craft, while heavier ships engaged enemy batteries which had already been subjected to bombardment from the air. Some of these were silenced. Allied forces continued to engage other batteries.

Landings were effected under cover of the air and naval bombardments and airborne landings involving troop-carrying aircraft and gliders carrying large forces of troops were also made successfully at a number of points. Reports of operations so far show that our forces succeeded in their initial landings. Fighting continues.

Allied heavy, medium, light, and fighter-bombers continued the air bombardment in very great strength throughout the day with attacks on gun emplacements, defensive works, and communications. Continuous fighter cover was maintained over the beaches and for some distance inland and over naval operations in the Channel. Our night fighters played an equally important role in protecting shipping and troop-carrier forces and in intruder operations. Allied reconnaissance aircraft maintained continuous watch by day and night over shipping and ground forces.

Our aircraft met with little enemy fighter opposition or anti-aircraft gunfire. Naval casualties were regarded as being very light, especially when the magnitude of the operation is taken into account.

As soon as Communiqué No. 1 was released to the Press at 1025 on the morning of June 6, a pre-recorded statement was broadcast to the people of Western Europe by the Supreme Commander: 'A landing was made this morning on the coast of France by troops of the Allied Expeditionary Force. This landing is part of the concerted United Nations plan for the liberation of Europe, made in conjunction with our great Russian Allies'. AFPU photographer Sergeant Jimmy Mapham, assigned to land on Sword, was on White Beach and 90 minutes earlier had taken this iconic picture looking towards Red Beach. These heavily-laden troops are from the 8th Field Ambulance, RAMC, attached to the 8th Brigade, who were most probably helping wounded from the wrecked carrier on the right belonging to the 2nd Battalion, the Middlesex Regiment. We may also be seeing men of No. 41 (RM) Commando in the background. The casualties of the 2nd Battalion, East Yorks on Red Beach are unknown, but the 1st Battalion of the South Lancs which landed on White Beach sustained 126 casualties during the assault phase of the landing. The soldier walking on the right is Fred Sadler of No. 84 Field Company, RE, who remembered the photographer walking past him and then turning to take the picture.

The next area to the west was Juno, the preserve of the 3rd Canadian Infantry Division, and it was here that one of the most famous images was taken by a cine camera on a landing craft touching down on Nan Red. Taken shortly after 0805, it shows either A or B Company of the North Shore Regiment. SHAEF even included the sequence in their own cinematic record covering the operations carried out to defeat Germany from Normandy to Berlin. *The True Glory* was released in August 1945 (see *After the Battle* No. 149). The same house still stands overlooking the holiday beach at La Rive.

At Bernières, also part of Juno, the high sea wall had to be breached to clear the beach and in this photo taken by Canadian photographer Lieutenant Gilbert Milne at around 1140 an assault bridge is already in place. The troops coming ashore are the Stormont, Dundas and Glengarry Highlanders which formed part of the reserve 9th Brigade. The battalion commented that 'the damage to the village [Bernières] is not as great as we imagined it might have been'. Points of interest are the prominent timbered house on the foreshore which still stands, and the railway station (with the white name board on its end wall) which also survives but is hidden in the comparison behind the new buildings.

The third area assaulted by the Eastern Task Force was Gold. Here men of No. 47 (Royal Marine) Commando were pictured coming ashore on Jig Sector. Their role was to advance through enemy lines and swing in an arc to capture Port-en-Bessin which lay at the junction with the US Western Task Force beaches of Omaha and Utah.

COMMUNIQUE No. 3   **June 7**

Allied forces continued landings on the northern coast of France throughout yesterday and satisfactory progress is being made. Rangers and Commandos formed part of the assaulting forces.

No further attempt at interference with our seaborne landings was made by enemy naval forces. Those coastal batteries still in action are being bombarded by Allied warships.

At twilight yesterday, and for the fourth time during the day, our heavy bombers attacked railways, communications, and bridges in the general battle area. There was increased air opposition and 26 enemy aircraft which attempted to interfere were shot down. One Allied bomber and 17 fighters failed to return from this operation. Other enemy air activity included an attack on our beach forces. This proved abortive and four of a formation of 12 Ju 88s were destroyed.

In addition to attacks on defended positions and other objectives in immediate support of land operations, railway centers, bridges, military buildings, and communications at ABANCOURT, SERQUEUX, AMIENS and VIRE were attacked repeatedly throughout yesterday by our medium and light bombers. Allied fighter-bombers and fighters flew low to attack enemy units and motor truck columns.

From dawn to dusk the vast Allied fighter force maintained vigil over our shipping and over the assault area. This air cover was again completely successful.

Airborne operations were resumed successfully last night. Coastal aircraft attacked German naval units, in the Bay of Biscay.

A strong force of heavy night bombers attacked bridges and road and rail communications behind the invasion area, including the junction at CHATEAUDUN. Thirteen heavy bombers are missing. Light bombers were also out against the same type of targets, and night intruders destroyed 12 enemy aircraft without loss.

This casemate containing an 88mm gun lay at the eastern end of King Red and caused heavy casualties to the 5th East Yorks.

Denuded of its armaments, the casemate still stands at La Rivière.

The capture of Port-en-Bessin was vital not only as point for the unloading of stores and supplies, but also because it was the key for linking up with the American landing on Omaha. The battle began early on June 7 (D+1) supported by fire from HMS *Emerald* and three squadrons of rocket-firing Typhoons. It was finally secured at 0400 on June 8 although the first contact between British and US forces had already occurred the previous evening between commandos and the American 3rd Battalion of the 16th Regimental Combat Team (RCT). This meeting was not recorded in the Army Commander's diary until 1630 on June 8.

25

However, on Omaha the 1st Infantry Division was having a hard time as the natural features of the area worked in favour of the enemy. Not only was the beach backed by rising ground some 100 feet high on which the Germans had constructed their defences but the course shingle precluded vehicle movement on the eastern end of the beach. Then the Sherman DD tanks were released up to nine miles offshore in a rough sea so that 27 of them floundered before reaching land. Finally, the German 352. Infanterie-Division had just been moved to the Omaha area to carry out defence exercises. Robert Capa, who landed with Company E (16th RCT) on Easy Red at 0631, took this memorable picture — one of only 11 frames which survived following a disaster later in the darkroom which ruined the rest of his film. Landing two minutes behind the first wave of infantry were the men of the special engineer task force, which included 16 joint Army-Navy combat demolition teams, whose job it was to clear 16 gaps through the obstacles, each 50 yards wide. Gap support teams would land not later than H+8 minutes to assist. Such was the plan and, following the overwhelming Allied bombardment of the German positions, the men were told that 'there will be nothing alive on the beach when you land'. The illusion did not last long. Because of the cloud cover, a safety margin had been introduced to prevent aircraft bombing short and, in the event, only two sticks of bombs landed within four miles of the shore defences. The engineers arrived amidst a storm of artillery, mortar and small-arms fire to find troops sheltering behind the very obstacles they were due to destroy.

Don Whitehead was a correspondent aboard the US vessel carrying Brigadier General Willard Wyman, the Assistant Commander of the 1st Infantry Division: 'The first and second waves of troops — scheduled to land at 6.30 and 7 a.m. — had been thown into disorder. Boats swung from their courses and drove through gaps wherever they could find them. This was possible because between 7 and 8 a.m. the tide rose eight feet in the Channel. But units landed far from their assigned sectors. Commanders were separated from their troops. Sections were fragmented. And those who landed were pinned to the beach by heavy machine-gun, artillery, and mortar fire. We rode the rising tide through one of the gaps and waded ashore at 8 a.m. As far as I could see through the smoke of battle, troops were lying along a shelf of shale. Ahead of us stretched mined sand dunes to the bluffs where the Germans were sheltered in their trenches, bunkers, and blockhouses. There was no cover for the men on the beach. The Germans were looking down on them — and it was a shooting gallery.'

COMMUNIQUE No. 4   June 7

Allied troops have cleared all beaches of the enemy and have in some cases established links with flanking beach-heads. Inland fighting generally is heavy.

An armoured counter-attack in the CAEN area on Tuesday evening was repulsed. Enemy resistance is stiffening as his reserves come into action. The landing of troops and seaborne military supplies continues on all beaches despite the north-westerly wind which has persisted since the assault.

Shortly before dawn today, light coastal forces, while sweeping to the eastward, encountered a superior force of enemy craft. Action was immediately joined and damage was inflicted on the enemy before he could make good his escape.

Enemy coastal batteries, which were still in action yesterday, have been silenced by Allied naval forces. It is not yet known whether all have been finally reduced.

Today Allied aircraft have been directing the fire of the USS *Texas* (Capt. C. A. Baker, USN) wearing the flag of Rear Admiral Carleton F. Bryant, USN and HMS *Glasgow* (Cap. C. P. Clarke, RN) who, together with other Allied warships, have been engaging inland targets behind the beaches.

Allied aircraft of all types and in great strength have again closely supported our land and sea forces.

Early this morning airborne operations were resumed on a very large scale, supplies and tactical equipment being delivered to our ground forces.

In two operations this morning, medium and light bombers attacked large troop concentrations and military buildings close behind the enemy line as well as gun positions in the battle area and railway lines south of the battle area.

The loss of life on Omaha was grievous, a total of 1,190 men killed being given for the 1st Division and 743 for the 29th Division on the first day. And it was here, right on the beach, that the first Allied cemetery was established in France. When the bodies were later exhumed, they were either buried in the permanent military cemetery in Normandy or repatriated at the request of the next of kin to the United States.

Road, rail and other targets, including armoured vehicles, troop concentrations, gun positions and ammunition dumps were also attacked during the morning by fighter-bombers.

Heavy bombers, in medium strength, attacked focal points on the road system in the area south of CAEN early this afternoon. Fighters escorted the bombers and also strafed and bombed railway yards, locomotives, trains of oil tank cars, flak towers, radio installations and airfields over a 40 to 50 miles arc south and south-east of the battle area.

Continuous patrols were maintained over shipping, the beaches and the battle area. More enemy aircraft were encountered than on Tuesday and a number of them were shot down.

In May 1945, T/Sergeant Robert Bradley returned to where the cemetery once lay. Bernard Paich pictured the present-day marker.

Then and Now. The promontory of Pointe du Hoc lay between Omaha and Utah and here the Germans had emplaced six large-calibre guns — believed to be 155mm — which had the ability of threatening the landings on both American beaches. So, like all the coastal fortifications, the position was subjected to severe bombing in April, May and June, this particular attack by the US Ninth Air Force (set up specifically to support the 'Overlord' operation) taking place on June 4. Although it was hoped that the bombing had neutralised the guns the risk was too great, so the 2nd Ranger Battalion was charged with their capture. To achieve this, they would have to land at the foot of the 100-foot cliffs and scale them using ropes and ladders. Scheduled to touch down at 0630, in the event the Rangers were 40 minutes late.

Unfortunately four DUKWs which had been specially fitted with 100-foot extending fire brigade ladders were hampered in driving ashore by the bomb-craters pitting the beach and when grappling hooks were fired, the rockets were unable to carry the waterlogged ropes to the top. Climbing was also made difficult as the bombing had brought down a huge mound of slippery clay which gave way too easily. In the end, a 16-foot ladder with toggle ropes was set up on top of the mound while a second Ranger climbed it with another section of ladder. The small force isolated from both Omaha and Utah had to then hold out for two days before being relieved. During that time they found that the Germans had removed the guns from the smashed casemates and re-positioned them in an orchard a few hundred yards further south. All were aligned on Utah beach.

Compared to Omaha, the casualties on Utah were very light, being reported as 197 — just one per cent of those coming ashore — perhaps aided by the fact that due to a navigational error the landing took place a mile further south from the intended beach. This picture was taken on June 8 with Red Beach HQ in the foreground.

Selected casualties were commemorated by having local roads named after them, this picture being taken on the first anniversary of D-Day in 1945. Although the original caption states that T/5 Stephen J. Olle of the 531st Engineer Shore Regiment was killed on Omaha, in fact he lost his life on Utah where a permanent road marker stands today. He was first buried at Sainte-Mère-Église but is now in Grave 33 in Row 17 of Plot F of the Normandy American Cemetery at Colleville-sur-Mer (see page 32).

Today, access to Utah beach is still via the opening on the right which was bulldozed in June 1944.

COMMUNIQUE No. 5   **June 8**

BAYEUX has fallen to our troops which have also crossed the BAYEUX—CAEN road at several points. Progress continues despite determined enemy resistance. Fierce armored and infantry fighting has taken place.

Contact has been established between our seaborne and airborne troops.

The steady build-up of our forces has continued. During the night, forces of E-Boats made unsuccessful attempts to interfere with the continual arrival of supplies. Support fire from Allied warships continued throughout yesterday.

Our air forces have given invaluable support to the ground troops on all sectors of the front. Advantage was taken of favorable weather over northern France yesterday afternoon and evening to attack enemy rail and road centers, concentrations of men and materiel, and to bomb airfields and other targets up to 100 miles in advance of our troops. More than 9,000 sorties were flown in tactical support of land and naval forces.

Out for the second time yesterday, heavy bombers with fighter escort in the late afternoon attacked airfields north-west of LORIENT, and railroad bridges and focal points in the area from the Bay of Biscay to the Seine. The bombers encountered no enemy fighter opposition but our fighters reported shooting down six enemy aircraft in combat and destroying more than a score on the ground.

After bombing rail and road objectives in the immediate zone of operations, medium and light bombers, flying as low as 1,000 feet just behind the enemy lines, strafed gun emplacements and crews, staff cars and trains. Allied fighter-bombers and fighters were also extremely active, flying armed reconnaissance over the assault area, covering naval operations and carrying out low-level attacks on bridges north of CARENTAN and in the Cherbourg peninsula.

Coastal aircraft attacked naval enemy units in the Bay of Biscay and Channel areas and at least two E-Boats were sunk.

Last night heavy bombers in strong force continued attacks on railroad centers at ACHERES, VERSAILLES and MASSY-PALAISEAU and JUVISY on the outskirts of PARIS and a concentration of enemy troops and transports some 12 miles south of the assault area.

Anti-tank guns, motor transports and considerable supplies were delivered to our troops by very strong air transport and glider forces.

Small enemy air formations attempted attacks on the beaches and night intruders appeared over East Anglia.

Bayeux has been liberated — this is Rue Saint-Martin then and now.

Within 24 hours of landing on Gold, the 56th Brigade had advanced seven miles inland and liberated the city of Bayeux. Then on June 14 — four years to the day when German troops had marched into Paris — Général Charles de Gaulle, the nominal French leader, set foot in France. Because there had been no formal agreement between Britain and the US as to the future civil government, his visit was to be low key with no public meeting. Nevertheless, de Gaulle later wrote that 'we proceeded on foot, from street to street. The inhabitants stood in amazement, then burst into cheers, or into tears. Coming out of their houses, they escorted me amidst an extraordinary display of emotion. The children surrounding me, the women smiling and sobbing. The men with hands outstretched. We thus walked on together, fraternally, overwhelmed, and we felt the joy, pride, and faith in the nation surging again from the abyss.' This photograph of de Gaulle was taken in Rue du Général de Dais.

Although the SHAEF communiqué is not specific, the heavy raid mentioned included an operation against the railway tunnel at Saumur. On June 7 a message decrypted by Ultra revealed that the 17. SS-Panzergrenadier-Division was to be moved to Normandy from Thouars, so it was perceived that an attack on the railway tunnel at Saumur, 25 miles to the north, just before the line crossed the River Loire, might stop the division in its tracks. A raid was quickly planned for the following night (June 8/9) using the RAF's latest weapon: the 12,000lb 'Tallboy' which had the explosive force of a high-capacity blast bomb coupled with the penetrative power of an armour-piercing missile. When it hit the ground, the Tallboy penetrated deep before exploding, displacing 5,000 tons of soil. Nineteen Tallboys were carried to the target by Lancasters of Bomber Command's specialist squadron, No. 617, led by Wing Commander Leonard Cheshire. Four Lancs from No. 83 Squadron were to mark the target and also attempt to hit the bridge over the river with ordinary 1,000lb bombs, but both these and the flares were dropped wide of the mark so Cheshire himself marked the south-western end of the tunnel. In this post-raid picture, 17 craters can be counted with one direct hit on the tunnel itself. The Germans made no attempt to repair the damage as the advance guard of the 17. SS-Panzergrenadier-Division had already crossed the river before the attack. Its SS-Panzer-Abteilung 17 was in action south of Carentan less than a week later.

COMMUNIQUE No. 6   June 8

British and Canadian troops are continuing to make progress. Repeated enemy attacks against the 6th Airborne Division have been held. The American bridgeheads are being gradually enlarged. The enemy is fighting fiercely. His reserves have now been in action along the whole front.

With the safe and timely arrival of merchant convoys and improvement in the weather, unloading of supplies is proceeding at a satisfactory rate. Development of the Allied beach-heads continues. The supply by air of arms to our airborne troops early this morning was completely successful.

Last night enemy E-Boats operating in four groups entered the assault area and attempted to interfere with our lines of communication. A series of running fights ensued and the attacks were successfully beaten off. Three of the enemy were seen to be repeatedly hit before they escaped. During the early hours of today, E-Boats were attacked off the French and Belgian coasts by coastal aircraft. One E-Boat was sunk and three others sunk or severely damaged.

Our air assault in support of the land and naval forces against a wide variety of tactical targets has continued uninterruptedly and in very great strength. The enemy air effort is as yet on a limited scale but some opposition from flak has been encountered.

Ceaseless patrols were maintained over the immediate battle positions by our fighters and fighter-bombers. As targets presented themselves, small units broke off from the main patrolling force to dive-bomb and strafe armored columns, troop movements, and gun positions. Other fighters covered shipping against air and sea attack.

Behind the combat zone, other fighter bombers ranged over the country in a deep belt many miles south and south-east of the battle area, attacking armored vehicles, motor transport, and troop concentrations. Other targets included railways, fuel dumps, airfields, and canal locks on the river Seine. Rocket-firing planes attacked a tank concentration west of CAEN.

Our heavy bombers in very strong force struck at railway focal points, railway yards, and airfields well beyond the battle area. This morning, medium and light bombers took advantage of the improved weather and made many sorties in the Normandy area against rail and road targets. Our aircraft have flown approximately 27,000 individual missions in the period from dawn June 6 to midday today. One hundred and seventy-six enemy aircraft have been destroyed in the air. In the same period our losses were 289 aircraft.

The line was still out of action when American forces captured Saumur at the end of August and it was not re-opened until 1948.

Back in May, the Allies launched the last phase of the 'Transportation Plan' designed to isolate Normandy from the rest of France by destroying all the rail and road bridges on routes leading to it, together with systematic attacks on bridges over the Seine, Oise and Meuse rivers. So as not to reveal where the invasion was to take place, no attempt had been made against the bridges over the River Loire until after the assault had taken place. In spite of initial doubts (experience in Italy had seemed to show that the weight of bombs required to knock out a bridge was out of all proportion to the value of the target), the attacks in northern France were largely successful.

The most spectacular operation was that aimed at the railway bridge at Vernon (reported in Communiqué No. 7) which was wrecked by eight Thunderbolts of the Ninth Air Force using only eight tons of bombs. More then one attack and far heavier bomb-loads were needed for the other bridges but in the end every crossing over the Seine between Mantes *(above)* and Rouen was destroyed at an average cost of only 220 tons per bridge. By June 12 it was reported that 21 out of the 24 road and rail bridges between Paris and the sea (some sources say all 24) had been put out of action, either by being cut or blocked.

COMMUNIQUE No. 7　　　　　June 9

Allied troops have continued to make progress in all sectors, despite further reinforcements of German armor.

Landings have continued on all beaches and bypassed strong points of enemy resistance are being steadily reduced.

During yesterday, there was desultory firing from some coastal batteries, which were again silenced by gunfire from Allied warships.

Allied aircraft continued to support naval and land forces by attacks on a variety of targets. Late in the day, weather over northern France caused a reduction in the scale of air operations.

Our heavy bombers, in strong force, attacked railway targets and airfields beyond the battle area yesterday morning. They were escorted by medium forces of fighters. These and other fighters strafed ground targets, shooting down 31 enemy aircraft and destroying more than a score on the ground. From these operations, three bombers and 24 fighters are missing.

Medium bombers attacked a road bridge over the Seine at VERNON. Fighter-bombers struck at troop and transport concentrations, gun positions, armoured vehicles, and railway and road targets behind the battle line.

Fighters patrolled over shipping and the assault area. Twenty-one enemy aircraft were destroyed. Eleven of our fighters were lost but two of the pilots are safe.

Rocket-firing fighters attacked German E-Boats in the Channel leaving one in sinking condition.

Last night heavy bombers, in force, attacked railway centers at RENNES, FOUGERES, ALENCON, MAYENNE, and PONTAUBAULT. Five heavy bombers are missing. Light bombers struck at railway targets behind the battle area during the night.

For the first time since 1940 Allied air forces are able to operate from French soil.

This first airfield to be constructed in France — codenamed A-21C — was simply an emergency landing strip comprising a graded earth surface 3,400 feet long by 120 feet wide located on the high ground behind Omaha beach. By 1800 hours on D+2 it was able to handle light observation aircraft but nothing larger than that until June 9.

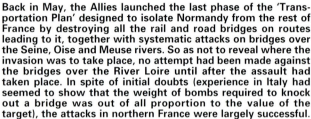

Over 90 airfields were deemed necessary in France to sustain 'Overlord' during the first three months, of which 27 were to be constructed in the Normandy countryside by the end of June. There were to be 12 in the US sector and 15 in the British where the more open landscape lent itself to better sites. In the event, only 17 had been completed by June 30: ten British and seven American, of which St Laurent, built on the bluffs behind Omaha by the 834th Aviation Engineer Battalion, was the first.

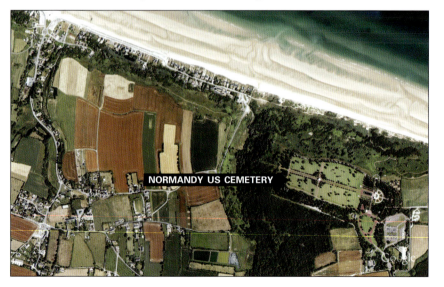

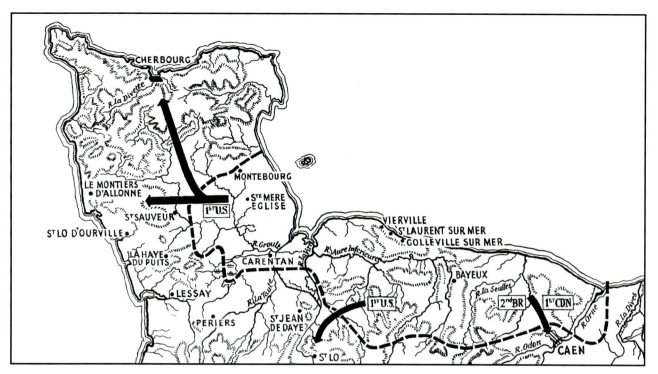

The developing campaign as depicted by SHAEF to illustrate the establishment and enlargement of the lodgement area.

COMMUNIQUE No. 8 June 9

American troops are across the CARENTAN—VALOGNES road in several places and have cut the broad-gauge railway to CHERBOURG. Further gains have been made west and south-west of BAYEUX.

Fighting is severe in the area of CAEN where the enemy is making a determined effort to stem the advance. The weight of armor on both sides is increasing and heavy fighting continues in all areas. The enemy strong points previously bypassed have now been eliminated. The weather has deteriorated but our beach-heads are being steadily developed.

Poor visibility and stormy weather reduced Allied air activity to a minimum over the battle area today.

Before dawn this morning, HMS *Tartar* (Commander B. Jones, RN), with HMS *Ashanti* (Lieutenant-Commander J. R. Barnes, RN), HM Canadian ships *Haida* (Commander H. G. de Wolf, RCN) and *Huron* (Lieutenant-Commander H. S. Rayner, RCN), ORP *Blyskawica*, HMS *Eskimo* (Lieutenant-Commander E. N. Sinclair, RN) ORP *Piorun* and HMS *Javelin* (Lieutenant-Commander P. B. N. Lewis, RN) in company, intercepted a force of German destroyers which had previously been reported off Ushant by coastal aircraft. The enemy were sighted and our ships turned towards them, avoiding their torpedoes. In the course of the action, at times conducted at point-blank range, HMS *Tartar* passed through the enemy's line. One enemy destroyer was torpedoed and blew up. A second was driven ashore in flames. Two others escaped after receiving damage by gunfire. HMS *Tartar* sustained some damage and a few casualties, but continued in action and has returned safely to harbor.

Unsuccessful attempts were again made after dawn by E-Boats to enter the assault area both from the east and west. They were intercepted and driven off by light coastal forces. Off the Pointe de Barfleur, in a short gun action, hits were observed on two of the enemy before they escaped.

During the night destroyers under the command of Rear Admiral Don Pardee Moon, USN, intercepted a force of heavily-armed enemy craft between the mainland and the Iles Saint Marcouf, and drove them off.

During the 24 hours to 0800 this morning, 46 targets were engaged by Allied warships. Spotting for these shoots was carried out both by aircraft and military Forward Observer Officers who had been landed with the assault troops.

HMS *Belfast* (Captain F. R. Parham, RN) wearing the flag of Rear-Admiral F. H. G. Dalrymple-Hamilton, and HMS *Frobisher* (Captain F. W. Mudford, RN) have done considerable execution on enemy concentrations. This morning HMS *Frobisher* neutralised two enemy batteries and destroyed an ammunition dump.

The capture of Isigny was vital to achieve the link-up between the two American beaches and when the 175th Infantry of the 29th Division landed on the afternoon of June 7, they were detailed to advance along the N13 towards the town. With the help of naval gunfire, Isigny was entered around 0300 on the morning of June 9. This is Rue Emile Demagny looking west towards Place Gambetta. SHAEF's Press Censor released the photograph for publication on June 13.

Meanwhile, at sea, RAF Coastal Command was tackling any German vessels posing a threat to the build-up convoys. *Above:* On the evening of June 9 (as SHAEF reported) three destroyers (*Z-24*, *Z-32* and *ZH-1*) were attacked by the Wick Wing (comprising Nos. 144 and 404 Squadrons) armed with 60lb rocket projectiles forcing *Z-32* to go aground off the Île de Batz *(right)*.

COMMUNIQUE No. 9 June 10

American troops have captured ISIGNY. Despite unfavorable weather conditions, the disembarkation of further men and materiel was uninterrupted.

Withstanding heavy enemy attacks delivered yesterday morning by infantry and armor, British and Canadian troops stood firm in the CAEN area.

Our forces have made contact with strong enemy forces near CONDE-SUR-SEULLES. There is continuous fighting in other sectors.

Adverse weather during daylight yesterday confined our air activity to limited patrols over the immediate battle area and to coastal aircraft operations. An enemy destroyer, driven ashore off BATZ in the Brest peninsula earlier in the day by naval surface forces, was attacked and left a smouldering hulk. One enemy aircraft was shot down 20 miles off BREST by anti-E-Boat patrols flown over western Channel waters.

Last night a strong force of heavy bombers, eight of which are missing, attacked enemy airfields at FLERS, RENNES, LAVAL and LE MANS in north-western France, and the railway center at ETAMPES. Light bombers pounded enemy communications in the rear of the battle zone. Weather conditions remained unfavorable.

Night fighters and intruder aircraft shot down four enemy planes over the beachhead.

Coastal aircraft are co-operating with naval surface forces in a vigorous offensive against U-Boats which are threatening to attack our lines of communication to the assault area.

Although Sainte-Mère-Église had been secured by paratroopers of the 82nd Airborne Division early on the morning of June 6, Carentan — the town at the base of the N13 highway north to Cherbourg whose capture was vital to the linking up of Omaha and Utah beaches — held out for six more days. Paratroops of the 101st Airborne Division made contact with men of the Omaha force on June 10 but Carentan did not fall until the night of June 11/12. With the link-up, the Allied lodgement area now stretched for 42 miles.

Claimed as the first French city to fall to the Allies, this is Rue Holgate at the junction with the D971 and 903.

Early on the morning of June 7, General Eisenhower left the SHAEF Advanced Command Post in Sawyer's Wood at Portsmouth to sail with Admiral Ramsay to see first-hand how the invasion was progressing, but it was not until the weekend that the SHAEF commanders actually stepped onto French soil. General Montgomery had arrived in France on June 8 to set up the 21st Army Group headquarters and two days later he called a conference with General Bradley and Lieutenant-General Sir Miles C. Dempsey of the British Second Army.

Left: This took place in a field alongside the Gendarmerie in Port-en-Bessin which lay on the dividing line between Omaha and Gold, the intention being to establish strategy to counter two strong German armoured divisions which were preventing the capture of Caen. *Right:* Unfortunately a house now stands in the field where Monty's Humber was parked, making for a difficult comparison. Then on Monday General Eisenhower accompanied General Marshall, the US Army Chief-of-Staff, to France to meet with General Bradley at Omaha beach *(below)*.

COMMUNIQUE No. 10   June 10

Allied progress continues along the whole of the beach-head. TREVIERES is in our hands.

On the eastern sector, severe fighting is in progress against strong enemy armoured forces. In the Cherbourg peninsula, our advanced patrols are west of the main railway in several places. In the CARENTAN sector, heavy fighting continues.

Intensive air operations in support of our ground and naval forces were resumed this morning in better weather.

Heavy bombers attacked enemy airfields in Brittany and Normandy. Their fighter escort remained in the zone of operations strafing enemy armour and transport. Other fighters attacked similar targets over a wide area.

Our medium bombers and their fighter escorts twice attacked targets close behind the enemy. These included road and rail transport, troop and tank concentrations, bridges and communication centers.

Widespread air cover was maintained over our beaches and the Channel.

Few enemy fighters were seen but flak was heavy at many points. According to reports so far received, three enemy aircraft have been destroyed. Seven of our fighters are missing.

Further troop-carrying and support operations to our forward formations were completed during the morning.

Allied warships have maintained their activity on the eastern and western flanks of the assault area in support of our ground forces.

Last night enemy E-Boats operated to the west of the assault area. They were intercepted by light coastal forces under the command of Lt. Collins RN and a number of brief engagements ensued. Some damage was inflicted on the enemy. Neither damage nor casualties were sustained by our forces.

Enemy patrol vessels heading toward the assault area this morning were attacked off Jersey by our coastal aircraft which also dispersed a cluster of E-Boats.

An unsuccessful attack was made by enemy aircraft on an Allied merchant convoy. One of the enemy was destroyed by gunfire from HMS *Wanderer* (Lt Comdr. R. F. Whinney, RN). There was no damage to the convoy or its escort.

Note that the German anti-tank ditch once lay in the left background.

COMMUNIQUE No. 11   June 11

As the result of an armoured thrust, British troops have reached TILLY-SUR-SEULLES. Naval guns yesterday lent effective support to our advance in this sector.

Further west, American forward troops are everywhere south of the flooded areas in the lower Aure valley. High ground between ISIGNY and CARENTAN has also been taken by American forces.

In the vicinity of CAEN, the enemy has made no progress against our positions despite continuous and vigorous attacks.

To the north-west of CARENTAN, we have crossed the Merderet river and, overcoming enemy resistance, have made further progress.

Allied aircraft pounded road and rail targets and airfields yesterday and last night in support of ground forces.

Over on the left flank, a bitter battle was being fought to advance on Caen. On the night of June 8/9, an armoured formation of Panther tanks from SS-Panzer-Regiment 12 advanced westwards along the N13 leading from Caen to Bayeux. One of the Panthers was knocked out just opposite the church in Bretteville-l'Orgueilleuse — reputedly the first Panther destroyed in the battle of Normandy. These photos were taken three weeks later when Bretteville was captured revealing that the tank had suffered a hit on the rear of the turret.

Heavy day bombers attacked airfields and inflicted considerable damage to rolling stock, bridges and armoured vehicles.

Thirteen enemy aircraft were destroyed. After escorting the bombers, formations of fighters attacked road and rail traffic, destroying an ammunition train. From these operations 23 fighters are missing.

Medium bombers, sometimes flying at 200 feet in the absence of enemy air opposition, bombed and strafed field guns and armoured vehicles. Considerable damage was inflicted in the FALAISE and ST LO area.

Fighter-bombers and fighters attacked rail yards at LAVAL and LE MANS at ground level. At AVRANCHES, armoured vehicles and a train were targets. In these operations, 15 enemy fighters were destroyed.

Last night heavy bombers attacked rail centers at ORLEANS, DREUX, ACHERES and VERSAILLES. There was strong opposition and 6 German aircraft were destroyed. Twenty bombers are missing.

Our night fighters were active, and 6 German bombers were destroyed, 5 of them over the battle area.

On June 9 the 38th Regimental Combat Team of the 2nd Division was charged with the advance across the N13 towards Trévières which they reached after some stiff fighting later that evening. The following morning the town was secured.

Allied warships also gave support to the armies yesterday by bombarding mobile batteries and enemy concentrations.

This morning the Allied air forces continued their supporting operations in spite of adverse weather. Strong forces of heavy day bombers attacked airfields, bridges, gun positions, and other targets ranging from the battle area to the vicinity of PARIS. Objectives in the Pas de Calais were also bombed. They were escorted by a strong force of fighters which attacked enemy tanks and lines of communication.

Medium bombers, fighter bombers and fighters attacked many targets behind the battle area including two railway bridges over the river Vire, military trains, railway sheds and yards, armored cars, and troop concentrations. Fighters maintained patrols over the battle area and shipping in the Channel. There was little enemy opposition in the air, though intense flak was met at some points.

Seaborne supplies are arriving at a satisfactory rate.

Enemy E-Boats were active again during the night and a number of brisk gun actions ensued during which one of the enemy was destroyed. Several of the enemy were damaged by gunfire before they evaded the pursuit. Early this morning our coastal aircraft attacked enemy E-Boats off OSTEND and left two of them on fire.

COMMUNIQUE No. 12   June 11

Good progress has been made on the right. Our troops are now fighting in the outskirts of MONTEBOURG. To the south-west, of the town we have held enemy counter-attacks attempting to stop our advance west of the main CHERBOURG railway.

American troops have liberated LISON and have advanced several miles southward on a broad front. In the vicinity of TILLY-SUR-SEULLES there is heavy fighting. The enemy has strong armored forces in this area and is stubbornly resisting our advance along the river Seulles. A particularly effective bombardment was carried out in this area by HMS *Argonaut* (Capt. E. W. L. Longley-Cook, RN) and HMS *Orion* (Capt. J. P. Gornall, RN).

Meanwhile in the effort to capture a port, the advance on Cherbourg was being led by the 8th Infantry Division and the 505th Parachute Infantry.

By June 11 they were closing on Montebourg, six miles north of Sainte-Mère-Église. Here, Signal Corps photographer Sergeant Peter J. Petrony pictured an M8 armoured car of the 801st Tank Destroyer Battalion entering the town during the northward advance toward the port of Cherbourg. In recognition of its suffering during the war, in June 1948 Montebourg was singled out for the award of the Croix de Guerre.

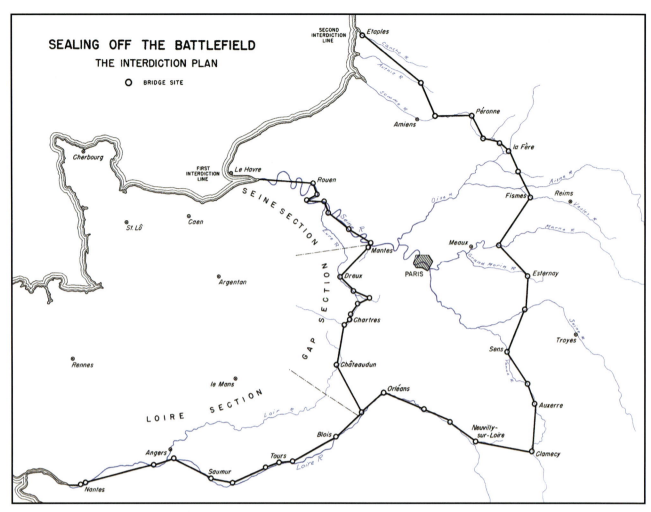

Operations to seal off the battlefield by destroying all the river bridges over the Seine and Loire (see also page 32), had made it difficult for the Germans to bring forward reinforcements.

Attacks on railway marshalling yards continued as well as on communication centres and Luftwaffe airfields maintaining Allied supremacy in the air.

COMMUNIQUE No. 13   June 12

The American advance east of the Vire river was continued into the FORET-DE-CERISY. Intense fighting against German armour continues in the TILLY-SUR-SEULLES area.

In the Cherbourg peninsula enemy mobile batteries have been under a heavy fire from Allied warships, and some further progress has been made west of the inundated valley of the Merderet river.

Air operations were curtailed sharply after midday yesterday when cloud and rain obscured much of the battle area.

After escorting heavy day bombers, our fighters joined fighter-bombers and rocket-firing fighters in attacking oil tanks, rail centers, and road and rail traffic, including several hundred railroad cars, tanks and armoured vehicles. From these operations 24 aircraft, including three heavy bombers, are missing.

During the night heavy bombers struck rail centers at NANTES, EVREUX and TOURS, and a railway bridge at MASSY PALAISEAU south of PARIS.

Allied medium and light bombers and rocket-firing aircraft hammered rolling-stock, a ferry terminal and road transport.

Intruder aircraft operated with success over enemy airfields in Holland and France.

However, the Luftwaffe had a surprise up its sleeve which was set in motion on the night of June 12/13 when the first four V1s — technically the FZG76 — were fired against Britain. The launch sites in northern France had already been spotted and bombed but with the air forces now currently devoted to supporting the troops ashore, no further attacks could be mounted until June 16. SHAEF made no mention of the V1 until June 20 in Communiqué No. 29. This site at Val-Ygot was refurbished in 1997 in memory of all the victims of the V-weapons (see *After the Battle* No. 122).

By June 7, the 6th Airborne Division had secured a large area east of the River Orne, repelling numerous attacks and bombardment from mortars and self-propelled guns. The small village of Bréville stands on high ground overlooking the plain towards Caen and it had to be taken. To this end, the 12th Battalion of the Parachute Regiment together with a company from the 12th Battalion, The Devonshire Regiment were detailed for the night attack on June 12 but the cost was high with nine officers and over 160 other ranks casualties and leaving much of the village in ruins.

ST NAZAIRE to LILLE. Armed reconnaissance, and medium-level bombing missions were flown from the tip of the Cherbourg peninsula over the battle area and south-eastward to JUVISY.

The largest single striking force of heavy day bombers ever dispatched from England struck this morning at a broad belt of 16 airfields, from DREUX to LILLE, and at six rail bridges in the ST NAZAIRE and PARIS areas, Strong forces of fighters, which escorted the bombers, scored against a variety of rail targets on their return flight.

The rail system focusing at RENNES was a major target for the day, with fighter-bombers severing in numerous places the railway lines leading to the city. Meanwhile, medium and light bombers carried out a succession of attacks on the railway installations there and highway junctions to the south of the battle area.

Rocket-firing aircraft attacked the military ferry at BERVILLE-SUR-MER. A ferry boat and a pier were left burning. Other rocket-firing planes on armed reconnaissance struck at a variety of armoured targets and motor transport in the combat zone.

Batteries at LA PERNELLE and at JOULINES, both near the tip of the Cherbourg peninsula, were attacked shortly before noon.

Our fighters continued their patrols over the beach and adjacent Channel waters. Eleven enemy aircraft were destroyed in this area, for the loss of eight of ours.

COMMUNIQUE No. 14   June 12

The fusion of our beach-heads is now complete and a coastal strip some 60 miles long is firmly in our hands. Its depth is being increased steadily.

Slight advances were made east of CAEN.

American troops in the Cherbourg peninsula have made further progress to the north and west. Additional road crossings over the coastal inundations are in our hands.

Further east the enemy was driven from the whole of the FORET-DE-CERISY. Fierce fighting between British and enemy armoured units continued between TILLY-SUR-SEULLES and CAEN.

Allied warships have been giving deep supporting fire in the centre and close support on the flanks of our armies.

Striking in very great strength, our aircraft today hammered enemy airfields and communications over a 400-mile arc from

Bréville was nearly all rebuilt after the war and is now much changed since 1944. This comparison was only made possible by the memories of older local residents.

Over on the western flank, the paratroopers of the 82nd Airborne Division were investing Pont-l'Abbé to the west of Sainte-Mère-Église. The village was subjected to a very heavy artillery and bombing regime and finally fell to the 358th Infantry on June 13 (see page 46). Meanwhile the dead were being buried but the SHAEF censor refused permission to release this photo.

Creuilly had been captured by the Canadians by the evening of D-Day, this shot of a Sherman flail mine-clearing tank seen thundering westwards past the church on the Rue de Bayeux being taken on the 14th.

COMMUNIQUE No. 15   **June 13**

After two days of hard fighting, American troops have liberated CARENTAN, the possession of which materially strengthens the link established between our two major beach-heads.

In the TILLY sector, strong enemy resistance continues. Steady progress has been made in other areas although there have been no marked advances.

The build-up is progressing satisfactorily. Railway targets and enemy troops and vehicles were the main objectives of our aircraft which struck again in great strength throughout the afternoon and evening yesterday.

Attacks were made by medium and fighter-bombers at various points on the railway system behind the enemy. The railway bridge over the Seine at MANTES-GASSICOURT was attacked. Tracks radiating from NOGENT LE ROTROU and LE MANS were cut at several places and oil tank cars and goods wagons were destroyed.

Other targets included troops and motor transport in the battle zone, radio installations and gun positions. A tank concentration in the FORET-DE-GRIMBOSQ, south-west of CAEN, was heavily bombed; in the course of this attack an ammunition dump blew up.

Fighters patrolled the beach areas and the Channel; other fighters destroyed a number of enemy aircraft on the ground.

Last night heavy bombers in great strength attacked the railway centers of AMIENS, ARRAS, CAMBRAI and POITIERS and bridges at CAEN. Twenty-three of these aircraft are missing. Medium and fighter-bombers bombed ferry installations over the Seine at CAUDEBEC, the rail center at MEZIDON, and other rail and road targets in the same area during the night. Four of these aircraft are missing.

Our night fighters destroyed 9 enemy aircraft over the beach-head and battle area.

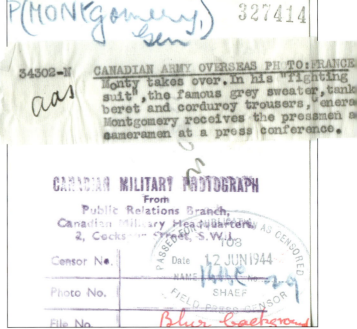

The château in the town had already been earmarked as the location for the Tactical Headquarters of the 21st Army Group and General Montgomery was based here from June 8 to June 22. He then moved his TAC HQ to Blay in the American sector, six miles west of Bayeux, to be closer to General Bradley's First Army HQ. This particular photograph is a good illustration of SHAEF's rigorous censorship, the picture being released the day following the press conference held in the grounds of the château but only with deletions to the background. On June 12 Churchill set foot in France with Field-Marshal Sir Alan Brooke, the Chief of the Imperial General Staff. Churchill later recalled that 'we lunched in a tent looking towards the enemy. The General was in the highest spirits. I asked him how far away was the actual front. He said about three miles. I asked him if he had a continuous line. He said "No". "What is there then to prevent an incursion of German armour breaking up our luncheon?" He said he did not think they would come.'

COMMUNIQUE No. 16   June 13

Allied troops have advanced generally in all sectors, particularly south of BAYEUX between the FORET-DE-CERISY and TILLY-SUR-SEULLES.

Two more towns have been liberated. They are TROARN on the left and LE HAM in the Cherbourg peninsula.

More than 10,000 prisoners have now been taken.

Attempts by enemy light craft were made last night to approach our lines of communication. The enemy was intercepted and driven off by our naval patrols.

Deteriorating weather today slowed down our air offensive. Nevertheless, escorted heavy day bombers continued their attacks on airfields to the west of PARIS at EVREUX FAUVILLE, DREUX and ILLIERS L'EVEQUE. A fuel dump at DREUX was set afire. Medium bombers were also active and again attacked the RENNES airfield.

Ranging from the Channel to TOURS, fighter-bombers swept the area for two and a half hours, destroying seven locomotives and some 50 vehicles, and strafing encampments.

E-Boats, which had been attacked off BOULOGNE early in the morning by coastal aircraft, were again hit later in the day by rocket and cannon-firing fighters. In these engagements, at least three enemy ships were sunk and others were left on fire or badly damaged.

Reconnaissance photographs show that severe damage was done to the railway centers of ORLEANS and RENNES, which were attacked by heavy bombers on the nights of June 10 and 11.

The Germans perceived the eastern end of the bridgehead to be the major threat and it was here that they concentrated their armoured units. Both the Panzer-Lehr-Division and the 12. SS-Panzer-Division had mounted fierce counter-attacks from the evening of June 8 onwards, sometimes supported by the 21. Panzer-Division. Elements of Panzer-Lehr are claimed to have reached within three miles of Bayeux on the night of June 10/11, demonstrating the potency of the German armour. However, by June 12 British and Canadian forces had regained the initiative, the British XXX Corps pushing inland towards Tilly-sur-Seulles and the 3rd Canadian Division towards Carpiquet. East of the Caen Canal, the 51st Highland Division had been used to reinforce the 6th Airborne Division and preparations were being made to push around the left flank. The effect of the pressure that Second Army was exerting meant that all of the German panzer divisions arriving at the invasion front were thrown into the battle to defend Caen. This they did in order to keep the British from expanding the lodgement area into the better tank country to the south. On June 13 a British armoured column broke through German lines to reach Villers-Bocage on the N175 between Vire and Caen but by the end of the day it proved to be one of the worst single actions suffered by any British armoured units during the war.

Most of the destruction had been caused — or was attributed to — the tank ace SS-Obersturmführer Michael Wittmann. As one might expect, no mention of the loss was made by SHAEF although one can read between the lines of Communiqué No. 17. Although the majority of the tanks knocked out were Cromwells of the 3rd County of London Yeomanry (the Sharpshooters), the Sherman Firefly with its very potent 17-pdr gun was much more effective and probably explains the interest of the Germans crowding round it at the junction at the top of the hill which leads down to the town. ('Allakafek' is Arabic slang for 'Can't be bothered' eminating from the days when the Sharpshooters were with the Eighth Army in the Western Desert.)

Already there had been instances of prisoners on both sides being shot but it was at Rots on the N13 just west of Caen that the first killings by Waffen-SS troops took place. The village lay in the path of the advance to take Carpiquet airfield by the North Nova Scotia Highlanders, over 20 prisoners being shot by the 12. SS-Panzer-Division after surrendering. When it was reported that over 40 Winnipeggers had also been murdered by SS Panzergrenadiers (see page 43), it created a no-holds-barred situation. Many British and American units routinely shot SS prisoners which was given as the reason why so few SS appeared in POW cages.

COMMUNIQUE No. 17   June 14

West of TILLY-SUR-SEULLES our armour found the enemy flank and struck south with great effect.

Advance patrols of our forces have now reached CAUMONT despite vigorous reaction on the part of the enemy.

In the sector between TILLY-SUR-SEULLES and CAEN, armoured clashes continued to take place. There is strong enemy pressure in the CARENTAN area.

Early yesterday evening, after a midday lull caused by bad weather, Allied aircraft resumed the offensive in one of the most concentrated efforts since the opening of the campaign. Enemy fighter opposition was sporadic but many of our aircraft encountered strong anti-aircraft fire.

Heavy day bombers with fighter escort attacked six bridges on the north-south railway system across the Brest peninsula and the airfields at BEAUVAIS/ NIVILLERS and BEAUMONT-SUR-OISE.

Further to the south-east, two large formations of fighter-bombers attacked railway bridges over the LOIRE at LA POSSONNIÈRE and PORT-BOULET; another formation patrolled the ETAMPES—ORLEANS railway seeking out traffic.

Throughout the Cherbourg peninsula, and in the immediate battle zone, large groups of fighter-bombers and rocket-firing aircraft attacked German troop concentrations, motor transport and other targets indicated by our ground forces.

Medium and light bombers in considerable strength bombed fuel dumps in the FORET D'ANDAIN and at DOMFRONT and ST MARTIN, and the highway junctions at MARIGNY and CANISY. Beach-head patrols continued throughout the day and evening.

During the night our fighters shot 3 enemy aircraft attacking the beach-head. Light bombers without loss attacked the railway yards at MEZIDON.

When Canadian war photographer Frank Dubervill entered Rots on June 15, he pictured two Shermans of the Canadian 10th Armoured Regiment (Fort Garry Horse) lost in the battle with the 12. SS-Panzer-Division on June 11-12 lying in front of the church.

Just 50 yards away on the Rue de l'Église lay this wreck of a German armoured car which possibly belonged to SS-Panzergrenadier-Regiment 26.

COMMUNIQUE No. 18   June 14

The armoured battle continued in the TILLY—CAEN area. The enemy has counter-attacked constantly in a furious attempt to stem our advance. We are holding firm and vigorously searching out weak points in his attack.

In the Cherbourg peninsula, the enemy is fighting fiercely. His heavy counter-attacks in the north have forced us to give some ground in the vicinity of MONTEBOURG. Further south we have made some gains. An enemy counter-thrust on CARENTAN has been repulsed.

In one of their most active mornings, Allied air forces today operated almost unopposed from the Brest peninsula to Belgium and Holland and penetrated deep into eastern France.

The effort of heavy day bombers exceeded even yesterday's figures. Targets included airfields at LE BOURGET, CREIL, ORLEANS/BRICY and ETAMPES/MONDESIR in France; BRUSSELS/MELSBROEK in Belgium and EINDHOVEN in Holland.

After escorting the bombers, our fighters hit numerous road, rail and military targets in France. Two enemy aircraft were destroyed. Fifteen bombers and eight fighters are missing from these widespread operations.

Before dawn, medium and light bombers hit communications targets near CAEN in close support of our ground forces. Attacks were made on a marshalling yard at MEZIDON and against bridges and traffic centers at AUNAY-SUR-ODON, FALAISE, VIRE, VIMOUTIERS and FLERS. Other formations struck far into the interior, bombing traffic points and moving targets in the CHARTRES region, south-west of PARIS, rail tracks west of LAVAL and railway guns south of the battle area.

No enemy fighters were encountered in these operations, but anti-aircraft fire was heavy. One medium bomber is missing.

Fighters, fighter-bombers, and rocket-firing fighters, some of them operating from bases in Normandy, gave close support to troops in the Cherbourg peninsula, cutting railroads and attacking large enemy convoys. Other fighters scored rocket hits on barges and batteries. Coastal aircraft harassed E-Boats near LE TOUQUET.

Shortly after midnight seven enemy M-class minesweepers were intercepted west of the Minquiers Rocks by ORP *Piorun* and HMS *Ashanti* (Lt Cdr. J. R. Barnes, RN) while on patrol. Action was joined at about 5,000 yards, the enemy being illuminated with star-shells. The enemy vessels were repeatedly hit and scattering, some of them sought shelter under the guns of the coastal batteries on the island of Jersey. Of the seven enemy vessels engaged, three were observed to sink and one was seen to receive such damage that its survival is considered unlikely. Of the remaining three, two were left stopped and burning fiercely.

North-east of CAP DE LA HAGUE, three enemy patrol vessels were intercepted and attacked early this morning by light coastal forces commanded by Lt H. Ascoli, RNVR. The first ship in the enemy line was as hit with a torpedo and the second set on fire.

The murdered Canadians have their memorial in Audrieu, some four miles west of Rots. This picture shows infantry from the Hampshire Regiment (49th Division) passing the ruined church on June 16.

The plaque on the wall of the church is dedicated to the memory of the men of the Royal Winnipeg Rifles, the 3rd Anti-Tank Regiment, the 6th Field Company, Royal Canadian Engineers, and the Cameron Highlanders of Ottawa who were murdered while prisoners of war at the Château d'Audrieu and near Le Mesnil-Patry and at Le Haut-du-Bosq.

COMMUNIQUE No. 19   June 15

On all parts of the front, Allied forces continue to carry the fight to the enemy.

The heaviest fighting has taken place in the CARENTAN, MONTEBOURG and CAEN areas. Airborne troops have successfully beaten off attempts made by the Germans to retake CARENTAN, and are again pushing southward from the town. They have also advanced further to the west in the LES SABLONS—BAUPTE vicinity.

Heavy armoured attacks and counter-attacks persist in the CAEN—TILLY-SUR-SEULLES areas.

The development of the beaches is making good progress and the unloading of troops and stores is steadily increasing.

Not far away lay the little village of Cristot which was right in the middle of the battles for Tilly-sur-Seulles. This knocked-out German half-track was photographed near the church. It was here that the 6th Canadian Armoured Regiment had fought a duel on June 11, losing 37 tanks and 96 killed, wounded and missing.

The Allied air forces continued their attacks yesterday afternoon and evening on communications and road convoys in the Cherbourg peninsula in support of our ground forces. Rail traffic was also bombed and in a surprise attack on the enemy airfield at LE MANS, about a dozen enemy aircraft were destroyed on the ground.

Before dusk heavy night bombers, with fighter escort, attacked E-Boats and the dockside at LE HAVRE. During the night they bombed railway centers at DOUAI, CAMBRAI and ST POL and troop concentrations at EVRECY and AUNAY-SUR-ODON. Five bombers are missing from these operations.

Light bombers made night attacks on enemy convoys end concentrations moving on the roads towards the battle area.

Reports as yet incomplete show that 17 enemy aircraft were destroyed in air combat since noon yesterday. Fourteen of our fighters are missing. Seven more enemy aircraft were shot down over Normandy during the night.

Perhaps this is the photographer's own Jeep parked a little further down the road.

COMMUNIQUE No. 20   June 15

Further steady progress has been made west of CARENTAN and between the rivers Vire and Elle.

Allied troops have repulsed several violent armoured attacks in the CAUMONT—TILLY sector with considerable loss to the enemy. In the Cherbourg peninsula, ground gained in the area of QUINEVILLE has made available a valuable new outlet from the beaches.

During yesterday mobile batteries on the flanks were engaged as necessary by Allied warships. On the eastern flank HMS *Belfast* (Capt A. H. Maxwell-Hyslop, RN) engaged the batteries of LE HAVRE.

During an unsuccessful enemy air attack in the western assault area, an enemy aircraft was shot down by the USS *Augusta* (Capt E. H. Jones, USN) wearing the flag of Rear-Admiral Alan Goodrich Kirk, USN.

Convoys of Allied merchant ships are arriving satisfactorily and the armies continue to build up with men, stores and equipment.

'Led by a white lieutenant, colored troops march forward along a dusty French road.' So runs the wartime caption approved by Censor No. 96 on June 13 although no location was given and a signpost was deliberately blotted out. Nevertheless, Jean Paul is never to be outdone and after a long investigation he pinpointed the spot as being the crossroads just west of Colleville-sur-Mer at a place called Le Bray. The squad is marching along the Gc 32 (now the D514).

Allied aircraft in great strength ranged from the Cherbourg peninsula southwards to the LOIRE and eastwards to CHARTRES and PARIS, continuing their attacks on communications, airfields, and tactical targets. Coastal aircraft kept up their attacks on enemy shipping in the Channel early today.

Heavy bombers in great strength attacked many targets in France this morning, including rail yards at ANGOULEME, airfields near BORDEAUX and PARIS, and railway bridges near TOURS. They were escorted by strong forces of fighters which also strafed ground targets. In these operations 12 enemy planes were destroyed. Three of our bombers and three of our fighters are missing.

Medium and light bombers attacked bridges at CONDE-SUR-NOIREAU, ST LO, LESSAY, CHARTRES and COLTAINVILLE, and a road junction at ARGENTAN. None of the bombers was lost.

Fighter-bombers and fighters provided close support for the ground forces and swept over Normandy attacking supply dumps, troop concentrations, tanks, convoys, and railway bridges. Other fighters attacked a ferry at QUILLEBEUF near the mouth of the Seine. In the course of a patrol this morning five enemy fighters were destroyed near EVREUX.

Photographic reconnaissance shows that the German naval forces in LE HAVRE suffered very severely from the attack by heavy night bombers on the evening of June 14.

The First Army's assault forces on D-Day at Omaha had less than 500 Negro soldiers out of the 29,714 men landing. These were one section of the 327th Quartermaster Service Company and the 320th Anti-Aircraft Balloon Battalion. At Utah there were 1,200 Negroes split between the second section of the 320th Balloon Battalion, the 582nd Engineer Dump Truck Company, the 385th Quartermaster Truck Company and the 490th Port Battalion. Representative of the intial use of Negro units in action was the 969th Field Artillery Battalion which landed at Utah on July 9 under the command of Lieutenant Colonel Hubert D. Barnes although the first armoured unit — the 761st Tank Battalion — did not reach France until October.

COMMUNIQUE No. 21   June 15

There has been no major change in any sector, but Allied troops have made further progress west of PONT-L'ABBE. All attempts by the enemy to gain the initiative have been frustrated and his counter-attacks have been successfully repelled. Our striking power grows steadily.

Despite rain and limited visibility over many parts of France yesterday, the Allied air forces flew 3,000 sorties, many of them by aircraft based in France attacking targets indicated by advanced air force and army headquarters.

In the afternoon medium bombers hit fuel and supply dumps, bridges and other communications targets from VALOGNES in the Cherbourg peninsula to LAVAL and DOMFRONT about 75 miles behind the enemy lines. One medium bomber is missing.

Fighter-bombers, fighters and rocket-firing fighters were active throughout the day. Their objectives included railway yards at LE MANS, FOUGERES, MAYENNE, VIRE, GRANVILLE, FOLLIGNY, HYENVILLE, CHARTRES and COLTAINVILLE, and a bridge over the Orne near AMAYE. East of CAEN fighter-bombers attacked enemy troops and tanks sheltering in woods and orchards. Others bombed Seine river ferries, observation posts, radio stations, artillery concentrations and several bridges and railway lines near ST LO. In these activities 14 enemy aircraft were destroyed for the loss of 7 of ours.

Last night our heavy bombers in great strength attacked concentrations of E- and R-Boats and minesweepers in BOULOGNE harbour as well as railway centers at VALENCIENNES and LENS and fuel dumps at CHATELLERAULT and FOUILLARD. Fourteen bombers are missing.

Four enemy aircraft were destroyed and others damaged over France by our night intruders.

Pont-l'Abbé fell to the 82nd Airborne Division on June 14, securing the bridge at the northern end of the town.

Bernard Paich, who took the comparison for us, comments that 'Pont-l'Abbé was mainly destroyed and the houses have been rebuilt a few metres behind the original plots. With the help of Loïc Dennebouy, I found that the troops in the picture are marching westward having entered the town via the roads now bearing the names Rue de la Libération and the Rue d'Utah Beach. The village has now been beautifully restored in typical Normandy style.'

When General Morgan was given the task of planning the invasion in August 1943, he realised that the armies would require around 40,000 tons of stores, fuel and ammunition per day. His plan submitted to the Chiefs-of-Staff relied on creating sheltered water on the beaches for unloading supplies which resulted in the creation of two prefabricated harbours to be towed to France in sections. Mulberry 'A' was to be positioned off Omaha and Mulberry 'B' on Gold, each covering an area equivalent to that of Dover harbour. They were to provide sheltered water by D+4 and to be fully established by D+14. The daily unloading target for the two Mulberries was 3,000 tons of stores by D+4; 7,000 tons and 2,500 vehicles by D+8, building to 12,000 tons and 2,500 unwaterproofed vehicles. Initially it was intended that they would have a life of 90 days at which point captured ports would take over. Blockships were to be provided using less elaborate 'Gooseberry' breakwaters on the other beaches. Although Mulberry 'A' *(above)* was not scheduled to be fully operational until D+18 (June 24), by D+12 a total of 314,504 out of the planned 358,139 men had crossed the American beaches and 11 of the planned build-up of 12 divisions were ashore.

COMMUNIQUE No. 22 June 16

Advances by Allied forces westward from PONT-L'ABBE in the Cherbourg peninsula have continued. Our troops had local successes in the TILLY sector, but the town remained in enemy hands. Active patrolling has been kept up by both sides.

Adverse weather during the morning once again restricted our air activity which was confined to limited patrols over the supply beaches and adjacent Channel waters and the immediate battle zone.

Yesterday HMS *Ramillies* (Capt G. H. Middleton, RN) engaged a battery at BENERVILLE on our eastern flank, which she silenced after an hour's duel, while HMS *Nelson* (Capt A. H. Maxwell Hyslop, RN) engaged an enemy battery north of LE HAVRE, which had been firing into the anchorage. Enemy batteries and concentrations were bombarded throughout the day by Allied cruisers.

On the western flank, the USS *Texas* (Capt C. A. Baker, USN), wearing the flag of Rear-Admiral Carleton F. Bryant, USN, the USS *Nevada* (Capt P. M. Rhea, USN) and the USS *Arkansas* (Capt F. G. Richards, USN) carried out heavy bombardments in support of the armies near ISIGNY and CARENTAN.

Mulberry 'B' *(above)* was located facing Arromanches, the main pierhead about three-quarters of a mile from the shore being completed by June 14. Within three days the discharge of cargo had reached 2,000 tons per day.

BRIDGE

Meantime, the drive to cut Cotentin Peninsula as the pre-requisite for the northward attack on Cherbourg continued. On June 14 a new offensive began along the road from Pont-l'Abbé towards St Sauveur-le-Vicomte, taken by troops of the 82nd Airborne Division. In a three-day operation, the division had advanced seven miles, captured a vital bridgehead, decimated the German 91. Luftlande-Division which suffered over 1,000 casualties, and hastened the fall of Cherbourg by at least two weeks.

COMMUNIQUE No. 23   **June 17**

Allied troops continue their advance with leading elements in ST SAUVEUR-LE-VICOMTE. Local advances were made in the face of heavy enemy opposition between CAUMONT and TILLY. East of CAEN a strong enemy attack was beaten off.

Throughout yesterday Allied cruisers and destroyers engaged gun batteries which the enemy had established on the eastern bank of the river Orne.

Concentrations of enemy armour north-east of CAEN were bombarded by HMS *Ramillies* (Capt G. H. Middleton, RN).

Merchant convoys continue to arrive at beaches steadily and in safety.

Adverse weather again restricted air operations yesterday afternoon and evening. Heavy bombers attacked enemy airfields near PARIS and LAON and objectives in the Pas de Calais. Railway targets, road transport and tanks behind the battle zone were attacked by fighters and fighter-bombers, and an ammunition dump near CAEN by medium bombers. Fighters also flew protective patrols and escorted the bombers.

During the night our light bombers attacked supply dumps in the Cherbourg peninsula. Two enemy aircraft were shot down over Normandy.

COMMUNIQUE No. 24   **June 17**

Allied forces have pushed deeper into Normandy. Villages east and west of TILLY-SUR-SEULLES have been freed of the enemy.

Advancing two miles south of ISIGNY, our troops have reached the Vire et Taute Canal.

In the Cherbourg peninsula, ST SAUVEUR-LE-VICOMTE has been liberated.

Air operations were sharply curtailed from dawn to midday when bad weather obscured much of the battle area. Nevertheless, fighter-bombers and rocket-firing fighters attacked railway yards, motor convoys and bridges leading to the Cherbourg peninsula.

A convoy of horse-drawn vehicles was destroyed at LA TRAVERSERIE and enemy machine-gun nests at FOLLIGNY were strafed. No enemy fighters were encountered during these operations. Shortly after noon, medium forces of heavy bombers, with fighter escort, attacked 7 enemy airfields in southern Normandy. Three enemy aircraft were destroyed. Two of our bombers and one fighter are missing.

Other fighters destroyed a railroad bridge across the Somme canal.

Early this morning coastal aircraft attacked enemy shipping in the Channel.

Saint-Sauveur-le-Vicomte had suffered grievously and all the buildings at the eastern end around the junction of the Coutances—La Haye-du-Puits roads have been completely rebuilt. (We told the detailed story of the battle for the town in *After the Battle* No. 103.)

```
SPECIAL COMMUNIQUE NO. 1        17 June 1944

     Since the 6th June, 1944, the Army of the French Forces of
the Interior has increased both in size and in the scope of its
activities. This army has undertaken a large plan of sabotage
which includes in part the paralysing of rail and road traffic
and the interruption of telegraph and telephone communications.
     In the majority of cases their objectives have been attained.
     The destruction of railways has been most effective. Bridges
have been destroyed, derailment effected and at least 70 locomo-
tives have been sabotaged.
     It is reported that both road and rail traffic is completely
stopped in the Valley of the RHONE.
     Canals have not been spared. One has been damaged, one cut
and another has been put out of action. Four consecutive locks of
another have been destroyed.
     Subterranean cables have been cut in many places, and, al-
though some were well defended, they have been attacked and des-
troyed.
     Many acts of sabotage have been carried out against transfor-
mer stations.
     It is neither possible nor desirable to enumerate all of the
many effective acts of destruction which have been carried out.
However, these multiple and simultaneous acts of sabotage, co-
ordinated with the Allied air effort, have delayed considerably
the movement of German reserves to the combat zone.
     Direct action also has been taken against the enemy. The
Maquis are reported to have taken 300 prisoners. German garri-
sons have been attacked. In some areas villages have been occu-
pied. Street fighting has occurred elsewhere. Enemy detachments
have been destroyed.
     Guerrilla operations against the enemy are in full swing and
in some areas the Army of the French Forces of the Interior are in
full control.
     At the end of the first week of operations on the shores of
FRANCE, the Army of the French Forces of the Interior has, with
its British and American comrades, played its assigned role in
the Battle of Liberation.
```

Up until now, the role of the Resistance forces — the French Forces of the Interior or FFI — had not been released to the public but a special communiqué (reproduced here in facsimile) was produced by SHAEF. No photographs were made available but this sequence of 'French partisans giving valuable assistance to GIs who are looking for Nazi snipers' was released on July 31.

COMMUNIQUE No. 25   June 18

Allied forces in the area of ST SAUVEUR-LE-VICOMTE have made further progress westwards. Local clashes continue in the TILLY and CAEN sectors.

Clearing weather in the late afternoon yesterday permitted the resumption of our tactical air operations on a considerable scale. Enemy air opposition was sporadic.

Heavy day bombers struck at 5 enemy airfields and landing strips in the TOURS—NANTES area. Their fighter escort later strafed targets of opportunity. Our medium and light bombers were brought into action with good results against fuel dumps in the BOIS DU HOMME (south of CAUMONT) and in the SENONCHES—LA LOUPE area (west of CHARTRES). Other medium bomber formations attacked the railway yards at MEZIDON and a 40-mile stretch of track between LE MERLERAULT and ST LUBIN on the PARIS—GRANVILLE line.

Five gun emplacements were attacked by fighter-bombers which were active during the afternoon against a variety of targets in an area from COUTANCES to LES PIEUX and eastward across the Cherbourg peninsula to QUETTEHOU. Constant armed reconnaissance patrols were flown over the combat zone in front of our troops. Other formations of fighter-bombers attacked military objectives in northern France.

Enemy communications were attacked at many points by light bombers on offensive patrols last night.

One of the most spectacular operations carried out by the FFI in Normandy was the destruction of the road bridge over the Seine at Vernon in August. The names of the 11 men who lost their lives are now immortalised in a plaque on the bridge.

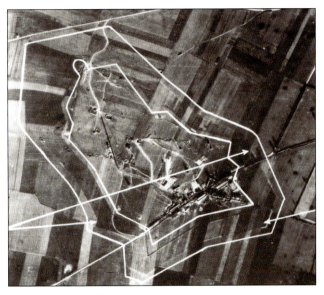 

In Eisenhower's 1946 report on 'Overlord' for the Combined Chiefs-of-Staff, he made particular mention of the German radar installation-cum-strong point at Douvres-la-Déliverande: 'Meanwhile, the Allies had their first experience of the enemy's skill and determination in holding out in fortified strong points behind our lines. Although German claims of the effects of these strong points in delaying the development of our operations were greatly exaggerated, it was undeniably difficult to eliminate the suicide squads by whom they were held. The biggest of these points was at Douvres in the Canadian sector, where the underground installations extended to 300 feet below the surface. It was not until June 17 that the garrison here was compelled to surrender.' *Left:* This early American reconnaissance photograph was taken during its construction in 1942. *Right:* The remains of the German installation have been preserved today as Le Musée Radar.

COMMUNIQUE No. 26   June 18

Allied troops have cut off the Cherbourg peninsula from the rest of Normandy, reaching the west coast near BARNEVILLE-SUR-MER. In the center, a steady advance east of the Vire has brought us within six miles of ST LO.

The strong point at DOUVRES, which had been holding out, was captured yesterday with over 150 prisoners. We lost one man killed in the final assault. More than 15,000 prisoners have been counted so far.

Low clouds over many parts of the battle area again restricted Allied air activity from midnight until noon today. Last night 10 enemy aircraft were destroyed by our fighters protecting the beaches.

This morning, medium and light bombers successfully attacked railway yards at RENNES. They also bombed objectives in the FORET-DES-ANDAINES, east of DOMFRONT, and other military and transport targets behind the enemy lines. All our bombers returned safely.

Fighter-bombers struck at MONTREUIL, BELLAY and SAUMUR damaging trains, locomotives, railway bridges and highways. Fighters maintained armed reconnaissance beyond the battle zone and attacked road and rail transport on the move at many points.

After initial attempts to capture the position on D+4 failed, the attack was called off and the installation bypassed. Ten days later the 26th Assault Squadron of the Royal Engineers was brought in with Churchill flails to tackle the minefield with support of No. 41 Commando and the 22nd Dragoons: 'In clouds of dust, and with a shattering clanking of chains, the flails moved into the minefield. German machine guns stuttered away here and there, swishing around them apparently at random. From a patch of dead ground, a group of supporting flails, hull down, loosed off machine guns and 75mm shell to keep the German heads down. For half an hour and more, the flails moved smoothly on, biting through the minefield and touching off mines that sent up tall pillars of heavy black smoke. Again a sudden quiet as the commandos closed in and then Germans began to pour out with hands up.'

The casualties suffered in the attempt to take the position were later given as three men killed and seven wounded — not as reported by the SHAEF communiqué.

COMMUNIQUE No. 27   June 19

The wedge across the base of the Cherbourg peninsula is being strengthened and widened.

In the TILLY-SUR-SEULLES area attacks by our troops have met strong opposition from enemy armour and infantry supported by heavy artillery fire. Further east a small counter-attack was thrown back.

The enemy battery at HOULGATE, east of OUISTREHAM, has been silent for 36 hours after an accurate bombardment by HMS *Ramillies*.

Weather again retarded air activity over the battle zone from noon yesterday until daybreak today. Nevertheless fighters and fighter-bombers ranged from the Cherbourg peninsula to LISIEUX in the east and to ALENCON in the south, striking at communications and transport.

Bridges, railway cars, locomotives and troops were attacked by fighters between VALOGNES, BRICQUEBEC and CARTERET. Rocket-firing planes and dive bombers attacked enemy ammunition dumps hidden in a forest; also canal bridges, ferries, motor lorries and a heavy concentration of troops between CAEN, FALAISE and MONTIGNY.

Sweeping from ARRAS and AMIENS to the outskirts of PARIS, long-range fighters searched out targets of opportunity throughout the day. They were unmolested by enemy aircraft. Attacks on road and rail targets were continued after dark by light bombers. Night fighters destroyed two enemy bombers over the beach.

COMMUNIQUE No. 28   June 19

The Allies' stranglehold on the Cherbourg peninsula has been strengthened by a series of local advances.

An enemy attack was repulsed near TILLY where heavy fighting continues. In the CAEN area enemy shelling has increased considerably.

No sooner had the two Mulberry ports began to bring ashore sizeable tonnage than the weather intervened. At 0330 on June 19, the north-easterly wind increased to Force 7 producing waves up to 12 feet high — twice the design strength of the components. Hundreds of vessels of all sizes were torn free of their moorings and tossed against the unloading piers adding to the destruction. Mulberry 'A' caught the full force of the sea although all this was downplayed by the SHAEF communiqué. Ten days later it was decided to abandon the Omaha Mulberry.

Allied warships continued to give support in the eastern flank yesterday by engaging enemy mobile batteries. North of CAEN successful shoots were carried out by HMS *Diadem* against a concentration of enemy armour.

Bad weather severely restricted the activity of the Allied Air Forces this morning.

Heavy bombers escorted by fighters attacked pilotless aircraft emplacements in the Pas de Calais and airfields in south-west France. Among the airfields were BORDEAUX/MERIGNAC, CAZAUX, LANDES-DE-BUSSAC, and CORME-ECLUSE. Seven bombers and 16 fighters are missing.

Fighter-bombers attacked an airfield near RENNES and fighters flew patrols over the beaches and the Channel.

Wreckage piled on the foreshore from Mulberry 'B' at Arromanches. With superhuman efforts, four days after the storm the overall discharge had risen to 40,000 tons and the backlog of ships waiting to be unloaded had been cleared.

Exit roads from the beaches had to be improved and narrow lanes widened and bomb damage repaired. *Left:* These Royal Engineers are working on the D112 leading from Crépon to Bayeux. *Right:* The improved road at Maronnes today.

COMMUNIQUE No. 29   June 20

Co-ordinated attacks all along the north front in the Cherbourg peninsula have brought the port under artillery fire. After liberating the town of BRIQUEBEC, Allied troops made further advances toward the village of RAUVILLE-LA-BIGOT.

East of VALOGNES our troops gained some ground. Another advance reached to within two miles of VALOGNES and cut the road from there to BRIQUEBEC.

Further east the enemy was once again driven from TILLY-SUR-SEULLES after fierce fighting.

Heavy day bombers attacked the Pas de Calais yesterday afternoon striking through thick clouds at the pilotless aircraft launching sites. From this second attack of the day, three bombers are missing. Small formation of medium bombers and fighter-bombers also attacked these targets.

In spite of bad weather, light aircraft escorted shipping and patrolled the beaches. Some fighters broke through the cloud screen to bomb and strafe locomotives, motor vehicles, barges and warehouses behind the lines. They encountered intense flak at low level. From these operations two medium bombers and 15 fighters are missing.

COMMUNIQUE No. 30   June 20

Allied troops are attacking the outer defences of CHERBOURG. MONTEBOURG has been liberated and our forces are on the three sides of VALOGNES, where heavy fighting is in progress.

Our positions in the area of TILLY are firm. Very heavy fighting continued near HOTTOT yesterday.

Bad weather in the battle area limited air operations until midday today. Fighter-bombers and bombers with fighter escort attacked flying bomb bases in the Pas de Calais area during the morning. Several hits were scored on these and other military installations. Other formations of fighter-bombers hit a bridge over the Loire near NANTES, destroyed a railway bridge at GRANVILLE, and bombed rolling stock and motor transport at TRAPPES, south-west of PARIS.

Fighter-bombers also successfully attacked railway tracks at a number of places both north and south of CHARTRES. Twelve FW 190's attempted to interfere with operation. Five of them were destroyed in the air combat for the loss of three of our aircraft.

Having encountered stiff resistance in front of Caen, the main effort was shifted to the Tilly-sur-Seulles area to try to out-flank the German positions from the east. The first attack on Tilly, four miles south-west from Bretteville, took place on June 10 supported by naval gunfire although it was not finally captured until June 19.

Further inland the struggle continued west of Caen as Eisenhower wrote in his report: 'In the British-Canadian sector, chief interest centred in the thrust by the British 3rd and Canadian 3rd Divisions toward Caen. Exploiting the success achieved on D-Day, they pushed southward and succeeded on June 7 in reaching points some two or three miles north and north-west of the city. However, the enemy fully appreciated the danger in this sector and employing the tanks of 21st Panzer and 12th SS Panzer Divisions, counter-attacked successfully in ideal tank country. This counter-attack penetrated nearly to the coast, and drove a wedge between the two Allied divisions, preventing a combined attack on Caen for the time being. Subsequent events showed that the retention of the city was the key to the main enemy strategy and during the struggles of the following weeks, the Germans fought furiously to deny us possession.' These Canadians are posting a warning in a side road at Bretteville on June 20.

COMMUNIQUE No. 31   June 21

Allied troops advancing on CHERBOURG have reached prepared positions defending the deep water port.

VALOGNES, LES PIEUX, COUVILLE and RAUVILLE-LA-BIGOT have been liberated. In the TILLY area three German attacks have been held. There has been active patrolling on all other sectors of the front.

Flying-bomb sites in the Pas de Calais, a coastal battery at HOULGATE and gun positions in the Cherbourg peninsula were targets for medium and fighter-bombers yesterday afternoon and evening.

Other fighter-bombers struck at locomotives, troop trains and railway installations in widespread areas of northern France. Preliminary reports show that eleven enemy aircraft were destroyed, while four of ours are missing.

Last night light bombers attacked railway centers at MEZIDON and CHARTRES and other enemy communications. Night fighters destroyed two enemy aircraft.

One of the most dramatic clashes took place in Lingèvres, a mile to the west of Tilly. These two Panthers belonging to Panzer-Regiment 6 were pictured on June 20 although the first tank attack by Panzer-Lehr-Regiment 130 against the town had taken place on June 11. Then on June 15, during a second attack, a Panther was knocked out by the church at the top of the hill. Driver R. S. Bullen of the Hertfordshire Yeomanry: 'The Panther stopped at the crossroads and started traversing its gun in our direction. Whether it was going to fire at us with its co-ax or finish off our Sherman we didn't know. Fortunately a Firefly of the 4/7 Dragoons, which looked as if it had been following the Panther, stopped where the German tank had originally halted. It fired two quick shots of AP at 300 yards. The Panther had no chance with two 17-pounders up its stern!'

Civilians stare in amazement at the Panther and Sherman lying at point-blank range on either side of the town's war memorial.

This photo of US aviation engineers laying Square Mesh Tracking (SMT) for an airfield on June 17 was specially released by SHAEF on June 21. Although no location was given — and there were several airstrips under construction by that date — A-6 at Beuzeville was the first to be opened so it may well illustrate that airfield as it was completed on June 18.

COMMUNIQUE No. 32   **June 21**

Allied forces have made further progress in the battle for CHERBOURG and the area held by the enemy is steadily diminishing. Our advance up the entire peninsula has been rapid. On the east we have driven forward astride the main road north from VALOGNES. To the west a broad thrust has taken us to within five miles of the sea, liberating the villages of TEURTHEVILLE-HAGUE and ACQUEVILLE.

Heavy fighting continues in the TILLY—CAEN area, where attacks and counter-attacks have left the front generally unchanged. In other sectors there has been patrol activity.

Dense cloud over the battle area limited air operations this morning. Five flying bomb sites between CALAIS and AMIENS were attacked by medium and light bombers.

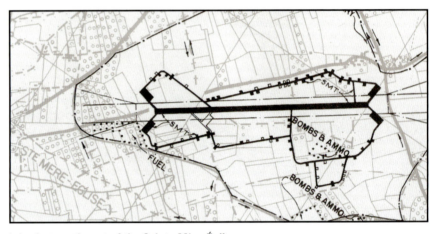

It lay just north-east of the Sainte-Mère-Église.

Valognes on the road to Cherbourg had been very heavily bombed from June 6 onwards, the worst raid being on the 8th when the centre of the town was destroyed, burying over 100 civilians under the rubble. More bombing and shelling followed and when the Americans finally entered the town on June 20, they found the streets so choked with debris that they were impassable for several days. *Left:* This picture was taken on June 24 when engineers were clearing a passage through the ruins. The Jeep named *Always Ruth* belonged to the 298th Engineer Combat Battalion. *Right:* The same spot today on the Rue de la Poterie, looking south towards the Place Vicq d'Azir. This part of Valognes was so utterly devastated that it had to be completely rebuilt after the war. However, the surviving parts of the Église Saint-Malo were incorporated into the new church.

COMMUNIQUE No. 33   June 22

The Allied drive on CHERBOURG has continued to make good progress with advances of two to three miles along the entire front.

On the right, Allied forces have reached the river Saire near the village of LE THEIL. On the left, they penetrated to within three miles of the sea in the vicinity of STE CROIX-HAGUE.

In the center, substantial gains have been made along the main road from VALOGNES to CHERBOURG.

In the TILLY sector enemy artillery and mortar fire was unusually heavy. Patrol activity continued in other areas.

Fighter-bombers operated successfully against the rail system leading west from PARIS, scoring hits on bridges at CHARTRES, COLTAINVILLE, CONCHES and CHERISY.

Slight enemy opposition was encountered in attacks on rail targets in the AUNAY and EVREUX areas. At least five enemy aircraft were destroyed without loss.

Flying bomb bases across the Channel were attacked by forces of heavy and medium bombers. Fighter escorts later strafed railway yards and canal barges at RIBECOURT, MONTDIDIER and CHAUNY. The bombing and strafing missions were without loss.

Six oil storage tanks at NIORT were in flames after a low-level attack.

COMMUNIQUE No. 34   June 22

The encirclement of the fortress of CHERBOURG is now almost complete. We have crossed the road leading east from the port to ST PIERRE-EGLISE and have liberated the town.

There is nothing to report from other sectors of the front.

In better weather hundreds of Allied fighter aircraft, many of them armed with rocket projectiles and bombs, swarmed over north-western France from dawn to midday to harass enemy reinforcements moving westward from the PARIS area.

Strong points in CHERBOURG were included in bombing and strafing missions in close support of ground forces.

Heavy day bombers continued the assault on flying bomb installations across the Channel. After escorting the bombers, fighters attacked locomotives, loaded freight and oil cars, barges and motor transport.

Except for heavy anti-aircraft fire in many areas, our aircraft encountered little opposition.

Private Malvin A. Gillespie, of Plymouth, Massachusetts, leading a group of German prisoners through a less-damaged section of Valognes on June 21.

The picture was taken in Rue des Religieuses and the prisoners were being marched south-eastwards in the direction of Montebourg. Jean Paul Pallud took the comparison.

COMMUNIQUE No. 35   June 23

Operations against the fortress of CHERBOURG are proceeding satisfactorily. Offensive action and local attacks have effectively pinned down enemy formations in the eastern sectors.

In preparation for our ground operations, waves of fighter-bombers attacked the strongly fortified German positions encircling CHERBOURG during the day and again at dusk yesterday. They went in, often at pistol range, to bomb forts, concrete pillboxes, ammunition dumps, oil stores and troop concentrations. Medium bombers also took part. Our aircraft flew through intense ground fire.

Strong forces of heavy bombers attacked rail and road transport, barges, and oil containers between the coast and PARIS, and the rail junctions at LILLE and GHENT. During these operations, six enemy aircraft were destroyed. Ten of our bombers and nine fighters are missing.

Light and medium bombers destroyed a steel works near CAEN. Fighter-bombers attacked bridges north-east of PARIS.

In Alderney, one of the Channel Isles, gun posts and barracks were the target for bombers and fighters. During the evening other formations raided fuel dumps at FORET-DE-CONCHES and BAGNOLES-DE-L'ORNE, railway yards at ST QUENTIN and ARMENTIERES and tracks and fuel tanks at DREUX and VERNEUIL.

After dark heavies attacked the rail centers at RHEIMS and LAON in force thus completing the biggest air effort for some days. Seven bombers are missing.

Rail targets at LISIEUX, DREUX and EVREUX were the night targets for our light bombers. Last night our fighters and intruders destroyed seven enemy aircraft over northern France.

The weather over the beach-head has moderated and unloading is proceeding.

COMMUNIQUE No. 36   June 23

Pressure on the CHERBOURG defences is increasing. Patrols east of CHERBOURG are finding little opposition in the sector between CAP LEVY and ST VAAST.

Local fighting continues in the CAEN—TILLY area.

Early this morning an escorted enemy convoy was intercepted south of Jersey by light coastal forces. One enemy armed trawler was sunk. One of the convoy was left ablaze and damage inflicted on the remainder by gunfire.

Weather restricted air operations this morning. Fighters and fighter-bombers attacked varied rail targets beyond the battle area including the yards at MÉZIDON and a junction north of LE MANS. Rail lines south of TOURS and ORLEANS were cut. Bridges and tracks at NANTES, LA ROCHE, SAUMUR and NIORT and to the east and south-east of GRANVILLE were attacked. Locomotives and other rail targets in the PARIS and CHATEAUBRIANT areas were shot up. Preliminary reports show 11 enemy aircraft destroyed. None of ours is missing.

Heavy day bombers, escorted by fighters, attacked, without loss, flying bomb installations in the Pas de Calais.

Coastal aircraft attacked E-Boats in the eastern Channel, sinking two, probably sinking three more and damaging several others. A minesweeper was also damaged.

Reconnaissance photographs show much rolling stock destroyed in attacks by heavy night bombers on railway yards at LAON and RHEIMS last night. Main lines were effectively blocked at many points by direct hits.

This Panther, somewhere on the road to Tilly, once belonged to the Panzer-Lehr-Regiment.

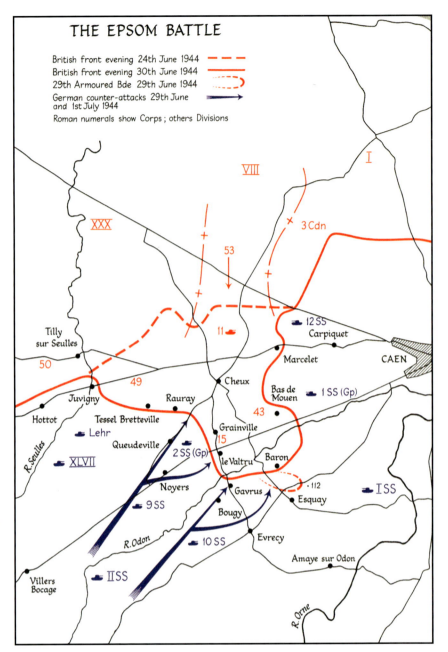

The storm, which had done so much damage to the prefabricated ports, had seriously interfered with the build-up of the armies ashore and for four days the Americans were prevented from landing one complete regiment plus other troops to complete formations already in France. The British were also two brigades behind schedule which meant that the major attack planned on the eastern side of the lodgement area — Operation 'Epsom' — had to be postponed until the 24th.

The storm had also made the capture of Cherbourg imperative, orders stressing that it was now to be 'the major effort of the American Army'. At the same time the Germans were methodically destroying the harbour installations. Here Fregattenkapitan Hermann Witt (left), with an unidentified harbour commander, and Konteradmiral Walther Hennecke (centre) discuss their plans to destroy the Gare Maritime. The 70-metre-high Campanile can be seen in the background shortly before it was blown up. On June 26, Hennecke was awarded the Knight's Cross for his work of destruction in the harbour of Cherbourg.

COMMUNIQUE No. 37   June 24

Fighting is heavy and resistance strong immediately before CHERBOURG. We are making steady progress and are now within a short distance of the north coast on both sides of the fortress. West of CARENTAN enemy resistance has increased.

North-east of CAEN our troops have made a local advance after fierce fighting.

To the east of the river Orne warships have bombarded enemy troops and armor. Intermittent shelling of the eastern anchorage continues and brief gun duels between Allied warships and mobile batteries ensue.

The Allied air forces yesterday concentrated their attacks on enemy reinforcements attempting to move westward from PARIS and up from southern France. Principal road and rail arteries and airfields from below the Loire Estuary to the Oise were bombed and strafed despite changeable weather and determined opposition by the enemy in some areas.

From noon till dusk fighter-bombers and fighters followed the main railways east and west of CHARTRES and to the south, hitting railway yards at NANTES and CHATEAU-DU-LOIR, cutting tracks in many places and destroying locomotives and freight cars especially at QUINCEY, SAUMUR and south of NANTES. Bridges and viaducts at CHARTRES, JUSSY, NOGENT and over the Oise and Somme rivers were also attacked.

At least 11 enemy aircraft were shot down, 10 of them in combat over the CAEN—EVREUX area. Eight of our fighters are missing from the day's operations. On their second mission of the day our heavy bombers, eight of which are missing, attacked airfields at ATHIES and JUVINCOURT near LAON. Their fighter escort hit rail and road and other targets east of PARIS.

Towards dusk medium and light bombers attacked military objectives in the Pas de Calais. Later, heavy night bombers attacked rail centers at SAINTES and LIMOGES, losing two aircraft.

COMMUNIQUE No. 38   June 24

Allied forces are steadily closing in on CHERBOURG. Despite fierce enemy resistance, each link in the chain of the defences is being systematically destroyed. In the center of the semi-circular front our troops are within two miles of the heart of the city.

In the river Orne sector, a strong Allied attack has liberated the village of STE HONORINE after hard fighting in which infantry and armor were engaged. Some enemy tanks were knocked out.

A convoy of seven small enemy ships, attempting to escape from CHERBOURG to the west under escort, was intercepted early this morning by light coastal forces. Two of the enemy vessels were destroyed and three more are believed sunk.

Rocket-firing aircraft and fighter-bombers damaged three 1,000-ton motor vessels near ST MALO and left one of them on fire.

Our air forces continued their program of obstructing the flow of enemy supplies and reinforcements to the battle area. Key points in a semicircle west and south of PARIS

The Quai de France was capable of berthing the largest ocean liners but the Kriegsmarine engineers made a good job of blowing out 600 metres of the quayside. *Right:* This access gallery was not damaged and is still in use today.

Above: The 39th and 47th Infantry Regiments of the 9th Division fought their way through the western half of Cherbourg on June 25. History was made by the 2nd Battalion of the 47th Infantry when its leaders entered the city at 12.55 p.m. Both Company E and the attached engineers from the 15th Engineer Combat Battalion could lay claim to having been the first to set foot inside the city but the accepted version is that Pfc John T. Sarao of Company E won. War photographer Robert Capa of *Life* entered Cherbourg with the 47th Infantry's 1st Battalion and he took this picture in the same quarter of Cherbourg the following day. *Below:* Rue Pierre de Coubertin, with Yannick Berton standing in for the surrendering Germans.

were under attack during the day by both heavy and fighter-bombers.

Armed reconnaissance in some force was flown over a broad belt extending from the line FALAISE—ARGENTAN—ST GERMAIN in the north to the ANGERS—SAUMUR line in the south to oppose military movements in this area. Railways east of FALAISE were bombed; a military train was attacked near DREUX and tank cars, ammunition cars, and armored vehicles were destroyed. In the AVRANCHES—COUTANCES area aircraft on patrol attacked targets of opportunity. Gun emplacements north of LA HAYE-DU-PUITS were attacked by fighter-bombers.

Heavy day bombers bombed railway bridges at SAUMUR and TOURS and airfields at CHATEAUDUN and ORLEANS/BRICY.

During the period, attacks were made on flying bomb sites.

Four Me 109s, of a formation of twelve which appeared in the CAEN area, were destroyed by our fighters without loss.

Reconnaissance shows that the bombing attacks on the night of 23/24 June on LIMOGES and SAINTES were highly successful.

'On the morning of 25th June, an attack was made by British troops on the village of Fontenay-le-Pesnel in an effort to straighten the line on the Tilly-sur-Seulles area. Heavy enemy opposition was encountered before the village was taken'.

So runs the official caption for this photograph released by the Press News Agency on June 27 for publication in the daily papers on the 28th showing 'a burnt-out German tank destroyed during the battle'.

The Panther at Fontenay, an Ausf G model, could have belonged to either the Hitlerjugend or Panzer Lehr as both were defending the area which lies ten miles west of Caen. When Bernard Paich arrived in the village to take the comparison of the burning tank he found it very difficult to pin down the location. However, he had a stroke of luck as he tracked down Henri Massinot who had lived in the village in 1944 and it turned out that the ruined house had belonged to his parents! However, it was not rebuilt after the war but Henri took Bernard to show where it had stood. Then the man produced this picture of British troops advancing through Fontenay which he was willing to trade for a copy of the other photograph.

COMMUNIQUE No. 39   June 25

Allied troops are in the outskirts of CHERBOURG and the final assault has begun. On a 10-mile front extending east and west of the city, our forces have advanced to within three miles of the sea. The enemy continues to fight desperately but relentless Allied pressure is steadily overcoming the defences throughout the entire length of the narrow coastal strip.

In other sectors, local fighting has left the front almost unchanged.

Taking advantage of the improved weather, our Air Forces were out in great strength yesterday afternoon and evening, concentrating largely on the enemy communication system.

Fighters and fighter-bombers attacked railway yards, tracks, bridges, tunnels and rolling stock in a belt at the base of the Cherbourg peninsula ranging from GRANVILLE and AVRANCHES in the west to ST LO on the river Vire. Similar attacks were made on targets more distant from the battle zone, including rolling stock in the yards at DREUX and at various points in the region of CHARTRES. Fighter-bombers also bombed the steel works at IJMUIDEN in Holland.

Our fighters destroyed at least 30 enemy aircraft on airfields in the area of ANGERS.

Medium bombers attacked a railway bridge over the Seine at MAISONS-LAFFITTE, and the railway centers at BEAUVAIS and HAZEBROUCK. They also bombed dumps in the FORET-DE-CONCHES and at BRUZ and BAGNOLES DE L'ORNE. Heavy bombers attacked a number of electrical switching stations near BOULOGNE. Attacks were continued on flying bomb sites.

According to reports so far received, 20 enemy aircraft were shot down. Nineteen of our aircraft are missing.

Last night light bombers attacked railway and road transport behind the battle area including the railway yards at MEZIDON.

Our night fighters, one of which is missing, destroyed 5 enemy aircraft over Northern France.

Three miles away lies Cheux which was entered on the 26th although Major Hugh Stewart, the AFPU photographer, explained that the village was still being shelled by the Germans when he took his picture.

The transport rounding the bend from Rue de Marchanville, turning right onto Rue Robert Courteheùse, is from the 2nd Fife and Forfar Yeomanry, part of the 29th Armoured Brigade (11th Armoured Division).

Left: Back in Cherbourg, Sherman tanks, most probably belonging to the 749th Tank Battalion, the armoured unit permanently attached to the 79th Division, entered the city. They are on Rue du Val de Saire at its junction with Rue Jean Fleury.

The centre of Cherbourg lies off to the right. Over on the left is Saint Clément Church and across the road to the right stands a large hospital, named the Hôpital Dieu in 1944. *Right:* Today the transformation from war to peace is complete.

COMMUNIQUE No. 40   June 25

The Allies now hold high ground overlooking CHERBOURG and are gradually pressing forward into the suburbs. The enemy is resisting bitterly, but is unable to stem our steady advance. Targets in the CHERBOURG area were subjected to a bombardment from seaward this afternoon by a force of Allied warships.

Local attacks have improved our positions in the eastern sector of the bridgehead after fierce fighting. Air bombardment has given invaluable aid to ground units.

Continuing the obstruction of enemy movements towards the battle zone, our fighter-bombers today attacked a series of rail targets including bridges, fuel tanks and rolling stock in the CHARTRES—DREUX—MANTES area and the rail crossings at CONCHES and MEZIDON.

On the railroad between CHARTRES and MANTES the tracks were severed at four points, and direct hits were registered on a tunnel.

The bridge at MAISONS-LAFFITTE and a radio installation at ST SAUVEUR were damaged.

There was an increase in enemy air activity. On one occasion a formation of German fighters gave battle, and nine were destroyed; seven of ours are missing.

Four airfields in southern France at FRANCAZAL, BLAGNAC, AVORD and BOURGES were targets for our heavy bombers. Escorting fighters destroyed locomotives, freight cars and vehicles. Medium bombers operating closer to the battle line hit fuel dumps in the FORET D'ECOUVES.

Coastal aircraft attacked E-Boats in the eastern Channel early this morning.

COMMUNIQUE No. 41   June 26

The liberation of CHERBOURG cannot be long delayed. Allied troops are fighting in the streets and by yesterday afternoon had reached the sea within a mile of the port on the east side. During a day of fierce fighting with the support of naval bombardment, enemy strong points were reduced one by one and the town was entered at many points simultaneously. The mopping-up of other portions of the original outer defences continues.

In the eastern sector our progress in the FONTENAY area was maintained and our positions were further strengthened.

Further enemy counter-attacks near STE HONORINE were beaten back.

Our Air Forces continued their attacks on the enemy's supply system during the afternoon and evening yesterday and also gave immediate support to the land and naval forces assaulting CHERBOURG.

Pushing forward in the early morning of June 26, the leading troops of the 313th Infantry reached the beach by 8 a.m.

The railway network east and south of Normandy was subjected to many attacks. Targets included the railway yards at DREUX and CHARTRES and bridges and embankments in the same area. Airfields at BRETIGNY and VILLACOUBLAY were bombed and a large formation of medium bombers attacked supply dumps in the SENONCHES area with good results.

Enemy opposition was on a limited scale yesterday though flak was intense at many points.

Troop concentrations south of CAEN were bombed last night.

Looking northwards at the junction of the Avenue de Paris and Avenue Etienne Lecarpentier.

COMMUNIQUE No. 42   June 26

Street fighting continues in CHERBOURG. The Germans are resisting desperately but the town is steadily being cleared.

In the north-eastern tip of the peninsula little opposition has been met. To the north-west in the CAP DE LA HAGUE area there is still some enemy strength.

Progress has been made in the FONTENAY sector, east of TILLY, after heavy fighting and our positions are improved.

More than 20,000 prisoners have been taken in the beach-head since the landings.

Dense cloud and fog over the continent today brought our air operations to a virtual standstill. Last night two enemy aircraft were destroyed by our patrols over northern France.

COMMUNIQUE No. 43   June 27

The fall of CHERBOURG ends the second phase in the campaign of liberation. Twenty days after the initial assault, Allied forces have established a firm beach-head which includes almost the whole of the Cotentin peninsula and a major port.

CHERBOURG's liberation came after a final day of fierce fighting in the northwestern part of the city. In the battle the enemy has lost the greater part of four infantry divisions, numerous naval and marine units and line of communication troops.

Lieutenant General Karl Wilhelm von Schlieben, commander of the Cherbourg garrison, and Konteradmiral Hennecke, sea defence commander of Normandy, have been captured.

A strong attack toward the VILLERS-BOCAGE—CAEN main road has secured CHEUX and FONTENAY and has advanced several miles in the face of heavy German armour and infantry. Progress continues.

Storms and dense clouds minimized air activity yesterday and throughout the night.

COMMUNIQUE No. 44   June 27

Allied forces in the TILLY—CAEN area have crossed the CAEN—VILLERS-BOCAGE railway near MOUEN. Our advance has been made in torrential rain and against determined resistance by enemy infantry and armour.

In the Cherbourg peninsula we are continuing our attacks against the last remnants of organized opposition. Elements of the enemy's forces are holding out in the MAUPERTUS airfield east of CHERBOURG and in the north-west tip of the peninsula. Prisoners taken in the peninsula total at least 20,000 and more are being brought in.

Bad weather during this morning severely curtailed air activity but fighter-bombers attacked a train at PARENNES (east of LAVAL) and road transport in the LAVAL and ALENCON areas.

Left: **The 79th Division drove into the city from the south-east with the 314th Infantry on the left and the 313th on the right. A Signal Corps photographer with the 314th pictured this dead German, still clutching a hand-grenade, in Rue Armand Levéel.** *Right:* **The Café Estasse has since closed but the building remains unchanged.**

The commander of 'Festung Cherbourg', Generalleutnant Karl-Wilhelm von Schlieben, surrendered on June 26 at his command post located in a deep tunnel in a quarry in the suburb of Saint-Sauveur.

Early this morning light coastal forces intercepted and engaged a force of enemy trawlers and minesweepers off Jersey. Considerable damage was inflicted on the enemy in a gun action in which coastal batteries from the island joined, and one minesweeper was hit by a torpedo. It is considered that this enemy ship may have sunk.

The tunnel entrance was covered with a rock fall — here the present-day owner of the quarry explains what happened and how a chicken coup now hides the spot. (The full story of the battle to capture Cherbourg was published in *After the Battle* **No. 147).**

Eisenhower: 'From the beginning it was the conception of Field-Marshal Montgomery (left), Bradley (right) and myself that eventually the great movement out of the beach-head would be by an enormous left wheel, bringing our front on to the line of the Seine, with the whole area lying between that river and the Loire and as far eastward as Paris in our firm possession. During the 20 days required by the US VII Corps to capture Cherbourg, the fighting was continuous throughout the remainder of the front, with only local gains anywhere, and almost stalemate in the Caen sector. As the days wore on after the initial landing the particular dissatisfaction of the Press was directed toward the lack of progress on our left. Naturally I and all of my service commanders and staff were greatly concerned about this static situation near Caen. Every possible means of breaking the deadlock was considered. Montgomery threw in attack after attack, gallantly conducted and heavily supported by artillery and air, but German resistance was not crushed.'

COMMUNIQUE No. 45   June 28

In the battle south-east of TILLY-SUR-SEULLES, Allied armour succeeded in widening the breach created by the infantry on Monday. Advancing on a 4-mile front our forces have driven across the main VILLERS-BOCAGE—CAEN road after particularly heavy fighting on the left in the area of TOURVILLE. The enemy is resisting stubbornly but the advance continues to make good progress.

In the vicinity of CHERBOURG Allied forces made progress in cleaning out enemy remnants hemmed in the horns of the peninsula.

After a two-day lull enforced by weather, the Allied Air Forces yesterday operated over a widespread area in north-west France, ranging from CHERBOURG and LA ROCHE-SUR-YON in the west to ORLEANS, PARIS and beyond in the east.

Operations in support of our ground forces were largely carried out by fighters and fighter-bombers. Attacks were concentrated on enemy reinforcements moving northward along several routes.

Successful attacks were made on numerous trains carrying troops and equipment between PARIS and ORLEANS. Other targets included marshalling yards at ARTENAY and TOURY, and road and rail traffic and focal points near RENNES, CHARTRES, ST NAZAIRE, LAVAL, NANTES, PARENNES, FLERS and east of PARIS.

West of Caen on June 27, these Churchill tanks are advancing northwards on the D83 with the shattered church at Norrey in the background.

The attacks were continued into the night by our light bombers. An enemy headquarters south of the battle area and a telephone center in the Brest peninsula were bombed with good results.

Other fighter-bombers attacked airfields at VILLENEUVE/VERTUS, CONNANTRE and COULOMMIERS.

Last night our heavy bombers struck at rail centers in VITRY LE FRANCOIS, and VAIRES east of PARIS. Others were over military installations at Pas de Calais, following up two daylight attacks on similar objectives. A small force of heavy day bombers also attacked an airfield at CREIL.

Twenty-three enemy aircraft were destroyed during the course of these operations. Thirteen of our bombers and eight of our fighters are missing.

Bayeux escaped without major damage, these troops being pictured on June 27 marching past the 12th-century cathedral.

COMMUNIQUE No. 46 June 28
The Allied attack south-west of CAEN is making steady progress in spite of more bad weather and intense opposition.

The enemy was driven out of RAURAY, south-east of FONTENAY, where resistance had been most stubborn. After further heavy fighting in GRAINVILLE and TOURVILLE, our armour and infantry crossed the river Odon south of TOURVILLE on a front of about two miles.

Our advance continues towards the high ground south of the Odon.

In the Cherbourg peninsula enemy strong points east and west of the city are being steadily cleaned up.

Early this morning two destroyers, HMCS *Huron* and HMS *Eskimo*, encountered three armed enemy trawlers near the Channel Islands. Action was joined and two of the enemy ships were destroyed by gunfire. The third which made off during the action was believed to be damaged.

Adverse weather this morning restricted air operations over the battle area to a limited number of patrols.

In the LAON district where better weather prevailed, our heavy bombers attacked airfields at COUVRON, ATHIES and JUVINCOURT. They also hit the railway yards at SAARBRUCKEN across the German frontier. Escorting fighters strafed and dive-bombed locomotives, railroad cars and trucks.

But not so on the road south towards Tilly-sur-Seulles where the men of the 6th Durham Light Infantry found this village in ruins. *Right:* **Royal Engineers from XXX Corps Headquarters Signal Section were called in on the 28th to restore communications.**

Although the wartime caption states that the photograph was taken in Condé-sur-Seulles, in fact the location was just to the west at Le Douet, the main crossroads on the D6 between Bayeux and Tilly.

Although organised resistance at Cherbourg had ceased, the final clearing of Cap de la Hague began on June 29 when the US 9th Division drove right up to the tip of the peninsula. On the way, all the strong points and coastal batteries like this one — Batterie Blankenese near Néville with its four 94mm Flak guns — were captured together with 6,000 prisoners.

COMMUNIQUE No. 47   **June 29**

More Allied forces have crossed the river Odon and the width of the bridgehead has been increased. Allied armour has been heavily engaged south of the river. There has also been heavy fighting, including armoured clashes, north and north-west of CAEN.

Enemy resistance has ceased in the area of the MAUPERTUS airfield east of CHERBOURG. A few strong points remain to be dealt with in the CAP DE LA HAGUE area.

Bad weather again restricted air activity during the afternoon and evening, but armed reconnaissance flights were carried out in the CAEN—LISIEUX—MEZIDON area. Attacks were made on enemy road transport at several points and a railway bridge at STE HONORINE-DU-FAY. According to preliminary reports 26 enemy aircraft were destroyed. Six of ours are missing.

Last night our heavy bombers, 20 of which are missing, attacked the railway centers of METZ and BLAINVILLE in eastern France.

During the night two enemy aircraft were shot down over northern France.

COMMUNIQUE No. 48   **June 29**

Our hold on the crossings of the river Odon has been strengthened after further heavy fighting in the TILLY—CAEN sector.

Enemy forces which had been bypassed in the area of MONDRAINVILLE and TOURVILLE were eliminated and counter-attacks against the base of our salient were firmly repulsed.

North of CAEN Allied troops have achieved small local gains against fierce opposition.

Fighting continues in the CAP DE LA HAGUE area.

Since the landing in Normandy 121 German tanks have been destroyed by our troops.

Thick cloud and rain squalls restricted air operations this morning.

Fighter-bombers however continued the attacks on enemy troops and transport moving towards the battle area. Their targets included road and rail bridges near MONTFORT-SUR-RISLE, CHERISY and ST PAUL-DE-COURTONNE (west of BERNAY), locomotives and trains at ORLEANS and near FLERS, and rail junctions at VIERZON.

Attacks were made on enemy R-Boats and minesweepers off LE TREPORT and on self-propelled barges at CAUDEBEC near the mouth of the Seine.

In a series of encounters eleven enemy planes were shot down for the loss of four of our aircraft.

Another huge burden on SHAEF had been caused by the introduction of the Luftwaffe flying bomb campaign. Hitler had ordered the long-range bombardment of England with the Vergeltungswaffe 1 (Revenge Weapon 1) as a reprisal for the hammering Germany was suffering from Allied air attacks and the first four V1s were fired at London on the night of June 12/13. The launch sites in France had already been subjected to prolonged air attacks but now there was the added pressure to capture them on the ground. The limited accuracy of the V1 led to widespread damage throughout southern England but on June 30 the Luftwaffe came close to scoring a bull's eye on the Air Ministry building on the corner of Kingsway. The bomb exploded in the road 40 feet in front of Adastral House, killing 48 and causing over 200 casualties.

Graphic photographs like this one showing the victims were banned by the censor.

Commenting after the war on the V-Weapon campaign, Eisenhower said that 'the effect of the new German weapons was very noticable upon morale. When the new weapons began to come over London in considerable numbers hopes were dashed. Indeed, the depressing effect of the bombs was not confined to the civilian population. Soldiers at the front began to worry about friends and loved ones at home, and many American soldiers asked me in worried tones whether I could give them any news about particular towns where they had previously been stationed in southern England. If the Germans had succeeded in perfecting and using these new weapons six months earlier than they did, our invasion of Europe would have proved exceedingly difficult, perhaps impossible. I feel sure that if they had succeeded in using these weapons over a six-month period, and particularly if they had made the Portsmouth-Southampton area one of their principal targets, "Overlord" might have been written off.'

COMMUNIQUE No. 49   **June 30**

The Allied bridgehead over the river Odon has been extended on both flanks. Elsewhere the situation remains unchanged.

Fighting continued north of EVRECY where the enemy brought up fresh troops.

The forts in the CHERBOURG breakwater have surrendered, and mopping up continues in the CAP DE LA HAGUE area.

Rail and road transport, bridges, railway tracks and crossings behind the battle line were attacked by our aircraft yesterday afternoon and evening.

Fighter-bombers, on armed reconnaissance in the DREUX, CHARTRES, and ARGENTAN areas, destroyed more than 100 railway cars. Other fighter-bombers strafed junctions and rolling stock near PARIS, at EVREUX and at BOLBEC, 20 miles east of LE HAVRE. The rail line at VITRY, 100 miles east of PARIS, was severed.

Medium and light bombers attacked the viaduct between ST HILAIRE and VITRE, and bridges in the RENNES area.

Coastal batteries on the CAP DE LA HAGUE were attacked by medium bombers.

The building became famous after the war when the Met Office measured London temperature and wind speeds on its roof for BBC weather reports. Then in 1954 the building was converted for use by commercial television. It was re-named St Catherine's House in 1967 for the General Register Office. The brave face of Adastral House today, now occupied by the London School of Economics.

Eisenhower: 'With the capture of Cherbourg the work of port rehabilitation was started immediately. The Germans had accomplished major demolitions and had planted in the harbour and its approaches a profusion and variety of mines. Some of the new types could be removed only by deep-sea divers, who had to descend to the bottom to disarm the mines before they could be moved. The work of the minesweepers and the deep-sea divers in Cherbourg harbour was one of the dramatic and courageous incidents of the war.' The photograph shows the Gare Maritime — the pride of Cherbourg — with the Darse Transatlantique basin and the Quai de France on the left. The Entrance to the Port de Commerce (right) has been blocked by sinking the coaster *Le Normand* in the Avant-Port. On June 28 a programme was established for opening those areas of the port as quickly as possible which could receive cargo with the least delay. Meanwhile, the Advance Section Communications Zone (ADSEC) was drawing up a plan for the port's reconstruction which was ready by July 4. Its most striking feature was the doubling of the tonnage discharge from 8,000 to 17,000 tons per day. The outer and inner roadsteads were declared free of mines by July 14 and two days later four Liberty ships entered the harbour. Port reconstruction, mine clearance, salvage and cargo discharge went on simultaneously throughout July and by the first week of August, just three weeks after the start of operations, Cherbourg was handling 6,000 tons per day with an eventual target of 20,000 tons by mid-September.

COMMUNIQUE No. 50   June 30

Allied forces, driving their salient towards the Orne river in the CAEN sector have compelled the enemy to throw in strong armoured reserves in an effort to halt our advance. In spite of repeated counter-attacks by these formations, our positions have not only been held but improved. Farther west, ground has been gained near ST JEAN-DE-DAYE. Resistance in the CAP DE LA HAGUE area of the Cherbourg peninsula has continued.

Weather severely restricted air operations between midnight and mid-morning, but improving conditions over the battle area, and southward, permitted Allied forces to complete some 1,000 sorties by early afternoon. Flying through clouds or under low ceilings, small forces of medium bombers before dawn attacked main thoroughfares in use by the enemy in the VILLERS-BOCAGE area.

From first light, fighter-bombers and fighters, based both in Britain and Normandy, harassed enemy movements in the area bounded by DREUX, CHARTRES, ALENCON and ARGENTAN, and carried out armed reconnaissance as far south as TOURS.

Small forces of medium bombers attacked road and rail junctions between MEZIDON and FALAISE. Fighter-bombers hit large warehouses at ARVILLE, east of LE MANS, and an important bridge at BEAUGENCY, as well as rail lines and machine gun emplacements in the ORLEANS area.

One of our fighters is missing.

The massive bombing campaign against all transport networks resulted in over 1,600 miles of railway track being destroyed and, of the 11,800 locomotives possessed by the French before the war, barely a quarter were still running. This is Alençon, a key station on the line to Brittany. It was bombed on June 6 and 8. This level of destruction meant that the Allies had to both repair the track and bring in locomotives — for example 400 American locos lent to British railways prior to the landings were shipped to France and later Belgium. By the end of the year there were 6,000 in service

At the end of the month there was good reason for the Allies to be pleased with their achievements. The 'Overlord' plan had been carried out successfully and a solid foothold had been established on the Continent for the bridge that was to carry men and weapons from across the Channel. Since D-Day 929,000 men, 586,000 tons of supplies, and 177,000 vehicles had been landed in France. American and British build-ups were roughly equal, General Bradley having four corps with 11 infantry and two armoured divisions while the British Second Army had four corps, ten infantry divisions, and three armoured divisions. However, the lodgement area was considerably smaller than had been planned for by this date as the forecast of operations anticipated by D+25 was for a front line running as far inland as Lisieux, Alençon, Laval and beyond Rennes and Saint-Malo. The failure to make anticipated territorial gains was the only major aspect in which the 'Overlord' operation had fallen short of the planning, and the success achieved by Allied arms generally exceeded expectations. The biggest surprise was the ability of the combined air forces and French Resistance to cripple the Germans' transportation system, the consequent lack of mobility of German forces being the primary reason why the counter-attack that figured largely in all Allied predictions never materialised. However, on June 6 such success was not guaranteed and the day before the landing General Eisenhower had drafted a communiqué to issue in case the cross-Channel operation should fail. He put the draft in his wallet and forgot about it until he came across it at the beginning of July. Commander Harry C. Butcher, Eisenhower's naval aide, described how one afternoon, the SHAEF commander called him into his office and handed him a sheet of notepaper. The note read: 'Our landings in the Cherbourg—Havre area have failed to gain a satisfactory foothold and I have withdrawn the troops. My decision to attack at this time and place was based upon the best information available. The troops, the air, and the Navy did all that bravery and devotion to duty could do. If any blame or fault attaches to the attempt it is mine alone.' Butcher told Eisenhower he wanted the note. 'He reluctantly assented, saying that he had written one in similar vein for every amphibious operation but had secretly torn up each one.' Now, with the lodgement on the coast of France secured, back in Britain SHAEF were on the point of opening their Forward Headquarters at Portsmouth. Code-named 'Shipmate', the actual location was Millard's Wood just to the south of Eisenhower's Advance Command Post 'Sharpener' in Sawyer's Wood. Admiralty headquarters remained in nearby Southwick House.

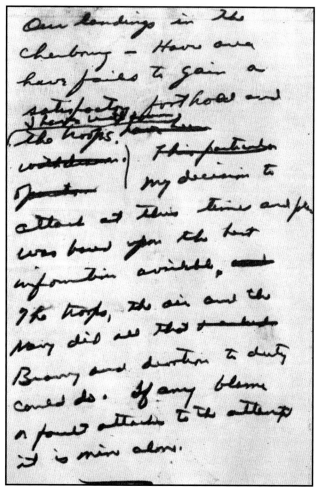

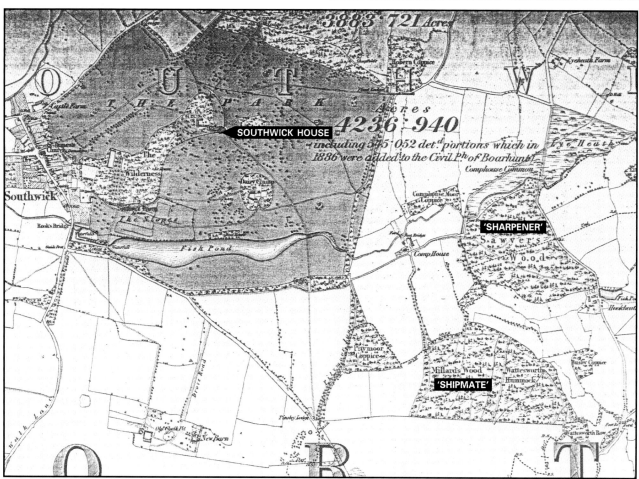

JULY 1944
STALEMATE

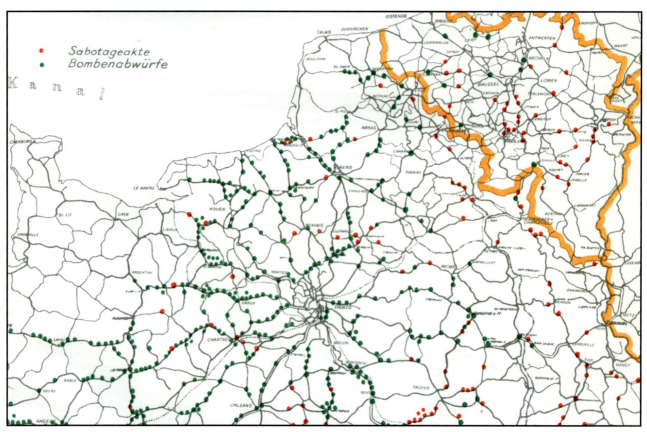

As with the rail network, so with bridges, some 4,000 having been destroyed. This German map shows the position in July indicating how difficult it was to transport units and supplies to the front. (The red dots signify bridges destroyed by sabotage and the green dots by bombing.) In OKW reserve in Belgium on D-Day, the 1. SS-Panzer-Division was soon directed to join the battle in Normandy and by the end of June the first elements were committed south of Caen together with the 12. SS-Panzer-Division. The other parts of the division arrived progressively including a company of Panther tanks from SS-Panzer-Regiment 1 which travelled to the front via Paris. Nevertheless, the whole division was not assembled with the I. SS-Panzerkorps south of Caen until July 9.

COMMUNIQUE No. 51   **July 1**

Allied troops are strengthening their positions on both banks of the Odon river. All enemy attempts to break in were frustrated in the CAEN—EVRECY sector. There is nothing to report on the rest of the front.

Enemy supply lines to the immediate battle area were constantly under attack by our aircraft yesterday. Further afield, focal communication points where enemy troops were on the move at CHARTRES, DREUX, ALENCON, L'AIGLE, and ARGENTAN were also bombed.

There were scattered encounters with enemy fighters throughout the day.

Five airfields in France and Belgium were the targets for some of our heavy day bombers while others attacked armoured vehicles around VILLERS-BOCAGE. Last night our heavies bombed the rail centers at VIERZON, south of ORLEANS. Sixteen heavy bombers are missing from these operations.

COMMUNIQUE No. 52   **July 1**

No further gains have been made in the strong Allied bridgehead across the Odon river.

Local enemy movement in the vicinity of ESQUAY and attempts by the enemy to infiltrate our positions from the east were unsuccessful.

In the Cherbourg peninsula a small area of enemy resistance in the CAP DE LA HAGUE has been further reduced.

Bad weather minimized air activity during the afternoon.

The bridge at La Possonnière over the river Loire, south-west of Angers, under attack on June 15.

To create choke-points to hinder the arrival of German reinforcements in the battle area, ten towns — such as Saint-Lô, Caen, Vire and Lisieux — were heavily bombed on D-Day. Hundreds of bombers of the Eighth and Ninth Air Forces had turned the centre of Caen into a mountain of rubble on June 6, killing 1,000 inhabitants in the process. *Left:* A lull took place in the afternoon before the second wave flew in around 4.30 p.m. *Right:* Rue Saint-Pierre near the junction with Rue Paul Doumer.

COMMUNIQUE No. 53 July 2

The liberation of the Cherbourg peninsula is now complete. The last enemy resistance in the CAP DE LA HAGUE ceased early yesterday morning

In the area south of TILLY-SUR-SEULLES the enemy has made repeated counter-attacks against the western flank of the river Odon bridgehead. The Allied positions remain firmly intact and the enemy has incurred serious losses in infantry and armour.

Unfavorable flying weather continued to restrict air activity from noon to midnight yesterday but in spite of low clouds our fighters attacked targets of tactical importance to our ground forces in the CAEN—EVRECY sector. Enemy guns and mortar positions near CARPIQUET and military transport near COUDRES, HARCOURT, ARGENTAN, and FALAISE were hit with good results by fighters based in Normandy. Other fighters and fighter-bombers operating from Britain, bombed and strafed moving targets east of the battle area and at CHARTRES and beyond PARIS.

Nine enemy aircraft were destroyed. Three of our fighters are missing.

COMMUNIQUE No. 54 July 2

The Allied bridgehead across the river Odon stands firm despite continuous enemy assault.

All day Saturday there was fierce fighting, particularly on the west of the deep salient. The enemy made repeated counter-attacks in a vain effort to cut off our wedge at its base. During the afternoon the enemy managed once to effect some penetration, but this temporary success was vigorously beaten back with heavy loss to the enemy of men and tanks.

Enemy units forming up for a major attack were broken up by a concentration of Allied artillery fire and the attack collapsed. Attacks by smaller forces, supported by a few tanks, have continued to prove very costly to the enemy. At least forty enemy tanks were knocked out.

The official count of prisoners taken since the initial landing now exceeds 40,000.

From midnight until noon today air operations were confined to patrols over the area occupied by our forces.

While personnel of the French civil defence helped victims to save what remained, the stunned inhabitants fled the city until only a third of Caen's pre-war 60,000 population were left behind. *Left:* Germans are clearing the way to enable convoys to reach the troops at the front, then some miles away to the north. *Right:* The Hôtel Malherbe, the large building in the background of Place du Maréchal Foch, still remains open for business today.

COMMUNIQUE No. 55   **July 3**

During yesterday morning our Odon river bridgehead was further strengthened. The enemy's activity was on a reduced scale owing probably to the severe mauling he received on Saturday. There were some enemy attacks but they were firmly repulsed. There is nothing to report from the remainder of the front.

Bad weather continued to restrict air activity yesterday, but fighter-bombers attacked bridges over the river Orne and fighters attacked vehicles on the roads behind the enemy lines.

Twenty one enemy aircraft were shot down. Three of ours are missing. One enemy aircraft was shot down over Normandy last night.

COMMUNIQUE No. 56   **July 3**

During Sunday afternoon there were only local clashes in the CAEN area. Our patrols penetrated deep into the enemy positions in some parts of the EVRECY sector. Contact was maintained along the whole front.

Today Allied forces gained some ground to the south in the Cotentin peninsula.

Air activity from midnight until noon today was again reduced by bad weather.

Our fighters destroyed eight enemy aircraft for the loss of two during the forenoon over the battle area.

COMMUNIQUE No. 57   **July 4**

Allied troops in the neck of the Cherbourg peninsula advanced at several points yesterday morning. Gains of up to two and one half miles were made in spite of heavy rains which severely restricted air support. The weather improved somewhat yesterday evening and defended localities, gun positions and a fuel dump in the LESSAY area were effectively attacked by fighter-bombers.

Our positions in the Odon salient remain firm.

Other air activity yesterday included successful attacks by medium bombers on a fuel dump near ARGENTAN and by rocket-firing aircraft on an electric power station near MUR-DE-BRETAGNE in the Brest peninsula.

The enemy railway system south of the battle area was further damaged during the night when a number of trains were bombed in the ORLEANS—CLOYES—MONTFORT area.

COMMUNIQUE No. 58   **July 4**

Allied forces made two major attacks this morning.

In the CAEN area, our troops, driving southeast astride the railway and main road from BAYEUX to CAEN, have captured CARPIQUET. Fighting is in progress on the airfield there.

Other Allied units, moving from the eastern flank of the Odon bridgehead, advanced several miles, capturing VERSON and joining with our troops on their left.

In the base of the Cherbourg peninsula, Allied forces moving south captured the high ground north of LA HAYE-DU-PUITS this morning. The successful assault of this dominating feature followed earlier advances near ST REMY-DES-LANDES, BLANCHELANDE and LA POTERIE where substantial gains have been made.

Weather continued to interfere with air operations from midnight until noon today but during the entire period our aircraft, taking advantage of favourable intervals, attacked a variety of targets in support of our troops.

All types of our fighters joined in supporting ground operations in the CAEN—EVRECY and Cherbourg peninsula sectors. Fighter-bombers made low level attacks on artillery positions, supply dumps, trenches and railways between COUTANCES and LESSAY. Troop concentrations on the railways at VILLEDIEU, VIRE, LE MANS and southeast of ARGENTAN were bombed and strafed in spite of poor visibility. Motor convoys, towing guns, were effectively hit near BETHON (south of ALENCON) as were railway targets and oil storage tanks in the Brest peninsula. Reports so far received show that twelve of our fighters are missing.

Heavy day bombers, escorted by fighters, this morning attacked a number of airfields in north and northwest France, bombing by instruments. No enemy aircraft were encountered. Two of our bombers are missing. Escorting fighters also bombed and strafed two Seine bridges and trains at LILLY.

Early this morning light coastal forces intercepted a small enemy convoy to the northeast of ST MALO. Two of the enemy were sunk, and damage inflicted on others.

Unsuccessful attempts were made by a number of enemy E-Boats to break in to our lines of communication from the eastward during the night. The enemy was finally driven off by light coastal forces after a succession of engagements which lasted throughout the night.

COMMUNIQUE No. 59   **July 5**

The Allied advance southwards in the Cotentin peninsula made further progress during the day, particularly in the vicinity of ST REMY-DES-LANDES and BLANCHELANDE.

Our troops to the west and north of LA HAYE-DU-PUITS, are now within four miles of the town. A small gain was also made southeast of ST JORES.

In the CAEN area, Allied forces were engaged in fierce fighting south of the village of CARPIQUET.

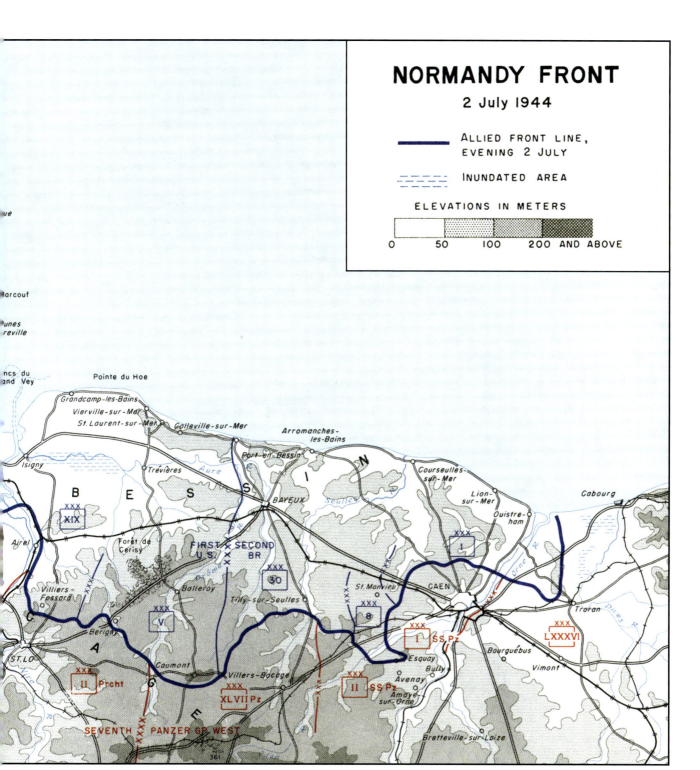

There was a considerable increase in air activity yesterday. The principal effort was directed by our fighter-bombers against enemy communications — road, rail and water — over a wide area extending from NANTES in the west to CAMBRAI in the east. Considerable damage was caused to trains, tracks, barges, motor transport and flak towers, in the ANGERS—TOURS—LAVAL area.

In the immediate battle zone south of CAEN, and at LESSAY on the extreme western flank, targets were attacked in direct support of our ground forces.

There was a series of encounters with enemy fighters during these operations and a number were destroyed. Our losses were small.

Last night the railways at VILLENEUVE-SAINT-GEORGES and ORLEANS were attacked by heavy bombers, fourteen of which are missing.

Light bombers also attacked successfully enemy reinforcements, particularly in the western battle sector. They also hit rail targets south of PARIS.

Coastal aircraft attacked enemy shipping off Brittany during the afternoon and in the Channel last night.

COMMUNIQUE No. 60   July 5

Further advances have been made by Allied forces in the base of the Cherbourg peninsula although resistance is strong and the enemy is well-positioned on high ground.

Most progress was made in the coastal sector. ST NICOLAS-DE-PIERREPONT and NEUFMESNIL have been liberated and some units are now approaching LA HAYE-DU-PUITS.

In the CAEN area the enemy is counter-attacking strongly. Our position at CARPIQUET remains firm.

During the night coastal aircraft heavily attacked concentrations of E-Boats and other vessels between DIEPPE and GRAVELINES. One armed auxiliary vessel blew up and several other craft were damaged.

Bad weather again interfered with air operations this morning.

Heavy bombers attacked airfields in Belgium and Holland. They were escorted by fighters which subsequently strafed a variety of ground targets including railway yards, power stations and airfields.

Medium bombers escorted by fighters bombed two bridges over the river Orne, a fuel dump at BENONCHES, a rail junction at L'AIGLE and a supply depot in a wood twenty-five miles southwest of DREUX. Two of the medium bombers are missing.

Fighter-bombers attacked flak positions in the CAEN area and railway targets near LAVAL.

Operation 'Charnwood'. With the objective of trying to clear the German defences up to the Orne river and, if possible, secure bridgeheads over it, British I Corps was directed to launch a frontal assault with three infantry divisions north of Caen on July 8. The previous evening, in the first use of its squadrons for the tactical support of ground operations, RAF Bomber Command despatched 450 heavy bombers to pound the rearmost German lines with 2,300 tons of bombs. One of the attacking Lancasters can be seen over the clouds of smoke rising from the target area.

COMMUNIQUE No. 61   July 6

Allied troops have taken the railway station at LA HAYE-DU-PUITS, and are pushing on to the south with the enemy contesting every foot of ground. Our positions at CARPIQUET have been held. Enemy attacks continue.

Fierce combats with strong formations of enemy fighters, which were engaged in varying weather over the battle area and to the south and east, marked our air operations yesterday afternoon and evening. Considerable numbers of our fighters and fighter-bombers, vigorously supporting our ground forces, joined in the air battles which took place along the entire front. Notable air victories were scored in the area bounded by CHARTRES, ROUEN, CAEN and ARGENTAN, by fighters out to attack road and rail transport. They also attacked tanks at CARPIQUET airfield and special targets indicated by ground commanders close behind the enemy lines and at ST LO, VIRE, FALAISE, PERIERS and DREUX. At least thirty-five enemy aircraft were shot down during the day and four more were destroyed on the ground. Fifteen of our fighters are missing.

During the night heavy bombers attacked the railway yards at DIJON. All our bombers returned safely. Light bombers also hit railway junctions and bridges at VILLEDIEU, HYENVILLE and GRANVILLE.

During Tuesday night a considerable force of enemy E-Boats and R-Boats attempted to enter the Eastern Anchorage. The enemy was intercepted, brought to action, and finally driven off by light coastal forces. Two enemy R-Boats were sunk and a third severely damaged.

COMMUNIQUE No. 62   July 6

Allied troops advancing east of LA HAYE-DU-PUITS have reached the edge of the FORET DE MONT-CASTRE and are threatening the last area of high ground which dominate the town. Our progress is maintained down the road southwest from CARENTAN in spite of enemy counter-attacks.

In the CAEN area the battle at CARPIQUET airfield continues with fierce armoured and infantry fighting. A number of enemy tanks have been destroyed.

The enemy's rail and road supply system in the huge triangle PARIS—DOL—LA ROCHE-SUR-YON was mauled severely today by our air forces operating in strength and without interruption. Our fighter-bombers maintained armed reconnaissance patrol in this triangle throughout the morning, severing rail lines at many points. Enemy troop concentrations southwest of CARENTAN and a road causeway near LESSAY were also dive-bombed.

Medium bombers attacked several rail bridges in the combat area with good results. Fuel dumps at CHARTRES, ARGENTAN and CERENCES were set afire.

Early this morning during an offensive sweep towards BREST, an enemy force of four armed trawlers was intercepted by destroyer patrols. Three of the enemy were left burning fiercely.

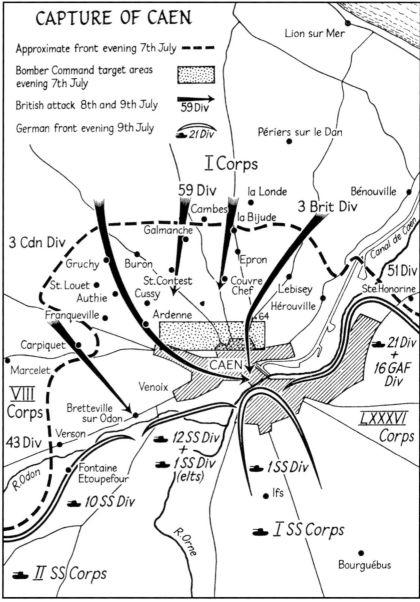

The attack was launched at 4.30 a.m. on July 8. On the left wing, the British 3rd Division swiftly cleared Lébisey and by evening had captured the high ground around Point 64 overlooking Caen. *Left:* The following day, AFPU photographer Sergeant Jimmy Christie pictured Shermans of the 33rd Armoured Brigade moving through the village. *Right:* Lébisey was largely destroyed by the fighting and it was a challenge for Bernard Paich to pinpoint where the photo had been taken. Fortunately he found another picture which showed the same ruined house seen in background, thus solving the mystery. QED Bernard!

COMMUNIQUE No. 63   July 7

The battle for LA HAYE-DU-PUITS continues. East of the CARENTAN—PERIERS road we have advanced towards SAINTENY. There is no change in the CAEN sector.

The enemy's supply system was again the principal target for our air forces which operated in strength throughout yesterday afternoon and evening. The attacks were mainly between PARIS and VIERZON in the east reaching west and northwest into Brittany and towards the battle area.

Heavy bombers, escorted by fighters, bombed railway bridges over the Loire, while medium and light bombers struck at other rail targets west of PARIS.

Fighter-bombers and fighters continued their armed reconnaissance, medium bombers joining them in attacks on fuel dumps and rail facilities.

Preliminary reports show that twelve enemy aircraft were shot down. Six of ours are missing.

During the night light bombers attacked rail targets behind the enemy line and in the neighbourhood of LE MANS.

COMMUNIQUE No. 64   July 7

Allied forces have made some progress southwest along the CARENTAN—PERIERS road.

West of AIREL our troops have captured a small bridgehead over the river Vire.

Air activity over the beaches and battle area up to noon today was confined to reconnaissance patrols.

The advance was more difficult in the centre and on the right wing where elements of the 12. SS-Panzer-Division fought hard at Buron and Saint-Contest, but in the evening, after the Canadian leaders pushed to Cussy, they managed to knock out six panzers that had attempted to counter-attack. One of them, a PzKpfw IV, was photographed the following day by Sergeant Jimmy Mapham. Note how a shot has hit its right track as the tank was moving causing the wheels on that side to dig in, so slewing it round on its axis.

Patrols infiltrated into Caen and the northern half of the city was at last under Allied control. This convoy has been forced to a halt by a bomb-crater.

In an area which has almost totally been rebuilt, it is fortunate that this house has survived at the end of Rue du Gaillon making a meaningful comparison possible.

Losses were heavy on both sides. These are men of the 16. Luftwaffen-Feld-Division crossing a ravaged Place Courtonne. By the time the battle for Caen ended, this particular unit had lost 75 per cent of its strength.

COMMUNIQUE No. 65   July 8

In the CARENTAN sector our troops advancing from the east have extended the bridgehead over the river Vire. Further north other Allied units have pushed down the road from CARENTAN towards ST JEAN-DE-DAYE. These two converging forces are now within two miles of the town.

Our air forces were active in close support of the land fighting yesterday afternoon and evening. Machine-gun nests and road junctions were under intermittent dive-bombing attacks throughout the period.

A strong force of heavy bombers effectively attacked a concentration of troops, tanks, guns, and strong points north of CAEN before darkness last night. Two thousand three hundred tons of explosives hit the target area.

Further damage was inflicted on the enemy's transport system from SAINTES and ANGOULEME, 200 miles south of Normandy, to MEAUX, east of PARIS. The TOURS-LA-RICHE railway bridge over the Loire was attacked by medium bombers, and fighter-bombers struck at railway yards, tracks, and motor convoys. An ammunition train on the NIORT—SAUMUR line exploded after a dive-bombing attack.

Early this morning heavy night bombers attacked railway yards at VAIRES on the eastern outskirts of PARIS.

COMMUNIQUE No. 66   July 8

Steady gains have been made on all active portions of the front.

Our patrols now are in the town of LA HAYE-DU-PUITS and we command all the high ground in the area. The bridgehead over the Vire river has been extended beyond ST JEAN-DE-DAYE, and between that village and CARENTAN, Allied troops have advanced to the Vire—Taute canal.

North of CAEN, in heavy fighting, the enemy has been driven from the villages of ST CONTEST, EPRON, and HEROUVILLE.

Our progress everywhere owes much to the Allied Air Forces which operated in strength. Medium and light bombers delivered low-level attacks with good results on troop concentrations, batteries and strong points just ahead of our troops near CAEN, and on communications targets as far south as NANTES. Others reported hits on a railway bridge over the river Eure at NOGENT-LE-ROI and another spanning the Loire at SAUMUR. One medium bomber is missing. Escorting fighters destroyed three enemy aircraft.

Heavy day bombers, with a strong escort of fighters, searched for openings in the clouds and bombed targets of opportunity east of the Seine.

Early Friday morning a force of enemy E-Boats and R-Boats with two M-Class minesweepers, and one other unidentified vessel, was intercepted in an attempt to enter the Eastern Anchorage and was brought to action. One German vessel was seen to blow up, one E-Boat or R-Boat was sunk and another set on fire.

Destruction was so great in this part of the city that it is difficult to comprehend that this is the same spot.

COMMUNIQUE No. 67 July 9

The attack on CAEN continues, with our infantry making steady progress covered by heavy artillery and air support. Every house and farm has been made into a center of resistance which is defended stubbornly.

On the west, further gains have been made on both sides of LA HAYE-DU-PUITS. Allied forces have advanced two miles southwest of ST JEAN-DE-DAYE.

Our fighters and fighter-bombers ranged from the Loire to the Channel, and from PARIS to NANTES, attacking enemy transportation. Tracks were severed on the main rail lines from PARIS to both LE HAVRE and ORLEANS. More than 150 railroad cars were destroyed. Near EVREUX direct hits were registered on the mouth of a rail tunnel.

Small formations of heavy day bombers struck at railway choke points at ETAPLES, junctions at L'AIGLE and the MANTES-GASSICOURT bridge, while medium and light aircraft hit a large railway bridge at NANTES.

Normandy-based aircraft, in close support of our troops, attacked earthwork fortifications and gun and mortar positions before our lines. Others strafed troops moving by rail towards the front and destroyed three tanks and other military vehicles.

During yesterday 24 enemy aircraft were destroyed on the ground and six in the air. Our losses were 12 heavy bombers and five fighters.

COMMUNIQUE No. 68 July 9

The town of CAEN has been liberated. Many pockets of enemy resistance remain but these are being systematically dealt with.

Local gains have been made in the Odon bridgehead and in the CAUMONT—TILLY sector.

In the base of the Cherbourg peninsula, German resistance in LA HAYE-DU-PUITS was crushed after the town had been bypassed on both sides.

Some ground has also been gained towards SAINTENY although enemy resistance is intense in both this area and beyond ST JEAN-DE-DAYE.

Heavy bombers attacked the airfield at CHÂTEAUDUN and bridges in the TOURS area this morning. Escorting fighters shot down one enemy aircraft, and bombed and strafed ground targets including locomotives, rolling stock and motor transport.

Medium bombers, one of which is missing, attacked a fuel dump at RENNES and a read bridge south of ORLEANS. They were escorted by fighters which also bombed gun positions south of RENNES and near ST MALO.

Naval patrols made contact with groups of enemy E-Boats off the mouth of the Seine early on Saturday morning. During the actions which followed two enemy E-Boats were severely damaged and one was set on fire before the enemy escaped into LE HAVRE.

Early this morning destroyers on patrol sighted and chased a force of five armed trawlers off CAP FREHEL. The enemy force escaped inshore under shelter of shore batteries, but not before they had received serious punishment.

Centre: **With two Shermans further down the street, this team from the 1st King's Own Scottish Borderers (9th Brigade, 3rd Division) have positioned their 6-pdr anti-tank gun to face any German threat arriving from the north-east.**
Right: **When so little remains of pre-war Caen, it is quite remarkable that these buildings on the corner of Rue Montoir Poissonerie and Rue Buquet still remain standing. Saint-Pierre Church can be seen in the background.**

Communiqué No. 68 of July 9 reported that 'Caen has been liberated'. These soldiers of the 2nd King's Shropshire Light Infantry of the 158th Brigade, 3rd Division, were photographed having just captured a German sniper.

After weeks of fighting to take the city, its final capture was of major symbolic importance for the Allies. *Left:* On July 11 General Montgomery came to personally inspect the prize and, significantly, visit the tomb of William the Conqueror. Here he is pictured outside Saint-Etienne Church acknowledging the cheers of the townspeople. *Right:* Fortunately the majestic church on the Place Monseigneur des Hameaux suffered only minor damage in the battle.

COMMUNIQUE No. 69   July 10

Following the devastating bombing yesterday morning, armor and infantry thrusting down all roads leading into CAEN from the north and west have forced the enemy out of the town back to the line of the river Orne. This advance was supported by naval gunfire and rocket-firing aircraft based in Normandy. Fighters from Britain ranged to the south and east of the town, effectively checking enemy attempts to bring up reinforcements. Reports received indicate that the enemy has suffered heavy casualties in this operation.

Patrols have crossed the river Odon a short distance above its junction with the Orne.

In the west an advance on both sides of the CARENTAN—PERIERS road brought Allied troops close to the village of SAINTENY.

The bridgehead over the river Vire was further widened and strengthened in spite of stiff enemy resistance.

Small formations of fighters and fighter-bombers on patrol in the area PARIS to ST LO and to the south attacked bridges and transport at MANTES-GASSICOURT, MONTFORT-SUR-RISLE and LESSAY. Rail embankments at BOURTH and bridges behind the enemy line were also attacked during the period from noon to midnight. Five enemy aircraft were destroyed for the loss of five of ours.

During the late evening, light bombers attacked a bridge and rail junction north of POITIERS, ferries between QUILLEBEUF and DUCLAIR and bridges, trains and road transport east of the battle area.

In yesterday morning's operations by escorted heavy bombers, six enemy aircraft were destroyed by our fighters. Three of our bombers and three fighters are missing.

COMMUNIQUE No. 70   July 10

In the CAEN sector the fighting has extended to the area south of the Odon river. From the Odon bridgehead our troops have advanced through the villages of ETERVILLE and MALTOT. Enemy strong points, which were bypassed in our advance yesterday, are being systematically eliminated.

Southwest of CARENTAN our troops advancing along the road toward PERIERS have liberated the village of SAINTENY. South of TILLY and south of LA HAYE-DU-PUITS strong German armored counter-attacks have been repulsed and a number of their tanks destroyed.

Widespread attacks on the enemy transportation system were carried out last night by our light bombers. Seventeen trains and associated targets on rail lines leading to the battlefront were damaged or set on fire.

Our fighter-bombers operated in the LESSAY and ST LO sectors this morning, attacking gun positions and strong points.

It was only after Operation 'Goodwood' had cleared the southern part of the city later in July that two Class 40 Bailey bridges — named 'Winston' and 'Churchill' — were built in Caen to carry traffic over the Orne river.

This modern span over the Orne is still named the Winston Churchill Bridge. The view is from the south bank with the church of Saint-Jean in the distance.

On the left wing of the 7. Armee, the LXXXIV. Armeekorps sector was weakly occupied but the defenders held their ground with tenacity. SHAEF Communiqué No. 72 reported on July 11 about the enemy 'delaying the advance toward Lessay'. *Above left:* PK photographer Koll first took this propaganda shot followed by another one *(above right)* showing the real misery of the soldiers. *Right:* By chance this second shot included a milestone and although it has now disappeared, the precise distance to Périers — 8.9 km — enabled us to trace where the picture had been taken. The sign marking the boundary of the municipality of Lessay makes for a fitting comparison.

COMMUNIQUE No. 71   **July 11**

Fighting has been particularly severe on the front of the Odon bridgehead where our advance to the high ground overlooking the river Orne was hotly contested.

South of the Vire bridgehead, Allied troops pushed forward towards PONT-HEBERT in the direction of ST LO.

Further west on the road to PERIERS an advance of more than a mile was made in the face of determined resistance.

South of LA HAYE-DU-PUITS local gains were made. The enemy has not repeated his counter-attacks in this area.

Yesterday, fighter-bombers and rocket-firing fighters attacked targets south of CAEN, including tank and troop concentrations and motor transport. One aircraft is missing from these operations.

Last night light bombers attacked enemy transport facilities in northeastern France.

COMMUNIQUE No. 72   **July 11**

The enemy south of LA HAYE-DU-PUITS is being pushed steadily southward. He is taking advantage of the close country to delay our advance toward LESSAY.

Allied thrusts southwest of CARENTAN and west from ST JEAN-DE-DAYE are converging on ST ANDRE-DE-BOHON.

In the Odon bridgehead area, fierce fighting has been going on. North of ESQUAY, Hill 112 has changed hands several times.

An enemy counter-attack from MALTOT towards ETERVILLE was repulsed. A number of enemy tanks were destroyed.

East of the Orne, Allied troops from the STE HONORINE area have advanced toward COLOMBELLES in the face of intense opposition.

In the area south of TILLY heavy fighting near HOTTOT has resulted in local Allied gains.

During the forenoon today fighters and fighter-bombers operating from bases in Normandy attacked targets in close support of the ground forces.

Allied troops, including French, of the Special Air Service regiments, have been operating well behind the enemy lines against communications and other military targets. Considerable success has attended their operations and a number of prisoners have been taken. These are being held pending transmission to this country.

COMMUNIQUE No. 73 July 12

German counter-attacks were many and severe all along the Allied front on Tuesday but they were held and we have made some gains.

There was an Allied advance on the road south from LA HAYE-DU-PUITS towards LESSAY and the bulge past SAINTENY was slightly enlarged.

Fighting in the vicinity of ST LO has been heavy and we now have PONT-HEBERT.

The strongest German counter-blow was in the area COLOMBELLES—STE HONORINE.

During the day our aircraft in support of ground forces destroyed 28 enemy tanks and damaged 16 others. Fighter-bombers destroyed or damaged 31 tanks in the LESSAY—ST LO area while rocket-firing aircraft accounted for 13 near HOTTOT and VIMONT.

Enemy artillery positions along the entire front were under air attack yesterday afternoon. Batteries in the PERIERS—LESSAY sector were attacked and direct hits registered on camouflaged gun positions.

Our medium bombers attacked fuel dumps at FLERS, FORET D'ECOUVES, CHATEAU-DE-TERTU and FORET D'ANDAINE, and a railway bridge at BOURTH yesterday afternoon.

East of PARIS aircraft on armed reconnaissance attacked transportation targets.

COMMUNIQUE No. 74 July 12

Steady Allied pressure in all the main areas of activity continues to force the enemy slowly back. Allied gains have been small but widespread, and the enemy has suffered considerable losses in abortive counter-attacks.

The FORET DE MONT-CASTRE is in our hands, and southwest of CARENTAN a further advance has been made down the road from SAINTENY. Allied troops also gained some ground south of the village of

Over in the American sector, the southern offensive by the US First Army was begun by VIII Corps on the right wing on July 3. However the Germans put up such a stubborn resistance that it took five days for the 79th Division to finally capture La Haye-du-Puits. What looks like a nice action shot was actually re-enacted the following day for the camera, Signal Corps photographer Corporal Billy Newhouse using these men from the 8th Division, which had just entered the line, for his picture.

The main road entering La Haye-du-Puits from the west has since been moved northwards at the point where it reaches the town. This has left the old road — the Route de Barneville — a quiet backwater.

ST ANDRE-DE-L'EPINE. Further east, fighting continued around the village of HOTTOT southwest of TILLY, and in the LOUVIGNY area near CAEN. More than 40 enemy tanks were claimed knocked out Tuesday by ground action.

From midnight until noon today, Allied aircraft ranged from BRUSSELS to BORDEAUX attacking transport and supply facilities and harassing troops.

During the night, light bombers patrolled the Seine crossings and the ORLEANS area, bombing power installations at BLOIS and the rail yards at TOURS.

The carts, carriages and wheelbarrows belonging to refugees fleeing the fighting have been moved aside to permit Allied armour to enter the town.

From first light, fighters and fighter-bombers gave close support to ground forces, attacking many targets indicated by Army Commanders. They also dive-bombed enemy troops and choke points at MANTES-GASSICOURT, ÉPERNON, CHARTRES and southwest of RAMBOUILLET. A railway bridge near CHERISY was attacked. Rail lines at TOURS, SAUMUR, LA FLECHE and CHERISY were cut.

In the ST LO area medium and light bombers destroyed a number of vehicles in a late morning attack on troop concentrations, fuel dumps and motor parks.

Coastal aircraft attacked enemy shipping off the coast, and bombs were seen to burst among enemy E- and R-Boats.

Rue du Château, the northern entrance to La Haye-du-Puits . . . then and now.

Left: **Another shot by Billy Newhouse, now looking in the opposite direction to his earlier shot on the facing page. This was obviously not a staged photo but were these exhausted GIs part of the 79th Division or from the 8th Division?** *Right:* **The same stretch of the bypassed road, looking east — the houses in the far background remain.**

From July 8, VII Corps pressed ahead with a two-division attack towards Périers. On the 9th, assisted by fighter-bombers, the 331st Infantry, 83rd Division, took Sainteny. A few days later, pilots of the 366th Fighter Group came to look at one of the Panthers that had been knocked out as a result of their 'accurate and deadly fire'. L-R: 1st Lieutenant Henry W. Collins, 1st Lieutenant Bayard B. Taylor, and 1st Lieutenant Joe F. Richmond.

COMMUNIQUE No. 75   **July 13**

The Allies continue to drive the Germans back in the base of the Cherbourg peninsula, and are now three miles south of LA HAYE-DU-PUITS.

LA SALMONNERIE, southeast of FORET DE MONT-CASTRE, was taken.

South of SAINTENY our units hold LA MAUGERIE and LA ROSERIE. Allied troops converging on ST ANDRE-DE-BOHON have met across the Taute river and most of the village is in our hands.

LA MEAUFFE, by-passed in the advance north of ST LO, has been mopped up, and ST PIERRE-LE-SEMILLY was occupied after we crossed the ST LO—BERIGNY road.

German counter-attacks, thrown repeatedly against our positions on the CAEN—EVRECY road, were beaten off by our forces.

Left: At Sainteny, Signal Corps photographer Arthur J. Ornitz must have been attracted by the symbolism of the ruined church framing the shattered memorial to the village dead of the First World War. *Right:* The memorial was rebuilt by re-assembling the original pieces . . . even the inscription remains the same. Also, although many of the ruined churches in Normandy were rebuilt along modern lines (see page 101), this particular church was restored traditionally.

This Panther of SS-Panzer-Regiment 2 abandoned in Sainteny provided a nice backdrop for a series of staged 'battle' photos re-enacted on July 13. Depicting a bazooka team in action, the caption to one photo explained that 'the camera records the instant when the bazooka gun scored direct hits on the German tank in the rear, and the vehicle goes up in a cloud of flame and smoke'. Additional 'colour' was provided by describing that the building behind was still being occupied by enemy snipers.

Attacking targets in close support of the land battles yesterday, our Normandy-based fighters, carrying bombs and rockets, scored many successes on convoys, enemy-occupied buildings, armored vehicles and a tank repair depot. Gun emplacements and mortar fire were silenced at army call.

Rail bridges at PONTORSON and CRAON were successfully attacked by fighter-bombers. At least nine enemy aircraft were destroyed in combat.

Despite unfavorable weather our medium bombers smashed the bridge at CINQ-MARS, 30 miles east of SAUMUR, and attacked other Loire river bridges at NANTES and SAUMUR and the span crossing the Eure river at NOGENT-LE-ROI.

The railway centers of TOURS and CULMONT-CHALINDREY were attacked by our heavy night bombers.

COMMUNIQUE No. 76 July 13

Allied forces are making slow but steady progress in the sector north of LESSAY.

South of CARENTAN, we have advanced 1,500 yards and driven the enemy from the village of ST ANDRE-DE-BOHON.

Further gains have been made along the BAYEUX—ST LO road near LA BARRE-DE-SEMILLY.

Coastal aircraft this morning attacked two small forces of enemy shipping in the eastern Channel area. Two of our aircraft are missing.

Fighter-bombers attacked a fuel dump at SENS southeast of PARIS and bombed railway tracks and yards in the area around CHARTRES.

Of the many shots that were restaged by Signal Corps photographers that day, the caption to this one states that 'a detachment of infantrymen under Sergeant James F. Kelly rush forward in their determined advance'. The impetus for this scenario prominently featuring a bazooka team in action could possibly have stemmed from higher up within VII Corps as it had struggled against German armour during the past week. Facing the corps' attack, the Germans had deployed tanks of the 2. SS-Panzer-Division to back their defensive line and Major General Robert C. Macon, commanding the 83rd Division, was worried when he saw his subordinate commanders concentrating on destroying individual panzers rather than advancing. On July 9 he ordered Colonel Ernest L. McLendon, the commander of the 330th Infantry, to push ahead with bazooka teams in the lead. However, when nothing changed, McLendon was relieved that evening. *Left:* Facing south, this Panther of SS-Panzer-Regiment 2 was obviously hit while withdrawing. *Right:* The highway near Sainteny (the centre of the village is off to the right in this photo) looking north in the direction of Carentan. With all the houses that were badly damaged in 1944 having been rebuilt in a more-modern style, it took some time to locate the same place but when we found it there was no doubt. Even the wall across the street, visible in the photo at the top of this page, was still standing, a hedge now having grown up where the bazooka team was lying.

COMMUNIQUE No. 77   July 14

On a ten-mile front south of LA HAYE-DU-PUITS, Allied forces have made good progress in an attack which brought our troops astride the main road to within two miles of LESSAY. Units on the right advanced about 2,000 yards near BRETTEVILLE and, on the left, the attack has overrun the village of VESLY.

In the CARENTAN sector the earlier advance has continued up both banks of the river Taute. Our troops have reached the outskirts of the village of TRIBEHOU and have pushed on two miles to the south and east through the BOIS DU HOMMET reaching the road near LE HOMMET-D'ARTHENAY.

Air operations were limited by weather from noon to midnight yesterday but Allied fighters and fighter-bombers continued their widespread attacks on enemy communications and flew many missions in direct support of our ground forces.

Gun positions and enemy headquarters near LESSAY, machinery loaded on trains near NOYANT, and a train loaded with armored vehicles in the LAVAL—ANGERS area were bombed and strafed with good results. Railway tracks were cut west and southeast of CHARTRES, and elsewhere deep behind the enemy lines. Successful attacks were made on locomotives, tanks, armored vehicles and loaded fuel and freight cars near TOURS and MANTES-GASSICOURT. Bridges at CHATEAUNEUF and ST FLORENTIN and a bridge and dam southwest of MAYENNE were hit. Near MONTARGIS and MEAUX, a number of freight cars were destroyed. A rail center at NANTES was bombed.

Six enemy aircraft were destroyed during the day. Seven of our aircraft are missing.

COMMUNIQUE No. 78   July 14

The Allied advance towards the LESSAY—ST LO road continues, and several small salients have been driven into the enemy's defences. LAULNE, northeast of LESSAY, has been taken.

Between LA MARTINIERE and AUXAIS we have made additional gains on both sides of the Taute river.

We are across the TRIBEHOU—LES CHAMPS-DE-LOSQUE road, southwest of BOIS DU HOMMET.

On the west bank of the Vire river, north of ST LO, another thrust has taken us to the outskirts of the village of LE MESNIL-DURAND. There is no change on the remainder of the front.

Our fighter-bombers operated in small force in difficult weather this morning against transportation targets at MONTDIDIER and BEAUVAIS and in the LISIEUX—BERNAY area.

Supporting the land forces, Normandy-based aircraft dive-bombed and strafed defended localities near ST LO.

Saint-Lô was the responsibilty of the II. Fallschirm-Korps which held the sector between the Vire and the Drôme rivers with three Kampfgruppen under the 352. Infanterie-Division on its left (west) wing and the 3. Fallschirmjäger-Division on the right. Some time in July PK photographer Wolfgang Vennemann pictured this road sign pointing to a detour to Sept-Vents, some 12 miles east of Saint-Lô. The proximity of the front can be gauged by the signs warning that the 'Enemy can see you'.

Left: **Another shot by Vennemann of an ambulance returning from the front with wounded men. The German field hospital in this particular sector was established in a manor house at La Mancellière, a mile south-east of Saint-Martin-des-Besaces.** *Right:* **The passing years have been kind to the building as it has hardly changed at all.**

COMMUNIQUE No. 79 **July 15**

More ground was gained by the Allies in the base of the Cherbourg peninsula. West of LESSAY, our patrols have advanced through ST GERMAIN-SUR-AY against light opposition to LES MEZIERES. We have approached more closely to LESSAY by taking BEAUVAIS and LA JOURDAINERIE. A few miles further east, we have taken LA LONDE and have reached the flooded basin of the Ay river.

Driving south through GORGES and ST GERMAIN, our units reached LES GRANGES and linked up south of LE HOMMET with troops advancing around the east of the GORGES marshes.

Between SAINTENY and the Vire river, and in the area east of ST LO, a number of local advances were made.

There is nothing to report from the remainder of the front.

Yesterday afternoon heavy bombers attacked targets in the AMIENS area and medium bombers attacked bridges at BOURTH and MEREY.

Fighters and fighter-bombers continued their attacks on transportation targets. Rail lines were cut in the ARGENTAN, LE MANS and ALENCON areas, and rolling stock in the Loire valley and at CHATEAUDUN and LA FERTE was attacked. Other targets included motor transport south of CAEN, enemy positions in the ST LO area and a radio installation near LE HAVRE.

During yesterday 25 enemy aircraft were shot down. Seven of ours are missing.

Last night the railway center of VILLENEUVE-SAINT-GEORGES was attacked by heavy bombers, while light bombers attacked barracks northeast of POITIERS.

Two enemy aircraft were destroyed last night, one by intruders over Belgium and the other over the battle area.

COMMUNIQUE No. 80 **July 15**

Allied troops, continuing their progress on the right of our front, have pushed forward to the immediate outskirts of LESSAY and reached the line of the inundations of the river Ay on a front of several miles.

The enemy was cleared from the villages of STE OPPORTUNE, PISSOT and ST PATRICE-DE-CLAIDS. Further east we have advanced through GONFREVILLE and NAY to the banks of the river Sèves.

Enemy artillery fire was heavier yesterday and during the night.

Fighter-bombers at minimum altitude bombed and strafed enemy troops and artillery positions in the ST LO area early this morning. Others, on reconnaissance patrols near CAEN, met a force of over thirty enemy aircraft and destroyed two of them without loss.

During the increased enemy air activity yesterday, anti-aircraft gunners in the eastern sector shot down five enemy aircraft and damaged others.

Early this morning enemy E-Boats were intercepted in the Seine Bay while attempting to break out to the westward from LE HAVRE. The enemy force was driven off and pursued. During the chase one E-Boat was set on fire. Patrol craft were later engaged off the harbor entrance and damage was inflicted on them.

Contact was also made with enemy E-Boats off CAP DE LA HEVE, and a short engagement took place before our force withdrew under fire from the shore batteries.

Centre: **On July 17, SS-Panzer-Regiment 12 reported that it was now down to 21 PzKpfw IVs and 18 Panthers.**
Right: **Bernard Paich discovered that the house, which lay on the corner of the junction near the church, has since disappeared.**

After four weeks of battle with heavy losses, the 12. SS-Panzer-Division was pulled back on July 9 to reorganise at Potigny, some 15 miles south of Caen. Here a command tank of SS-Panzer-Regiment 12 halted in front of the church at Soumont-Saint-Quentin. The 'Staudinger' sign, bottom right, identifies the HQ of SS-Brigadeführer Walter Staudinger, commander of artillery at Panzergruppe West.

COMMUNIQUE No. 81   July 16

Hard infantry fighting in close country continued yesterday all along the western sectors of the Allied front. Limited advances were made at a number of points notably south of the SAINTENY—PERIERS road and on the northern and eastern approaches to ST LO.

In a dusk attack in the EVRECY area the village of ESQUAY was captured and at midnight our troops had advanced some little distance beyond it.

Fighter-bombers penetrated 150 miles south of PARIS yesterday evening to attack transportation and supply targets in the NEVERS—BOURGES—ORLEANS—TOURS area.

Last night the rail centers at NEVERS and CHALONS-SUR-MARNE were attacked by a force of heavy bombers.

Nine enemy aircraft were destroyed in the air during yesterday's operations. Fourteen of ours are missing.

COMMUNIQUE No. 82   July 16

Allied advances have continued on the western sector of the front. Troops moving south on the CARENTAN—MARIGNY road have taken the village of LA TIBOTERIE. Gains have been reported south of LE HOMMET-D'ARTHENAY.

Attacking towards ST LO from the northeast, our troops have advanced more than a mile, taking the village of EMELIE. They have reached a point within 1,500 yards of ST LO itself, where enemy infantry today was also subjected to attack by our medium bombers.

Further east, in the TILLY—EVRECY area, our troops have occupied BRETTE-VILLETTE. Last night's attack through ESQUAY was developed to the west some 4,000 yards along high ground north of EVRECY. The enemy salient created by this attack was eliminated this morning with the occupation of GAVRUS and BOUGY.

In addition to attacking enemy front line positions, our medium bombers, escorted by fighters, struck at rail targets at PARIS, DREUX, GRANVILLE and near ARGENTAN. Bridges at BOISSEI-LA-LANDE, AMBRIERES and near DREUX were also attacked. None of our aircraft is missing.

Fighters which had escorted heavy day bombers to Germany this morning, attacked rail traffic at LUNEVILLE and strafed airfield installations in Belgium.

Coastal aircraft attacked enemy shipping in the eastern Channel early this morning.

Luckily one building by the edge of the cratered area has survived to this day enabling a perfect comparison.

Following SHAEF's plan to try to hinder the movement of German forces to the bridgehead, Saint-Lô had been heavily bombed on June 6 leaving almost 800 civilians dead under the ruins. The bombers returned every day for a week and the devastation was such that the German propaganda machine used the town as an example of how the Allies were 'liberating France'. With over 95 per cent of its buildings destroyed, after Saint-Lô was captured it became known as the 'Capital of the Ruins'. This is the road to Carentan.

On the same day, the German photographer pictured this long column of American prisoners being marched through the city. As they were arriving from the north, logically coming from the front, then some three miles away, the photo must have been taken around July 10.

This street running in front of the old Ecole Normale is the Rue Saint-Georges and is only 100 yards east of the ruined area seen in the photo at the top of the page, so it is amazing to see how this one street escaped unharmed amidst so much destruction.

COMMUNIQUE No. 83   July 17

Allied forces have made progress south of LE HOMMET-D'ARTHENAY and PONT-HEBERT. Our troops have established and widened a bridgehead across the Lozon river. Other small gains have been made against heavy enemy resistance. Allied pressure north and east of ST LO continues,

The village of CAHIER in the TILLY—EVRECY sector has been taken. About three miles west of CAHIER our forces have advanced southward, against fierce enemy resistance, to the vicinity of NOYERS on the CAEN—VILLERS-BOCAGE railroad.

Communications were principal targets for the Allied air forces from noon yesterday until dawn. Medium bombers severed the steel rail bridge at NANTES and fired a fuel dump in the forest of GUERCHES, south of RENNES. Bridges at ST HILAIRE-DU-HARCOURT and at L'AIGLE were attacked by light bombers.

Rail facilities in the PARIS area were hit by fighter-bombers which inflicted considerable damage to rolling stock and tracks.

COMMUNIQUE No. 84   July 17

Pressure by the Allied forces has led to further minor penetrations in the enemy positions in Normandy.

Some of our patrols are across the flooded basin of the Ay river near LESSAY, and to the east, just north of PERIERS, LES MILLERIES has been taken after a short advance.

We are threatening the lateral road PERIERS—ST LO in the vicinity of LE MESNIL-VIGOT after taking REMILLY-SUR-LOZON. Our patrols are now east and southeast of EVRECY, although we have not occupied the town.

Strong forces of heavy bombers this morning attacked railway yards at BELFORT and more than a dozen river bridges in a wide circle around PARIS, including bridges over the Loire, Yonne, Ailette and Somme rivers. Fighters which escorted the heavy bombers also attacked locomotives, railway cars and motor transport.

On July 10, XIX Corps began their attack to take Saint-Lô, the leaders of the 29th Division finally entering the town on the afternoon of the 18th. At 'Mortar Corner', so named because it had been subjected to a rain of artillery and mortar fire, Signal Corps photographer Sergeant James A. Ryan pictured two M10 tank destroyers which had been knocked out by the 88mm gun they had tried to silence.

The historic 'Mortar Corner' is now named Place du Major Howie in honour of the fallen commander of the 3rd Battalion of the 116th Infantry. All houses that lined the junction have disappeared with just a single building in the background remaining as a link with the past.

Medium bombers, one of which is missing, bombed a fuel dump at RENNES while fighters and fighter-bombers attacked rail facilities in the ALENCON, ARGENTAN, DOMFRONT, and NONANT areas and troops behind the enemy lines.

The speed with which Task Force C, the leading battle group of the 29th Division, had entered Saint-Lô caught the German defenders by surprise and by 5.30 p.m. — just 90 minutes after the leaders had entered it — the town was safely in American hands. *Left:* Having photographed 'Mortar Corner', Sergeant Ryan crossed the junction to Rue de Neufbourg where he pictured another M10 of the 803rd Tank Destroyer Battalion and Shermans of the 747th Tank Battalion rolling along the ruined street. *Right:* Looking westwards along Rue du Neufbourg today, with Place Sainte-Croix on the right.

COMMUNIQUE No. 85   July 18

Sporadic fighting from LESSAY to NOYERS has brought further gains of important and commanding ground for the Allies.

North of REMILLY-SUR-LOZON we overran the villages LA SAMSONERIE and L'ABBAYE and they are now firmly in our hands.

On the west bank of the Vire river there was a mile-deep advance south of LE MESNIL-DURAND. MARTINVILLE on one of the approaches to ST LO has been taken.

There has been heavy fighting north of NOYERS and EVRECY. HAUT-DES-FORGES has been captured.

Enemy airfields, troops, gun positions, rail centres, and fuel and ammunition dumps were targets yesterday afternoon and evening for Allied aircraft which ranged through comparatively clear skies southward to the Loire and eastward to the Somme.

In operations in close support of our ground forces fighters and fighter-bombers hit many pinpoint targets in the path of our troops near ST LO and blocked a highway in use by the enemy south of the town. Others successfully attacked guns and an ammunition dump near PERIERS. Airfields at LE MANS and at CORNE and VALADE on the outskirts of ANGERS, were bombed and strafed with good results. Railway tracks were cut at SABLE-SUR-SARTHE and near CHARTRES and a railway bridge northeast of MAMERS was severed.

Our fighters attacked an enemy headquarters south of CAEN, destroyed motor transport south of HOTTOT, and made a number of sweeps deep into France.

Medium bombers in the afternoon attacked a fuel dump on the outskirts of ALENCON and bombed trains and a transformer station near ARGENTAN.

COMMUNIQUE No. 86   July 18

Allied forces have broken through the enemy positions east of the river Orne. In an attack which commenced early this morning, supported by a terrific and accurate air bombardment, our troops have driven along the east bank of the river into the open country southeast of CAEN where armored and mobile forces are now in action against strong enemy forces.

Along the Orne our troops are steadily clearing the enemy out of the area, including the town of VAUCELLES on the south bank of the river opposite CAEN. Heavy fighting continues.

In preparation for the advance, the massive weight of Allied air power was concentrated in the heavily defended CAEN sector at dawn today.

Waves of escorted heavy, medium and light bombers, numbering more than 2,200, showered enemy troops, artillery and strong points south and southeast of CAEN with 7,000 tons of high explosive and fragmentation bombs. The attack continued for almost four hours with the bomb line moving gradually southward ahead of our troops on prearranged schedule.

Fighter-bombers operating in great strength, in even more direct support of our advancing troops, sought out individual targets which might have impeded their progress. Others stabbed to the east and southeast of the target area to interfere with enemy air and ground movement.

No enemy aircraft appeared during the entire bombardment. Nine of our bombers are missing.

On the western sector Allied troops have made another important advance at ST LO. The high ground to the east of the town was captured by our forces this morning after very stiff resistance. Fighting continues in the vicinity of ST LO itself.

 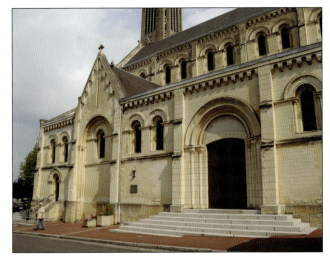

After Major Tom Howie was killed the previous day by a mortar burst, Major General Charles Gerhardt, the 29th Division commander, directed that his body should accompany the first US troops into Saint-Lô in a gesture of respect to the 5,000 Americans who had died to capture the town. *Left:* Draped in the Stars and Stripes, his body was then symbolically placed on the top of the debris from the shattered wall of Sainte-Croix Church. Thus a legend was born. On the July 19 SHAEF Communiqué No. 87 reported the final capture of Saint-Lô. *Right:* Damage to the church has been nicely repaired and a plaque now recalled that 'here was placed the body of Major Howie'. (See also *After the Battle* No. 138.)

COMMUNIQUE No. 87   July 19

Fierce fighting is going on in FAUBOURG-DE-VAUCELLES and in the plain south and east of CAEN. Enemy armored formations have been thrown in in an attempt to block the breach made in the German positions in this area.

In the JUVIGNY area, south of TILLY, our troops have advanced about half a mile and the enemy is fighting desperately to retain his hold on NOYERS.

ST LO was finally cleared of the enemy during yesterday evening.

The road from ST LO to PERIERS has been cut between the Taute and Vire rivers south of the village of AMIGNY which is in our hands.

Allied aircraft, in great strength, continued their support of our ground forces throughout yesterday afternoon. Bridges across the rivers Seine and Eure and railway lines in the ROUEN area were attacked during the afternoon by medium and light bombers.

Fighters and fighter-bombers, in great force, attacked enemy batteries, mortar positions, strong points and troop concentrations near the battle zone. Farther afield they struck at communications, airfields, supply dumps and transport from AMIENS in northeastern France to the west coast of the Cotentin peninsula.

During the day, first reports show 15 enemy aircraft were shot down and a number destroyed on the ground. Twenty-four of our aircraft are missing.

In the evening the rail yards at VAIRES, on the eastern outskirts of PARIS, were successfully attacked by escorted heavy bombers. Two bombers are missing.

During the night heavy bombers, 29 of which are missing, attacked the railway junction at REVIGNY, about 100 miles due east of PARIS, and AULNOYE, about 20 miles west of the Franco-Belgian frontier. Preliminary reports indicate that both attacks were well concentrated.

Two enemy aircraft were destroyed over the battle area and one by our intruders over Germany during the night.

Early Tuesday morning light coastal forces fought three brief gun actions close to the enemy coast between CAP GRIS-NEZ and the mouth of the river Authie. The enemy received considerable punishment. Two of his craft were last seen on fire.

Over on the eastern side of the battlefield, the British Second Army was about to begin the long-awaited Operation 'Goodwood'. Preliminary operations were launched west of Caen when the 50th Division captured Hottot. Here AFPU photographer Sergeant Norman Midgley follows a patrol as it moves cautiously into the village in search of snipers.

The wall and gate have remained unchanged in the main street.

On the left wing of the XII Corps attack, Gavrus was taken by the 15th Division and Esquay was entered but, after repeated attacks and counter-attacks, the village still remained in German hands. *Left:* Sergeant Mapham pictured infantry moving into Tourville which lies just north of Gavrus. *Right:* The main street in Tourville, yesterday and today.

Operation 'Goodwood' began at daylight on July 18 with a massive bombardment of the German lines when over 2,000 British and American aircraft dropped 8,000 tons on the sector south-east of Caen. *Right:* **Positions occupied by the 21. Panzer-Division (with schwere Panzer-Abteilung 503 under command), were heavily hit and 20 of their panzers were later found abandoned midst a cratered landscape, like this PzKpfw IV near Émiéville, and it was midday before the dazed survivors were rescued.** The VIII Corps then launched its attack led by three armoured divisions. However German resistance soon stiffened, the advance was stopped, and by July 20 the British gain appeared to be only some seven miles. This failure led to widespread disappointment and discontent at SHAEF, and Commander Butcher, Eisenhower's naval aide whose job it was to keep an unofficial daily diary, noted Ike's grim comment: 'Can we afford a thousand tons of bombs per mile?'

COMMUNIQUE No. 88   July 19

Fierce armoured and infantry fighting continued this morning in the area south and east of CAEN.

FAUBOURG-DE-VAUCELLES is now entirely in our hands, and the enemy has been cleared from the villages of LOUVIGNY on the west bank and FLEURY on the east bank of the river Orne.

The breach in the enemy defences has been widened and Allied troops have occupied the villages of TOUFFREVILLE, DEMOUVILLE and GIBERVILLE. Pockets of enemy resistance which had been by-passed have been eliminated. Progress continues in spite of stubborn enemy opposition.

Throughout yesterday and today Allied warships and landing craft have been engaging enemy batteries on the eastern flank in support of the Army. Allied aircraft based in Normandy maintained their patrols and close support of our troops this morning.

One thousand two hundred fifty prisoners were taken yesterday in the CAEN area, and the total taken since the beginning of the campaign is now over 60,000.

Allied troops have made local advances in the HOTTOT area and north of REMILLY-SUR-LOZON.

COMMUNIQUE No. 89   July 20

The battle south and east of CAEN continues. Allied troops striking towards TROARN have reached the railway half a mile from the town while other forces which had taken part in the clearing of LOUVIGNY and VAUCELLES have driven the enemy from the villages of CORMELLES and IFS. To the south and east of these villages our armour has been in action against enemy armour and anti-tank defences based on villages and farmsteads.

Further west a systematic advance has been made along the front between GRAINVILLE and ST GERMAIN-D'ECTOT.

Seven bridges and enemy fuel dumps at ORLEANS and BRUZ were the principal objectives for our medium bombers yesterday. Loire river bridges at LES PONTS-DE-CE, TOURS-LA-RICHE, LA POISSONIERE and NANTES, and other bridges at MANTES-GASSICOURT, COMBOURG and ST HILAIRE-DU-HARCOURT were attacked. Results could not be observed in all cases but three of the bridges attacked are believed to have been made impassable.

Armed reconnaissance patrols ranged southward to BORDEAUX and eastward from Normandy to the PARIS area to attack rail traffic. Many locomotives and goods wagons were damaged during widespread strafing and bombing of trains and railyards.

The Canadian II Corps seized the southern part of Caen and soon established a firm bridgehead over the Orne. On July 19 Communiqué No. 88 reported that 'Faubourg-de-Vaucelles is now entirely in our hands'. A few days later these Churchill AVREs were pictured just after they had crossed over to the right bank.

This is Boulevard Leroy in Faubourg-de-Vaucelles just south of Caen.

Although the destruction of this PzKpfw IV in Faubourg-de-Vaucelles on July 18 looks spectacular, the main purpose of the operation which, in Montgomery's words, was to engage the German armour in battle and 'write it down', was not achieved.

COMMUNIQUE No. 90   July 20

A series of infantry thrusts to the east and south of CAEN have steadily extended the area, which is firmly in our hands. BOURGUEBUS and FRENOUVILLE have been freed of the enemy and we are in possession of the villages of BRAS and HUBERT-FOLIE and of the ridge to the north of ST ANDRE-SUR-ORNE.

Enemy attempts to counter-attack were repulsed and our threat to TROARN was increased by an advance towards ST PAIR on the high ground to the south of the town.

Northwest of ST LO Allied troops advanced to the line of the Vire and also improved their positions to the south of the town.

Visibility limited air operations over the immediate battle area from midnight until noon, but several successful attacks were made in northeast France.

Near AMIENS, two trains loaded with enemy tanks were effectively bombed by our fighter-bombers which also damaged a bridge over the Somme and destroyed railroad rolling stock at ABANCOURT and at SABLE-SUR-SARTHE, northeast of ANGERS. A highway bridge at GISORS was attacked and rail lines were cut in several places north of LAVAL and LE MANS and southwest of DREUX.

Escorted light bombers hit the rail center at CHAULNES, near AMIENS, destroying much rolling stock.

Coastal aircraft attacked enemy surface craft in the Channel.

One enemy aircraft was shot down near ST QUENTIN. Two of our fighters are missing.

On the 19th Lieutenant-General Sir Miles Dempsey, the British Second Army commander, directed that the Canadian II Corps relieve the VIII Corps so that the armoured divisions which had lost 271 tanks in the operation could refit. *Left:* Canadian engineers sweep the verge of a road for mines in Faubourg-de-Vaucelles. *Right:* A French veteran of the First World War greets carriers of the South Saskatchewan Regiment pushing through Fleury-sur-Orne, just south-west of Caen.

On July 20, Eisenhower, frustrated with the failure of Operation 'Goodwood', decided that he had to visit Montgomery and Bradley in France. However, the weather was poor and all aircraft were grounded. Eisenhower drove to the airfield where he impatiently waited clearance, Butcher recording in his diary that Ike said he had to get across, 'even if he had to swim'. The meeting with Montgomery was difficult as was borne out in the letter Eisenhower sent to him the following day to question whether they saw 'eye to eye on the big problems'. Ike wrote that he had been 'extremely hopeful and optimistic that Operation "Goodwood", assisted by the tremendous air attack', would have a decisive effect on the battle in Normandy but 'that did not come about'. He pointed out that 'while we have equality in size we must go forward shoulder to shoulder, with honours and sacrifice equally shared.' At SHAEF, speculation now began as to who might succeed Montgomery if he was sacked, Butcher noting how the Americans discussed the British system of taking care of unsuccessful generals. 'There was 'in fact a number of methods of kicking a man upstairs. Montgomery could be made a peer and sit in the House of Lords or even given a governorship, such as Malta.' This picture was taken less than a week after the July 20 meeting when Eisenhower visited Montgomery again on the 26th. Signal Corps photographer Lieutenant Eugene Moore wrote humorously in his caption that Montgomery's dog in background was called 'either Hitler or Rommel'! In fact the Fox Terrier was named Hitler, Rommel being a Spaniel Monty acquired shortly after D-Day.

As Eisenhower was visiting Montgomery on July 20, over in East Prussia an attempt was made to kill Hitler at his Rastenburg Führerhauptquartier. The bomb exploded at 12.42 p.m. but Hitler suffered only minor wounds — a cut to his hand and ruptured ear drums. *Left:* Pictured with Hitler less than a week before (July 15), this is Oberst Claus von Stauffenberg (left), the officer who placed the briefcase bomb in the conference room. Second from left is Konteradmiral Karl-Jesko von Puttkamer, naval liaison officer to the Führer, and, right, Generalfeldmarschall Wilhelm Keitel, head of the OKW. *Right:* That day, Mussolini was due to arrive any minute for a scheduled meeting so Hitler, having changed his clothes which had been ruined, took the Duce to inspect the damaged conference room. This was less than four hours after the explosion. Behind the two men is Hitler's interpreter, Paul Schmidt. The following day Hitler broadcast over national radio so that the German people 'should hear my voice and should know that I am unhurt and well'. He announced that 'a very small clique of ambitious, irresponsible and stupid officers had formed a conspiracy to kill me and eliminate at the same time the command of the Wehrmacht'. In their Weekly Intelligence Summary, SHAEF commentated that there was no reason to disbelieve Hitler's assertion that it was 'an Army Putsch cut to the 1918 pattern and designed to seize power in order to come to terms with the Allies'. SHAEF found it 'encouraging' that German officers had been planning to liquidate Hitler. 'The very fact that plotters reckoned that the time was ripe for a venture so complicated as the assassination of the Führer argues that they had good reason to hope for success. How else save something, at least, from the chaos? How else save the face of the German Army, and, more important still, enough of its blood to build another for the next war?' The Military Governor of France, General Carl-Heinrich von Stülpnagel, was a dedicated member of the conspiracy, but with Generalfeldmarschall Hugo Sperrle and Admiral Theodor Krancke, the commanders of the Luftwaffe and the Kriegsmarine, both loyal to Hitler and his regime, the success of the coup depended very much on the support of the Commander-in-Chief in the West, Generalfeldmarschall Hans-Günther von Kluge.

Without a caption there was no clue as to where Propaganda-Kompanie photographer Arthur Grimm pictured von Kluge relaxing with junior members of his staff . . . that is until Jean Paul tracked down the venue to the Villa David on the Rue Alexandre Dumas in Saint-Germain-en-Laye, outside Paris, where the German HQ in the West was located (see *After the Battle* No. 141).

COMMUNIQUE No. 91   July 21

Attacking from the ridge north of ST ANDRE-SUR-ORNE, Allied infantry have captured the village. Between there and BOURGUEBUS we have extended our hold on the high ground from the river Orne to the vicinity of VERRIERES.

Air operations over the immediate battle area yesterday were limited by poor visibility.

A strong force of heavy bombers, nine of which are missing, made an accurate and concentrated attack last night on the railway yards at COURTRAI in Belgium.

COMMUNIQUE No. 92   July 21

Allied troops yesterday continued the advance south of ST ANDRE-SUR-ORNE against heavy enemy resistance, which developed into an enemy counter-attack near ST MARTIN-DE-FONTENAY. This counter-attack, which was supported by armour, was repulsed with loss to the enemy.

In the area east of CAUMONT our troops have made a slight advance.

Allied forces in the western sector have made small local gains north of PERIERS and along the PERIERS—ST LO road south of REMILLY-SUR-LOZON. An enemy counter-attack near RAIDS was repulsed.

COMMUNIQUE No. 93   July 22

There is nothing to report.

COMMUNIQUE No. 94   July 22

A number of enemy counter-attacks on both western and eastern sectors of the front have been repulsed with a total of at least 14 enemy tanks knocked out.

A limited number of aerial patrols were operated during the period from midnight to noon today.

Having visited the Panzergruppe West command post at Mittois, 20 miles south-east of Caen, for a conference, von Kluge returned to his headquarters around 6 p.m. where he heard the news that Hitler was dead although conflicting reports said he was alive. At that point, a call came through from the conspirators in Berlin but von Kluge held back from doing anything until a telex from Keitel reached him at 8 p.m. confirming that Hitler was in full health. Later in the evening, von Kluge learned from von Stülpnagel, whom he had summoned from Paris, that about 1,200 Nazi officials had been arrested in the French capital. Von Kluge immediately sent von Stülpnagel back to Paris to have them freed. In the early hours of the 21st, he sent a letter of congratulations to Hitler, praising the 'gracious dispensation of Providence' which had saved the Führer's life. 'In the name of the three services subordinate to me as Ob. West, congratulate you and assure you, my Führer, of our unchangeable loyalty, come what may'. However, in spite of these efforts to disassociate himself from the conspiracy, von Kluge would still soon fall under suspicion.

However, the assassination attempt and subsequent arrest and execution of the conspirators had no effect at all on the military situation in the West. At the front, German soldiers were too busy trying to remain alive to do more than speculate about the truth behind the news. This paratrooper was photographed in Torigni-sur-Vire.

Left: Under the protection of a .50-calibre machine gun, an outdoor Mass was held in a farmyard at Couvains, in the sector of the VII Corps, some five miles north-east of Saint-Lô. Veterans have identified these two men as belonging to the 4th Cavalry Group. *Right:* The Commune farm, just north-west of the village.

Since the second week in July when the First Army had begun to display definite signs of bogging down in the Cotentin, General Bradley had begun to envisage mounting an operation that combined concentrated land power with an overwhelming bombardment from the air. By July 13 his idea became the First Army's plan for Operation 'Cobra'. The planners were careful to eliminate one factor that had just hampered Operation 'Goodwood' which was the long interval between the bombing and the ground troops jumping off. The 'Cobra' plan called for 2,500 aircraft to obliterate the German defences along the Périers—Saint-Lô road by dropping 5,000 tons of bombs. Three infantry divisions of the VII Corps were to make the main effort with the 4th Division in the centre flanked by the 9th and the 30th Divisions. They were to secure the towns of Marigny and Saint-Gilles, thereby sealing off the flanks. The 2nd and the 3rd Armored Divisions and the 1st Infantry Division would then drive through the gap and towards the west coast of the peninsula near Coutances and surround the German forces opposite the neighbouring VIII Corps. *Left:* Major General Manton S. Eddy, the commander of the 9th Division, discusses the situation with some of his men.

COMMUNIQUE No. 95   July 23

In the CAEN sector, east of the Orne, Allied troops have cleared the enemy from the village of ETAVAUX. Our forces advanced southeast of ETERVILLE and MALTOT is in our hands.

North of PERIERS we have crossed the Seves river in the vicinity of the village of SEVES.

Fuel dumps at FORET DE CONCHES, MESSEI and CHATEAU-DE-TERTU were attacked by medium bombers early yesterday evening. Escorted night bombers attacked rail lines at BOURTH and military buildings near VANNES.

Bridges near BREST and CHOLET were hit by fighters and fighter-bombers. Locomotives were attacked, tracks severed and trucks destroyed in the areas of LORIENT, CHARTRES and ANGERS. Two of our aircraft are missing.

COMMUNIQUE No. 96   July 23

Allied troops east of CAEN have cleared the enemy from the village of EMIEVILLE. Enemy counter-attacks were repulsed in the regions of yesterday's advance near MALTOT and near SEVES in the western sector.

Medium and light bombers this morning attacked six rail targets leading to the battle zone. Results were unobserved.

Other bombers, before dawn, harassed enemy communications at ROUEN, VIERZON and a number of Seine crossings.

With no indication in the wartime caption as to the location, it was a real challenge to trace it to this farm — La Cour-Miette — at Les Champs-de-Losque, nine miles north-west of Saint-Lô.

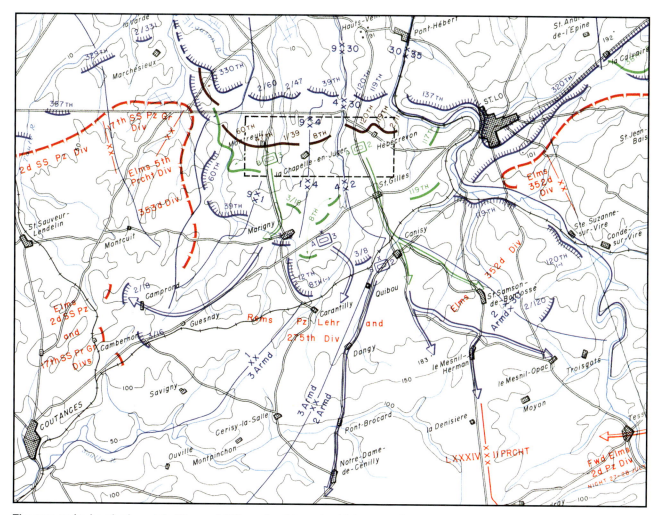

The area to be bombed on July 25 was 7,000 yards wide and 2,500 yards deep immediately south of the Périers—Saint-Lô highway and to prevent accidents, the troops in the front line were pulled back 1,200 yards from the road.

COMMUNIQUE No. 97   July 24

Sharp local engagements took place south of the river Sèves in the area north of ESQUAY and on the river Orne south of MALTOT. Our forward positions remain substantially unchanged.

Enemy supply system and airfields northeast of PARIS were attacked by our air forces during yesterday. In addition close support was given to the land forces in Normandy.

Medium bombers attacked a railway bridge north of the Seine at MIRVILLE and a railway crossing at the Risle southwest of ROUEN, and the Charentonne at SERQUIGNY. Other targets were fuel dumps in the FORET DE CONCHES and a railway yard near MONTFORT.

Direct hits were registered by our fighter-bombers on two double-span highway bridges crossing the Sienne river at COUTANCES.

Other fighter-bombers, patrolling southward below the valley of the Loire, severed rail lines in many places and damaged numerous railroad cars and locomotives.

Last night heavy bombers attacked oil storage depots at DONGES, near ST NAZAIRE.

SHAEF Communiqué No. 100 reported of the 'great weight of Allied air power employed in conjunction with our ground troops'. Near Amigny, a mile north of the Périers—Saint-Lô highway, GIs from the 8th Infantry Regiment, 4th Division, gaze skyward at the bombers releasing their loads on the German lines. The wristwatch of the soldier in the middle conveniently reveals the time: 1035.

COMMUNIQUE No. 98   July 24

Early today, Allied light bombers harried enemy troops and attacked rail movements in a broad belt behind the enemy line from east of the Seine to the battle area. A supply dump in the FORET DE CINGLAIS was bombed. Two of our aircraft are missing.

Enemy coastal craft were intercepted and engaged off CAP D'ANTIFER by our naval patrols early yesterday. Three enemy R-Boats were severely damaged and one was set on fire.

There is nothing to report from our ground forces.

COMMUNIQUE No. 99 July 25

An Allied attack began early this morning astride the FALAISE road south of CAEN. First reports indicate that some progress already has been made.

Rail bridges and other communications facilities north of the river Loire and west of TOURS were successfully attacked yesterday by our medium and light bombers.

Ammunition and fuel dumps southeast of CAEN and rail targets in the ARRAS and LE MANS areas were attacked by low-flying fighter-bombers.

An enemy cargo ship was damaged by coastal aircraft last evening off GUERNSEY.

Last night an oil storage depot at DONGES, near ST NAZAIRE was attacked by our heavy bombers, two of which are missing.

Left: **On the left wing of the attack, the 30th Division met determined resistance just across the highway and it was around midnight when they finally entered Hébécrevon, the first of their objectives. Here men of the 120th Infantry Regiment move up through the ruins of the village.** *Right:* **The church was so badly damaged that almost all of it had to be demolished before rebuilding.**

COMMUNIQUE No. 100 July 25

Heavy fighting has followed our attack south of CAEN this morning. In spite of stubborn enemy resistance with armour and infantry, the advance has been maintained and fighting is in progress in the area of MAY-SUR-ORNE and TILLY-LA-CAMPAGNE.

In the western sector an attack was launched at noon west of ST LO.

A great weight of Allied air power was employed in conjunction with our ground troops. Very large forces of heavy, medium, light and fighter-bombers joined in a concentrated attack preceding the ground operations near ST LO, dropping very great numbers of fragmentation and high explosive bombs.

More medium and fighter-bombers attacked targets in the zone beyond CAEN. Fighters provided escort and carried out offensive sweeps.

At least 12 enemy aircraft were shot down in these operations. According to reports so far received six of our bombers and three fighters are missing.

Coastal aircraft this morning attacked enemy surface craft in the Channel.

Further south, the bombing smashed a sector held by elements of the Panzer-Lehr-Division and attached units. Near the destroyed church of Saint-Gilles, which is just out of this picture to the right, Signal Corps photographer Norbie took this shot of engineers bulldozing wrecked PzKpfw Vs off to clear the road.

Armageddon. The bombardment buried men and equipment, overturned tanks, cut communications and turned the sector into a frightening moon-like landscape. About one third of the men holding the main line of defence and assembled on the immediate reserve line were killed or wounded, the survivors dazed and with barely a dozen tanks or tank destroyers undamaged. This Panther was half buried in a large crater.

Air Chief Marshal Leigh-Mallory personally went to Normandy to check the weather conditions for July 24. Finding the sky overcast, he signalled for the bombing to be aborted, but it was too late and one formation released bombs north of the road killing 25 men and wounding 131. The following day over 1,500 B-17s and B-24s of the Eighth Air Force and 380 medium bombers from the Ninth carried out the main bombing operation, but once again some bombs fell north of the road, killing another 111 troops and wounding 490. With the Americans now having suffered over 900 casualties in two days, Eisenhower resolved that he would never again use heavy bombers in a tactical role. Some official observers and newspaper reporters had also been killed, among them Lieutenant General Lesley J. McNair, the commanding general of the US Army Ground Forces. A bomb had landed squarely on his slit trench, blowing his body 60 feet away and mangling it beyond recognition. (It was only identified by the three stars on his collar.) McNair was the commander of the 1st US Army Group, the notional unit created in 1943 as part of the Allied deception plan for the invasion. Therefore, as news of General McNair's death might compromise the deception, he was buried secretly with only senior officers in attendance. Commander Butcher wrote: 'McNair's death came as a shock. He had been wounded in Africa while observing in Tunisia. The Germans seem to have his number but that doesn't quite make sense either, assuming an American bomb killed him'. In 1954 McNair was posthumously promoted to the rank of a four-star general by the US Congress although the gravestone in the Normandy American Cemetery was not changed to reflect his final rank until November 2010.

Left: On the right wing, Marigny was finally cleared during the morning of the 27th. These horses were spooked by the sound of armour rumbling through town and they suddenly bolted into the street which caused 'a little diversion for US troops as they pass on to the front'. *Right:* The houses lining the left-hand side of Rue Auguste Eudeline were never rebuilt.

COMMUNIQUE No. 101   July 26

In the area west of ST LO, Allied troops have advanced up to 3,000 yards on a wide front and have crossed the PERIERS—ST LO road at a number of places. South of CAEN, fighting has been very bitter and enemy counter-attacks, some supported by armor, have continued all day. Our initial gains have been held and fighting continues in the area of MAY-SUR-ORNE, VERRIERES and TILLY-LA-CAMPAGNE.

Following yesterday morning's operations in support of ground forces in both the CAEN and ST LO sectors, smaller formations of Allied aircraft continued close support of our ground forces throughout the day.

Numerous tanks, gun positions, strong points and motor transport just forward of our line and an enemy headquarters west of ST LO were among targets attacked by fighter-bombers and fighters.

Other formations of both fighters and medium bombers attacked communications targets, including bridges, fuel dumps, supply depots, rail yards and trains behind the enemy lines.

At least 25 enemy aircraft were destroyed yesterday. Seventeen of ours are missing.

Searching for snipers in Marigny. The 'Heintz' sign identifies Kampfgruppe Heintz, a battle group from the 275. Infanterie-Division that was annihilated during the fighting near Hébécrevon on the 25th. The sign at the top refers to the 3. Kompanie of SS-Panzer-Pionier-Bataillon 2, which was the engineer unit of the 2. SS-Panzer-Division.

COMMUNIQUE No. 102   July 26

In the western sector the Allied advance has continued to make steady progress and the battle area has been extended.

East of the Orne the enemy is making every effort to block our entry to the open country southeast of CAEN, and additional enemy reinforcements have been brought into the area.

Allied attacks have been heavily engaged by defensively-sited armor, artillery and mortar fire. In one locality our forces have repulsed a heavy enemy counter-attack which was strongly supported by tanks.

Small forces of medium bombers operating in poor weather bombed enemy positions in the ST LO area and a fuel dump near ALENCON this morning.

Formations of fighter-bombers struck at enemy bivouac areas, machine-gun positions and other tactical targets which were indicated by our land forces.

Left: Recognising a photo opportunity, Sergeant William Spangle of the Signal Corps quickly snapped this shot which he captioned as a 'Yank infantryman taking a nap among the debris littering a sidewalk in Marigny'. *Right:* The picture was taken near the church on Avenue du 13 Juin 1944. This building can also be seen in background of the photo in the middle of the page.

With the breakthrough now beginning to gather speed, Spangle then pictured this Howitzer Motor Carriage M8 passing a tank and a Jeep which had been knocked out on July 27. Unfortunately the SHAEF censor has heavily obliterated the marking on the M8 before releasing the print for publication but it most probably belonged to the 3rd Armored Division.

COMMUNIQUE No. 103   July 27

In the area west of ST LO Allied forces have made good gains through enemy positions. One armored column has driven south some five miles from the PERIERS—ST LO road to take MARIGNY. Another armored prong thrust across the ST LO—COUTANCES road through ST GILLES. The advance is continuing. Elsewhere in the western sector local gains have been made.

South of CAEN there has been heavy fighting, with the enemy continuing a stubborn defense. All attacks by our forces in this sector have met strong concentrations of enemy tanks, artillery and mortars. Several enemy counter-attacks have been repulsed.

Yesterday afternoon and evening fighter-bombers attacked enemy gun positions, strong points, tank and troop concentrations in and around the battle areas. Other fighter-bombers and fighters kept up the attack on transportation targets over a wide area from DOUAI to VENDOME, cutting railway tracks and strafing locomotives, rolling stock and vehicles.

Sixteen enemy aircraft were shot down. Thirteen of ours are missing.

Fuel dumps at FONTAINEBLEAU and SENONCHES and railway bridges at EPERNON and L'AIGLE were attacked early yesterday evening by medium bombers.

Heavy bombers, six of which are missing, attacked the railway center of GIVORS-BADIN, 12 miles south of LYON, last night.

Three enemy aircraft were shot down during the night, two over Normandy and one by intruders.

Centre: While there were no constraints on releasing photos of enemy dead, if the censor did approve the release of pictures showing American dead, the faces were always blotted out to prevent identification. *Right:* The road sign gives the clue as to where this picture was taken: on the N172 between Coutances and Saint-Lô. There are several junctions along this road but the only one that matches the directions given by the signpost — left to Coutances and right to Marigny — unfortunately shows houses that appear old enough to appear in the 1944 photo. So it would appear that the sign may have been turned round so we chose this alternative comparison.

COMMUNIQUE No. 104   **July 27**

Allied armoured thrusts in the western sector continue to make rapid progress. One column has cut the road from ST LO to PERCY in the neighbourhood of LE MESNIL-HERMAN while another has advanced four miles to the southwest of CANISY. A third has driven some distance west from MARIGNY down the COUTANCES road. Between the Sèves and the Ay rivers, an advance of some 2,000 yards has cut the PERIERS—LESSAY road.

Between ST LO and CAUMONT, the enemy salient is being steadily eliminated and advanced troops after occupying BERIGNY have reached the outskirts of NOTRE-DAME-D'ELLE. Other forces moving west from the CAUMONT area have reached the village of MOUFFET.

A strong enemy counter-attack towards VERRIERES was repulsed last night. The enemy has made no further effort in the CAEN sector.

Fighter-bombers, supporting advancing ground forces in the ST LO sector, attacked enemy guns and transport.

Military targets at BRUSSELS and GHENT were attacked by small forces of heavy bombers this morning. Escorting fighters strafed roads and railway facilities in the same area.

Enemy shipping off the Pas-de-Calais coast was attacked by coastal aircraft early today.

Top: The leaders of the Combat Command B of the 4th Armored Division cleared Coutances on July 29 before pushing southwards to Cérences and Lengronne. The censored caption to this photo released by SHAEF on July 31 simply stated: 'American anti-snipers in action in Coutances'. *Left:* This photograph is captioned as 'Medics give first aid to soldiers wounded in the first Jeep to enter Coutances which hit a mine and overturned in the middle of the street'. *Right:* Now renamed Avenue de la Division Leclerc, this is the main road from Périers just as it enters Coutances which gives some credence to the claim in the original caption that the Jeep could well have been the first vehicle to enter the town.

Left: The Germans heavily mined the stretch of the road where it entered the town and, less than 100 yards further down the same street, an M5 light tank belonging to the 25th Cavalry Reconnaissance Squadron also struck a mine. *Right:* Avenue de la Division Leclerc, named in honour of the commander of the French 2ème Division Blindée.

COMMUNIQUE No. 105   July 28

In the western sector Allied forces have maintained their rapid advances.

Our troops have pushed forward west of MARIGNY to the vicinity of CAMPROND and southwest to the vicinity of CERISY-LA-SALLE. Other formations have advanced south of PERIERS. Ground has also been gained west of CAUMONT. South of CAEN our positions remain firm.

A number of attempts by the enemy to develop counter-attacks have been broken up by our artillery and supporting aircraft which were active throughout yesterday on both sectors.

In the western sector, fighter-bombers patrolled ahead of the advancing armoured columns, attacking tank units, gun positions, defended hedgerows and observation posts as far as COUTANCES and southward to VILLEBAUDON.

In the eastern battle sector rocket-firing aircraft scored hits on tanks and motorised infantry targets.

East and south of the battle area fighter-bombers in strength attacked rail targets. In the AMIENS—ST QUENTIN area in ammunition train was blown up. Other rolling stock was attacked and rails cut in many places.

During yesterday at least 23 enemy planes were destroyed in the air. Twenty-one of our aircraft are missing from all operations.

The 5x4 Speed Graphic camera was standard issue to Signal Corps photographers, producing beautiful 10x8 prints from the 5x4 negatives. Usually the wartime captions identify the photographer concerned although not in this case.

Left: On July 28 the leaders of CCB of the 2nd Armored Division pushed westwards to Saint-Denis-le-Gast, trapping large German forces near Roncey. Fuel shortages and congestion caused them to abandon their equipment and instead organise themselves into haphazard groups to try to escape southwards on foot. On July 29, pilots of the IX Tactical Air Command discovered this mass of vehicles — a 'fighter-bomber's paradise' — and for six hours that afternoon waves of aircraft had a field day. Over 100 German tanks and 250 vehicles were later counted knocked out in the Roncey area alone. This French family are returning home past the ruined church and wrecked German equipment which includes two Marder III tank destroyers. *Right:* The church was so badly damaged that it was replaced in the late 1950s by a completely new building.

Left: During the night of the 29th, the trapped Germans resumed their withdrawal and shortly before midnight they reached Saint-Denis-le-Gast. Their arrival surprised the Americans who quickly pulled back leaving the Germans free to escape through the gap but US troops rallied and retook the village at daybreak on the 30th. This PzKpfw IV probably belonged to the 2. SS-Panzer-Division. *Right:* Bernard Paich took this timeless comparison at the southern entrance to the village.

While American troops on Operation 'Cobra' were now seeing positive results, over on the eastern flank Montgomery directed British Second Army on July 27 to regroup and shift its weight to attack from the Caumont area — and the sooner it began the better. The offensive, code-named Operation 'Bluecoat', was launched on July 30, the XXX Corps leading, with VIII Corps on their right. On the first day, AFPU photographer Sergeant Jock Laing pictured Shermans passing through Caumont.

Another shot by Sergeant Laing of an M10 tank destroyer loaded with infantrymen passing through the devastated streets of Caumont. However, the operation did not quite go as planned and while the VIII Corps advanced, the XXX Corps attack stalled. The 11th Armoured Division established a bridgehead across the Souleuvre river on July 31 and on August 1 it captured Le Bény-Bocage. Armoured car patrols ranged over the country well to the south, coming to within two miles of Vire where they found the Germans building up strong resistance. However, as that town lay across the boundary between the US and British armies, the capture of Vire was left to the Americans.

COMMUNIQUE No. 106　　　July 28

In the western sector there has been some progress south of LESSAY where Allied troops have advanced down the LESSAY—COUTANCES road to the vicinity of MARGUERIN. Further east our forces have advanced up both banks of the river Ay to the area of CORBUCHON.

On the PERIERS—COUTANCES road a strong armored thrust has joined the westward drive from MARIGNY in the outskirts of COUTANCES. Our forces have passed through NOTRE-DAME-DE-CENILLY and are continuing down the road to the southwest. Another force has passed through MAUPERTUIS, north of PERCY. Our forces have taken TESSY-SUR-VIRE and have continued along the road southwest of the town. We are eleven kilometers from GAVRAY.

South of ST LO our forces hold the high ground east of the river. In the area between ST LO and CAUMONT we have improved our positions.

Our aircraft continued their support of the ground forces, concentrating on road and rail targets, as weather permitted. Light and medium bombers cut rail lines radiating from PARIS to MONTARGIS, DIJON, MOULINS, TOURS, and ROUEN. Supply stores near BRECEY and CAILLOUET were hit. Fighter-bombers later destroyed rolling stock in rail yards at BUEIL and near MAINTENON.

COMMUNIQUE No. 107   July 28

COUTANCES is now clear of the enemy and Allied armored forces have reached the sea south of the estuary of the Sienne river. Areas of enemy resistance north of the town are being rapidly cleared.

Further progress has been made by the thrust southwest from NOTRE-DAME-DE-CENILLY.

In support of ground operations, yesterday, fighter-bombers attacked an ammunition distribution point, enemy gun positions, enemy reserves and vehicles. Other fighter-bombers and long-range fighters, on armed reconnaissance over northwest France attacked locomotives, rolling stock and road transport.

Targets for our medium and light bombers were eight rail bridges northwest of PARIS, an important ammunition dump in the FORET DE SENONCHES near CHARTRES, and rail centers north of BERNAY. Last night light bombers attacked 18 trains and many road targets in northern France.

Coastal aircraft attacked small enemy vessels off ST MALO yesterday. One boat carrying troops was sunk.

Five enemy aircraft were shot down over the beach-head last night.

The Guards Armoured Division took Saint-Martin-des-Besaces on July 31 where this Sherman and Carrier with a 6-pdr anti-tank gun in tow were pictured.

Left: **Just to the west, across the boundary with the US First Army, V Corps launched an attack near Vidouville on the 28th** by the 2nd Infantry of the 5th Division. *Right:* **A remarkable comparison at La Croix-Prie, five miles west of Caumont.**

Left: Some six miles further south, still with the 2nd Infantry, Signal Corps photographer Lieutenant Mark A. Freeman pictured radio operator Private Paul Berkebile catching a brief rest as he waited for orders for his unit to resume the advance. *Right:* The Vauviel crossroads just south-east of Placy-Montaigu.

COMMUNIQUE No. 108 July 29

Allied armored columns in the western sector continue to advance against stiffening resistance. One column has reached the coast west of COUTANCES and has taken the town of PONT-DE-LA-ROQUE. Another column has reached HYENVILLE south of COUTANCES. Pockets of resistance at CERISY-LA-SALLE and MONTPINCHON have been mopped up.

The salient between VILLEBAUDON and ST DENIS-LE-GAST has been cleared of the enemy. The town of HAMBYE has been taken.

Enemy forces are astride the Vire south of TESSY. Southeast of ST LO the Allied forces have advanced several kilometers.

German military buildings near MORLAIX were attacked by fighter-bombers this morning.

COMMUNIQUE No. 109 July 30

Allied forces pushing south from COUTANCES have linked up with our forces in LENGRONNE. The whole of the road between these two towns is in our hands.

An enemy force south of the river Seulles has been surrounded and is being steadily eliminated in spite of determined efforts to break out.

'Heavy armour and artillery roll through a French town as Allied forces advanced on all fronts'. This picture of a High Speed Tractor M4 towing a 155mm Long Tom was taken on the American left wing in the Torigni-sur-Vire sector, the censor again deliberately obliterating the unit marking in red ink. So, without more information, it could have belonged to either a unit in V Corps or XIX Corps. Picture released by SHAEF on July 31.

Left: **The lead tank having rammed a steel gate forming a roadblock at the entrance of the town, CCB of the 6th Armored Division rolled into Bréhal on July 30.** *Right:* **Rue du Général de Gaulle, in front of the Town Hall.**

Our troops advancing to the west have crossed the river Sienne in several places. PERCY and the PERCY—HAMBYE road are in our hands. Heavy fighting continues in the area of TESSY. Further east an advance of a mile has been made astride the river Seulles in the area of ST VAAST.

Throughout yesterday, in changeable weather, Allied fighters and fighter-bombers closely supported our advancing troops. At least 20 tanks were destroyed; fighters trapped an enemy convoy crossing a bridge over the river Sienne near GAVRAY and destroyed 12 tanks.

Enemy troops, gun positions, and bridges were hit in attacks southwest of COUTANCES, and near AVRANCHES and ST LO.

Many railway cars and armoured and motor vehicles were set on fire by fighters operating in rear of the immediate battle zone and at VENDOME and in the ROUEN—AMIENS—ARRAS area.

Escorted heavy bombers, using instruments, attacked airfields at JUVINCOURT and LAON-COUVRON. Five enemy aircraft were destroyed during the day's operations. Five of our fighters are missing.

COMMUNIQUE No. 110   July 30

The Allied advance continues in the western sector. BREHAL, CERENCES, and GAVRAY have been occupied and Allied troops are pushing on beyond these towns.

Pockets of enemy infantry and armor which had been bypassed are being steadily eliminated. Attempts to break out with tank support by enemy encircled in the areas of LENGRONNE and ST DENIS-LE-GAST were frustrated, and more than 30 tanks were knocked out. A strong counter-attack in the area of TESSY-SUR-VIRE was beaten back.

In the CAUMONT area an advance of three miles has been made south of the town, and Allied troops have reached ST JEAN-DES-ESSARTIERS and LES LOGES. To the east of CAUMONT our troops have gained ground in spite of strong enemy resistance, very difficult ground and extensive minefields.

A force of heavy and medium bombers attacked tactical targets in the CAUMONT area this morning in support of the ground action there. Both visual and pathfinding techniques were employed due to the cloud layer which extended to within 2,000 feet of the ground.

Fighter-bombers continued to support our advancing columns in the western sector.

Armed reconnaissance patrols were flown as far eastward as AMIENS, PARIS and CHARTRES.

The US bridge was just downstream from the one destroyed by the Germans.

Meanwhile, in the early afternoon of the 30th, the leaders of CCA, 3rd Armored Division, had reached the Sienne river near Gavray. The bridge had been blown but, after infantry waded across under the protection of artillery, engineers began to construct a treadway bridge. This M5 light tank belonging to the HQ of the 32nd Armored Regiment cautiously crosses over, followed by an M3 half-track of the armoured infantry.

COMMUNIQUE No. 111   **July 31**

An Allied armoured column has entered AVRANCHES after an advance of more than 12 miles.

Another column moving south from BREHAL is within three miles of GRANVILLE.

Heavy fighting continues in the area of GAVRAY, PERCY and TESSY-SUR-VIRE.

In the CAUMONT sector the Allied advance has made further progress and we have captured the high ground east of ST MARTIN-DES-BESACES.

An enemy attack in the NOYERS area was beaten off yesterday evening after hard fighting.

Medium bombers attacked tactical targets in the CAUMONT area and fuel dumps near ARGENTAN and CHATEAUDUN.

Fighter-bombers and fighters attacked targets in close support of the ground forces, road transport behind the battle zone, and rail targets in the region of BLOIS and ORLEANS.

Six enemy aircraft were destroyed during the day. Eight of ours are missing. Four enemy aircraft were shot down over France during the night.

COMMUNIQUE No.112   **July 31**

Allied troops in the western sectors have entered the town of GRANVILLE and are mopping up the whole area between AVRANCHES, GRANVILLE and BREHAL. Other pockets of resistance are being cleared and heavy fighting continues northwest of TESSY and in the PERCY area.

The enemy has been driven from the ground immediately south of GAVRAY and Allied troops have also advanced on each side of TORIGNI-SUR-VIRE.

In the CAUMONT area Allied progress continues and we have taken ST GERMAIN-D'ECTOT, CAHAGNES and ST MARTIN-DES-BESACES. Hill 309, east of ST MARTIN, remains in our hands in spite of several enemy counter-attacks.

Rail targets south of the battle area were attacked by escorted medium and light bombers. Rail bridges at FORGES, CHARTRES, south of DOMFRONT, and across the Loire, south of TOURS, were bombed with good results. Elsewhere, poor visibility prevented immediate assessment of results.

Fighter-bombers were active in close support of our ground troops.

Two airfields in northern France were attacked by small formations of heavy bombers shortly after noon.

The picture was taken at Le Repas, a crossroad south of Bréhal. Avranches is 15 miles away to the south.

On the afternoon of July 30, CCB of the 4th Armored Division moved rapidly through La Haye-Pesnel, reaching Avranches by evening. On July 31, this decisive movement made the opening statement in SHAEF Communiqué No. 111. This M8, belonging to the 25th Cavalry Reconnaissance Squadron, was photographed passing a disabled Opel Blitz that had belonged to the 2. SS-Panzer-Division.

Left: **Breakthrough becomes break-out! On July 31, the leaders of the VIII Corps burst out into open France. Shermans of the 68th Tank Battalion, 6th Armored Division, were pictured passing through Avranches, the destruction here having been caused when the town was bombed by the Allies on June 7.** *Right:* **Place Littré with the Saint-Gervais Church in background.**

By late afternoon on July 31 a task force of the 4th Armored Division swept over the Pontaubault bridge crossing the Sélune and occupied the important road intersections immediately south of it. By the morning of August 1 the VIII Corps possessed three crossing sites over the Sée river and four over the Sélune — more than enough routes to enter Brittany. It was vital to prevent jams building up at the crossing points so strict priorities were established with great attention to proper compliance. Commanders engaged themselves at vital crossroads and Major General Robert W. Grow, the commander of the 6th Armored Division, later commented that he had spent most of his time there as 'a traffic cop'. This gave exceptional results for in less than two days, the 4th and 6th Armored Divisions had reached Brittany. The Luftwaffe tried hard to stop them and from August 3 through 7, the vital Pontaubault bridge was bombed several times yet suffered only one near miss; the flow of traffic was never really stopped. *Below:* The old stone bridge at Pontaubault survives to this day.

Having smashed the French railway system through repeated bombing, now it all had to be repaired as quickly as possible. Throughout north-eastern France bomb damage at rail centres had been extensive and had been combined with serious demolition south of the Seine. In spite of the efforts of the railway operating organisation, it was not until the end of September that the railway system began to show signs of providing a reliable service. There was also a shortage of rolling stock which had to be imported through Cherbourg although the first American locos to reach the Continent arrived at Utah Beach on July 10, already pre-loaded on trailers. By the end of the month 48 locomotives and 184 railway cars had been received from the UK and captured equipment included 100 steam locos and over 1,500 freight cars. With the 21st Army Group, it was not until the Dieppe train ferry opened on September 29 that the shortage was overcome in the British sector. Caen became the main traffic and communications centre in spite of the damage being inspected here by a Railway Construction Company of the Royal Engineers.

TOWARDS COUTANCES: Armoured division moves along the road into St. Sauveur Lendelin.

AUGUST 1944
BREAK-OUT

The US Third Army was put under the command of General George S. Patton in late 1943 but it was not until July 1944 that the plan for the break-out required its employment in France. On July 25 Eisenhower announced that US forces were to be regrouped under General Bradley commanding the 12th Army Group which was to become active on August 1. That same day the Third Army became operational, this press conference being held on July 11 near its command post which had been set up in an apple orchard at Néhou, just north of Saint-Sauveur-le-Vicomte.

Other photos taken on August 24 showing Patton's headquarters were stopped by the censor for publication until June 1945. The communications trailer was the nerve centre.

COMMUNIQUE No. 113   **August 1**

In the western sector Allied forces which entered GRANVILLE have now cleared the town. An advance on a broad front towards the main PERCY—AVRANCHES road has brought our troops close to VILLEDIEU. There is heavy fighting near PERCY.

Strong enemy resistance continues northwest of TESSY. We have made substantial gains in the TORIGNI—ST MARTIN area. Isolated pockets of resistance throughout the sector are being steadily eliminated.

Escorted heavy bombers attacked naval vessels at LE HAVRE and the railway centre of LA ROCHE last night, as our air forces kept up their pounding of enemy supply and communication.

Medium bombers hit rail bridges crossing the SEINE at MANTES-GASSICOURT and LE MANOIR and over the LOIRE river at NANTES, TOURS and PONTS DE CE. Fuel dumps in the FORET DE LA GUERCHE and at TOURS and ammunition stores southeast of CAEN were bombed effectively.

Fighter-bombers, on armed reconnaissance, attacked railways, rolling stock, airfields and motor transport over a wide area.

COMMUNIQUE No. 114   **August 1**

Allied progress in the western sectors continues. Armored forces pushing on from AVRANCHES have captured the dams southeast of DUCEY and near VEZINS, while others have taken BRECEY and reached the river See in this area. Fighting is going on south of VILLEDIEU though the town itself has not yet been taken.

Our forces have driven further forward in the TESSY area and are now within a mile of the town. There has also been some progress south of TORIGNI-SUR-VIRE.

In the area south of CAUMONT Allied troops, after clearing the FORET L'EVEQUE, have crossed the river SOULEUVRE and taken LE BENY-BOCAGE.

Poor visibility limited air activity from midnight until noon. During the morning Normandy-based aircraft attacked targets in advance of our troops.

On June 11, 1994, a memorial was dedicated in the orchard by Patton's granddaughter, Helen Ayer Patton.

On August 1, as the Third Army was sliding into Brittany, the US First Army started to swing left to drive to the Seine in conjunction with the British Second Army and Canadian First Army. Commander Butcher, Eisenhower's naval aide, noted in his diary that: 'We are to hell and gone in Brittany and slicing them up in Normandy'. *Above:* Signal Corps photographer Root pictured an M10 tank destroyer moving through the junction in the centre of Percy.

COMMUNIQUE No. 115   August 2

In the AVRANCHES sector Allied armored forces continue to push forward to the south and east. South of VILLEDIEU further progress has been wide.

Allied forces have captured TESSY after heavy enemy resistance. Our hold on LE BENY-BOCAGE and the crossings over the river Souleuvre have been strengthened.

Enemy vehicles, ammunition dumps and other battlefield targets were attacked by fighter-bombers in close support of our ground forces yesterday.

Better weather during the afternoon made possible a step-up in the Allied air offensive and large-scale attacks were launched on enemy bridges and airfields.

Airfields at CHATEAUDUN, ORLEANS/BRICY, TOURS, CHARTRES and MELUN, bridges over the Seine and Marne rivers, and an oil dump at ROUEN were attacked by heavy bombers.

Rail bridges crossing the Loire, other rail bridges in the LE MANS, CHARTRES and DREUX areas, a fuel store at ST MALO and an ammunition dump south-east of CAEN were targets for medium and light bombers.

COMMUNIQUE No. 116   August 2

Allied formations have continued to fight their way forward during the day and have now reached VIRE and the road from VIRE to CONDE. The village of ESTRY has been taken and progress continues. There is also heavy fighting in the area of ONDEFONTAINE. Our troops are approaching AUNAY.

In the CAEN area bitter fighting continues against enemy armored formations in the region of TILLY-LA-CAMPAGNE.

In the western sectors, Allied armored formations have progressed beyond PONTORSON while other forces are approaching ST POIS and advancing south-east of BRECEY. The town of VILLEDIEU has been captured and further progress has been made south of TORIGNI.

Our air operations were limited by the weather.

SHAEF reported the capture of Le Bény-Bocage in Communiqué No. 114, though it only refers to 'Allied troops'. The captors were the leaders of the 11th Armoured Division in the British VIII Corps. With their hands raised above their heads these two German prisoners are brought into the town.

COMMUNIQUE No. 117   August 3

Little change was reported from the front during the night. South-east of BRECEY enemy opposition was overcome at LE MESNIL-ADELEE and fighting continues a few miles south-east of PERCY. Fighting was also heavy in the neighborhood of VILLERS-BOCAGE and AUNAY. The advance beyond PONTORSON continues.

Bridges, armored vehicles, ammunition and oil dumps, road and rail transport, and enemy shipping were primary targets for Allied aircraft which ranged from Belgium to the Bay of Biscay and deep into southern France in varying weather yesterday.

Railway bridges at LISLE, NANTES, EPONE, MAINVILLIERS, NOYEN and CINQ-MARS were attacked with good results by escorted medium bombers. Barges on the Seine and ammunition dumps at CAUDEBEC, MONTREUIL and LE LUDE were also hit.

Fuel dumps at SENS, ST OUEN and GENNEVILLIERS were targets for escorted heavy day bombers which also attacked bridges in the PARIS area and the Loire valley and other tactical targets in northern and central France. Escorted heavy night bombers struck by day at naval vessels in LE HAVRE.

Railway yards were attacked by fighter-bombers which also destroyed locomotives, munitions cars and motor transport over a wide area.

Throughout the day, fighters and fighter-bombers provided close support for our armies along the entire front.

Ten enemy aircraft were destroyed during these operations. Seventeen of ours are missing.

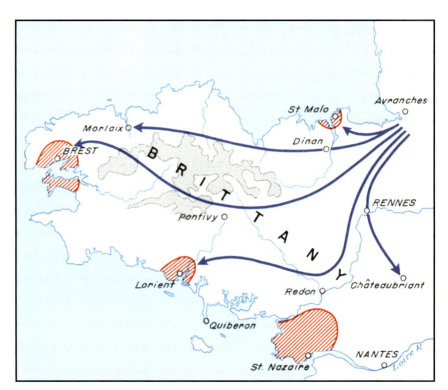

Patton launched two armoured columns into Brittany, the 4th Armored Division to cut the neck of the peninsula and the 6th to go all the way to Brest. Meanwhile, a provisional Task Force A was to secure the railway line that follows the northern shore of the peninsula. The armoured commanders were far from enthusiastic about advancing westward, 'winning the war the wrong way' as Major General John S. Wood of the 4th Armored complained, preferring to head east towards Germany. *Right:* **The leading tanks of the 4th Armored reached the outskirts of Rennes during the evening of August 1 although the attack they then launched failed. Additional infantry was committed and the German garrison finally withdrew in the early hours of August 4. The 13th Infantry Regiment marched into Rennes the following morning welcomed by the cheers and kisses of the population crowding the Place de la République.**

Left: **At Dinard, on the western bank of the Rance estuary, GIs were pictured crouching alongside the Casino, trying to move forward 'despite the harassing fire of German snipers'. On the other** side of the estuary, the garrison in Saint-Malo was still holding strong. *Right:* **This is Boulevard Wilson in Dinard photographed for us by Jacques Launay. The Casino is still in business.**

Originally, development of the 'Overlord' plan implied that the Allies first needed to capture the Breton ports. However, after the break-out at Avranches, SHAEF realised that it might be possible to secure two objectives simultaneously and by August 2 Eisenhower believed it was 'unnecessary to detach any large forces for the conquest of Brittany'. Instead, it would be more advantageous to 'devote the greater bulk of the forces to the task of completing the destruction of the German Army, at least that portion west of the Orne, and exploiting beyond that as far as [possible].' On August 3, Bradley announced that the Third Army was to clear Brittany using only 'a minimum of forces', its primary mission now being to drive eastward in a sweeping manoeuvre toward Paris. As the XV Corps had already advanced around the German left, it was directed to initiate the operation. *Right:* On August 5 the corps took Mayenne where Pfc Bernard T. Godin was photographed inspecting a makeshift American flag hung out to greet the liberators. So the story goes, this flag was made during the First War and kept hidden during the German occupation. The lad on the left is Pierre Jousse.

COMMUNIQUE No. 118   August 4

Allied forces have reached RENNES and have elements to the south of the town. Another column advanced through DOL and moving westward along the north side of the Brittany peninsula has reached the area of DINAN.

Other Allied formations east of the PERCY—VILLEDIEU road have captured BEAUMESNIL and are in the area of ST SEVER-CALVADOS. Further south our forces have captured MORTAIN.

In the area south-east of CAUMONT Allied troops have made progress towards VILLERS-BOCAGE and AUNAY where there has been some hard fighting. We hold the BOIS DE BURON.

There has been a series of enemy counter-attacks along the entire front from the north and east of LE BENY-BOCAGE.

Good weather yesterday afternoon and evening allowed Allied fighters and fighter-bombers, some carrying rockets, to give close support to the ground forces. Barges on the Seine, an ammunition dump south-east of CAEN, gun positions, and a considerable number of enemy vehicles, were destroyed.

Bridges near PARIS, ORLEANS, CHARTRES and ROUEN were bombed with satisfactory results by medium and light bombers. Other formations attacked an ammunition dump at MAINTENON.

Three marshalling yards and an oil dump in Alsace-Lorraine, objectives near PARIS and BRUSSELS and a synthetic oil plant and a storage depot near DOUAI were hit by strong forces of heavy bombers. Accompanying fighters attacked rolling stock, power stations and other targets.

Rail communications were attacked during the night by our light bombers.

One of a formation of five E-Boats was sunk by a direct bomb hit by coastal aircraft in an attack off the Channel Islands.

A force of enemy E-Boats was intercepted on Thursday morning west of CAP DE LA HEVE by light naval coastal forces. In the short action which followed one of the enemy was sunk and another damaged before he made good his escape towards LE HAVRE.

According to the original caption, the leaders of the 90th Infantry Division entered Mayenne as the 'Germans were still shelling the town'. This is Rue Du Guesclin at the western entrance.

Meanwhile, over on the right wing of the British Second Army, Operation 'Bluecoat' had turned out to be a big disappointment. Stiffening German resistance had halted the advance, so with XXX Corps lagging behind, VIII Corps was forced to protect its exposed left flank. As a result heads had to roll and the commander of XXX Corps, Lieutenant-General Gerard Bucknall, went on August 2 and the CO of the 7th Armoured Division, Major-General George Erskine, the following day. *Above:* This is Sergeant Jock Laing's picture of Churchill tanks making their way across country near Saint-Pierre-Tarentaine, two and a half miles north of Le Bény-Bocage.

The photograph was taken here, just south of Saint-Pierre-Tarentaine, proving that the tanks had bypassed the village across the open country to the east. They were now just rejoining the main road.

COMMUNIQUE No. 119   August 5

Allied troops have made rapid progress in Brittany, fanning out to the neighborhood of LOUDEAC, MAURON, DERVAL and CHATEAUBRIANT. RENNES is in our hands, and DOL has been cleared of enemy. Our forward troops are already beyond FOUGERES.

Other forces are advancing south-east of LANDIVY and while fighting continues for MORTAIN, advanced troops have reached the area of BARENTON. A large part of the FORET DE ST SEVER is in our hands.

ESQUAY and EVRECY have been cleared of enemy and leading troops are reported in the area of VACOGNES and AMAYE-SUR-ORNE. Further south, our position has been improved by the capture of ONDEFONTAINE. Determined enemy counter-attacks in the area east and north-east of VIRE have been frustrated.

Yesterday, escorted heavy bombers attacked targets in widely separated districts of France, including airfields at LILLE and ACHIET, a railway bridge at ETAPLES, a coastal battery in the Pas-de-Calais and oil storage depots at PAUILLAC and BEC D'AMBES, near BORDEAUX.

Medium bombers attacked railway yards at MONTFORT, and BEAUVAIS, a railway embankment at EPERNON and a concentration of enemy troops south of AUNAY. Light bombers went for rail targets in western France, blowing up an ammunition train near BORDEAUX.

Fighter-bombers flew reconnaissance beyond the battle area and in north-eastern France in addition to attacking an oil dump at ANGERS, barges on the Seine and an airfield near AMIENS. In these operations, locomotives, rolling stock and motor transport were destroyed.

A coastal vessel was blown up during an attack by rocket-firing fighters on a convoy off the Dutch coast.

During last night road and rail transport and enemy concentrations were attacked by medium and light bombers. Five enemy aircraft were shot down over Normandy.

Infantry of the Royal Scots Fusiliers, 15th (Scottish) Division, hitch a lift on a Churchill of the 4th Grenadier Guards of the 6th Guards Tank Brigade. The circle identifies the tank belonged to C Squadron. Brigadier Sir Walter Bartellot took command of the brigade on August 3 only to be killed on the 16th. Positive identification of the disabled PzKpfw IV is not possible but one can guess by the location that it once belonged to SS-Panzer-Regiment 10.

Surrounded by its churchyard, the repaired church still stands in the heart of Le Tourneur.

COMMUNIQUE No. 120   August 6

In Brittany, an Allied armored force has driven to REDON. Another force has continued its attack north-west of DOL. VITRE and PONTIVY have been cleared of the enemy.

RENNES, PONTORSON and AVRANCHES were bombed by the enemy early yesterday. Damage was slight.

SS Panzer troops were captured at DINAN, RENNES and VITRE. An Allied task force has engaged the enemy near ST MALO.

In Normandy, we have moved through the FORET DE ST SEVER. The forest is not entirely clear of the enemy, and in approaching CHAMP-DU-BOULT, our troops are encountering pockets of machine guns and small arms resistance. Enemy Panzer units and paratroops are opposing our advance in the town LE MESNIL-GILBERT.

Near VIRE, our forces are encountering enemy artillery fire. We are 1,500 yards from the center of the town. Further north, enemy pockets of resistance left behind by our advance have now been eliminated. Leading troops have entered AUNAY-SUR-ODON.

On the west bank of the Orne, our advance southwards has continued. All the high ground as far south as the village of LE HOM, a mile north of THURY-HARCOURT, is in our hands.

At midday yesterday, heavy bombers attacked a railway bridge at ETAPLES and submarine pens at BREST. Hits were scored on the pens with 12,000-pound bombs. In the evening oil storage depots at BASSENS and BLAYE near BORDEAUX, and at PAUILLAC, were attacked by other heavy bombers. Two heavy bombers are missing.

Eight railway bridges and embankments on an arc extending from ELBEUF on the Seine to BRIOLLAY near ANGERS, were attacked by medium and light bombers. Other medium bombers attacked railway yards at COMPIEGNE, SERQUEUX and VERNEUIL, and flak barges in the harbor at ST MALO.

Locomotives and rolling stock in the CHARTRES—ORLEANS area and motor transport were targets for fighter-bombers. Direct support was given our ground forces by fighter-bombers. Fighters provided bomber escort.

Two enemy aircraft were destroyed over northern France during the night.

This was then the N177, now the D577, near Beaulieu, looking north.

Above left: **Tank crews of the 23rd Hussars, 29th Armoured Brigade, 11th Armoured Division, crowd onto a Sherman to celebrate the destruction of another PzKpfw IV at Le Bény-Bocage.** *Above right:* **This street is now aptly named Rue de la 11ème Division Blindée.**

The advance goes on, Shermans and armoured cars passing a road junction just south of Le Bény-Bocage.

Above: The village school still survives and this was the clue that enabled Bernard Paich to track down the location to Le Plessis-Grimoult. The photo shows that the prisoners were marching northwards in the direction of Aunay-sur-Odon.

Infantry of the 129th Brigade and tanks from the 13th/18th Hussars reached the top of Mont-Pinçon on the evening of the 6th where they dug in for the night. They cleared the last of the defenders the next morning, taking 200 prisoners. SHAEF was quick to report the capture of this remarkable tactical feature in Communiqué No. 121. *Above:* Sergeant Midgley pictured this column of prisoners being marched past 'Jacko', a Light Reconnaissance Morris Mark II armoured car from the 43rd (Wessex) Division displaying the 'Wyvern' badge of the division.

COMMUNIQUE No. 121   August 7

In the Brittany peninsula, Allied troops continue to strengthen their positions in the vicinity of BREST. Our armor has freed CARHAIX, VANNES and REDON and other units have reached the Vilaine river at various points from RENNES to the sea.

CHATEAU-GONTIER and HOUSSAY have been cleared of the enemy. Mayenne river has been crossed 17 miles south of LAVAL. MAYENNE is in our hands.

Allied armor is in the outskirts of VIRE. The FORET DE ST SEVER is being cleared of light enemy resistance. The strong point of ST POIS has been taken. Two enemy counter-attacks in that area were unsuccessful.

To the north-east, the high ground at MONT-PINCON was captured yesterday by Allied troops after heavy fighting.

Between this area and VIRE, enemy resistance was stubborn and a strong enemy counter-attack was repulsed. The advance continues.

South of CAEN, a local attack on the east bank of the Orne met heavy enemy resistance in MAY-SUR-ORNE. Railway bridges at OISSEL, ST REMY-SUR-AVRE, COURTALAIN and BEAUMONT-SUR-SARTHE, and ammunition and fuel dumps in the forests of BLOIS, ANDAINE and PERSEIGNE, and at LIVAROT, were attacked by escorted medium and light bombers. Other formations attacked Panzer division concentrations near THURY-HARCOURT.

Submarine pens near LORIENT were attacked by escorted heavy night bombers.

Fighter-bombers hit an ammunition train at BELLEVILLE, south of NANTES, and tanks near SAUMUR, and attacked gun positions, rolling stock and vehicles throughout the day. Rail lines were cut near CHARTRES, TOURS, LE MANS, ST CYR and ORLEANS.

Four enemy aircraft were destroyed. Eight of ours are missing.

Meanwhile, the German garrison at Le Plessis-Grimoult resisted strongly and it was nearly midnight when they were finally overwhelmed in hand-to-hand fighting. About 120 prisoners were counted on the morning of the 7th and amongst the spoils was this Tiger II from schwere Panzer-Abteilung 503.

This stretch of the main street has completely changed, only the church tower in the background providing a link with the past.

COMMUNIQUE No. 122   August 8

The largest attack against the western sector since D-Day was launched by the enemy Sunday night on a front extending from MORTAIN to SOURDEVAL. At least four German armored divisions are being employed in the drive. MORTAIN has changed hands for the third time and is now held by Allied troops.

The enemy penetrated some three miles in the area of CHERENCE-LE-ROUSSEL where a tank battle is in progress. Armor of both sides is involved. Another enemy penetration has been made to ST BARTHELEMY.

More than 100 tanks and 90 motor vehicles were destroyed in a series of attacks in the MORTAIN area by our fighter-bombers and rocket-firing aircraft. Other tanks and trucks were damaged.

In the Brittany peninsula, Allied troops have freed CHATEAUNEUF, and fighting is in progress outside ST MALO, which is now cut off. ST BRIEUC has been taken and the advance is continuing beyond the town.

No changes are reported in the areas of BREST and LORIENT. AURAY has been reached by Allied forces.

CHATEAUBRIANT has been freed. Sporadic fighting continues over the peninsula. In Normandy Allied troops have taken VIRE.

Across the river Orne, a bridgehead was established yesterday in the neighborhood of GRIMBOSQ. Counter-attacks against this bridgehead, and further west, were repulsed. In the MONT-PINCON area, mopping-up of the ground won is nearly completed.

Allied troops are attacking south of CAEN.

Heavy bombers, in very great strength, attacked the hinge of the enemy's defense line just south of CAEN before midnight last night. The attack was in clear weather, and a great weight of bombs was dropped on targets indicated by our ground forces.

Earlier in the day strong forces of heavy bombers, operating in small units, attacked fuel storage points, bridges and rail targets in a wide arc north-east and east of PARIS and south-east of BORDEAUX.

Fighter-bombers, sweeping east and south-east of PARIS, destroyed 32 locomotives, 350 railway cars and 80 military vehicles.

Ammunition dumps at LIVAROT, LA FOLLETIERE, LE LUDE and BAUCHES-DU-DESERT were attacked by medium and light bombers. Other formations bombed shipping in BREST harbor and bridges at NOGENT-LE-ROI, NEUVY-SUR-LOIRE, and CORBIE, east of AMIENS.

At least 20 enemy planes were destroyed in the air during encounters throughout the day and last night.

From all operations, 22 of our aircraft are reported missing.

Early Sunday morning, a force of enemy E-Boats was intercepted close to the port of LE HAVRE by light coastal forces and brought to action. The last R-Boat in the enemy's line received very heavy damage and many hits were observed on another.

One hour before midnight on August 7, the First Canadian Army launched Operation 'Totalize' aiming at the capture of Falaise. After a massive bombardment of the German positions by a thousand aircraft of RAF Bomber Command, two attacking forces of tanks and armoured personnel carriers moved on on each side of the Caen—Falaise road. After another heavy air raid by 500 heavies of the Eighth Air Force, at midday on the 8th, the 1st Polish Armoured Division attacked on the left wing with the 4th Canadian Armoured Division on the right. This Canadian battle group was pictured that day near Cintheaux.

A German counter-attack began after midday on the 8th while Shermans of the 1st Northamptonshire Yeomanry, 33rd Armoured Brigade, destroyed three Tigers near Gaumesnil. One was the mount of tank ace SS-Hauptsturmführer Michael Wittmann although at the time he was simply posted as missing in action. His precise fate remained unclear for decades until 1982 when Jean Paul traced the exact spot where the Tiger had been knocked out. A sketch plan sent by *After the Battle* to the German War Graves Commission led them to mount a search of the field and in March 1983 the remains of Wittmann and his crew were recovered and buried in the German cemetery at La Cambe (see *After the Battle* No. 48).

Hitler directed a counter-attack to be launched towards Mortain to cut through the rear of the Third Army forces pushing into Brittany. The panzer divisions earmarked for the operation code-named 'Lüttich' were pulled out of the line on three successive nights beginning on August 3/4. *Left:* In early August, Kriegsberichter Theobald pictured elements of the 84. Infanterie-Division moving in to relieve the 116. Panzer-Division. *Right:* The cross-roads at Beauchêne, 12 miles east of Mortain.

COMMUNIQUE No. 123 August 9

Allied forces in Brittany are closing in on the ports of ST MALO, BREST and LORIENT. Converging columns have pushed to within five miles of LORIENT, and other forces have engaged the enemy four miles from BREST. Fighting is now in progress in the outskirts of ST MALO. Large fires are burning at both ST MALO and LORIENT, indicating destruction by the Germans of their supplies in both ports.

Confused fighting is in progress around MORTAIN on the Normandy front. To the north-west of MORTAIN, a German counter-attack, with tanks and infantry, was broken at GATHEMO, which has been freed. The drive penetrated about one mile into our lines, but heavy losses were inflicted on the enemy by Allied troops, assisted by planes and artillery. The front line in this area now extends generally along the road between GATHEMO and VIRE. In the vicinity of VIRE, the enemy is offering stubborn resistance south and south-west of the town.

The Allied drive south of CAEN progressed some 7,000 yards yesterday. After heavy and accurate preliminary bombing the first objectives were secured by first light and a number of pockets of enemy, which had been bypassed in this first advance, were cleared up during the day. The advance continued at midday in face of determined enemy resistance, supported by armor. The villages of LA HOGUE, HAUT-MESNIL, CINTHEAUX and ST AIGNAN and the town of BRETTE-VILLE-SUR-LAIZE are in our hands.

The attack forces were assembled hastily at night with great difficulty and some of the infantry units that were to replace the armoured forces were late in arriving. Theobald featured this camouflaged StuG III manoeuvring during the build-up phase for Operation 'Lüttich'. The tower of the church identifies this village as Lonlay L'Abbaye which lies three miles south of Beauchêne. The 1. SS-Panzer-Division and the 2. SS-Panzer-Division both possessed assault guns (their anti-tank battalion was actually equipped with them instead of tank destroyers), but as Theobald photographed SS-Oberscharführer Johann Thaler of SS-Panzer-Regiment 2 on the same roll of film, it is reasonable to assume that this StuG III belonged to SS-Sturmgeschütz-Abteilung 2.

Left: Theobald followed the advance of this unit westwards until he reached Ger, four miles west of Beauchêne. There, he pictured a Panzerknacker (tank hunter) crossing the village. These shots are of particular interest for the front was then only a few miles away and the 84. Infanterie-Division is seen deploying its units to take over the whole length of the front allocated to it. *Right:* Some parts of Normandy have changed little over the intervening years.

Although German successes were usually played down by SHAEF, Communiqué No. 123 goes so far as to say that there was 'confused fighting in progress around Mortain'. This picture perfectly illustrates a battle group of the 2. SS-Panzer-Division emerging from the fog on the morning of August 7 only to suddenly come under fire from the anti-tank guns of the 120th Infantry Regiment. Six SdKfz 251 armoured personnel carriers were disabled with the grenadiers being machine-gunned as they tumbled out of their stricken vehicles to try to reach cover.

The bridgehead over the river Orne has been extended, and local advances were made to improve our positions east of MONT-PINCON.

Targets in immediate support of the ground forces south-west of CAEN and airfields at LA PERTHE, CLASTRES, VILLACOUBLAY and ROMILLY-SUR-SEINE were attacked successfully by heavy bombers in a day of great air activity.

By last light, and during darkness, heavy bombers also attacked fuel dumps in forests at CHANTILLY, AIRE-SUR-LA-LYS and LUCHEUX.

Road and rail bridges were attacked by medium and light bombers, with satisfactory results reported over nine widespread targets, most of them east of the Seine. Rail yards at IGOVILLE, south of ROUEN, were also attacked.

Long-range and short-range fighters, in considerable numbers, swept the area south and east of the battle zone throughout the day, taking heavy toll of enemy transport and attacking gun positions.

Three enemy minesweepers in the Bay of Biscay were attacked by rocket-firing coastal aircraft and were left ablaze.

During the night, fires were started among oil tanks south of FONTAINEBLEAU and a crane at DIJON was also set afire by light bombers.

COMMUNIQUE No. 124   August 10

LE MANS has been liberated by Allied forces, and our troops are in the vicinity of ANGERS in the Loire valley.

The city of NANTES has been reached and our columns are converging on LORIENT.

In the Brittany peninsula we are now in ST MALO but the enemy at DINARD is resisting stubbornly.

Along the north coastal road we have passed through MORLAIX. At BREST the enemy garrison has rejected an ultimatum to surrender and fighting is proceeding outside the city. Lt. Gen. Karl Spang, commanding the German 266th Infantry Division, was captured near BREST.

On the Normandy front there has been no major change in the line.

Vigorous patrolling is being carried out in the MAYENNE area.

Although the censored caption simply states that this scene was pictured 'on the road to Mortain', nevertheless careful research by Jean Paul led Bernard to this spot on the road passing the railway station at Le Neufbourg, the northern suburb of Mortain.

The German counter-attack managed to advance west of Mortain but it soon stalled enabling the Americans to recover the lost ground. *Left:* On August 12, troops of the 120th Infantry re-entered the town. *Right:* **Rue du Bourglopin** . . . then and now.

The enemy holds MORTAIN and heavy fighting has been going on north and west of the town. A German counter-attack at GATHEMO was checked by our forces, with the destruction of five of the 25 enemy tanks participating. South of ST GERMAIN-DE-TALLEVENDE our troops advanced 1,000 yards.

The Allied advance toward FALAISE has penetrated the first and second German positions and reached the neighborhood of POTIGNY. The villages of POUSSY-LA-CAMPAGNE and ST SYLVAIN have been taken and armored columns have reached ESTREES-LA-CAMPAGNE and SOIGNOLLES.

Our troops in the bridgehead over the river Orne repulsed further counter-attacks yesterday and have driven the enemy back. Further west, more ground was gained south-east of MONT-PINCON and between ESTRY and VIRE.

Yesterday afternoon, heavy bombers attacked with 12,000-pound bombs the U-Boat base at LA PALLICE. A fuel dump in the FORET DE MORMAL, south-east of VALENCIENNES, was also attacked in the afternoon, and last night heavy attacks were made on two more fuel depots at CHATELLERAULT, some 40 miles south of TOURS, and in the FORT D'ENGLOS near LILLE. None of our heavy bombers are missing.

Railway bridges in the valley of the OISE, and at EPERNON, L'ISLE-ADAM and CHAUNY were attacked by medium and light bombers, as was a rail junction at EPONE-MEZIERES. An ammunition dump in the FORET DE LYON; military building at TONNEINS on the Garonne river; a radio installation in the ARGENTAN area and two freighters in BREST harbor were also bombed.

Tanks, gun positions, rolling stock as well as barges on the Seine were attacked by fighter-bombers. Fighters provided escort for bombing missions. Barges on the Seine were also attacked last night by light bombers.

PT-Boats, on offensive patrol off the island of JERSEY, intercepted a southbound enemy convoy off la CORBIERE in low visibility early yesterday morning. One enemy vessel was hit by torpedo and one other damaged by gunfire before the convoy escaped.

Shortly after daylight, with visibility further reduced by fog, other PT-Boats entered the roadstead of ST HELIER and attacked two M-class minesweepers with gunfire. Many hits were observed on the enemy before our forces withdrew.

Off the port of LE HAVRE, light coastal forces intercepted an enemy vessel under escort of six E-Boats. The vessel was sunk. One of the escorts was also hit by torpedo and its destruction is considered probable.

This picture of Americans advancing through Juvigny-le-Tertre, five miles west of Mortain, could easily illustrate the American response to the German counter-attack but in fact the photo was taken one week earlier when troops of the 1st Infantry Division fought through the village on August 2. Remarkably, this Sherman and Sturmgeschütz III were knocked out on either side of the road within a few feet of each other.

This is Rue d'Avranches, looking eastwards, a few hundred yards before reaching the main road junction in the centre of the village.

COMMUNIQUE No. 125   August 11

Allied troops have entered the city of NANTES and ANGERS. Enemy resistance was slight at NANTES, but there is extensive enemy mining in the area of both cities.

In the Brittany peninsula, mopping-up is proceeding in the area of HENNEBONT, AURAY and QUIBERON on the south coast.

LORIENT has been completely surrounded by Allied troops on the land side.

The enemy is maintaining strong resistance at BREST, where elements of three German divisions are located. Our forces outside the city have been joined by another force which proceeded along the north coastal road of the peninsula.

The enemy defense at ST MALO has been reduced mainly to a single strong point which still is offering stubborn resistance. A total of 3,000 prisoners has been taken thus far in the port. DINARD, in the ST MALO area, is still being strongly defended by the Germans.

Hard fighting continues in the MORTAIN—VIRE area of Normandy. Stubborn enemy resistance is being encountered north and south of MORTAIN, particularly in the vicinity of ST BARTHELEMY. Gains of one to one-and-one-half miles were made in a southerly direction by Allied forces in the area of VIRE, and other units are attacking towards GATHEMO against strong German resistance.

While the German counter-attack threatened to widen northwards, V Corps held on firmly to the town of Vire that had been captured on the 7th, the day the German operation began. It had previously been reduced to ruins by a strong Allied aerial bombardment and Signal Corps photographer Hugh McHugh pictured GIs moving 'past heaps of rubble that once formed part of the town of Vire'.

Left: Men of the 82nd Engineer Combat Battalion at work clearing piles of rubble blocking the street in front of the railway station. *Right:* Rue de la Gare today although the Hôtel du Chemin de Fer was never rebuilt.

Left: Having checked this stretch of road leading east from Vire for mines, Sergeant Charles T. Lynch and Private Louis Motte pinned their 'cleared to hedge' notice under the prophetic sign: 'To Paris'. *Above:* At the eastern end of Rue Emile Desvaux, the junction has been transformed into a large roundabout, with the D512 (the N812 in 1944) leading east to Condé-sur-Noireau and Falaise and the D524 (then the N24bis) south-eastwards to Flers, Alençon and Paris.

The operation by the V Corps to put pressure on the trapped German forces had to be postponed for three days due to the counter-attack, but on the 12th the situation in the Mortain sector was cleared up which enabled the corps to revert back to the original plan. The 29th and 2nd Divisions now attacked alongside each other and three days later they had captured Tinchebray, nine miles south-east of Vire. *Left and right:* Rue de Paris in Tinchebray . . . 1944 and 2014.

Enemy resistance to the Allied thrust toward FALAISE increased considerably yesterday. A strong screen of anti-tank guns and heavily defended positions in the areas FONTAINE-LE-PIN, QUESNAY, ESTREES-LA-CAMPAGNE, ST SYLVAIN and VIMONT slowed the advance and heavy fighting resulted. ESTREES-LA-CAMPAGNE was captured, SOIGNOLLES changed hands several times and fighting in and around VIMONT continued all day.

Allied forces have enlarged the bridgehead over the Orne with an advance of 4,000 yards, capturing ESPINS, on the fringe of the FORET DE CINGLAIS, and the villages of CROISILLES and FORGE-A-CAMBRO.

Driving down from LE PLESSIS-GRIMOULT, Allied armor and infantry have captured a number of villages including CAUVILLE and LENAULT, and have reached the vicinity of ST PIERRE-LA-VIEILLE.

Despite variable weather and unusually intense anti-aircraft fire in many sectors, Allied aircraft continued their close support of our Armies, especially near LE MANS where 15 tanks were destroyed. Throughout the day, our planes ranged from Belgium to BORDEAUX to attack supply centers and road and rail targets.

Eight enemy aircraft were shot down and 26 others were destroyed or damaged on the ground by our fighters after they had escorted heavy bombers to attack several bridges in the PARIS area and the oil storage center at DUGNY, near the metropolitan airport of LE BOURGET. An estimated 150 locomotives, 1,000 railway cars and scores of vehicles were shot up by other strong forces of fighter-bombers and fighters which also hit numerous rail centers, bridges, barges on the Seine and two ammunition trains.

Good results were reported from medium bomber attacks designed to destroy or halt repairs on rail bridges and embankments at NOGENT-SUR-SEINE, ANIZY-LE-CHATEAU, PERONNE, EPONE/MEZIERES, EPERNON, and MEREY.

Submarine oil storage depots at BORDEAUX and LA PALLICE and the DIJON rail center were hit by heavy bombers in a series of midnight attacks.

Enemy rail movements westward from ANTWERP, BRUSSELS, METZ, STRASBOURG, LILLE, SEDAN and other points east of the Seine were attacked incessantly by fighter-bombers. During the evening five enemy aircraft were shot down over the battle area. Twenty-two of our aircraft are missing.

The First Army hoped to capture a considerable number of prisoners in the Tinchebray sector but the haul only amounted to a disappointing 1,200 — even less than the V Corps casualties. *Above:* This M3 half-track of the 41st Armored Infantry Regiment was photographed in Lonlay L'Abbaye leading the 2nd Armored Division.

Place Saint-Sauveur looking westwards at the D56 arriving from Ger.

In the south, as XV Corps was approaching Argentan, VII Corps was advancing from the Mayenne area. The 1st Infantry Division on the left and the 3rd Armored Division on the right advanced over 20 miles on the first day of this operation.

This 3-inch anti-tank gun is rolling through Couterne which lies eight miles south of the town of La Ferté-Macé. The convoy is proceeding from the west (Rue de Domfront) to east (Rue d'Alençon).

COMMUNIQUE No. 126   August 12

Allied troops have crossed the Loire river and have reached a point ten miles south of NANTES. Some fighting continues in the areas of NANTES and ANGERS.

In the Brittany peninsula, a small part of the enemy's one remaining strong point at ST MALO is still holding out. Heavy fighting is in progress in DINARD. The situations at BREST and LORIENT remain unchanged.

In Normandy, the enemy is maintaining a stubborn defense in the MORTAIN—VIRE sector. Near MORTAIN, an Allied attack is meeting strong resistance from German armored units east and north of the town. Farther north, our troops have pushed beyond GATHEMO to the vicinity of VÉNGEONS, on the GATHEMO—TINCHEBRAY highway. Further gains have been made below VIRE, and the enemy has been pushed back to a point 1,000 yards south of MAISONCELLES-LA-JOURDAN.

East of VIRE, Allied troops advanced from 1,000 to 2,000 yards on a six-mile front in spite of determined enemy opposition. Further east, in the vicinity of ST PIERRE-LA-VIEILLE, Hills 266 and 229 were captured. Patrols operating from the Orne bridgehead through the FORET DE CINGLAIS and from east of the Laize penetrated to BARBERY.

THURY-HARCOURT and ST MARTIN-DE-SALLEN were cleared of enemy, and south-east of THURY-HARCOURT the village of ESSON was taken. Fighting continues in the town of VIMONT.

During the 24 hours ending midnight August 9, the total of prisoners taken, in the western sectors, mostly in Brittany, reached 4,822.

In a day of widespread air activity, harbor defense, fuel depots, railway yards and bridges, locomotive depots, submarine shelters and airfields were under attack by many formations of our heavy bombers.

The stubbornly-resisting harbor defenses of BREST were bombed at more than 20 points by small formations.

Fuel depot targets included ST FLORENTIN, PACY, STRASBOURG, LA PALLICE and BORDEAUX.

Railway yards attacked were at STRASBOURG, MULHOUSE, BELFORT, SAARBRUCKEN, LENS, DOUAI and GIVORS.

Airfield targets included VILLACOUBLAY, TOUSSUS-LE-NOBLE and COULOMMIERS. Still other targets were the submarine shelters at LA PALLICE and BORDEAUX, the locomotive depots at SOMAIN and the ETAPLES rail bridge, which was attacked last night.

Our medium bombers also operated against a variety of targets. Coastal batteries, which were holding out in the ST MALO area, were attacked in support of our ground forces. In the FALAISE sector, mortar and artillery positions were bombed. Other targets included an ammunition dump in the FORET DE ROUMARE, rail targets at ST MAXIMIN and at FISMES, and a temporary bridge at OISSEL.

Fighter-bombers operated both in close support of our forces and also on strafing missions in the EVREUX area and from PARIS south-eastward to DIJON.

The advance of the VII Corps continues. Signal Corps photographer Sergeant Warden F. Lovell pictured a truck pulling a Long Tom through Bagnoles-de-l'Orne.

A nice spa town, it remains remarkably unchanged; this is Rue des Casinos.

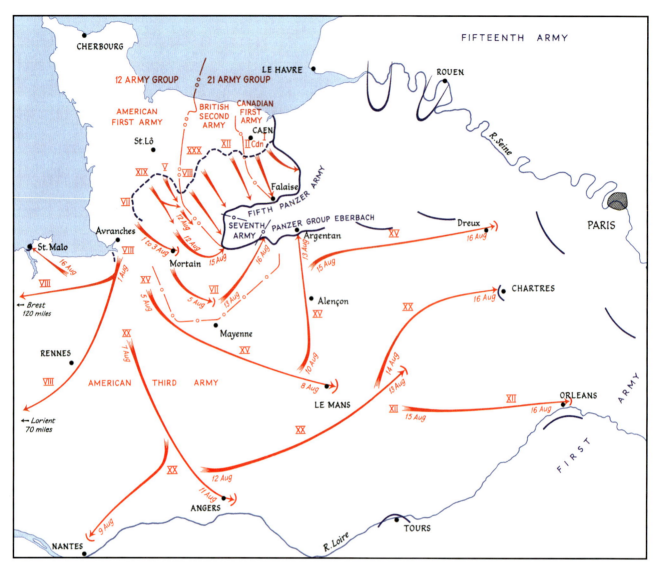

Eisenhower: 'By 10 August, following a conference at General Bradley's Headquarters, it was decided to seize the opportunity for encirclement offered by the enemy tactics. XV Corps of the Third Army already had pushed eastward to capture Le Mans on August 9 and had thence turned north according to plan to threaten the rear of the armoured forces battling at Mortain.

At the same time XX Corps drove beyond Châteaubriant toward the Loire and captured Angers on August 10, thus effectively guarding the southern flank of our encircling movement. On August 11 XV Corps was north of the Sées-Carrouges road, and on the night of August 12 the US 5th Armored Division was in the outskirts of Argentan.'

Although strong opposition slowed the advance, VII Corps finally made contact with British troops at several points along its front, so closing the gap on the XV Corps left flank. In the five-day operation, the corps had taken more than 3,000 prisoners and destroyed a mass of equipment. *Left:* A Sherman of the 3rd Armored Division loaded with GIs entered La Ferté-Macé. *Above:* Looking northwards along Rue Félix Désaunay at the outskirts of the town in the south-west.

COMMUNIQUE No. 127 August 13

South of CAEN contact has been made by Allied forces converging between the rivers Orne and Laize. A thrust from BRETTEVILLE-SUR-LAIZE through BARBERY reached MOULINES, while another advance from the Orne bridgehead captured BOIS HALBOUT.

Fighting continued all day in the ST SYLVAIN area where a number of counter-attacks were beaten off and local advances were made.

West of the Orne fighting continued around Hill 229, which remains in our hands. An Allied advance down the CONDE road made some progress beyond ST PIERRE-LA-VIEILLE.

East of VIRE an advance of a mile was made in the face of heavy resistance.

Forces advancing south-eastward in the VIRE area are experiencing decreasing enemy resistance. Progress has been made to a position east of MAISONCELLES-LA-JOURDAN, and along the GATHEMO—TINCHEBRAY road east of VENGEONS. Patrols have penetrated as far as SOURDEVAL in the sector between VIRE and MORTAIN. MORTAIN has been reoccupied by our troops, but the enemy is still offering strong resistance in the vicinity of the town.

In Brittany our forces are attacking the citadel at ST MALO where remnants of the enemy garrison are still resisting. Heavy fighting continues in DINARD. In the area of BREST a local enemy counter-attack was repulsed north of the city. The situation at LORIENT remains unchanged.

In the Loire valley mopping up is proceeding in ANGERS which is now in our hands.

A large area north, east and south of PARIS was swept continuously yesterday by our long-range fighters which reported great destruction of enemy rolling stock, ammunition trains and lorries, barges, marshalling yards and bridges. There was some air opposition and six enemy fighters were shot down.

U-Boat shelters at BREST, LA PALLICE and BORDEAUX, a petrol dump at FORET DE MONTRICHARD, rail yards at METZ and nine airfields were attacked by heavy bombers.

At OISSEL the only usable Seine bridge north of PARIS was successfully attacked by our medium bombers, which also operated against road junctions and other targets near ARGENTAN.

Normandy-based aircraft operated throughout the day, giving immediate support to ground forces.

Enemy shipping off the west coast of France was attacked by coastal aircraft which reported setting fire to a medium-sized vessel and blowing up a minesweeper.

Last night, enemy troop concentrations in the FALAISE area were attacked by our heavy bombers.

COMMUNIQUE No. 128 August 14

Further progress was made west of the river Orne, where Allied troops entered CLAIR-TISON and DONNAY. South of ST PIERRE-LA-VIEILLE the advance continued along the high ground on each side of the road to CONDE.

South-east of VIRE ground was gained in heavy fighting.

Further south, toward MORTAIN, our forces, following up the German withdrawal, encountered mines and long-range artillery fire.

In Brittany the Allied attack on DINARD continues to meet strong resistance and remnants of the German garrison at ST MALO still hold out in the citadel. Slight advances have been made by our units in the vicinity of BREST There has been no change in the situation at LORIENT.

Highways and road junctions on both sides of the Seine from PARIS to the sea, and westwards to LISIEUX and RUGLES, were attacked by heavy and medium bombers. Medium bombers also attacked rail bridges at PERONNE, BEAUTOR, DOULLENS and CHERISY, rail facilities at CORBEIL, and enemy gun positions in the FALAISE area.

A railway bridge over the Seine at LE MANOIR, U-Boat shelters at BREST, an oil storage depot for U-Boats at BORDEAUX and gun positions at ST MALO and on the Ile de Cezembre were other targets for heavy bombers. From these operations fourteen heavy and two medium bombers are missing.

Fighters, fighter-bombers and rocket-firing fighters provided cover for the ground forces and bombed and strafed tanks, motor transport, strong points and troop concentrations in the battle zone.

Fighters also ranged over north-eastern and central France attacking locomotives, railway cars, motor transport and canal barges while other fighters provided escort for bombing missions.

Light bombers last night continued their attack on transport targets behind the enemy's lines.

The German defenders facing the British VIII Corps finally pulled back permitting the 4th Battalion King's Shropshire Light Infantry to take Vassy, nine miles east of Vire, without a fight on August 15. Sergeant Laing pictured this Cromwell of the 2nd Northamptonshire Yeomanry, 11th Armoured Division, but the unit was so depleted after the fighting of the last ten days that it soon had to be disbanded.

This is the main square in Vassy looking eastwards along Rue Joseph Requeut.

On August 15 a second front opened in the West when the Allies landed on the Riviera beaches in southern France. Operation 'Dragoon' — a three-division assault — began with an air and naval bombardment of the landing areas from 5.50 a.m. with the first troops touching down, largely unopposed, about three hours later.

None of the SHAEF communiqués in August refer to operations in the south of France as initially Operation 'Dragoon' came under the control of the Supreme Allied Commander, Mediterranean Theater, General Sir Henry Wilson. This arrangement had been agreed because of the distance and lack of communications with SHAEF.

COMMUNIQUE No. 129   August 15

Advances were made yesterday on both sides of the FALAISE—ARGENTAN gap. Allied troops attacking towards FALAISE from the north quickly gained their first objectives and, having crossed the river Laizon, are now firmly established within 7,000 yards of the town.

On the other side of the gap, the thrust northward from LE MANS and ALENCON has reached the vicinity of ARGENTAN. Pockets of resistance left behind in this advance are being mopped up near ALENCON.

Inside the Normandy pocket advances were made.

Between the Laize and the Orne an advance of some 5,000 yards brought our forward elements to the vicinity of the village of BONNOEIL. In the Orne valley, THURY-HARCOURT was cleared of enemy.

North of CONDE the village of PROUSSY was taken and our troops are approaching ST DENIS-DE-MERE.

Further west, Allied troops advanced to within a mile of MASSY, and south-east of VIRE an advance of a mile has brought us to a point about one mile from TINCHEBRAY.

Other units advancing south of VIRE are moving along the GATHEMO—TINCHEBRAY road against moderate resistance. Troops pushing eastward from MORTAIN have reached GER.

Along the southern boundary of the pocket our columns moving from the BARENTON area are approaching DOMFRONT and units which reached RANES are encountering increasing resistance.

In Brittany fighting is still in progress at ST MALO where the situation remains unchanged, and at DINARD, where we have made advances towards the port. At BREST and LORIENT there is nothing new to report.

Throughout the third consecutive day of clear weather, massive formations of all types of Allied aircraft hammered at German forces in the Normandy pocket and attacked airfields, bridges and communications targets from western Germany to BORDEAUX, virtually without opposition.

Seven enemy strong points massing tanks, guns and troops north of FALAISE were attacked by more than 700 escorted heavy bombers in a concentrated bombardment preceeding an advance of our ground forces. Three other strong points south of MEZIDON were hit by medium bombers in a precision operation only 3,000 yards in advance of our troops.

Well before daylight, paratroopers of the 1st Airborne Task Force jumped inland to prevent German forces moving down to the beach-head. However, ground fog blanketed the landing areas and the men were scattered while the first flight of gliders had to turn back. Sergeant Irwing Leibowitz was on hand to picture glidermen moving towards their command post.

Left: **On Delta Red, a 45th Infantry Division's beach just east of Sainte-Maxime, the *US 513* (a Landing Craft, Infantry) and the *US 1143* (a Landing Craft, Tank) were able to land men and vehicles straight onto the beach.** *Right:* **This is the same beach at La Nartelle, now a popular venue for nicely undressed sunbathers.**

Six highway bridges over the Touques river north and south of LISIEUX were attacked by more than 250 medium bombers which also pounded bridges and railway junctions at NOGENT-LE-ROI, LES FOULONS, EPONE MEZIERES, FREVENT, ST MARTIN and PONTOISE.

Escorted heavy bombers struck shipping and harbor installations at BREST in two attacks, and others ranged from eastern France to the BORDEAUX area, hitting three airfields near DIJON and the ANGOULEME and SAINTES railway yards with good results.

The day-by-day fighter-bomber and fighter onslaught against enemy communications entered its second week with widespread attacks on road and rail targets in areas on both sides of the Seine. At least 750 railway cars and hundreds of motor vehicles were destroyed and damaged in the areas of FALAISE, L'AIGLE, DOMFRONT, EVREUX, CHARTRES, ST ANDRE and east of the Seine.

Light bombers harried enemy movements during the night, causing large fires and explosions at several points near FALAISE and south of PARIS. Twenty-nine enemy aircraft were destroyed. Twenty-four of ours are missing. A heavy battery on the island of ALDERNEY has been subjected to naval bombardment.

On the right wing, three beaches — Camel Green, Red and Blue — had been allocated to the 36th Infantry Division. The primary beach was Camel Green, near Cap du Dramont, where two battalions of the 141st Infantry began landing at 9 a.m., also encountering little opposition. There was some sporadic artillery fire but by 10 a.m. the beaches had been cleared. As soon as the troops began to advance inland, the weak German defenders — actually Osttruppen who were conscripts from the occupied eastern territories recruited into the German Army — were quick to surrender. *Above:* **This shot taken on D + 1 shows LCT *US 1141* unloading DUKWS onto rocky Camel Green. In the background lies the Ile d'Or (Golden Island) where Auguste Lutaud had a tower residence built for himself in the early 19th century. Naming himself King of the Ile d'Or, for 20 years the eccentric Auguste I organised sumptuous parties on his small kingdom that were much frequented by the jet-set.** *Right:* **Today, the Dramont beach is another of the popular beaches on the French Riviera although the Ile d'Or still remains privately owned.**

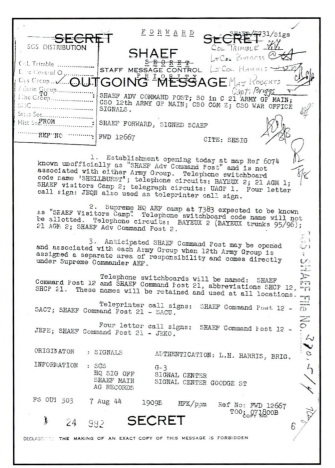

COMMUNIQUE No. 130   August 16

Allied troops are in the outskirts of FALAISE and dominate the communications in this area. All along the northern flank of the enemy pocket our forces are driving steadily forward in spite of attempts to delay us with mines and booby traps.

The villages of COSSESSEVILLE and TREPREL between the rivers Orne and Laize were taken.

CONDE was by-passed by a thrust across the river Noireau a few miles east of the town. TINCHEBRAY has been captured.

Our troops along the western and southern flanks of the pocket have also advanced generally.

DOMFRONT, GER and LA FERTE-MACE have been freed. Our forces have entered YVRANDES, three miles south of TINCHEBRAY.

Further east, other units are pushing northward beyond RANES where strong enemy opposition is being met. South-east of RANES and in the vicinity of ALENCON, mopping-up operations are proceeding against enemy groups cut off by the advance northward.

In ARGENTAN, we hold a portion of the city and enemy resistance is stubborn.

In Brittany, the citadel at ST MALO continues to hold out. Organized resistance has ceased at DINARD. There are no changes to report from BREST or LORIENT.

A massive force of Allied heavy bombers was thrown against key German air force stations in western Germany and the Low Countries yesterday. Twenty-one main Luftwaffe headquarters, control stations and airfields were attacked by 1,900 four-engined bombers, with fighter escort in great strength.

Key installations bombed were at COLOGNE/OSTHEIM, WIESBADEN and FRANKFURT, all in the Rhine valley; air force stations at WITTMUND, BAD ZWISCHENAHN, VECHTA, HANDORF,

Exactly two months after D-Day, General Eisenhower moved his Advance Command Post, now re-named 'Shellburst', to Normandy. Although he had been commuting regularly from 'Sharpener' to France, Tedder had been pressing the Supreme Commander to establish a tactical headquarters on the Continent to permit closer liaison with the forces on the battlefield. Eisenhower's first press conference was to be held there on August 16 at which it was planned to officially release the names of Lieutenant General Patton as commander of the US Third Army and Lieutenant General Courtney H. Hodges as that of the First. Within two weeks, Patton had already achieved a spectacular advance through Brittany — moving so fast that the spearheads had run off their maps — and Eisenhower was being pressed to announce the name of the commander responsible. However, at first, he was reluctant to agree, telling Butcher, 'Why should I tell the enemy?'

The field where 'Shellburst' had been located, 12 miles south-west of Bayeux off the D15 near Tournières, was pinpointed by Madame Bouvier-Muller of the French-American Ninth Air Force Normandy Airfields Association. This memorial was unveiled on June 6, 1990 but unfortunately it was placed 300 yards away in front of the wrong field (see *After the Battle* No. 84).

The German garrison of Saint-Malo fought a bitter battle against the 83rd Division. Here GIs of the 331st Infantry are pictured advancing in the Paramé suburb on the east side of the town. On August 11 medium bombers were called in to bomb the Citadel, with 100 B-24s following up on the 13th, and yet another raid two days later. Only on the 17th did the garrison commander, Oberst Andreas von Aulock, finally agree to surrender.

HOPSTEN and PLANTLUNNE in north-west Germany; FLORENNES in Belgium, and TWENTE/ENSCHEDE and VENLO in Holland.

Other targets attacked were at LE CULOT, ST TROND, TIRLEMONT, and BRUSSELS/MELSBROEK in Belgium and GILZE-RIJEN, DEELEN, SOESTERBERG, VOLKEL and EINDHOVEN in Holland.

Communications targets and an ammunition dump in northern France, and defenses in the ST MALO area, were attacked by medium bombers.

Heavy damage resulted from the bombing of the AUVERS-SUR-OISE and L'ISLE ADAM bridges over the Oise. The SERQUEUX rail center was attacked and fires resulted from a medium bomber mission against a fuel dump in the FORET DE CHANTILLY, twenty miles north of PARIS.

Fighter-bombers and rocket-firing aircraft continued to seek out targets in the Normandy pocket. Eighteen tanks and more than 175 vehicles, including half-tracks, were destroyed, and an equal number damaged in the area.

Thirty locomotives were put out of commission in a fighter-bomber sweep against the rail yard at BRAINE-LE-COMTE in Belgium. Thirty-seven enemy planes were destroyed in the air.

From all of these operations 20 bombers and 16 fighters are missing.

Von Aulock emerged from the Citadel with about 400 of his men displaying an insolent attitude towards his captors. This photo was captioned as 'Saluting his officers and men just before being driven away to a POW camp' but, in actual fact, the officer depicted was not von Aulock but one of his staff!

Just offshore, the island of Cézembre was still holding out so it was shelled 'day and night' by heavy artillery, HMS *Warspite* adding salvoes from her 15-inch guns. Finally bombed into submission, the garrison gave in on September 2. *Left:* Apart from sea birds, Cézembre is uninhabited, still littered with the smashed concrete of the German gun positions. *Right:* In spite of repeated mine-clearing operations, the island has not yet been completely declared safe, so access to most of the northern part is prohibited, being fenced off with barbed-wire and warning notices.

The withdrawal of German forces from Normandy began after dark on August 16 when the westernmost troops of the 7. Armee pulled back to the Orne river. The deteriorating situation soon made it necessary to carry out the retreat during the day as well, regardless of the Allied fighter-bombers that swarmed over the battlefield. Kriegsberichter Zwirner pictured an attack by a Typhoon that was followed seconds later by a pall of thick smoke erupting from behind a wood.

Zwirner then reached a section of the road where a column of ambulances had been caught in the open. He proceeded all along the shattered convoy to investigate, taking photos of wrecked vehicles and ambulances containing dismembered corpses. In 1975 SS-Sturmmann Rudi Cihotzki recalled that 'on the hill, a column of German ambulances has been shot to pieces by fighter-bombers. This is the most gruesome sight I've seen throughout the whole war. The ambulances are burned out, and in the melted hulks you can make out the remains of men — shrivelled to such an extent by the heat that they look like dolls.' Zwirner took a total of 27 pictures of the shattered column but without recording the location. To trace where the convoy had been shot up was a challenge but thanks to Cihotzki's description of the road 'curving to the left and coming to a hill' Jean Paul finally found the spot in 1993 (see *After the Battle* No. 133 and *Rückmarsch Then and Now*, pages 64-75). *Right:* It proved to have taken place six miles east of Vimoutiers — right here on this innocent stretch of the D46 in the Bois de Meulles.

Following orders from General Bradley to stop all further movement northwards to respect the boundary with the 21st Army Group, the XV Corps was halted in front of Argentan on August 13. Bradley then sent parts of the corps eastward, with the Seine river as the objective, leaving the Argentan sector in the hands of the French 2ème Division Blindée, the 90th Infantry Division and the incoming 80th Infantry Division. Then on August 16 Montgomery telephoned Bradley to propose that American troops should move further north to meet up with the Canadians on the line between Chambois and Trun. To this Bradley readily agreed and so he ordered Patton to push northwards. *Above:* This armour is moving through Écouché, five miles west of Argentan.

Looking westwards along Rue Pierre Pigot today. The French military policeman was directing the convoy northwards, i.e. in the direction of Falaise.

COMMUNIQUE No. 131   August 17

Allied troops have made further gains in the Normandy pocket. Our forces are clearing the last enemy from the town of FALAISE. East of the town heavy fighting continues.

Most of the road from FALAISE to CONDE is in our hands and the town of CONDE has been captured.

Forward elements advancing from the west and north-west have reached FLERS. To the east, enemy opposition was bitter and the Allied advance was made more difficult by the enemy's large-scale use of mines, booby-traps, and demolitions.

Further west advances have been made east of TINCHEBRAY, which has been freed, and east from GER.

Mopping-up has been completed in the vicinity of JUVIGNY and in the FORET D'ANDAINE, east of DOMFRONT. North of LA FERTE-MACE and north-east of DOMFRONT gains of up to six miles have been made against resistance which varies from light to moderate.

North of RANES, which has been bypassed, our units are encountering heavy opposition.

In ARGENTAN, the enemy still holds most of the city and fighting is in progress.

In Brittany the port of DINARD has been completely occupied. The German garrison at ST MALO is maintaining stubborn defense in the citadel.

Bad weather limited the Allied air effort over northern France yesterday.

Five bridges over the river Risle, which flows parallel to the Seine on the western side, were attacked by our medium bombers, and an ammunition dump near ROUEN was bombed by light bombers.

Last night crossing points on the Seine and road transport near DIJON, were successfully attacked by our light bombers.

Night fighters destroyed seven enemy aircraft over the battle area.

For one week, the Germans grimly held on to Argentan and it was only on August 19 that the 80th Infantry Division finally managed to enter the town. This symbolic photo was taken to signify its capture.

Rue Victor Hugo lies in the southern quarter of Argentan. The school on the right survived virtually undamaged.

131

The sign of victory. On August 20 men of the 318th Infantry (80th Infantry Division) admire the American flag on the town hall.

COMMUNIQUE No. 132   August 18

Allied forces driving east have liberated DREUX, CHARTRES, CHATEAUDUN and ORLEANS. East of CHARTRES, the Aunay river has been crossed and at DREUX a bridgehead has been established over the Eure. ST CALAIS and AUTHON, both in the path of the eastward drive, have also been liberated.

In the Normandy pocket heavy opposition is being encountered north of RANES. FROMENTEL, north-west of RANES, has been freed. Our troops north of LA FERTE-MACE have advanced 3,000 yards against light and scattered resistance. American patrols have made contact with British forces along the line north and north-east of DOMFRONT.

Allied troops advancing from the FLERS area have taken ATHIS and crossed the river Rouvre east of LA CARNEILLE.

East of the Orne, our forces pushing to RAPILLY and to the vicinity of ST PHILBERT, further compressed the area still occupied by the enemy.

FALAISE was cleared of enemy yesterday morning and our troops are established on the high ground south of the town while to the south-east they advanced down the railway from DAMBLAINVILLE to take FRESNE-LA-MERE.

After capturing BAROU and NORREY-EN-AUGE, our forces drove on to the area of TRUN and CHAMBOIS. ST PIERRE-SUR-DIVES and MEZIDON are in our hands and we are pushing eastward along the whole of our northern sector. North of MEZIDON our troops have reached the line of the Dives as far as BURES and we have taken TROARN and BAVENT.

In Brittany, the citadel at ST MALO has fallen. At DINARD, which has now been liberated, the German commander and his staff were captured. Numerous enemy pockets, which were isolated in the drive through the peninsula, are being mopped up along the north and south coast with the aid of French resistance forces.

Heavy bombers attacked shipping at BREST yesterday afternoon.

Sixteen bridges spanning the river Risle, from FOULBEC near its mouth to LA FERRIERE-SUR-RISLE, 35 miles upstream, were attacked by medium and light bombers in two operations during the day. A fuel dump near LA MAILLERAYE-SUR-SEINE was the target for other medium bombers.

Rail lines from Belgium to France were systematically patrolled by fighters as far as the Seine.

They successfully attacked locomotives, tunnels, bridges, and large numbers of railway cars.

Enemy road transport, particularly in eastern Normandy, was heavily attacked by fighters, which also hit tanks, strong points, troop concentrations and barges on the Seine.

During the night, light bombers attacked transportation targets in Normandy and south-east of PARIS.

The day after the capture of Argentan, a Signal Corps camera-man recorded battle damage on the main square in the centre of the city. In the background, the badly broken spire of the Saint-Germain Church. The Hôtel de Ville is just off to the left.

Dusty and tired GIs of the 80th Infantry Division gather for a little swing played by Corporal H. C. Medley. In the background is the former German employment office.

COMMUNIQUE No. 133   August 19

The net around the German forces in Normandy was drawn tighter yesterday.

American and British troops established contact near BRIOUZE. From the west an advance was made to approximately the line of the river Orne. Advances were also made towards the escape route of German troops streaming eastwards in an attempt to avoid complete encirclement.

Our forces, moving from the south, made progress east and west of ARGENTAN against enemy opposition. A thrust down the ARGENTAN road from the north took us to PIERREFITTE. Our hold on TRUN and the area near CHAMBOIS was extended eastward to CHAMPEAUX.

Further north, the advance continued and our troops have crossed both the river Dives and the river Vie near NOTRE-DAME-D'ESTREES. ST JULIEN-LE-FAUCON has been taken and in the coastal area we have reached DOZULE and the outskirts of CABOURG and DIVES-SUR-MER.

In the DREUX area, our troops have widened their bridgeheads across the river Eure north and south of the city. Farther south, VENDOME has been freed.

The last enemy resistance on the north coast of Brittany has been overcome with the elimination of a German pocket in the LANNION—PAIMPOL area.

Around-the-clock attacks by Allied aircraft against enemy troops and transport, airfields, communications systems, and supply centers has been maintained from Thursday midnight.

The first attacks began with medium and light bombers harassing enemy movements on both sides of the upper Seine. From first light Friday, fighter-bombers and fighters repeatedly swept the area from the immediate battlefront to east of the Seine and deep into Belgium and Holland. They destroyed or damaged many hundreds of railway cars and motor vehicles, at least 10 tanks and numerous locomotives and armored vehicles especially at the mouth of the Normandy pocket. A convoy of 500 vehicles was successfully attacked by rocket-firing fighters north-east of TRUN, and a large number were destroyed or damaged.

On the Seine, two river steamers and many barges were sunk.

At least 51 enemy aircraft were destroyed in combat or on the ground by fighter, which had escorted heavy bombers to attack five key airfields at MÉTZ, NANCY/ESSEY, ROYE/AMY, ST DIZIER, ROMILLY-SUR-SEINE. Sixteen other enemy planes were shot down in a single engagement near BEAUVAIS. Other heavy bomber targets included ships and oil storage tanks at BORDEAUX, submarine shelters at LA PALLICE, and fuel depots near GHENT, NANCY, PACY-SUR-ARMANCON, the railway center of CONNANTRE and bridges over the Meuse river at MAASTRICHT, NAMUR and HUY.

Heavy and medium bombers made three co-ordinated attacks on an important ammunition dump in the forest of L'ISLE-ADAM north of PARIS. Rail embankments at VERBERIE, GOURNAY-EN-BRAY and RIVECOURT and a fuel dump at VALENTON were attacked by other medium and light bombers.

Last night, light bombers and fighters, working in close support of our troops, dropped flares on enemy forces retreating eastward from the FALAISE area and continued to harry them. From all of these operations 39 of our aircraft are missing.

Photographers or caption writers seem to have had a fixation about identifying all large German tanks as Tigers even if it is a Panther!

Argentan, Rue Aristide Briand, looking westwards with the nicely repaired Saint-Germain Church. The shop is now a grocery.

COMMUNIQUE No. 134   August 20

Allied forces have advanced to the vicinity of the Seine and have closed the enemy escape corridor south of FALAISE.

Leading elements moving north and north-east from DREUX have reached a point 18 miles beyond the city to the vicinity of MANTES-GASSICOURT.

Allied forces from north and south have met in CHAMBOIS, sealing the exit south of FALAISE. The area of the enemy pocket has again been reduced substantially by advances from all directions, particularly southwards towards MONTABARD and north to ECOUCHE, where heavy fighting has taken place. West of ARGENTAN, in the area south-east of PUTANGES, we have completed the mopping up of enemy groups behind the southern edge of the pocket.

Further north, in the area east of ST PIERRE-SUR-DIVES, our troops have continued to thrust eastwards and have established three bridgeheads over the river Vie at LIVAROT, COUPESARTE and GRANDCHAMP.

No changes are reported in the areas of CHARTRES and ORLEANS or in the Brittany peninsula.

Our Normandy-based planes continued the heavy attacks on tanks and motor vehicles of all types retreating eastward, and against river barges on the Seine. They also provided close support for our advancing columns.

Roads in the escape corridor in the vicinity of ORBEC are strewn with knocked-out vehicles, often making it difficult for our pilots to select active targets. More than 800 motor trucks were destroyed and 600 damaged yesterday from the line FALAISE—ARGENTAN north-eastward to the Seine, in addition to 40 tanks destroyed and many others damaged.

Twenty-six large river barges on the Seine were sunk by fighter-bombers during the day. Fifty-nine were destroyed the previous day.

Direct hits were registered during an attack by coastal aircraft on small groups of enemy E-Boats in the eastern Channel early yesterday.

A small force of heavy bombers attacked the LA PALLICE oil storage depot yesterday morning.

Other operations by aircraft based in England were curtailed by weather.

A force of enemy E- and R-Boats was intercepted off CAP DE LA HEVE by light coastal forces early Saturday. After a short engagement, during which damage was inflicted on the enemy, our force withdrew leaving the enemy craft firing upon each other in some confusion.

An armed trawler and an M-class minesweeper were also attacked by light coastal forces off the entrance to the harbor of LE HAVRE despite the fire of the shore batteries, which prevented observation of results.

Left: **Leaders of the 4th Canadian Armoured Division entered Saint-Lambert-sur-Dives, six miles north-east of Argentan, on August 18. There Major David V. Currie was pictured rounding up prisoners at pistol point. Later he was awarded the Victoria Cross, the first Canadian VC of the campaign.** *Right:* **A memorial now stands beside the northern entrance to Saint-Lambert-sur-Dives to record this iconic photograph.**

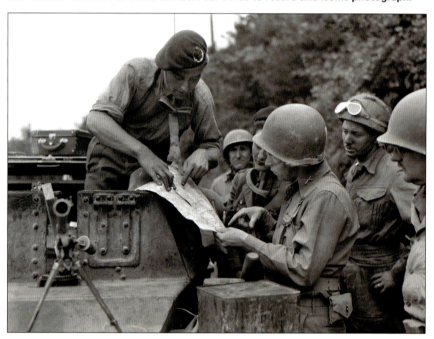

On August 20, Communiqué No. 134 reported that 'Allied forces from north and south have met in Chambois'. The link-up took place at 7.45 p.m. on the 19th when Canadians of the 4th Armoured Division joined hands with Americans of the 90th Infantry Division.

Battle trophies! In Chambois, these GIs purloin binoculars, hand-guns and other souvenirs from an abandoned Luftwaffe vehicle.

From a head-count carried out by the survey teams from the Bombing Analysis Unit of the RAF, German losses in motor vehicles in the 'Pocket' (the area bounded by a line passing through Falaise, Vassy, Barenton and Argentan) and the 'Shambles' (a triangular area in between Falaise, Argentan and Vimoutiers) totalled about 8,000. *Above:* Just two of the casualties were pictured in Chambois: a PzKpfw IV of the 8. Kompanie of an unknown panzer regiment and a SdKfz 7 heavy tractor. *Right:* Rue Emile Combes, looking northwards, with the bridge over the Dives river in middle distance. *Below:* At the eastern exit of the Moissy ford, in between Saint-Lambert-sur-Dives and Chambois, the field by the lane was strewn with equipment of every description. Visiting the battlefield, 'one of the greatest killing grounds of any of the war areas' just two days after the closing of the gap Eisenhower said that he encountered 'scenes that could be described only by Dante'.

Looking over the sea of wheat that now lines the field belonging to the Jacqueau farm.

The RAF survey determined that about one quarter of the motor vehicles lost during the retreat were damaged directly by air attacks. This column was bombed and strafed when it was halted by a bomb-crater which was blocking the road in front of the underpass beneath the railway line crossing a secondary road just west of Clinchamps, eight miles south-east of Falaise. However, in addition, a sizeable number of the German vehicles were estimated to have been abandoned owing to the indirect effects of air attack such as lack of petrol and congestion. It was just here in 1975 that Winston Ramsey recovered the smashed arm from the road sign broken off by the same air attack that disabled this column.

COMMUNIQUE No. 135   August 21

Further progress in the Allied drive toward LISIEUX has been made. A thrust north-east of GRANDCHAMP brought us to within five miles of the town.

Gains were made on the right bank of the river Vie against determined opposition. The town of LIVAROT was taken and a successful attack was made south of DOZULE.

Mopping-up continued south of FALAISE, where several strenuous attempts by enemy armor to break out were frustrated. ARGENTAN is in our hands. Allied troops occupying CHAMBOIS have held an enemy counter-attack toward the town from the north-west.

Enemy forces caught in the trap, including elements of at least 14 divisions, are being subjected to heavy artillery fire.

Allied units are on the Seine in the vicinity of MANTES-GASSICOURT. To the south, our forces in the DREUX area are mopping up pockets of resistance. The elimination of isolated German units around ORLEANS has been completed.

Heavy rainstorms and low clouds limited our air operations. Nevertheless, Normandy-based fighters and fighter-bombers continued to harass the enemy withdrawal in the BERNAY area.

There was some enemy air reaction and we shot down 12 enemy aircraft.

Concentrations of troops waiting to cross the Seine near ROUEN were attacked by our medium bombers.

Last night, Seine ferry crossings at four points between ELBEUF and the coast were attacked by our light bombers. Several barges were hit.

Considerable damage was done to road transport in the BERNAY area where bombing by flares was carried out.

On Saturday and Sunday enemy batteries at HOULGATE and BENERVILLE, which had been interfering with our advance on the northern flank were engaged and neutralised by HMS *Erebus*. Early Sunday morning, a coastal patrol of six E-Boats was intercepted by light coastal forces. The enemy was brought to action under cover of his shore defences off LE HAVRE and considerable damage was inflicted upon his craft before our patrols withdrew to seaward.

One has difficulty comprehending that this quiet stretch of country road could have been the scene of such devastation in August 1944. The view is looking westwards along the D29E between Pierrefitte and Clinchamps which lies beyond the railway embankment in the background.

COMMUNIQUE No. 136   August 22

Good progress has been made between LISIEUX and the sea where Allied troops have captured DOZULE and DIVES-SUR-MER and advanced to ANNEBAULT and BONNEBOSQ. West of LISIEUX we have taken CAMBREMER, while an advance north of ST MARTIN-DE-LA-LIEUE has brought our troops within a mile of LISIEUX itself.

Fighting is going on in the vicinity of VIMOUTIERS.

Further south, an advance has been made east of CHAMBOIS and GACE is in our hands.

Determined enemy efforts to break out of the encirclement were again checked effectively. Mopping-up continues.

There is nothing further to report from the remainder of the front.

Weather severely restricted air operations yesterday, but during the evening, coastal aircraft attacked enemy shipping near the mouth of the Gironde river.

Doubting von Kluge's loyalty after what had happened in Paris on July 20 (see page 92), by mid-August Hitler had removed him from command. Having taken over on August 17, the following day the new German C-in-C in the West, Generalfeldmarschall Walter Model directed that the 7. Armee was to extricate itself from the pocket and pull back to the Touques river where an attempt to stabilise the front was to be made. Altogether the Allies captured over 40,000 to 50,000 men in the pocket while several thousand others had lost their lives while trying to escape, later estimates ranging up to 10,000. Also, it is not possible to put an accurate head-count on how many Germans succeeded in escaping before the pocket was closed, estimates varying from 30,000 to 40,000. *Above:* It was during the four-day period after August 20, when poor visibility and rain prevented SHAEF air forces from operating, that Kriegsberichter Kurth, another photographer from Propaganda-Kompanie 698, pictured this Sturmgeschütz III rattling through at Orbec, 13 miles east of Vimoutiers. *Right:* **Rue de la République, pictured from Rue du Pont-Guernet.**

The German withdrawal towards the Seine continued in full swing. At the approach of fighter-bombers, this particular column has taken cover by the side of the road enabling war photographer Hans Scheck to take some interesting shots of the crew of an SdKfz 251. These men belong to the 9. SS-Panzer-Division.

To trace this very stretch of road was a tempting challenge, if a seemingly impossible one.

Another *After the Battle* success was finding the location where Kriegsberichter Genzler took this sequence showing a convoy caught in the open by Allied aircraft. It came down to detailed detective work by Jean Paul to find the clues and track it down. *Above:* Here we see Waffen-SS troopers studying a map by the side of the road while armoured vehicles stand parked in the background under the trees. Another frame on the roll shows one of the men pointing his finger at a spot on the map. Jean Paul identified the relevant Michelin sheet and then visited the sector being indicated. Once on the battlefield, he finally traced the only shot in the series which showed an identifiable feature *(top right)*. This proved to be at La Haye-du-Theil, eight miles north-east of Brionne. *Above right:* Jean Paul took his comparison on the D80, a half-mile south of the village. *Right:* Another frame shows a Panther tank stopped in the open in a rather perilous position (see also *Rückmarsch Then and Now*, pages 129-134).

When the aircraft appeared approaching the spot, the driver of this Kübelwagen quickly drove off the road to get under cover.

We found that the picture had been taken on Rue Lemarrois, looking north. In the background stands the new bridge that now sends the main road eastwards out of town, leaving this street a quiet backwater.

Above: Allied fighter-bombers constantly roamed the battlefield looking for targets of opportunity and the crew of this SdKfz 251 have just spotted 'Jabos' overhead on the outskirts of Brionne, 19 miles north-east of Orbec. *Right:* In the centre of the town, PK Kurth pictured more armoured personnel carriers but not all of them would succeed in reaching the Seine. In what the RAF called the 'Chase' area leading to the river, German losses were estimated at 6,400 motor vehicles and 600 tanks, armoured vehicles and SP guns. *Below:* On the outskirts of the town Kurth also found a pair of Jagdpanthers of schwere Panzerjäger-Abteilung 654. This was quite a rare beast in Normandy for this was the only formation which possessed them, the unit reporting at the end of July that they only had 25 Jagdpanthers left. It was another rainy day, hence it must have been sometime between August 20 and 23 when really bad weather prevailed.

Jagdpanther '302' had another casualty in tow, apparently bearing the number '301'.

Left: **At the Seine, all the bridges were down having been cut by Allied air attacks and many of the ferries sunk. German engineers struggled to provide emergency crossings and at Rouen, they operated this ferry to the Ile Lacroix, an island in** the middle or the river. Once on the island, men and vehicles could then reach the northern bank via a small bridge which was still intact. *Right:* **From Ile Lacroix, looking downstream across the Seine with the Quai d'Elbeuf on the left bank.**

COMMUNIQUE No. 137   August 23

Allied forces have liberated SENS, on the east bank of the river Yonne. PITHIVIERS and ETAMPES are also in our hands.

North of DREUX, other units are moving north-westward between the rivers Seine and Eure. A drive northward between DREUX and VERNEUIL has liberated NONANCOURT, and the advance has carried to a point north of ST ANDRE-DE-L'EURE.

To the west considerable advances have been made along the whole Allied front between L'AIGLE and the sea. In the center of this wide sweep our forces are fighting in LISIEUX.

North of the town our forces have surged forward all along the line, captured CABOURG, HOULGATE, VILLERS-SUR-MER and DEAUVILLE along the coast and have reached TROUVILLE, PONT-L'EVEQUE and the line of the river Touques further south.

South of LISIEUX, our troops have established a broad bridgehead extending for several miles further east across the Orbec river.

Other troops have advanced across the river Vie through VIMOUTIERS, crossed the river Touques and have reached the area of the town of ORBEC.

Continuing the advance from GACE our troops have captured L'AIGLE. The FALAISE pocket has been eliminated.

Allied fighter-bombers and fighters continued to pound the enemy at Seine crossings, destroying more than 200 vehicles, 15 boats and barges and six tanks. These attacks, made through rain and cloud, were often delivered at 200 feet despite heavy anti-aircraft fire and strong air opposition.

More than 150 railway cars were destroyed or damaged by other formations operating to the east and south-east of PARIS. Marshalling yards at DIJON and CHARNY were attacked with good results.

At least 31 enemy aircraft were destroyed in the air and six on the ground. Preliminary reports show two of ours are missing.

During a gun action fought Monday morning south of CAP D'ANTIFER between light coastal forces of the Royal Navy and an enemy patrol of armed trawlers and E-Boats, one trawler was severely damaged and an R-Boat destroyed. Two other E-Boats received serious damage.

Right: **Saint-Nicolas-de-Bliquetuit, on the left bank of the Seine, across from Caudebec-en-Caux that is seen on the far bank. The ferry service was resumed after the war but it finally closed down in 1977 when the Brotonne bridge was opened just upstream from this site.**

At Caudebec-en-Caux, the large steam ferry had been sunk during an air attack on August 27 so instead pontoons were improvised using two pneumatic boats tied on each side of a motorised storm boat although the structure could only carry one vehicle at a time.

The railway bridge at Eauplet, upstream from Rouen, had been bombed although only one span had collapsed. The other three were nearly intact and German engineers quickly carried out a temporary repair of the broken span with timber. This made the bridge passable and from August 22 motor vehicles were crossing at the rate of about a thousand a day. By the end of the month 6,000-7,000 vehicles and thousands of men had made it across to the northern bank. *Left:* Around August 24, Kurt Müller took this shot of a battered Kübelwagen carefully negotiating the patched-up bridge. *Right:* It was rapidly repaired and re-opened to traffic in 1945 — this is how it looks today.

COMMUNIQUE No. 138   August 24

South-east of PARIS, Allied forces have reached the vicinity of CORBEIL and MELUN, and reconnaissance elements are 15 miles east of SENS. Farther south units are east of MONTARGIS, after crossing the Loing river.

The Allied enveloping drives towards the lower Seine continue.

Units advancing northwards have liberated EVREUX and are now several miles beyond the city. Other units have reached CONCHES after freeing VERNEUIL.

A thrust north-east from MONNAI progressed about five miles and a drive north-eastwards from ORBEC reached the village of LA THIBOUTIERE.

Several bridgeheads have been made across the river Touques. Fighting continued in the area of LISIEUX where the enemy had taken up strong positions dominating the eastern exit from the town. In the PONT-L'EVEQUE area, enemy resistance was stubborn and between there and LISIEUX heavy mortar fire was brought down on our troops crossing the river.

The enemy's dwindling road, rail and water transport systems were attacked by our aircraft yesterday. Fighter-bombers destroyed more than 500 motor transport in the woods and on the roads in the ELBEUF—LOUVIERS area, and sank 15 river barges at TOURNEDOS-SUR-SEINE.

Both flak and enemy air opposition were encountered along the river and as far east as SENS where our fighters gave support to the ground forces. Seventeen enemy planes were destroyed in the air in this sector and 12 others damaged. Fifteen of our aircraft are missing.

In the CAMBRAI—LILLE area, rail yards and canal barges were attacked effectively and without loss.

Fires resulted from an attack by a small force of medium bombers on a fuel dump near ROUEN.

Left: German engineers also assembled makeshift ferries to replace those sunk, this by mounting a platform on cargo barges. When the ferry landing stages were also bombed out, they constructed new ones using other barges so that the platform would rise and fall in unison as the Seine was a tidal river.

This large ferry at Petit-Couronne could transport between 100 and 150 vehicles per day, plus hundreds of men, and it turned out to be one of the major crossing points for the withdrawing German forces. *Right:* This is where an army escaped: Petit-Couronne today.

Eisenhower's move to France marked the beginning of a new phase in the conduct of the war in which politics came increasingly to the fore. The Allied victory at Falaise, and the subsequent rout of the German forces in the West, led the top political players to look to their futures. The first major problem to beset the Supreme Commander was that of Général de Gaulle, who now expected to be installed as France's political leader. Roosevelt opposed such automatic recognition without the French people having their say but the impending liberation of Paris meant that the matter could no longer be avoided. As word reached Paris that the Allied formations were approaching the city, on August 19 the Resistance movement decided to take a hand in the liberation of their capital. The Germans were leaving — now was the time for action. An informal truce was agreed with the German commander, General Dietrich von Choltitz, while envoys were sent to the Americans warning them that an uprising was about to take place in the city and to speed up their advance. Général de Gaulle had only just arrived in France and on the 21st he came to see Eisenhower in his tented office at 'Shellburst' with Général Pierre Koenig, the commander of the French Forces of the Interior (FFI), with an ultimatum: if SHAEF did not send troops into Paris at once, the French were prepared to so unilaterally.

COMMUNIQUE No. 139   August 25

After overcoming considerable enemy opposition, elements of the 2nd French Armored Division, under General Leclerc, have entered the outskirts of PARIS. South and south-east of the capital, Allied troops have crossed the Seine near MELUN and in the FONTAINEBLEAU area. Further up river, we have occupied MONTEREAU. East of MONTARGIS, now in our hands, American units have made further gains.

Our forces now closing in towards the Seine estuary have made further advances.

A thrust from the south has brought us to the southern outskirts of ELBEUF and to GAILLON, south-east of LOUVIERS.

The advance from the west gained fresh impetus yesterday after the last enemy resistance at LISIEUX and PONT-L'EVEQUE had been overcome.

Allied forces moving north-east from MONNAI have reached the area of BROGLIE. In a rapid thrust from the ORBEC area, our troops have captured THIBERVILLE and advanced several miles to the banks of the river Risle, east of BERNAY, which is in our hands. Other troops from LISIEUX have reached the Risle, near BRIONNE.

South-east of PONT-L'EVEQUE, our forces, after seizing the high ground at BLANGY, have advanced to the line of the river Calonne from the area of MOYAUX, on the right, to LES AUTHIEUX, on the left. Further north, we have captured the FORET DE ST GATIEN and have reached the main road south of BEUZEVILLE. On the coast we have captured TROUVILLE and are approaching HONFLEUR.

Enemy escape lines in the Seine area were attacked yesterday by fighters and fighter-bombers as weather permitted. The attacks were continued last night by light bombers which also struck at motor transport in the DIEPPE—BEAUVAIS area and bombed railways in Belgium and north-east France.

E-Boat and R-Boat pens at IJMUIDEN in Holland and shipping at BREST were attacked with good results in daylight yesterday by heavy bombers.

On August 22 Eisenhower finally gave orders to march on Paris and the French 2ème Division Blindée and US 4th Infantry Division led out from the Argentan sector. The 2ème Division Blindée reached the capital late on the 24th and the western outskirts were cleared next morning but not before some sharp exchanges had taken place with the small German rearguard. In the meantime, the US 12th Infantry had taken the eastern part of the city without encountering much resistance.

Residents of the suburb of Rambouillet wave and cheer the French armour as it roars down Rue Georges Clemenceau on its way to liberate the capital.

The plan was for a truly Allied force to liberate Paris and the 2ème Division Blindée was to enter the city accompanied by American cavalry and British troops, all displaying their national flags but whether by accident or design, the British force failed to appear. While the US 4th Infantry Division seized a bridge over the Seine to the south, the French armour crossed the river via the Pont d'Austerlitz. *Left:* Breaking through a barricade on the Rue de Rivoli, a Sherman named *Douaumont* entered the Place de la Concorde, just a few yards from where this Panther was exchanging shots with other Shermans up on the Avenue des Champs-Élysées. *Douaumont* fired but its high-explosive shell had no effect on the Panther so the French tank deliberately rammed the German. With its turret jammed, the panzer crew quickly bailed out and ran off through the Jardin des Tuileries. Sadly the *Douaumont* commander, Sergent Marcel Bizien, was killed shortly afterwards by a sniper. *Right:* Where one of the last skirmishes for Paris took place.

As the gun-fire had not yet completely died away, French cameraman Gaston Madru of Paramount News played safe and fixed a warning on the top of his car as he toured the streets.

COMMUNIQUE No. 140   August 26

More Allied armor and infantry are in PARIS following the entrance of the 2nd French Armored Division Friday morning, and all resistance in the southern and southwestern outskirts has been overcome. By noon yesterday, one armored column had crossed the SÈVRES bridge over the Seine and another column had progressed into the southern part of the city. Infantry followed the armor and advanced to the Cathedral of Notre Dame.

South of PARIS, the enemy holds the east edge of the Seine between VILLENEUVE-SAINT-GEORGES and CORBEIL. Between CORBEIL and MELUN reconnaissance elements have crossed the river. No changes have been reported from the areas of MONTEREAU, or MONTARGIS, both of which are in our hands.

The enemy is withdrawing north-east from MONTARGIS and we have patrols as far east as TROYES.

ELBEUF has been liberated and Allied troops between there and the sea are rapidly approaching the Seine. The river Risle has been crossed at many places and our troops hold both banks as far north as MONTFORT-SUR-RISLE. We have taken HONFLEUR and BEUZEVILLE.

Further to the south-east, EPAIGNES and ST GEORGES-DU-VIEVRE are in our hands, and British and Canadian forces have made contact with American troops.

BREST was subjected to attack by land, air and sea. Enemy strong points, including the arsenal, were attacked by medium and heavy bombers yesterday afternoon and last night. Coastal batteries and selected targets were bombarded from the sea.

A fuel dump at CLERMONT, east of BEAUVAIS, was attacked by medium bombers during the afternoon.

Fighters and fighter-bombers attacked tanks, motor vehicles and barges, particularly in the lower Seine and eastward from the river. Medium bombers also hit concentrations of motor vehicles near ROUEN.

There was more opposition in the air, and 51 enemy aircraft were shot down, and others were destroyed on the ground. Twenty-one of our aircraft are missing.

Motor transport and trains in north-eastern France were attacked during the night by our light bombers.

He was photographed on the Boulevard du Palais on the Ile de la Cité, the picture being taken looking westwards over the Pont Saint-Michel.

While enthusiastic crowds thronged the streets of Paris, Colonel R. Ernest Dupuy, the SHAEF Public Relations Officer, was not a happy man, as Captain Butcher explains: 'Today Paris seems finally to have fallen, after a premature announcement to the press by the French some three days ago. Poor Colonel Dupuy has been unable to give the correspondents confirmation that Paris has been liberated. His last several press conferences have been most difficult. SHAEF would not confirm the French announcement, and Colonel Dupuy has been on the battle line with the correspondents, particularly the Americans, who insist that if the French say their capital is liberated, why must SHAEF be so far behind the news? He is handicapped by slowness of communications. Telephone connexions with SHAEF Forward (at Jullouville) are hard to get, and once a connexion is obtained one has to shout to be heard. Official information about progress on the various battle fronts percolates slowly from company to battalion, to regiment, to division, to corps, to armies and then to army groups, and finally to SHAEF Forward — each step being slowed by necessary coding and decoding of official messages.'

The German commander von Choltitz surrendered at the Hôtel Meurice, the German headquarters in Paris *(left)*, whereupon he was taken to Général Leclerc's command post situated at the Montparnasse railway station (since demolished and relocated some 300 metres away). *Right:* There, in Room 32 on Platform 3, von Choltitz signed acts of capitulation to avoid further bloodshed and copies were then quickly circulated to various German strong points still holding out in the city. All surrendered during the day except for a force of about 2,500 men stationed in the Bois de Boulogne — a wooded area to the west of the city — which only finally emerged the following day. According to Capitaine Alfred Betz who was present, the photo actually shows von Choltitz signing a chit to enable his personal possessions to be retrieved from the Hôtel Meurice.

Général de Gaulle arrived in Paris at 4 p.m. and went straight to see Général Leclerc. He was not pleased to see that the head of the FFI, Colonel Rol, had countersigned the capitulation document as it implied that the Communists had been chiefly responsible for the defeat of the Germans in Paris. The following day, Saturday, August 26, the Général arrived at the Arc de Triomphe, his appearance having been announced on the airwaves. After re-kindling the Eternal Flame on the memorial to the Unknown Soldier at 3 p.m., he began his victory march as a million Parisians cheered wildly . . . from the roadside, balconies, windows and roof-tops. Ahead of de Gaulle rumbled four tanks while Jeeps moved along with him on either side to keep back the crowds. However, the day was not to be without incident as shots rang out as he entered the Place de la Concorde. While the crowd ran for cover neither de Gaulle nor Leclerc wavered from steadfastly leading the procession.

General Bradley: 'The day after we had liberated Paris I returned from a hurried flight to Brest to find Eisenhower camped on my doorstep in our barnyard CP near Chartres. Although he had come with more pressing issues in mind, Ike suggested we slip quietly into Paris for a glimpse of the city on the following morning, "It's Sunday", he said. "Everyone will be sleeping late. We can do it without any fuss." He radioed Monty an invitation to join us but Monty replied with regrets; he was much too busy pushing his British troops on to the Seine. It was not yet eight the following morning when we wedged our column into a convoy trundling through the shuttered boulevards of Chartres. Ike's OD Cadillac with its British, French and American flags had been placed in between two armoured cars. We drove to the headquarters de Gaulle had established in the Prefecture of Police. Inside de Gaulle waited. He creased his long mournful face into a smile of welcome. This was my first meeting with France's dour soldier. De Gaulle spoke of the urgent need to reassure the Parisians that this time the Allies had come with forces strong enough to drive the German into his homeland and there destroy him. To impress the people with this strength and give them heart, he suggested that we parade a division or two of troops through Paris. Ike turned to me and asked what we could do. Since we had already planned to attack eastward out of Paris, I told him that we could probably march a division straight through the Etoile rather than around the city's fringes. With General Joseph-Pierre Koenig, whom de Gaulle had named French military governor of Paris, we drove up the Boulevard des Invalides to where the gilded Dome des Invalides stood over the tomb of Napoleon. After halting briefly at the crypt, we crossed the Seine to the broad Place de la Concorde and drove up the leafy Champs Elysées. A huge Tricolor filled the Arc de Triomphe from its arch to the street. As Eisenhower dismounted to salute France's unknown warrior, a jubilant crowd bore down on him. His way back to the car was blocked and a wedge of MPs struggled to clear a path to its door.'

Bradley continues: 'On the sunny afternoon of August 29 the 28th Division's freshly scrubbed columns with loaded guns and full bandoliers swung down the Champs Elysées from the Arc de Triomphe to the crowded Place de la Concorde. There to the division's own tune of *Khaki Bill*, the procession parted into two columns, each moving into assembly preparatory to attack. What appeared to the Parisians to be a division on parade was actually a tactical movement into battle. Within 26 hours from the moment it had been alerted for this march, the division had moved up from Versailles to a bivouac in the Bois de Boulogne. There it scrubbed from its uniforms and trucks the encrusted dirt of 36 days in the line, issued instructions for the "parade" and battle orders for the end of the line of march.' Later, General Eisenhower presented a bronze SHAEF badge to be added in front of the tomb to mark the liberation of Paris.

In the north, the 21st Army Group advanced to the Seine with the First Canadian Army on the left and British Second Army on the right. On the right wing of the Second Army, leaders of the XXX Corps pushed eastwards via Gacé and L'Aigle and by the afternoon of August 25 the assault group of the 43rd (Wessex) Division was assembled behind Vernon on the Seine bank, ready to force the crossing. *Left:* Sergeant Midgley pictured people of Gacé giving a great welcome to the British troops. *Right:* Timeless comparison in Rue de Rouen at Gacé.

COMMUNIQUE No. 141   August 27

Allied troops advancing eastwards towards the upper Seine valley have reached the river in the northern outskirts of TROYES and at a point 12 miles farther north.

Nearer PARIS, armored units have launched an attack between MELUN and CORBEIL where a bridgehead had been previously established.

Approximately 10,000 enemy troops including the German commander and his staff were taken prisoner in PARIS. One enemy strong point has been holding out in CHAMPIGNY on the south-east edge of the city and small enemy groups still operate in the north-east and north-west suburbs. Within the city, formal resistance has ceased but some sniping continues.

In the Seine valley armored elements have advanced along the south side of the river in the area between MANTES-GASSICOURT and PARIS encountering slight opposition.

Allied forces have closed in towards the south bank of the Seine and have crossed the river at VERNON and PONT-DE-L'ARCHE. Further west our troops have captured BOURGTHEROULDE and are clearing the enemy from the FORET DE LA LONDE. In the coastal area the enemy has been driven over the lower Risle and PONT-AUDEMER is in our hands.

Referring to the British I Corps figthing against strong opposition to force the Touques river on the left wing of the First Canadian Army, Communiqué No. 139 reported their advance gaining 'fresh impetus' after this 'last enemy resistance' had been overcome. Troopers of the 49th (West Riding) Division took another group of prisoners.

The I Corps had yet to overcome opposition in the Brotonne Forest from German forces covering the crossings in this loop of the Seine. This rearguard finally withdrew enabling British troops to continue the advance to Bourneville.

Jean Paul's comparison was taken in the early morning light, some four miles from the river bank. Apart from cosmetic changes, time has stood still on this stretch of road leaving it completely unchanged.

In the British XXX Corps' sector, the 43rd (Wessex) Division launched the first British assault of the Seine on the evening of August 25. The assaulting troops — the 4th Somerset Light Infantry on the left and the 5th Wiltshire Regiment on the right — crossed in storm boats under German fire and, in spite of losses and difficulties, the division had the best part of three battalions across the river when dawn broke on the 26th. A first bridge, a Class 9 folding-boat bridge named 'David', was completed by late afternoon on the 26th and by nightfall the division had two brigades on the far bank. The first tanks were ferried across early on the 27th, just in time to beat off German infantry and some tanks trying to push down to the bridgehead. Taken on the 27th by Sergeant Bill Ginger, the SHAEF censor has been at work on this shot of an ambulance and infantry crossing the 'David' bridge before it was released on the 29th. On the left is the Class 40 Bailey pontoon bridge 'Goliath' built on August 26-27.

Heavy fighting is in progress in the area north of BREST on the Brittany peninsula where the enemy garrison is offering stubborn resistance. Gun positions and fortified targets at BREST were again attacked without loss by escorted heavy bombers.

Attacks on enemy transport in north-east France by our fighter-bombers and fighters are being extended into Belgium and Germany. Locomotives and hundreds of motor vehicles and railway cars — some loaded with ammunition and oil — have been destroyed or damaged during the last 24 hours, especially near the Seine at ROUEN. Marshalling yards at GISORS and CHARLEROI also were hit. Rail movements in the LILLE—AMIENS—DIEPPE area have been pounded incessantly.

Concentrations of enemy troops and vehicles seeking passage over the Seine were hit throughout the day by waves of escorted light and medium bombers which dropped fragmentation and high-explosive bombs. Their targets also included four fuel dumps to the east and south-east of ROUEN.

Enemy air opposition was slight, but heavy anti-aircraft fire has been concentrated at many points to the east of the Seine. Six enemy aircraft were shot down and at least twelve others were destroyed on the ground. Seven of our bombers and 17 fighters are missing.

A photo symbolic of the German defeat in the West. On September 1, Montgomery crossed the Seine via the 'Goliath' bridge at Vernon. In 1992, on the 48th anniversary of the crossing, a memorial was unveiled at the spot where Royal Engineers constructed 'David' and 'Goliath' bridges in August 1944.

Left: In the British XII Corps' sector, the 15th (Scottish) Division crossed the Seine at Saint-Pierre-du-Vauvray, 12 miles south of Rouen, and the construction of a Class 40 Bailey pontoon bridge was started upstream from the destroyed bridge. *Right:* This is the exact comparison although trees now hide the houses on the far bank.

Following the establishment by the US XV Corps of the first Allied bridgehead across the Seine near Mantes, 30 miles downstream of Paris, on the 20th the US Third Army achieved three more bridgeheads upstream of Paris within four days. At Melun the 7th Armored Division tried to cross on what remained of the destroyed bridge on the 23rd but the action was stalemated by German defenders entrenched on the far bank. In the meantime, other elements of the division crossed the Seine at Tilly, eight miles downstream from Melun. Engineers worked on through the night to build a treadway bridge and on the 24th a combat command turned south and drove into Melun, putting an end to the fight for the town on the morning of the 25th. On the XX Corps right flank, the 5th Infantry Division established one bridgehead at Samoreau, near Fontainebleau, on the 24th and another at Montereau. *Above:* Though German machine guns were still active on the far bank, during the morning of the 25th rafts were in operation ferrying vehicles across at Montereau.

COMMUNIQUE No. 142   August 28

Allied forces which crossed the Seine south of PARIS are continuing their eastward drive between the Marne and the Seine. At the southern end of this sector, elements have advanced beyond TROYES, and other units are in the immediate vicinity of MILLY-SUR-SEINE. NOGENT-SUR-SEINE is in our hands. Our troops are approaching PROVINS, and, to the north-west, they have advanced to the vicinity of LAGNY.

The enemy has been cleared from BOURDENAY and ST LUPIEN, south of NOGENT-SUR-SEINE.

In the PARIS area, the situation is now generally quiet although resistance continued on Sunday at CHAMPIGNY. The BOIS DE BOULOGNE has been cleared of Germans but minor isolated groups have been operating in the BOIS DE MEUDON, on the south-western outskirts of the city.

Elimination of enemy forces between PARIS and MANTES-GASSICOURT has been proceeding mainly in the vicinity of VILLENNES-SUR-SEINE, near POISSY.

The Allied bridgeheads over the Seine at MANTES-GASSICOURT, VERNON and east of ELBEUF were strengthened and enlarged.

Our troops pushed eastwards from PONT-AUDEMER in face of stubborn enemy resistance, and the road from that town to BOURG ACHARD is now in our hands. The clearing of the FORET DE LA LONDE is now almost complete.

In Brittany, gains have been made by forces fighting near BREST.

Enemy troops, vehicles and barges concentrated on the west bank of the Seine at ROUEN have been attacked throughout the last 24 hours by hundreds of Allied airplanes. Waves of light and medium bombers dropped thousands of fragmentation and high-explosive bombs in their second consecutive day of operations against these targets, despite intense anti-aircraft fire. Attacks lasting several hours were also delivered by strong formations of fighters and fighter-bombers. Results were excellent.

Other formations of light and medium bombers hit two fuel dumps at BUCY-LES-PIERREPONT and in the FORET DE SAMOUSSY, north-west of REIMS, as well as radio installations near BOULOGNE.

Locomotives, military vehicles and hundreds of railway cars were destroyed or damaged by other fighters which bombed and strafed over a wide territory from the mouth of the Seine to Luxembourg, Germany and into Denmark.

Escorted heavy bombers again hit shipping targets at BREST without loss.

At least 16 enemy aircraft were destroyed in the air and 14 on the ground. Seventeen of ours are missing.

The houses that were visible in 1944 on the far bank of the Seine are still there although new houses and mature trees hide most of them. At this spot of the Chemin de Halage there is now a barge repair yard.

The Waffen-SS soldier was perched on bollard No. 230 waiting to cross but Jean Paul took this shot a little further along the quay to have this nicer comparison with a ship tied alongside Quai Jean de Béthencourt.

Above left: At Rouen, Kriegsberichter Müller pictured the western bank of the Seine crammed with vehicles waiting to cross on another ferry that had been improvised by German engineers. With a large platform built across two cargo barges tied side by side, this heavy ferry could carry up to 25 vehicles in one go. Müller probably took these pictures on August 25 when the troops were queuing up for their turn to board the ferry after four days of bad weather that had protected them from interference by Allied aircraft. *Right:* When the sky cleared on the 25th, Mitchells and Bostons suddenly appeared overhead and bombed the hundreds of vehicles cramming the western bank. Kriegsberichter Jesse pictured the carnage from the right bank with the whole left bank burning fiercely. Three days of bombing — August 25, 26 and 27 — left an impressive mass of burnt-out vehicles lying all along the left bank of the river, and a later survey reported a total of 680 vehicles, including 20 armoured vehicles, and 48 guns.

Speeding away from the Seine along Boulevard des Belges, only a few hundred metres from the river bank.

COMMUNIQUE No. 143   August 29

Allied forces which crossed the Seine at TROYES have reached a point approximately 15 miles north-east of the town, and another crossing has been made several miles to the north. Other elements are in the immediate vicinity of ARCIS-SUR-AUBE.

Troops advancing north and east below the Marne have reached MONTMIRAIL. LA FERTE-SOUS-JOUARRE has been liberated. Forces north of the river have advanced to within six miles of CHATEAU-THIERRY. North of MEAUX, Allied armored units have reached CUVERGNON, 14 miles from the Marne, in a rapid advance against light resistance.

The bridgeheads over the Seine below PARIS, at MANTES-GASSICOURT, VERNON and PONT-DE-L'ARCHE, have all been extended. Varied enemy resistance was encountered on the north side of the river near MANTES-GASSICOURT. Our forces in the two other bridgeheads have made good progress. Another bridgehead east of LOUVIERS has now been established. Our troops are firmly along the general line of the Seine and the only ground south of the river remaining in enemy hands is in the loop between ELBEUF and the sea.

In Brittany, Allied forces closing in on BREST from three sides continue to make slow, steady progress against heavy opposition.

Our long-range fighters, operating well ahead of the advancing Allied armies, carried out low-level attacks on road, rail and water communications in north-eastern France, Belgium, Holland, Luxembourg, and western Germany. Extensive destruction was wrought, including some 320 locomotives, 279 railway cars, and three ammunition trains. Many barges were damaged, two railway marshalling yards were attacked, and 17 enemy aircraft were destroyed in combat in addition to some on the ground.

Twenty-three of our long-range fighters are missing.

The area between the Seine and the Somme was swept by our close-support fighters and fighter-bombers. There were fewer targets but much damage was inflicted on road transport.

Fuel dumps at HAM, DOULLENS and south of AMIENS were the principal targets for medium and light bombers and a successful attack was carried out on an ammunition dump in the FORET DE LAIGLE near COMPIEGNE. The Seine ferry at DUCLAIR was also raided and great destruction was caused to barges and massed vehicles.

Small groups of enemy shipping off the Pas-de-Calais were attacked by our coastal aircraft yesterday morning and some vessels were left ablaze.

Left: **Though the situation was anything but joyful, the three top German commanders in the West — SS-Oberstgruppenführer Josef Dietrich of the 5. Panzerarmee; Generalfeldmarschall Walter Model, C-in-C in the West, and General der Panzertruppen Heinrich Eberbach commanding 7. Armee — were still able to raise a smile for the camera. Behind stands Oberst Rudolf-Christoph von Gersdorff, Chief-of-Staff of 7. Armee, who had just been awarded the Knight's Cross, with Generalleutnant Alfred Gause, Chief-of-Staff of 5. Panzerarmee.** *Right:* **The château which was once the German headquarters is at Metz-en-Couture, 11 miles south-west of Cambrai.**

Yesterday evening, heavy bombers attacked shipping at BREST and a battery on the island of Cezembre near ST MALO.

Last night, low-level attacks from the battlefront to STRASBOURG were continued by our light bombers. Targets included marshalling yards near METZ, rail installations at CHARLEVILLE, ABBEVILLE, ARRAS and DOULLENS, a large horse-drawn convoy at LAON, and other road transport.

On August 29 the XXX Corps attacked out from the Vernon bridgehead and had reached Beauvais by late afternoon on the 30th. This M10 tank destroyer belonged to the Guards Armoured Division. Then, driving through the night by moonlight, the leaders pushed on to Amiens which was entered at dawn on the 31st.

The crossroads on Boulevard Docteur Lamotte is a major road junction in Beauvais.

German forces of the 19. Armee started to withdraw from southern France on August 17. Transport was in short supply and many of the men just had to make their way on foot up the N7. These men are at Fiancey, 19 miles north of Montélimar.

COMMUNIQUE No. 144   August 30

Allied forces, continuing their sweep beyond PARIS, have crossed the Aisne and the Marne rivers. In the upper Marne valley, mopping-up is in progress in VITRY-LE-FRANCOIS, and our troops have reached MARSON and LEPINE, south-east and east of CHALONS-SUR-MARNE. Other units are less than one mile south of CHALONS on the west side of the river.

CHATEAU-THIERRY, on the Marne, has been occupied, and our armored units have moved north to take SOISSONS and establish a bridgehead across the Aisne at PONT-ARCY, 14 miles to the east.

Other troops are advancing through the area between the Marne and the Aisne, north of MEAUX and CHATEAU-THIERRY.

In the PARIS area, advances have been made through the north-eastern outskirts of the city beyond LE BOURGET and MONTMORENCY, and further west elements have cleared the FORET DE ST GERMAIN and moved northward to a point less than two miles south of PONTOISE.

The bridgehead across the Seine in the vicinity of MANTES-GASSICOURT has been further enlarged to the north and to the east beyond MEULAN. Contact was made with troops from the bridgeheads to the north.

Advancing from the VERNON bridgehead, our troops pushed across the PARIS—ROUEN road to the town of ETREPAGNY and from there to the village of LONGCHAMPS.

The PARIS—ROUEN road was also cut near the village of ECOUIS by troops from the LOUVIERS bridgehead. In the evening, contact was established between these two bridgeheads.

South-east of ROUEN, our forces advanced in the face of persistent opposition and captured the village of BOOS, some five miles from the center of ROUEN. In the CAUDEBEC area, fighting was heavy, but the FORET DE BROTONNE was cleared and the whole of this loop of the river is now in our hands.

In Brittany, hard fighting continues at BREST as Allied forces close in slowly on the port.

Air operations yesterday were restricted by weather. Fighters and fighter-bombers attacked enemy rail and road movement over a wide area in the Low Countries, western Germany and in France as far south as LYON. Large numbers of locomotives, railway cars and motor transport were attacked successfully, and 20 enemy aircraft were destroyed on the ground near BRUSSELS. Six of our aircraft are missing.

Left: On the 25th and 26th, a battle group from the 11. Panzer-Division successfully mounted a counter-attack to stop the advance of Task Force Butler which was threatening to cut the N7 highway. The battle group then pulled back, abandoning this PzKpfw III that had broken down. *Right:* The mountain skyline in the background enabled Jean Paul to trace this field by the side of the D538 just north of Crest. The Germans still pushed on northwards throughout the 27th and 28th but losses were mounting and the large rearguard group was then overrun south of Montélimar, the Americans taking 500 prisoners. Over 1,200 men were captured during the final battles on August 28-29 and 3,000 more when the area north-east of Montélimar was captured on the 30th. By now the battle of southern France was over.

In mid-August, Eisenhower was astounded when Montgomery 'proposed to me that he should retain tactical co-ordinating control of all ground forces throughout the campaign but this, I told him, was impossible.' On August 19, Butcher said that a premature article in *Stars and Stripes* indicating that Bradley had taken over the two American armies in the field, and would have equal rank with Montgomery, started a row in the Press. Reactions came from both sides of the Atlantic. In London the reports were that Montgomery had been 'demoted' by being placed on an equal footing with Bradley, while the *Washington Times Herald* wrote about 'British dominance' of the invasion command. SHAEF promptly denied the premature announcement on the command set-up which had created such confusion in America. In a telegram to General Marshall, Eisenhower expressed his irritation, pointing out that 'it wasn't enough for the public to obtain a great victory, the manner in which it was gained seemed to be more important'. On August 23, Eisenhower informed Montgomery of his decision. Churchill then informed the Supreme Commander that Montgomery's promotion to Field-Marshal would run from the termination of his command of Allied ground forces. This, the Prime Minister said, was a necessary concession to British public opinion, and on August 31 Montgomery officially ceased to act as ground forces commander. Eisenhower took over direct control on September 1.

COMMUNIQUE No. 145   August 31

Allied armor yesterday drove swiftly northward from the bridgeheads over the lower Seine. Bypassing scattered areas of enemy resistance, our forces captured GOURNAY-EN-BRAY, BEAUVAIS and MARSEILLE-EN-BEAUVAISIS and leading troops are now within 20 miles of AMIENS.

Further west, we have reached a point eight miles north-east of ROUEN, and FLEURY-SUR-ANDELLE is in our hands. Opposite DUCLAIR, our troops cleared the enemy from the south bank of the Seine.

Troops from the MANTES-GASSICOURT bridgehead are advancing northward along the Epte river and have reached a point less than two miles south of CHAUMONT-EN-VEXIN. Other advances were made beyond the northern suburbs of PARIS.

In the drive to the east of the capital, Allied forces have reached REIMS. Armored units, moving towards the Aisne river, are ten miles north of REIMS, and elements which crossed the Vesle river are now several miles south-east of the city.

Our reconnaissance elements have penetrated to points two and one-half miles north and north-east of LAON and to MONTAIGU, ten miles south-east. The bridgehead across the Aisne near SOISSONS has been extended east and north.

In the Marne valley, our troops have crossed the river and are opposite EPERNAY, with some elements one mile south of the town. Up river, forces which made another crossing have reached LES GRANDES-LOGES, eight miles north-west of CHALONS-SUR-MARNE on the CHALONS—REIMS road.

Allied air activity was sharply curtailed yesterday by thick clouds over north-east France. Light and medium bombers attacked by instruments the enemy forces still occupying the small but strongly fortified island of Cezembre off the entrance to ST MALO harbor. Others bombed a large enemy oil storage center in the FORET D'ARQUES near DIEPPE.

Following the collapse of German forces in Normandy, the speed of the Allied advance across France surprised everyone. SHAEF Forward had no sooner become established at the 'Shipmate' site near Portsmouth, (see page 67) than steps were being taken to transfer the headquarters to the Continent. Locations were considered at Saint-Lô and Granville at the base of the Cherbourg peninsula, the choice eventually falling on the latter with the provisional commencement date of mid-September.

While the SHAEF signals centre was installed in the Hotel Normandie *(left)* in the town, the headquarters itself was centred on the 'Château' *(right)*, a children's holiday camp eight miles down the coast at Jullouville. This manor house was built in 1907 but the town of Saint-Ouen, near Paris, bought it in 1929. A new brick building was built in the park and the 'Château' was from then on a holiday home for 600 children. The centre was completely renovated in early 2000.

Eisenhower's personal quarters were the Villa Montgomery, eight miles further down the coast at Saint-Jean-le-Thomas, and it was here that Commander Butcher joined him early in September: 'I spent the weekend at Granville [*sic*] with General Ike who is confined to his bed by a wrenched knee. He is in a small villa named Montgomery overlooking Mont-Saint-Michel, the ancient abbey on a rock surrounded by water at high tide but by almost flat sand at low.' Butcher was currently seconded to public relations in Britain and much of the conversation concerned the proposal to bring in a new director of administration which would permit Colonel Dupuy to devote himself primarily to briefing correspondents. Eisenhower was also concerned that the move of the US supply organisation zone (COM Z) had led to a large number of staff officers and personnel taking over every hotel room in Paris.

Several enemy aircraft were shot up on the ground near COPENHAGEN by fighter-bombers which also operated over the Skagerrak. Other small forces harassed enemy movements in the ROUEN—ABBEVILLE—GOURNAY area as weather permitted.

So why was Eisenhower confined to bed in an out-of-the-way villa at such an important time? Major Larry Hansen, Eisenhower's pilot, explains: 'On September 2, 1944, we took off early in the morning in the B-25 to Laval to pick up General Hoyt Vandenburg. General Eisenhower was aboard en route to a meeting with General Bradley at Chartres. Upon landing at Laval, we found nothing but a mud hole and the field was very rough so I radioed the four P-47 escorts not to land. From there we flew our passengers into Chartres and met General Bradley. We were informed by General Smith that a heavy storm was kicking up at our destination, Pontorson [across the bay from Granville], and that we should not waste too much time at Chartres. We took off as quickly as possible and, right after take-off, we noticed the right engine was on fire. Flames were shooting out around the engine nacelle and we immediately turned and landed again at Chartres. We found due to the rough field at Laval, we had broken several exhaust stacks and the fire was burning the ignition harness and other flammable items within the nacelle. In the meantime, Dick Underwood, my co-pilot, rode with Major Robinson, who was General Bradley's pilot, and they flew General Eisenhower back to Pontorson. Upon landing, the weather was very bad but Dick elected to fly the General back to Granville across the water in an L-5 which we kept at Pontorson in order to commute between there and Granville. Dick took off but the weather became so bad he had to land on the beach. In order to save the plane from the incoming tide, the General and Dick pulled the airplane higher on the beach and in so doing the General wrenched his knee badly.'

PNA   Em 36680

U.S. TROOPS CROSS INTO BELGIUM
A column of U.S. vehicles passes the marker indicating the Franco-Belgian border, which was crossed by Allied troops September 2, 1944. U.S. Signal Corps Photo ETO-HQ-44-13806.
SERVICED BY LONDON OWI TO LIST B
CERTIFIED AS PASSED BY SHAEF CENSOR

SEPTEMBER 1944
OVER THE FRONTIERS

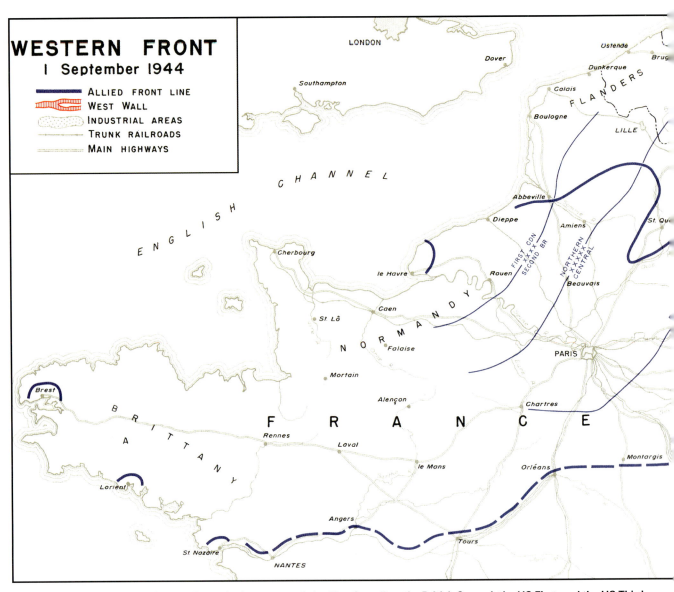

On September 1, SHAEF had four armies under its command: the First Canadian, the British Second, the US First, and the US Third.

COMMUNIQUE No. 146   September 1

Driving on northward from the BEAUVAIS area, Allied forces yesterday reached AMIENS and established a firm bridgehead over the river Somme. CORBIE, VILLERS-BRETONEUX and MOREUIL were among the towns taken by this advance.

Further to the west our troops reached FORMERIE, BUCHY and FORGES-LES-EAUX. North of ROUEN we have captured TOTES, halfway to DIEPPE, while other forces which crossed the Seine near CAUDEBEC have passed through LILLEBONNE and reached the area of ST ROMAIN-DE-COLBOSC.

The commander of the Seventh German Army was among prisoners taken yesterday. In the BEAUVAIS area, Allied armored units have pushed northeastward along the Brèche river, occupying BRESLE and FOUQUEROLLES.

Allied troops advancing north from PARIS have taken the towns of SENLIS, CREIL and CREPY. The forces that took CREPY have advanced to BETHAN-COURT and HARAMONT. East of CREPY, our troops have reached VAUMOISE. Reconnaissance elements are within 2,000 yards of COMPIEGNE.

Gains of about 10 miles have been made by Allied troops moving north and east of REIMS. Other troops have entered LAON where a stiff fight occurred when our forces accounted for three trainloads of German

Leading the Second Army, XXX Corps was pushing forward through northern France. On September 1, Sherman and Cromwell tanks of the 8th Armoured Brigade passed through Doullens after having overcome slight resistance on reaching the town. Meanwhile, on the right wing, the Guards Armoured Division had captured the high ground north of Arras by midday. That afternoon the 1st Welsh Guards, who had been the last British troops to leave Arras in May 1940, re-entered the town.

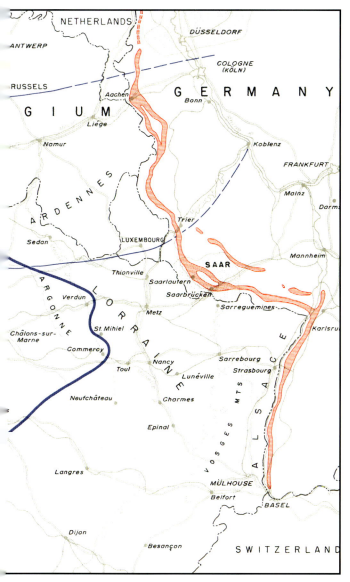

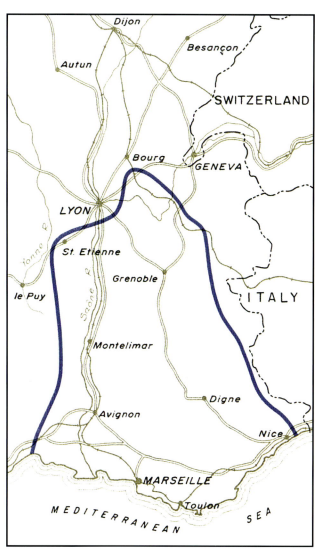

In southern France the US Seventh Army was not yet under SHAEF command.

troops who were attempting to withdraw from the town.

Allied troops advancing beyond ST DIZIER have crossed the upper Aisne river several miles north of STE MENEHOULD. Other troops moving east and southeast of TROYES have made gains to points over 20 miles from the town reaching the area just east of BAR-SUR-SEINE.

In Brittany, Allied troops closing in on BREST have advanced almost to the coast west of the port in the area south of ST RENAN. The enemy has been cleared from the Daoulas peninsula south of BREST.

Clouds over France hindered Allied air activity early yesterday, but operating under improved conditions later in the day, fighters and fighter-bombers attacked enemy road and rail movements in northern France and Belgium. Motor transport numbering in hundreds was destroyed and locomotives and trucks were hit.

Coastal guns on the island of Cezembre were attacked by medium and heavy bombers. Fuel dumps in the FORET D'ARQUES and at MOMEXY were hit by light bombers which also attacked military buildings at VINCEY.

During the night of 30-31 August, enemy shipping in Channel waters stretching from DIEPPE to DUNKIRK was attacked by coastal aircraft. One large merchant vessel and a small ship were hit.

The same day, the First Army was turned north to carry out General Bradley's plan to cut the Lille—Brussels highway near Tournai. *Left:* Task Force Lovelady was pictured some 30 miles short of the Belgium frontier, one of their M8 howitzer motor carriages (a 75mm howitzer mounted on a M5 light tank chassis) passing an M8 armoured car through Vervins. *Right:* Rue du Général Déville where tanks of the 3rd Armored Division had thundered through in September 1944.

COMMUNIQUE No. 147   September 2

DIEPPE, ARRAS and VERDUN were liberated yesterday by Allied forces.

On the Channel coast, Allied troops entered DIEPPE, where the enemy offered only slight opposition, and pushed northward to LE TREPORT. Further west, our troops have taken BOLBEC, FAUVILLE-EN-CAUX and have entered YVETOT.

Armored thrusts northward from AMIENS passed through ARRAS soon after midday, and by evening were established in strength north of the town. Another thrust captured the town of DOULLENS, and further west our leading elements have reached the Somme southeast of ABBEVILLE.

Light enemy resistance was met by Allied troops advancing northeast of BEAUVAIS and we have taken COULLEMELLE and VILLERS-TOURNELLE, six miles west of MONTDIDIER. Our advance through the FORET DE COMPIEGNE to the southwestern edge of the town of COMPIEGNE met heavy resistance.

North of the Aisne river, armored elements have taken MONTCORNET, 18 miles northeast of LAON. Other units have entered RETHEL, 20 miles northeast of REIMS, and have made gains to the edge of the FORET DE SIGNY.

Allied troops have occupied VERDUN. They have crossed the Meuse river in the town and also between ST MIHIEL and COMMERCY. West of the Meuse, forces which advanced through the ARGONNE forest are in the areas of BAULNY, VARENNES and CLERMONT.

Troops moving through the area north of ST DIZIER have reached a point near the Marne—Rhine canal. Southeast of ST DIZIER, armored units have advanced to the vicinity of JOINVILLE.

Enemy transport in the Low Countries and northern France was attacked throughout yesterday by fighters and fighter-bombers. Targets included motor and horse-drawn transport, tanks, locomotives and barges. Fighter-bombers also bombed an ammunition dump near ST QUENTIN.

Targets for medium bombers were gun posts, strong points and a motor park in the BREST area, troop concentrations near ABBEVILLE and railway yards at GIVET on the Franco-Belgian border.

Fighter-bombers continued the attack on the island of Cezembre, off ST MALO, which has also been bombarded by HMS *Malaya*. Air observation was provided.

At 9.30 a.m. on September 2, leaders of the 2nd Armored Division, XIX Corps, crossed the frontier, the first Allied soldiers to set foot in Belgium. Signal Corps photographer Sergeant Bill Augustine was on hand to record the historic occasion at Rongy. Here the crew of an M5 light tank of the 113th Cavalry Group are cheered at the first village they entered.

The first US infantrymen to cross into Belgium pause at the border post at Maquenoise on the N99 between Hirson and Chimay.

Leading the VII Corps drive northwards, the 3rd Armored Division advanced on Mons on September 2-3. However, neither the Germans nor the Americans were aware of the approach of each other, and both stumbled into an unforeseen meeting that resulted in a short, sharp clash. It started in the early hours of September 3, while it was still pitch dark, when an American detachment guarding a crossroads south of the city gave the first alarm of the approach of a long enemy column. The small detachment was unable to stop the Germans and even more escaped across country during the night. At daybreak, with German troops pouring headlong into the 3rd Armored Division road obstacles, the crews of tanks and tank destroyers had a field day. *Above:* Here, later that day, an American medic treats wounded German prisoners in Frameries on the outskirts of the city. *Above right:* Rue Ferrer, near the junction with Rue du Bois Bourdon. Within a matter of three days, the Americans had annihilated the pocket, destroying masses of matériel — some 40 armoured vehicles, tanks and SP guns, 100 half-tracks, 120 artillery pieces, 100 anti-tank and flak guns, and nearly 2,000 vehicles — capturing in the process about 25,000 prisoners, the remnants of 20 disorganised divisions and a multitude of miscellaneous units and services. Among the prisoners were three generals: Generalmajor Rudiger von Heyking, commander of the 6. Fallschirmjäger-Division; Generalmajor Carl Wahle of the 47. Infanterie-Division, and Generalmajor Hubertus von Aulock, of the divisional battle group carrying his name.

COMMUNIQUE No. 148   September 3

Allied forces expanding their drive north from ARRAS have crossed VIMY RIDGE and occupied LENS and BULLY-GRENAY. To the east, we have taken DOUAI and a thrust westward has brought us to the area of ST POL.

On the Channel coast ST VALERY-EN-CAUX is in our hands. We have reached ABBEVILLE and closed on the Somme between there and the sea.

In the area of the FORET DE COMPIEGNE, northeast of PARIS, advances were made against varying resistance. The Aisne river was crossed west of SOISSONS.

A thrust northeast of MONTCORNET has put us across the Belgian frontier.

Further south, progress continues east of VERDUN.

Bad weather again hindered air operations over northeastern France. A force of heavy bombers attacked shipping at BREST.

Eisenhower wrote that 'in ordinary times this would have been acclaimed as a great victory. But the times were far from ordinary and the incident passed almost unnoticed in the press.' Yet, in numbers of troops and equipment lost, Mons was the second-largest German defeat of the whole campaign in the West, and the Allies would not experience such mass surrenders again until the final days of the war. At Quévy-le-Grand, six miles south of Mons, a captured Hauptmann knocks at the window of a house to call his men out.

Allied losses at Mons were minimal. Between September 2-4, the 3rd Armored and 1st Infantry Divisions lost less than 100 men, and just two tanks, one tank destroyer, and about 20 other vehicles. The Germans on the other hand were still using horse-drawn transport and at Ghlin, just north-west of Mons, Signal Corps photographer Sergeant J. A. DeMarco pictured locals cutting up the carcasses of dead horses for meat.

Left: **On September 3, the leaders of the Guards Armoured Division also crossed the Belgian border, encountering little opposition until later in the morning when they came across some** anti-tank guns near Chapelle-à-Wattines, mid-way between Tournai and Ath on the N8. The prisoners were marched to Leuze. *Right:* **No. 2 Chaussée de Bruxelles.**

At Hondzocht, nine miles from Brussels, a point of resistance had just been dealt with by the time that Sergeant Charles Hewitt was on hand to photograph a Stuart tank passing prisoners drawn up on the Edingense Steenweg.

COMMUNIQUE No. 149 September 4

BRUSSELS has been liberated. Allied troops which crossed the Belgian frontier early yesterday morning rapidly freed TOURNAI, and pushed on to the north and east to enter the capital in the late evening.

Further west other armored forces drove north through BETHUNE and LILLERS and reached the neighbourhood of AIRE. In the ABBEVILLE area the river Somme was crossed on both sides of the town which is now in our hands after some fighting. Our troops pushed on northward from the river.

North and east of LE HAVRE we closed in on the main defences of the port.

Some 40 miles southwest of BRUSSELS, the Belgian frontier has been crossed by other columns advancing northeast. Elements are in the area of CHARLEROI.

Further south the advance eastward has brought our troops to the vicinity of NANCY. Units following up this thrust have made other crossings of the Meuse river near CHALAINES, 10 miles southeast of COMMERCY, and our troops are in ST MIHIEL.

Enemy road and rail movements in Belgium and the Pas-de-Calais were attacked by fighters and fighter-bombers yesterday. Considerable numbers of motor vehicles, locomotives and railway cars were destroyed or damaged.

Six airfields in Holland were attacked by a strong force of heavy bombers.

The fortified area of BREST was the target for medium forces of heavy, medium and light bombers which made a series of attacks in the morning and evening. Gun positions, ammunition and fuel dumps and strong points were hit.

The advance into Belgium resumed with the Grenadier Guards on the left and the Welsh Guards on the right, and before nightfall on the 3rd, the latter had entered Brussels. An hour before the Belgian capital had been deserted and silent but now it suddenly erupted with flags and banners everywhere and a huge crowd cheered their liberators. The following afternoon, the Guards Armoured Division commander, Major-General Allan Adair, made a triumphal entry in the city swamped by a huge cheering crowd. On September 8, Prime Minister Hubert Pierlot and his government returned to Brussels after being exiled in London for four years, making Belgium the first liberated country in Europe with a restored constitutional government.

COMMUNIQUE No. 150 September 5

ANTWERP has been liberated. After a two-day drive across Belgium, Allied armor entered the city yesterday and by evening was clearing the dock area.

Earlier in the day, our troops to the south captured LOUVAIN, MECHELEN and ALOST. Other forces operating near the Franco-Belgian frontier took LILLE.

North of the Somme, steady progress is being made. Our troops reached HESDIN, MONTREUIL and ETAPLES.

Allied forces in the MONS area of Belgium have eliminated a large German pocket southwest of the city. An estimated 9,000 prisoners were taken. Some 40 tanks and 1,500 motor vehicles were captured or destroyed by ground and air forces.

Local enemy pockets were mopped up south of TOURNAI and in the areas of MARCHIENNES, northwest of VALENCIENNES, and VILLEROT, northwest of MONS. Gains were made south of CHARLEROI as far as FLORENNES and BEAUMONT.

In the upper Meuse valley, our forces have advanced northeast of ST MIHIEL. Further south, there are no changes to report. Weather restricted air operations yesterday.

In the meantime, the 11th Armoured Division pushed on to Antwerp which it reached the following day, September 4, capturing most of the harbour facilities in working order. 'We were electrified', recorded Eisenhower later, 'to learn that the Germans had been so rapidly hustled out of the place that they had had not time to execute extensive demolitions.' In all, some 6,000 prisoners were rounded up including the German commander of Antwerp sector, Generalmajor Christoph von Stolberg-Stolberg. On September 5, AFPU photographer Bert Hardy pictured this group of prisoners being marched across the Koningin Astridplein.

By now the British XII Corps, on the left of the advance, was aiming at Ghent with the 7th Armoured Division in the lead and on the 4th the leaders over-nighted at Oudenaarde, 20 miles short of Ghent. At dawn on September 5, the 11th Hussars and the 5th Royal Inniskilling Dragoon Guards entered the city, meeting only sporadic resistance from the odd rear-guards that remained behind. *Left:* These Shermans are crossing Avelgem, 12 miles south-east of Oudenaarde. *Right:* This is Doorniksesteenweg today, photographed looking southwards.

COMMUNIQUE No. 151   September 6

In the BRUSSELS—ANTWERP sector, Allied forces were engaged yesterday in mopping up operations. Further west, forward elements of our armor have reached the southern outskirts of GHENT.

Allied troops continued to make good progress north of the Somme river, reaching the line AIRE—ST OMER yesterday evening. Other forces by-passing BOULOGNE have reached the area FORET DE GUINES.

Further south our troops advancing into Belgium have freed CHARLEROI and NAMUR. Crossings of the Meuse river have been made at DINANT and GIVET where enemy opposition was light.

mopping up continues in the area southwest of MONS where more enemy troops are surrounded.

Fighters and fighter-bombers strafed and dive-bombed enemy airfields, road convoys and railway trains in Holland and western Germany yesterday. One hundred and forty-three enemy aircraft were destroyed on the ground and 28 were shot down in combat.

Enemy shipping off the Dutch Islands was attacked by rocket-firing fighters. One medium-sized vessel was sunk, another left on fire and three smaller craft were damaged.

During the night railway targets in Holland and Germany were attacked by light bombers.

Aerial bombardment of the fortified area of BREST was continued during the day by heavy, medium and light bombers.

Troop concentrations at LE HAVRE were attacked by heavy bombers which dropped more than 1,000 tons of high explosives.

Left: South of Brussels, citizens in Nivelles went wild with joy when the US cavalry rode into town. Damage from the battle in 1940 had still not been repaired, leaving an open space in front of the Collégiale. *Right:* As the left side of Rue de Mons has been rebuilt, an exact comparison is somewhat difficult to achieve.

The leaders of the 3rd Armored Division reached Namur on September 5. While infantry crossed the Meuse via a damaged bridge to disperse the weak German forces defending the town, by the morning of the 6th tanks were able to roll across the river via a 505-foot floating treadway bridge which had been thrown across upstream from the lock and weir at La Plante. A second floating bridge was under construction further up the river.

Left: On the left wing of VII Corps, men of Company B, 16th Infantry, 1st Division, advance along a street in the centre of Battice, 13 miles east of Liège. It is now about September 10 and the Germans were in the process of disengaging to take up new positions in the 'Westwall', the band fortifications shielding Germany that the Allies referred to as the Siegfried Line. *Right:* Battice today at the junction of the Rue de Hervé and Rue de Verviers.

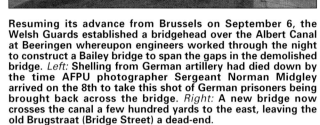

Resuming its advance from Brussels on September 6, the Welsh Guards established a bridgehead over the Albert Canal at Beeringen whereupon engineers worked through the night to construct a Bailey bridge to span the gaps in the demolished bridge. *Left:* Shelling from German artillery had died down by the time AFPU photographer Sergeant Norman Midgley arrived on the 8th to take this shot of German prisoners being brought back across the bridge. *Right:* A new bridge now crosses the canal a few hundred yards to the east, leaving the old Brugstraat (Bridge Street) a dead-end.

COMMUNIQUE No. 152   September 7

GHENT has been captured and COURTRAI is reported clear of enemy.

Allied forces have taken ARMENTIERES and the area west of LILLE as far as MERVILLE.

Our armor has thrust eastward from ST OMER to the vicinity of CASSEL. Our troops are in the outskirts of BOULOGNE and forward elements have surrounded CALAIS.

Mopping-up continues in the BRUSSELS—ANTWERP area.

To the south our forces are advancing beyond the Meuse, southeastward from NAMUR and northeastward from GIVET. They are encountering mortar and small-arms fire.

Troops moving through the forest of Ardennes are east of AUCHAMPS.

Enemy strong points in LE HAVRE and BREST were attacked by heavy, medium and light bombers yesterday. Targets over a wide area in the Low Countries and western Germany were bombed and strafed by fighters and fighter-bombers which successfully attacked motor transport, locomotives, rail cars and troops.

During the night a small force of light bombers attacked road and rail movements in Holland and on the Dutch-German border.

Montgomery with his plan of a single thrust to the Ruhr was still at odds with Eisenhower's 'broad front' strategy, even going so far as to tell the Supreme Commander that 'he should not descend into the land battle and become a ground C-in-C'. Montgomery also criticised the siting of SHAEF Forward at Granville '400 miles behind the battlefront and useless for a ground commander to give quick decisions in rapidly changing situations'. On September 4 Montgomery sent Ike a nine-point plan based around his single thrust proposal, either via the Ruhr or further south through the Saar. However, communications with Granville were poor and Eisenhower's reply sent on the evening of the 5th reached Montgomery in two portions, the second part on September 7 followed by the first part two days later! So one can understand Montgomery's frustration when he signalled back asking Eisenhower to fly to Brussels for a meeting to sort things out. Ike's knee was still troubling him so the meeting at Melsbroek airfield took place aboard his B-25 on Sunday, September 10. Although Montgomery failed to convince Eisenhower for forces to be concentrated for a thrust by the left wing to the Ruhr, he was given permission for the Arnhem operation to go ahead. (General Eisenhower's executive transport started life on March 31, 1943 as a B-25J-1-NC, but it was sent to North American at Inglewood to be modified specifically for the Supreme Allied Commander. The work included covering over the bombardier's position; adding additional windows; moving the entry hatch at the rear to obtain more floor space for chairs and including a drop-leaf desk for the General. The interior olive drab fabric used to line the aircraft was replaced with General's blue upholstery and luggage racks were installed above the seats. Long-range fuel tanks were installed in the bomb bay along with additional luggage space.)

Meanwhile, with its cavalry units leading the way, the Third Army had reached the west bank of the Moselle river on September 1 but lack of fuel due to Eisenhower's decision to make the main effort in the north, left Patton virtually immobilised. On September 4 Eisenhower finally gave him the green light for the XII and XX Corps to seize bridgeheads over the Moselle. On September 8, the XX Corps carried out an assault crossing of the river at Dornot, south of Metz, and by late afternoon four companies of the 11th Infantry, 5th Division, were across. However, the Germans counter-attacked and the Americans, struggling to hold on to their minuscule bridgehead, eventually had to evacuate it on the night of September 10/11.

COMMUNIQUE No. 153   September 8

Allied forces pressing northeast from LOUVAIN crossed the Albert Canal in the vicinity of BEERINGEN and advanced elements reached the area of BOURG-LEOPOLD yesterday evening.

YPRES has been captured and our forces have advanced to the vicinity of ROULERS. Another armored column has reached a point 10 miles northwest of the town.

We have continued to close in on BOULOGNE and CALAIS. The area of these ports was further sealed off yesterday by an advance of our troops from the area of FORET DE GUINES to GRAVELINES.

Troops operating further south in Belgium have taken WAVRE, southeast of BRUSSELS. Other forces moving along the Meuse from NAMUR have freed HUY and elements are in the area immediately west of LIEGE.

East of DINANT gains have been made and troops advancing through the forest of Ardennes have taken LOUETTE-SAINT-PIERRE and BIEVRE.

Our forces are near the Moselle river a few miles north of METZ. Further south we have crossed the Moselle north of PONT-A-MOUSSON against stiff enemy resistance.

Adverse weather yesterday restricted air operations.

Left: On the morning of September 8, Signal Corps photographer Lieutenant Mark A. Freeman pictured men of the 11th Infantry and half-tracks of the 23rd Armored Infantry Battalion moving down Dornot's steep main street on their way to the river. *Above:* Dornot stands remarkably unchanged after seven decades. This is the main street pictured from near the church which stands just off to the right.

The 10th Infantry forced another crossing near Arnaville, three miles south of Dornot, in the early hours of September 10. This caught the Germans by surprise and a solid bridgehead was established which stood up to repeated German counter-attacks. However, because of the accurate German artillery fire, US engineers could only work at night to carry across reinforcements using a ferry service, working steadily during the hours of darkness. Division had ordered that a bridge must be put across the river before morning but nothing was in position when daylight came on September 10. During the following night engineers worked on establishing a treadway bridge and this was finally completed under a smoke-screen by noon on the 12th. Tanks of the 31st Tank Battalion then joined the troops in the bridgehead followed by a company of tank destroyers. By the 14th, a heavy pontoon bridge had been built some 400 yards further upstream. This is the treadway bridge as seen from the eastern bank of the Moselle with the far bank still hazy from the smoke. A memorial to the 5th Division now stands beyond the trees on the far side of the river.

The Third Army's XII Corps now launched a pincer movement to capture Nancy. A first bridgehead across the Moselle was established near Bayon, south of the city, on September 11, and the following day the 80th Division carried out another crossing at Dieulouard to the north. *Above:* While the original caption to this photo states the date (September 12) and the unit involved (318th Infantry), it gives no precise location, only the 'Moselle area'. However, although Jean Paul quickly recognised the house that appears in the photograph, he could not understand how the river (where the 318th Infantry crossed) now appeared in the foreground. Then he discovered that in the 1970s the Moselle and the canal at that point had been completely rerouted to eliminate the bends, a new stretch of the river being excavated and canalised after which the old riverbed and canal was filled in. *Right:* So the house, known as the Château Matharel, was still standing but where it was then on the eastern bank of the river, it is now west of it!

Men of the 317th Infantry, 80th Division, cautiously observe the eastern bank of the Moselle which was still in German hands on September 5.

Saint-Martin's Church in Pont-à-Mousson photographed from Maidières which lies on the west bank. Remarkably, the stairway was retained when the bridge was rebuilt.

COMMUNIQUE No. 154   September 9

Expansion of the Allied bridgehead over the Albert Canal has met growing enemy resistance. The capture of BOURG-LEOPOLD was completed against strong opposition.

Our troops continued the advance through ROULERS and reached THIEL yesterday where sharp fighting continues. Another armored thrust from this area advanced some miles towards BRUGES. Further north Allied armor has captured DIXMUIDE.

Our troops continue to close in on the ports of CALAIS and BOULOGNE.

In eastern Belgium Allied troops have occupied LIEGE, 21 miles from the German frontier, after advancing along the north bank of the Meuse river against scattered enemy resistance. Elements have moved to ROMSEE, three miles southeast of LIEGE. In the area south of the Meuse between NAMUR and LIEGE, our troops have reached the village of NEUVILLE-EN-CONDROZ, 10 miles east of HUY.

In the Ardennes forest, our troops are advancing eastward between GIVET and SEDAN against resistance from isolated strong points. Elements have reached HAUT-FAYS and MAISSIN. East of SEDAN, we are at STE CECILE after an advance of 12 miles.

Allied bombers were sent against three resisting harbour defences in France yesterday while fighters and fighter-bombers continued to harass enemy movements, transport and communications in the Low Countries and in western Germany.

Yesterday morning heavy bombers attacked LE HAVRE and strong points and gun positions at BREST were targets for fighter-bombers. In the evening medium bombers attacked fortifications at BOULOGNE.

Ten enemy aircraft were destroyed on the ground during attacks by fighters and fighter-bombers on enemy movements in the Low Countries and against airfields and transport in western Germany.

A road bridge east of ROTTERDAM was attacked during the night by light bombers.

Meanwhile, in the advance from the Riviera, the US Seventh Army was now pushing northwards on the heels of the withdrawing German forces at a quickening pace. Lyon, over 180 miles from the coast, was reached on September 3 and Mâcon, 40 miles further north, the next day. The caption to this photo dated September 9 simply states: 'a long convoy of tanks move up to the front'.

The picture was taken on the then N492, less than a mile from Ornans which lies 15 miles south of Besançon. The tanks have already crossed half of France and are moving northwards in the direction of Baume-les-Dames.

COMMUNIQUE No. 155   September 10

Allied forces clearing the Channel coast area have made considerable progress around BERGUES, southeast of DUNKIRK. Farther east units are approaching BRUGES. Gains have been made north of ANTWERP.

Development of the bridgeheads over the Albert Canal is continuing to meet stiff resistance.

Our forces have advanced to KERMPT, four miles west of HASSELT, and to NODUWEZ, MARILLES, and FOLX-LES-CAVES, in the TIRLEMONT—HUY sector. Other forces moving east and southeast of LIEGE are in LIMBOURG after a 14-mile advance.

After thrusting through the forest of Ardennes to points 15 to 20 miles east of the Meuse river, our troops reached the vicinity of ST HUBERT. Elements further south have entered ECOUVIEZ, east of MONTMEDY.

The west bank of the Moselle river has been cleared of enemy in the vicinity of POMPEY, six miles north of NANCY.

Allied forces continue to close in on the port of BREST where the enemy is maintaining a stubborn defense.

Transport, communications and airfields in Holland and western Germany were bombed and strafed by fighters and fighter-bombers yesterday. Nine enemy aircraft were shot down in combat and five others were destroyed on the ground.

Gun positions and strong points at BREST were again attacked by fighter-bombers and similar objectives at BOULOGNE were targets for medium bombers.

While SHAEF's four armies in the north were advancing towards the frontier of Germany, soon to be joined from the south by the US Seventh Army, a new American army became operational on September 5. This was the US Ninth Army under Lieutenant General William H. Simpson which took over the now remote battlefield in Brittany as the capture of Brest had turned out to be far more difficult than anticipated. Though three American divisions were deployed against the German fortress — the 2nd, 8th and the 29th — with massive air support, their attacks were making little progress. Communiqué No. 155 merely reported that 'Allied forces continue to close in on the port of Brest', these GIs being pictured on September 10 pushing through Gouesnou north of the city on the left wing of the 8th Division's sector.

Jean Paul took the comparison in the centre of Gouesnou from in front of the church, looking north towards Rue de la Gare.

The Ninth Army quickly released the 6th Armored Division and despatched it eastwards to reinforce the Third Army. Here elements of the division were pictured having travelled right across France to reach Clamecy, 50 miles north-west of Autun.

COMMUNIQUE No. 156   September 11

The city of LUXEMBOURG has been liberated by Allied forces advancing towards the Moselle. Northwest of NANCY, our troops are in the northern part of LIVERDUN.

Further north, in the Ardennes, we are at NEUFCHATEAU, 22 miles northeast of SEDAN.

Units are along the Ourthe river in the area east of MARCHE and elements have moved east of ST HUBERT.

Southeast of LIEGE, our troops are in the vicinity of THEUX, and enemy resistance has increased in the area immediately to the southeast. Northwest of LIEGE, our forces have occupied REMICOURT and have reached HEX, 7 miles southeast of ST TROND.

Stiff German opposition continues in our Albert Canal bridgeheads.

Enemy resistance at GHENT has been overcome and our troops are in possession of the town.

OSTEND and NIEUPORT have been cleared of the enemy and the coast between OSTEND and FURNES is in our hands.

In Brittany, house-to-house fighting is in progress in the outskirts of BREST. The German commander at LOCHRIST has surrendered, but isolated enemy groups continue to resist in the area. Resistance also continues on the Crozon peninsula, which forms the southern shore of the bay of BREST.

HMS *Warspite* and *Erebus* yesterday subjected the defenses of LE HAVRE to a heavy bombardment in support of ground operations.

The attack against the garrison and fortified positions at LE HAVRE was also continued yesterday morning, afternoon and evening by heavy bombers. Visibility was excellent and the bombing was highly concentrated.

Fighter and fighter-bombers gave support to ground forces and attacked locomotives and motor transport in the Low Countries, barges in Holland and an airfield at LEEUWARDEN.

Coastal aircraft attacked enemy shipping in the North Sea between the HOOK OF HOLLAND and AMELAND.

During the night light bombers attacked motor transport, a bridge and a train in Holland, and small surface vessels near FLUSHING.

By September 10, the escape door was closing on the German forces struggling to withdraw from the Atlantic coast. *Left:* The French Groupement Demetz reached Autun on the night of September 8/9 and continued to push on northwards towards Dijon but renewed opposition from German forces led to a squadron of the 2ème Régiment de Dragons being sent back to secure the town. *Right:* Place Anatole de Charmasse at Autun . . . then and now.

As with other link-ups, the time and place of the first contact between Seventh Army advancing from the Riviera and the forces coming from Normandy is a subject of controversy. Reconnaissance elements of both forces were reported to have met near Sombernon, 15 miles west of Dijon, in the late evening of the 10th and at least one courier plane of the 2ème Division Blindée landed near the same town the following afternoon. Formal contact was carried out next day at Montbard and Aisy, 30 miles north-west of Dijon. The Supreme Allied Commander Mediterranean gave September 11 as the date of the first meeting while the French accepted September 12. *Above:* On September 13 an unidentified American command organised this particular 'meeting' between 'Dragoon' and 'Overlord' forces at Autun, 45 miles west of Dijon, to be able to claim the headline in the US forces newspaper *Stars and Stripes*. On the left is *Champs Elysées*, an M8 of the 2ème Régiment de Dragons, Seventh Army, crewed by Adjudant Emile Lancery, Dragon Emile Lalanne and Dragon Jean Quignon, while on the right stands *Butch*, an M8 of the 86th Cavalry Reconnaissance Squadron, Third Army, with Sergeant Louis Basil, Corporal Edgar Ellis and Corporal Carl Newman. On September 15, in accordance with the order of the Combined Chiefs of Staff, the 6th Army Group became operational under Lieutenant General Jacob L. Devers to take command of the forces from the Mediterranean — the US Seventh Army and the French 1ère Armée — which thus passed to SHAEF control.

Eisenhower now commanded a continuous front from the North Sea to the Swiss border, with three army groups about to enter Germany — the 21st Army Group in the north, the 12th Army Group in the centre, and the 6th Army Group in the south. Though it was taken later in the winter, this picture of General Patton, Third Army, shaking hands with General Alexander M. Patch, commander of the Seventh Army, is symbolic of the new situation.

Crossing the frontier into Germany was a symbolic act and there were several claims as to who was the very first Allied soldier to set foot on German soil. It was later determined that it was a five-man patrol from the 85th Cavalry Reconnaissance Squadron of the 5th Armored Division under Sergeant Warner W. Holzinger *(left)* which crossed the Our river that marks the frontier between Luxembourg and Germany near Stolzembourg, just north of Vianden, at 1805 hours on September 11. This plaque on the river bank now commemorates the event although the dragon's teeth are not original.

Also claiming to be 'one of the first original photos from Germany', this shot was taken on September 13 at Grosskampenberg in the sector of operations of the 28th Division in V Corps area.

On the other hand, this picture was also released by the SHAEF Field Press Censor on September 15 and stated that: 'The first infantrymen to set foot on German soil use a smashed bridge to cross a river separating Belgium and Germany as Allied forces carry the war into the Reich. American troops crossed into Germany in force, September 12, 1944.' No location was allowed to be published in the censored version but on the original print it was given as Winterspelt.

COMMUNIQUE No. 157   September 12

Allied troops have crossed the Luxembourg-German frontier, and to the south, we have established contact with our forces advancing from southern France.

In the Moselle valley, we are continuing to meet stubborn resistance along the river.

Further north, troops which made the crossing of the German frontier in force are now in the area northwest of TRIER. Earlier, forces which liberated the city of LUXEMBOURG had encountered enemy delaying acting northeast of MERSCH.

In the Ardennes, gains have been made in the vicinity of BASTOGNE.

Advances south of LIEGE have taken our troops across the road between HARRE and AYWAILLE. Ten miles east of LIEGE we have occupied HERVE after encountering scattered enemy resistance. We have also reached JUPRELLE on the LIEGE—TONGRES road.

The bridgeheads over the Albert Canal have been enlarged in spite of stubborn enemy resistance.

East of GHENT we have liberated LOKEREN and ST NICHOLAS.

On the coast, Allied troops have reached BLANKENBERGHE. Between CALAIS and CAP GRIZ-NEZ we have taken WISSANT and SANGATTE.

Enemy gun positions and strong points between METZ and THIONVILLE were attacked by strong forces of medium and light bombers yesterday. There was no opposition in the air, but heavy flak was encountered. One bomber is missing.

Railway targets from SAARBRUCKEN to COLOGNE were hit by fighter-bombers which destroyed and damaged many locomotives and railway cars. Other fighter-bombers attacked enemy guns and fortifications in eastern Belgium. The airfield at LEEUWARDEN and ferry installations at BRESKENS were targets for medium and light bombers over Holland.

The fortified area of LE HAVRE was again pounded by heavy bombers, and fighters continued the attack on BREST.

Coastal aircraft yesterday afternoon attacked four large minesweepers off CHRISTIANSAND and left them on fire. Late Sunday evening, a formation of trawler-type auxiliaries was hit with rockets and cannon. One vessel was probably sunk and four others damaged. One coastal aircraft is missing.

During the night light bombers attacked transportation targets in Holland and Germany.

The railway line was closed after the war and the bridge was never rebuilt but the two abutments still stand on either side of the river.

It is not generally appreciated that the defeat of Germany entailed a huge price to be paid in the occupied countries of Europe where there was massive collateral damage to property and countless deaths of civilians. Occupied France had been on the receiving end of heavy attacks during the previous two years — examples being the raid by the RAF Bomber Command in March 1942 on the Renault factory at Billancourt which killed nearly 400 civilians and that by the US Eighth Air Force on the harbour at Nantes in September 1943 that missed the actual target but still killed over 1,100 — and from the end of that year the whole of the country was under attack. In the preparation for D-Day, a concentrated bombing campaign was begun in 1944 against airfields, the railway network, bridges and marshalling yards. One devastating raid by the US Fifteenth Air Force operating from Italy took place on the railway station at Saint-Étienne on May 26. It missed the target and instead hit the town killing over 1,000 civilians. The same thing happened at Lyon the same day with over 700 dead, and the regional commander of the Resistance sent a radio message to the Allies stating that such operations which had no military gain and only resulted in heavy civilian losses, had a hugely negative effect on the population. Well over half a million tons of bombs were dropped on France by the Allied air forces during the war, eight times the total tonnage that had been dropped by German aircraft and V-weapons on the United Kingdom. Estimates of the numbers of civilians killed during these raids are believed to be more than 65,000. With the pre-invasion bombing of key targets, most of the destruction and casualties occurred in 1944 causing nearly 70 per cent of the civilian casualties suffered throughout the war.

COMMUNIQUE No. 158   September 13
   LE HAVRE is now in Allied hands.
   On the Belgian coast, mopping up continues between FURNES and ZEEBRUGGE.
   Further progress has been made beyond the Albert Canal.
   North of LIEGE we have taken FORT EBEN-EMAEL. Forces advancing east and southeast of LIEGE, after meeting strong resistance from German infantry, anti-tank guns, and mines in the LIMBOURG area, captured EUPEN and MALMEDY. Units crossed the German frontier east of EUPEN.
   In the Ardennes our troops which liberated BASTOGNE have advanced to the vicinity of CLERVAUX in northern Luxembourg.
   In the Moselle valley we have enlarged our bridgeheads across the river against heavy enemy resistance.
   Concrete emplacements in the Siegfried Line in the neighbourhood of SCHEID, some 50 miles west of COBLENZ, were attacked by medium and light bombers yesterday. Other formations struck at a railway yard at ST WENDEL, artillery positions and observation posts in the vicinity of NANCY and a railway and road bridge between South Beveland and the Dutch mainland.
   Enemy transportation was attacked by fighters and fighter-bombers operating from Holland to the Moselle river and from STRASBOURG to KARLSRUHE. Close support to our ground forces was also given by attacks on gun positions. According to reports so far received, 30 enemy aircraft were shot down and nine were destroyed on the ground. Two of our aircraft are missing.

Possibly one of the worst raids of all took place on Le Havre when 9,800 tons were dropped between September 5 and 11, 1944. With a death toll in excess of 5,000, it was understandable that the stunned survivors showed little enthusiasm greeting their liberators when the leaders of I Corps entered the city on September 12.

The centre of Le Havre was erased from the map on September 5 by high explosive and incendiaries dropped from 348 aircraft of RAF Bomber Command. The attack resulted in few German casualties but French civilians suffered grievously. In all, the port was the target for 117 Allied raids during the war that left over 80 per cent of the town in ruins with 10,000 homes destroyed.

The rebuilt area just north of the Bassin du Roi and the Bassin du Commerce.

COMMUNIQUE No. 159   September 14

On the Channel coast mopping up continues. Allied troops have taken a strong point in the vicinity of NIEUPORT-BAINS.

In northeastern Belgium we have enlarged our bridgeheads over the Albert Canal at GHEEL and to the southeast more enemy counter-attacks against our bridgehead brought no result. Mopping-up in the area of HECHTEL has been completed and elements have reached the Escaut canal.

Other Allied troops, after crossing the Albert Canal, have pushed on to cross the Dutch frontier. The frontier has also been crossed further south near MAASTRICHT.

In Luxembourg our forces have made gains in the area northeast of the capital.

The bridgehead over the Moselle river continues to be strengthened in face of heavy enemy resistance and we now hold high ground in one area on the east bank.

In Brittany progress is being made at BREST against stubborn defenses which includes small arms, mortars, machine guns and some artillery. A fort about two miles east of the town has been taken. Fighter-bombers supported yesterday's attack.

Attacks on the Siegfried Line and against strong points near NANCY and METZ were made yesterday by fighter-bombers. Other fighter-bombers hit rail targets in the NANCY area, destroying and damaging a number of locomotives and railway trucks.

Communications and transportation targets on railways and water-ways of Holland were bombed and strafed by medium, light, and fighter-bombers. Hits were scored on the causeway between Walcheren and South Beveland. Fortified positions at BOULOGNE were targets for other medium and light bombers.

Coastal aircraft attacked an enemy convoy in the anchorage off DEN HELDER Tuesday night. Five vessels were left on fire and a sixth apparently sinking. Shore installations were also hit. Other formations attacked shipping between the HOOK OF HOLLAND and AMELAND. Two coastal aircraft are missing.

Right: **The attack through the 'Laura' gap was in full swing on September 10. Riding on the deck of one of the Churchill tanks of the 7th Royal Tank Regiment, Sergeant Max Collins pictured a section of the 2nd South Wales Borderers moving into the assault behind a Crocodile. The last strong points in the outer defences surrendered on the second day of the operation and the two divisions advanced into Le Havre on September 12.**

On the Channel coast, Allied forces were now closing on the first major port after Cherbourg — Le Havre. The attack to capture the port at the mouth of the Seine (Operation 'Astonia' — see *After the Battle* No. 139) relied on the massive use of special armour to create breaches in the German minefields and form crossings over the anti-tank ditches. Provided by the 79th Armoured Division, these comprised Crabs (mine-sweeping flail tanks); Crocodiles (flame-throwing tanks); and AVREs armed with a heavy Petard mortar that could throw 40lb projectiles against concrete fortifications but which could also carry an assault bridge. This bridgelayer with a Churchill tank of the 34th Tank Brigade was pictured by Sergeant Bert Wilkes, one of the AFPU photographers who covered the 49th Division attack.

The garrison commander, Oberst Eberhard Wildermuth, was captured together with over 11,000 of his men. *Left:* **Having cleared the waterfront, troops of the 2nd Gloucestershire Regiment, 49th Division, take leave of Le Havre.** *Right:* **This is Rue George Lafaurie with Chapelle d'Ingouville in the background.**

On September 3, Hitler had ordered an armoured force to be assembled in Lorraine in front of the Vosges mountains to counter-attack 'the deep eastern flank of the enemy' and he earmarked a strong attack force for the operation including three new panzer brigades brought in from Germany. *Left:* Engaged west of Épinal to stop the advance of the XV Corps, Panzerbrigade 112 clashed on September 13 with a combat command of the 2ème Division Blindée but the fight turned into such a débâcle that the brigade lost nearly all of its Panthers. This one was disabled at Madonne, just east of Dompaire. *Right:* This street is now aptly named Rue du Maréchal Leclerc after the commander of the 2ème Division Blindée.

COMMUNIQUE No. 160   September 15

Allied troops in northeastern Belgium have reached the line of the Leopold Canal north of MALDEGEM. Mopping-up continues in the area south of our bridgehead over the Escaut canal.

Further south, Allied troops have taken several small towns inside Germany and are meeting increasing resistance from prepared enemy positions.

South of AACHEN, enemy resistance is strong. East of ST VITH we have pierced an outer section of the Siegfried Line defences on a six-mile front. Other units encountered extensive road-blocks and pillboxes but progress was maintained.

In the Moselle valley, strong enemy counter-attacks against our bridgeheads were contained.

Further advances have been made in the area south of NANCY, where the Germans are putting up a stubborn defence with heavy mortar, small-arms, machine-gun and sporadic artillery fire.

The enemy garrison at BREST has rejected demands for surrender and fighting continues in the city where fires are burning and loud explosions have been heard. Enemy guns in the area were attacked yesterday by fighter-bombers.

Scattered enemy fire was also encountered on the Crozon peninsula, south of BREST, where strong points were attacked by medium and light bombers.

Fighters and fighter-bombers provided support for ground forces and attacked transportation in Holland.

Strong points near BOULOGNE were targets for medium and light bombers.

On September 15 Montgomery went to confer with General Horrocks of XXX Corps and to inspect the Guards' bridgehead at Beeringen. Sergeant Bill Morris pictured the Field-Marshal with Major-General Adair (left), the commander of the Guards Armoured Division, General Horrocks, and Major-General George Roberts (right), commander of the 11th Armoured Division.

Two months later, General Eisenhower had the opportunity to pose at the same spot with Lieutenant General Bradley for this symbolic photo.

From September 15 the breaching of the Siegfried Line was mentioned daily in the SHAEF communiqués although the first crossing had taken place on the 13th at Roetgen, a small village astride the Belgian—German border just south of Aachen. Here, GIs of the 39th Infantry, 9th Division, hitch a ride through the dragon's teeth on a Sherman bulldozer but unfortunately trees now planted beside the L238 have now completely hidden the line of dragon's teeth from view (see *After the Battle* Nos. 42 and 163).

COMMUNIQUE No. 161   September 16

Allied troops are now thrusting eastward along the 500 miles from the Swiss frontier, south of BELFORT, to the Channel coast around the Scheldt estuary.

Near the Swiss border, Allied troops advancing from southern France have made further progress since contact was established near DIJON with patrols from our forces operating to the north. The enemy is fighting stubbornly from prepared positions to protect the southern hinge of his withdrawal movement towards the BELFORT gap. Northeast of VESOUL we have advanced several miles against increasing resistance.

Elements have pushed to the vicinity of FAY-BILLOT and south of the town an enemy column was attacked and destroyed. Northwest of DIJON we have reached MONTBARD in the BRENNE valley without meeting serious opposition.

CHATENOIS, six miles from NEUFCHATEAU, has been captured and units are in the vicinity of MIRECOURT.

In the Moselle valley, our troops have entered NANCY and EPINAL. Fighter-bombers were active against enemy transportation in the Moselle valley.

In northern Luxembourg, east of ST VITH, our advance has continued against strongly-held pillbox defenses.

Allied troops closing on AACHEN from three sides are meeting stubborn opposition. MAASTRICHT has been liberated and our troops have moved beyond the city.

Fighting continued throughout yesterday in our bridgeheads over the Meuse—Escaut canal and a number of enemy counter-attacks were beaten off. The coastal areas north of the Albert Canal are being steadily cleared of enemy.

Fighter-bombers hit enemy transport in Holland. Ships and shore installations at BRESKENS, FLUSHING and ELLEWOUTSDIJK on the west Scheldt were attacked by medium and light bombers.

On the 13th, Task Force Lovelady of the 3rd Armored Division moved out of Roetgen, northwards to Rott.

Eisenhower's strategy for the defeat of Germany was to advance across France on a broad front but Montgomery disagreed, arguing that if SHAEF supported his 21st Army Group with all the supply facilities available, 'he could rush right on into Berlin and end the war'. Montgomery's plan called Operation 'Market-Garden' was designed to seize a crossing of the Neder-Rijn at Arnhem and open a gateway to the Ruhr by outflanking the Siegfried Line. Eisenhower agreed that it was certainly worth trying and gave his approval at the meeting on September 10 (see page 163), allocating Montgomery the First Allied Airborne Army that had been recently formed under Lieutenant General Lewis H. Brereton. The plan consisted of two operations: 'Market', an airborne operations to seize bridges over the watercourses and other important terrain features between the starting line and the objective, and 'Garden' employing powerful ground forces of the British Second Army driving north to join with the airborne units. Operation 'Market' would be the largest airborne operation in history, delivering nearly 35,000 men of the British 1st Airborne Division, the US 82nd and 101st Airborne Divisions, and the 1st Polish Parachute Brigade. *Left:* September 17 morning: a final salute before take off at Welford airfield for Major General Maxwell Taylor, the 101st Airborne Division commander. *Right:* At Barkston Heath, British paratroopers of the 1st Battalion, 1st Airborne Division, carry out final checks of their gear.

COMMUNIQUE No. 162   September 17

Advances were made by Allied troops yesterday between ANTWERP and the sea. Our bridgeheads over the Meuse—Escaut canal continue to be subjected to enemy counter-attacks, but we are holding firm.

Further south, on the German frontier, our forces are fighting in the southern outskirts of AACHEN and strong elements have broken through the Siegfried defences east of the city against heavy resistance. We have also pierced the defences below ROTT, southeast of AACHEN, and have advanced into the ROETGENWALD.

Moderate resistance is being met across the frontier east of ST VITH but our forces further south near BRANDSCHEID are encountering heavy resistance.

In the Moselle valley, our forces are now across the river in strength and elements have advanced a considerable distance east of NANCY.

The advance from southern France is making progress against varying resistance. Elements have pushed without opposition to CHAUMONT but advances northeast of VESOUL, at the western approach to the BELFORT GAP, were made against defences which the enemy has been strengthening.

In the Alps, troops have entered MODANE at the western entrance of the MODANE railway tunnel linking France and Italy. The enemy is withdrawing in the direction of the high MONT-CENIS PASS.

The ARNEMUIDEN and BATH dykes, linking by road and rail the island of Walcheren to the Dutch mainland, were attacked yesterday by medium and light bombers; other medium bombers struck at two strong points north of BOULOGNE. Fighters and fighter-bombers attacked transportation targets in Holland.

Invasion from the sky. On the first day of the operation, 424 C-47 troop carriers and 70 Waco gliders were to deliver nearly 6,700 men of the 101st Airborne Division to the sector north of Eindhoven, while 480 troop carriers dropped about 7,250 men from the 82nd Airborne Division south of Nijmegen and 50 gliders brought in anti-tank guns and reconnaissance detachments. At the same time, over 320 gliders and 143 troop carriers were to land about 5,800 men of the 1st Airborne Division near Arnhem which lay 50 miles north of the start line for the ground forces. William Jenks, one of the paratroops of the 505th Parachute Infantry Regiment, 82nd Airborne Division, took this impressive shot as he descended to Dutch soil. The number of men jumping in this A-5 serial dropped over Groesbeek, south of Nijmegen, was about 740.

Left: Operation 'Garden' began in early afternoon of the 18th when the Irish Guards battle group that was to lead the XXX Corps' advance north to Arnhem crossed the Maas—Scheldt canal at Neerpelt. *Right:* The present-day bridge was built to replace 'Joe's Bridge' (just off to the left) but the old approach to the Bailey bridge laid alongside remains unchanged.

COMMUNIQUE No. 163   September 18

Allied airborne troops were landed in Holland yesterday after powerful air preparation in which the Allied air forces operated in great strength. First reports show that the operation is going well.

Our ground forces near the Belgian—Dutch frontier are continuing to make progress.

Further south we have mopped up pockets of resistance on the outskirts of AACHEN. Heavy fighting continues in the city. Elements pushing on east of the town are encountering determined resistance. Advances have also been made across the Luxembourg—German frontier.

In the Moselle valley our troops are clearing the area west of the river of isolated enemy groups. North of NANCY progress has been made and enemy counter-attacks near PONT-A-MOUSSON were repulsed.

The Germans are fighting hard in the BELFORT GAP. Our troops have occupied the town of ST LOUP-SUR-SEMOUSE and cleared LURE of the enemy. North of LURE the enemy used tanks in resisting the advance. Local engagements took place in the area of PONT-DE-ROIDE.

At 2 p.m. over 300 guns started the massive artillery preparation and at 2.35 p.m. the Irish Guards Group began to advance along the Hechtel—Valkenswaard road. Typhoons circled overhead, in direct radio contact with an RAF liaison team travelling with the leading armour. German defenders quickly knocked-out nine of the leading tanks but by 4.30 p.m. this resistance was overcome and the advance continued.

Left: Darkness was falling when the leaders entered Valkenswaard but as neither the corps nor the division urged the troops to move on, the column halted for the night. (There is still controversy over the reason why the British force halted rather than pressing on through the night.) This shot was taken next morning when the battle group was preparing to resume the advance to Eindhoven. *Right:* Valkenswaard today. Comparison taken by Jurgen van Hoof.

During the night engineers completed building a bridge over the Wilhelmina Canal at Son and, taking the lead, the Grenadier Guards Group began crossing early on the morning of the 19th. The leaders pushed on at full speed, passing American paratroops at every junction, cheering and beckoning the way to Nijmegen and by 6.45 a.m. the Household Cavalry had reached Veghel held by the 501st Parachute Regiment. *Left:* The drawbridge over the Zuid Willems Canal there was too narrow to be used by large vehicles so most had to use an improvised trestle and log bridge constructed alongside it by paratroop engineers. *Right:* With a new bridge now just to the east, the old bridge at the lock has been dismantled.

Striking in advance of our airborne forces yesterday, heavy, light and fighter-bombers in very great strength attacked anti-aircraft batteries, gun positions, communications, troops and transport through a wide area of Holland while fighters swept a path for the aerial transports and gliders, and provided umbrella cover for the landing. As the enemy's guns opened fire, our fighters and fighter-bombers dived to silence them in low-level strafing and bombing attacks.

Many motor vehicles, locomotives, railway cars and barges were destroyed or damaged, and bridges and supply dumps were hit. According to reports so far received, nine enemy aircraft were shot down in combat by our fighters.

Later in the day, gun positions and troops on the island of Walcheren were attacked by a strong force of heavy bombers. Coastal aircraft struck at shipping off the Frisian Islands.

Fortified positions and garrison troops at BOULOGNE were bombarded for four hours by other heavy bombers which dropped more than 3,500 tons of high explosives. Intense anti-aircraft fire was encountered at times, but there was no opposition in the air.

Strong points at BREST were attacked during the day by small forces of fighter-bombers. Other fighter-bombers hit locomotives and railway cars in western Germany.

The leading tanks of the Grenadier Guards soon appeared: these are Shermans from the 1st Squadron. *Below:* This is Schoonenburgseweg at the western entrance of Overasselt. The tall chimney in the background has gone but the building, a former dairy factory, still stands.

The advance northwards resumed and at 8.30 a.m. the Household Cavalry had reached Grave and made contact with the 82nd Airborne Division which had captured intact the huge nine-span bridge over the Maas. Lieutenant-General Frederick Browning of the I Airborne Corps and Major General James Gavin commanding the 82nd Airborne Division had driven down from Nijmegen to Overasselt, some three miles from the Grave bridge, to await the arrival of the ground forces.

While the operation in Holland was continuing, 350 miles away to the south-west the campaign in Brittany to wrest the port of Brest from the Germans was in full swing, and to assist the Americans had secured the support of a squadron of flame-throwing Churchill tanks from the British 141st Royal Armoured Corps. On September 14, the US 29th Division advanced on Fort Montbarey, a key point in the German defences on the western side of the perimeter. After battling for two days, supported by the flame-throwing tanks and point-blank fire from tank destroyers, the position was finally taken on the 16th. This cracked the German defence and soon thereafter resistance began to disintegrate. Here an M18 tank destroyer of Company B, 705th Tank Destroyer Battalion, fires at another position holding out in Brest.

COMMUNIQUE No. 164   September 19

The landing of Allied airborne troops in Holland continued yesterday. Supplies were also landed and positions were consolidated and strengthened. Operations are proceeding, and in one area our ground forces have already linked with the airborne troops.

In advance of the airborne operations, fighters and fighter-bombers attacked flak boats and positions, troops and transport. Other fighters maintained patrols and provided escort and cover for the transport aircraft and gliders. More than 70 flak boats and positions were put out of action. Many motor and horse-drawn vehicles were destroyed and an ammunition dump was blown up.

Opposition to the advance of our ground troops was stubborn. In the area west of ANTWERP, Allied troops, now fighting on Dutch soil, are advancing in spite of stiff opposition.

Fighting continues in BOULOGNE where we have made further progress into the town.

In southern Holland, our troops have advanced northeast of MAASTRICHT against stiff resistance from enemy infantry, artillery and dug-in tanks.

Elements further east have reached UBAGSBERG and SIMPELVELD against moderate resistance. In AACHEN, hard fighting continues. Southeast of the city we have cleared the town of BUSBACH and units to the northeast have met strong opposition.

Mopping-up of German elements is in progress east of ROETGEN, across the border from EUPEN, and we have captured HOFEN. East of ST VITH, our troops in Germany are meeting stiffening resistance and increasing artillery fire. BRANDSCHEID has been taken and we have advanced to HONTHEIM, six miles east of the border.

Armored units moving across the Luxembourg—German frontier have taken the town of HUTTINGEN.

In the Moselle valley, we have further reinforced our troops to the east of the river.

West of BELFORT GAP, our troops, in an advance of more than five miles eastward from ST LOUP-SUR-SEMOUSE, have entered the town of FOUGEROLLES. An enemy attack near PONT-DE-ROIDE was repulsed.

According to reports so far received, 32 enemy aircraft were destroyed in yesterday's overall air operations. Thirty-three of our fighters are missing.

Brest is quite a large city, with hundreds of junctions all looking much the same, so it was a real challenge for Jean Paul to find where the photograph had been taken. He finally tracked it down to the junction of Rue Kerfautras and Rue Duret, the tank destroyer was firing south-westwards down the length of the latter street.

Another shot taken in the same sector by Signal Corps photographer T/5 George Herold who captioned it as 'infantrymen advancing under machine-gun fire into outskirts of Brest'.

Jean Paul found that the GIs were crouching in Rue de la Duchesse Anne, looking southwards down Rue Albert de Mun. A somewhat more peaceful scene today.

COMMUNIQUE No. 165   September 20

The advance of the Allied forces in Holland has continued rapidly. Ground troops made contact yesterday with more airborne formations. EINDHOVEN is in our hands and our armored units have advanced nearly 40 miles to the area of NIJMEGEN. Strong enemy counter-attacks were beaten off near BEST and in our bridgehead north of GHEEL.

Fighters and fighter-bombers again supported and covered airborne operations

The German forces in Brest surrendered on September 18, the 2nd and 29th Divisions taking about 10,000 prisoners between them.

Apart from its port facilities so completely wrecked by Allied bombing and German demolitions, Brest of course was a very important U-Boat base with massive bomb-proof pens.

Though it can be seen from Route de la Corniche, the huge U-Boat shelter pictured here by Jean Paul now lies inside the Marine Nationale installation which is off limits.

and attacked road and rail transport over a wide area of Holland. According to reports so far received, 26 enemy aircraft were shot down for the loss of nine of our fighters.

To the west, the enemy is still resisting stubbornly south of the Scheldt, but our troops made progress in the area of the AXEL—HULST canal. On the coast we have captured the citadel and Mont-Lambert in BOULOGNE.

In southern Holland our troops have liberated SITTARD and AMSTENRADE, northeast of MAASTRICHT, meeting moderate opposition.

East of AACHEN, fighting is in progress in the factory area of STOLBERG, and enemy pressure is being met near BUSBACH. Operating in advance of our ground forces, medium and light bombers hit railway yards at ESCHWEILER, DUREN and MERZENICH on the AACHEN—COLOGNE line.

Mopping-up of enemy pillboxes and pockets of resistance continues east of ROETGEN and in the HOFEN and ALZEN areas, south of MONSCHAU. Enemy counter-attacks in this area were unsuccessful.

Heavy and determined resistance has been encountered east of the German—Luxembourg border. East of BLEIALF, an enemy pocket was wiped out.

In the Moselle valley, we have made gains south of METZ against stubborn resistance. Mopping-up is in progress six miles northeast of PONT-A-MOUSSON. Further south, our forces have liberated GERBEVILLER, 14 miles northeast of CHARMES.

In Brittany, all organized resistance has ceased in BREST and RECOUVRANCE, and our troops have cleared the enemy from the Crozon peninsula.

The commander of the fortress, Generalleutnant Hermann Ramcke, had managed to escape across the harbour to the Crozon peninsula and he was not captured until the afternoon of the 19th.

Left: **On September 20, Major General Troy H. Middleton, commander of the VIII Corps, formally presented the liberated city to Jules Lullien, the acting Mayor of Brest following the death of Victor Eusen killed in the night of September 8/9.** *Right:* **Though badly damaged, the main Post Office in the Rue de Siam was rebuilt along its previous lines.**

Though Armeegruppe G had succeeded in extricating about 60 per cent of its forces from western and southern France, its losses still amounted to nearly 100,000 men, plus the 25,000 garrison troops cut off in 'fortresses' around Lorient, Saint-Nazaire and Royan. One remarkable event concerning these retreating troops took place 100 miles south of Paris when a large force of 20,000 men, withdrawing from the Atlantic coast under Generalmajor Botho Elster, marched into captivity of their own free will without firing a shot! *Left and right:* First contacts with Elster had been established by French officers of the FFI on September 8 when the Germans made it clear that they were only willing to surrender to the Americans, not the FFI, so officers of the 83rd Infantry Division took over to discuss terms. On September 15 Lieutenant Colonel Jules K. French was pictured discussing details of the formal surrender with Generalmajor Elster and his staff. As the Ninth Army was eager to extract every ounce of propaganda from the occasion, Elster was forced to accept a public surrender, set to take place on September 16. *Below:* A long procession of Germans then marched north along an agreed route to the Loire. The Germans were allowed to retain their weapons until they had reached the northern bank of the river in case of an attack by the FFI.

COMMUNIQUE No. 166 September 21

There has been heavy fighting in the area of NIJMEGEN where Allied land and airborne forces have linked up. The base of the Allied salient has been widened and airborne landings have been further reinforced.

Fighters and fighter-bombers provided escort and support for these airborne operations and also provided support for the ground forces.

Allied troops in Belgium advanced to the line of the Leopold Canal and made substantial gains to the Scheldt west of ANTWERP.

Mopping-up continues in the area of BOULOGNE south of the Liane river.

The German garrison and fortified positions at CALAIS were subjected to a strong and concentrated attack yesterday afternoon and evening by heavy bombers, one of which is missing.

In southern Holland our ground forces have crossed the German border to SCHERPENSEEL, five miles northeast of HEERLEN, under heavy German artillery fire. Stubborn fighting is in progress at other points along the front, particularly at STOLBERG, east of AACHEN, and on the outskirts of BIESDORF, east of the Luxembourg town of DIEKIRCH, where, earlier, a strong enemy counter-attack was repulsed and 17 German tanks knocked out.

In the Moselle valley, heavy enemy resistance is being encountered south of METZ, with fighting centering around SILLEGNY. Our forces also are engaged in the vicinity of CHATEAU-SALINS, 18 miles northeast of NANCY. Our troops advancing northeast of CHARMES have reached the towns of MOYEN and MAGNIERES.

Gains have been made along the entire sector northwest of BELFORT. Opposition has been slight and the enemy is relying principally on lightly-defended road-blocks to stay our advance. Several small towns have been occupied.

The enemy south of BELFORT has confined his activity to patrolling with moderate support from artillery and mortars.

A force of 19,312 enemy troops under General Elster has been taken prisoner after a mass surrender south of the Loire river.

The Americans picked a suitable venue at the southern end of the bridge at Beaugency, near Orléans, and even specified 3 p.m. to give the best light for filming.

Jean-Paul researched the story for *After the Battle* and found that this picture had taken at Neung-sur-Beuvron, 25 miles south of Orléans (see issue No. 48).

This is where the engineers' bridge once crossed the canal beside Lock No. 11.

Meanwhile, on September 21 back in Holland, British VIII Corps had established a bridgehead across the Zuid Willems Canal at Someren, 12 miles east of Eindhoven. During the night engineers built this Bailey bridge across the canal to allow the 4th King's Shropshire Light Infantry and tanks of the 2nd Fife and Forfar Yeomanry to proceed to Asten at daybreak.

COMMUNIQUE No. 167   September 22

The Allied drive northwards through NIJMEGEN continued yesterday against increasing enemy opposition. Our armored forces, having captured the bridge at NIJMEGEN in conjunction with airborne troops, crossed to the north bank of the Waal and pushed on north. The town of NIJMEGEN has been cleared of the enemy.

The base of the Allied salient has been widened on both sides of EINDHOVEN. We have reached SOMEREN on the east and we are fighting in the area of WINTELRE on the west.

Fighters and fighter-bombers supported the operations in Holland. Some enemy aircraft were encountered, principally in the areas of NIJMEGEN and LOCHEM. Twenty enemy aircraft were shot down for the loss of four of our fighters.

In the Scheldt estuary we have captured TERNEUZEN and are steadily mopping up the southern bank east of the Leopold Canal.

In the BOULOGNE area, the enemy has been confined to the high ground southwest of the town. An enemy strong point in the FORET DE LA CRECHE on the outskirts of the town was attacked by medium and light bombers.

Troops crossing into Germany from southern Holland have advanced to within 3 miles of GEILENKIRCHEN. In the STOLBERG—BUSBACH area east of AACHEN, mopping up is in progress and we are engaged in house-to-house fighting in STOLBERG. East of the town our troops have gained high ground.

Further south, Allied troops are clearing the HURTGEN FOREST against moderate artillery fire and are also mopping up in the area of LAMMERSDORF. Numerous counter-attacks have been repulsed near DIEKIRCH and one unit has destroyed 28 enemy tanks.

South of METZ, our forces advanced to within miles of the city. Along the Meurthe river we have cleared LUNEVILLE and our troops have taken the high ground along the west bank five miles to the southeast. Other units are in the vicinity of FLIN on the Meurthe river, five miles northwest of BACCARAT.

Railway centers at EHRANG, GEROLSTEIN and PRONSFELD in Germany were attacked yesterday by medium bombers.

At Nijmegen, the Germans mounted a strong defence of the road and rail bridges until the 504th Parachute Regiment crossed the river under fire — an exploit often hailed as one of the most daring feats of the entire war. This manoeuvre enabled the paratroops to approach the defenders from the rear and force them to withdraw. The huge bridge was then rushed by tanks of the Grenadier Guards and the 2nd Battalion, 505th Parachute Infantry, secured the bridge that evening.

Except for an extra bicycle lane which has been added on the downstream side, the road bridge at Nijmegen remains unchanged.

On September 22, maintaining a positive stance, SHAEF announced in Communiqué No. 167 the successful crossing of the Waal while keeping quiet on events further north where the last British paratrooper positions at Arnhem had been overwhelmed on the morning of the 21st. One day later, Communiqué No. 168 reported troops reaching the 'southern bank of the Neder-Rijn' but still nothing concerning the defeat at Arnhem that spelt the end of Montgomery's grand plan. *Right:* When the 1st Airborne Division landed outside Arnhem on September 17, the march to the city by the 1st and 3rd Parachute Battalions had been intercepted en route by small German units which prevented them from reaching the bridge. Only Lieutenant-Colonel John Frost's 2nd Parachute Battalion found its route largely undefended and it arrived at the bridge that evening. However, following two unsuccessful attempts to capture the bridge itself and its southern approach, Frost's men set up defensive positions in houses at the northern end. Early on the morning of the 18th, SS-Panzer-Aufklärungs-Abteilung 9, on its way back from Nijmegen, attempted to rush the bridge but they were beaten back with heavy losses. The wrecks left by the German battle group can be seen on this aerial shot of the northern end of the bridge.

COMMUNIQUE No. 168   September 23

The clearing of the BOULOGNE area has been completed with the capture of LE PORTAL.

Fierce fighting continued all day yesterday in the area of the Allied northward thrust. Other troops crossed to the north of the Waal and after bitter fighting between NIJMEGEN and ARNHEM our troops reached the southern bank of the Neder-Rijn (north branch of the Rhine river).

The enemy attacked the eastern side of our salient strongly but the base was further widened by a crossing of the BOIS-LE-DUC canal and on the west by fresh advances beyond VESSEM.

Our forces have captured STOLBERG, east of AACHEN, and are now mopping up isolated enemy pockets in the town.

There has been little change from the Dutch—German border south to the LUNEVILLE area. Enemy counter-attacks were repulsed at a number of places. German tanks and infantry were driven back by our artillery northwest of GEILENKIRCHEN after an unsuccessful counter-attack.

Southeast of STOLBERG we inflicted heavy losses in repulsing German counter-attacks. Stubborn resistance was met from enemy pillboxes and defended road-blocks.

In the area east of DIEKIRCH our units were forced to give some ground. Active patrolling and mopping up continue in other sectors along the line.

In the Moselle valley an enemy counter-attack was repulsed at COIN-SUR-SEILLE, five miles south of METZ.

Our troops have reached EPINAL and have forced crossings of the Moselle at many points against stiffened resistance. The roads southeastward toward REMIREMONT are heavily defended.

Further south, in the vicinity of MELAY, counter-attacks have been repulsed. The town of MELISEY, in the LURE area, has been taken.

In the Riviera, the resort town of MENTON is in our hands.

Transportation targets in northern France, Holland and western Germany were attacked yesterday by our fighters and fighter-bombers which also provided close support for troops.

Bridges and barges in Holland were the targets for our light bombers last night.

As the last British positions at the bridge were being overwhelmed, the remainder of the 1st Airborne Division, some 3,600 men all told, had established themselves in the houses and woods around Oosterbeek, a suburb just west of Arnhem, with the intention of holding a bridgehead on the north side of the Rhine until XXX Corps arrived.

A timeless comparison taken at the corner of Klingelbeekseweg in western Arnhem.

COMMUNIQUE No. 169 September 24

Heavy engagements continued yesterday in the Allied salient in Holland.

Fighting was particularly fierce in the vicinity of ARNHEM where the enemy is exerting strong pressure. We have increased our hold on the area between the Neder-Rijn and the Waal. Our positions in the NIJMEGEN area have been improved and we have strengthened the bridgehead over the BOIS-LE-DUC canal near the base of the salient.

Our airborne operations were further reinforced during the day.

Ahead of the transport aircraft and gliders, fighters and fighter-bombers in strength dropped fragmentation bombs on numerous gun positions, and carried out low-level strafing attacks. Many batteries were silenced. Other fighters provided escort and cover for the airborne operations: the enemy was active in the air and a number of combats with our fighters resulted. According to reports so far received 27 enemy aircraft were shot down, fourteen of our fighters are missing.

East of ANTWERP our forces advanced after establishing a bridgehead across the Meuse—Escaut canal. Northwest of the city we have made a slight advance.

The entire front from GEILENKIRCHEN area to the Meurthe valley remains relatively unchanged, with stubborn enemy resistance and numerous counter-attacks in all sectors.

In the AACHEN area, our patrols are meeting fire from the outskirts of the city, where the enemy appears to be well entrenched. STOLBERG is being cleared of isolated German pockets, but southeast of the town our troops are meeting stubborn resistance in their advance. East of BUSBACH a counter-attacking German force was driven off with an estimated loss of 40 per cent of its strength.

German pockets are being mopped up in the sector bordering northern Luxembourg, and our units along the entire German-Luxembourg frontier are receiving moderate artillery fire from the enemy.

South of METZ, stubborn enemy resistance continues, and a small counter-attack at POURNOY was broken up by our artillery. We have made gains nine miles north of NANCY, where the town of MOREY was freed. Enemy tanks and infantry are offering strong opposition in the area east of NANCY.

Our troops have advanced to the vicinity of BENAMENIL, ten miles east of LUNEVILLE.

Gun emplacements on the island of Walcheren in the Scheldt estuary were attacked by a small force of heavy bombers.

Strong points at CALAIS were attacked by medium and light bombers.

Fighter-bombers hit fortified positions in the TRIER area.

Left: **Major-General Robert E. Urquhart pictured at the rear of the Hartenstein Hotel in Oosterbeek which had been taken over for the command post of his 1st Airborne Division.** *Right:* **The hotel was closed in 1978 to convert it into a museum dedicated to the battle of Arnhem.**

The Germans inexorably closed in on the positions held by the paras in and around Oosterbeek. This picture has been described as 'the most famous 3-inch mortar team of World War 2', with Private Ron Tierney (facing the camera), Corporal Jim McDowell (foreground), and Private Norman Knight, all of the 1st Border.

German PK photographer Jacobsen pictured a German battle-group advancing up Utrechtsestraat to the airborne perimeter.

Though Communiqué No. 170 claimed that 'some reinforcements' were passed to the north bank under cover of darkness, the attempt to support the bridgehead turned out to be a complete failure. Now it was just a case of trying to rescue as many men as possible and get them back across the river.

Left: **The Germans close in — this is Oberwachtmeister Joseph Mathes, commander of the 3. Batterie of Sturmgeschütz-Brigade 280.** *Right:* **Onderlangs in western Arnhem. A much embattled hotel in September 1944, the building in the left background is now the Golden Tulip Rijnhotel.**

COMMUNIQUE No. 170   September 25

Fierce fighting continues in the ARNHEM area where we have succeeded in passing some reinforcements to the north bank of the river under cover of darkness.

East of NIJMEGEN, Allied troops have entered German territory in the neighbourhood of the REICHSWALD forest. The area north of VEGHEL, where enemy pressure was strong, has been cleared after the repulse of a counter-attack from the village of ERP.

East of EINDHOVEN, our bridgehead over the BOIS-LE-DUC canal was extended to the neighbourhood of DEURNE. Further west, we have pushed the retreating enemy from the Escaut canal to the general line of the ANTWERP—TURNHOUT canal.

In the GEILENKIRCHEN area, our troops met concentrated medium artillery fire, which was countered, and patrol activity continued in the sector. In the area of ROETGEN, south of AACHEN, one of our units reduced a German strong point, and slight gains were made against stubborn enemy resistance.

A German counter-attack was repulsed east of AACHEN with heavy enemy losses.

In the METZ area, the enemy is still strongly entrenched on the west side of the Moselle river, and south of METZ our troops are continuing to meet strong opposition.

Allied forces have cleared LEYR, eight miles northeast of NANCY, and are clearing the BOIS DE FAULX and the FORET DE CHAMPENOUX, to the east of NANCY.

In the Meurthe valley, our units have made further gains in the FORET DE MONDON, northwest of BACCARAT.

Enemy fortified positions at CALAIS were attacked early yesterday evening by heavy bombers.

Support for the ground forces in Holland and eastern France was provided by fighters and fighter-bombers, which attacked tanks and armored vehicles near NANCY and mortar positions and infantry in the ARNHEM area.

Locomotives, railway trucks and motor transport in Holland were also attacked by fighters.

The remnants of the airborne force finally withdrew across the Rhine during the night of the 25th. Here, some days before the end, Jacobsen pictured wounded being evacuated from a house in Oosterbeek, No. 151 Utrechtseweg. On the left is Captain Sandy Flockhart. The Germans allowed him and three other medical officers and ten orderlies to return to the British line after the patients were evacuated. Of approximately 10,600 men of the 1st Airborne Division and other units who set out on the operation at Arnhem, 2,400 survivors escaped to the southern bank; 1,485 lost their lives and 6,414 were taken prisoner.

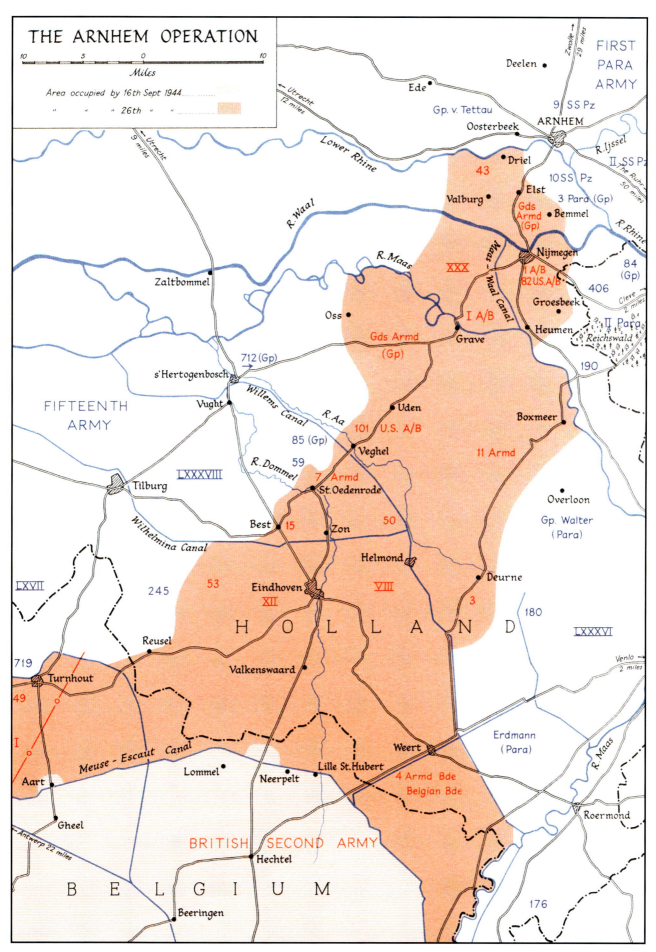

A bridge too far! While Operation 'Market-Garden' created an impressive salient into Holland, it failed in its main objective of securing a bridgehead over the Rhine at Arnhem and opening a gateway to the Ruhr by outflanking the Siegfried Line.

During August and September, traffic between the War Department and the European Theater of Operations was extremely heavy — so heavy that it even put a strain on the War Department facilities in the United States handling overseas business. A total of 356,669 messages containing more than ten million words flowed between the two points. Moreover, there were 75 high-level secrecy telephone conversations and 95 teletypewriter conferences, not to mention 736 telephotographs transmitted. This was more traffic than the amount carried across the Atlantic by all the existing pre-war commercial facilities in any comparable period. Only extensive and complicated semi-automatic and automatic equipment of the most modern type could handle such loads. Furthermore, in the theatre, a telephone system to serve a large headquarters such as SHAEF required as much equipment as that necessary to serve a city of 30,000 people.

COMMUNIQUE No. 171   September 26

Allied troops have made good gains on the east of the EINDHOVEN—NIJMEGEN salient. HELMOND and DEURNE have been captured and we have advanced several miles to the north.

In the SCHIJNDEL area enemy attacks against the supply corridor have been repulsed.

West of TURNHOUT our troops have gained a bridgehead over the ANTWERP—TURNHOUT canal.

From the area north of AACHEN to the Meurthe valley there has been little change. Sporadic artillery fire and patrolling by the enemy continue in the northern half of this sector. East of AACHEN our patrol activity has met strong enemy reaction.

In the Moselle valley slight advances have been made by our troops northeast of NANCY. Southeast of LUNEVILLE our forces have made gains in the BENAMENIL area.

In the EPINAL area, our troops have advanced several miles east of the Moselle. The village of JEUXEY has been taken and the occupation of EPINAL completed.

West of BELFORT gains of several miles were made by our armour and infantry against stiff opposition.

Gun positions and strong points in the ARNHEM area were attacked by medium, light and fighter-bombers yesterday. Four enemy aircraft which attempted to intercept the bombers were shot down by escorting fighters.

Road and rail transport in the Ruhr was strafed by fighters.

Fortified positions at CALAIS were bombarded for over an hour by heavy bombers which dropped more than 1,000 tons of high explosives.

In September, SHAEF began sending out the daily communiqués by teleprinter, No. 171 being reproduced here in facsimile. They were issued under the signature of Lieutenant Colonel D. R. Jordan of the Communiqué Section of the Public Relations Division (see page 511) with a distribution list covering the Adjutant General in the US and all the various Allied headquarters.

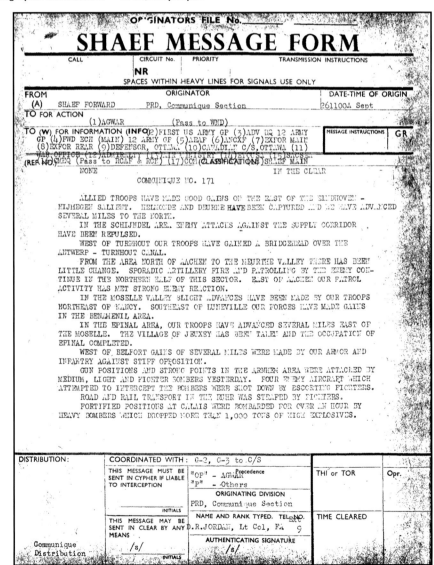

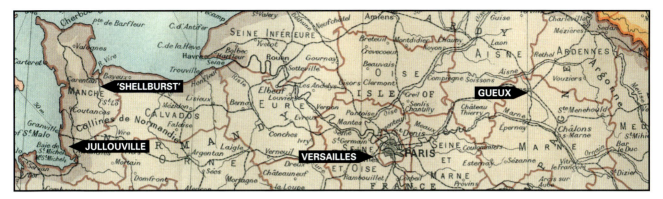

Although all eyes were currently focussed on the airborne operations taking place in Holland, behind the scenes SHAEF was on the move again. However, this was easier said than done and, in the two months that it had taken to choose a site on the Continent and organise the move of the 3,000 personnel concerned to Granville, the front had moved a further 150 miles to the east. Supreme Headquarters never really caught up with itself: in a way, it was a victim of its own success.

'Shellburst' was Eisenhower's Advanced CP (see page 128) and the map shows the next three moves across France, By September, his personal headquarters was temporarily merged on the same site as SHAEF Forward at Jullouville (see page 152), but the move proved abortive with poor communications and on September 20 SHAEF Forward opened at the Trianon Palace Hotel at Versailles, just outside Paris, with the Advanced Command Post at Gueux.

COMMUNIQUE No. 172   September 27

Allied troops have again repulsed enemy moves threatening our communications along the EINDHOVEN—NIJMEGEN road.

Our salient has been further secured south of the Meuse by advances to OSS, on the west, and to the area of BOXMEER, on the east. A stretch of some five miles of the Meuse south of BOXMEER is in our hands.

Gains have also been made on both sides of the base of the Allied salient. On the west, we have reached the ANTWERP—TURNHOUT canal, along a considerable portion of its length. On the east, around MAESEYCK, we control the west bank of the Meuse between WESSEM and DILSEN.

To the south, as far as LUNEVILLE, active patrolling continues with little change of position. Light to moderate artillery fire was encountered in the AACHEN and STOLBERG area and our units engaged German pillboxes and strong-points northeast of ROETGEN.

In southern Luxembourg we occupied GREIVELDANGE.

An enemy counter-attack in the vicinity of MARSAL, east of NANCY, was repulsed.

Considerable enemy artillery fire has been directed against our troops in the Meurthe valley.

North of EPINAL our forces have crossed the Moselle in strength and have occupied CHATEL-SUR-MOSELLE and a number of towns to the south.

The enemy is fighting stubbornly in the vicinity of DOCELLES and TENDON to slow our advance east of EPINAL.

West and northwest of BELFORT further progress has been made and several villages have been liberated.

On the Channel coast ground operations against CALAIS continue successfully. Yesterday fortified positions in the town and heavy guns and radio installations at CAP GRIS-NEZ were attacked by heavy bombers.

Other heavy bombers attacked rail centers at OSNABRÜCK and HAMM in northwest Germany, and industrial targets at BREMEN. Twelve bombers are missing.

Fortifications and strong points at BRESKENS and rail and road targets at CLEVE were attacked by medium bombers.

Fighters provided escort for the heavy bombers to Germany and also for supply missions to the Low Countries, while fighters and fighter-bombers gave support to the ground forces and also attacked transportation targets in Holland. Thirty-eight enemy aircraft were destroyed in the air. Seven of our fighters are missing.

Last night light bombers attacked road, rail and river transport in Holland and western Germany.

In the midst of war, the Supreme Commander had to find time to meet members of the US House of Representatives. This visit led by Congressman Walter Horan took place on October 3. Eisenhower's aide Harry Butcher, about to be promoted to captain, stands on the far right of the steps of the Trianon Palace Hotel.

The Trianon Palace Hotel has fortunately preserved Eisenhower's suite of rooms (Nos. 102-106) situated on the first floor just to the right of the main entrance, although room numbers in 1944 were different.

The communiqués continually refer to the use of fighter-bombers which were being used for close support on the battlefield and to attack road and rail transportation targets. Fighter-bombers often strafed from tree-top height either using cannons or rockets. Back in 1941, when the question of attacking tanks from the air was being addressed, one suggestion was to use the Army's 3-inch rocket for the purpose. Two types of warhead were designed for RAF use, either a 25lb armour-piercing round or 60lb high-explosive shell. The rockets were mounted on rails in groups of four and were electrically fired, either in a salvo of eight or in four pairs. When the Second Tactical Air Force put in an urgent request for some means of increasing the number of rockets carried, a modified launcher allowed for eight under each wing. However, targeting the unguided missiles with some accuracy was very difficult, trajectory drop being a major problem at longer ranges. When the No. 2 Operational Research Section of 21st Army Group surveyed Normandy to study the German vehicles and equipment left behind, they came to the conclusion that few of them had actually been knocked out by rocket strikes, certainly many less than the hundreds claimed by Typhoon pilots.

In Lorraine, the ambitious German scheme for a counter-attack (see page 174) was now considered out of the question and by September 20 the German headquarters in the West had drawn up an alternative operation on a smaller scale to be mounted in the Lunéville sector. Here, General Hasso von Manteuffel, commanding the 5. Panzerarmee, confers with the staff of Panzerbrigade 111.

In 1994 Jean Paul had the honour of leading a tour of the battlefields with three former officers of the brigade (see *After the Battle* No. 83). Gerhard Tebbe, former Major commander of the brigade's Panther battalion, and Horst Gittermann, former Oberleutnant and battalion adjutant, check the map just as they had done 70 years previously, watched by Walter Schubert, then Oberleutnant and commanding the battalion's staff company.

COMMUNIQUE No. 173   September 28

The withdrawal of our forces from north of the Neder-Rijn has been completed.

Fighting continued throughout yesterday in the area north of NIJMEGEN where Allied troops made some progress to the northeast against stiff opposition. On the west of the salient, an advance was made south of OSS and the villages of HEESCH and NISTELRODE were freed.

Fighters and fighter-bombers attacked strong points and gun positions in the ARNHEM—NIJMEGEN area and strafed road and rail transport behind the enemy lines in Holland. There were many combats and, according to reports so far received, 41 enemy aircraft were destroyed. Ten of ours are missing. To the east of the Allied salient, an attack was made by medium bombers on communications at GOCH near the German frontier.

Last night, intruders attacked road and rail transport over a wide area in Holland and western Germany.

In northern Belgium our ground forces have further extended the bridgehead over the canal west of TURNHOUT.

Active patrolling by both sides continues from north of AACHEN to the LUNEVILLE area. Our troops are meeting stiff opposition from German pillboxes and strong points near HURTGEN, southeast of STOLBERG.

West of METZ, an enemy counter-attack was contained in the vicinity of GRAVELOTTE. Other counter-attacks were dispersed near COINCOURT and BEZANGE, northeast of LUNEVILLE, with heavy losses to the enemy.

In the CALAIS area, our troops closing in on the town across the flooded ground to the west, were given close support by fighter-bombers. A concentrated attack or fortified positions in the town was made by heavy bombers, one of which is missing.

Over 1,100 heavy bombers with a strong fighter escort attacked industrial targets at COLOGNE, a synthetic oil plant at LUDWIGSHAFEN, a tank factory at KASSEL, an ordnance factory at MAINZ and railway yards at LUDWIGSHAFEN, MAINZ and COLOGNE. Strong fighter opposition and intense flak were encountered.

Thirty-six enemy aircraft were destroyed in combat and five more on the ground. Forty-two bombers and seven fighters are missing.

Beginning on September 22, the 5. Panzerarmee launched several attacks but American counter-attacks halted them all. The German battle-groups suffering heavy losses and on September 28 Communiqué No. 173 did not exaggerate the facts when it reported that 'counter-attacks were dispersed near Coincourt and Bézange with heavy losses to the enemy'.

With the left wing of the Allied armies having captured Le Havre (see page 173), and found Dieppe undefended, the First Canadian Army went on to clear the coastal area up to Bruges. *Left:* Men of the South Saskatchewan Regiment, 2nd Canadian Infantry Division, pause for a break in Nieuwpoort. L-R: Corporal S. J. R. Wilson, Private P. J. Kraft and Private H. E. Looker. *Right:* The first house at the end of Pelikaanstraat, the western entrance of Nieuport, still stands unchanged.

COMMUNIQUE No. 174 September 29

Allied troops have continued to strengthen the flanks of the NIJMEGEN salient. Enemy counter-attacks from SCHIJNDEL were driven back and our forces made a limited advance towards HERTOGENBOSCH.

Our bridgehead over the ANTWERP—TURNHOUT canal was extended.

Fighters and fighter-bombers gave close support to our ground forces in Holland and attacked railway targets and shipping in the Scheldt estuary. Two enemy aircraft were destroyed. Road and rail communications at EMMERICH, across the German frontier east of NIJMEGEN, were hit by medium bombers.

In southeastern Luxembourg our troops have liberated REMICH. Further south we have freed PONT-SUR-SEILLE, northeast of PONT-A-MOUSSON.

East of NANCY several enemy counter-attacks were repulsed near PETTONCOURT, BEZANGE and COINCOURT and our troops, in an advance of three miles, have seized high ground in the FORET DE PARROY. A concentration of enemy troops, tanks and supplies in the forest was heavily bombed.

In the EPINAL—BELFORT sector, we have made substantial advances despite increased enemy aggressiveness. Northeast of EPINAL the villages of BULT and DESTORD were taken in an advance of several miles. A number of villages in the northwest approaches to the BELFORT pass are also in our hands. A strong counter-attack was repulsed with heavy loss to the enemy.

Our troops continued to close on CALAIS yesterday against heavy opposition. We hold all the high ground dominating the city and have captured the citadel. German fortifications in the port were attacked by heavy bombers during the morning. Gun positions at CAP GRIS-NEZ were heavily bombed in the evening.

More than 1,000 heavy bombers with a strong fighter escort, attacked industrial plants at MERSEBURG, a synthetic oil plant and railway yards at MAGDEBURG and a tank factory at KASSEL yesterday. Thirty-six enemy aircraft were destroyed in combat. Forty-nine bombers and 12 fighters are missing.

The Germans had established 'fortresses' at Boulogne, Calais and Dunkirk. The 3rd Canadian Division captured Boulogne on September 22 and then turned to Calais which fell on the 30th. As far as Dunkirk was concerned, the use of the small port was not essential and Eisenhower decided that 'it would be preferable to contain the enemy with the minimum forces necessary rather than to attempt an all-out attack'. To the north-east, the coast was in Canadian hands as far as Zeebrugge — the western bastion of the German defences south of the Scheldt. The German line there was based along two canals and although the 4th Canadian Armoured Division succeeded in establishing a bridgehead across the canals, five miles south-east of Zeebrugge, it could not be held; consequently the troops had to be withdrawn. Ken Bell pictured carriers of the Royal Regiment of Canada at Blankenberge, three miles west of Zeebrugge.

COMMUNIQUE No. 175 September 30

Enemy resistance in the CAP GRIS-NEZ area has ceased, and the long-range batteries there have been silenced.

At Calais, a truce has been arranged while the remaining civilians are evacuated from the city.

In the Scheldt estuary, enemy movements were under attack last night by light bombers.

Our troops are advancing steadily on a six-mile front west of TURNHOUT in face of stubborn opposition. German counter-attacks against our NIJMEGEN salient were repulsed north of BEST and in the vicinity of NIJMEGEN. Allied forces advancing towards HERTOGENBOSCH from the southeast are within four miles of the town.

Fighters and fighter-bombers closely supported our ground forces and attacked transportation targets in Holland. There was considerable opposition in the air and according to reports so far received, 31 enemy aircraft were shot down by our fighters, four of which are missing.

Patrol activity continued from the AACHEN area to the Luxembourg— German frontier, with enemy artillery fire on a slightly decreased scale.

Troop concentrations and strong points southeast of AACHEN were attacked by medium and fighter-bombers.

Allied units made a local attack near HURTGEN, southeast of STOLBERG. Further south our troops made limited progress southwest of PRUM against enemy fortifications, eight of which were reduced in one attack.

In southeastern Luxembourg we have liberated MOMPACH and WASSERBILLIG. HAUTE-KONTZ, six miles south of REMICH, has been freed.

West of METZ, an enemy thrust in the vicinity of GRAVELOTTE was repulsed. Concentrated enemy artillery, mortar and small-arms fire were later directed against our troops in this area. Two German counter-attacks were repulsed near the FORET DE GREMECEY, 14 miles northeast of NANCY.

In the VOSGES foothills, the village of ST GORGON, just south of the communication center of RAMBERVILLERS, was taken. Our positions west and northwest of BELFORT were improved against intensified enemy resistance.

The offensive against the enemy's railway system supplying the battle zone was continued. Medium and light bombers struck at railway targets at GELDERN, EUSKIRCHEN, PRUM, BITBURG and SAARBRUCKEN and rolling stock in the Rhineland was hit by fighter-bombers.

After weeks of painful combat in the hedgerows followed by the break-out and swift pursuit across France, by the end of September the Allies appeared close to strike at the heart of Germany. *Left:* September had seen the symbolic moment when Allied soldiers first crossed the frontier into Germany (see pages 170-171), another historic photo being this one of T/5 Charles D. Hiller driving the first Jeep onto German soil. *Right:* The Roetgen railway station has since been demolished though an old signal pylon remains standing.

In 1943 when the cross-Channel invasion of France was being planned, due regard was given to the end product — the occupation of Germany. The staff of COSSAC (Chief-of-Staff to the Supreme Allied Commander), meeting in London, put forward their plan for the division of Germany between Britain, the United States and the Soviet Union. Germany proper would be divided into three 'Zones', while Berlin would be sub-divided into three further areas to be called 'Sectors'. The plan used the existing boundaries of the various German Länder (or states), giving the Soviet Union Mecklenburg, Pomerania, Brandenburg (the state surrounding Berlin), Saxony-Anhalt, Thuringia, Saxony, Silesia and East Prussia. Because US forces were to be assigned the western landing beaches in France, American forces advanced to Germany on a southern axis with the British to the north. This determined that the United States would end up occupying southern Germany — the states of Bavaria, Baden-Württemberg, Hesse and the Rhine Palatinate, while Great Britain would be in possession of the north-west: Schleswig-Holstein, Lower Saxony, the Ruhr, North Rhine-Westphalia. The Soviet Army was already entering the German territory of East Prussia although the fate of Eastern Europe had been sealed in 1943 when Roosevelt and Churchill failed to stand up to Stalin at the Teheran Conference. Using the Soviet victory in the battle of Kursk, as well as key positions on the German front, Stalin dominated the conference. Roosevelt attempted to cope with Stalin's onslaught of demands but was able to do little, and Churchill mostly argued for his Mediterranean plan instead of Operation 'Overlord'. These weaknesses and divisions played into Stalin's hands and the Western leaders agreed to accept his demands regarding Poland's post-war boundaries. The Soviet Union would keep the territory of eastern Poland which had been annexed in 1939 while Poland would be compensated for that by extending its western border at the expense of Germany.

OCTOBER 1944
PROBLEMS OF SUPPLY

On October 1 came a brief moment of frivolity. At Batterie Todt this soldier bravely demonstrated the sheer size and scale of this cross-Channel weapon, captured by the Canadians on their way to liberate Calais (see also *After the Battle* No. 29).

Shortly after the capture of Turm III (Turret 3), two French road workers decided to explore the interior using burning sticks of cordite to light the way. These ignited the cartridge store which exploded and blew the casemate apart!

COMMUNIQUE No. 176   October 1

CALAIS has been captured. The commander of the garrison was taken prisoner last midnight and by early morning the main body of defenders had surrendered. Mopping-up of scattered elements continues.

The advance northwest of TURNHOUT continued to make progress.

In all sectors in Holland there was steady fighting during yesterday, with the situation generally unchanged. Fighters and fighter-bombers attacked railway wagons and transportation targets. Enemy counter-attacks on the west of our salient continued and northeast of NIJMEGEN there has been heavy fighting. Communications at ARNHEM and near GOCH, across the German frontier to the east, were attacked by escorted medium bombers. Trains, barges and motor transport in the Ruhr and northern Holland were attacked by light bombers during last night.

Yesterday strongly escorted heavy bombers, in very great strength, pounded the railway yards at HAMM, MUNSTER, and BIELEFELD in western Germany. Along the German frontier bordering southern Holland and Belgium, slight advances were made southeast of ROETGEN and southwest of PRUM, where several pillboxes were destroyed and a number of prisoners taken.

Several small enemy counter-attacks northeast of NANCY and at JALLAUCOURT were repulsed.

Northeast of EPINAL, the town of RAMBERVILLERS has been reached by our forces against light resistance. Local gains were made east of the Moselle river in this sector. The enemy has been launching counter-attacks and has intensified artillery fire.

Then at Calais itself the tallest man in the German army — a 7ft 3in circus performer named Jakob Nacken — was taken prisoner by a Canadian soldier, the 5ft 6in Corporal Bob Roberts *(above)*. 'I never knew his name', says Bob, 'only that he was a lance-corporal. But he spoke very good English and one of my mates later asked him where he learned it and he said he used to be in the circus in America.'

Northwest of BELFORT a number of violent counter-attacks were repulsed and our positions improved.

And the 'human cannonball' act was demonstrated at Batterie Lindemann by Private C. D. Walker to the amusement of Lieutenant M. G. Aubut. Unfortunately the whole of the battery now lies beneath the spoil excavated to bore the Channel Tunnel.

COMMUNIQUE No. 177   October 2

Allied troops have strengthened the Dutch salient, by an advance north of OSS which cleared the enemy from the banks of the river Maas. Northeast of NIJMEGEN we have repulsed attacks by enemy infantry and armor.

To the southwest, our forces making further progress west of TURNHOUT, captured the village of BRECHT and are three miles north of MERKSPLAS.

Fighters and fighter-bombers attacked troop concentrations, guns, and transportation targets in support of our ground forces in Holland. Other fighters flew offensive patrols.

Active patrolling was maintained along the German border from AACHEN to southeastern Luxembourg.

Air Marshal Sir Arthur Coningham, AOC of the RAF's Second Tactical Air Force, was sceptical of the 'wasteful destruction of habitations and the unavoidable heavy loss of life of friendly nationals in the occupied areas'. Experience of heavy bombing in Sicily, at Cassino, and more recently, at Caen, Saint-Lô, Villers-Bocage and Le Havre led to, as he phrased it, 'the damaged areas [being] actually improved as centres of defence by snipers and special detachments of the enemy.' And, as occurred at Boulogne, the ground over which the troops had to cross was so choked with rubble and craters that it impeded and even halted the advance of the armoured columns. This is the Quai Gambetta where in spite of the devastation, the bunkers were still intact. This Canadian soldier still appears wary of hidden snipers two days after the surrender. Other fortresses on the Atlantic coast like Lorient and St Nazaire were isolated and left to surrender in May 1945 (see *After the Battle* Nos. 48 and 55).

In the area northeast of NANCY our troops advanced into the FORET DE GREMECEY and occupied the high ground around FRESNES-EN-SAULNOIS and COUTURES. A strong counter-attack near JALLAUCOURT was repulsed.

Local gains were made in the EPINAL sector against strong resistance. Artillery fire was particularly heavy. The town of ST JEAN-DU-MARCHE is in our hands.

Mopping-up at CALAIS has been completed.

'The bombing of friendly towns during the campaign, and the insistence by the Army Commanders that it was a military necessity, caused me more personal worry and sorrow than I can say. My resistance, apart from humanitarian grounds, was due to a conviction, since confirmed, that in most cases we were harming Allies and ourselves eventually more than the enemy. I thought, also, of the good name of our forces, and particularly of the Air Force. It is a sad fact that the Air Forces will get practically all the blame for destruction which, in almost every case, was due to Army demands. On many occasions, owing to the organisation of command, I was over-ruled and then came the "blotting" by strategic bombers who, on their experience with German targets tended to over-hit. Ample factual evidence will now be forthcoming, and I hope that, in future, it will not be thought that the sight and sound of bombers, and their uplift effect on morale, is proportional to the damage they do to the enemy.'

Overloon, ten miles inside Holland north of Venray, was badly damaged by the time it fell on October 2, these first pictures not being released until later in the month. The unit marking for the Royal Ulster Rifles was deleted by the censor.

Literally every house in Overloon has been replaced since October 1944. Even the church no longer stands on this corner.

COMMUNIQUE No. 178   October 3

Allied infantry and tanks have launched an attack in the area north of AACHEN. Our troops have crossed the Wurm river and the attack is meeting strong resistance from pillboxes and enemy artillery and mortar fire. In the area west of HURTGEN an enemy counter-attack was contained with no ground lost.

The attack across the Wurm river followed an intensive air bombardment and artillery barrage. Escorted medium and fighter-bombers gave close support by attacking gun positions, troop concentrations and communications. Other fighter-bombers went for transportation targets in the Ruhr and in Holland, and approximately 1,200 escorted heavy bombers attacked industrial targets in the KASSEL and COLOGNE areas and a rail yard at HAMM. From these operations 12 bombers and seven fighters are missing. Last night, light bombers continued attacks on transportation targets in northwestern Germany.

Our ground forces in the Dutch salient advanced several miles towards MEIJEL and other units freed OVERLOON in an advance against heavy resistance. Several enemy tanks and numerous anti-tank guns have been destroyed in the area and we are in contact with strong bodies of enemy.

Southeast of ARNHEM, escorted medium bombers attacked strong points and fighters and fighter-bombers gave close support to ground troops.

On the west of the salient, we have extended our hold on the north bank of the ANTWERP—TURNHOUT canal west of ST LENAARTS. Progress was also made northwest of TURNHOUT.

In southeastern Luxembourg, our troops have reached the outskirts of GREVENMACHER on the Moselle river. Northeast of NANCY, the FORET DE GREMECEY has been cleared.

Our troops have pushed ahead at a number of places in the EPINAL sector, encountering stiff opposition.

Further south, RONCHAMP, west of BELFORT, was freed.

German efforts to move reinforcements to advanced units were checked with heavy losses to the enemy.

In 1945 members of the British 3rd Division, which had been responsible for the capture of Overloon, helped local Dutchmen set up a museum on the actual battlefield to the east of the village. The first exhibits were this Sherman 'flail' *(left)* and Panther *(right)*, both of which had been knocked out in the fighting (see *After the Battle* No. 9).

General Eisenhower: 'With the completion of the Market-Garden operation the Northern Group of Armies was instructed to undertake the opening of Antwerp as a matter of the first priority. While the city and port installations had fallen virtually intact to XXX Corps on 4 September, the harbor had proved and was to continue to prove useless to us until the Scheldt Estuary had been cleared of mines and South Beveland and Walcheren Island, commanding the sea lane to the harbor, had been reduced. The operation to achieve this involved the employment of amphibious forces, and the joint naval, air and ground force planning was immediately undertaken and worked out during the latter part of September and early October at the Headquarters of the Canadian First Army.' The dykes themselves had been constructed over a period of hundreds of years; now they were to be demolished in an instant. Although the territory belonged to one of the Allies, the Dutch government-in-exile in London was not given prior information on the full extent of the bombing operation before its execution, possibly because they would have refused to give permission. On October 2, the day before the first raid, the civilian population were warned by a leaflet drop and by radio that an attack was imminent and that they should take shelter.

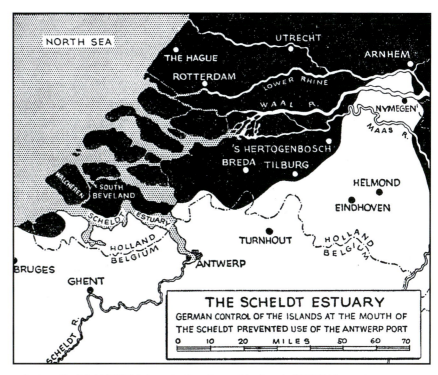

COMMUNIQUE No. 179   October 4

Allied troops advancing north of the ANTWERP—TURNHOUT canal have reached a point eight miles northeast of ANTWERP on the road to BREDA. North of TURNHOUT, we have taken BAARLE-NASSAU. East of TURNHOUT, our forces are in the village of REUSEL.

Between the Maas and the Waal the villages of WAMEL and DREUMEL have been freed. In the area of OVERLOON, a German counter-attack was repulsed by our troops with an estimated 50 per cent loss to the enemy.

Allied forces attacking in the area north of AACHEN are advancing slowly against varying resistance from German artillery and small arms, and from pillboxes.

Our troops have penetrated to UBACH three miles south of GEILENKIRCHEN and have advanced against heavy resistance in the area immediately southwest of UBACH. Gains have been made in the vicinity of MERKSTEIN, north of KERKRADE.

Just south of AACHEN, intense tank and mortar fire has been directed against our units, and in the area west of HURTGEN small enemy counter-attacks were repulsed at three points.

Fighters and fighter-bombers supported ground forces and attacked transportation targets in Holland and the Rhineland.

In southeastern Luxembourg, our troops have gained high ground just west of ECHTERNACH and GREVENMACHER. Farther south, high ground was taken in the vicinity of MAIZIERES-LES-METZ, on the west side of the Moselle northwest of METZ.

Five miles southwest of METZ, our forces have entered FORT DRIANT after a successful assault.

East of NANCY, the enemy has been forced back in the FORET DE PARROY by our advance which has gained more than a mile in some sectors. Our armored elements repulsed a counter-attack by enemy infantry and tanks in the vicinity of ANGLEMONT, five miles southwest of BACCARAT.

Northeast of EPINAL, our troops, favored by clearing weather, made new gains and occupied several villages. These included GRANDVILLERS, DEYCIMONT and LEPANGES.

Farther south, resistance was more stubborn and enemy counter-attacks have been more frequent.

Limited progress was made in the area northwest of BELFORT.

The sea dyke near WESTKAPELLE on the Dutch island of Walcheren was breached yesterday in a two-hour attack by waves of heavy bombers escorted by fighters. A gap 120 yards wide was made in the dyke and extensive flooding of enemy positions resulted. None of the aircraft is missing from this operation.

More than 1,000 heavy bombers, with a strong fighter escort, attacked the Daimler-Benz factory at GAGGENAU, tank works at NURNBERG and airfields at LACHEN SPEYERDORF and GIEBELSTADT. The escorting fighters also strafed airfields in Germany. Eleven bombers are missing.

The opening shot of Operation 'Infatuate' was the preparatory bombing of the sea wall at Westkapelle on October 3 when a breach was made of over 100 yards. (For more details on the Walcheren operation see *After the Battle* No. 36.)

October 5 and Canadian troops — Essex Scottish, 2nd Infantry Brigade — of the 2nd Canadian Division, move north for the coming operation. Here they are crossing the frontier at Putte on the highway from Antwerp to Bergen op Zoom.

On the same day but 100 miles away at Frelenberg between Aachen and Geilenkirchen in Germany, GIs — most probably from the 30th Division — warily cross deserted Geilenkirchener Strasse as XIX Corps break through the Siegfried Line.

COMMUNIQUE No. 180   October 5

North of ANTWERP, the enemy is being driven from the perimeter forts. KAPELLEN and STABROEK are in our hands.

Further progress has been made north and northeast of TURNHOUT and we are advancing north of POPPEL and BAARLE-NASSAU. The capture of HILVARENBEEK has brought us to within five miles of TILBURG.

South of ARNHEM our troops have gained some ground in heavy fighting. On the east of the salient in the area of OVERLOON, we are moving ahead slowly, hindered by marshy terrain and enemy mines.

Allied infantry, supported by armor, is making slow progress near UBACH, north of AACHEN, against heavy opposition from enemy small arms, mortars, anti-tank guns and artillery. A German tank attack was repulsed by our infantry in the vicinity of HERBACH.

Fighters and fighter-bombers supported ground forces during the day and went for transportation targets in western Germany. Night bombers attacked trains and barges in Holland and northwestern Germany.

Southwest of METZ, our troops fighting within FORT DRIANT are meeting stubborn resistance from the enemy who is defending from dug-in positions and pillboxes.

Further south, an enemy counter-attack was repulsed in the vicinity of SIVRY, north of NANCY.

In the EPINAL sector we made slight local gains southeast of ST AME. Elsewhere, strong enemy resistance was encountered.

West of BELFORT, a pocket of resistance has been mopped up in the RONCHAMP area where the enemy continued to fight stubbornly.

At DUNKIRK, a truce has been arranged to allow the evacuation of civilians.

Eupen, a Belgian frontier town which was incorporated into the Reich in 1940, was retaken in the drive on Aachen. A *Planet News* photographer was on hand on October 6 to record the removal of the Nazi insignia from the front of the police station.

COMMUNIQUE No. 181   October 6

Allied troops have crossed the Dutch frontier north of ANTWERP in the neighborhood of PUTTE. We have continued to make progress north of BAARLE-NASSAU and POPPEL. Gains made along the HILVARENBEEK road have brought us within three miles of TILBURG.

Stubborn German resistance from strong points is impeding our forces in the area of OVERLOON. Two enemy counter-attacks southwest of the town were contained.

Fighters and fighter-bombers and a small force of medium bombers, operating in close support of our ground forces in Holland, attacked enemy troops and strong points and destroyed a number of locomotives, railway trucks and barges in Holland and Germany. According to reports so far received, six enemy aircraft were destroyed in the air.

North of AACHEN, our forces have advanced about a mile east of HERBACH against strong opposition. Near UBACH, we have made progress against heavy artillery and anti-tank fire, and our troops have reached BEGGENDORF, one and one-half miles to the east.

South of AACHEN, patrol activity continues along the front, and considerable enemy artillery fire has been falling in and around MONSCHAU.

Our troops fighting in FORT DRIANT have been mortared and shelled by the enemy. Fighting has been in progress near SIVRY, north of NANCY, where earlier an enemy counter-attack was repulsed.

In support of our troops near NANCY, fighter-bombers attacked troops and fortified buildings. Other fighter-bombers hit the railway station at SARREBOURG, destroyed a number of motor vehicles in this same area, and struck at barges and canal installations on the Marne—Rhine canal east of NANCY.

Heavy bombers in very great strength, strongly escorted by fighters, bombed railway yards at COLOGNE and RHEINE and German air force installations at HANDORF, LIPPSTADT, PADERBORN and MUNSTER/LODDENHEIDE. The escorting fighters destroyed 15 enemy aircraft on the ground and one in the air, and strafed locomotives and goods trucks. Thirteen bombers and five fighters are missing.

WILHELMSHAVEN was attacked by a strong force of heavy bombers with fighter cover. One bomber is missing.

Nineteen thousand civilians have been evacuated form DUNKIRK under a truce arranged for that purpose.

The building still stands at Herbesthalerstrasse 12-14 as the local and federal police station for Eupen. The eagle was sculpted by a local stonemason and has been preserved although not on public display. (Photo by Patrick Schumacher.)

All the while the ground forces were pressing ahead, the war was being pursued overhead. On October 7, anti-aircraft claimed to have destroyed around 25 German aircraft the previous day. Meanwhile the Eighth Air Force despatched over 850 B-17s and 400 B-24s to bomb industrial targets in northern Germany. The 1,200 bombers were escorted by nearly 800 fighters.

COMMUNIQUE No. 182   October 7

Allied troops have crossed the Leopold Canal in spite of heavy mortar and machine-gun fire. North of ANTWERP our troops continued to advance into Holland. Progress has also been made north of POPPEL and HILVARENBEEK.

Northwest of NIJMEGEN, there has been heavy local fighting between the Neder-Rijn and the Waal.

Our forces in the UBACH area, north of AACHEN, have gained ground to the north and northeast reaching a point a half mile north of BEGGENDORF. We have also advanced one and a half miles along the road running southeast from UBACH. A counter-attack in strength by enemy infantry and tanks was repulsed during the morning near HERBACH, with no material change in the line. Out of nearly 50 enemy planes over the UBACH area, an estimated 25 were destroyed by our anti-aircraft artillery.

Our troops within FORT DRIANT continue to meet stubborn resistance, and have been subjected to heavy artillery fire. Near SIVRY, north of NANCY, the enemy regained some ground in a counter-attack. To the east of NANCY, sporadic artillery fire has been directed against our forces.

Sterkrade, north of Oberhausen, was a manufacturing centre for steel products like turbines, compressors, pumps, lifts and coal-mining equipment, and the Gutehoffnungshütte concern alone was producing five million tons of coal each year. It was also the location of a vitally important synthetic oil plant that British Naval Intelligence believed was producing 130,000 tons of fuel per annum from coal, lignite or tar oil. RAF Bomber Command followed up the American daylight raid on the night of October 6/7 which marked the opening shot of the Second Battle of the Ruhr.

Allied troops have advanced more than half way through the FORET DE PARROY, east of LUNEVILLE, against stubborn resistance. A counter-attack by enemy infantry with some armored support was repulsed in the southeastern part of the forest. ANGLEMONT, southwest of BACCARAT, has been freed after bitter fighting.

Southeast of EPINAL, in the vicinity of CLEURIE, the enemy has been driven from a heavily fortified stone quarry which was delaying our advance. Elsewhere resistance to our progress is stiff.

In the Vosges foothills our troops are now on three sides of the town of LE THILLOT.

West of BELFORT further progress has been made through wooded terrain.

A fuel dump at AMERSFOORT, railway targets at HENGELO and DUREN, an airfield and barracks at DUREN, and communications at ARNHEM were attacked by medium and light bombers yesterday. Fighters and fighter-bombers also attacked locomotives, barges and motor transport in Holland and western Germany. After dark, light bombers attacked railway yards at AMERSFOORT and trains and barges in northern Holland and western Germany.

Very strong forces of escorted heavy bombers in daylight yesterday attacked oil plants at SCHOLVEN-BUER, STERKRADE and HARBURG; an aircraft engine plant and an ordnance depot in HAMBURG; a tank assembly plant, a military depot, and ordnance depot and an aircraft engine plant in BERLIN; airfields at STARGARD and WENZENDORF and a fighter assembly plant at NEUBRANDENBURG. In the course of these operations 20 enemy aircraft were shot down. Thirty-six seaplanes were destroyed at Baltic stations and three enemy aircraft were destroyed on the ground by fighters which had provided a part of the escort. Twenty-eight bombers and ten fighters are missing.

Last night heavy bombers in great strength attacked DORTMUND and BREMEN. BERLIN was also bombed.

The first set-piece attack against the German Westwall in the Übach-Palenberg sector, eight miles north of Aachen, was preceded by carpet-bombing the defences although officers of the 30th Division were nervous following the disastrous incident near Saint-Lô (see pages 95-97). Although no American soldiers were killed in the bombing on October 2, one group of medium bombers hit a town in Belgium, 28 miles away, killing 34 civilians! The attack on Übach by the 117th Infantry began the following day. The Germans poured round after round of mortar and artillery fire into the town, some of the GIs believing that it was the heaviest shelling they had experienced since Normandy. In house-to-house fighting, the 117th suffered heavy casualties before the town was taken.

COMMUNIQUE No. 183   October 8

Allied troops moving towards the southern bank of the Scheldt estuary from our bridgehead over the Leopold canal, are engaged in heavy fighting. North of ANTWERP further progress has been made towards the road leading to the island of Walcheren. Here the sea dykes at FLUSHING were attacked yesterday without loss by a strong force of escorted heavy bombers.

North of NIJMEGEN we have freed the village of MALDEREN. Fighting continues in the area of OPHEUSDEN.

Fighters and fighter-bombers closely supported our ground forces in Holland and attacked transportation targets in Holland and western Germany. Rocket-firing fighters sank a medium-sized coastal vessel near the HOOK OF HOLLAND.

Medium bombers struck at bridges in the ARNHEM area and a railway yard at HENGELO. Heavy bombers, in very great strength with fighter escort, struck at enemy supplies and communications at EMMERICH and CLEVE. Five bombers are missing.

In the AACHEN sector, our troops have captured BEGGENDORF and BASWEILER east and southeast of UBACH. Forces which advanced to the outskirts of ALSDORF encountered decreasing resistance and lessening artillery fire. On the northern fringe of this advance, we have occupied WALDENRATH.

Good progress in the forest of HURTGEN has taken our troops to less than two miles of the village of HURTGEN.

In Luxembourg, we have cleared the enemy from ECHTERNACH and WORMELDANGE.

North of METZ our troops have entered MAIZIERES-LES-METZ. Heavy fighting continued in FORT DRIANT where we hold the northwest and southwest corners of the fort.

Along the whole front from AACHEN to NANCY, fighter-bombers in strength supported our troops and attacked transportation targets behind enemy lines. Medium bombers hit railway targets at EUSKIRCHEN, TRIER and DILLINGEN.

In the Vosges foothills our troops captured two villages but lost ground to a strong enemy counter-attack northeast of EPINAL.

Further south, newly-won positions in the LE THILLOT area were consolidated and numerous counter-attacks were repulsed.

More than 1,400 heavy bombers, escorted by 900 fighters, hit synthetic oil plants at POLITZ, RUHLAND, MAGDEBURG, BOHLEN, MERSEBURG and LUTZKENDORF; tank plants at MAGDEBURG and KASSEL; aero-engine, locomotive and chemical works at KASSEL and CLAUSTHAL ZELLERFELD; an aircraft repair depot and motor transport plant at ZWICKAU; and an airfield at NORDHAUSEN. In the course of these operations 33 enemy aircraft were shot down and 16 destroyed on the ground. Fifty-six bombers and 15 fighters are missing.

October 7 and the battle is over. Pfc William Gregory takes stock of captured booty in Baesweiler, four miles east of Übach. The 30th Division and 2nd Armored Division had suffered more than 1,800 casualties including nearly 200 killed but the breach in the Westwall was now six miles long and four and a half miles deep.

COMMUNIQUE No. 184   October 9

In the advance around the Scheldt estuary, our troops north of ANTWERP have freed HOOGERHEIDE and KALMPTHOUT. To the south of the estuary there has been very heavy fighting in the bridgehead over the Leopold Canal.

On the west side of our Dutch salient there was some local fighting east of HERTOGENBOSCH.

Allied forces have closed the gap northeast of AACHEN to about four miles. Troops moving from the north have gained about a mile southwest and southeast of OFDEN, and units which attacked northward on Sunday morning, after a preliminary bombardment, have advanced 3,000 yards to VERLAUTENHEIDE, three miles northeast of AACHEN, and to a hill half a mile east of HAAREN.

Just north of this area, our forces have overcome stubborn enemy resistance to seize OIDTWEILER, one and one-half miles northeast of ALSDORF which was captured earlier.

Throughout the AACHEN sector, we are encountering considerable enemy artillery, small-arms and machine-gun fire.

Southwest of HURTGEN, we have renewed our advance in rugged terrain, meeting stubborn opposition from German field defenses. An enemy counter-attack was repulsed.

In the METZ sector, we have cleared the enemy from the northern half of MAIZIERES-LES-METZ. Hard fighting continues at FORT DRIANT.

Our forces have attacked north and northeast of NANCY and have liberated the towns of MOIVRONS, AJONCOURT, JEANDELAINCOURT and CHENICOURT.

In the Vosges foothills, we have taken prisoners and gained more ground against stubborn resistance around LE THILLOT. The village of RAMONCHAMP was taken after hard fighting.

Fighters and fighter-bombers attacked enemy troops and gun positions yesterday. In addition, locomotives, rail cars and airfields were strafed and rail tracks cut in western Germany. Three enemy aircraft were destroyed on the ground.

One hundred and twenty-five miles to the south, the Third Army was locked with an assortment of German troops manning the fortress city of Metz in Alsace which Hitler had annexed in 1940. A series of forts built between 1899 and 1912 ringed the town, one of the most fought over being Fort Driant, named Feste Kronprinz by the Germans. It proved a very hard nut to crack and although it was shelled and bombed from September 27 on, and Company B of the 11th Infantry (5th Division) actually entered the south-western corner of Driant on October 3, the GIs were forced to pull out ten days later. The failure to capture the fort was the first publicised reverse of the Third Army.

Medium and light bombers attacked railway bridges at BAD MUNSTER, EUSKIRCHEN and AHRWEILER; a railway junction at NOHFELDEN and enemy strong points at METZ, JULICH and BAAL.

Total American casualties in the Fort Driant battle were 64 killed, 547 wounded and 187 missing. They left the fort on the night of October 12/13, the garrison finally surrendering on December 8. Today, because of uncleared explosives, the fort is off limits.

By October 10, Aachen (Aix-la-Chapelle in French), largely in ruins from air attacks, was encircled by the First Army so its commander, Lieutenant General Courtney Hodges, decided to give the Germans a chance to give up. Marching under the protection of a white flag carried by Pfc Kenneth Kading, 1st Lieutenant Cedric Lafley (right) with 1st Lieutenant William Boehme as interpreter, advance along Trierer Strasse bearing a copy of the surrender terms: 'Aachen is completely surrounded by Americans who are sufficiently equipped with both planes and artillery to destroy the city if necessary. We shall take the city, either by surrender or by attacking and destroying it. Unconditional surrender will require the surrender of all armed bodies, the cessation of all hostile acts, the removal of mines and prepared demolitions. It is not intended to molest the civil population and needlessly sacrifice human lives. But if the city is not completely and promptly surrendered the ground forces and air forces will proceed ruthlessly to reduce it to submission. There is no middle course of choice, and the responsibility is yours. Your answer must be delivered within 24 hours.' The military commander of Aachen was Oberstleutnant Maximilian Leyherr, one of the 246. Infanterie-Division's regimental commanders, and he dutifully rejected the ultimatum in accordance with Hitler's orders that the city must be held to the last man.

When the deadline for a reply expired on October 11, four groups of IX Tactical Air Command P-38s and P-47s — about 300 aircraft — opened the assault, dropping over 60 tons of bombs on targets in the outskirts. At the same time, 12 battalions of VII Corps and 1st Division artillery opened up a bombardment of over 5,000 rounds (170 tons). Not to be left out, combat engineers on the heights south of the city, towed a tram to the top of a hill where they loaded it full of explosives set with a time fuze before sending it back down the tram lines into the city. The new weapon which the engineers dubbed the 'V-13' exploded prematurely but not to be outdone they tried again and this time the tram detonated in the city proper. Meantime, a more conventional approach was being made by these M10s of Company A of the 634th Tank Destroyer Battalion to shell German observation posts with their 3-inch guns.

VERLAUTENHEIDE. In the HURTGEN area we made slight gains southeast of the town against very heavy resistance.

Weather curtailed air operations over the battle area. A small force of medium bombers attacked a railway bridge at EUSKIRCHEN. Armed reconnaissance was flown by fighters and fighter-bombers.

North of METZ, an enemy counter-attack was repulsed at MAIZIERES.

Advances in the area north of NANCY have reached LETRICOURT. The BOIS DE LA FOURASSE, two miles west of LETRICOURT, is being cleared of the enemy. Several more towns in this sector including SIVRY, LIXIERES and SERRIÈRES, have been liberated.

In the Vosges foothills, our advance has freed more villages. Hard fighting continues particularly in the LE THILLOT sector where a number of strong points were overcome. Heavy losses were inflicted and several hundred prisoners taken.

East of EPINAL, the enemy was forced from LAVELINE and HERPELMONT.

More than 1,100 heavy bombers, escorted by very strong forces of fighters, yesterday attacked military targets in southwest Germany. Most of the bombing was concentrated in the FRANKFURT, COBLENZ and MAINZ regions. Bombing was by instrument, through heavy clouds. In the course of these operations, two enemy aircraft were destroyed. Five bombers and three fighters are missing.

Last night, BOCHUM, in the Ruhr, was strongly attacked by heavy bombers. Objectives in WILHELMSHAVEN were also bombed.

COMMUNIQUE No. 185   October 10

Heavy fighting continues in the Allied bridgehead over the Leopold Canal. Enemy attempts to eliminate the bridgehead were repulsed.

Our troops which made a landing early on Monday morning of the south shore of the Scheldt estuary have made good progress.

North of ANTWERP, local gains were made.

There has been little change in position in the AACHEN area. In the vicinity of OFDEN, north of AACHEN, we made an advance of about 600 yards and later contained a counter-attack by enemy tanks. Our forces advancing from the south in the area east of AACHEN, held their positions against several counter-attacks near

With no location given, this picture took us some time to track down to the suburb of Forst just south of the railway at Rothe Erde. Signal Corps photographer T/4 Leo B. Moran took his picture from an upstairs window on Schönrathstrasse but we had to make do with a ground level shot.

The American Ninth Air Force, charged primarily with support of the ground forces, began to be established in France from June 17. By the end of July, all the Ninth Air Force fighter groups had bases in Normandy and the bomber groups moved to the Continent following the Saint-Lô break-out. The airfields in France were mostly those which had been used by the Luftwaffe and the first bomb group to move from England was the 394th on August 28. They took over Tour-en-Bessin airfield (A-13) near Bayeux and then moved on September 25 to Orléans-Bricy (A-50). On October 10 the 394th moved further north to Cambrai/Niergnies (A-74) *(right)* where they remained for the next seven months, carrying out 132 missions. Ironically, this very airfield had been bombed by the group a month before D-Day! Each of the American armies had a Tactical Air Command (TAC) in direct support, just as the 21st Army Group had the Second Tactical Air Force at its disposal. In addition to the IX and XIX TACs which had supported the First and Third Armies in the drive across France, on September 14 the XXIX TAC was activated in anticipation of the Ninth Army's move from Brittany to the main battlefront. This new air command then became operational on October 1. Depending on the demands of the ground forces, units of the Ninth Air Force were transferred from one command to another and at times the fighter-bombers were combined to meet critical situations. On September 21, IX and XIX TAC were told to concentrate on the German railway system west of the Rhine, rail-cutting being the priority. Fair weather from October 6-8 enabled medium bombers to interdict in the Aachen operation but later missions during the battle for the city were either cancelled, abandoned or recalled because of bad weather at their bases or cloud cover at the target. Nevertheless IX TAC mounted 6,000 sorties during the Aachen campaign.

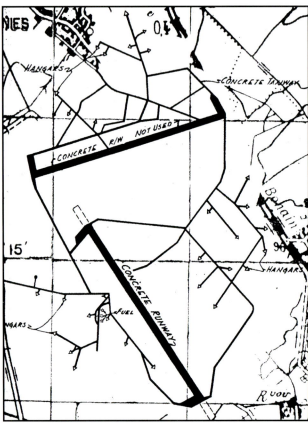

This map was drawn by IX Engineer Command in October 1944.

Cambrai/Niergnies airfield has since been very much enlarged.

COMMUNIQUE No. 186 October 11

The Allied force which landed on the south bank of the Scheldt estuary has improved its positions east of BRESKENS. Fighters and fighter-bombers attacked enemy strong points in the area yesterday. Elsewhere air operations were restricted by weather.

Heavy fighting continues in the area of the Leopold Canal bridgehead. North of ANTWERP, we have cut the main road leading from the mainland to Zuid Beveland.

A sharp enemy attack near DODEWAARD, on the Waal, was repulsed yesterday morning.

A 24-hour ultimatum to surrender was served on the German forces in AACHEN at 1015 hours Tuesday. Earlier, units in the northern arm of our encircling movement had captured SCHAUFENBERG and BARDENBERG and advanced to WURSELEN. Other units moving up from the south and east had reached HAAREN and had cut the main AACHEN—COLOGNE highway. By noon, the enemy was being mopped up in the northern part of HAAREN. German counter-attacks were repulsed at Crucifix Hill, southeast of HAAREN, and in the area of BARDENBERG.

Hard fighting is in progress southwest of HURTGEN, and our troops have made gains. Patrol activity and sporadic artillery fire are reported along the frontier in the area of MONSCHAU.

House-to-house fighting is in progress in MAIZIERES-LES-METZ.

East of LUNEVILLE, our troops in the FORET DE PARROY have advanced about 1,500 yards.

East of EPINAL, our positions were improved despite increased enemy artillery fire.

After hard fighting in the LE THILLOT sector, our troops established a substantial bridgehead across the Moselotte river. Heavy losses were inflicted on the enemy. Several strong points near LE THILLOT have been taken against stiff resistance.

The forests of LONGEGOUTTE and GEHAN have been largely mopped up.

Progress has been made in the CHAMPAGNEY region west of BELFORT.

Bridges on the roads to Aachen. It appears that railway bridges became vulnerable to both sides: the Allied air forces knocking them down to hinder the retreat and the Germans destroying them during their withdrawal to block the Allied advance.

COMMUNIQUE No. 187　　OCTOBER 12

The Allied bridgehead over the Leopold Canal was held firmly yesterday and our landings on the south shore of the Scheldt were reinforced. Fighter and fighter-bombers continued their support of our troops in the BRESKENS area. Fortified positions at OOSTBURG, SLUIS and SCHOONDIJKE were hit with rockets and bombs. Heavy bombers with fighter cover attacked a dyke near VEERE and gun emplacements on the island of Walcheren and the Dutch mainland opposite FLUSHING. One bomber is missing.

West of ARNHEM, the enemy has withdrawn from one area of the south bank of the Neder-Rijn. Strong points, troop concentrations and tanks in the ARNHEM area were attacked by fighters and fighter-bombers in support of our ground forces.

Our troops encircling AACHEN renewed their attack on the city following the refusal of the German garrison to surrender. The city was bombarded for five hours by medium bombers. Fighter-bombers attacked enemy troops southeast of the city.

North of AACHEN, enemy infantry and tanks were engaged in BARDENBERG. Counter-attacks were beaten off in the HAAREN area and heavy losses were inflicted by our infantry, with close artillery support.

Southeast of AACHEN, our troops have advanced against stubborn resistance to cut the MONSCHAU—DUREN road about one mile southwest of HURTGEN.

Hard fighting continues in MAIZIERES-LES-METZ. The enemy is using the basements of houses as anti-tank positions.

We repulsed a strong counter-attack in the vicinity of LETRICOURT, north of NANCY.

'Wounded Yank is moved on a litter by companions from barnyard to medical aid station near Bardenberg'. This is the caption released with this picture although the censor has cut 'by mortar' from the original and obliterated the rank markings from the men's helmets. (For more on censorship, see SHAEF and the Press on page 510.)

In the Vosges foothills limited advances were made northeast of EPINAL and in the LE THILLOT area where, in hard fighting, enemy counter-attacks have been repulsed. The village of SAPOIS is in our hands.

The bridgehead over the Moselotte river has been extended.

Transportation targets in the Rhineland were hit by fighter-bombers. Canal locks and railway bridges in the SAARBRUCKEN area were also attacked. Heavy escorted bombers struck at military targets in the region of COLOGNE and COBLENZ. Five bombers and one fighter are missing.

Meanwhile in Holland, British infantrymen advancing along a side road near Deurne, 12 miles east of Eindhoven, come across the body of an American soldier which, the caption says, was 'killed by a Nazi sniper'. The unit markings on the armoured car have been blotted out by the SHAEF Field Press Censor. The American must have been a member of the 7th Armored Division which was in the area during the opening phase of the battle for Overloon (see page 198), possibly part of Combat Command B. The British troops could be either from the 11th Armoured Division or 15th Scottish Division.

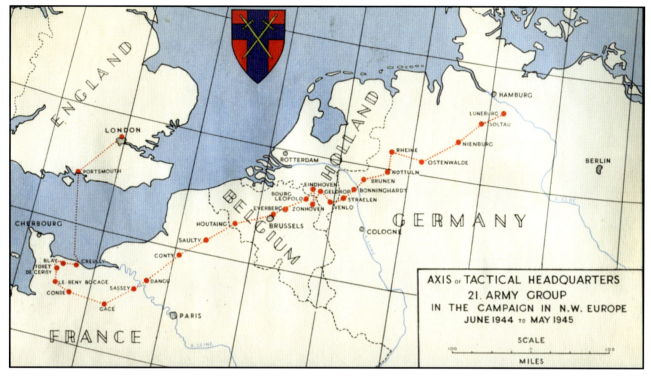

COMMUNIQUE No.188   October 13

Further reinforcements have been landed on the south shore of the Scheldt estuary east of BRESKENS. In the Leopold Canal bridgehead, the village of BIEZEN was cleared of the enemy. Heavy fighting continues in both areas. Near ANTWERP, an enemy counter-attack was repelled.

Fighters and fighter-bombers continued to support our ground forces in the BRESKENS area. Troops and strong points were hit. Fortified positions at OOSTBURG, SLUIS and SCHOONDIJKE were again attacked by rocket-firing fighters. Heavy bombers struck at gun emplacements at FORT FREDERIK-HENDRIK.

Batteries north of KNOCKE were bombed, without loss, by medium bombers. Other fighters and fighter-bombers provided support for our troops near ARNHEM and NIJMEGEN and attacked transportation targets in the AMERSFOORT and APELDOORN areas and elsewhere in Holland.

On the east side of the Dutch salient, Allied troops have retaken OVERLOON. Medium and light bombers hit road junctions at VENRAY, south of OVERLOON.

AACHEN was dive-bombed and strafed yesterday by hundreds of fighter-bombers. Other fighter-bombers attacked tanks east of AACHEN. Enemy fighters came up to give battle over the city and 12 were shot down and others damaged for the loss of four of our aircraft.

Northeast of AACHEN, a heavy enemy counter-attack, with infantry and tanks, has been launched in the BARDENBURG area. Earlier, counter-attacks from the east in the vicinity of VERLAUTENHEIDE and HAAREN were repulsed by our artillery. Fighting is still in progress at HAAREN and WURSELEN where an enemy pocket has been cleaned up. Air attacks were made during Wednesday night on our troops in the area of SCHAUFENBERG and SIERSDORF, east of ALSDORF, and increased artillery fire has been encountered in the area southeast of GEILENKIRCHEN. Four miles east of STOLBERG, our forces have advanced slightly against heavy resistance.

Further south, in the HURTGEN sector, we reached VOSSENACK but were pushed back slightly by a counter-attack.

Striking at communications in the AACHEN sector, medium and light bombers, with fighter escort, bombed a railway bridge across the river Erft at GREVENBROICH and the towns of ALDENHOVEN and LANGERWEHE. At AHRWEILER also, a rail bridge was bombed.

South of MONSCHAU, patrol activity continues and our troops are encountering sporadic artillery and mortar fire.

Near NANCY, fighter-bombers, in advance of our infantry, dropped fragmentation bombs in wooded country.

East of LUNEVILLE, our patrols have advanced to the eastern edge of the FORET DE PARROY and the town of PARROY has been cleared of enemy. Local counter-attacks have been met near COINCOURT.

In the EPINAL—BELFORT sector, our troops have made substantial gains over rugged country in the bend of the Moselotte river, north of LE THILLOT. Several villages have been taken. Heavy enemy counter-attacks were repulsed in this area as well as in the vicinity of LE THILLOT where our positions were improved.

Elsewhere in the Vosges foothills activity was limited mostly to artillery exchanges and patrolling.

Strong forces of heavy bombers, with fighter escort, attacked an aircraft component factory at BREMEN and other targets in northwest Germany. Other escorted heavy bombers struck at the synthetic oil plant at WANNE-EICKEL. Medium and light bombers attacked targets in HENNINGEN.

As the battle moved forward, so did the various army, corps and divisional headquarters. With winter approaching, tented camps were givng way to the requisition of buildings and by October the First Army was the only senior HQ still under canvas. On October 13, the 21st Army Group TAC HQ was outside Eindhoven, already having moved over a dozen times, when King George VI and General George C. Marshall, Chief-of-Staff of the US Army, was due to visit Montgomery and carry out an investure.

COMMUNIQUE No. 189   October 14

North of the Leopold Canal, Allied troops have made some progress southwards from the BIERVLIET area. The bridgehead over the canal has been slightly extended. Fighters and fighter-bombers renewed their attacks on gun emplacements and strong points in the BRESKENS area.

In the neck of the Zuid Beveland peninsula, the enemy continues to counter-attack fiercely.

In the Dutch salient, a local enemy counter-attack southeast of HERTOGENBOSCH was repulsed. North of the salient, medium bombers struck at rail targets at UTRECHT and AMERSFOORT.

Allied troops, south of OVERLOON, have advanced some 1,500 yards through difficult wooded country in the face of stiff opposition. In support of our troops in this sector, light bombers cut the railway line leading to a bridge at VENLO and destroyed the western end of the Meuse bridge at ROERMOND.

Our troops are advancing slowly in house-to-house fighting in the northeast section of AACHEN.

Fighter-bombers continued the air attack on AACHEN and also struck at rail communications in this sector. Enemy aircraft were sent up and our fighters shot down 18 of them for the loss of eight.

North of the city, in the region of BARDENBERG, the Germans, reinforced by armor, have increased their pressure, but several counter-attacks have been dispersed by our planes and artillery. Just south of KOHLSCHEID and WURSELEN, our forces are moving forward slowly against stubborn resistance from both mobile and dug-in tanks.

In the HURTGEN FOREST, near GERMETER, we are making slow progress against stiff opposition to regain ground lost earlier in a strong enemy counter-attack. Two miles southwest of GERMETER, slight advances have been made and pillboxes are being mopped up.

Medium and light bombers hit LANGERWEHE on the AACHEN—DUREN road. The bridges at MAYEN, west of COBLENZ, and at EUSKIRCHEN, were also attacked. One medium bomber is missing from these operations. Fighter-bombers struck at rail communications at a number of points in western Germany.

East of NANCY, our patrols have penetrated the FORET DE PARROY and three-quarters of the forest has now been cleared of the enemy.

Our forces have made further progress against heavy resistance in the Moselotte river bend southeast of EPINAL and have advanced over rugged terrain to the vicinity of CORNIMONT. Pressure has been maintained near LE THILLOT. Elsewhere in the Vosges foothills, activity was limited chiefly to artillery exchanges and vigorous patrolling.

Left: General Bradley: 'On October 14 as Hodges completed encirclement of the roofless city of Aachen, we assembled the US senior command at First Army's CP to greet the King of England then touring the Allied front. Hodges had pitched his CP in the mud surrounding a dilapidated chateau near the Belgian city of Verviers.' *Right:* The Château de Maison-Bois at Ensival lies on high ground two miles south of the town.

Brigadier General Charles Hart, Hodges' chief of artillery, was sent north to Montgomery's command post to escort the King across Belgium, down to the US sector. 'En route over the gutted brick roads after having breakfasted on several cups of tea', wrote General Bradley, 'Hart squirmed uncomfortably with the knowledge that his Jeep outriders would soon require a pause for roadside relief. Uncertain as to how he might explain the necessity for this stop to the King, Hart murmured that he was stopping the convoy "for a sanitary halt". When the vehicles were once again under way, the King looked to Hart and chuckled, "A sanitary halt, you say?" He turned to his equerry and laughed. "Now be sure to include that in the diary".'

Bradley continues: 'At lunch in the barren dining room where "Master" had made a grudging concession to comfort by moving it inside, Patton held the guests with a recital of his experiences in the African campaign. He spoke of the thievery of Tunisian Arabs, sipped his coffee, and declared to the King, "Why I must have shot a dozen Arabs myself". Ike looked up with a wink toward me. "How many, did you say, George?", he asked. Patton pulled on his cigar. "Well maybe it was only a half a dozen", he replied with a mischievous grin. "How many?" Ike repeated the question. George hunched his shoulders, laughed, and turned to the King. "Well, at any rate, Sir, I did boot two of them squarely in the—ah, street at Gafsa.'"

The formal line-up photo of the 13 American commanders hosting the King. Front row, L-R: General Patton, General Bradley, General Eisenhower, General Hodges, Lieutenant General William H. Simpson. Second row: Major General William B. Kean, Major General Charles E. Corlett, Major General J. Lawton Collins, Major General Leonard P. Gerow, Major General Elwood R. Quesada. Third row: Major General Leven C. Allen, Brigadier General Charles C. Hart, Brigadier General Truman C. Thorson.

COMMUNIQUE No. 190   October 15

A further crossing of the Leopold Canal was made yesterday near WATERVLIET and our troops north of the canal have been reinforced. Further east, we have advanced northwesterly around the southern end of the SAVOJAARDSPLAAT towards other Allied units which have continued to move southwards from the BIERVLIET area. Our hold on the neck of the Zuid Beveland peninsula remained firm.

Strong points, gun emplacements and communications in the BRESKENS area and in the Zuid Beveland peninsula were attacked by fighters and fighter-bombers. Railway facilities at WOENSDRECHT were bombed by fighter-bombers.

Fighters and fighter-bombers supported our ground forces in the ARNHEM—NIJMEGEN areas. Northeast of ARNHEM, medium and light bombers hit the railway bridge crossing the river at ZUTPHEN.

Southeast of OVERLOON, our forces advanced about 1,000 yards over a front of several miles against stiff opposition.

Fighters and fighter-bombers attacked artillery positions northeast of AACHEN where our troops were subjected to heavy fire in the vicinity of ALSDORF.

Nearer AACHEN we continued to advance slowly against fierce resistance from pillboxes, dug-in tanks and artillery fire and have reached points about one-half mile south of KOHLSCHEID and WURSELEN.

Our troops within the northeastern edge of the city of AACHEN have made some progress in house-to-house fighting.

In the HURTGEN area we have made gains against very heavy resistance.

General Eisenhower: 'During the month of October an administrative change had been placed in effect which was to bring the Tactical Air Forces more closely under the control of my headquarters. Prior to 15 October the Allied Expeditionary Air Force, under Air Chief Marshal Leigh-Mallory, had maintained its separate headquarters, reporting to me through my deputy, Air Chief Marshal Tedder. In October, however, we were informed that the Air Ministry desired to transfer Air Chief Marshal Leigh-Mallory to a post of greater responsibility in the China-Burma-India Theater, where, because of his long experience, his presence could be best employed to further the ends of the war. It was with great reluctance that I agreed to this change, but once it had been made I felt that the AEAF, without Air Chief Marshal Leigh-Mallory, might better function as an integral part of my own Headquarters. SHAEF Air Staff thus came into being on 15 October and the planning and operational staffs became part of my headquarters.' Back in July, SHAEF approved a project suggested by the British Chiefs-of-Staff to break German civilian morale through epochal bombing although General Carl Spaatz, the Chief of the US Strategic Air Force, secured an agreement from Eisenhower that the Americans should not be deflected from precision bombing. On September 9, orders were issued by SHAEF for Operation 'Thunderclap' — a massive joint Eighth Air Force/RAF Bomber Command mission to wipe out Berlin. Spaatz raised the moral issue with Washington which supported that such operations 'were contrary to air force policy and national ideals'. Spaatz insisted that his own forces be sent only to what he considered legitimate military targets so a British counter-proposal was agreed instead. Code-named Operation 'Hurricane', the directive stated that 'in order to demonstrate to the enemy in Germany generally the overwhelming superiority of the Allied Air Forces in this theatre, the intention is to apply within the shortest practical period the maximum effort of the Royal Air Force Bomber Command and the VIIIth United States Bomber Command against objectives in the densely populated Ruhr.'

Northeast of LE THILLOT, our units continued to advance over rugged country and took the village of CORNIMONT. There was sharp fighting over the height just north of the town. The forest of GEHAN, south of CORNIMONT, also is in our hands.

Gun batteries in the COLOGNE area and rail and river transportation targets at DUSSELDORF and elsewhere in the Rhineland were hit by fighter-bombers. Industrial targets at PRUM were also attacked.

More than 1,000 heavy bombers, escorted by fighters, dropped over 4,500 tons of high explosives and incendiaries on the inland port and industries of DUISBURG. Fourteen bombers are missing.

Another force of over 1,000 heavy bombers with strong fighter escort struck targets at COLOGNE, SAARBRUCKEN and other objectives in western Germany.

During the night, heavy bombers, in very great strength, again struck at DUISBURG and attacked BRUNSWICK. Objectives in BERLIN and HAMBURG were also bombed.

Duisburg-Hamborn at the confluence of the Ruhr and Rhine rivers was the largest inland river port in Europe as well as a huge nucleus for iron, steel and zinc works and engineering and machine tool plants as well as coal mines. The picture shows the Aussenhafen waterway which leads to the inner harbour.

COMMUNIQUE No. 191   October 16

Driving from north and south, Allied troops joined up yesterday along the western shore of the SAVOJAARDSPLAAT. Later the combined force advanced westward to merge with the bridgehead in the WATERVLIET area. Fighters and fighter-bombers gave support to our troops in the BRESKENS sector and bombed FORT FREDERIK-HENDRIK. North of ANTWERP, our forces operating with close air support, took the village of WOENSDRECHT. Other formations of fighter-bombers struck at communications deeper in Holland, including DORDRECHT and the area north and east of ARNHEM where rail tracks were cut at several points. Medium and light bombers hit a railway bridge at DEVENTER.

In the Dutch salient, our forces made a local advance towards VIERLINGSBEEK. Bridges, embankments and other rail and road targets east and southeast of the salient at EMMERICH, WESEL, GELDERN and RHEINDAHLEN and elsewhere in the Rhineland were hit by fighter-bombers.

Pressure on AACHEN continued with house-to-house fighting in the outskirts. To the north of the city, our units advanced against stubborn resistance from mortar fire and dug-in tanks.

WURSELEN, north of AACHEN, and fortified positions in the enemy's defenses southeast of the city were bombed and strafed by fighter-bombers. Tank concentrations, entrenchments, gun emplacements and other strong points were hit.

There has been no substantial change in the HURTGEN area or in the Moselle valley.

In the Vosges foothills our advance eastward gained momentum. Gains were made against strong resistance along a wide front, and several towns were freed.

Northwest of the communications center of BACCARAT, the towns of GLONVILLE and FONTENOY were taken. Further south, our forces have cleared FREMIFONTAINE, the scene of recent heavy fighting.

Northeast of LE THILLOT, our advance has progressed further over rugged terrain, reaching to within two miles of LA BRESSE.

Attacks by fighter-bombers on rail transport and communications were made in the vicinity of LANDAU and elsewhere.

More than 1,200 heavy bombers with a strong escort of fighters, attacked military targets at COLOGNE.

Other escorted heavy bombers struck at oil refinery plants at REISHOLZ and MONHEIM, south and southeast of DUSSELDORF.

Heavy bombers, without loss, made a daylight attack with 12,000-pound bombs on the SORPE DAM at the eastern end of the Ruhr valley.

Last night other heavy bombers attacked the naval base of WILHELMSHAVEN. Objectives in HAMBURG were also bombed. Four of our aircraft are missing.

Over the two attacks, the Eighth Air Force recorded a loss of eight B-17s and four B-24s and a thousand aircraft returned damaged. Twenty-nine crew were killed but over 100 more were missing. This B-17 of the 398th Bomb Group (43-38172) was hit by an anti-aircraft shell which exploded in the nose killing the bombadier, but the pilot, 1st Lieutenant Lawrence De Lancey, managed to get the machine back to Nuthamstead.

The RAF lost 17 bombers on the daylight raid on the 14th and 12 the following night. Due to measures taken to distract enemy night-fighters, Luftwaffe records indicate that without the advantage of their radar on the coast and in Belgium and France, the raid was not registered until the bombers had been over Duisburg for two minutes. Even so over 130 crewmen were lost. Flying Officer F. H. Greenhalgh, a wireless operator with No. 158 Squadron, contemplates his lucky escape when the propellor from the damaged port inner engine of his Halifax (MZ928 coded NP-S), smashed into his position during the raid. The aircraft was hit by anti-aircraft fire over the target, putting the engine out of commission and shooting away two of his toes. As the aicraft completed its bombing run and turned for home, the propellor and reduction gear sheared off and smashed a large hole in the fuselage just where Greenhalgh's legs would have been had he not shifted position in order to bandage his wounded foot. The pilot brought the damaged aircraft back, making a safe landing at Carnaby where this photo was taken.

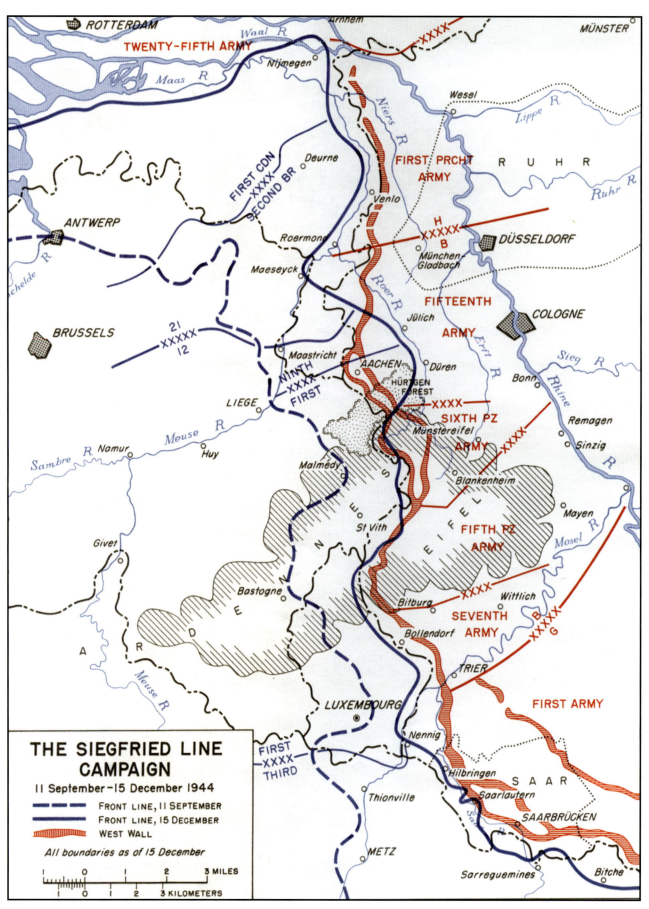

THE SIEGFRIED LINE CAMPAIGN
11 September – 15 December 1944

- — — — FRONT LINE, 11 SEPTEMBER
- ———— FRONT LINE, 15 DECEMBER
- ▨▨▨▨ WEST WALL

All boundaries as of 15 December

Although the Germans had a defensive line in France called the Siegfried-Stellung in the First World War, the band of fortifications built by Nazi Germany along its western frontier was called the Westwall. The term Siegfried Line came into everyday use through the popular song written by Captain Jimmy Kennedy while he was serving in France during the 'Phoney War' in 1939-40 which mocked the 630-kilometre-long chain of fortifications. Constructed in several stages between 1936 and 1940, it was later improved in several stages with additions. Initially, Aachen was left isolated forward of the line but in October 1938, Hitler ordered a second line to be built around its western side.

'Hanging out the washing on the Siegfried Line' The road from Eupen to Aachen crosses the Belgian-German frontier at Köpfchen just south of the city. Here the dragon's teeth of the line ran just in front of the two housing blocks built for German customs' personnel. On September 12, troops of the 16th Infantry of the 1st Infantry Division breached the Westwall in this sector, penetrating into the Aachen Forest and forcing back the defending troops of the 353. Infanterie-Division. Some time later, Press photographer Bert Brandt of the Acme photo agency pictured Captain Max Zera and Private Jim Spilker of the 1st Division hanging out their washing outside the customs' barracks which the GIs had taken over as quarters. As we have seen on page 175, on September 13, troops of the 3rd Armored Division achieved a first penetration in strength of the Westwall at Roetgen, south of Aachen, followed a day later by another sizeable indent into the line by the 5th Armored Division at Wallendorf in the Schnee Eifel further south. This was the beginning of a bitter campaign along the entire length of the Siegfried Line that would last for seven months, interrupted only by the German Ardennes offensive from mid-December to mid-January. There would be heavy and costly fighting in many sectors: on both sides of Aachen in October (see *After the Battle* No. 42); in the Hürtgenwald forest from September to December (see *After the Battle* No. 71); at Geilenkirchen in November (see *After the Battle* No. 140); at the Orscholz-Riegel from November to February; along the Saar river in December; in the Reichswald forest in February (see *After the Battle* No. 159); in the Saar-Palatinate Triangle in February and March, and at many other places along the 630-kilometre line (see *After the Battle* No. 163).

COMMUNIQUE No. 192   October 17

Steady progress continues north of the Leopold Canal. Gains of up to 1,000 yards were made against somewhat decreased enemy opposition. A small counter-attack on EEDE was repulsed. Fighter-bombers supporting our ground forces concentrated their attack mainly on the village of OOSTBURG. Many fortified buildings were destroyed. Strong points in SLUIS and SCHOONDIJKE were also hit.

Enemy counter-attacks in the WOENSDRECHT area were held and military targets at BERGEN OP ZOOM were bombed by fighter-bombers.

On the east of the Dutch salient, we made gains in the VENRAY area. East of VENRAY, an enemy battery of field guns was hit by rocket-firing fighters. Fighters flew offensive patrols over the battle zones in Holland.

Our units continue to make slow progress in AACHEN in house-to-house fighting. To the northeast, in the vicinity of WURSELEN, stiff opposition of all types is being met, and near OFDEN we are encountering heavy artillery and mortar fire.

East of AACHEN we have repulsed several counter-attacks in the area of VERLAUTENHEIDE with no loss of ground.

Southwest of GERMETER, our forces mopped up pillboxes with no substantial changes in the line.

Our units have met many enemy counter-attacks in the Vosges foothills where our gains were mostly slight. Two counter-attacks were repulsed in the LUNEVILLE sector.

Northeast of LE THILLOT, further progress was made east of the Moselotte river. Fighting has been heavy at several points in this sector.

Neatly repaired, today the old customs' quarters at Aachen-Köpfchen have been turned into private housing, and the moss-covered dragon's teeth form part of their gardens.

'House-to-house fighting continues in Aachen' run the communiqué. This 57mm anti-tank gun is positioned outside the court house on Adalbertsteinweg and is firing towards a target near St Adalbert Church.

COMMUNIQUE No. 193   October 18

In the Scheldt pocket, Allied units have reached the area of IJZENDIJKE. North of the town we advanced westward about a mile. Good progress also was made further south.

Fighter-bombers gave support to our ground forces which repulsed counter-attacks against the neck of the Zuid Beveland peninsula.

Escorted heavy bombers, none of which is missing, attacked the sea dyke at WESTKAPELLE on the island of Walcheren.

In the BRESKENS sector, supply dumps, strong points, and road transport were hit by fighter-bombers.

Our forces have reached the outskirts of VENRAY where heavy fighting continues. In another thrust to the southwest our units have crossed the VENRAY—DEURNE road.

Rail targets were hit over a wide area in Holland in western Germany by fighter-bombers. Attacks were made in the areas of VENLO and KEMPEN, east of the Dutch salient, at NEUSS near DUSSELDORF, BAD KREUZNACH, BELLHEIM and RHEINZABERN in the Rhineland, and at MUNSTER.

Our units are mopping up northeast of AACHEN and are maintaining lines completely encircling the city where house-to-house fighting continues. Northwest of AACHEN we have mopped up segments of the Siegfried Line.

Light bombers, without loss, attacked a railway bridge at EUSKIRCHEN.

In the Moselle valley, fighting continues in MAIZIERES-LES-METZ.

Military targets at COLOGNE were attacked in daylight by more than 1,300 heavy bombers escorted by 800 fighters. Thirteen bombers and three fighters are missing.

In the Vosges foothills, despite stubborn resistance and strong enemy counter-attacks in several areas, our troops have made substantial advances just south of the road junction at BRUYERES, and northeast of LE THILLOT. Hard fighting continues in both of these areas.

The village of LAVAL near BRUYERES was taken. Counter-attacks were repulsed in the LUNEVILLE—EPINAL sector.

The machine-gunners were firing in the same direction from the westernmost doorway of the Justizvollzugsanstalt (State Penitentiary).

Venray in Holland, three miles south of Overloon, was captured on the morning of October 18. These infantrymen — unfortunately with their shoulder patches censored — are searching for any remaining snipers.

COMMUNIQUE No. 194   October 19

South of the Scheldt, Allied forces made progress westward to within 3,000 yards of BRESKENS. We have made good gains east of SCHOONDIJKE and southwest of IJZENDIJKE.

On the east side of the Dutch salient, we captured VENRAY yesterday morning, and to the southwest, our forces are now some two miles south of the VENRAY—DEURNE road. Gains have also been made along the north side of the railway east of DEURNE.

Fighters and fighter-bombers supported our ground forces in Holland. Other fighter-bombers, striking at the enemy's supply routes to Holland, attacked railway targets north and west of the Ruhr.

Our units are continuing the battle in AACHEN, meeting stubborn resistance in house-to-house fighting. Fighters and fighter-bombers made a concentrated attack on a building in the northwest section of the city where enemy forces are holding out.

Just to the northwest of AACHEN our forces have destroyed a large number of pillboxes and have made gains against strong opposition. Units which closed the gap northeast of the city repulsed two counter-attacks by infantry and tanks.

Railway targets along the DUSSELDORF—DUREN—AACHEN line and elsewhere on lines leading westward to AACHEN were attacked by fighter-bombers.

Northeast of HURTGEN, small counter-attacks were repulsed.

We consolidated and improved our positions at several points in the Vosges foothills where the enemy continued to oppose our advances stubbornly and made more vain counter-attacks.

Two hundred enemy prisoners were taken in a series of successful local actions southeast of CORNIMONT.

A strong force of heavy bombers, with fighter escort, attacked industrial targets and railway yards in the COLOGNE and KASSEL areas. Other escorted heavy bombers struck the railway center of BONN.

Sixty miles away, American forces were battling their way into Aachen. These GIs advancing down Luisenstrasse towards the city centre are from Company M of the 26th Infantry (1st Division). In the last ten days fighting, exploits in and around the city had led four men to receive Medals of Honor: Captain Bobbie E. Brown on October 8; Sergeant Jack J. Pendleton (posthumously) on the 11th; Captain James M. Burt on the 13th and Sergeant Max Thompson on the 18th.

By now warning signs had been erected to alert troops that they were entering enemy territory. No detail is given for this picture other than it was taken on October 20 for release to the Press the following day.

COMMUNIQUE No. 195   October 20

Good progress was made south of BRESKENS and our troops are now within two miles of SCHOONDIJKE and OOSTBURG. Other units, advancing from the original bridgehead over the Leopold Canal, took the villages of MIDDELBURG and AARDENBURG. Patrols from the two forces made contact in the area south of OOSTBURG.

Fighter-bombers and rocket-firing fighters, supporting our operations in the BRESKENS sector, attacked communications and strong points and hit supply dumps at FORT FREDERIK-HENDRIK.

In the area south of VENRAY, some progress was made against determined resistance west and southwest of OVERBROEK.

Our units made gains in the fighting inside AACHEN. We continue to mop up the area north of the city.

The enemy reoccupied several pillboxes in the HAAREN area, but was later driven out. A fairly strong counter-attack with tanks and infantry north of HAAREN was broken up by our artillery during the afternoon.

In the Moselle valley, fighting continues in MAIZIERES-LES-METZ.

East of LUNEVILLE, a concentration of enemy tanks was attacked by fighter-bombers. Other formations, striking across the German frontier to the east, went for rail targets at KAISERSLAUTERN.

In the EPINAL sector, we made gains near BRUYERES and occupied the high ground just north of the town.

Further progress was made in the Vosges foothills. Six enemy counter-attacks were thrown back northeast of LE THILLOT and more prisoners were taken.

Heavy bombers, in very great strength with strong fighter escort, attacked in daylight military targets at MAINZ and in the LUDWIGSHAFEN—MANNHEIM area in southwestern Germany.

Last night, heavy bombers, again in very great strength, struck at STUTTGART and NUREMBERG. A lighter attack was made on WIESBADEN in the Rhineland. Nine of our aircraft are missing.

COMMUNIQUE No. 196   October 21

In an attack which began yesterday morning north of ANTWERP, Allied forces advanced more than three miles to the area of LOENHOUT. West of KALMPTHOUT, we made good gains, and southeast of the village we advanced on both sides of the ANTWERP—ROOSENDAAL road.

In the Scheldt pocket, more ground was taken south of SCHOONDIJKE, and the original bridgehead was merged with the main westward drive.

Fighters and fighter-bombers attacked fortifications in the BRESKENS area and continued their close support of our ground forces. Other attacks were carried out in the neighbourhood of BERGEN OP ZOOM, at ESSCHEN, GIESBEEK, STEEG and MAASHEES. The fighter-bombers also attacked transportation targets, cutting rail lines and attacking trains and motor transport in Holland and western Germany in the areas of ZWOLLE, ZUTPHEN, AMERSFOORT, NEUSS, KREFELD, HAMM and LISSENDORF.

Medium bombers, none of which is missing, hit a railroad bridge at MOERDIJK, 15 miles southeast of ROTTERDAM, and a road bridge at GEERTRUIDENBERG, ten miles further east.

Most of AACHEN is in our hands. Our forces have forced their way through the main part of the city and are now encountering resistance in its outskirts.

Fighting continues in MAIZIERES-LES-METZ.

Some 25 miles east of NANCY our fighter-bombers successfully attacked the dam at DIEUZE. Other formations attacked enemy troop concentrations and rail supply lines along this sector.

We have made gains east and north of BRUYERES following the capture of that stubbornly defended strong point. Counter-attacks were thrown back.

In the Vosges foothills further south, reinforced enemy units counter-attacked in a vain attempt to halt our advance east of the Moselotte bend area. The opposition is being cleared rapidly from forests in this sector.

During the day, 18 enemy aircraft was shot down and two were destroyed on the ground. Eleven of our aircraft are missing.

And there were those of a more humorous nature, although the original caption to this photograph claims that it was actually 'a Nazi propaganda sign'!

Back in September, Generalleutnant Gerhard Graf von Schwerin, commander of the 116. Panzer Division, had been relieved of the command of Aachen when an incriminating letter he had written to the opposing US commander fell into the wrong hands. Oberstleutnant Maximilian Leyherr had taken his place and was in charge when the American ultimatum was delivered on October 10 but it fell to Oberst Gerhard Wilck to surrender the city. *Left:* Here he is being driven into captivity, his command of the garrison having lasted a mere nine days. *Right:* Wilck's command post was in this huge bunker on Rütscherstrasse which still bears the marks of shelling from one of the American 155mm guns. (For more on the Aachen battle see *After the Battle* No. 42.)

COMMUNIQUE No. 197   October 22

In the BRESKENS area, Allied troops are fighting in the outskirts of the port. Fighter-bombers struck at the port installations there yesterday and attacked FORT FREDERIK-HENDRIK and other military buildings west of BRESKENS. Heavy bombers, one of which is missing, bombed gun batteries near FLUSHING. Medium bombers hit gun positions at CADZAND.

Further good progress was made north of ANTWERP. We have driven along the roads from WUUSTWEZEL and ACHTERBROEK to within three miles of ESSCHEN. Enemy forces in the wooded area north of WITHOF were bypassed and later mopped up. Fighters and fighter-bombers gave close support to our troops.

The enemy's rail system serving the Dutch battle zone was again under attack. At TERHEIJDEN, a bridge carrying the BREDA—DORDRECHT line over the river Mark was destroyed by fighter-bombers. Other fighter-bombers ranged over the frontier into Germany to strike targets near HALDEN and VREDEN.

Last night, light bombers struck at road and rail targets in Holland and Germany.

In AACHEN, the commander of the German garrison surrendered the remainder of its forces at 1206 hours yesterday after our troops had fought their way through the city to its western edge. Minor fighting continued in parts of the city for some time after the formal surrender but by mid-afternoon resistance had ceased.

Fighter-bombers, operating in the AACHEN sector, attacked fortified villages and bombed and strafed enemy artillery. Other fighter-bombers struck at railway targets from points near AACHEN to the area east of NANCY and also in the Rhine valley. Near HERMESKEIL a bridge was hit.

House-to-house fighting is still in progress in MAIZIERES-LES-METZ.

East of EPINAL, activity increased in the area of BROUVELIEURES and BRUYERES. Our troops made further gains against stiff resistance. In the BRUYERES area, fighters swept over the battle zone and fighter-bombers attacked troop concentrations.

East of the Moselotte river bend, a lull has followed the heavy fighting of the past few days.

Enemy fighters in some strength were encountered yesterday over the Ruhr valley and in combats 21 enemy aircraft were shot down for the loss of three fighter-bombers.

As one battle ends, another begins. By now the Allied armies faced serious supply problems and some units were even grinding to a halt for lack of ammunition. Although Antwerp had been captured by the 11th Armoured Division on September 4, the port was useless as the Germans held the north bank of the River Scheldt leading to it. So on October 16, Eisenhower instructed Montgomery to make the opening of Antwerp the sole priority for the 21st Army Group. The plan was to clear the Germans from the area south of the Maas river using units of the Canadian First Army attacking northwards and the British Second Army moving westwards. The latter thrust had three divisions: the 53rd Welsh aiming at 's-Hertogenbosch; the 51st Highland with the objective of Boxtel, and the 15th Scottish at Tilburg. At 2.30 a.m. on October 22, a three-hour bombardment began from over 200 guns and at 6.30 a.m. the men moved off. This is Geffen, jump-off point for the 4th Welch Regiment.

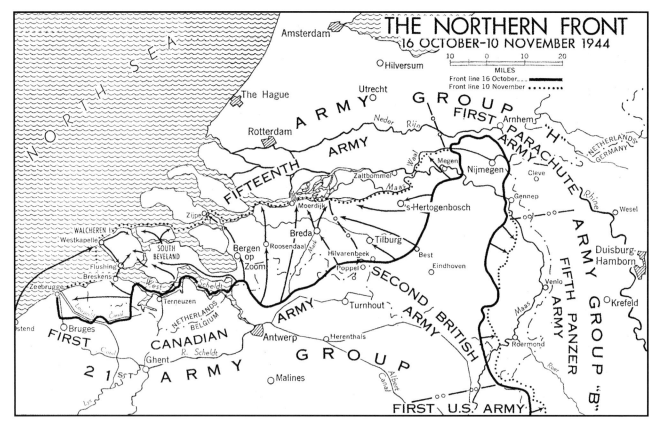

Communique No. 198 October 23

Inside the Scheldt pocket, Allied forces have taken BRESKENS and FORT FREDERIK-HENDRIK. We have also made progress from AARDENBURG to the vicinity of DRAAIBRUG. Units from the east have taken SCHOONDIJKE.

North of ANTWERP the enemy has been cleared from ESSCHEN. We have made gains on both sides of the railway to the southwest and along the roads from WUUSTWEZEL and ACHTERBROEK.

Early yesterday morning, an Allied attack was launched in the area east of HERTOGENBOSCH. The attack is continuing and good progress is being made. Fighters and fighter-bombers gave close support to our troops.

Our forces are clearing the enemy from areas of WURSELEN, northeast of AACHEN. In AACHEN, we continued to search for stragglers. Approximately 1,600 prisoners were taken when fighting in the city ceased.

Transportation targets were attacked by fighters and fighter-bombers in the METZ sector in immediate support of operations by our ground forces. West of the RHINE in this region fighter-bombers cut rail tracks in many places.

Fighting is still in progress in MAIZIERES-LES-METZ.

Further south we have made gains in the area of BEZANGE, COINCOURT and EMBERMENIL northeast and east of LUNEVILLE.

Northeast of EPINAL, gains were made against heavy resistance. BROUVELIEURES was taken and DOMFAING, VERVEZELLE and BELMONT were entered by our forces.

East of EPINAL a concentration of enemy troops was hit by fighter-bombers.

Heavy pressure was maintained by our forces against the enemy in the Vosges sector.

Industrial targets and communications in the HAMM, MUNSTER, HANNOVER and BRUNSWICK areas were attacked in daylight by a force of more than 1,100 heavy bombers escorted by some 750 fighters.

Other escorted heavy bombers, none of which is missing, made a heavy attack on the inland port and railway centre of NEUSS near DUSSELDORF.

Over on the coast, not much was left of Breskens which fell to the Canadians on October 22.

Left: This is the railway embankment along which the 1st East Lancashire Regiment made a daring march on the night of October 23/24. They reached 's-Hertogenbosch in complete surprise, to be followed an hour later by men of the Royal Welch Fusiliers. This photo was taken the following morning. The train visible in the distance at Rosmalen station was a German hospital train that had remained there having been immobilised by Allied strafing early in September. *Right:* A new station has since been built further east but the old railway building still stands.

COMMUNIQUE No. 199   October 24

In the area south of BRESKENS, Allied troops continue to make progress in spite of waterlogged country. We are within a mile of the village of GROEDE.

North of ANTWERP, gains were made west of the ROOSENDAAL—ANTWERP railway and a fresh advance into Holland was made in this area. West of WOENSDRECHT, we have again crossed the road and railway leading to Beveland and Walcheren. Weather restricted air operations yesterday, but during the afternoon, heavy bombers, escorted by fighters, attacked gun emplacements on Walcheren island. Four bombers are missing.

Allied forces have reached the edge of HERTOGENBOSCH. South of the town, we have reached ST MICHIELSGESTEL and are within a mile of BOXTEL.

There have been no major changes along our front from AACHEN to the upper Moselle valley. In MAIZIERES-LES-METZ, house-to-house fighting continues, with the enemy holding approximately one-fourth of the town.

Northeast of LUNEVILLE, our forces are consolidating gains made in a push to the immediate vicinity of MONCOURT. Several tank-supported counter-attacks were repulsed by our units in the LUNEVILLE sector.

Northeast of BROUVELIEURES, our forward elements forced crossings of the Mortange river at several points and continued to push eastward.

Slight gains were made in the Vosges mountains against stiff resistance.

Last night heavy bombers in great strength attacked ESSEN.

Although the code-name for the overall offensive in Holland was Operation 'Pheasant', the assault on 's-Hertogenbosch (the Dutch just call it Den Bosch) received one of its own: Operation 'Alan'. The town was divided by a triangle of waterways where the Zuid Willems Canal and the Aa and Dieze rivers met before flowing north to the Maas.

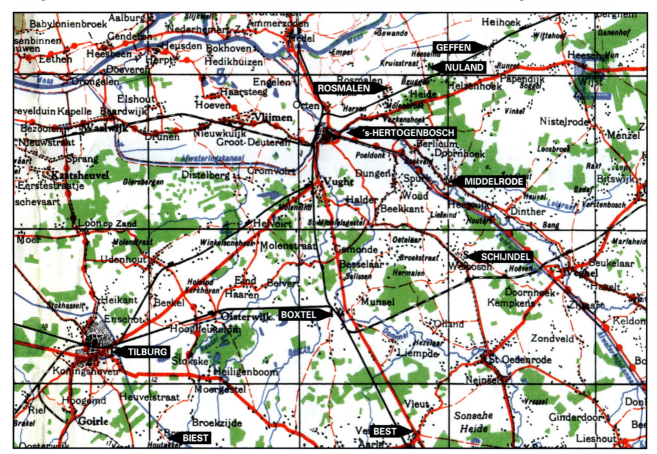

This map, produced by the Geographical Section of the General Staff, dates from June 1944. The patches are ours.

Aided by civilians, one of whom is armed with a German rifle, men of the 1st Battalion, East Lancashire Regiment, advance through 's-Hertogenbosch towards the canal bridge. When the photograph was released at the end of October, the Resistance man in the shop doorway had his face blotted out with red ink by the censor to prevent him from being identified.

COMMUNIQUE No. 200   October 25

South of BRESKENS, the road from SCHOONDIJKE to OOSTBURG is in Allied hands, and our troops are on the edge of OOSTBURG.

South of ROOSENDAAL, further gains have brought us to the neighbourhood of PINDORP. Some progress was also made north and northeast of WOENSDRECHT.

Our troops are fighting in the outskirts of HERTOGENBOSCH and have cut the main road and railway both north and a few miles south of the town.

Fighters and fighter-bombers supported our ground forces in the Zuid Beverland peninsula and hit military buildings at DORDRECHT. Other fighter-bombers attacked strong points northeast of NIJMEGEN. Road and rail transportation targets in Holland in western Germany were attacked by fighter-bombers in strength. In the areas of HANNOVER and KASSEL. More than 100 locomotives are many freight cars were destroyed.

In the area from north of AACHEN to LUNEVILLE, there were no substantial changes. Patrol activity continued throughout the area, and in the Moselle valley, our units encountered sporadic artillery and small arms fire.

In the BACCARAT sector, MENARMONT has been freed.

Northeast of EPINAL we have made further gains and have taken the villages of MORTAGNE and BIFFONTAINE after house-to-house fighting.

Our forces in the Vosges mountains are improving their position.

Evidence of the huge bombardment on the road from Nuland to Rosmalen. The Germans were still relying on horse-drawn transport, these beasts and the gunner belonging to the 712. Infanterie-Division.

With the troops having gained a foothold in Den Bosch, the 51st (Highland) Division had moved out from Veghel towards Schijndel. The town was successfully taken by the 5th Black Watch and the 1st Gordon Highlanders. This is the main street looking south-east although André von Hilst's grocery store is now a fashion shop.

This is the Dommel bridge on Rechterstraat in the centre of the village blown by the Germans on the morning of October 24, just before the Allies arrived.

Above left: **Next to fall was Boxtel . . . and here lies a very interesting story as explained in Army Training Memorandum No. 51 of 1944: 'In 1794 the young Colonel Arthur Wellesley stood beside a soldier dying of wounds received in a savage attack by the French at Boxtel in Holland. The man's name was Thomas Atkins and seeing the grief on his Colonel's face he gasped, "It's all right, Sir, it's all in the day's work". Fifty years later the Duke of Wellington, by then Commander-in-Chief of the British Army, was asked to suggest a name for printing as a specimen signature on a form relating to soldiers' pay. The Duke paused long, thinking of the campaigns he had fought in, and remembering the spirit shown by the dying soldier at Boxtel he replied "Private Thomas Atkins" . . . a nickname which has been given ever since to soldiers of the British Army.'**

COMMUNIQUE No. 201   October 26

Allied forces are fighting in HERTOGENBOSCH where they have driven the enemy from the north and east sections of the town. BOXTEL has been freed and gains have taken us several miles to the northwest. On the OIRSCHOT—TILBURG road we have reached the area of MOERGESTEL.

There has been general progress northward in the area east of the ANTWERP—BREDA road.

In the approach to Zuid Beveland, we have taken the village of RILLAND and have moved forward three miles further west along the south side of the isthmus. Further ground has been gained in the area between PINDORP and WOENSDRECHT.

In the Scheldt pocket, Allied forces have made progress in the direction of POLDERTJE. FORT FREDERIK-HENDRIK, from which we withdrew after initial entry four days ago, has been taken. Further south, we have reached the outskirts of GROEDE. We have also gained some ground west and northwest of SCHOONDIJKE.

Northeast of EPINAL, our advance was slowed by stiffened resistance. In the Vosges mountains sector further south, counter-attacks were thrown back with severe losses to the enemy.

Fighters and fighter-bombers gave support over the battle zones and went for road and rail transport in western Germany.

In daylight, heavy bombers in very great strength, escorted by fighters, attacked ESSEN and the synthetic oil plant at HOMBERG. Four bombers are missing.

More than 1,200 heavy bombers, escorted by some 500 fighters, again in daylight, attacked the railway yard at HAMM, an oil refinery in the HAMBURG area, and other military targets in northwestern Germany.

Further up the road from Schijndel lay Sint-Michielsgestel with its bridge over the River Dommel. However, a mile short of the village, the attack was held up by a series of road-blocks constructed with fallen trees so by the time the Black Watch came within sight of the bridge, it was blown in their faces. Under cover of darkness, a platoon then rowed across the river to establish a toe-hold on the opposite bank while Royal Engineers worked through the night of October 23/24 to construct a Class 40 Bailey bridge which they had ready by the following morning.

A Sherman of the East Riding Yeomanry enters 's-Hertogenbosch on October 25, at the point where Graafseweg enters the town.

COMMUNIQUE No. 202   October 27

Most of HERTOGENBOSCH is in Allied hands and progress has been general in the whole sector from there to the sea. The enemy defenses between HERTOGENBOSCH and TILBURG have been deeply penetrated. After hard fighting, our troops are within 4,000 yards of ROOSENDAAL and the enemy has been forced to withdraw all along the line from there to TILBURG. Our units are in the eastern and southern outskirts of TILBURG.

Further gains have been made in the neck of the Beveland peninsula. In the Leopold canal area our troops are fighting in OOSTBURG.

We have bypassed GROEDE on the north and south.

In the area north of AACHEN, our units have made minor gains against stubborn resistance. South of MONSCHAU patrol activity continues.

In the Moselle valley we encountered sporadic enemy artillery fire. Northeast of LUNEVILLE we cleared the Germans from the FORET DE MONCOURT and the high ground north of the forest. Several counter-attacks were repulsed in the LUNEVILLE sector.

Northeast of EPINAL we made gains against strong resistance. Further slight progress was made in the Vosges sector and counter-attacks were repulsed.

Yesterday, more than 1,200 heavy bombers, escorted by over 650 fighters, attacked industrial targets at BIELEFELD, MUNSTER, HANNOVER and elsewhere in Germany. Other heavy bombers, also escorted by fighters, attacked the I.G. Farbenindustrie chemical works at LEVERKUSEN.

Fighter-bombers hit rail targets in the Rhineland and in the METZ area. A rail bridge at RHEINBACH, a railway yard at MUNICH, west of DUSSELDORF, and a round-house and locomotives in the METZ area were attacked. Rail tracks were cut in many places west of the Rhine.

Two enemy aircraft was shot down and six of ours are missing.

The capture of South Beveland to help clear the Scheldt was entrusted to the 2nd Canadian Infantry Division (see map page 220). The operation began on October 20 with the support of the 4th Canadian Armoured Division. En route, Esschen was captured with the help of a fighter-bomber attack and the troops reached Bergen op Zoom on the 27th. This was the scene in the town square as Dutch policemen greeted the Canadians. Note more censoring of particular individuals.

COMMUNIQUE No. 203   October 28

In Zuid Beveland, Allied forces now hold the south side of the isthmus as far as the canal west of KRUININGEN. Our bridgehead on the southern coast of the peninsula has been reinforced and expanded.

GROEDE, in the Scheldt pocket, is in our hands and we are on the coast to the northwest of the village.

Northeast of the Zuid Beveland isthmus we have taken BERGEN OP ZOOM. North of ESSCHEN our units are within two miles of ROOSENDAAL. On the ANTWERP— BREDA road we have progressed to the area of ZUNDERT.

We are in the eastern outskirts of TILBURG and north of the town our troops have reached the vicinity of LOON OP ZAND. To the south, we have made good gains, and on the west, forward elements have cut the TILBURG-BREDA road.

The enemy has been cleared from HERTOGENBOSCH and we have made some progress further west.

On the east side of the Dutch salient we checked a counter-attack in the vicinity of MEIJEL where fighting is still in progress.

Light artillery fire was directed against our units in the AACHEN area and along the Belgian-German frontier in the sector east of ST VITH.

Near RAMBERVILLERS we made local gains at several points. The village of HOUSSERAS has been taken.

Farther south, limited progress was made between BRUYERES and LE THOLY.

In the Vosges mountains, attempts to infiltrate our positions were frustrated and losses were inflicted on the enemy.

Adverse weather restricted air operations yesterday.

On October 24 the 15th Scottish Division, supported by the 6th Guards Tank Brigade, began the attack to capture Tilburg, the town falling on the 27th. This photo of a troop of the King's Own Scottish Borderers was captioned as being taken in Best which lies 12 miles east of Tilburg. However, being quite familiar with that village, Karel knew it must have been taken elsewhere and on consulting the index of the 15th Scottish Division history he spotted that there was another village, just three miles south-east of Tilburg, named Biest (see map page 221). He drove there to check and it all immediately fell into place although unfortunately the church is hidden by the trees in his comparison. (When Best, the other village, was liberated a British officer proposed a toast to the health of Queen Wilhelmina. An elderly Dutchman immediately replied in English: 'Ladies and Gentlemen — Lloyd George'!)

COMMINIQUE No. 204   October 29

In Zuid Beveland the Allied bridgehead over the Beveland canal has been extended. Fighters and fighter-bombers bombed and strafed gun positions and troops near KAPELLE and supported our ground operations on the peninsula.

South of the Scheldt we have reached the outskirts of ZUIDZANDE. Near CADZAND our fighter-bombers hit gun positions and fortified buildings housing enemy troops.

Escorted heavy bombers attacked gun emplacements on the island of Walcheren. Two bombers are missing. Fighter-bombers and rocket-fighting fighters went for similar targets on the island.

On the east of the Dutch salient our forces repulsed counter-attacks north and west of MEIJEL.

The enemy's communications system in Holland and the Rhineland was under attack throughout the day. Medium and light bombers hit the rail bridge over the IJssel river at DEVENTER, a bridge carrying the road and railway over the Meuse at VENLO, and destroyed the central span of a road bridge over the river at ROERMOND.

From AACHEN to the FORET DE PARROY there were no important changes. Our patrols were active in the AACHEN and MONSCHAU areas.

Fighter-bombers in strength attacked railway bridges in the Rhineland from WESEL in the north to KARLSRUHE in the south. Over 40 locomotives and a large number of rail trucks were destroyed or damaged and rail tracks west of the Rhine were cut in some 60 places.

Medium and light bombers struck at railway bridges at AHRWEILER and SINZIG. One light bomber is missing. During the day, fighter-bombers shot down 13 enemy aircraft.

The Canadians had fought their way up the coast from Antwerp as far as Woensdrecht opposite the eastern end of the isthmus connecting the mainland with South (Zuid) Beveland. This connecting neck of land had originally been drained from the sea and was five miles wide at the point where the ship canal bisected it. The Canadian assault to capture South Beveland had begun on the 24th and by the evening of the second day they had fought through minefields, mud, wire and water to within five miles of the canal. There the bridge had been blown so Buffaloes of the 79th Armoured Division crossed the river to land beyond the canal and establish a bridgehead on the southern shore. By the 27th engineers had bridged the canal allowing reinforcements to cross and Goes to be captured without difficulty.

COLOGNE was attacked in daylight by a strong force of heavy bombers escorted by fighters.

Heavy-caliber German artillery shelled the city of LUXEMBOURG early yesterday. Sporadic artillery and small-arms fire were encountered by our units in the Moselle valley. In the EPINAL sector we made limited gains east of BRUYERES. The village of JUSSARUPT was taken against strong opposition. Enemy artillery fire was strong at several points in this area and also in the Vosges mountains.

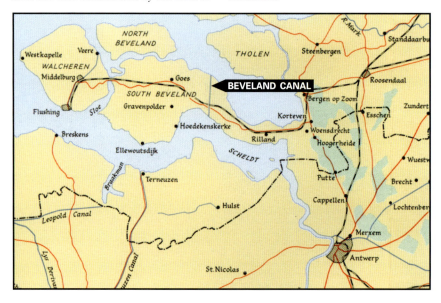

Today the Beveland Canal is crossed not only by the road and rail bridges but also by the motorway . . . although below the water!

COMMUNIQUE No. 205 October 30

CADZAND and ZUIDZANDE, south of the Scheldt, have been taken by Allied troops.

In Zuid Beveland, our troops freed GOES and linked up with our seaborne forces in the area of HOEDEKENSKERKE. The seaborne bridgehead was also enlarged to the westward. Defences on the island of Walcheren were attacked yesterday by heavy bombers, one of which is missing, and by fighter-bombers. Fighters which escorted the heavy bombers made low-level attacks on flak positions.

Allied forces continued their advance along the whole front south of the Maas. BREDA was freed by troops advancing from the east. Other forces driving from the south cut the road between BREDA and ROOSENDAAL. Fighter-bombers strafed road transport north of these two towns and medium bombers attacked a bridge at MOERDIJK.

In the area north of TILBURG our forces are some miles north and west of LOON-OP-ZAND. Fighter-bombers cut railway lines between AMERSFOORT and ZWOLLE in the VENLO area, and elsewhere behind the battle areas in Holland.

In southeastern Holland, medium bombers also attacked communications at VENLO and a bridge at ROERMOND.

Our ground forces held further enemy attacks in the MEIJEL area.

Bridges at KONZ-KARTHAUS, EUSKIRCHEN, MAYEN and ELIER were the targets for medium bombers, and fighter-bombers destroyed three bridges and damaged a fourth across the river Ahr, south of BONN, and sealed two nearby railway tunnels. Fighter-bombers hit highways radiating northward from DUREN, a railway yard at KERPEN, and cut rail lines in many places between MUNSTER and the Dutch-German frontier and in the areas of BONN and COBLENZ. They also attacked locomotives, rail cars and barges over a wide area and silenced gun positions.

Our units made slight gains in the LUNEVILLE sector. East of RAMBERVILLERS, we took FRAIPERTUIS and held the village against strong counter-attacks. Other counter-attacks against our positions in the Vosges mountains were repulsed.

Yesterday morning heavy bombers, one of which is missing, attacked the battleship *Tirpitz* near TROMSO.

According to reports so far received, 28 enemy aircraft were shot down during yesterday. One medium bomber and nine fighter-bombers are missing.

Yet with the German defences on Walcheren still active, the Scheldt was still not usable. Fighter-bombers pounded the gun positions, this attack on the 30th being carried out by a Polish squadron on positions north of Flushing (Vlissingen).

Back in September the Royal Netherlands Brigade 'Princess Irene', which had been raised in Britain in 1941, had the joy of liberating Uden, a town on the 'Market-Garden' corridor route. There they found that the Germans had created a cemetery for Allied dead — mostly unidentified airmen — in the garden of the parish priest which lay next to the Roman Catholic church. This picture, released on October 31, shows the early beginnings of a tradition, now firmly established in Holland, of involving school children in caring for the graves of the war dead.

COMMUNIQUE No. 206   October 31

Zuid Beveland is in Allied hands. Early yesterday GOES was taken and later our forces, pushing westward along the railway, reached the causeway leading to Walcheren. By evening the enemy had been driven from the country north and south of the railway. Gun emplacements, strong points and ammunition dumps on the island of Walcheren were attacked by heavy and fighter-bombers.

In the Scheldt pocket, RETRANCHEMENT was freed. There was heavy fighting in the area of SLUIS where our troops have reached the outskirts of the village. Fighters and fighter-bombers supported the ground forces west of BRESKENS and rocket-firing fighters hit fortified buildings and pillboxes at KNOCKE.

In the BERGEN OP ZOOM—ROOSENDAAL sector, good gains were made in spite of enemy mines and booby-traps. Our troops are within three miles of STEENBERGEN. ROOSENDAAL was taken, we reach the area of OUD-GASTEL.

There has been some progress northeast of BREDA and we are across the whole of the road between BERGEN OP ZOOM and BREDA. Transportation targets in the BREDA area and a road bridge at TERHEIJDEN were hit by fighter-bombers.

Northwest of TILBURG, our advance continued on a broad front. We have reached the outskirts of OOSTERHOUT and further east we are in the vicinity of CAPELLE.

Further east, the enemy counter-attack in the MEIJEL area made no headway during the day.

The synthetic oil plant at WESSELING, near COLOGNE, was the target for heavy bombers with fighter escort.

MAIZIERES-LES-METZ has been cleared of the enemy. In other regions, from AACHEN to LUNEVILLE, patrolling continued.

Slight gains were made east of RAMBERVILLERS and the villages of JEANMENIL and BRU were freed. Activity from LUNEVILLE to the Swiss border otherwise consisted largely of patrolling. A number of counter-attacks were repulsed without difficulty.

These graves on what is today a grassy area on Pastor Spieringstraat have now all been moved to the Uden War Cemetery on Burgermeester Buskensstraat.

Canadians move through Boekhoute, a village on the Belgian-Dutch border south-east of Breskens. This particular picture was released through Canadian Military Headquarters in London on October 24.

Switching now to Germany, a Jeep patrol (believed to be from the 29th Division) has entered Birgden. According to the original caption a mine, thought to have been placed in the street by civilians, caused the death of three American soldiers.

NOVEMBER 1944
THE BATTLE BOGS DOWN

1er char (EVREUX) entré dans Strasbourg. (S/gpt Rouvillois)

COMMUNIQUE No. 207 November 1

Heavy fighting went on all day yesterday on the causeway linking Zuid Beveland and Walcheren.

Between OUDENBOSCH and BREDA we have reached the line of the River Mark. Crossings have been made due north of OUDENBOSCH and on the main road to DORDRECHT, northwest of BREDA.

Northeast of OOSTERHOUT our forces have continued to make good progress. We have reached the river Maas north of CAPELLE. RAAMSDONK, SPRANG and WAALWIJK have been taken and we are in the outskirts of WASPIK.

In southeastern Holland there is been heavy fighting in the vicinity of LIESSEL.

RAF Bomber Command despatched nearly 500 heavy bombers on the night of October 31/November 1 to attack Cologne. The target was covered with thick cloud so bombing was carried out using Oboe-marking leading to scattered results. Photo shows the eastern bank of the Rhine between the Hohenzollern railway bridge and the post-war Zoobrücke. Today an exhibition hall and the Rheinpark occupy the riverside site.

The enemy has been driven from the town.

Although weather curtailed their activities over the greater part of the battle areas, fighter-bombers attacked a supply dump to the northwest of SAARBURG. One fighter is missing.

In the afternoon, heavy bombers escorted by fighters attacked the synthetic oil plant at BOTTROP in the Ruhr. One bomber is missing.

Last night, heavy bombers in strength attacked COLOGNE; this bombing was preceded by an attack on the city by light bombers. Heavy artillery exchanges took place north of BACCARAT.

Our troops have entered ST BENOIT, east of RAMBERVILLERS, against stubborn resistance.

East of BRUYERES, the village of LES POULIERES was freed.

The SHAEF censor has been at work on this print released on November 1 — an MP directing traffic in liberated Holland.

After the Battle editor Karel Margry re-stages the occasion in Schijndel — one village away from 's-Hertogenbosch.

We have already seen on page 199 that the operation to capture Walcheren had begun at the beginning of October with the breaking of the dyke at Westkapelle, so flooding a large part of the island. Now a combined air/sea assault with warships and fighter-bombers paving the way was planned against the port of Flushing.

In fact it was like a re-run of D-Day in miniature, with 150 vessels of various kinds escorted by a support squadron of 27 gun and rocket-firing craft plus the 15-inch guns of *Warspite*, *Erebus* and *Roberts*. The troops themselves travelled by Buffaloes (tracked vehicles called Amtraks by the Americans) and LCA landing craft.

COMMUNIQUE No. 208   November 2

Allied forces landed yesterday morning on Walcheren island and have made good progress. Two beach-heads are firmly established. Some miles of the coast and a large part of the town of FLUSHING are in our hands.

At FLUSHING, an army commando was successfully landed under cover of bombardment from the south shore of the Scheldt estuary. At WESTKAPELLE, Royal Marines secured a beach head under cover of long-range bombardment by HM ships *Warspite*, *Erebus* and *Roberts*, and close bombardment by a squadron of support craft.

Preparing the way for these landings, light bombers during the night of Tuesday/Wednesday attacked enemy gun positions and strong points on Walcheren. At daylight yesterday, fighter-bombers renewed the attack on gun positions and strong points, and struck at enemy troop movements, while fighters provided cover for land and sea forces. No enemy opposition was encountered in the air and none of our aircraft are missing from the operations.

Heavy fighting continues at the western end of the Beveland Walcheren causeway. In the Scheldt pocket, our troops are fighting in KNOCKE. SLUIS and WESTKAPELLE have been cleared of the enemy.

There has been stiff fighting in the area of our crossings over the river Mark. Farther east we have increased our hold on the south bank of the river Maas in the KAPELLE area.

We have made further progress east and southeast of LIESSEL.

Transportation targets in Holland were hit by fighter-bombers.

Objectives in the Ruhr were attacked in the afternoon by heavy bombers escorted by fighters. In the late evening, a strong force of heavy bombers attacked, through clouds, the industrial and railway centre of OBERHAUSEN in the Ruhr, and light bombers hit COLOGNE and BERLIN.

Communications, rail transport and power facilities in the Rhineland and the Saar were the objectives for fighter-bombers. Other formations hit a dam near DIEUZE.

North of NANCY our forces have cleared the enemy from LETRICOURT and ABAUCOURT.

Our units have made gains southeast of LUNEVILLE and freed the villages of BURIVILLE, HABLAINVILLE and AZERAILLES.

Substantial gains were also made in the wooded country southeast of RAMBERVILLERS.

No. 4 Army Commando led the way ashore at Flushing with elements of 155th Infantry Brigade following on. *Left:* **Here men of the 4th King's Own Scottish Borderers advance down** Molenstraat. *Right:* **They came this way. Seventy years later the re-developed street is a shady retreat from the bustle of the port.**

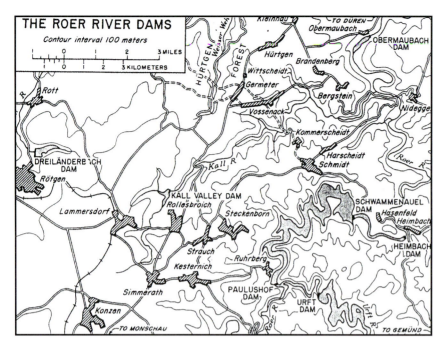

Meanwhile the First Army, having punched two holes in the Siegfried Line at Aachen and Roetgen, was about to launch its next operation to cross the Roer river and so reach the Rhine. The initial objective was to be Schmidt which was not only an important road junction but it overlooked the Schwammenauel Dam, one of seven dams on the Roer, any one of which the Germans might blow to flood and isolate any troops east of the river. On November 2 the 28th Infantry Division under Major General Norman D. Cota found itself the only Allied attacking force along more than 170 miles of the front from Holland to Metz.

COMMUNIQUE No. 209   November 3

Progress on the island of Walcheren continues. Allied forces moving from WESTKAPELLE have now bypassed DOMBURG, while others have reached a point within two miles of FLUSHING. Fighting continues in FLUSHING itself and at the western end of the Walcheren causeway. All resistance in the area of KNOCKE and ZEEBRUGGE has ceased.

Fighters and fighter-bombers attacked enemy troops and positions in the region of KNOCKE during yesterday morning. Coastal guns and strong points on Walcheren island were also attacked, and close support was given to our ground forces north of BREDA. In southern Holland, bridges, locomotives and barges were attacked and rail lines cut.

In the MEIJEL area, Allied troops advanced to within 2,000 yards of the town.

Our troops, attacking in the HURTGEN sector after heavy artillery preparation, made gains of 2,500 yards. The town of VOSSENACK, one and one-half miles south of HURTGEN, was taken, and our drive is continuing against stiffening resistance.

A factory south of BONN and an airfield to the east of TRIER were targets for fighter-bombers, which also attacked locomotives and freight cars and cut rail lines in the COLOGNE and DUSSELDORF areas.

Heavy bombers, escorted by fighters, attacked the synthetic oil plant at HOMBERG in the Ruhr.

Three enemy aircraft were shot down. Four heavy bombers and three fighters are missing.

Five rail bridges behind the enemy lines were the targets for medium and light bombers; the bridges attacked were in the Moselle valley at KONZ-KARTHAUS, EHRANG and BULLAY, over the Nette at MAYEN, and over the Erft at EUSKIRCHEN. The medium bombers were escorted by fighters.

Last night more than 1,000 aircraft were over western Germany with DUSSELDORF as the main objective. Light bombers attacked OSNABRUCK.

BACCARAT in the Vosges foothills has been freed and the villages of GELACOURT and DENEUVRE, near BACCARAT, are in our hands.

Gains were also made farther south where the village of LA BOURGONCE was taken against heavy resistance.

In the Moselotte bend our positions have been improved.

All through October the 9th Infantry Division, in particular its 39th Infantry, had been fighting in the Hürtgen Forest just south of Aachen attempting to capture Schmidt. Casualty rates were very high and even losses due to non-battle causes had reached unprecedented levels. By the time the 9th was relieved by the 28th they had suffered 2,500 casualties and still not reached Schmidt. War correspondent Ernest Hemingway likened the fighting in the forest to 'Passchendaele with tree bursts'. The 112th Infantry Regiment began its attack on Vossenack on November 2 but after four days, one panicking platoon led a whole battalion to flee to the rear. *Left:* **This picture of the town under attack was not released until March 1945.** *Right:* **This was all that was left of St Josef Church in Vossenack. It changed hands seven times before the 146th Engineers recovered it on November 7.**

Back in Holland, now all of Middelburg was under water. This is Park van Nieuwenhove . . . then and now.

COMMUNIQUE No. 210 November 4

On Walcheren island Allied troops have cleared DOMBURG of the enemy. The regimental command of the enemy troops in FLUSHING was captured yesterday, but there is still some resistance in the northern part of the town and mopping-up continues in the docks area.

To the west of FLUSHING our troops have joined with forces advancing along the coast from WESTKAPELLE.

Early yesterday morning Allied units from Zuid Beveland landed on the east side of the island and have made good progress.

Gun positions and strong points near MIDDELBURG were bombed and strafed by fighter-bombers.

The build-up of supplies on Walcheren island is being satisfactorily maintained. During the earlier stages of the landing operation, HM ships gave support to the land forces by bombardment of enemy guns and positions, and the landings were successfully completed in spite of severe opposition from enemy batteries.

North of OUDENBOSCH, our bridgehead over the River Mark has been widened and deepened. Northwest of OOSTERHOUT the two bridgeheads established earlier have merged, and our troops have advanced to the vicinity of DEN HOUT in spite of enemy opposition.

Concentrations of enemy troops and military buildings north of BREDA were attacked by fighter-bombers. Road and rail transport in Holland and the Ruhr were the targets for other fighter-bombers.

Northeast of WEERT, the enemy has been driven out of an area between the Bois-le-Duc canal and in the Noorder canal.

Southeast of AACHEN, fighter-bombers, in close support of our ground forces, attacked enemy units and tanks. Our forces made small gains south of VOSSENACK against moderate to heavy resistance and have entered the town of SCHMIDT, two miles to the southeast. In the forest southwest of VOSSENACK, we are clearing out pillboxes against stubborn opposition.

Communications in the Rhine valley and westward to the enemy line, and in the Moselle valley were attacked by medium, light and fighter-bombers. Among the targets were seven bridges and a railway tunnel.

Additional gains have been made in the BACCARAT sector where the village of REHERREY has been freed.

East of REMIREMONT, our troops in the Vosges mountains launched an attack which has made progress against stiff resistance.

In the Maritime Alps, SOSPEL, and several nearby villages and heights overlooking the Italian frontier north of MENTON have been taken without resistance.

Flushing was in Allied hands by October 4 and final resistance on Walcheren ceased with the surrender of General der Infanterie Wilhelm Daser at his HQ at No. 6-8 Dam in Middelburg. Once the Scheldt had been cleared of mines — a job which took the navy two weeks — the first ships began unloading urgently needed supplies there on November 26, yet the cost of opening up Antwerp had been high. For all the operations in the area, British and Canadian casualties totalled 27,633 which compared to less than 25,000 in the capture of Sicily where the Allies defeated a garrison of over 350,000. (For more on Walcheren see *After the Battle* No. 36.)

After being occupied for over four years, Breda (inland of the Beveland isthmus) gives a joyful welcome to Allied troops as they pass through the town although SHAEF censor No. 102 has still found a reason to cut it! The 49th Division had begun to move towards the town back on October 22 but had been blocked by a new German unit rushed in from northern Holland and it was not until the 29th that the 1st Polish Armoured Division cleared Breda after house-to-house fighting.

COMMUNIQUE No. 211   November 5

FLUSHING is now clear of the enemy, and Allied forces have made some gains north of the town. Our units which landed on the east side of Walcheren island have now joined with our troops at the west end of the causeway.

On the Dutch mainland, STEENBERGEN, NIEUW VOSSEMEER and KLADDE have been freed. Our bridgehead over the Mark north of OUDENBOSCH has been enlarged and we are within a mile of KLUNDERT. Enemy troop movements in this area were attacked by fighters and fighter-bombers. Rocket-firing fighters destroyed enemy observation posts at DINTELOORD and strafed defence positions. Fighter-bombers also attacked an ammunition dump at ZEVENBERGEN.

In the OOSTERHOUT sector, our bridgehead has expanded to the north where we are within a mile of GEERTRUIDENBERG. WAGENBERG has been freed and good gains have been made further west.

Fighter-bombers, striking deeper into Holland, bombed and strafed an ordnance factory at UTRECHT. Other fighter-bombers and fighters, operating over a wide area of Holland and in the Ruhr, went for rail and water transport and cut rail communications in some 40 places.

Medium and light bombers, with fighter cover, attacked a road and rail bridge over the River Meuse at VENLO.

To the west of VENLO, our ground forces continued to advance eastward along the Noorder canal and some progress has been made farther north.

An enemy counter-attack in the village of SCHMIDT, from which we had been forced to withdraw, was repulsed yesterday afternoon, and our troops are again making progress towards SCHMIDT. Pillboxes are being mopped up in the area west and northwest of the town, which was dive-bombed and strafed by our fighter-bombers yesterday.

In the area of HURTGEN we continue to make slow progress against mines, infantry and artillery. Less than a mile to the southeast our advance is meeting strong resistance from tanks and infantry.

East of AACHEN, medium and light bombers, attacking in waves, bombed enemy strong points at ESCHWEILER. Fighters and fighter-bombers went for railway yards at DUREN, HAMM and BRUHL; an airfield west of NEUSS, and an ammunition dump at LECHENICH, southwest of COLOGNE. Other targets for fighter-bombers were rail bridges at BAAL, northeast of AACHEN, and at BERGHEIM, west of COLOGNE.

Yesterday afternoon, heavy bombers with fighter escort, attacked the industrial town of SOLINGEN, a few miles south of the Ruhr. In the evening, heavy bombers in very great strength went again to Germany with BOCHUM in the Ruhr as the main target. Medium and light bombers attacked ordnance supply depots near TRIER.

In the LUNEVILLE sector, slight gains were made northeast of MANONVILLER. Our troops are mopping up resistance pockets in the BACCARAT area and in the Vosges heights southeast of GERARDMER.

On November 4 the 893rd Tank Destroyer Battalion, attached to the 28th Division, were pictured moving up to Vossenack preparing to cross the Kall river gorge and reinforce the defenders in Schmidt and nearby Kommerscheidt. These M10s are in the Hürtgen Forest west of Germeter. (For more on the Hürtgen battle, see *After the Battle* No. 71.)

No precise location was given to this sequence taken on November 5 other than the Monschau area, i.e. just inside Germany in the northern Ardennes. The original caption adds that 40mm Bofors were now being used against ground targets having been released due to the non-activity of the Luftwaffe. The unit concerned is the 461st Anti-Aircraft Artillery Battalion.

COMMUNIQUE No. 212   November 6

Excellent progress has been made in western Holland. Allied forces are approaching the line of the Maas and the Hollandsche Diep. HEUSDEN, GEERTRUIDENBERG, KLUNDERT and DINTELOORD were cleared of enemy and we are operating in the island of Tholen and on the St Philipsland isthmus.

On Walcheren, progress was made northeast of DOMBURG. NIEUWLAND was freed and we are within 1,000 yards of MIDDELBURG to the south. Fighters and fighter-bombers gave support to our forces in this area.

Other fighters and fighter-bombers attacked troop concentrations, strong points, ammunition dumps and flak positions in the DUNKIRK area. Rail lines in northern and eastern Holland were cut.

In southeastern Holland heavy fighting continues in the MEIJEL area.

In the areas of AACHEN, BONN, KAISERSLAUTERN and VIERSEN, fighter-bombers attacked dumps and military buildings.

Our forces made small gains in the HURTGEN FOREST sector against stubborn resistance. Extensive minefields covered by artillery and small-arms fire hindered our progress southwest of the town of HURTGEN and our units near KOMMERSCHEIDT, three-fourths of a mile northwest of SCHMIDT, continued to meet strong resistance from tank, infantry and artillery fire. Mopping-up continued in the forest approximately one mile west of SCHMIDT. Our fighter-bombers attacked tanks and troops near SCHMIDT.

Other fighter-bombers attacked airfields near HALLE, CRAILSHEIM and SACHSENHAUSEN and a dam near FRITZLAR. Rails were cut at several places in the Rhineland: rail yards near DUSSELDORF were bombed, and an ammunition train south of KASSEL was blown up.

Medium and light bombers, using Pathfinder technique, attacked an ordnance depot at HOMBURG.

Four enemy aircraft were shot down and 34 destroyed on the ground. Seven of our aircraft are missing.

During the afternoon, escorted heavy bombers attacked the industrial town of SOLINGEN, just south of the Ruhr. One bomber is missing.

In the Moselle valley, our units freed BERG on the Moselle river, eight miles northeast of THIONVILLE.

Farther south, our troops maintained good progress in the BACCARAT sector and have taken the village of STE BARBE.

As Holland is a country full of rivers, waterways and canals, the engineers had their work cut out building Bailey bridges as inevitably the Germans blew all the existing ones . . . from the largest like the Nijmegen railway bridge *(left)* to some of the smallest like this rail bridge *(right)* over the Wilhelmina Canal at Best. The latter had been demolished by cutting charges at the mid-span and blowing one of the abutments. No. 3 Railway Construction and Maintenance Group of the Royal Engineers started work on the replacement on October 30 and a single line opened on December 15 and a double by January 31.

COMMUNIQUE No. 213   November 7

On Walcheren island, Allied troops have taken MIDDELBURG and, after cutting the road between there and VEERE, have freed VEERE itself. Other units are fighting their way northeastwards from the DOMBURG area.

Gains on the Dutch mainland have taken our troops to the outskirts of WILLEMSTAD and fighting continues on the approaches to the MOERDIJK bridges, which have been blown by the enemy.

Communications and supply lines in Holland and over the Dutch-German frontier were attacked yesterday by fighter-bombers. Targets included railway yards at UTRECHT and GOUDA and railway tracks over widespread areas of northern and eastern Holland. Rocket-firing fighters hit military buildings east of ZUTPHEN.

Our units continued to meet strong opposition in the HURTGEN FOREST. A German counter-attack was repulsed west of HURTGEN, but a thrust by enemy infantry and tanks in VOSSENACK forced us to withdraw a short distance in the town. The enemy attack was contained and our units resumed the offensive to regain their former positions.

We made small gains two miles west of SCHMIDT against heavy opposition.

Fighter-bombers, supporting our ground units in the SCHMIDT area, made a series of attacks on the enemy troops and armored units. They also bombed and strafed military buildings northeast of GEILENKIRCHEN and hit targets at JULICH and fuel and ammunition dumps at DUREN.

Other fighter-bombers attacked communications and transport in the Rhineland and elsewhere in Germany.

GELSENKIRCHEN was bombed during the afternoon by a very strong force of escorted heavy bombers, five of which are missing. In the evening, other heavy bombers attacked COBLENZ.

East of LUNEVILLE, the village of HERBEVILLER was taken. Our units have freed several additional towns north and southeast of BACCARAT. These include VACQUEVILLE, BERTRICHAMPS, LACHAPELLE, ST REMY, NOMPATELIZE and LA SALLE. New gains were made against stubborn resistance in the Vosges heights west of GERARDMER.

In the Maritime Alps, we have made gains at several points and now hold the high ground along the Italian frontier.

The two bridges at Moerdijk — a road and rail over 1,000 yards long — lay on the direct route from Breda to Rotterdam but the attempt to capture them intact was thwarted when the Germans managed to hold up the 1st Polish Armoured Division at the River Mark for several days. By the time they battled through Moerdijk — demolishing an anti-tank wall at point-blank range — the town was in ruins and the bridges were down.

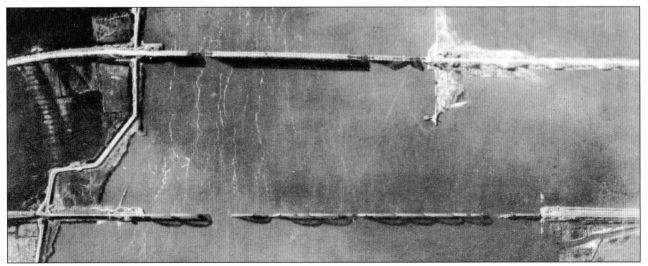

Two military buildings in DUNKIRK were destroyed yesterday in attacks by rocket-firing fighters.

Air attacks on enemy communications were continued. Fighter-bombers cut railway lines in the areas of AMERSFOORT, APELDOORN and ZWOLLE. A railway bridge at GOCH, an oil storage tank and railway buildings at EMMERICH were hit by a rocket-firing fighters and fighter-bombers. Railway lines were cut in several other places along the Dutch-German frontier.

Action continues in the HURTGEN FOREST sector with a little change in positions. Fighting still is in progress in the village of VOSSENACK. Farther south, we have repulsed two counter-attacks from the vicinity of SCHMIDT. West of SCHMIDT our units improved their positions and mopped up pockets of resistance.

Enemy defence positions near SCHMIDT were attacked by fighter-bombers. Other targets were buildings, railway lines and bridges in the Ruhr.

Rain slowed ground operations in the LUNEVILLE—REMIREMONT sector. A strong counter-attack was repulsed west of GERARDMER after stiff fighting.

And this is another example of the importance of bridges in war. On November 7 fighter-bombers attacked the railway bridge over the River Niers at Goch — as reported in this communiqué — but they failed to demolish it. That was left to the Germans who destroyed both spans and also the brick abutments.

COMMUNIQUE No. 214   November 8

With the freeing of WILLEMSTAD, Allied forces now hold the entire south shore of the Hollandsche Diep and the Maas river with the exception of an area south and east of the destroyed MOERDIJK bridges where a small isolated force of the enemy is still holding out.

On Walcheren, fighting is continuing northeast of DOMBURG. Gun positions in this area were hit by rocket-firing fighters. Elsewhere on the Island, resistance has ceased.

No. 607 Railway Construction Company, Royal Engineers, did not begin work to construct a replacement until March 3, 1945, the new single-track being completed by March 19.

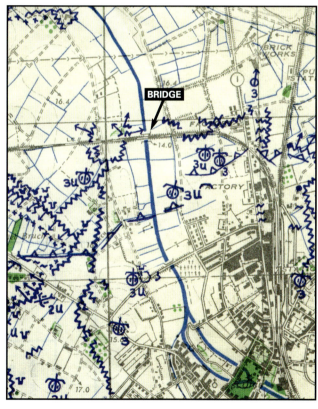

The map from the same period shows the bridges protected by several AA guns and machine gun positions.

After the war the Germans finally demolished the bridge a second time when this line was taken out of service.

Fifty miles west of Moerdijk lies the 16th-century fort of Willemstad protecting the entrance to the Hollandsche Diep (or Lower Rhine). Approaching the fort on November 8, the 4th Battalion, Lincolnshire Regiment, sent forward the ADC of the 49th Division with a Dutch interpreter to call on the German garrison of some 300 troops to surrender. Here a patrol from A Company is pictured passing a wrecked gun in the centre of the fortress.

COMMUNIQUE No. 215   November 9

On Walcheren island, Allied forces have freed VROUWENPOLDER. Only a few pockets of resistance are holding out and mopping-up continues.

There has been bitter fighting for the MOERDIJK bridge approaches. We penetrated the concrete defences and made some advance in the face of fierce opposition. The enemy has been driven out of the area east of the town.

Gun positions at DUNKIRK were attacked yesterday by rocket-firing fighters.

Fighter-bombers continued the attacks on transportation targets in Holland, principally in the UTRECHT area. Rail tracks were cut in numerous places and motor transport destroyed. The railway station and a factory at WEEZE, south of GOCH, and strong points north and south of the REICHSWALD FOREST, were attacked by rocket-firing fighters.

Fighter-bombers attacked the communications center of GEILENKIRCHEN where many fires were started, bridges near DUSSELDORF and COLOGNE, and a rail yard near EUSKIRCHEN. Locomotives and freight cars in the Rhineland were also attacked.

Airfields at WIESBADEN and SACHSENHEIM were hit by fighter-bombers.

In the HURTGEN FOREST sector our forces are attacking against strong enemy pressure, and are gaining ground slowly in the area south of VOSSENACK. Gains have been made against very heavy resistance southwest of the town of HURTGEN. West of SCHMIDT enemy pockets are being mopped up

In the Seille valley, our units made gains east and northeast of NANCY after an artillery preparation yesterday morning. The following towns northeast and east of NANCY have been freed: AULNOIS-SUR-SEILLE, MAILLY-SUR-SEILLE, FRESNES-EN-SAULNOIS, MALAUCOURT, JALLAUCOURT, MONCOURT and BEZANGE.

Between NANCY and METZ, nine enemy command posts were bombed and fighter-bombers, supporting our ground forces in the area east of PONT-A-MOUSSON, bombed gun positions and troop concentrations.

North of BACCARAT the enemy has been cleared from MIGNEVILLE.

Gains have been made in the wooded area west of ST DIE and we have taken the village of LES BARAQUES.

Several enemy counter-attacks were repulsed in the Vosges mountains southwest of GERARDMER.

Eight enemy aircraft were shot down and two destroyed on the ground in tactical air operations yesterday. Seven of our aircraft are missing.

Yesterday morning, heavy bombers attacked the synthetic oil plant at HOMBERG in the Ruhr. Fighters escorted the bombers and flew supporting sweeps. From this operation one bomber and one fighter are missing.

On November 8, the Americans began the envelopment of Metz from the north when the 90th Division crossed the Moselle downstream of Thionville and began to push southwards. Elements of the 25. Panzergrenadier-Division launched two strong counter-attacks in an attempt to contain the bridgehead. On the 12th, a Kampfgruppe attacked near Kerling aiming for the bridge at Malling and on the 15th another battle-group struck from Metzervisse, leading to a fierce battle in the village of Distroff. Having driven back the Germans, the Americans captured Metzervisse on the 16th. The following day Signal Corps photographer Warren J. Rothenberger pictured men of the 358th Infantry moving through the village.

The same junction at the eastern end of the village, looking down the Kédange road,

On October 28, Eisenhower confirmed his decisions made ten days earlier at a meeting in Brussels favouring a two-pronged strategy rather than Montgomery's single thrust. He then began a two-week tour to visit every division in the First and Ninth armies. The 28th Division's commander, General Cota, was having a bad time with his struggle to capture Schmidt and on November 7, tired from long days and sleepless nights and mentally exhausted from what was happening to his division, he nearly had a fit when one of his regimental commanders — whom Cota expected to be at the front — suddenly appeared at his HQ in Rott. Two days later General Eisenhower, together with Generals Bradley, Hodges and Gerow, arrived and during the meeting Hodges of First Army drew Cota aside for a 'short sharp conference' in which he remarked on the fact that division HQ appeared to have no precise knowledge of the location of its units and was doing nothing to obtain the information. The picture of the tormented Cota and the worried-looking Eisenhower (left) was taken outside the division CP, which was at 23 Quirinus-strasse, a village inn owned by the Emonts family. Right: This nicely-staged comparison was taken some years ago by one of our American readers, Cyrus Lee.

COMMUNIQUE No. 216   November 10

Allied forces are advancing east of the Moselle valley in the METZ—NANCY sector and units are now in the vicinity of VIVIERS, 17 miles east of PONT-A-MOUSSON. Our operations yesterday were supported by heavy, medium and fighter-bombers in very great strength. Enemy troops, strong points, artillery, transport and communications were bombed and strafed.

In the area southeast of PONT-A-MOUSSON, our units have reached MORVILLE-LES-VIC east of the Seille river and are in the BOIS D'AULNOIS, two and one-half miles north of the FORET DE GREMECEY.

Northeast of PONT-A-MOUSSON, our forces have passed through CHEMINOT and are making gains beyond town.

Farther north, we have made some progress across the Moselle river, northeast of THIONVILLE.

Bitter fighting continues in the HURTGEN area and our units have made local gains against heavy resistance west of SCHMIDT and in the area southwest of the town of HURTGEN. In VOSSENACK our units consolidated and improved their positions.

Objectives in the Ruhr were attacked by escorted heavy bombers, two of which are missing.

In southwestern Holland, resistance has ceased on the approaches to the MOERDIJK bridges and on Walcheren island.

Rocket-firing fighters attacked gun positions and strong points in DUNKIRK.

In the LUNEVILLE sector the enemy reinforced his forward positions and intensified his artillery fire.

Northwest of ST DIE the village of DEYFOSSE in the Meurthe valley has been taken.

To the south, our advance has reached the eastern edge of the FORET DOMANIALE DE CHAMP where resistance continues to be heavy.

Eisenhower: 'With the opening of Antwerp our supply problem was considerably eased, but the Germans had profited by our earlier logistical handicap to reinforce their Siegfried defenses with hurriedly formed Volksgrenadier divisions. These divisions initially had very low combat value, but both General Bradley and I felt that unless the Siegfried positions could be speedily attacked the relative strength of the opposing forces would gradually become more favorable to the enemy. My plan of campaign at this peirod included an advance on the fronts of the Northern and Central Groups of Armies to the Rhine, which it was necessary to hold from its mouth to Düsseldorf at least, if not to Bonn or Frankfurt, before a large-scale penetration beyond the river into Germany could be attempted. With the strong defensive barrier which the Rhine would afford our armies, it would become more easily possible to concentrate power at one point for the breakthrough, leaving relatively thinly held positions along the rest of the front.'

Bradley: 'This decision of Eisenhower's to resume the offensive in November resurrected once more the perennial dispute between Montgomery and me over the old issue of *single* versus the *double* thrust. My reasoning on the *double* thrust was quite simple. Were Eisenhower to concentrate his offensive north of the Ardennes, the enemy could also concentrate his defenses there the better to meet that single attack. On the other hand, if we were to split our effort into a double thrust with one pincer toward Frankfurt, we might both confound the enemy and make better use of the superior mobility of our armies. Patton had the most at stake for if Montgomery's views were to prevail, Third Army would be consigned to the defensive south of the Ardennes and there perhaps wait out the war behind the Moselle river. Could not those divisions be better employed against the Saar, I asked SHAEF?' Above: Now in the sector of Patton's Third Army, this is all that was left of Cheminot, between Metz and Nancy, when patrols entered on November 9.

Eisenhower chatting to men of a signal company attached to the 8th Infantry Division in Wiltz, Luxembourg, on November 9. Bradley wrote that 'Ike apparently agreed, for this time he decided in favor of our double-pronged offensive. In his plan, 12th Army Group was to attack north of the Ardennes with the First and Ninth Armies, and south of that wooded barrier with the Third. All three were to push on to the Rhine and seize crossings there if they could. Meanwhile Monty was to clean out his sector west of the Meuse where he had previously by-passed the enemy on his lunge toward Arnhem. Thereafter he was to sweep south from Nijmegen toward the Ruhr down the wedge between the Rhine and Meuse rivers. Target date for the First and Ninth Armies' offensive was fixed for November 5. Third Army was to go by the tenth. In preparation for this new offensive I pulled Simpson [Ninth] out of the Ardennes and shifted him north of Hodges [First] adjacent to Montgomery's British front in Holland.'

COMMUNIQUE No. 217   November 11

Allied forces continued their advance in the METZ—NANCY sector against light to moderate resistance yesterday. CHATEAU-SALINS has been freed and our units have pushed on to AMELECOURT and HAMPONT. DELME ridge, six miles east of NOMENY has been reached. We have also reached VIGNY and SECOURT east of LOUVIGNY.

Small gains were made in the area of MAIZIERES-LES-METZ. Fighter-bombers attacked enemy positions east of METZ.

In the Moselle river bridgehead northeast of THIONVILLE, we have made gains south and east of KOENIGSMACKER and have repulsed a minor counter-attack east of the town.

In the HURTGEN area, our units continued their attack against heavy resistance from dug-in enemy positions. Many mines are being encountered. A counter-attack was repulsed in this sector. West of SCHMIDT we have made progress and are clearing pillboxes.

In the area north of AACHEN and west of COLOGNE, fighter-bombers went for freight yards, railway lines, roundhouses and trains. Among fighter-bomber targets were a freight yard at AMELN, a roundhouse three miles south JULICH, two trains at WEGBERG and a railway control station at RHEINDAHLEN. Other fighter-bombers bombed MERSEBURG and the rail and road centre of SAAL, starting a number of fires, and a warehouse near ERKELENZ was also attacked.

An enemy strong point north of the forest of REICHSWALD and a factory at WEEZE were hit by rocket-firing fighters.

Fighters and fighter-bombers supported ground operations and continued attacks on enemy communications in eastern Holland and across the frontier into Germany. Rocket-firing fighters attacked a railway junction south of EMMERICH.

In the Meurthe river valley slight gains were made northwest of ST DIE. The villages of LE MENIL and BIARVILLE have been taken.

A local counter-attack was repulsed east of BRUYERES, and in the Vosges, enemy attempts to infiltrate were frustrated.

To avoid a complex physical transfer of troops and supplies, Bradley directed the two army headquarters simply to exchange corps, with the First Army receiving the VIII Corps and the Ninth Army obtaining the XIX Corps. This is General Bradley's own map to show the change when the 8th Division passed from the Ninth to the First.

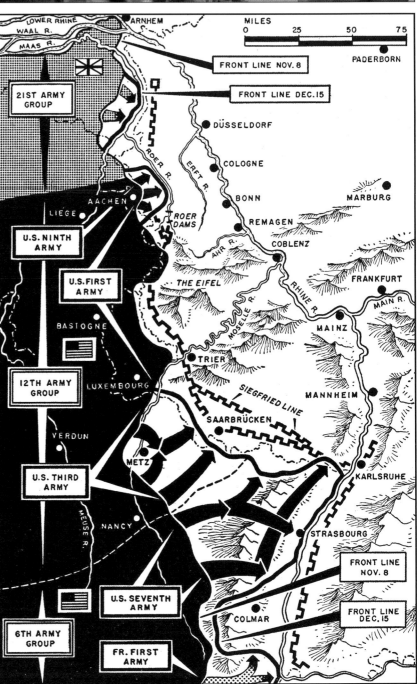

242

Of all the Armistice Day parades held that November, none was more appropriate than the one held in Luxeuil-les-Bains on the edge of the Vosges mountains in south-eastern France. In April 1916, the Escadrille Américane — Squadron No. 124 — was deployed here with volunteer flyers from the USA, although the name had to be changed in December to Lafayette Escadrille following a complaint from the Germans that the original name implied that the United States was allied to France, rather than being neutral. Therefore it was very fitting that the 36th 'Texas' Division liberated Luxeuil as the unit had fought in the Meuse-Argonne in 1918. Now, having landed in the south of France, it was attached to the French First Army. Major General John E. Dahlquist and General Alexander Patch of the Seventh Army were present at the ceremony in the Place de l'Abbaye when a second plaque was dedicated beneath the original.

COMMUNIQUE No. 218   November 12

Allied forces attacking in the METZ—NANCY sector continue to make progress. Our armored units have advanced to HABOUDANGE, seven miles northeast of CHATEAU-SALINS, and infantry elements are clearing GERBERCOURT, on the eastern edge of the FORET DE CHATEAU-SALINS.

Southeast of METZ, the villages of BECHY and TRAGNY have been freed, and our units have reached REMILLY and SANRY-SUR-NIED.

In the HURTGEN sector, our forces west of SCHMIDT are making slow progress in cleaning out pillboxes against heavy mortar and machine-gun fire.

Fighter-bombers supporting our ground forces in the regions of NANCY, CHATEAU-SALINS, METZ, THIONVILLE and MONTENACH heavily attacked strong points, gun positions, tanks, troop concentrations and motor transport. Medium bombers attacked strong points and gun concentrations northeast of AACHEN.

Other medium bombers attacked rail bridges at SINZIG, EUSKIRCHEN, AHRWEILER and MAYEN. Fighter-bombers went for rail targets in Germany around GELSENKIRCHEN, TRIER, EUSKIRCHEN and COLOGNE.

Transportation targets in Holland were attacked by fighter-bombers and rocket-firing fighters with rail tracks, bridges and trains as the principal targets. Three bridges at WOERDEN, ZWOLLE and NIJKERK were attacked, and rail tracks, chiefly in the areas of UTRECHT, ARNHEM, ZWOLLE and ZUTPHEN were cut. Loaded trains in the AMERSFOORT area were successfully attacked. Other targets were lock gates at SNEEK and ferries on the lower Rhine and the Maas. Medium bombers went for rail targets at OLDENZAAL and ROERMOND. Two enemy aircraft were shot down and eight of ours are missing.

Heavy bombers, escorted by fighters, yesterday afternoon attacked the synthetic oil plant at CASTROP-RAUXEL in the Ruhr. None of our aircraft is missing from this operation.

In the LUNEVILLE—BRUYERES area gains were made at many points and several more towns have been occupied.

Our troops have reached the Meurthe river between RAON L'ETAPE and ST DIE. Farther south the forests of MORTANGE and DOMANIALE DE CHAMP have been virtually cleared of the enemy.

In the Vosges heights our positions were improved.

COMMUNIQUE No. 219   November 13
Allied forces continued to advance in the NANCY—METZ area with thrusts to the east of PONT-A-MOUSSON. Armor and infantry units have reached the villages of CONTHIL and LIDREZING, approximately seven miles north of DIEUZE. Other units are in CHATEAU-BREHAIN, DALHAIN and VAXY, north of CHATEAU-SALINS. Armored elements have crossed the Nied Francais river and are in HERNY, three miles east of HAN-SUR-NIED.

In the KOENIGSMACKER area our infantry has restored its line after a counter-attack, and a newly-won bridgehead across the Moselle below THIONVILLE was reinforced.

Farther south, small advances were made west of ST DIE and east of BRUYERES. The villages of LA BOLLE and LES MOITRESSES have been taken.

Adverse weather yesterday restricted our air operations.

COMMUNIQUE No. 220   November 14
Allied forces continued to advance yesterday north and south of METZ. Our armor is astride the rail line southeast of METZ in the vicinity of HERNY and BAUDRECOURT. Infantry units have reached HERNY and are a mile northeast of ANCERVILLE.

Following towns are in Allied hands: CORNY, on the Moselle river; POMMERIEUX, VERNEY and LIEHON, southeast of CORNY.

Our units are in the FORET DE BRIDE at DE KOECKLING and also are north of the FORET DE CHATEAU-SALINS.

A fort northeast of THIONVILLE has been cleared.

Gains of approximately two miles were made in the sector east of LUNEVILLE, despite strong resistance and hampering snow. LEINTREY was freed. Farther south, the village of MONTIGNY was taken.

Southeast of BACCARAT an enemy counter-attack was broken up by our artillery which inflicted severe casualties.

Substantial gains were also made southeast of BRUYERES where the villages of AUMONTZEY and CHAMPDRAY were freed, and nearby high ground was occupied.

Activity in Holland was restricted to patrolling artillery duels in bad weather. Air operations were again restricted by weather.

Eisenhower: 'On the 6th Army Group front, the November offensive of the French First Army was launched on the 14th. Within a week the Belfort Gap had been breached and our troops had reached the Rhine. Belfort was cleared of all resistance by the 22nd. The breakthrough, accomplished on the 18th, turned the flank of the German positions in the Vosges and forced a general withdrawal in front of the Seventh Army sector to the north, where Seventh Army troops, after launching their attack simultaneously with that of French First Army, had been struggling slowly forward along the roads leading through the Vosges passes. The towns of Blâmont, Raon-l'Étape, Gérardmer, and St-Dié, with other lesser villages which controlled the passes through the hills, had been stubbornly defended by the enemy, for as long as they remained in his hands the High Vosges stood as an impassable wall protecting the Rhine plain to the east. With the outflanking movement to the south these towns fell to advancing Seventh Army troops, and the 44th Infantry Division, rapidly exploiting the strategic possibilities, advanced to Saarebourg, which fell on the 21st.' This Sherman of the 756th Tank Battalion bogged down at Rouges-Eaux, six miles west of St-Dié.

The York was due to touch down at Pomigliano near Naples at around 2 p.m. but when it failed to appear after another two hours, a flurry of signals alerted SHAEF, HQ Mediterranean Air Forces, Overseas Aircraft Control, Air/Sea Rescue and air forces on the Continent. The Second Tactical Air Force was asked to mount a search 30 miles on either side of the planned route but bad weather prevented the operation starting for another two days. Over the next six days more that 100 aircraft searched an area of 61,000 square miles but the York had disappeared without trace. Séraphin Mathieu, an electricity worker in the tiny hamlet of Le Rivier d'Allemont, east of Grenoble in south-eastern France, heard an aircraft crash in the mountains above the village yet he had to wait until the snow had melted before he could climb to the crash site. It was over seven months later, after the war in Europe was over, that he discovered the wreckage still covered with a layer of snow. The authorities were notified on June 4, 1945 and the Deputy Chief Inspector of Accidents despatched to France. He determined that the York had struck the mountainside at 8,500 feet under full power.

Although the communiqué for November 15 makes no mention of it, behind the scenes General Eisenhower must have been very anxious as Air Chief Marshal Leigh-Mallory was overdue on the first leg of his flight to take over as the Air Commander in South-East Asia. Sir Trafford had been notified about his new appointment back in August and Eisenhower had reluctantly agreed his release from SHAEF in October. His last public appearance in the UK was on October 16 to meet ten aircraft identifiers of the Royal Observer Corps who had just been mentioned in despatches for their work in the invasion of Normandy. He is seen here congratulating Observer J. W. Reynolds of Coventry. After a brief spell of leave, Sir Trafford, his wife and members of his staff arrived at Northolt early on the morning of November 14. The weather was already severely restricting operations on the Continent yet the flight went ahead and the Avro York with ten persons aboard took off at 9.07 a.m. Initially a Spitfire escort was provided as far as the Channel but thereafter the aircraft was on its own across France, taking a wide berth to avoid areas still being fought over.

In 1982 we decided to research the story for issue 39 of *After the Battle* and Jean Paul was a natural choice to do the on-the-spot investigation as he not only lived in the area but was also a trained mountaineer. The spot was bleak and remote with pieces of wreckage still scattered across the landscape, denoting the sad end to SHAEF's Air Force Commander.

COMMUNIQUE No. 221   November 15

Allied forces attacks in the sector east of WEERT against moderate opposition. The village of NEDERWEERT EIND was freed and bridgeheads were established over the Noorder and Wessem canals.

In the METZ sector our forces have repulsed counter-attacks and have increased pressure on the city from the north and south. Bridgeheads across the Moselle in the KOENIGSMACKER and THIONVILLE areas have been joined. Our units have reached FRECHING and KUNTZIG, and patrols or in the vicinity of LEMESTROFF.

Other forces have taken ORNY and are in the BOIS DE L'HOSPITAL. We have reached the DESTRICH—BARONWEILER area northeast of DIEUZE.

Northeast of BACCARAT, gains up to approximately two miles were made against light opposition.

East of BRUYERES the enemy was forced to withdraw more than a mile and GRANGES-SUR-VOLOGNE and several nearby villages were freed.

In the BELFORT sector, limited gains were made against stiff resistance along flooded Doubs river.

Weather severely restricted air operations.

The smashed and decomposed bodies were brought down to the village and laid to rest in the small local cemetery on June 15.

COMMUNIQUE No. 222 November 16

Allied forces continued to advance in the WEERT area yesterday, pushing forward to a depth of 7,000 yards despite difficult roads and enemy mines.

Transportation targets and gun positions in the THIONVILLE area were attacked by a small number of fighter-bombers. In this sector our ground forces cleared ILLANGE, and further south FEVES and QUARAILLE have been liberated.

We have repulsed counter-attacks in the ENSCHWEILER—LANDORF area.

Our forces are in MORCHINGEN, BARONWEILER and GUEBLING, and other units have reached the MARSAL area and the village of HARAUCOURT.

The French Ier Corps d'Armée started its offensive to breach the Belfort Gap on November 14 with the 2ème Division d'Infanterie Marocaine attacking at midday. Two days later, advance units of the division, with elements of the 5ème Division Blindée in support, reached a point half a mile short of Héricourt and the Lizaine river. These two Shermans of the 5ème Division Blindée were knocked out that day as they entered Issans, three miles south of Héricourt. The picture was taken two days after the battle by which time the two tanks had alrady been moved to clear the road.

Northeast of BACCARAT our troops freed STE POLE after hard fighting. In this sector, the enemy holds commanding ground and our progress is slow.

Constant pressure continued to force the slow enemy withdrawal southeast of BRUYERES.

In the BELFORT sector, our troops advanced several miles in the DOUBS river area. A number of villages have been liberated including MARVELISE, MONTENOIS, LOUGRES, ECOT and ECURCEY. Several hundred prisoners have been taken.

A synthetic oil plant at DORTMUND was attacked by escorted heavy bombers. BERLIN was hit by a force of light bombers yesterday evening.

COMMUNIQUE No. 223   November 17

The Allied advance towards the Maas in southeastern Holland continued yesterday. Opposition was light and fighter-bombers gave support by attacking enemy positions west of VENLO. We have taken WESSEM and are within a mile of ROERMOND. Three miles farther north, BUGGENUM has been freed, while other troops have reached the Canal de Derivation in the BROEKHEIDE area. Contact has been established between the forces south of the Noorder canal and the troops which captured MEIJEL.

In the GEILENKIRCHEN sector our units launched attacks and made gains of several thousand yards. We are in FLOVERICH and IMMENDORF.

These operations were preceded and supported by air attacks in very great strength by heavy, medium and fighter-bombers.

In support of our ground forces in the GEILENKIRCHEN area, fighter-bombers attacked at least 12 German towns and bombed and strafed dug-in enemy troops, gun positions and communications. In the DUREN—ESCHWEILER area, 1,200 heavy bombers, escorted by 480 fighters, attacked enemy strong points, field batteries and anti-aircraft guns. Some of the escorting fighters also strafed enemy transport in the FRANKFURT and GIESSEN region. Bombing generally was in adverse weather, although some crews reported seeing good results through breaks in the clouds. Medium bombers, none of which is missing, hit gun positions at ECHTZ and LUCHEM, east of ESCHWEILER.

Another force of heavy bombers, numbering 1,150 with an escort of 250 fighters, struck at the towns of DUREN, JULICH and HEINSBERG, immediately behind the enemy lines. The bombing was controlled throughout by Master Bombers, who claim that all attacks were highly concentrated.

VI Corps renewed its attack in the Vosges on November 12. On the corps' northern wing the 100th Division started south-eastwards through a forested area. It was the first time the 'Century' Division was going into combat. Hindered by rain and muddy mountain trails, on the 16th the GIs finally reached the crest of a hill from where they overlooked the Plaine river valley in the rear of the German defences at Raon-l'Étape. These men of the division's 398th Regiment were pictured on November 17 when the American attackers started to pour down the hills. By November 18, Raon-l'Étape was clear of German troops.

Striking deeper into Germany, other fighter-bombers attacked railway targets in the vicinity of COLOGNE. Eight fighters and fighter-bombers are missing from the day's operations.

Further south our forces continued the attack enlarging the Moselle bridgeheads. We have troops in the vicinity of MONNEREN, LACROIX and METZERVISSE in the THIONVILLE area. STUCKANGE is in our hands and our forces are in AUGNY and MARLY, south of METZ.

In the BLAMONT—ST DIE area, resistance was moderate but progress was slow. ST DIE and several other villages in the path of our advance was set afire by the enemy and many explosions were heard.

In the approaches to the BELFORT GAP the momentum of our drive was maintained. Several towns have been freed north and south of the Doubs river.

Woippy, on the north-western outskirts of Metz, was taken on the 16th when the 377th Regiment (95th Division) drove out the last defenders belonging to Grenadier-Regiment 1215 reinforced by a company from SS-Panzergrenadier-Regiment 38.

On the following day Signal Corps photographer Pfc Cyril F. Colwell was on hand to picture men of the sister regiment, the 378th, advancing up a street which has since been renamed Rue Général de Gaulle.

COMMUNIQUE No. 224 November 18

Progress continued in the Allied advance towards the Maas. Opposition was generally light. We have established a bridgehead over the Canal de Derivation at the junction of the Noorder canal. Northwest of ROERMOND, the village of HORN was freed.

Trains in the Dutch-German frontier zone at several points between LEGDEN and MUNCHEN-GLADBACH were attacked by fighter-bombers.

In the sector between GEILENKIRCHEN and BLAMONT our forces continued to advance in the face of heavy artillery fire and stiffening resistance. We have taken GRESSENICH, eight miles southwest of DUREN.

In the THIONVILLE area our units are in BUDING, METZERVISSE and REINANGE. Other units have entered NORROY LE VENEUR, LORRY, MARLY and FRONTIGNY in the METZ area.

Fighter-bombers gave support to the ground forces, attacking fortified towns and ground defences, and rail and road targets behind the enemy lines. Gun positions, strong points, troop concentrations and supply dumps were attacked, and locomotives, railroad cars, and road transport were destroyed. The action ranged from DUREN, JULICH and AACHEN in the north through the area of the Saar valley and METZ to COLMAR and MULHOUSE in the south.

Medium bombers attacked a supply depot at HAGUENAU.

Five enemy aircraft were shot down in the course of the day's operations, while 15 were destroyed on the ground near FRANKFURT. Twelve of our aircraft are missing

Advances were made by our ground forces at many points along the 100-mile sector between BLAMONT and the Swiss border.

Several villages were taken in the vicinity of BLAMONT and south of ST DIE. Other villages in the path of our advance were burned by the enemy.

In the BELFORT GAP, our armored and infantry forces made new gains reaching MONTBELIARD, and a number of other towns southwest of BELFORT.

With the move of the newly operational Ninth Army under Lieutenant General William H. Simpson closer to the First Army, the boundary with the British Second Army now ran through Geilenkirchen. Capturing the town would require at least one division, probably two, and Simpson had only one available, the untried 84th Infantry Division, so he decided to ask the neighbouring British to do the job. On November 10, Simpson visited General Sir Brian Horrocks of XXX Corps at his headquarters at Beek in Holland and put the proposal to him. Horrocks initially declined, explaining that, as much as he would like to help, he, too, had only one division, the 43rd, at his disposal. A few days later, Simpson invited Horrocks to his headquarters in Maastricht for an evening with him and Eisenhower. After dinner, Eisenhower jokingly asked: 'Well Jorrocks [his nickname], are you going to take on Geilenkirchen for us?' Horrocks again explained that he had just one division for what was clearly a two-division task. Eisenhower turned to Simpson and said 'Give him one of ours' so Simpson offered him the 84th. The American generals brushed aside Horrocks' objections that it was unfair to give such a difficult task to an untried division but nevertheless Geilenkirchen became a XXX Corps responsibility. The joint Anglo-American operation began on November 18 and for the British Army it was to be their first major battle on German soil. (For more see *After the Battle* No. 140.)

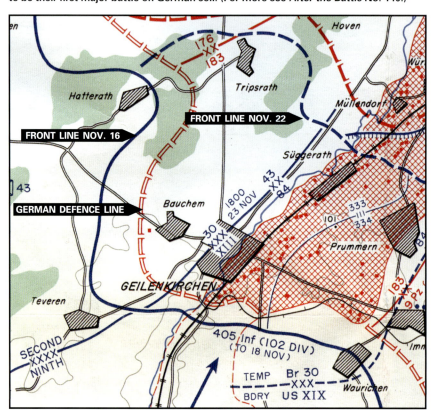

The battle began before dawn when flail tanks of the Lothians and Border Yeomanry (79th Armoured Division) opened up two tracks through the minefields to allow the US 334th Infantry to assault German positions south-east of the town. Here, on the Geilenkirchen to Immendorf road, a Tellermine explodes just beyond the bulldozer which appears to have struck another mine.

COMMUNIQUE No. 225 November 19

The Allied bridgeheads across the Canal de Derivation have been enlarged. We have cut the MEIJEL—PANNINGEN road and reached the vicinity of HELDEN. Opposition was light but many mines were encountered.

Progress north and south of GEILENKIRCHEN has now completed the encirclement of the town, except for a narrow escape corridor northeast along the railway. Units to the north freed NIEDERHEIDE and made gains of 1,500 yards farther east. Units to the south launched an attack at first light yesterday, in the face of moderate opposition, and freed HUNSHOVEN and PRUMMERN. We are in the outskirts of SUGGERATH. Farther south we have taken a number of towns including PUFFENDORF and contained two counter-attacks.

Our forces made slight gains against the mortar and small-arms fire in the area south of WURSELEN and moderate progress against stubborn resistance in the STOLBERG area. Wire obstacles and minefields delayed our advance.

Farther south Allied forces have entered Germany near the Luxembourg border and in the town of BUSCHDORF. Other elements are at RITZING and in the HALSTROFF area. We also have units in SCHWERDORFF and HECKLING.

Our forces are at the north and south edges of METZ.

Gains of up to two miles in the BLAMONT—ST DIE sector have freed 12 towns including RAON L'ETAPE, in the Meurthe valley, which was found heavily mined. More villages have been set on fire by the enemy.

Our forces in the BELFORT GAP freed many towns and drove to within four miles of BELFORT. Along the Swiss border we have advanced nearly 20 miles in three days.

Communications and supply lines behind the enemy lines from NIJMEGEN to BELFORT were attacked by medium and fighter-bombers in strength yesterday. Bridges, rail and road focal points and transport vehicles were among the targets.

MUNSTER, center of rail and water transport, was hit by a strong force of escorted heavy bombers.

Close support for our attacking troops was given in all sectors by fighter-bombers.

In the areas of ESCHWEILER and DUREN, fortified villages, troop concentrations and military barracks were hit by medium and light bombers.

Near the towns of GEILENKIRCHEN, JULICH, DUREN, STOLBERG, and GREVENBROICH, troops, armored units, gun positions and strong points was strafed in low-level attacks by fighter-bombers.

Oil storage and transport facilities in MUNICH, HANAU and ULM areas were hit by fighter-bombers. Airfields at LECHFELD, LEIPHEIM and MENGEN were strafed by other fighter-bombers which destroyed more than 60 enemy aircraft on the ground and damaged others. Enemy fighters were encountered principally in the FRANKFURT and NEUSTADT areas and, in combats which ensued, 25 of them were shot down.

The synthetic oil plant at WANNE-EICKEL was attacked last night by a force of heavy bombers.

Meanwhile, 300 miles to the south, it was an auspicious day for the French as the 1ère Division Blindée of the First French Army reached the Rhine near Rosenau just to the north of Basel where the French-German-Swiss borders meet. More troops followed and one of their tanks even ceremoniously loosed off a few shells across the river to land in Germany! The final liberation of Alsace, a French province which had been annexed by the Third Reich in 1940, came when Strasbourg was occupied on November 26.

COMMUNIQUE No. 226   November 20

In the VENLO area of southeastern Holland, Allied forces have cleared the wooded area between HELDEN and KESSEL, and reconnaissance elements have reached the Maas at KESSEL. North of MEIJEL, crossings were made over the Deurne canal

Medium, light and fighter-bombers, and rocket-firing fighters operating in strength, again struck at the enemy's rail and road supply routes to the battlefront. In northern and eastern Holland and beyond the frontier into Germany northwest of the Ruhr and in the Rhineland, railway lines were cut in some 50 places. Many locomotives and a large number of railway trucks and road vehicles were either destroyed or damaged.

Medium and light bombers attacked the road and railway bridge at VENLO and railway targets at KEMPEN and VIERSEN.

Further progress has been made in our attacks in the GEILENKIRCHEN—AACHEN sector. The town of GEILENKIRCHEN was taken yesterday. Several counter-attacks were contained in the vicinity of PRUMMERN, and we have made gains east of SETTERICH which has been cleared of the enemy.

Farther south, HONGEN, KINZWEILER and ST JORIS are in Allied hands. Our patrols, advancing through wire entanglements and minefields, are in the southern outskirts of ESCHWEILER, and we have reached the town of ROHE. HAMICH and HASTENRATH, northeast of STOLBERG, have been freed and we have made substantial progress in this area.

In close support of our troops in the GEILENKIRCHEN—AACHEN sector, fighter-bombers dive-bombed and strafed nine towns including WELZ, GEREONSWEILER, ALDENHOVEN, NIEDERMERZ and GUSTEN. Medium bombers attacked four defended villages near DUREN. Light bombers struck at troop concentrations at BAAL.

Northeast of KOENIGSMACKER our forces have reached LAUNSTROFF and advanced across the border to WELLINGEN.

Medium bombers attacked MERZIG, five miles northeast of LAUNSTROFF.

Our forces have completed the encirclement of METZ. Troops are on the eastern edge of the city, and units from the north and south have established contact at VALLIERES and VAUDREVILLE east of METZ. On the northwestern side of the city, our forces are advancing across St Symphorien island between the Moselle river and the lateral canal, while other units have crossed the Seille river on the northeastern edge of the city.

Farther south we are in the northern outskirts of DIEUZE and have reached GROSSTANCHEN, 11 miles to the north.

Advances of several miles were made against moderate resistance in the offensives north and southeast of BLAMONT. Eleven more towns have been freed in the area farther south, including RECHICOURT, HARBOUEY and BADONVILLER.

In the Vosges mountains, GERARDMER has been freed.

Our troops have thrust almost through the BELFORT GAP, reaching SAPOIS, within 20 miles of the Rhine. Other units have driven to within three miles of BELFORT.

East of the BELFORT GAP, medium bombers went for the Rhine bridge at NEUENBURG.

A storage depot at ZABERN, 20 miles northwest of STRASBOURG, an ordnance depot at PIRMASENS, and two enemy radio stations were among the day's targets for other medium, light and fighter-bombers and rocket-firing fighters.

From all air operations, 29 fighters and three bombers are missing, but four of our fighter pilots are safe. At least 16 enemy aircraft were destroyed in the air during the day.

A sharp attack by enemy ground forces on MARDYCK in the DUNKIRK area was firmly repulsed on Saturday morning [18th]. Yesterday, strong points and gun positions in the area were attacked by fighter-bombers.

Also on the 19th a link-up took place at Metz where men of the 95th Division met a patrol from the 5th Division coming up from the south, so closing the pincer around the city.

The 95th had been involved in the assault on Fort de Plappeville just west of the city, and this soldier could well be a member of the 1st Battalion of the 378th Infantry as they managed to get right inside the fortress on the 18th but were withdrawn at midnight. The garrison did not finally give up until December 7, some two weeks after Metz itself had surrendered. (For the full story of the battle for Metz see *After the Battle* No. 161.)

COMMUNIQUE No. 227   November 21

Allied forces have made good progress west of VENLO over heavily mined ground against light opposition. North of MEIJEL we have reached the vicinity of HELENAVEEN on the Canal de Helena. Northeast of the BERINGE—HELDEN road our troops advanced about 2,000 yards. Gains were also made east of HELDEN.

Northeast of GEILENKIRCHEN an enemy counter-attack supported by tanks was beaten off. East of the town our forces are meeting fierce enemy resistance in the vicinity of GEREONSWEILER and in the town of FREIALDENHOVEN. DURBOSLAR has been captured and our troops have advanced beyond SCHLEIDEN.

Substantial gains have been made east of AACHEN and we are fighting in the western and southern outskirts of ESCHWEILER. WENAU has been taken, and fighting is in progress north of the town.

Our forces have entered METZ from three sides. Enemy resistance is centered in two pockets in the northern part of the city.

Southeast of METZ we are in LELLINGEN east of FALKENBERG. DIEUZE has been freed and our patrols are at INSVILLER, ten miles northeast.

In an advance of more than six miles, our troops pushed forward against broken resistance close to SARREBOURG.

More than a score of villages in the BLAMONT area were freed.

Substantial gains were also made farther south in the ST DIE area.

Our forces have driven through the BELFORT GAP and reached the upper Rhine. ALTKIRCH and several other towns have been freed.

Weather restricted air operations yesterday, but fighter-bombers attacked transportation targets behind the enemy lines, principally in the region from MERZIG to ST DIE, destroying locomotives, railway cars and road transport vehicles. In the same region, close support was given to the ground forces by attacks on gun positions, troop concentrations and strong points. Medium bombers, escorted by fighters, attacked a rail bridge near HAUSEN, north of COLMAR. From these operations, three fighter-bombers are missing.

Yesterday afternoon, escorted heavy bombers attacked objectives in the Ruhr.

The British 79th Armoured Division, commanded by Major-General Percy Hobart, had a unique role in the defeat of Germany. Equipped with a wide variety of assault armour, it was called upon to clear minefields with its 'Crabs', flame pillboxes with its 'Crocodiles', blast bunkers with its heavy Petard mortars, bridge ditches with bundles of chespale and cross waterways with folding bridges. A mixed force were ordered to Geilenkirchen and two AVREs (Armoured Vehicle Royal Engineers) of No. 617 Squadron were the very first Allied troops to enter the town which they did by mistake on the 19th. These two pictures could show the Churchills concerned . . . but are they coming or going?

The location is near the junction of the Immendorf and Übach-Palenberg roads, the building in the background being the town's Volksschule — now the Janusz Korczak School.

'American Ninth Army captures another town'. So reads the caption to this photo released by SHAEF on November 22. The official US Army history explains more: 'At Immendorf, the Germans employed a battalion of the 10th Panzer Grenadier Regiment supported by tanks variously estimated at from three to ten. Soon after the fight began, General Harmon [2nd Armored Division] placed the commander of the 406th Infantry, Colonel Bernard F. Hurless, in command of Task Force X and authorised him to use all his regiment, if necessary. As events developed, Colonel Hurless needed no more than the one infantry battalion and a company each of tanks and tank destroyers already in the village. Using mortar, artillery, and small-arms fire with deadly effect, the task force threw back the Germans after a fight lasting most of the morning [November 17]. Guns of the 771st Tank Destroyer Battalion knocked out three Panther tanks.'

COMMUNIQUE No. 228   November 22

Allied forces, after freeing HELENAVEEN, have pushed four miles east of the town. To the southeast the advance continued in the neighbourhood of MAASBREE, and we are within four miles of VENLO.

Fighter-bombers supported our troops in southeastern Holland and struck at communication and transport targets in northern and eastern Holland and western Germany. Rail lines were cut at a number of places including UTRECHT and ZWOLLE in Holland and GELDERN and COESFELD in Germany. At GELDERN, two enemy aircraft were shot down.

Heavy fighting continues in the GEILENKIRCHEN sector. Our advance towards WURM and BEECK is being bitterly opposed. The following towns are in our hands: GEREONSWEILER, EDEREN, MERZENHAUSEN, ENGELSDORF, ALDENHOVEN and LAURENZBERG. Escorted medium bombers attacked road junctions immediately ahead of our ground forces in this area, and fighter-bombers hit enemy transport.

Our troops have penetrated some distance into ESCHWEILER. Strong enemy resistance is being encountered by our forces northeast of STOLBERG and in the northern portion of the HURTGEN FOREST. HEISTERN, two miles northeast of GRESSENICH has been captured and other elements have advanced beyond the town.

East of ESCHWEILER, medium and fighter-bombers attacked communications and transport. Other medium bombers hit the fortified town of DUREN.

Over DUSSELDORF a formation of 60 enemy fighters was encountered by 16 of our fighters. Ten enemy aircraft were shot down for the loss of one of our aircraft.

Northeast of THIONVILLE, troops across the German border are encountering enemy road blocks, mines, anti-tank obstacles and artillery fire. West of MERZIG an enemy counter-attack was repulsed.

In METZ enemy resistance continues on the Ile du Saulcy. The German garrison at FORT QUELEU in the southeastern part of the city has surrendered.

Southeast of METZ our forces have made gains north of FALKENBERG. HELLIMER, ten miles southeast of FALKENBERG, has been freed and farther south, TORCHEVILLE and INSVILLER are in our hands.

Against crumbling resistance, our armor and infantry drove eight miles east of SAARBURG on a wide front. The defences in front of the SAVERNE GAP through the Vosges have been passed. Much equipment was abandoned by the rapidly withdrawing enemy, and many villages in the area of more than 100 square miles were freed by our advance.

Fighters and fighter-bombers gave close support to our units in the BLAMONT—GERARDMER area.

Our advance elements made additional progress in the upper Alsace plain in the MULHOUSE area.

The synthetic oil plant at HOMBERG in the Ruhr was attacked in the afternoon by escorted heavy bombers.

Last night heavy bombers were out in very great strength with ASCHAFFENBURG, a railway key point 25 miles southeast of FRANKFURT, and two synthetic oil plants in the Ruhr, as the main objectives.

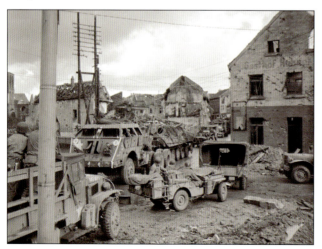

The Americans claim their prize. The 464th Ordnance Evacuation Company use an M26 Pacific truck-tractor to pull a trackless Panther along Jülicher Strasse into Geilenkirchen. The Volksschule building stands at the top of the street.

COMMUNIQUE No. 229   November 23

The Allied advance continues in the VENLO sector. We have captured MAASBREE and are less than four miles from VENLO. Farther north our forces have taken the village of AMERIKA on the DEURNE—VENLO railway.

West of ROERMOND, our troops have advanced to the bank of the Meuse river opposite the town and have captured the village of WEERD.

In the GEILENKIRCHEN sector, our forces advancing towards the Roer river have taken HOVEN and are on the high ground beyond GEREONSWEILER. We are approaching KOSLAR, two miles west of JULICH.

In the area northeast of ESCHWEILER, fighting is in progress in LOHN. DURWISS and ESCHWEILER have been cleared of the enemy.

We are making slow gains in the HURTGEN FOREST against intense small-arms, mortar and artillery fire.

Northeast of THIONVILLE, Allied armored elements are advancing northward beyond the German border in the area of TÜNSDORF.

METZ has been entirely cleared of the enemy, but several outlying forts continued to resist.

Gains have been made by our forces north of FALKENBERG, and east and northeast of DIEUZE we have reached ROHRBACH, ANGWEILER and BISPING. Forward elements are beyond KUTTINGEN and are in the vicinity of MITTERSHEIM.

Our units drove into the lower Alsace

Trooper Fred Smith takes a victory shot for the boys . . . and those back home.

plain within 20 miles of STRASBOURG and the Rhine. SAVERNE, eastern gateway of the SAVERNE GAP, was occupied and our forward elements advanced elsewhere in this area

ST DIE, burned by the enemy, has been entered and extensive gains made east of the Meurthe river.

In the BELFORT GAP, a strong enemy counter-attack has been repulsed. Most of BELFORT has been cleared. Gains were made in the area of MULHOUSE which has been freed.

Fighter-bombers yesterday attacked a road and railway transport in the COLMAR and STRASBOURG areas but generally bad weather throughout the day prevented other air operations.

Technically Geilenkirchen was claimed to have been captured by the 84th Division by November 21 but the fight for the surrounding villages lasted for another four weeks. General Miles Dempsey, the commander of British Second Army, had visited General Horrocks at his XXX Corps headquarters on the 21st and decided that the command and administrative set-up had become too complex and confusing. The American 84th Division was fighting under British XXX Corps, but its 335th Regiment was attached to the US 2nd Armored Division as part of US XIX Corps. In its place, the 405th Infantry was attached to the 84th Division from the 102nd Division which itself was part of US XIII Corps. Dempsey decided it was time to return the 84th Division to American control and sort out the units.

The 84th and 102nd Divisions were to be united under XIII Corps. General Alvan C. Gillem, commander of that corps, said he needed extra time for the reshuffle, so it was agreed that the change in operational control would occur at 1800 hours on the 23rd. Reviewing the progress of the battle, Dempsey judged that the operation had achieved its main objective, the removal of the Geilenkirchen salient, and could therefore be terminated at the same time. Therefore, late on November 23, General Alexander R. Bolling ordered his 84th Division to go over to the defensive. In six days of fighting, it had incurred some 2,000 battle casualties, including 169 killed and 752 missing. Non-battle losses, primarily from trench foot, raised the total by another 500. The 43rd Division had lost some 270 men.

Somewhere near Nancy a GI has triggered an S-Mine and an engineer from the 35th Infantry Division has swept a path so that members of the Graves Registration Service can recover the body.

COMMUNIQUE No. 230   November 24

Allied forces made further progress in the VENLO sector where our units are within three miles of the town. North of the HELMOND—VENLO railway we have advanced about one mile over very difficult country, and have taken METERIK and HORST. South of the railway our forces have gained about 1,000 yards on a 5,000-yard front.

Northeast of GEILENKIRCHEN there has been bitter fighting in the areas of HOVEN and BEECK where the enemy is resisting fiercely.

Small enemy counter-attacks have been repulsed by our units in the GEREONSWEILER area, northeast of JULICH, while very slow progress has been made towards KOSLAR and BOURHEIM, in the JULICH area. North of WEISWEILER, our forces are fighting in LOHN and PUTZLOHN.

Other elements are west, south and southeast of WEISWEILER and gains have been made towards the town. To the southeast, bitter fighting continues in the HURTGEN FOREST where our forces are slowly gaining against very stubborn resistance.

In the area east of METZ, our armored elements have reached JOHANNS-ROHRBACH, and our infantry is in the vicinity of LEYWEILER. An enemy counter-attack has been repulsed near FREMERSDORF. Other armored units farther south have reach FINSTINGEN.

'The war is over for these American soldiers who have paid its price in full in this apple orchard.' Initially the SHAEF Field Press Censor stamped this photo with its caption 'Not to be published' but then relented once the faces had been obliterated.

After the breakthrough in the SAVERNE GAP our troops reached STRASBOURG and freed many towns in the northern Alsace plain. More than 3,000 prisoners, including two generals, and much enemy material have been taken in the rapid advance.

Unfavourable weather slowed progress in the southern Vosges and the BELFORT GAP area, but limited gains were made.

Weather severely curtailed air operations yesterday, but heavy bombers, with fighter escort, attacked the Nordstern synthetic oil plant near GELSENKIRCHEN in the Ruhr.

But German dead were not afforded the same treatment by the censor. This crewman was blasted from his tank at Immendorf.

This machine-gunner was photographed beside his weapon near Heistern, east of Geilenkirchen, without masking his face.

COMMUNIQUE No. 231   November 25

The Allied advance continues northeast of VENLO despite very extensive enemy mining and road demolitions. In the GEILENKIRCHEN area fighting continues.

Stubborn opposition is being met west of JULICH around the villages of BOURHEIM and KOSLAR, both of which are still in enemy hands. Our forces have taken PATTERN and LOHN. In the southwest outskirts of WEISWEILER we are engaged in house-to-house fighting.

Slow but steady progress is being made against very strong enemy resistance in the HURTGEN FOREST. Several enemy counter-attacks have been repulsed in the area northeast of HEISTERN.

To the east of METZ, we have cleared the enemy from REININGEN, INSMINGEN and KAPPELKINGER. Armored units have advanced to HILSPRICH and repulsed an enemy counter-attack in the area. East of FINSTINGEN our forces have crossed the Saar river and are in the vicinity of POSTDORF.

Our forces have cleared the enemy from the major portion of STRASBOURG and have taken some 2,000 prisoners. Many additional prisoners are being rounded up in the vicinity of the city. A counter-attack northwest of the SAVERNE GAP, which caused us to make some slight withdrawals, was beaten off and most of the lost ground was regained.

Steady progress was made towards clearing the enemy from the Vosges mountains in the SAALES PASS area and on the slopes of the BALLON D'ALSACE, north of BELFORT. Adverse weather yesterday restricted air operations.

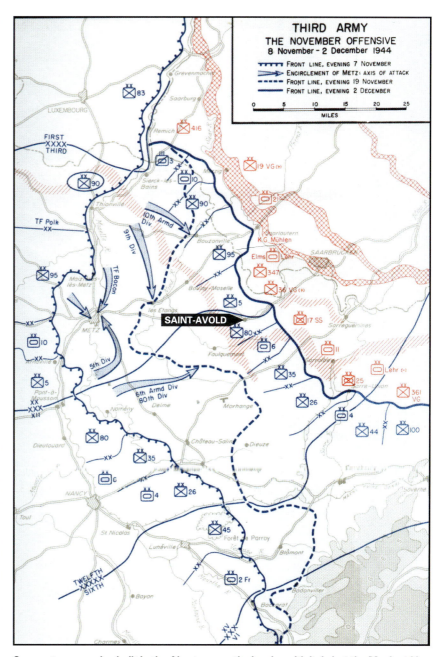

By November 17, the Third Army's 80th Division had been in continuous contact with the enemy for over 100 days. It was now holding a blocking position 50 miles east of Metz near Saint-Avold, close to the Maginot Line — the line of fortifications built by the French in the 1930s facing Germany. Named after the Minister of War André Maginot, the line covered the whole of the north-eastern border of France from the North Sea to Switzerland although much weaker along the border with the neutral countries of Belgium and Luxembourg (see *After the Battle* No. 60). The weakest link was Sector 5 covering the Ardennes which were believed to be impassable. However, by 1944 the defences were in a poor state of repair with much of the artillery unusable. In any case, the Germans were not familiar with the workings, and of course all the casemates faced the wrong way!

Casemates were also built in the Alps to cover the border with Italy but the Maginot Line was far from a continuous front as was the Siegfried Line with its dragon's teeth.

The Faulquemont Fortified Sector comprised five individual fortresses, Bambesch lying close to the N3 near Saint-Avold. The 80th Division along with armoured support went in on

November 25, capturing the fort at Bambiderstroff, a mile west of Bambesch, together with 600 prisoners. But was the damage caused by German shells in 1940 or American in 1944?

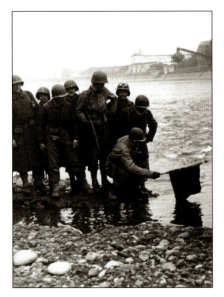 

Lieutenant General Jacob L. Devers commanding the 6th Army Group had under him the Seventh Army (Lieutenant General Alexander Patch) and the First French Army (Général Jean de Lattre de Tassigny). We have seen that an advanced patrol had reached the Rhine on the 19th (page 249) and actually dipped the unit flag of the 1ère Division Blindée into the water *(left)* as a symbolic gesture. On the 21st, the French leading elements entered Mulhouse, the main city in southern Alsace.

COMMUNIQUE No. 232   November 26

Allied forces have closed up to the western defences of VENLO. Farther north, the advance continued and we are approaching the villages of SWOLGEN and GRUBBENVORST.

Rocket-firing fighters, operating in support of our ground forces in Holland yesterday, attacked defended positions to the east of NIJMEGEN. Fighter-bombers bombed barracks south of HILVERSUM and cut rail tracks in the AMERSFOORT, ZWOLLE, UTRECHT and ARNHEM areas.

Strong points, and gun and mortar positions in the DUNKIRK area were also attacked by rocket-firing fighters.

In the GEILENKIRCHEN sector there is no change in the ground situation. Troop concentrations north of GEILENKIRCHEN were attacked by other formations of rocket-firing fighters.

Our forces west of JULICH are fighting in the immediate vicinity of KOSLAR and have captured BOURHEIM. Farther south, PUTZLOHN has been taken and the advance to the southeast continues. House-to-house fighting is in progress in the outskirts of WEISWEILER, and at one point we have reached the WEISWEILER—LANGERWEHE road. On a hill south of LANGERWEHE we are fighting to regain a small amount of ground lost in an enemy counter-attack. Our forces north of the HURTGEN are within a few hundred yards of GROSSHAU and HURTGEN itself is under fire from our artillery.

Strong points and transportation targets in the area north of DUREN were attacked, fighter-bombers attacking a number of pillboxes and gun positions in this area. Medium bombers, which were covered by fighters and fighter-bombers, went for the rail yards at RHEYDT. The rail yards at MUNCHEN-GLADBACH, HARFF and GREVENBROICH were also attacked by fighter-bombers.

Northeast of THIONVILLE our forces across the German border have reached TETTINGEN, three miles southeast of REMICH. BIRGINGEN, southwest of MERZIG, has been taken and we are advancing north of BOUZONVILLE.

A number of enemy positions in the villages near the meeting point of the French—Luxembourg—German border were the targets for fighter-bombers. Behind the enemy lines in the same area, rail cars and motor transport were destroyed and tracks cut in many places, while the rail yards at GEMUNDEN, northwest of KARLSTADT, were also attacked.

Medium and light bombers went for the arsenal at LANDAU and ammunition dumps at KAISERSLAUTERN.

In the area east of METZ we have reached NARBEFONTAINE, seven miles northwest of ST AVOLD.

The ALBESDORF forest, northwest of FINSTINGEN has been cleared of the enemy, and patrols are in the BOIS GIVRYCOURT to the east. Units which crossed the Saar river in the FINSTINGEN area have liberated BARONDORF.

Substantial gains were made against light resistance in the north Alsatian plain and in the Vosges mountains.

STRASBOURG has been cleared of the enemy except for the defenders of the Rhine bridges. The prisoner count in the city has reached 5,000.

In eastern Alsace, fighter-bombers attacked tanks, motor vehicles, locomotives and rail cars, and cut rail lines. Eleven enemy aircraft were shot down during these operations.

According to reports so far received, six of our aircraft are missing from yesterday's operations.

Our units advancing from the ST DIE region towards STRASBOURG pushed almost through the SAALES PASS in the northern Vosges.

In the southern Vosges and BELFORT GAP the enemy has been cleared from additional areas northeast and east of BELFORT.

The French attackers pushed into Mulhouse and the final clearing of the strong German force holding the Lefèbvre Barracks on the 23rd marked the end of the fighting in the southern part of the city. This is the corner of Rue Aristide Briand. However, the German defenders would hold the suburbs north of the Doller river until February.

On the morning of November 23, Task Force Rouvillois of the 2ème Division Blindée entered Strasbourg right on the Rhine.

COMMUNIQUE No. 233   November 27

Allied forces, continuing to clear the Maas pocket, have reached the river between BLITTERSWIJCK and BROEKHUIZEN. North of the VENLO defences, only scattered pockets of enemy remain west of the Maas.

Fighters and fighter-bombers, supporting our ground forces in Holland, hit gun positions, strong points and fortified buildings. Medium and fighter-bombers struck at communications, transport, airfields and military barracks in northern and eastern Holland and over the German frontier.

In the GEILENKIRCHEN area enemy troop concentrations and armoured units were attacked by fighter-bombers.

In the area west of JULICH, we contained counter-attacks by infantry and tanks. Farther south, WEISWEILER has been cleared after stubborn house-to-house fighting and we have advanced to the east. Fighting continues for high ground south of LANGERWEHE and our forces continue to make slow progress in the forest south of HURTGEN.

South of JULICH, fighter-bombers broke up a counter-attack by enemy armor. Other fighter-bombers bombed DUREN and LANGERWEHE and troops and gun positions in the area.

Communications and transport behind the enemy line in Germany were attacked by fighter-bombers which hit rolling stock in the COLOGNE, COBLENZ and GIESSEN areas. Railway yards at RHEYDT were the target for escorted medium bombers.

Fortified towns along the Saar river were bombed by fighter-bombers. Southwest of MERZIG in the Saar valley our forces have reached OBERESCH.

General gains were made in the area east of METZ despite enemy counter-attacks. FORT SOMMY and FORT ST BLAISE were captured, and FORT MARIVAL was abandoned by the enemy. Allied units made gains of one and one-half miles to take RIORANGE, 17 miles northeast of METZ, and other elements are in ZIMMINGEN, northwest of ST AVOLD.

The GUTENBRUNNER WALD north of FINSTINGEN is being cleared. We have advanced up to three miles to reach HUNKIRCH.

North of SAARBURG we have repulsed counter-attacks and regained lost ground.

Our forces, advancing from the ST DIE region, have pushed through the SAALES PASS in the Vosges mountains and reached the Alsace plain west of STRASBOURG. Our grip on STRASBOURG was tightened with the capture of a dozen forts near the city. Prisoners included two generals.

In the southern Vosges, further progress was made toward clearing the enemy from mountain passes and narrowing his salient in the BELFORT GAP.

Ammunition and fuel dumps at HOMBURG, GIESSEN and BERGZABERN were attacked without loss by medium and light bombers. Escorted heavy bombers without loss attacked objectives in western Germany.

As the capital of Alsace-Lorraine, Strasbourg is a large city and Jean Paul had considerable difficulty in finding this particular street. He finally tracked down the location in the Stockfeld part of the city. As this is a southern quarter of Strasbourg it means that the wartime picture was not taken during the initial advance into the city by Task Force Rouvillois but sometime later in the battle. It just shows how wartime captions, having passed through the censor for obvious reasons cannot be relied on. This is Allée David Goldschmidt today.

General Patch was elated by the success of the Seventh Army to have advanced to the Rhine and was following current SHAEF directives that provided for the seizure of bridgeheads across the river if the opportunity arose. However, Eisenhower now ruled against such a move. Furthermore he proposed transferring two divisions from the 6th Army Group to Bradley's 12th to strengthen Patton's Third Army. To this General Devers strongly objected, particularly as plans had already been initiated for the Rhine crossing at Rastatt, north of Strasbourg, and by November 24 the specialised river crossing units were already on the move. As yet no firm date had been set for the Rhine assault but Devers and Patch were looking forward to a crossing between December 10 to 20. There had already been criticism over Eisenhower adopting the role of tactical ground commander back in September, and of SHAEF taking over Leigh-Mallory's role as head of the Tactical Air Forces. Coupled with the on-going row with Montgomery, now Ike was at odds with American generals. This picture was taken at the command post of the French Ier Corps d'Armée at Beaucourt on November 25. L-R: Bradley; Général Jean de Lattre de Tassigny, 1ère Armée; Général Emile Béthouart, Ier Corps d'Armée; Devers and Eisenhower.

On 24 November, the Allied high command initiated a series of decisions that would have a major impact on the course of the war in Europe.

Eisenhower and Bradley began a tour of the Allied southern front. The two American generals first visited the Third Army command post at Nancy.

During the brief stopover, Patton urged that either a portion of his seventy-mile front be assigned to Devers [6th Army Group] or the XV Corps be returned to Third Army control, preferably the latter. Although Eisenhower was apparently noncommittal, he also seemed to have made up his mind that something drastic had to be done to assist Patton.

Eisenhower and Bradley next traveled to Lunéville. There, after joining Devers and Patch [commanding the Seventh Army], they proceeded first to Major General Wade H. Haislip's new XV Corps headquarters at Sarrebourg and then to Major General Edward H. Brooks [VI Corps] who had recently opened his command post at St. Dié. At Sarrebourg the energetic Haislip proved an anxious host, exuberant over the capture of Strasbourg but concerned over the southward progress of the Panzer Lehr through the Sarre river valley. At St. Dié, the usually serious Brooks was more relaxed, elated over his success in finally pushing his command over the Vosges and urging all of his scattered forces to continue the pursuit. Within both headquarters Eisenhower and Bradley found the corps staffs busily planning to push their forces farther east, seize bridgeheads over the Rhine, and cross into Germany itself. Eisenhower, however, quickly ended these preparations. Concerned about Patton's flagging offensive, he wanted the Seventh Army's axis of attack reoriented from the east to the north, through the Low Vosges and against the German First Army's southern flank.

At Haislip's command post, he even issued verbal orders on the 24th directing the XV Corps to halt all preparations for a Rhine crossing, change direction immediately, and advance generally northward astride the Low Vosges Mountains in close support of the Third Army. Supporting Patton's advance into the Saar basin was to have first priority.

Somewhat stunned by the new orders, Devers was determined to challenge them. Returning to the 6th Army Group headquarters at the Héritage Hotel in Vittel that evening, the three principal American ground commanders had a late formal dinner and then retired to Devers' private office to talk over the entire matter. The ensuing discussion lasted until the early hours of the following day and saw a heated argument between Eisenhower, Bradley and Devers.

Eisenhower continued to insist that Devers halt all preparations for a Rhine crossing and turn the Seventh Army north to assist Patton's forces as quickly as possible. Devers objected bitterly to each of these measures, arguing that the Seventh Army was the force that ought to be strengthened and not the Third. If assisting Patton was the primary objective then, he contended, a Seventh Army Rhine crossing at Rastatt followed by a drive north to envelop the Saar basin was the best solution. On this point, however, Bradley strongly disagreed: attempting to force the Rhine against the prepared defensive positions of the West Wall was foolhardy and would only lead to failure.

Exasperated, Devers countered that the Germans currently had few if any troops in front of the Seventh Army and that Patch's reconnaissance patrols across the Rhine had found the defenses there completely unmanned. Eisenhower was unmoved. He instructed Devers to use whatever strength was necessary to clean up the area between the Vosges and the Rhine but to turn the Seventh Army north as quickly as possible, attacking west and east of the Low Vosges. There would be no Rhine crossing.

But none of the three commanders was fully satisfied with the results of the meeting, and all were stung by the tenor of the discussions. The Supreme Commander reportedly came out of the conference 'mad as hell' over Devers' open criticism of his operational strategy, while Devers emerged equally angry, wondering if he was 'a member of the same team'. Thus, instead of abating, the tension between Eisenhower and Devers seemed only to have grown.

The following day Eisenhower and Bradley concluded their visit, touring the French front before returning north via Vittel on the morning of the 26th. Nothing Eisenhower saw in the southern sector of the 6th Army Group altered his decisions. Therefore, between 25 and 26 November, Patch's Seventh Army staff drew up new plans based on Eisenhower's instructions.

RIVIERA TO THE RHINE,
CENTRE OF MILITARY HISTORY, 1993

COMMUNIQUE No. 234 November 28

Allied forces made slow progress yesterday in the JULICH—HURTGEN sector. House-to-house fighting continues in KOSLAR, and farther south we have advanced to the vicinity of ALTDORF. Northeast of WEISWEILER we have captured FRENZ. Our units have reached the outskirts of LANGERWEHE, and we have driven the enemy from the high ground near the village. House-to-house fighting is in progress in HURTGEN.

Fighter-bombers supporting our troops in this sector attacked enemy artillery, flak positions and troops near DUREN, and troop concentrations in the JULICH area and damaged a railway bridge crossing the Roer south of JULICH. Other fighter-bombers went for transportation targets near COLOGNE and disabled locomotives, railway cars and horse-drawn vehicles. Heavy bombers, escorted by fighters, attacked a railway yard in the KALK district of COLOGNE.

We have made gains of up to several miles in the area east of METZ. Our units have reached TETERCHEN, approximately 20 miles northeast of METZ, and we have entered ST AVOLD and a number of small towns in this area.

North of SAARBURG we have taken HONSKIRCH and WOLFSKIRCHEN and have reached DURSTEL and GUNGWILLER. Considerable enemy armour has been encountered in some parts of this sector.

Fighter-bombers attacked troop concentrations in the area north of SAARBURG and in the vicinity of STRASBOURG they struck at tanks and road vehicles. West of STRASBOURG our units cleared MUTZIG and continued their drive eastward through MOLSHEIM on the Alsatian plain.

A rail bridge over the Rhine at BRIESACH, a pontoon bridge in the same area, and the rail centre of FREIBURG were bombed by fighter-bombers. Two of our aircraft are missing from yesterday's operations.

In the Vosges mountains additional gains were made against scattered resistance.

Our advance northeast of BELFORT continued and several villages were freed.

An enemy salient south of the Rhone—Rhine canal was virtually wiped out. The town of DANNEMARIE and several nearby villages were taken after stiff fights in which many enemy tanks were destroyed and 1,000 prisoners were taken.

Last night heavy bombers were over Germany in great strength with FREIBURG and NEUSS, railway centres and advance supply bases for the enemy's western front, as the main objectives. Berlin was attacked by a force of light bombers.

Eisenhower's decision on November 24 to turn the 6th Army Group's main effort north required a major regrouping of the Seventh Army and it was not before November 27 that the VI Corps finally moved off southwards with plans to clear the area from the Vosges mountains to the Rhine. Here, elements of the 2ème Division Blindée move through the town of Entzheim, six miles south-west of Strasbourg, on the 27th. As if Eisenhower's problems were not great enough, now President Roosevelt stepped in proposing that a joint Anglo-American statement be issued to try to bring down German morale. Captain Butcher comments that 'after a considerable exchange of ideas, the conclusion finally was reached, on recommendation of the Supreme Commander, that no such proclamation be issued at this time. General Ike cabled General Marshall that any such statement preferably should follow some successful military operation. The Supreme Commander felt that the statement at this moment probably would be interpreted as a sign of weakness rather than an honest statement of intent.'

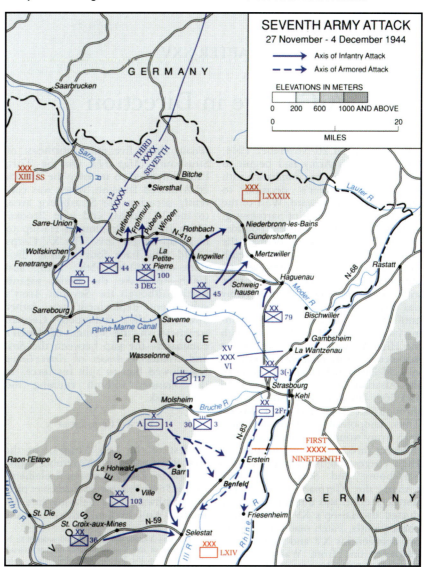

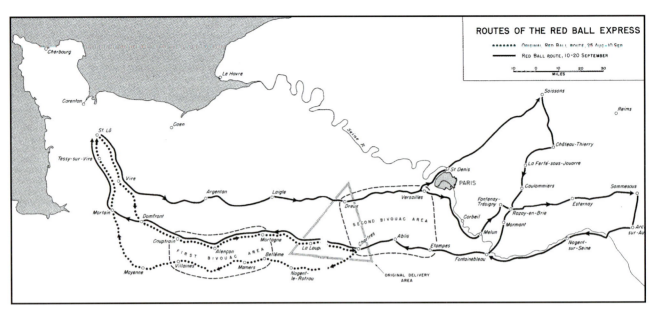

SHAEF had not anticipated such a swift advance across France and the battles at the front were now being severely affected through lack of fuel and ammunition. Initially, in August-September, a one-way route dubbed the Red Ball Express had been established to carry supplies from Normandy and up until it was officially closed on November 16, the trucks had moved over 400,000 tons. But now it was self-defeating at the expense of fuel expended for the 600 miles to the front and wear and tear on the trucks and fatigue of the drivers which was leading to more accidents. On October 6 a White Ball Express route was initiated from Le Havre and Rouen but once Antwerp was operational, the ABC (Antwerp-Brussels-Charleroi) Express Route began on November 30. This transported supplies about 90 miles to dumps where the First and Ninth Armies could access via the use of semi-trailers.

COMMUNIQUE No. 235   November 29

Allied forces north of VENLO are in contact with the few remaining enemy strong points west of the Maas.

Gun positions and defended buildings in Holland were attacked by fighter-bombers yesterday and cover was given to our ground forces. Other fighter-bombers hit railway targets in Holland and over the German frontier to MUNSTER, and struck at the Ruhr valley railway system. At ZWOLLE the railway yards were bombed and strafed and near BORKEN, station buildings were set on fire.

In the GEILENKIRCHEN area increased mortar fire was encountered by our ground forces, and mortar positions at BIRGDEN were destroyed by rocket-firing fighters.

South of JULICH, we have taken high ground and attacked the village of BARMEN. Fighting continued in KOSLAR, and the enemy was cleared from MERZENHAUSEN and KIRCHBERG. Farther south, our units were fighting in five German towns: INDEN, LANGERWEHE, JUNGERSDORF, HURTGEN and LAMMERSDORF.

In this sector, medium, light and fighter-bombers destroyed a number of tanks near BARMEN and attacked fortified villages including RURICH, MERKEN and BIRGEL. Railway yards at ERKELENZ and ELSDORF were among the other targets hit.

Our forces have extended their action in the Saar valley and occupied a number of towns. We have reached WILLINGEN and BERUS, southwest of SAARLAUTERN.

Gains have been made in the ST AVOLD area where we are beyond OBER-HOMBURG and armored elements have reached VAHL-EBERSING and DIEFENBACH. Infantry has advanced to HINSINGEN, and farther south armored forces have almost completely cleared the GUTENBRUNNER WALD and cleared WOLFSKIRCHEN. Other elements are at BURBACH and BERG.

In the northern Alsace plain our advances reached within three miles west of HAGUENAU. Farther north, the Moder river was crossed and INGWEILER and the outskirts of ZUTZENDORF reached. Other elements completed their drive through the Vosges mountains south of MOLSHEIM.

In the BELFORT GAP area a large enemy salient between BELFORT and MULHOUSE was cut by forces which joined south of the Doller river after an eight-mile drive. Main enemy escape routes were severed.

Fighter-bombers attacked strong points and gun positions at DUNKIRK. In the late evening the industrial town of NUREMBERG was bombed by light bombers.

The German High Command were very much alive to the chance of stemming the Allied advance by attacking transportation targets and on October 7 the first V1 flying bomb fell on Antwerp. Launched from the Cologne-Trier-Coblenz area of Germany, 131 V1s and 160 V2s landed on the city in October alone, and over 850 in November. By March 1945 when the launch sites had been overrun, 3,752 civilians and 731 Allied servicemen had been killed. One of the worst incidents occurred on November 27 when a military convoy was hit in Teniers Square killing 157.

COMMUNIQUE No. 236   November 30

In the GEILENKIRCHEN—JULICH sector, Allied forces launched an attack west of LINNICH. We have troops in BEECK and gains were made in the vicinity of LINDERN. KOSLAR has been cleared and other advances have been made in this sector.

Fighter-bombers, supporting our ground forces, attacked enemy targets in the LINNICH area and destroyed an ammunition dump at STETTERNICH.

Farther north, air attacks ranged from the Channel coast to the Ruhr valley. Around DUNKIRK, medium, light and fighter-bombers attacked fortifications and enemy positions. Fighter-bombers and rocket-firing fighters went for transportation targets in northern and eastern Holland, and across the frontier. They attacked road vehicles, locomotives, railway trucks and barges, and cut railway lines in many places. Medium and light bombers struck at the railway bridges at ZWOLLE and DEVENTER.

During the afternoon light bombers attacked targets in the DUISBURG area, and escorted heavy bombers went for targets in DORTMUND.

Hürtgen has finally fallen. Charles B. MacDonald: 'For a long time, the village would bear the terrible stench of war'.

In the DUREN—HURTGEN sector our ground forces repulsed counter-attacks at INDEN and LAMMERSDORF north of FRENZ, and fighting continues for both towns. Resistance ended in JUNGERSDORF and, after bitter fighting, LANGERWEHE was cleared. Gains were made in attacks in the MERODE area west of DUREN. Farther south, our forces continued to push out of the HURTGEN FOREST. KLEINHAU and HURTGEN were captured.

In this sector enemy troop concentrations immediately northwest of DUREN and at ELSDORF and PIER were attacked by medium bombers. Fighter-bombers dive-bombed and strafed targets in the villages of LUCHERBERG, MERODE, WINDEN and GEICH.

In the Saar valley we consolidated previous gains and pushed eastward. We have troops near KARLINGEN, west of SAARLAUTERN, and other units reached the vicinity of SAARUNION where we hold the high ground.

Medium and light bombers struck at ordnance and motor transport depots at LIMBURG, east of COBLENZ, targets at WITTLICH, northeast of TRIER, and supply depots at LANDAU and RASTATT.

Gains were made against spotty resistance at many points west of HAGUENAU, in the Vosges mountains, and on the Alsace plain west of the Rhine.

Elements which crossed the Vosges captured ANDLAU and ST MAURICE at the edge of the plain against strong resistance.

In a drive southward from STRASBOURG, ERSTEIN was captured and our units have reached MATZENHEIM. Gains were also made in the southern Vosges heights.

DECEMBER 1944
COUNTER-ATTACK

With operations continuing from Holland to the Swiss border, Colonel Jordan and his staff must have had their work cut out to prepare their daily communiquès by 11 a.m. each day. December begins with a report about the capture of the castle at Broekhuizen on the west bank of the River Maas in south-eastern Holland. It was one of three bridgeheads that the Germans were still occupying across the river to stop any Allied attempt to cross and use them as springboards for possible future offensives. 'Brückenkopf Broekhuisen' — based around a 15th-century castle and farmhouse *(left)* — had been turned into a veritable fortress with elaborate trench systems, minefields and with artillery support from the far side of the Maas. The position was being held by a mere 15 young paratroopers of the 6. Kompanie of Fallschirmjäger-Regiment 20 but they inflicted severe casualties on the 3rd Battalion of the Monmouthshire Regiment whose job it was to capture it. They had 12 flail tanks available to clear a path through the minefield but several bogged down and one was knocked out by a Panzerfaust (now at Overloon Museum, see page 198). The frontal attack by the infantry across open ground took place on November 30 and of the 300 men taking part, 140 became casualties with 27 killed. (For more, see *After the Battle* No. 107.) *Right:* This was the castle and farm after the battle.

COMMUNIQUE No. 237   December 1

Allied forces, continuing to clear the Maas pocket, have occupied enemy strong points in the two castles near WANSSUM and BROEKHUIZEN. The village of BROEKHUIZEN was cleared of the enemy.

Railway transport and communications in northern and eastern Holland were again under attack by fighter-bombers. At SUCHTELN factory buildings were hit by fighter-bombers.

In the area of LINNICH our forces have reached the Roer river north of KOSLAR. We are fighting in BEECK, LINDERN and FLOSSDORF. Fighters and fighter-bombers, closely supporting our ground forces in this sector, attacked enemy troops and mortar positions, and bombed and strafed strong points at BAAL, RURICH, GLIMBACH, GEVENICH and BOSLAR.

Farther south we have cleared LAMMERSDORF after hard fighting and have entered the section of INDEN west of the Inde river. High ground east of GROSSHAU was occupied. In MERODE heavy fighting continued.

Medium, light and fighter-bombers destroyed a number of enemy tanks at PIER and INDEN, attacked the fortified villages of STOCKHEIM, VETTWEISS and ERP, bombed and strafed strong points and gun positions at BRANDENBERG, BERGSTEIN and BERG, and bombed an armoured vehicle repair depot at GEMUND.

Other medium and light bombers went for railway yards at ZWEIBRUCKEN. Escorted light bombers attacked a benzol plant at DUISBURG during the afternoon and two other benzol plants at OBERHAUSEN and BOTTROP were the targets for escorted heavy bombers which made concentrated attacks through cloud. Last night heavy bombers were over Germany in strength with DUISBURG as the main objective.

FORT PRIVAT, in the METZ defense ring, was taken, and 500 prisoners were captured. In the Saar valley further gains were made. We occupied high ground west of MERZIG and are fighting in the BUREN area northwest of SAARLAUTERN. In clearing out the ST AVOLD area we occupied KARLINGEN and L'HOPITAL and entered ADAMSWILLER, southeast of SAARGEMUND.

Limited advances were made by our ground forces east and west of the Vosges mountains north of the SAVERNE GAP, and near the Rhine river in the vicinity of HAGUENAU.

STRASBOURG was shelled heavily by enemy guns across the Rhine.

On the northern Alsace plain our units have reached GERSTHEIM and STOTZHEIM, meeting little opposition.

The advance in the southern high Vosges continues on a wide front and our forces are within a mile of URBES and ST AMARIN.

We inflicted heavy losses on the enemy in repulsing a counter-attack at BURBACH, just south of THANN. East of MULHOUSE deep penetrations have been made into the Harth forest. On the Channel coast strong points at DUNKIRK were hit by medium and fighter-bombers.

Seventy years later nature is taking over the crumbling ruins.

COMMUNIQUE No. 238   December 2

Allied forces are encountering stubborn resistance all along the LINNICH—HURTGEN sector. In the northern part of the sector, we have cleared WELZ and are fighting in LINNICH, FLOSSDORF and BEECK. A counter-attack at LINDERN was repulsed and house-to-house fighting continues at INDEN. Small gains were made in the face of stubborn opposition in an attack towards GEY and BRANDENBERG.

Tanks and fortified positions in the LINNICH and JULICH areas and troops in the HAMBACH FOREST were attacked by fighter-bombers yesterday. Around DUREN other fighter-bombers struck at fortified villages, a rail yard, buildings housing armored vehicles, and a supply dump.

In the Saar valley we now dominate the west bank of the Saar north and south of MERZIG, and we are in the area two miles west of SAARLAUTERN. Towns taken in the advance include FITTEN, FREMERSDORF and OBERLIMBERG. We have entered BUREN and ITZBACH and have elements in FELSBERG.

Fighter-bombers, supporting our ground forces, went for strong points south of MERZIG and fortified positions near SAARLAUTERN and SAARBRUCKEN. Medium bombers attacked fortifications in the SAARLAUTERN area and rail bridges at RASTATT and BANTZENHEIM. Fighter-bombers went for a rail bridge at GERMERSHEIM.

Our ground forces continued to advance in the Alsace plain. SCHWEIGHAUSEN, west of HAGUENAU, was freed after stiff fighting, and gains were also made to the northwest. South of STRASBOURG armored forces reached KOGENHEIM and BOOFZHEIM in a gain of approximately four miles against enemy delaying tactics. Two villages immediately west of SELESTAT were cleared

Fighter-bombers silenced German gun positions in Alsace and struck behind the enemy lines at transportation targets. The rail yards at OFFENBURG were strafed and locomotives and rolling stock destroyed.

On the upper Rhine below the Swiss frontier, ROSENAU was occupied and further slight advances were made in the southern Vosges heights.

In the course of the day's operations, which also included a fighter-bomber attack on a strong point in the DUNKIRK area, four enemy aircraft was shot down. Eight of ours are missing.

Last night bombers attacked the rail centre and supply base of KARLSRUHE.

This is Dorfplatz in Ederen today, looking south-west into Aachener Ende on the left and Denkmalstrasse on the right.

Meanwhile the drive to the Roer river was nearing its objective. From November 16 — before Geilenkirchen had been taken — units of the Ninth Army had advanced up to six miles and now the front line stood just north of Ederen. Linnich fell on December 1 to the 102nd Division.

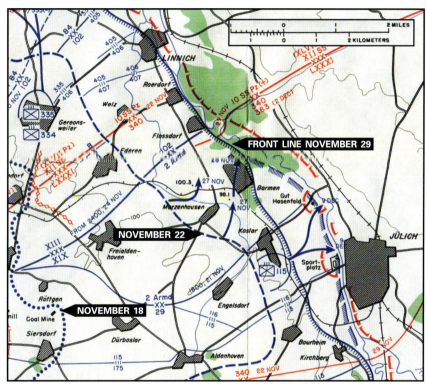

Following the Franco-Prussian War of 1870-71, the Sarre region of France became part of the German Empire being renamed the Saar. In 1920, under the Treaty of Versailles, the Saar was occupied by Britain and France under a 15-year mandate from the League of Nations but when this expired in 1935, a referendum resulted in an overwhelming vote to return to Germany. In 1936, the town of Saarlouis was renamed Saarlautern by the Nazi regime, and this is the name used by SHAEF in their communiqués. This picture shows troops of the 95th Division preparing to move into the front line near Saarlautern early in December.

COMMUNIQUE No. 239   December 3

Allied forces which entered LINNICH were mopping up in the town yesterday. To the south, we have cleared RURDORF, and fighting continued in FLOSSDORF and in INDEN where the action was fierce.

Fighter-bombers went for road, river and railway targets over a wide area in the Rhineland. They destroyed or disabled a large quantity of enemy rolling stock and cut railway lines in many places. Fortified towns immediately behind the enemy lines in the DUREN—LINNICH areas, and troop concentrations near DUREN, were attacked, and a railway bridge 20 miles east of EUSKIRCHEN was destroyed.

Our ground forces enlarged their control of the Saar river bank above and below MERZIG and entered the town of REHLINGEN. Other forces were in the outskirts of SAARLAUTERN on the west side of the river. Farther south, moderate gains were made and mopping up is in progress in SAARUNION.

Medium, light and fighter-bombers struck at enemy positions and other targets in the SAARBRUCKEN region, destroyed a railway bridge near SAARGEMUND and set on fire an oil and ammunition dump at PIRMASENS.

Southeast of SAARUNION our forces made gains of approximately two miles and reached the vicinity of MACKWEILER. Two enemy counter-attacks were repulsed.

The enemy was forced from an area on the west bank of the Rhine near STRASBOURG. In his retreat he blew up three bridges across the Rhine.

Fighter-bombers attacked railway yards at RASTATT and OFFENBURG.

On the Alsace plain we have reached SELESTAT where house-to-house fighting continues.

In the southern high Vosges, our forces pushed into the upper Thur river valley and occupied several villages. Units which crossed to the north bank of the Doller river near MULHOUSE repulsed a strong counter-attack.

During the day's air operations, which included an attack by rocket-firing fighters on an enemy strong point in the VENLO area of Holland, four enemy aircraft were destroyed in the air and seven on the ground. According to reports so far received, we lost one light bomber and 13 fighter-bombers.

Yesterday afternoon a force of escorted heavy bombers attacked a benzol plant in the outskirts of DORTMUND. Last night heavy bombers were over Germany in strength with HAGEN as the main objective.

Following the defeat of Germany in 1945, the name was changed back to Saarlouis and France once again took over administration of the 'Saar Protectorate' until it joined the Federal Republic of Germany on January 1, 1957. Although the sign on the right of the wartime photograph says 'Saarlautern', Karel actually found that the picture had been taken at Ober-Felsberg, two miles west of the city.

Just one bridgehead now remained over the Maas. Blerick is a suburb of Venlo and the river can be seen beyond the buildings on Antoniusplein.

Southeast of HURTGEN, our forces have taken BRANDENBERG, and are threatening BERGSTEIN, about a mile to the east, where targets were attacked by fighter-bombers.

In the Saar valley, our troops have crossed the river at SAARLAUTERN and are fighting in the eastern part of the town. A bridge across the Saar was taken intact, but is under enemy artillery fire.

Farther south we have reached WILHELMSBRONN and two miles southeast of the town we have crossed the German border. SAARUNION has been cleared of the enemy. Fighter-bombers operating across the German frontier, struck at targets in ZWEIBRUCKEN.

Gains of two miles were made east of SAARUNION and several villages were taken including WINGEN on the TIEFFENBACH—INGWEILER pass. To the southeast, our units are approaching the outskirts of HAGUENAU.

In the STRASBOURG area fighters and medium and fighter-bombers, silenced gun positions, and attacked rail transport deep behind the enemy lines.

In the southern high Vosges, our units have pushed eastward north of COL DE LA SCHLUCHT. After violent fighting, the high ground dominating the lower Thur valley was taken. Our artillery set afire and armored train in this area.

COMMUNIQUE No. 240   December 4

Allied forces have made good progress in an attack on the last remaining enemy bridgehead over the Maas, west of VENLO. We reached the river in the area of the bridge and mopped up all but a few small pockets. Enemy strong points in the WANSSUM area have also been cleared.

In this sector, road intersections at STRAELEN and KALDENKIRCHEN were bombed by medium and light bombers. Farther north, rocket-firing fighters hit machine-gun and mortar positions north and east of NIJMEGEN. Fighter-bombers struck at enemy communications at ARNHEM and AMERSFOORT and elsewhere in Holland. They also flew into Germany to attack rail transport at STADTLOHN, DULMEN and KREFELD, and railway yards at GREVENBROICH.

Our ground forces in the Roer valley have cleared the village of LEIFFART, and have repulsed a counter-attack in the LINDERN area. ROERDORF and FLOSSDORF, on the Roer river, are in our hands.

South of JULICH, we have crossed the Inde river at INDEN and have cleared the eastern portion of the town. The spearhead of the force which crossed the river advanced 1,500 yards southeast of INDEN and captured LUCHERBERG after heavy fighting. Troops driving north from LANGERWEHE have captured LUCHEM and advanced beyond to reach the autobahn which connects AACHEN and COLOGNE.

When the town was entered by the Royal Scots there was no sign of the enemy which had escaped to the eastern bank. Blerick had the appearance of utter desolation but even so Private Tosh of the 6th Battalion, King's Own Scottish Borderers, is still wary of possible sniper fire.

In this sector fighter-bombers attacked enemy troops and fortifications north of JULICH, and hit artillery positions north of DUREN.

The Sint Antonius Monastery that stood on the left has been pulled down but the house standing on the corner of Helling and Antoniusplein remains.

COMMUNIQUE No. 241   December 5

Allied forces in Holland have now cleared the enemy from the entire area west of the Maas.

Transport in eastern Holland and western Germany and targets in the battle areas were attacked yesterday by fighter-bombers. Rail lines were cut northeast of AMERSFOORT, and north and northwest of the Ruhr, in the DORSTEN area, at VARSSEVELD, at XANTEN and northwest of BORKEN. Attacks were also made on a troop train northeast of AHAUS, locomotives east of GELDERN, rail tank cars at HALTERN, railway station buildings at MUNSTER, and barges, locomotives and trains between MUNSTER and MEPPEN.

On the west bank of the Roer river our ground forces are meeting stubborn resistance in the outskirts of JULICH. East of the Inde river, we have consolidated our positions in LUCHERBERG and LUCHEM. In the BRANDENBERG area, southeast of HURTGEN, slight progress has been made.

Fighter-bombers attacked fortified villages in the area of DUREN, the towns of EUSKIRCHEN and UXHEIM, rail yards at LOVENICH and ZULPICH and factories at KIERDORF.

In the Saar valley we now hold the entire west bank of the river from the MERZIG area south to SAARLAUTERN. The town of WALLERFANGEN has been cleared, and our troops across the river in SAARLAUTERN are meeting strong enemy opposition.

Farther south, we have reached the towns of THEDINGEN and DIEBLINGEN and have advanced beyond PUTTLINGEN. Northeast of SAARUNION, our troops are meeting stubborn opposition in the vicinity of VOELLERDINGEN and DOMFESSEL.

In the Saar area fortified villages were attacked by fighter-bombers. Locomotives and rail cars behind the enemy lines were destroyed and rail lines cut in many places. Fighter-bombers also struck at railway yards at REICHSHOFFEN and east of STUTTGART.

By now the lack of replacements was becoming extremely bad, Patton commenting that in the Third Army he was only at 55 per cent strength in his rifle companies. Overall, his six infantry and three armoured divisions were short of 11,000 men, much due to trench foot. Patton had already attempted to solve the problem in his own way by taking five per cent of the corps and army HQ personnel to train as infantry. Naturally this caused wails of complaint from the section chiefs who declared they could not run their offices if such a cut was implemented. Nevertheless it went ahead, as did a further five per cent cut early in December. Here the 95th Division passes through Felsberg on its way to the Saar front.

Several villages were cleared east and west of the lower Vosges in our northward advance. On the Alsace plain, slight gains were made. Fighting was in progress for the third day in SELESTAT. The methodical advance continued in the southern high Vosges.

During yesterday afternoon heavy bombers, escorted by fighters, continued the offensive against the railways of the Ruhr district with a concentrated attack on OBERHAUSEN.

Last night heavy bombers, in very great strength, attacked the railway industrial centres of KARLSRUHE and HEILBRONN.

At Saarlautern, in the late afternoon of December 2, an artillery observation plane discovered that a bridge spanning the River Sarre between the centre of the city and the suburb north of the river was still intact, and the air photo showing this was sent to the commander of the 379th Infantry. After interrogating prisoners on details of the city plan, and consulting General Twaddle (95th Infantry Division), Colonel Robert L. Bacon sent his 1st Battalion to seize the bridge.

The Sarre makes a loop at the north-western corner of the city of Saarlautern, and Colonel Bacon decided to take advantage of this configuration by sending the battalion across the near segment of the loop. After this move the attack would dash inland through the northern suburb and take the bridge from the rear or north side. In the early morning hours of December 3, the 1st Battalion (Lieutenant Colonel Tobias R. Philbin) moved to the river. Philbin's troops were fresh, for the battalion had not been engaged since the fighting at Metz. At 0545 the first assault boats shoved off to make the 125-foot crossing. Ten minutes later the whole battalion was on the opposite bank. The noise of the American guns shelling Saarlautern had drowned out all sounds of the crossing. Company B and a platoon of Company C, 320th Engineer Combat Battalion, led the surprise attack, double-timing a distance of about 1,000 yards through an empty park and down the road to the bridge. Here a light German tank was discovered, sitting beside the bridge exit. A German inside the tank suddenly awoke to the danger and started frantically working his radio, persisting until he was knifed by the commander of Company D. Another made a dash for the switch connected with the demolitions on the bridge and was shot by Colonel Philbin. The engineers, commanded by Lieutenant Edward Herbert, raced onto the bridge, cut the demolition wires, and surprised and killed four German guards at the opposite end of the bridge. (The white circles on the photo indicate pillboxes.)

COMMUNIQUE No. 242   December 6

There have been no substantial changes along the Roer river in the JULICH—LINNICH areas where Allied forces have been under moderate enemy artillery fire. Stubborn resistance continues at the outskirts of JULICH. A German counter-attack with infantry and tanks against LUCHERBERG, east of the Inde river, was broken up by our artillery. Farther south we made gains against strong opposition and captured BERGSTEIN, southeast of HURTGEN.

In the Saar valley, our forces east of the river repulsed an enemy counter-attack northwest of SAARLAUTERN. We have crossed the Saar river at a second point in this area. Our armored elements have freed RUHLINGEN and reached HUNDLINGEN, west of SAARGEMUND. Other forces have occupied WUSTWEILER. Northeast of SAARUNION we are advancing in the vicinity of OERMINGEN and DEHLINGEN. Northwest of HAGUENAU our forces entered MERTZWEILER against strong resistance.

The garrison of an enemy fort which held out for more than a week at MUTZIG, west of STRASBOURG, surrendered after the walls had been breached.

In the high Vosges gains of several miles were made. The HOHNECK height and COL DE LA SCHLUCHT were cleared.

Heavy, medium and fighter-bombers made attacks yesterday on the enemy's railway system in western Germany over a wide area from STROHEN and points between OSNABRUCK and DETMOLD north of the Ruhr to the region of DARMSTADT and MANNHEIM in the southern Rhineland. In the afternoon escorted heavy bombers, one of which is missing, attacked the railway marshalling yards at HAMM.

Medium bombers attacked the railway yards at KEMPEN and fighter-bombers went for railway yards at LIBLAR, southwest of COLOGNE, and the railway station at MAYEN-KOTTENHEIM. Railway lines were cut in some 80 places during the day. Last night a strong force of heavy bombers struck at the marshalling yards at SOEST.

Fighter-bombers and rocket-firing fighters went for targets in northern and eastern Holland. Fighter-bombers destroyed a bridge near GOUDA and bombed and strafed an enemy troop train near HILVERSUM and another between APELDOORN and AMERSFOORT.

Rocket-firing fighters hit gun positions near GRAVENDEEL and an enemy strong point and an observation post east of NIJMEGEN.

Medium, light and fighter-bombers made attacks against targets in western Germany. Fighter-bombers bombed and strafed gun positions, hangars, barracks and factories in the RHEINE-MUNSTER area, and medium bombers attacked a fuel storage dump and a road junction near DULMEN.

Medium and light bombers hit enemy troops quarters and a bomb dump at DREMMEN, north of GEILENKIRCHEN, the village of HUCHEM north of DUREN, and KALL, a fortified industrial town southwest of EUSKIRCHEN.

Fighter-bombers strafed and bombed gun positions southeast of GELDERN. They also attacked troop concentrations at AHRWEILER and MAYEN, a factory at WICKRATHBERG, south of MUNICH, a fuel dump at DUSSELDORF and storage tanks at MONHEIM.

In the area of DUPPENWEILER, north of SAARLAUTERN, medium bombers attacked enemy positions, and fighter-bombers struck at targets in SAARBRUCKEN and other defended areas in this sector, and farther south hit an ammunition dump near SENHEIM, northwest of MULHOUSE.

Word of the German failure at the bridge reached Hitler the following day, OB West reporting that 'the Führer was enraged'. An immediate investigation was demanded but it was concluded that the Americans had engineered surprise by using a captured German tank!

During the autumn, differences in opinion as to the best strategy to further the defeat of German forces in the west tested General Eisenhower's abilities to mediate between his commanders to the utmost. In one letter to Montgomery in September he said that 'I regard it as a great pity that all of us cannot keep in closer touch with each other because I find, without exception, when all of us can get together and look the various features of our problems squarely in the face, the answers usually become obvious'. Then in October he had to tell Montgomery that 'it would be quite futile to deny that questions of nationalism often enter our problems. It is nations that make war, and when they find themselves associated as Allies, it is quite often necessary to make concessions that recognise the existence of inescapable differences.' Nevertheless Montgomery was still championing his favoured single-thrust strategy to the Ruhr which, at the end of November, led him to write a critical letter to Eisenhower stating that in his opinion the Supreme Commander had failed and that consequently the Allies had suffered 'a strategic reverse'. In reply Eisenhower stated that 'I do not agree that things have gone badly since Normandy, merely because we have not gained all we had hoped to gain'.

COMMUNIQUE No. 243   December 7

Allied forces in the HURTGEN sector have repulsed attempts by enemy infantry and armor to retake the village of BERGSTEIN. German tanks east of BERGSTEIN were bombed and strafed by fighter-bombers yesterday. The fortified town of NIDEGGEN, two miles to the east, was attacked by medium and fighter-bombers which also struck at gun positions, troops and strong points in JULICH; targets in BROICH, ERKELENZ and MUNSTEREIFEL; five bridges in the area of FUCHSHOFEN; and the railway junction of DAUN.

In the Saar valley, our forces have made a third crossing of the Saar river and are fighting in DILLINGEN. We are attacking enemy strong points in SAARLAUTERN and south of the town we have reached the river near WEHRDEN.

Allied units have entered ROSSBRUCKEN and WELFERDINGEN and are engaged in house-to-house fighting against stiff resistance in SAARGEMUND. Farther southeast, we have entered LE GRAND BOIS, five miles from SAARGEMUND, and armored elements have reached BININGEN.

East of the Saar, gun positions at BETTINGEN, AUSSEN and elsewhere were hit by fighter-bombers. Other fighter-bombers, striking deeper into Germany, attacked rail transport near LEBACH and BAD KREUZNACH and four railway yards near SPEYER. In advance of more than three miles against scattered resistance, our forces occupied eight villages on the western slope of the lower Vosges east of SAARUNION.

The enemy is resisting our advance stubbornly northwest of HAGUENAU and has heavily shelled MERZWEILER where fighting continues.

In the Alsace plain further gains were made and OSTHEIM, five miles north of COLMAR, was freed.

Last night heavy bombers, in very great strength, attacked the railway centres of OSNABRUCK and GIESSEN and a synthetic oil plant at MERSEBURG. BERLIN was also bombed.

On November 28 Eisenhower visited Montgomery in Holland. The Field-Marshal had still not given up on his personal plan for ending the war — the single thrust by him to Berlin — which had been argued over since September. He still felt that Eisenhower's strategy was wrong and he bluntly told him so. The visit ended with Monty requesting a further meeting between himself, Tedder, Bradley and Eisenhower which was fixed for December 7 in Maastricht in southern Holland. In the meantime, Churchill had been in touch with Roosevelt voicing similar concerns that the Allies 'had failed to achieve the strategic object we gave our armies five weeks ago'. Having just visited all the corps, army and army group commanders, Eisenhower reported to General Marshall in Washington that his plan was to keep up a number of limited attacks towards the Rhine while preparing for an all-out offensive. At Maastricht, Montgomery reiterated his plan that the Ruhr should be the strategic objective and that the main effort had to be made in the north. He said that he disagreed widely on fundamental issues and that he could not endorse Eisenhower's plan of two offensives in 1945: one north of the Ruhr and one aimed at Frankfurt-Kassel. *Top:* The two viewpoints were never reconciled yet it was all smiles for the Press on the steps of the Ninth Army headquarters although the host, Lieutenant General William H. Simpson on the right, is often cropped out of the photo! *Left:* Bradley looks rather glum on leaving. *Right:* The headquarters was located in a school on Aylvalaan — now it is apartments.

For obvious reasons, SHAEF's communiqués can only tell the wider picture so the tank battle on December 6 at Singling, a small village six miles southeast of Sarreguemines, does not get a mention, yet it was the last action in Lorraine for the 4th Armored Division. The official report reads as follows: 'Combat Command A began their attack on Bining around noon. The 38th (*sic*) Tank Battalion and 53rd Infantry formed a base of fire to the south of town and the 37th Tank Battalion hit Bining from the west. As the attack on Bining progressed, Combat Command B passed Combat Command A and attacked Singling. The opposition here consisted of infantry, tanks, and anti-tank fire from numerous pillboxes, and artillery fire which came in 30- to 40-round concentrations. The fighting at Singling and Bining was very difficult, but by nightfall Combat Command A was in Bining and Rohrbach. Singling was not clear as of 1730.' By the end of the day the Americans had lost five Shermans and the Germans two Panthers *(below)*. The official historian commented that 'the battle of Singling was neither a big action nor a startling one. In itself, the action was a stalemate', yet it was described by Generalleutnant Fritz Bayerlein, the commander of the Panzer-Lehr-Division, who ought to know, as 'an outstanding tank attack such as I have rarely seen'.

The main street at Singling pictured on December 12 — an unusual shot as it shows the official historian, Master Sergeant Gordon A. Harrison, making notes for the *American Forces in Action Series* produced under Eisenhower's signature by the Historical Department of the US War Department in April 1946.

COMMUNIQUE No. 244   December 8

In Holland ground activity yesterday was confined to a number of patrol clashes. Weather severely curtailed air operations, but fighter-bombers cut rail lines in Holland and successfully attacked two goods trains, one northeast of ZWOLLE and the other between ZWOLLE and AMERSFOORT.

Farther south our forces in the Roer valley, from LINNICH to JULICH, encountered moderate enemy artillery and mortar fire. Southeast of HURTGEN, we have made small gains to the east, south and southwest of BERGSTEIN. Our units north of the town made little progress against stiff resistance.

In the METZ area, we have captured FORT ST QUENTIN and FORT PLAPPEVILLE, west and northwest of the city.

In the Saar valley, Allied forces east of the river have penetrated into the PACHTENER BUCHWALD. Southeast of SAARLAUTERN, we have taken HOSTENBACH and reached FURSTENHAUSEN and GROSSROSSELN. House-to-house fighting continues in SAARGEMUND. Our forces to the southeast have taken ETTINGEN. Other units have entered ENCHENBERG, and occupied several nearby villages against stiffening resistance.

Heavy fighting took place in MERZWEILER farther east, where part of the town was lost to a counter-attack.

North of COLMAR in the Alsace plain we made a slight advance despite vigorous enemy resistance and counter-attacks.

In the southern high Vosges, the Thur river valley is being cleared and our units have reached THANN where fighting continues.

Early last night light bombers attacked COLOGNE.

This photo is a very good illustration of the inaccuracy of wartime captioning. The photographer stated in his caption that 'an American LVT of the 95th Division moves down a street in Saarlautern' but we failed to trace it anywhere in what is now the German town of Saarlouis, even after consulting the city archives. So we passed it to Jean Paul who has a nose for these things and he very cleverly tracked it down to Bouzonville, a town 20 kilometres west of the city . . . in France!

COMMUNIQUE No. 235   December 9

Allied forces in the JULICH—LINNICH area continued to encounter moderate artillery fire along the Roer river. In the immediate vicinity of JULICH the enemy holds two small pockets west of the river.

Fighter-bombers strafed targets in the JULICH—LINNICH area and in the region of DUREN.

Farther south, our units have gained high ground about one mile east of GROSSHAU, and have repulsed a small counter-attack southeast of BERGSTEIN.

In the METZ area, our forces have captured FORT DRIANT.

In the Saar valley, we are fighting in the forward defenses of the Siegfried Line in the DILLINGEN area and in SAARLAUTERN where enemy artillery fire is extremely heavy. Targets north of SAARLAUTERN and east of MERZIG were hit by fighter-bombers.

We have crossed the Saar river at SAARGEMUND and are fighting house-to-house in the city east of the river. Another crossing has been made in the vicinity of WITTRINGEN. Our forces have reached ACHEN and a point slightly to the east of DIEDINGEN.

Slight progress continued to be made in the region of LEMBERG and near the Rhine northeast of STRASBOURG.

Our units edged forward northwest of COLMAR and made progress in the high Vosges.

Fighting continued in the vicinity of THANN where the Thur valley is being cleared.

Fighter-bombers maintained attacks on transportation targets in Holland and deep into Germany yesterday cutting rail lines in many places.

Among the targets inside Germany were a factory at BURGSTEINFURT, and railway yards northeast of KAISERSLAUTERN, at HANAU, in the region of KARLSRUHE—LANDAU and near OFFENBURG.

During the day, escorted heavy bombers attacked the marshalling yard at DUISBURG.

A synthetic oil plant in the MEIDERICH district of DUISBURG was also attacked.

In yesterday's air operations, 12 enemy aircraft were shot down for the loss of six of our fighters.

Rue de Saarlouis in Bouzonville with the Hôtel de Ville (town hall) on the left.

COMMUNIQUE No. 240   December 10

Organised resistance has ceased west of the Roer river in the JULICH area with the clearing of the Sportplatz and the Husenfeld Gut. Allied units in this area are encountering light artillery and mortar fire. Enemy attempts to regain Hill 400, east of BERGSTEIN, have been repulsed.

Defensive positions at ZULPICH and bridges crossing the river Erft at EUSKIRCHEN were attacked by fighter-bombers yesterday.

In the Saar valley, our units are strengthening their bridgeheads across the Saar river in the DILLINGEN and SAARLAUTERN areas. We have cleared SAAREINSMINGEN, and patrols have reached the village of NEUENKIRCHEN just east of SAARGEMUND. Other units have reached WEISWEILER and WOLFLINGEN.

Supporting our ground forces in the Saar valley, medium and light bombers struck at fortified positions at LOSHEIM, OBERTHAL, THOLEY, LEBACH, WIESBACH and SAARWELLINGEN, and attacked military barracks at BAUMHOLDER.

Tank concentrations and gun positions southeast of SAARGEMUND, targets at ZWEIBRUCKEN and the supply center of PIRMASENS were the objectives for other medium and fighter-bombers.

Our ground forces made gains on both sides of the lower Vosges. NIEDERBRONN was cleared, and the main bridge over the Zinsel river at BISCHWILLER was seized intact when we entered the city.

Most of THANN has been cleared after the two days' fighting and further progress has been made in this area of the southern high Vosges. The enemy is resisting stubbornly our efforts to extend the bridgehead over the Doller river at MULHOUSE.

Fighter-bombers struck at rail communications west of FREIBURG.

BERLIN was attacked by a force of light bombers last night.

A little further east, Rohrbach-les-Bitche lies on the N62 about ten miles east of Sarreguemines where Signal Corps' photographer Miller took this picture on December 9. Pvt William Meador of Gallatin, Tennessee, and Pfc William Hahn of Brooklyn, New York, were members of the 80th Division. SHAEF passed the photo for publication on the 11th, although Karel found that the church had been completely demolished (see also page 521).

Since November 25, the 80th Division (we last saw them on page 255) had fought non-stop for 18 miles and during the last month had suffered 513 killed, 2,215 wounded and 373 men missing. The weather was so bad with the men having difficulty keeping dry (this was one of Patton's units suffering badly from immersion or trench foot) that the General told the Third Army chaplain: 'I'm tired of these soldiers having to fight mud and floods as well as Germans. See if we can't get God to work on our side.' Chaplain O'Neill replied: 'May I say, General, that it usually isn't the customary thing among men of my profession to pray for clear weather to kill fellow men.' Patton's reply was typical: 'Chaplain, are you teaching me theology or are you the Chaplain of the Third Army? I want a prayer' . . . and this is what he got: 'Almighty and most merciful Father, we humbly beseech Thee, of thy great goodness, to restrain these immoderate rains with which we have had to contend. Grant us fair weather for Battle. Graciously hearken to us as soldiers who call upon Thee that, armed with Thy power, we may advance from victory to victory, and crush the oppression and wickedness of our enemies, and establish Thy justice among men and nations. Amen.'

COMMUNIQUE No. 247   December 11

Allied forces moved forward yesterday in the area east of AACHEN. Units pushing beyond INDEN made a 2,500-yard gain towards SCHOPHOVEN and are fighting in PIER. Gains have been made one mile east of LUCHEM, and fighting is in progress in OBERGEICH, east of LANGERWEHE.

Medium bombers attacked the fortified villages of BIRKESDORF, HUCHEM and STAMMELN near DUREN, and fighter-bombers supported our ground forces in this sector.

Three miles northeast of HURTGEN our units are fighting house-to-house in GEY, and in the village of STRASS. SCHAFBERG, in the same area, has been cleared.

In the Saar valley, where fighter-bombers have supported our ground forces, two counter-attacks by enemy infantry and tanks have been repulsed in the DILLINGEN area. At SAARLAUTERN, our forces are still fighting in the town and improving their positions east of the Saar river in that area.

Another crossing of the Saar has been made in SAARGEMUND, and house-to-house fighting is in progress in the town east of the river. Two enemy counter-attacks with infantry and armor were repulsed near SAAREINSMINGEN, and our troops have advanced through LE GRAND BOIS. We have reached GROS REDERCHINGEN, seven miles southeast of SAARGEMUND.

Our troops have entered HAGUENAU against stiff resistance and the fighting continues. Gains were also made north and south of the town.

We should now break away from the Saar sector for a moment to look back at what the Seventh Army was doing further south. Following Eisenhower's orders to turn and face north, General Patch had begun to redeploy his forces. However, the 1ère Armée of de Lattre stayed put, continuing its eastward drive to try to eliminate what later became known as the Colmar Pocket. Thus, at the beginning of December, the Seventh Army's advance in northern Alsace was split into two directions: east through the high Vosges mountains and north towards the German border east of Haguenau *(above)*. (See the map on page 259.)

Aiming at Wissembourg on the German frontier, General Patch's forces pass through Soufflenheim.

country south of DUREN were attacked by fighters-bombers supporting the ground forces. Other fighter-bombers hit bridges at NIDEGGEN and southwest of DUREN, and struck at gun positions and strong points at ERKELENZ, BOSLAR, SCHOPHOVEN, STOCKHEIM, WEILERSWIST and EUSKIRCHEN.

Numerous local counter-attacks against our bridgeheads over the Saar river have been repulsed in the area of DILLINGEN and SAARLAUTERN. Mopping-up is proceeding in SAARGEMUND, and our forces east of the town have reached BLIESBRUCKEN. Southeast of SAARGEMUND we have advanced to within one mile of RIMLINGEN.

Snipers are being mopped up in HAGUENAU which is in our hands. In coordinated attacks beyond the city we have reached WALBOURG to the north, and the southern outskirts of SOUFFLENHEIM to the east. Further progress was made in the Vosges mountains, and in the vicinity of THANN toward reducing the enemy-held area west of the Rhine.

Limited progress was made at the foot of the Vosges mountains northwest of COLMAR. Farther south, THANN has been cleared.

Medium bombers attacked a railway bridge at NEU-BREISACH.

Transportation targets in northern and eastern Holland and in Germany were objectives yesterday for fighter-bombers. Among the targets hit were railway yards at WIERDEN and BORKEN. Medium bombers attacked a canal lock at ZUTPHEN.

COMMUNIQUE No. 248   December 12

Allied forces driving towards the Roer river, southeast of JULICH, are fighting house-to-house in PIER. Elements driving 2,000 yards east from LUCHERBERG, have reached MERKEN. In the area east and southeast of LANGERWEHE, the villages of ECHTZ, OBERGEICH, SCHLICH and MERODE have been cleared of the enemy. Fighting continues in GEY, and we have taken STRASS.

Troop concentrations in the wooded

On the left flank, infantrymen of the 45th Division (3rd Battalion, 157th Regiment) are pictured cautiously moving through Niederbronn-les-Bains, ten miles north-west of Haguenau. At the precise moment when Signal Corps photographer T/4 Bennett Fenberg took this photo on December 10, a shell was heard coming towards them as the town was still within range of German artillery fire. One of the GIs in the photo made a humorous comment: 'We were fighting up the street and I had the damdest thought. I had a little German in school and noticed the little sign above our heads "Ladies and Gentlemen's Hairdressers". I said to myself: That last sniper's bullet curled my hair but thank God it wasn't a permanent wave.'

Half-an-hour before Fenberg took this picture, one of the men from the 1st Battalion manning this .30-calibre machine gun on Adolf-Hitler-Strasse was injured by an exploding shell — the blast mark can be seen in the wall.

The enemy's rail transport and communications in eastern Holland and in western Germany were again under attack yesterday by fighter-bombers which ranged over the Dutch frontier eastward to OSNABRUCK and southward to STADT MECKENHEIM. Locomotives and freight cars were destroyed and tracks cut at a number of places.

Heavy and light bombers with fighter escort attacked marshalling yards and a benzol plant at OSTERFELD, and benzol plants at MEIDERICH and BRUCKHAUSEN.

Karel visited Niederbronn in France in August 2014 and was disappointed to find that the shell-marked wall on what is today Avenue Foch at the eastern end of town had been repaired.

Now just five miles short of the French-German border, this is the small village of Keffenach just off the main road to Wissembourg.

COMMUNIQUE No. 249   December 13
Allied forces advancing towards the Roer river in the JULICH—DUREN sector have captured PIER, MERKEN and HOVEN. We are meeting stubborn resistance in MARIAWEILER, and are fighting house-to-house in DERICHSWEILER.

Farther south, fighting continues in GEY, and in the area just to the southeast.

Targets in JULICH, DUREN, VETTWEISS and EUSKIRCHEN and in the vicinity of the Roer river, south of DUREN, were hit by fighter-bombers yesterday.

Our units across the Saar river have repulsed numerous counter-attacks in the vicinity of DILLINGEN, and are engaged in fierce fighting in FRAULAUTERN, on the eastern edge of SAARLAUTERN.

Four miles northeast of SAARGEMUND, our forces have crossed the Blies river which here forms the Franco-German border and have entered HABKIRCHEN. East of SAARGEMUND, we have advanced to within a mile of OBERGAILBACH.

Northeast of HAGUENAU, our forces overcame enemy delaying efforts, and drove forward through the Rhine valley as much as eight miles.

The Maginot Line defenses were penetrated and SELZ was reached before any determined resistance was met. At several points our units are within five miles of the Franco-German border.

Fighter-bombers, striking into Germany, blew up a fuel dump at ZWEIBRUCKEN and attacked railway targets between LANDAU and KARLSRUHE, and at MONSHEIM west of WORMS.

Yesterday afternoon, escorted heavy bombers attacked WITTEN, an industrial and railway town in the Ruhr. Last night a strong force of heavy bombers attacked ESSEN and light bombers struck at OSNABRUCK.

In all air operations yesterday 21 enemy aircraft were shot down.

From December 11 the Seventh Army offensive along the west bank of the Rhine had gained momentum with weakened German forces now fighting with their backs to the much-vaunted Westwall. But even that was not that strong in this sector and by December 14 von Rundstedt expected 'hourly' to receive news that the Americans had broken through as he estimated that the Americans had a numerical superiority of ten to one. However, in reality, the combat strength of the US formations was barely 50 per cent — the 90th Division for example reporting only 43 per cent effectiveness with an acute shortage of replacements. This is the 36th Division on the road to Wissembourg.

Looking from France into Germany, the border at Wissembourg lay just beyond the town, and the censored captioning could not hide the euphoria that 'the new offensive has placed five Allied armies inside the Reich, with the US First, Third and Ninth Armies and the British Second Army already battling in Germany.' The caption further claimed that 'the Seventh Army liberated almost all the towns on the French side of the border during their rapid advance in northern Alsace which brought American troops to the edge of the plain before the Rhine'.

COMMUNIQUE No. 250   December 14

In the JULICH—DUREN sector, Allied troops after overcoming heavy resistance, have cleared SCHOPHOVEN. The villages of MARIAWEILER and DERICHSWEILER, west of DUREN, and GEY further south, are also in our hands.

Gains have been made in the areas north and south of MONSCHAU. East and southeast of ROETGEN, our troops have taken ROLLESBROICH and SIMMERATH. Progress has been made in the forest area about four miles southeast of MONSCHAU. Supporting our ground forces, medium, light and fighter-bombers attacked fortified positions at SCHONESEIFFEN, HELLENTHAL, BLUMENTHAL, SCHLEIDEN and KALL.

And now to the First Army east of Aachen. The spirits of these Germans appear to have been raised — as well as their hands — as now for them the war was over. Gürzenich was taken on December 14 in the drive east to Düren, just a mile or so down the road.

Medium and fighter-bombers struck at targets in the ZULPICH area and a railway yard at EUSKIRCHEN.

In the Saar valley, our ground forces in the DILLINGEN bridgehead are being subjected to considerable enemy artillery fire.

We have crossed the Blies river between HABKIRCHEN and BLIESBRUCKEN in the area northeast of SAARGEMUND. House-to-house fighting continues in HABKIRCHEN. FORT JEANNE D'ARC, the last of the METZ forts held by the enemy, has been captured.

In northern Alsace, just west of the lower Vosges, gains of up to three miles were made. Northwest of BITSCH our forces went through the Maginot Line to KAPELLENHOF.

In the drive north of the HAGUENAU FOREST, SULZ and several nearby villages were freed, and to the east fighting continued at SELZ near the Rhine.

The attack on the enemy's rail transport and communications in Holland and western Germany was continued yesterday by fighter-bombers.

Looking east on Schillingstrasse at the extreme western end of Gürzenich.

We left the 1ère Armée behind south of Strasbourg where the Germans still held a sizeable pocket west of the Rhine, centred on Colmar — hence its name. On December 15, Général de Lattre de Tassigny renewed his offensive against the pocket, one attack with his Ier Corps d'Armée in the south towards Cernay and the other using his IIème Corps d'Armée in the north at Sélestat, but on the first day neither corps was able to achieve much in the strengthened German defences. These Shermans of the 2ème Régiment de Cuirassiers belonged to the 1ère Division Blindée.

COMMUNIQUE No. 251   December 15

Allied forces now hold the left bank of the Roer river from its junction with the Inde to a point just northwest of DUREN, except for two small pockets of resistance in a castle near SCHOPHOVEN, and a factory southeast of MARIAWEILER. Units which cleared the area south of the junction of the two rivers captured the village of VIEHOVEN.

Southwest of DUREN, we have reached GURZENICH and have pushed approximately half a mile east of GEY.

Fighting is in progress in the town of KESTERNICH. Slow progress against stubborn resistance is being made by our forces southeast of MONSCHAU.

Fighter-bombers cut rail lines in the BOCHOLT and COESFELD areas and attacked rail bridges at several places behind enemy lines from DUSSELDORF to the EUSKIRCHEN area. Rocket-firing fighters struck at gun positions at ROERMOND.

In the Saar valley, bitter fighting continues in our bridgeheads across the Saar river in the areas of DILLINGEN and SAARLAUTERN. Near SAARGEMUND, our forces east of HABKIRCHEN made gains across the Blies river into Germany.

Fighter-bombers operating in the Saar region attacked troop concentrations in the area of DILLINGEN and rail yards at HOMBURG, VOGELBACH and NEUENKIRCHEN.

In northern Alsace our units pushed north as much as six miles and reached RIEDSELTZ, two miles from the border town of WISSEMBOURG. In this area, and eastward towards the Rhine, more than twelve villages were taken against scattered resistance. Our forces moved down the Rhine to less than a mile from the Franco-German frontier in the vicinity of LAUTERBURG.

Medium bombers attacked defences in the Siegfried Line north of the WISSEMBOURG, and fighter-bombers struck at rail yards at LANDAU and locomotives and rolling stock in the upper Rhine valley.

On the Alsace plain south of STRASBOURG, we gained approximately two miles near the Rhine.

In yesterday's air operations seven enemy aircraft were shot down. Three of ours are missing.

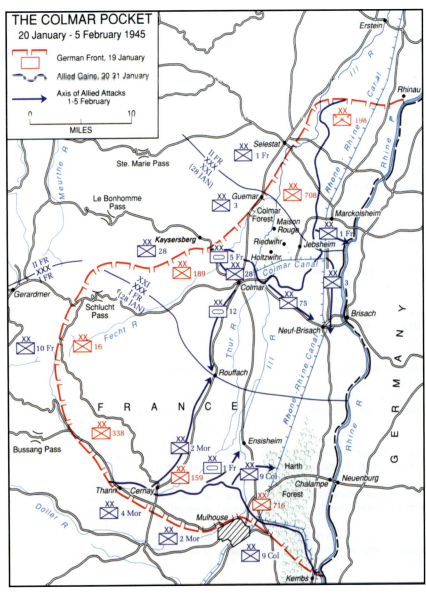

Saturday, December 16, was wedding day at SHAEF headquarters in Versailles as General Eisenhower's faithful orderly Sergeant Mickey McKeogh was getting married. He had met his bride, WAC driver Pearlie Hargreaves, in North Africa and had been engaged for a year before he asked his boss if he could tie the knot. Ike gave his approval and Special Services provided a white gown which they loaned out for servicemen's weddings. The setting could not have been grander, or more historic -- the beautifully ornate chapel where Marie Antoinette had married Louis XVI in 1770. Eisenhower broke off from a meeting to attend and then went to the reception that had been laid on at his residence (which had previously been used by von Rundstedt) at Saint-Germain. General Bradley arrived to discuss with Eisenhower the pressing problem of getting more reinforcements from the States so they both adjourned to the SHAEF war room at the Trianon Hotel. And it was there that evening the first fragmentary reports began coming in about a series of German attacks which had taken place at dawn in the Ardennes.

COMMUNIQUE No. 252   December 16

Allied progress towards DUREN has given us control of the high ground dominating the Roer river on the southwest side of the town. The villages of GURZENICH, BIRGEL and KUFFERATH are in our hands and enemy counter-attacks against both GURZENICH and BIRGEL have been repulsed. Targets in the village of KREUZAU, across the Roer from KUFFERATH, were hit by fighter-bombers.

Farther north the two remaining pockets of resistance west of the DUREN—LINNICH sector of the Roer river have been cleared. Our units mopped up the factory area southeast of MARIAWEILER and captured the castle near SCHOPHOVEN.

Fighter-bombers struck at military objectives in BAAL and other villages in the JULICH—LINNICH area; BUIR northeast of DUREN; and railway yards at RHEYDT, GREVENBROICH, EUSKIRCHEN and COLOGNE.

Southeast of LAMMERSDORF our ground forces are mopping up KESTERNICH. In this sector we are encountering minefields and wire entanglements.

Medium and light bombers attacked fortifications in five villages in the area east and southeast of MONSCHAU.

In the Saar valley, the enemy continues to direct heavy artillery fire into our bridgeheads across the river at DILLINGEN and SAARLAUTERN. A small counter-attack in the SAARLAUTERN area was repulsed by our artillery.

East of SAARGEMUND, mopping up continues in HABKIRCHEN. We have entered NIEDERGAILBACH and ERCHINGEN.

Fighter-bombers supported our ground forces in the Saar valley, striking at defended positions and communications behind enemy lines.

Farther into Germany ammunition dumps were attacked.

West of the lower Vosges mountains where the enemy is manning Maginot fortifications, resistance continued to be stubborn.

On the east side of the lower Vosges our units have crossed the Franco-German frontier north of KLIMBACH which has been freed.

Heavy fire is coming from the Siegfried Line at many points between WISSEMBOURG and the Rhine.

An additional slight advance has been made on the Alsace plain northeast of SELESTAT.

Fighter-bombers attacked troop and ammunition trains and other railway targets north of the Ruhr and in Holland. Railway bridges at ZWOLLE and DEVENTER were targets for medium and light bombers. Medium bombers attacked an oil storage depot at RUTHEN east of the Ruhr.

Yesterday afternoon heavy bombers, escorted by fighters, attacked the E- and R-Boat pens at IJMUIDEN with 12,000-pound bombs. Last night a strong force of heavy bombers made a heavy and concentrated attack on LUDWIGSHAFEN.

In an all-out gamble to wrest the initiative from the Allies, Hitler conceived the idea of a major counter-offensive in the West.

The objective of Operation 'Wacht am Rhein' was to split the Allied armies by a Blitzkrieg-type thrust right through the Ardennes to Antwerp. Four armies were tasked for the operation: on the right wing, the 6. Panzerarmee was entrusted with taking Antwerp; in the centre, the 5. Panzerarmee was to push through the Brussels area and reach the coast west of Antwerp, while the 7. Armee on the left was to protect the south and south-western flank of the operation. Just to the north, on the right flank of the 6. Panzerarmee, the 15. Armee was first given a secondary role of holding American forces in place, and then to launch attacks 'as soon as the least opportunity arises'. When they first heard of Hitler's plan, Generalfeldmarschall Gerd von Rundstedt *(left)*, the commander-in-chief in the West, and Generalfeldmarschall Walter Model *(right)*, the commander of Heeresgruppe B, were far from enthusiastic and they joined forces to propose a more realistic 'small solution' plan but Hitler dismissed anything less than his strategic counter-blow and the operational goals remained largely as originally planned. The operation was launched on the morning of December 16.

This still from a German newsreel shows Tiger IIs moving through an unidentified village a few days before the offensive, on its way to join Kampfgruppe Peiper (1. SS-Panzer-Division), the spearhead battle-group of the 6. Panzerarmee.

After much searching, in 1979 Jean Paul Pallud managed to trace where this sequence had been filmed: at Tondorf, six miles east of Blankenheim. Today, the 'Gasthaus zum Weissen Ross' is still in business in the main street.

Two special operations were organised to support the advance of the 6. Panzerarmee. Operation 'Stösser' involved a night paratroop drop behind the Allied lines aimed at capturing road junctions in the forested areas on the right wing. Then Operation 'Greif' under SS-Obersturmbannführer Otto Skorzeny comprised teams of English-speaking German soldiers, dressed in American uniforms, which were to infiltrate behind the lines and disrupt US convoys by changing signposts and mis-directing traffic, while others were to reach bridges across the Meuse and capture them intact. According to Skorzeny, six 'commando' teams were committed in the first days of the offensive, plus six 'lead commandos' attached to divisions and battle-groups of the 6. Panzerarmee. When questioned after the war, Skorzeny said that 'of the 44 men sent through our lines, all but eight returned'. *Left:* 'Greif' operatives captured in American uniforms were judged guilty of spying and Oberfähnrich Günther Billing, Gefreiter Wilhelm Schmidt and Unteroffizier Manfred Pernass were the first to meet their deaths in front of a firing-squad. *Right:* They were shot at the rear of what was then an army barracks but now the logistical base of a truck company on the Chaussée de Liège at Henri-Chapelle.

On the right wing of the 6. Panzerarmee, two infantry divisions attempted to break through the American lines to enable the panzer divisions to race ahead. However the US 2nd and 99th Infantry Divisions held their ground on the Elsenborn ridge and by nightfall the breakthrough had still not been achieved. As a result the I. SS-Panzerkorps had to commit further elements from the panzer divisions. Fighting raged throughout the 17th and by evening the Americans were finally forced to pull back from endangered positions near Mürringen and the village was abandoned that night. *Above left:* **This truck from the 372nd Field Artillery Battalion, 99th Infantry Division, was pictured withdrawing through Wirtzfeld while the M10 tank destroyer is facing in the direction from where German armour might appear.** *Above right:* **This is the road leading north-westwards to Elsenborn a few hundred metres from the main junction in the centre of Wirtzfeld.**

COMMUNIQUE No. 253   December 17

Allied forces yesterday repulsed a number of local counter-attacks in the areas of BRACHELEN and MARIAWEILER, northwest of DUREN; near ROLLESBROICH, east of ROETGEN, and in the forest southeast of MONSCHAU.

Increased enemy artillery fire preceded the attack in the DUREN sector, particularly in the area of KUFFERATH.

In the Saar valley, we are steadily enlarging our bridgeheads across the river in the DILLINGEN and SAARLAUTERN sectors.

Extremely heavy enemy artillery fire was encountered in the SAARLAUTERN bridgehead.

Northeast of SAARGEMUND, we made gains near HABKIRCHEN, and farther east reached GERSHEIM.

Supporting our ground forces, fighter-bombers attacked troop concentrations and gun positions between SAARLAUTERN and SAARBRUCKEN, and southeast of MERZIG, and struck at rail and road transport behind the enemy lines. Many locomotives, freight cars and motor vehicles were destroyed.

West of the lower Vosges, gains were made in heavy fighting in the vicinity of BITSCH. To the northwest, HOTTVILLER was entered.

Nearer the Rhine, the town of WISSEMBOURG, just south of the Franco-German frontier, and SCHEIBENHARD in Germany were taken.

In the high Vosges, a slight advance was made north of MUNSTER.

Railway targets in the upper Rhine Valley from LANDAU southward to MULHOUSE were attacked by medium and fighter-bombers. Locomotives and railroad cars were hit and the rail line was cut in several places.

Targets in the railway center and industrial town of SIEGEN were attacked in the afternoon by escorted heavy bombers.

On the morning of the 17th tank destroyers arrived just in time to establish a roadblock on the southern side of the village. There they knocked out two PzKpfw IVs pushing northwards from a small reconnaissance team sent towards Wirtzfeld after the leaders of Kampfgruppe Peiper took Büllingen.

The wartime photo was taken 300 yards south of the bridge over the small stream just south of Wirtzfeld, looking south up Zur Holzwarche in the direction of Büllingen. Since we were last there in 1979 (see *Battle of the Bulge Then and Now*, pages 92 and 93), new houses have been built in the field.

COMMUNIQUE No. 254   December 18

Fighting has increased in intensity from the MONSCHAU area southward to the southern end of the Luxembourg-German border, with the enemy continuing his attacks. Both infantry and armor are now in action, and in some sectors the enemy has made use of small groups of parachutists. Gains were made by the Germans near HONSFELD, southwest of VIANDEN, and south of ECHTERNACH.

The enemy's efforts to give air support to his attacking ground forces resulted in aerial battles in which we destroyed 108 of his aircraft for the loss of 33 of our fighters. Most of the action took place over the Monschau Forest and adjoining areas, though combats also developed farther north in the RHEINE, MUNSTER and BOCHOLT regions.

Fighter-bombers, operating mainly against road traffic in the Monschau Forest area, and rail traffic radiating from COLOGNE, destroyed or damaged large numbers of locomotives, rail cars, armored fighting vehicles and motor and horse-drawn vehicles. Much of the road traffic was moving eastward on the road running along the Roer river to the east of MONSCHAU; other operations against road traffic were carried out between MONSCHAU and PRUM.

In the Saar valley, Allied forces are making steady progress in the DILLINGEN and SAARLAUTERN areas. Northeast of SAARGEMUND, we have made gains north of WALSHEIM. Fighter-bombers attacked fortified towns in the Saar region and bombed an ammunition dump east of COBLENZ. In the BITSCH area, heavy fighting continues round Maginot forts. Enemy resistance slackened slightly, but remains stubborn.

Northeast of WISSEMBOURG, our units have captured a half-dozen villages inside Germany, including SCHWEIGHOFEN and KAPSWEYER. Our forces are now facing the Siegfried Line at many points.

Meanwhile, the leaders of Kampfgruppe Müller belonging to the 12. SS-Panzer-Division were fighting hard to capture Rocherath and Krinkelt, suffering in the process painful losses in the so-called 'twin villages'. Panther '126' managed to break through by itself and press on westwards until it was finally disabled by three rounds into its thinner rear armour from an M10 of the 644th Tank Destroyer Battalion.

It was knocked out here on the main road between Büllingen and Krinkelt, a few hundred yards north of the bridge over a small stream.

Medium bombers, two of which are missing, attacked Siegfried Line defences between OBEROTTERBACH and STEINFELD, including fortifications, pillboxes, tank traps and wire entanglements.

Fighter-bombers operating in the KAISERSLAUTERN, SPEYER and PFORZHEIM areas shot down four enemy aircraft and attacked rail lines, locomotives, rail yards and cars and motor transport.

In the high Vosges mountains, our ground forces freed KAISERSBERG. On the Alsace plain some ground was lost to strong enemy counter-attacks.

Fighter-bombers, one of which is missing, struck at barges, bridges, road-blocks and barracks in the COLMAR, FREIBURG and NEUSTADT areas. A rail bridge at FREIBURG was attacked by medium bombers.

Heavy bombers attacked industrial and railway targets in ULM.

Just to the south, Kampfgruppe Peiper was ruthlessly trying to extricate itself from the massive log-jam of traffic east of Losheim. Having done so it advanced to Lanzerath where the leaders of the 3. Fallschirmjäger-Division had already broken through. In the early hours of the 17th, the battle-group pressed on under black-out conditions so as not to warn the Americans with men holding white handkerchiefs walking beside each vehicle to guide the drivers. Just before daybreak the leaders reached Honsfeld, quietly driving into the village and joining the stream of American traffic that was trundled through. The American troops — elements of the 99th Infantry Division and men of the 14th Cavalry Group — were taken by surprise and most were caught in their attempt to get out of the village. *Left:* Next morning, a German war photographer pictured this Kübelwagen passing a disabled 76mm anti-tank gun. *Right:* Time marches on yet the chapel has withstood the passage of time at Merlscheid, a road junction just south of Lanzerath.

Left: Then in Honsfeld he took a series of photos showing men of the 3. Fallschirmjäger-Division removing the boots from American dead to replace their own footwear. *Right:* The road junction in Honsfeld with its drinking trough has since become an iconic image of the Bulge battlefield. A memorial stands nearby dedicated to 'the 612th and 801st TD Battalions and attached units of the 99th Division', adorned with the checkerboard emblem of the latter.

COMMUNIQUE No. 255   December 19

Heavy fighting continues in the sectors where the enemy launched his attacks between the MONSCHAU area and the southern part of the German-Luxembourg border. Supporting Allied ground forces, fighter-bombers knocked out 95 enemy armored vehicles and struck at rail and road transport. Medium and light bombers attacked targets at HERHAHN, OLEF, HARPERSCHEID, BLUMENTHAL and HELLENTHAL, east of MONSCHAU. Forty-six enemy aircraft were shot down in the air. From these operations, 11 fighters are missing; all the bombers returned.

Our forces in the LINNICH area are mopping up in WURM and MÜLLENDORF.

In the DILLINGEN and SAARLAUTERN bridgeheads our troops continue to make slow progress in wiping out enemy strong points. In the area northeast of SAARGEMÜND, we have reached the wooded area one mile north of HABKIRCHEN and gains were made in the vicinity of WALSHEIM and MEDELSHEIM.

Fighter-bombers destroyed or damaged many fortified buildings and attacked road and rail transport in the area of LANDAU.

In the vicinity of BITSCH our units have taken a large portion of two stubbornly defended Maginot fortifications.

Northwest of WISSEMBOURG we advanced two miles and entered the German villages of BUNDENTHAL and NIEDERSCHLETTENBACH.

Farther east, heavy fire was received from the Siegfried Line.

Stiff fighting continues northwest of COLMAR. Further limited advances have been made in the high Vosges mountains.

Last night a strong force of heavy bombers attacked enemy ships in the Baltic port of GDYNIA.

COMMUNIQUE No. 256   December 20

Fighting continues in the area between MONSCHAU and southern Luxembourg where the enemy has launched his attacks.

Despite poor flying conditions, German armor and truck convoys in the Monschau Forest and in the SCHLEIDEN area were attacked by fighter-bombers yesterday. Farther east, targets at MARMAGEN and MUNSTEREIFEL were hit.

North of MONSCHAU, Allied forces continued mopping up enemy elements in WURM and MULLENDORF.

Fighter-bombers attacked railway yards at LIBLAR, east of DUREN.

Farther south escorted heavy bombers attacked targets at TRIER in the afternoon and fighter-bombers hit rail transport east of the city. In the TRIER area our fighters encountered enemy aircraft, 11 of which were shot down for the loss of three of ours.

Our forces in the Saar valley have cleared all of DILLINGEN except the factory district on the east side of the town, and we have made progress in the SAARLAUTERN bridgehead against stubborn resistance. Northeast of SAARGEMUND, our units have made small gains north of HABKIRCHEN and WALSHEIM.

Rail lines between NEUENKIRCHEN and HOMBURG were cut in several places by fighter-bombers. In the same area a number of locomotives and many railway cars were hit.

After several days' heavy fighting, FORT SIMSERHOF in the Maginot Line, just northwest of BITSCH, was occupied. The enemy continued to resist stubbornly at nearby FORT SCHIESSECK.

Northwest of WISSEMBOURG our troops encountered stiff opposition. Two strong counter-attacks were repulsed.

Medium and fighter-bombers struck at rail transport and communications north of WISSEMBOURG, principally at NEUSTADT and LANDAU, and bombed the fortified villages of SCHAIDT and KANDEL, south of LANDAU. Other fighter-bombers flew deeper into Germany to attack an airfield north of STUTTGART where two enemy aircraft were destroyed on the ground and others damaged.

Our ground forces made further small gains northwest of COLMAR and in the high Vosges.

A small number of fighter-bombers attacked rail targets in northern Holland.

Today this stretch of the Saint-Vith to Malmedy road has been bypassed and the old T-junction has been left as quiet backwater in a nondescript industrial area. The old road to Recht is just off the photo to the right.

Prior to 1870, also from 1914 to 1918 and again from 1940, this region of eastern Belgium including Saint-Vith was German territory. The local language was — and still is — German, so the attacking troops were assured of a friendly welcome from the villagers. Jean Paul first discovered the location where this sequence, taken from a German newsreel, was shot back in 1980; it proved to be at Deidenberg, six miles north of Saint-Vith.

Another famous photo often used to illustrate the Battle of the Bulge: Tiger '222', the mount of SS-Oberscharführer Kurt Sowa. In 1979 Jean Paul traced the route of the Tiger with its load of Fallschirmjägers when it was pictured by the German cameraman at four different locations as it proceeded on its westerly course: Tondorf (see page 281); Merlscheid; Deidenberg (top); **Kaiserbaracke** (above) **and Ligneuville.**

This well-known series of action photos was included in many publications since the war but always without meaningful captions . . . that is until Jean Paul pinpointed the location where they were taken back in 1979. Once that had been established, he was then able to trace which units had been present at the time, and even try to put a name to a face. *After the Battle* published the results of his research in issue 37 in 1982. It turned out that elements of Kampfgruppe Knittel (1. SS-Panzer-Division) had ambushed Task Force Mayes of the 14th Cavalry Group as it moved north out of Poteau, just west of Saint-Vith, on the morning of December 18. The photographer, who was SS-Unterscharführer Max Büschel, and the movie cameraman, SS-Unterscharführer Schaefer, asked some of the men to stage 'attacks' for them against the background of the burning American vehicles. For convenience to describe the men who appeared in different shots, Jean Paul originally used code-letters of his own, like 'SS-Schütze V', but since publication of the story in *After the Battle*, other historians have identified several of them like SS-Unterscharführer Josef Priess of the Staff Company of SS-Panzer-Aufklärungs-Abteilung 1 and also SS-Unterscharführer Wilhelm Gilbert, a platoon commander in the 2. Kompanie. The reason why this sequence of photographs received so much publicity is that the film was captured by the Americans on December 18. Two couriers dispatched from Cologne to bring back the photos and footage exposed during the first days of the offensive, lost their way on their return journey and ended up in Waimes which was still in American hands.

Above: **One 'attack' was staged across the road although in actual fact the 'attackers' were filmed advancing in the wrong direction, back from where they had just come from!** *Right:* **The battlefield today at Poteau, looking in a northerly direction.**

These men were part of a force from SS-Panzer-Aufklärungs-Abteilung 1 driving westwards behind Kampfgruppe Hansen to link up with Kampfgruppe Knittel via Kaiserbaracke and Stavelot. Although one name has been put forward to try to identify the individual in the centre, unfortunately positive identification has not been forthcoming. His legacy is nevertheless assured as his portrait has now become synonymous with the offensive in the Ardennes.

It is difficult to see how an M8 could get stuck on this bank but possibly panic set in after German fire struck the leading vehicle.

On the morning of December 18, the leaders of Kampfgruppe Peiper advanced on Stavelot and reached the northern bank of the Amblève river although they failed to capture the whole of the town. *Left:* The following day, Tiger '105' was hit just as it reached the top of the steep Rue Haut-Rivage. The driver tried to back away from the danger but, losing control, crashed into a building which then collapsed on top of it. *Right:* From 1944 to 2014; here the Tiger met its end.

vicinity of MASPELT, five miles to the south.

In the ECHTERNACH area, an enemy penetration was made to CONSDORF, and ECHTERNACH itself was surrounded.

The enemy force involved in the attack on the front includes five to six armored divisions and eight or nine infantry divisions.

There have been no changes in our positions to the north of MONSCHAU along the ROER river from LINNICH to DUREN

In the Saar valley fighting continues in our DILLINGEN and SAARLAUTERN bridgeheads. Two small enemy counter-attacks northeast of SAARGEMUND were repulsed.

FORT SCHIESSECK, second major Maginot Line fortification to be reduced in the vicinity of BITSCH, was cleared.

Farther east the enemy was aggressive and several of his patrols crossed the Rhine.

Northwest of COLMAR limited progress was made in the high Vosges mountains, and in a series of local operations approximately 800 prisoners were taken.

Weather reduced air activity yesterday to a minimum.

Unable to pass through Stavelot, the battle-group that was following instead sent a battalion west along the southern bank of the Amblève river, soon establishing a bridgehead at Petit-Spai which lies just east of Trois-Ponts. On the morning of the 21st, a Jagdpanzer IV/70 tried to cross to the northern bank but its weight brought down the flimsy bridge. These engineers were pictured working on a new bridge which was constructed just upstream from the one that had collapsed.

COMMUNIQUE No. 257   December 21

Fighting continues in the area where the enemy attacked westward from the German borders of Belgium and Luxembourg. Our positions east of MONSCHAU were restored after a German force which entered the town was surrounded.

Enemy units, making two thrusts from the east in the general direction of MALMEDY reached STAVELOT, southwest of MALMEDY, and BUTGENBACH, east of MALMEDY.

Another enemy driving into the area of ST VITH cut off some of our forces east of the town, and enemy elements moved to within two miles of ST VITH and to the

Apart from the new bridge, Petit-Spai has seen little change since the war. It remains one of those places where one can really feel the atmosphere of 1944.

Alerted on December 17, the 30th Infantry Division was rushed south from the Aachen area to help reinforce the Amblève sector. Its 120th Infantry arrived at Malmédy on the 18th, joining with the 291st Engineer Combat Battalion and the 526th Armored Infantry Battalion when they began erecting road-blocks on the approaches to the town. *Right:* Few American photographers were on hand in the early days of the German offensive but fortunately one from the Signal Corps was following the 30th Division as it rushed southwards. This is one of the pictures he took showing the south-eastern entrance of Malmédy near the bridge over the Warchenne river. It was probably taken on December 22, the day before a heavy American bombing raid hit the town. Malmédy had been wrongly reported as having been captured by the Germans so the Ninth Air Force first attacked the town on December 23 though 'not very accurately' according to Sergeant Arthur P. Wiley of the 120th Infantry who witnessed the attack. Another raid took place the following day (December 24), this time by B-24 heavies from the 458th Bombardment Group which believed they were dropping their bombs on Schönecken, 25 miles away to the south-east! Their 'accuracy was deadly', noted Wiley, 'and it was beyond our belief that our own planes could bomb us two days in a row'. In spite of the fact that Malmédy remained firmly in American hands throughout, American aircraft raided the town for a third time later the same day, though doing little more damage, and even returned on Christmas Day for a fourth and final raid. Malmédy was never taken by the Germans but, as a result of the bombing, the entire centre of the town was laid waste, the final death toll being 37 GIs and over 200 civilians.

By December 22, the Germans had halted their attack on Malmédy and pulled back but Sergeant Wiley wrote that 'we did not know this for sure so we remained on 100 per cent alert all day'. *Above left:* A Signal Corps photographer recorded infantry pushing south-eastwards from the town. *Above:* Remarkably, the houses lining Avenue Monbijou have all survived, enabling this perfect comparison.

Left: At Vielsalm, ten miles south-west of Malmédy, elements of the 7th Armored Division controlled the western bank of the Salm river. Here they are placing an anti-tank gun in position to cover the bridge on the road out of town. *Above:* Now Rue des Chasseurs Ardennais, this was the main road leading to the west in the direction of Lierneux.

Although the Americans were still unaware of what had taken place at the Baugnez crossroads, a mile and a half south-east of Malmédy, it was here that the leaders of Kampfgruppe Peiper had shot 86 American prisoners on December 17. Lying in the field beyond the site of the massacre, these two men may have been cut down while trying to escape.

COMMUNIQUE No. 258   December 22

Several small enemy attacks have been repulsed by Allied forces in the vicinity of MONSCHAU, and we have regained a few small towns in that area.

On the north flank of the German thrust we have stemmed the enemy advance and have retaken STAVELOT, southwest of MALMEDY. Fighting is in progress for MALMEDY itself. Enemy armored elements have reached HABIEMONT, eight miles west of STAVELOT, and enemy parachutists were dropped a few miles to the southwest of HABIEMONT.

Our forces have slowed down the enemy pincer movement directed at ST VITH, which is still in our hands.

The enemy drive west from VIANDEN has penetrated to a point just east of WILTZ, and a force operating about six miles farther north reached the vicinity of CLERVAUX.

Fighting continues in the ECHTERNACH area, where our troops have denied the enemy control of ECHTERNACH and other towns in immediate vicinity. The enemy thrust to CONSDORF, southwest of ECHTERNACH, made further progress to the west.

In the Saar valley, our forces have cleared DILLINGEN.

North and northwest of WISSEMBOURG, two counter-attacks, one supported by tanks, were beaten off. Repeated patrol clashes took place further east nearer the Rhine.

Further slight gains were made in the high Vosges. We are now two miles south of Lake Noir, near MUNSTER.

Weather restricted air operations yesterday. Targets in TRIER were attacked by heavy bombers. Fighter-bombers which provided the escort, also struck at objectives in the city and at SPEICHER, a main road junction twelve miles north. Anti-aircraft positions east of LEBACH were targets for other fighter-bombers. From these operations one fighter-bomber is missing.

Last evening heavy bombers attacked the marshalling yards at COLOGNE and BONN.

```
                    ORDER OF THE DAY
                                      22 December 1944

TO EVERY MEMBER OF THE A.E.F.:

The enemy is making his supreme effort to break out of the
desperate plight into which you forced him by your brilliant
victories of the summer and fall. He is fighting savagely
to take back all that you have won and is using every
treacherous trick to deceive and kill you. He is gambling
everything, but already, in this battle, your gallantry has
done much to foil his plans. In the face of your proven
bravery and fortitude, he will completely fail.

But we can not be content with his mere repulse.

By rushing out from his fixed defenses the enemy may give
us the chance to turn his great gamble into his worst de-
feat. So I call upon every man, of all the Allies, to
rise now to new heights of courage, of resolution and of
effort. Let everyone hold before him a single thought --
to destroy the enemy on the ground, in the air, everywhere --
destroy him! United in this determination and with un-
shakable faith in the cause for which we fight, we will,
with God's help, go forward to our greatest victory.


                              (Signed)

                              DWIGHT D. EISENHOWER
```

SHAEF issued this special communiqué to all members of the Allied Expeditionary Force under the signature of the Supreme Commander on December 22.

The nature of the terrain in the sector of the 5. Panzerarmee gave it comparatively better roads compared to those of the 6. Panzerarmee but nevertheless they first had to cross the Our river. One of the major crossing points was at Dasburg where a major road arrived from Germany and a direct route ran westwards. Engineers quickly constructed a heavy bridge for the 2. Panzer-Division and the army commander, General Hasso von Manteuffel, helped personally to direct traffic there. By midnight on December 16, the leaders of the 2. Panzer-Division had passed Marnach and were well on their way to Clervaux. The Panzer-Lehr-Division crossed the Our river some distance to the south, its engineers establishing a bridge in front of Gemünd, about mid-way between Dasburg and Vianden. *Above left:* This snapshot was taken of Hauptmann Kunze, the battalion commander of Panzer-Pionier-Bataillon 130, as he urged on his men to complete the bridge on the morning of the 16th. *Above right:* The crossing was ready by midday. This is the view from the German side of the river, with Luxembourg on the far side. However the site was not ideal as it had a muddy winding road on the exit side so one battle-group of the Panzer-Lehr-Division was redirected to cross at Dasburg instead.

Whereas in the 6. Panzerarmee and the 5. Panzerarmee the advance was by armoured formations moving together with infantry troops, on the left wing the 7. Armee had to work only with infantry units whose most-efficient weapon against tanks was the Panzerfaust.

On the morning of December 17 a platoon of Shermans was sent from Clervaux to try to stop the panzers but they were quickly dealt with whereupon the leading PzKpfw IVs rolled into the town.

Although this image was poor as it was lifted from a German cine, it proved to have been filmed looking north along Grand Rue, the matching shot being taken by Jean Paul.

Meanwhile, at Bastogne, the VIII Corps commander, General Troy H. Middleton, strove to organise the defence of the town. He directed two armoured combat commands — CCR of the 9th Armored Division and CCB of the 10th Armored — to set up road-blocks on the roads east of Bastogne. Positioned on the Allerborn—Bastogne road, the forces of CCR were cut to pieces by the Germans during the night of the 18th. Meanwhile, CCB formed three battle groups, Team O'Hara going east to Wardin, Team Desobry north to Noville and Team Cherry north-east to Longvilly. *Above:* On the 19th, elements of Team Cherry were caught up in a battle with leaders of the 2. Panzer-Division east of Mageret, subsequently losing all their vehicles. Taken in January 1945 when much had already been cleared, this photo still shows wrecks of tanks and vehicles that had been knocked out on December 19. *Right:* The road from Mageret looking towards Longvilly.

Left: Meanwhile, stragglers from the 110th Infantry (28th Division) who managed to reach Bastogne after the regiment was virtually wiped out in Luxembourg, were re-organised and re-equipped. Picture taken on December 19. *Right:* No. 12 Rue du Marché.

The 101st Airborne Division, then in SHAEF reserve in the Reims area of France, was ordered to Bastogne with all speed and began to arrive late on December 18. That night the division's acting commander, Brigadier General Anthony McAuliffe, met General Middleton at the VIII Corps command post to confer on the uncertain tactical situation. The next morning Middleton left Bastogne after giving McAuliffe a simple instruction: 'Hold Bastogne!'

Left: On the 19th, Signal Corps photographer T/5 Wesley B. Carolan pictured men of the 506th Parachute Infantry Regiment moving 'to stem the German drive'. *Right:* Chaussée de Houffalize at the northern entrance of Bastogne.

COMMUNIQUE No. 259   December 23

Allied forces in the MONSCHAU sector continued local engagements with no substantial change in position. In the vicinity of HOFEN, the enemy gained a small amount of ground.

No further attempts have been made by the enemy to break out in the STAVELOT area, and the northern German thrust has been confined temporarily to the area of ST VITH, STAVELOT and MALMEDY. All three of these towns are in our hands.

An enemy drive that outflanked BASTOGNE from the north reached as far as LA ROCHE. Fighting continues in that sector.

A large-scale thrust is being made by the enemy in the WILTZ—BASTOGNE area. WILTZ has been encircled, and the enemy is pushing on after an action at the town. German armour continued its advance to cut roads north, south and east of BASTOGNE, while a portion of the force bypassed BASTOGNE and continued west.

In the ECHTERNACH area, the line has been stabilised. The enemy has been checked in the areas of DICKWEILER, OSWEILER and BERDORF, west and south of ECHTERNACH.

In the sector east of SAARGEMUND, we have occupied UTWEILER.

Activity in the Alsace plain was generally limited to patrol clashes. Further local gains were made in the high Vosges south of LAPOUTROIE where the village of LA CHAPELLE was cleared.

Continued adverse weather yesterday again prevented the weight of our air power being brought to bear on the enemy.

Bombing through cloud, escorted medium bombers attacked enemy troop concentrations and supply dumps while fighters and fighter-bombers flew offensive patrols in support of our ground forces.

Enemy troops, communications and rail transport in the upper Rhine valley were struck at by fighter-bombers. East of FREIBURG, six enemy aircraft were shot down by our attacking aircraft. According to reports so far received, four of our fighters are missing from these operations, but the pilot of one is safe.

Shortly after dark yesterday evening, heavy bombers attacked the marshalling yards at COBLENZ and BINGEN.

By December 21 Bastogne was completely surrounded and German artillery was shelling the town from all points of the compass. Then on Christmas Eve the Luftwaffe mounted two bombing raids on the town and surrounding area leaving the main square strewn with wrecks.

Now a focal point of the town square, this is said to be the first tank to enter Renuamont on January 2. On the right stands one of the 'Voie de la Liberté' marker obelisks which mark every kilometre of the Liberty Highway across France, Luxembourg and Belgium, beginning at Utah beach.

```
                                            December 22nd 1944

To the U.S.A. Commander of the encircled town of Bastogne.

        The fortune of war is changing.  This time the U.S.A.
forces in and near Bastogne have been encircled by strong
German armored units.  More German armored units have crossed
the river Ourthe near Ortheuville, have taken Marche and
reached St. Hubert by passing through Hompré-Sibret-Tillet.
Libramont is in German hands.
        There is only one possibility to save the encircled
U.S.A. troops from total annihilation: that is the honorable
surrender of the encircled town.  In order to think it over
a term of two hours will be granted beginning with the
presentation of this note.
        If this proposal should be rejected one German
Artillery Corps and six heavy A. A. Battalions are ready
to annihilate the U.S.A. troops in and near Bastogne.  The
order for firing will be given immediately after this two
hours' term.
        All the serious civilian losses caused by this
artillery fire would not correspond with the wellknown
American humanity.

                                            The German Commander.
```

At 11.30 a.m. on December 22, four Germans under a white flag approached an American outpost south of Bastogne to demand 'honourable surrender'. Colonel Joseph H. Harper, commanding the 327th Glider Infantry Regiment, took the note to division headquarters. McAuliffe, reading the message, laughed and according to the history books said: 'Aw, nuts!' although some say his language was a little more basic!

Thinking how he should respond, his G-3 (Operations Officer), Lieutenant Colonel Harry Kinnard, then suggested: 'That first remark of yours would be hard to beat' so McAuliffe wrote a one-word reply yet it was 'Nuts!' that became legend. The German envoy, Leutnant Hellmuth Henke, asked whether the reply was negative or affirmative. 'The reply is decidedly not affirmative', said Colonel Harper.

After days of poor weather, December 23 dawned bright and clear enabling 241 C-47s from the IX Troop Carrier Command to drop over 144 tons of assorted supplies just west of Bastogne. The drop zone lay just beyond the town cemetery which was across the road from the Belgian barracks where General McAuliffe had set up the HQ for the 101st Airborne Division.

Another massive supply drop involving 160 aircraft took place on December 24 but poor flying weather on Christmas Day cancelled other supply missions apart from 11 gliders that managed to land within the perimeter. The biggest operation to resupply the troops in the town comprising 289 aircraft occurred on the 26th.

COMMUNIQUE No. 260   December 24

There have been no substantial changes in the Allied positions in the MONSCHAU sector.

In the area northeast of MARCHE enemy forces have cut the road northeast of HOTTON. The town of HOTTON remains in our hands but there is considerable resistance south of the road between HOTTON and SOY, three miles to the northeast.

Farther south enemy forces have reached MORHET, six miles southwest of Bastogne.

In the area north of MERSCH our troops have made gains on the southern flank of the enemy penetration.

Allied forces in the Saar valley repulsed a counter-attack by enemy infantry who crossed the Saar river south of SAARLAUTERN.

East of WISSEMBOURG, enemy artillery and mortars were active. More than 1,000 rounds fell on BERG within a few hours.

Slight further progress was made in the Vosges west of COLMAR.

Improved weather yesterday permitted the resumption of air operations on a large-scale. Fighter-bombers in great strength struck at motor transport, tanks, rolling stock, troop concentrations, gun positions and other targets in and behind the area of the enemy counter-offensive, while fighters flew offensive sweeps. Medium and light bombers in force attacked bridges, railheads and communication centers behind this area. Great numbers of aerial combats ensued in the course of these operations.

The targets for the medium and light bombers were rail bridges at EUSKIRCHEN, AHRWEILER, MAYEN and ELLER, railheads at ZULPICH, PRUM and TYLLBURG and communication centers in the neighbourhood of ST VITH and at HERGARTEN, LUNEBACH, WAXWEILER and NEUERBURG.

Farther to the south medium bombers attacked bridges at NECKARGEMUND and BREISACH, also dropping anti-personnel bombs on enemy troops in the latter area.

Fighter-bombers went for rail yards, rolling stock and rail lines in the areas of LANDAU, RINGSHEIM and COLMAR, destroying locomotives and rolling stock.

Escorted heavy bombers attacked objectives in the railway and garrison town of TRIER and seven other rail and road

Meanwhile, on the right wing, Kampfgruppe Peiper was leading the advance of the 6. Panzerarmee. Although the battle-group took Stoumont on December 19, its leading Panther was destroyed at the eastern entrance of the village by a direct hit from a 90mm anti-aircraft gun positioned near the church.

Decades have passed and the fields on both sides of the road have now been built up.

Left: **As American prisoners were rounded up in Stoumont, ready to be marched eastwards to La Gleize, SS-Sturmbannführer Werner Pötschke was filmed talking to his men in front of a house at the eastern end of the village. Although the film taken at Poteau on the 18th had been captured by the Americans (see page 286), this sequence taken by the same team at Stoumont on the 19th successfully made it back to Germany.** *Right:* **While the house across the road was burned down during the battle, the clapboard house opposite remains unscathed.**

Having run out of fuel and food, Peiper (above) had to set up a static defence in a pocket around Stoumont and La Gleize, waiting for follow-up units and supplies to arrive. On December 22, American artillery started to shell the pocket and although the Luftwaffe flew a resupply mission during the night, many of the containers fell into American hands. After every effort to reach and sustain him had failed (see page 287), and with supplies down to zero, Peiper had no option but to abandon all his vehicles and equipment. He led the party through the Allied lines on foot during the night of December 24/25 and some 800 men managed to return to Germany. (Joachim Peiper was awarded the Swords to the Knight's Cross for his brilliant, if vain, performance in the Ardennes.)

Nevertheless over 300 Germans, most of them wounded, were captured when the pocket was cleared on Christmas Day at which point 170 American prisoners were freed. About 25 panzers and 50 armoured half-tracks were found abandoned in the area. *Above:* Not counting those at Stoumont, 13 Panthers lay in La Gleize alone, including '221' in the centre of the village.

communications centers in western Germany including rail yards at EHRANG, KAISERSLAUTERN, HOMBURG and rail and road junctions in an area between COBLENZ and the Belgian border.

Last night light bombers attacked rail targets near BONN and COBLENZ.

In the course of all these operations 178 enemy aircraft were shot down and nine destroyed on the ground; eight of our heavy bombers, 26 fighters and fighter-bombers, and 39 medium and light bombers are not yet reported, though some of the medium bombers may have landed away from base. During the night our night fighters shot down nine enemy aircraft.

This is the road junction at the northern entrance to La Gleize, the main road turning off to the left running to Stoumont. The building in background now houses the hotel 'Aux Écuries de la Reine' (The Queen's Stables).

Seven Tiger IIs were left in La Gleize and the surrounding area. In January, these paratroops of the 82nd Airborne Division no doubt enjoyed some target practice using a bazooka against the dreaded German tank. None of their shots pierced the front armour though better success was achieved through the side armour of the turret.

On the left wing of the 6. Panzerarmee, the leaders of the 2. SS-Panzer-Division swept through the important junction of Manhay, 25 miles north of Bastogne, on Christmas Day, catching elements of Combat Command A of the 7th Armored Division by surprise just as they had received orders to pull out.

Left: This photo of a Sherman disabled at the crossroads was taken after the recapture of the village two days later. *Right:* Jean Paul tried to get access to the same upstairs window but without success so he had to be satisfied with a comparison from street level.

COMMUNIQUE No. 261   December 25

The MONSCHAU and STAVELOT sectors have been relatively quiet although both Allied and enemy artillery fire has been heavy. No further progress has been made by the enemy in these sectors. The Germans dropped parachutists in small groups in several places in the area north and northwest of STAVELOT. These are being dealt with.

Very heavy enemy attacks directed to the northwest in the areas of HOTTON and MARCHE have been successfully held.

Enemy forward elements have moved westward and tanks and troop-carrying vehicles been reported between MARCHE and ROCHEFORT.

There has been only local ground activity in the area of BASTOGNE, but enemy pressure continues to be strong southwest of the town. German tanks are in the vicinity of ROSIERE, seven miles southwest of BASTOGNE.

CHAUMONT, about six miles south of BASTOGNE, has been cleared, and fighting continues near the town following an enemy counter-attack. Farther to the south, MARTELANGE on the BASTOGNE—ARLON road is half cleared of the enemy and we have made gains to the vicinity of BIGONVILLE, three miles northeast.

In the area west and northwest of DIEKIRCH, our troops have cleared the enemy from HEIDERSCHEID. A German counter-attack launched with tanks and infantry near TADLER resulted in heavy fighting. Further progress has been made by our forces a few miles west of the DIEKIRCH.

There have been no substantial changes in the area south and southwest of ECHTERNACH where fighting is underway in the vicinity of CONSDORF.

Allied air operations were continued in very great strength yesterday. German armour, troops, fortified positions, gun positions and road and rail transport in and behind the battle area were hit by fighter-bombers operating from first light. Attacks were also resumed on the enemy's reinforcement routes.

Medium and light bombers struck at railheads and communications at NIDEGGEN, ZULPICH and elsewhere in the area, while farther south, bridges at KONZ-KARTHAUS and TRIER-PFALZEL were targets for other medium and light bombers.

Forty-four enemy aircraft were destroyed in the air in the course of these operations. According to preliminary reports, 45 of our fighters are missing but the pilots of two are safe.

Their advance having ground to a standstill, the SS grenadiers were then attacked by fighter-bombers on the 26th. After they had pulled back the following night, Corporal James R. Gordon and Private L. C. Rainwater were pictured with one of the division's Panthers abandoned near the church at Grandménil, a mile west of Manhay.

Although almost certainly not the same tank, one of the Panthers left behind by the 2. SS-Panzer-Division was retained by the village which set it up at the same junction.

Having left Kampfgruppe 901 to stiffen the infantry assault against the Americans holed up in Bastogne, the Panzer-Lehr-Division bypassed the town and pressed on westwards. Advancing across country, the leaders took Saint-Hubert 12 miles away without a fight on the 22nd and then swept a battalion of the 335th Infantry Regiment, 84th Division, from Rochefort, a further 12 miles to the north-west, on the 24th. *Left:* Grenadiers supported by Panthers pictured in the main street of Rochefort amid a detritus of abandoned American equipment. In eight days the Panzer-Lehr-Division had advanced over 40 miles since they had crossed the Our river. *Right:* This is the main junction in the centre of the town.

More than 2,000 heavy bombers, escorted by over 900 fighters, attacked 11 airfields in the FRANKFURT area and road and rail junctions, bridges and supply centers from EUSKIRCHEN south to TRIER.

Seventy enemy aircraft were shot down by the escorting fighters and 18 by the bombers. From incomplete reports, 39 bombers and six fighters are missing, but some of them are believed to have landed away from their bases.

Yesterday afternoon, small strong forces of enemy bombers with fighter escort attacked two airfields in the Ruhr. In the evening, heavy bombers struck at railway targets at COLOGNE and an airfield at BONN.

Enemy patrols which crossed the Rhine northeast of STRASBOURG were repulsed. North of COLMAR, a counter-attack forced a slight withdrawal of our forward elements at SIGOLSHEIM.

Medium bombers striking deep into Germany attacked a bridge at LANGENARGEN on the north shore of Lake Constance, and hit a railway yards at EMMENDINGEN, north of FREIBURG. Night fighters shot down six enemy aircraft last night.

The German offensive may have gone under the code-name 'Wacht am Rhein' yet it stalled just 15 miles short of another river — the Meuse. 'The dream is over' wrote a grenadier on a 76mm anti-tank gun captured in the centre of Rochefort.

The unit that advanced closest to the river was the 2. Panzer-Division; they reached Foy-Notre-Dame, just six miles short of the Meuse at Dinant. *Left:* Stranded with no fuel, on Christmas Day the division attempted to pull back but it was too late for the battle-group in Foy where 150 men were captured along with 20 vehicles, including this Puma. *Above:* Foy-Notre-Dame . . . then and now.

COMMUNIQUE No. 262   December 26

Allied forces in Holland have encountered enemy patrol activity along the River Maas north of TILBURG, and in the VENLO area.

South of DUREN, we have pushed forward into the village of WINDEN, where fighting is still going on against strong opposition, and cleared OBERMAUBACH, one mile farther south.

In the MONSCHAU—MALMEDY sector, following a quiet day, the Germans launched an attack in the evening with armor and infantry near BULLINGEN. This was repulsed with heavy losses to the enemy. Our troops have cleared LA GLEIZE, three miles northwest of STAVELOT. MALMEDY, STAVELOT and STOUMONT remain in Allied hands.

In the area northwest of LIERNEUX, our troops made a slight withdrawal and the enemy has reached GRANDMENIL a few miles west. More enemy paratroops have been dropped in the area a few miles southwest of STAVELOT and north of BEAURAING, five miles southeast of GIVET. All these were mopped up.

ROCHEFORT has been occupied by the enemy and enemy pressure has been increasing east of HOTTON, near ROCHEFORT and near MARCHE.

BASTOGNE is still held by our forces despite heavy pressure. The enemy has launched an attack with tanks and infantry near MARVIE, and after making gains southwest of BASTOGNE, now holds ROSIERE and LIBRAMONT.

Along the southern flank of the enemy penetration, gains have been made and enemy attacks repulsed. Fighting is still in progress near CHAUMONT and we have cleared the enemy from WARNACH. Ground has been gained just north of BIGONVILLE, and in the areas of NEUENHAUSEN, HEIDERSCHEID and ARSDORF, which has been cleared of the enemy. German attacks near HEIDERSCHEID and at KEHMEN were repulsed. Progress was also made south and east of DIEKIRCH, where we took MOSTROFF, and south of ECHTERNACH, despite enemy counter-attacks.

Air operations were continued yesterday on a large scale. Ground targets in the battle area, including motor transport, armor, strong points and gun positions were attacked throughout the day by fighter-bombers.

The enemy's supply and reinforcement routes in and behind the battle zone were the objectives for heavy, medium and light bombers.

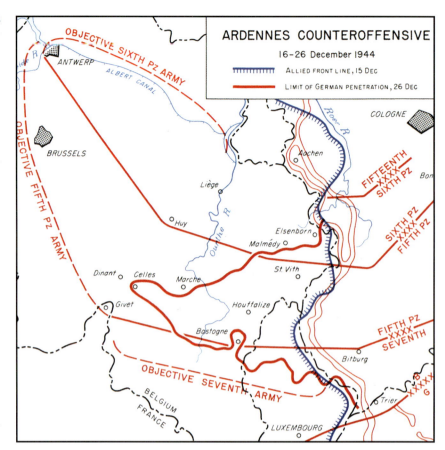

By December 26, the German advance was effectively at an end, still 75 miles short of Antwerp, the objective of the counter-offensive, having been brought mainly to a halt by the lack of fuel. In the south, although the 4th Armored Division made contact with the garrison of Bastogne at 4.50 p.m., SHAEF only announced the link-up on the 28th (see Communiqué No. 264).

Rail bridges and road and rail junctions in the battle area were attacked by medium forces of escorted heavy bombers.

Road junctions at MUNSTEREIFEL, in the BITBURG area and at VIANDEN were attacked by medium and light bombers; at the latter place a fuel storage depot was also hit. Rail bridges at KONZ-KARTHAUS, TABEN and KEUCHINGEN, as well as rail facilities in the ST VITH area and at WENGEROHR, and communications centers at HILLESHEIM and AHUTTE were also attacked by medium and light bombers.

Farther south, medium bombers went for a rail bridge at SINGEN, while fighter-bombers attacked locomotives and rolling stock in the region of the upper Rhine. In the COLMAR area fighter-bombers gave close support to our ground forces.

Seventy-eight enemy aircraft was shot down yesterday, 13 heavy bombers, seven medium and light bombers and 43 fighters are missing. Some fighters are believed to have landed safely in friendly territory.

Ground patrols were active in the WISSEMBOURG area and along the Rhine. NOTHWEILER and SCHWEIGEN were shelled by enemy artillery. North of COLMAR our troops have re-entered BENNWIHR.

As the Ardennes crisis developed, the First and Ninth Armies practically lost all communication with Bradley's headquarters at Luxembourg, so on December 20 Eisenhower decided to put Montgomery in temporary command of the two American armies north of the German salient. *Left:* On the 26th, Montgomery came for a conference with Generals Collins and Ridgway at the headquarters of VII Corps then located in the Château de Bassinnes in Méan, ten miles north of Marche. *Right:* Unfortunately, the château was demolished in 1984 but the majestic entrance gate still stands, pictured here by André Dessaint.

Breaking the encirclement. On the 27th, two photographers of the 166th Signal Corps Photographic Company, Pfc Sam Gilbert and Pfc Donald R. Ornitz, pictured men of the 10th Armored Infantry Battalion, 4th Armored Division, advancing over snowy terrain.

COMMUNIQUE No. 263   December 27

Allied forces in Holland continued to encounter enemy patrols along the Maas river north of TILBURG.

South of DUREN the village of WINDEN has been cleared by our forces against stiff opposition. The MONSCHAU—MALMEDY sector has been quiet except for a small unsuccessful attack by the enemy near BULLINGEN, and there is no change in our positions. Northwest of STAVELOT our units cleared up an enemy pocket near LA GLEIZE and captured 150 prisoners, 38 tanks, 70 half-track vehicles, eight armoured cars and six self-propelled guns.

The enemy attacked strongly at MANHAY, ten miles southwest of STAVELOT, and succeeded in capturing the village. Our troops later counter-attacked and the situation was restored, though the village itself remains in enemy hands.

Enemy pressure continues to be heavy between HOTTON and MARCHE but our positions have been maintained. A few enemy tanks and troop carriers pushed forward in the direction of CELLES. These were engaged by our forces and driven back, some tanks being knocked out.

Our forces maintain their hold on BASTOGNE despite heavy German pressure from all sides, and numerous enemy tanks have been destroyed in attempts to enter the town. Southwest of BASTOGNE, we have advanced to the vicinity of COBREVILLE, and fighting continues just north of CHAUMONT.

South of BASTOGNE the towns of HOLLANGE and TINTANGE have been cleared of the enemy. Our forces are fighting in the vicinity of ARSDORF and have entered LULTZHAUSEN. Fighting is in progress in ESCHDORF, where the enemy is offering stubborn resistance with infantry and tanks, and in KEHMEN and RINGEL.

We have reached high ground west of EPPELDORF, four and one-half miles southeast of DIEKIRCH, and have repulsed an enemy counter-attack in the vicinity of HALLER and have taken WALDBILLING. Additional gains have been made by our units in the area south of ECHTERNACH.

Heavy, medium and fighter-bombers were out yesterday attacking targets in the immediate battle zone and striking at communications and supply routes behind the enemy lines. Our fighters flew protective patrols and escort missions.

Communications and rail transport in northern Holland were attacked by fighter-bombers. Other fighter-bombers hit barracks at ZWOLLE and bombed enemy aircraft on the ground near CLEVE.

A strong force of escorted heavy bombers made a heavy attack on enemy troop concentrations, armor and supplies in the ST VITH area. Fighter-bombers in strength, maintaining a day-long attack on the enemy's mechanised forces, destroyed or damaged 857 motor vehicles and 146 armoured vehicles including a number of tanks.

Other escorted heavy bombers bombed two railway yards in the COBLENZ area and railway bridges north of COBLENZ, while fighter-bombers struck at railway targets along the Rhine valley from COBLENZ to KARLSRUHE. Many locomotives and railway cars were hit and rail lines cut in a number of places. Medium and light bombers attacked railway bridges at AHRWEILER, KONZ-KARTHAUS, BAD MUNSTER and RASTATT.

According to reports so far received, 71 enemy aircraft were shot down during the day. Thirty of our fighters and one bomber are missing.

Our ground forces made a slight gain in the wooded area west of WISSEMBOURG, but this sector was generally inactive.

In the southern high Vosges mountains an attempted enemy raid on THANN was repulsed.

Moving up from the south, the vanguard of Third Army broke through the German siege on December 26, and the following day General Maxwell Taylor arrived in Bastogne to resume command of his 101st Airborne Division. (He had been on leave in the States when the German attack began whereupon he rushed back to Europe.) Patton visited Bastogne on December 30 when he awarded the Distinguished Service Cross to General McAuliffe (right). In January McAuliffe was given command of the 103rd Infantry Division.

Advancing north from the Rochefort area, on December 25 the Panzer-Lehr-Division tried to relieve the trapped battle-group of the 2. Panzer-Division but without success. Meanwhile, off to their right with the same objective, the 9. Panzer-Division was moving out from the Marche sector. *Left:* This Panther of the latter division was knocked out in Humain which lies midway between Rochefort and Marche. *Right:* A nice comparison in front of the school where little has changed over the following 70 years.

COMMUNIQUE No. 264   December 28

Allied forces in Holland continued to encounter active patrolling by the enemy along the River Maas north of TILBURG and north of VENLO.

The enemy made a small local attack at GERBROEK, three miles southeast of MAESEYCK. Our troops after a slight withdrawal counter-attacked to regain their original positions.

The MONSCHAU—MALMEDY sector remains quiet, with both sides carrying out active patrolling.

The enemy attacked at a number of places on the northern flank of his salient. Heavy fighting continues at GRANDMENIL and MANHAY, and we repulsed strong German attacks two miles northeast of LIERNEUX and near HUMAIN and HAVRENNE.

Small groups of enemy tanks have been observed in the triangle ROCHEFORT—BEAURAING—ST HUBERT, but enemy armored patrols pushing from ROCHEFORT towards CELLES have been less active. Those that have been encountered have been severely dealt with. In the area of ST HUBERT, which is in enemy hands, we encountered mines, road-blocks and blown bridges.

Allied forces advancing from the south have made contact with units holding BASTOGNE at a point about three miles south of the town. During the period of encirclement, the units in BASTOGNE inflicted severe damage on the enemy, and on the day before their relief, they repulsed two German attacks. In the first attack, made by an estimated two regiments of infantry and a large number of tanks, an estimated 27 enemy tanks were destroyed and 250 prisoners taken. A similar attack was contained later, and in the third attack the enemy lost four out of five tanks taking part.

In the area southeast of BASTOGNE we have cleared the enemy from BONNAL and INSENBORN and have crossed the Sure river in three places near BONNAL. ESCHDORF was cleared of the enemy after heavy fighting, and a strong enemy counter-attack with infantry was repulsed in the vicinity of RINGEL. Northwest of ECHTERNACH, we have encircled BEAUFORT and are mopping up in BERDORF.

Strong formations of fighters and fighter-bombers operated in close support of our ground forces and attacked German armor, troops, gun positions and road and rail transport.

Medium bombers attacked a railhead at KALL and railway bridges at AHRWEILER, and at NONNWEILER southeast of TRIER. Light bombers went for objectives at LA ROCHE and HOUFFALIZE.

More than 600 heavy bombers with an escort of over 400 fighters attacked railway communications in western Germany. Targets included a railway junction at GEROLSTEIN, 40 miles west of COBLENZ, and marshalling yards at EUSKIRCHEN, ANDERNACH, KAISERSLAUTERN, HOMBURG and at FULDA, 60 miles south of KASSEL. Some of the escorting fighters also strafed railway transport near TRIER and east of BONN.

Fighter-bombers attacked railway transport and communications over the area from ST WENDEL southeast to STUTTGART and struck at road bridges at COLMAR and ENDINGEN and an ammunition dump at FREIBURG.

Road and rail transport in the RHEINE area were targets for fighter-bombers and rocket-firing fighters. Yesterday afternoon escorted heavy bombers made a concentrated attack on the railway center at RHEYDT.

During the night our intruder aircraft were over the battlefront attacking railway and road transport.

In day and night operations, according to preliminary reports, 90 enemy aircraft were destroyed in the air. Five heavy bombers and 23 fighters are missing.

Ground action in the WISSEMBOURG area near the Rhine was limited to patrol clashes and artillery exchanges. North of COLMAR we made local gains.

The trapped units of the 2. Panzer-Division made two attempts to break out — on December 26 and 27 — leaving behind large quantities of vehicles and equipment which soon fell into Allied hands. These Panthers stood at the Ferme de Mahenne, on a high ground just east of Foy-Notre-Dame, probably with empty tanks. A squadron of P-38 Lightnings then targeted both the armour and the farm leaving the building in flames.

COMMUNIQUE No. 265   December 29

Enemy patrols are still active across the River Maas in Holland. Along the northern flank of the German salient in the Ardennes, enemy pressure between STAVELOT and HOTTON has decreased, and MANHAY, GRANDMENIL, and HUMAIN have been retaken after hard fighting. An enemy attack between HOTTON and MARCHE was repulsed with heavy losses to the Germans. Farther west an enemy force which had been surrounded was mopped up. More than 1,000 prisoners and much equipment, including tanks and vehicles, were taken.

Isolated enemy units are offering stubborn resistance in the area of ST HUBERT. Allied forces which made contact with our units in BASTOGNE have entered the town. To the southwest we have reached the outskirts of SIBRET and to the south we have cleared HOMPRE and SALVACOURT. Heavy fighting is in progress in the woods north of ASSENOIS. Our units continuing the advance along the southern flanks of the salient have taken SAINLEZ, LIVARCHAMPS, SURRE, BOULAIDE, BASCHLEIDEN, BAVIGNE and KAUNDORF. We have crossed the Sure river near ESCH.

Between DIEKIRCH and ECHTERNACH, we continued to make gains south of the Sauer river. East of ECHTERNACH, our patrols have reached the Sauer at three points, including ROSPORT.

Unfavourable weather yesterday caused a stepping down of our air attack. Operations were directed mainly against rail targets.

A small number of fighter-bombers attacked road and rail transport in northern Holland and north of the Ruhr.

Heavy bombers, in great strength, with strong fighter escort, struck at railway targets between COLOGNE and SAARBRUCKEN including railway yards and bridges in the vicinity of COLOGNE, BONN, COBLENZ, NEUENKIRCHEN and KAISERSLAUTERN.

Fighter-bombers attacked rail and road transport and communications in the areas of KAISERSLAUTERN, KARLSRUHE and STUTTGART.

Last night, heavy bombers attacked railway targets at BONN and MUNCHEN-GLADBACH. Light bombers attacked communications in the LA ROCHE area.

Activity in the WISSEMBOURG area was generally limited to patrolling.

In the high ground east of COLMAR we improved our positions by occupying LE GRAS, southeast of LAPOUTROIE.

Putting Montgomery in command of the two American armies north of the German salient could easily have caused trouble but, as Eisenhower wrote later, 'the command plan worked and there was generally universal acceptance of its necessity at the time'. *Above:* On December 29, the Field-Marshal met with Lieutenant General Simpson, the Ninth Army commander, together with corps and division commanders at the XIX Corps headquarters. However smiles soon turned to anger following an interview given by Montgomery to the Press at his headquarters at Zonhoven on January 7. He started by giving credit to the 'courage and good fighting quality' of the American troops and praised Eisenhower, stating 'on our team, the captain is General Ike'. However, as he made a lengthly analysis of the battle, he focused exclusively on his own generalship with an attitude that his own Chief-of-Staff characterised as a 'what a good boy am I'! Insisting that he 'was thinking ahead', he said he had 'employed the whole available power of the British Group of Armies; this power was brought into play very gradually. Finally it was put into battle with a bang. You thus have the picture of British troops fighting on both sides of the Americans who have suffered a hard blow.'

The overall impression given by the Field-Marshal at the interview was that Eisenhower had placed him in command in the north when the situation 'began to deteriorate' and that he had rescued the besieged Americans. Montgomery failed to mention the contribution of any American general beside Eisenhower, gravely belittling the part played by Bradley, Patton and other American commanders. Also he gave a total misrepresentation of the relative share of the fighting played by the British and American troops in the Ardennes as for every British soldier involved, there were over 30 Americans. The US commanders, particularly at the 12th Army Group headquarters, were outraged by the interview. Eisenhower commented in his own memoirs that 'the incident caused me more distress and worry than did any similar one of the war. I doubt if Montgomery ever came to realise how resentful some US commanders were. They believed he had belittled them — and they were not slow to voice reciprocal scorn and contempt.' Much damage had been done to the relation between the American and British commanders and the incident effectively killed off any chance of a single ground commander — as proposed by Montgomery (see page 152) — being seriously considered by the Americans. Bradley even made absolutely clear to Eisenhower that he would ask to be relieved if he were placed under Montgomery's command.

Montgomery's headquarters at Zonhoven had been established at Villa Magda at Houthalenseweg 9. The villa still stands and a plaque was unveiled beside the gatepost in September 1994.

Now that the German offensive had ground to a halt, SHAEF made plans to eliminate the deep salient in the Allies' line by ordering Patton's Third Army to advance north from the Bastogne sector while Montgomery's forces would strike south.

Left: Erezée lies ten miles north-east of Marche where these engineers were pictured using a horse's manger for a sledge. *Right:* At the eastern entrance, this corner of the village has changed little.

COMMUNIQUE No. 266   December 30

Allied forces have driven back an enemy attack launched with infantry near GANGELT, on the German-Dutch frontier, northwest of GEILENKIRCHEN. The attack gained some initial success. Enemy losses were about 100 killed and wounded and we took 70 prisoners.

In the Ardennes salient we have made some gains, especially along the southern flank, and repulsed a number of enemy attacks. Near the northern hinge of the salient south of MONSCHAU, the enemy formed up for an attack east of ELSENBORN. This was broken up by our artillery before it reached our positions.

On the northern flank of the salient, our forces made a successful raid on an enemy position north of LIERNEUX, disorganizing the enemy and killing 30 including the commanding officer. Enemy troops which attempted to infiltrate our lines west of GRANDMENIL, were mopped up and more than 100 prisoners were taken. Farther southwest we have advanced to the outskirts of ROCHEFORT where stiff opposition is being met.

Along the southern flank, in the ST HUBERT—BASTOGNE sector, we have entered MOIRCY, cleared REMAGNE, MAGEROTTE, MORHET and SIBRET and pushed northwards to the wooded area a mile beyond SIBRET.

The Allied corridor leading into BASTOGNE has been strengthened against enemy resistance on both sides and we have made gains west and east of the BASTOGNE—ARLON road in the areas and northeast of ASSENOIS, east of HOMPRE, and around VILLERS-LA-BONNE-EAU, where we have encountered moderate small-arms and mortar and rocket fire.

Farther east we have pushed about a mile north of BAVIGNE and have encountered sporadic resistance along a line approximately two miles southwest and south of WILTZ. Near RINGEL we repulsed a counter-attack by infantry supported by artillery and took a small number of prisoners.

On the southern hinge of the salient our advance towards the Sauer river in the BIGELBACH area was met initially by strong enemy resistance, but this became scattered. EPPELDORF was cleared though the enemy holds the high ground east and southeast of the town. A group of German tanks in the area of BOLLENDORF was dispersed by artillery fire. Our patrols have penetrated into ECHTERNACH.

In the Saar valley, enemy patrols were encountered by our troops in FRAULAUTERN, east of SAARLAUTERN.

The enemy rail communication system north of and leading into the Ruhr was heavily attacked yesterday by fighter-bombers which destroyed many locomotives and rail trucks.

Other fighter-bombers flew in an arc extending from the Ardennes forest to the Saar and ranged as far east as FRANKFURT, attacking motor transport, armor and gun positions in Belgium and Luxembourg and striking at rail and road transport targets in Germany.

Escorted heavy bombers in great strength attacked road and rail junctions, railheads, bridges and marshalling yards in western Germany, severing communications to the enemy units in the Ardennes salient. Targets included two marshalling yards at COBLENZ and marshalling yards at FRANKFURT, BINGEN and ASCHAFFENBURG.

Medium bombers attacked the communications center of ANNWEILER while fighter-bombers attacked a storage dump at ACHERN and rail yards in the upper Rhine valley.

Enemy troops and guns on the Dutch island of Schouwen were attacked by fighter-bombers, while rocket-firing fighters struck at barges between Schouwen and the island of Overflakkee. Escorted heavy bombers attacked the E- and U-Boat pens of ROTTERDAM.

In the day's operations 32 enemy aircraft were shot down; 10 of our heavy bombers and 25 of our fighters are missing.

Last night heavy bombers attacked the railway junction and yards at TROISDORF near BONN, and the synthetic oil plant at SCHOLVEN-BUER in the Ruhr.

East and west of WISSEMBOURG, artillery exchanges and patrol clashes were the principal activity.

North of COLMAR enemy troops infiltrating SIGOLSHEIM were mopped up. A German foray across the Rhine north of the Swiss border was broken up.

Left: **Just east of Erezée, the II. SS-Panzerkorps launched a new attack just down the road at Sadzot late on December 27 and the village was in German hands on the 28th. However, the Americans quickly counter-attacked and by dawn on the 30th the village had been recaptured.** *Right:* **Sadzot was given the nickname 'Sad Sack' by the GIs after the popular cartoon character of this name that appeared in the *Stars and Stripes* newspaper.**

The Third Army now widened the axis of its advance with the III Corps on the right, effectively in Luxembourg, while VIII Corps headed out of Bastogne. Fifteen miles east of the town, Heiderscheid revealed the wrecks of a German battle-group of the Führer-Grenadier-Brigade which had been wiped out there a few days earlier.

COMMUNIQUE No. 267 December 31

The enemy has continued sending patrols across the River Maas north of TILBURG. These withdrew when fired upon by Allied forces.

The northern flank of the Ardennes salient has been quiet. A small enemy pocket west of GRANDMENIL is surrounded and is being mopped up. At ROCHEFORT our troops still are meeting strong opposition and enemy artillery and mortar fire is heavy.

On the southern flank of the salient we have reached the vicinity of LAVASELLE and CHENOGNE and we are near SENONCHAMPS, two and one-half miles west of BASTOGNE. The enemy is strongly dug in along the line of ST HUBERT—MOIRCY—REMAGNE—LAVASELLE where he is supported by tanks and self-propelled guns.

Continued strong enemy resistance is being met by our forces widening the corridor into BASTOGNE. The ARLON—BASTOGNE road was cleared and we have taken REMOIFOSSE, MARVIE and LUTREBOIS. Our units have reached the southeastern edge of HARLANGE. The enemy in this area is taking advantage of high ground to fight a delaying action.

We have made gains in the vicinity of BERLE, southeast of WILTZ, and have cleared NOTHUM. A small-scale enemy counter-attack made in the area one mile southwest of WILTZ was broken up by our artillery.

In the DIEKIRCH area, we have cleared the enemy from high ground just north of ETTELBRUCK. Most of the right bank of the Sauer river between DIEKIRCH and ECHTERNACH is now in our hands with the exception of a short stretch northwest of BIGELBACH.

There has been only patrol activity and sporadic enemy artillery fire in the Saar valley.

Yesterday heavy bombers, in very great strength, with a strong escort of fighters, attacked a number of bridges and marshalling yards in western Germany, including those at KAISERSLAUTERN, MANNHEIM and KASSEL.

Weather prevented the full employment of our medium and fighter-bombers. In attacks by fighter-bombers 32 tanks were knocked out and others were damaged, mostly in the BASTOGNE area. Enemy road transport also was hit. Fighter-bombers struck at railway stock and communications between BONN and KAISERSLAUTERN and farther south in the areas of HOMBURG, LANDAU, KARLSRUHE and COLMAR.

Medium bombers hit supply stores, fuel dumps and barracks at OOS, four miles south of RASTATT, and a marshalling yard at FREIBURG.

Five enemy aircraft were shot down during the day. From all air operations eight heavy bombers and eight fighters are missing.

Active patrolling and artillery exchanges continued in the WISSEMBOURG sector. Several towns in the Alsace plain were shelled by the enemy.

Anxious for souvenirs, GIs clamber over a disabled Sturmgeschütz knocked out by the Shermans of the 702nd Tank Battalion. The main street on the left by-passes the centre of Heiderscheid. Am Eewischteneck lies to the right.

JANUARY 1945
THE TIDE TURNS

COMMUNIQUE No. 268   January 1

The northern flank of the Ardennes salient has been quiet. Allied troops have occupied ROCHEFORT after heavy fighting in the area.

On the southern flank of the salient west of BASTOGNE, Allied armor and infantry have launched an attack to the northeast. Several enemy counter-attacks by tanks and infantry near CHENOGNE and another north of LUTREBOIS have been repulsed. In the engagement at LUTREBOIS our forces destroyed 18 enemy tanks. Enemy artillery in this area has been more active.

South of WILTZ, we made gains against heavy enemy resistance.

In the area south of the Sauer river between DIEKIRCH and ECHTERNACH, we have occupied REISDORF.

There is aggressive patrolling by our forces along the Moselle and Saar rivers.

In the SAARLAUTERN bridgehead, there has been increased enemy artillery fire.

The main emphasis of our air attack yesterday was laid on the enemy's communications and oil supplies. Fighter-bombers attacked the railway bridges between HERTOGENBOSCH and UTRECHT, and struck at road and rail transport in the AMERSFOORT area; to the southeast of VENLO, and over the German border northeastward to DORSTEN and COESFELD. Railway yards at HAMM also were attacked. Near AMERSFOORT vehicle repair sheds were bombed. Railway yards at VOHWINKEL were attacked by escorted heavy bombers in the afternoon. Fighters shot down seven enemy aircraft in the RHEINE-MUNSTER area.

In the Ardennes salient fighter-bombers and a small number of medium and light bombers attacked enemy armor and motor vehicles and struck at his communications.

Farther south fighter-bombers struck at rail transport and communications and bombed rail yards at BAD KREUZNACH, KAISERSLAUTERN, HOMBURG, PIRMASENS and NEUSTADT. Near KAISERSLAUTERN six enemy aircraft shot down.

More than 1,300 heavy bombers escorted by 700 fighters, attacked oil refineries in the HAMBURG-HARBURG area and at MOISBURG; submarine yards at HAMBURG; a jet plane factory at WENZENDORF, two railway yards near DUSSELDORF and junctions and detraining points between the Rhine and the Ardennes salient. In the course of these operations 78 enemy aircraft were shot down.

Targets in enemy-occupied villages in the area north of the Maas and gun positions west of DULKEN were attacked by fighter-bombers. According to reports so far received 35 of our bombers and 19 of our fighters are missing.

Last night light bombers bombed BERLIN and heavies attacked the railway yards at OSTERFELD. During the night five enemy aircraft were shot down by our fighters.

Enemy counter-attacks north and west of COLMAR were repulsed. Nearly 300 prisoners have been taken in this sector during the past two days.

On January 3, east of Bastogne in the VIII Corps sector, Pfc Ornitz pictured a Sherman of the 4th Armored Division passing machine-gunners of the 104th Infantry, 26th Division.

His colleague, Pfc Sam Gilbert, captured this winter setting in Luxembourg depicting men from the same regiment returning to their own lines after having carried out an attack in the woods during the night.

Communiqué No. 269 of January 2, 1945: 'Light bombers attacked targets in the Ardennes salient'. Operating B-26s from Laon airfield in France, the 454th Bomb Squadron received a Distinguished Unit Citation for having effectively hit German transportation installations used to bring reinforcements to the Ardennes during the period December 24-27. This particular Marauder coded RJ-A was of the G-5-MA type.

COMMUNIQUE No. 269   January 2

Allied artillery has dispersed enemy patrols which have again been active across the river Maas in the area of ROERMOND.

There has been increased enemy artillery fire in the area north of DUREN.

In the Ardennes salient, Allied forces along the southern flank have reached points less than two miles south of ST HUBERT. Progress has been made northeast of MOIRCY; we have entered REMAGNE and taken HOUMONT and CHENOGNE.

Two enemy counter-attacks in the BASTOGNE sector were repulsed, one in the area of CHAMPS, the other near VILLERS-LA-BONNE-EAU. We are in the vicinity of WARDIN, three miles southeast of BASTOGNE. Stiff fighting is in progress near NOTHUM, southeast of WILTZ, following an enemy counter-attack. Enemy artillery was active in the vicinity of RÖLLINGEN just south of WILTZ.

We have made small gains in the SAARLAUTERN bridgehead.

Yesterday morning between 250 and 300 enemy aircraft, mainly single-engined fighters, strafed our aircraft on a number of airfields in Holland and Belgium. A few bombs were also dropped. Fighters and anti-aircraft guns engaged the enemy and 125 of the attacking force were shot down.

In Holland enemy troop quarters north of the river Maas, barges east of DORDRECHT, and two bridges near UTRECHT were among the targets for our rocket-firing fighters.

Escorted heavy bombers in great strength attacked railway bridges and marshalling yards in the COBLENZ area and an oil refinery at DOLLBERGEN, east of HANNOVER, and other targets in north-central Germany. Heavy bombers operating with fighter cover again breached the DORTMUND-EMS canal.

Medium and light bombers attacked targets in the Ardennes salient including objectives at ST VITH, LA ROCHE and DASBURG, and fighter-bombers struck at railway communications and armored vehicles south and west of PRUM. Other fighter-bombers hit railway yards and focal points in the enemy's supply and reinforcement routes in the areas of TRIER, KAISERSLAUTERN, HOMBURG and south to HAGUENAU.

Light bombers attacked a number of railway tunnels on main lines leading to the salient. Medium bombers struck at a railway bridge at KONZ-KARTHAUS, southwest of TRIER, a road and railway bridge over the Moselle river at BULLAY, and barracks, storage dumps and workshops at KAISERSLAUTERN.

Thirty-five enemy aircraft were shot down in addition to the 125 destroyed in the airfield attacks. From all of our air operations during the day, according to incomplete reports, two medium bombers and 27 fighters are missing.

Last night heavy bombers were over Germany with a marshalling yard at VOHWINKEL, and a benzol plant among the objectives. Our intruder aircraft attacked enemy movement in the area of ZULPICH, MAYEN and CLERVAUX. Night fighters shot down four enemy aircraft.

From the area of BITCHE to the Rhine the enemy ground forces were aggressive. One of a series of enemy attacks made a slight gain in the wooded area south of BANNSTEIN. Other attacks in the vicinity of BITCHE and DAMBACH were repulsed.

Enemy artillery harassed towns in the Alsace plain. Hostile patrols were turned back at several points west and east of MULHOUSE.

On New Year's Day, the Luftwaffe launched Operation 'Bodenplatte', a surprise attack against 16 Allied air bases in Belgium, the Netherlands and France, with the object of regaining air superiority in the West. Over 1,000 aircraft were involved, mostly single-engine Bf 109 and Fw 190 fighters and fighter-bombers. Planning for the operation was marred by extreme secrecy as none of the German anti-aircraft batteries were pre-warned and many aircraft were shot down by their own Flak. Also the execution of the attack was in part poor as a sizeable number of the pilots were young and inexperienced. Nevertheless the operation achieved tactical surprise although Allied loss records are confused making it difficult to ascertain the number of Allied aircraft destroyed. The most-recent research gives around 300 destroyed and 190 damaged. However, while the military effect on the Allies was negligible as these losses were soon made up, the operation was a disaster for the Germans with 300 aircraft shot down and 210 pilots failing to return — the largest loss in a single day for the Luftwaffe. As a result the German Air Force had sacrificed its last reserves and was now no longer able to mount an effective defence of German air space during the Allied advance into Germany.

In General Eisenhower's own report on the campaign in western Europe published in 1946, he made special reference to two of his SHAEF commanders who had not survived to see the final victory. 'I pay tribute to the memory of two very senior and gallant officers who started the campaign with us and who lost their lives before its conclusion. These were Admiral Sir Bertram H. Ramsay of the Royal Navy, and Air Chief Marshal Sir Trafford Leigh-Mallory of the Royal Air Force. At the beginning of the operation these officers were respectively my Naval Commander-in-Chief and my Air Commander-in-Chief.

The former lost his life in an airplane accident near Versailles, France, while still serving in the same capacity [see *After the Battle* No. 87]. The latter, relieved from my command to take over the Allied Air Forces in Southeast Asia, was lost in an airplane accident near Grenoble, France [see page 245]. The war service, the devotion to duty, and the sacrifice of these two outstanding men typify the irreplaceable cost of the campaign represented in the lives of thousands of officers and enlisted men and members of the women's services, of the American, British, and French forces.'

COMMUNIQUE No. 270   January 3

Allied forces in the Ardennes salient have made some gains and repulsed a number of enemy counter-attacks.

In the ST HUBERT—BASTOGNE sector of the southern flank, we have made progress in the areas of BONNERUE and HUBERMONT, against resistance varying from moderate to heavy. We have taken GERIMONT and MANDE. Fighting is in progress in SENONCHAMPS.

Northeast of BASTOGNE, we have reached a point on the railway three miles beyond the town. MAGERET is in our hands and we are in the immediate vicinity of MICHAMPS. Heavy fighting is going on in the areas of NEFFE and WARDIN. We have made some gains east and south of LUTREBOIS and are encountering heavy shelling in HONVILLE.

In the Saar valley enemy activity has increased. Southeast of SAARLAUTERN, a small-scale infantry attack in the area of BIESLAUTERN was repulsed and our units cleared the area northeast of WERBELN against strong resistance. Northeast of SAARGEMUND, near NEUENKIRCHEN, an infantry attack supported by one tank was contained. Between HABKIRCHEN and BLIESBRUCKEN enemy attempts to cross the Blies river were repulsed. German units are in BLIESBRUCKEN but we have cleared the wooded area just south of the town across the Blies river. Farther east five companies of German infantry gained about one kilometer from the area south of OBERGAILBACH to a point just west of RIMLINGEN.

Enemy attacks supported by tanks southeast of BITCHE forced our units to give some ground initially but all the thrusts were either slowed down or halted.

Strong enemy pressure continued in the lower Vosges mountains where hostile attacks were launched, and attempts to infiltrate were made at several points in the area about five miles north of REIPERTSWILLER.

Farther east patrolling was active and was particularly aggressive in the vicinity of BERG near the Rhine.

The enemy pocket west of the Rhine farther south was generally quiet. Our troops captured a strong point north of KAMBS and held it against a counter-attack.

In the Ardennes salient fighter-bombers attacked enemy armor in the BASTOGNE and ST VITH areas. Medium and fighter-bombers struck at communications and transport in the salient including a rail junction at GOUVY.

Other medium bombers bombed railway bridges at SIMMERN and BAD MUNSTER.

More than 1,000 heavy bombers escorted by 650 fighters attacked six rail bridges, mainly in the COBLENZ area; communication centers including road and rail junctions and de-training points at PRUM, BITBURG, KYLLBURG, DAUN and MAYEN; railway yards at GEROLSTEIN, EHRANG and BAD KREUZNACH; tank and equipment concentrations northeast of SAARLAUTERN, and other targets in western Germany.

Fighters and fighter-bombers attacked troop concentrations and defense positions in the NEUNKIRCHEN and KAISERSLAUTERN areas, destroyed several tanks near PIRMASENS, and struck at rail and road transport and communications in the HOMBURG and KAISERLAUTERN areas. Medium bombers attacked supply dumps and troop barracks at NUNSCHWEILER, THALEISCHWEILER and OOS.

In the course of these operations 13 enemy aircraft were shot down. Eleven of our fighters and ten bombers are missing, according to reports so far received.

A very strong force of heavy bombers last night attacked the industrial and railway center of NUREMBERG and chemical works at LUDWIGSHAFEN. BERLIN was also bombed.

Admiral Ramsay's Hudson crashed on take-off at Toussus-le-Noble aerodrome near Paris for a flight to Brussels on January 2 for a meeting with Montgomery regarding the Scheldt defences. The five men who were killed in the crash were buried at Saint-Germain-en-Laye on January 8 in the presence of General Eisenhower.

Meanwhile in the north, Montgomery had postponed the beginning of the operation to erase the salient until January 3. *Left:* The next day, men of the 51st Highland Division were pictured entering Hotton, five miles north-east of Marche. *Right:* **Though redeveloped, Jean Paul found the main street still sports some of the buildings of 1944.**

COMMUNIQUE No. 271   January 4

Active patrolling by Allied forces and by the enemy continues in Holland.

In the Ardennes salient, we counter-attacked yesterday morning in the GRANDMENIL area. Good progress is being made against stiff opposition.

Gains were made to the south of ROCHEFORT where some commanding ground and a village have been taken against strong enemy resistance.

On the southern flank of the salient, our forces have gained ground about one mile south of VESQUEVILLE and are fighting in the wooded area two and one-half miles east of ST HUBERT. We have made some gains northeast of BONNERUE and are meeting stubborn opposition on the high ground one and one-half miles southwest of TILLET.

In the BASTOGNE bulge, SENONCHAMPS has been taken and we are fighting in the area of LONGCHAMPS, BOURCY and BOIS DU MAISTER. Resistance has been stiff at ARLONCOURT and on the high ground southwest of VILLERS-LA-BONNE-EAU.

Heavy enemy artillery fire was directed against LUTREBOIS.

Yesterday, escorted medium and light bombers struck at the communications center of HOUFFALIZE in the Ardennes salient, and last night light bombers attacked targets at HOUFFALIZE and ST VITH.

Our forces in the Saar valley have cleared the area two and one-half miles northwest of VOLKINGEN. Strong resistance met our efforts to force the enemy back towards the Saar river in the LUDWEILER area.

East of SAARGEMUND, a small force of enemy, after several attempts, crossed the Blies river just south of HABKIRCHEN, but our artillery prevented him from making further gains. The enemy penetrated to GROS REDERCHINGEN, and there is fighting in the vicinity of ACHEN.

In the wooded area south and southeast of BITCHE enemy pressure lessened somewhat. Three small-scale attacks were repulsed.

PHILIPPSBURG was shelled by the enemy after his attack on the town failed.

In the Alsace plain north of COLMAR, our troops repulsed an enemy attack and gained some ground in a counter-attack. Enemy attempts to infiltrate the Lake Noir region of the Vosges were turned back.

More than 1,100 heavy bombers, escorted by approximately 600 fighters, attacked enemy communications yesterday. The targets included railway and road centers near the Belgian-German frontier and northwest of KARLSRUHE, the railway marshalling yards at ASCHAFFENBURG, FULDA, and in the vicinity of COLOGNE.

Escorted heavy bombers attacked two benzol plants in the Ruhr at CASTROP-RAUXEL and the Hansa works near DORTMUND.

Other airborne operations were on a very small scale due to adverse weather. Railway yards at EMMENDINGEN, north of FREIBURG, and gun positions around COLMAR were attacked by fighter-bombers. Fighters destroyed three enemy aircraft. Three of the heavy bombers and nine fighters are missing according to reports so far received.

Launched between the Ourthe and Salm rivers, the First Army offensive involved four divisions: the 84th Infantry with the 2nd Armored on the right, and the 83rd Infantry and 3rd Armored on the left. Near Trou de Bra, six miles north of Manhay, these Shermans of the 3rd Armored are shelling German positions on the far side of the hill.

On January 5, T/5 William E. Williams of the 167th Signal Corps Company pictured men of Company I, 333rd Infantry Regiment, 84th Division, 'moving cautiously through the snowy streets of the recently captured town of Forge à l'Aplé'.

COMMUNIQUE No. 272   January 5

Allied forces in the Ardennes salient continued their attack southeast of GRANDMENIL. Bad visibility, snow and rough terrain made movement difficult. Slow, steady progress has been made.

In the BOIS DE TAVE and ARBREFONTAINE areas enemy counter-attacks have been held. Southeast of MARCHE we made gains of 1,500 yards against opposition.

Fighting continued around the BASTOGNE bulge, with the enemy making numerous counter-attacks. One near MANDE was repulsed and another, made by an estimated 35 tanks and a regiment of infantry near LONGCHAMPS, was followed by heavy fighting. Farther east, a smaller enemy force made some progress from the direction of BOURCY towards BASTOGNE, but was forced to withdraw.

South of BASTOGNE, we are clearing the northeast edge of LUTREBOIS and have made slight gains east of HARLANGE against strong enemy resistance.

In the Saar valley our artillery broke up a small force of enemy infantry attacking from GEISLAUTERN toward LUDWEILER. In the area west of SAARBRUCKEN, east of SAARGEMUND, our troops repulsed an enemy counter-attack south of BLIESBRUCKEN. Farther south, the enemy units, which had penetrated to GROS REDERCHINGEN and ACHEN, were driven back.

In the lower Vosges mountains southeast of BITCHE, the enemy kept up pressure by repeated small-scale attacks and by attempts to infiltrate. South of BITCHE our troops regained the village of MEISENTHAL which changed hands several times. Hard fighting continued in the vicinity of BARENTHAL and PHILIPPSBURG.

Far from a town, Forge à l'Aplé was — and still is — just a small hamlet comprising a few houses tucked away at the T-junction between the north-south road from Erezée to Dochamps and a smaller road coming from Grandménil.

In the COLMAR area our reconnaissance elements were active. An enemy attack at KEMBS on the upper Rhine was repulsed.

Unfavourable flying conditions yesterday confined our air operations to fighter and fighter-bomber missions. Enemy-occupied factory buildings at SLIEDRECHT in Holland were hit by rocket-firing fighters. Fighter-bombers attacked rail and road transport and struck at communications in northern and eastern Holland and over the German border to MUNSTER and OSNABRUCK.

The area of BITCHE fighter-bombers attacked gun positions and defended buildings and struck at the enemy's transport and communications.

Ten enemy aircraft were shot down in these operations. Three of our aircraft are missing.

Berlin was attacked last night by light bombers.

COMMUNIQUE No. 273   January 6

Allied patrols were active yesterday along the Maas river.

Our attack from the northern flank of the Ardennes salient continued in the face of stiff and determined opposition. Progress has been slow but gains up to 1,000 yards have been made in several sectors, notably southwest of STAVELOT, where several enemy counter-attacks were beaten off.

On the southern flank of the salient heavy enemy pressure consisting of tank and infantry counter-attacks continues. A small enemy thrust was repulsed in the area two miles west of TILLET. A strong counter-attack by a force including 15 to 20 enemy tanks resulted in heavy fighting two miles west of MANDE.

Our forces made a withdrawal from the MICHAMPS area to high ground about two miles northeast of BASTOGNE. Southeast of BASTOGNE, a strong counter-attack by infantry tanks was repulsed by our artillery in the vicinity of WARDIN and a smaller counter-attack was beaten off at HARLANGE.

Communications and supply lines in the area of ST VITH and in and behind the Ardennes salient were the targets for fighter-bombers, which struck at road junctions and road and rail transport and also attacked armored fighting vehicles and enemy-held buildings. In addition they went for rail centers at EDENKOBEN and SIMMERN, and the enemy-occupied town of WARDIN. Escorted medium and light bombers, as well as going for communications near ST VITH, attacked bridges at AHRWEILER and SIMMERN. Last night, light bombers harassed enemy movement behind the salient.

In the lower Vosges mountains the enemy's attempts to enlarge his salient southeast of BITCHE were frustrated in a day of hard fighting. Enemy elements which infiltrated southward to the vicinity of WINGEN were virtually disposed of. North and east of this sector fighter-bombers attacked road and rail transport in the areas of KAISERSLAUTERN, KARLSRUHE and NEUENKIRCHEN.

Enemy ground forces crossed the Rhine about eight miles below STRASBOURG and entered GAMBSHEIM and OFFENDORF. Fighting followed in both localities.

German troop quarters in the island of Schouwen and north of the river Maas were attacked by fighter-bombers, which also hit a rail bridge at CULEMBOURG and a road bridge at VIANEN, south of UTRECHT. Fighter-bombers, ranging over an arc from HENGELO through MUNSTER and HAMM down to COBLENZ, went for locomotives, rail cars and road transport.

More than 1,000 heavy bombers, escorted by more than 500 fighters, attacked rail centers over a broad area extending from COLOGNE south to KARLSRUHE and from the Siegfried Line east to beyond FRANKFURT. Among the rail yards attacked were those at HANAU, FRANKFURT, COBLENZ, SOBERNHEIM and KIRN and among the rail centers were those at KAISERSLAUTERN, PIRMASENS and NEUSTADT. In addition a number of other rail and road targets and enemy fighter landing grounds were attacked. Some of the escorting fighters attacked locomotives, rail cars and an airfield in the FRANKFURT area, shooting down one enemy aircraft and destroying four on the ground.

Other escorted heavy bombers attacked the rail yards at LUDWIGSHAFEN. Last night heavy bombers in very great strength, made two attacks on HANNOVER. Light bombers attacked BERLIN. Before dawn this morning, heavy bombers attacked concentrations of German troops and armor in and around HOUFFALIZE.

Having just joined the VII Corps on January 2, the 75th Division began moving in a southerly direction towards La Roche. En route, men of the 290th Infantry entered the shell-torn village of Beffe.

For his second shot taken a few seconds later, the photographer has just swung round to picture the same column marching through the mud and slush covering the main road.

However these photos are a good example that things are not always what they seem! On visiting Beffe, Jean Paul established that the troops seen on both these photos are not marching towards La Roche but in the opposite direction as if coming from La Roche!

COMMUNIQUE No. 274   January 7

Allied forces continued to maintain pressure on the northern flank of the Ardennes salient southwest of STAVELOT. An attack across the river Ambleve by our units achieved an initial gain of 3,000 yards. Further west the villages of ODEIGNE and LIERNEUX have been taken.

We have made small gains north of the ST HUBERT—BASTOGNE road two miles east of ST HUBERT and have reached TILLET. Two miles southeast of TILLET, our artillery broke up a counter-attack by enemy infantry.

Northeast of BASTOGNE, an enemy counter-attack with eight tanks and an estimated battalion of infantry was broken up by fire from our tanks and artillery just north of MAGERET. Probing activity by enemy tanks and infantry continues along the east side of the BASTOGNE bulge, particularly in the MAGERET area.

South of WILTZ, our troops have crossed the Sure river one and one-half miles northeast of ESCHDORF and have cleared GOESDORF and DAHL.

Our units have made progress towards reducing the enemy salient southeast of BITCHE against strong resistance. We have made gains of more than 1,000 yards in an attack north of REIPERTSWILLER near the southernmost point of the salient. The remaining elements of the enemy force which infiltrated WINGEN are surrounded.

On the west bank of the Rhine, enemy units which crossed the river Thursday [January 4] were mopped up at all points of penetration except at GAMBSHEIM where stubborn opposition was still being met.

Heavy bombers in great strength with a strong fighter escort attacked bridges across the Rhine at COLOGNE and BONN, railway marshalling yards at COLOGNE, COBLENZ and LUDWIGSHAFEN and other railway yards and junctions behind the battle areas. Some of the escorting fighters strafed railway transport between STUTTGART and WURZBURG and an airfield near GIEBELSTADT. Thirteen enemy aircraft were destroyed on the ground.

Weather restricted air operations over the battle zones yesterday. Railway transport in the ZUTPHEN area and between ARNHEM and ROERMOND were attacked by rocket-firing fighters and fighter-bombers which also struck at enemy troop quarters at VIANEN, south of UTRECHT. Other fighter-bombers hit a radio station at KALVERDIJK, south of DEN HELDER. Medium bombers struck at a highway bridge crossing the Prum river at PRUM. From these operations seven heavy bombers and 11 fighters are missing.

Early last night heavy bombers, again in great strength, were over Germany with the important railway and industrial center of HANAU as the main objective.

In the south, XII Corps on the Third Army's right wing, was ordered to launch a limited-objective attack across the Sûre river from the sector of Eschdorf, a village 12 miles east of Bastogne that had been bitterly fought for by the 26th Infantry Division earlier in December.

After the 166th Engineer Combat Battalion completed a bridge over the river at Heiderscheidergrund on January 6, the 319th Infantry (80th Division) were able to cross over and capture Goesdorf and Dahl. The next day, Signal Corps photographer Corporal Harry Miller pictured men of the 317th Infantry advancing over the temporary bridge.

Although since rebuilt and widened, the bridge at Heiderscheidergrund still carries the main road between Bastogne and Ettelbruck. This is a view from the southern bank, looking north-west.

COMMUNIQUE No. 275　　　January 8

Lierneux lies just under 20 miles due north of Bastogne on the left wing of the First Army's attack and it was here that men of the 83rd Infantry Division were pictured waiting to move out.

Along the Maas river there have been some sharp patrol clashes. East of GEERTRUIDENBERG an enemy outpost on the south bank of the river was attacked by Allied forces and after spirited fighting mopping-up is in progress.

On the northern flank of the Ardennes salient our attack has been continued with advances in most sectors against stubborn enemy resistance. Southeast of LIERNEUX we have gained two and one-half miles. Farther west we have captured LA FALIZE and FRAITURE and cut the main ST VITH—LA ROCHE highway in three places.

Southeast of MARCHE our units gained 2,000 yards. Under heavy enemy pressure the village of BURE was evacuated.

Northwest of BASTOGNE our forces have cleared the enemy from FLAMIERGE, one and one-half miles northeast of MANDE. Southeast of BASTOGNE we have made limited gains in the area one to two miles east of HARLANGE. In the WILTZ area, a small counter-attack moving from the vicinity of NOCHER towards DAHL was repulsed by our artillery.

In the salient southeast of BITCHE we continued mopping up enemy groups and made small local gains. German troops surrounded in WINGEN attempted to escape and many were captured.

South of WISSEMBOURG enemy infantry supported by tanks made four attacks in which some ground was lost by our forward elements. In one attack three of nine enemy tanks were knocked out.

On the west bank of the Rhine an attack against ROHRWILLER by enemy units that had crossed the river was repulsed. Other hostile elements entered DRUSENHEIM after we had inflicted losses and destroyed three of five enemy tanks. Fighting continued at GAMBSHEIM. Enemy transport near GAMBSHEIM was attacked by a small number of fighter-bombers.

Rue du Centre in Lierneux, looking eastward, with Rue des Marcadènes branching off to the right in the middle distance.

In the Alsace plain, 20 miles south of STRASBOURG, an enemy force supported by tanks which drove northwards along the Rhine-Rhone canal forced our troops from WITTENHEIM and FRIESENHEIM. Fighting continued north of these towns.

Weather again restricted air operations over the battle zones yesterday. More than 1,000 heavy bombers escorted by 650 fighters attacked railway yards, bridges and communications in western Germany from HAMM in the north to RASTATT in the south. Among the targets attacked were railway yards at HAMM, BIELEFELD, PADERBORN, COLOGNE and RASTATT, and road and rail junctions east of the Ardennes salient.

Heavy bombers in great strength attacked the industrial railway center of MUNICH last night.

On the right wing of the attack, Sergeant Charles Tesser pictured an M5 light tank of the 4th Cavalry Squadron passing a disabled Panther being inspected by ordnance personnel on January 9. Unfortunately no precise location is given in the wartime caption but the sector where this shot was taken suggests that this tank may have belonged to the 116. Panzer-Division.

COMMUNIQUE No. 276   January 9

Allied forces have attacked and destroyed the enemy position recently established on the west bank of the river Maas at WANSSUM.

On the north flank of the Ardennes salient we have cleared the west bank of the river Salm as far as VIELSALM. We have extended our hold on the ST VITH—LA ROCHE highway east of REGNE which we have now captured. The villages of SART and VERLEUMONT also are in our hands. In the sector southwest of GRANDMENIL we have taken DOCHAMPS and cleared the east bank of the river Ourthe as far south as MARCOURT which we have occupied.

On the southern flank of the salient BONNERUE, six miles east of ST HUBERT, has been cleared after having changed hands twice in the past few days. Increasingly heavy resistance is being met just east of TILLET.

Southeast of BASTOGNE, four enemy columns were dispersed by our artillery, tank and automatic weapons fire, as they converged about half a mile north of WARDIN. Southeast of WILTZ, an enemy counter-attack was repulsed by our troops in the vicinity of DAHL. Enemy artillery has been active in the area of DICKWEILER, three miles south-east of ECHTERNACH.

Our units entered RIMLINGEN in a local advance eight miles east of SAARGEMUND. The gain of one-half mile was made west of BITCHE at the western base of the enemy salient in the lower Vosges mountains. Fighters and fighter-bombers, which operated on a very small scale owing to adverse weather, strafed two enemy transport columns in the BITCHE area and hit objectives at MUTTERHAUSEN. Towns on the perimeter of the enemy salient were shelled by his artillery.

The upper Alsace plain was mostly quiet. South of STRASBOURG enemy armor and infantry elements continued to be aggressive. Southeast of STRASBOURG fighter-bombers attacked a railway station at GENGENBACH and a bridge at ZELL.

More than 700 heavy bombers escorted by over 200 fighters attacked a railway marshalling yard at FRANKFURT and marshalling yards, bridges and road and railway junctions inside the enemy lines in Luxembourg and Belgium, and on routes leading to the Ardennes and Saar areas.

Having taken the high ground lying to the north-west of Dochamps on the night of January 6/7, the leaders of the 84th Division moved into the village, which lies between La Roche and Manhay, later the following night. Some days later, Fred Ramage pictured tanks of the 2nd Armored Division moving along Rue du Lavoir.

COMMUNIQUE No. 277 January 10

Allied forces in the Ardennes salient continue to make progress in some sectors of the northern flank, notably south of DOCHAMPS where enemy armour has been engaged by our artillery. Operations have been hampered by deep snow.

Around MARCOURT mopping-up has continued while the village of CIELLE to the south has been taken and Allied units are now thrusting in the direction of LA ROCHE.

Southeast of MARCHE we have cleared the BOIS DE NOLAUMONT and have occupied the village of FORRIERES southeast of ROCHEFORT.

West of BASTOGNE, bitter fighting continues in the areas of BONNERUE and TILLET. About two miles west of MANDE an enemy counter-attack was repulsed with the destruction of nine of the 18 enemy tanks engaged.

Southeast of BASTOGNE, our troops have made gains against strongly defended enemy positions. Enemy attacks were broken up in the RIMLINGEN area and also near REYERSWEILER and LEMBERG in the enemy lower Vosges salient.

In the Rhine valley north of the HAGUENAU FOREST a strong enemy attack supported by tanks was repulsed. Heavy losses were inflicted on the enemy and he withdrew northward.

We have made some progress on the Rhine river bank and re-entered GAMBSHEIM.

Weather severely restricted air operations yesterday, but a small force of medium bombers attacked a railway embankment and bridge at RINNTHAL, west of LANDAU, and fighter-bombers attacked rail yards at NEUSTADT and RASTATT.

South of STRASBOURG the enemy continued aggressive attempts to exploit the gains he made on Sunday [January 7]. We have withdrawn from BOOFSHEIM.

In the Vosges west of COLMAR our troops occupied high ground near TURCKHEIM.

Fighter-bombers attacked a bridge across the Rhine-Rhone canal near HIRTZFELDEN.

An enemy ground force attack in the outskirts of MULHOUSE was beaten off.

In all air operations five enemy aircraft were shot down; one of our fighters is missing.

By January 10 the German 'Bulge' was being assailed on three sides: from the north by the First Army; from the west by the British XXX Corps, and by the Third Army from the south.

When the XVIII Airborne Corps was committed to the battle (see page 292), its two airborne divisions (the 82nd and 101st) were initially directed to the Bastogne area. However the First Army was forced to divert the 82nd Airborne Division to Werbomont in the north to counter the swift advance of Kampfgruppe Peiper. Teamed up with elements of the 3rd Armored Division, the airborne division soon found that the German battle-group had been immobilised, having run out of fuel (see page 295). So at the beginning of January, when the main offensive on the north flank was launched by the VII Corps between the Ourthe and Salm rivers, the XVIII Airborne Corps launched limited-objective attacks in the sector south-west of Trois-Ponts. *Left:* Men of the 508th Parachute Infantry wait ready to move out . . . but from where? *Right:* With the SHAEF censor not giving any clue as to where this photo had been taken, it was a challenge to find this lone farm. In the end, Hubert Stembert succeeded in tracking it down for us by the side of the small road to Haute-Bodeux and Jean Paul took the comparison a few hundred yards off the main road between Manhay and Trois-Ponts.

On January 11, the leaders of the 84th Division made their way down to La Roche from the north while the 1st Black Watch, 51st Highland Division, arrived from the other side of the Ourthe river. *Above:* Rue de l'Eglise in La Roche today. The old Hôtel du Luxembourg now houses the Musée de la Bataille des Ardennes.

COMMUNIQUE No. 278   January 11

On the northern flank of the Ardennes salient, Allied forces have cleared the west bank of the Salm river as far south as SALMCHATEAU. The village of SAMREE has been taken after heavy fighting.

Father west our units continued to follow up the withdrawing enemy. HODISTER has been captured and we are patrolling forward to the LA ROCHE—MARCHE road. South of MARCHE we have crossed the river Homme and occupied AMBLY. Opposition has been slight, but mines are plentiful.

On the southern flank of the salient, TILLET is in our hands after hard fighting. In the wooded area just west of the town, our troops have made gains of about a quarter of a mile. We have been forced back from FLAMIERGE. Our units have reached points four and a half miles directly north of BASTOGNE and have taken RECOGNE.

In the sector south and east of BASTOGNE, our forces have cleared the enemy from VILLERS-LA-BONNE-EAU and HARLANGE. Farther east we have taken BERLE and our units are one-half mile north of the town. We hold high ground one and a half miles southwest of WILTZ. Fighter-bombers operating in this sector attacked enemy transport and troop barracks.

More than 1,100 heavy bombers escorted by 300 fighters attacked bridges, and railway yards and airfields in western Germany and road bridges and junctions on the German-Belgian frontier at the base of the Ardennes salient. Targets included road and rail bridges over the Rhine at COLOGNE, airfields in the areas of COLOGNE, BONN and EUSKIRCHEN and marshalling yards at KARLSRUHE.

South-west of SAARBRUCKEN, we gained more than 2,000 yards against moderate resistance and entered OETINGEN.

Progress also was made on the east side of the enemy wedge in the lower Vosges mountains where OBERMUHLPHAL was occupied by our forces.

In the Rhine valley north of the HAGUENAU FOREST, fighting continued at HATTEN where a strong enemy thrust was turned back on Tuesday [January 9]. Along the Rhine nearby, there was fighting at several points in the enemy bridgehead north of STRASBOURG.

Enemy attacks were repulsed in the Alsace plain between STRASBOURG and COLMAR.

Supply dumps at ZWEIBRUCKEN and PIRMASENS were destroyed by fighter-bombers.

Striking along the Rhine valley from LANDAU southward to MULHOUSE other fighter-bombers destroyed an ammunition dump at LANDAU and hit a supply dump at DURLACH; bombed and strafed targets at RASTATT, FREISTETT and WITTENWILLER; destroyed ten enemy tanks and damaged others northeast of COLMAR and east of EMMENDINGEN; hit a bridge at RIEGEL, and cut the railway line in a number of places between COLMAR and MULHOUSE.

Early last night a force of light bombers attacked HANNOVER.

Left: Some days later, Signal Corps photographer Carmen A. Corrado pictured the link-up between the First and Third Armies when a patrol from the 507th Parachute Infantry, 17th Airborne Division, Third Army, met men of the 24th Cavalry Squadron, VII Corps, First Army. *Right:* The Ourthe river bridge with the ruins of the 11th-century castle beyond.

In the south, the III Corps renewed its attack from January 9 and the 90th Infantry Division seized Doncols on the 12th while the 6th Armored Division captured Wardin. These men from the 359th Infantry, 90th Division, are passing the wreck of a PzKpfw IV disabled in December when the Panzer-Lehr-Division was trying to break through to the west (see page 290).

COMMUNIQUE No. 279 January 12

On the northern flank of the Ardennes salient Allied forces have taken BIHAIN and LA ROCHE farther to the west. Enemy opposition was generally less severe.

The enemy has continued his withdrawal from the extremity of the salient and our units, following up, have occupied GRUNE and cut the LA ROCHE—CHAMPLON road in the vicinity of RONCHAMPS.

On the southern flank of the salient we have entered ST HUBERT and our forces have cleared the enemy from VESQUEVILLE, three miles to the southeast. Farther east, our units advancing northward have cut the ST HUBERT—BASTOGNE road northeast of TILLET.

Southeast of BASTOGNE, our forces are reducing the small enemy pocket north of HARLANGE. The only road from the pocket has been cut near the village of DONCOLS, which is now in our hands, and our units at the southern end of the pocket have taken TARCHAMPS.

On the Luxembourg-German border, an attempt by enemy infantry to cross the Sauer river southeast of WALLENDORF was broken up by our artillery.

Bad weather continued to limit air operations over the battle zones yesterday. Medium and light bombers attacked road junctions at HOUFFALIZE and CLERVAUX. Fighter-bombers hit rolling stock near PRUM. East of the Ardennes salient other fighter-bombers destroyed an ammunition dump at MAYEN and light bombers attacked a railway bridge spanning the Simmer river at SIMMERN.

In the afternoon, escorted heavy bombers attacked the railway marshalling yards in the UERDINGEN district of KREFELD.

South of SAARBRUCKEN we made another local gain and took BEHREN against light resistance. In the southern part of the BITCHE salient the enemy attempted to infiltrate our positions without success.

A strong hostile attack supported by approximately 15 tanks, of which we destroyed four, was launched in the Rhine valley in the HATTEN area where hard fighting continues. The enemy attempted to infiltrate towards RITTERSHOFFEN.

The enemy also continue to be aggressive in the Rhine bridgehead north of STRASBOURG where we withdrew a short distance west of HERRLISHEIM to more-favourable positions.

In the Alsace plain south of STRASBOURG, the village of OBENHEIM was overrun by a tank-supported enemy force, after our troops had been supplied by air.

There was hard fighting at ROSSFELD and HERBSHEIM.

Southeast of STRASBOURG, fighter-bombers attacked targets at HAUSACH in Germany.

Time has stood still at Wardin, barely three miles east of Bastogne, this picture taken looking west from the neighbouring hamlet of Harzy.

In the north, the VII Corps encountered heavy German artillery, mortar and rocket fire but the 83rd Infantry Division finally took Langlir on January 12, Communiqué No. 280 reporting its capture on the 13th. That day, Private W. B. Allen pictured a tank destroyer of the 703rd TD Battalion, 3rd Armored Division, moving past a wrecked PzKpfw IV, elements of Task Force Lovelady attacking toward Lomré, south along this road.

COMMUNIQUE No. 280   January 13

On the northern flank of the Ardennes salient Allied forces made slight progress southeast of BIHAIN and have taken LANGLIR. We are meeting strong resistance in this area and have repulsed several local counter-attacks with heavy losses to the enemy.

We have advanced about a mile towards the BOIS DE WIBRIN, southeast of SAMREE, and also along the road from LA ROCHE to BERTOGNE. South of LA ROCHE, progress has been made but a number of road-blocks and many mines are being encountered. We have occupied HIVES and MIERCHAMPS and have reached the outskirts of CHAMPLON.

Our units which encircled a small enemy pocket southeast of BASTOGNE continue to close in from east and west and the link-up of our forces was made near BRAS. WARDIN and BRAS are now in our hands and we have made gains beyond DONCOLS. An enemy convoy attempting to leave the pocket was heavily damaged by our artillery. Southeast of WILTZ we gained more than a mile in the vicinity of NOCHER.

East of Luxembourg, our units cleared the village of MACHTUM, on the west bank the Moselle river, one and one-half miles south of GREVENMACHER.

In the lower Vosges salient we occupied ALTHORN and made limited gains north and south of the village despite continued stubborn enemy resistance. Local gains were also made on the southern flank of the enemy bulge.

We have frustrated enemy break-through attempts and inflicted heavy losses during hard fighting in the Maginot Line positions north of the HAGUENAU FOREST. The enemy has been cleared from RITTERSHOFFEN except for a strong point in the southern outskirts. Fighting continues in HATTEN.

In the Alsace plain, south of STRASBOURG, hostile attacks in the vicinity of ROSSFELD, HERBSHEIM and BENFELD were repulsed.

Whether again severely limited air operations yesterday, but fighter-bombers attacked a supply dump near FRECKENFELD, east of WISSEMBOURG.

During the afternoon escorted heavy bombers attacked the U-Boat shelters and enemy shipping at BERGEN. Three of our bombers are missing.

Langlir presents a new face in 2014 but luckily the house in middle distance provides the link between past and present. This would have been the German's view, looking north along the small road from Montleban (behind the photographer) to Joubieval.

Meanwhile, the Third Army had reached a point three miles north of Bastogne. This is Foy on the road to Houffalize. Looking east from the main road . . . then and now. The building on the left is the local chapel.

COMMUNIQUE No. 281   January 14

Allied forces in Holland have taken the village of GEBROEK in a local attack north of SITTARD.

In the Ardennes salient east of the river Salm, good progress has been made south of STAVELOT and MALMEDY. Heavy fighting continued south of LANGLIR where our troops advanced in the direction of MONTLEBAN against stiff opposition.

East of LA ROCHE, we have made limited progress against moderate resistance. An enemy counter-attack by a small number of tanks supported by infantry was repulsed to the southeast of the town.

South of LA ROCHE our units continued to follow up the withdrawing enemy and have occupied ORTHO. Other forces pushing northward have cleared the enemy from LAVACHERIE, JFRIMONT, AMBERLOUP and FOSSET, and we have reached ROUMONT in the woods east of the BASTOGNE—MARCHE highway. In the general area of these villages enemy resistance has been confined largely to minefields, booby traps and sniper activity. Farther east we have reached GIVES and our units are just south of BERTOGNE. Our forces made progress northeast of BASTOGNE, reaching the point on the railroad three and one-half miles from the city, and FOY, on the road to HOUFFALIZE.

Fighter-bombers struck at rail and road transport in the ST VITH area and elsewhere in the Ardennes salient, destroyed several tanks and armoured vehicles, and strafed enemy infantry south of PRUM. Escorted medium and light bombers attacked communications at MANDERFELD. During the night light bombers attacked road and rail transport.

Our units kept up pressure against the western and southern flanks of the lower Vosges salient, and were meeting strong resistance.

In heavy fighting in the Maginot Line positions north of the HAGUENAU FOREST we made progress in the vicinity of HATTEN. The enemy fought stubbornly to maintain his last strong point in RITTERSHOFFEN against our attacks.

More than 900 escorted heavy bombers attacked railway bridges over the Rhine at RUDESHEIM, MAINZ, MANNHEIM, WORMS, GERMERSHEIM and KARLSRUHE, and railway yards at BISCHOFSHEIM and KAISERSLAUTERN. Other escorted heavy bombers attacked enemy communications at SAARBRUCKEN.

Bridges at STEINBRUCK and DASBURG and a bridge over the Simmer at SIMMERN were attacked by medium and light bombers.

Fighter-bombers striking at German communications and supplies in the KAISERSLAUTERN and BITCHE areas attacked railway yards at BEEDEN and NEUSTADT; hit rail transport near LANGMEIL and OTTERBERG; bombed two tunnels and cut the rail line in a number of places between KAISERSLAUTERN and NEUSTADT, and started fires in an ammunition dump at DURLACH.

Fighters and fighter-bombers flew offensive patrols over Holland and into Germany eastward of MUNSTER.

Last night heavy bombers in strength attacked the synthetic oil plant at POLITZ, near STETTIN and again attacked communications at SAARBRUCKEN.

According to the caption, this Sherman of the 42nd Tank Battalion, 11th Armored Division, was 'the first down the Houffalize road'.

The junction of the First and Third Armies was officially achieved on the morning of January 16 at a place named Moulin de Rensiwez on the bank of the Ourthe river, four miles west of Houffalize. These photos claim to depict the moment 'when the two patrols met'. T/5 Ancel Casey of the 11th Armored Division stands in the turret while Sergeant Rodney Himes and Pfc Alfred Gernhart of the 84th Infantry Division were two of the other men named in the wartime caption.

COMMUNIQUE No. 282   January 15

On the northern flank of the Ardennes salient, south of STAVELOT and MALMEDY, opposition has stiffened. Allied forces have taken the villages of HENUMONT, HEDOMONT and THIRIMONT.

To the southwest we have cleared MONTLEBAN and cut the main HOUFFALIZE—CHERAIN road south of CHERAIN. In the area west of the LA ROCHE—BERTOGNE road mopping-up operations continue and reconnaissance elements have reached the river Ourthe and contacted Allied patrols from the southern flank of the salient.

Northwest of BASTOGNE, Allied units, advancing against moderate resistance, captured GIVROULLE and BERTOGNE and pushed two miles beyond both towns to a point on the Ourthe river. Earlier an enemy counter-attack, made by a force of infantry and 25 tanks, was repulsed just east of BERTOGNE. Farther east we advanced to the edge of COMPOGNE and have entered the town of NOVILLE, four and one-half miles northeast of BASTOGNE.

East of BASTOGNE, our forces pushed one mile past MAGERET. We have made additional gains on the high ground just southwest of WILTZ.

Southeast of REMICH, near the Luxembourg-German border, we have cleared the enemy from TETTINGEN.

Fighter-bombers destroyed fortified buildings in the region of HOUFFALIZE and hit road and railway bridges at PRUM and east of MALMEDY. Medium and light bombers attacked communications west and south of ST VITH, at SCHLEIDEN, east of MONSCHAU, and at BITBURG. Other medium, light and fighter-bombers attacked bridges at AHRWEILER, MAYEN and BULLAY and fighter-bombers struck at motor vehicles and tank concentrations between TRIER and MERZIG.

Against stubborn resistance in rugged terrain we made gains of up to 1,000 yards at the southern edge of the lower Vosges salient.

Fighting continues in the Maginot Line in upper Alsace and we made headway despite intermittent enemy attacks. Part of HATTEN has been cleared, and in RITTERSHOFFEN the enemy still holds one strong point.

At the western end of a bridge, three plaques fixed on a natural rock now commemorate the link-up. The top one shows a picture of the meeting while the two others contains a text in English and French: 'Here on 16 Jan 1945 the Bulge was wiped out by the junction of the 84th Inf. Div. and the 11th A.D.'.

As a major road centre, Houffalize suffered daily from attacks by Allied aircraft. A raid on January 6 devastated the town which suffered seven more attacks before being finally liberated on the 18th. This Panther was found lying in the Ourthe near the bridge on the road to La Roche at the western entrance of Houffalize, although it is difficult to determine if the original caption claiming that it was 'knocked out by Allied air bombardment' is correct.

In Saturday's fighting [January 13] in this area, 17 tanks and six other enemy armoured vehicles were knocked out.

Fighter-bombers cut railway lines south and southeast of KAISERSLAUTERN, destroyed a bridge at FRANKENSTEIN and attacked railway tunnels between FRANKENSTEIN and LAMBRECHT. Medium and light bombers attacked a railway embankment at RINNTHAL, west of LANDAU.

Escorted heavy bombers again hit the railway yards at SAARBRUCKEN.

South of STRASBOURG, fighter-bombers struck at enemy positions in BENFELD.

Fighter-bombers and rocket-firing fighters attacked barges off the Dutch island of Schouwen; hit railway lines west of UTRECHT and in the area of DORDRECHT and AMERSFOORT, and struck across the frontier at railway targets north of the Ruhr. Fighters flew on offensive sweeps in the ENSCHEDE—RHEINE—OSNABRUCK region.

More than 900 heavy bombers with an escort of over 850 fighters attacked the HEMMINGSTEDT oil refinery near HEIDE in the Danish peninsular; a synthetic oil plant at MAGDEBURG, oil storage depots at DERBEN, northeast of MAGDEBURG, and at EHMEN, northeast of BRUNSWICK, and a benzol plant and steel works at HALLENDORF. Attacks were also made on three bridges across the Rhine at COLOGNE.

In the day's air operations 235 enemy aircraft were shot down and eight others were destroyed on the ground. Nineteen of our heavy bombers, one medium bomber and 33 fighters are missing.

While GIs check the road for mines, stunned refugees emerged from the cellars with their few possessions. We have already commented on the huge loss of life suffered by citizens of the occupied countries during Operation 'Overlord' and Houffalize is no exception. Over 190 persons had lost their lives in the bombing and by late January, only 130 people remained in the town, living in glacial cellars among hundreds of bodies lying unburied in the ruins.

Early last night heavy bombers attacked a railway junction at GREVENBROICH southwest of DUSSELDORF. Later heavy bombers in very great strength were again over Germany with the Leuna synthetic oil plant near MERSEBURG and a fuel depot at DULMEN as the main objectives. BERLIN was also bombed.

Saved from the scrapman, the Panther now stands by the side of Rue de Bastogne, just off to the right of this comparison.

Nine miles north of Houffalize, T/4 Leo Moran of the 165th Signal Corps Company featured men of Company B, 329th Infantry, 83rd Division, as they entered Bovigny after having crossed the Bois de Ronce, a large wooded area east of Langlir.

COMMUNIQUE No. 283   January 16

In the STAVELOT—MALMEDY sector on the northern flank of the Ardennes salient the Allied attack has been extended to the area of FAYMONVILLE, southeast of MALMEDY, and LIGNEUVILLE has been occupied by our forces. Bitter fighting has taken place in this area, particularly in the vicinity of THIRIMONT. Numerous counter-attacks by enemy tanks and infantry have been repelled.

Farther to the southwest our forces are now fighting on the outskirts of BOVIGNY, about four miles south of VIELSALM. To the south we have strengthened our hold on the BOVIGNY—CHERAIN road. Just northwest of HOUFFALIZE, the village of WIBRIN has been cleared and we have advanced southeast beyond ACHOUFFE, two miles northwest of HOUFFALIZE.

North of BASTOGNE we have pushed north of the BERTOGNE—COMPOGNE road and have taken VILLEREUX, one mile northeast of COMPOGNE. Southeast of COMPOGNE the villages of COBRU and NOVILLE have been taken and our units have advanced one-half mile farther north despite heavy resistance from enemy tanks and infantry.

East of BASTOGNE, our armor has reached a point one and one-half miles east of MAGERET, and we are making slow progress against very stubborn enemy resistance one and one-half miles east of WARDIN.

Southeast of REMICH, our units east of the Moselle river have taken the German town of NENNIG.

Enemy transport and communications in the Ardennes salient, and to the east and southeast, were attacked by fighter-bombers and a small force of light bombers. Targets

The picture was taken at the western end of the village on the small local road.

included railway bridges near BITBURG, BAD KREUZNACH, LEBACH and KAISERSLAUTERN and several railway yards. Fighter-bombers attacked rail and road transport north of BITCHE.

Bitter fighting continued at HATTEN following an enemy attack supported by artillery and armor. Two other hostile attacks within the same 24-hour period were beaten off.

Enemy losses for the first two weeks of the Alsace—Lorraine offensive are estimated at more than 10,000 killed and wounded, 4,000 prisoners, and 100 tanks knocked out.

Other losses have been inflicted in the central Alsace plain.

More than 600 heavy bombers escorted by 675 fighters attacked railway yards at FREIBURG, REUTLINGEN, AUGSBURG and INGOLSTADT. Other escorted heavy bombers bombed benzol plants near BOCHUM and RECKLINGHAUSEN.

Casualties in the Battle of the Bulge were heavy on both sides, in the order of over 80,000 respectively though estimates vary widely, some ranging as high as 100,000. At Wiltz, Signal Corps photographer Pfc Cam Gilbert pictured these German graves. Georg Felsner was a sailor transferred to the infantry who fought and died serving with the 9. Volksgrenadier Division. Moved from his field grave, Felsner now lies in Grave 403 in the German War Cemetery at Lommel.

No complete report was produced so losses in matériel can only be estimated but it is believed that the Germans lost upwards of 500 tanks like this Panther claimed by the Ninth Air Force. Eisenhower gives a figure of 733 for Allied losses in armour.

Eisenhower: 'Now that the time was approaching for what, we trusted, would be the final blow to Nazi Germany, a closer co-ordination with the Russian High Command and mutual understanding of our respective plans became essential. Our first liaison with Moscow had been effected late in 1944 when air operations necessitated the establishment of a co-ordinated bomb-line, but little further had been accomplished. The only link between my headquaters and that of Marshal Stalin was through the medium of the Allied Military Mission in Moscow, and it appeared most difficult to learn of Soviet intentions. Up to the end of 1944 I had received no information on matters affecting the Russian grand strategy, although I had expressed my willingness to afford any such information concerning my own overall plans as the Red Army might desire. At Christmas time, however, following upon a message which I sent to the Combined Chiefs-of-Staff explaining the difficulty with which I was faced in attempting to evolve plans while still ignorant of the Russian intentions, President Roosevelt secured from Marshal Stalin his agreement to receive our representative in order to discuss the correlation of our respective efforts in the forthcoming spring. Accordingly, in January, my deputy, Air Chief Marshal Tedder, accompanied by Major General Bull (G-3) and Brigadier General Betts (G-2), journeyed to Moscow for this purpose. The conference proved conspicuously successful. In the course of a discussion ranging over many aspects of the forthcoming campaigns, Marshal Stalin was acquainted with the nature of our own plans, including the timing. He, in turn, responded with a full explanation of the great four-pronged offensive, involving from 150 to 160 divisions, which the Red Army was preparing to launch. He further gave us an assurance that, in the event of the main offensive being halted by bad weather, the Red Army would still conduct local operations which he believed would so pin down German armies as to permit no major movement of divisions from east to west during the difficult period of the spring thaw. As events showed, the success of this gigantic offensive proved even greater than had been anticipated. In the meantime, fortified by Marshal Stalin's assurances, we were able to proceed with our own operational planning.'

COMMUNIQUE No. 284   January 17

Allied forces in southern Holland have launched an attack in the area north of SITTARD, near the Dutch-German border. Fighters and fighter-bombers, flying patrols ahead of our ground units, struck at enemy positions.

Escorted medium and light bombers attacked the communications centers of ERKELENZ and HALLSCHLAG, road and railway bridges at SINZIG, NEUWIED and BULLAY, and a motor repair depot at KEIBERG.

In the Ardennes salient, heavy fighting continues south of MALMEDY. FAYMONVILLE has been cleared of the enemy and we have taken ONDENVAL to the south. Farther southwest, our units are engaged in heavy fighting on the outskirts of BOVIGNY which is still held by the enemy. CHERAIN, south of BOVIGNY, is in our hands

Our units which entered HOUFFALIZE are engaged in mopping-up operations. Contact has been made at HOUFFALIZE and at a point two miles to the west by elements of our forces from the northern and southern flanks of the salient.

South of HOUFFALIZE our units pushed one mile north of NOVILLE, on the BASTOGNE—HOUFFALIZE road. In the area northeast of BASTOGNE, our armoured units have taken MICHAMPS and have advanced about a mile beyond the town. Considerable enemy anti-tank fire has been encountered in this sector.

East of BASTOGNE we have taken LONGVILLY, OBERWAMPACH and NIEDERWAMPACH.

In and behind the salient, fighter-bombers hit enemy armour, gun positions and road and rail transport. Other fighter-bombers struck at road transport from TRIER south to SAARBRUCKEN, and road and rail traffic eastward to the Rhineland.

In the BITCHE salient a small enemy attack in the REIPERTSWILLER area was repulsed.

Our troops made progress in HATTEN and now hold three-fourths of the town as a result of heavy fighting.

We also made gains of a mile or more in the enemy's Rhine bridgehead in the vicinity of HERRLISHEIM.

The commander of the 17th SS-Panzergrenadier-Division is among the prisoners we have taken in the Alsace-Lorraine action.

Medium bombers attacked a marshalling yards and a railway bridge at RASTATT. Fighter-bombers struck at enemy positions north of STRASBOURG and communications east of the Rhine. More than 600 heavy bombers escorted by over 650 fighters attacked a synthetic oil plant at RUHLAND northeast of DRESDEN, a tank plant at MAGDEBURG and railway marshalling yards at DRESDEN and DESSAU north of LEIPZIG.

Railway lines west of UTRECHT at VLEUTEN and east of UTRECHT at VECHTEN and GROEP were hit by fighter-bombers.

Fifteen enemy aircraft was shot down during the day. Fighters which attacked an airfield south of BERLIN destroyed at least 25 enemy aircraft on the ground.

Last night heavy bombers were out in very great strength. The objectives were in the industrial and railway center of MAGDEBURG and synthetic oil plants at BRUX in Czechoslovakia, ZEITZ near LEIPZIG and WANNE-EICKEL.

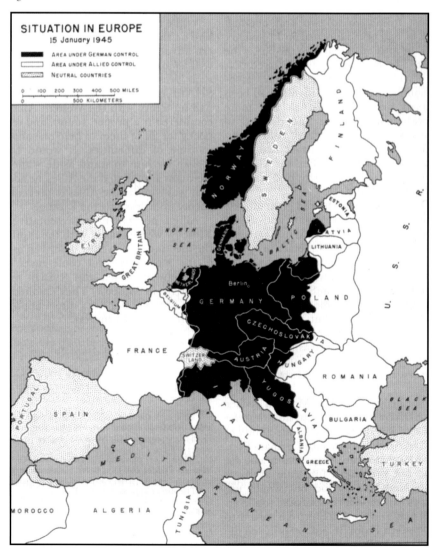

COMMUNIQUE No. 285   January 18

In the area north of SITTARD, the village of DIETEREN has been captured and Allied forces made limited progress against heavy enemy opposition and in poor visibility.

During the night light bombers operating from dusk to dawn in the SITTARD battle area bombed fortified buildings in HEINSBERG, WEGBERG and ERKELENZ and attacked enemy movement.

In the Ardennes heavy fighting continues south of FAYMONVILLE and ONDENVAL. THIRIMONT is now firmly in our hands, and enemy counter-attacks in the area have been repulsed. In the Salm river sector we have occupied VIELSALM, and the high ground to the east against lighter resistance. South of BOVIGNY and CHERAIN heavy fighting continues.

East of BASTOGNE our forces have taken BOURCY and cut the BOURCY—LONGVILLY road about one mile north of LONGVILLY. Strong enemy counter-attacks were repulsed north of OBERWAMPACH which is just southeast of LONGVILLY.

Southeast of REMICH near the Luxembourg-German border our units are clearing up an enemy force cut off just south of NENNIG.

In the BITCHE salient we made limited gains near REIPERTSWILLER but our progress was halted by counter-attacks.

The enemy put reinforcements into the battle in the HATTEN area in a renewed attempt to break through our Maginot Line positions. Our troops stood firm and inflicted severe losses including more than 200 dead. A hostile thrust in the forest south of HATTEN was checked.

In tank-supported attacks the enemy fought aggressively to enlarge his Rhine bridgehead. Our forces lost the villages of STATTMATTEN and DENGOLSHEIM, and during a see-saw engagement SESSENHEIM, which we now control, changed hands several times. There was heavy street fighting at HERRLISHEIM.

Weather over the battle areas yesterday was bad. Fighter-bomber missions were flown against enemy positions and fortified villages in northern Holland. Other fighter-bombers attacked enemy transport from UTRECHT to HENGELO.

Seven hundred escorted heavy bombers attacked a large oil refinery at HARBURG, oil refineries and submarine building yards at HAMBURG, and transportation targets in northwest Germany including marshalling yards and railway repair facilities at PADERBORN. Some of the escorting fighters strafed railway targets.

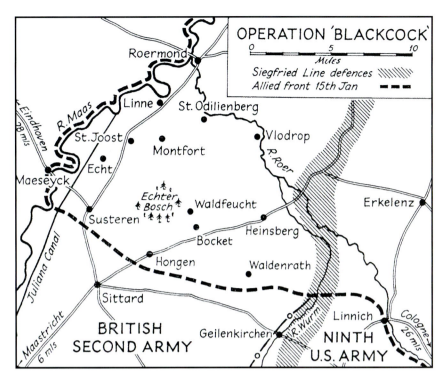

Meanwhile, in the West, Operation 'Blackcock' finally began on January 16 having been delayed by bad weather in November and the German offensive in December. This was designed to eliminate the German salient between Roermond and Geilenkirchen.

The British 7th Armoured Division opened the attack with the 131st Infantry Brigade clearing the road from Susteren to Roermond.

Susteren was cleared by the evening of the 17th and by midnight Echt had also fallen after a sharp fight. These men of the 2nd Battalion, the Devonshire Regiment, were pictured clearing the latter town of stragglers.

Susteren has fallen, these photographs being released for publication in the *Daily Sketch* on January 19.

COMMUNIQUE No. 286   January 19

Along the Maas front north of NIJMEGEN, there has been a renewal of activity by both Allied and enemy forces.

North of SITTARD, our units have made further progress. ECHT, north of SITTARD, has been captured and we are attacking eastward across the main ROERMOND—SITTARD road. SUSTEREN, south of ECHT, has been taken, and our attack has been extended by a thrust northeast from SITTARD in the direction of HONGEN. Vigorous enemy opposition is being encountered.

In the FAYMONVILLE area, our units holding high ground just south of ONDENVAL defeated enemy attempts to advance northward. Southwest of ONDENVAL we have made further progress against moderate resistance to about two miles east of RECHT.

South of VIELSALM our forces are clearing the woods northeast of the village of STERPIGNY and our armor has reached a point less than a mile northwest of RETTIGNY.

East of BASTOGNE, more counter-attacks by enemy tanks and infantry have been repulsed in the OBERWAMPACH area. Just southeast of WILTZ, we are mopping up in NOCHER.

Our units have launched an attack across the Sauer river in the DIEKIRCH-BETTENDORF area, against moderate resistance. ERPELDANGE to the west of DIEKIRCH is being cleared, and we have pushed to the western edge of DIEKIRCH and to the high ground just northeast of the town. Farther east our units have reached points north and northeast of BETTENDORF. East of ECHTERNACH the town of ROSPORT has been cleared of the enemy.

Southeast of REMICH, our forces in the TETTINGEN area have repulsed a counter-attack by enemy tanks.

In the BITCHE salient the enemy renewed attempts to infiltrate our forward positions near REIPERTSWILLER and stiff fighting followed.

We made slight gains in RITTERSHOFFEN where the enemy is clinging to a strong point. Fighting continued in HATTEN.

Near the junction of the Maginot Line and the Rhine, our troops occupied the village of AUENHEIM and LEUTENHEIM, but have withdrawn from SESSENHEIM and HERRLISHEIM after hard fighting.

Escorted heavy bombers attacked railway yards at KAISERSLAUTERN yesterday. Some of the escorting fighters strafed railway transport in the area of HEIDELBERG. Bad weather prevented air operations elsewhere.

Accredited War Pool photographer Harold Tetlow of the *Daily Sketch* took these pictures of tanks and other vehicles of the British 7th Armoured Division moving up through Susteren.

This is Markstraat, looking in a southerly direction at its crossing with Willibrordusstraat (left) and Dieterderweg (right). We are in fact looking back to the marketplace seen in the top picture.

Twenty miles due south, Stanley Maxted was in the village of Schilberg not far from the Dutch-German border recording a report for the BBC. Today's communiqué comments on the capture of Schilberg making a mockery of the empty words on the wall: 'With our Führer to Victory'. On the evening of D Day, the BBC had launched 'War Report' immediately after the 9 p.m. news and in the months that followed the programme had an audience of ten to fifteen million listeners in the British Isles. It had been introduced to link civilians with the Services — 'a window on the war through which the combatant and the folk at home could catch a glimpse of each other'. The exciting words 'And now, over to Normandy' which began the early broadcasts and the familiar voices of the correspondents — Robert Barr, Richard Dimbleby, Frank Gillard, Chester Wilmot to name just a few — became almost household friends.

COMMUNIQUE No. 287   January 20

In Holland northwest of NIJMEGEN, the enemy continued to attack Allied forward positions in the area of ZETTEN, and made a slight local gain. The situation was later restored and fighting continues.

In the SITTARD area, our forces continue to make progress. An enemy counter-attack at SCHILBERG, southeast of ECHT, was beaten off and the village is in our hands. Over the German border our units have occupied the villages of SCHALBRUCH, HAVERT, HEILDER, and have made gains beyond HONGEN.

Southeast of MALMÉDY, we are clearing SCHOPPEN and have advanced to a point more than two miles south of ONDENVAL against light resistance. RECHT is in our hands and we have pushed on to a point one and one-half miles east of the town on the LIGNEUVILLE—ST VITH road.

East of VIELSALM, we are clearing the wooded area of GRAND BOIS and have reached a point just south of POTEAU on the VIELSALM—ST VITH road. South of VIELSALM, our units are in BOVIGNY, and we have made gains in the area south of the town. RETTIGNY and BRISY, northeast of HOUFFALIZE, have been occupied by our armored units and we have reached the high ground half a mile south of RETTIGNY against light resistance.

We have cleared NOCHER southeast of WILTZ. DIEKIRCH and BETTENDORF, on the Sauer river, have been cleared, and we have reached points about one mile north of both towns.

In the TETTINGEN area, southeast of REMICH, our forces have repulsed numerous counter-attacks by enemy tanks and infantry.

We repulsed strong enemy attacks in the BITCHE salient northeast of REIPERTSWILLER without loss of ground.

At HATTEN, following a lull, the enemy attempted again to break through our Maginot Line positions with a tank-supported assault from three directions, and again was turned back.

Enemy efforts to advance in his Rhine bridgehead north of STRASBOURG were also checked. Our forces reached SESSENHEIM in an attack but were unable to hold their gain and retired.

Weather curtailed air operations yesterday. Targets northeast of ST VITH and south of TRIER were bombed by small formations of fighter-bombers. Other fighter-bombers, operating from BITCHE to the south of STRASBOURG, attacked road and rail transport and communications and destroyed a number of fortified buildings. A small number of fighter-bombers hit several locomotives near MUNSTER.

The slogan . . . the wall . . . and the sign to the border . . . all gone.

COMMUNIQUE No. 288   January 21

The ZETTEN area northwest of NIJMEGEN is quiet and Allied forward elements have re-occupied their positions following recent enemy attacks.

North of ECHT our units have occupied the town of STEVENSWEERT without opposition.

In the area between STEVENSWEERT and SITTARD we continued to make gains to the eastward and have occupied more villages, including PEIJ, two miles to the east of ECHT. BREBEREN, two miles east of HONGEN, also is in our hands. The area west of the line ECHT—BREBEREN is clear of the enemy except for small pockets of resistance which are being mopped up.

Fighter-bombers and rocket-firing fighters attacked enemy gun positions in the SITTARD battle area. Fighter-bombers also bombed a road bridge near KORRENZIG, north of LINNICH.

Southeast of MALMEDY, our forces have cleared SCHOPPEN and have made slight gains south of the town. DEIDENBERG, four miles north of ST VITH, has been taken by our armored units. Northwest of ST VITH, we have made small gains against light resistance in the wooded area one and one-half miles east of POTEAU.

Farther to the southwest COURTIL, one-half mile south of BOVIGNY, is in our hands and a small enemy pocket one mile southeast of the town is being mopped up.

In the area east of BASTOGNE, our units gained 1,200 yards east and north of OBERWAMPACH.

North and northeast of DIEKIRCH, we have reached the edge of BASTENDORF and are in the vicinity of LONGSDORF.

Southeast of REMICH, a number of enemy pillboxes south of NENNIG have been reduced, while farther to the east our units are in the vicinity of ORSCHOLZ, after an advance of half a mile.

Enemy artillery was active against our forces in the SAARLAUTERN bridgehead area.

In the BITCHE salient our forces and hostile elements were active. There were infantry engagements and patrol clashes northeast of REIPERTSWILLER which the enemy shelled.

Heavy fighting ceased in the HATTEN—RITTERSHOFFEN section of the Maginot Line but Allied and enemy patrolling was aggressive.

Enemy pressure in his Rhine bridgehead continued to be heavy. Our forces still hold a major portion of DRUSENHEIM.

A strong Allied attack, supported by artillery, was launched between the Rhine and ST AMARIN in the Vosges, and we have made gains of up to three miles in some sectors.

Fighter-bombers, flying in weather which restricted their operations in all areas yesterday, attacked transportation targets in Holland, the Rhineland and elsewhere. They cut railway lines at many places in the UTRECHT and AMERSFOORT areas, struck at railway transport across the frontier beyond MUNSTER, hit enemy material moving by road and rail mainly around EUSKIRCHEN, bombed trains near COBLENZ and TRIER and struck at railway yards at AALEN, some 30 miles east of STUTTGART.

Railway traffic centers at RHEINE, north of MUNSTER, and at HEILBRONN, north of STUTTGART, and a rail and highway bridge across the Rhine at MANNHEIM, were attacked by more than 750 escorted heavy bombers. Some of the fighter escort also strafed transportation targets near OSNABRUCK. During the day seven enemy aircraft were shot down.

As we have seen on page 279, the German salient at Colmar still had to be eliminated but General Devers requested that SHAEF give him two additional divisions to carry out the attack. His 6th Army Group was given the 10th Armored and 28th Infantry Divisions although the latter was still licking its wounds suffered in the Ardennes and was only capable of limited action. The operation to eliminate the pocket began on January 20 when the Ier Corps d'Armée attacked the southern flank.

This French armour was moving through Rosheim, 15 miles south-west of Strasbourg.

The dragon's teeth of the Siegfried Line ran almost continuously from the village of Tettingen 12 miles south-east of Luxembourg, eastwards along the border interrupted only by stretches of impenetrable woodland. Tettingen was attacked twice, first by the 358th Infantry of the 90th Division back in November and then — after the Americans had been forced to relinquish the ground due to the outbreak of the Ardennes counter-offensive further north — again by the 376th Infantry of the 94th Division on January 14. On January 18, the 11. Panzer-Division counter-attacked from Sinz, and Tettingen was almost lost yet again but the Americans held on. Signal Corps photographer Heimberger pictured men of the 94th Division 'racing for cover across the dragon's teeth' on the 19th.

COMMUNIQUE No. 289   January 22

Allied mortar fire dispersed a small enemy force which was forming up at MIDDELAAR on the right bank of the Maas river south of NIJMEGEN.

The area between the Juliana Canal and the Maas river in the vicinity of STEVENSWEERT and ECHT has been cleared following a link-up of our forces in that sector.

Northeast of ECHT our units have met determined resistance in the area of ST JOOST and fighting continues. BOCKET and WALDFEUCHT to the southeast have been taken after our forces gained more than two miles. An enemy counter-attack with infantry supported by self-propelled guns was beaten off at WALDFEUCHT.

A German observation post near HANK, southeast of DORDRECHT, was hit by rocket-firing fighters.

In the SITTARD battle area medium, light and fighter-bombers bombed targets at MONTFORT and enemy heavy guns in the wooded country at WILDENRATH. During the night light and heavy bombers struck at two fortified villages and attacked enemy transport and communications.

Our armored units are fighting in BORN, three and one-half miles north of ST VITH, and have seized the high ground just east of the town. Minor gains have been made in the wooded area two and one-half to three miles west and northwest of ST VITH, where operations are hampered by difficult terrain, snow and icy roads. CIRREUX, one mile north of BOVIGNY, is in our hands.

East and southeast of HOUFFALIZE our forces have taken the towns of VISSOULE, TAVIGNY, CETTURU and BURET. Northeast of BASTOGNE, our armored elements have taken MOINET, TROINE, LULLANGE and HOFFELT. Our forces have reached the Wiltz river in the area three miles west of the town of WILTZ.

Northwest of the DIEKIRCH, the towns of BOURSCHEID and BURDEN, on the west side of the Sauer river, have been cleared of the enemy. North of DIEKIRCH, we have cleared BASTENDORF and advanced to LANDSCHEID.

Fighter-bombers, in some strength, struck at road and rail transport, communications, tanks and armored vehicles east of the Ardennes salient. Medium and light bombers attacked railway bridges at EUSKIRCHEN and MAYEN and a railway junction west of EUSKIRCHEN.

Southeast of REMICH, an enemy counter-attack with tanks and infantry made slight progress just north of NENNIG, and another tank-infantry attack in the vicinity of TETTINGEN was repulsed.

A counter-attack by a force of approximately 450 enemy infantry in the SAARLAUTERN area was repulsed by our troops.

In the BITCHE salient recent enemy aggressiveness subsided to normal patrol clashes.

Our forces repulsed an attack in the enemy's Rhine bridgehead north of STRASBOURG and knocked out four of 18 supporting tanks.

Targets at HERRLISHEIM were bombed by a small number of fighter-bombers.

On the southern flank of the COLMAR sector our forces pressed their attack vigorously despite stubborn opposition and heavy snow. Several hundred prisoners have been taken.

Nine hundred escorted heavy bombers attacked railway yards at MANNHEIM, ASCHAFFENBURG and HEILBRONN. Some of the escorting fighters strafed railway targets and aircraft on the ground. Fighter-bombers attacked locomotives and railway cars in the areas of DORSTEN, HALTERN and OSNABRUCK.

At Tettingen, although there is little to confirm the comparison except the lay of the land, this is certainly the same spot. The dragon's teeth have been demolished but Karel Margry found the concrete foundations still in place on the left. The picture was taken at the southern exit of Tettingen, just beside the main road to Wochern.

The Third Army's 94th Infantry Division — known as 'Patton's Nugget' — had been stationed in Brittany until New Year's Day when it was moved up to the front. The division was spoiling for a fight and its 376th Infantry fought a running battle at Tettingen as indicated in Communiques 287, 289 and 290. According to the caption on this picture of January 20, this particular German soldier charged to within a dozen yards of an American outpost before he was cut down.

A month ago this road between Saint Vith and Nieder-Emmels was crowded with advancing Germans . . . now their bodies lie in the snow alongside their abandoned armour as American troops regain the ground lost. Picture taken at the northern entrance of Nieder-Emmels looking south-east by Signal Corps photographer Private John P. Salis on January 23.

COMMUNIQUE No. 290   **January 23**

North of ZETTEN Allied forces have driven the enemy across the Linge canal.

Northeast of ECHT heavy fighting continues in the area of ST JOOST where the enemy has reinforced his units with local reserves. We have repulsed counter-attacks against WALDFEUCHT, and farther to the southeast our units have occupied the villages of HONTEM and SELSTEN.

Fighter-bombers attacked a factory at ALBLASSERDAM, southeast of ROTTERDAM, enemy barracks at WAGENINGEN and in the NIJMEGEN area, and targets at BOCHOLT, yesterday.

Northeast of SITTARD, fighter-bombers struck at fortified buildings at HEINSBERG, and targets at MONTFORT, while escorted medium bombers bombed a road junction at WASSENBURG. Rail targets north and northeast of the Ruhr were also bombed by fighter-bombers.

Our forces have cleared BORN, and against light resistance have pushed to a point two miles north of ST VITH. We have entered HINDERHAUSEN, three and a half miles west of ST VITH, and our troops, meeting slightly stiffening opposition, have taken the high ground southwest of HINDERHAUSEN. We have gained up to 1,500 yards east of a line HINDERHAUSEN—ROGERY, and our elements east and southeast of BOVIGNY have driven 3,000 yards eastward, meeting little resistance. Along the HOUFFALIZE—ST VITH road our units have cleared GOUVY, three miles east of CHERAIN. Other elements moving northeast from the BASTOGNE area took HACHIVILLE and advanced one and a half miles to the northeast. Our units on the BASTOGNE—ST VITH road are less than a mile southwest of TROIS VIERGES. BOEVANGE, three miles west of CLERVAUX, has been taken.

WILTZ has been cleared of the enemy and our troops have taken NOERTRANGE, two miles to the northwest. Northeast of BOURSCHEID, our forces east of the Sauer river have taken LIPPERSCHEID and have gained more than a mile farther north.

Rail yards at NEUSS, on the route from the Ruhr to DUREN, where there was a heavy concentration of rail cars, were attacked by fighter-bombers. In the course of this and other attacks more than 650 rail cars were destroyed, and many others damaged. Enemy motor transport, in two dense concentrations leading from the Ardennes salient, was bombed and strafed by fighter-bombers operating in great strength. Approximately 1,600 vehicles were destroyed and many others were damaged. Following an attack by medium bombers on a bridge across the Our river at DASBURG, one concentration was attacked on the west bank of the river on the roads leading to the bridge, while the other concentration was attacked in an area some 10 miles southwest of PRUM. Fighter-bombers also successfully went for tanks, armored fighting vehicles, gun positions, locomotives and strong points in and behind the salient, and cut rail lines in many places.

In the area southeast of REMICH, more enemy counter-attacks have been repulsed in the vicinity of TETTINGEN.

In the BITCHE salient the enemy made aggressive attempts to infiltrate. Our forces mopped up hostile elements which had penetrated our forward positions.

Patrols were active on the Rhine west bank north of STRASBOURG but no major fighting developed. Late reports disclose that 12 rather than four tanks were knocked out in Sunday's actions [see Communiqué No. 289].

On the south side of the COLMAR sector the principal suburbs of MULHOUSE have been cleared in our attacks of the last three days and gains have been made in the vicinity of CERNAY. This progress was made against stiff enemy resistance, through snowstorms and icy roads.

The forest of NONNENBRUCH south of CERNAY has been cleared. More than 1,000 prisoners have been counted.

Medium and light bombers attacked the railhead of BLANKENHEIM, rail bridges at SINZIG, SIMMERN and BULLAY, and rail yards and a supply depot at GEROLSTEIN. Farther south fighter-bombers struck at rail yards at HOMBERG, ELMSTEIN, BERGZABERN and NEUSTADT, and fuel dumps near KAISERSLAUTERN and BERGZABERN.

Escorted heavy bombers attacked the synthetic oil plant at STERKRADE in the Ruhr. Some of the escorting fighters also strafed an airfield and rail targets in the HANNOVER area. During the day seven enemy aircraft were shot down and eight destroyed on the ground. From the day's operations nine heavy bombers, two medium bombers, and 21 fighters are missing.

Last night a strong force of heavy bombers attacked targets in western Germany, with the synthetic oil plant at DUISBERG as the main objective.

Ten miles south-east of Aachen, the pillbox-studded valley between Lammersdorf and Rollesbroich remained a static front for over four months, both sides holding on while the battle of the Hürtgen Forest raged to the north and then the Battle of the Bulge erupted in the Ardennes to the south. For most of this period the front was held by the 78th Infantry Division. In January 1945, Fred Ramage of Keystone pictured a five-man ski patrol of the 310th Infantry, being led through the dragon's teeth by Tech/Sergeant James R. Weik (an American of Norwegian descent).

COMMUNIQUE No. 291   January 24

Allied forces extended their hold on the river Maas north of STEVENSWEERT, and occupied MAASBRACHT. Farther south, we have cleared ST JOOST and are fighting on the outskirts of MONTFORT.

Northeast of SITTARD our forces continued to press forward against strong opposition. We have taken OBSPRINGEN, about two miles northeast of WALDFEUCHT, and to the southeast, the villages of LAFFELD and WALDENRATH.

Fighters and fighter-bombers hit railway yards and bridges in the LEIDEN—UTRECHT—DORDRECHT area, attacked railway lines and enemy troops moving by road between AMERSFOORT and APELDOORN and struck at road and rail transport north of the Ruhr. Rocket-firing fighters attacked targets in the area south of ARNHEM.

Escorted medium and light bombers attacked communication centers at NIEDERKRUCHTEN and WEGBERG east of ROERMOND. Fighter-bombers bombed enemy gun positions in the fortified village of UETTERATH, east of WALDENRATH.

Our forces have taken ST VITH. Southwest of ST VITH we have reached the edge of WEISTEN and cleared the enemy from COMMANSTER and BEHO. In the BEHO area our units made gains of up to one mile northeast of the town against slight opposition, while other elements moved one mile to the southeast meeting artillery, small-arms and mortar fire.

North of CLERVAUX, we have cleared the enemy from BOXHORN and have taken high ground in the vicinity of ELSENBORN.

ESCHWEILER, two and one-half miles north of WILTZ, is in our hands and we have reached the south side of WILWERWILTZ on the Clerf river.

In the area north of DIEKIRCH, our troops have gained approximately two miles north of LANDSCHEID.

WALSDORF, one and one-half miles southwest of VIANDEN, has been cleared of the enemy, and fighting is in progress in FOUHREN, where a small enemy counter-attack has been repulsed. Fighting continues in the area of NENNIG, southeast of REMICH.

Light and fighter-bombers continued the attack of enemy motor transport in the Ardennes area and southwest of EUSKIRCHEN. Nearly 1,000 vehicles and 39 tanks and armoured vehicles were destroyed.

Near BITCHE approximately half of an enemy column of 30 vehicles was destroyed by our artillery. Groups of hostile infantry and tanks were dispersed by artillery fire east of the BITCHE salient.

In northern Alsace we have made a limited withdrawal to more advantageous positions in the general area east and north of HAGUENAU. The movement was carried out according to plan and without enemy interference. No large towns were yielded.

Four hundred prisoners were taken by our forces in repulsing enemy attacks Sunday night and Monday [January 21/22] at KILSTETT near the Rhine north of STRASBOURG. North of COLMAR our forces launched a surprise attack. Further limited progress against stiff resistance was made in our attack which continues along the southern edge of the COLMAR sector in the MULHOUSE area. A number of enemy tanks have been knocked out or captured in these engagements.

Fighter-bombers struck at enemy transport east of BITCHE, railway yards at GERMERSHEIM, a fuel dump at ZELL northeast of STRASBOURG and targets at OHNENHEIM, ELSENHEIM and MACKENHEIM northeast of COLMAR.

Railway yards at NEUSS were attacked by escorted heavy bombers.

During the day 32 enemy aircraft were destroyed in the air and three on the ground. Two other enemy aircraft were shot down last night by night fighters. Six of our heavy bombers, four light bombers and 18 fighters are missing, but five of the fighter pilots are safe.

Karel discovered that the picture was taken just south-east of Lammersdorf, looking south to Paustenbach, the first houses of which can be seen on the ridge. The dragon's teeth at this point are now completely overgrown, forcing him to take his comparison from their edge (note the iron rods sticking out). The section rising to Paustenbach can just be made out among the trees in the distance.

On January 22 the 6th Army Group launched the second part of its offensive at Colmar using the IIème Corps d'Armée to attack the northern part of the salient. French forces tried hard to turn the German defences of the Cernay sector (five miles west of Mulhouse) and cut them from the rear but, aided by heavy snowfalls and overcast skies that limited Allied air support, German forces held on stubbornly. Four kilometres east of Cernay, the sector of Wittelsheim was hotly contested from January 22 and it was not before February 3 that the town was finally secured. This Sherman M4A2 of the 5ème Régiment de Chasseurs d'Afrique was pictured in Cité Graffenwald, a mile south of Wittelsheim.

COMMUNIQUE No. 292   January 25

Allied forces in southern Holland have occupied MONTFORT against moderate resistance. Across the German border to the southeast our units have entered HEINSBERG where they are mopping up enemy pockets in the face of artillery and mortar fire.

Fighter-bombers attacked gun positions northeast of ROERMOND, enemy-occupied factory buildings east of HEINSBERG and German troops in UETTERATH.

Our units, advancing in deep snow against moderate resistance, have cut the BULLINGEN—ST VITH road about one mile southwest of BULLINGEN. We have repulsed several enemy counter-attacks near ST VITH. South-west of the town, we have made gains against moderate opposition to take NEUNDORF, CROMBACH, WEISTEN and MALDINGEN and are fighting in ALDRINGEN. We have taken the town of OURTHE, on the upper Ourthe river, southwest of ALDRINGEN.

North of CLERVAUX, our forces are in the vicinity of WILWERDANGE, on the BASTOGNE—ST VITH road, and have pushed beyond BINSFELD. Farther south, we have taken high ground overlooking the Clerf river two miles north of CLERVAUX, and ESELBORN is in our hands. At a point three miles east of WILTZ we have reached the Clerf river.

Northwest of VIANDEN we have made gains to the vicinity of PUTSCHEID. South of VIANDEN, fighting continues at FOUHREN, where an enemy counter-attack was repulsed.

In the Ardennes sector enemy transport, armored vehicles and tanks continuing their withdrawal were attacked by fighter-bombers which operated from northwest of EUSKIRCHEN southward to PRUM and over a rectangle area formed by CLERVAUX, PRUM, BITBURG and VIANDEN. Troop concentrations, gun positions, fortified buildings and communications were also struck at while a small number of medium and light bombers hit targets at SCHLEIDEN and STADTKYLL.

In the northern Alsace plain, small enemy attacks were repulsed northeast of INGWEILER in the BISCHOLTZ area. Hostile groups were dispersed by our artillery northwest and southeast of HAGUENAU.

North of COLMAR our forces have crossed the Ill river and have made progress on the eastern side against moderate resistance.

Limited gains have been made in the MULHOUSE—CERNAY sector against stiff resistance.

Communications and enemy transport in the Rhine valley from DARMSTADT to MULHOUSE were attacked by fighter-bombers striking along the Rhine valley. Road bridges at KARLSRUHE and near FREIBURG were hit, the rail line between LANDAU and WISSEMBOURG was cut, and targets at WINDEN were attacked.

Railway targets and communications in northern and eastern Holland were attacked by fighter-bombers. Between LEEUWARDEN and GRONINGEN the rail track was cut in several places, and at BARNEVELD, road and rail bridges were hit. Other fighter-bombers bombed a pier at HELLEVOETSLUIS, sheds at MAASSLUIS and enemy troop billets near NIJMEGEN.

Flying eastward into Germany as far as GOTTINGEN, fighter-bombers struck at rail and road transport in the areas of MUNSTER and OSNABRUCK and elsewhere.

One cannot fail to reflect on the significance that in January 1945, of the two divisions occupied in the battle at Colmar, the 3rd Infantry Division saw one of the bravest actions by an individual while the 28th Division the most ignominious. It was on January 14 that Lieutenant Audie Murphy rejoined his regiment, the 15th Infantry, after having been confined to hospital for two months after being wounded. Now the main effort in the north was to be made by Major General 'Iron Mike' O'Daniel's 3rd Division using his four infantry regiments in a leap-frog movement to capture the bridge over the Rhine at Neuf-Breisach. Two rivers stood in the way — the Fecht and the Ill — and Murphy crossed the footbridge over the Fecht on the night of January 22/23. Meanwhile, a bridge over the Ill at Maison Rouge had collapsed under the weight of a tank so the 15th had to protect the engineers while they built a new treadway bridge. This was completed by the morning of the 25th. The following day Murphy assumed command of his company — Company B of the 1st Battalion — after 1st Lieutenant Ernest Leake was wounded. Orders were to advance with other companies of the 1st Battalion to the southern end of the Riedwihr woods facing Holtzwihr. The citation for the award of the Medal of Honor describes Murphy's exploit: 'Company B was attacked by six tanks and waves of infantry. Lieutenant Murphy ordered his men to withdraw to prepared positions in a woods, while he remained forward at his command post and continued to give fire directions to the artillery by telephone. Behind him, to his right, one of our tank destroyers received a direct hit and began to burn. Its crew withdrew to the woods. Lieutenant Murphy continued to direct artillery fire which killed large numbers of the advancing enemy infantry. With the enemy tanks abreast of his position, Lieutenant Murphy climbed on the burning tank destroyer, which was in danger of blowing up at any moment, and employed its .50-caliber machine gun against the enemy. He was alone and exposed to German fire from three sides, but his deadly fire killed dozens of Germans and caused their infantry attack to waver. The enemy tanks, losing infantry support, began to fall back. For an hour the Germans tried every available weapon to eliminate Lieutenant Murphy, but he continued to hold his position and wiped out a squad which was trying to creep up unnoticed on his right flank. Germans reached as close as ten yards, only to be mowed down by his fire. He received a leg wound, but ignored it and continued the singlehanded fight until his ammunition was exhausted.' (For more information see *After the Battle* No. 3.)

COMMUNIQUE No. 293   January 26

Allied forces have wiped out an enemy party which crossed the Maas river near BOXMEER, south of NIJMEGEN. Farther south our troops have occupied LINNE, north of MONTFORT. The wooded area south of MONTFORT has been cleared of the enemy.

Across the German border, mopping up operations in HEINSBERG have been completed and the town is in our hands.

A crossroads at the German town of BIRGELEN, southeast of ROERMOND, was attacked by rocket-firing fighters.

Our forces between BULLINGEN and ST VITH have gained a half a mile southeast of MÖDERSCHEID and have taken high ground approximately two miles east of BORN. Deep snow continued to hamper our operations in this area. We have made small gains just southeast of ST VITH. South-west of ST VITH, we have cleared ALDRINGEN and WATTERMAL. To the southeast, WILWERDANGE has been taken despite strong resistance from the enemy and we have occupied BREIDFELD, one mile east of BINSFELD.

We have crossed the Clerf river north and south of CLERVAUX. North of the town our troops have taken HUPPERDANGE and are in the vicinity of URSPELT. One and one-half miles south of CLERVAUX, our units have gained high ground across the river. Farther to the south we have cleared the enemy from ALSCHEID, three miles east of WILTZ.

We have captured HOSCHEID, four miles west of VIANDEN, after a battle in which three enemy tanks were knocked out. Four other enemy tanks were destroyed when we repulsed a counter-attack at PUTSCHEID, two miles northwest of VIANDEN.

House-to-house fighting is in progress in WASSERBILLIG at the junction of the Sauer and Moselle rivers.

In the Ardennes sector fighter-bombers continued their attacks on withdrawing enemy transport and armored vehicles, destroying 679 motor vehicles and 52 armored vehicles and damaging many others. In addition, a number of gun positions were knocked out and rail cars destroyed or damaged.

Medium and light bombers attacked roads at KALL, STADTKYLL and HILLESHEIM and rail bridges at EUSKIRCHEN, SINZIG and ELLER. Elsewhere weather restricted air operations.

East of SAARGEMUND, one of our ground patrols destroyed five enemy-held bunkers and inflicted personnel losses.

In the northern Alsace plain the reinforced enemy launched a series of attacks against our new positions and scored initial gains, but by the end of the day these were largely offset by our counter-attacks.

Hostile forces penetrated more than a mile to SCHILLERSDORF and occupied nearby MUHLHAUSEN. They were halted in hard fighting which continued in SCHILLERSDORF. West of HAGUENAU, our counter-attacks resulted in retaining sections of wooded areas which the enemy entered after crossing the Moder river.

East of HAGUENAU, 80 of an enemy company which crossed the river were captured and the rest forced back.

Stiff fighting continued north of COLMAR and along the southern edge of the COLMAR sector with little change in the situation.

Meanwhile, ten miles north-west of Holzwihr, Private Eddie Slovik of Company G of the 109th Infantry Regiment, was awaiting execution by firing-squad for desertion. According to the evidence presented at his court-martial, Private Slovik had arrived in France in August when he was assigned to the 28th Infantry Division. Arriving at Elbeuf, 60 miles north-west of Paris, Slovik went missing on August 26 and when he returned to his unit on October 8 he asked his company commander if he could be tried for being absent without leave. An hour later he asked: 'If I leave now will it be desertion' before disappearing again. The following morning Slovik handed himself in to the Military Government Detachment in Rocherath, handing over a signed confession. Having been found guilty of desertion at his court-martial at Roetgen on November 11, on November 27 Major General Norman D. Cota, the CG of the 28th Infantry Division, approved the sentence of death which was to be carried out in view of and by his own unit. (By that stage of the war executions were normally carried out in Disciplinary Training Centres — usually civilian prisons taken over by the military.) On December 9, Slovik wrote to General Eisenhower, pleading for clemency but on January 6, the Assistant Judge Advocate General reported to Eisenhower that: 'This is the first death sentence for desertion which has reached me for examination. It is probably the first of the kind in the American Army for over 80 years — there were none in World War I. In this case, the extreme penalty of death appears warranted. This soldier had performed no front line duty. He did not intend to. He deserted when about to join the infantry company to which he had been assigned. His subsequent conduct shows a deliberate plan to secure trial and incarceration in a safe place. The imposition of a less severe sentence would only have accomplished the accused's purpose of securing his incarceration and consequent freedom from the dangers which so many of our armed forces are required to face daily. His unfavorable civilian record indicates that he is not a worthy subject of clemency.' Eisenhower approved the execution and Private Slovik was taken to the little town of Sainte Marie-aux-Mines in the Vosges mountains, 15 miles north-west of Colmar. Enlisted men from various components of the division were detailed as witnesses with 12 men being selected to form the firing-squad. Just after 10 a.m. on January 31 the execution took place in the garden of No. 86 Rue Général Bourgeois. (See also *After the Battle* No. 32.)

COMMUNIQUE No. 294 January 27

Allied forces continued their advance between LINNE and HEINSBERG. Southeast of HEINSBERG our units have occupied the villages of GREBBEN, DREMMEN, HORST and NIRM on the west bank of the river Wurm. East of the Wurm our attack has been extended and our units have occupied BRACHELEN and advanced beyond it to the north.

Northeast of ST VITH we have made gains of up to 2,000 yards against light resistance and have taken MIRFELD, AMBLEVE and MEYERODE. The town of WALLERODE, two miles northeast of ST VITH, is in our hands after our units overcame determined opposition, and we have taken high ground between WALLERODE and MEYERODE.

In the area north and northeast of CLERVAUX, our forces are clearing the wooded area east of WILWERDANGE, near the northern border of Luxembourg, and have entered WEISWAMPACH. Farther south we have reached HEINERSCHEID, on the ST VITH—DIEKIRCH road, and are in the vicinity of FISCHBACH.

South of CLERVAUX, we are in the vicinity of BOCKHOLTZ and have cleared PINTSCH, after having repulsed a counter-attack near the town. Farther southeast our troops are fighting at HOSCHEIDERDICKT.

Southeast of REMICH, we are meeting resistance from small-arms and mortar fire in the area of NENNIG.

Bad weather somewhat restricted air operations yesterday. However fighter-bombers continued the destruction of enemy armor and vehicles in the Ardennes, mainly in the area around PRUM.

In northern Alsace enemy forces which penetrated to SCHILLERSDORF and crossed the Moder river farther east were driven back at all points. Our positions were restored and heavy losses inflicted on the enemy. We have reoccupied MUHLHAUSEN and BISCHOLTZ.

Northeast of COLMAR we have made a slight gain and have entered RIEDWIHR.

Further local gains have been made northwest of MULHOUSE where our forces are clearing the enemy from the potash-mining area.

Fighter-bombers destroyed a railway bridge over the Moselle, 16 miles northeast of TRIER, attacked a railway yard northeast of KAISERSLAUTERN, and road and rail transport in the BITCHE and COLMAR areas; bombed and strafed convoys west of KARLSRUHE and struck at targets northwest of HAGUENAU.

Brachelen, six miles north-east of Geilenkirchen, was captured on January 26 during the Ninth Army's final push to reach the Roer river. A combined operation invloving American infantry, British tanks and Scottish soldiers, the wartime caption commented that this was the first important battle fought by British and American troops in snow suits.

Other fighter-bombers and rocket-firing fighters hit road and rail transport north of the Ruhr and between OSNABRUCK and BREMEN and attacked railway yards at RHEYDT, MUNCHEN-GLADBACH and GREVENBROICH. Medium bombers hit a railway bridge crossing the Erft river at EUSKIRCHEN.

In the approach to Brachelen, the US 102nd Infantry Division had to overrun around 75 pillboxes of the Siegfried Line.

COMMUNIQUE No. 295   January 28

Allied forces have reached ST ODILIENBERG, two and one-half miles southeast of LINNE. Elsewhere in southern Holland and across the German border in the HEINSBERG vicinity, activity was confined to patrolling. Our patrols have reached the Roer river at a number of places in this area.

In the ST VITH area our forces gained 1,000 yards against light small-arms and mortar fire to reach a point one and one fourth miles southeast of the town. Halfway between ST VITH and CLERVAUX, we have pushed more than a mile east of LENGELERN, and have reached LIELER, three miles east of BINSFELD. CLERVAUX is in our hands.

Southeast of CLERVAUX, our forces advanced against strong resistance to NEIDHAUSEN while other units reached the vicinity of HOSINGEN on the ST VITH—DIEKIRCH road. Advancing from the south, Allied elements have reached the vicinity of WEILER, and a point one mile north of HOSCHEIDERDICKT.

Southeast of REMICH, our forces have advanced just north of TETTINGEN.

Weather curtailed air operations again yesterday, but fighter-bombers continued their attack on enemy transport and armored vehicles withdrawing from the Ardennes sector, and struck at fortified buildings and communications. Railway yards at AHRWEILER and targets at MAYEN were bombed.

Although Operation 'Blackcock' had taken longer than expected, by the 28th British troops had entered Heinsberg, five miles to the north-west of Brachelen. Casualties in the operation were in the order of 1,500, more than half being from the 52nd Lowland Division and its attached 8th Armoured Brigade. Over 100 tanks had been lost, a quarter of them flame-throwing and mine-clearing vehicles from the 79th Armoured Division. Prisoners taken numbered over 2,500.

In northern Alsace, activity subsided to patrolling and light artillery exchanges following the repulse of the enemy's attacks across the Moder river.

Northeast of COLMAR our troops gained more than a mile north of the East-West Colmar canal.

On the south side of the COLMAR sector we have reached the outskirts of CERNAY after stiff fighting.

A small number of fighter-bombers attacked rail transport in eastern Holland and in the areas of HALTERN and BIELEFELD in Germany.

Not much chance of matching up these shots taken by Harold Tetlow of the *Daily Sketch*.

Meanwhile, away to the south, the battle to reduce the Colmar Pocket was continuing. At Jebsheim, five miles north-east of Colmar, the 254th Infantry (63rd Division) and Combat Command 6 (5ème Division Blindée) were involved in violent fighting throughout the 27th and 28th but by evening the village was finally in Allied hands.

the lower Vosges and northern Alsace a lull in activity continued. Heavy snowfalls hampered operations.

Northeast of COLMAR our forces have reached the East-West Colmar canal. On the southern edge of the COLMAR sector we have made further limited gains.

Mortar positions southwest of MEEUWEN and a strong point southeast of NIJMEGEN were attacked by fighter-bombers yesterday. Communications in Holland and northwest Germany were also targets for fighter-bombers; rail lines were cut in the UTRECHT-DEVENTER area, and also to the northwest of RHEINE, while locomotives and rolling stock to the north and northeast of the Ruhr were attacked.

Escorted heavy bombers in very great strength attacked two benzol plants near DORTMUND, Rhine bridges at DUISBURG and COLOGNE, and rail yards near COLOGNE and DUISBURG. Escorted medium and light bombers attacked rail bridges at REMAGEN, SINZIG, ELLER and KAISERSLAUTERN and the communications centers of MAYEN and WENGEROHR.

Last night heavy bombers were over Germany in great strength with railway communications near STUTTGART as the main objective. BERLIN was also bombed.

COMMUNIQUE No. 296   January 29

Allied forces launched an attack in the area northeast of ST VITH against light to moderate resistance.

We have captured HEPSCHEID and HEPPENBACH. Gains were also made east of AMBLEVE and to high ground two miles southeast of ST VITH. South-west of ST VITH, we have cleared the enemy from GRUFFLINGEN.

Farther southeast, our units have advanced to the vicinity of BRACHT after encountering enemy mines and road-blocks west of the town.

Northeast of WEISWAMPACH we have made gains to within one mile of the Our river, and our patrols have reached KALBORN, five miles northeast of CLERVAUX. MUNSHAUSEN, southeast of CLERVAUX, is in our hands. In the area four miles northwest of VIANDEN, our units have occupied WAHLHAUSEN and WEILER and have reached the high ground northeast of WEILER.

In the area southeast of REMICH, we repulsed a small enemy counter-attack in the vicinity of SINZ.

From the SAARBRUCKEN area across

Left: Nevertheless, elements of Gebirgsjäger-Regiment 136 with some Jagdpanthers of Panzerjäger-Abteilung 654 in support mounted an attack on Jebsheim on the morning of the 29th and again that afternoon. However, American infantry were able to resume their advance from the Jebsheim eastwards in the direction of the next village to the east — Artzenheim. *Right:* No snow and a much nicer weather when Jean Paul took this comparison.

COMMUNIQUE No. 297   January 30

Allied forces, continuing their eastward drive, have taken BULLINGEN. In the area northeast of ST VITH, we have made gains of nearly two miles against scattered resistance to take HERRESBACH, and have reached the vicinity of HOLZHEIM, three miles northeast of HERRESBACH.

Our units have made gains in the vicinity of MASPELT, four miles south of ST VITH. Farther south we have taken OBERHAUSEN on the Our river, and some of our elements have crossed the river in the OBERHAUSEN area against very strong resistance. KALBORN has been cleared of the enemy and we have taken RODER. PUTSCHEID, three miles northwest of VIANDEN, is in our hands.

West of the lower Vosges mountains and northern Alsace a lull continued for the third day with heavy snow hampering all movement. Long-range artillery fire fell in the vicinity of SAVERNE. Northeast of COLMAR we made local gains. Our forces drew closer to CERNAY from the west and east of the town.

Rail transportation targets over a wide area in western Germany were under air attack yesterday. Fighter-bombers struck at rail traffic in the region of RHEINE, OSNABRUCK and HERFORD in northwest Germany, railway yards in the areas of DUSSELDORF, DUREN, COLOGNE and PRUM and farther south in the areas of FRANKFURT, KAISERSLAUTERN, TRIER, PIRMASENS, MANNHEIM and STUTTGART.

Escorted heavy bombers, in very great strength, attacked marshalling yards at HAMM, MUNSTER, COBLENZ, NIEDERLAHNSTEIN, SIEGEN east of BONN, and KASSEL. A tank plant at KASSEL also was bombed. Rail traffic was strafed by many of the escorting fighters. Other escorted heavy bombers attacked marshalling yards at KREFELD.

Concentrations of motor vehicles in the triangle formed by ST VITH, TRIER and BONN were attacked by fighter-bombers throughout the day. Nearly 700 vehicles were destroyed.

Escorted medium and light bombers struck at communication centers at RHEINBACH, KALL, BLANKENHEIM, AHRWEILER, MAYEN and WITTLICH; and railway yards at BUNDENTHAL; fortified positions at HABSCHEID southeast of ST VITH, and railway bridges at NONNWEILER, southeast of TRIER, and RINNTHAL, east of PIRMASENS.

Alsace-Lorraine (German Elsass-Lothringen) has long been disputed territory between France and Germany, having changed hands five times in the last 100 years. Re-annexed by Hitler in 1940, by the end of 1944 the majority of the area was occupied by American forces. It was on the northern sector of this front that the Germans launched Operation 'Nordwind' as an adjunct to 'Wacht am Rhein' then being fought some 100 miles to the north-west. As the Allies' main concern in January was to counter the offensive in the Ardennes, when 'Nordwind' began on New Year's Eve, Eisenhower simply ordered General Devers to pull back the majority of the 6th Army Group. However, this order was unacceptable to the new French Government as it would leave Strasbourg — the capital of Alsace — exposed, and the symbolic city, which had been lost to Germany from 1870 to 1918 and again from 1940 to 1944, could not be lost again without damaging political repercussions. General de Gaulle immediately protested to Eisenhower and indicated that the commander of the French First Army, Général de Lattre de Tassigny, had been advised to defend Strasbourg with French forces even if the American units withdrew. The Seventh Army had actually begun the operation to evacuate the city but the French protests caused Eisenhower to modify his orders; nevertheless the city lay undefended for a day. By January 25 the Allies had gained the upper hand and by the end of the month German forces had been withdrawn from the area and sent to the Eastern Front.

Northeast of COLMAR, fighter-bombers made a number of attacks on targets at ELSENHEIM and on enemy units outside the town. In Holland, fighter-bombers attacked railway lines east of DORDRECHT and in the area between ZWOLLE and ZUTPHEN.

During the day seven enemy aircraft were destroyed on the ground.

According to reports so far received five of our heavy bombers and 10 fighters are missing. Last night objectives in BERLIN were bombed.

Left: Meanwhile, in the Ardennes, American artillery plastered Büllingen for days before it was finally retaken late in January as reported in Communiqué No. 297. *Right:* Now looking spick and span, this is the Hauptstrasse as it appears today.

COMMUNIQUE No. 298 January 31

Allied forces attacking in the vicinity of SIMMERATH, northeast of MONSCHAU, made gains of one to three miles to reach KESTERNICH and capture KONZEN.

We have taken ROHREN, two miles east of MONSCHAU, in an advance of 3,000 yards against increasing resistance.

East of MALMEDY, we have taken WIRTZFELD and have pushed on to ROCHERATH and KRINKELT, where fighting is in progress against stiffening opposition. East of BULLINGEN, our infantry made gains of 3,000 yards against moderate resistance to take MURRANGE. The towns of HUNNINGEN and HONSFELD also are in our hands. Farther to the south, we have cleared the enemy from HOLZHEIM and have gained one mile northeast of the town.

South of ST VITH, our units are fighting in the vicinity of STEFFESHAUSEN, east of the Our river near the Belgian-German border. Farther to the south we have cleared the German town of WELCHENHAUSEN on the east bank of the Our river. Our patrols are along the west bank of the Our in the area east and southeast of CLERVAUX.

As we have seen on pages 170 and 171, the first footing on German soil by the western Allies took place on September 11 but what happened on the Eastern Front? The Red Army had already crossed the East Prussian border on August 17, although the single platoon was wiped out the same day and it was not until two months later that two Soviet Armies of the Third Byelorussian Front charged across the borders into East Prussia between Schirwindt and the Romintener Heide. Five days later, on October 21, the Soviets massacred villagers in Nemmerdorf. However, it was not until the Soviet winter offensive (the so-called Vistula-Oder Offensive) began on January 12 that the German frontier proper was crossed. The Red Army began on the Vistula river east of Warsaw and within a matter of days had advanced deep into Poland and across the border into Germany. On January 31, having secured bridgeheads across the River Oder, the Soviets voluntarily halted their forces even though Berlin was now only 40 miles away. At that stage of the war, the western Allies were still over 300 miles from the German capital and they had not even crossed the Rhine. As early as December 1941, Stalin had stated that Poland should receive all the German territory up to the Oder river, a point which was raised again at the Teheran Conference with Roosevelt and Churchill in late 1943. In January 1944, at the first meeting of the European Advisory Commission, Britain stated that the Poles should be given East Prussia and extend its western border to the Oder. Discussed again at the Yalta Conference in February 1945, the decision as to the 'new' Polish borders was not finally agreed until August 1945 at Potsdam. Poland inherited 43,000 square miles of Germany but lost 72,000 square miles to the Soviet Union. The so-called 'Border of Peace and Friendship' was agreed by the German Democratic Republic in 1950 but not by the Federal Republic until 1970. The new borders resulted in a huge shift of population — some 14 million Germans expelled from eastern Europe — and it was only in November 1990 after German reunification that a final treaty was signed between the Federal Republic of Germany and the Republic of Poland accepting that the eastern border of Germany would be defined by the line of the Oder-Neisse rivers.

Weather curtailed air operations yesterday. However, rail and road transport, communications and troops in a triangular area formed by HEIDELBERG, KARLSRUHE and STUTTGART were attacked by fighter-bombers. Included among the targets hit were railway yards at BRUCHSAL, road and rail bridges in the area of HEILBRONN and PFORZHEIM, and troops and horse drawn artillery in the KARLSRUHE and PFORZHEIM areas.

From the SAARBRUCKEN area to the Rhine in northern Alsace, activity was confined to patrolling and minor exchanges of small-arms and scattered artillery fire.

Northeast of COLMAR our forces gained more than a mile after crossing the Colmar canal and entered WIHR-EN-PLAINE, BISCHWIHR and MUNTZENHEIM. Southeast of BISCHWIHR stiff resistance was met in the vicinity of FORTSCHWIHR where hard fighting is in progress. East and southeast of FORTSCHWIHR, fighter-bombers struck at the fortified villages of DURREM, ENZEN and WIDENSOLEN, and road junctions west of the Rhine—Rhone Canal.

On the southern edge of the COLMAR sector, local gains tightened the ring around CERNAY. Farther east we have reached the outskirts of WITTELSHEIM and have entered WITTENHEIM.

Fighter-bombers destroyed a pontoon bridge over the Rhine northeast of MULHOUSE.

So it is interesting that in Kienitz, on the western bank of the Oder river, this T-34 was set up by the government of the now-defunct German Democratic Republic with the inscription on the plaque reading: '31 January 1945 — Kienitz, the first place in our country to have been liberated from Fascism. Glory and honour to the fighting soldiers of the 5th Shock Army and the 2nd Guards Tank Army'. To the Communists in East Germany, this was obviously how they viewed the situation but in reality the First Ukrainian Front entered the Upper Silesian region of Germany proper on January 29. Ironically, one of the first towns to be captured in the East would have been Gleiwitz where German special forces staged a fake border incident in 1939 designed to give Nazi Germany an excuse for invading Poland (see *After the Battle* No. 142).

339

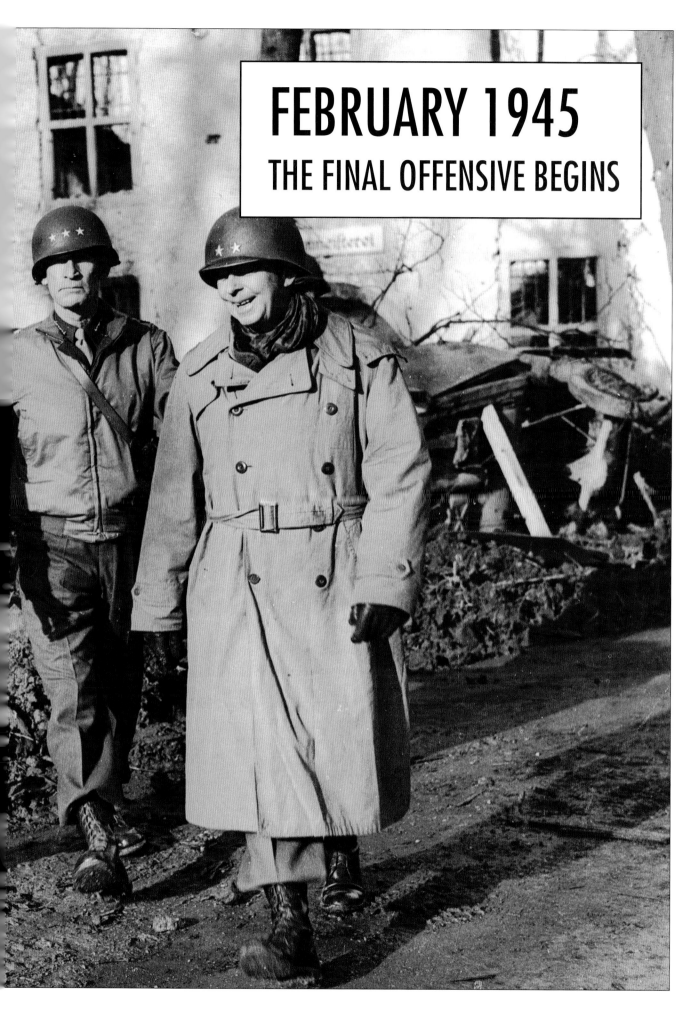

FEBRUARY 1945
THE FINAL OFFENSIVE BEGINS

When this picture was taken on February 1 of Eisenhower and Bradley meeting in Ike's office in Versailles, one of the worst rows of the war was brewing between the American and British Chiefs-of-Staff then conferring in Malta with Roosevelt and Churchill before flying on to meet Stalin at Yalta. The British were openly criticising Eisenhower's strategy, raising the old argument concerning his 'broad front' and his refusal to appoint an overall ground commander. 'I repudiated this suggestion, as I always had before. I was certain that our plans for the completion of the German defeat were the best that could be devised. Entirely aside from my feeling that the proposed arrangement would be futile and clumsy, I was determined to prevent any interference with the exact and rapid execution of those plans.' When it was implied that his plans were drawn up on nationalistic lines, Eisenhower retorted: 'I am certainly no more anxious to put Americans into the thick of the battle and get them killed than I am to see the British take the losses. I have strengthened Montgomery's army group by a full American army, since in no other way can I provide the strength north of the Ruhr that I deem essential for the rapid execution of my plans. I have not devised any plan on the basis of what individual or what nation gets the glory, for in my opinion there is no glory in battle worth the blood it costs.'

COMMUNIQUE No. 299   February 1

Allied forces have completely cleared the enemy from the island of KAPELSCHEVEER in the River Maas east of GEERTRUIDENBERG after heavy and prolonged fighting. Farther south, our units continued their attacks northeast of MONSCHAU and have captured EIGELSCHEID and IMGENBROICH.

Between MONSCHAU and the area northeast of CLERVAUX, we have made general gains, advancing 5,000 yards in some places.

In the forest southeast of HOFEN, our forces gained up to 4,000 yards, and pushed 1,000 yards east of ROCHERATH through deep snow and occasional minefields. Our infantry elements have crossed the Belgian-German border in a 5,000-yard advance to within a mile west of UDENBRETH. Another crossing of the border was made five miles southeast of BULLINGEN.

East and southeast of ST VITH, our units have taken SETZ, SCHLIERBACH and LOMMERSWEILER and have cleared the enemy from STEFFESHAUSEN, three miles farther south.

In the bridgehead across the Our river east of WEISWAMPACH, our artillery repulsed an infantry counter-attack, and we have advanced to a point one and one-half miles northeast of WELCHENHAUSEN, on the east bank of the river.

West of the lower Vosges mountains and in northern Alsace activity was confined to patrolling and exchanges of small-arms fire.

Northeast of STRASBOURG we have occupied GAMBSHEIM and BETTENHOFEN against light resistance.

South of STRASBOURG forces progressed about four miles to the Rhine-Rhone canal in the area east of BENFELD.

Our bridgehead south of the Colmar canal was enlarged with the aid of armor to a depth of approximately three miles. Resistance was spotty. On the southern edge of the COLMAR sector, the enemy continued to defend CERNAY and WITTELSHEIM stubbornly. Violent street fighting has been in progress in both towns.

Weather drastically restricted air operations yesterday.

Eisenhower was still suffering from his injured knee so he sent his Chief-of-Staff instead, and Smith forcefully presented Eisenhower's plan to advance to the line of the Rhine. General Marshall was so adamant that he said if the Prime Minister and President approved the British plan, he would recommend to Eisenhower that he resign. Marshall later described the débâcle as 'a terrible meeting' which ended with a closed session with no minutes being taken. The argument ended when Roosevelt approved Eisenhower's plan whereupon Churchill endorsed it.

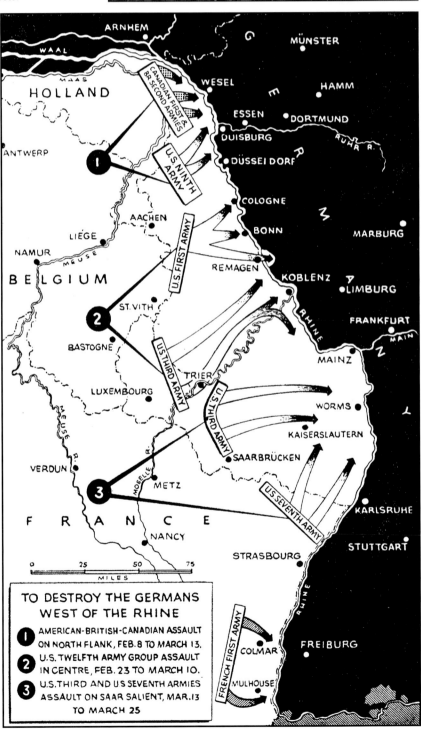

Mürringen lies just a mile east of Büllingen which was one of the first villages captured on December 16 by the combined efforts of the 12. and 277. Volksgrenadier-Divisions. Now the tables have been turned as prisoners are lined up outside a German first-aid post. Two dead Germans lie in the snow . . .

Escorted heavy bombers in great strength struck at objectives in Germany, including the railway marshalling yards at MANNHEIM-LUDWIGSHAFEN and Rhine bridges at WESEL, northwest of the Ruhr. Other escorted heavy bombers attacked the railway junction of MÜNCHEN-GLADBACH west of DUSSELDORF.

Medium and light bombers with fighter escort attacked communication centers at SCHLEIDEN, BRANDSCHEID and PRUM; rail bridges spanning the Rhine at ENGERS, the Lahn river at NASSAU and the Moselle river at ELLER, and road junctions at BLANKENHEIM, southeast of SCHLEIDEN, and at WITTLICH. Several barges on the Rhine northeast of COBLENZ were destroyed.

Rail traffic north of the Ruhr in the areas of BOCHOLT, DULMEN, COESFELD and BURGSTEINFURT and gun positions east of COESFELD were attacked by fighter-bombers and rocket-firing fighters.

Last night heavy bombers in very great strength made heavy attacks on the main railway centers at MAINZ, LUDWIGSHAFEN and SIEGEN and light

COMMUNIQUE No. 300   February 2

In the area northeast of MONSCHAU, Allied forces continued mopping-up operations. Southeast of MONSCHAU we have made gains of from 800 to 3,000 yards against light resistance from pillboxes in the MONSCHAU forest.

Our units made additional gains in the forest east of ROCHERATH and KRINKELT and are within a few hundred yards of the German border.

SCHOENBERG, six miles east of ST VITH, is in our hands and we have advanced two miles farther east and crossed the Belgian-German border to capture LAUDESFELD. Farther south our elements are within one mile of WINTERSCHEID and have taken EIGELSCHEID and HECKHALENFELD east of the Our river.

Southeast of HAGUENAU near the Rhine our forces broke a six-day lull in the northern Alsace plain with an attack which gained up to two miles against strong resistance. We crossed the Moder river in these operations. Hard fighting is in progress at OBERHOFFEN.

Farther south the forest of STEINWALD, north of GAMBSHEIM was cleared.

South of STRASBOURG the area between the Ill and the Rhine rivers has been largely cleared by our infantry and armor. We have reached the Rhine at several points northeast of COLMAR.

Gains up to three miles were made in our continuing drive south of the Colmar canal. In this area fighter-bombers attacked targets at ARTZENHEIM, BALZTENHEIM and

. . . and in front of a house across the street lies a dead GI.

BIESHEIM, close to the west bank of the Rhine.

Our artillery has been firing on the enemy-held BREISACH railway bridge over the Rhine. Enemy resistance continued strong on the southern edge of the Colmar sector where only local gains were made.

bombers struck at the rail network north of the Ruhr. BERLIN was also bombed.

One enemy aircraft was shot down during the day and night fighters destroyed another during the night. One of our heavy bombers and three fighters are missing from the daylight operations.

One of the soldiers raises the corner of the cover to see if he can recognise the casualty. See how the censor has tried to

delete the background to hide the identity of the location . . . but he did not bargain with Jean Paul tracking it down!

Ten miles north of Mürringen soldiers of the 2nd Infantry Division march prisoners out of Harperscheid which they cleared on February 4. The Americans took 150 Germans captive in the battle for the town. According to SHAEF, German losses in December and January totalled 220,000 of whom 110,000 had been taken prisoner and 860,000 Germans had been captured on the Western Front since D-Day. Enemy dead and wounded amounted to over 400,000.

COMMUNIQUE No. 301   February 3

Allied infantry gained from 1,500 to 2,000 yards in the MONSCHAU forest against light to moderate resistance to points three and one-half miles east of HOFEN. Other infantry elements reached the eastern edge of the forest along the main road running southeast from MONSCHAU.

Farther to the south we pushed eastward through the dragon's teeth obstacles of the Siegfried Line against increasing resistance from small-arms and machine-gun fire, and reached the high ground west of RAMSCHEID. Five and one-half miles east of BULLINGEN, the German town of NEUHOF has been taken, and heavy fighting is in progress in UDENBRETH to the north.

Across the German border, east and southeast of ST VITH, we have captured AUW, MUTZENICH, and have reached the vicinity of BLEIALF after taking GROSSLANGENFELD. HECKHUSCHEID, three miles southwest of GROSSLANGENFELD, is also is in our hands.

At OBERHOFFEN, southeast of HAGUENAU, we made slow progress in fighting which continued to be heavy for the second day.

Our infantry and tanks drove to the center of COLMAR, and we also made gains on the eastern and western sides of the city.

To the east near KUNHEIM our units reached the Rhine. We now hold the west bank of the Rhine for about 35 miles south of STRASBOURG. Progress was made in the Colmar forest, while heavy fighting took place at nearby APPENWEIER and BIESHEIM.

Local gains were made on the southern side of the COLMAR sector against strong resistance.

Continuing the offensive against the enemy's communications and transport, medium and fighter-bombers in strength struck at targets from GRONINGEN in the north of Holland, to NEU-BREISACH, southeast of COLMAR. They operated in the battle areas and eastward into Germany. Railway yards and bridges were bombed, rail lines were cut in many places, and large numbers of locomotives and railway cars were destroyed or damaged. A considerable number of motor and armored vehicles also were hit.

In the COLMAR area fighter-bombers bombed and strafed the enemy from dawn to dusk and inflicted heavy losses on his transport.

An oil refinery and fuel dump near EMMERICH and targets at EUSKIRCHEN, GEMUND, STADTKYLL and HILLESHEIM were attacked by other medium bombers.

During the day's operations 64 locomotives, 1,312 railway cars and 274 motor vehicles, including several armored vehicles and tanks, were destroyed or damaged and rail lines were cut in 125 places. Three enemy aircraft were destroyed in the area and several others on the ground. According to reports so far received, two of our bombers and 13 of our fighters are missing.

Last night heavy bombers in very great strength, attacked WIESBADEN, KARLSRUHE and the synthetic oil plant at WANNE-EICKEL. Light bombers struck at rail transport over wide areas in Germany.

As we have seen, many of the wartime captions are not accurate as to the place depicted. Karel visited Harperscheid and took this comparison although he was not entirely convinced with it as none of the present-day houses matched.

On February 3, the Eighth Air Force mounted a 1,000-bomber raid on Berlin, reportedly the heaviest of any attack on the city to date with more than 2,000 tons of bombs landing on a concentrated area, killing 20,000. Werner Girbig, writing in *Im Anflug auf die Reichshauptstadt*, states that 'the German people came to know about this heavy attack on Berlin only through eyewitnesses and those that had experienced it. Any disclosure in the Press or on the radio about the extent and results of air attacks remained, as before, strictly forbidden.' Twenty-five B-17s and eight of the escorting fighters failed to return.

COMMUNIQUE No. 302   February 4

Allied forces in the MONSCHAU area pushed from one to three miles deeper into Germany to capture the towns of HAMMER and HARPERSCHEID and enter DREIBORN. Resistance from small-arms and mortar fire was heavy. UDENBRETH, about seven miles south of HARPERSCHEID, was cleared after heavy fighting in the town.

In the border area 11 miles northeast of ST VITH, we have taken LOSHEIM and MANDERFELD.

Southeast of ST VITH we captured BLEIALF after overcoming strong resistance in the town.

Our units which pushed eastward in the area of the Luxembourg—Belgium—German border intersection have reached the vicinity of GROSSKAMPENBERG. German positions in this area are strongly defended.

East of DIEKIRCH we have cleared the enemy from HOESDORF on the west bank of the Our river.

Southeast of HAGUENAU we have cleared ROHRWILLER, and after three days of hard fighting have taken most of OBERHOFFEN. Stiff resistance and flooded terrain resulted in our withdrawal in the vicinity of HERRLISHEIM and from OFFENDORF.

All of COLMAR has been liberated and we have driven some four miles south of the city. We have freed WINZENHEIM, west of COLMAR, and several other towns nearby. To the east hard fighting continued in the approaches to fortified NEU-BREISACH. Fighter-bombers struck at targets in the city and enemy communications leading to this sector.

Gains on the southern side of the COLMAR sector, where we have reached the outskirts of PULVERSHEIM, have narrowed the distance from our forces in the north to those in the south to less than 12 miles.

Twenty-five hundred tons of bombs were dropped with good results on military objectives in BERLIN yesterday by more than 1,000 escorted heavy bombers. Objectives included important military and governmental offices, the Anhalter railway station and the Tempelhof rail yards. Large fires were started in the target areas.

More than 400 escorted heavy bombers attacked rail yards at MAGDEBURG, and a synthetic oil plant in the MAGDEBURG suburb of ROTHENSEE with unobserved results. Escort for these attacks was provided by more than 900 fighters. The escort shot down 21 enemy fighters in the air and destroyed 14 on the ground and strafed ground targets in northwest Germany, destroyed or damaged locomotives, freight cars and other objectives. Other fighters patrolled airfields in northwest Germany. Thirty-five bombers and five fighters are missing from these operations.

The E-Boat shelters at IJMUIDEN and naval establishments at PORTERSHAVEN near MAASSLUIS were attacked by other escorted heavy bombers with 12,000-pound bombs. Last night heavy bombers attacked targets in western Germany with synthetic oil plants at BOTTROP and DORTMUND as the main objectives.

German billets at DUNKIRK and the rail bridge at ZWOLLE were attacked yesterday by medium bombers.

Mortar positions and troops in the neighbourhood of BABYLONIENBROEK, transportation targets in Holland and northwest Germany, particularly to the north and northeast of the Ruhr, were attacked by fighter-bombers. Locomotives and rolling stock, as well as motor transport and barges were attacked and rail lines were cut in several places.

Farther south fighter-bombers struck at rail yards in the areas of ZULPICH and EUSKIRCHEN and also attacked a number of trains, particularly in the EUSKIRCHEN area, and motor transport to the northeast of BONN. A motor transport repair and storage depot at BERG-GLADBACH, rail bridges at AHRWEILER and SINZIG and a rail yard at JUNKERATH, as well as communications centers at DAHLEN and WITTLICH were targets for medium and light bombers. Fourteen fighter-bombers are missing from the day's operations.

Jean Paul took the comparison on Stresemannstrasse with the Anhalter Bahnhof behind his right shoulder.

Although the siege of Bastogne had ended on December 26, it was not until January 18 that Major General Maxwell Taylor of the 101st Airborne Division formally handed over the town.

In a unique ceremony, held in front of this corner building, a receipt had been prepared for Major General Middleton to accept Bastogne 'used but serviceable, Kraut disinfected'.

COMMUNIQUE No. 303   February 5

Allied forces northeast of MONSCHAU gained up to 3,000 yards to reach the edge of RUHRBERG, and our infantry advanced 3,500 yards to the south shore of the Urftstausee, the large lake formed by the Urft river dam. Southwest and south of the lake, we have cleared the enemy from the towns of EINRUHR, WOLLSEIFEN, and MORSBACH, and have pushed one-half mile east of MORSBACH.

Southeast of MONSCHAU in the vicinity of HOLLERATH, we have encountered rifle and machine-gun fire from enemy pillboxes, and a number of pillboxes just west of the town have been neutralized. In the area two miles southeast of UDENBRETH a group of enemy infantry forming for a counter-attack was dispersed by our artillery.

ROTH, 11 miles northeast of ST VITH, has been cleared of the enemy, and our infantry elements have advanced into the Schnee Eifel forest east of BUCHET.

On the eastern edge of the Hardt mountains, we entered ROTHBACH, inflicted casualties and took prisoners and then withdrew to positions southwest of the town.

Near the Rhine in the HAGUENAU area, fighting continued in OBERHOFFEN. Farther east, advances were made in the BOIS DE DRUSENHEIM, northeast of ROHRWILLER.

In the COLMAR sector, WOLFGANTZEN, one mile west of NEU-BREISACH, was cleared after hard fighting, and mopping-up was in progress in BIESHEIM to the north. South and west of COLMAR, the towns of OBERMORSCHWIHR, VOEGTLINSHOFFEN, TURCKHEIM and LABAROCHE were liberated.

Farther south, CERNAY was completely cleared and STEINBACH and UFFHOLTZ in the same area were occupied.

East of CERNAY we crossed the Thur river near STAFFELFELDEN which was occupied. The advance here reached BERRWILLER, two miles northwest of STAFFELFELDEN.

Weather curtailed air operations yesterday. However fighter-bombers strafed enemy motor transport and troops in the COLMAR area, hit the railway bridge at BREISACH and bombed targets in BREMGARTEN and GRISSHEIM, villages on the German side of the Rhine river southeast of BREISACH. Other fighter-bombers attacked railway yards at OFFENBURG, ROTTWEIL, DONAUESCHINGEN and STEIG.

Last night heavy bombers in strength, were over Germany with BONN as the main objective. Light bombers attacked road and rail targets over a wide area in western Germany.

Then on February 5, Generals Bradley and Patton met Eisenhower at Bastogne. Patton wrote that 'as I was trying to keep the [Third Army's] impending Bitburg offensive a secret so it would not be stopped from above, I was quite perturbed when I received a telephone call directing me to report to General Eisenhower at Bastogne. When I got there, I was relieved to find it was simply a photographic mission so to speak. It was rather amusing, though perhaps not flattering, to note that General Eisenhower never mentioned the Bastogne offensive, although this was the fist time I had seen him since the nineteenth of December, when he seemed much pleased to have me at the critical point.'

COMMUNIQUE No. 304   February 6

Allied armored elements have taken the towns of STRAUCH and STECKENBORN in the area six miles northeast of MONSCHAU. Our units have cleared the high ground east of RUHRBERG and are on the Roer river below the URFTTALSPERRE DAM. Other elements have reached the dam and control it.

Our infantry units two miles north of UHLLIDEN have made a 1,500 yard gain to the east. Other units are fighting in HELLENTHAL, two and one-half miles southwest of SCHLEIDEN. Farther south, BRANDSCHEID has been cleared of the enemy and we have made gains in the Schnee Eifel forest, two miles east of BUCHET.

The area north of STRASBOURG and west of the Rhine was the quietest it has been in recent weeks.

The COLMAR sector has been split by juncture of our units from the north and south sides at ROUFFACH.

Near the Rhine, the road from NEU-BREISACH to the Rhine bridges at VIEUX BREISACH was cut and the village of VOGELSHEIM, just south of the road and one mile east of NEU-BREISACH, was reached.

The west bank of the Ill river has been almost completely cleared of the enemy.

In the high Vosges mountains, enemy units which were cut off are being pursued through difficult terrain. MITTLACH and MUHLBACH in the upper Fecht river valley were liberated, and WALBACH in the lower valley was cleared.

In the south GUEBWILLER and a number of nearby towns were liberated. During the four days ending with February 3, Allied forces in the West captured 6,912 prisoners.

Bad weather prevented air operations yesterday. Last night BERLIN was bombed by a force of light bombers.

Members of the 517th Parachute Infantry Regiment, attached to the 82nd Airborne Division, carry one of their wounded to be evacuated near Bergstein, Germany. When this photograph was released, the SHAEF censor chose the opportunity to give figures for US armed forces casualties since the American declaration of war in December 1941. Up to February 9, 1945, 163,458 had been killed, 436,424 wounded, 101,349 missing and 63,353 taken prisoner.

Link-up in the Colmar Pocket (see map page 279). In the early hours of February 5, Combat Command A of the 12th Armored Division entered Rouffach having driven south from Colmar which had been liberated on the 3rd. A battle-group of the 1ère Division Blindée then reached the town from the south but when its commander, Chef d'Escadron Jacques de Bertereche de Menditte (left), met Brigadier General Riley F. Ennis (right) commanding CCA of the 12th Armored Division, Ennis pointed out that Rouffach lay within the XXI Corps sector of action, not that of the Ier Corps d'Armée. He therefore asked that the French combat command be moved beyond the boundary. The French commander immediately concurred and issued orders to resume the advance east using another route more to the south which ran through Munwiller.

COMMUNIQUE No. 305   February 7

Allied forces northeast of MONSCHAU have pushed 1,000 yards south from BERGSTEIN against minefields and defended pillboxes, and to the southwest we have gained 500 yards to a point approximately one mile west of SCHMIDT. Our infantry elements have pushed another 1,000 yards to the east of STECKENBORN.

South of Urftstausee, we have reached the area one and one-half miles east of MORSBACH. SCHEUREN, one-half mile northwest of SCHLEIDEN, is in our hands and heavy fighting continues in HELLENTHAL, three miles southwest of SCHLEIDEN.

Our forces have captured SCHLAUSENBACH on the edge of the Schnee Eifel forest and we have made small gains in the forest southeast of SCHLAUSENBACH. Southwest of the forest a counter-attack in the vicinity of BRANDSCHEID resulted in stiff fighting. Farther southwest our units have taken HABSCHEID. Southwest of HABSCHEID, we have captured GROSSKAMPENBERG and LUTZKAMPEN.

East of the Moselle river in the REMICH area, we repulsed a small counter-attack in the woods one-half mile south-east of TETTINGEN.

Between the battle area and the Rhine, medium and light bombers attacked the communications centers of SOTENICH, MUNSTEREIFEL and WITTLICH, and an ammunition dump at RHEINBACH. Fighter-bombers struck at fortified places in the EUSKIRCHEN—MAYEN area.

In the southern Alsace plain we have occupied NEU-BREISACH. The western approaches to the Rhine bridges leading to VIEUX BREISACH were taken and further progress was made to the south between the Rhine and the Rhine-Rhone canal.

To the southwest, the Ill river was crossed at a number of points and we continued to make gains in the direction of the Rhine-Rhone canal. The villages of BATTENHEIM, BALDERSHEIM and SAUSHEIM, northeast of MULHOUSE were liberated.

Enemy troops in the HARDT FOREST were strafed and a rail yard at VIEUX BREISACH was attacked by fighter-bombers.

Communication targets in Holland and northwest Germany were attacked yesterday by medium and fighter-bombers. A bridge at DEVENTER was the target for escorted medium bombers, whilst fighter-bombers struck at bridges, locomotives and rolling stock and cut rail lines, particularly in central Holland and to the north and northeast of the Ruhr. A fuel dump at EMMERICH was attacked by medium bombers, and fighter-bombers attacked an ammunition dump at AMERSFOORT and an oil storage plant north of LINGEN. A vehicle depot at BERG-GLADBACH was attacked by medium and light bombers.

Fighter-bombers struck at motor transport, rail yards and rolling stock in the DUSSELDORF area; rail yards in the region of WURZBURG, LANDAU and TRIER; and rolling stock and motor transport in the TRIER and KARLSRUHE areas.

Rail yards at RASTATT and OFFENBURG and a rail bridge at RASTATT were targets for fighter-bombers, which also attacked rolling stock near RASTATT and MAHLBERG.

More than 1,300 heavy bombers escorted by more than 850 fighters attacked rail yards and industrial targets at MAGDEBURG and CHEMNITZ and other points over a wide area of central Germany. Many of the escort strafed ground targets in western Germany, destroying three enemy aircraft on the ground and destroying or damaging locomotives, freight cars and military vehicles.

Late on February 5, the 15th Infantry (3rd Division) reached the Rhine — the first American troops to touch the river marking the official end of the battle. However, both the road and rail bridge *(above)* had been blown by the retreating Germans. Four days later when the count had been finalised, SHAEF claimed to have taken 17,400 prisoners while German casualties were over 5,000 — half of whom had been killed.

Before the war, Breisach was the frontier station on the Freiburg to Colmar international railway line. But the railway bridge was never rebuilt. A new road bridge using the same piers was opened in 1961.

In the lower Alsace plain the advance down the corridor between the Rhine and the Rhine-Rhone canal reached points seven miles south of NEU-BREISACH. The villages of HEITEREN, BALGAU and FESSENHEIM were liberated.

The west bank of the Rhine-Rhone canal has been entirely cleared of the enemy. Crossings were made near Ile Napoleon at the junction of the Rhine-Rhone and Huningue canals.

In the Vosges mountains organised enemy resistance has been broken. Mopping-up of isolated enemy groups continues.

Allied forces in the west captured 2,905 prisoners 5 February.

Bad weather severely restricted air operations yesterday.

An enemy railhead at LIPP, 16 miles west of COLOGNE, was attacked without loss by a small force of medium bombers. Escorted heavy bombers struck at objectives in western Germany.

Last night enemy troops and equipment in CLEVE and GOCH between the Maas and Rhine rivers were attacked by heavy bombers operating in great strength. Targets at MAGDEBURG, KASSEL, MAINZ, COBLENZ, BONN, HANNOVER, DUSSELDORF and DUISBURG were struck at by light bombers.

COMMUNIQUE No. 306   February 8

Allied forces in the area northeast of MONSCHAU have encountered heavily defended minefields between BERGSTEIN and the Kall river. Our infantry elements have advanced more than 1,000 yards to the edge of KOMMERSCHEIDT, one-half mile northwest of SCHMIDT, and our armor has pushed to within 500 yards of SCHMIDT, west of the town. In this area we have taken 159 enemy pillboxes during the past three days.

Southwest of SCHLEIDEN our forces have cleared the enemy from HELLENTHAL, after several days of fighting in the town against stubborn resistance.

In the area north and northwest of PRUM, our infantry has reached WASCHEID, and the towns of HONTHEIM and SELLERICH are in our hands. Southwest of PRUM we have taken HOLLNICH.

Our forces have launched attacks across the Our and Sauer rivers at several places on a front extending from the area northeast of CLERVAUX to the vicinity of ECHTERNACH. The crossings were impeded by high water and enemy obstacles on the eastern bank. We have made gains over the Our near DASBURG, four miles east of CLERVAUX, and in the area of WALLENDORF, six miles east of DIEKIRCH. Other infantry elements crossed in the vicinity of ECHTERNACH and have made gains of more than 800 yards in the area northeast of the town.

Southeast of REMICH our forces have captured SINZ.

East of SAARGEMUND an enemy attack by an estimated 100 infantry was repulsed without loss of ground. Our forces raided BUCHHOLZ east of the Hardt mountains, inflicted casualties and took prisoners.

Our efforts to clear the northern part of OBERHOFFEN, near HAGUENAU, were stubbornly resisted. Farther east, our forward elements received considerable fire from DRUSENHEIM.

These photos of a rocket assembly mounted on a Sherman were taken on February 8 when the 80th Division was fighting in the Wallendorf area although they were not released for publication by the SHAEF censor in London until March 10.

Eighty 4.5-inch rockets could be fired independently or as a salvo and when all had been fired the empty rack would be jettisoned. This night shot was taken somewhere on the Seventh Army front in northern Alsace.

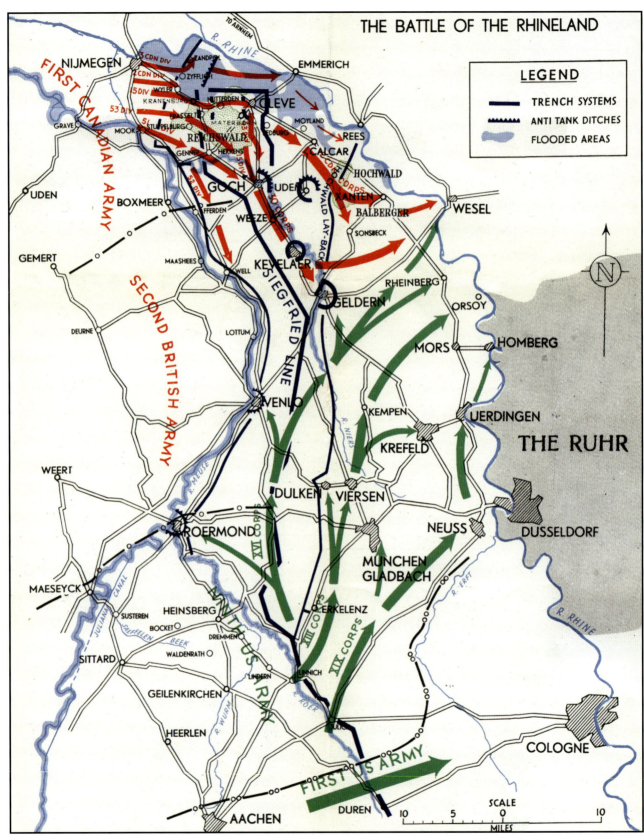

On February 8, the First Canadian Army launched Operation 'Veritable', a massive offensive designed to conquer the northern half of the German Rhineland and obtain positions favourable for a later assault across the Rhine. From jump-off positions near Nijmegen in the Netherlands, British XXX Corps (operating under Canadian command) launched three British and two Canadian infantry divisions in a concentrated assault towards the south-east and into Germany. Their area of operations was narrow and constricted by the Rhine river in the north and the Maas river in the south. Prime obstacles to their advance was the Reichswald Forest, an impenetrable area of dense woodland right on the Dutch-German frontier, stretching some nine miles from east to west and five miles from north to south. Through it ran the northern spur of the Siegfried Line, its defensive fortifications anchored on the towns of Cleve in the north and Goch in the south. In two weeks of grim and costly fighting, the British and Canadians battled their way through and past the forest, overcoming mud, rain, floods and fierce German resistance. By February 21 they had emerged from the woods, broken through the Siegfried Line and captured both Cleve and Goch. This is Field-Marshal Montgomery's own map — the US Ninth Army having been transferred to 21st Army Group to carry out Operation 'Grenade' — the assault across the Roer.

The North Shore Regiment of the 3rd Canadian Division move out from Nijmegen on February 8. Because the Germans had blown the Rhine dykes, much of the land bordering the river was flooded and torrential rain, which had been falling for four days, caused the water level to rise even further — hence the troops had to use DUKWs and tracked Alligators.

COMMUNIQUE No. 307   February 9

Allied forces have launched an attack in the area southeast of NIJMEGEN. Heavy air support was provided during the night preceding the attack when GOCH and CLEVE were bombed. Good initial progress has been made and our forward elements have reached the western edges of the REICHSWALD forest. Fighting is in progress in the outer defences of the Siegfried Line.

The enemy's supply lines, strong points, gun positions, troop concentrations, armor and transport in the NIJMEGEN battle area were attacked yesterday by medium, light and fighter-bombers, in considerable strength. Fighters provided protection overhead and patrolled the enemy's airfields.

We have taken the town of KOMMERSCHEIDT, and are fighting in SCHMIDT and HARSCHEIDT in the area northeast of MONSCHAU.

Farther to the south, our infantry elements have captured OBERMEHLEN, two miles northwest of PRUM.

In the area northeast of CLERVAUX, our armored elements have made gains to a point about one and one-half miles from DAHNEN and other forces have reached DASBURG.

WALLENDORF, at the junction of the Our and Sauer rivers, is in our hands. We repulsed a counter-attack by enemy infantry and tanks one and one-half miles north of ECHTERNACH.

Fighter-bombers attacked rail communications, railway yards and rolling stock between COLOGNE and MAYEN and in the Cologne plain, and hit the railway bridge at LIMBURG.

In the Luxembourg sector, other fighter-bombers hit fortified positions, tanks and armored vehicles and attacked targets at FERSCHWEILER and ERNZEN.

East of the Hardt mountains our ground forces raided KINDWEILER, inflicted casualties and took prisoners.

The enemy was driven from several of his strong points in the OBERHOFFEN area, southeast of HAGUENAU. Near the Rhine in this sector, HERRLISHEIM and OFFENDORF were found to have been evacuated by the enemy.

In the lower Alsace plain the enemy was pressed back to a narrow strip along the line between the Hardt forest and the river. Advance elements reached CHALAMPE in the center of this strip. The villages of MUNCHHAUSEN, ROGGENHAUSEN, NAMBSHEIM, BLODELSHEIM and RUMERSHEIM, northwest and north of CHALAMPE, and HOMBURG to the southwest were liberated.

Allied forces in the West captured 4,063 prisoners 6 February.

Medium and fighter-bombers struck at communications in the upper Rhine valley and eastward. Railway bridges at RASTATT, HORNBERG, LOFFINGEN and NEUENBURG and marshalling yards at FREIBURG were bombed, and communications, transport and troop barracks in the COLMAR area were attacked. Targets at STAUFEN, southwest of FREIBURG, also were hit.

Escorted heavy bombers attacked with 12,000-pound bombs the E-Boat shelters at IJMUIDEN.

During the night heavy bombers were over Germany in very great strength. The synthetic oil plant at POLITZ and other targets were attacked. Light bombers attacked BERLIN. Other light bombers attacked German movements from NIJMEGEN to DUREN and eastward.

Karel Margry's comparison taken on Ubbergseweg shows the same pumping station on the Waal river at Nijmegen.

Then, as soon as the attack began, German engineers blew the sluices of the Quer-Dam which gave way under the pressure. Whole areas then disappeared under water. This is Leuth between the Waal river and the Nijmegen—Cleve road.

COMMUNIQUE No. 308   February 10

The Allied offensive in the area southeast of NIJMEGEN continues to make good progress.

In spite of stiff enemy resistance from his prepared positions, difficult terrain, numerous minefields and anti-tank obstacles, our units have captured ZYFFLICH, NIEL, KRANENBURG, FRASSELT and BREDEWEG and are fighting in the western fringe of the REICHSWALD forest.

Southeast of the battle area enemy troops and equipment just east of the REICHSWALD forest and at GOCH, GELDERN and RHEINBERG were attacked by medium, light and fighter-bombers. East of WESEL a road bridge spanning the railway line was destroyed by rocket-firing fighters which also hit Rhine river traffic in the area.

Our forces have cleared the towns of HARSCHEIDT and SCHMIDT in the area northeast of MONSCHAU, against stiff resistance and have advanced to HASENFELD, two miles southeast of SCHMIDT.

Farther south, in the area north of PRUM, our infantry captured OLZHEIM and entered the town of NEUENDORF. Other elements have captured the towns of GONDENBRETT, HERMESPAND and NIEDERMEHLEN. West of PRUM, our forces are three-fourths of a mile from the town.

Across the Our river in the area five and one-half miles northeast of CLERVAUX, our units have gained one-half mile. Other elements farther southeast have pushed 1,000 yards in the area one and one-half miles southeast of WALLENDORF. North of the Our river, one and one-half miles northwest of WALLENDORF, two infantry counter-attacks were repulsed.

The BANNHOLZ wood, one-half mile northeast of SINZ, has been cleared by our troops. A counter-attack by tanks and infantry in this area was repulsed.

Enemy artillery activity was increased along the sector east of the Hardt mountains.

East of HAGUENAU in the Rhine valley, OBERHOFFEN was cleared except for a few houses in the northwestern section of the town. Patrols in the DRUSENHEIM region farther east drew strong hostile reactions.

In southern Alsace all organised enemy resistance on the west bank of the Rhine has ceased. Allied forces in the West captured 1,049 prisoners 7 February.

The communications centre of KEMPEN and railway yards at VIERSEN, RHEYDT, and GREVENBROICH were struck at by medium and light bombers. Fighter-bombers attacked railway yards at EUSKIRCHEN, COBLENZ, TRIER, KAISERSLAUTERN and WURZBURG, and a rail junction at WENGEROHR, northeast of TRIER. Rail bridges at SINZIG and NEUWIED, northwest of COBLENZ, were attacked by small formations of medium and light bombers.

Rail traffic over a wide area ranging from MANNHEIM south to the German-Swiss frontier, rail bridges at RASTATT, HORNBERG and OFFENBURG, enemy barracks at DONAUESCHINGEN and road traffic near OBERKIRCH were targets for medium and fighter-bombers.

Escorted heavy bombers in very great strength attacked the synthetic oil plant at LUTZKENDORF, south of HALLE; an ordnance and motor transport factory at WEIMAR; oil installations and railroad marshalling yards at MAGDEBURG and other communications targets in Germany. Escorting fighters shot down 23 enemy aircraft, destroyed 41 others on the ground and strafed rail transport.

From all operations, according to reports so far received, 19 heavy bombers and five fighters are missing. Last night light bombers attacked a road and rail movement in Holland in western Germany.

The peaceful Steenheuvelsestraatweg today with No. 16 on the right.

Across the frontier! Here soldiers of the 5th/7th Gordon Highlanders pass the 'Reichs-Grenze' sign at Grafwegen about six miles south-east of Nijmegen. They are just about to enter the Reichswald Forest at its western extremity.

Somehow the thrill of crossing a frontier has been lost with the opening of European borders. All that remains today to mark the division between Holland and Germany on Alte Grafwegener Strasse is Boundary Marker Post 593.

COMMUNIQUE No. 309   February 11

The Allied offensive southeast of NIJMEGEN continues over very difficult terrain. South of WYLER the town of HEIKANT has been captured and our units have penetrated the REICHSWALD forest and captured SCHOTTHEIDE. More than 3,000 prisoners have been counted to date.

In the NIJMEGEN sector supply dumps, gun positions and enemy troops and transport south and southeast of the REICHSWALD forest and between GOCH and GELDERN were attacked by fighter-bombers. Farther to the rear of the enemy lines, factory buildings near WESEL and BOCHOLT were hit by rocket-firing fighters while medium and fighter-bombers struck at communications at XANTEN and BORKEN and attacked rail and road transport in the GUTERSLOH and BIELEFELD areas.

Allied forces have reached the northern end of the SCHWAMMENAUEL DAM despite heavy artillery and mortar fire. All flood-gates have been blown by the enemy, but the dam itself remains intact. Conduits leading from the backed-up waters of the URFTTALSPERRE DAM to a point downstream from the SCHWAMMENAUEL DAM have been blown open, causing a rise of three feet in the Roer river. The town of HASENFELD, 1,200 yards east of SCHWAMMENAUEL DAM, has been captured, and patrols have pushed to the Roer river east and northeast of the town.

In the area north of PRUM we have captured NEUENDORF, and have reached WILLWERATH. Other units made gains up to three-quarters of a mile and are a little more than one-half mile northwest of PRUM, and have reached the high ground two and one-half miles northeast of the town. In the NIEDERMEHLEN area two enemy counter-attacks, each made by two to three infantry companies and led by five tanks, were repulsed. Four of the ten tanks were knocked out.

Allied elements across the Sauer river, in the area two and one-half miles northwest of BOLLENDORF, have gained three-quarters of a mile to the northeast.

Communications and rail and road transport from KEMPEN to TRIER and eastward to the Rhine were attacked by medium, light and fighter-bombers. Motor repair depots at BERG-GLADBACH and MUNSTEREIFEL were bombed by other medium and light bombers.

Fortified towns of METTENDORF, KRUCHTEN, BETTINGEN and PEFFINGEN were hit by fighter-bombers.

Southeast of HAGUENAU near the Rhine, our forces crossed the Moder river and captured a railway station northwest of OBERHOFFEN. Further progress was made towards clearing OBERHOFFEN. Our attack on nearby DRUSENHEIM was met by determined resistance and a strong tank-supported counter-attack which forced us to withdraw.

Several groups of prisoners were taken in mopping up operations in the COLMAR area.

Communications in northern Holland were attacked by fighter-bombers. A fuel depot at DULMEN and submarine pens at IJMUIDEN were targets for escorted heavy bombers.

Railway yards at KAISERSLAUTERN, ZWEIBRUCKEN and FREIBURG were bombed by fighter-bombers. HANNOVER was attacked during the night by light bombers. Other light bombers struck from dusk to dawn at enemy movements in the quadrilateral area formed by CLEVE, RHEINE, HAMM and COLOGNE.

Below: **This splendid photograph was released on February 11 with the caption: 'Monty speeds up Big Offensive'.**

COMMUNIQUE No. 310   February 12

Allied forces have occupied MILLINGEN, on the Dutch-German border east of NIJMEGEN, and KEEKEN across the border south of MILLINGEN. Our advance continues despite difficult ground conditions and stiffening resistance.

Fighting continues in the devastated town of CLEVE. We have made further progress in the REICHSWALD forest and have taken the towns of MIDDELAAR, OTTERSUM, and ZELDERHEIDE to the south.

Enemy troop concentrations northeast of the REICHSWALD forest and focal points for communications at KEVELAER and SONSBECK north of GELDERN were attacked by medium, light and fighter-bombers.

Our forces have cleared the enemy from the area north and west of the Roer river between the SCHWAMMENAUEL DAM and HEIMBACH.

West and southwest of PRUM, we have captured STEINMEHLEN and WEINSFELD and have pushed to the Prum river in several places from three-fourths of a mile to two miles southwest of PRUM.

Farther south, our units have cleared the enemy from BIESDORF, one mile northeast of WALLENDORF, and have advanced in the area north of ECHTERNACH to reach the outskirts of FERSCHWEILER.

Our forces in the SINZ area, southeast of REMICH, have repulsed two counter-attacks by infantry and tanks.

Southeast of HAGUENAU a tank-supported enemy counter-attack was repulsed in OBERHOFFEN after it had made initial gains. In stiff fighting our forces regained the lost ground and took 150 prisoners including a battalion commander. Hard fighting also continued in the vicinity of nearby DRUSENHEIM.

South of STRASBOURG enemy raids from east of the Rhine were repulsed.

Northeast of MULHOUSE harassing enemy artillery fire was received in the CHALAMPE-BANTZENHEIM area.

Transportation targets in northwest Germany were hit by fighter-bombers and rocket-firing fighters. Many locomotives and rail cars were destroyed or damaged and barges, tugs and road vehicles were shot up.

Medium and light bombers struck at railway yards at MODRATH and KIERBERG near COLOGNE and at BINGEN. Bridges, rolling stock and railway lines mainly west of the Rhine in the areas of COLOGNE, BONN and COBLENZ, and rail traffic in the upper Rhine region northwest and southwest of MANNHEIM, and at HEILBRONN, were the principal targets for other fighter-bombers.

In Holland fighter-bombers struck at rail supply routes, German units moving in the ROTTERDAM area and an airfield and barracks at STEENWIJK, north of ZWOLLE.

Escorted heavy bombers attacked a motor fuel depot at DULMEN southwest of MUNSTER.

One enemy aircraft was destroyed during the day. Eight of our fighters are missing.

Spoils of war! Five miles north of Grafwegen in Kranenburg the crooked cross comes rolling down Adolf Hitler Strasse. According to the caption, Privates H. McIvor of Glasgow, W. Harton of Durham and D. Mills of Dumbartonshire of the Highland Light Infantry, told the photographer that they intended to use the sign for firewood.

Although frontages have been modernised, the Hotel zur Post is still open for business on what is now renamed Grosse Strasse.

The Highlanders were then pictured in Nütterden, the next village just a mile further east, where they displayed a Nazi Party flag and guild standard outside the Wilhelm Vinck pub/restaurant — remarkably unchanged seven decades later.

Cleve, north-east of the Reichswald, was entered from the west by Scottish troops. This photograph was taken on Tiergarten-Strasse.

COMMUNIQUE No. 311   February 13

Allied forces have reached the line of the railway running north from CLEVE to the Rhine. CLEVE has been cleared except for a few snipers, and to the south of the town our forces have reached HAU.

Further progress has been made through the REICHSWALD forest and to the southwest we have occupied HEKKENS and GENNEP.

East of the Belgian-German border the town of PRUM has been virtually cleared. Some enemy mortar, artillery and small-arms fire is being received in the town. WATZERATH, three miles southwest of PRUM has been captured. Our units have gained one-half mile to a point two miles southeast of HABSCHEID. Other elements pushed to an area four and one-half miles southwest of PRUM near the Prum river. Farther southwest HARSPELT has been taken and we are fighting in SEVENIG four miles east of WEISWAMPACH.

Farther south, our forces have entered VIANDEN where fighting continues. BOLLENDORF has been cleared and our units are one-fourth mile west of FERSCHWEILER. Other elements have reached the vicinity of ERNZEN, two miles north of ECHTERNACH.

The enemy forced his way into the factory area of OBERHOFFEN, near the Rhine in northern Alsace. Additional small enemy units which infiltrated other parts of the town were dispersed. Hard fighting has been in progress in OBERHOFFEN for ten days.

An explosion damaged the superstructure of the MARKT DAM across the east channel of the Rhine near the Swiss border.

Allied forces in the West captured 2,536 prisoners 9 February.

Bad weather yesterday restricted air operations. STUTTGART and targets in western Germany were attacked last night by a force of light bombers.

Left: Meanwhile, on the other side of the Reichswald, having broken out into the open countryside south of the forest, the 153rd Brigade of the 51st Division attacked and captured the town of Gennep on the night of February 10/11. This was an important objective as it was where an extra Bailey bridge across the Maas was planned to ease supply for the 'Veritable' offensive. However, heavy fighting broke out immediately to the south of it, which lasted for the next four days. On the 12th, Sergeant Johnny Silverside pictured a platoon of the Black Watch rushing the next house up the main street under cover of smoke.

With Cleve taken, the Allies prepared to break out south to Goch and east to Calcar. Blocking the way towards the latter town was Moyland Wood, a forested spur stretching eastwards from a point just east of Cleve to just south of the village of Moyland which was named after Schloss Moyland *(left)*, an 18th-century castle which stood just north of the Cleve-Calcar road. It took the Canadians six days of bitter and costly fighting to capture both the wood and castle. *Right:* Gutted by fire in 1956 and now restored, it presently houses a museum of modern art.

Of the many raids that assailed German towns and cities during Operation 'Overlord', none came close to the destruction wrought on Dresden in February 1945. For several months the Air Ministry had been considering dealing knock-out blows to selected targets and now that Germany was fighting to defend its own territory on two fronts, the time had come to put what was called Operation 'Thunderclap' to the test. The cities on the Eastern Front that were considered the best to attack, both to help the Soviet Army and also prevent reinforcements being switched to the west, were Berlin, Chemnitz, Dresden and Leipzig. As Dresden had been largely untouched, it was singled out for the opening shot in a combined attack to be carried out by Bomber Command and the Eighth Air Force. However, the weather on February 13 was too poor to carry out the opening daylight raid by the Americans so it fell to the RAF to follow that night. In the first phase, over 800 aircraft dropped more than 2,600 tons of high explosive and incendiaries, followed three hours later by a further 1,800 tons from over 500 Lancasters in the second wave. The combined effect was to create a firestorm which was stoked the following day by more that 300 B-17s dropping over 750 tons. At the same time, fighter-bombers strafed traffic on the surrounding roads. The death toll has never accurately been determined as Dresden was full of refugees retreating in front of the approaching Red Army but a figure of 50,000-plus has been suggested, certainly making it the most destructive raid since D-Day. Symbol of the devastation was the ruin of the Frauenkirche which caught fire and collapsed on the 15th.

COMMUNIQUE No. 312   February 14

Allied forces east of NIJMEGEN have occupied GRIETHAUSEN south of the Rhine river. We have also made progress to the east of CLEVE and have cleared most of the REICHSWALD forest despite stronger enemy resistance.

East of GENNEP our troops have extended their bridgehead across the Niers river.

Enemy positions east of the REICHSWALD forest and troop concentrations at KAPELLEN and SONSBECK to the southeast were repeatedly attacked by rocket-firing fighters and fighter-bombers. Focal communication points at WEEZE, UDEM, KEVELAER and XANTEN were struck at by medium and light bombers.

We have cleared the enemy from PRUM, and have repulsed two counter-attacks by infantry and tanks, one and one-half miles northeast of the town.

Farther to the south, our forces have taken VIANDEN, on the Our river. Our infantry east of the river has captured AMMELDINGEN, two miles northwest of WALLENDORF, against stiff resistance.

North of ECHTERNACH, we have taken FERSCHWEILER and have reached a point one-fourth mile west of ERNZEN.

Across the Sauer river from ECHTERNACH the town of ECHTERNACHERBRUCK has been captured, and we have captured a number of pillboxes in the vicinity of the town. Our bridgehead across the Sauer and Our rivers is now ten and one-half miles wide and two and one-fourth miles deep.

Fighter-bombers attacked targets in the battle area east of VIANDEN and north of ECHTERNACH.

Enemy activity increased somewhat in the Hardt mountains and northern Alsace plain. The enemy was particularly active north of PFAFFENHOFEN where our patrols encountered heavy small-arms fire. At OBERHOFFEN, southeast of HAGUENAU, the factory area which German forces penetrated was cleared.

Harassing enemy artillery fire was received at several points on the upper Rhine.

The enemy's rail system for the supply and reinforcement of his forces were strongly attacked throughout the day. Northeast and east of the Ruhr fighter-bombers and rocket-firing fighters disabled or damaged a large number of locomotives and hit other rail and road transport.

Rail yards and other communication targets mainly west of the Rhine from DÜSSELDORF to COLOGNE, and rail traffic concentrations at NEUENKIRCHEN, ZWEIBRUCKEN and GRUNSTADT, and from KARLSRUHE south to the German-Swiss frontier were hit by formations of fighter-bombers. Other fighter-bombers struck at rail transport and supply routes in Holland.

Medium, light and fighter-bombers attacked motor vehicle depots at SCHWELM and ISERLOHN in the Ruhr, railway bridges at EUSKIRCHEN, SINZIG, NEUWIED-IRLICH, and southwest of NEUSS and targets at WITTLICH, northeast of TRIER, and SOBERNHEIM, north of KAISERSLAUTERN.

Last night heavy bombers in very great strength attacked DRESDEN and the synthetic oil plant at BOHLEN, south of LEIPZIG. MAGDEBURG was also bombed. Light bombers continued attacks on rail and road communications north and west of the Ruhr.

The Communist regime decided to leave the ruin which was officially declared a war memorial in 1966, possibly as a counterpart to the remains of Coventry Cathedral destroyed by the Luftwaffe in November 1940. Each year citizens came to pay their respects on the anniversary of the raid but it was not until the East German government fell in 1989 — leading to the reunification of Germany — that a project was launched to rebuild the cathedral. Back in the 18th century, the Frauenkirche had taken 17 years to construct but the replacement, following the original plans and using as much of the original stonework as possible, took 11 years from the laying of the foundation stone to topping out with a British-made gilded cross. It was finished in time to be dedicated on the 800th anniversary of the founding of Dresden in 2006.

COMMUNIQUE No. 313   February 15

Allied forces northeast of CLEVE continued to advance despite flooding in the area. Our units have cleared the REICHSWALD forest and have repulsed counter-attacks to the south of BEDBURG. South of GENNEP we made further progress against strong resistance.

Troop concentrations, transport, gun positions, and strong points in the REICHSWALD forest area, and at KEVELAER, GELDERN, XANTEN and east of WESEL, were heavily attacked by medium, light and fighter-bombers.

A strong patrol was dispersed by Allied artillery in the vicinity of HELLENTHAL, southwest of SCHLEIDEN. In the northern part of PRUM our forces repulsed a counter-attack made by enemy units which crossed the river from the east.

In the ECHTERNACH sector we have reached the area two and one-half miles north of BOLLENDORF. Other elements pushed northeast of HERSCHWEILER to a point one-half mile from the PRUM river. ERNZEN, north of ECHTERNACH, has been cleared of the enemy after stiff fighting, and our units are three-fourths of a mile northeast of the town.

Southeast of REMICH we continued to make gains in the area northwest of SINZ.

The sector west of the Hardt mountains and in the northern Alsace plain was quiet. OBERHOFFEN has been cleared.

The estimate of prisoners taken in clearing the COLMAR area has increased to approximately 20,000. Allied forces in the West captured 5,087 prisoners 10, 11 and 12 February.

Throughout yesterday communications and rail and road transport behind the enemy front in western Germany from EMMERICH in the north to FREIBURG in the south, eastward into Germany and along the Rhine valley were struck at by medium, light and fighter-bombers in very great strength. A large number of locomotives, railway cars and motor vehicles were destroyed, rail lines were cut in very many places and several bridges were bombed.

Trains and transport targets at DRESDEN, CHEMNITZ and MAGDEBURG and a road bridge across the Rhine at WESEL were attacked by 1,350 escorted heavy bombers. Locomotives, railway cars and rail lines over a wide area of

Oberhoffen, on the eastern outskirts of Haguenau, reported captured today, was a tough nut to crack. Having successfully crossed the River Moder, the 142nd Infantry of the 36th Division and CCB of the 14th Armored Division then had to fight for the town street by street. By February 9, SHAEF reported that a 90-mile stretch of the Rhine — from Strasbourg south to the Swiss border — was in Allied hands as well as another 14,000 prisoners.

Germany were strafed by the escorting fighters.

Supply dumps, troop barracks and a railway yard at LABACH, near SAARBRUCKEN, and a factory near KARLSRUHE were attacked by medium bombers.

Last night heavy bombers were out in very great strength. CHEMNITZ, the main objective, was attacked twice and another strong force attacked the synthetic oil plant at ROSITZ, south of LEIPZIG. BERLIN also was bombed. Enemy movements in northwest Germany were attacked by light bombers.

Oberhoffen today, looking south down Rue Principale from the main village crossroad. Only a few of the original houses remain.

Schmidt, at the crossroads of the Hürtgen Forest, had been captured on February 9 by troops of the First Army advancing on the huge Schwammenauel Dam. Just as T/4 Moore was taking this shot in the ruins of the town on February 17, a shell burst in the background yet the men of the 82nd Airborne Division did not flinch and just kept on marching unconcerned.

STRASBOURG and SAVERNE underwent hostile shelling.

Allied forces in the West captured 1,499 prisoners 13 February.

Rail bridges at SINZIG, MAYEN and BREMM, rail traffic and other communications targets west of the Rhine from COLOGNE to southwest of COBLENZ were attacked by medium, light and fighter-bombers.

North of Alsace and east of the upper Rhine other medium and fighter-bombers in strength attacked six railway yards, including those at OFFENBURG, which were hit twice during the day. Other targets were road transport, armored vehicles, supply dumps and barracks.

Transportation targets in DRESDEN and COTTBUS and a synthetic oil refinery near MAGDEBURG were attacked by more than 1,100 escorted heavy bombers. Rail transport was strafed by some of the escorting fighters.

In other areas bad weather restricted air operations.

During the day six enemy aircraft were shot down and five others were destroyed on the ground. Fifteen of our heavy bombers, one medium bomber and nine fighters are missing.

COMMUNIQUE No. 314   February 16

Allied forces have captured WARBEYEN, northeast of CLEVE, and advanced beyond it toward the Rhine. South of the REICHSWALD forest we have extended our bridgehead across the river Niers and captured KESSEL and HOMMERSUM, despite stiffening enemy resistance.

Fortified towns in the PRUM sector were attacked by our fighter-bombers.

In the area northwest of ECHTERNACH, our ground units gained one-half mile northward against strong resistance to reach high ground one mile southeast of CRUCHTEN. A quarter-mile gain was made to the area one and a half miles north of FRESCHWEILER and one mile west of the Prum river. Our units just north of ECHTERNACH continue to clear enemy pillboxes.

In the area southeast of REMICH we gained three-fourths of a mile against small-arms and mortar fire to reach a point one mile southeast of SINZ. A number of pillboxes were cleared in this operation.

In northern Alsace, west of HAGUENAU, an enemy raid across the Moder river following an artillery concentration was repulsed.

The Americans came into town from the south-west, advancing up Monschauer Strasse. Only one original house — No. 30 on the right — remains, as all the others are post-war.

The dam was finally reached after dark on February 9 when the 309th Infantry (78th Division) sent their 1st Battalion in to capture it. The party was split into two groups: one to gain the top of the dam while the other advanced on the lower level to take the power house. Engineers then went forward to check for demolition charges expecting it to be blown by the Germans at any moment. When the men found the entrance to the inspection tunnel on top blocked, there was no other way but to slide down the 200-foot face of the dam to the bottom exit of the tunnel. Although this was slow and treacherous, it was accomplished only to discover that the Germans had already destroyed the machinery in the power room and blown the discharge valves. So although there would be no major cascade of water, a steady flow would still create a long-lasting flood in the Roer valley.

Four miles north-west of Schmidt engineers have strung up camouflage netting to hide the heavy vehicle movements along the Germeter road. Taken by T/5 Edward Norbuth of the 165th Signal Photographic Company on February 17, SHAEF initially stamped the reverse of this print 'Confidential — not to be published' but then released it ten days later.

COMMUNIQUE No. 315   February 17

Allied forces have captured HUISBERDEN east of CLEVE. Farther south, heavy fighting continues along the CLEVE—CALCAR road, and to the east of the Cleve forest. Several enemy counter-attacks, with strong artillery support, were beaten off. Our bridgeheads over the Niers river have been extended.

In the NIJMEGEN sector communications centers and supply centers at REES, WEEZE, UDEM and WESEL were attacked by medium, light and a strong force of escorted heavy bombers while rocket-firing fighters and fighter-bombers went in immediately ahead of our advancing ground forces to attack blockhouses, earthworks, gun positions and fortified buildings south and southeast of the REICHSWALD forest.

Our ground units repulsed an attempt by the enemy to retake the bridge over the Prum river at HERMESPAND, northeast of PRUM.

North of ECHTERNACH, our forces gained one fourth mile to occupy high ground overlooking the Enz and Prum rivers. Northeast of ECHTERNACH, our units astride the ECHTERNACH—IRREL road cleared some enemy pillboxes and pushed to a point one-half mile from IRREL. East of ECHTERNACH, we gained one-half mile against strong resistance along the Sauer river, and other elements reached a point one-half mile northwest of MINDEN.

Fortified localities in the area of PRUM, BITBURG and SAARBURG were attacked by fighter-bombers.

Our patrols entered WASSERBILLIG, at the junction of the Sauer and Moselle rivers, but were forced to withdraw under enemy pressure. In the SINZ area, southeast of REMICH, enemy infantry and tanks made two counter-attacks against our forces and retook several pillboxes.

Allied forces in the West captured 1,258 prisoners 14 February.

Troop barracks and supply areas in the outskirts of LANDAU were hit by medium bombers. Fighter-bombers attacked fortified buildings northwest of HAGUENAU.

More than 1,000 escorted heavy bombers attacked railway yards at RHEINE, OSNABRUCK and HAMM, oil refineries at SALZBERGEN and near DORTMUND and benzol plants near DORTMUND and GELSENKIRCHEN. Medium, light and fighter-bombers, in strength struck at communications, railway yards and rail and road transport north and east of the Ruhr and along the Rhine valley from EMMERICH in the north to OFFENBURG in the south. Rail lines were cut in many places and a large number of locomotives, railway cars and motor vehicles were destroyed.

An aircraft factory at SOLINGEN, and an ordnance factory at UNNA were attacked by a strong force of medium and light bombers and a chemical plant at LEVERKUSEN was hit by fighter-bombers.

At Lindern, five miles north-east of Geilenkirchen, things were more peaceful with Pfc Raleigh Campbell, a military policeman with the 84th Division, directing traffic. Taken on February 18, this picture was released without any restrictions on the 20th.

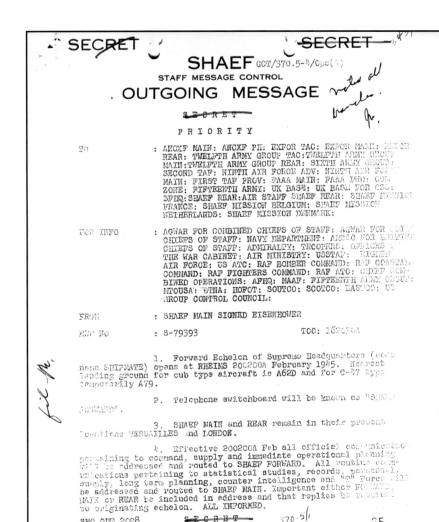

enemy from numerous concrete strong points, we captured HASSUM and AFFERDEN.

Our forces repulsed a counter-attack in the HERMESPAND area, northeast of PRUM, and our artillery fire broke up a concentration of tanks, vehicles and infantry one mile farther northeast.

Northwest of ECHTERNACH, we have entered ROHRBACH and SCHANKWEILER, and other elements have reached the high ground northwest of SCHANKWEILER. The bridgehead across the Sauer river at this point is now three and one-half miles in depth.

Along the ECHTERNACH—IRREL road we have made a half-mile gain and have occupied the high ground, two and one-fourth miles northeast of ECHTERNACH, overlooking the Prum river. During this push, our units captured a number of pillboxes against heavy machine-gun and mortar fire.

Two enemy attacks were repulsed in the SAARGEMUND area, one south of FORBACH and another in the vicinity of RIMLINGEN. One of them was made by armored forces, the other by infantry in battalion strength. Our forces, aided by accurate artillery fire, inflicted heavy losses on the enemy.

Allied forces in the West captured 1,090 prisoners 15 February.

Weather severely restricted air operations in many areas yesterday. Railroad yards at FRANKFURT ON MAIN and GIESSEN were attacked by heavy bombers. Fighters which provided the escort, and fighter-bombers, struck at transportation targets in the region of FRANKFURT and LIMBURG and in the MUNICH and ULM areas. A railway bridge at MAYEN spanning the Nette river was attacked by medium bombers. An enemy troop train near BITBURG, northeast of ECHTERNACH, was hit by fighter-bombers. From these operations two heavy bombers and two fighters are missing.

COMMUNIQUE No. 316   February 18

Southeast of CLEVE the Allied advance has made good progress against stiff opposition. After capturing LOUISENDORF our units cut the main road between CALCAR and GOCH, bastion town in the Siegfried defense belt. We are converging on GOCH from the north and northwest having taken HERVORST and ASPERDEN. Our bridgehead over the Niers river has been further extended, and after clearing the

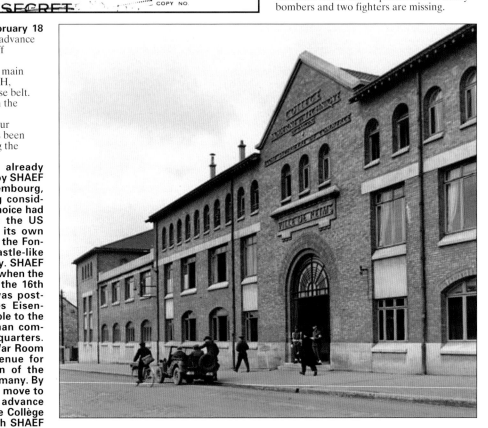

A modern, three-storey building, constructed in 1931 on the Rue Henri Jolicoeur, this was the building which is often referred to in contemporary accounts as the 'little red schoolhouse'.

Back in October, plans were already being made for the next move by SHAEF Forward, Verdun, Reims, Luxembourg, Liège, Metz and Spa all being considered. By early December, the choice had fallen on Luxembourg where the US Third Army was establishing its own headquarters and war room in the Fondation Pescatore, a large castle-like building in the centre of the city. SHAEF wanted the same building but, when the Germans counter-attacked on the 16th in the Ardennes, the move was postponed and even at Versailles Eisenhower was considered vulnerable to the perceived threat from a German commando assault on his headquarters. In the event, the Third Army War Room became a useful front-line venue for planning the final elimination of the Bulge and the advance into Germany. By mid-February, SHAEF began its move to Reims and on the 20th the advance party began operating from the Collège Moderne et Technique although SHAEF records the name of the school as the 'École Professionelle'. (Now it is the Lycée Franklin Roosevelt.)

On February 19 at Warden, seven miles north-east of Aachen, the 1st Battalion of the 117th Infantry Regiment (30th Infantry Division) claimed to have held the first battle parade on German soil. The unit had its origins with National Guard units from Tennessee, Georgia, and North and South Carolina. As the 1st Battalion had distinguished itself in the battle at Saint-Barthélemy near Mortain on August 7, so every member was being awarded a Presidential Citation Medal Ribbon for their 'outstanding courage and performance in frustrating the enemy attack'.

COMMUNIQUE No. 317 February 19

Between the Rhine and the Maas, Allied forces are advancing against stronger enemy opposition. Fierce fighting continues in the outskirts of MOYLAND, and to the north of GOCH, where our troops cleared the Cleve forest and advanced to a point one mile from the town. Heavy fighting continues in the AFFERDEN area.

Communications at WESEL were heavily attacked by heavy bombers.

There was some patrol activity by the enemy in the vicinity of GEMUND and east of HELLENTHAL and Allied forces contained a small-scale counter-attack by enemy infantry in the area of UDENBRETH.

Southwest of PRUM, our elements reached high ground overlooking the Prum river, four and one half miles from PRUM.

Southeast of GROSSKAMPENBERG, our forces cleared KESFELD, and in the area southwest of KESFELD, we gained 1,000 yards. Other elements crossed the Our river and pushed one-half mile to the high ground three miles north of VIANDEN.

Northwest of ECHTERNACH our elements captured CRUCHTEN, and ROHRBACH, and entered HOMMERDINGEN. Farther east, we captured SCHANKWEILER and reached a point one mile north of the town. Other elements pushed one-half mile to the high ground overlooking the Prum river one mile east of SCHANKWEILER. Northeast of ECHTERNACH we captured a number of pillboxes in the area between PRUM and the Sauer rivers.

In the SAARLAUTERN bridgehead, two small counter-attacks by enemy infantry were repulsed.

A rail bridge at DOTTESFELD, north of COBLENZ, and the communications center at DAUN, east of PRUM, were attacked by escorted medium bombers.

In the SAARGEMUND area we repulsed two armor-supported attacks north of nearby AUERSMACHER, and our units captured 94 prisoners from three enemy infantry companies which infiltrated the wooded section.

Last night light bombers attacked MANNHEIM and bombed objectives in BERLIN.

Here Major General S. Leyland Hobbs, the commanding general of the 30th Infantry Division, pins the ribbon on Sergeant David M. Cantrell of the 1st Battalion Colour Party.

Every man in the battalion also received a copy of the Presidential Citation. According to the press report, machine-gun and artillery fire could be heard during the ceremony.

In the north, finally, with the help of two squadrons of AVRE tanks, Goch — the objective for Operation 'Veritable' — was captured. The German garrison commander surrendered on the 19th but confused fighting continued for another 48 hours. Here troops of the 53rd Division proceed down Bahnhofstrasse, the damage having been caused by a heavy raid by RAF Bomber Command on February 7/8.

COMMUNIQUE No. 318   February 20

Between the Rhine and the Maas rivers heavy fighting continues in the MOYLAND area where Allied forces made slight advances towards CALCAR. GOCH has been entered and most of the town has been cleared despite strong enemy opposition.

The communications center of WESEL again was attacked by heavy bombers.

Southwest of PRUM, our forces pushed more than a mile and captured the towns of UTTFELD and MASTHORN. Farther west, other elements captured LEIDENBORN.

Northwest of ECHTERNACH we have cleared NUSBAUM and NIEDERSGEGEN and have entered STOCKIGT. North of ECHTERNACH we have pushed to a point one and a fourth miles north of SCHANKWEILER and to the Prum river overlooking HOLSTHUM.

Northwest of BOLLENDORF, we have repulsed counter-attacks. East of ECHTERNACH, our elements pushed to within a mile of MINDEN.

Gains of up to one mile have been made by our units southeast of REMICH in the vicinity of MUNZINGER. In this operation we took 207 prisoners and 14 pillboxes.

Objectives from PRUM south to SAARBURG, in the battle zone southeast of SAARBRUCKEN, and in the KARLSRUHE area were attacked by fighter-bombers.

In the vicinity of FORBACH our forces have occupied OETINGEN and ETZLINGEN. Heavy losses were inflicted on the enemy. We are on high ground overlooking FORBACH.

North of SAARGEMUND the enemy was driven from the German town of AUERSMACHER where our units crossed the Sauer river.

Farther east we have occupied FRAUENBERG and FOLPERSVILLER. Barracks and supply dumps at LAHR, southeast of STRASBOURG, were hit by waves of escorted medium bombers.

Twelve rail centres, including RHEINE, MUNSTER, OSNABRUCK and SIEGEN, and industrial targets mainly in the Ruhr, were attacked by heavy bombers in very great strength. Rail and road traffic over an area of central Germany was heavily hit by many of the escorting fighters.

A motor depot at MECHERNICH, southwest of BONN, an ordnance depot at WIESBADEN, and rail bridges at NEUWIED-IRLICH and other areas east of the Rhine, were attacked by medium and light bombers. Fighter-bomber targets were rail yards east of COBLENZ, north of SAARBRUCKEN and in the region of the upper Rhine.

During the day eight enemy aircraft were shot down. One of our heavy bombers, one medium bomber, and nine fighters are missing according to reports so far received. Last night light bombers attacked targets at ERFURT in Saxony.

Members of the 51st Highland Division march down Mühlenstrasse and are about to reach Markt. Since the devastation of

1945, Goch has been largely rebuilt. (The full story of the Battle of Reichswald Forest was published in *After the Battle* No. 159.)

Reminiscent of a First World War battlefield with continuous trenches and shell-holes, this picture shows Hekkens crossroads (mis-spelt 'Heppens' in the wartime caption) on the southern edge of the Reichswald Forest which had been the scene of bitter fighting. It was an important road junction leading to the front but when the photograph was submitted to the SHAEF censor on February 22 publication was denied.

Our forces in the bridgehead at SAARLAUTERN repulsed a small counter-attack without loss of ground.

In the southern outskirts of FORBACH, stiff fighting resulted when we surrounded an enemy strong point.

South of SAARBRUCKEN, our elements have occupied several towns including ALSTINGEN, ZINZINGEN, HESSLING and GROSS BLITTERSDORF. Farther east, KLEIN BLITTERSDORF, on the German bank of the Saar river, has being cleared.

Supply dumps near PIRMASENS and LANDAU, and a train loaded with vehicles near EUTINGEN as well as rail centers at HASLACH, HAUSACH and VILLINGEN were attacked by fighter-bombers.

During the day strong forces of escorted heavy bombers attacked the rail center at NURNBERG. The escorting fighters shot down 14 enemy aircraft and strafed airfields and rail targets in southern Germany. They destroyed 39 enemy aircraft on the ground and destroyed or damaged large numbers of locomotives and rail cars.

From all of yesterday's operations, 16 bombers and 24 fighters are missing. Last night very strong forces of heavy bombers attacked DORTMUND, while light bombers attacked BERLIN and road and railways in and to the west of the Ruhr.

COMMUNIQUE No. 319   February 21

Allied forces between the Rhine and Maas river have beaten off infantry and armored counter-attacks launched in the area west of CALCAR. Our units in GOCH are mopping up the last remaining pockets of resistance in the southern part of the town.

East of the GOCH-CALCAR highway, we have captured the villages of HALVENDOOM and BUCHHOLT. Approximately 10,000 prisoners have been taken since the attack in the northern sector began.

Tanks and gun positions in the DUREN area and fortified buildings at BUIR to the northeast were attacked by fighter-bombers which also struck at rail yards near COBLENZ and in the region around KAISERSLAUTERN.

Our ground forces have entered BINSCHEID, about four miles east of the intersection of the Luxembourg-Belgium-German border, where they encountered fire from small arms and self-propelled guns, and resistance from pillboxes on the high ground near the town. To the southwest, our forces reached the DASBURG—LUTZKAMPEN road along a two-mile stretch north of DAHNEN.

In the VIANDEN area, we entered BIVELS to the north, and to the southeast we cleared OBERSGEGEN and took KORPERICH. Our units have captured STOCKEN about five miles to the east.

Allied elements, after a surprise crossing of the Moselle river north of REMICH, occupied WINCHERINGEN, while other units captured PALZEM, just north of REMICH, and advanced to the vicinity of ROMMELFANGEN four and a half miles southwest of SAARBURG. Farther to the southeast our troops have captured WEITEN and are clearing FREUDENBURG. Fierce fighting is in progress in ORSCHOLZ, two miles south of WEITEN. Fighter-bombers struck at the fortified towns of TABEN and TRASSEM.

It was not until April that the picture appeared in the *Daily Sketch*. Today, vague tracks of disturbed ground are still evident. The village on the crossroads is actually called Grunewald. The shattered remains of a row of bunkers from the Siegfried Line remain in the edge of the forest

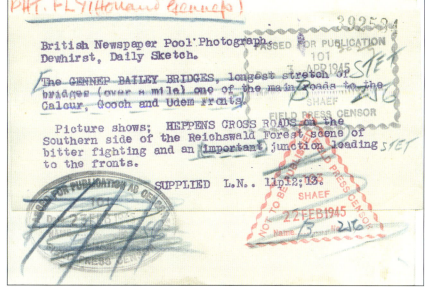

Operation 'Clarion', which began on February 22, was one of the most successful missions conducted by the Eighth Air Force. It was designed to give the German transport system a paralysing blow with the minimum of risk, to restrict the flow of men and materials to the fighting front. Because large marshalling yards required an inordinate tonnage to cripple them, 25 secondary rail centres, which also had the advantage of possessing only light flak, were selected to cut rail lines between eastern and western Germany. In this example at Ludwigslust, 60 miles east of Hamburg, the main station and large storage buildings received direct hits and were left burning by 48 aircraft of the 401st Bomb Group. The aircraft bombed from 12,000 feet which was almost half the usual height. Seventy hits on the rail lines were recorded and railway cars and two rail bridges were severely damaged.

COMMUNIQUE No. 320   February 22

Between the Rhine and the Maas, Allied forces continue to make good progress. In the MOYLAND sector, the woods to the south of the town have been cleared of the enemy.

Our forces driving down from the north have reached the line of the GOCH—UDEM railway and a point about two and a quarter miles west of UDEM. GOCH is now clear of the enemy. Southeast of HOMMERSUM we have made gains up to 2,000 yards.

Strong points and gun and mortar positions in wooded country west of CALCAR and near GOCH were attacked by rocket-firing fighters and fighter-bombers which went in just ahead of our ground forces. The fortified village of CALCAR was subjected to repeated bombing and strafing attacks by other fighter-bombers. Behind the enemy line communications targets in WEEZE, UDEM, LABBECK, SONSBECK, GELDERN and XANTEN were attacked by medium, light and fighter-bombers.

In the area southwest of PRUM, our forces have captured the town of HUF and are fighting in BINSCHEID. Farther southwest near the Luxembourg-German border we have captured DAHNEN and have entered DASBURG.

In the VIANDEN area, our units have reached the German border one-half mile northeast of the town. Just southeast of VIANDEN we have taken ROTH. In the METTENDORF area, east of VIANDEN, our forces have repulsed a heavy counter-attack. Our units now overlook the Prum river on a six-mile stretch in the area north of ECHTERNACH.

In the Saar-Moselle triangle our forces have cleared TEMMELS just northeast of GREVENMACHER and our armor has pushed beyond ONSDORF to a point three and one-half miles northwest of SAARBURG, which has been entered by other armored elements. Our forces have reached the Saar river south of SAARBURG and have taken HAMM and TABEN. The towns of FREUDENBURG and ORSCHOLZ also are in our hands after heavy fighting.

Two counter-attacks were repulsed by our units in the SAARLAUTERN bridgehead area.

Fortified towns in the SAARBURG area, including PELLINGEN, SERRIG, TABEN, GREIMERATH and KRETTNICH were attacked by fighter-bombers.

Our forces are fighting from house-to-house in FORBACH. The enemy is resisting stubbornly and has reinforced the defenders with local members of the Volkssturm. The nearby village of SPICHEREN was cleared despite stiff opposition.

An armor-supported enemy attack was repulsed in the ST ARNUAL forest, northeast of FORBACH.

In the northern Alsace plain our artillery dispersed a group of enemy armoured vehicles.

One thousand eight hundred prisoners have been taken in the past six days in the sector between SAARBRUCKEN and the Rhine.

Communications and rail and road transport in western Germany north and northeast of the Ruhr and between the Rhine and the Roer were attacked by medium, light and fighter-bombers. Targets included the rail bridge at BAD OEYNHAUSEN and VLOTHO, HERFORD and LAGE and several railway yards in the DUREN area and elsewhere. Locomotives, railway cars and motor vehicles were destroyed and damaged and rail lines cut in many places.

Farther south, medium and fighter-bombers attacked railway yards at ZWEIBRUCKEN, KAISERSLAUTERN, MANNHEIM and DARMSTADT and a rail bridge at BAD MUNSTER. Communications at FREIBURG and to the south were bombed by other fighter-bombers.

Rail and industrial targets at NURNBERG were attacked by escorted heavy bombers in very great strength. Targets included railway yards, locomotive repair shops, a tank factory and a large electrical equipment plant. Some of the escorting fighters strafed railway targets in southern Germany.

South of SAARBRUCKEN, fortified buildings were hit by other fighter-bombers.

Last night the railway centre of WORMS was heavily attacked by heavy bombers and another strong force bombed DUISBURG. BERLIN also was bombed twice during the night.

At the same time that German bridges were being demolished, Allied bridges were being built to keep the troops on the move.

'Bristol Bridge' was constructed at Maaseik over the Maas river on the Belgian-Dutch border next to the blown road bridge.

A 'tourist' attaction then . . . and a tourist attraction now — the 'Three-Country Point' where Germany, Belgium and the Netherlands meet on the Vaalserberg, just west of Aachen. Although this photograph was taken back in September, it was only released for publication on January 27.

FORBACH. Two-thirds of the town is in our hands. In the vicinity of STIRING-WENDEL we cut the main FORBACH—SAARBRUCKEN highway.

To the east, gains of up to 1,000 yards were made north of SPICHEREN. Woods in the area were cleared and we took heights which give us observation of SAARBRUCKEN.

An enemy railway gun, estimated to be firing from a distance of 25 miles, shelled SAVERNE.

The enemy's communications system was under very heavy and widespread air attack throughout yesterday, during which some 8,000 sorties were flown.

Medium, light and fighter-bombers struck at marshalling yards, rail junctions and other communications targets in northern Holland and from north to south over western Germany.

Escorted heavy bombers attacked communications over a wide area of central Germany and in southern Germany, Austria and northern Italy. Targets included viaducts at BIELEFELD and ALTENBEKEN near PADERBORN and benzol plants at SCHOLVEN and OSTERFELD in the Ruhr.

Last night BERLIN was bombed by light bombers. During the day 39 enemy aircraft were shot down and 24 others were destroyed on the ground. Eight heavy bombers, five medium bombers, 21 light bombers and 40 fighters are missing according to reports so far received.

COMMUNIQUE No. 321   February 23

Allied forces have entered MOYLAND, southeast of CLEVE. Our troops astride the GOCH—UDEM railway have maintained their positions against strong enemy reactions.

Strong points, mortar and gun positions south of CALCAR and in the areas of WEEZE, KEVELAER and SONSBECK and rail lines between EMMERICH and WESEL were struck at by fighter-bombers and rocket-firing fighters.

An attempt by a large enemy patrol to cross the Roer river in the area east of SCHMIDT was broken up by our artillery.

East of the intersection of the Belgium-Luxembourg-German border we have cleared BINSCHEID. We have captured LICHTENBORN, two miles to the east, and northeast of the town we have made gains eastward to within three-quarters of a mile of the Prum river. To the south and southwest, ARZFELD, IRRHAUSEN, DALDEIDEN and DASBURG have been taken. Forty more enemy pillboxes were knocked out by our forces in the area northeast of DASBURG.

We have taken VIANDEN and thus cleared the enemy entirely from Luxembourg. In the area east of VIANDEN, we have captured GEILCHLINGEN and OBERGECKLER where we met very stiff resistance from enemy forces which employed tanks. In the METTENDORF area a small enemy counter-attack was repulsed.

Our elements have now cleared the enemy from the Saar-Moselle triangle, have taken the towns of FELLERICH and TAWERN and occupied the part of SAARBURG west of the Saar river. Our units have made two crossings of the Saar in the area south of SAARBURG. SERRIG on the east side of the river, has been entered, and house-to-house fighting is in progress. Our troops east of the river in the vicinity of TABEN are encountering enemy small-arms and mortar fire. Our troops made steady progress against stubborn resistance toward clearing

To the Dutch it is Drielandenpunt; to the Germans Dreiländereck, and Trois Frontières to the French-speaking Belgians.

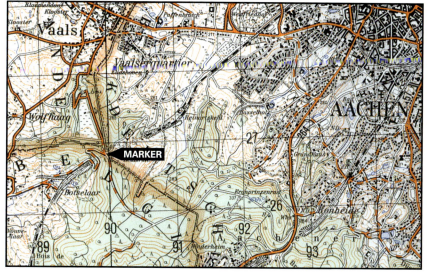

365

Jülich, 15 miles north-east of Aachen, was captured by the US 29th Division — or rather what was left of it! Operation 'Grenade' began in the early hours of February 23 as XIII and XIX Corps attacked across the Roer (see map page 350). Although the 175th Infantry Regiment was initially held up, by the end of the day a large part of the town had been cleared.

COMMUNIQUE No. 322 — February 24

Between the Rhine and the Maas, Allied forces have occupied MOYLAND while other units have made further progress south of the GOCH-UDEM railway.

We have resumed the offensive across the Roer river and have captured RURICH, GLIMBACH, GEVENICH and BOSLAR in the LINNICH area. Our elements have cleared JULICH except for the Citadel and northern part of the town and have occupied SELGERSDORF.

North of DUREN we have cleared HUCHEM-STAMMELN, and are fighting in BIRKESDORF and DUREN against increasing resistance.

The attack was preceded by a heavy artillery preparation. River crossings were made in assault boats, storm boats, and by ferry. Opposition to this crossing was in the form of small-arms and mortar fire.

MERSCH and STETTERNICH, fortified towns at junctions on the main roads leading to the northeast and east of JULICH, were attacked several times by fighter-bombers. Many other targets west of the Rhine between KREFELD and ANDERNACH were bombed by other fighter-bombers.

Our elements, in gains of a mile and one-half on a six-mile front southwest of Prum, have captured KOPSCHEID, LAUPERATH, HOLZCHEN, KRAUTSCHEID, HEILBACH and AMMELDINGEN.

Enemy armored vehicles, principally in the area between PRUM and BITBURG, were attacked by fighter-bombers. More than 170 vehicles were destroyed and many others were damaged.

Armored elements have captured the town of JUCKEN, four miles east of DASBURG on the Luxembourg-German border, and have pushed three-fourths of a mile beyond the town. Our armor also has made gains of up to one-half mile on a four-mile front, capturing the towns of PREISCHEID and AFFLER in the area south of DASBURG.

We have reached the wooded area two and one-half miles northeast of VIANDEN. Farther northeast, our units captured OBERGECKLER and SINSPELT.

There is house-to-house fighting in OCKFEN, on the east bank of the Saar river, north of SAARBURG. In this area we have crossed the river, and an enemy counter-attack by tanks and infantry has been repulsed. SERRIG, on the east bank of the Saar river, south of SAARBURG, has been cleared with the exception of four houses.

The communications center and industrial town of ESSEN and the Alma-Pluto benzol plant at GELSENKIRCHEN were attacked by escorted heavy bombers.

West of the Rhine, bridges near KREFELD and MUNCHEN-GLADBACH were targets for medium bombers. Road facilities in several towns ranging from ERKELENZ and GREVENBROICH in the north to ZULPICH and STADT MECKENHEIM in the south, where heavily bombed by medium and light bombers. Rail targets, principally on the Cologne plain and along the Rhine valley from KREFELD to ANDERNACH, were successfully attacked by fighter-bombers in great strength. In the course of these attacks nearly 1,500 rail cars as well as a number of locomotives, were destroyed and rail lines were cut in many places. Road transport in the same general area also was bombed and strafed.

Here Pfc Tom Snyder and Pvt Paul Mattox, both of Company C of the 175th, display the banner that they are about to mount above the entrance to the Hexenturm — the Witch's Tower. However, the 'Blue & Grey' Division did not cause all the destruction — that was as a result of the Americans asking RAF Bomber Command to wipe out Jülich (along with Düren and Heinsberg) to soften them up prior to the assault by the First and Ninth Armies. Although that raid had taken place on November 16, there was a three-month delay in the execution of the ground plan.

The symbol of the town — the Hexenturm or Witch's Tower — was rebuilt between 1949 to 1956.

The 16th-century Citadel was not captured until the following day, this picture being released for publication on February 26. The inscription over the arch stated: Heeres-Unteroffizier-Schule (Army NCO's Schule — non-commissioned officer's school).

On Thursday, March 1, Captain Butcher was with General Eisenhower when he visited Aachen and Jülich where Ike was pictured with General Simpson and Major General Raymond S. McLain, the CG of the XIX Corps. Photo released by SHAEF on March 5.

Our forces clearing FORBACH made further progress in hard fighting. The remaining enemy troops have been pushed into the eastern section of the town.

Four enemy attacks, two of which were supported by armor, were repulsed farther east. We have occupied SCHONBACH on the west bank of the Saar river. On the east bank, three miles south of SAARBRUCKEN stiff fighting continued in the southern outskirts of BUBINGEN.

Allied forces in the West captured 2,700 prisoners 21 February.

Bridges, locomotives, rail cars and other communications targets were attacked by fighter-bombers in the KAISERSLAUTERN area.

Escorted heavy bombers in very great strength carried out widespread attacks on rail yards and other communications targets in south, central and southeast Germany, while many of the escorting fighters strafed transportation targets and airfields, destroying 14 enemy aircraft on the ground.

Last night heavy bombers attacked the communications and industrial center of PFORZHEIM in the upper Rhineland. Light bombers attacked BERLIN.

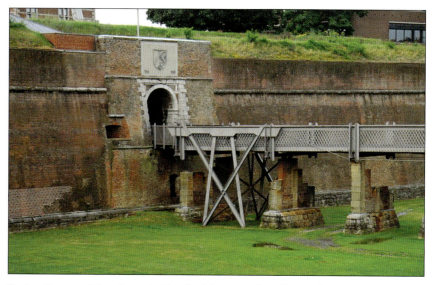

Today the moat has been bridged with a metal walkway. Peter Haas took the comparisons.

And now . . . nine miles to the south-east . . . Düren.

COMMUNIQUE No. 323   February 25

Allied forces south of the REICHSWALD forest, have made limited advances toward WEEZE against strong enemy resistance. Strong points, gun and mortar positions and troop concentrations in wooded country in the areas of CALCAR, UDEM and GOCH were attacked by rocket-firing fighters while medium and light bombers bombed targets at RHEDE, RHEINBERG and GELDERN. Artillery positions near VENLO were attacked with fragmentation bombs and rockets.

Our units have extended their bridgeheads across the Roer river, encountering moderate opposition from the enemy who launched several infantry and tank counter-attacks, all of which were repulsed. Northeast of LINNICH we have occupied several villages including BAAL and HOMPESCH. JULICH has been completely cleared and our units have progressed eastward to the outskirts of STETTERNICH.

In the area north of DUREN, our units have cleared OBERZIER and BIRKESDORF and are fighting in ARNOLDSWEILER. Half of DUREN is in our hands, and the enemy is resisting in the remaining portion from scattered strong points in houses and other buildings. Fighting is in progress in NIEDERAU two miles south of DUREN.

Fortified buildings in many towns between the Rhine and the Roer and particularly in the triangle formed by MUNCHEN-GLADBACH, EUSKIRCHEN and COLOGNE were struck by fighter-bombers.

We have captured WAXSWEILER, OBERPIERSCHEID, RINGHUSCHEID and NEUERBURG, southwest of PRUM. Our units driving from the northwest have met our elements advancing from the south in the vicinity of OBERGECKLER. South of NEUERBURG we have taken SINSPELT. Our armored elements driving to the northeast beyond the town have encountered road-blocks and mines.

Strong points and enemy armor in the PRUM, WAXWEILER and BITBURG areas were attacked by fighter-bombers.

In the lower Saar valley, our units have captured OCKFEN, two miles southeast of SAARBURG on the east side of the river. SERRIG is now completely in our hands, and we have taken high ground two and one-half miles east of the town.

Railway yards, communication centers and rail and road transport north and northeast of the Ruhr and between the Rhine and the Roer rivers were attacked by medium, light and fighter-bombers. Among the targets were the communications centers of VIERSEN, RHEINDAHLEN, BLATZHEIM, ZULPICH and VLATTEN. A large number of locomotives, railway cars and motor vehicles were destroyed and railway lines were cut in many places.

Fighting continued in FORBACH with resistance still stubborn in the western section of the town. Enemy artillery and mortar fire increased considerably in the area.

Three counter-attacks were repulsed on the high ground south of SAARBRUCKEN with heavy losses to the enemy.

BUBINGEN, on the east bank of the Saar river, was cleared. Farther east, the town of BLIESRANSBACH was captured.

Allied forces in the West captured 2,330 prisoners 22 February.

The aerial offensive against the enemy's communications also was continued elsewhere yesterday with heavy and widespread attacks by heavy, medium, and fighter-bombers.

Railway bridges at NEUWEID and MAYEN were attacked by medium bombers while railway communications and transport in the areas of NEUSTADT, HOMBURG, FREIBURG and to the south were struck at by medium and fighter-bombers.

Railway yards at BIELEFELD and rail targets elsewhere in northwestern Germany; oil refineries at MISBURG, HAMBURG and HARBURG; a synthetic oil plant at KAMEN and submarine building yards at HAMBURG and BREMEN were attacked by escorted heavy bombers in very great strength.

Some of the escorting fighters flew low to strafe rail, road and canal transport. An oil refinery northeast of HANNOVER was hit by fighter-bombers which set fire to many storage tanks and three oil trains.

Communications and rail, road and water transport in northern Holland were struck at by fighter-bombers. BERLIN was attacked by light bombers last night.

With Düren in American hands, prisoners are being escorted to the rear in Karlstrasse.

Now on the road to München-Gladbach (since re-named Mönchengladbach), troops of the Ninth roll through Erkelenz, 12 miles north of Jülich. The town was taken on the 26th.

COMMUNIQUE No. 324   February 26

Allied forces are now across the Roer on a wide front and have continued to make good progress against moderate enemy resistance. North and northeast of LINNICH we have occupied DOVEREN, LOVENICH and RALSHOVEN, and east of JULICH our units have cleared the HAMBACH forest and have captured STEINSTRASS.

In the DUREN area the towns of ELLEN, MERZENICH, BINSFELD, STOCKHEIM and KREUZAU have been captured. We repulsed a tank-supported counter-attack near ELLEN. The castle of RATH, between ELLEN and MERZENICH, was captured and more than 250 prisoners were taken from the castle.

Northeast and east of VIANDEN we have taken SCHFUERN, WEIDINGEN, OBERRADEN, UTSCHEID, BRIMINGEN and METTENDORF.

Our forces have crossed the Prum river in the area seven miles north of ECHTERNACH, and have pushed two miles northeast of the crossing point. The towns of WETTLINGEN and HOLSTHUM have been captured and we are fighting in PEFFINGEN.

In the SAARBURG area our units have extended their bridgehead to a width of four miles and a depth of two miles. Two counter-attacks in this area have been repulsed. We have cut the main highway out of SAARBURG at a point three and one-half miles east of the town.

In the SAARBRUCKEN area our elements on the east side of the Saar river in Germany cleared the remaining enemy from the HINTERWALD, just east of BUBINGEN, after three enemy counter-attacks were repulsed. North of nearby BLEISRANSBACH we wiped out a 40-man enemy patrol.

At STRASBOURG two attempted enemy raids on the FORT OF COMMERCE were turned back. Farther south the group of prisoners were taken from a hostile force which crossed the Rhine at MARKOLSHEIM.

Allied forces in the West captured 3,149 prisoners 23 February.

Medium and light bombers attacked the communications centers of UDEM and XANTEN. At WEEZE a formation of enemy tanks was successfully attacked and dispersed by rocket-firing fighters which also hit enemy troops and fortified buildings in the UDEM area. Other medium and light bombers struck at targets at WEGBERG, north of ERKELENZ and just east of DUREN.

Enemy rail communications were again heavily attacked. Rail lines and rolling stock in Holland, eastward to north central Germany, and as far south as PFORZHEIM in the upper Rhineland were hit by fighters and fighter-bombers. Communications centers in the region of COLOGNE and rail bridges at AHRWEILER, south of BONN, and east of the Rhine at COLBE and NIEDERSCHELD were attacked by medium and light bombers. Escorted heavy bombers in very great strength struck at rail yards at MUNICH, ASCHAFFENBURG and ULM. Other targets for heavy bombers were tank plants at FRIEDRICHSHAFEN and ASCHAFFENBURG, air bases west of NURNBERG, and an oil storage depot at NEUBURG.

The synthetic oil plant at KAMEN, near DORTMUND, was attacked by other escorted heavy bombers for the second consecutive day.

Looking up Kölner Strasse from its junction with Ostpromenade in rebuilt Erkelenz.

A large ammunition dump at SIEGELBACH, southeast of HEIDELBERG, and barracks and supply dumps at DONAUESCHINGEN were struck at by medium bombers. During the day 39 enemy aircraft were shot down and 20 others were destroyed on the ground. From incomplete reports three medium and light bombers and 28 fighters are missing.

Last night light bombers attacked the important communications center of ERFURT and bombed targets at BERLIN. Other light bombers struck at rail targets in Holland and north of the Ruhr and objectives west of the Rhine from EMMERICH to COLOGNE.

Meanwhile, Sergeant Wayne Grier of Company F, 385th Infantry of the 76th Division (US Third Army) was pictured leading his squad through the remains of a road block at Binsfeld.

Karel first went to the town of that name east of Düren but after a fruitless search there, he eventually found it in Binsfeld, north of Trier — 75 miles away!

Now we should turn to catch up with events in the north. Höst, a village just south of Goch, was captured by soldiers of the Royal Welch Regiment on the 26th. Here members of the 4th Battalion clear a farmhouse in the hamlet.

COMMUNIQUE No. 325   February 27

Allied infantry, supported by tanks, advanced against strong opposition to KEPPELN, southwest of CALCAR, where heavy fighting continues. Enemy gun positions west of XANTEN were attacked by medium bombers.

East of the Roer our troops have made further good progress.

In the area north of LINNICH we have captured GOLKRATH, GRANTERATH and KUCKHOVEN. Northeast of JULICH we have occupied AMELN and OBEREMBT and to the east, most of the HAMBACH forest is in our hands.

In the JULICH-DUREN area we have reached the outskirts of ELSDORF, and have entered BLATZHEIM, ESCHWEILER and FRAUWULLESHEIM. A number of towns were captured during including BUIR, GOLZHEIM, ROMMERSHEIM, DROVE and BOICH. DUREN has been completely cleared of the enemy. Resistance in the area was centered mainly in the towns.

Armored elements have crossed the Nims river in the vicinity of BITBURG. In this area we have captured LIESSEM, OBERWEIS, BETTINGEN and MESSERICH, and have entered WOLSFELD. A strong enemy counter-attack was repulsed six miles southwest of BITBURG.

Northeast of SAARBURG, our armored units have cleared SCHODEN, and have reached a point five and one-half miles east of SAARBURG. We repulsed a strong tank-supported counter-attack five miles east of SAARBURG.

North of FORBACH our forces repulsed two attacks near STIRING-WENDEL.

Enemy patrols were turned back in the northern Alsace plain and farther south along the west bank of the Rhine.

Allied forces in the West captured 3,500 prisoners on February 24.

Three BERLIN rail stations, their sidings and traffic-handling facilities, were attacked yesterday by more than 1,200 heavy bombers escorted by more than 700 fighters. The targets were the Schlesischer station which has freight car repair shops and extensive sidings and storage depots; the Berlin North station, a large freight terminal with important facilities; and the Alexander Platz, which serves several lines. More than 3,000 tons of bombs were dropped. Some of the escorting fighters strafed ground targets, destroyed two enemy aircraft on the ground and shot up locomotives and trucks.

The Hoesch-Benzin synthetic oil plant at DORTMUND was attacked by other escorted heavy bombers.

Medium and light bombers struck at junctions of rail and road lines in the DUSSELDORF area and south of EUSKIRCHEN.

Rail lines and other rail targets in the KAISERSLAUTERN and MANNHEIM areas, a troop train near WURZBURG, and a barracks at RUMBACH were attacked by fighter-bombers, which also struck at an airfield at ROHRDORF, west of ROTTENBURG, rail yards near FREUDENSTADT, and objectives in FREIBURG.

From yesterday's operations 16 heavy bombers and eight fighters are missing. Last night light bombers attacked BERLIN and NUREMBERG.

Karel was amazed to find that the Polzenhof farm on Vornicker Weg had been beautifully restored.

Another town which had been subjected to continual aerial attack was Bitburg in First Army territory. Lying midway between Trier and Prüm, it was taken by the 5th Infantry Division on February 27. Evidence of the interdiction meeted out by fighter-bombers was clearly evident from this photograph taken at the town's railway station.

COMMUNIQUE No. 326   February 28

Allied forces have captured UDEM and have advanced to the western edge of the HOCHWALD where heavy opposition has been met.

Weather limited our air operations in the battle zones yesterday. However targets at MARIENBAUM and SONSBECK were bombed in the morning and again in the afternoon by medium and light bombers. Fighter bombers hit targets at WINNEKENDONK.

East of the Roer river we have made good progress. Our units have cleared ERKELENZ and have advanced to WALDNIEL and RHEINDAHLEN. Farther east we have occupied KUCKUM and BORSCHEMICH, east of ERKELENZ, and have entered KONIGSHOVEN on the left bank of the Erft river.

Farther to the southeast our armored units, after a six-mile advance, entered the town of SINDORF, ten miles west of COLOGNE. Armored infantry elements cleared the towns of BERRENDORF, WULLENRATH and HEPPENDORF in the area northeast of SINDORF, and fighting continues in ELSDORF and in the nearby towns of GIESENDORF, ANGELSDORF and GROUVEN.

South of SINDORF, the towns of BERGERHAUSEN and BLATZHEIM have been captured. Other elements in the course of a two-mile push captured NIEDER BOLHEIM and crossed the Neffel river north of the town.

In the area east and southeast of DUREN, the towns of ESCHWEILER, FRAUWULLESHEIM and JAKOBWULLESHEIM have been captured and we are fighting in VETTWEISS following a 4,000-yard gain. In the area east of HURTGEN, we have cleared NIDEGGEN.

We have crossed the Prether river and cleared DICKERSCHEID, six miles south SCHLEIDEN, and are fighting in GIESCHEID.

The communications centers of GLESSEN, west of COLOGNE, and MUNSTEREIFEL to the south were bombed by medium and light bombers whilst fighter-bombers struck at fortified places ahead of our ground forces.

North of BITBURG, armoured elements have captured the towns of NATTENHEIM and MATZEN and have cleared FLIESSEM. Infantry and armoured elements have entered BITBURG.

In the area south of BITBURG, the BITBURG—TRIER road has been cut in three places and we have cleared the towns of OBERSTEDEM, ESSLINGEN and MECKEL. Other units have entered IRREL and GILZEM and have cleared NIEDERWEIS and KASCHENBACH. Targets in the BITBURG area were attacked by fighter-bombers.

Farther south we have entered WASSERBILLIG, near the junction of the Moselle and Saar rivers.

Our forces have extended the crossing of the Saar river to a depth of six miles. BEURIG has been cleared and armored elements have captured NIEDER ZERF, six and a half miles east of SAARBURG.

In FORBACH, our units were harassed by increased enemy artillery and mortar fire. Activity slackened farther east and along the Rhine. Allied forces in the West captured well over 8,000 prisoners 26 February.

The rail centres of MAINZ and LEIPZIG and HALLE were attacked by escorted heavy bombers in very great strength. Another force of escorted heavy bombers attacked a benzol plant near GELSENKIRCHEN. Some of the escorting fighters on the LEIPZIG and HALLE missions strafed enemy airfields and rail lines. A considerable number of enemy aircraft were destroyed on the ground and locomotives and rail cars were shot up.

Rail communications in the areas of HEILBRONN, STUTTGART and PFORZHEIM were struck at by fighter-bombers. Among the targets were railway yards at KOCHENDORF and ERNSBACH.

Farther south other fighter-bombers bombed railway yards at LOFFINGEN, VILLINGEN, ROTTWEIL and SIGMARINGEN, and hit rail lines between the upper Rhine and Lake Constance. BERLIN was attacked last night by light bombers.

Bitburg was left a complete shambles as the troops head east towards the Rhine.

MARCH 1945
OVER THE RHINE

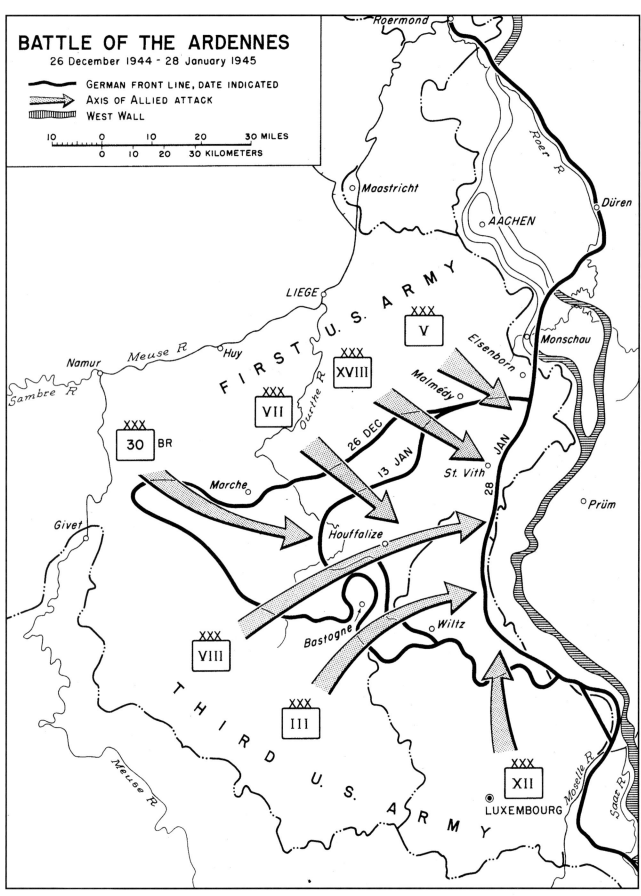

The official US historian wrote that as the tempo for the Third Army advance accelerated, General Patton became increasingly impatient to stage a break-through on the 1944 scale. On February 20 he pressed General Bradley to give him additional divisions for an attack in the area of Trier and the Saar. He pointed out that the great proportion of US troops in Europe were not fighting and warned that 'all of us in high position will surely be held accountable for the failure to take offensive action when offensive action is possible'. General Bradley agreed that advances were possible in the Third Army sector, but added that higher authority had decided to make the thrust elsewhere. He reminded General Patton: 'Regardless of what you and I think of this decision, we are good enough soldiers to carry out these orders.'

At the end of February, General Eisenhower had to decide how the Allies should proceed with the next phase of Operation 'Overlord' and he drove with General Bradley to have a meeting with Field-Marshal Montgomery at the latter's headquarters in Holland. Also present were Lieutenant-General Henry Crerar, the Canadian commander (rear left); General Simpson of the Ninth and General Dempsey, British Second Army. Monty favoured crossing the Rhine on a broad front between Rheinberg and Emmerich — an operation which would take several weeks to plan — while Simpson stated that as seven of his 12 divisions had nothing to do, he proposed to carry out a surprise crossing. Meanwhile Bradley said he proposed to complete his support of the Ninth Army by investing Cologne from the north and to advance to secure the Coblenz sector and so close the Rhine north of the Moselle. This offensive began on March 1.

COMMUNIQUE No. 327   March 1

Allied forces have occupied CALCAR which was found to be clear of the enemy. Farther south there has been heavy fighting in the HOCHWALD and along the UDEM—XANTEN railway. We have occupied a number of villages between GOCH and the Maas.

Ferry and barge traffic on the Rhine between REES and WESEL, troop concentrations at WINNEKENDONK and SONSBECK, and strong points near WEEZE were hit yesterday by fighter-bombers and rocket-firing fighters. Medium and light bombers attacked targets at GELDERN, KAMP and RHEINBERG. Other fighter-bombers struck at the railway yards at WESEL.

We have continued our operations across the Roer river against slight to moderate resistance which has stiffened in the area west of COLOGNE.

Our forces have driven to within seven miles of COLOGNE and have established three bridgeheads over the Erft river and canal west of the city. West of the Erft, we have cleared ESCH, and have reached MODRATH to the southeast after crossing the river west of the town.

East and southeast of DUREN, we have taken NORVENICH, HOCHKIRCHEN, GLADBACH, and VETTWEISS, and our units have driven to the edge of MULDENAU encountering heavy enemy artillery fire.

Fighter-bombers attacked fortified villages in the area of MUNCHEN-GLADBACH and near EUSKIRCHEN.

South of SCHLEIDEN, we have cleared RESCHEID. Northeast of PRUM, our forces made gains of up to one mile, repulsing a counter-attack four and one-half miles from the town.

Southwest of PRUM, our armored elements crossed the Prum river, captured PRONSFELD, LUNEBACH and MERLSCHEID, and made penetrations of one mile east of the river. WAXWEILER has been taken. BITBURG is now clear of the enemy, and our units have advanced to the Kyll river and have captured ROHL, SULM and IDENHEIM. We have taken IRREL and HELENENBERG, seven miles northwest of TRIER.

WASSERBILLIG, at the junction of the Saar and Moselle rivers, is now in our hands. Armored elements, advancing one mile against enemy strong points, anti-tank guns and road blocks, have entered PELLINGEN, five and one-half miles southeast of TRIER. In the wooded area five and one-half miles east of SAARBURG, our infantry gained up to one and one-half miles southward.

Fortified towns and strong points in the PRUM area and along the main road from BITBURG south of TRIER were attacked by fighter-bombers.

From SAARBRUCKEN to the Rhine and south to the Franco-Swiss border, patrol clashes were the only activity. Allied forces in the west captured 7,168 prisoners 27 February.

Rail bridges at COLBE and NIEDERSCHELD, north and northwest of GIESSEN, at MAYEN, and traffic centers at SIEGEN and ST WENDEL, northeast of SAARBRUCKEN, were targets for medium and light bombers.

Fighter-bombers struck at rail lines in the areas of SAARLAUTERN, KAISERSLAUTERN and ZWEIBRUCKEN and NEUSTADT. Objectives in the industrial area of EMMENDINGEN east of COLMAR were bombed by medium bombers.

Rail yards at KASSEL, SOEST, SCHWERTE, HAGEN and SIEGEN were attacked by escorted heavy bombers in very great strength. Fighters strafed rail transport over a wide area. Other escorted heavy bombers made a concentrated attack on the Nordstern benzol plant near GELSENKIRCHEN. An ordnance depot at UNNA, east of DORTMUND, was attacked by a strong formation of light bombers.

From the days' operations three of our heavy bombers and 20 fighters are missing according to incomplete reports.

Last night light bombers again attacked targets at BERLIN.

This picture was taken at Montgomery's 21st Army Group headquarters — then located at No. 52 Nieuwedijk at Geldrop, just east of Eindhoven. Unfortunately the rear of the house has since been extensively modified with an extension added covering the spot where the commanders were sitting.

COMMUNIQUE No. 328　　　　March 2

Heavy fighting continues in the area between the HOCHWALD FOREST and WEEZE. South of UDEM Allied forces have entered KERVENHEIM against strong opposition.

Enemy troops on the northwest fringe of the HOCHWALD FOREST were strafed by fighters. Strong points and gun positions near LABBECK and the village of SONSBECK were attacked by fighter-bombers. Targets at XANTEN and KEVELAER were attacked by medium and light bombers and rail lines in the WESEL area were cut by fighter-bombers.

Our ground units across the Roer have maintained good progress. MUNCHEN-GLADBACH has been captured.

Fighter-bombers struck at rail yards north of DUSSELDORF and rail and road targets between MUNCHEN-GLADBACH and DUSSELDORF.

We are meeting stubborn enemy resistance east of the Erft river. Our units have entered BERGHEIM, ICHENDORF, HORREM and MODRATH.

East of DUREN we have crossed the Neffel river, cleared PINGSHEIM and DORWEILER and have entered WISSERSHEIM. Farther to the south MUDDERSHEIM and DISTERNICH have been captured. Our units, driving south on the east side of the Roer river, have met strong enemy resistance south of NIDEGGEN.

Rail and road targets on both sides of the Rhine near COLOGNE and to the south were struck at by fighter-bombers. Medium and light bombers attacked eight communications centers, most of them west of the Rhine in the COLOGNE area, and a rail bridge east of the city.

South of SCHLEIDEN, we have taken OBERREIFFERSCHEID. Our forces have gained one-half mile against stubborn resistance in the area nine miles northeast of PRUM, and we have taken high ground just east of WILLWERATH four miles northeast of PRUM. South of PRUM we have expanded our bridgehead across the Prum river, and have captured LASCHEID and LAMBERTSBERG.

In the area north of BITBURG we have taken SCHEID and EHLENZ and our armored elements have repulsed a strong, tank-supported counter-attack. Fighter-bombers operating in this area struck at fortified towns and armored columns.

North of TRIER, our infantry has taken MOHN and BUTZWEILER. Our armored elements advancing from the south against enemy small-arms, mortar and artillery fire have entered the outskirts of TRIER and have cut the main highway one and one-half miles northeast of the city. South of TRIER, we have taken KRETTNACH-OBERMENNIG and OBEREMMEL in an advance to the northwest. Our forces in the area five and one-half miles east of SAARBURG have gained one mile to the south.

There was little activity in the sector from SAARBRUCKEN to the Franco-Swiss border. Two enemy raids were repulsed near the Rhine northeast of STRASBOURG.

Allied forces in the west captured 7,507 prisoners 28 February.

Rail yards at HEILBRONN, BRUCHSAL, GOPPINGEN, REUTLINGEN, NECKARSULM, INGOLSTADT, ULM and AUGSBURG, all in southern Germany and the communications center and industrial town of MANNHEIM were attacked yesterday by escorted heavy bombers in very great strength. By strafing in the vicinity of STUTTGART, MUNICH, NURNBERG and KASSEL, the escorting fighters destroyed nine enemy aircraft on the ground and shot up large numbers of locomotives, rail cars and road transport. Other escorted heavy bombers attacked the synthetic oil plant at KAMEN near DORTMUND.

Two rail bridges over the Moselle and an ordnance depot at GIESSEN were targets for medium and light bombers. Fighter-bombers attacked rail yards in the DARMSTADT area and at ALZEY, northwest of WORMS, and cut rail lines in the KAISERSLAUTERN area.

Twenty-three enemy aircraft were shot down. Twelve heavy bombers and 22 fighters are missing.

Last night light bombers attacked targets in BERLIN and ERFURT.

The industrial centre of München-Gladbach fell to the Ninth Army on March 1. Much was already in ruins from prolonged aerial bombardment prior to its capture.

In actual fact the picture was taken in Rheydt, a suburb which became part of München-Gladbach in 1975, the same year that the city changed its name to Mönchengladbach. This is the crossroads of Horst-Wessel-Strasse and Dr Frick-Strasse — now renamed respectively Friedrich-Ebert-Strasse and Stresemannstrasse.

The following day the Prime Minister accompanied by the Chief of the General Staff, Field-Marshal Sir Alan Brooke, and General Sir Hastings Ismay, Churchill's Chief-of-Staff, arrived at Montgomery's HQ. There was already behind-the-scenes intrigue to get Field-Marshal Alexander appointed Deputy Supreme Commander but Montgomery stated that 'a change like this at this stage will merely raise a storm'.

COMMUNIQUE No. 329   March 3

Allied forces have fought their way through the HOCHWALD FOREST despite strong resistance, and farther west have taken the strongly defended villages of KERVENHEIM and WEEZE.

Targets in KEVELAER, a communications center, were bombed by medium and light bombers, while fighter-bombers attacked enemy troops and gun positions near WEEZE.

Other fighter-bombers attacked rail and road transport and communications in the Ruhr, to the north and northeast of the Ruhr, and barges on the Rhine between WESEL and DINSLAKEN.

To the south, our advance has now reached STRAELEN, and ROERMOND and VENLO have been captured.

North of MUNCHEN-GLADBACH we have occupied DULKEN and VIERSEN. Our units have entered KREFELD and have captured NEUSS. Our forces west of COLOGNE have advanced to BEDBURG and BUCHHOLZ. BERGHEIM has been cleared, and we have reached NIEDERAUSSEM and HABBELRATH. Fighting continues in MODRATH. Enemy resistance is stiff in the area east of the Erft river and canal.

Communications and other targets at COLOGNE were bombed yesterday morning and again in the afternoon by escorted heavy bombers in great strength. More than 3,000 tons of bombs were dropped in the target areas.

East of DUREN our units entered GYMNICH after a gain of about two and one-half miles. WISSERSHEIM and ERP have been cleared and our armored elements are in BORR and FRIESHEIM. In the ZULPICH area, we have reached BESSENICH, JUNTERSDORF and EMBKEN. We have cleared HEIMBACH and advanced 1,500 yards farther south on the east side of the Roer river.

In the PRUM area, our forces reached high ground two and one-half miles northeast of the town, and to the south and southeast have captured WINRINGEN, PLUTSCHEID and SEFFERN.

Fighter-bombers attacked fortified places east of PRUM, and targets in the towns of BADEM and EISENSCHMITT to the south.

TRIER has been captured by armored and infantry units. Our forces advancing from the northwest are two and one-half miles from the city after taking KERSCH and NEWEL. Southwest of TRIER we have captured KONZ-KARTHAUS at the junction of the Saar and Moselle rivers.

Fighter-bombers attacked targets in SCHILLINGEN, GREIMERATH and LOSHEIM and fortified towns south of TRIER.

Enemy patrols which crossed the Rhine north and south of STRASBOURG were repulsed. Allied forces in the west captured 7,053 prisoners 1 March.

Communications and transport west of the Rhine from KREFELD southward to LANDAU and east of the Rhine from DORTMUND southward to HASLACH were struck at by medium, light and fighter-bombers in strength. Among the targets were communications centers at SINNERSDORF and MECKENHEIM, and bridges at SINZIG, ELLER, ZELL, BERNKASTEL-KUES and SIMMERN.

The following day they visited Simpson's HQ. Brooke described what happened: 'As we were leaving Simpson's headquarters, Simpson asked Winston whether he wished to make use of the lavatory before starting. Without a moment's hesitation, he asked, "How far is the Siegfried Line?" On being told about half-an-hour's run, he replied that he would not visit the lavatory but that we should halt on reaching the Siegfried Line! On arrival there the column of some 20 or 30 cars halted, we processed solemnly out and lined up along the Line. As the photographers had all rushed up to secure good vantage points, he turned to them and said, "This is one of the operations connected with this great war which must not be reproduced photographically." To give them credit, they obeyed their orders and, in doing so, missed a chance of publishing the greatest photographic catch of the war! I shall never forget his childish grin of intense satisfaction that spread all over his face as he looked down at the critical moment.'

A motor repair depot at ISERLOHN and ordnance depots at GIESSEN and WIESBADEN were hit by medium and light bombers.

Railway yards at CHEMNITZ and DRESDEN, synthetic oil plants at MAGDEBURG and BOHLEN, an oil refinery at ROSITZ and the Krupp works at MAGDEBURG were attacked by escorted heavy bombers in very great strength. Airfields near LEIPZIG and MAGDEBURG were strafed by some of the escorting fighters.

Targets in BERLIN and KASSEL were bombed last night by light bombers.

None of the captions of the many press photos taken on this occasion identified the exact spot where Churchill watered the dragon's teeth but it was somewhere between Simpson's command post at Maastricht in the Netherlands, and the recently captured German town of Jülich which the Prime Minister visited in the afternoon. The logical route would be via Vaals and Aachen which meant the motorcade would cross the Siegfried Line at Vaalserquartier. Although the dragon's teeth at this spot have been completely cleared away, the lay of the land on the north side of the Vaalser Strasse is still recognisable.

Venlo is a Dutch town on the border with Germany and in their retreat German engineers blew both the road and rail bridges. The town spans the River Maas, the actual frontier running just to the east of the built-up area.

Although the town lay about 20 miles north of the Ninth Army's zone, a task force from the 35th Infantry Division — in particular the 320th Infantry Regiment — was assembled to take the town which fell almost without a fight on March 2 after Major General John Anderson *(left)*, the XVI Corps commander issued probably one of the shortest orders of the war: 'Take it'!

Much of the damage had been caused by the constant aerial bombardment of enemy-held towns in recent weeks, but today all has been swept away at the junction of Spoorstraat and Vleesstraat.

Having crossed the river the 35th Division task force headed out north-east, the climax of its three-day, 50-mile drive being a swift night assault on Sevelen 12 miles beyond Venlo. Here the crews pause for a break before pushing on to the Rhine.

Sevelen today. This is Dorfstrasse, at its junction with Issumer Strasse (right), looking in the direction of Geldern.

Sixty miles south of Venlo, Trier was another border town but this time east of the Moselle inside Germany. It fell to the 76th Infantry and 10th Armored Divisions on March 2 and a photographer was fortunately on hand to picture a unique moment. One of the officers had been sent a Stars and Stripes flag by his wife in the mail and it arrived just in time to be flown over captured Trier. Standing on left, holding the swastika banner which it replaced, is Colonel J. E. Raymond of Washington, DC. Standing in the door panel on the left, is Captain R. Wilson, of Newark, New Jersey, who was the man who got the flag from his wife in exchange for the Nazi swastika. On the right, holding the other side of the flag, is Captain Steve Lang, of Chicago, and pulling on the halyard is Brigadier General Edwin W. Piburn. And helping him to do the job is T/5 Leon Sours of Maine, Indiana. This ceremony happened in front of the Porta Nigra Hotel, which had been a Nazi headquarters.

The hotel was named after the Porta Nigra — one of the oldest monuments in the world having been built by the Romans in 186-200 AD. According to the caption it was spared by US artillery fire . . . but the same cannot be said for the historic hotel opposite, demolished in 1966 and now replaced by the ultra-modern Mercure Hotel.

German street names have often been altered on political grounds, this particular one in Trier being changed in May 1945.

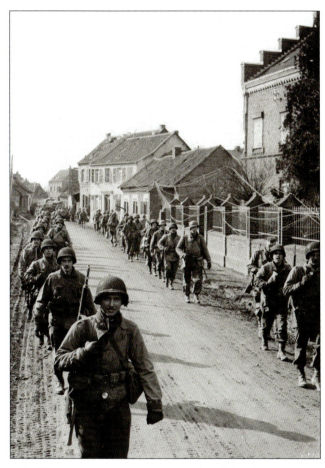

Left: All eyes were now on the great prize of the city of Cologne which was the objective of VII Corps of the First Army but first the troops had to cross the Cologne plain which lay between the Roer and Rhine rivers. Heppendorf, 11 miles west of Cologne, had been entered by Task Force Kane (of Combat Command A, 3rd Armored Division) on February 27; now this picture taken on March 3 shows infantry marching through that town on their way to Cologne. *Right:* Aleſstrasse, looking west.

Meanwhile the roads leading west were filled with increasing numbers of prisoners — SHAEF now including daily totals in their communiqués. Up to March 3, the Ninth Army had taken 20,000 prisoners since crossing the Roer. In the background troops of the 83rd Infantry Division continue their drive to capture Neuss (15 miles north of Cologne) and to try to capture intact bridges over the Rhine. (For some unexplained reason the censor has blanked out the faces of the leading prisoners.)

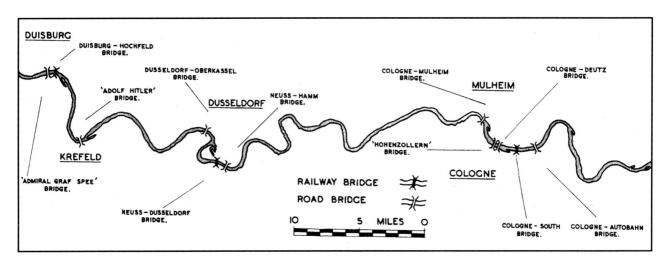

COMMUNIQUE No. 330 March 4

Allied forces east of the HOCHWALD FOREST are fighting against fierce enemy resistance. We have occupied KEVELAER and to the west have advanced beyond the villages of BERGEN and LANGSTRAAT on the right bank of the Maas. Contact has been made between elements of our forces advancing from the Roer and our units moving southward from the REICHSWALD. Farther south we have occupied GELDERN, SEVELEN and KEMPEN.

Enemy troops, defense positions, observation posts, road transport and barges in an area around XANTEN and near SONSBECK; objectives in the WESEL area, and rail and road traffic to the eastward were targets for medium, light and fighter-bombers and rocket-firing fighters.

The city of KREFELD has been completely cleared of the enemy. Three bridges across the Rhine in the NEUSS—DUSSELDORF area were blown by the Germans.

We are fighting in FRIMMERSDORF, southwest of GREVENBROICH, and in STOMMELN, northwest of COLOGNE

On March 1, Major General Raymond S. McLain, commanding the XIX Corps, gave the 83rd Infantry Division the task of capturing Neuss and attempting to take intact the two rail and two road bridges beyond the town. Although the 83rd attacked with two regiments throughout the night of March 1/2 and cleared Neuss, the troops found three of the four bridges destroyed. One of these was the road bridge connecting Neuss with the Düsseldorf suburb of Hamm on which the cantilever spans and four of the flood spans had been blown.

The Düsseldorf-Oberkassel road bridge was constructed in 1896-98 and later altered in 1925-26. It was a twin, bowstring arch with the two arches supported on a central pier. There were three lattice steel approach spans on each bank with overtrack. It was renamed the Skagerrak-Brücke in commemoration of the naval battle in 1916. General McLain decided to try to take the Oberkassel bridge by subterfuge. On the night of March 2/3, a task force was organised comprising parts of the 736th Tank Battalion and the 643rd Tank Destroyer Battalion with riflemen from the 330th Infantry. The men were dressed in German uniforms and the tanks and vehicles disguised as Wehrmacht transport. German-speaking troops were put up front to bluff the column through. The ruse worked better than anyone had hoped. The column passed through the German lines and successfully outwitted German sentries. At one point, the Americans actually passed German foot soldiers moving in the opposite direction down the other side of the road. As dawn broke, the column was passing through the outskirts of Oberkassel but then their luck gave out. A German motor cyclist challenged the Americans and, not believing the answer he was given, turned his machine towards the bridge. The Americans tried vainly to bring the motor cyclist down with gun-fire but only succeeded in raising the alarm still further. Although the Americans were strong enough to fight their way forward, the town's air raid warden, aroused by the firing, set off the warning siren. Undaunted, the task force pushed on, some tanks actually reaching the western end of the bridge, whereupon the Germans fired the demolition charges in the faces of the Americans.

The other two demolished bridges reached by the 83rd Division at Neuss were in fact only 50 metres apart. This was a twin railway bridge, one for passenger traffic the other for goods trains.

while other units have reached PULHEIM, four miles from the outskirts of COLOGNE. In this area BUSDORF, FLIESTEDEN, MANSTEDTEN and GEYEN have been cleared.

MODRATH, on the DUREN-COLOGNE road, and HERRIG, LECHENICH, AHREM and WEILERSWIST, southwest of COLOGNE also have been cleared.

Enemy positions north of KREFELD, communications on both sides of the Rhine and rail traffic around COLOGNE were hit by fighter-bombers. ZULPICH has been cleared.

Our forces across the Erft river north of EUSKIRCHEN repulsed a counter-attack supported by tanks and self-propelled guns after a hard fight.

We have crossed the SCHWAMMENAUEL DAM and have mopped up the area between Schwammenauel lake and the Urft lake to the south. Numerous minefields were encountered.

Northeast of PRUM we have entered WEINSHEIM and repulsed a small counter-attack in that area. South of PRUM our armor has crossed the Nims river. We have captured OBERLAUCH, NIEDERLAUCH, SCHONECKEN and DINGDORF. A bridge at SCHONECKEN was taken intact.

Our units hold the high ground overlooking the Nims river in the area ten miles northwest of BITBURG. We have captured HEILENBACH.

Armored elements have reached the junction of the Kyll and Moselle rivers northeast of TRIER. Southwest of TRIER, we have taken LANGSUR, IGEL, ZEWEN and EUREN.

Two counter-attacks were repulsed by our units in the area two miles southwest of ZERF.

Fortified towns in the area of BITBURG and TRIER were attacked by fighter-bombers.

Breaking a week's lull, our forces made limited gains in an attack in FORBACH against stiff resistance. Farther east, a slight gain was made north of BUBINGEN on the east bank of the Saar river in Germany.

Fighter-bombers set on fire a large ammunition dump at ESCHRINGEN east of FORBACH, and attacked rail traffic in the KAISERSLAUTERN area.

In northern Alsace and along the Rhine, there was little activity. Allied forces in the west captured 9,599 prisoners 2 March.

Medium and light bombers attacked supply and communications targets in the Ruhr and western Germany, including ordnance and motor repair depots at SCHWELM, BERGISCH-BORN, northeast of COLOGNE, GIESSEN, and WIESBADEN; rail bridges at REMAGEN and HEIMERSHEIM between BONN and COBLENZ, and at SIMMERN; an ammunition dump at RHEINBACH; road-blocks at KIRN and a storage depot at NAHBOLLENBACH to the southwest.

Oil, rail, and industrial targets over a wide area of Germany were attacked by escorted heavy bombers in very great strength. They included rail yards at CHEMNITZ, synthetic oil plants at MAGDEBURG and RUHLAND, north of DRESDEN, oil refineries and other factories in the BRUNSWICK and HANNOVER areas and a road and rail bridge spanning the Weser river at NIENBURG, northwest of HANNOVER. Fighters strafed rail transport and destroyed 20 enemy aircraft on the ground. Ten enemy aircraft were destroyed in the air.

Last night heavy bombers were over Germany in strength with KAMEN as the main objective. WURZBURG was also bombed. Light bombers again attacked targets in BERLIN.

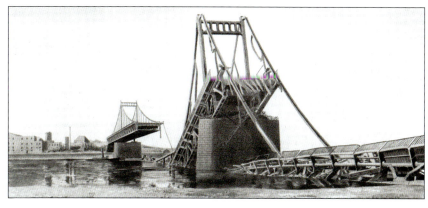

All the other bridges on the plan opposite had been blown save the 'Adolf Hitler' road bridge at Krefeld. After the 2nd Armored Division reached the bridge on the afternoon of March 3, an engineer party under Captain George L. Youngblood ventured onto the bridge, cutting all the wires they could see. Although they went right across in a gallant effort, after they retired the Germans detonated charges at 7 a.m. the following morning, so dropping the centre span in the Rhine.

Once Krefeld was in American hands, now came the street-naming routine although this time with a difference. *Left:* Sergeant George A. Kaufman renames Adolf-Hitler-Strasse after the US President while Warrant Officer Richard W. Geger replaces one songwriter for another as Francis Scott Key wrote *The Star Spangled Banner*.

The assault is underway on Rheindahlen which lies south-west of Rheydt.

COMMUNIQUE No. 331   **March 5**

Allied forces are meeting determined resistance in the XANTEN area, but elsewhere we have made good progress. The WEEZE-GELDERN-VENLO pocket is being mopped up and to the east of the towns of KAPELLEN, ISSUM and RHEURDT have been cleared of the enemy. Farther east and south our forces are fighting in MOERS, HOMBERG and UERDINGEN.

Southeast of NEUSS we have reached DERIKUM, less than two miles from the Rhine river, after an advance of more than five miles.

Northeast of COLOGNE our forces reached RAMRATH and ANSTEL, cleared STOMMELN and SINNERSDORF, and have sent patrols to the Rhine north of COLOGNE. We reached WIDDERSDORF, two miles west of COLOGNE, and fighting is in progress at FRECHEN, on the COLOGNE—DUREN road, against strong enemy resistance.

Southwest of COLOGNE, our infantry is fighting in LIBLAR and we have cleared WEILERSWIST and DERKUM on the east bank of the Erft river.

FRAUENBERG, northwest of EUSKIRCHEN, is in our hands. To the southwest we are fighting in GEMUND, and our units have taken SCHLEIDEN.

In the PRUM area we have captured REUTH, BUDESHEIM and SEIWERATH. North of BITBURG we captured BALESFELD and our units advancing from the north and south made contact in this area between the Nims and Kyll rivers.

North of TRIER, our infantry crossed the Kyll river and entered HOSTEN, encountering enemy small-arms, mortar and artillery fire. Northeast of TRIER, we captured PFALZEL. In the ZERF area east of SAARBURG our units repulsed a counter-attack by a strong force of enemy infantry.

We have cleared almost all of FROBACH against stubborn resistance. House-to-house fighting continued in the nearby village of MARIENAU.

Gains of more than a mile were made between FORBACH and SAARBRUCKEN. Our forces partially cleared STIRING-WENDEL. We cut the SAARBRUCKEN—METZ highway two miles southwest of SAARBRUCKEN.

Along the Rhine south of STRASBOURG hostile patrols were forced back across the river. Allied forces in the west captured 9,769 prisoners 3 March.

Adverse weather yesterday limited air operations which were confined mainly to attacks on the enemy communications. Communication centers at WINTERSWIJK in Holland, BARLO, northeast of BOCHOLT, BRUHL and SECHTEM, near COLOGNE, and rail yards at LENKERBECK, RECKLINGHAUSEN and WANNE-EICKEL were attacked by escorted heavy, medium and light bombers.

Farther south rail targets in a wide arc from PIRMASENS to DONAUESCHINGEN were struck at by fighter-bombers. Among these were rail yards at GERNSBACH and KARLSRUHE and the rail station at DONAUESCHINGEN. Communications at FREIBURG and a fuel dump near the city also were attacked.

Rail yards, ordnance depots and industrial targets at ULM and elsewhere in southwest Germany were attacked by escorted heavy bombers in great strength. Targets in BERLIN were bombed last night by light bombers.

This close-up shows four Panzer Mk IVs and an American M5 light tank which had been captured and used by the Germans to defend the town against the Ninth Army attack. Zig-zag personnel trenches and an anti-tank ditch were part of the in-depth defences.

When the Ninth Army reached the Rhine at Neuss, this effectively protected the American left flank so late on March 3 General Collins issued the order to capture Cologne. The assault was to be spearheaded by the 3rd Armored Division aided by the 13th Infantry Regiment of the 8th Division.

By March 6 the armour had reached the city centre with the twin steeples of the cathedral visible ahead. Two Shermans advancing down Zeughaus-Strasse were fired on by a Panther, scoring a direct hit and blowing two of the crewmen into the street.

COMMUNIQUE No. 332   March 6

Allied forces continue to make good progress in reducing the enemy bridgehead west of the Rhine. Our units have occupied WARDT and advanced to the approaches of XANTEN. Mopping-up operations in the area of GELDERN have been completed and farther east we have reached RHEINBERG and captured ORSOY. MOERS and HOMBERG have been cleared of the enemy and we hold the left bank of the Rhine from HOMBERG to NEUSS.

Farther south our units reached the Rhine at GRIMLINGHAUSEN and have captured the town. South and southeast of GRIMLINGHAUSEN, the towns of SCHLICHERUM and NIEVENHEIM were captured, and we reached DORMAGEN after a four-mile advance. In the same area, cavalry elements cleared BENRATH CHORBUSCH, a forest, and occupied STRABERG and DELHOVEN.

We reached the Rhine at WORRINGEN, cleared ROGGENDORF, and pushed south to occupy LONGERICH.

COLOGNE has been entered by our armor which has penetrated more than one mile within the city limits. Other units are fighting in the western suburbs of MUNGERSDORF and JUNKERSDORF.

To the south, we have taken GLEUEL and BURBACH. Farther south of COLOGNE we have occupied SCHMARZMAAR and our armor cleared EUSKIRCHEN and pushed 800 yards southeast of the town.

BILLIG and KREUZWEINGARTEN, south of EUSKIRCHEN, have been taken.

East of the GEMUND FOREST we have taken BERG and entered GLEHN. The town of GEMUND has been captured.

Northeast of PRUM we captured SCHONFELD, DUPPACH and SCHWIRZHEIM. East and south of PRUM we captured KOPP, MALBERG and NEUHEUENBACH.

Our units have reached the Kyll river on a two-mile stretch in the area nine miles southeast of PRUM.

East of BITBURG our forces crossed the Kyll river and captured PICKLIESSEM and ORDORF.

In the SAARBRUCKEN area we have cleared FORBACH and nearby MARIENAU after hard fighting. Our units also have driven the enemy from a large part of STIRING-WENDEL. Some 1,250 allied prisoners of war were liberated at STIRING-WENDEL, most of them were ill.

In northern Alsace, and along the Rhine south of STRASBOURG enemy patrols were repulsed. Allied forces in the west captured 7,454 prisoners 4 March.

Rail lines in Holland and north of the Ruhr were attacked by fighter-bombers. Medium and light bombers attacked rail communications over a wide area mainly east of the Rhine. Targets were rail yards at NUTTLAR, 45 miles west of KASSEL; ALTENHUNDEM and KREUZTAL, north of SIEGEN; MARBURG, WETZLAR and BINGEN; a rail junction at WESTERBURG, and the communications center of STADT MECKENHEIM, southwest of BONN. An ordnance depot at UNNA, east of DORTMUND, also was attacked.

Rail yards at KAISERSLAUTERN and NEUSTADT and rail traffic in the ZWEIBRUCKEN area were targets for fighter-bombers.

Escorted heavy bombers attacked railway marshalling yards at CHEMNITZ and oil refineries at HARBURG, near HAMBURG.

Other escorted heavy bombers made a concentrated attack on a benzol plant near GELSENKIRCHEN. Last night CHEMNITZ was again attacked by heavy bombers which were over Germany in very great strength. Targets in BERLIN also were bombed.

The German crew of the Panther were captured in a shelter beneath the cathedral. Leutnant Barthell Bortr had three leg wounds, Obergefreiter Otto Koenich a burned face, while the third man lay dying on his bed. They surrendered to the first Americans they saw: war correspondent Mike Levin of ONA and three cameramen of the 165th Signal Company, Captain Charles Malley, Staff Sergeant Voight Carrell and Sergeant Harold Robert, who had boldly ventured out in front of the infantry. The photographs they took symbolised the battle for the city . . . and Germany. (For more, see *After the Battle* No. 104.)

Left: As part of the Ninth Army's northwhard drive to link up with the British and Canadians struggling to eliminate the last German troops west of the Rhine at Xanten, the 8th Armored Division captured Rheinberg late on March 5, but only after losing 39 tanks in stiff fights on the approaches to the town. *Right:* Rheinstrasse — then and now.

COMMUNIQUE No. 333   March 7

Allied forces are meeting fierce resistance along the approaches to XANTEN. SONSBECK, southwest of XANTEN, has been captured against moderate resistance and farther south our troops have made advances of two miles to the BONNINGHARDT FOREST. The town of RHEINBERG has been cleared.

Continued bad weather yesterday again limited our air operations, however enemy troops, armor and transport at WESEL were attacked by escorted light bombers.

Our forces cleared the area west of the Rhine river from a point eight miles south of NEUSS to COLOGNE, with the exception of ZONS and the area in the river bend just north of ZONS.

COLOGNE has been captured but sporadic fighting continues in the southern outskirts of the city. Resistance in the city came mainly from houses converted into strong points.

South of COLOGNE, resistance is stronger and fighting is in progress in HERMULHEIM. We captured the Goldenberg power station on the northwest edge of KNAPSACK and have reached PINGSDORF and HEIMERZHEIM. Our units are within six miles of BONN. East of EUSKIRCHEN, we have taken NIEDERDREES and OBERDREES. Farther to the southwest the towns of STOTZHEIM, SATZVEY and GLEHN are in our hands. South of GEMUND, we have crossed the Olef river and have taken the town of OLEF.

Northeast of PRUM, our units reached the Kyll river, captured LISSENDORF and entered NIEDERBETTINGEN. An enemy counter-attack was repulsed in this area. East and southeast of PRUM, we crossed the Kyll, captured MICHELBACH and MURLENBACH, and entered DENSBORN.

An armored column, striking northeast and east from the BITBURG area, drove 25 miles to reach the vicinity of SCHONBACH. The towns of GINDORF, MEISBURG and OBERSTADTFELD were over-run by this force, which reached a point 20 miles from the Rhine river in one area.

East of BITBURG we reached the vicinity of BINSFELD. East of TRIER, our troops have crossed the Ruwer river to clear KENN and EITELSBACH. Enemy counter-attacks were repulsed north, east and southeast of TRIER.

West of FORBACH stiff fighting continued in the BOIS DE LA RESERVE where the enemy established strong points. Hostile infiltrations were mopped up. North of FORBACH we repulsed a tank-supported counter-attack.

Sharp fighting also took place on the east bank of the Saar river north of BUBINGEN.

Along the Rhine enemy patrols were turned back. Allied forces in the west captured 6,485 prisoners 5 March.

An oil refinery at SALZBERGEN was bombed by escorted heavy bombers. Rail yards at LENKERBECK, RECKLINGHAUSEN, RAUXEL, OPLADEN and SIEGBURG were attacked by medium and light bombers.

During the night heavy bombers made two separate attacks and light bombers made repeated attacks on enemy concentrations at WESEL.

Targets at SASSNITZ, on the island of Rugen in the Baltic, were attacked by heavy bombers which also attacked targets in BERLIN.

The procedure for the burial of the dead was well established. Graves concentration units had the task of giving honourable burial to both their own and enemy dead. While Britain made some use of space in cemeteries laid down after the First World War, many temporary burial grounds were created like the one on page 228. As far as British dead in Germany were concerned, after the war scattered graves were exhumed and concentrated in 14 permanent cemeteries, the largest of which is in the Reichswald Forest with over 7,500 dead. However one huge difference between the United States and Britain and the Commonwealth was that America permitted the repatriation of the dead after the war whereas the Imperial War Graves Commission did not. On September 25, 1944, the American Graves Registration service opened a central cemetery in Belgium at Henri-Chapelle (ten miles west of Aachen) which by May 1945 contained over 46,000 American and more than 25,000 German dead in a separate plot. In July 1947 the first shipment of US dead was made to the next of kin in the States so that today only 7,992 remain at Henri-Chapelle. Seven more US cemeteries for the Second World War were established in France, Belgium, Luxembourg and the Netherlands for dead in northern Europe as no American soldiers were permitted to lie in enemy territory.

Although the advantages of seizing a bridge across the Rhine had been discussed by SHAEF, no one entertained more than a vague hope that such an opportunity would present itself, and no specific order had been issued or plan made for this eventuality. When on March 7 US armour reached the town of Remagen, 30 miles south of Cologne, to their amazement they found the Ludendorff railway bridge still intact.

COMMUNIQUE No. 334 — March 8

Allied forces are still meeting fierce resistance in the approaches to XANTEN. We have advanced to the outskirts of VEEN where heavy fighting continues. BONNINGHARDT has been occupied and farther east our units are fighting in OSSENBERG. The west bank of the Rhine has now been cleared between RHEINBERG and ORSOY.

Enemy troop concentrations west of WESEL, and barges in the RHEINBERG area were attacked by fighter-bombers.

South of DUSSELDORF we have captured ZONS.

In COLOGNE our units continued to mop up sporadic resistance in the southeast section of the city. South of COLOGNE we cleared RONDORF, IMMENDORF, MESCHENICH and FISCHENICH, and reached BRUHL.

Northwest of BONN we have reached BRENIG, and have captured BORNHEIM and BOTZDORF.

Southeast of EUSKIRCHEN we occupied RHEINBACH, SCHWEINHEIM and KIRCHHEIM and are fighting in the FLAMERSHEIMWALD.

East of SCHLEIDEN we occupied KALL, KELDENICH and SOTENICH.

East of PRUM we have captured BOLSDORF, DOHM, GEROLSTEIN and PELM, and our armor pushing more than 11 miles northeast of PELM has captured HINTERWEILER, DREIS and BOXBERG.

Another armored unit has reached the Rhine in the area north of COBLENZ after overrunning a number of towns including UDERSDORF, SCHONBACH and MONREAL.

Infantry units are mopping up behind the armored thrust.

Southeast of BITBURG we have captured BINSFELD and HERFORST. Northeast of TRIER we have cleared QUINT, EHRANG and MERTESDORF.

In our Saar bridgehead we repulsed five counter-attacks.

We met continued stubborn resistance in the FORBACH area. The sector farther west and along the Rhine was quiet. Allied forces in the west captured 6,467 prisoners 6 March.

A railroad viaduct near BIELEFELD, marshalling yards at BIELEFELD, SOEST, SIEGEN, and GIESSEN, the Castrop-Rauxel benzol plant, the Harpen refinery and two other benzol plants in the DORTMUND area were attacked by escorted heavy bombers in great strength.

Rail lines and traffic north of the Ruhr were attacked by fighter-bombers. Four enemy aircraft were shot down. One of our heavy bombers and two fighters are missing.

Last night heavy bombers were over Germany in very great strength with DESSAU and oil refineries at HARBURG, near HAMBURG, and HEIDE in Schleswig-Holstein, as the main objectives. Targets in BERLIN were bombed by light bombers.

Although the bridge had been wired for demolition, as German troops were still using it to cross to the eastern bank, the charges had not been fired. However, as a squad led by Lieutenant Karl Timmerman approached the western end, a 30-foot gap was blown in the approach, preventing it being used by vehicles. Brigadier General William M. Hoge, the 9th Armored CCB commander, promptly gave the order for it to be taken which was relayed to Timmerman at the bridge. The Germans then made a second attempt to blow the charges but having had insufficient explosive of the correct military quality to bring the structure down, when the smoke cleared the bridge was still standing . . . a gateway across the river as was proudly announced by the 9th Armored. However, no mention of its capture appeared in the following day's communiqué.

Even two days later, the precise location of the crossing had not been released by SHAEF. Here, Eisenhower describes the moment he was told of the capture of the Remagen bridge: 'This news was reported to Bradley. It happened that a SHAEF staff officer was in Bradley's headquarters when the news arrived, and a discussion at once took place as to the amount of force that should be pushed across the bridge. If the bridgehead force was too small it would be destroyed through a quick concentration of German strength on the east side of the river. On the other hand, Bradley realized that if he threw a large force across he might interfere with further development of my basic plan. Bradley instantly telephoned me. I was at dinner in my Rheims headquarters with the corps and division commanders of the American airborne forces when Bradley's call came through. When he reported that we had a permanent bridge across the Rhine I could scarcely believe my ears. He and I had frequently discussed such a development as a remote possibility but never as a well-founded hope. I fairly shouted into the telephone: "How much have you got in that vicinity that you can throw across the river?" He said: "I have more than four divisions but I called you up to make sure that pushing them over would not interfere with your plans." I replied: "Well, Brad, we expected to have that many divisions tied up around Cologne and now those are free. Go ahead and shove over at least five divisions instantly, and anything else that is necessary to make certain of our hold." His answer came over the phone with a distinct tone of glee: "That's exactly what I wanted to do but the question had been raised here about conflict with your plans, and I wanted to check with you." That was one of my happy moments of the war'. This is Eisenhower's own map.

COMMUNIQUE No. 335   March 9

Allied forces have surrounded XANTEN despite strong enemy resistance and are fighting in the town. Heavy fighting continues in the area of VEEN.

We captured RODENKIRCHEN and entered SURTH near the Rhine south of COLOGNE.

Our units have reached the Rhine and crossed it to establish a bridgehead on the east bank, south of COLOGNE.

Northwest of BONN we captured BERZDORF, ECHTEM and ROISDORF, and have cleared half of the city of BONN. West of BONN, we occupied DRANSDORF, and entered DUISDORF. Three-fourths of the city of BAD GODESBERG, south of BONN, has been cleared.

Our infantry units, in gains of up to three and one-half miles, captured WIESBAUM and LEUDERSDORF northwest of PRUM. Our armored elements have advanced to the vicinity of BOOS, nine miles west of MAYEN. Other armored elements are patrolling the Rhine, northwest of COBLENZ, and are not in contact with the enemy in this area.

Our infantry, mopping up behind the armored thrusts in the area east of PRUM, has occupied DARSCHEID, NEROTH, SALM, EISENSCHMITT, and SCHWARZENBORN.

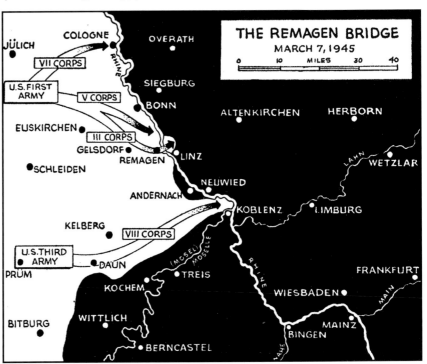

Even though engineers had constructed a pontoon bridge alongside the Ludendorff bridge within 96 hours to help cross, traffic still queued bumper to bumper to reach the far bank. This jam stretched five miles from Bad Bodendorf.

East of BITBURG other infantry units have captured several towns, including ARENRATH and NIERSBACH.

Four enemy counter-attacks in the vicinity of the junction of the Saar and Moselle rivers near TRIER were repulsed by our armored elements. We also repulsed a counter-attack in the area seven miles southeast of TRIER.

In the FORBACH area enemy resistance continued from dug in positions. Hostile patrols were repulsed along the Rhine. Allied forces in the west captured 6,753 prisoners 7 March.

Six benzol plants and a synthetic oil plant in the Ruhr, mainly in the GELSENKIRCHEN and DORTMUND areas, and rail yards at ESSEN, BETZDORF, SIEGEN, DILLENBURG, and GIESSEN were attacked by escorted heavy bombers in very great strength.

Striking at the enemy's communications leading to the area of our bridgehead over the Rhine south of COLOGNE, medium and light bombers attacked targets in a number of towns. Other medium and light bombers bombed targets at BERG-GLADBACH and ALTENKIRCHEN and a motor vehicle depot and repair pool at WULFRATH. One heavy bomber is missing from the day's operations.

Last night heavy bombers made heavy attacks on the communications center and industrial town of KASSEL, and on submarine building yards at HAMBURG; while targets in BERLIN, and enemy movements north and south of the Ruhr, were attacked by light bombers.

Frank Cornely of the Remagen Museum took the comparison from the very busy B266.

Military police kept the vehicles moving once they reached the river. Unfortunately a new shopping mall, since built at this spot, would make a comparison meaningless so Frank took his shot from across the river, looking in the reverse direction.

Not much left of Xanten — key town on the Rhine facing Wesel — whose capture was vital for Montgomery's forthcoming crossing of the river in the north.

COMMUNIQUE No. 336   March 10

Allied forces have captured XANTEN after bitter fighting and advanced beyond it to the south. In the area of VEEN our units are meeting strong enemy resistance. We have captured ALPEN and MILLINGEN and the town of OSSENBERG has been cleared.

Enemy troops west of the Rhine, near WESEL, were attacked by fighter-bombers.

Farther south the cities of BONN and BAD GODESBERG have been captured. Some mopping-up continues in the southern sector of BONN.

Our crossing of the Rhine was made at REMAGEN where a railway bridge was captured intact by our armor. ERPEL, on the east bank of the Rhine, was captured by our forces before they proceeded inland. Fighter aircraft gave cover yesterday to our operations in the bridgehead.

Armored units striking northeast in a 19-mile advance, captured BROHL on the Rhine, while another armored column, moving parallel, has captured MAYEN and advanced 11 miles farther to take ANDERNACH on the Rhine. Our armored units advancing from the south have linked up along the Rhine with other units advancing from the north.

Other armored elements, mopping up in the COBLENZ plain, have captured KARLICH, northwest of COBLENZ.

Northwest of MAYEN we captured several towns including ADENAU, REIFFERSCHEID and HOFFELD.

Infantry units mopping up in the area east of PRUM, reached the vicinity of WALDKONIGEN and other elements reached MANDERSCHEID.

In the area east and south of BITBURG, we captured BURG, LANDSCHEID and GLADBACH, and crossed the Salm river on a three and one-half mile stretch, and reached a point one mile east of the river. Our armor advancing one and one-half miles to the east on a five-mile front, entered FOHREN. Most of the resistance consisted of road-blocks and mines.

Rail yards west of the Rhine in the MANNHEIM area, at GRUNSTADT, BAD DURKHEIM and SCHIFFERSTADT, and fortified villages in the SAARBRUCKEN area were attacked by fighter-bombers.

Along the Rhine, northeast of STRASBOURG, we repulsed an enemy raid which followed a violent artillery and mortar barrage. Enemy patrols also were turned back south of STRASBOURG.

Allied forces in the west captured 5,944 prisoners 8 March.

Just look how beautifully the old Roman town has been restored. St Victor's Cathedral was begun in 1263 but not finished until 1544. It was extensively damaged in the battle. The town was eventually taken by Canadian troops after losing 400 men in the attempt. Restoration of Xanten was completed by the mid-1960s.

The Hotel Dreesen at Bad Godesberg was one of Hitler's favourite watering holes and it was from there that he set out on the night of June 29/30, 1934 to carry out the 'Blood Purge' of the SA. *Left:* Four years later, on September 22, 1938, he chose it as the venue for his second meeting with the British Prime Minister Neville Chamberlain to solve the Sudeten question which led to the dismemberment of Czechoslovakia. Chamberlain had called the outcome 'peace for our time' but Churchill viewed it as 'a total unmitigated defeat'. *Right:* In March 1944 Hitler's favourite hotel saw another surrender of sorts when a party of Germans were rounded up following the capture of the city on March 9. By now, the Führer had only a few weeks left to live.

Rail yards at FRANKFURT, KASSEL, MUNSTER, RHEINE and OSNABRUCK; the Henschel tank works at KASSEL, and the Hedderheim propeller and casting plant at FRANKFURT, were attacked by escorted heavy bombers in very great strength.

Enemy road and rail movement and communications east of the Rhine and barge traffic on the Rhine were attacked by fighter-bombers. Medium and light bomber targets were rail yards at DORSTEN, HALTERN, ARNSBERG, BUTZBACH and in the WIESBADEN area; armored vehicle depots at WIESBADEN and the communications centers of WESTERBURG and NASTATTEN, southeast of COBLENZ. Ammunition factories at WULFEN, north of DORSTEN; and LUNEN, north of DORTMUND, were attacked.

Fighter-bombers hit rail supply routes in eastern Holland and water traffic off the Dutch island of Overflakkee.

Escorted heavy bombers made concentrated attacks on two benzol plants at DATTELN on the northeastern outskirts of the Ruhr.

Fifteen enemy aircraft were shot down during the day. Ten of our heavy bombers, four medium and light bombers and 15 fighters are missing according to reports so far received.

Last night targets in BERLIN were bombed by light bombers. Other light bombers struck at road and rail targets north of the Ruhr eastward to MAGDEBURG and east of COLOGNE and BONN.

Bonn was cleared the same day by the 1st Infantry Division. Although the German commander of the city, General Richard von Bothmer, escaped across the Rhine, he was court-martialed and stripped of his rank at which point he shot himself. Yet Bonn's claim to fame is that it is the birthplace *(left)* of Ludwig van Beethoven in December 1770 (the precise date is not known). Ironically, it was the opening notes of his Fifth Symphony which were adopted as the signature for the BBC's European Service. Churchill had already adopted the V-sign as his personal symbol of victory and on January 14, 1941 Victor de Lavelaye, a Belgian programme maker at the BBC, encouraged his listeners on the Continent to show their defiance to the Germans by painting the letter 'V' wherever they could. The European Service also got its own 'sound' as the letter 'V' in Morse code is three dots and a dash — the same as the opening notes of the Fifth Symphony. These notes, played on the timponi, were adopted to give the station identification for the BBC's services to occupied Europe.

COMMUNIQUE No. 337   March 11

Allied forces have virtually eliminated the German bridgehead west of WESEL and only mopping-up operations remain to be completed. The enemy has blown both bridges at WESEL.

Farther south we have expanded our Rhine bridgehead at REMAGEN with gains of 500 to 1,500 yards eastward toward high ground. Considerable artillery fire is being directed against the rail bridge crossing the Rhine to the bridgehead. Fighter patrols were maintained throughout yesterday over the bridgehead. A small number of escorted enemy fighter-bombers which attempted to bomb the rail bridge were driven off by our fighters. Two of the enemy aircraft were shot down.

Twenty-three thousand Germans are estimated to be in a pocket created by the link-up along the Rhine of our armored elements advancing from the north and south. We captured 75 artillery pieces and a dump containing 20 carloads of materiel, mostly ordnance, in the vicinity of AHRWEILER, southwest of REMAGEN.

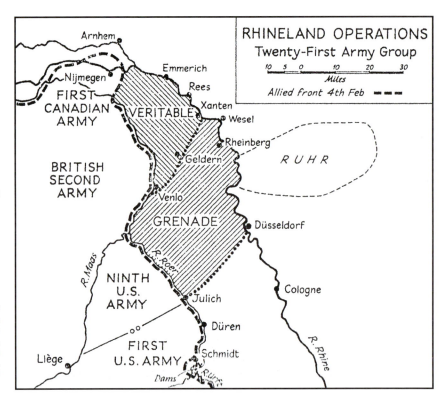

The four-week Rhineland operation by the 21st Army Group came to a close with the capture of Xanten. Here victorious Canadians march through Sonsbeck, five miles to the south-west. With an assault crossing of the Rhine imminent, the two bridges at Wesel were blown by the Wehrmacht on March 10.

Farther to the south, in the area west of MAYEN, we captured BAULER, ROTHENBACH, BODENBACH and HEYROTH. East of BITBURG, we have captured MANDERSCHEID, BETTENFELD, MUSWEILER, WITTLICH and NEUERBURG.

Northeast of TRIER, our armor advancing against moderate resistance, has reached SALMROHR after capturing BEKOND, FOHREN and RIVENICH.

Other armored units, pushing east of TRIER, repulsed a counter-attack and reached the vicinity of FELL.

From the SAARBRUCKEN area to the Rhine and southward to Switzerland, activity was limited to patrolling and scattered artillery fire. Allied forces in the west captured 6,012 prisoners 9 March.

The enemy's communications in an area stretching from BURGSTEINFURT, south of RHEINE, to COBLENZ and eastward, were heavily attacked yesterday by heavy, medium, light and fighter-bombers.

Left: **The Büderich road bridge seen from the left bank and** *(right)* **the Menzelen railway bridge which dated from 1874.**

Striking in and near the Ruhr, escorted heavy bombers in very great strength bombed rail yards at COESFELD, DORTMUND, SCHWERTE, SOEST and PADERBORN, and other objectives including rail viaducts. Rail yards at BURGSTEINFURT, LIPPSTADT, LENNEP, ERNDTEBRUCK and NIEDERSCHEID, and the communications centers of ALTENKIRCHEN and SIEGEN were attacked by other medium and light bombers.

Farther south, communications at KAISERSLAUTERN, HOMBURG, ZWEIBRUCKEN and WISSEMBOURG, and rail stations at DONAUESCHINGEN and TUTTLINGEN were attacked by fighter-bombers. Near LANDAU, medium bombers struck at a supply dump.

A synthetic oil plant at GELSENKIRCHEN was attacked by escorted heavy bombers.

According to reports so far received, one bomber and ten of our fighters are missing.

Targets in BERLIN were attacked by light bombers last night.

Although the road bridge on the right was rebuilt, the rail bridge in the foreground on the left was not.

The steelwork blocking the river was cleared and the track lifted, yet the brickwork remains as a graphic legacy of the war.

By March 11, the Third Army had eliminated German forces in the mountainous Eifel region west of Mayen and Allied units now held the east bank of the Rhine from Emmerich on the Dutch border, through Andernach (above) to Coblenz.

COMMUNIQUE No. 338   **March 12**

Allied forces have eliminated the enemy bridgehead west of the Rhine at WESEL.

We have extended our REMAGEN bridgehead to a width of nine miles and a depth of three miles. Two small enemy counter-attacks were repulsed. Our units in the bridgehead are fighting in BAD HONNEF and have captured the towns of RHEINBREITBACH, BRUCHHAUSEN, UNKEL, OHLENBERG and LINZ.

Our anti-aircraft claimed 23 enemy planes destroyed and five probables out of a total of 47 planes over the bridge site. Fighter aircraft patrolled the bridgehead area yesterday.

Farther south along the Rhine our armor cleared another six-mile stretch of the west bank of the river reaching a point about one mile north of COBLENZ.

Southwest of COBLENZ we cleared the north bank of the Moselle river from the vicinity of COBLENZ to COCHEM, capturing nearly a score of towns and villages including GUIS, WINNIGEN, KOBERN, GONDORF, HATZENPORT, CARDEN, POMMERN, LANDKERN and COCHEM.

North of WITTLICH, our infantry, mopping up behind our armored units, captured a number of towns including GILLENFELD, DIERFELD, FLUSSBACH, LUXEM and DORF.

In the area northeast of TRIER our armor captured LONGUICH and LONGEN and cleared WENGEROHR.

In the SAARBRUCKEN area our artillery knocked out a small number of enemy armored vehicles. Along the Rhine south of STRASBOURG enemy patrols were repulsed.

Allied forces in the west captured 4,719 prisoners 10 March.

Yesterday afternoon, escorted heavy bombers in very great strength, struck at ESSEN. The attack was controlled by a master-bomber and a great weight of high-explosive bombs was dropped.

Other escorted heavy bombers, also in very great strength, attacked submarine building yards at BREMEN, HAMBURG, and KIEL, and oil refineries at BREMEN and HAMBURG.

During February, General Patton had been planning the next move for his Third Army's attack towards — and he hoped — over the Rhine to upstage Montgomery, but first there was the job of eliminating the huge triangle of enemy-held territory west of the river. This area was protected in the north-west by the Moselle and the south-west by the Siegfried Line.

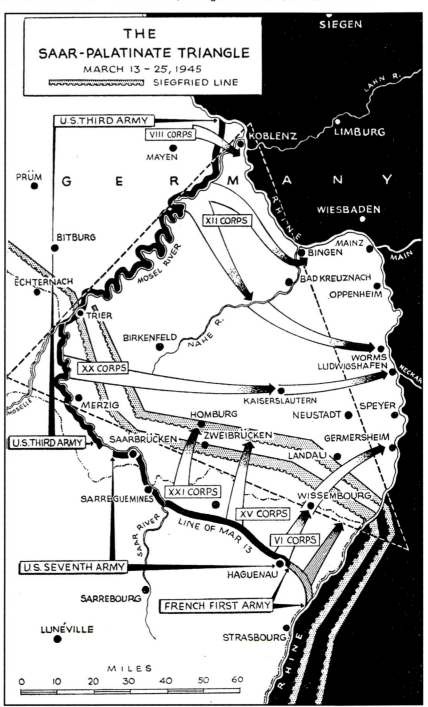

Trucks of the Third Army roll through Mayen on March 12 towards the front. Patton explains his plan: 'The scheme devised, and later executed, was as follows: to attack with two corps with the purpose of seizing bridgeheads over the Rhine river in the vicinity of Mainz, Oppenheim and Worms. The XX Corps, consisting of the 94th, 26th and 80th Infantry Divisions and the 10th Armored Division, later reinforced by the 65th Infantry and the 12th Armored, was to attack from Trier—Saarburg in the direction of Kaiserslautern. The XII Corps, consisting of the 4th Armored, the 5th, 76th, 90th and 89th Infantry Divisions, was to attack south across the Moselle river southeast of Mayen, heading initially on Bingen and Bad Kreuznach, with the purpose of cutting off the recrossing of the Rhine by the enemy and securing a crossing for us somewhere between Mainz and Worms. The VIII Corps, with the 87th and 4th Infantry and 11th Armored, was to continue mopping up north of the Moselle and west of the Rhine, with the distinct understanding that if we could secure a crossing over the Rhine, it was to be exploited.'

The communications centers of AHAUS and STADTLOHN, northwest of COESFELD, and ammunition factories at WULFEN, north of DORSTEN, and SYTHEN, northeast of HALTERN, were attacked by medium and light bombers. Other medium and light bombers struck at communications centers at HACHENBURG and WESTERBURG, east of REMAGEN; targets at WEYERBUSCH and WISSEN, northeast of REMAGEN; at SIERSHAHN, northeast of COBLENZ; and four enemy airfields in the areas south and southeast of SIEGEN and east and southeast of GIESSEN.

A rail bridge at BAD MUNSTER, a road bridge northeast of SAARGEMUND and rail targets in and near SAARBRUCKEN, ST INGBERT, NEUENKIRCHEN, HOMBURG and ZWEIBRUCKEN were targets for medium and fighter-bombers.

Targets in BERLIN were bombed by light bombers last night.

COMMUNIQUE No. 339   March 13

The Allied bridgehead across the Rhine has been extended, against increasing enemy resistance, to a depth of four miles and a length of ten miles. In the northern part of the bridgehead fighting continues in BAD HONNEF. Our units cleared the towns of HARGARTEN and GINSTERHAHN, northeast of LINZ, and fighting is in progress in HONNINGEN in the southern portion of the bridgehead.

Mayen had been 90 per cent destroyed in raids by the Eighth Air Force on December 12 and January 2, and it was only after a special referendum was offered to the surviving townspeople that a decision was made to rebuild.

Enemy artillery directed at the bridgehead decreased after we captured several hills which were being used for observation. Fighter aircraft continued to provide umbrella cover for the bridgehead. On the west bank of the Rhine, our units continued to reduce the enemy pocket in the Laacher See area southwest of ANDERNACH, clearing the towns of EICH, NICKENICH and KRETZ.

We now control all of the north bank of the Moselle river between TRIER and COBLENZ with the exception of a ten-mile stretch between COCHEM and REIL. West of COCHEM, we captured DRIESCH and LUTZERATH, and our armor reached the vicinity of REIL, to the south. Southeast of WITTLICH, we captured URZIG and cleared MARING.

Northeast of TRIER, our forces south of the Moselle captured RIOL in a one-mile gain. An enemy counter-attack with armor and infantry succeeded in recapturing some high ground in the area of WALDBACH, five miles east of TRIER.

In the SAARBRUCKEN area and the Hardt mountain sector farther east our troops repulsed several small enemy attacks and attempts at infiltration. Harassing enemy artillery fire fell along the Rhine.

Allied forces in the west captured 4,980 prisoners 11 March.

The enemy's communications in and around the Ruhr were subjected to heavy air attacks yesterday. The communications center of DORTMUND was attacked by escorted heavy bombers in very great strength. Four thousand nine hundred tons of bombs were dropped in a concentrated attack which lasted less than half an hour.

Other escorted heavy bombers in great strength struck at rail yards at BETZDORF, SIEGEN, DILLENBURG, WETZLAR, MARBURG and FRIEDBERG.

Nine rail yards and a communications center in the quadrilateral area formed by DORSTEN, GESEKE, FRANKENBERG and MARIENBERG, and rail yards at LORCH, east of STUTTGART, were attacked by medium and light bombers in strength.

Farther south fighter-bombers struck at communications and other targets from NEUENKIRCHEN northeastward to SCHWEINFURT.

An ammunition filling depot east of WESEL and an ammunition dump at KIRKEL, northeast of SAARBRUCKEN, were attacked by other medium bombers.

Naval and military installations in the Baltic port of SWINEMUNDE were attacked by escorted heavy bombers in great strength.

Four enemy aircraft were shot down during these operations. According to reports so far received three bombers and three of our fighters are missing.

Targets in BERLIN were bombed by light bombers last night.

Now, on the south-western corner of the Saar-Palatinate Triangle, men of Troop B, 116th Cavalry Reconnaissance Squadron, of the XXI Corps (Seventh Army), have rounded up these prisoners in the Ludweiler area, six miles south of Saarlautern (now Saarlouis).

COMMUNIQUE No. 340   March 14

Allied forces in the REMAGEN bridgehead have made gains of up to 1,000 yards eastward over rugged terrain and against stubborn resistance. We reached a point four miles northeast of REMAGEN after an 800-yard push. BAD HONNEF has been cleared but fighting continues in the suburbs.

We cut the north-south road due east of LINZ and reached a point two and one-half miles from the autobahn which parallels the Rhine east of the bridgehead.

A tank-supported enemy counter-attack was repulsed near HARGARTEN. We knocked out four of the six tanks in the attack. We repulsed another counter-attack made by infantry northeast of HONNINGEN. Fighting continues in HONNINGEN.

A pontoon bridge capable of handling light vehicular traffic to the bridgehead is in operation. The bridgehead is now four and one-half miles deep and ten and one-half miles long. Our fighter aircraft maintained patrols over the bridgehead throughout the day and shot down ten enemy planes.

The enemy pocket in the Laacher See area, southwest of ANDERNACH, has been mopped up. Our forces now control the north bank of the Moselle river between TRIER and COBLENZ, with the exception of a four-miles stretch from EDIGER to a point across the river from BULLAY.

In the area northwest of EDIGER, our units cleared DOHR, FAID, GEVENICH, WEILER, URSCHMITT, KLIDING, and STROTZBUSCH. Northeast of WITTLICH we captured KINDERBEUREN, BENGEL and REIL.

A small enemy counter-attack with armor and infantry was repulsed without loss of ground in the area seven miles east of TRIER. Our units have pushed eastward two and one-half miles in the wooded area nine and one-half miles east of SAARBURG. They crossed the Ruwer river against light resistance. In the area seven miles southeast of SAARBURG we captured GREIMERATH.

Between SAARBRUCKEN and the Hardt mountains enemy artillery and mortar fire increased.

In a raid on the northern part of HAGUENAU we took prisoners and captured additional houses.

Enemy patrols were repulsed on the west bank of the Rhine south of STRASBOURG.

Allied forces in the west captured 5,416 prisoners 12 March.

The communications center and industrial town of BARMEN on the southern outskirts of the Ruhr was attacked by escorted heavy bombers yesterday.

Medium and light bombers struck at rail yards and communications centers at NIJVERDAL in eastern Holland; LENGERICH, STADTLOHN and BORKEN north of the Ruhr, and other rail yards east of DORTMUND. Rail and river traffic between LIPPSTADT, SIEGEN and the Rhine, rail targets northeast of COLOGNE, south to the northern Alsace frontier region, supply installations and ammunition dumps in the SAARBRUCKEN area and a motor transport depot at BAD KREUZNACH were attacked by medium, light and fighter-bombers. Rail lines were cut in very many places both in Holland and Germany.

Enemy airfields at RHEINE and southwest of FRANKFURT were bombed by medium and light bombers. Fighter-bombers attacked another airfield south of STUTTGART.

Fortified towns between the Moselle and Saar rivers were hit by fighter-bombers.

During the day 24 enemy aircraft were shot down including the ten in the REMAGEN bridgehead area. According to reports so far received five of our medium and light bombers and 11 fighters are missing.

Objectives in the Ruhr were attacked by heavy bombers last night. Light bombers bombed targets in BERLIN. Enemy movement east of the Ruhr was attacked by other light bombers.

The wartime caption states that in their latest attack the Seventh Army were reported to have taken 3,000 prisoners.

With prisoners now being rounded up in their thousands it was a huge logistic task to move them from the front line. These men assembled at Welsfeld, seven miles north of Echternach, are being loaded for transportation to France. On March 9, it was announced that 1,009,631 prisoners had been taken by the Allies since June 6, 1944.

At the same time, civilians had to be informed about military occupation regulations as soldiers now had to become governors. Eisenhower was already well aware of the problems having broached the subject with General Marshall a few weeks after the North African campaign in 1942: 'The sooner I can get rid of these questions that are outside the military in scope, the happier I will be. Sometimes I think I live ten years each week of which at least nine are absorbed in political and economic matters.' Here, officers of the US Counter Intelligence Corps belonging to the 80th Infantry Division (Third Army) address the people of Kyllburg, seven miles north-east of Bitburg.

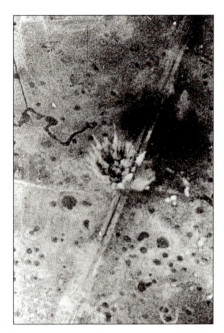

COMMUNIQUE No. 341   **March 15**

Allied forces have increased the depth of the bridgehead over the Rhine at REMAGEN to more than five miles. In the northern portion of the bridgehead, our infantry advanced 1,500 yards northward to reach a point one and one-half miles northeast of BAD HONNEF. Other elements drove to a point one and one-fourth miles from the autobahn in the area three miles east of BAD HONNEF.

Northeast of LINZ our units are in the outskirts of KALENBORN and NOTSCHEID. Our infantry pushed into the wooded area three and one-half miles due east of LINZ against stiff resistance.

Mopping-up operations continue along the north side of the Moselle river. South of COCHEM, we have captured ELLER, BREMM and ALDEGUND. Three more bends in the river northeast of TRIER have been cleared with the taking of CUES, MINHEIM and TRITTENHEIM.

Southeast of TRIER, our infantry made gains of one and one-half miles eastward, capturing MORSCHEID, HOLZERATH, HENTERN and FROMMERSBACH. Enemy Nebelwerfer and artillery fire against our forces increased in the area southeast of TRIER.

West of SAARBRUCKEN our forces advanced up to three miles on a five-mile front. The Franco-German border was crossed and the Saar river reached at several points. Towns occupied include SCHAFFHAUSEN, WEHRDEN, GEISLAUTERN, FURSTENHAUSEN, KLARENTHAL and SCHONECKEN.

Farther east, at HAGUENAU, an armor-supported enemy attack failed to dislodge our units from newly-won positions on the north side of the Moder river.

Allied forces in the west captured 2,413 prisoners 13 March.

Enemy communications in Holland, western Germany and along the entire length of the battle area and eastward, were under heavy attack from the air yesterday. Rail yards at GUTERSLOH, HOLZWICKEDE, LOHNE, southwest of OSNABRUCK; SEELZE and GIESSEN; rail bridges at BAD OEYNHAUSEN and VLOTHO; armored vehicle plants at HANNOVER; oil refineries at MISBURG and NIENHAGEN, a casting plant at HILDESHEIM; benzol plants near BOCHUM and RECKLINGHAUSEN, and a viaduct at ARNSBERG were attacked by escorted heavy bombers in very great strength.

At Bielefeld, a 400-metre viaduct on the main rail line from the Ruhr to Hannover and Berlin carried the four tracks across the Johannisbach valley. Its strategic importance had already led it to be the subject of over 50 attempts to bomb it since 1940 but none had succeeded, other than pitting the surrounding area with hundreds of craters. In February 1945, SHAEF wanted to isolate the Ruhr so cutting the rail line at Bielefeld was top priority. Conventional bombs were no match for the massive masonry so No. 617 Squadron were given the task using their 12,000lb 'Tallboy' bombs which had already been successfully used against targets in France (see page 31). However, an attack by 18 Lancasters on February 22 failed to bring the viaduct down so the squadron returned on March 14 with 14 more Tallboys and also the first two 22,000lb Grand Slam bombs, designed to create an earthquake effect. That did the job magnificently! (See also *After the Batttle* No. 79.)

The rail viaduct at BIELEFELD was attacked with 22,000-pound bombs by other escorted heavy bombers.

Rail yards at HALTERN and BOCHOLT; rail bridges at NIEDERMARSBERG, PRACHT, COLBE, NIEDERSCHELD and BAD MUNSTER; communications centers at HAIGER, BAD KREUZNACH and WALLHAUSEN; and enemy airfields at BABENHAUSEN and GROSSOSTHEIM were the targets for medium and light bombers.

Enemy transport on roads leading to REMAGEN, and an airfield at LIPPE were attacked by fighter-bombers. Fifty-eight enemy aircraft were destroyed on the ground and many others were damaged.

Rail targets in Holland; fortified towns, strong points and transport in the TRIER sector; supply centers at FRANKFURT and MONTABAUR; rail yards at DONAUESCHINGEN; communications at KAISERSLAUTERN, and ammunition dumps at NEUENKIRCHEN and near LANDAU also were attacked by fighter-bombers.

During the day a large number of rail cars, locomotives and motor vehicles were destroyed and rail lines were cut in many places.

E-boat pens at IJMUIDEN were attacked by heavy bombers. Twenty-seven enemy aircraft were shot down during these operations. According to reports so far received, 14 of our bombers and 20 fighters are missing.

Last night a synthetic oil plant at LUTZKENDORF and objectives in ZWEIBRUCKEN and HOMBURG were heavily attacked by heavy bombers. Targets in BERLIN were bombed by light bombers.

Over 75 unexploded bombs were uncovered during the rebuilding of the viaduct.

Patton's troops push on across the Triangle. These men of the 11th Infantry (5th Infantry Division) have already reached Korweiler over ten miles east of the Moselle. Next stop Kastellaun three miles down the road.

COMMUNIQUE No. 342   March 16

The Allied bridgehead over the Rhine has been increased to a depth of six miles and a width of eleven miles, against stiff resistance. In the northern portion of the bridgehead, we captured RHONDORF on the Rhine north of BAD HONNEF. To the east, our units entered AEGIDIENBERG at a point 1,000 yards from the autobahn, which is within their view.

Farther south, we captured a road junction at ROTTBITZE and fighting continues in the town. A tank-supported enemy counter-attack was repelled at KALENBORN and our units are fighting in the outskirts of the town. Our forces captured LORSCHEID after repelling an enemy counter-attack.

In the southern sector of the bridgehead we captured 125 prisoners in an enemy strong point in a quarry and cleared HEDDELN after repelling a counter-attack. Other advances of 400 yards were made to the south.

Of a total of 555 enemy planes observed over the Ludendorff bridge since the bridgehead was established, our anti-aircraft claims 111 destroyed and 26 probably destroyed.

Our forces have crossed the Moselle river in the area southwest of COBLENZ and now hold a bridgehead nine miles wide and six miles deep at a point nine to eighteen miles southwest of COBLENZ. Resistance is moderate. In this area we have cleared numerous towns and villages including UDENHAUSEN, HERSCHWIESEN, OPPENHAUSEN, MORSHAUSEN, NIEDER-GONDERSHAUSEN, OBER-GONDERSHAUSEN and LUTZ, and captured DOMMERSHAUSEN.

Two small enemy pockets remain north of the Moselle river. Our units captured an enemy hospital at BAD BERTRICH, northeast of WITTLICH, taking 171 prisoners. Five American patients were freed.

Southeast of TRIER, our forces gained up to two and one-half miles to the east, captured HEDDERT and SCHILLINGEN, and entered KELL. Resistance was spotty. The terrain was the toughest obstacle. Southeast of SAARBURG, our units advancing southeast against strong resistance from road-blocks and pillboxes, entered WEISKIRCHEN, SCHEIDEN, BERGEN and BRITTEN. We repulsed seven small counter-attacks in the area nine miles southeast of SAARBURG.

Between SAARBRUCKEN and the Rhine our units attacked at many points and gained up to three miles in several areas. Our forces are along the Saar river in the SAARBRUCKEN vicinity and are patrolling within one-half mile of the city.

Enemy fortified positions and troop concentrations in the areas of SAARBRUCKEN and ZWEIBRUCKEN were heavily attacked by medium and fighter-bombers. Farther east, fighting was in progress in ENSHEIM and HABKIRCHEN. UTWILLER was cleared.

SCHORBACH, north of the Maginot defenses at BITCHE, was occupied. In the Hardt mountains, we met strong resistance, but made substantial gains.

In northern Alsace our troops moved across the Moder river and advanced into OFFWILLER. BITSCHHOFFEN was bypassed. Only a small section of the northern part of HAGUENAU remains to be cleared.

Enemy communications in Holland and in western Germany from north of the Ruhr to the German-Swiss frontier were subjected to heavy air attack yesterday. Rail yards at OMMEN, east of ZWOLLE, and at DORSTEN, HALTERN and DULMEN; rail bridges near BORKEN; rail lines and rolling stock in the Ruhr valley; and road and rail targets between DUSSELDORF and HAGEN were struck at by medium, light and fighter-bombers.

The rail viaduct at ARNSBERG was attacked with 22,000-pound bombs by escorted heavy bombers, while benzol plants near ESSEN and RAUXEL were hit by other escorted heavy bombers.

Farther south, medium, light and fighter-bombers attacked the rail and communications centers of ERBACH, due east of the REMAGEN bridgehead, NOHFELDEN, north of ST WENDEL, SAARBRUCKEN, NEUENKIRCHEN, HOMBURG, ZWEIBRUCKEN, and PIRMASENS.

Communications targets at RASTATT, ROTTWEIL, DONAUESCHINGEN and TUTTLINGEN also were struck at by fighter-bombers. Five enemy airfields, including one at LIPPE; a number of fortified towns and supply dumps in the WIESBADEN and FRANKFURT areas, and other supply depots near COBLENZ and DARMSTADT were targets for other fighter-bombers.

Escorted heavy bombers in very great strength attacked rail yards at ORANIENBURG and objectives at ZOSSEN, south of BERLIN. Last night, the industrial and communications center of HAGEN and the oil refinery at MISBURG, east of HANNOVER, were heavily attacked by heavy bombers. Targets in BERLIN also were bombed.

Bundesstrasse 327 which runs through Kastellaun had been built as a military road on Göring's instructions — its popular name being the Hunsrückhöhenstrasse (Hunsrück Heights Road).

Meanwhile SHAEF announced that another 4,500 prisoners were in the bag, a problem which was to escalate dramatically during the last weeks of the war.

Although the Seventh Army was fighting with one foot in France, it still managed to break through the Siegfried Line on a wide front. Here the men of Company A of the 255th Infantry (63rd Division) cross the dragon's teeth near Oberwürzbach just east of Saarbrücken.

COMMUNIQUE No. 343   March 17

The Allied bridgehead across the Rhine is 13 miles long by seven miles deep. Our units in the northern part of the bridgehead are fighting in KONIGSWINTER after clearing RHONDORF. The autobahn has been cut in two places northwest and southeast of HOVEL. We are fighting in HOVEL and AEGIDIENBERG. A small enemy counter-attack was repulsed just southeast of AEGIDIENBERG.

In the center of the bridgehead, stiff enemy resistance has been encountered in KALENBORN, and near VETTELSCHOSS. To the south, we entered BREMSCHEID and reached the west bank of the Wied river to the east. HONNINGEN is virtually clear of the enemy.

Communications in four towns east of the REMAGEN bridgehead, a rail bridge at NIEDERSCHEID and rail yards at HERDORF were attacked by medium and light bombers yesterday. Fighter-bombers hit rail and road transport from REMAGEN east to WURZBURG, and attacked airfields at LIMBURG, SCHWEINFURT, WURZBURG and FRANKFURT.

Our infantry crossed the Moselle river southwest of COBLENZ and captured WALDESCH. Other elements advanced to a point two miles south of BOPPARD and two miles west of the Rhine river. We repulsed a tank-supported counter-attack near HERSCHWIESEN, west of BOPPARD. In the BOPPARD sector, we cleared EHR, BELTHEIM, BUCH and MORSDORF.

Our armor made swift gains to the southeast. One column gained 11 miles to enter RHEINBOLLEN and ELLERN on the edge of the SOONWALD. To the west, another column advanced 12 miles to enter SIMMERN, captured a bridge intact, and pushed on to the southeast. Resistance to these advances was light.

Additional crossings of the Moselle were made by our infantry in the vicinity of NEEF and BULLAY.

Southeast of TRIER, we captured REINSFELD, HERMESKEIL, GUSENBURG and GRUNBURG against decreasing enemy resistance.

Farther to the southwest we captured WEISKIRCHEN and reached LOSHEIM. We repulsed several tank-supported counter-attacks in this area.

Our infantry, advancing south along the east side of the Saar river, entered SAARHOLZBACH where house-to-house fighting is in progress. Other elements are within three miles of MERZIG.

Enemy armored columns, and troops in the area east of TRIER were attacked by fighter-bombers.

Our drive northward between the SAARBRUCKEN area and the Rhine continued to make steady progress against spotty resistance. East of SAARBRUCKEN we cleared ENSHEIM and pushed on more than two miles into the outer belt of the Siegfried Line. OMMERSHEIM was taken in the northernmost advance in this area. Advances up to two miles were made farther southeast, and MEDELSHEIM and several other villages were captured in this vicinity.

BITCHE, scene of heavy fighting in recent weeks, is being mopped up.

Additional progress was made in the Hardt mountain area over difficult terrain. Our troops entered BARENTHAL and cut the BARENTHAL—ZINSWILLER road.

In the northern Alsace plain, advances of more than a mile at several points took our forces to the Zinsel river at GUMBRECHTSHOFFEN.

HAGUENAU has now been cleared and we have advanced northward into the HAGUENAU FOREST.

Allied forces in the west captured 4,983 prisoners 15 March.

Fortified positions, mainly south of ZWEIBRUCKEN, and communications in the areas of NEUENKIRCHEN, KAISERSLAUTERN, MANNHEIM and east of HEIDELBERG were heavily attacked by medium and fighter-bombers. The rail yards at KAISERSLAUTERN were hit twice, and a large concentration of motor vehicles near MANNHEIM was bombed and strafed.

Barracks, ordnance depots and rail and road targets at LANDAU were attacked by strong formations of medium and light bombers. In these operations 15 enemy aircraft were shot down, seven were destroyed on the ground and others damaged. Eleven of our fighters are missing.

Last night heavy bombers were over Germany in strength with the important communications centers of NUREMBERG and WURZBURG as the main objectives. Targets in BERLIN also were bombed.

No visible signs of the defence line beside the Oberwürzbach-Manderbachtal road today but the concrete foundations still remain in the nearby undergrowth.

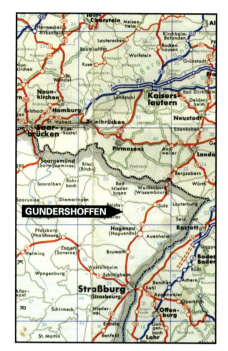

Back in France, the army was only a few miles from the frontier. Gundershoffen (four miles north-west of Haguenau) was captured by the US 103rd Division on March 17, two days after the offensive opened in northern Alsace.

COMMUNIQUE No. 344   March 18

The Allied bridgehead across the Rhine is now 14 miles long by seven and one-half miles deep. Another cut in the autobahn has been made east of KONIGSWINTER. We have entered ITTENBACH west of the highway, and HUSCHEID and BRUNGSBERG on the east side. We control four and one-half miles of the autobahn.

In the center of the bridgehead, VETTELSCHOSS and STRODT were cleared, but our forces are encountering fire from enemy self-propelled guns east of the towns. In the southern sector of the bridgehead, REIFERT and BREMSCHEID have been captured. In the vicinity of HAUSEN we took 200 prisoners, including ten officers. HONNINGEN was cleared and our forces have advanced 1,500 yards east of the town. An enemy counter-attack was broken up by our artillery in this area.

Our units have virtually cleared the city of COBLENZ. Our infantry, advancing east and southeast, has reached the Rhine river on a six-mile stretch in the area nine to 15 miles south of COBLENZ and has entered BOPPARD and captured the towns of BAD SALZIG, HOLZFELD and ST GOAR.

Farther west armored elements advancing southeast have captured MAISBORN, LAUDERT, RHEINBOLLEN and ELLERN. Another armored unit advancing southeast of SIMMERN, against light resistance has reached the Nahe river. Our infantry following up the armor has captured numerous towns including WUSCHHEIM, REICH, KULZ and NANNHAUSEN. East of the Moselle river town of ZELL, other units moving south captured BLANKENRATH, PANZWEILER, WURRICH and BUCHENBEUREN.

MERL, north of ZELL, and BRIEDEL to the southwest, have been cleared and our units are on the high ground overlooking the two remaining enemy pockets on the north bank of the Moselle.

Southeast of TRIER, we captured THOMM. Southeast of SAARBURG, the towns of STEINBERG, KONFELD, WADERN, THAILEN, MITLOSHEIM, LOSHEIM and BACHEM were cleared, RIMLINGEN was entered and our units reached a point less than one mile north of MERZIG, on the Saar river.

Enemy troops, armor, transport and artillery in the Moselle battle area were attacked by fighter-bombers.

Advances of up to seven miles were made from the SAARBRUCKEN area east toward the Rhine.

The Siegfried Line was reached and the outer defenses entered at several points. Among the towns entered were NIEDERWURZBACH, eight miles east of SAARBRUCKEN in the Siegfried Line; MIMBACH and ALSCHBACH farther east and in front of the Siegfried defenses; HORNBACH and DIETRICHINGEN, ten miles northwest of BITCHE in Germany; and ROBLINGEN, French border town, ten miles north of BITCHE.

In the Rhine valley, NIEDERBRONN was cleared and advances of six miles were made northwest of HAGUENAU. In the Rhine sector we are fighting in SCHIRRHEIM.

Allied forces in the west captured 4,299 prisoners 16 March.

Northeast of ST WENDEL 175 motor vehicles were destroyed and many others were damaged by fighter-bombers. Targets at NEUENKIRCHEN, ST INGBERT, and PIRMASENS were also attacked. Other fighter-bombers bombed and strafed an enemy troop concentration and command post near ZWEIBRUCKEN.

Looking south down the Grand Rue, the main road through the town.

An ammunition dump northeast of STRASBOURG was attacked by fighter-bombers.

Communications in Holland were the objectives for other fighter-bombers.

A supply dump east of WESEL and enemy-held buildings northeast of BOCHOLT were bombed by fighter-bombers. Synthetic oil plants at BOHLEN and RUHLAND, a benzol plant at MOLBIS, tank factories at HANNOVER, and other industrial targets and rail yards at MUNSTER were attacked by escorted heavy bombers in very great strength. Benzol plants near HULS and DORTMUND were bombed by other escorted heavy bombers.

The attack on the enemy's communications was continued. Medium, light, and fighter-bombers operating in strength from north of the Ruhr southward to ETTLINGEN struck at 13 rail yards, and the communications centers of WEILBURG and IDSTEIN. Ordnance and storage plants at GIESSEN also were attacked. Last night light bombers attacked targets in BERLIN.

As soon as the bridge at Remagen had been captured, engineers began to build two floating bridges, upstream and downstream. Once these were finished the Ludendorff bridge was closed to traffic to undergo repairs, caused not only by earlier Allied attempts to destroy it but from constant German shelling and bombing by the Luftwaffe. By March 17, the flooring had been largely repaired and several girders had been replaced. A number of suspension cables from the central arch of this lattice bowstring bridge had been spliced and work was beginning on the main damage above the eastern pier. At 3 p.m. about 200 engineers were at work on the bridge when there was sharp crack followed by another and the bridge began to tremble. It was obvious to the men working on the bridge that it was about to collapse but the warning came too late. With a grinding roar the massive structure swayed and twisted before plunging into the Rhine.

COMMUNIQUE No. 345   **March 19**

Allied forces in the Rhine bridgehead pushed north to the outskirts of NIEDERDOLLENDORF and east, against intense heavy-caliber enemy artillery fire, to high ground one mile north of BRUNGSBERG. Other elements crossed the autobahn to reach the outskirts of WINDHAGEN. We now control six miles of the highway.

East of LORSCHEID, in the central sector of the bridgehead, our forces crossed the Wied river. In the southern sector we have taken high ground four miles east of HONNINGEN. The bridgehead is 15 miles long by nearly eight miles deep. The railroad bridge at REMAGEN has collapsed into the Rhine.

In the Moselle-Rhine sector, street fighting continues in COBLENZ. South of the city we have cleared RHENS and captured BREY and BOPPARD. Our units control the west bank of the Rhine for a stretch of 17 miles from BOPPARD to a point six miles northwest of BINGEN. We entered BINGEN after an advance of seven miles.

Farther to the south, our armored elements are mopping up in BAD KREUZNACH after dispersing a counter-attack in the vicinity of the city. Other units entered SOBERNHEIM, southwest of BAD KREUZNACH. A number of towns have been taken in the SIMMERN-BAD KREUZNACH area.

Southwest of SIMMERN our units cleared KIRCHBERG, RHAUNEN and WICKENRODT; entered KELLENBACH and pushed on to the vicinity of BERGEN.

East of TRIER we cleared BEUREN and RASCHEID.

MERZIG, on the Saar river, is in our hands and to the south we have entered BECKINGEN and DILLINGEN. In the area northeast and east of MERZIG we cleared KRETTNICH and captured AUSSEN and HUTTERSDORF.

Between SAARBRUCKEN and the Hardt mountains our advance was slowed by stiffening resistance from the outer Siegfried Line defenses.

In the Hardt mountain area gains of up to eight miles were made. STURZELBRONN, near the frontier and LUDWIGSWINKEL, across the border in Germany, were cleared. Farther east WINGEN and several nearby towns were liberated.

Rapid advances were made in the Alsace plain north of the HAGUENAU FOREST where the enemy appeared to be in full retreat. SULZ, a communication center, was reached. Farther east we drove to the Maginot Line at RITTERSHOFFEN and HATTEN.

Along the Rhine we continued to make progress. FORSTFELD and BEINHEIM were taken.

Allied forces in the west captured 5,146 prisoners 17 March.

Military targets in the BERLIN area including the Schlesischer and north rail yards and stations; the Rheinmetal armament plant at TEGEL and the Borsig locomotive works at HENNIGSDORF were heavily attacked by escorted heavy bombers in very great strength. A benzol plant north of HATTINGEN and another east of BOCHUM were bombed by other escorted heavy bombers.

The attack on the enemy's communications was continued. Rail lines in Holland and north of the Ruhr; a rail bridge southeast of UTRECHT; rail yards at BOCHOLT and near HALTERN, and the rail center of BORKEN were struck at by medium, light and fighter-bombers.

Rail yards near DORTMUND, at KREUZTAL, north of SIEGEN, and at WETZLAR; rail traffic in the Ruhr and near GIESSEN, MARBURG and WURZBURG were attacked by other medium, light and fighter-bombers.

Farther to the south, rail and road traffic and other communications targets in the area from MAINZ to ST WENDEL and southeast to KARLSRUHE were under heavy attack by medium, light and fighter-bombers. Included among the targets were large concentrations of motor and horse-drawn vehicles at MAINZ and ST WENDEL; a rail bridge at WEIDENTHAL, east of KAISERSLAUTERN; road junctions and rail yards at BAD DURKHEIM and rail yards at WORMS, NEUSTADT and LANDAU.

A large enemy troop concentration at FISCHBACH, southeast of PIRMASENS, was attacked by fighter-bombers.

During the day a large number of rail cars, locomotives and motor vehicles was destroyed and rail lines were cut in many places. Last night the communications centers of WITTEN, southeast of BOCHUM; and HANAU, east of FRANKFURT, were attacked by heavy bombers in strength.

Targets in BERLIN and enemy movements over a wide area of Germany were attacked by light bombers.

Frantic attempts were made to rescue the men in the fast-flowing river and although most were saved, 25 had been killed, 18 of whom were never found. A further three of the 93 injured died of their wounds.

COMMUNIQUE No. 346   March 20

Allied forces continue to expand the REMAGEN bridgehead. We have pushed north to OBERKASSEL on the Rhine, and to the east have cleared STOCKHAUSEN and WINDHAGEN against heavy enemy artillery fire. Another 1,500 yards of the autobahn southeast of WINDHAGEN is in our hands. In the southern sector of the bridgehead we cleared ROCKENFELD, against moderate resistance, and reached HAMMERSTEIN. The bridgehead is 18 miles long and eight miles deep.

Armored vehicles and transport in the REMAGEN bridgehead area were attacked by our aircraft.

COBLENZ has been cleared of the enemy and we control the west bank of the Rhine from COBLENZ to BINGEN. BINGERBRUCK, across the Nahe river west of BINGEN, has been captured.

In the area south of BINGEN and east of BAD KREUZNACH heavy fighting is in progress. We have cleared WOLFSHEIM and SPRENDLINGEN and entered WOLLSTEIN.

BAD KREUZNACH and SOBERNHEIM, to the southwest, are in our hands. Between SOBERNHEIM and KIRN to the west, our amored units crossed the Nahe river and pushed southeastward to clear MEISENHEIM and to reach the vicinity of MERZWEILER. Towns cleared in these advances include MEDDERSHEIM, MERXHEIM and SCHMIDTHACHENBACH.

Our armored columns advancing from the north and west met in the vicinity of MERZWEILER. The resulting pocket, which extends northwest almost to the Moselle river, is estimated to contain about 2,000 enemy troops.

Farther to the southwest our units cleared ST WENDEL and DIRMINGEN. We captured the personnel and guns of an entire field artillery battalion in the DIRMINGEN area.

Troop concentrations and transport south and east of BAD KREUZNACH and ST WENDEL were attacked by Allied planes.

In the SAARLAUTERN bridgehead our units made gains northeastward against heavy resistance.

Our forces breached the Siegfried Line defenses at more than a dozen points along the sector between SAARBRUCKEN and the Rhine. Some units are through the fixed fortifications. Resistance continued to be stubborn. Except for stragglers, the enemy has been entirely expelled from French soil in this area.

West of ZWEIBRUCKEN, ALSCHBACH was cleared and 21 pillboxes were knocked out. Gains were made in the immediate ZWEIBRUCKEN area.

Farther east, the enemy's main defense line was reached in the Hardt mountain area. Fighting continued in NIEDERSCHLETTENBACH.

In the northern Alsace plain, we cleared OBERHOFEN, ALTENSTADT and WISSEMBOURG, and advance elements drove northward three miles to OBEROTTERBACH. LAUTERBURG, near the Rhine, was taken after hard fighting.

Enemy defenses in the Siegfried Line south of PIRMASENS and LANDAU were bombed by medium bombers.

Allied forces in the west captured 5,040 prisoners 18 March.

Medium, light, and fighter-bombers hit enemy road and rail traffic yesterday over an area ranging from north of the Ruhr to the Saar valley. About 4,000 motor and horse-drawn vehicles, rail cars and locomotives were destroyed and a very large number were damaged. Rail lines were cut in approximately 280 places including some in Holland. Among the day's targets were rail yards at COESFELD, DULMEN, BARMEN, LANDAU, around OSNABRUCK and MUNSTER, southwest of KASSEL and east of the upper Rhine and rail traffic in and south of the Ruhr. Five bridges were attacked, two between OSNABRUCK and HANNOVER and three west of KASSEL. Fighter-bombers hit a large motor repair depot north of EMMERICH, an ammunition dump near TERBORG, both in Holland, and airfields north and east of the Ruhr valley.

Hitler's ambitious plan, announced on National Labour Day in 1933, was to build over 6,000 miles of motor roads to be called Reichsautobahns that would not only solve Germany's crippling unemployment but also create a network of military highways. The initial plan was for six principal autobahns, two running north to south, three from east to west, and one north-west to south-east. The new highways began and ended at strategic points on the frontiers of the country and served all the important industrial cities. Dr Fritz Todt masterminded the project and at the end of the first Four-Year Plan in February 1938, Hitler announced that 1,500 miles were under construction and that 'a mammoth work must give witness to our will, our dilligence, our talent and our strength'. Ironic words when in a few short years the Germans would begin demolishing what had been achieved! This bridge at Rottbitze was just one of the 3,400 bridges which had been built over the autobahns. (Sorry, no comparison, as it would be somewhat dangerous to stand in the middle of the road!)

Escorted heavy bombers in very great strength, attacked industrial objectives at PLAUEN, JENA, ZWICKAU, jet aircraft factories at NEUBURG, LEIPHEIM and BAUMENHEIM, west of NEUBURG, and marshalling yards at FULDA. A benzol plant at GELSENKIRCHEN, the railway viaduct at ARNSBERG and another railway viaduct in the BIELEFELD area were attacked by other escorted heavy bombers.

In all the day's operations, 47 enemy aircraft were shot down and 20 others were destroyed on the ground. Nineteen of our fighters are missing, according to reports so far received.

Last night bombers attacked targets in BERLIN and rail communications from the Ruhr to HANNOVER and south to COBLENZ.

As announced in Communiqué 346, Coblenz was finally cleared of the enemy on March 19. The battle for the city — defended almost to the last man by Kampfgruppe Koblenz — had been a desperate struggle throughout the 17th.

COMMUNIQUE No. 347   March 21

Enemy resistance west of the Rhine and south of the Moselle rivers has been almost completely disorganized by swift Allied advances.

Our units have reached the Rhine, or points near it, at several places. We have reached the vicinity of MAINZ and BODENHEIM and have captured WORMS. Numerous towns have been overrun and captured including ALZEY, southeast of BAD KREUZNACH, and NIEDERHAUSEN, ST ALBAN and ROCKENHAUSEN, south of KREUZNACH.

Elements of our armies advancing from the north and west made contact 12 miles west of KAISERSLAUTERN. The city, initially bypassed by an armored spearhead, has been entered by both armored and infantry units. Enemy supply installations have been overrun at some points and numbers of weapons and vehicles have been captured.

In the SAARLAUTERN area our units cleared the towns of RODEN, FRAULAUTERN, ENSDORF and VOLKINGEN and advanced eastward to a point ten miles west of NEUENKIRCHEN.

Northeast of NEUENKIRCHEN we captured OTTWEILER and FURTH.

SAARBRUCKEN, chief city of the Saar basin, was taken in the rapid advance of our units which crossed the Saar river west of the city. ZWEIBRUCKEN, 20 miles farther east, also was captured.

We are through the Siegfried Line on a wide front in this area with enemy resistance disorganized at some points.

Progress was slower in the rugged Hardt mountain area. In the Rhine valley, KAPSWEYER, northeast of WISSEMBOURG, was captured.

In the triangle formed by SAARBRUCKEN, MAINZ and KARLSRUHE, fighter-bombers struck throughout the day at enemy transport, guns and tanks retreating toward the Rhine.

In a dawn attack between BAD DURKHEIM and FRANKENSTEIN, 141 vehicles were destroyed and many others damaged.

Our Rhine bridgehead at REMAGEN has been expanded to a length of 22½ miles and a depth of eight miles. In the north end of the bridgehead we cleared OBERKASSEL and entered the outskirts of BEUEL, across the Rhine from BONN. East of BEUEL we reached HOLZLAR and STIELDORF against light resistance.

By contrast, 70 miles due south, the 319th Infantry (80th Division) of the Third Army entered Kaiserslautern on the 20th without encountering any opposition, and then linked up with armour of the Seventh Army 12 miles to the east. The memorial on Schillerplatz is to the First World War dead of the Bayrische Infanterie-Regiment 23.

The formal occupation of Germany lasted for ten years and from 1950 to 1955 Kaiserslautern became the largest US base in the country. Dubbed 'K-Town' by the millitary, today it has the largest American population outside of the United States with accommodation for 50,000 military personnel and families. The huge Ramstein Air Base is also located close by.

Fifteen miles to the east lies Bad Dürkheim, today a pleasant watering hole in the wine-drinking country of the Palatinate. This enemy convoy retreating there from Frankenthal was attacked by fighter-bombers at dawn on March 20. As it was at the junction of the two US armies, the caption to the top photo claims it for the Third and the one below for the Seventh!

Northeast of HONNEF we captured EUDENBACH and an airfield near the town. We repulsed two tank-supported counter-attacks at the airfield.

The enemy directed heavy artillery and mortar fire at the center of the bridgehead. Farther south resistance was light and our units gained 1,000 yards to reach the vicinity of LEUTESDORF.

Allied forces in the west captured 13,873 prisoners 19 March.

The offensive against the enemy's communications was continued yesterday by heavy, medium, light and fighter-bombers. Targets in Holland and in western Germany from north of the Ruhr southward to KARLSRUHE were attacked. Among the objectives were the rail centers of BOCHOLT and DORSTEN; rail yards at RECKLINGHAUSEN, HAMM, GESEKE, PADERBORN and KASSEL, and road junctions at GRONAU, VREDEN and WESTERBURG.

German airfields at AHLEN, HANDORF, HALTERN, GUTERSLOH, LIPPSTADT, GESEKE and PADERBORN were attacked by fighter bombers. Fifty enemy aircraft were destroyed on the ground and over 100 damaged in the course of these attacks.

An ammunition dump at SYTHEN was attacked by medium and light bombers while fighter-bombers hit an ordnance depot at MARBURG. Oil refineries at HEMMINGSTEDT and HAMBURG, submarine yards at HAMBURG, and other targets in the port of HAMBURG, were attacked by a strong force of escorted heavy bombers. Eleven enemy aircraft were shot down in the course of these operations. According to reports so far received four of our bombers and nine fighters are missing.

Last night heavy bombers were over Germany with the synthetic oil plant at BOHLEN and the oil refinery at HEMMINGSTEDT as the main objectives. Light bombers again attacked targets in BERLIN.

Worms — the historic cathedral where Martin Luther was declared a heretic in 1521 — was claimed in the SHAEF caption to this photograph to have been 'spared from destruction by the precision bombing of US planes' yet the town had already been the subject of RAF Bomber Command's first and only large raid on the city on the night of February 21/22 when the cathedral was damaged! The 4th Armored and 5th Infantry Divisions took the city on March 20, one of their number being photographed lying on the Ernst Ludwig Bridge which had already been blown before the troops arrived.

Two other 'bridge' towns were captured on March 20. This is Saarbrücken on the French border, named after the crossing over the River Saar (a tributary of the Moselle) dating from 1546.

This photograph taken a few days later shows men of the US 70th Division crossing to the western bank over a Bailey bridge spanning a gap in the town's Alte Brücke.

COMMUNIQUE No. 348   **March 22**

Allied forces have reduced the German-held area south of the Moselle and west of the Rhine to little more than a bridgehead. Enemy units remaining in the area are generally disorganized.

BINGEN, on the Rhine west of MAINZ, has been completely cleared of the enemy and several towns to the east have been mopped up. GONSENHEIM, one and one-half miles west of MAINZ, and DEXHEIM, near the Rhine south of MAINZ, have been captured. We repulsed two small counter-attacks in the area between DEXHEIM and MAINZ.

Our armored units have entered LUDWIGSHAFEN and reached the Rhine one mile north of the city.

Farther southwest our forces are fighting in NEUSTADT and have cleared KAISERSLAUTERN and ENKENBACH to the northwest.

Another link-up by Allied armies advancing from the north and west was made in the area south of OTTWEILER. Our units occupied ST INGBERT, south of OTTWEILER, and HOMBURG, east of ST INGBERT.

Between PIRMASENS and the Rhine the enemy is fighting stubbornly in an attempt to keep open an escape route.

Fighter-bombers bombed and strafed targets west of the Rhine including a convoy stretching for ten miles between PIRMASENS and LANDAU. In the KARLSRUHE area fighter-bombers struck at rail lines and motor transport.

In our REMAGEN bridgehead we have cleared BEUEL, opposite BONN, and reached the Sieg river on a seven-mile front from the Rhine east to NIEDERPLEIS after capturing a number of villages.

Several counter-attacks were repulsed at the airfield near EUDENBACH and the enemy continued to direct heavy artillery and mortar fire at the center of the bridgehead.

In the southern sector we repulsed a small counter-attack north of LEUTESDORF. The bridgehead is approximately 25 miles long and eight miles deep. Enemy armor near the bridgehead was attacked by fighter-bombers.

Allied forces in the west captured 8,683 prisoners 20 March.

Ten airfields in western Germany and a tank plant at PLAUEN, south of LEIPZIG, were attacked by 1,400 escorted heavy bombers yesterday.

Escorting fighters dive-bombed and strafed the airfields. Forty-three enemy aircraft were destroyed on the ground.

Rail yards at MUNSTER and RHEINE and an oil refinery at BREMEN were heavily attacked by other escorted heavy bombers. A rail bridge spanning the WESER river in the neighborhood of BREMEN was attacked with 22,000-pound bombs.

Medium and light bombers attacked the rail yards and communications centers north of the Ruhr at ANHOLT, ISSELBURG, BOCHOLT, BORKEN, DORSTEN, AHAUS, VREDEN, STADTLOHN, HALTERN, COESFELD and DULMEN. Fighter-bombers attacked rail yards at WINTERSWIJK, northeast of BOCHOLT, and struck at the enemy's main rail routes east and west of MUNSTER and in Holland. Enemy barracks and an ammunition and oil dump at WEZEP, southwest of ZWOLLE, were hit by rocket-firing fighters.

Rail traffic in the Ruhr and in the LIMBURG area, bridges in the region of KASSEL and rail lines and rolling stock around FRANKFURT were targets for fighter-bombers.

An oil refinery at UETZE, east of HANNOVER, was bombed.

An ammunition factory and a storage dump at EBERSTADT, south of DARMSTADT, were hit by medium bombers. Farther south in the FREIBURG area medium bombers attacked rail yards at RIEGEL, west of EMMENDINGEN, and at SCHRAMBERG. In all operations, 19 enemy aircraft were shot down. According to reports so far received, nine of our heavy bombers, five medium and light bombers, and 21 fighters are missing.

Targets in BERLIN were attacked twice during the night by light bombers. Transport and other objectives northeast of the Ruhr and south to COLOGNE were attacked by other light bombers.

Fifteen miles east of Saarbrücken lies Zweibrücken whose two bridges cross the River Schwarzbach. The town was one of the last Siegfried Line strong points in the Saar region, the ruins being taken by the Seventh Army. SHAEF's caption, passed for publication on March 29, says that 'these pictures give you an idea of the tremendous destruction suffered by German towns and cities which had to pay an enormous price for Hitler's stubbornness'.

Charles MacDonald, the renowned American military historian, graphically described the closing stages of the battle in the Palatinate: 'As American armored spearheads appeared without warning, seemingly over every hill and around every curve, and as American planes wreaked havoc from the air, hardly any semblance of organization remained in German ranks. It was less withdrawal than it was *sauve qui peut*. Camouflage, anti-aircraft security, dispersal — those were fancy terms from some other war, without meaning in this maelstrom of flight. Highways were littered with wrecked and burning vehicles and the corpses of men and animals. Road-blocks at defiles and on the edges of towns and villages might halt the inexorable onflow of tanks and half-tracks temporarily, but the pauses were brief and in the long run meaningless. Improvised white flags flying from almost every house and building along the way added a final note of dejection to the scene.'

COMMUNIQUE No. 349 March 23

Allied forces continue to reduce the German bridgehead west of the Rhine. We control the west bank of the river from COBLENZ to LUDWIGSHAFEN, although our forces have not reached the river at all points along this stretch.

MacDonald: 'From the first, Patton had hoped to exploit his part in the Saar-Palatinate campaign into a crossing of the Rhine. He wanted a quick, spectacular crossing that would produce newspaper headlines in the manner of the First Army's seizure of the Remagen bridge. He wanted it for a variety of reasons, no doubt including the glory it would bring to American arms, to the Third Army, and possibly to himself, but most of all he wanted it in order to beat Montgomery across the river. Patton remained concerned lest the Supreme Commander put the First and Third Armies on the defensive while farming out US divisions to the 21 Army Group. It was this concern, shared by Bradley and Hodges, that hovered specterlike over the meeting of the three American commanders at Bradley's HQ in Luxembourg on 19 March. Having received Eisenhower's permission to increase the First Army's strength in the Remagen bridgehead and an alert to be ready to break out from 23 March onward, Bradley told Patton to do the very thing the Third Army commander wanted to do — take the Rhine on the run.'

CROSSING THE RHINE

1.	March 7, 1600	Remagen	US First Army, 27th Armd. Inf. Batt.
2.	March 22, 2200	Oppenheim	US Third Army, 5th Div. 11th Inf. Reg., 3rd Batt.
3.	March 22, 2200	Nierstein	US Third Army, 5th Div., 11th Inf. Reg., 1st Batt.
4.	March 23, 2100	Rees	Second British Army, 51st Highland Division
5.	March 23, 2200	Wesel	Second British Army, 1st Commando Brigade
6.	March 24, 0200	Büderich	US Ninth Army, 30th Inf. Div., 119th Inf. Reg.
7.	March 24, 0200	Wallach	US Ninth Army, 30th Inf. Div., 117th Inf. Reg.
8.	March 24, 0200	Rheinberg	US Ninth Army, 30th Inf. Div., 120th Inf. Reg.
9.	March 24, 0200	Xanten	Second British Army, 15th Scottish Division
10.	March 24, 0300	Walsum	US Ninth Army, 79th Inf. Div., 315th Inf. Reg.
11.	March 24, 0300	Orsoy	US Ninth Army, 79th Inf. Div., 313th Inf. Reg.
12.	March 25, 0001	Boppard	US Third Army, 87th Inf. Div., 345th Inf. Reg.
13.	March 25, 0001	Rhens	US Third Army, 87th Inf. Div., 347th Inf. Reg.
14.	March 26, 0200	St. Goar	US Third Army, 89th Inf. Div., 354th Inf. Reg.
15.	March 26, 0200	Oberwesel	US Third Army, 89th Inf. Div., 353rd Inf. Reg.
16.	March 26, 0230	Hamm	US Seventh Army, 45th Inf. Division
17.	March 26, 0230	Frankenthal	US Seventh Army, 3rd Inf. Division
18.	March 28, 0100	Mainz	US Third Army, 80th Inf. Div., 317th Inf. Reg.
19.	March 31, 0230	Speyer	1ère Armée, 3ème Régiment de Tirailleurs Algériens
20.	March 31, 0600	Germersheim	1ère Armée, 4ème Régiment de Tirailleurs Marocains
21.	March 31, 0600	Mechtersheim	1ère Armée, 151ème Régiment d'Infanterie
22.	April 2,	Leimersheim	1ère Armée, 9ème Division d'Infanterie Coloniale
23.	April 15, 1100	Strasbourg	1ère Armée, 23ème Régiment d'Infanterie

Meanwhile, oblivious of Patton's scheme, Montgomery was perfecting his own plans for his set-piece assault crossing in the north.

This meeting took place at General Simpson's Ninth Army HQ in the courthouse on Höhenzollernstrasse in München-Gladbach.

In MAINZ the enemy is still resisting in a small area along the river in the northwest part of the city. Between MAINZ and WORMS our units pushed toward the Rhine on a broad front. Fighting continues in LUDWIGSHAFEN.

Our armored elements have reached points five miles northwest and seven miles west of SPEYER. NEUSTADT and ANNWEILER have been cleared and our units are within three miles of LANDAU. Fairly strong enemy resistance was encountered east of NEUSTADT where some of our tanks were knocked out by enemy artillery. Farther to the west, we cleared NEUENKIRCHEN.

In ZWEIBRUCKEN, which was partly bypassed two days earlier, several hundred prisoners were taken. PIRMASENS, ten miles farther east, was captured. Several thousand Allied nationals were freed by our advances.

The enemy continued to fight stubbornly in the remaining section of the Siegfried Line to keep open an escape route, but we are through the fortifications at several more points. RUMBACH has been cleared, and BIRKENHORDT and BOLLENBORN reached.

In the northern part of our REMAGEN bridgehead our units reached BUISDORF, and cleared half of HENNEF, three miles southeast of SIEGBURG. In the area south of HENNEF our infantry cleared several towns and encountered moderate resistance from enemy artillery and mortar fire.

Resistance continued to be stiff in the northeast sector of the bridgehead. Advances by our troops in the south lengthened the bridgehead to 31 miles along the Rhine river. We reached NEUWIED after capturing several towns including LEUTESDORF and IRLICH. Numerous enemy mines were encountered in this advance.

Allied forces in the west captured 16,400 prisoners 21 March.

The aerial offensive against the enemy's communications continued yesterday and enemy airfields and other objectives were attacked.

Communications targets in Holland and in western Germany from BREMEN southward to STUTTGART were targets for heavy, medium, light and fighter-bombers.

Rail bridges at BREMEN and NIENBURG, the communications and supply centers of BOCHOLT, DORSTEN and DULMEN, and targets at HILDESHEIM were attacked by escorted heavy bombers in great strength.

Twenty-four communications centers north of the Ruhr; two others in Holland, and enemy airfields at MUNSTER, HANDORF, GUTERSLOH and PADERBORN were attacked by other medium and light bombers.

Escorted heavy bombers in very great strength bombed nine German army encampments and concentration centers in the Ruhr and attacked enemy airfields including those at GIEBELSTADT, AHLHORN and KITZINGEN. Rail bridges at HEIDELBERG and NECKARGEMUND were attacked by medium bombers.

More than 50 rail yards were attacked during the day's operations. A large number of rail cars and motor vehicles were destroyed and locomotives were disabled. Rail lines were cut in many places.

Tanks and armored vehicles in the ALTENKIRCHEN area were attacked by fighter-bombers. Targets in BERLIN were attacked last night by light bombers. Other light bombers struck at enemy movements around the Ruhr.

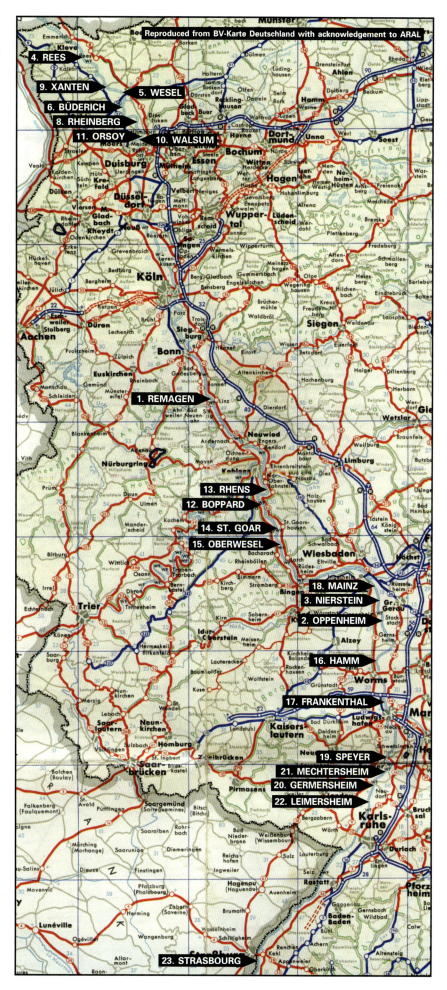

Having stolen Monty's thunder, Patton congratulates his engineers for the speed in which they bridged the Rhine after his men paddled across in assault boats just after 10 p.m. on March 22. The double crossing was made some eight miles south of Mainz by the 5th Division's 11th Infantry, the 1st Battalion crossing at Nierstein and the 3rd Battalion a mile or so to the south at Oppenheim. Patton telephoned the news of the successful crossing to Bradley at breakfast time. 'Brad, don't tell anyone but I'm across', said Patton. 'I sneaked a division over last night. But there are so few Krauts around here they don't know it yet. So don't make any announcement — we'll keep it a secret until we see how it goes!' During the morning, Patton's liaison officer at 12th Army Group could not conceal his smile as he announced that, 'Without benefit of aerial bombardment, ground smoke, artillery preparation and airborne assistance' (giving a direct dig at Monty) 'the Third Army at 2200 hours, Thursday evening, March 22, crossed the Rhine River.' Just hours before Montgomery's crossing began, Patton phoned Bradley again: 'Brad', he shouted, 'for God's sake tell the world we're across . . . I want the world to know Third Army made it before Monty starts across!'

COMMUNIQUE No. 350   March 24

Allied forces have established another bridgehead across the Rhine in an area south of the REMAGEN bridgehead. The crossing was made at 2200 hours Thursday without air or artillery preparation and our forces have since been engaged in enlarging the bridgehead.

Meanwhile other forces are in the process of mopping up the remaining German pockets in the Saar. The last such pocket between COBLENZ and LUDWIGSHAFEN is being reduced at a point eight lines miles north of WORMS. Fighting continues in LUDWIGSHAFEN and RHEINGONHEIM, on the southern edge of the city, has been cleared.

SPEYER and LANDAU have been captured and our units are mopping up in EDENKOBEN north of LANDAU and in SPIRKELBACH to the east.

Our forces have broken through another section of the remaining Siegfried defenses and are rapidly reducing the last enemy elements along the Alsace border near the Rhine.

KLINGENMUNSTER, BAD BERGZABERN and OBERHAUSEN have been captured and our units have reached WINDEN. Enemy elements remaining in this area have been squeezed into a strip ten miles deep along the Rhine east and southeast of LANDAU. Resistance is stubborn and we repulsed a counter-attack near STEINFELD, five miles west of WISSEMBOURG.

HENNEF, in the northern part of our REMAGEN bridgehead, has been captured. In the central sector we reached the autobahn east of RAHMS, extending the bridgehead to a depth of ten miles at that point. Farther south our units are across the Wied river on a 14-mile front north of NEUWIED. BREITSCHEID, WALDBREITBACH, NIEDERBREITBACH, NIEDERBIEBER and SEGENDORF have been captured and NEUWIED has been cleared.

Enemy artillery fire was heavy in the vicinity of BREITSCHEID. Enemy armor and road transport northeast of the bridgehead were bombed by fighter-bombers.

Allied forces in the west captured 14,056 prisoners 22 March.

On March 24, Patton arrived at the Nierstein crossing site (always incorrectly stated as being at Oppenheim), his ADCs Colonel Charles R. Codman and Major Alexander Stiller, were with him as he crossed the engineers' bridge. 'Time out for a short halt', Codman reported Patton as saying. Then the General walked to the edge of the bridge and surveyed the slow-moving surface of the river. 'I have been looking forward to this for a long time', the General said, unbuttoning his trousers and straightaway showing his disdain for the mighty Germany Empire by relieving himself into the Rhine. Reaching the far side where the grassy bank had been churned up, as the history-minded Patton stepped off the last pontoon, he deliberately stumbled onto the soft ground in an imitation of William the Conqueror (who is supposed to have said as he fell flat on his face as he stepped out of his boat, 'See, I have taken England with both hands'). Patton, kneeling, steadied himself against the bank with both hands and, rising, opened his fingers to let two handfuls of earth fall, exclaiming: 'Thus William the Conqueror!'

The air attack on enemy communications was again very heavy yesterday. Marshalling yards at OSNABRÜCK, RHEINE, MUNSTER, COESFELD, RECKLINGHAUSEN and GLADBECK and east and southeast of the Ruhr at UNNA, GESEKE, HOLZWICKEDE, SIEGEN and NARBURG were attacked by escorted heavy bombers in very great strength. A rail bridge northeast of BIELEFELD and another over the Weser river at BREMEN were attacked with 22,000- and 12,000-pound bombs by other escorted heavy bombers.

More than 20 communications centers between MUNSTER and the Rhine were hit by medium and light bombers which operated in very great strength throughout the day. Fighter-bombers ranged over a wide area mainly north and east of the Ruhr attacking rolling stock, rail lines and road transport. Many gun positions also were hit. Road traffic was bombed in the FRANKFURT, GIESSEN, FULDA area.

Farther south, rail yards at HEIDELBERG and NECKARGEMUND, rail bridges at NECKARELZ and near MOSBACH, southeast of HEIDELBERG, rail lines and other targets east of the Rhine were attacked by medium and fighter-bombers.

Two enemy airfields in Holland, a factory west of MEPPEN and an ammunition dump and other objectives in the ARNHEM area were hit by fighter-bombers and rocket-firing fighters.

During the day a very large number of rail cars, locomotives, motor and horse-drawn vehicles was destroyed or damaged. Twenty-five enemy aircraft were shot down and ten others were destroyed on the ground.

Targets in BERLIN were attacked by light bombers last night.

Monty's plan — Operation 'Plunder' — for the 21st Army Group's huge Rhine crossing north of the Ruhr on the night of March 23/24 involved close on a million men in five distinct set-pieces. The 51st Highland Division was to assault Rees at 2100 hours and an hour later the 1st Commando Brigade was to cross to Wesel. Then the 15th Scottish Division would go in at 0200 from the Xanten area. There was considerable acrimony from General Simpson when he found that the Ninth's contribution was for a supporting role on the right flank so Monty modified his plan for the US force so that the 30th and 79th Divisions would cross south of Wesel at 0200 and 0300 hours respectively

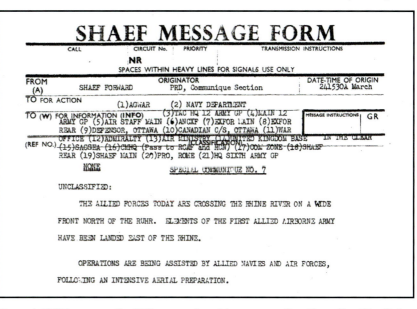

Then, at 1000 hours on the 24th, a massive airborne assault — Operation 'Varsity' — would transport 17,000 men comprising the British 6th Airborne Division flying in from Britain and the US 17th Airborne Division from airfields around Paris. The paratroopers were to drop first, followed by the gliderborne troops, with the object of protecting the bridgehead crossing sites from a German counter-attack, and securing eight bridges over the Issel river, five miles east of the Rhine.

One of the British Horsa gliders employed in 'Varsity' crashed in the railyards of Hamminkeln station.

Eisenhower: 'The March 24 operation sealed the fate of Germany. Already, of course, we had secured two bridgeheads farther to the south. But in each of those cases surprise and good fortune had favoured us. The northern operation was made in the teeth of the greatest resistance the enemy could provide anywhere along the long river. Moreover, it was launched directly on the edge of the Ruhr and the successful landing on the eastern bank placed strong forces in position to deny the enemy use of significant portions of that great industrial area. With the arrival of daylight I went to a convenient hill from which to witness the arrival of the airborne units, which were scheduled to begin their drop at ten o'clock. Fog and the smoke of the battlefield prevented a complete view of the airborne operation but I was able to see some of the action. A number of our planes were hit by anti-aircraft, generally, however, only after they had dropped their loads of paratroopers. As they swung away from the battle area they seemed to come over a spot where anti-aircraft fire was particularly accurate. Those that were struck fell inside our own lines, and in nearly every case the crews succeeded in saving themselves by taking to their parachutes. Even so, our loss in planes was far lighter than we had calculated. Operation 'Varsity' was the most successful airborne operation we carried out during the war.'

Eisenhower continues: 'During the morning I met the Prime Minister with Field-Marshal Brooke [for an alfresco lunch at the US XVI Corps HQ at Kamp Lintfort]. Mr Churchill always seemed to find it possible to be near the scene of action when any particularly important operation was to be launched.

On that morning he was delighted as indeed were all of us. He exclaimed over and over, "My dear General, the German is whipped. We've got him. He is all through." The Prime Minister was merely voicing what all of us felt and were telling each other.'

'About noon of March 24, it was necessary for me to rush down with Bradley to his headquarters to confer on important phases of his own operations. After I left, the Prime Minister persuaded the local commander to take him across the Rhine in an LCM. He undoubtedly derived an intense satisfaction from putting his foot on the eastern bank of Germany's traditional barrier. Possibly he felt the act was symbolic of the final defeat of an enemy who had forced Britain's back to the wall five years before. However, had I been present he would never have been permitted to cross the Rhine that day.' (For more see *After the Battle* No. 16.)

We met Eisenhower before noon. Here a number of American generals were gathered. After various interchanges we had a brief lunch, in the course of which Eisenhower said that there was a house about ten miles away on our side of the Rhine, which the Americans had sandbagged, from which a fine view of the river and of the opposite bank could be obtained. He proposed that we should visit it, and conducted us there himself. The Rhine — here about four hundred yards broad — flowed at our feet. There was a smooth, flat expanse of meadows on the enemy's side. The officers told us that the far bank was unoccupied so far as they knew, and we gazed and gaped at it for a while. With appropriate precautions we were led into the building. Then the Supreme Commander had to depart on other business, and Montgomery and I were about to follow his example when I saw a small launch come close by to moor. So I said to Montgomery, 'Why don't we go across and have a look at the other side?' Somewhat to my surprise he answered, 'Why not?' After he had made some inquiries we started across the river with three or four American commanders and half a dozen armed men. We landed in brilliant sunshine and perfect peace on the German shore, and walked about for half an hour or so unmolested.

As we came back Montgomery said to the captain of the launch, 'Can't we go down the river towards Wesel, where there is something going on?' The captain replied that there was a chain across the river half a mile away to prevent floating mines interfering with our operations, and several of these might be held up by it. Montgomery pressed him hard, but was at length satisfied that the risk was too great. As we landed he said to me, 'Let's go down to the railway bridge at Wesel, where we can see what is going on on the spot.' So we got into his car, and, accompanied by the Americans, who were delighted at the prospect, we went to the big iron-girder railway bridge, which was broken in the middle but whose twisted ironwork offered good perches. The Germans were replying to our fire, and their shells fell in salvos of four about a mile away. Presently they came nearer. Then one salvo came overhead and plunged in the water on our side of the bridge. The shells seemed to explode on impact with the bottom, and raised great fountains of spray about a hundred yards away. Several other shells fell among the motor-cars which were concealed not far behind us, and it was decided we ought to depart.

WINSTON S. CHURCHILL, *Triumph and Tragedy*, 1954

On Friday, March 23, the Prime Minister, together with his private secretary John Colville and Flag Officer Commander 'Tommy' Thompson, accompanied the Chairman of the Chiefs-of-Staff Committee, Field-Marshal Sir Alan Brooke, on a two-hour flight from Northolt. Their Dakota landed at Venlo close to Montgomery's TAC HQ which had for the first time been pitched on German soil. Saturday was spent touring the battlefields at Xanten, Marienbaum, Hochwald and Calcar. The next day was Palm Sunday and after attending a church service Churchill moved on to General John Anderson's XVI Corps headquarters at Kamp Lintfort where he was met by Eisenhower, Bradley and Simpson.

The first woman to cross the Rhine was war correspondent Rhona Churchill (no relation), seen here following her namesake on the east bank. The party had come ashore just opposite a hotel appropriately-named Rheinterrasse Wacht am Rhein at Büderich. 'I crossed in the same boat with the Premier', wrote Rhona in her front-page article in the *Daily Mail*. 'An infantry landing craft used less than 36 hours previously to carry over the river part of the third wave of assault troops of the Ninth Army. He first drove to an observation post on the west bank which had been under heavy shell-fire all the morning. He sat watching the far bank through his field glasses, puffing his cigar and discussing the various phases of the operation with the divisional generals. It seemed as though he would not cross the river. Nobody suggested such a move, so I asked General Simpson whether he proposed taking the Premier across. Simpson observed with a half smile that Mr Churchill had no business over the river, but that he had been asking to go over ever since he got into the Ninth Army area, and that Mr Churchill had a way of getting what he wanted. Mr Churchill did. He got up from his chair, put on his famous bulldog expression, and addressed Field-Marshal Montgomery in an undertone. The next moment he was striding to the river beach, his face lit up with a contented smile. The Prime Minister crossed, spent 15 minutes on the far side, and then cruised a short way down river.'

413

Men of the 1st Commando Brigade crossed the Rhine on the night of the 23rd/24th under a barrage from 1,500 guns.

COMMUNIQUE No. 351   March 25

The Allied attack across the Rhine southeast of NIJMEGEN and north of the Ruhr is making good progress. Enemy resistance, which varied from light to moderate at the beginning of the attack, is stiffening but our forces are firmly established.

Fighting is in progress in the towns of REES and DINSLAKEN. The locks of the Lippe canal have been cleared. Also the towns of WESEL, SPELLEN, LOHNEN, VORDE, MOLLEN, OVERBRUCH and WALSUM have been captured. At some points our units have pushed as much as five miles east of the Rhine.

Airborne units, which landed ahead of the attacking forces, captured their objectives and linked up with the advancing ground units in at least two places. These forces were transported by more than 3,100 tow planes and gliders. The airborne units captured intact six bridges over the Issel river and have taken a number of prisoners.

Ahead of the airborne forces, medium, light and fighter-bombers attacked enemy gun positions with fragmentation and high-explosive bombs. As the German guns opened fire, fighter-bombers dived to silence them in low-level attacks. Fighters patrolled the enemy's airfields and provided escort and protective cover for the aerial transport.

German troops, strong points and armor in the battle area were bombed and strafed by heavy medium, light and fighter-bombers operating in very great strength. Other heavy bombers, flying very low, dropped supplies to our forces on the ground.

In the REMAGEN bridgehead our units met stiffened resistance in the northeast sector and repulsed several enemy counter-attacks in the vicinity of HENNEF. In the central sector we reached points 500 yards beyond the autobahn in the area east of RAHMS. Farther to the south, we captured KURTSCHEID and RENGSDORF, and advanced east along the Rhine river to within 1,000 yards of ENGERS. The REMAGEN bridgehead is now 33 miles long and ten miles deep.

Our forces are strengthening and expanding their bridgehead over the Rhine in an area between MAINZ and WORMS against scattered resistance. The bridgehead is now more than four miles deep and considerably more than four miles long. A bridge has been constructed across the river. The towns of ASTHEIM, GEINSHEIM, LEEHEIM and ERFELDEN, all in the area west of DARMSTADT, have been captured. Naval units assisted in the crossing of the river, and some of our tanks and tank destroyers are now operating in the bridgehead.

By 2 a.m. on the morning of the 24th the major town of Wesel had been captured. This picture shows follow-up troops of the Cheshire Regiment who crossed that afternoon.

According to the caption, 300 prisoners were taken, this group being confined in a convenient bomb crater. The wartime caption explains that 'the town no longer exists — there is not one habitable dwelling in it'.

And photographs were now being released by SHAEF of operations further south. This one shows the first elements of the 4th Armored Division being ferried across at Oppenheim to back up the 5th Infantry Division which made the initial crossing.

Nearly all organized resistance was overcome in the small enemy pocket left in the Saar-Palatinate west of the Rhine. Only a few Siegfried Line positions were still being defended.

Our forces drove to the Rhine at LEIMERSHEIM north of KARLSRUHE. Many other Rhine valley towns were taken.

Allied forces in the west captured 20,963 prisoners 23 March.

Our air forces flew more than 10,000 sorties yesterday striking at enemy troops, armor and strong points in the WESEL battle area severing the enemy's communications, bombing his airfields and attacking other objectives.

Communications and transport in and around the Ruhr and southward to STUTTGART were heavily attacked. Objectives included communications centers at STADTLOHN, BORKEN and DORSTEN, rail yards at STERKRADE and PFORZHEIM; bridges at VLOTHO, PRACHT, COLBE, GERMERSHEIM, KOCHENDORF, PFORZHEIM and a rail viaduct at BIETIGHEIM.

Sixteen enemy airfields east of the Rhine were attacked by heavy bombers in very great strength. Supply dumps at PFORZHEIM were hit by fighter-bombers. An oil refinery near DORTMUND, and a benzol plant near BOTTROP were bombed by heavy bombers.

Targets in BERLIN were bombed by light bombers last night.

Eisenhower: 'We now had crossings over the Rhine in every main channel we had selected for invasion. The ease with which these were accomplished and the light losses that we suffered incident to them were in great contrast to what certainly would have happened had the Germans, during the winter, withdrawn from the west bank and made their decisive stand along the river. It is a formidable obstacle and the terrain all along the eastern bank affords strong defensive positions. Frontal assaults against the German Army, even at the decreased strength and efficiency available to it in early 1945, would have been a costly business. We owed much to Hitler. There is no question that his General Staff, had it possessed a free hand in the field of military operations, would have foreseen certain disaster on the western bank and would have pulled back the defending forces, probably no later than the beginning of January. At that time the abortive attack in the Ardennes was a proven failure and the participating German troops were being driven back in defeat. Moreover, on January 12 the Russians began a great offensive that was to carry them all the way from the Vistula to the Oder, within thirty miles of Berlin. Militarily, the wise thing for the German to do at that moment would have been to surrender. His position was hopeless and even if he could have saved nothing on the political front, he could have prevented the loss of thousands on the field of battle and avoided further destruction of his cities and industries. Even Hitler, fanatic that he was, must have had lucid moments in which he could not have failed to see that the end was in sight. He was writing an ending to a drama that would far exceed in tragic climax anything that his beloved Wagner ever conceived.'

So there was something to shout about. On the 25th Eisenhower flew to Remagen to confer with Patton, Bradley and Hodges as the advance out of the bridgehead was to begin the following day. The V Corps, now under Major General Clarence R. Huebner, was to join with the converging thrusts of the First and Third Armies. The same day General Haislip's XV Corps of the Seventh Army forced a crossing of the river near Worms (see table page 408). Taking up the advance, it linked up with the Third to capture Mannheim.

Meanwhile, although the censor tried to hide the location with the deletion mark, the Field-Marshal was pictured conferring with Lieutenant-General Sir Brian Horrocks of XXX Corps just north of Xanten at Marienbaum . . .

COMMUNIQUE No. 352   **March 26**

Allied forces continue to make good progress in their bridgehead over the Rhine north of the Ruhr. REES is virtually clear, and to the north we have captured SPELDORF. Southeast of REES, HAFFEN and MEHR have been taken and south of WESEL we have captured LIPPEDORF, FRIEDRICHSFELD and DINSLAKEN. We hold over 25 miles of the east bank of the Rhine and our units have pushed eastward more than seven miles at some points.

Enemy artillery positions and strong points, tanks, troop concentrations and road transport in the bridgehead area were attacked by medium, light and fighter-bombers operating from first light and in very great strength. Close co-operation was maintained throughout the day with our forward units. Fighters flew constant patrols over the whole area. Targets in the ARNHEM area and farther north were also hit with rockets and bombs.

We made advances to the east along almost the entire length of the REMAGEN bridgehead. More than a dozen towns and villages were captured. After repulsing several counter-attacks in the northeast sector, our units captured UCKERATH. In the central sector we reached FIERSBACH and FLAMMERSFELD southeast of UCKERATH.

Farther south our infantry units, after meeting stiff resistance from infantry and tanks, captured ELLINGEN and DASBACH.

In the southern sector our armor captured ENGERS, cleared BENDORF and reached VALLENDAR.

Fighter-bombers gave close support to ground units in the REMAGEN area. Concentrations of enemy armor were hit northeast of the bridgehead and six communications centers were bombed.

Our infantry made new crossings of the Rhine between COBLENZ and BOPPARD. The crossings were made in assault boats and our units met strong resistance from anti-aircraft guns and dug-in enemy positions.

Fast moving armored spearheads advanced 27 miles from the bridgehead between MAINZ and WORMS and captured a bridge intact over the Main river.

RUSSELSHEIM, on the Main river ten miles southwest of FRANKFURT, has been captured.

Farther south the bridgehead has been expanded to a depth of 13 miles. DARMSTADT has been captured and our units have entered GRAFENHAUSEN and WEITERSTADT to the northwest. West of DARMSTADT we have captured GRIESHEIM and to the southwest GODDELAU, PFUNGSTADT, JUGENHEIM and HAHNLEIN are in our hands.

We have cleared the enemy from the last portion of the west bank of the Rhine between Switzerland and Holland. Final resistance was overcome with the silencing

. . . on the very same day that Patton's army did it again at Boppard, Rhens, Oberwesel and St Goar! Here traffic clogs the main street of St Goar as men of the 354th Infantry of the 89th Division await their turn to cross.

With the Rhine two miles behind them, these infantrymen of the 5th Division, Third Army, take a break at Geinsheim after having crossed at Oppenheim.

On March 26, General Eisenhower wrote to his boss, General Marshall, in Washington: 'Naturally I am immensely pleased that the campaign west of the Rhine that Bradley and I planned last summer and insisted upon as a necessary preliminary to a deep penetration east of the Rhine, has been carried out so closely in accordance with conception. You possibly know at one time the CIGS [Field Marshal Brooke] thought I was wrong in what I was trying to do and argued heatedly on the matter. Yesterday I saw him on the banks of the Rhine and he was gracious enough to say that I was right, and that my current plans and operations are well calculated to meet the current situation. The point is that the great defeats, in some cases almost complete destruction, inflicted on the German forces west of the Rhine, have left him with very badly depleted strength to man that formidable obstacle. It was those victories that made possible the bold and relatively easy advances that both the First and Third Armies are now making toward Kassel. I hope this does not sound boastful, but I must admit to a great satisfaction that the things that Bradley and I have believed in from the beginning and have carried out in the face of some opposition from within and without, have matured so splendidly.'

of snipers on the west bank between SPEYER and KARLSRUHE.

Allied forces in the west captured 31,348 prisoners 24 March.

The main railway centers of MUNSTER, OSNABRUCK and HANNOVER were heavily bombed by escorted heavy bombers in strength. Seven rail yards between the Rhine and BRUNSWICK were hit by strong formations of fighter-bombers.

Rail and road traffic from WIPPERFURTH, northeast of COLOGNE, over a wide area southeast to ASCHAFFENBURG and FULDA, were hit by fighter-bombers.

Medium and light bombers in great strength operated between the REMAGEN bridgehead and FRANKFURT attacking rail yards, communications centers and defense installations. Transportation targets were numerous and the destruction of enemy materiel in these attacks was very heavy.

Communications and transportation east of the upper Rhine were attacked by fighter-bombers. Two bridges, one at WEIHER, between HEIDELBERG and KARLSRUHE, and another west of MOSBACH, were destroyed. Medium bombers attacked a tank and motor repair depot at MORSCH, southwest of KARLSRUHE.

Underground oil storage depots at EHMEN, northeast of BRUNSWICK; BUCHEN, east of HAMBURG, and at HITZACKER farther south, were attacked by escorted heavy bombers.

In all the day's operations well over 6,000 sorties were flown by the Allied air forces. Nineteen enemy aircraft were shot down and 14 others were destroyed on the ground. Ten of our heavy bombers, one medium bomber and 28 fighters are missing.

Targets in BERLIN were attacked by light bombers last night.

On the afternoon of March 24, Combat Command A of the 4th Armored Division led the advance from the Oppenheim bridgehead. Pressing on through Wolfskehlen *(centre)*, they thrust on half-circling Darmstadt prompting General der Infanterie Hans Felber, the commander of the 7. Armee, to abandon the town. This is Oppenheimer Strasse.

On March 27, 1945, after a short but intense two-day battle, troops of the Third Army captured Frankfurt-am-Main. The operation involved two American divisions, the 6th Armored and 5th Infantry Divisions, which were opposed by an assorted collection of German garrison, training and police troops, backed up by strong artillery. Here men of the 5th Division advance towards the city along the Frankfurt to Darmstadt autobahn, the viaduct marking the Frankfurt South exit. This section of the road was the first of Germany's new motorways to be brought into use.

COMMUNIQUE No. 353 — March 27

Allied forces continued to strengthen their bridgehead over the Rhine north of the Ruhr. REES has been completely cleared and to the north, BIENEN has been captured. North of WESEL we occupied HAMMINKELN and advanced beyond it. Good progress has been made between the Lippe canal and DINSLAKEN, and HUNXE, BRUCKHAUSEN and HIESFELD have been captured.

In the WESEL area enemy armor, gun positions and troops were attacked by medium, light and fighter-bombers, operating in strength immediately ahead of our ground forces. Single enemy tanks, being used as forward gun positions, were hit by rocket-firing fighters. Other fighter-bombers took a heavy toll of motor transport in and behind the battle area and attacked airfields at DORSTEN and DORTMUND.

Our forces have broken out of the REMAGEN bridgehead. In the north we gained 4,000 yards to reach the outskirts of EITORF on the Sieg river, and to the southeast other elements advanced up to seven miles to reach a point one mile southeast of ALTENKIRCHEN. Tanks and armored vehicles north of ALTENKIRCHEN were attacked by fighter-bombers.

In the central sector of the bridgehead we pushed eight miles eastward and reached MAXSAIN, while to the south our units gained 15 miles to reach STAUDT, two miles north of MONTABAUR.

Our forces in a 22-mile advance drove east of GRENZHAUSEN, and then southeastward along the COLOGNE-FRANKFURT autobahn to LIMBURG.

East of the Rhine between COBLENZ and BOPPARD, we cleared FILSEN and advanced southeast against varying resistance to take LYKERSHAUSEN. Our units pushing out seven miles to the northeast from the bridgehead in the MAINZ-WORMS area have entered the outskirts of FRANKFURT. We now control the south bank of the Main river for a stretch of seven miles upstream from its junction with the Rhine.

East of FRANKFURT, our units reached the Main river opposite HANAU. Two enemy counter-attacks, one to the south of HANAU and the other at ASCHAFFENBURG, were repulsed. Targets at ASCHAFFENBURG were bombed by aircraft co-operating closely with our ground forces.

In the area between FRANKFURT and DARMSTADT, we have entered LANGEN and have cleared WIXHAUSEN.

Farther south our units made another Rhine crossing without air or artillery preparation.

Allied forces in the west captured 15,132 prisoners 25 March.

Communications and rail targets in and around the Ruhr were attacked by fighter-bombers. Objectives included rail yards at DORSTEN, RECKLINGHAUSEN, LUNEN, AHLEN, HAMM, ESSEN and HAGEN, and 13 rail yards in the SIEGEN and GIESSEN areas.

A strong force of medium and light bombers bombed rail yards at FLIEDEN, GEMUNDEN and WURZBURG while fighter-bombers struck at rail traffic in the FRANKFURT and FULDA areas.

Road and rail transport, strong points and communications were attacked by fighter-bombers flying missions ahead of our ground forces in the battle areas south of FRANKFURT. In the HEIDELBERG-KARLSRUHE-STUTTGART triangle motor vehicles were hit.

An armored vehicle plant at PLAUEN and a synthetic oil plant and refinery at ZEITZ were attacked by a strong force of escorted heavy bombers.

Railroad and water transport in widespread areas of Holland were attacked by fighter-bombers.

South of ENSCHEDE a train of petrol tank cars was destroyed. Strong points southwest of ARNHEM and other military objectives northwest of NIJMEGEN were hit with rockets and bombs.

Targets in BERLIN were attacked last night by light bombers.

The official opening ceremony on May 19, 1935 was an elaborately staged propaganda event, with Hitler opening the road in his open Mercedes and then saluting a column of trucks carrying those who had worked on its construction. Unfortunately no comparison as the autobahn at this point has now been widened to eight lanes and the bridge has been demolished. (See also *After the Battle* No. 154.)

The Joint Anglo-American Film Planning Committee was set up in March 1944 for the purpose of producing a film showing Allied operations from an integrated viewpoint. A draft script with the working title *A Single Instrument* was already in being and during transatlantic discussions over the next months, it was developed into SHAEF's account of Operation 'Overlord' — the Defeat of Germany. It was to be a six-reeler (60 minutes) and be ready eight weeks after D-Day when it was thought the battle would be over!

COMMUNIQUE No. 354   March 28

The heavy enemy resistance in the northern sector of the Allies' lower Rhine bridgehead shows signs of slackening.

Northeast of REES our hold on the EMMERICH-WESEL railway has been extended. To the east, our forces have crossed the Issel river and entered DINGDEN.

North of WESEL, our units pushing up from HAMMINKELN have taken RINGENBERG, and to the east we have captured BRUNEN. East of WESEL, along the Lippe canal, KRUDENBERG and GAHLEN are in our hands and we are within three miles of DORSTEN. To the south, other units have taken WALSUMERMARK and HOLTEN and are within a thousand yards of the main Ruhr autobahn.

In the northern sector of our bridgehead east of REMAGEN we met stiff resistance along the Sieg river. Elsewhere our units continued to break from the bridgehead. Armored elements cleared ALTENKIRCHEN and WAHLROD and advanced eastward 27 miles to reach the vicinity of HERBORN.

To the south another armored column reached ALTENBERG, two miles west of WETZLAR, after a 14-mile advance.

Armored elements reached the outskirts of WEILBURG, about ten miles northeast of LIMBURG, and another unit crossed the Lahn river to AUMENAU, ten miles east of LIMBURG.

Infantry units following up the armor have cleared LIMBURG and another armored unit advancing along the autobahn to the southeast, reached a point five miles north of WIESBADEN.

Along the east bank of the Rhine our units pushing from the south and from the north linked up at NIEDERLAHNSTEIN, four miles south of COBLENZ, after capturing a number of towns and villages.

Our armored units are fighting in FRANKFURT after crossing the Main river on a railroad bridge which had been damaged but not destroyed. The FRANKFURT suburbs of SCHWANHEIM, NIEDERRAD and SACHSENHAUSEN have been cleared. To the east our units are fighting in HANAU.

Concentrations of motor vehicles in the GIESSEN area and near DILLENBURG and FRANKFURT were bombed by fighter-bombers. More than 600 vehicles were destroyed. A number of rail yards and fortified towns also were bombed. Troop concentrations at BENSHEIM and east of DARMSTADT at BREITENBACH also were attacked.

In our bridgehead near WORMS our units captured more than 2,500 prisoners. Eastward advances of up to about nine miles have been made and a number of towns have been cleared. Among the places occupied were LANGWADEN, KLEINHAUSEN, BURSTADT and LAMPERTHEIM, and our forces have generally crossed the autobahn which runs north and south throughout the zone.

Our units mopping up on the west bank of the Rhine captured a divisional commander, Generalleutnant Franz Sensfuss, and his Chief-of-Staff. Allied forces in the west captured 19,712 prisoners 26 March.

The railway center of PADERBORN was heavily bombed by escorted heavy bombers yesterday.

The concrete U-Boat shelters under construction at FARGE, near VEGESACK on the Weser river, were attacked with 22,000-pound bombs. A large oil storage depot in the same area and the Konigsborn and Sachsen benzol plants near HAMM were attacked by other escorted heavy bombers. Fighter-bombers attacked targets at NECKARSTEINACH and NEU LUSSHEIM in the HEIDELBERG area.

Targets in BERLIN were attacked last night by light bombers.

Two experienced film directors were appointed: Carol Reed to represent British interests and Garson Kanin those of the US, and over the next three months the project moved forward helped by the release of a copy of the 'Overlord' plan by SHAEF in August. By late November it was agreed that the film should cover the period from pre-invasion to German capitulation, one of the highlights being that the linking commentary would be given by actors speaking as participants. Of the 700 cameramen whose film was used, 32 had lost their lives. General Eisenhower was shown the film on March 28 and a visual prologue and sections of his commentary were shot and recorded on the 29th. With regard to the content, he made the following observations: '(i) General Bradley should appear in at least one shot; (ii) the commentary describing the Omaha landing was not good in that it indicated something went wrong due to mistakes, etc., whereas resistance experienced at Omaha was expected everywhere; (iii) that the Mortain fighting should not be presented as a "retreat"; (iv) the commentary should indicate that the brass hats gave to the Leclerc Division the opportunity to enter Paris first; (v) more space should be given

to the landings in Southern France and the advance of General Devers' 6th Army Group up the Rhône Valley.' In conclusion, Eisenhower stated that he and senior members of his staff wanted a preview before the film's public release. The Supreme Commander wanted the emphasis to be 'teamwork and unity' between the Allies. The British and Canadian view was that the film was of 'inestimable value' for releasing in all three countries as an 'outward and visible manifestation of the integrated effort which alone has enabled the Allied Expeditionary Force to reach present positions'. British opinion was that the keynote of victory 'will be the completeness of unity among the victorious armies of all three nations.' Although the war was not yet at an end, a final review of *The True Glory* was to be held on May 18. In the end the final post-production was laid out during transatlantic telephone conference on July 12. It was to be shown to Eisenhower (then based in SHAEF headquarters in Frankfurt) before its premiere in London on August 4. (The US release was held up until September through objection by the American censor about the inclusion of swear words (see also *After the Battle* No. 149).

COMMUNIQUE No. 355   March 29

Allied forces breaking out of their bridgehead across the Rhine north of the Ruhr have made good progress in all sectors. North of REES our units reached the outskirts of EMMERICH and captured ISSELBURG. Farther east, we advanced rapidly to BORKEN, ERLE and the part of DORSTEN that is north of the Lippe canal. South of the canal we occupied BESTEN and KIRCHHELLEN and cleared HAMBORN.

In the northern sector of our lower Rhine bridgehead fighter-bombers attacked enemy transport, troops, tanks and guns. At AHAUS a petrol-laden convoy was destroyed. Other fighter-bombers bombed an artillery observation post east of ISSELBURG.

Farther south our armored units driving eastward have entered GIESSEN, 65 miles east of the Rhine river, and BELLNHAUSEN, eight miles north of GIESSEN. One unit reached the vicinity of LICH, six miles southeast of GIESSEN, after an advance of 27 miles. WEILBURG, southwest of GIESSEN, has been captured, and our armor crossed the Lahn river there, and at AUMENAU, six miles farther south. Infantry units, mopping up behind the armor west of the GIESSEN-WEILBURG area, reduced enemy strong points and units bypassed by the armor.

Our forces across the Rhine east of BOPPARD reached the vicinity of HENNETHAL, ten miles northwest of WIESBADEN. Farther south our units, after making another crossing of the Rhine, have cleared KASTEL, HOCHHEIM and BIEBRICH, and have entered WIESBADEN.

Our infantry and armor have cleared half of FRANKFURT against stiff opposition. HANAU and ASCHAFFENBURG farther to the east have been cleared. North of HANAU our armor reached the vicinity of NIEDER FLORSTADT, six miles southeast of BAD NAUHEIM.

Road and rail transport and communications south and east of the Ruhr in the areas of HAGEN, WIPPERFURTH, BERGNEUSTADT and WARBURG and south and east of GIESSEN were struck at by fighter-bombers. Rail yards at ENGELSKIRCHEN and OLPE; targets at ATTENDORN; a road junction at KITZINGEN and oil storage depots at NEUENHEERSE and EBRACH were bombed by medium and light bombers.

We continued to expand our bridgehead in the DARMSTADT-MANNHEIM area. The bridgehead area is now more than 200 square miles. Several bridges are in operation across the Rhine.

Units pushing out of the bridgehead reached NIEDERNBERG, on the Main river south of ASCHAFFENBURG, after occupying GROSS-UMSTADT.

The last major raid on Duisburg by RAF Bomber Command took place on the night of February 21/22 when over 350 Lancasters carried out an area bombing attack. The city had suffered constant air raids since 1940, evidence of the devastation being only too apparent to the troops of the Ninth Army when they entered the largest inland port in Europe on March 27.

Progress was slower in the ODENWALD area but more than a score of towns were taken. The northern half of MANNHEIM has been cleared. Fourteen hundred additional prisoners have been taken in this area east of the Rhine. On the west bank of the Rhine some 700 more enemy stragglers have been picked up. Allied forces in the west captured 17,039 prisoners 27 March.

Armored vehicle plants at SPANDAU and FALKENSEE, industrial suburbs of BERLIN, and rail yards and armored vehicle plants in the HANNOVER area were bombed by strong forces of escorted heavy bombers. Communications in Holland were attacked by fighter-bombers.

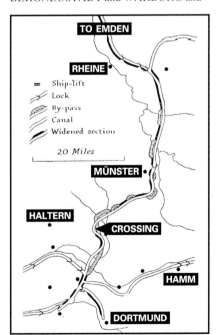

Another vital waterway in western Germany was the canal constructed between Dortmund and Ems in the 1890s to connect the heart of the industrial district of the Ruhr with Emden where another canal gave access to the naval base at Wilhelmshaven. The RAF tried on numerous occasions to breach it but it was the US 2nd Armored Division that first crossed it. They moved out from Haltern just before midnight on March 29 and reached the canal early next morning but as the bridge had been blown they had to wait for a pontoon bridge to be thrown across. The 83rd Division followed in trucks and in the late afternoon of the 31st they had cut the autobahn between the Ruhr and Berlin at Beckiem, 40 miles from their line of departure.

COMMUNIQUE No. 356   March 30

North of the Ruhr Allied forces continue to make good progress in the break-out from their Rhine bridgehead. Several armored thrusts have achieved gains of more than ten miles. In the area of EMMERICH heavy fighting continues. Gun positions north of EMMERICH were attacked by medium and light bombers.

Our armored units, thrusting deeper into Germany over a wide area east and southeast of the Ruhr, have reached numerous points on a line extending roughly from PADERBORN on the north to ASCHAFFENBURG on the south. One unit driving north advanced 55 miles to reach a point ten miles south of PADERBORN. To the south other units have reached LELBACH, TITMARINGHAUSEN, LANGEWIESE and HALLENBERG.

WALBACH, south of SIEGEN and northwest of GIESSEN, has been cleared by our infantry. Northeast of GIESSEN our armor has captured WARBURG and reached AMONEBURG, 85 miles east of the Rhine.

East of GIESSEN we have entered ULRICHSTEIN and LAUTERBACH. Small-arms and sniper fire, scattered mines and road-blocks were encountered in this advance.

To the south between GIESSEN and FRANKFURT our units have reached LANGGONS, BAD NAUHEIM and cleared a number of towns including RENDEL and MASSENHEIM. The city of FRANKFURT has been cleared.

In the area between the Rhine and the GIESSEN-FRANKFURT road, units moving from the north and from the south linked up along the COLOGNE-FRANKFURT autobahn at KAMBERG, IDSTEIN and NIEDERHAUSEN.

The city of WIESBADEN has been cleared.

Germans were now surrendering in droves . . . these scenes were pictured at Limburg *(above)*, 20 miles east of the Rhine at Coblenz, and *(below)* at Giessen, 30 miles further to the east. The average bag of prisoners captured was now running at 15,000 to 20,000 per day.

East of DARMSTADT our units reached the Main river on a 12-mile front and hold the east bank for a distance of eight miles south of ASCHAFFENBURG. Resistance stiffened in this area with the enemy fighting from prepared positions.

Farther south, armored elements advanced beyond MICHELSTADT. Other units are northeast of BEERFELDEN.

MANNHEIM on the Rhine has been captured. The Neckar river has been crossed at several points in this area.

LADENBURG to the east has been cleared and our units are within three miles of HEIDELBERG.

Allied forces in the west captured 18,719 prisoners 28 March.

A benzol plant near BRUNSWICK was attacked by escorted heavy bombers.

Whereas American forces had made huge advances after crossing the Rhine, the British and Canadians in the north were fighting against stubborn resistance and repeated counter-attacks with the 15th Division, for example, suffering over 800 casualties in four days. Emmerich, 20 miles north-west of Wesel, was the objective of the 3rd Canadian Division. The town had been smashed to pieces following a very heavy Bomber Command raid on October 7, a German report stating that 2,424 buildings had been destroyed and nearly 700,000 cubic metres of rubble had to be cleared from the streets. The Canadians faced stiff opposition, battling their way through the ruins with constant artillery support adding to the destruction.

COMMUNIQUE No. 357   March 31

North of the Ruhr Allied forces continue to make rapid progress in all sectors. In the area east of EMMERICH the towns of NETTERDEN, ANHOLT and DINXPERLO have been cleared.

Farther to the east BOCHOLT, BORKEN and DULMEN are in our hands and substantial advances have been made beyond these points.

In the area south of the Lippe canal, DORSTEN, GLADBECK, BOTTROP and HAMBORN have been captured.

Gun positions north of EMMERICH were attacked by medium and light bombers. Enemy troops and gun positions in the MUNSTER-DUSSELDORF-PADERBORN area; an airfield east of DUSSELDORF, and another at GUTERSLOH, were hit by fighter-bombers.

East of the Ruhr our units have entered PADERBORN and HUSEN. In the area southwest of KASSEL we reached a point just west of FRANKENAU. Farther east our units advanced up to 30 miles to reach ALTWILDUNGEN and FRITZLAR.

Other elements reached BORKEN on the KASSEL-FRANKFURT railroad line. All these advances were made by armored elements followed by infantry which continued mopping-up operations.

In the Sieg river sector our infantry units reached a point two miles south of the town of SIEGEN.

Armored units striking north and northeast from the vicinity of BAD NAUHEIM advanced up to 42 miles to reach the vicinity of TREYSA and ALSFELD, some 30 miles northeast of GIESSEN. Enemy planes strafed our units making these advances.

Armored elements pushed northeast from LAUTERBACH to the vicinity of GREBENAU and south of LAUTERBACH we entered HERBSTEIN.

An armored unit moving northeast from HANAU reached the vicinity of BUDINGEN against resistance which decreased from severe to scattered during the advance. Infantry elements are mopping up northeast of HANAU behind our armored spearheads. Other infantry elements pushed to points five miles east and southeast of HANAU, repulsing two enemy counter-attacks in the sector.

Mopping-up operations continue in the pocket west of WIESBADEN; and in the area between FRANKFURT and GIESSEN. Strong resistance was encountered by our units in the WIESBADEN pocket.

South of ASCHAFFENBURG we have a 12-mile bridgehead across the Main river as deep as three miles. In this area the enemy is fighting stubbornly from prepared positions.

Farther south armored elements drove eastward beyond AMORBACH in an advance hindered by rugged terrain and blown bridges. Eight miles still farther south MUDAU was reached.

The ancient university city of HEIDELBERG was taken after surrender negotiations failed. Our units crossed the Neckar river east and west of the city.

Advances of some six miles also were made south of MANNHEIM along the east bank of the Rhine. The day's prisoners included the German 719th Infantry

By the end of the month the 21st Army Group's bridgehead measured some 35 miles wide and 20 miles deep. The British Second Army had suffered nearly 4,000 casuaties and the US Ninth Army just under 3,000. *Left:* Canadian infantry were pictured entering Emmerich after facing 'fierce resistance from fanatical Nazi paratroopers'. *Right:* The prisoner total was at least 15,000 including these two exhausted Germans pictured at Emmerich on the 31st.

Bulldozers had to be brought in to clear the streets — this is all that was left of Kass-Strasse.

Division commander who was taken on the west bank of the Rhine. Allied forces in the west captured 18,542 prisoners 29 March.

Five submarine yards and other targets in the port areas of WILHELMSHAVEN, BREMEN, FARGE, northwest of BREMEN, and HAMBURG were heavily attacked yesterday by escorted heavy bombers in very great strength.

Road and rail transport and other communications targets in Holland and north and east of the Ruhr were struck at by fighter-bombers and rocket-firing fighters.

A tank assembly plant at BAD OEYNHAUSEN; an ordnance depot at HANNOVERSCH MUNDEN; and an oil storage factory at EBENSHAUSEN north of EISENACH were attacked by medium and light bombers. In the day's operations, seven enemy aircraft were shot down and 42 others were destroyed on the ground. Nine of our heavy bombers, one light bomber and 12 fighters are missing.

Light bombers attacked targets in BERLIN and enemy communications over a wide area of Holland and northern Germany last night.

PNA EA 60393
NAZIS WATCH U.S. ADVANCE
Captive German officers watch from the side of the autobahn as vehicles of the Sixth Armored Division, Third U.S. Army, approach Giessen, Reich city 30 miles north of Frankfurt, which was entered March 28, 1945. By April 3, 1945, racing armored columns of the Third Army drove through the Fulda Gap, parallel with the Frankfurt-Dresden autobahn, to reach a point 155 miles southwest of Berlin and 185 miles from the advancing Soviet First Ukrainian Army.
U.S. Signal Corps Photo ETO-HQ-45-24489.
SERVICED BY LONDON TO LIST B-1
CERTIFIED AS PASSED BY SHAEF CENSOR

APRIL 1945
OVER-RUNNING GERMANY

COMMUNIQUE No. 358   April 1

North of the Ruhr Allied forces continue to make rapid progress and the momentum of the advances has been maintained. Our units are more than 65 miles east of the Rhine at some points. Several of our armored units gained more than 15 miles yesterday. North of BORKEN we captured STADTLOHN and made substantial advances beyond the town.

Gun positions north of EMMERICH were attacked by medium and light bombers.

Our armored elements are fighting in the southern outskirts of PADERBORN against stiff resistance from enemy infantry and dug-in tanks. Farther southeast, our armor has reached WARBURG, after an 18-mile advance. Infantry units continue to mop up behind the armor and have entered BRILON and BUREN, south of PADERBORN. Southwest of KASSEL our forces captured BERGHEIM and the EDERSEE DAM on the Eder river.

Our infantry entered SIEGEN and cleared the area south of the Sieg river between SCHONSTEIN and ELSENFELD.

Armored elements advancing north gained up to 35 miles and reached a point five miles south of KASSEL. Other elements, advancing northeast, are in the area of KAPPEL, 15 miles southeast of KASSEL.

Our armor, advancing 23 miles northeast from LAUTERBACH, reached the area south of BAD HERSFELD. We liberated 10 American airmen in ASBACH, two miles south of BAD HERSFELD. To the southeast near ELTRA we knocked out several tanks.

Armored units have reached the vicinity of GIESEL, six miles southwest of FULDA. Our units met strong tank and infantry resistance near GELNHAUSEN, 20 miles northeast of FRANKFURT, but bypassed the town and entered BIRSTEIN, 20 miles southeast of FULDA. Infantry continues to mop up and is in the area 12 miles west and southwest of FULDA, while other units have reached a point 18 miles northeast of HANAU.

The area west of WIESBADEN has been cleared and mopping-up continues north and northwest of FRANKFURT. We entered BAD SCHWALBACH, 12 miles northwest of MAINZ, and captured an enemy hospital complete with 12 enemy medical officers, 38 nurses, 63 enlisted men and 900 enemy patients.

Enemy gun positions, strong points, armor and road and rail transport ahead of our ground forces in the areas of RECKLINGHAUSEN, east of COLOGNE, KASSEL, HERSFELD and ERFURT were attacked by fighter-bombers in strength. Seven hundred motor vehicles were destroyed and others were damaged.

Much of ASCHAFFENBURG was in flame as enemy forces continued to resist stubbornly our efforts to clear the city with ground and air attacks. Gains of up to six miles were made east of the main river south of ASCHAFFENBURG.

Armored elements drove eastward 25 miles to within six miles of WURZBURG on the upper Main river, more than 60 miles east of the Rhine. A number of towns including TAUBERBISCHOFSHEIM and WALDBRUNN were taken in this drive.

As early as the end of March, it was seen that there was a danger that the forces of the Western powers might drive headlong into Soviet troops. By now the advance eastwards had reached a point at which divisional commanders were not always sure just how far their leading elements had travelled and a clash between friendly ground forces had to be avoided. Other than the meeting between SHAEF officers and Stalin (page 324), there had been no direct communication with the Russians, but the line of the Rivers Elbe and Mulde was deemed a suitable natural feature at which Western forces could be halted. It was also felt that there would be no advantage in capturing territory which would subsequently have to be handed over to the Soviets as part of their previously agreed Zone of Occupation (see page 193). However, Eisenhower explained that 'this future division of Germany did not influence our military plans for the final conquest of the country. Military plans', he believed, 'should be devised with the single aim of speeding victory. A natural objective beyond the Ruhr was Berlin but I decided that it was not the logical nor the most desirable objective for the forces of the Western Allies.'

When the Western Allies stood on the Rhine in the last week of March, they were 300 miles from Berlin while Russian forces were firmly established at Küstrin on the Oder with a bridgehead on its western bank only 30 miles from the German capital.

Gun positions near WURZBURG were hit by fighter-bombers and rail yards and storage installations in the area were attacked by medium and light bombers.

Our units advancing southeastward along the Neckar river reached DALLAU. South of HEIDELBERG we reached WALLDORF.

South of SPEYER our forces made another crossing of the Rhine on a ten-mile front.

Elements of this force joined at HOCKENHEIM with our units pushing southward from the MANNHEIM area.

Allied forces in the west captured 19,166 prisoners 30 March.

Enemy transport moving from the Zuider Zee area of Holland towards northwest Germany in considerable numbers was attacked by fighters and fighter-bombers in strength. In the ENSCHEDE area more than 350 motor vehicles were destroyed or damaged.

Communications and transport in the RHEINE-OSNABRUCK areas, and a column of enemy troops and motor vehicles farther to the north between HASELUNNE and CLOPPENBURG, were attacked by fighter-bombers.

An oil storage depot at EBRACH, rail yards at HEILBRONN and a motor transport depot at BOBLINGEN, near STUTTGART, were bombed by meduim and light bombers.

Transport and communications in the triangular area formed by ASCHAFFENBURG, STUTTGART and NUREMBURG, and airfields southeast of MUHLHAUSEN, west of GOTHA, and near NUREMBURG were attacked by fighter-bombers. A number of enemy aircraft were destroyed on the ground and others were damaged.

Rail and industrial objectives at HALLE, BRANDENBURG and BRUNSWICK and a synthetic oil plant at ZEITZ, southwest of LEIPZIG, were attacked by escorted heavy bombers in very great strength. A strong force of escorted heavy bombers bombed submarine building yards at HAMBURG.

According to reports so far received, 14 enemy aircraft were shot down during these operations. Seventeen of our bombers and 22 fighters are missing.

Eisenhower: 'The Ruhr had been isolated by air action early in 1945. In addition to the direct damage to factories, the transportation system had been wrecked, and the coal and steel produced there, on which the German war economy largely depended, had been, for the time being, denied the enemy. Before operations deep into the German interior could be safely undertaken, however, the Allies had, following the Rhine crossings, to complete the encirclement of the Ruhr and the elimination of any danger from the pocket which would be thus created. I determined, therefore, before launching any further offensive eastward into Germany, to carry out the policy originally envisaged of enveloping the Ruhr by converging thrusts from the two bridgeheads at Wesel and Frankfurt. Under the Ninth Army [still part of the 21st Army Group] in the north, while XVI Corps probed southward into the industrial area, XIX Corps swung around its left flank and drove eastward. Meanwhile VII Corps of the First Army, spearheaded by the 3rd Armored Division, struck north from Marburg, which had been taken on 28 March. The operation constituted the largest double envelopment in history. Inside the pocket we had trapped the whole of the German Army Group B and two corps of Army Group H, including the picked troops who had been massed in March to defend the southern approaches of the Ruhr.'

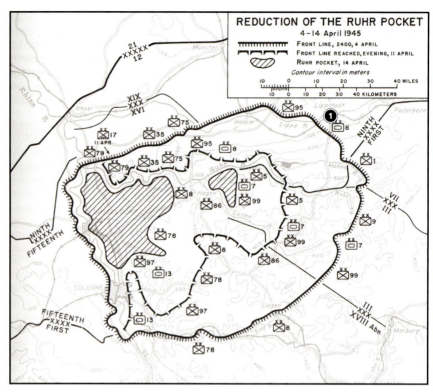

COMMUNIQUE No. 359   April 2

Allied forces advancing from the west and from the south have linked up in the vicinity of LIPPSTADT, 75 miles east of the Rhine, and encircled the whole of German Army Group B. The destruction of this large enemy force in the densely populated area of the Ruhr and in the mountainous district to the south, will take time but will not preclude the advance of Allied armored columns farther into Germany.

North of the Ruhr our forces continued to make good progress advancing more than 15 miles in some sectors.

GESEKE, southeast of LIPPSTADT, has been captured and our units are mopping up in PADERBORN where resistance from enemy tanks, bazookas and small-arms fire has been stiff.

Farther to the southeast, our armored elements advanced three and one-half miles east of WARBURG. In the vicinity of RIMBECK, northwest of WARBURG, our infantry encountered resistance from an estimated 1,000 enemy troops.

Our infantry in a six-mile advance, reached a point north of BESSE, six and one-half miles south of KASSEL. Armored units crossed the Fulda river in the area 15 miles south of KASSEL and entered ADELSHAUSEN. We encountered strong enemy resistance in this area from assault guns and tanks.

On April 1, the First and the Ninth made contact near Lippstadt, [1] on map, and the operation which might be said to have begun with the air forces' interdiction program in February, was completed. *Left:* A symbolic photo to mark the encirclement of the Ruhr — Colonel Paul A. Disney, the commanding officer of the 67th Armored Regiment of the 2nd Armored Division, with Major Robert Coughlin of the 32nd Armored Regiment of the 3rd Armored Division. *Above:* Only the front part of the former Bergschneider car dealership and garage on the Erwitter Strasse remains.

Brigadier General Felix L. Sparks: 'On the morning of March 27, the day after the regiment had crossed the Rhine River, I received an order to move my battalion (3rd Battalion, 157th Infantry) to the high ground immediately beyond Aschaffenburg, about 40 miles distant. The assigned mission was to secure the ground for the anticipated advance of the 45th Division through the area on the following day. Almost simultaneously with the crossing of the Rhine by the 45th Division on March 26, the boundaries between the Seventh Army and the Third Army were changed with the Aschaffenburg area being assigned to the Seventh Army. As a result of this sudden boundary change, a strange and illogical event occurred. General Patton, in great secrecy, ordered a small task force from the 4th Armored Division to make a raid deep into German territory for the purpose of liberating American PWs then believed to be held in a prison camp near Hammelburg, some 50 miles from Aschaffenburg (see *After the Battle* No. 91). General Patton's son-in-law, Lieutenant Colonel John Waters, was reported to be a prisoner there. As it turned out, three officers from the 157th Infantry Regiment were also prisoners at Hammelburg, Lieutenants John E. Floyd, Richard Baron and William Meiggs, all having been captured at Reipertswiller in January. I was told nothing about Task Force Baum, then operating somewhere in my assigned area. From subsequent events it would appear that the 45th Division had been told nothing about this task force. My orders, however, did include one bit of curious information. I was told that I must not fire on any American tanks that I might encounter to my front. There was no further information, and I assumed that I would encounter elements of the Third Army in the Aschaffenburg area. About the same time my battalion reached the Main river on March 27 Task Force Baum reached Hammelburg prison camp some 50 miles behind German lines. On the following morning, March 28, my battalion resumed its attack on Aschaffenburg with bitter fighting against a fanatical garrison determined to fight to the last man. The battle lasted five days until the enemy finally capitulated on April 3.'

The Kampfkommandant of Aschaffenburg was Major Emil Lamberth and during the battle he charged about 40 of his men with desertion and cowardice, five of whom were executed as an example. The white notice reads: 'Cowards and traitors are hanged! Yesterday, an officer candidate from Alsace-Lorraine died a hero's death while destroying an enemy tank. He lives on! Today, a coward in officer's uniform is hanged because he betrayed the Führer and the people. He is dead forever.'

Leutnant Friedel Heymann was found by GIs hanging outside the Cafe Höfling at No. 5 Herstallstrasse. According to the story he was recovering in the local military hospital from wounds and was on home leave as he had just got married on March 23. A patrol came to check up which resulted in him being court-martialed on the 27th and executed the following day. His widow Anneliese campaigned for his exoneration and he was finally officially pardoned in 2003.

Farther to the southeast, our armored elements advanced eight miles to the vicinity of NESSELRODEN, west of EISENACH, while other units reached the vicinity of HERINGEN, 13 miles southwest of EISENACH. In these advances, we encountered road-blocks and resistance from assault guns and tanks.

HERSFELD has been cleared by our infantry, and north of FULDA we captured LANGENSCHWARZ and entered LUDERMUND. Northeast of FULDA we reached the vicinity of OBERNUST.

In the area northeast of HANAU, our cavalry entered EIDENGESASS. Mopping-up proceeds in the area north of FRANKFURT against strong resistance from enemy groups.

Rail and road communications in the areas of ISERLOHN, HOLZMINDEN, SIEGEN, MUHLHAUSEN, EISENACH, ERFURT and east of FULDA were attacked by fighter-bombers.

Fanatical resistance continued in ASCHAFFENBURG. At SCHWEINHEIM the enemy continued to resist by infiltrating after the town had been cleared.

Our rapid armored advance up the Main river continued and gains of up to 18 miles were made. Our forces control more than 14 miles along the Main river southeast of WURZBURG and generally have broken out of the ODENWALD into the WURZBURG-HEILBRONN plain.

In the action near BAD MERGENTHEIM we captured a lieutenant general, commander of a corps.

South of MANNHEIM, the last units which crossed the Rhine advanced eastward up to 18 miles and crossed the autobahn.

Allied forces in the west captured 22,877 prisoners 31 March.

Strong points, gun positions and fortified buildings impeding the progress of our forces in the sector east and northeast of the Main river were heavily bombed by fighter-bombers in great strength. Targets were in an area extending from ASCHAFFENBURG to KONIGSHOFEN, some 60 miles to the northeast.

Barracks and supply areas near STUTTGART, including targets at VAIHINGEN and LUDWIGSBURG, were attacked by medium bombers.

Rocket-firing fighters hit a convoy of more than 100 vehicles, some loaded with ammunition, attempting to move northeast from ENSCHEDE on a partially blocked road. Scattered motor transport was attacked in the LINGEN area.

Twenty rail yards were hit during the day. Nearly 800 transport vehicles and 43 tanks and armored vehicles were destroyed.

A number of airfields including those at HERZBERG and at GROSSEN BEHRINGEN south of MUHLHAUSEN also were bombed. Forty-seven aircraft were destroyed on the ground and others were damaged. One enemy aircraft was shot down.

From all operations 31 of our fighters are missing.

The moated Schloss Nordkirchen is renowned as being one of the finest palaces in Europe. Located 15 miles north of Dortmund in the Ruhr, it became known as the Versailles of Westphalia when completed for the Prince-Bishops of Münster in 1734. The 2nd Armored Division took it in the big breakthrough by the Ninth Army, this picture being released on April 3.

COMMUNIQUE No. 360 — April 3

Allied forces north and west of EMMERICH continue to make good progress and in some areas have reached points 15 miles north of the Dutch-German border. Farther north the line of the Twente canal has been reached. To the east we captured ENSCHEDE and reached the outskirts of RHEINE.

East of the Dortmund-Ems canal our troops are fighting in the IBBENBUREN and LENGERICH areas. North of the Lippe river our armor reached LIPPSTADT and made substantial gains to the north and east.

Our forces are consolidating their positions and closing in on the sides of the Ruhr pocket. Our armor cleared PADERBORN and infantry units advancing west reached ALTENRUTHEN southwest of PADERBORN.

Farther south our units are clearing the enemy from the vicinity of WINTERBERG and LANGEWIESE, and from the woods four miles southwest of BAD BERLEBURG. We are fighting in SIEGEN and repulsed a counter-attack at NETPHEN, northeast of SIEGEN.

East of the Ruhr pocket our units repulsed a tank-supported counter-attack north of WARBURG and reached PECKELSHEIM and BORGENTREICH.

We are fighting in the outskirts of KASSEL and our units have reached the vicinity of HELSUNGEN, 12 miles to the south. Resistance southeast of KASSEL along the east bank of the Fulda river continues to be strong.

Our armor crossed the Fulda river and reached the Werra at a point 17 miles northwest of EISENACH. Other armored elements reached a point three miles northwest of EISENACH.

Our infantry entered FULDA and very severe street fighting is in progress. Armored units which bypassed FULDA on the south, advanced 25 miles eastward to the area of MITTELSDORF and KALTENNORDHEIM. Farther east our armor reached the Werra river at a point two miles north of MEININGEN.

Our units continue to mop up in the area north and northeast of FRANKFURT. Groups of the enemy are ambushing supply lines along the autobahn.

Northeast of ASCHAFFENBURG we drove 12 miles to BAD ORB where some 6,500 Allied personnel were released from an enemy prisoner of war camp.

Hard fighting continued in ASCHAFFENBURG which is almost completely destroyed.

Substantial advances were made northwest of WURZBURG. To the southeast we are along the Main river almost to MARKTBREIT. The GIEBELSTADT airfield south of WURZBURG was captured.

In the drive up the Neckar river our armor and infantry reached the vicinity of BAD WIMPFEN, eight miles north of HEILBRONN.

South of HEIDELBERG approximately 100 anti-tank and other artillery pieces were knocked out in heavy fighting. Our advance in this area has reached UNTEROWISHEIM and we are near BRUCHSAL.

Allied forces in the west captured 12,446 prisoners 1 April.

Fortified buildings and strong points at ASCHAFFENBURG; EPPINGEN, east of BRUCHSAL; GOTTINGEN, northeast of ULM, and ammunition dumps east of HEILBRONN and near SCHWABISCH HALL were hit by fighter-bombers.

Barracks, supply and motor transport maintenance installations in the STUTTGART area; and at BOBLINGEN and TUBINGEN, southwest of STUTTGART, were attacked by medium bombers.

Road and rail transport in Holland, in the OSNABRUCK area, and farther to the east between CHEMNITZ and DRESDEN were attacked by fighter-bombers and rocket-firing fighters. Other rocket-firing fighters hit a gun position and strong points near ARNHEM.

Targets in BERLIN and MAGDEBURG as well as enemy communications over a wide area of Holland and northwest Germany were attacked last night by light bombers.

In 1903 the schloss was purchased by Duke Engelbert Marie von Arenberg and 30 years later — for tax reasons — the Duke's asset management company took possession. It was rather ironic therefore that in 1959 the State of Nordrhein-Westfalen purchased it for a training college for their tax inspectors! In the picture, Lieutenant William Gibson has called on the Duke and his wife Princess Valéria-Maria von Schleswig-Holstein (great granddaughter of Queen Victoria) informing them that they have to vacate the castle. She had been born out of wedlock in Hungary in 1900 to a Prussian noblewoman, Baroness Berta von Wernitz, who died of complications the following day. Valéria was brought up by a Jewish family with the name of Schwalb and it was not until 1938 that she received a letter from Duke Albert of Schleswig-Holstein admitting that she was his illegitimate daughter. She divorced her first husband the same year and married the 10th Prince of Arenberg in Berlin in June 1939. Torn between her early life in poor surroundings and the death of her adoptive mother in a concentration camp, she took her own life in 1953. The Duke died in 1974.

Now 65 miles east of the Rhine, infantrymen of the 42nd Division (Seventh Army) pick their way over rubble in Würzburg on April 2.

COMMUNIQUE No. 361   April 4

Allied forces north of NIJMEGEN have cleared a large area between the Waal and the Neder-Rijn. To the northeast along the Twente canal we have cleared LOCHEM and have advanced beyond the town to the west.

Northeast of ENSCHEDE we captured NORDHORN. Farther east our forces advanced through difficult country and have reached the outskirts of OSNABRUCK.

MUNSTER has been cleared. Northeast of BIELEFELD we crossed the Werra river south of HERFORD and have advanced to the northeast. Our units crossed the BIELEFELD-PADERBORN road and pushed beyond it to the east.

Rail yards at HOLZMINDEN and HAMELN were bombed by medium and light bombers.

On the northern side of the Ruhr pocket our forces crossed the Lippe Seiten canal and are fighting in the outskirts of HAMM. To the southeast we captured OESTEREIDEN and RUTHEN.

WINTERBERG is in our hands, and in the area to the south we made gains of up to two miles toward the west. We repulsed a counter-attack southwest of WINTERBERG and are fighting in BAD BERLEBURG.

Our forces pushing northward along the southern edge of the Ruhr pocket crossed the Sieg river ten miles north of SIEGEN which is in our hands. NETPHEN, to the northeast, was taken after a three-hour battle.

Southeast of PADERBORN, our infantry is advancing into the HARDEHAUSEN FOREST where an estimated 1,000 German infantrymen and 20 tanks were bypassed by our spearheads. This enemy force made two unsuccessful counter-attacks in the vicinity of BLOMENBERG and eight of its tanks were knocked out in the first attack. We have cleared HELMERN and BORGENTREICH northwest and northeast of WARBURG which has been captured. Fighting continues in KASSEL.

German barracks and troop concentrations at NORDHAUSEN, east of KASSEL, were bombed by heavy bombers. Airfields at THAL and west of ERFURT were attacked by fighter-bombers.

Fanatical enemy resistance in ASCHAFFENBURG was overcome after several days' severe fighting. We made gains of up to 10 miles to the northeast, reaching FLORSBACH.

At WURZBURG our infantry, with armor support, crossed the Main river in assault boats and entered the city. Another crossing was made some eight miles to the south. We drove two miles beyond the river but an enemy counter-attack cost some of the gains.

Armored columns advancing up to the Neckar river closed on HEILBRONN farther north and west.

Among 4,400 prisoners taken, mostly in the HEILBRONN-WURZBURG-ASCHAFFENBURG sector, was another German general who was a hospital patient.

Allied forces in the west captured 27,771 prisoners 2 April.

Artillery positions east of ASCHAFFENBURG and enemy armor and strong points in the outskirts of WURZBURG were bombed and strafed by fighter-bombers. Rail yards at WURZBURG and STUTTGART were attacked by other fighter-bombers.

Three large U-Boat bases, the naval base and the ship-building center of KIEL were attacked yesterday by escorted heavy bombers in great strength.

Road and rail transport in wide areas stretching from AMERSFOORT, Holland, to BREMEN, Germany, and motor transport and armor in the Ruhr were attacked by fighter-bombers.

Targets in BERLIN and enemy movements in the areas of BREMEN, HAMBURG, STENDAL and MAGDEBURG were attacked last night by light bombers.

The southern end of Petererpfarrgasse at its junction with Zwinger has now been completely rebuilt.

During April, the 21st Army Group was undertaking widely separated operations. While the Second Army was advancing north towards the River Elbe, the Canadian Army was moving north into occupied Holland, while the US Ninth Army was closing the northern face of the Ruhr (see page 428). Here, at the beginning of the month, the Régiment de Maisonneuve line up ready to move north. Although the caption says Terborg, 12 miles east of Arnhem, the picture was actually taken in Gaanderen, the next village to the north-west.

COMMUNIQUE No. 362   April 5

Allied forces north of NIJMEGEN reached the line of the Neder-Rijn on a broad front. In the ZEVENAAR area north of EMMERICH we made further progress to the northwest.

North of the Twente canal, we cleared HENGELO and made gains to the north and west. Farther north, armored units, advancing northeast from NORDHORN, reached the line of the Ems river at several points.

Southeast of RHEINE, our troops crossed the Dortmund-Ems canal. Northeast of OSNABRUCK we crossed the Ems-Weser canal and advanced beyond it.

OSNABRUCK has been entered, but is not yet clear. Other units bypassed the town to the south and reached a point seven miles east of it.

MUNSTER has been cleared with the exception of snipers. Over 1,700 prisoners were taken in the city.

Our armor reached the Weser river in the vicinity of BAD OEYNHAUSEN, and other elements reached a point five miles northeast of BAD SALZUFLEN. Other armored units reached the Bega river on the outskirts of LEMGO capturing more than 4,000 prisoners.

Our infantry is mopping up a bypassed hill in the TEUTOBURGERWALD. In the DETMOLD area we are meeting resistance from the remnants of an SS tank battalion.

Enemy strong points near GUTERSLOH were attacked by fighter-bombers.

KASSEL has been cleared after heavy house-to-house fighting.

Our armor reached the vicinity of OBERDORLA, four miles south of MUHLHAUSEN. Other armored elements are in the vicinity of HELDRA, northwest of KREUZBURG. Infantry, advancing behind the armor, crossed the Fulda river and reached a point 14 miles northwest of EISENACH. EISENACH, bypassed by our spearheads, is an enemy strongpoint defended by tanks and infantry.

Armored spearheads cleared GOTHA and entered OHRDRUF, seven miles to the south. Farther south of GOTHA our armored units reached the vicinity of OBERHOF and cleared SUHL.

German troop concentrations at NORDHAUSEN were attacked by escorted heavy bombers. Fighter-bombers hit enemy airfields at SCHWEINFURT and JENA.

Meanwhile, troops had been racing against time to try to cut off the V2 launch sites in central Holland which were still wreaking havoc right through March, the last rocket falling on London and Antwerp on the 27th. The Press dubbed the operation as being against 'V-country'. This armour is being cheered on its way at liberated Hummelo en route for Zutphen which was captured on the 14th.

On March 27 Montgomery had issued orders to his army commanders on the assumption that the US Ninth Army would remain with the 21st Army Group on the right flank of the drive to the Elbe. The leading troops had already begun the advance when he received the following message from Eisenhower on the evening of the 28th: 'I agree generally with your plan up to the point of gaining contact with Bradley to the east of the Ruhr. But thereafter, my present plans are now being co-ordinated with Stalin. As soon as you and Bradley have joined hands in the Kassel—Paderborn area, Ninth Army will revert to Bradley's command. He will then be responsible for occupying and mopping up the Ruhr and with minimum delay will make his main thrust on the axis Erfurt—Leipzig—Dresden and join hands with the Russians. Your Army Group will protect Bradley's northern flank with the inter-army group boundary similar to Second Army's right boundary, Münster—Hannover inclusive to Bradley, thence Wittenberge or Stendal as decided later.' Eisenhower's message came as a great shock to Montgomery who immediately sent this reply: 'I note from FWD 18272 that you intend to change the command set-up. If you feel this is necessary I pray you do not do so until we reach the Elbe as such action would not help the great movement which is now beginning to develop.' However, Eisenhower would not be moved and the Ninth Army reverted to General Bradley's 12th Army Group on April 4. Lying 40 miles north of Dortmund, the garrison town of Münster possessed five large complexes of barracks for the Wehrmacht. The US 17th Airborne Division — now being used in an infantry role — attacked the city assisted by the 771st Tank Battalion and the British 6th Guards Tank Brigade on April 2, its capture being reported in today's communiqué.

On the northern side of the Ruhr pocket, our infantry crossed the Dortmund-Ems canal, captured ICKERN and WALTROP, and advanced to a point one and a half miles west of LUNEN after repulsing several small counter-attacks. Resistance continues in HAMM with considerable artillery fire coming from the city.

On the eastern side of the pocket, northeast of WINTERBERG, our armor reached HILDFELD and GRONEBACH against tank and self-propelled gun-fire. We cleared OBERKIRCHEN to the southwest and repulsed two small counter-attacks.

Southwest of SIEGEN we cleared a number of small towns including MUDERSBACH and KATZENBACH and repulsed several counter-attacks.

Targets at ESSEN and LUDENSCHEID, in the pocket, were attacked by fighter-bombers.

It is estimated that our ground units inflicted 4,600 casualties in breaking the enemy resistance at ASCHAFFENBURG.

Northeast of ASCHAFFENBURG we gained ten miles in rugged terrain, advancing past OBERSINN. BURGSINN and RIENECK were cleared. Our forces made another crossing of the Main river south of LOHR.

About a half of WURZBURG has been cleared.

Our armor, driving south of the Main river bend at OCHSENFURT, gained some ten miles. Farther west our armor reached IGERSHEIM on the Tauber river.

MOCKMUHL, BAD WIMPFEN and a number of other towns northeast of HEILBRONN were captured. Enemy resistance around HEILBRONN was strong and we repulsed a counter-attack north of the city.

Completely rebuilt, this is Münster's Prinzipalmarkt, looking north from in front of the St Lamberti Church. The tall spire of the Town Hall in the background forms the link between then and now.

The distance between the fronts in the West and East was now only about 200 miles with the Third Army being the closest to the Soviet lines. At Kassel, 115 miles east of the Rhine, the battle was costly and it took the 80th Division three days to advance just three miles, before finally clearing the city on April 4. But now it was Patton's turn to be annoyed when Bradley told him that the Third would have to slow down until the First and Ninth were in line with it. Patton protested that it would mean more casualties as it would give the Germans time to lay mines ahead of his advance. Bradley replied that he didn't think they had many mines left but Patton retorted: 'Well, they had a hell of a lot of them at Kassel. 6th Armored and 80th had a great deal of trouble with mines there. I don't like this constantly being sat down. Everytime we've been sat down it has cost us heavily. We've got the Germans on the run and the only way to end this war is to kill them or run them to death. Just disconnect me from a telephone connection with SHAEF', Patton said, 'and I'll contact them for you in two days.' Bradley shook his head. 'It isn't as simple as that, I wish it were but a lot of high-level politics are involved.'

KARLSRUHE was captured against stiff resistance.

Between the ASCHAFFENBURG area and HEILBRONN, 2,594 prisoners were taken. Allied forces in the west captured 28,817 prisoners 3 April.

Supply depots at EBRACH, east of WURZBURG, and GROSSASPACH, northeast of STUTTGART, were targets for medium and light bombers.

Enemy troop concentration and fortified positions in the area from HEILBRONN northeastwards to BAMBERG and NUREMBERG, and a barracks area at CRAILSHEIM, were struck at by medium, light and fighter-bombers.

Submarine yards at KIEL and HAMBURG and airfields in northwest Germany were attacked by escorted heavy bombers in very great strength.

Road and rail transport in Holland in the MEPPEN and CLOPPENBURG areas northwest of OSNABRUCK; near OLDENBURG and BREMEN; and in the area of MUHLHAUSEN and HALLE, and rail yards at ERFURT, SCHWEINFURT and CRAILSHEIM were heavily attacked by medium, light and fighter-bombers.

In all the day's operations, 31 enemy aircraft were shot down and 32 others were destroyed on the ground. According to reports so far received, nine of our heavy bombers, three medium bombers and 17 fighters are missing.

Once surrounded by ruins, the statue of Prince Karl Hesse-Kassel is now restored in front of the Karlskirche.

Last night heavy bombers were over Germany in very great strength with synthetic oil plants at MERSEBURG and HAMBURG as the main objectives. Light bombers again attacked targets at BERLIN.

With Kassel in the bag, troops of the 80th Division's 318th Infantry move out east on April 5.

At the same time that the battle at Kassel was taking place, Patton's two Combat Commands of the 4th Armored were 60 miles to the south-east advancing on Gotha. There, on the morning of April 4, they found a huge underground communication centre constructed for the German High Command but that afternoon they made an even more important discovery . . . one which was to shock the free world and tarnish forever Hitler's Germany. On the fringe of Ohrdruf, they came across their first Nazi concentration camp. The men were appalled at what they saw . . . horrors that distressed even the battle-hardened GIs. The repercussions would prove to be immense.

The measured tone of Colonel Jordan's communiqué (page 432) is in stark contrast to what the name 'Ohrdruf' would forever mean. Bruce Nickols was a member of the Headquarters Company of the 354th Infantry Regiment belonging to the 89th Infantry Division operating with the 4th Armored: 'From the outside, the camp was unremarkable. It was surrounded by a high barbed-wire fence and had a wooden sign which read, "Arbeit Macht Frei." [Work Sets you Free] The swinging gate was open, and a young soldier, probably an SS guard, lay dead diagonally across the entrance. The camp was located in the forest and was surrounded by a thick grove of pine and other conifers. The inside of the camp was composed of a large 100-yard-square central area which was surrounded by one-story barracks painted green which appeared to house 60-100 inmates. As we stepped into the compound one was greeted by an overpowering odor of quick-lime, dirty clothing, faeces, and urine. Lying in the centre of the square were 60-70 dead prisoners clad in striped clothing and in disarray. They had reportedly been machine-gunned the day before because they were too weak to march to another camp.'

Now located on a Bundeswehr army training ground, all has been swept away . . . but, as we will see, Eisenhower would soon visit the camp personally.

'The idea was for the SS and the prisoners to avoid the approaching US Army and the Russians. Adjacent to the "parade ground" was a small shed which was open on one side. Inside, were bodies stacked in alternate directions as one would stack cordwood, and each layer was covered with a sprinkling of quicklime. I did not see him, but someone told me that there had been a body of a dead American aviator in the shed. This place reportedly had been used for punishment, and the inmates were beaten on the back and heads with a shovel. My understanding is that all died following this abuse. I visited some of the surrounding barracks and found live inmates who had hidden during the massacre. They were astounded and appeared to be struggling to understand what was happening. Further into the camp was evidence of an attempt to exhume and burn large numbers of bodies. I became very upset when we got back to our quarters, but the whole experience was far beyond my understanding. I wrote a letter to my parents describing the experience which was read at a local gathering of businessmen. It was widely disbelieved.'

The next major waterway to be crossed was the River Weser, over 450 miles long, running from its estuary at Bremen south past Verden, Nienburg, Minden and beyond Hameln to Kassel. And it was near the Pied Piper town that Ninth Army engineers prepared a pontoon bridge for the 30th Division to continue their eastward drive. Here an M4 medium tank of the 2nd Armored Division crosses the bridge at Ohsen, four miles south of Hameln.

COMMUNIQUE No. 363   April 6

Allied patrols north of NIJMEGEN crossed the Neder-Rijn west and east of ARNHEM. In the ZUTPHEN area fierce opposition was encountered and the town is still in enemy hands.

Northwest of HENGELO we captured ALMELO and made good gains to the north and east. Farther east there is fighting in the LINGEN area but the town is not yet clear. Southeast of RHEINE, the Dortmund-Ems canal bridgehead has been further extended and DREIERWALDE has been captured.

In the IBBENBUREN area resistance remains strong but armored elements bypassed the town to the south and advanced to a point five miles south of DIEPHOLZ. OSNABRUCK is in our hands and armored units, which previously bypassed the town, advanced to the line of the Weser river north of MINDEN. Another column reached the Weser in the PETERSHAGEN area and virtually cleared MINDEN.

We have cleared BIELEFELD, and the garrisons in HERFORD and

Two-way traffic! As the armour rolled eastwards, prisoners were brought back to the western bank.

'The Rats come out of Hamlin [*sic*] town.' The Press were quick to draw a parallel with the fable as Pfc Clifton Baker 'pipes' the column of prisoners through the town of Hameln with his walkie-talkie. This is Bäckerstrasse looking north to Am Markt.

Left: The 2nd Fife and Forfar Yeomanry (11th Armoured Division) en route for Osnabrück sporting the ubiquitous street sign souvenir for every town in Germany had its Adolf-Hitler-Strasse. The city was taken during the night of April 4/5 by the combined efforts of No. 3 Commando, No. 45 Royal Marine Commando and the 12th Battalion of the Parachute Regiment. *Right:* The victory was marked by the raising of the unit flag bearing its unofficial motto: 'Bash on regardless'.

The infantry were supported by the Churchills of No. 3 Squadron of the 4th Grenadier Guards. However, as the city had been rendered uninhabitable by Allied bombing, the tanks could only assist in the western suburbs.

Fierce fighting is in progress in HAMM. East of the city our units crossed the Lippe river and reached the HAMM-SOEST rail line. On the east side of the pocket, we are in the vicinity of RUTHEN.

Southwest of WINTERBERG our forces reached points near WINKHAUSEN and LATROP. We repulsed numerous counter-attacks between SIEGEN and SIEGBURG, one of which reached the outskirts of SIEGEN before it was repelled.

Fighter-bombers attacked targets in the pocket including a large formation of enemy troops on a road near ARNSBERG. South of FULDA our armor and infantry drove through the Spessart hills to reach SPEICHERZ and BAD BRUCKENAU. Farther south on the Main river, east of LOHR, we reached WIESENFELD.

Heavy fighting is in progress in WURZBURG and most of the city has been cleared. An enemy counter-attack forced us back in the northern part of the city, but the attack was repulsed and the lost ground was regained. More than 1,000 prisoners have been taken in the city.

BAD OEYNHAUSEN have surrendered. Armored elements pushed to within two miles of RINTELN. Another armored spearhead advanced to the Weser river opposite HAMELN. DETMOLD, and VELDROM in the TEUTOBURGERWALD, were cleared and we are fighting in ALTENBEKEN. The HARDEHAUSEN FOREST, northwest of WARBURG was cleared.

Our units entered MEIMBRESSEN northwest of KASSEL and pushed beyond NIENHAGEN, east of the city. MUHLHAUSEN was cleared by armored elements which pushed eight miles farther northeast to the vicinity of SCHLOTHEIM. Our infantry reached the vicinity of ALTENGÖTTERN, northeast of MUHLHAUSEN, and MIHLA, farther southwest. We entered the southern outskirts of EISENACH, and reached points seven miles west of SCHMALKALDEN. Armored units cleared ZELLA MEHLIS, capturing three small-arms ammunition factories. Seven small-arms factories were taken in SUHL.

Our forces made further gains into the Ruhr pocket from the north and east. On the north, we captured BRAMBAUER, four miles north of DORTMUND.

Despite the damage wrought to Osnabrück, the view in the rebuilt Hauptbahnhof remains remarkably unchanged from when the Royal Marine commandos were photographed there by Herbert Dewhirst of *The Times*. This is Platfom No. 2 looking back to No. 1.

Allied forces in the west captured 32,616 prisoners 4 April.

Enemy transport in the areas of PFORZHEIM, HEILBRONN, STUTTGART, LEIPZIG, NUREMBERG and GERA was attacked by fighter-bombers. An ammunition store southeast of STUTTGART, and an oil storage depot at GEISLINGEN, northwest of ULM, were bombed by medium bombers.

Enemy transport, supply dumps, troops and strong points in the DEVENTER, ZWOLLE and GRONINGEN areas of Holland and in wide areas of northwestern Germany, including HAMBURG, BREMEN, MEPPEN, CELLE and HANNOVER, were attacked yesterday by fighter-bombers.

Airfields in the WEIMAR area and farther south also were attacked by fighter-bombers. Seventy-one enemy aircraft were destroyed on the ground and many others were damaged in the course of these attacks.

Military equipment depots at INGOLSTADT, northeast of MUNICH, at GRAFENWOHR, southeast of BAYREUTH, and at FURTH; railway yards at PLAUEN, BAYREUTH and NUREMBERG; and an airfield southwest of NUREMBERG, were attacked by escorted heavy bombers in very great strength.

With the return of Simpson's Ninth Army to the 12th Army Group, General Bradley had under his command four armies, 12 corps and 48 divisions — more than 1,300,000 men making it the largest American command in US history. Now a new central thrust aimed at Leipzig and Dresden would be the main role of General Hodges' First Army, its 1st Division seen here making an assault crossing of the Weser at Wehrden, 20 miles north of Kassel, on April 8. The offensive south of the Harz mountains got under way by April 11 but all organised resistance did not cease for another ten days.

Substantial advances were made by our armor and infantry northeast and southeast of OCHSENFURT. KITZINGEN, northeast of OCHSENFURT, was cleared.

The enemy is fighting stubbornly to hold the line of the Neckar and Jagst rivers, and in front of HEILBRONN. West of HEILBRONN, we captured a number of villages. SCHWAIGERN was cleared.

Allied forces which made the latest Rhine crossing below SPEYER and captured KARLSRUHE, reached the Neckar river more than 30 miles east of the Rhine.

Heidelberg was the one large city to escape virtually undamaged. Straddling the Neckar river, a tributary of the Rhine just south of Mannheim, it fell within the jurisdiction of the Seventh Army, in particular the 44th Infantry Division. As the telephone system was still operational, Major General William F. Dean gave the task of negotiating with the Germans to his German-speaking artillery commander, Brigadier General William Beiderlinden, who was familiar with the city and its famous university which he wanted to try to save from destruction. Having made contact, a party of German parliamentaries crossed the river in a white ambulance flying a white flag. While negotiations were taking place, a German threat to blow the two remaining bridges was carried out. Nevertheless, the surrender was agreed and the 10th Armored Division entered the city on April 1. The following day, these prisoners were photographed crossing the market square to the POW cages.

Hamm on the north-eastern end of the Ruhr Pocket was reported as cleared on April 7. These prisoners are marching into what remains of the marshalling yards which had been the subject of air attacks for months — even as far back as 1940.

COMMUNIQUE No. 364   April 7

Allied forces have broken out of their bridgehead across the Twente canal and are astride the ZUTPHEN-DEVENTER highway within two miles of DEVENTER.

To the northeast our forward elements have reached MEPPEN following a 15-mile advance. LINGEN has been cleared and we have gained a bridgehead across the Ems river in the LINGEN area.

We captured IBBENBUREN, east of RHEINE, and reached DIEPHOLZ, northeast of OSNABRUCK. Our units secured a bridgehead north on MINDEN on the right bank of the Weser river. MINDEN is in our hands.

Our forces are at a point five miles south of BUCKEBERG. We are fighting in HAMELN, and to the south we have crossed the Weser river near TUNDERN and continued eastward.

In the area northeast of WARBURG our units reached the vicinity of BRUCHHAUSEN, and we are at TIETELSEN and BORGENTREICH.

We captured HOFGEISMAR, ten miles east of WARBURG, and to the southeast we reached HANN MUNDEN after repulsing a counter-attack.

Our forces advanced 12 miles on a five-mile front east and southeast of KASSEL. We repulsed a counter-attack in the vicinity of OSTERODE, 13 miles southwest of KASSEL.

Our infantry entered BAD LANGENSALZA and other elements are in the area four to seven miles north of GOTHA. Infantry units, mopping up behind our armor, are in an area 13 to 18 miles southwest of GOTHA.

We cleared EISENACH and MEININGEN and our armored elements have reached the vicinity of STUTZERBACH.

We made gains into the Ruhr pocket from the north and east. HAMM has been cleared, and to the east we captured NORDDINKER and SUDDINKER. Our armor took BETTINGHAUSEN and SCHMERLECKE, northeast of SOEST.

We reached OLSBERG and captured SIEDLINGHAUSEN north of WINTERBERG, and our armor is beyond WINKHAUSEN, west of the city. Considerable opposition is being met in the SIEGEN area.

We advanced to the outskirts of FULDA and cleared a substantial area to the south. WURZBURG has been cleared and gains were made north and south of the city.

Farther south our units gained more than six miles south of BAD MERGENTHEIM. We cleared one-third of HEILBRONN.

East and southeast of KARLSRUHE we captured BRETTEN, and reached STEIN.

Allied forces in the west captured 40,107 prisoners 5 April.

Rail yards at LEIPZIG, HALLE and GERA, southwest of LEIPZIG, were attacked by escorted heavy bombers in strength. Other rail yards at NORTHEIM, GOTTINGEN, in the area south of NORDHAUSEN and north of BAYREUTH, and at STUTTGART; and an ammunition dump at GAILENKIRCHEN, east of HEILBRONN, were targets for medium, light and fighter-bombers.

Fortified positions and troop concentrations at GOLLHOFEN, southeast of WURZBURG; LOWENSTEIN and SCHWABISCH HALL, east of HEILBRONN; at ELLWANGEN; and in the area northeast of STRASBOURG were attacked by fighter-bombers.

Enemy airfields at BINDERSLEBEN, west of ERFURT, and at ILLESHEIM, northeast of ROTHENBURG, were targets for other fighter-bombers.

Back in September, SHAEF issued this proclamation to the German press concerning the military government of Germany: 'The Allied Forces serving under my Command have now entered Germany. We come as conquerors, but not as oppressors. In the area of Germany occupied by the forces under my Command, we shall obliterate Nazism and German militarism. We shall overthrow the Nazi rule, dissolve the Nazi Party and abolish the cruel and oppressive and discriminatory laws and institutions which the party has created. We shall eradicate that German militarism which has so often disrupted the peace of the world. Military and party leaders, the Gestapo and others suspected of crimes and atrocities, will be tried, and if guilty, punished as they deserve.' So now that large areas of Germany had been taken, Psychological Warfare Teams were on hand to broadcast Allied occupation regulations. This visit was pictured in the Duisburg suburb of Hamborn on the western edge of the pocket. The regulations included the surrender of all warlike materials and stores, firearms including sporting guns, wireless and signalling equipment, and carrier pigeons.

While the 4th Canadian Armoured Division presses on through Delden in eastern Holland *(above)*, the British 3rd Division enters Lingen, 12 miles inside Germany *(below)*.

COMMUNIQUE No. 365 **April 8**

Allied forces entered MEPPEN on the Ems river. Farther south, the bridgehead over the river at LINGEN has been extended against moderate resistance.

Northeast of RHEINE we occupied HOPSTEN and pushed east of the town. South of BREMEN our forces passed through SULINGEN and SIEDENBURG.

In the area of STOLZENAU on the Weser, we met determined enemy opposition. To the south we advanced more than 12 miles beyond the river near MINDEN.

Strong points, gun positions and enemy troops in the areas of DEVENTER, RIJSSEN, LEESE, HASELUNNE, FURSTENAU and FREREN were hit with rockets and bombs by fighter-bombers. Rail lines were cut in many places including the AMERSFOORT and ZWOLLE areas, and a bridge was destroyed west of RIJSSEN.

Our armor broke out of the Weser bridgehead in the HAMELN area, took SCHULENBERG and ELZE, and reached HASEDE. Mopping-up continues in HAMELN. Farther south, our infantry captured STAHLE, across the Weser river from HOLZMINDEN.

Armored elements reached a point two miles from HELMARSHAUSEN, and other units are in the vicinity of TRENDELBURG, on the Diemel river. We have taken VECKERHAGEN on the west bank of the Weser north of HANN MUNDEN, and just southeast of the city our units are on the autobahn in the vicinity of LAUBACH. Our infantry is in the area four miles southwest of WITZENHAUSEN.

West of MUHLHAUSEN we have retaken STRUTH after it was lost in an enemy counter-attack. We have reached the vicinity of KEULA, northeast of MUHLHAUSEN, and to the southeast of the city we cleared LANGERNSALZE.

Our armor in the area south of SUHL captured SCHLEUSINGEN.

Enemy troops and other targets in the Ruhr pocket, and armor east of KASSEL, were hit by fighter-bombers. Other fighter-bombers attacked airfields in the areas of HANNOVER, DORTMUND, HILDESHEIM, ERFURT, LAUCHA, ZWICKAU and BAYREUTH.

On the northern side of the Ruhr pocket our armor captured OST ONNEN, west of SOEST, which has been cleared, and reached MULLINGSEN to the southeast.

The photo, which is believed to be a re-enactment, was taken outside what is today the dental practice of Dr Elizabeth Horrix at No. 13 Castellstrasse.

As the communiqués increasingly show, the number of prisoners captured each day now ran into thousands, over 40,000 on the day this photo was taken of the Seventh Army POW cage at Worms which contained over 24,000 men. The picture was submitted to the censor but SHAEF initially denied publication on April 18.

Along the eastern side of the pocket we are fighting in GLEIDORF, two miles northeast of SCHMALLENBERG, and we repulsed a counter-attack in that area. We have taken FLECKENBERG and WINGEHAUSEN, south of SCHMALLENBERG.

On the southern flank of the pocket our forces reduced all enemy strong points in SIEGEN, and made a new crossing of the Sieg river two and one-half miles west of the town.

Southeast of FULDA we gained up to ten miles against spotty resistance.

Our armored elements reached CRAILSHEIM, east of HEILBRONN, after a 20-mile advance. A number of enemy motor convoys were trapped in CRAILSHEIM.

In HEILBRONN the enemy continued to resist stubbornly.

East of KARLSRUHE gains of more than eight miles were made. Resistance was strong from Siegfried Line defenses in the direction of RASTATT.

Allied forces in the west captured 42,888 prisoners 6 April.

Strong forces of medium, light and fighter-bombers attacked rail and road transport, communications and rail facilities at NORTHEIM and GOTTINGEN; along the GOTHA, ERFURT, WEIMAR rail line; between HILDESHEIM and CALBE; between KASSEL and HALLE; and in the triangle formed by GOTTINGEN, BAYREUTH and CHEMNITZ.

Escorted heavy bombers in very great strength bombed objectives in northern Germany including airfields at WESENDORF, PARCHIM and KALTENKIRCHEN, an oil storage depot at HITZACKER, an ordnance depot at GUSTROW and rail yards at LUNEBURG and NEUMUNSTER.

Strong points in and near ODHEIM, north of HEILBRONN, were attacked by fighter-bombers.

In the course of the day's operations 105 enemy aircraft were shot down, 116 were destroyed on the ground and many others were damaged. Twenty-two of our bombers and 16 fighters are missing.

Enemy movements from HANNOVER to BERLIN were attacked during the night by light bombers.

The camp lay here alongside the Pfortenring leading to the Rhine. The church in the distance is the Liebfrauenstift.

Located on the eastern bank of the IJssel river, Zutphen, 20 miles north of Arnhem, fell to the Canadians after a stiff fight.

An anti-tank barrier lay at the end of the bridge which had been partially demolished acros the moat that surrounds the town.

COMMUNIQUE No. 366   **April 9**

Allied airborne forces have been dropped over a wide area in northwest Holland. ZUTPHEN, on the IJssel river, has been captured.

Enemy resistance continues to be strong in the MEPPEN area. East of LINGEN we occupied LENGERICH and FREREN and are continuing to advance eastward. To the south, we captured HALVERDE.

Gun positions and strong points at DEVENTER, in the areas of LINGEN, HASELUNNE and QUAKENBRUCK, and road and rail transport over wide areas in Holland and northwest Germany were struck at by fighter-bombers and rocket-firing fighters.

Our armored forces advancing northeast from the Dummersee, continued to make good progress. SYKE has been captured and we are less than 12 miles from BREMEN.

East of the Weser river we occupied LOCCUM and BAD REHBURG and are on the outskirts of NEUSTADT after passing through SACHSENHAGEN.

We reached the northern outskirts of STADTHAGEN. Our armor captured SARSTEDT and HIMMELSTHUR, north of HILDESHEIM, and MARIENBURG, two miles south of the town.

To the southwest we are fighting in CAPELLENHAGEN, and we captured ESCHERSHAUSEN. Fighting continues in HOXTER.

The rebuilt crossing spanning the Coehoornsingel on Deventerweg is today named the 'Canadians' Bridge'.

Northeast of KASSEL our infantry reached a point three miles west of HARDEGSEN. We took GOTTINGEN and VARLOSEN, while other units cleared HANN MUNDEN and pushed beyond the town.

Our armor reached DINGELSTADT, ten miles northwest of MUHLHAUSEN. In the vicinity of STRUTH, west of MUHLHAUSEN, we repulsed a counter-attack, knocked out nine of the 16 enemy tanks employed and killed or captured approximately half of the estimated 1,000-man infantry force. Another counter-attack was repelled southwest of MUHLHAUSEN.

Our infantry reached a point four miles northeast of GOTHA, and other units mopping up behind the armor cut the OHRDRUF—SUHL road eight miles north of SUHL. Our forces reached a point three miles southeast of SUHL.

German prisoners were quickly employed in digging graves for the Canadian soldiers killed in the fighting. These photos taken on April 10 were not approved for publication, not that such work was disallowed by the Geneva Convention.

As the advance swept across the country, a ploy which was increasingly being used to prevent unnecessary loss of life was to telephone the town or village ahead to demand its surrender, a good example taking place at Werl, just east of the Ruhr, the birthplace of Franz von Papen *(left)*. Captain William E. Hensel *(right)* of the 8th Armored Division used a telephone in the Inn Stewen in the nearby village of Westönnen to call the German command post in the cellars of the Ursulinen Nunnery to negotiate the capitulation of Werl. Dr Fritz Leimgardt acted as parliamentary and, after the departure of Stadtkommandant Dunker, Chief of Police Hochstul approved the surrender of the town without opposition. (Before the war von Papen was the German military attaché in Mexico and Washington, but when Paul von Hindenburg became President in 1933, von Papen became his Vice-Chancellor. He was appointed ambassador to Austria from 1936-38 and Turkey from 1939-1944. He stood trial at Nuremberg in 1946 but was acquitted and died in Obersasbach in 1969.)

South of MEININGEN our infantry and armor advanced eastward about 15 miles to reach KONIGSHOFEN.

In mopping up the area between salients farther south, we occupied many towns and villages south and southeast of BAD KISSINGEN.

East of WURZBURG our troops have cleared the west bank of the Main river for a distance of some 12 miles.

Armor, driving westward from CRAILSHEIM, reached GEISLINGEN.

House-to-house fighting continues in HEILBRONN.

The town of PFORZHEIM, southeast of KARLSRUHE, has been captured and our forces have made good gains to the east.

On the northern sector of the Ruhr pocket our infantry extended its bridgehead over the Rhine-Herne canal and entered KATERNBERG and GELSENKIRCHEN. We are meeting strong resistance in CASTROP. To the west a number of towns were cleared including MERKLINGEN and RAHM, and we entered the northwest outskirts of DORTMUND. Farther west our armor entered WERL, captured GUNNINGEN and entered WARSTEIN.

On the eastern edge of the pocket we are within two miles of MESCHEDE.

West of SIEGEN our forces captured several towns including FREUDENBERG, MORSBACH and MERTEN.

Allied forces in the west captured 39,662 prisoners 7 April.

Rail yards at STENDAL, PLAUEN, and CHEB, southeast of PLAUEN; ordnance depots at BAYREUTH and

Sergeant Edward M. Gorman lost no time in claiming this souvenir from the wall of the building across the street from von Papen's birthplace *(below)*. **(Comparison by Helmuth Euler.)**

GRAFENWOHR, southeast of BAYREUTH; an aircraft repair factory at FURTH and airfields at SCHAFSTADT, southwest of HALLE, and at ROTH, south of NUREMBERG, were attacked by escorted heavy bombers in great strength.

Rail and road transport, rail yards and other communications targets at CELLE, northeast of HANNOVER, MAGDEBURG, SONDERSHAUSEN, LEIPZIG, SCHLEIZ, northwest of PLAUEN, BAMBERG and in the area of NUREMBERG were attacked by strong forces of medium, light and fighter-bombers.

Sixteen enemy airfields including those at NORDHAUSEN, DESSAU, HALLE, MERSEBURG, ERFURT and HOF, and others in the NUREMBERG area, also were targets for medium, light and fighter-bombers.

An oil refinery at NIENHAGEN, northeast of HANNOVER; an oil storage depot at MUNCHENBERNSDORF, southwest of GERA; and an ammunition dump at KLEINENGSTINGEN, south of STUTTGART, were hit by medium and light bombers.

During the day's operations, 35 enemy aircraft were shot down, 66 were destroyed on the ground and many others were damaged. According to reports so far received, ten of our heavy bombers, one medium bomber and six fighters are missing.

Last night heavy bombers in great strength attacked submarine building yards at HAMBURG, and a synthetic oil plant at LUTZEN west of LEIPZIG. Targets in BERLIN were also bombed.

Closing the noose around the Ruhr, the US 17th Airborne Division entered Essen on April 10. As the home of the Krupp factories with the largest steel works in Europe, it had long been a prime target for Bomber Command and the RAF were especially keen to inspect the damage wrought to 'the arsenal of Germany'. *Left:* Here an Air Ministry photographer inspects a bronze statue of the man himself, Alfred Krupp, blasted from its plinth. *Right:* Meanwhile troops of the 79th Division push on through the rubble.

COMMUNIQUE No. 367   April 10

Allied forces overcame enemy resistance at MEPPEN and after crossing the Ems river made good advances northward beyond LATHEN. East of LINGEN our units occupied FURSTENAU.

South of BREMEN we captured BASSUM and RIEDE where enemy resistance is stiffening. Armored elements have captured NIEDERNSTOCKEN on the Leine river and farther south other units have secured bridges intact across the river in the area of NEUSTADT and have continued their advance.

Our units crossed the Leine river at RICKLINGEN, northwest of HANNOVER, and other elements reached a point five miles from the western edge of the city. To the south our armor captured GESTORF and cleared HILDESHEIM, while infantry crossed the Leine river south of the town and pushed seven miles eastward.

Northwest of GOTTINGEN we took DIEMARDEN and REINHAUSEN. We are across the Leine river on an 11-mile front from GOTTINGEN south to a point just northeast of WITZENHAUSEN.

East of MUHLHAUSEN, our armor and infantry entered ALTENHAUSEN and reached the vicinity of KLETTSTEDT.

Looking down Richard-Wagner-Strasse. The church-like building in the distance in the wartime shot is actually the headquarters of the regional water supply company on Kronprinzenstrasse. Although hidden in our comparison, it still stands.

East of GOTHA, our infantry is in the vicinity of NOTTLEBEN, while farther south other elements are near CRAWINKEL and STUTZHAUS. To the west, we repulsed a counter-attack near TAMBACH.

Northeast of SUHL, we reached the vicinity of STUTZERBACH after repulsing a small counter-attack. In the area 15 miles south of SUHL our armored elements occupied BEDHEIM.

The Allied air forces were still hammering towns ahead of the troops and as Communiqué 366 on page 443 states, Stendal was attacked on April 8. Lying just this side of the Elbe, some 70 miles west of Berlin, it still lay well inside the future Soviet Zone of Occupation (see page 426). One of the aircraft on Mission 932 was a veteran of 129 missions with the 91st Bomb Group based at Bassingbourn. A crewman in another B-17 described what he saw: 'We were flying over the target at 20,500 feet altitude when I observed aircraft B-17G, 42-31333, to receive a direct flak hit approximately between the bomb bay and No. 2 engine. The aircraft immediately started into a vertical dive. The fuselage was on fire and when it had dropped approximately 5,000 feet the left wing fell off. It continued down and when the fuselage was about 3,000 feet from the ground it exploded and then exploded again when it hit the ground. I saw no crew member leave the aircraft or parachutes open.' In fact, the pilot, 1st Lieutenant Robert E. Fuller, had managed to escape from the stricken machine but his eight fellow crewmen were killed.

GOMPERTSHAUSEN and RIETH, south of BEDHEIM, were reached by our armored elements after a 12-mile advance.

We are within four miles of SCHWEINFURT on both the north and south sides.

East of OCHSENFURT our armor reached DORMHEIM after a six-mile gain.

The southern point of the CRAILSHEIM salient was widened against strong ground resistance supported by enemy air attacks.

Farther west our troops have pushed south from the Jagst river and forced the enemy back toward the Kocher river.

House-to-house fighting continued in HEILBRONN. BRACKENHEIM, southwest of HEILBRONN, has been captured.

South of KARLSRUHE the enemy continues to hold out in the Siegfried Line fortifications.

Targets at NIDERSTETTEN, NEUENSTADT and KOCHENDORF were attacked by fighter-bombers operating ahead of our ground forces.

In the Ruhr pocket our infantry entered the northwestern part of ESSEN after meeting fairly stiff resistance. Southwest of SOEST we cleared WERL and reached WIEHAGEN.

On the eastern side of the pocket our forces reached HIRSCHBERG and took MESCHEDE, both southwest of RUTHEN. Our armor cleared FREDEBURG, northwest of SCHMALLENBERG, while southwest of the city we captured SAALHAUSEN and HEINSBERG.

North of SIEGEN we entered HILCHENBACH and BUSCHHUTTEN.

Ten airfields in an area 60 miles square around MUNICH, an oil storage depot at NEUBERG, and an explosive plant at WOLFRATSHAUSEN were attacked yesterday by escorted heavy bombers in very great strength while 13 airfields from north of HANNOVER southward to INGOLSTADT were bombed and strafed by fighter-bombers. One hundred sixty-eight enemy aircraft were destroyed on the ground and many others were damaged in these attacks.

On April 8 and 9, Allied forces captured over 50,000 prisoners. Nothing could be more graphic than the looks on the faces in these two photographs: the dejection shown by these young boys that the Nazi dream had come crashing down, compared with the smiles from the officers who appear to be relieved that it is all over.

Rail yards at JENA, SAALFELD, BAMBERG, STUTTGART and near LEIPZIG and road and rail transport north of NORDHAUSEN and in the NUREMBERG area were attacked by medium, light and fighter-bombers.

Other medium and light bombers attacked an oil refinery at DEDENHAUSEN, oil storage depots at BAD BERKA and WEISSENHORN, an armored vehicle depot southwest of LEIPZIG, and an ordnance depot at AMBERG while supply and ammunition dumps near ERFURT and at KLEINENGSTINGEN were hit by medium and fighter-bombers.

Gun positions in the ZUTPHEN sector were silenced by medium bombers. Enemy transport and communications in Holland and northwestern Germany were attacked by fighter-bombers.

U-Boat shelters and oil storage depots at HAMBURG were bombed by escorted heavy bombers. Twenty-two thousand-pound and 12,000-pound bombs were dropped.

During the day's operations 21 enemy aircraft were shot down. According to reports so far received, 11 of our bombers and ten fighters are missing.

Last night heavy bombers were over Germany in very great strength with the shipbuilding yards at KIEL as their main objective. Targets in BERLIN, and enemy movement over a wide area of Germany, were attacked by light bombers.

COMMUNIQUE No. 368   April 11

Allied forces occupied DEVENTER against strong opposition. Farther east, RIJSSEN and NIJVERDAL have been captured.

East of the Ems river we captured SOGEL, and HASELUNNE.

Troop concentrations, gun positions and strong points at ARNHEM and in the DEVENTER area and rail transport and other communications targets in northern Germany from CLOPPENBURG eastward to BREMEN were attacked by medium and fighter-bombers and rocket-firing fighters.

More crossings of the Weser have been made at HOYA and NIENBURG and we advanced several miles east.

North and east of NEUSTADT we gained ten miles.

We cleared HANNOVER, cut the HANNOVER—BRUNSWICK autobahn midway between the two cities, and are within five miles of BRUNSWICK. Our armor captured OTHFRESEN about seven and one-half miles north of GOSLAR which was entered by our infantry. Other elements were fighting near MUNCHEHOF to the southwest.

Our forces captured EINBECK. Armored units reached a point 14 miles northeast of NORTHEIM and fought a tank battle at GIEBOLDEHAUSEN to the south.

Armored task forces are in the area eight miles east of DUDERSTADT and have entered NORDHAUSEN to the east, and CLINGEN, north of ERFURT.

Infantry following the armor cleared towns northwest of GOTTINGEN, captured DUDERSTADT and DEILIGENSTADT and reached DINGELSTADT, east and southeast of the city.

Other infantry advanced east of BAD TENNSTEDT, southwest of CLINGEN, and our units are in the vicinity of DACHWIG farther south.

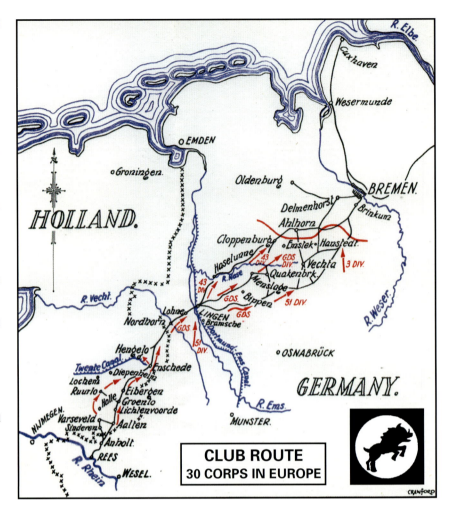

CLUB ROUTE
30 CORPS IN EUROPE

On April 10, Montgomery decided that he would push on to the Elbe river without pause. He instructed Lieutenant-General Dempsey, the commander of Second Army, to have his two leading corps — XII and VIII — outflank Bremen, and leave it to be dealt with by the army's third formation — XXX Corps. At that time, XXX Corps, led by Lieutenant-General Sir Brian Horrocks, was advancing with three divisions abreast: the 51st (Highland) Division on the left, the Guards Armoured Division in the centre, and the 43rd (Wessex) Division on the right. Following Montgomery's new orders, there was a reshuffling of units within Second Army. To provide XXX Corps with four infantry divisions for the capture of Bremen, Dempsey ordered the 3rd and 52nd (Lowland) Divisions to be transferred to it, and the Guards Armoured Division to move from XXX Crops to XII Corps and join the race to Hamburg. The 3rd Division came under command of XXX Corps on April 11 and the 52nd Division followed on the 19th. Although Nienburg on the River Weser had been entered by XII Corps on April 9, it was here at the end of the war that a symbol of the XXX Corps' achievements was unveiled. According to the story related to your editor by a member of the Intelligence Corps, someone spotted a bronze statue of a boar in a front garden of the town and, as the insignia of XXX Corps was a rampant boar, it was thought that the statue of a boar at rest would be perfect to illustrate the long journey from the beaches in Normandy. So it was quietly purloined and the XXX Corps memorial was unveiled by General Horrocks in December 1945 in Nienburg *(left)* which lay in the centre of British-controlled Germany. However, following the withdrawal from northern Germany, the memorial was dismantled and re-erected on the parade ground at Sandhurst *(right)* in 1958.

As early as April 8, the Americans had become aware of the existence of another Nazi death camp when a broadcast was picked up saying 'SOS Buchenwald'. This had been transmitted by one of the inmates on a home-made radio set, but it was not until three days later that Combat Team 9 of the 9th Armored Infantry Battalion of the 6th Armored Division of the Third Army arrived at the main gate on their drive to Weimar, some ten miles away. They found that the inmates had already taken over the camp and were holding the guards prisoner. At 5.30 p.m. on the afternoon of April 11 two Psychological Warfare Division officers, Lieutenants Edward Tenenbaum and Egon Fleck, arrived to meet the 'Inmate Committee' made up of all the nationalities incarcerated at Buchenwald. It was reported that around 21,000 prisoners had been rescued — 3,000 French, 2,000 Poles, 2,000 Czechs, 5,000 Russians, 600 Yugoslavs, 200 Italians, 200 Spaniards, 2,200 Germans and 6,000 others.

We entered GOTTSTEDT and are near SCHMIRA in the ERFURT area. To the south we entered PLAUE and are in the vicinity of RODA, and reached UNTERNEUBRUNN.

Our armor entered BAD RODACH, northwest of COBURG, while other units reached WOHLSBACH northeast of the city.

Our armor advanced southeast of MEININGEN, reaching points within six miles of COBURG and 15 miles of BAMBERG.

We have closed around SCHWEINFURT from three sides against heavy artillery fire.

Buchenwald — literally 'Beech Forest' — never existed as a village, the innocuous-sounding name being coined for the concentration camp built north of Weimar, in 1937. Units of the US Army's 4th and 6th Armored Divisions reached the camp on April 11, 1945 but, based on arrangements worked out at Allied meetings at Malta (January 1945) and Yalta (February 1945), the Americans turned over the area to the Soviets when the zoning of Germany came into effect on July 1. The Soviets then used it as an internment camp until 1950, shortly after the German Democratic Republic was established. Between 1954, when the GDR earmarked it for memorialisation, and 1958 when Otto Grotewohl, the Prime Minister, dedicated it as the first anti-Nazi memorial on German soil, a large monument, incorporating three mass graves, was erected on the south flank of Ettersberg Hill. During the 40 years under GDR control, literature available at the camp emphasised the 'anti-fascist' nature of Buchenwald as a memorial site; now, like all historical sites in the former GDR, Buchenwald has been subjected to a 'revision of the basic concept' or, as the Germans put it so well: 'Über-arbeitung der Gesamtkonzeption'. (See also *After the Battle* No. 93.)

Armor driving toward SCHWEINFURT from the south cleared 15 miles of the east bank of the Main river.

Strong enemy pressure was exerted against our CRAILSHEIM salient.

House-to-house fighting continues in HEILBRONN, and to the northwest we forced the enemy back more than three miles from the line of the Jagst to the Kocher river. We established a bridgehead over the Kocher.

Gains up to five miles were made southeast of KARLSRUHE. We have a bridgehead some five miles deep across the Enz river east of PFORZHEIM.

Fortified positions and troop concentrations in and near SCHWEINFURT, and at ROTHENBURG and BEUERBACH, north of CRAILSHEIM, were targets for medium and fighter-bombers.

In the Ruhr pocket we advanced southward to the Ruhr river just east of ESSEN, and captured several small towns on the western edge of DORTMUND. Two fairly strong counter-attacks northwest and west of DORTMUND were contained. To the northeast and east, our armor took HOINGEN, and our infantry reached a point one and one-half miles west of MESCHEDE. A small counter-attack was repulsed at BONACKER. We entered COBBENRODE, and to the southwest gained six miles and cleared OLPE. SIEGBURG, southeast of COLOGNE, has been cleared and we advanced five miles northeast of the town.

Allied forces in the west captured 54,395 prisoners 8 and 9 April.

Enemy airfields at ZERBST, BRIEST, NEURUPPIN, ORANIENBURG, PARCHIM and LARZ, and a supply depot at ORANIENBURG were attacked by escorted heavy bombers in very great strength. The escorting fighters destroyed 284 enemy aircraft on the ground. Other escorted heavy bombers attacked rail yards at LEIPZIG.

Rail yards at TRIPTIS, east of NEUSTADT; EGER, NUREMBERG, ANSBACH, and in the triangular area of COBURG, BAYREUTH, and HOF; rail and road traffic in the WEIMAR and LEIPZIG areas were attacked by medium, light and fighter-bombers.

An oil storage depot at STASSFURT-LEOPOLDSHALL; a motor transport repair depot at RUDOLSTADT; and a rail viaduct and a rail bridge at EGER were hit by other medium and light bombers.

Fortified positions and troop concentrations in the area of NORDHAUSEN, and objectives at BRUNSWICK were attacked by medium and fighter-bombers.

Airfields near BRUNSWICK, WEIMAR, HOF, EGER, NUREMBERG, ILLESHEIM, and in the MUNICH area were struck at by other fighter-bombers.

During the day's operations 57 enemy aircraft were shot down, 339 were destroyed on the ground and many others were damaged. According to reports so far received 25 of our heavy bombers and 18 fighters are missing.

The camp mortuary on the left and crematorium as they appear today, photographed for us by Claus Bach of the Sammlung Gedenkstätte Buchenwald.

The following day, Eisenhower, together with Generals Bradley and Patton, visited Ohrdruf: 'My first horror camp was near the town of Gotha. I have never felt able to describe my emotional reactions when I first came face to face with indisputable evidence of Nazi brutality and ruthless disregard of every shred of decency. I am certain that I have never at any other time experienced an equal sense of shock. I visited every nook and cranny of the camp because I felt it my duty to be in a position from then on to testify at first hand about these things in case there ever grew up at home the belief or assumption that "the stories of Nazi brutality were just propaganda". Some members of the visiting party were unable to go through the ordeal. I not only did so but as soon as I returned to Patton's headquarters that evening I sent communications to both Washington and London, urging the two governments to send instantly to Germany a random group of newspaper editors and representative groups from the national legislatures. I felt that the evidence should be immediately placed before the American and British publics in a fashion that would leave no room for cynical doubt.'

COMMUNIQUE No. 369   April 12

Allied forces have launched an attack westwards across the IJssel river.

We pushed beyond FURSTENAU, crossed the Hase canal and captured BADBERGEN, ANKUM and BERSENBRUCK. North of OSNABRUCK we occupied BRAMSCHE and VORDEN.

Southwest of BREMEN our forces are in WILDESHAUSEN and HARPSTEDT but farther east we are meeting strong enemy opposition.

Our armored elements, advancing more than 50 miles eastward, have reached the Elbe river at MAGDEBURG after enveloping WOLFENBUTTEL, just south of BRUNSWICK, and passing through EILENSTEDT and WULFERSTEDT, southwest of OSCHERSLEBEN.

Other armored units have reached MEINE, north of BRUNSWICK, while infantry is heavily engaged in and around the city against stubborn enemy delaying action.

Our infantry made rapid progress to the vicinity of HALBERSTADT.

Armored and infantry units reached HERZBERG and OSTERHAGEN, northwest of DUDERSTADT. Armored elements cleared NORDHAUSEN, and east of MUHLHAUSEN reached BILZINGSLEBEN, eight miles northeast of CLINGEN, and are one mile from KOLLEDA to the southwest after a 22-mile advance.

Southwest of COBURG we made limited advances against scattered resistance.

SCHWEINFURT was entered after being practically surrounded and heavy house-to-house fighting is in progress. Armored units pushed along the Main river to the east and also made gains to the south.

To the southeast we advanced four miles along the highway between OCHSENFURT and ANSBACH, occupying UFFENHEIM and RUDOLZHOFEN.

Our armor withdrew from a part of the CRAILSHEIM wedge after more than 1,500 prisoners and important enemy materiel were taken.

Our bridgehead over the Kocher in the vicinity of NIEDERNHALL was extended to a depth of three miles.

Progress was made in HEILBRONN and north of the city two bridgeheads over the Neckar river have been joined.

We made advances up to three miles southeast of KARLSRUHE and have reached the BLACK FOREST. Our bridgehead across the Enz river east of PFORZHEIM has been expanded.

Allied forces in the west captured 24,846 prisoners 10 April.

In the Ruhr pocket our infantry cleared ESSEN, captured GELSENKIRCHEN and entered BOCHUM. We took FRONDENBERG, south of UNNA. West of MESCHEDE we captured FREIENOHL. Our infantry advancing in the area north of SIEGEN took ATTENDORN, while armored elements made limited gains north of SIEGBURG.

Enemy armor and artillery around DORTMUND and in the triangle formed by REMSCHEID, GUMMERSBACH and MESCHEDE were attacked by fighter-bombers.

In Holland fighter-bombers attacked bomb factory buildings at HEVEADORP, west of ARNHEM; enemy transport withdrawing northward in the ZWOLLE area; communications between UTRECHT, AMERSFOORT and ZWOLLE, and a number of gun positions.

In Germany an oil storage depot, an ordnance depot and an airfield at REGENSBURG; an airfield and rail yard at INGOLSTADT; an explosives plant at KRAIBURG, east of MUNICH; an ordnance depot at LANDSHUT; an oil storage depot at FREIHAIM, west of

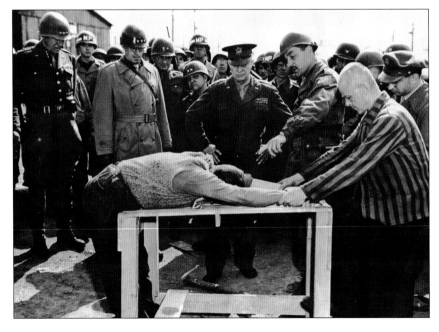

Patton: 'Our guide then took us to the whipping table, which was about the height of the average man's crotch. The feet were placed in stocks on the ground and the man was pulled over the table, which was slightly hollowed, and held by two guards, while he was beaten across the back and loins. The stick which they said had been used, and which had some blood on it, was bigger than the handle of a pick. Our guide claimed that he himself had received twenty-five blows with this tool. It later developed that he was not a prisoner at all, but one of the executioners. General Eisenhower must have suspected it, because he asked the man very pointedly how he could be so fat. He was found dead next morning, killed by some of the inmates. Just beyond the whipping table there was a pile of forty bodies, more or less naked. All of these had been shot in the back of the head at short range, and the blood was still cooling on the ground. In the shed nearby was a pile of forty completely naked bodies in the last stages of emaciation. These bodies were lightly sprinkled with lime — not, apparently for the purpose of destroying them, but to reduce the smell.'

MUNICH, and rail yards at TREUCHTLINGEN, NEUMARKT, DONAUWORTH and AMBERG were attacked by escorted heavy bombers in very great strength.

Enemy troop transports and oil and ammunition supplies in the BREMEN area were attacked by fighters and fighter-bombers. Medium and fighter-bombers struck at rail and road targets in the areas of EMDEN, BREMEN, HAMBURG and HANNOVER. Rail yards at ROTENBURG and SOLTAU were hit and an oil train was blown up at WESTEN.

Fortified buildings in BRUNSWICK, heavy artillery and road transport in the area formed by HALLE, JENA, HOF and CHEMNITZ, and airfields in the BRUNSWICK, HALLE, ERFURT and JENA areas and at EGER in Czechoslovakia were attacked by fighter-bombers. Many enemy aircraft were destroyed or damaged in the attacks on the airfields.

Rail yards at KOTHEN and ZWICKAU and a motor vehicle plant at BAMBERG were attacked by medium and light bombers in strength. Fighter-bombers bombed rail yards at NUREMBERG and BAYREUTH.

Fuel and ammunition dumps at GEISLINGEN and in the ULM area were attacked by medium bombers.

Targets in BERLIN were attacked last night by light bombers.

Horrified at what he had seen, the Supreme Commander immediately requested that reporters from the Allied press be sent to record and publicise the ghastly scenes . . . but more was yet to come. Three days after Eisenhower had visited Ohrdruf, the British forces entered Belsen, 40 miles north of Hannover. If anything could be more shocking, the conditions at this camp were even more horrendous with thousands of unburied dead. The photographs and cine film taken as the camp was cleared, the bodies being buried in 11 huge pits, defy description . . . they speak for themselves. Sapper Frank Chapman is filmed bulldozing bodies into a mass grave.

On April 24 all the SS men and women who had been put to work to move the rotting corpses, together with local civil officials, were lined up beside Grave No. 3 to listen to a speech by a British officer from a loudspeaker van: 'You who are the fathers of German youth, see in front of your eyes some of the sons and daughters who carry a small part of the responsibility for these crimes. Only a small part and yet more difficult to carry than the human soul possibly can. But who carries the real responsibility? You, who allowed your Führer to carry out this flagrant madness; you, who could not get enough of these degenerate triumphs; you, who heard about these camps.'

Ohrdruf, Buchenwald and Belsen were not the first camps to be liberated as the Red Army had captured Maidanek in Poland as far back as July 1944 and Auschwitz on January 27, 1945. However the Germans had evacuated those camps — as they would do with numerous others before the approaching armies — systematically trying to remove or destroy as much as possible of the physical evidence of mass genocide. At Auschwitz, for example, the Russians found only 5,000 survivors and the ruins of the gas chambers. (See *After the Battle* No. 157.) The reports on these camps in the East did not have the impact in the West compared with those overrun in April 1945, and of those Bergen-Belsen was undoubtedly the worst. After the camp had been totally cleared, all the buildings were destroyed by fire as the only sure way of getting rid of the typhus germs. On May 21, a special parade was held to set fire to the last hut, Colonel Johnston of No. 32 Casualty Clearing Station firing a flare-pistol at a picture of Hitler. (For more, see *After the Battle* No. 89.)

COMMUNIQUE No. 370 April 13

The Allied attack across the IJssel river between DEVENTER and ZUTPHEN is progressing well against stiffening resistance. Between the IJssel and the Ems rivers we advanced up to 20 miles and occupied SPIER, EXLOO and WEERDINGE.

In the area east of HASELUNNE where the enemy still is offering stubborn opposition from rear guards, we captured WACHTUM and LONINGEN. Between FURSTENAU and the Dummersee we made good progress to the north and occupied LOHNE and HOLDORF.

RETHEM, on the left bank of the Aller river, has been captured after heavy fighting and we established two bridgeheads across the river. We repulsed a tank-supported counter-attack which was launched against one of the bridgeheads.

CELLE, northeast of HANNOVER, has been occupied.

We have reached the vicinity of CLAUSTHAL-ZELLERFELD, northeast of NORTHEIM. Farther southeast our armor and infantry are clearing the Harz mountains. An armored column in a 20-mile advance east of NORDHAUSEN reached a point two and a half miles beyond SANGERHAUSEN. Another column is at NIEDERROBLINGEN to the south.

Our armor crossed the Saale river south of NAUMBURG. Infantry reached the river in the vicinity of CAMBURG and at points farther south. Other elements are at the outskirts of APOLDA, while another crossing of the Salle river was made by our armor south of JENA.

Fighting continues in ERFURT and WEIMAR has been cleared. Our forces reached DIENSTEDT, east of ARNSTADT, and SCHWARZBURG, seven and a half miles west of SAALFELD.

Our armor captured COBURG, and reached GESTUNGSHAUSEN, southeast of the city, while infantry advanced in the area to the northeast.

South of COBURG our armor and infantry made gains of up to 15 miles. LICHTENFELS, southeast of COBURG was reached. Other elements reached a point within five miles of BAMBERG.

Following the capture of SCHWEINFURT, our infantry advanced eastward on both sides of the upper Main river, taking many towns in the HASSFURT area.

East of OCHSENFURT on the WURZBURG-NUREMBERG highway, our armor drove as far as MARKT BIBART. To the southwest our units are within five miles of ROTHENBURG on the Tauber river.

East of HEILBRONN, our bridgehead over the Kocher river is eight miles deep. The city of HEILBRONN has been cleared of all but isolated pockets of resistance.

Near the Rhine we took RASTATT and the resort town BADEN BADEN. Approximately 1,000 prisoners were taken at RASTATT.

Allied forces in the west captured 40,159 prisoners 11 April.

In the Ruhr pocket our forces continue to make steady progress. In the northeast corner we reached a point one mile west of ARNSBERG, and our armor is on the southern end of the Sorpetalsperre lake. Farther south we reached the area six miles north of ATTENDORN. Other forces gained up to 12 miles in the area northwest of SIEGEN and we reached MUCH, northeast of SIEGBURG. Armor advancing north along the Rhine on the western side of the pocket has reached a point near BURSCHEID, northeast of COLOGNE.

Road traffic in the Ruhr pocket was attacked by fighter-bombers.

Road traffic in the triangular area formed by LEIPZIG, PLAUEN, DRESDEN; rail transport east of LEIPZIG and other rail targets in the areas of JENA, PLAUEN and CHEMNITZ were heavily attacked by fighter-bombers.

Enemy airfields near DESSAU, SCHAFSTADT, LEIPZIG, WEIMAR, ORLAMUNDE, JENA, EGER and BAYREUTH, were targets for other fighter-bombers.

Fortified positions near ARNHEM, in Holland; a rail bridge at HOF; the communications center of LAUPHEIM, southwest of ULM; and an ordnance depot at KEMPTEN, were attacked by medium and light bombers.

Road and rail transport near UTRECHT, ZWOLLE, EMDEN, BREMEN and UELZEN and an airfield at BROCKZETEL, east of AURICH, were hit by fighter-bombers and rocket-firing fighters.

Targets in BERLIN were attacked last night by light bombers.

And fanatical SS commanders were still trying to enforce a 'no surrender' order on soldiers who realised that by now the game was up. At Schweinfurt, some 90 miles east of Mainz, troops of the Seventh Army found 11 Germans hanged by the SS Mayor of the city. He was put under guard but committed suicide shortly afterwards by jumping from a window. Here, Lieutenant Colonel Downard and Private Rosser cut down one of those executed for attempting to surrender. Although the unit formation patch has been censored — in this case by scratching out the negative — the men would have belonged to either the 12th Armored or 42nd Infantry. The 42nd Division had been delayed in the battle to capture Würzburg, 22 miles to the southwest, so the 12th Armored Division's Combat Command A was despatched instead to the frequently-bombed centre of the German ball-bearing industry. However, hardly had the armor begun to advance on April 5 when the tanks ran into a defensive position erected across the main highway to Schweinfurt by a regiment formed from students and staff of an infantry school. These troops had hurriedly gone into position only the night before. The German infantry was still holding CCA's tanks at bay when on April 7 men of the 42nd Division arrived to help. As the Germans at last fell back, the 42nd Division commander sent one regiment to seize high ground north of Schweinfurt, cutting the German escape routes in that direction, while CCA crossed the Main river and on April 10 cut a remaining major road to the south-east of the city. Medium bombers of the 9th Bombardment Division at the same time were giving the city a final working-over. Then on April 11, infantry cleared the bulk of resistance from the rubble that Schweinfurt had become.

In Holland, the 49th (West Riding) Division were finally coming to grips with the long-awaited recapture of Arnhem from which British and Polish forces had been evacuated in September. Now, on April 12, after fighter bombers and artillery had softened up the defences, the division assaulted across the IJssel river in Buffaloes and storm boats at Westervoort. There was little oppostion and rafts and a bridge enabled Canadian tanks to cross to support the infantry.

COMMUNIQUE No. 371 April 14

Allied forces made a second crossing of the IJssel river and are fighting in ARNHEM. We expanded our bridgehead south of DEVENTER and captured TEUGE. Between the IJssel and the Ems rivers we captured DALFSEN and ASSEN.

In the area north of OSNABRUCK we reached FRIESOYTHE and CLOPPENBURG and occupied VECHTA.

In the RETHEM area we expanded our bridgeheads over the Aller river.

Northeast of HANNOVER we made another crossing of the Aller at CELLE, from which our forces advanced ten miles and captured ESCHEDE and ELDINGEN.

Other units pushing from the south have reached the vicinity of CELLE.

BRUNSWICK has been cleared, and our infantry gained 15 miles to reach MEINE to the north. Infantry units pushed east of BRUNSWICK and reached the vicinity of CALVORDE. Other elements reached HASSELBURG.

Eisenhower: 'Arnhem was captured April 15. The fall of Arnhem was the signal for the enemy in that sector to withdraw into the Holland fortress behind flooded areas which posed a serious obstacle to an advance into western Holland. Montgomery believed, and I agreed, that an immediate campaign into Holland would result in great additional suffering for that unhappy country whose people were already badly suffering from lack of food. Much of the country had been laid waste by deliberate flooding of the ground, by bombing, and by the erection of German defences. We decided to postpone operations into Holland and to do what we could to alleviate suffering and starvation among the Dutch people.'

Our armor advanced more than 50 airline miles to the Elbe river at a point southeast of STENDAL. Infantry units reached the Elbe near BARBY. We now control ten miles of the west bank of the river in the vicinity of MAGDEBURG. We crossed the Elbe and are meeting enemy small-arms and artillery fire. The crossing was made in assault boats.

On the edges of the HARZ FOREST our armor has cleared OSTERODE, HERSBERG and SANGERHAUSEN and pushed five miles northeast of SANGERHAUSEN.

Infantry following the armor has reached the vicinity of SCHWENDA and WOLFSBERG in the forest, and is fighting against fanatical resistance.

Our armor advancing 25 miles from WEISSENFELS reached a point seven miles from LEIPZIG. Infantry is mopping up in WEISSENFELS. Armored units entered PEGAU, 11 miles south of LEIPZIG. ZEITZ, southeast of WEISSENFELS, has been entered.

ERFURT has been cleared and our forces are fighting in JENA. Our armor reached a point 11 miles east of JENA. South of JENA we are along the Saale river on a 40-mile front. We have entered RUDOLSTADT and reached a point three miles southeast of SAALFELD. We entered GRAFENTHAL. Northeast of COBURG we cleared STEINACH and SONNEBERG. East of COBURG our armor has cleared KRONACH, and other elements are four miles south of the town.

Our infantry and armor closed about BAMBERG after advances of more than 15 miles. Fighting is in progress in the vicinity of HALLSTADT, two miles north of BAMBERG.

To the west our troops south of the Main river have cleared most of the area between SCHWEINFURT and BAMBERG. In clearing SCHWEINFURT, the number of prisoners taken there was increased to approximately 2,500.

Northeast of HEILBRONN our bridgehead across the Kocher river was expanded and we captured many more towns. North and south of HEILBRONN enemy resistance weakened. The east bank of the Neckar river was cleared to HORKHEIM, three miles south of HEILBRONN.

Some 2,000 prisoners were taken in the capture of RASTATT and BADEN BADEN. Allied forces in the west captured 50,177 prisoners 12 April.

Thirty miles north-east of Arnhem the Fort Garry Horse received a rapturous welcome in Rijssen. Photo taken on April 9 and released by SHAEF on April 12.

This is Grotestraat in the centre of Rijssen, 70 years later.

Left: **Ten miles to the east, the first British patrol from the 7th Hampshires, 43rd Wessex Division, was pictured marching into Hengelo. They entered the town from the north-east along Oldenzaalsestraat.** *Right:* **A few of the original houses remain.**

However, this picture which was taken the following day, April 13 — even though heavily censored — was not passed for publication until the war had ended. Taken when the 21st Army Group Tactical Headquarters was located at Ostenwalde, it shows a typical briefing by Montgomery. 'My team of liaison officers which I organised to keep me in touch with events on the battlefront, were young officers of character, initiative and courage; they had seen much fighting and were able to report accurately on battle situations. I selected each one personally, and my standard was high. It was dangerous work and some were wounded, and some killed. Winston Churchill knew them intimately and one of his greatest delights was to sit in my map caravan after dinner at night and hear these young officers tell me the story of what was happening on the battle front. In April 1945, one was killed (John Poston) and another wounded (Peter Earle); both had been engaged on the same task, given them by me. The Prime Minister heard about it and he sent me a message which ended with the following words: "I share your grief. Will you kindly convey to their gallant comrades the sympathy which I feel for them and you."'

In the northwest edge of the Ruhr pocket, our infantry is meeting stiff resistance north of the Ruhr river. Farther east we reached the southeastern outskirts of DORTMUND. On the eastern side, infantry reached NEUENRADE and LUDENSCHEID. Farther southwest we captured WIPPERFURTH. On the western edge tanks gained five miles east of COLOGNE. Enemy armor and troops in the pocket were attacked by fighter-bombers.

Rail yards at NEUMUNSTER, north of HAMBURG, were attacked yesterday by escorted heavy bombers. The escorting fighters strafed enemy airfields at NEUMUNSTER and destroyed enemy aircraft on the ground.

Enemy troops, transport and armored vehicles in the area formed by EMDEN, CUXHAVEN, WISMAR and SALZWEDEL were bombed and strafed by fighters and fighter-bombers.

Coastal guns at DEN HELDER; troops, strong points and gun positions in the APELDOORN area; rail yards at ZEITZ, HAINICHEN, NEUSTADTEL, WILDSTEIN and in the GERA area; an oil dump at ZERBST and airfields at WITTENBERG and BAYREUTH were attacked by fighter-bombers. In the attacks on the airfields enemy aircraft were destroyed and damaged on the ground.

Last night heavy bombers were out in great strength with KIEL as the main objective.

General Bradley had visited the Field-Marshal on April 10 to co-ordinate plans for the final drive to the Elbe, Generals Dempsey and Simpson also being present. To prevent Bradley's armies from colliding with the Soviets along this 200-mile front, the Supreme Commander had issued a 'stop line'. This basically followed the Elbe and Mulde rivers. Eisenhower explained that 'while the Central Group of Armies had been pushing eastward to divide Germany, the Northern and Southern Groups had each in their respective sectors been carrying out the operations assigned to them during this period. Under 21st Army Group, Second Army was, by my instructions, to advance towards Bremen and Hamburg, thereafter thrusting to the Elbe (gaining a bridgehead if the opportunity offered) and thereby protecting the northern flank of the Ninth Army in the 12th Army Group. Meanwhile the Canadian Army was to open up a supply route to the north through Arnhem and then to operate to clear Northeast Holland, the coastal belt eastward to the Elbe, and West Holland, in that order of priority. The operations were, in many respects, similar to those carried out in France by the same Army Group in the preceding summer, when the Second Army drove across the rear to the Pas-de-Calais while the Canadian Army mopped up the enemy along the coast.' *Left:* These Canadian troops of the Lincoln and Welland Regiment (4th Canadian Armoured Division) were pictured taking a breather on Wehmer Strasse in Werlte . . . just 40 miles to go to Bremen.

Ahead of the Ninth Army lay the cities of Hannover, Brunswick (Braunschweig) and Magdeburg. Hannover lay on the River Leine which was crossed by the 84th Infantry Division on the 8th, capturing in the process a German soldier who was carrying a map of the city's defences. The map revealed that these were concentrated in the south and south-west facing the direction from which an Allied attack was expected, so instead the division decided to attack through the back door! Moving in from the north and north-west on April 10, by mid-afternoon Hannover had been secured.

COMMUNIQUE No. 372 April 15

Allied forces are clearing the last pockets of enemy resistance in ARNHEM. Farther north, we reached the outskirts of APELDOORN.

Good advances were made between the IJssel and Ems rivers and we reached the outskirts of ZWOLLE, GRONINGEN and WINSCHOTEN.

To the east, FRIESOYTHE and CLOPPENBURG have been cleared of the enemy. Several counter-attacks launched against our bridgehead over the Aller river near RETHEM were repulsed.

We advanced 30 miles beyond CELLE and are fighting in UELZEN.

Our armor reached the Elbe river near WERBEN, north of MAGDEBURG. Infantry units following the armor reached WITTINGEN and GLADDENSTEDT, 30 miles north of BRUNSWICK, and the vicinity of BISMARK, northwest of STENDAL.

We also have reached the Elbe near TANGERMUNDE and are fighting in the town. North of MAGDEBURG we have taken WOLMIRSTEDT and BARLEBEN and we are on the river northeast of BARLEBEN.

We have made two crossings of the Elbe. Our forces on the east bank repulsed several counter-attacks and we are receiving artillery fire.

We reached ALTENAU and BREITENSTEIN in the HARZ FOREST. Our armor, advancing up to 30 miles, is at a point three miles southwest of DESSAU. Infantry units following the armor reached areas three miles north and four miles south of HALLE.

We have reached the Pleisse river at BERGISDORF, 15 miles south of LEIPZIG.

Looking back down Georgstrasse from Georgplatz with the building of the Landeszentralbank Hannover remaining on the left as a link with the past.

ZEITZ has been cleared and our armor is 16 miles east of the town. Southeast of ZEITZ we are meeting heavy artillery, small-arms and bazooka fire.

Armored elements crossed the Mulde river and reached the vicinity of MEINSDORF and HOHENSTEIN, west of CHEMNITZ.

We cleared the enemy from JENA and are fighting in GERA. Our infantry is mopping up in the area south of JENA. RUDOLSTADT has been cleared with the exception of a fortified castle, and we are in the area 16 miles east of SAALFELD.

Our armor is fighting in BAYREUTH and infantry is ten miles north of the city.

BAMBERG has been completely cleared of the enemy. Some 1,850 prisoners were captured there. Our armor advanced 15 miles northeast and east of the city.

To the southwest we are within six miles of ROTHENBERG.

In the HEILBRONN area our units advanced eight miles east of the city and six miles southward toward STUTTGART.

Near the Rhine we gained more than ten miles southwest of BADEN BADEN. STEINBACH and BUHL were captured.

Allied forces in the west captured 57,187 prisoners 13 April.

In the Ruhr pocket we have cleared DORTMUND and the enemy controls only

Next stop Brunswick. Although the city was first entered on the 11th, it took the 30th Division another two more days to clear it after a stiff fight as the western approaches were protected by 88mm flak guns. Over 60 of the weapons, now being used as ground artillery, were sited around the Hermann Göring Steelworks south-west of the city. Pictured here are troops of the 117th Infantry Regiment on their way to Brunswick.

five square miles north of the Ruhr river. HAGEN has been entered by our forces, and we captured EISBORN and ASBECK. LUDENSCHEID has been cleared and we took 3,600 prisoners from the town.

Enemy gun positions, strong points and other installations in the Gironde area of France, near ROYAN, and an ammunition storage area north of ULM in Germany, were attacked by medium bombers.

Rail and road traffic in the large triangular area formed by DESSAU, DRESDEN and NUREMBERG; rail yards at SCHWABACH, SCHORNDORF, HERBRECHTINGEN, northeast of ULM, and at NORDLINGEN; rail communications near PILSEN, ROKYCANY, BEROUN and PRAGUE; objectives at LEITZKAU, southeast of MAGDEBURG; airfields at BRANDIS, east of LEIPZIG; near BAYREUTH and NORDLINGEN; and fortified positions and strong points at BARSSEL, HARKEBRUGGE, and KAMPE, west of OLDENBURG; STUTTGART and INGOLSTADT were attacked by fighter-bombers.

The communications center of POTSDAM was heavily attacked last night by heavy bombers. Objectives in BERLIN also were bombed.

Infantry of the 117th and Shermans of the 745th Tank Battalion entering the city along Madamenweg on April 15.

Now the armour belonging to the Ninth Army rolls through the burning village of Born and on towards the Elbe at Magdeburg, which, as the sign says, is still some 23 miles further away. On April 12 the river was reached by the 83rd Division, 15 miles to the south of Magdeburg at Barby, and by the 84th Division 35 miles north of the city at Tangermünde. Now the Allies were just 60 miles west of Berlin. Then, just after nightfall on the 12th, news arrived that the 2nd Armored Division had stolen a march and slipped two battalions of armoured infantry across the river at Westerhausen, just south of Magdeburg.

COMMUNIQUE No. 373 April 16

Allied forces completely cleared ARNHEM and advanced beyond the town to DEELEN. Fighting continues in APELDOORN. Farther north we occupied ZWOLLE, MEPPEL and HEERENVEEN.

Reconnaissance elements have reached the sea north of TERNAARD. We captured the southern half of GRONINGEN and occupied WINSCHOTEN.

In our bridgehead over the Aller river north of RETHEM we pushed four miles against determined enemy resistance. To the southeast we occupied MINSEN on the right bank of the river and advanced north to BERGEN.

Heavy fighting continues in UELZEN.

Our armored units now hold a 12-mile stretch of the west bank of the Elbe river

At Magdeburg, the 30th Infantry Division faced the strongest resistance since they had crossed the Rhine. The 2nd Armored, which had been ousted from the city having entered it, joined with the 30th to recapture it. This picture was released on April 20.

But now the Russians stepped in. Having got wind of Montgomery's proposal — subsequently turned down by Eisenhower — to aim at capturing Berlin, Stalin was determined not to let the Allies claim the glory of being the first in the German capital. On April 1, Stalin had ordered that Operation 'Berlin' should begin on the 16th with the aim of reaching the Elbe by May Day. This gave the two Fronts — the First Byelorussian commanded by Marshal Georgi Zhukov and the First Ukranian under Marshal Ivan Koniev — barely two weeks to prepare. Marshal Zhukov's forces were then 40 miles east of Berlin on the Oder, some units having managed to cross the partially frozen river to establish a bridgehead on the western bank (see page 339). Facing them were three hotch-potch German armies: the 3. Panzerarmee, 9. Armee and 4. Panzerarmee. Some two-and-a-half million Soviet troops would face about a million defenders. At the beginning of the assault on Berlin, a special Victory Flag was prepared by the Third Shock Army, and a hand-picked squad was charged with the honour of raising the banner above the Reichstag — the building which, to the Soviets, epitomised Imperial Germany — by May Day.

In the ideology of the National Socialist Party, Bayreuth was the Hauptstadt der Kultur — the Cultural Capital of the Third Reich. 'For me', said Hitler, 'Wagner is someone godly and his music is my religion. I go to concerts as others go to church.' Although Richard Wagner was born in Leipzig, it was the annual Bayreuth Festival with its Festspielhaus built specially for performances of his operas that established the city in Nazi 'Kultur'. The Third Army captured Bayreuth on April 15, these tanks belonging to the 11th Armored Division are preceeding along Bahnhofstrasse.

near SEEHAUSEN. We cleared STENDAL and advanced eight miles beyond. Our forces mopping up in the rear areas reached WITTINGEN and SALZWEDEL and cleared BISMARK.

Our armor withdrew from the northern bridgehead across the Elbe river because of heavy enemy pressure, but farther south infantry continues to expand its bridgehead in the vicinity of BARBY.

Armored elements reached the Mulde river two miles southeast of DESSAU and other units are on the main DESSAU—LEIPZIG railroad, eight miles south of DESSAU. We are fighting in KOTHEN.

Northeast of NORDHAUSEN we entered GUNTERSBERGE and SIPTENFELDE.

House-to-house fighting continues in HALLE and we captured LEUNA.

Our armor established a six-mile front on the Mulde river, 20 miles north of CHEMNITZ.

South of LEIPZIG our armored units are fighting in HAGENEST and ALTENBERG, and infantry entered ZIEGELHEIM and GLAUCHAU.

We reached the vicinity of WEISSBACH, entered PILLINGSDORF and ROSENDORF, northeast of NEUSTADT, and we are in BAHREN to the southwest. Our forces cleared BAD LOBENSTEIN, entered HIRSCHBERG, and captured SCHLEGEL, all northwest of HOF. Other units are in the area ten to 13 miles southwest of the city. Our armor captured BAYREUTH and entered WEIDENBERG.

In a 20-mile advance our armor reached CREUSSEN, seven miles south of BAYREUTH.

We have closed to within 15 miles of NUREMBERG. To the north, FORCHHEIM was taken; to the northwest we are across the Aisch river, and to the west we reached HERRNNEUSES.

On a wide front from north of ROTHENBURG to the HEILBRONN area we gained several miles.

Southeast of BADEN BADEN our advance extended to BESENFELD in the BLACK FOREST. Pushing along the Rhine plain southeast of KEHL, opposite STRASBOURG, we gained some eight miles to the vicinity of OFFENBURG.

Allied forces in the west captured 87,779 prisoners 14 April.

The Ruhr pocket was cut in two when our units advancing from the north and from the south met at WETTER. We are in the vicinity of WUPPERTAL. HAGEN was cleared of the enemy, and we are near ISERLOHN.

Allied forces which launched an attack to clear the enemy from the Gironde estuary in France captured MESCHERS, SEMUSSAC, MEDIS, and are one mile from ROYAN.

Gun positions, strong points and other enemy installations on both sides of the estuary were attacked without loss by our heavy and medium bombers in very great strength. Enemy batteries at the mouth of the estuary were subjected to severe bombardment by an Allied naval task force supporting the ground operations.

Rail lines between BREMEN and HAMBURG were severed in several places and motor transport on the west and east sides of the Elbe were attacked by fighter-bombers.

Rail yards at HERSBRUCK and DONAUWORTH, GUNZBURG and ULM were attacked by medium, light and fighter-bombers. Rail and road transport in the areas of DESSAU, MUHLBERG, LEIPZIG, BORNA, DRESDEN and CHEMNITZ, and airfields near DESSAU, LEIPZIG and at MARIENBAD in Czechoslovakia, were attacked by fighter-bombers which destroyed and damaged enemy aircraft on the ground.

Enemy troops and strong points ahead of our ground forces in central Germany, and strong points in the LOWENSTEIN area, at NEUHAUS, and east of STUTTGART were hit by fighter-bombers.

Nineteen enemy aircraft were shot down during the day. According to reports so far received four of our fighter-bombers are missing.

Targets in BERLIN were attacked by light bombers last night.

COMMUNIQUE No. 374   April 17

Allied forces, breaking out from the ARNHEM area, advanced beyond OTTERLO. They also joined with units in the most northerly bridgehead across the IJssel in the area southwest of ZUTPHEN. Heavy fighting continues in APELDOORN and in GRONINGEN to the north.

We occupied LEEUWARDEN and reached the North Sea coast at several places. Our armor broke out of our bridgeheads over the Aller river and advanced up to 15 miles, capturing WALSRODE, BERGEN and MUDEN.

Eisenhower: 'With Bradley's army group firmly established on the Elbe, the stage was now set for the final Allied moves of the campaign. With his world collapsing about him, the German soldier lost all desire to fight. Only in isolated instances did commanders succeed in maintaining cohesion among their units. During the first three weeks of April the western Allies captured more than a million prisoners. Even before the Allied advance across central Germany began, we knew that the German Government was preparing to evacuate Berlin. The administrative offices seemed to be moving to the southward, possibly, we thought, to Berchtesgaden in the National Redoubt. Continuation of the movement was no longer possible after Bradley's speedy advance barred further north-south traffic across the country. We knew also that Hitler had been unable to go south and that he was making his last stand in Berlin. Nevertheless, the strong possibility still existed that fanatical Nazis would attempt to establish themselves in the National Redoubt, and the early overrunning of that area remained important to us.' (Map courtesy of General Bradley.)

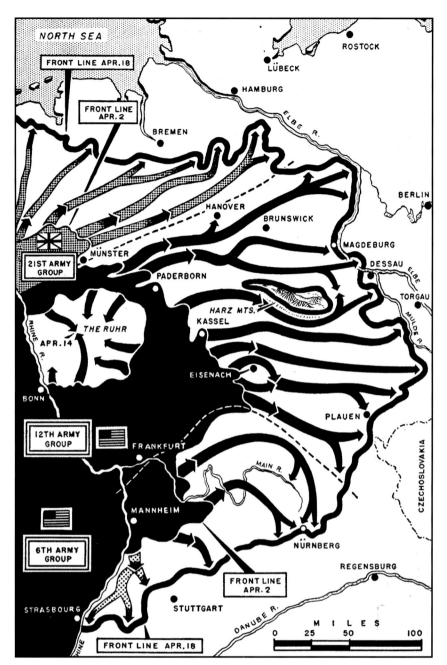

A symbol of the surrounding of the Ruhr Pocket. 'Colonel Edson D. Raff of the 507th Parachute Infantry Regiment turns over an un-named Nazi colonel to the Military Police after he had surrendered the city of Duisburg on April 17.'

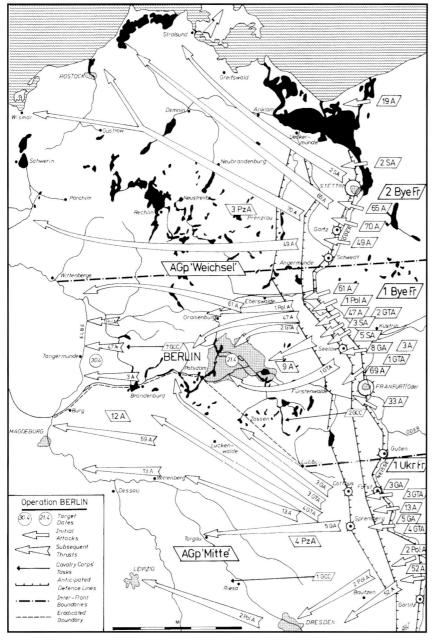

The Soviets had a sufficiently large bridgehead opposite Küstrin from which to launch their offensive but first came a decisive battle for the Seelow Heights. Zhukov had four combined armies for his main thrust, attention being concentrated on the Eighth Guards Army astride the main road to Berlin running through Seelow. The attacks on April 16 suffered tremendous casualties and failed to penetrate the main line of defence running along the Seelow Heights. Progress was so slow during the course of the day that Zhukov committed his two tank armies, adding to the confusion on the already congested battlefield. On the 17th and 18th, the Soviet armour eventually broke through and bypassed Seelow, which fell on the afternoon of the 18th. A German counter-attack at Diedersdorf that day caused further heavy casualties but could not prevent the much stronger Soviet forces breaking through. Finally, on April 19, the last of the German lines of defence was breached near Müncheberg and Batzlow, the German 9. Armee being split asunder and the remains of the LVI. Panzerkorps driven back on Berlin.

Fighter-bombers attacked road movement over a wide area from the Zuider Zee to EMDEN, BREMEN and HAMBURG and heavily bombed road and rail transport in the BREMEN—HAMBURG—BERLIN triangle. West of OLDENBURG a number of targets, including infantry and pillboxes, were hit by rocket-firing fighters.

We control the west bank of the Elbe river, except for a few small pockets, from WITTENBERGE to the Elbe—Saale junction, south of BARBY.
MAGDEBURG is not yet clear of the enemy. Our bridgehead across the Elbe is five miles deep.

Our armor entered BERNBURG and reached a point two and one-half miles southeast of DESSAU where the autobahn crosses the Mulde river. KOTHEN was cleared. East of KOTHEN our units moving south met others advancing north, thus closing a long narrow pocket of about 350 square miles which extends westward into the Harz mountains.

Infantry units mopping up behind our armor reached HASSELFELDE in the Harz mountains and cleared ALSLEBEN, south of BERNBURG.

Our armor is at BITTERFELD, north of LEIPZIG. We are still fighting in HALLE.

MERSEBURG, to the south, has been cleared. East of LEIPZIG our armor reached the outskirts of WURZEN, the vicinity of STOCKHEIM and BORNA to the southwest, and cleared COLDITZ. Our armored units occupied ALTENBURG, and after a 23-mile advance are in the area north of CHEMNITZ. Southwest of RONNEBERG we entered WEIDA, LINDA and WILDETAUBE and to the east we cleared GLAUCHAU, except for a small pocket of resistance. We cleared SCHLEIZ and reached the vicinity of JOSSNITZ north of PLAUEN. We reached GROBAU, north of HOF, which has been cleared and to the south our infantry is in the vicinity of SCHWARZENBACH and WEISSENSTADT.

Rail and other communications targets at WITTENBERG; ZERBST, northwest of DESSAU; HERZBERG and RIESA, northwest of DRESDEN, and in Czechoslovakia, were heavily attacked by medium, light and fighter-bombers. Heavy road movement was bombed around RIESA, DRESDEN and CHEMNITZ. Objectives ahead of our forward ground elements near DESSAU and LEIPZIG were attacked by other fighter-bombers.

Our infantry entered NUREMBERG after a 20-mile advance from the northeast.

Our forces are just northeast of ROTHENBERG after a gain of five miles.

Southwest, towards HEILBRONN, gains were made on a wide front. Fighter-bombers attacked targets ahead of our ground forces in the HEILBRONN and SCHWABISCH HALL areas.

In the BLACK FOREST north of FREUDENSTADT, a six-mile gain put our units in IGELSBERG. In the Rhine valley we took OFFENBURG and several other towns to the northwest toward STRASBOURG. Forward elements drove 12 miles to the vicinity of KURZELL.

Allied forces in the west captured 66,767 prisoners 15 April.

In the Ruhr pockets our armor reached HILDEN and HAAN. The one-time crack German Panzer-Lehr-Division, including its commanding general, his staff and 3,000 men surrendered to us at ISERLOHN. An enemy corps, consisting of the remnants of three divisions and including four generals, 23 other officers and 5,000 men, also surrendered.

On the French west coast the town of ROYAN is now in our hands. Our infantry and tanks are clearing the fortified area surrounding the town.

The Arvers peninsula is being mopped up. In the POINTE DE GRAVE sector our units forced the enemy to withdraw beyond the ST VIVIEN L'HÔPITAL line.

An Allied naval task force operating off the mouth of the Gironde continued to bombard enemy positions. Spotting aircraft directed the warships' fire. Artillery positions northwest of POINTE DE LA COUBRE and other targets along the estuary were attacked with high-explosive and fragmentation bombs by strong formations of medium bombers.

In southern Germany, medium, light and fighter-bombers hit rail yards at GUNZENHAUSEN, REUTLINGEN, ULM and HERBERTINGEN, and an ordnance depot at KEMPTEN some 60 miles southwest of MUNICH.

In attacks on enemy airfields, fighters and fighter-bombers destroyed at least 827 aircraft on the ground and damaged a large number of others. During the day 47 enemy aircraft were shot down.

German naval units at SWINEMUNDE, on the Baltic coast, were attacked by escorted heavy bombers.

Last night heavy bombers in strength attacked railway targets on each side of the German—Czechoslovak border. Targets in BERLIN were bombed by light bombers.

If Bayreuth was a significant venue in the Nazi calendar, then Nuremberg was top of the list. All political parties hold annual rallies to publicise their policies, encourage their delegates, and fire up their supporters, but none have surpassed the huge National Socialist gatherings in Nuremberg in the 1930s. The first Nazi Party rally was held in Munich in 1923 and Weimar in 1926 but from 1927 onwards they were always staged in Nuremberg. It was Julius Streicher (seen here, bald-headed in civilian attire) with his Nuremberg background who was instrumental in promoting *his* city with its beautiful walled old town — the Altstadt — and castle, steeped in Teutonic legend, something which always appealed to the Nazi ideologists. So Nuremberg became the Hauptstadt der Partei — the NSDAP capital — with the first Reichsparteitag being held from August 19-21, 1927. The saluting base for the street parade was Hitler's Mercedes parked in the market place — the Marktplatz — naturally renamed the Adolf-Hitler-Platz in 1933.

The battle to capture the city began on April 16, the 3rd Infantry Division moving in from the north while the 45th Division approached from the east and southeast, both from General Patch's Seventh Army. It was a gruelling fight for the ring of anti-aircraft guns protecting the city were used against the ground forces; only when this ring had been broken could the troops begin the costly business of house-to-house clearance . . . only that in bomb-blasted Nuremberg it was more rubble-to-rubble! With fighter-bombers blasting the ruins, by the 19th the 3rd Division's 30th Infantry Regiment had penetrated the mediaeval walls and entered the Altstadt. There on the Adolf-Hitler-Platz stood a platform from which Karl Holtz, the Nazi gauleiter, only a few days previously had announced to the local civilians that victory was in sight. He had vowed to Hitler to fight to the death and early the following morning he directed a last counter-attack, his dead body being found later in a cellar although it is unclear whether he died in battle or by his own hand. It was April 20 — Hitler's birthday.

COMMUNIQUE No. 375   April 18

Allied forces south of the IJsselmeer in Holland captured BARNEVELD and VOORTHUIZEN and occupied APELDOORN.

In north Holland we captured HARLINGEN and cleared the last of the enemy from GRONINGEN.

North of FRIESOYTHE in Germany we established a bridgehead over the Kusten canal against which the enemy launched two unsuccessful counter-attacks.

South of HAMBURG, our armor advanced across the Luneburg moor and captured SCHNEVERDINGEN and EBSTORF. Fighting continues in UELZEN, but we have advanced beyond the town to the northeast.

Our infantry and armor launched an attack on MAGDEBURG following heavy bombardment by artillery and medium, light and fighter-bombers.

In the bridgehead area south of MAGDEBURG our forces east of the Elbe repulsed a heavy counter-attack, and destroyed 15 to 20 of the estimated 30 enemy tanks participating.

There were no changes in the DESSAU area where we are meeting resistance from German civilians as well as troops.

Farther south, our forces advanced to BITTERFELD, where we have been held up by enemy tank and artillery fire. HALLE is half cleared.

Our units are enveloping LEIPZIG from the west, south and east.

The enemy commander at CHEMNITZ refused a surrender demand by our forces, which are two miles west of the city. To the southwest, we have taken WERDAU and cleared GREIZ after heavy street fighting. Our units have entered NETZSCHKAU, captured PLAUEN, and cleared OELSNITZ.

On April 21, the Americans staged their own victory parade in the very place where Hitler had celebrated coming to power in 1933. Now surrounded by ruins that were still smouldering, General Patch and his corps commander, Major General Wade Haislip, personally thanked the men of the two divisions. The Stars and Stripes was raised to the top of a flagpole specially installed, but it was then lowered to half-mast in observance of the death of President Roosevelt who had died suddenly the previous week.

In the HOF area we advanced to within four and one-half miles of the Czechoslovakian border.

In the Harz pocket, our forces on the north side captured WERNIGERODE and are meeting stiff resistance as they pushed southward from the town. Other elements advancing from the southern edge entered BRAUNLAGE and pushed four miles northeast from GUNTERSBERGE.

Our armor reached HOPFENOHE, 15 miles southeast of BAYREUTH, in an advance of some ten miles.

NUREMBERG was almost encircled while stubborn resistance continued in the outskirts. To the north, ERLANGEN was captured.

Nazi parade in the Zeppelinwiese stadium, completed in time for the 1937 rally in September that year.

ROTHENBURG was taken after negotiations for surrender failed. Farther west, gains up to five miles were made against varying resistance.

Strong points near ROTHENBURG and in the HEILBRONN and SCHWABISCH HALL areas, and a troop concentration northwest of CRAILSHEIM were hit by fighter-bombers.

Southwest of STUTTGART, NAGOLD was reached after an advance of some 12 miles. In the BLACK FOREST and the Rhine plain up-river from STRASBOURG further gains were scored.

In the Maritime Alps several peaks have been taken and BRIEL, near the Italian border, was entered.

Allied forces in the west captured 112,033 prisoners 16 April.

In the Ruhr the enemy has been confined to a single pocket of about 125 square miles in the DUSSELDORF area. We are fighting in the eastern section of DUSSELDORF. To the northeast our armor advanced to a point just south of KETTWIG and met our units moving from he north.

On the French Atlantic coast the enemy pockets at POINTE DE GRAVE and POINTE DE LA COUBRE were subjected to heavy artillery concentrations and were bombed by medium bombers.

Our ground forces made a deep penetration into the LA COUBRE FOREST where enemy resistance was broken and mopping-up is proceeding rapidly.

The German admiral commanding enemy forces in the ROYAN pocket and his entire staff were captured.

Rail targets in the DRESDEN area, at FALKENAU, KARLSBAD, BEROUN, KLADNO and AUSSIG; and an oil storage depot at RAUDNITZ, north of PRAGUE, were attacked yesterday by escorted heavy bombers in very great strength. The escorting fighters destroyed a large number of enemy aircraft on the ground in both Germany and Czechoslovakia.

Heavy rail movement in an area south and east of BAYREUTH; rail yards in the area from DRESDEN to PILSEN and others at NORDLINGEN, ESSLINGEN, EPFENDORF, northest of ROTTWEIL, and at PUTTLINGEN, and airfields at NORDLINGEN and in the area of EGER were attacked by fighter-bombers.

Fast-forward eight years and Hitler's Thousand Year Reich has marched into the pages of history as infantrymen of the 3rd Division follow in the footsteps of the defeated Wehrmacht. General Patch and Major General John O'Daniel, the commanding officer of the 3rd Division, take the salute from Hitler's tribune.

The Nazi wreath on top of the grandstand was later blown off in a spectacular explosion, and the columns demolished by the authorities post-war. Now the stadium is used for motor racing. (For more, see *The Third Reich Then and Now*.)

Ammunition dumps at ALTENDETTELSAU and GUNZENHAUSEN east and southeast of ANSBACH, and warehouses and rail communications at AALEN, TUBINGEN and WEINGARTEN were targets for medium and light bombers.

Road and rail transport in Holland and in northern Germany near SCHWERIN and in the area of WITTSTOCK and KYRITZ;

The Luitpoldhain — literally 'Holy Forest of Luitpold' — was a park in front of the First World War Memorial. Hitler had it transformed into a showcase stadium which became the focus of the huge parade by the SA and later SS. A wide paved pathway — Die Strasse des Führers — linked the memorial with the speaker's podium along which Hitler would march between the serried ranks. What better place to entertain the men of the 80th Division.

enemy shipping in the Frisian Isles area; and gun positions and troop concentrations west of OLDENBURG were struck at by fighter-bombers and rocket-firing fighters. Last night light bombers attacked targets in BERLIN.

The show on April 26 featured the 'Yankee Doodlers' of the XIX Tactical Air Command, part of the Ninth Air Force.

COMMUNIQUE No. 376   April 19

All organized resistance in the Ruhr pocket has ceased and Allied forces have virtually completed mopping up the last enemy stragglers in this area.

In Holland our forces advancing from the ARNHEM area have occupied WAGENINGEN and EDE and reached the Zuider Zee north of BARNEVELD.

West of the Ems river near its mouth, and around our bridgehead over the Kusten canal, the enemy is offering stiff resistance.

Beyond the Aller river, VERDEN and SOLTAU have been captured and our columns advanced ten miles north of SCHNEVERDINGEN. UELZEN, now almost cleared of the enemy, has been surrounded and we advanced north of the town to the outskirts of LUNEBURG, and east to ROSCHE.

Our units attacking south into the Harz mountains gained two to four miles. MAGDEBURG has been cleared to the Elbe river. In the bridgehead across the Elbe we repulsed two small counter-attacks.

We entered LEIPZIG from the west with infantry and tanks and reached the west bank of the Elster canal. In the CHEMNITZ area our units encountered small-arms and bazooka fire at AUERSWALDE.

At the same time that Nuremberg was being subjugated, one of the last major towns to be captured by the American army was under attack, a battle for a city which lay deep in the future Soviet Zone of Germany. However, as has been explained, Eisenhower did not let his strategy be influenced by the zones of occupation, and Leipzig, which lay 85 miles south-west of Berlin, was still west of the nominal 'stop-line' of the River Elbe. Nevertheless the two divisions concerned in the Leipzig battle — the 2nd and the 69th — hoped to keep casualties to a minimum. Initial resistance appeared light as the troops entered the city, this column having pulled up in Merseburger Strasse.

Left: However, Oberst Hans von Poncet was determined to mount a last-ditch defence and as the troops advanced into the city, danger lurked around every corner. As this Sherman of the 741st Tank Battalion turned from Zschochersche Strasse into Karl-Heine-Strasse it was hit by a Panzerfaust fired by a youth of the Hitlerjugend. Two of the crew were killed; the body of one can be seen in front of the tank covered with a blanket and the other lies slumped against the door on the right. An Associated Press photographer pictured the locals swarming around the still-smouldering Sherman. *Right:* The Felsenkeller restaurant on the corner was one of Leipzig's best-known beer halls and meeting places.

South of NUREMBERG we reached SCHWAND, and to the west, ANSBACH has been largely cleared. Farther west towards HEILBRONN we reached JOCHSBERG, WESTHEIM and GRAB.

South of PFORZHEIM we reached HORB, on the upper Neckar river. FREUDENSTADT, communications center in the SCHWARZWALD, was captured and the advance extended five miles farther south.

In the Rhine plain, our units pushed as far south as DINGLINGEN. Enemy resistance in OBERKIRCH was overcome and long-range guns which had been firing on STRASBOURG were silenced.

Allied forces in the west captured 37,427 prisoners 17 April bringing the total prisoners captured in the west since D-Day to 2,093,002.

On the French Atlantic coast we have cleared the entire north side of the Gironde estuary. The attack continues on the southern side of the estuary where we have pushed the enemy into his last defensive positions on the VERDON plain.

The naval base and fortress island of Heligoland and an airfield on the island of Dune, near Heligoland; rail yards, transformer stations and other rail facilities at ROSENHEIM, TRAUNSTEIN, PASSAU and STRAUBING in southern Germany and at HOLIN and PILSEN in

Meanwhile, 150 miles to the north-west, the 15th Scottish Division were finally clearing Uelzen after several days of stiff street fighting.

Our infantry gained up to 12 miles on a 14-mile front in the ZWICKAU area and ZWICKAU and LENGENFELD have been cleared. We met strong resistance at LENGENFELD from dug-in tanks and infantry.

South of LENGENFELD we cleared TREUEN. East of ZWICKAU we reached the vicinity of WILDENFELS and cavalry elements are near THIERFELD.

Farther south we reached the vicinity of SACHSGRUN and our patrols advanced six miles east, crossed the Czechoslovakian border, and reached GOTTMANNSGRUN.

South of HOF we entered SCHWARZEN-BACH and WEISSENSTADT.

In NUREMBERG our units which entered from the north and from the east joined, and other elements drove into the city from the south. Resistance decreased as we knocked out enemy gun positions. The suburb of FURTH and a nearby airfield were captured.

Little changed after seven decades, this is Louisenstrasse, the house on the corner being No. 10.

And in northern Holland the Royal Hamilton Light Infantry caught a party of Germans perparing to pull out in trucks. Flame-throwers accounted for the German vehicles, still burning as Canadian armour presses onward to Assen.

Czechoslovakia were attacked by escorted heavy bombers in very great strength.

Fighter-bombers hit targets ahead of our ground forces and attacked rail targets elsewhere in northwest Germany; rail and road transport and airfields in central Germany and as far east as PILSEN and PRAGUE in Czechoslovakia, and rail targets in southern Germany including the yards at GUNZENHAUSEN, EICHSTATT, INGOLSTADT and DENKINGEN.

Enemy barracks at OLDENBURG were attacked by medium bombers; an oil storage depot at NEUBURG, communications targets at JUTERBOG and FALKENBERG were hit by medium and light bombers, and enemy airfields in the ULM area were attacked by medium and fighter-bombers.

Targets in BERLIN were attacked last night by light bombers.

The huge number of Germans now being captured in droves — SHAEF reported over 37,000 on April 17 and over 50,000 on the 18th — put an incredible strain on the logistics for feeding and housing tens of thousands of prisoners. SHAEF announced that up to April 22, 2,378,000 had been captured since D-Day, more than a million of these on the Western Front in April alone. This photo was taken of a POW enclosure at Remagen. German servicemen taken after the capitulation in May were deemed 'Disarmed Enemy Personnel' because they belonged to a State that had ceased to exist. This effectively removed them from the protection of the Geneva Convention for by not classing another four million captured troops as POWs, it simplified the problem. Nineteen holding camps were set up by the US Army: A1 at Büderich, A2 Rheinberg, A3 Wickrathberg, A4 Remagen, A5 Sinzig, A6 Siersahhn, A7 Andernach, A8 Diez, A9 Urmitz, A10 Koblenz, A11 Dietersheim, A12 Heidesheim, A13 Hechtsheim, A14 Winzenheim/Bretzenheim/Biebelsheim, A15 Bad Kreuznach, A16 Ludwigshafen, A17 Böhr-Iggelheim, A18 Heilbronn. Due to the numbers involved, the Americans delegated internal control of the camps to the Germans themselves and all administration such as medical and cooking was undertaken by the prisoners. Even the armed guards were ex-Wehrmacht Feldgendarmerie. The International Committee of the Red Cross were prevented from visiting the camps. In June the camps at Büderich and Rheinberg were taken over by British forces while Sinzig, Andernach, Siershahn, Bretzenheim, Dietersheim, Coblenz, Hechtheim and Dietz were given to France as Général de Gaulle wanted 1.75 million prisoners of war for use as forced labour in France.

By the end of September 1945 nearly all the Rhine camps had been closed, just Bretzenheim and Bad Kreuznach remaining open for another three years acting as transit camps for German prisoners released from France. The death rate in the camps has been the subject of controversial data, the US giving a figure of 3,000; the Germans 4,537, and some post-war reports as high as 10,000.

By the 20th Leipzig was reported as being nearly cleared of the enemy but it would be amiss of us to move on and not include mention of a remarkable series of photographs taken by Robert Capa of *Life*. He was with Company F of the 23rd Infantry as it attacked the Zeppelin Bridge — the main crossing over the Weisse Elster. Capa went into a corner house overlooking the bridge where a machine-gun crew had set up their water-cooled .30-calibre Browning on the balcony. Both men were wearing looted Luftwaffe sheepskin helmets. Routinely, he began photographing as they fired several belts of ammunition at the Germans across the river but suddenly the gunner fell, hit by a sniper. What Capa had envisaged as being 'the last picture of the war for my camera' instead became the symbolic image of the 'last soldier to be killed in the war'. *Life* magazine printed Robert Capa's picture in its issue of May 14, although the censor had insisted that the gunner's face be blanked out. (See also *After the Battle* No. 130.)

COMMUNIQUE No. 377   April 20

Allied forces in Holland occupied HARDERWIJK on the Zuider Zee, and reconnaissance patrols to the northeast entered KUINRE and KAMPEN. Virtually the whole of northeastern Holland is liberated.

Defense positions, gun and infantry concentrations in the PAPENBURG area, were hit by fighter-bombers and rocket-firing fighters. An enemy barracks at LEER was bombed by medium bombers.

The enemy has maintained his pressure on our bridgehead over the Kusten canal but to the east we took ADELHEIDE and closed up to the outskirts of DELMENHORST, six miles west of BREMEN.

At OLDENBURG a counter-attack which was forming was attacked by rocket-firing fighters.

Strong points and troop entrenchments ahead of our forward positions in the area were hit.

East of the Aller river the enemy suffered a decisive defeat on the LUNEBURG HEATH and, though we are still experiencing heavy opposition inside the village of VISSELHOVEDE, our armored units advanced to within ten miles of HAMBURG and are along the HAMBURG—BREMEN autobahn for a distance of more than 12 miles.

Rail targets between HAMBURG and BREMEN were bombed.

Armored columns captured LUNEBURG and pushed on to the Elbe river south of LAUENBURG where the enemy is offering strong opposition.

In the area 35 miles northeast of BRUNSWICK the enemy launched a counter-attack in approximately division strength, supported by 25 tanks, half-tracks and self-propelled guns.

Attacking rapidly to the southeast, enemy task forces bypassed our units and penetrated 15 miles in the direction of the KLOTZE FOREST before our forces brought the situation under control.

We repulsed two small counter-attacks in our bridgehead across the Elbe river south of MAGDEBURG where our fighter-bombers attacked enemy armor and troop positions. South of ZERBST, in the bridgehead area, fighter-bombers destroyed or damaged a large number of enemy fortified buildings and five heavy guns.

Enemy pockets of resistance west of the Elbe river between LUNEBURG and WITTENBERGE were hit with bombs and rockets.

In the HARZ FOREST pocket we entered QUEDLINBURG, ELBINGERODE and BALLENSTEDT.

South of DESSAU we are near BOBBAU-STEINFURTH after heavy fighting. An enemy counter-attack near BITTERFELD was repulsed. Our units cleared HALLE, and LEIPZIG is almost clear of the enemy.

Thanks to research by Peter Hendrikx (see *After the Battle* No. 142, page 24), we are now able to put a name to a face. Pfc Raymond J. Bowman, ASN 3284651, was born on April 2, 1924. He joined up on June 21, 1943 and was assigned to Company D of the 23rd Infantry. Landing with the 2nd Division in Normandy on June 7, 1944, he was wounded in action west of Saint-Lô, being admitted to hospital on July 28. Fatally hit at Leipzig on April 18, 1945, his burial report states that he died from a bullet-wound in the right shoulder (not by a bullet between the eyes as Capa described it in *Slightly out of Focus*). He was initially buried in a temporary cemetery at Breuna near Kassel on April 21 but his remains were soon transferred to the military cemetery at Margraten, Netherlands, where he was re-interred on July 27. Later, at his mother's request, his remains were repatriated to the United States to be buried at Holy Sepulchre Cemetery in Rochester (Section 13, North Division, Veterans' Plot, Grave 482).

The Harz is the highest mountain range in northern Germany covering an area of 1,500 square miles. During the Nazi era the Harz became an important location for the armaments industry with associated forced-labour camps like Mittelbau-Dora at Nordhausen where V1s and V2s were manufactured in the underground factory. During the advance of the First Army, more than 11,000 Germans were cut off in the mountains. They fought stubbornly for ten days in the wooded terrain, with winding roads blocked at defiles with mines or log barriers. Finally, on April 23, the Americans came across the German command post near Blankenburg, capturing the entire staff, including the commander of the 11. Armee, General Walter Lucht. These infantrymen of the 8th Armored Division were pictured passing a German fire crew in the ruined streets of the town.

We reached the area of CHEMNITZ and our infantry entered OBERLUNGWITZ southwest of the city. South and southeast of HOF we cleared SCHWARZENBACH and WEISSENSTADT, and entered PILGRAMSREUTH and KIRCHENLAMITZ.

Farther south we entered BISCHOFSGRUN and reached an area five miles northeast of BAYREUTH.

Our units advancing from the west and from the east made contact eight miles south of NUREMBERG to completely encircle the city. Inside NUREMBERG the enemy has been driven into an area one mile square where house-to-house fighting is in progress.

Southeast of NUREMBERG our units reached NEUMARKT. We captured two airfields near FURTH, west of NUREMBERG, and to the southwest we reached MERKENDORF.

We captured a number of towns in a five-mile advance south of ROTHENBURG. East of HEILBRONN we captured FICHTENBERG and MITTELROT.

Between HEILBRONN and NUREMBERG we captured 8,101 prisoners in 24 hours including three generals, 150 firemen who were in NUREMBERG defense units, and a trainload of German women auxilliaries.

TUBINGEN, southwest of STUTTGART, was captured. We hold a 20-mile stretch of the upper Neckar river and the road from STRASBOURG to TUBINGEN, through the BLACK FOREST, is in our hands.

In the Maritime Alps we made additional progress in the area of the town of BRIEL which we captured.

Allied forces in the west captured 50,626 prisoners 18 April.

On the French Atlantic coast our units clearing the Gironde area continue to make progress. Additional gains have been made in the POINTE DE GRAVE sector over flooded, marshy ground and against stubborn resistance.

Rail facilities at FALKENBERG and ELSTERWERDA; between BERLIN and DRESDEN; at PIRNA, southeast of DRESDEN, at KARLSBAD and AUSSIG in Czechoslovakia, were attacked by escorted heavy bombers in strength. Rail targets in the TORGAU area and along a broad front southeastwards to PRAGUE were hit by fighter-bombers.

Rail yards at ULM and NEU ULM, an ordnance depot at NEU ULM, a rail bridge at DONAUWORTH on the ULM-NUREMBERG line, and a supply depot at DONAUESCHINGEN, 50 miles southeast of STRASBOURG, were attacked by medium and light bombers. At PASING, near MUNICH, escorted heavy bombers attacked a transformer station serving electric railways leading to the Bavarian mountains.

Gun positions and ammunition dumps at DUNKIRK were attacked by medium bombers.

Shipping on the Zuider Zee and around the Ems estuary was hit by fighter-bombers and rocket-firing fighters.

Two ships were left sinking and another was damaged. Objectives on the island of Heligoland were attacked with 12,000-pound bombs. A number of enemy airfields were bombed during the day. In addition to many enemy aircraft destroyed on the ground, 30 were shot down in combat.

According to reports so far received six of our heavy bombers and 13 fighters are missing from the day's operations.

Targets in BERLIN were bombed last night by light bombers.

The ruin of the Blankenburger Hof hotel on the left and the Kurhaus café in the far right background have all been cleared away, leaving just a bland traffic roundabout at the junction of Mauerstrasse and Hasenfelder Strasse.

The Nordhausen complex was reached first on April 11 by Combat Command B of the 3rd Armored Division but it later came under the control of the 5th Armored Division of the Ninth Army. Nordhausen lay in the Soviet Zone and officially the Allies were not permitted to remove any industrial machinery, equipment or scientific information but, between its capture and May 6, close on 100 V2s together with documents and blueprints were removed for shipment to the USA. The British were then invited to share the spoils before Nordhausen was handed over to the Soviets on July 1. This is the exit to the V1 factory — note the spherical compressed-air bottles. After they had removed what they wanted, the Soviets blew up the entrance in 1948. (See *After the Battle* No. 101.)

COMMUNIQUE No. 378   April 21

Allied forces in Holland advanced in the sector west of BARNEVELD, despite stubborn enemy opposition, and captured the village of HOEVELAKEN, two miles east of AMERSFOORT.

West of BREMEN we captured DELMENHORST and closed farther around the defenses of BREMEN. East of the Weser river, Allied armored elements in a series of outflanking thrusts took VISSELHOVEDE and HEMSLINGEN, cut the main railway north of ROTENBURG, and rushed down the HAMBURG—BREMEN autobahn for more than 20 miles. We are in the vicinity of ZEVEN, about midway between BREMEN and HAMBURG.

Our armor is on the outskirts of HARBURG, just south of HAMBURG, we captured WINSEN, thus extending our hold on the Elbe river.

Rail lines between BREMEN and HAMBURG; road and rail transport in the BREMEN—HAMBURG—BERLIN area; enemy shipping north of Wangerooge; fortified positions and strong points near PAPENBURG, west of OLDENBURG, and near STADE were hit by fighter-bombers and rocket-firing fighters.

Northeast of BRUNSWICK the enemy counter-attack of estimated division strength, launched to the southeast in the direction of the KLOTZE FOREST on 19 April, has been sealed off and our troops are attacking to regain lost ground.

South of DESSAU our armor and infantry elements are fighting in BOBBAU-STEINFURTH, WOLFEN, and the vicinity of BITTERFELD against strong enemy resistance including self-propelled guns.

Our cavalry elements captured a 94-car enemy railroad supply train near HALLE.

LEIPZIG is now completely in our hands and our armored units northeast of the city gained 1,500 yards to reach a point on the Mulde river south of EILENBURG.

Southeast of HOF our infantry cleared SELB, THIERSHEIM, and WUNSIEDEL and advanced to the vicinity of OBER REDWITZ.

Farther south other elements reached the vicinity of KEMNATH while our armor captured GRAFENWOHR.

Our infantry captured an enemy airfield nine miles southeast of BAYREUTH seizing some bombs and other equipment.

In the Harz Pocket our units south of HALBERSTADT have taken THALE, QUEDLINBURG, and BALLENSTEDT. West of THALE we entered HUTTENRODE where an enemy counter-attack was repulsed.

All organized resistance in NUREMBERG has ceased. Twelve miles to the southeast we are encountering stubborn resistance in NEUMARKT.

Southeast of ROTHENBURG, we captured FEUCHTWANGEN after a six-mile advance.

STUTTGART was virtually encircled as armored units from the northeast advanced 25 miles to OHMDEN, east of KIRSCHHEIM, and other forces swung north to AICH, ten miles south of STUTTGART.

To the southwest, a broad wedge was pushed 20 miles to ROTTWEIL, north of the Swiss-German border, and more than 25 towns were taken in the area. Gains up to five miles southward were made in the BLACK FOREST and south of DINGLINGEN. In the Rhine plain, we advanced to FORCHHEIM.

Allied forces in the west captured 64,667 prisoners 19 April.

On the French Atlantic coast all resistance in the Gironde estuary pocket ceased and the German commander and his staff were captured.

Rail yards and other rail facilities at NEURUPPIN, ORANIENBURG, NAUEN, WUSTERMARK, BRANDENBURG, SEDDIN and TREUENBRIETZEN were attacked by escorted heavy bombers in strength. Other escorted heavy bombers made a heavy attack on a fuel depot at REGENSBURG, and at KLATOVY, ZWIESEL, and MUHLDORF.

Rail and road traffic near JESSNITZ, RIESA, DRESDEN, PILSEN and WITTENBURG; rail yards at AULENDORF, north of WEINGARTEN; MEMMINGEN, NORDLINGEN, WITTENBURG and EBENHAUSEN, south of INGOLSTADT, were hit by medium, light and fighter-bombers.

Fuel depots at ANNABURG, DEGGENDORF; an ordnance depot at STAUBING, and an ammunition dump at INGOLSTADT, were attacked by medium and light bombers. A large oil storage dump near TORGAU was hit by fighter-bombers.

Enemy airfields near LUDWIGSLUST, BRANDENBURG, RIESA, DRESDEN, PILSEN, ULM, EHINGEN, LAUPHEIM, AUGSBURG, INGOLSTADT and RIEM, east of MUNICH, were bombed and strafed by medium and fighter-bombers. Many aircraft were destroyed on the ground and others were damaged.

Targets in BERLIN were attacked last night by light bombers.

Having crossed to the Aller river at Verden, 25 miles south-east of Bremen, on April 18 the 52nd (Lowland) Division began its drive on the city with the 1st Glasgow Highlanders in the lead. For the first two days progress was slow so on the 20th Lieutenant-General Sir Brian Horrocks commanding XXX Corps decided to offer the city the chance of surrendering via this message: 'The choice is yours. The British Army is lying outside Bremen supported by the RAF and is about to capture the city. There are two ways in which this can take place. Either by the employment of all the means at the disposal of the Army and the RAF, or by occupation of the town after unconditional surrender. The choice is yours as to which course is followed. Yours is the responsibility for the unnecessary bloodshed which will result if you choose the first way. Otherwise you must send an envoy under the protection of a white flag over to the British lines. You have 24 hours in which to decide.' When no positive reply was received — the view of the Nazi faction in the city had prevailed — the Lowland Division resumed its advance and by April 23 forward elements had reached Mahndorf, a village just inside the official city boundary.

COMMUNIQUE No. 379   April 22

Allied forces reached the line of the Eem river northwest of AMERSFOORT.

East of the Ems river, PAPENBURG was entered. We enlarged our bridgehead over the Kusten canal despite strenuous opposition.

Our forces closed in nearer to ZEVEN and ROTENBURG and repulsed a counter-attack in the vicinity of ELSDORF. Mopping-up operations continue in the wooded areas west of LUNEBURG.

In the area west of WITTENBERGE our forces have gained up to seven miles in the GARTOWER FOREST, capturing PREZELLE.

Northeast of BRUNSWICK we have pocketed the enemy force which counter-attacked us April 19. We have retaken DIESDORF and ABBENDORF.

In the Harz Pocket we captured BLANKENBURG. All organized resistance in the pocket has ceased.

Enemy swimmers failed in an attempt to blow a bridge leading to our bridgehead across the Elbe river and some of the swimmers were captured.

Farther south our armored task forces entered DESSAU. South of the city we cleared BOBBAU-STEINFURTH and WOLFEN and entered JESSNITZ and GREPPIN against stiff resistance. We are fighting in BITTERFELD.

Northeast of LEIPZIG our armor occupied KROSTITZ and our troops are mopping up along the Mulde river.

In Czechoslovakia we cleared ASCH and advancing to the east reached a point five miles north of the town. In Germany, south of ASCH, we entered SCHIRNDING and cleared ARZBERG. Farther south we entered FUCHSMUHL, ERBENDORF and PRESSATH and entered RIGGAU.

Mopping-up in NUREMBERG has been completed. More than 14,000 Allied prisoners were liberated when we cleared a concentration camp in the area.

In the ROTHENBURG area, our armor drove 18 miles southward to BOPFINGEN. CRAILSHEIM, from which we withdrew two weeks ago, was captured and we made further gains southward.

A four-mile gap remained in the link around STUTTGART with approaching columns at KIRCHHEIM and UNTERENSINGEN. A score of towns were taken in the area as we drove towards STUTTGART from all sides. Forward elements were at ESSLINGEN.

South of STUTTGART, our units thrust 18 miles to DONAUESCHINGEN, on the headwaters of the Danube, ten miles north of the German-Swiss border. TUTTLINGEN and MUHLHEIM farther east were also taken.

In the BLACK FOREST several more towns fell to our forces. In the Rhine plain, BREISACH was reached in a five-mile gain.

Between the Rhine and NUREMBERG more than 11,000 prisoners were taken in 24 hours.

Allied forces in the west captured 46,334 prisoners 20 April.

The rail center at OLDENBURG was attacked by medium bombers.

Rail communications between PRAGUE and PILSEN; motor transport between NUREMBERG and AUGSBURG; enemy strong points east of HEILBRONN, southeast of STUTTGART, and east of STRASBOURG; and a number of airfields were attacked by fighter-bombers. Many enemy aircraft were destroyed on the ground and a number were damaged. Fifty vehicles were destroyed in a depot in the NUREMBERG-AUGSBURG area.

Rail yards and facilities at MUNICH and INGOLSTADT and an airfield at LANDSBERG, 30 miles west of MUNICH, were bombed by escorted heavy bombers. Light bombers hit a rail yard at ATTNANG-PUCHHEIM, 35 miles northeast of SALZBURG.

Five enemy aircraft were shot down in the day's operations. According to reports so far, six of our heavy bombers and two fighters are missing.

Targets at KIEL were attacked last night by light bombers.

Meanwhile events some 200 miles to the east were reaching their inevitable conclusion. Having been joined in Berlin by Eva Braun on April 15, on his birthday five days later Hitler had declared his intention of remaining at his Chancellery with its secure underground bunker. The first Russian shells had fallen in the capital the same day and Soviet troops — vanguards of the Third and Fifth Shock Armies — entered northeastern Berlin on the 21st. Stalin's command had been to raise the Red Flag over the Reichstag by May Day in just over a week's time.

In the south, the Seventh Army was continuing the advance over the River Danube to Austria. General Devers' plan for the 6th Army Group was for the 1ère Armée under Général de Lattre de Tassigny to take Stuttgart but only after American troops were first positioned east and south of the city. However, de Lattre de Tassigny had other ideas and, having quickly captured Karlsruhe on April 4 and Pforzheim on the 8th, on April 15 he sent a corps across the Rhine at Strasbourg aimed at the Black Forest. Despite Devers' orders, de Lattre de Tassigny felt that with American forces still some 20 miles short of Stuttgart, to delay his attack was to invite the Germans to escape from the city, so he ordered one corps to launch a double envelopment of the southern half of the forest, while the other began to surround Stuttgart from the south and east. This operation began on April 18, forcing Devers to legitimise the French move into the Seventh Army zone by changing the inter-army boundary. By April 22, the city had been taken. This picture shows the junction of Tübinger Strasse with Eberhard-Strasse.

COMMUNIQUE No. 380   April 23

Allied forces continue to make progress north of PAPENBURG and have beaten off additional enemy counter-attacks against our bridgehead over the Kusten canal.

In the BREMEN—HAMBURG area we captured ROTENBURG and BUXTEHUDE, and cleared a large area southeast of ROTENBURG.

Escorted heavy bombers attacked objectives in BREMEN. Enemy strong points southeast of BREMEN were attacked by medium bombers.

Our forces spread farther down the south bank of the Elbe river and entered BLECKEDE, and to the south we cleared most of the GOHRDE FOREST.

Two-thirds of DESSAU has been cleared and fighting continues against strong resistance.

BITTERFELD, JESSNITZ and RAGUHN have been cleared and infantry elements advanced east to the Mulde river.

Southeast of LEIPZIG our patrols crossed the Mulde river and advanced several kilometers without resistance.

Some sniping activity is being met northwest of NAUMBURG.

South of NUREMBERG our infantry made gains up to five miles, reaching LAFFENAU and GROSSWEINGARTEN.

To the southeast, we cleared BOPFINGEN and drove six miles farther south. South of CRAILSHEIM, we reached ELLWANGEN.

STUTTGART was occupied, and numerous towns in the surrounding area were taken. Southeast of STUTTGART, we made gains up to five miles.

Forces to the south drove ten miles to the German-Swiss border, near EPFENHOFEN, thus sealing off a BLACK FOREST pocket of more than 1,000 square miles.

The bridgehead across the Danube was expanded to a width of nearly 40 miles, reaching SIGMARINGEN, which was captured. Along the German-Swiss border, a drive eight miles to the east brought our forces to WORBLINGEN.

In the southwest corner of the BLACK FOREST pocket, in thrusts of up to ten miles, we reached WALDKIRCH, FREIBURG and GREZHAUSEN.

An enemy airfield at MEMMINGEN, 30 miles southeast of ULM, was attacked by fighter-bombers.

Allied forces in the west captured 37,276 prisoners 21 April.

As Charles MacDonald admitted in the official US Army History: 'In an imaginative, aggressive maneuver, de Lattre's First French Army in twelve days had swept the northern half of the Black Forest, trapped the bulk of the German LXIV Corps, and seized Stuttgart, in the process taking some 28,000 prisoners at a cost of 175 French troops killed and 510 wounded.'

On April 23 the 395th Infantry Regiment of the 90th Division were approaching the Czech border east of Nuremberg when they came across another death camp at Flossenbürg but, in this case, almost empty. Just three days earlier the SS had marched away over 14,000 of the inmates towards the camp at Dachau near Munich leaving behind only those too sick and weak. They had erected this banner at the entrance.

South of NUREMBERG our armor and infantry made gains up to ten miles and reached WEISSENBURG.

Our forces crossed the Danube at DILLINGEN, 15 miles northwest of AUGSBURG, and we advanced five miles south of the river.

Upstream along the Danube we reached EHINGEN, 12 miles southwest of ULM. Other units driving east from SIGMARINGEN advanced to within six miles of EHINGEN, virutally sealing off an area of 500 square miles southeast of STUTTGART.

From LUDWIGSHAFEN we drove 25 miles eastward to a point 18 miles north of FRIEDRICHSHAFEN on Lake Constance. A 40-mile stretch of the German-Swiss border is now in our hands.

West of the BLACK FOREST we gained eight miles southward along the Rhine to reach MULLHEIM.

Allied forces in the west captured 32,642 prisoners 22 April.

Enemy shipping off the Frisian Islands and in the Ems estuary; rail lines and traffic between the Ems and Weser estuaries and in the Elbe estuary area, and airfields in both northern and southern

COMMUNIQUE No. 381   April 24

Allied forces in north Holland beat off an enemy counter-attack near WAGENBORGEN and are fighting in APPINGEDAM.

Our forces in Germany, advancing down the right bank of the Weser, captured UPHUSEN, five miles from the outskirts of BREMEN.

Enemy defense positions around BREMEN were attacked by medium bombers. West of OLDENBURG fighter-bombers hit a concentration of field guns.

West of HAMBURG we have occupied HARSEFELD and ESTERBRUGGE.

Enemy forces which penetrated the KLOTZ area April 19, and subsequently were pocketed, have been mopped up except for a few stragglers.

DESSAU has been cleared and our forces are fighting in the western part of EILENBURG. Our patrols crossed the Mulde river in the vicinity of EILENBURG.

In Czechoslovakia our troops liberated THONBRUNN and DOLREUTH.

To the south, in Germany, our infantry cleared TIRSCHENREUTH after meeting strong resistance from 1,500 Hungarian troops who ultimately surrendered.

Our armor cleared WEIDEN and advanced south to enter NABBURG and SCHWARZENFELD. Our infantry, advancing with the armor, reached the

Now pleasantly landscaped, its present-day apperance belies the horrors found within its walls.

vicinity of MANTEL and entered ASCHACH.

Southwest of AMBERG we reached the vicinity of KASTL and cleared NEUMARKT after repelling a small counter-attack.

Germany were attacked by fighter-bombers. Many aircraft were destroyed or damaged on the ground.

Four enemy aircraft were shot down during the day. According to incomplete reports eight of our fighters are missing.

Sixty corpses were found stored in the mortuary. A War Crime Investigation Team from the Third Army was sent in to produce a full report and 90 former guards were brought to trial of whom 17 were executed. (See *After the Battle* No. 131.)

Two days later American forces liberated another camp, this time in Austria. A soldier from Patton's 11th Armored wrote that 'no description can do justice to the stench, the filth and the human misery that we found at Mauthausen'.

COMMUNIQUE No. 382   April 25

Allied forces in north Holland occupied APPINGEDAM and cleared the whole of the coastline as far east as the mouth of the Ems estuary.

Southeast of BREMEN we captured ARBERGEN and TYTEN. We entered ZEVEN, between BREMEN and HAMBURG, and fighting continues in the town.

Enemy strong points in the BREMEN area were attacked by medium bombers. Gun positions and troop concentrations in the area of the Ems estuary and around OLDENBURG were hit by fighter-bombers.

Targets in the communications center of BAD OLDESLOE, northeast of HAMBURG, were attacked by escorted heavy bombers.

Southwest of WEIDEN our infantry units reached the vicinity of VOHENSTRAUSS. In the area north of REGENSBURG we captured SCHWANDORF and BURGLENGENFELD.

Other units in the area north of REGENSBURG reached the vicinity of RODING and entered NITTENAU. Several bridges were captured intact across the Regen river in the course of these operations.

To the west our forces entered LAUTERBACH and BERATZHAUSEN and reached the vicinity of THUMHAUSEN, four miles west of REGENSBURG and three miles from the Danube river.

In a rapid advance to the southeast our armored elements reached the vicinity of ARNETSRIED, three miles northwest of REGEN and 35 miles from the Austrian border.

South of NUREMBERG, our armor and infantry advanced up to ten miles on a broad front to within seven miles of the Danube. Forces in this area were within 13 miles of units pushing downstream from the DILLINGEN bridgehead. Our hold south of the river at DILLINGEN was expanded to a width of ten miles and a depth of six miles.

The 500-square-mile pocket south of STUTTGART is being steadily reduced.

ULM was captured by units making simultaneous thrusts from the northwest and from the southwest. Units advancing from the north reached the city in a drive of 15 miles.

Twenty miles to the south, our forces advanced 25 miles eastward to reach the Iller canal.

Additional penetrations were made into the BLACK FOREST pocket. Another crossing of the Rhine, at KEMS, put our forces within eight miles of BASLE, Switzerland.

Allied forces in the west captured 39,089 prisoners 23 April.

An airfield at FLENSBURG; road and rail traffic in the BERLIN area and from EGGENFELDEN, southeast of LANDAU, to PRAGUE; strong points in DILLINGEN; airfields at AUGSBURG, LANDSBERG and MUNICH; rail yards at INGOLSTADT, LANDAU, PLATTLING and in Czechoslovakia and the Danube valley were attacked by fighter-bombers. Many enemy aircraft were destroyed or damaged on the ground.

An oil depot near SCHROBENHAUSEN, northeast of LANDSBERG, was attacked by medium and light bombers.

Eight enemy aircraft were shot down during the day. According to incomplete reports, two of our medium bombers and ten of our fighters are missing.

From 1938 to 1945 Mauthausen was a name synonymous with fear and terror. Historian Derek Penton explains that 'it evolved from a ringed enclosure of barbed wire into a citadel consisting of granite gateways, courtyards, watch towers and high-voltage fencing. The camp was constructed by the prisoners themselves over a period of six years from granite blocks hewn in the quarry below. The appearance of Mauthausen was probably more forbidding than any other concentration camp. At night it was depicted by brilliant but sinister floodlights. Such a sight must have struck fear into the hearts of thousands of prisoners as they approached the fortress after a two and a half mile trek from the railway station. The entrance into the camp was through the main outer gateway, under whose arch countless men, women and children passed only once in their lifetime. Newly arrived prisoners were initiated into camp life in the yard just inside the main gate. Here the commandant, Franz Ziereis, would often welcome the newcomers with the words "Here is only a marching in; the way out is through the chimney of the crematorium".' *Left:* On May 6, 1945, the inmates had the supreme pleasure in toppling the symbol of Nazism from over the main gate. *Right:* The supports still remain to be seen.

Having captured Stuttgart, Général de Lattre was still not satisfied as he had two specific targets on his wish list. The first was the town of Sigmaringen, 50 miles south of the city, to which the collaborationist Vichy government had fled the previous August and where they had since set up a French government-in-exile, and the second was the city of Ulm, scene of Napoléon's victory over the Austrians in 1805. Although Ulm lay 44 miles east of the 1ère Armée's zone, de Lattre de Tassigny was still determined to be in Ulm by April 25. By the 21st the southern half of the Black Forest had been cleared and an armoured column had reached the first goal at Sigmaringen although too late to capture Marshal Philippe Pétain, head of the Vichy government, or Pierre Laval, the Deputy Prime Minister. Ordering his division to keep going to Ulm, de Lattre declared that 'the Americans will perhaps dislodge us from it but the French flag will have flown there'. However, the US 10th Armored Division stood in their way, raising the possibility of a clash with American troops who would be unaware of the French in their area. Fortunately the French armour was identified by the outposts of the 10th Armored and its commander raised no objection to the French: 'Among tankers, we always understand each other'.

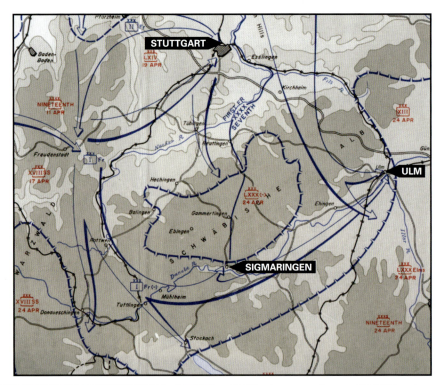

Nevertheless, General Devers was furious and sent an officer to de Lattre ordering him to withdraw immediately. De Lattre ignored the order and at dusk on April 23 the leading platoon reached Ulm to be joined at dawn by the 324th Infantry of the 44th Division. Both French and American forces launched their attack the following morning and by nightfall all resistance had ceased. The day ended with the French raising the Tricolour over the fort, just as Napoléon had done 140 years earlier.

COMMUNIQUE No. 383   April 26

Allied forces have reached the sea near the Dutch-German frontier, isolating a pocket of the enemy in the area of DELFZIJL.

We have launched an attack on BREMEN from the south and the east and are fighting in the eastern suburbs.

Enemy gun positions, an ammunition dump and several supply dumps in the BREMEN area, and infantry entrenched with self-propelled guns at WEHLDORF, north of BREMEN, were attacked by rocket-firing fighters and fighter-bombers. Medium bombers attacked defended positions in BREMEN.

ZEVEN has been cleared of the enemy and we advanced beyond it to the north and captured SELSINGEN.

Enemy ships in the Ems and Elbe estuaries and at CUXHAVEN, and road and rail traffic in northern Germany were hit with rockets and bombs. Strong points at LEER, oil storage plants at BRAKE, and a camp and defense works at OLDENBURG were attacked by fighter-bombers.

Coastal guns and fortified positions on Wangerooge Island, near the mouth of the Weser river were bombed by escorted heavy bombers.

Our infantry units cleared ESLARN and advanced southeast to the vicinity of SCHONTHAL. Other elements reached the vicinity of LAMBERTSNEUKIRCHEN and entered WENZENBACH in the area northeast of REGENSBURG.

To the east our armor cleared REGEN and entered ZWIESEL. Other armor advanced to a point 15 miles southeast of REGEN and 18 miles from the Austrian border.

In the area north of REGENSBURG our infantry reached the vicinity of REGENSTAUF and KARETH.

Our forces are along a ten-mile stretch of the Danube river from a point two miles west of REGENSBURG to KELHEIM.

South of NUREMBERG we entered SULZBURG and reached the Altmuhl river in the vicinity of HIRSCHBERG and GUNGOLDING. Several crossing of the Altmuhl river were made in the vicinity of GUNGOLDING and one bridge was captured intact.

With entry roads to Ulm now all converted to autobahns, it took Karel much time and effort to find the match on Stuttgarter Strasse — the old approach from the north.

474

West of GUNGOLDING we reached the vicinity of NEUDORF and captured RUPERTSBUCH.

South of RUPERTSBUCH we reached HARD and GAMMERSFELD, and to the southwest we are in the vicinity of DONAUWORTH on the Danube.

East and south of DILLINGEN we captured WERTINGEN and KNORINGEN, and reached ANHAUSEN.

German aircraft made 25 attempts to bomb a two-lane bridge we captured at DILLINGEN, but the span was undamaged and ten enemy planes were shot down. Enemy efforts to destroy the bridge with mines also failed.

A number of towns were taken in the collapsing Swabian Pocket south of STUTTGART.

Our units are approaching the Danube north of GUNZBURG.

We entered WIBLINGEN, on the Iller canal three miles south of ULM, and farther south we established bridgeheads across the canal at VOHRINGEN and ILLERTISSEN.

To the west in the Rhine plain, the Swiss border was reached in the vicinity of BASLE. We captured LORRACH and advance elements pushed ten miles northeast of the town.

Allied forces in the west captured 43,405 prisoners 24 April.

Rail traffic between LINZ and PRAGUE; communications targets in the PRAGUE-LINZ-MUNICH triangle; horse-drawn and motor vehicles moving southward in the INGOLSTADT area and in the Danube valley, and airfields in the MUNICH, AUGSBURG and LINZ areas were heavily attacked by fighter-bombers. A very large number of aircraft were destroyed or damaged on the ground.

Large ammunition dumps south of ULM and northwest of MUNICH, and an ordnance depot northwest of SALZBURG were bombed by medium and light bombers.

The Skoda armament works and an airfield at PILSEN; rail yards and facilities in the BERCHTESGADEN region at TRAUNSTEIN, SALZBURG, HALLEIN and BAD REICHENHALL were attacked by escorted heavy bombers in strength.

Uncertain as to Hitler's precise whereabouts, and with the knowledge that the Nazis were reported to be preparing to make a last stand in an Alpine redoubt, a massive knockout blow was planned by the RAF for Hitler's mountain retreat using over 350 Lancasters from Nos. 1, 5 and 8 Groups including No. 617 Squadron carrying 12,000lb Tallboys — their last mission of the war. Low cloud and snow covering the ground also made positive identification of the individual buildings extremely difficult. [1] Berghof. [2] SS Barracks. [3] Platterhof Hotel. [4] Göring's House. [5] Guest house. [6] Bormann's House. [7] Hotel Zum Türken (the SS headquarters). [8] Bomb-burst.

Twelve thousand-pound and other high-explosive bombs were dropped on the German Fuhrer's chalet near BERCHTESGADEN, the SS barracks in the grounds and his mountain refuge at the top of the Kehlstein five miles from the chalet by other escorted heavy bombers.

Eleven enemy aircraft were shot down during the day. Eighteen of our heavy bombers and 14 fighters are missing according to incomplete reports.

The oil storage depot at VALLO, in the OSLO fjord, was attacked last night by heavy bombers. The transformer station at PASING near MUNICH and the naval base of KIEL were bombed by light bombers.

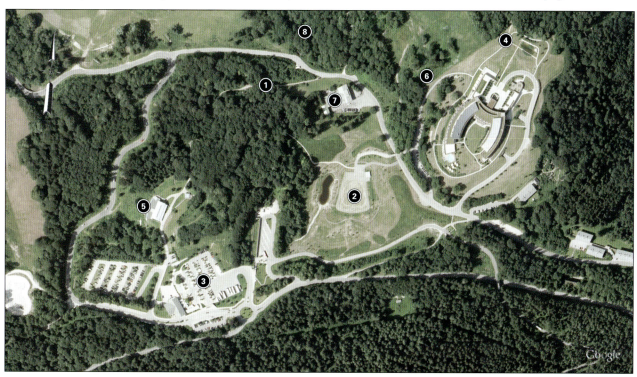

In efforts to expunge the history of the Third Reich from the map, virtually all has been swept away save for the Hotel Türken [7].

As we saw on page 470, when no reply was forthcoming to General Horrocks's message to the Bremen commander, from April 20, four infantry divisions — the 3rd, 43rd, 51st and 52nd — closed in around the city. Against stubborn defences, the fighting continued for five days, heavy and medium bombing attacks going in on the 25th. Bremen was finally clear of the enemy on the 27th. These infantrymen of the 3rd Division are marching along the Neuenlander Strasse just as a column of prisoners are led to the rear. (For more details see *After the Battle* No. 135.)

COMMUNIQUE No. 384   **April 27**

Allied forces west of DELMENHORST advanced three miles to reach RETHORN. We occupied the greater part of BREMEN where enemy opposition weakened.

Enemy gun positions and strong points east of LEER and north of BREMEN; shipping off the Frisian Islands and in the Ems estuary; road and rail transport and other communications targets in the area of FLENSBURG and RENDSBURG and west of OLDENBURG, and objectives south of OLDENBURG, were attacked by other fighter-bombers and rocket-firing fighters.

Medium bombers attacked rail yards at BUCHEN east of HAMBURG.

Our units have liberated EGER in Czechoslovakia and reached a point 27 miles to the south. West of the Czech-German border, 16 miles farther south we reached the vicinity of STADLERN.

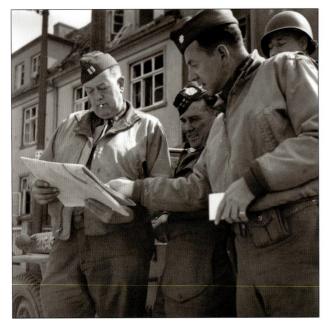

Left: Long before its capture, Bremen had been designated part of an American enclave to be established along the Weser in order to provide the American army of occupation with a deep-water seaport to supply its zone direct from the States. The first US military entered the city with the forward British troops.

On April 26, Lieutenant Colonel D. W. Mersevey of the American Military Government Detachment entered the city with the 3rd Division and was pictured here conversing with a British officer outside No. 304 Langemarckstrassse near the intersection with Neuenlander Strasse.

With the link-up between the Western Allies and Soviet forces now imminent, Eisenhower was well aware that he had to get the Russians to agree on the Rivers Elbe and Mulde as the stop-line. However, bridgeheads had already been established over the Elbe by the 83rd Division at Barby; the 6th Armored and 76th Division near Rochlitz; the 87th and 89th Divisions west of Chemnitz; the 69th Division east of Leipzig and the 2nd Division south-east of the city.

To the southeast, in Germany, our armor has entered ROHRNBACH and reached the vicinity of TITTLING, 11 miles northwest of the Austrian border.

In the area north and east of STRAUBING, we entered NEUKIRCHEN and reached the vicinity of GSCHWENDT.

Our units crossed the Danube river in several places between FRENGKOFEN and REGENSBURG and entered IRL.

Other troops crossed the Danube in the vicinity of KAPFELBERG and reached a point three miles south of REGENSBURG. Our cavalry elements have cleared that part of KELHEIM on the north bank of the Danube.

Farther west, we captured DIETFURT and entered EICHSTATT and INGOLSTADT.

In the area north of AUGSBURG our units moved to the Danube and are mopping up the north bank for a stretch of 11 miles. To the southwest, we advanced ten miles beyond the river on a front paralleling it for 20 miles. MUNSTERHAUSEN, 15 miles south of the Danube, was reached.

Two counter-attacks, one in battalion strength supported by armor, were beaten off at an autobahn bridge over the Danube near GUNZBURG. NEU ULM, across the river from ULM, was entirely cleared.

Along the Iller canal running south from ULM our units fanned out to the east, west and south. We reached a point 15 miles south of ULM.

The pocket south of STUTTGART was considerably reduced.

Our forces reached a point on the north shore of Lake Constance within 13 miles of FRIEDRICHSHAFEN, and are along the Swiss border from BASLE to the lake.

Deep penetrations were made into the BLACK FOREST. A 12-mile thrust to the east almost cut it in two.

From north of AUGSBURG to south of ULM, 11,335 prisoners were taken. Between ULM and the Rhine, 6,000 were captured.

Allied forces in the west captured 34,237 prisoners 25 April.

Road and rail communications in an area east of NUREMBERG to south of MUNICH and in a triangular area formed by MUNICH-PRAGUE-LINZ, and a motor convoy north of BERCHTESGADEN, were attacked by fighter-bombers.

Airfields east of MUNICH, southeast of STRAUBING and near PLATTLING were attacked by light and fighter-bombers. Many aircraft were destroyed or damaged on the ground.

Although troops of the 21st Army Group had reached the river in the north on the 19th it was not until the 29th that a brigade of the 15th (Scottish) Division accompanied by a Commando brigade crossed near Lauenburg. The 82nd Airborne Division, attached to the British Second Army, crossed the following day at nearby Bleckede.

On April 25 there were three contacts by Americans with the Soviets. The first took place at 11.30 a.m. here in this yard at Leckwitz, about 17 miles south of Torgau when a patrol led by 1st Lieutenant Albert Kotzebue met a rather un-communicative Soviet soldier on horseback. An hour later they crossed the Elbe near Strehla, three miles away, to make contact with the Russians. No photographers were present so the meeting was restaged the following day at the ferry site at Kreinitz. Later on the 25th another patrol from the 1st Battalion, 273rd Infantry, led by 2nd Lieutenant Bill Robertson, made contact with the Soviets at Torgau at 4 p.m. Then, 45 minutes later, a Jeep patrol led by Major Fred Craig met up with a Soviet patrol looking for the Americans near the village of Clanzschwitz, not far from where Kotzebue had come across the lone horseman earlier in the day.

COMMUNIQUE No. 385   April 28

Allied forces east of the Dutch-German frontier cleared the Rheiderland peninsula. We occupied the whole of BREMEN including the docks. West of ZEVEN we captured KIRCHTIMKE.

Enemy ships and barges off CUXHAVEN; road and rail traffic in the areas of WILHELMSHAVEN, OLDENBURG and BREMEN; motor transport between KIEL, WISMAR and WITTENBERGE, and a convoy on the PERLEBERG—KYRITZ road were attacked by fighter-bombers and rocket-firing fighters.

Our forces have effected a firm juncture with elements of the Russian First Ukrainian Army at TORGAU on the Elbe river.

To the south, our units reached a point two miles north of EGER in Czechoslovakia.

Our infantry captured FURTH, near the German-Czech frontier, and other elements reached the vicinity of DRACHSELSRIED in the area northwest of REGEN.

Our armor entered Austria at a point two miles south of the intersection of the German, Czechoslovakian and Austrian borders. Other armored elements entered GEGENBACH one mile west of the Austrian border.

In the area east of STRAUBING, our units reached a point one mile northwest of DEGGENDORF, the Danube river near BOGEN, and the vicinity of STRAUBING north of the river.

South of the Danube, we captured REGENSBURG. East of REGENSBURG our bridgehead across the Danube is eight miles wide and four miles deep. West of the town our bridgehead across the Danube is six miles wide and two and one-half miles deep.

Farther southwest we reached the Danube on an 11-mile front and crossed at EINING and at a point five miles southwest of EINING.

It was the Robertson meeting at Torgau which got the glory the following day when photographers arrived to record the event, symbolically staged on the broken road bridge. (For more, see *After the Battle* No. 88.) The delay in releasing the SHAEF communiqué covering the meeting was due to the necessity to wait for simultaneous announcements in Washington, London and Moscow.

INGOLSTADT has been captured. In the area east and northeast of the town, our armor captured MENNING and entered FORCHHEIM and MAILING. In an advance along the MUNICH—NUREMBERG autobahn our infantry reached a point three and one-half miles south of INGOLSTADT.

West of INGOLSTADT our units pushed five miles south of the Danube and to the southwest, we closed on AUGSBURG from north, west and south. Forward elements are within five miles of the city on the northwest and within eight miles of it to the south.

A number of points were reached on the Lech river along a front of 20 miles to the north and 20 miles to the south of AUGSBURG. From east of the Iller canal, armored units advanced 25 miles eastward to cross the Lech at LANDSBERG.

South of MEMMINGEN, armored spearheads thrust 20 miles southward to KEMPTEN, 12 miles from the Austrian border.

The pocket south of STUTTGART has been eliminated except for stragglers who are being mopped up.

Although the bridge had been blown, the Germans had also built a road-block at the eastern end.

The road bridge at Torgau was repaired and remained in use until a new single-span bridge was opened in July 1993. The following June German engineers blew up the original bridge amid much protest that a piece of history was being destroyed just months before the 50th anniversary of the meeting between East and West.

On the Swiss border, CONSTANCE was captured.

The BLACK FOREST pocket, now an area of about 250 square miles just north of the Swiss frontier, is being steadily reduced.

From ten miles east of INGOLSTADT to the Iller canal area, 11,346 prisoners were taken. Between the Iller canal and the Rhine, 6,500 were captured.

Allied forces in the west captured 46,694 prisoners 26 April.

Road and rail traffic in the PRAGUE-PILSEN—MUNICH triangle; enemy armor, motor transport, fortified buildings and an ammunition dump in the MUNICH and AUGSBURG areas; airfields near MUNICH, STRAUBING and SALZBURG; and a collection point for enemy troops at SCHROBENHAUSEN, between AUGSBURG and INGOLSTADT, were bombed by fighter-bombers.

During the day's operations two enemy aircraft were shot down. Seven of our fighters are missing.

This memorial was erected by the Soviets at Torgau in 1945.

For the first time, on April 29 the communiqué refers to events in the Alps where French forces had been fighting since August using both conventional infantry and the FFI. By January the Germans had halted to face their pursuers on a front along the Franco-Italian frontier. With them were elements from four Italian divisions. By April 24 the 1ère Division d'Infanterie Marocaine was advancing in the mountainous region bordering Italy along with a platoon of six M5 light tanks from the 1er Régiment de Fusiliers Marins — surely a first for the employment of armour at an altitude of over 6,000 feet!

COMMUNIQUE No. 386 — April 29

Allied forces advancing along both banks of the Weser river in the BREMEN area have occupied SEEHAUSEN and GROPELINGEN. Northwest of ROTENBURG we have advanced seven miles and reached HORSTEDT and VORWERK. Southwest of ZEVEN we captured KIRCHTIMKE.

Enemy strong points south of LEER and other objectives in LEER were attacked by fighter-bombers.

Our forces advanced three miles into Czechoslovakia and entered KARLSBACH, 16 miles south of TACHAU. Farther south we entered MAXBERG against strong enemy resistance.

North of REGEN, in Germany, we reached the vicinity of NEUKIRCHEN and entered OBER REID.

We captured DEGGENDORF and entered SCHOFWEG and OBERAUERBACH, east of DEGGENDORF.

Southeast of REGENSBURG, we reached the outskirts of AITERHOFEN and PERKAM and cleared ALTEGLOFSHEIM and THALMASSING.

In the area southwest of REGENSBURG, our troops cleared TEUGN and ABENSBERG and advanced six miles into the DURRENBUCHER FOREST.

South of INGOLSTADT we repulsed a small enemy counter-attack and reached the vicinity of MAINBERG and HIRNKIRCHEN.

Our units are closing in on MUNICH in a wide arc extending from north to southwest of the city. Advance elements are within 20 miles of the city.

Mechanized cavalry drove 15 miles southeast from the vicinity of NEUBERG to PFAFFENHOFEN. Infantry across the Danube, west of NEUBURG, was within 20 miles of MUNICH to the northwest after capturing HAAG and TANDERN.

Our forces across the Lech river north of AUGSBURG reached AINDLING and WILLPRECHTSZELL. We captured AUGSBURG including the garrison and the major general commanding it, and advanced to FRIEDBERG four miles farther east.

East and south of LANDSBERG we captured several towns including SCHOFFELDING, FINNING and STADL. Farther south along the Lech river, we reached SCHONGAU after a 20-mile advance from the northwest.

Other elements advanced 25 miles east from the KEMPTEN area to the vicinity of the Lech river between SCHONGAU and the Austrian frontier. BURGGEN, LECHBRUCK and DIETRINGEN were captured.

To the south FUSSEN was taken and we crossed into Austria in that vicinity. All organized resistance in the BLACK FOREST ceased and the area is being mopped up.

On the Maritime Alps front, our forces were at or across the Italian frontier for a stretch of 50 miles from the Ligurian sea. At some points we pushed ten miles into Italy.

From the vicinity of NEUBURG to the Iller canal area we captured 24,887 prisoners, including three generals, and between the Iller canal and the Rhine, more than 7,000 were taken.

Allied forces in the west captured 57,533 prisoners 27 April.

Following the crossing of the River Po on April 24 by the Eighth Army, also advancing towards the Alps, German forces were ordered to withdraw to northern Italy. Five days later Generalleutnant Max Pemsel, the Chief-of-Staff of the Armee Ligurien, signed an order that all units under his command were to surrender to the Allies. The same day a general surrender was signed at the headquarters of the Supreme Allied Commander in the Mediterranean at Caserta (see *After the Battle* No. 48). According to the terms of the armistice which had been signed with the Italians in September 1943, only British and Americans were permitted to occupy Italy but the French had already crossed the border and refused to pull back. Arguments continued for several weeks until the best part of the contested territory was vacated on July 10. (Some slight adjustments were made to France when Italy signed a peace treaty in 1947.)

COMMUNIQUE No. 387   April 30

Allied forces crossed the Leda river near its junction with the Ems river and occupied most of LEER. Good advances were made in the area northwest of ROTENBURG where the enemy salient between BREMEN and ZEVEN is being reduced.

Farther east we are mopping up in LAUENBURG after crossing the Elbe river upstream from HAMBURG against moderate resistance.

Enemy positions southeast of HAMBURG and near LAUENBURG, and road and rail transport between LAUENBURG and LUDWIGSLUST and east of SCHWERIN, were attacked by fighter-bombers and rocket-firing fighters. Thirteen enemy aircraft were shot down over our Elbe bridgehead.

In Czechoslovakia our forces captured an airfield one mile northeast of EGER which was strongly defended by 1,000 enemy troops. Three hundred and fifty prisoners were taken.

Northeast of STRAUBING, in Germany, our troops captured LAM.

Southeast of REGENSBURG our armor captured PLATTLING, entered HAADER and advanced eight miles southeast of the town.

Our infantry elements cleared STRAUBING and reached the vicinity of FIERLBRUNN. Other units captured MALMERSDORF, entered SCHATZHOFEN and reached the vicinity of MOOSBURG.

At MOOSBURG a POW camp of 27,000 British and American troops was liberated.

Farther west our infantry reached the vicinity of HIRSCHBACH, 22 miles north of MUNICH.

Our forces captured and cleared the concentration camp near DACHAU. Approximately 32,000 persons were liberated. three hundred SS guards at the camp were quickly overcome.

General Patton, later Military Governor of Bavaria, destroyed all the evidence and today even the wall has been demolished.

En route to Munich on April 29, the 42nd and 45th Divisions arrived at Dachau, eight miles to the north-west. The conditions within the camp were horrendous with piles of cadavers heaped outside the crematorium. The official US history would have us believe that 'delirious with joy, some of the pitiful survivors of the camp rushed the electrically-charged wire enclosure and died in their moment of liberation. Others hunted down their wardens, many of whom had changed into prison garb to hide among the inmates, and beat them to death with stones, clubs, fists.' However, Signal Corps photographer T/4 Arland B. Musser took this photo which SHAEF released with this caption: 'Soldiers of the 45th Infantry Division, US Seventh Army, order SS men to come forward after one of their number tried to escape from the Dachau concentration camp after it was liberated by US Forces. Men on the ground feign death by falling as the guards fired a volley at the fleeing SS man. 157th Regiment 29 April 1945'. However, the truth, revealed by Colonel Howard A. Buechner in his book *Dachau* published in 1986, is rather different. During the war, 1st Lieutenant Dr Buechner was a medical officer with the 3rd Battalion 157th Infantry of the 45th Division: '1st Lieutenant Jack Busheyhead was the Executive Officer. He was in command of the camp and a small cadre of men armed with rifles, pistols, a Browning automatic rifle and two machine guns. He could no longer reject the role which fate had fashioned for him and for which he seems to have been predestined. Acting with what he believed to be compelling justification, he became an instrument of vengeance and recompense for the atrocities which he had witnessed. In a matter of minutes, he ordered his prisoners to line up along a high brick wall and disposed of them with a few bursts of machine-gun fire. He then armed three or four inmates with pistols and allowed them to the satisfaction of completing the execution.'

Just as Hitler was making his final farewells to those loyal members of his staff in the Führerbunker in Berlin, 300 miles to the south in Munich the 20th Armored Division was rolling into the city from the north-west.

Our armor entered the outskirts of MUNICH.

We reached the northern end of the Ammersee. Armored spearheads swung around its southern tip and pushed five miles northward along the eastern shore to HERRSCHING.

To the south, other armor reached SPATZENHAUSEN. We captured SAULGRUB and drove southward into the Bavarian Alps to OBERAMMERGAU.

South of FUSSEN we expanded our hold in Austria and advanced to the vicinity of ROSSSCHLAG.

In the area north of the eastern end of Lake Constance our units pushed southeast along a front of nearly 25 miles. Advances of up to 15 miles brought our forces to LEUTKIRCH and WEINGARTEN. From the MUNICH area to the Iller canal, we took 35,890 prisoners, and between the Iller canal and the Rhine, 3,500, including two generals.

Allied forces in the west captured 74,986 prisoners 28 April.

Several large road convoys mainly moving southward in the area east and south of PILSEN, and a large number of rail cars, many of them loaded with motor transport, in the same area were attacked by fighter-bombers. Throughout the day more than 900 road vehicles and rail cars were destroyed or damaged.

Enemy strong points west of MUNICH, at HATTENHOFEN, MAMMENDORF and FURSTENFELDBRUCK, scattered road and rail traffic moving southward from MUNICH and airfields in the area east and southeast of the city were bombed by other fighter-bombers. Many enemy aircraft were destroyed or damaged on the ground.

Yesterday afternoon unescorted heavy bombers dropped over 600 tons of food supplies for the Dutch population in enemy-occupied Holland.

In the day's operations 17 enemy aircraft were shot down including those destroyed in the Elbe bridgehead area. Nine of our fighters are missing.

Elements of the 3rd and 42nd Divisions reached the city centre by midday, this picture being taken on Dachauer Strasse.

Where it all began — the Bürgerbräukeller on Rosenheimer Strasse. It was from here on November 9, 1923 that Hitler and his NSDAP followers set out on their revolutionary attempt to gain power. In 1935, two years after achieving his goal, Hitler explained what had gone wrong. 'I was following Mussolini's example too closely. I had meant the Munich Putsch to be the beginning of a "March on Berlin" which should carry us straight to power. From its failure I learnt the lesson that each country must evolve its own type and methods of national regeneration.'

The final ignominy. The 157th Infantry Regiment (the unit that we last saw clearing Aschaffenburg) of the Thunderbird Division have commandeered the beerhall for their CP. The GIs are Private Samuel Banz and Pfc Edward De Young with three released British POWs.

The National Socialist Party was given birth in Bavaria so it was only natural for its capital to be located in Munich. Here the embryo movement had tried to seize power and here the Party gave honour to its revered dead. Central to that aim was the King's parade ground — the Königsplatz — burial place of the Party's putsch martyrs killed in November 1923, the twin tombs lying just a few yards from its headquarters: the Brown House at No. 45 Brienner Strasse *(above left)*. The building, originally known as the Barlow Palace, was erected in 1828 and the Nazi Party purchased it on July 5, 1930. *Above right:* By 1945 the building was in a sorry state and the ruin was demolished, the empty site being earmarked for a historical centre documenting the city's Nazi era — a praiseworthy initiative in itself for a city that was seen as the ideological capital of the Third Reich. *Right:* In 2007 the foundations were exposed but the argument given for their demolition was that they dated from 1830, completely ignoring their historical significance to the Nazi era which was the very period to be recorded — a very German paradox!

By midday on that Monday, Soviet troops in Berlin were reported right outside the Chancellery in the Voss-Strasse and it was obvious that it might be overrun at any moment. After taking their formal leave of those remaining in the bunker, Eva Braun led the way to Hitler's study. The armoured door was closed and Otto Günsche took up station to prevent anyone entering. After an interval of ten minutes or so no sound had been heard and eventually Heinz Linge opened the door but when he was assailed by the strong smell of cordite and bitter almonds, Linge called for Bormann to lead the way. Linge describes the scene that was presented to them: 'Hitler was sitting on the left of the sofa, with his face bent slightly forward and hanging down to the right. With the 7.65mm he had shot himself in the right temple. The blood had run down on to the carpet and from this pool of blood a splash had got on the sofa. Eva Braun was sitting on his right. She had drawn both her legs up onto the sofa and was sitting there with cramped lips so that it immediately became clear to us that she had taken cyanide.' (See *Berlin Then and Now*.)

MAY 1945
SURRENDER

In his 'political statement', Hitler had nominated Grossadmiral Karl Dönitz, the head of the Kriegsmarine, as his successor. Thus on April 30, Dönitz became the Head of State of the German Reich and Supreme Commander of the Armed Forces, although a confirming telegram did not arrive from Berlin until the afternoon of May 1. (See *After the Battle* No. 128.) The situation of the German forces was dire: the army in the West was disintegrating; German forces in Italy had already surrendered, the Navy had suffered crippling losses and the air force had ceased to exist. Dönitz's headquarters were located 50 miles north of Hamburg in the Stadtheide Barracks (since demolished) at Plön.

COMMUNIQUE No. 388 May 1

Allied forces captured LEER on the right bank of the Ems river and advanced to the east. In the OLDENBURG area we occupied HUDE.

North of ZEVEN we reached the outskirts of BREMERVORDE. West of HAMBURG we are fighting in HORNEBURG.

We expanded our bridgehead over the Elbe at LAUENBURG and ten miles upstream made a second crossing in the vicinity of BLECKEDE.

An enemy airfield at BANZKOW, southeast of SCHWERIN and road transport in the area of SCHWERIN and PARCHIM were attacked by fighter-bombers. Twenty enemy aircraft were shot down near the airfield and others were destroyed on the ground.

Another link-up was made by our units with Russian forces in the town of APOLLENSDORF west of WITTENBERG.

Northeast of CHAM, our forces crossed the Czechoslovakian border in the vicinity of VSERUBY and farther south, in Germany, reached the vicinity of ECKERSBERG.

Our armor entered WEGSCHEID, one mile from the Austrian border, and entered GRIESBACH in the area southeast of DEGGENDORF.

Farther west, armored elements crossed the Isar river and reached a point two miles south of PLATTLING. Southeast of PLATTLING, our infantry entered KLEEGARTEN.

Northeast of LANDSHUT our units reached the Isar river in the vicinity of ALTHEIM and other elements entered ERGOLDSBACH. We entered LANDSHUT and reached the vicinity of OBERGLAIM, EDENLAND and BRUCKBERG.

In the area northeast of MUNICH, our infantry cleared FREISING and reached the vicinity of BERGLERN.

It is estimated that 110,000 Allied prisoners of war were liberated at MOOSBURG by our forces. Earlier estimates placed the figure at 27,000.

Organized resistance in all of MUNICH west of the Isar river has ceased. This is more than three-fourths of the city. Snipers are being cleared.

South of AUGSBURG an airfield with six jet-propelled planes and other aircraft was taken intact. Several pilots were in the cockpits preparing to take off when captured.

In the approaches to the Bavarian Alps, armored spearheads driving south made contact with others advancing east in the vicinity of OBERAU. From this area we pushed southeast of MITTENWALD on the German-Austrian border. Other advances to the west expanded our hold in Austria to a width of 20 miles and an average depth of five miles.

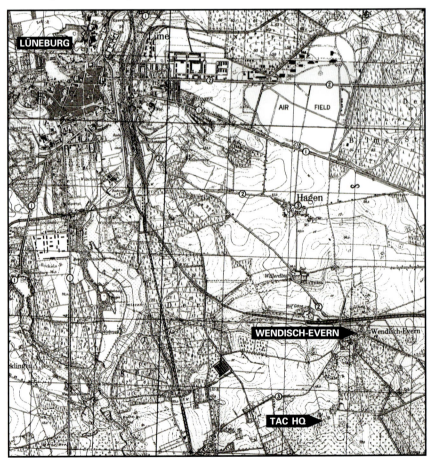

Also on May 1 Montgomery moved his 21st Army Group TAC HQ from Soltau (see map page 209) to Lüneburg Heath near the village of Wendisch-Evern. A flat area had been chosen on the top of the Timeloberg — soon to be renamed by the Field-Marshal: 'Victory Hill'.

From the Iller river westward to WANGEN we advanced up to ten miles southward. In a 15-mile drive through WANGEN we pushed about one mile across the Austrian border near the southeastern tip of Lake Constance. LINDAU was captured. Farther west, FRIEDRICHSHAFEN was occupied. Allied forces in the west captured 59,739 prisoners 29 April.

On the French Atlantic coast our forces have launched an attack to clear the Germans from the Ile d'Oleron. We captured ST TROJAN LES BAINS on the southeastern tip of the island and took a number of prisoners. Allied naval and air units supported the attack.

Rail and road transport in the area east and southeast of MUNICH, and from SALZBURG to PRAGUE and near PILSEN, and an airfield east of PILSEN were attacked by fighter-bombers.

Yesterday afternoon heavy bombers dropped some 1,250 tons of food supplies for the Dutch population in enemy-occupied Holland.

German soldiers were now anxious to avoid being captured by the Russians so made strenuous efforts to surrender to the Western Allies. When advancing US forces reached the Elbe they found the opposite bank lined with Germans desperate to reach the Americans before being overtaken by Soviet units.

This was the scene at Tangermünde, 50 miles west of Berlin, on May 1 where a signboard erected by the 405th Infantry Regiment welcomed the Red Army. The SHAEF censor has obliterated the identification of the division concerned — the 102nd.

COMMUNIQUE No. 389   May 2

Allied forces advanced seven miles beyond LEER to HESEL. We are two miles from the outskirts of OLDENBURG. West of HAMBURG we occupied HORNEBURG and STADE meeting no resistance. The Elbe bridgehead, east of HAMBURG, is now 30 miles in length and armor has broken out to the north. We captured GEESTHACHT and BOIZENBURG and crossed the HAMBURG—BERLIN autobahn.

Two airfields in the LUBECK area and road transport around LUBECK and SCHWERIN were bombed by our medium and fighter-bombers.

Northeast of GRAFENAU, our forces crossed the Czechoslovakian border at two points.

Farther south, our armor crossed the Austrian border in the vicinity of OBERKAPPEL and entered OPPING northwest of LINZ.

We reached the vicinity of KOLLERSBERG, northeast of PASSAU, and an armored column advanced into Austria to reach a point 23 miles southeast of PASSAU. West of PASSAU we entered KRIESTORF and reached the vicinity of PORNDORF south of DEGGENDORF.

Advancing rapidly against light resistance, our armor reached the Inn river in the vicinity of BRAUNAU. Other armored elements captured EGGENFELDEN and entered KOSSLARN northeast of BRAUNAU.

Eighteen miles north-east of Plön lies Oldenburg on the promontory separating the ports of Kiel and Lübeck in the Baltic. This photo of Canadian troops — the Fusiliers Mont Royal — mounting a combined infantry/tank attack was taken sometime during the period from April 25 to May 4 when the town fell. The customary technique was for the infantry to move within striking distance of the enemy and then for the armour, including flame-throwing 'Crocodiles', to move in to soften up the target.

Whereas the US-Soviet link-up on the Elbe was mainly a delicate tactical operation to avoid the two Allies clashing with each other, the British-Soviet link-up on the Baltic, which occurred a week later, was governed by real military, strategic and political considerations. As a result, it had all the characteristics of a race as to who would arrive there first as both sides were about equal distance from Wismar. About mid-April, Eisenhower ordered Montgomery to advance to the Baltic shore as quickly as possible to seal off Schleswig-Holstein and Denmark, partly in order to cut off the German forces there, partly to intercept the mass of fugitives trying to escape from the Red Army, but also in order to prevent the approaching Soviets from advancing into Denmark. To accomplish this, the Allies needed to cross the Elbe and reach the Baltic port of Wismar, located some 30 miles east of Lübeck (see map page 486), even though it lay 35 miles within the future Soviet zone of occupation. The thrust to the Baltic to forestall Russian entry into Denmark was a remarkable departure from Eisenhower's normal policy. The stated US military doctrine followed generally throughout the war was to concentrate everything on achieving military victory over the armed forces of the enemy, and not risk any lives for purely political purposes. It was for that reason that Eisenhower had halted the advance to Berlin and also decided not to advance to Prague, but instead concentrate on a thrust into Austria to deny the Germans a National Redoubt. However, and in contrast, his decision for a drive to the Baltic, resulting from a request by the British Chiefs-of-Staff, was clearly chiefly motivated by political considerations. The 6th Airborne Division, albeit that at the beginning of May it was part of the US XVIII Airborne Corps, was the only British unit to meet the Russians face to face.

From the very north of Germany to the border with Austria. Garmisch-Partenkirchen had been the venue for the Nazi Winter Olympics in 1936. Hitler's showpiece games were intended to show the Third Reich at its grandest, yet nine years later Garmisch was the scene of its demise as weary troops surrendered in their droves.

We captured OBERHOCKING, south of LANDAU, and pushed 12 miles to the southwest.

Our units cleared LANDSHUT and repulsed an enemy counter-attack of 200 infantry southwest of the town. South of LANDSHUT we cleared HUBENSTEIN and reached the vicinity of DORFEN.

The capture of MUNICH was completed. Southeast of MUNICH our units reached the Mangfall river and south of the city we circled around the Wurmsee from north and south and continued five miles east of it.

Our forces crossed the Austrian frontier north of SCHARNITZ, ten miles northwest of INNSBRUCK. GARMISCH-PARTENKIRCHEN, north of the border to the west, was reached.

Near the Plansee in Austria, we took a prison camp and liberated a number of high-ranking French and Belgian civil and military officials including seven French generals. Gains southward were made generally through difficult alpine terrain in Austria. South of FUSSEN we advanced ten miles along the Lech river to within 35 miles of the Italian border.

West of the Iller river along a 20-mile front from IMMENSTADT to BREGENZ, we gained up to eight miles southward. South of BREGENZ we pushed five miles into Austria.

From the MUNICH area to the Iller canal 26,946 prisoners, including five German generals, were taken during the 24 hours ending midnight 30 April.

Enemy resistance on the Ile d'Oleron on the French Atlantic coast has been eliminated. The enemy was overcome rapidly following the liberation of the capital, ST PIERRE D'OLERON. The commandant of German defenses on the island surrendered and numerous prisoners were taken.

An ammunition plant near STOD, 16 miles southwest of PILSEN, was attacked by light bombers.

During the day 13 enemy aircraft were shot down, five of them in the Elbe bridgehead area. One of our fighters is missing. Food supplies for the Dutch population were dropped at THE HAGUE and ROTTERDAM yesterday by approximately 400 heavy bombers.

These Hungarian troops fighting for the German cause were captured by the 103rd Infantry Division of the Seventh Army. The photo was taken at Garmisch on May 1 but not released until the 7th.

COMMUNIQUE No. 390   May 3

Allied forces, breaking out of their bridgehead over the Elbe river near LAUENBURG, completely overcame enemy resistance and drove to the Baltic coast and captured WISMAR. Between the Elbe and WISMAR we captured a number of towns including LUDWIGSLUST, HAGENOW, SCHWERIN and MOLLIN. Farther west we captured LUBECK.

North of BREMEN we occupied BREMERVORDE. East of LEER we captured REMELS and GROSSSANDER.

In Holland we eliminated the pocket near DELFZIJL, on the Ems estuary.

Enemy road movement in the triangular area of LUBECK, WISMAR and SCHWERIN was repeatedly attacked by fighter-bombers and rocket-firing fighters. More than 1,500 road vehicles were destroyed or damaged.

The communications center of ITZEHOE was attacked by medium bombers. Last night light bombers attacked objectives at KIEL.

During the day 32 enemy aircraft were shot down and others were destroyed or damaged on the ground. Four of our fighters are missing.

Our forces effected another juncture with Russian forces along the Elbe river at a point five miles southeast of WITTENBERGE.

Farther south our cavalry patrols reached the Czechoslovakian border at several points southeast of CHAM. In Austria our forces crossed the Inn river in the area west of BRAUNAU.

Our units are clearing the area 12 miles east of MUNICH along a 20-mile front. Huge quantities of enemy materiel were taken in the MUNICH area. About 85 planes, including ten jet-propelled aircraft, and more than 137,000 gas and smoke shells were captured. In this area a Hungarian infantry division surrendered intact.

South of MUNICH armored spearheads advanced rapidly to the east to reach the Inn river at two points south of ROSENHEIM.

In the Austrian alps our forces met increased resistance but advanced to a point eight miles west of INNSBRUCK and within 25 miles of the Italian border.

Thirty miles to the west we advanced along the Lech river to within 20 miles of Austria's southern border.

East of Lake Constance we pushed south from BREGENZ to DORNBIRN. Field-Marshals von Rundstedt, Freiherr von Weichs and von Sperrle and 18 German generals were captured.

Allied forces in the west captured 93,797 prisoners 30 April and 1 May.

Approximately 900 heavy bombers dropped food supplies for the Dutch population in enemy-occupied Holland. In the period 30 March to 30 April, 61,764 long tons of supplies were carried by air supply missions to our battle units and 64,076 casualties and 104,739 repatriates were evacuated.

On May 2 word had gone out from Dönitz at Plön to commanders facing the Russians to try to pull back west and negotiate local surrenders to the Allies. General der Infanterie Kurt von Tippelskirsch *(above)*, the commander of the 21. Armee, complied that afternoon and contacted General Gavin, the CO of the 82nd Airborne Division, which was now fighting in a ground role. Gavin accepted the capitulation but only for those troops who passed through Allied lines. *Below:* This shot was taken on May 3 at Grabow, the only trouble being that there are two villages of that name in area of the American airborne corps; one 15 miles east of Hamburg and the other ten miles north of the city. And with little background detail, it would be guesswork matching it up. The original caption explains that the men from the 21. Armee struggling to get away from the Russian army, capitulated to the 82nd Airborne Division. When released by SHAEF on May 14, additional information given was that 'thousands of prisoners were taken in the mopping-up area between the British Airborne Division and the 11th Armoured Division drive to Lübeck'.

COMMUNIQUE No. 391   May 4

OLDENBURG surrendered to Allied forces after fighting had taken place in the outskirts of the town. HAMBURG surrendered and we have occupied the city.

In the LUBECK area we captured BAD SEGEBERG and TRAVEMUNDE on the Baltic.

Our units have effected junctions with forces of the Second White Russian Army Group near WISMAR and GRABOW. Large and medium-sized enemy vessels and smaller craft off FLENSBURG, ECKERNFORDE, KIEL and LUBECK and in Kiel Bay and Lubeck Bay were attacked by rocket-firing fighters and fighter-bombers. Nine ships were sunk and over 100 others were left in a damaged condition, some of them in flames. Enemy road transport heading towards Denmark between FLENSBURG, KIEL, NEUMUNSTER and LUBECK was hit by fighter-bombers. Some 1,200 vehicles were destroyed or damaged. Many enemy aircraft were destroyed or damaged on the ground in attacks on airfields by other fighter-bombers. Eleven enemy aircraft were shot down.

Our forces crossed the Czechoslovakian border and reached a point one and one-half miles south of TAUS. Southeast of TAUS, other elements crossed the border and reached the area ten miles south of WALLERN.

On April 29, Major-General Lewis Lyne, commander of the 7th Armoured Division which had reached the outskirts of Hamburg, sent a message to the garrison commander, Generalmajor Alwin Wolz demanding the city's surrender. Consequently Hamburg was entered without bloodshed on May 3. Here the division's armour crosses the first bridge into the city.

The Alte Harburger Elbbrücke (left), built in 1892-99, was the very first bridge constructed across the Elbe in Hamburg. The span on the left is now named the Brücke des 17. Juni (recalling the 1953 uprising in East Berlin). Today, there is yet a third bridge off to the right.

Farther south, in Austria, we reached the vicinity of HASLACH and our armor advanced to a point seven miles northwest of LINZ.

Our infantry elements captured PASSAU, in Germany, and to the east, in Austria, our armor crossed the Muhl river in the vicinity of NEUFELDEN.

No doubt much to the astonishment of the local police, the British soon Anglicised the city streets!

491

By now Hitler's body had been partially cremated along with his bride in the Chancellery garden in Berlin. Marshal Zhukov wrote later that they had already started looking for the place where they had been buried but so far they could find no trace.

Meanwhile, on May 4, the 80th Infantry Division of the Third Army crossed the River Inn, which marked the frontier between Germany and Austria, via this pontoon bridge to enter Braunau, Hitler's birthplace on April 20, 1889.

Watched by a crowd lining the city wall, GIs of the 1st Battalion, 317th Infantry Regiment, set foot on Austrian soil.

Infantry, south of PASSAU, reached the Inn river in the vicinity of SCHARDING and OBERNBERG.

Our armor captured BRAUNAU and crossed the Inn river in that vicinity. Infantry elements crossed the Inn river at points northeast and east of BRAUNAU. East of the Inn river we captured HAUSERDING and reached a point 15 miles east of BRAUNAU.

Farther west, we advanced to the vicinity of NEUOTTING and reached the Inn river southwest of MUHLDORF.

Our infantry advanced rapidly to the southeast and captured WASSERBURG, 26 miles east of MUNICH.

Thirty-five miles east and southeast of MUNICH, our units were disposed along the Inn river over a front of 30 miles where crossings were effected at several points.

From the vicinity of ROSENHEIM we drove eastward along the autobahn to reach a point south of the Chiemsee, 25 miles west of SALZBURG and 28 miles northwest of BERCHTESGADEN.

In the Austrian alps, our forces approaching INNSBRUCK from the west met stubborn resistance after negotiations for the surrender of the city failed.

Forty miles to the west of INNSBRUCK, our units were slowed in their southeastward drive along the Lech river by difficult terrain and snow up to four feet deep.

The building where Hitler had been born, which later became a Nazi shrine (see *The Third Reich Then and Now*), was now shorn of its Nazi impedimentia and was taken over as the command post of the 80th Division. Its commander, Major General Horace McBride, is pictured here arriving in his specially armoured Jeep.

Russian generals Vishnevsky and Tonkogonov were liberated. Allied forces in the west captured 85,283 prisoners 2 May.

The large ammunition plant near STOD, southwest of PILSEN, was attacked by strong formations of light bombers. Fighter-bombers bombed road transport near the Chiemsee. From the day's operations, ten of our fighters are missing. Approximately 800 heavy bombers dropped over 1,500 long tons of food supplies for the Dutch population in enemy-occupied Holland.

After 1945 the building served in turn as a school, a bank and a library, later becoming a workshop for the disabled. The municipality was always uncomfortable over the connection with Hitler so just prior to the 100th anniversary of his birth, a memorial stone quarried from the former Mauthausen camp was placed in front, its inscription reading: For Peace, Freedom and Democracy. Never again Fascism, Millions of dead serve as a warning'. In 2014, the Austrian authorities announced that they had decided to turn the building into a museum called 'House of Responsibility'.

On the evening of Wednesday, May 2, Dönitz had moved his headquarters as far north as possible to Flensburg, right on the border with Denmark. There he took over the sports school building of the Naval Cadet School in the suburb of Mürwik. He then detailed Generaladmiral Hans-Georg von Friedeburg (his successor as C-in-C of the Navy) to make contact with Montgomery to offer to surrender all German forces in north-western Germany. Von Friedeburg was to be accompanied by General der Infanterie Eberhard Kinzel, Chief-of-Staff to the Oberbefehlshaber Nordwest, Generalfeldmarschal Ernst Busch; Konteradmiral Gerhard Wagner, military representative on Dönitz's staff; and one OKW staff officer, Major Hans Jochen Friedel. *Left:* Dönitz is pictured emerging from his headquarters building with his personal adjutant Korvettenkapitän Walter Lüdde-Neurath. *Right:* When we visited the building it was undergoing refurbishment (see *After the Battle* 128).

COMMUNIQUE No. 392   **May 5**

All German armed forces in northwest Germany, Holland and Denmark, including the garrisons on Heligoland and the Frisian Islands, have surrendered unconditionally to Allied forces. Hostilities ceased at 0800 hours British Double Summer Time today.

Enemy shipping off Wangerooge and FLENSBURG, in Kielforde and Eckernforde bay and south of the island of Aero, was attacked yesterday by fighter-bombers and rocket-firing fighters. Attacks were made on large and medium-sized surface vessels as well as on smaller craft and barges, and also on submarines. Seven ships were sunk and more than 70 damaged.

Airfields at LECK, HUSUM and GROSSENBRODE were hit by fighter-bombers which also attacked motor transport in the Schleswig-Holstein area north of BREMEN.

In the STENDAL area, the remnants of two German armies, the Ninth and Twelfth, surrendered to our units. North of REGEN our forces reached GRUN in Czechoslovakia. Other elements advanced to a point 22 miles northeast of REGEN and ten miles inside the Czechoslovakian border.

Farther south, our units crossed the Czechoslovakian border and reached a point 25 miles northeast of PASSAU.

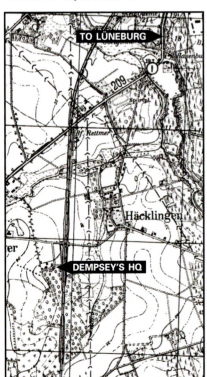 

On May 3, a German delegation seeking surrender terms — on the one hand for the city of Hamburg and the other for all German forces in northern Germany — was escorted to Lieutenant-General Dempsey's headquarters, then located in a villa at Häcklingen, just south of Lüneburg. In this heavily censored photo, the seven German parliamentaries are (L-R): Major Andrae, Generalmajor Alwin Wolz, Major Hans Jochen Friedel, Konteradmiral Gerhard Wagner, Generaladmiral von Friedeburg, Hauptmann Link (in front of von Friedeburg) and General der Infanterie Kinzel.

Fifteen minutes later four of the seven Germans — (L-R) Friedeburg, Wagner, Friedel and Kinzel — leave to be taken to see Montgomery at his TAC HQ on the Timeloberg hill.

Vacated by the psychiatric clinic that used the building until 2007, Dempsey's headquarters is today a rather sorry sight although it has been placed on the protected buildings list.

Lieutenant-Colonel Trumbull Warren, Montgomery's Personal Assistant, witnessed their arrival: 'At 0800 hours on May 3, Colonel Christopher Dawnay [Monty's Military Assistant] received a phone call from Colonel Michael Murphy [General Dempsey's Intelligence Officer] to say that he had received a delegation of four officers and, although General Dempsey had not spoken to them, it was thought that they wanted to try and compromise a surrender if they could get certain terms for Germany. Dawnay went immediately to Field-Marshal Montgomery and reported this to him. He told Dawnay to have Dempsey send them to his headquarters and when this was done to report back to him. He then pushed the buzzer in his caravan, sending for me.' Having been conducted to the Field-Marshal, the German party was lined up beside the Union flag flying from a temporary flagpole. After keeping them waiting (no doubt for the customary psychological period) Montgomery appeared. They saluted, and through his interpreter, Captain Derek Knee, the Field-Marshal asked: 'Who are these men?' and then on receiving an answer: 'What do they want?'

In his own inimitable style, Montgomery described what happened next: 'They said, "We've come here from Feldmarschall Busch to ask you to accept the surrender of the three German armies that are now withdrawing in front of the Russians in Mecklenburg between Rostock and Berlin. They are the 3rd Panzer, the 12th and 21st Armies". I said, "No, certainly not. These armies are fighting the Russians and therefore if they surrender to anybody it must be to the Russians — it has nothing to do with me and I am not going to have any dealings with anything on my eastern flank from Wismar to Domitz on the Elbe, on which flank we are now in close contact with the Russians. This is the Russians' business. A Russian peace, therefore you surrender to the Russians. Now this subject is closed." I then said to them, "Are you prepared to surrender to me the German forces on my western and northern flanks — that is to say, all the German forces between Lübeck and Holland, and all those forces that they have in support of them? These forces including the German army in Denmark — will you surrender those?" They said, "No". So far it had been a very good discussion. Then they said, "We are most anxious about the condition of civilians in the areas of Lübeck and on the northern flank — we are very anxious about them and we would like to come to some agreement with you by which these civilians can be saved slaughter in battle. We thought perhaps you would make some plan with us whereby you would advance slowly and we would withdraw slowly and all the civilians would be all right." So far we had not got very far. I said, "No. There is nothing doing. I am not going to discuss any conditions at all as to what I am going to do. I wonder whether you officers know what is the battle situation on the Western Front? In case you don't I will show it to you." I produced a map which showed the battle situation. That situation was a great shock to them. They were quite amazed and very upset. I was perfectly frank and held back no secrets. They were in a condition — and in a very good, ripe condition — to receive a further blow.' At this stage, however, the Field-Marshal considered a break for lunch would give the German officers time to reflect on what he had said. In a tent by themselves, they had their lunch in the presence of one British officer.

When Montgomery advised Eisenhower that overtures for negotiations were being made, the Supreme Commander declared that only unconditional surrender would be accepted. He added that an offer to give up Denmark, the Netherlands, the Frisian Islands, Heligoland, and Schleswig-Holstein could be considered as a tactical matter and the surrender accepted. Any larger offer, such as a proposal to give up Norway or forces on another front, would have to be handled at SHAEF headquarters. After lunch the Field-Marshal sent for the German delegation. 'I said to them, "You must clearly understand three points. One. You must surrender to me unconditionally all the German forces in Holland, in Friesland, including the Frisian Islands, Heligoland, and all other islands, in Schleswig-Holstein and in Denmark. Two. Once you have done that I am then prepared to discuss with you the implications of the surrender — that is to say I am prepared to say to you how we will dispose of the German forces, how we will occupy the area concerned, how we will deal with the civilians and so on. Once you have done Point Number One I will discuss Point Number Two. (You see, they wanted me to do Point Number Two first.) Three. If you don't agree to Point Number One I shall go on with the war and will be delighted to do so and am ready. All your soldiers will be killed. These are the three points — there is no alternative — one, two, three. Finished!" Then they said to me, "We came here entirely for the purpose of asking you to accept surrender of these German armies on your eastern flank and we have been given powers to agree to that subject only. We have no power to agree to what you now want. That is a new one on us. But two of us will now go back again to where we came from, get agreement and come back again. Two will stay here with you".' The Field-Marshal then drafted a minute on what had been discussed and proposed, this being signed by himself and von Friedeburg. Von Friedeburg and Major Friedel then took the document back to Dönitz at Flensburg, escorted through Hamburg and into the German lines by Lieutenant-Colonel Trumbull Warren. They had instructions to return by 6 p.m. the next day. The other two German officers remained at the Field-Marshal's headquarters.

Early the following morning, Friday, May 4, D Squadron of the 11th Hussars, stationed at Quickborn, ten miles north of Hamburg, were warned to expect the delegation returning. The Germans arrived in the afternoon and were halted by No. 4 Troop.

Captain Toby Horsford went forward to investigate and shortly afterwards 21st Army Group staff officers arrived to escort the German officers back to Montgomery. *Right:* The meeting took place here on the Kieler Strasse just north of Quickborn.

Meanwhile, at his headquarters, Field-Marshal Montgomery was confident the Germans would return with full powers to sign the surrender. At 5 p.m. he called a press conference at which he outlined fully what had taken place the previous day and what he hoped would happen at 6 p.m. Here the Field-Marshal reads the terms of surrender. Of the five Germans sitting round the table three were to die shortly afterwards in violent circumstances. Major Friedel (just out of the picture to the left) was killed in a motor accident while being driven to Reims on May 20, and Generaladmiral von Friedeburg (behind the microphones) committed suicide on May 23. After the surrender General der Infanterie Kinzel (right) was detailed to set up a small liaison HQ to relay 21st Army Group instructions to the German Army. He was permitted to retain his sidearm — and also wangled an attractive blonde as his personal assistant. When Montgomery's Chief-of-Staff, Major-General Sir Francis de Guingand, heard of the appointment, it was swiftly terminated and on June 25 Kinzel shot both the girl and himself (see *After the Battle* No. 128). After the war, Konteradmiral Wagner (on von Friedeburg's right) served in the Naval Department of the West German Defence Ministry. Odd man out with his back to the camera, and a late arrival: Oberst Fritz Poleck from the staff of OKW. Captain Knee in the spectacles stands beside Montgomery ready to translate.

In 1958 the British forces handed over military control of the area to the new Bundeswehr and Victory Hill then became part of a battle training area. Today nothing marks the spot where Montgomery's headquarters once stood.

Instrument of Surrender

of

All German armed forces in HOLLAND, in northwest Germany including all islands, and in DENMARK.

1. The German Command agrees to the surrender of all German armed forces in HOLLAND, in northwest GERMANY including the FRISIAN ISLANDS and HELIGOLAND and all other islands, in SCHLESWIG-HOLSTEIN, and in DENMARK, to the C.-in-C. 21 Army Group. This to include all naval ships in these areas. These forces to lay down their arms and to surrender unconditionally.

2. All hostilities on land, on sea, or in the air by German forces in the above areas to cease at 0800 hrs. British Double Summer Time on Saturday 5 May 1945.

3. The German command to carry out at once, and without argument or comment, all further orders that will be issued by the Allied Powers on any subject.

4. Disobedience of orders, or failure to comply with them, will be regarded as a breach of these surrender terms and will be dealt with by the Allied Powers in accordance with the accepted laws and usages of war.

5. This instrument of surrender is independent of, without prejudice to, and will be superseded by any general instrument of surrender imposed by or on behalf of the Allied Powers and applicable to Germany and the German armed forces as a whole.

6. This instrument of surrender is written in English and in German.

    The English version is the authentic text.

7. The decision of the Allied Powers will be final if any doubt or dispute arises as to the meaning or interpretation of the surrender terms.

B. L. Montgomery
Field-Marshal

4 May 1945
1830 hrs

Top left: The following day an oak plaque commemorating the signing was placed on Victory Hill but this was soon stolen, then replaced, yet vandalised again. *Top right:* In November 1945 a permanent stone memorial was erected by Royal Engineers, but this too was subjected to damage and graffitti and the bronze plaque stolen. As a consequence, a round-the-clock guard had to be employed, using five Germans in shifts, but after ten years the cost had become prohibitive, and with the imminent withdrawal of BAOR (the post-war successor to the 21st Army Group) from northern Germany, the safety of the monument could no longer be guaranteed, so it was dismantled and re-erected on the parade ground at Sandhurst. The foundation was still visible in 1975 but it has since been ground into dust by German tanks!

Today an inscribed boulder has been placed at the base of Victory Hill but it, too, has had its inscription defaced.

The ultimate prize: Hitler's private residence on the mountain above Berchtesgaden captured on May 4. The 101st Airborne Division and the 2ème Division Blindée had specific orders to take the town but Major General John O'Daniel was determined that his men of the 3rd Infantry Division should have the glory. Sending the 7th Infantry ahead with all speed, a patrol headed by 2nd Lieutenant William Miller entered Berchtesgaden at 3.58 p.m. (see *After the Battle* No. 9). They soon found the Berghof, badly damaged from the raid by No. 617 Squadron on April 24. All has now been totally expunged from the map, see page 475.

In Austria, we are along the west bank of the Muhl river in the area 20 miles northwest of LINZ. North of LINZ our armor cleared ZWETTL, REICHENAU and GRAMASTETTEN and reached ALTENBERG, three miles northeast of LINZ.

Our infantry elements crossed the Inn river at a point eight miles south of PASSAU and cleared WAIZENKIRCHEN, 22 miles to the southeast.

Other infantry units advanced rapidly to clear SULZBACH, 18 miles southwest of LINZ. West of LINZ we cleared RIED and AICHKIRCHEN.

Fourteen miles northeast of SALZBURG our units made rapid advances to clear STRASSWALCHEN. SALZBURG surrendered to our mechanized cavalry forces. We captured BERCHTESGADEN.

To the southwest, in Austria, our forces took INNSBRUCK, and drove through the BRENNER PASS to link up at VIPITENO, Italy, with Fifth Army units pushing northward. Other forces fanning out from INNSBRUCK advanced 18 miles northeast along the Inn river.

Following our juncture in Italy practically all organized resistance collapsed along a 70-mile front extending from 30 miles east of Austria's western border with Germany to 15 miles east of INNSBRUCK.

We took 48,100 prisoners between SALZBURG and the Iller river and 1,500 from the Iller river to Lichtenstein. Prisoners included 14 generals. Allied forces in the west captured 412,493 prisoners 3 May.

Airfields, rail yards and rail and motor transport in southwestern Czechoslovakia and northern Austria, and motor transport between SALZBURG and INNSBRUCK were attacked by fighter-bombers. In the attacks on airfields a number of aircraft were destroyed on the ground and others were damaged. One enemy aircraft was shot down. Five of our fighter-bombers are missing.

Heavy bombers dropped over 400 long tons of food for the Dutch population in enemy-occupied Holland.

A 50th birthday present to himself. Hitler's mountain-top retreat — officially the Kehlsteinhaus but targeted by the Allied air forces as far back as October 1944 as 'The Eagle's Nest' — proved to be a lasting tourist attraction . . . then as now.

In September 1945, General Eisenhower had the opportunity of visiting Hitler's eyrie with General Mark Clark who commanded the Fifth Army in Italy. Cigarette in hand, the Supreme Commander appears to be in a thoughtful mood as he ponders on past days in the Eagle's Nest before adding his signature to the table.

COMMUNIQUE No. 393 May 6

Allied forces in Czechoslovakia reached the vicinity of DURNBACH northwest of PILSEN, and DARMSCHLAG, 25 miles southwest of PILSEN.

South of KLATTAU, we entered BRUNST and reached a point 32 miles east of REGEN. In Austria, armored and infantry elements entered the cities of URFAHR and LINZ on the Danube. We captured a bridge intact across the Danube river.

North of the Danube, to the east of LINZ, our units reached the vicinity of WARTBERG and RIED. South of the Danube, our infantry advanced rapidly to capture STEYR and WARTBERG southeast of LINZ. We captured bridges intact across the Krems and the Enns rivers.

West of LINZ, we occupied EFERDING and reached HORSCHING. Southwest of LINZ, along the Ager river, we captured VOCKLABRUCK and LAMBACH.

The German Army Group G, composed of two armies which were spread over an area of some 9,500 square miles from the Rhine east to about 20 miles beyond SALZBURG, and south of our lines to the Italian and Swiss borders, surrendered. The capitulation is effective at noon May 6, but immediate announcements made to troops of both sides, ordered all combat to cease at once. One army within the group surrendered effective 1800 hours May 5.

The unconditional surrender terms included the provision that all troops were to stand fast in place with their arms and equipment.

Josef Thorak was an Austrian-German sculptor who had joined Arno Breker in 1933 as one of the two 'official sculptors' of the Third Reich. Albert Speer, Hitler's architect, had built him this mansion at Baldham near Munich which the XV Corps took over for their headquarters. On May 5 this became the setting for the surrender ceremony of Heeresgruppe G.

Generalleutnant Hermann Foertsch signed on behalf of Generalfeldmarschall Kesselring.

Thorak died in 1952 and today his estate is owned by the government of Bavaria. The grounds are overgrown, protected by security fencing, the building now being used as the storage depot of the Archaeological Collection of the City of Munich.

Two more local surrenders took place, the first at 3 p.m. on May 5 in the civic centre *(right)* in Innsbruck, Austria.

A secret prison camp deep in the Alps was captured and several world-famous prisoners of Nazis were liberated. They included Edouard Daladier and Paul Reynaud, former Premiers of France, and Generals Gamelin and Weygand. Kurt Schuschnigg, former Chancellor of Austria, and Leon Blum, former socialist Premier of France, had been imprisoned there but were hurried away a few hours before the camp was captured.

Colonel Wilhelm Buchner, former aide to Hitler, and Reichminister Frank, former Gauleiter of Poland, have been captured. Allied forces in the west captured over 176,000 prisoners 4 May.

During the first four days of May more than 3,800 long tons of supplies were carried by air supply missions to our battle units and more than 3,700 casualties and over 11,300 repatriates were evacuated.

Yesterday heavy bombers dropped 1,100 long tons of food supplies for the Dutch population in enemy-occupied Holland.

Below: **There, General der Panzertruppen Erich Brandenberger surrendered the 19. Armee (a part of Heeresgruppe G) to Major General Edward H. Brooks of VI Corps.**

Then, on May 6 at Wageningen in Holland, Generalleutnant Paul Reichelt, the Chief-of-Staff to Generaloberst Johannes Blaskowitz, surrendered all German forces in the Netherlands to Lieutenant-General Charles Foulkes, commander of the I Canadian Corps.

The capitulation ceremony took place in the lounge bar of the Hotel de Wereld on what has now been renamed 'Liberation Street'. The room is now back in use as a hotel lounge. (For more detail on all the German surrenders, see *After the Battle* No. 48.)

COMMUNIQUE No. 394 May 7

Our forces liberated PILSEN, reached the vicinity of MAIERSGRUN and entered WESENAU, northwest of PILSEN.

To the west and south, our units reached TSCHERNOSCHIN and BISCHOFTEINITZ and freed STRIBRO and KLATTAU. Our infantry reached KUNKOWITZ and GUTWASSER. Other elements reached to the Otava river in the area 20 miles northeast of REGEN.

Southeast of PILSEN, we occupied WINTERBERG and crossed the Muldau river to reach SCHATTAWA.

In the area 22 miles north of LINZ our units advanced to the Muldau river. South and east of LINZ we reached LEONDING and ENNS. Other elements advanced to WALDNEUKIRCHEN, southeast of LINZ.

In the vicinity of ROITHAM 2,000 Hungarians surrendered to our forces.

An order by SS-Reichsfuhrer Heinrich Himmler on 14 April that no prisoners in notorious Dachau concentration camp 'shall be allowed to fall into the hands of the enemy alive' has come into Allied possession. He had ordered the camp evacuated 'immediately'.

Distinguished Allied prisoners released by Nazis included Lieutenant The Viscount Lascelles, nephew of King George VI; Captain John Alexander Elphinstone, nephew of Queen Elizabeth; First Lieutenant John G. Winant, Jr., son of the American ambassador to Great Britain, and General Bor-komorowski who commanded the uprising in WARSAW. All had been released under Swiss diplomatic protection.

Prisoners taken in Austria included former German ambassador von Mackensen, ex-Foreign Minister von Neurath and General Beck.

Our forces in accordance with the terms of the German surrender in Holland, northwest Germany and Denmark are proceeding with the occupation of enemy-held territory. Allied forces in the west captured 398,630 prisoners 5 May. More than 350 heavy bombers dropped food for the Dutch population yesterday.

SHAEF's HQ, the so-called 'little red schoolhouse', was located on Rue Henri Jolicoeur, since renamed Rue du President Franklin Roosevelt (see page 360). Unfortunately the main entrance further up the street, through which the Germans entered the building to ascend to the War Room on the first floor, has been closed and replaced by a new one in the foreground.

Following von Friedeburg's appearance at the 21st Army Group surrender on Friday, May 4, arrangements had been made for him to proceed to SHAEF headquarters in Reims. Bad weather on Saturday morning delayed his arrival with Oberst Poleck so instead of landing at Reims their aircraft had to divert to Brussels which meant a journey by road of 125 miles. *Left:* They arrived just after 5 p.m. Von Friedeburg's intention was just to surrender the forces facing the Western Allies (as by then negotiations in the Netherlands were already over), but Eisenhower refused to continue discussions unless the Eastern Front was included. It was to be the total unconditional surrender of all German forces and there was to be no bargaining. When von Friedeburg explained that he did not have authority to surrender both fronts, a message was relayed to Flensburg asking that either he be given permission to sign or the head of the OKW be sent for that purpose. *Right:* Generaloberst Jodl arrived with his aide, Major Wilhelm Oxenius, at 6 p.m. Sunday evening wearing a somewhat frosty face as he passed von Friedeburg in the corridor. The escorting officer is Major-General Kenneth Strong, head of the intelligence section (G-2) at SHAEF. Jodl's letter of authority from Dönitz used the word 'Waffenstillstand' (armistice) and he tried to explain why an overall capitulation was impossible but this ploy was given short shrift by Eisenhower. Giving Jodl an ultimatum, the latter sent a signal to Dönitz asking permission to agree to the Allied terms of unconditional surrender. The reply was received just after midnight.

Seated around the table in SHAEF's War Room, at the rear are (L-R): Lieutenant-General Sir Frederick Morgan, Deputy Chief-of-Staff; Général François Sevez representing Général Alphonse Juin, Chief-of-Staff of French Forces; Admiral Harold M. Burrough, C-in-C Allied Naval Expeditionary Forces; Lieutenant General Walter Bedell Smith; Major General Ivan Susloparoff, the Soviet liaison officer at SHAEF; and Lieutenant General Carl Spaatz, Commanding General of the US Tactical and Strategic Air Forces. Standing behind Général Sevez is Captain Harry Butcher, Naval Aide to General Eisenhower. Jodl put his signature to the document on behalf of the German High Command at 2.41 a.m. Sunday morning. It was then counter-signed by Smith on behalf of Eisenhower, Susloparoff and Sevez.

At the concusion of the signing, General Jodl got to his feet and stood to attention. Addressing General Smith he said in English; 'I want to say a word'. Then he lapsed into German, which was later interpreted as: 'General! With this signature the German people and German armed forces are — for better or worse — delivered into the victor's hands. In this war, which has lasted more than five years, both have achieved and suffered more than perhaps any other people in the world. In this hour I can only express the hope that the victor will treat them with generosity.'

SPECIAL COMMUNIQUE May 8
All German land, sea and air forces in Europe were unconditionally surrendered to the Allied Expeditionary Force and simultaneously to the Soviet High Command, at 0141 hours Central European Time, 7 May. The surrender terms, which will become effective at 2301 Central European time, 8 May, were signed by an officer of the German High Command. Allied Expeditionary Forces have been ordered to cease offensive operations, but will maintain their present positions until the surrender becomes effective.

Jodl was brought to trial before the International Military Tribunal at Nuremberg and found guilty on each of the four indictments of which he was accused. On the night of October 15/16, 1946, he was the last but one to die on the gallows. The other executed men were Joachim von Ribbentrop, Ernst Kaltenbrunner, Alfred Rosenberg, Hans Frank, Wilhelm Frick, Fritz Sauckel and Arthur Seyss-Inquart. (For more see *The Third Reich Then and Now*.)

Men and women of the Allied Expeditionary Forces:
The crusade on which we embarked in the early summer of 1944 has reached its glorious conclusion. It is my special privilege, in the name of all Nations represented in this Theater of War, to commend each of you for valiant performance of duty. Though these words are feeble they come from the bottom of a heart overflowing with pride in your loyal service and admiration for you as warriors.

Your accomplishments at sea, in the air, on the ground and in the field of supply, have astonished the world. Even before the final week of the conflict, you had put 5,000,000 of the enemy permanently out of the war. You have taken in stride military tasks so difficult as to be classed by many doubters as impossible. You have confused, defeated and destroyed your savagely fighting foe. On the road to victory you have endured every discomfort and privation and have surmounted every obstacle ingenuity and desperation could throw in your path. You did not pause until our front was firmly joined up with the great Red Army coming from the East, and other Allied Forces, coming from the South.

Full victory in Europe has been attained.

Working and fighting together in a single and indestructible partnership you have achieved a perfection in unification of air, ground and naval power that will stand as a model in our time.

The route you have travelled through hundreds of miles is marked by the graves of former comrades. From them has been exacted the ultimate sacrifice; blood of many nations — American, British, Canadian, French, Polish and others — has helped to gain the victory. Each of the fallen died as a member of the team to which you belong, bound together by a common love of liberty and a refusal to submit to enslavement. No monument of stone, no memorial of whatever magnitude could so well express our respect and veneration for their sacrifice as would perpetuation of the spirit of comradeship in which they died. As we celebrate Victory in Europe let us remind ourselves that our common problems of the immediate and distant future can best be solved in the same conception of cooperation and devotion to the cause of human freedom as have made this Expeditionary Force such a mighty engine of righteous destruction.

Let us have no part in the profitless quarrels in which other men will inevitably engage as to what country, what service, won the European War. Every man, every woman, of every nation here represented, has served according to his or her ability, and the efforts of each have contributed to the outcome. This we shall remember — and in doing so we shall be revering each honored grave, and be sending comfort to the loved ones of comrades who could not live to see this day.

DWIGHT D. EISENHOWER,
VICTORY ORDER OF THE DAY, MAY 8, 1945

When Stalin heard about the ceremony which had taken place in Reims he was furious. Not only was the Soviet representative not empowered to sign anything but he insisted that the surrender must be enacted in Berlin, the 'centre of Nazi aggression', and before the 'Supreme Command of all the countries of the anti-Hitler coalition'. He sent Andrei Vyshinsky from Moscow with the agreed document to organise a re-signing the following day; meanwhile Major-General Susloparoff was recalled to Moscow in disgrace and never heard of again. The venue for the ratification ceremony was the Officers' Mess of the Wehrmacht's military engineering school at Karlshorst which had been taken over by Colonel-General Nikolai Bezarin, commander of the Fifth Shock Army, for his headquarters. After the war it became part of the main Soviet headquarters in Berlin but the mess was opened in 1967 as a combined museum and memorial to the Red Army's achievements in defeating Germany. Since the withdrawal of Russian forces in 1994, the museum has been managed by a combined German-Russian foundation and the display altered to cover relations between the two countries since 1917.

Nevertheless, there were considerable delays before the signing could take place while various protocol problems were resolved and it was just past midnight, Moscow time, before the German delegation was marched in for the ceremony, surrounded by a scrum of pressmen. Generalfeldmarschall Wilhelm Keitel was the main German signatory, with Generaloberst Hans-Jürgen Stumpff signing for the Luftwaffe (Generalfeldmarschal Ritter von Greim, the newly-appointed head of the air force, was currently in hospital in Kitzbühel as he had been injured while flying into Berlin), and von Friedeburg for the Kriegsmarine. Marshal Georgi Zhukov, Commander-in-Chief of the First Byelorussian Front and nominal Deputy Supreme Commander of the Soviet Forces, signed for the Red Army and Air Chief Marshal Sir Arthur Tedder for the Western Allies, while General Carl Spaatz of the USAAF and Général Jean de Lattre de Tassigny of the French 1ère Armée added their names as witnesses. The war in Europe was officially over and the defeat of Germany absolute.

UNDERTAKING
GIVEN BY CERTAIN GERMAN EMISSARIES
TO THE ALLIED HIGH COMMANDS

It is agreed by the German emissaries undersigned that the following German officers will arrive at a place and time designated by the Supreme Commander, Allied Expeditionary Force, and the Soviet High Command prepared, with plenary powers, to execute a formal ratification on behalf of the German High Command of this act of Unconditional Surrender of the German armed forces.

Chief of the High Command
Commander-in-Chief of the Army
Commander-in-Chief of the Navy
Commander-in-Chief of the Air Forces.

SIGNED

Jodl

Representing the German High Command.

DATED 0241 7th May 1945
Rheims, France

Both documents stated the same time and date that hostilities must cease: 2301 hours Central European Time on May 8 save that the Berlin document had a few significant changes from the one signed a day earlier at Reims. The phrase 'Supreme

ACT OF MILITARY SURRENDER

1. We the undersigned, acting by authority of the German High Command, hereby surrender unconditionally to the Supreme Commander, Allied Expeditionary Force and simultaneously to the Supreme High Command of the Red Army all forces on land, at sea, and in the air who are at this date under German control.

2. The German High Command will at once issue orders to all German military, naval and air authorities and to all forces under German control to cease active operations at 2301 hours Central European time on 8th May 1945, to remain in the positions occupied at that time and to disarm completely, handing over their weapons and equipment to the local allied commanders or officers designated by Representatives of the Allied Supreme Commands. No ship, vessel, or aircraft is to be scuttled, or any damage done to their hull, machinery or equipment, and also to machines of all kinds, armament, apparatus, and all the technical means of prosecution of war in general.

High Command of The Red Army' was substituted for 'Soviet High Commmand'; Article 2 was altered to require that Germany 'disarm completely' and the demand that ships and military equipment not be damaged was made more detailed.

3. The German High Command will at once issue to the appropriate commanders, and ensure the carrying out of any further orders issued by the Supreme Commander, Allied Expeditionary Force and by the Supreme High Command of the Red Army.

4. This act of military surrender is without prejudice to, and will be superseded by any general instrument of surrender imposed by, or on behalf of the United Nations and applicable to GERMANY and the German armed forces as a whole.

5. In the event of the German High Command or any of the forces under their control failing to act in accordance with this Act of Surrender, the Supreme Commander, Allied Expeditionary Force and the Supreme High Command of the Red Army will take such punitive or other action as they deem appropriate.

6. This Act is drawn up in the English, Russian and German languages. The English and Russian are the only authentic texts.

Signed at Berlin on the 8. day of May, 1945

Friedeburg Keitel Stumpff

On behalf of the German High Command

IN THE PRESENCE OF:

Tedder
On behalf of the
Supreme Commander
Allied Expeditionary Force

On behalf of the
Supreme High Command of the
Red Army

At the signing also were present as witnesses:

J. de Lattre-Tassigny
General Commanding in Chief
First French Army

Carl Spaatz
General, Commanding
United States Strategic Air Forces

SHAEF MESSAGE FORM

ORIGINATORS FILE No. _____

CALL	CIRCUIT No.	PRIORITY	TRANSMISSION INSTRUCTIONS
	NR		

SPACES WITHIN HEAVY LINES FOR SIGNALS USE ONLY

FROM (A): SHAEF FORWARD
ORIGINATOR: PRD, Communique Section
DATE-TIME OF ORIGIN: 081505B May

TO FOR ACTION: (1) AGWAR (2) NAVY DEPARTMENT

TO (W) FOR INFORMATION (INFO): (3) TAC HQ 12 ARMY GP (4) MAIN 12 ARMY GP (5) AIR STAFF MAIN (6) ANCXF (7) EXFOR MAIN (8) EXFOR REAR (9) DEFENSOR, OTTAWA (10) CANADIAN C/S, OTTAWA (11) WAR OFFICE (12) ADMIRALTY (13) AIR MINISTRY (14) UNITED KINGDOM BASE (15) USASTAF (16) HQ SHAEF (PRESS C) (REF: RCAF & RCN) (17) COM ZONE (18) SHAEF REAR (19) 6 ARMY GP MAIN (20) HQ SIXTH ARMY GP (21) WOIA FOR OWI WASHINGTON FOR RELEASE TO COMBINED US AND CANADIAN PRESS AND RADIO AT 0900 HOURS GMT (22) AFHQ ROME FOR PWB

MESSAGE INSTRUCTIONS: IN THE CLEAR
GR: NONE

SPECIAL COMMUNIQUE NO. 8

UNCLASSIFIED:

ALL GERMAN LAND, SEA AND AIR FORCES IN EUROPE WERE UNCONDITIONALLY SURRENDERED TO THE ALLIED EXPEDITIONARY FORCE AND SIMULTANEOUSLY TO THE SOVIET HIGH COMMAND, AT 0141 HOURS CENTRAL EUROPEAN TIME, 7 MAY.

THE SURRENDER TERMS, WHICH WILL BECOME EFFECTIVE AT 2301 CENTRAL EUROPEAN TIME, 8 MAY, WERE SIGNED BY AN OFFICER OF THE GERMAN HIGH COMMAND.

ALLIED EXPEDITIONARY FORCES HAVE BEEN ORDERED TO CEASE OFFENSIVE OPERATIONS, BUT WILL MAINTAIN THEIR PRESENT POSITIONS UNTIL THE SURRENDER BECOMES EFFECTIVE.

DISTRIBUTION:- Communique Distribution

COORDINATED WITH: G-2, G-3 to C/S

Precedence: "OP" - AGWAR & WOIA "P" - Others

ORIGINATING DIVISION: PRD, Communique Section

NAME AND RANK TYPED. TEL. NO.: D.R. JORDAN Lt Col FA 4655

AUTHENTICATING SIGNATURE: /s/

THIS MESSAGE MUST BE SENT IN CYPHER IF LIABLE TO INTERCEPTION — INITIALS /s/

THIS MESSAGE MAY BE SENT IN CLEAR BY ANY MEANS

THI or TOR | **Opr.** | **TIME CLEARED**

The daily battle communiqués issued by SHAEF (Supreme Headquarters Allied Expeditionary Forces) in Europe between D-Day on June 6, 1944 and the German surrender on May 7, 1945 were designed mainly as a guide for press, radio, and newsreel correspondents covering the battlefront activities. Descriptions of the horror, the suffering, and the destruction that go with each shell fired and each bomb dropped were purposely left to the scores of talented news and photo reporters assigned by the worldwide news media to cover the day-to-day carnage of the war.

The communiqués were issued under the signature of Lieutenant Colonel D. Reed Jordan, the Chief of the Communiqué Section of SHAEF. Initially, they were released at 11 a.m. and 11.30 p.m. each day — the frequency later reduced to one per day at 11 a.m. They were issued to the British media in Europe and to the Office of War Information in the United States which forwarded them to American and Canadian journalists. *Right:* David Reed Jordan was born in 1909 in La Grande, Oregon, and worked as editor of the *Daily Post* in Butte, Montana, and at the *Sacramento Bee* in Sacramento, California. He was called up for service in the Army and, because of his career as a journalist, was assigned to the Presidio of San Francisco military base as an information officer. In April 1944 he was posted to General Eisenhower's staff in London. After the war, when the Army Air Corps split from the Army, he transferred to the USAF, retaining his rank as Lieutenant Colonel. In the Korean war, he was information officer at the Wright-Patterson Air Force Base. Reed died in March 2006. (Photo courtesy of Keith S. Taylor.)

SHAEF and the Press

Forrest C. Pogue
OFFICIAL US ARMY HISTORIAN

The story of public relations in the European Theater of Operations, 1944-45, is that of an attempt by SHAEF and its subordinate headquarters to keep the public informed of operational developments without compromising the security of operations. A brief of SHAEF's efforts in that direction makes clear the difficulties confronting any agency which tries to reconcile these opposing interests.

To inform the Allied peoples of the D-Day landing, SHAEF began preparations weeks in advance to facilitate maximum coverage of the story. Colonels Joseph B. Phillips and David Sarnoff installed special communications for the rapid transmission of news from northern France. In addition, the Press Signal Center was established at the Ministry of Information in London with direct teleprinter circuits to SHAEF (Main) and the air, ground, and naval advance headquarters. Teletype and radio links from London to Washington permitted quick transmission to the War Department.

Before D-Day, correspondents were permitted to file 'colour' stories which were censored and ready for transmission when the assault began. Early on June 6 newsmen met at Macmillan Hall at the University of London where they were locked in the Press Room and furnished maps and background material on the attack. At 0830 Colonel R. Ernest Dupuy, an American member of the SHAEF Public Relations Division (PRD), read the brief official communiqué which had been written several days previously and carefully censored to prevent the enemy from learning anything of the Allies' future plans. The correspondents then wrote their stories, had them censored, and were ready to send their copy when G-3 flashed the code-word 'TOPFLIGHT' which was the signal for release of information. Teams of censors at the Ministry of Information, at the beach-head, and on naval assault craft passed more than 700,000 words on D-Day.

In Britain, the Ministry of Information was based in Senate House, the University of London building in Malet Street, London, and it was here that Colonel R. Ernest Dupuy, deputy head of SHAEF's Public Relations Division, gave the first news of the Normandy landings to the press on the morning of June 6. The Allies should have won the race to be first with the news as statements had been prepared and approved weeks in advance. General Eisenhower's pre-recorded message to the 'People of Western Europe', broadcast after Communiqué No. 1 (see page 20), had been issued for broadcasting to the people of Norway, Denmark, the Netherlands, Belgium and France in their own languages. However, Joseph Goebbels, the German propaganda chief, broadcast the news to the world at 7 a.m., pre-empting the Allies by some two hours. SHAEF's Communiqué No. 1 was not put out by the BBC until 9.32 a.m., John Snagge reading the bulletin.

Naturally, in the initial period of the invasion, the press coverage of D-Day could not be maintained. Like everything else in the beach-head, press communications were limited and many newsmen were unable to file all their copy for transmission to the United States and the United Kingdom. The opening of new transmitters in late June and early July improved the situation, but the breakthrough and rapid pursuit which followed put additional burdens on SHAEF, the army groups, and the armies, with the result that not until the Allies reached Paris were sufficient facilities available to meet the need of correspondents in the field.

Besides attempting to equalise opportunities for transmitting copy dealing with the various armies in Normandy, SHAEF also took steps during the first week of the invasion to avoid invidious comparisons between national armies. On June 13, the authors of SHAEF communiqués were informed that the Supreme Commander desired 'that in the future references to American and British troops, as such, be held to the very minimum and the term "Allied troops" be used instead'. As an example, they were told that a previous reference to 'American' troops liberating Carentan should have read 'Allied' (see page 36). Thus, in August, on the eve of the drive to Paris, Colonel Dupuy warned General Walter Bedell Smith that unless the approaching American break-out was summarised and depicted as part of an integrated assault, 'the importance of the British-Canadian offensive in its zone may be minimised,

With D-Day being the greatest news story of the war, virtually every one of the 500-odd newsmen accredited by SHAEF applied for the top assignment: attachment to General Eisenhower's headquarters at Portsmouth. With so many correspondents competing for what could only be a limited number of places, on Thursday, June 1, Colonel Dupuy told Eisenhower that press coverage at 'Sharpener' would be limited to four reporters, two American and two British, to be chosen by drawing lots. Here, Eisenhower holds a press conference with the lucky winners: Front L-R: Major W. R. Carr of SHAEF; Stanley Birch representing the British news agency Reuters; Robert Barr for the BBC; Merrill 'Red' Mueller of NBC; Edward 'Ned' Roberts of United Press, and Lieutenant Colonel Thor Smith, the SHAEF public relations officer for the Advanced Command Post. Behind stand Captain Victor J. Meluskey, the SHAEF press censor, and Commander Butcher. The reporters have just presented Eisenhower with an old Royal Horse Artilery print to hang on the bare wall of his office tent.

The paving stone which once lay in front of the tent in Sawyer's Wood. (For the story of how we found the location of 'Sharpener', see *After the Battle* No. 84.)

Chief of the Public Relations Division at SHAEF was Brigadier General Thomas J. Davis *(left)* who had previously been the adjutant-general at Supreme Headquarters. Appointed in April 1944, in the summer he asked to be released of his duties as he had been ill for a number of weeks but General Eisenhower asked him to remain at his post until a suitable replacement had been found. *Right:* An early press conference held in the European Theater of Operations Public Relations office.

with resultant embarrassment to Anglo-American relations, as well as distortion of the overall picture'. He urged the SHAEF Chief-of-Staff to give an interview which would put the contributions of the various armies into the proper perspective.

Holding the view that democratic peoples must be told as much as possible concerning the accomplishments of their armies, the Supreme Commander went as far as he could, consistent with security, toward announcing full details of his forces' activities. Despite curbs on interviews by senior officers, the way was left open for frank comments in the form of 'off the record' statements which were not attributable to the commander concerned. These were used, in particular, for guidance to correspondents on matters which had to be kept secret but on which they wished to be able to comment intelligently once the ban of secrecy was removed. The device was also exceedingly valuable in dealing with questions of military policy which might otherwise be misunderstood. In the latter case, an interesting example was shown in the handling of reports on the reception given Allied troops in Normandy by the French. After the enthusiasm of the first week of the invasion had passed, correspondents began to report stories of French unfriendliness. Evidence of well-filled shops in Bayeux was interpreted as meaning that the French had prospered under German rule. French citizens were charged with sniping at Allied troops and giving aid to German troops. General Eisenhower found it necessary in late June to issue a special press release declaring that investigation had shown 'no authenticated use of French civilian snipers'. He emphasised on the contrary that French Resistance had been 'a great contribution in support of Allied operations'.

Unfavourable reactions from the Allied governments to certain types of stories were responsible for changes in SHAEF censorship rules during the early weeks of invasion. The public relations director was reminded officially of Mr Churchill's earlier reaction to reports of the chivalrous treatment by Germans of US wounded. The Prime Minister had felt that, since for one good deed they committed 400 bad ones, there was no need of singling out the unique experience for publicity.

With the liberation of Paris, the SHAEF Public Relations Division entered a new phase. Until that time, the number of correspondents permitted on the Continent had been limited, and a rotation system had been imposed on all correspondents except those from news agencies and major independent newspapers. Correspondents were subject to recall to the United Kingdom after 30 days in the combat zone.

The main offices of the PRD remained in London during this period with the result that it was somewhat out of touch with the situation on the Continent. In late August the division was able to get General Smith to withdraw his usual opposition to placing SHAEF agencies in Paris and approve the establishment of PRD in the French capital, where it was possible to receive a greater number of newsmen. The Hotel Scribe, near the Opera, was reserved for billets, messing, and accommodations for Allied correspondents in addition to SHAEF censorship, briefing, and information services.

The perfect location for newsmen with SHAEF in Paris — the Hotel Scribe!

General Eisenhower had a personal dislike of censorship and he said that 'I had to be convinced that the reason for such action was important, and from August on, the friendly relationship between the press and the military was strengthened by the presence of Brigadier General Frank A. Allen, Jr, as my public relations officer'. In carrying out its task of censoring news and photographs, SHAEF followed British and US practices developed in the United Kingdom after the outbreak of war. American censors had been appointed in 1942 shortly after US troops arrived in the United Kingdom, and worked in close contact with the British censors. In late April 1944, a Joint Press Censorship Group, headed by Lieutenant Colonel Richard H. Merrick and including officers from the Allied ground, sea, and air forces was organised. Its purpose was to advise the British Ministry of Information on censorship of press and radio material originating in the United Kingdom which dealt with contemplated operations, and to censor material returned to the United Kingdom from the Continent. The chief of the Public Relations Division was made responsible for the censorship of press material originating in the United Kingdom which dealt with the US forces.

The number of correspondents accredited to SHAEF for the European Theater of Operations grew steadily after the invasion. From 530 on June 7, the number had risen to 924 by January 1945 and to 996 shortly before the war's end. Although the vast majority of this group was attached to units in the field, the task of furnishing censorship guidance, providing communications for copy filed at SHAEF, the accreditation of all correspondents for the ETO, and the outlining of broad policy for public relations throughout the theater imposed a heavy burden on SHAEF PRD.

The shift of the Public Relations Division from London to Paris was made gradually, and it was not until October 10 that the first briefing conference was held in Paris. An Army broadcasting line which connected Paris with the British Broadcasting Corporation in London was replaced by a BBC transmitter in the Hotel Scribe. By the end of November the daily average of copy sent from Paris to the United States and United Kingdom had risen to about 108,000 words. More facilities were added in December with the laying of a BBC submarine cable, initiation of voice casts from the city of Luxembourg, and the installation of an additional teleprinter line to the United Kingdom.

Sometimes the censors went over the top and it is difficult to understand the thinking behind the deletion of the wallpaper in this photo of Staff Sergeant Walter D. Ehlers (left) being interviewed by a group of correspondents in December. Ehlers of the 18th Infantry, 1st Infantry Division, had been awarded the Medal of Honor for gallantry near Goville on June 9-10.

Censorship problems arose for the Public Relations Division even before its movement to the Continent. An advance party of SHAEF censors, going into Paris shortly after the first Allied forces had entered the city, reported that six American and British correspondents had broadcast details of the liberation of the French capital without submitting their copy to Allied censors (see page 144). SHAEF suspended for 60 days the right of the correspondents to remain on the Continent, but permitted them to carry out their normal duties in the United Kingdom.

Press activities declined slightly during the period of the German counter-offensive in the Ardennes as security blackouts were imposed. For the first time since D-Day the number of words sent in a given month dropped below that of the previous month. After mid-January the volume of words began to rise and continued to increase until the end of the war.

The Public Relations Division expanded its censorship services and telecommunication facilities to take care of new demands. The army groups had their own teleprinter connections to Paris and London, and by the beginning of February the Ninth Air Force and army press camps had set up five commercial mobile transmitters. The BBC had its own mobile transmitters with the British and Canadian armies, and regular Army sets with the American armies. A special short-wave transmitter was opened at Luxembourg on Christmas Day for press voice-casting and direct broadcasting to the United States.

To provide for a sudden news development, such as the entry into Berlin, the Public Relations Division built flying radio stations into two Flying Fortresses for use to the United States and the United Kingdom. Through the Communications Zone, SHAEF also had the use of the world's largest mobile radio station, housed in 17 vans. Under construction by a French firm for the Luftwaffe, the apparatus had been seized by American forces and completed by them. The 60-kilowatt transmitter was capable of communicating

General Allen officially took over from Davis in September. Eisenhower wrote that 'he had been a successful leader of an armoured combat command in North Africa and France but I believed that his ability to maintain military security and at the same time to assure the public the information it wanted and needed would prove most valuable to the war effort. By his assignment to headquarters duty, although I lost a proved combat commander thereby, I was relieved of many worrisome problems.'

with Washington over three teletype channels, which could be used simultaneously with a fourth channel that provided voice or picture transmission. General Eisenhower's train was also fitted up with radio equipment in case it should be needed for surrender negotiations.

SHAEF also continued to send an impressive amount of material from London. Some concept of the Public Relations Division's task may be seen in a breakdown between the two cities during the last four months of the war. Paris censored over 15 million words of text and checked over 100,000 photographs while nine million words and nearly a million photos were censored in London, but these statistics do not tell the entire story, since censors were also on duty at army groups and armies, while others dealt with copy in liberated newspapers, and with amateur photographers' film. An example may be found in a busy, but not a peak, month such as February 1945 in which copy handled by censors at SHAEF and the three army groups totaled 13,075,600 words; public relations officer copy to be mailed home 9,529,345 words; scrutiny of domestic press 44,221,377 words; still pictures 208,965 and 1,128,155 feet of film.

SHAEF's Public Relations Division had the task not only of censoring stories to prevent breaches of security and the disturbance of good relations between Allies, but also of publicising the exploits of various units to aid morale. This became difficult when commanders like General Patton by their personal colour and their slashing advances overshadowed the hard work of other commanders and armies. SHAEF was concerned less by the disparity in coverage than by the possible harm done to the morale of units whose efforts had not been adequately recognised. General Smith reminded the Public Relations Division of this problem in early September and asked that briefing officers call especial attention to the work of General Hodges' First Army. 'In other words', he said, 'try to attract a little more attention to Hodges and Bradley as against Patton's colourful appeal to the press. This without detriment to Patton.'

From time to time the Allied correspondents protested to SHAEF because of news blackouts, delays in passing stories, failure of censors at various headquarters to follow a consistent pattern, release of information at SHAEF which army headquarters were not allowed to release, use of censorship for political rather than security purposes, and refusals to release 'horrifics' and stories of reverses. On the question of 'horrifics' and reverses, the censors acted in accord with the policy followed by both the War Department and

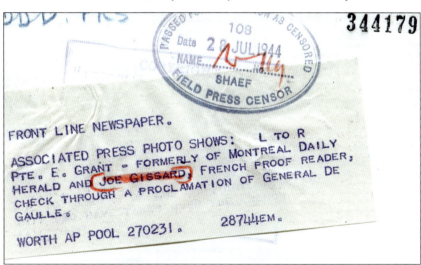

Names of civilians which could put a life in danger were deleted as illustrated by this War Pool photo of July 1944.

Supreme Headquarters of passing any story which did not give information to the enemy. Statistics on casualties were issued rather regularly, although a time lag was maintained to prevent the enemy from determining the effectiveness of any current defence the Allies might be making. SHAEF applied a temporary stop to the report of more than 8,600 casualties in the 106th Division at the outset of the German counter-offensive in the Ardennes.

SHAEF censors discovered that radio broadcasting, in particular, created a number of special censorship problems. Especially serious were premature releases of information on coming attacks. Because of the speed with which information from a BBC broadcast could be picked up, breaches of security by it were more helpful to the enemy than similar statements in the press. It was charged that enemy fire fell on Allied troops just 17 minutes after a casual newscast indicated that they were entering the factory district of Aachen.

A particularly embarrassing episode for SHAEF came in late April when the BBC made a premature announcement of the link-up of the Russians and Americans near Torgau (page 478) despite elaborate precautions to have the announcement made simultaneously in Moscow, Washington and London. In this instance, a French news agency had sent out by radio the announcement to be held for a release date. The information was monitored by the BBC, which interrupted a scheduled programme to announce the news. SHAEF officials submitted sharp protests to the governors of the BBC as a result of this action.

The most widely publicised breach of censorship involved an American newsman who prematurely announced the signing of the instrument of surrender at Reims. One of the 17 correspondents to witness the event, Edward Kennedy, chief of the Associated Press bureau in Paris, made use of an open wire from the Hotel Scribe to give the story of the surrender to the Associated Press bureau in London. Unaware that the story had not been released, the London bureau flashed it to the United States. Kennedy, who had been in difficulties with SHAEF as recently as February 1945 (over a story that President Roosevelt was coming to Paris to investigate scandals in the Army's handling of the relief programme for French civilians), held that the story had been broken by the German radio which was broadcasting Admiral Dönitz' orders to his forces to cease fighting. Since the German high command was supposedly acting under the orders of SHAEF, he felt that this action absolved him from his promise not to release the story until it had been released by SHAEF. Such an interpretation was not followed by the other 16 correspondents at Reims nor by the other newspapermen in Europe, all of whom were aware of the surrender story. The story was branded as unofficial, and the Associated Press and its representatives in London and Paris were suspended until an investigation could be held. The Associated Press protested the suspension of its entire organisation, and the War Department ruled that, since all agreements relative to censorship were made between correspondents and SHAEF, responsibility had to be placed on the individual news man. The ban against the Associated Press was lifted despite the bitter protests of more than 50 correspondents at an indignation meeting in Paris on May 8 in which they attacked Brigadier General Frank A. Allen, Jr, and the Public Relations Division of Supreme Headquarters. After investigation it was announced on May 12 that there were no grounds for court-martial proceedings but recommended that the credentials of Mr Kennedy and his assistant, Morton Gudebrod, be withdrawn and that the two correspondents be returned to the United States. This action was carried out on May 14, the Associated Press expressed its regrets, and on the following day SHAEF, in a statement praising the other correspondents for not releasing the story, declared the incident closed. In 1948, through the aid of Senator Sheridan Downey, Mr. Kennedy's case was presented to General Eisenhower, then US Army Chief-of-Staff, who restored the newsman's credentials as war correspondent.

```
                    Chief of War Room
                    Col. S. H. Negrotto

                    Official Press Party
                        May 6, 1945

Associated Press                    Edward Kennedy
United Press                        Boyd Lewis
International News Service          James L. Kilgallen
Reuters                             H. C. Montague Taylor
Exchange Telegraph                  Price Day
Canadian Press                      Margaret Ecker
Australian Press                    Osmar E. White
Agence Francaise Presse             Jean E. Lagrange
TASS                                Michael Litvin-Sedoy
BBC                                 Thomas Cadett
NBC                                 W. W. Chaplin
CBS                                 Charles Collingwood
Blue Network                        Herbert M. Clark
Mutual Bdcst. System                Paul Manning
CBC                                 Gerald Clark
Stars and Stripes                   S/Sgt. Charles Kiley
Maple Leaf                          Sgt. Ross D. Parry


Brigadier General Frank A. Allen, Jr.   Captain Harry Butcher
Col. George Warden                      Lt. Col. S. R. Pawley
Group Captain G. W. Houghton            Lt. Col. Burrows Matthews
Lt.Col. Richard Merrick                 Col. P.H. Lash
Lt.Col. Thor M. Smith                   Capt. R. L. Hays
Lt.Col. Reed Jordan
Capt. Don Davis


                    Official Pictorial Party

U.S. Still Pool                     Ralph Morse
British Still Pool                  Fred S. Skinner
U.S. Newsreel Pool                  Yves Naintre
British Newsreel Pool               Roni Read

Col. Kirke B. Lawton                Lt. Leo S. Moore
Lt. H. W. Schmidt                   T/Sgt. Jack M. Howell
Lt. Robert McWade                   Sgt. A. B. Messerlin
Lt. Andrew G. Burt Jr.              Cpl. Ardean Miller
Lt. Robert C. Scrivner              Pfc Albert N. Stephens
T/Sgt. Harold Lee
T/5 Charles Corn
T/5 Roger Davis
Pfc Bruce Chin

                    Radio Technicians

Lt. Col. Walter Brown
Capt. Ted Bergmann
```

The end of war 'wrap' party for the Press was held on May 6 although two days later the man at the top of the list was disgraced for jumping the gun over the premature announcement of the signing of the surrender. Edward Kennedy was returned to the States and the Associated Press agency was suspended by SHAEF.

Then, to make matters worse, *Stars and Stripes* stole a march on the British press by producing an 'extra' issue on *The Times* presses at 9 p.m. on May 7. Resurrected in April 1942 after it had ceased publication in 1919, the US forces' newspaper had grown from a London edition to being produced at over a dozen sites on the Continent by 1945. (See also *After the Battle* No. 157.)

```
               " THE S.H.A.E.F.   COMMUNIQUE "
```

   Melody like "MANDALAY" -
                                 Lyrics like nothing you ever heard before.

```
Lis't to SHAEF's COMMUNIQUE -           Still it's SHAEF'S COMMUNIQUE
All the war news every day,             Never matter what the day.
Can't you hear the words a-tumblin'     It's the umpteenth High Commandment
From Verdun to Biscay Bay.              Written in the Four-Star Way!

It's today's COMMUNIQUE -               Come ye back to PAREE gay
Nothing new in what we say.             Where for smokes you got a lay
G-3 scorns us - G-2 loathes us          Come ye back ye correspondents
PR hates to give us pay.                It's the LAST COMMUNIQUE!

It's last week's COMMUNIQUE,            It's the LAST COMMUNIQUE
Hot from out old Monty's way            Talisman has come to stay,
Can't you see it's "Most Immediate"     And the General goes to Berlin
Signals paused to have some "tay"!      While we fly to U - S - A!!!!!

Christmas Day's COMMUNIQUE
Came out on the third of May.
Brown had routed it to London
But it went to Santa Fe -
```

SHAEF even penned their own tribute to over 400 communiqués issued between June 6, 1944 and May 8, 1945.

Casualties

According to Michael Clodfelter's exhaustive statistical reference *Warfare and Armed Conflicts*, the total number of Allied soldiers who served in the 11 months of the campaign in Western Europe in 1944-45 was 5,412,219. By VE-Day Allied forces numbered 4,581,000 spread between three army groups, nine armies, 23 corps and 93 divisions. The armies were the US First, Third, Seventh, Ninth and Fifteenth, the First Allied Airborne, the British Second, the First Canadian and the French First.

Total Allied casualties for the campaign in Western Europe were stated in 1968 by the official British historian, Major L. F. Ellis, as being 782,374 for the ground forces, 61,624 in the air and 10,308 at sea, split up as shown in the tables. These figures differ from those given by his US counterpart, Forrest C. Pogue of the Office of the Chief of Military History, as during the war the United States Air Force was part of the Army. And the air casualties include those suffered during the preparatory operations for 'Overlord' from April 1.

German losses on the Western Front between June 2, 1944 and April 10, 1945 (excluding those suffered by the Luftwaffe and Waffen-SS) were reported as 80,819 killed, 265,526 wounded, 490,624 missing with 2,057,138 prisoners of war. As a large number of the missing had to be presumed dead, this raises the German total deaths to around 263,000. In addition, several thousand died in the so-called Rhine Meadow Camps (see page 466) which existed from April to September 1945. Of the million prisoners spread between the 19 US-run camps, some sources say that up to 10,000 died from malnutrition and exposure to the elements.

Even after the surrender had been ratified, the war was still claiming more casualties. While escorting a German admiral from Kiel on May 9, Major Charles Sweeny, one of Field-Marshal Montgomery's liaison officers (see page 453), was killed when his car ran off the road and crashed near Celle. Monty had him buried on Victory Hill in a piece of ground a little higher up from where his caravan stood, but today Major Sweeny lies in Grave 2 of Row F in Plot 2 in Becklingen War Cemetery at Soltau. By May 1945 the 21st Army Group reported that British and Canadian Grave Registration Units had recorded a total of 48,506 graves during the campaign in 79 permanent UK and Commonwealth cemeteries and 28 plots in communal burial grounds. The official cut-off date for American deaths in the Second World War was December 31, 1946 while Britain included deaths due to war operations up to December 31, 1947.

ALLIED ARMIES, JUNE 6, 1944 TO MAY 7, 1945

Nationality	Killed or died of wounds	Wounded	Missing or captured	Total
British	30,276	96,672	14,698	141,646
Canadian	10,739	30,906	2,247	43,892
American	109,824	356,661	56,632	523,117
French	12,587	49,513	4,726	66,826
Other Allies	1,528	5,011	354	6,893
Total	**164,954**	**538,763**	**78,657**	**782,374**

ALLIED NAVIES, JUNE 6, 1944 TO MAY 7, 1945

Navies	Killed or died of wounds	Wounded	Total
Royal Navy	4,230	3,334	7,564
US Navy	1,102	1,642	2,744
Total	**5,332**	**4,976**	**10,308**

ALLIED AIR FORCES, APRIL 1, 1944 TO MAY 7, 1945

Air Forces	Killed or died of wounds	Wounded	Missing or captured	Total
Royal Air Force	16,589	1,746	5,314	23,649
US Army Air Force	14,034	5,545	18,067	37,646
French Air Force	222	49	58	329
Total	**30,845**	**7,340**	**23,439**	**61,624**

German prisoners of war landscaped the American cemetery at Saint-Laurent, Normandy, seen here in May 1945. The whole cemetery was reconstructed by the American Battle Monuments Commission in 1948 at which point approximately 60 per cent of the dead were repatriated to the United States. Other burials were then brought in to Saint-Laurent which today contains 9,387 graves. Private William Johnson, whose grave can be seen in the left foreground, was a member of the 306th Railhead Company who lost his life on September 7. He still remains buried in Normandy in Plot D, Row 28, Grave 8.

After the war, the United States did not permit its servicemen who had been killed to lie in enemy soil, so no permanent cemeteries were established in Germany. Instead 12 war cemeteries were built by the American Battle Monuments Commission for the European Theater of Operations: one each in Britain, Holland and Luxembourg, two in Belgium and Italy, and five in France.

Credits

This book could not have been produced without the help of two individuals, both of whom are now deceased.

First the communiqués. As has been explained on page 511, these were issued under the signature of Lieutenant Colonel Reed Jordan, and it was only due to his foresight that he preserved copies for posterity as daily press releases so often get quickly discarded. In December 1998 Mr Jordan's nephew Keith S. Taylor donated a complete set of the originals to the Harold B. Lee Library of Brigham Young University in Provo, Utah, where the digitisation of the 609 pages was carried out by Richard D. Hacken, the European Studies Bibliographer. (Gail Ramsey tracked down their existence, see http://www.paperlessarchives.com)

And then the photographs to illustrate each day. In 1972 Roger Bell established The Society for the Studies of the European Theater of Operations and over the following years built up an extensive photographic archive, as well as a large library containing unit histories and many other publications covering the 1944-45 period.

Thus I felt a marriage of Jordan's communiqués with Roger's photographs was a perfect way to tell the story of the defeat of Germany, although it is a real shame that neither is alive to see the end result, Reed Jordan having died on February 26, 2006 and Roger Bell on June 7, 2012 (see *After the Battle* No. 158).

As with all *After the Battle* publications, we revisit the original locations to match the wartime photographs with 'then and now' comparisons, and Karel Margry, Bernard Paich and Jean Paul Pallud worked hard for several weeks during 2014 to tackle the project which covers France, Belgium, Holland, Luxembourg and Germany.

Roger Bell, founder of the Society for the Studies of the ETO, who died just before D-Day in 2012, in action photographing the remains of German defences at Breisach (see page 348).

We must also not overlook the huge debt we owe to the wartime photographers who risked — and many lost — their lives endeavouring to record history. The captions that they supplied are not always accurate and a good example of the difficulty our photographers faced is illustrated by the photo on page 273. Karel explains:

'I was about to leave Saarbrücken for Rohrbach-lès-Bitche, 50 kilometres to the east, when I noticed the official caption of that picture said "US 80th Division". Don't ask me how I know, but I recalled that that division could not have been in that Seventh Army area. Went back into the hotel, checked *The Lorraine Campaign* on the internet and, the 80th was indeed never there.

Bernard Paich, who resides in Normandy, is steeped in its history and he was the ideal choice for photography in that region covering the period from June to August.

Jean Paul's forté is the Battle of the Bulge and he revisited the area for the December and January chapters. He also took comparisons from Brest to Stuttgart and Berlin, and from Cherbourg to the Riviera.

Karel Margry, Editor of *After the Battle* ranged right across Europe, undertaking comparison photography in the Netherlands, Belgium, Luxembourg, France and all over Germany.

Autographed photograph from the archive of the late Roger Bell. United Press photographer Boyd Dewolf Lewis pictured in the French town of Lauterbourg, east of Wissembourg, on the Lauter river. The 2nd Battalion, 315th Infantry, of the 79th Division put a footbridge across the river to the west of town in the early afternoon of December 15 and to them fell the honour of having the first 79th Division soldier to set foot on German soil; he was Staff Sergeant Dewey J. White.

'In early December 1944 they were south-east of Saarbrücken, advancing to Völkingen. However, there was no place named Rohrbach in that area. The closest were villages named Rosbruck and Morsbach. I took the gamble and drove west instead of east. Got to Rosbruck and found it had indeed a modern church but the background didn't look quite right. I asked a local Frenchman and he said there was a grotto further down the main road at a spot where there had been a church. Checked it out and, lo and behold, a plaque beside the grotto showed a picture of the same church as shown in the Signal Corps picture!! The church was pulled down in 1967 but the houses in the background confirm the match. So not "Rohrbeck in Germany" (official caption) but Rosbruck in France, over 60 kilometres away!'

WINSTON RAMSEY,
FEBRUARY 2015

The frontier crossing on the D468/L540 at the northern end of the town. The houses in the background are in Neulauterburg in Germany.

INDEX
COMPILED BY PETER GUNN

Note: Page numbers in *italics* refer to illustrations. There may also be textual references on these pages.

Aa, River *221*
Aachen
  September, sector fighting 174–177, 179, 181–186, 188, 189, 191, 193
  October
    Allied capture *219*, 220, 516
    battle for 199, *201*, *205*–*207*, *208*–*209*, *210*, 212–213, *215*–*217*, 218, 250
    sector 197, 198, *200*, 202–204, 221, 222, 224, 225, 226, 228
  November
    Allies bomb area 235, 236, 237, 242, 243, 248
    sector 251
  December 267, 274, *278*, *288*
  February *361*, *366*, *367*
  March *377*
  see also Siegfried Line; Vaalserberg, The: 'Three-Country Point'
Aalen 328, 463
Aardenburg 218, 220
Abancourt, Allied bombing 24, 91
Abaucourt 233
Abbendorf 470
Abbeville
  Allied bombing 150, 158
  Allies reach 158, 159, 160
Abensberg 480
Abrefontaine 310
Achen 272, 309, 310
Achères, railway centres bombed 30, 36
Achern 302
Achouffe 322
Achterbroek 219, 220
Acme photo agency *215*
Acqueville, Allies liberate 54
Adair, Maj.-Gen. Allan *160*, *174*
Adamswiller 264
Adastral House, London *65*
Adelheide 467
Adelshausen 428
Adenau 390
Aegidienberg 399, 400
Aero Island 494
Afferden 360, 361
Affler 366
Ager, River 502
Ahaus 268, 395, 407, 420
Ahlen 418
Ahlhorn 409
Ahr, River 227
Ahrem 383
Ahrweiler
  October 204, 209, 226
  November 243
  December 269, 294, 299, 300
  January 311, 320, 335, 337
  February 345, 369
  March *392*
Ahütte 298
Aich 469
Aichkirchen 500
Ailette, River 87
Aindling 480
Aircraft
  Avro York (ACM Leigh-Mallory's death in crash) *245*
  B-17 Flying Fortress (42-31333) 91st BG *444*
  B-17 Flying Fortress (43-38172) 398th BG *213*
  B-25 (Eisenhower's transport) *163*
  Hawker Typhoon *190*
  Marauder G-5-MA type RJ-A *307*
Aire-sur-la-Lys 119, 160, 162
Airel 75
Airfields
  Achiet 114
  Ahlen 405
  Amiens 114
  Angers 59
  Athies 57, 63
  Augsburg 469, 473, 475, 486
  Avord 60
  Babenhausen 398
  Banzkow 486
  Barkston Heath *176*
  Bassingbourn *444*
  Bayreuth 450, 453, 455
  Beaumont-sur-Oise 42
  Beauvais-Nivillers 42
  Beuzeville (A-6) *54*
  Bindersleben 439
  Blagnac 60

Bordeaux-Mérignac 51
Bourges 60
Brandenburg 469
Brandis 455
Brétigny 60
Briest 447
Brockzetel 450
Brunswick 447, 449
Brussels-Melsbroek 43, 129, *163*
Cambrai-Niergnies (A74) *206*
Carpiquet *42*, *72*, 74
Cazaux 51
Chartres 111
Châteaudun 58, 77, 111
Clastres 119
Cologne Ostheim 128
Connantre 62
Corme-Écluse 51
Corne 88
Coulommiers 62, 123
Crailsheim 237
Creil 43, 62
Deelen 129
Dessau 443, 450, 458
Dijon 127
Düne island 465
Eger, Czechoslovakia 447, 449, 450, 462, 481
Ehingen 469
Eindhoven 43
Erfurt 443, 449
Étampes-Mondésir 43
Eudenbach 407
Évreux-Fauville 41
Flensburg 473
Flers 34
Florennes 129
Francazal 60
Geseke 405
Giebelstadt 199, 430
Gilze-Rijen 129
Greenham Common *18*
Grossenbrode 494
Grossostheim 398
Gütersloh 405, 409, 422
Halle 237, 443, 449
Haltern 405
Handorf 128, 405
Hof 443, 447
Hopsten 129
Husum 494
Illesheim 439, 447
Ingolstadt 469
Jena 449, 450
Juvincourt 57, 63, 105
Kaltenkirchen 441
La Perthe 119
Lachen-Speyerdorf 199
Landes de Bussac 51
Landsberg 470, 473
Laon-Couvron 63, 105, *307*
Larz 447
Laupheim 469
Le Bourget 2, 43
Le Mans 34, 44, 88
Lechfeld 249
Leck 494
Leeuwarden 168, 171
Leipheim 249
Leipzig 377, 450, 458
Lille 114
Lippe 398, 399
Lippstadt 405
Lübeck 488
Ludwigslust 469
Marienbad 458
Maupertus 61, 64
Melun 111
Memmingen 471
Mengen 249
Merseburg 443
Metz 133
Munich 447, 473, 475, 477, 479
Münster-Loddenheide 201
Nancy-Essey 133
Neuruppin 447
Nordhausen 203, 443
Nördlingen 455, 462
Northolt *245*, *413*
Nürnberg (Nuremberg) 447
Nuthamstead *213*
Oranienburg 447
Orlamünde 450
Orléans-Bricy (A50) 43, 58, 111, *206*
Paderborn 405, 409
Parchim 441, 447

Pilsen 475
Plantlunne 129
Plattling 477
Ramstein *404*
Regensburg 448
Rennes 34, 41, 51
Riem 469
Riesa 469
Rohrdorf 370
Romilly-sur-Seine 119, 133
Roye-Amy 133
Sachenhausen 237
Sachsenheim 240
Saint-Dizier 133
St Laurent-sur-Mer (A-21C) *32*
Salzburg 479
Schafstädt 450
Stargard 202
Straubing 477, 479
Thal 431
Tour-en-Bessin (A13) *206*
Tours 111
Toussus-le-Noble 123, *308*
Twente Enschede 129
Vaires 62
Valade 88
Vechta 128
Venlo 129, *413*
Villacoublay 60, 119, 123
Villeneuve-Vertus 62
Weimar 447, 450
Welford *176*
Wenzendorf 202
Wesendorf 441
Wick (Wing at) *34*
Wiesbaden 240
Wittenberg 453
Wittmund 128
Wright-Patterson AFB, USA *511*
Zerbst 447
Zwischenahn 128
Aisch, River 457
Aisne, River 151, 152, 157, 158, 159
Aisy *169*
Aiterhofen 480
Aix-la-Chapelle *see* Aachen
Ajoncourt 204
Albert Canal 172, 175
  Allied bridgeheads over *163*, 164, 166, 167, 168, 171, 173
Albesdorf 256
Ablasserdam 330
Aldegund 398
Aldenhoven 209, 250, 252
Alderney, Channel Islands 56, 127
Aldringen 332, 333
Alençon
  Allied front *67*
  June, Allied bombing 32, 51, 61, *66*
  July, Allied bombing 70, 72, 85, 87, 88, 98
  August *121*, 126, 128
Alexander, FM Sir Harold *377*
Allen, Brig. Gen. Frank A., Jr. *514*, *515*, 516
Allen, Maj. Gen. Leven C. *211*
Allen, Pte W. B. *318*
Aller, River 450, 451, 454, 456, 458, 464, *470*
Allerborn *291*
Almelo 436
Alost 161
Alpen 390
Alsace
  November 252, 253, 254, 256, 259, 260, 261
  December 265, 266, 270, 271, *274*, 277, 278, 279, 280, 283, 292, 303
  January 309, 313, 314, 317, 322, 331–336, *337*, 339
  February 342, 343, 348, *349*, 351, 352, 355, 356, 357, 358, 364, 370
  March 383, 385, 396, 399, 400, *401*, 402, 403, 410
  see also Metz
Alsace-Lorraine *337*, *429*
  Allied bombing 113
  see also Ardennes; Strasbourg
Alschbach 401, 403
Alscheid 333
Alsdorf 203, 204, 209, 212
Alsfeld 422
Alsleben 459
Alstingen 363
Altdorf 259
Alteglofsheim 480
Altenau 541
Altenbeken 365, 437
Altenberg 419, 457, 500
Altenburg 459
Altendettelsau 463
Altengöttern 437
Altenhausen 444

Altenhundem 385
Altenkirchen 389, 393, 409, 418, 419
Altenrüthen 430
Altenstadt 403
Altheim 486
Althorn 318
Altkirch 251
Altmühl, River 474
Altwildungen 422
Alzen 181
Alzey 376, 404
Amayé-sur-Orne 114
  bridge bombed 46
Amberg 445, 449, 472
Amberloup 319
Amblève
  Allied capture 334
  sector *288*, 336
Amblève, River *287*, 312
Ambly 316
Ambrières 86
Ameland 168, 173
Amelécourt 242
Ameln 242, 370
American Battle Monuments Commission *8*, *519*
Amerika 253
Amersfoort
  October 202, 209, 210, 218, 227
  November 239, 243, 256
  December 267, 268, 269, 271
  January 309, 321, 328, 331
  February 348
  April *431*, 440, 448, 469, 470
Amiens
  air reconnaissance 105
  Allied advance from 158
  Allied advance to *150*, 152
  Allied air attacks 24, 40, 51, 85, 89, 91, 101, 105, 117, 147, 150
  Allies establish bridgehead 156
Amigny 89, *95*
Ammeldingen 356, 366
Ammersee 482
Amoneburg 421
Amorbach 422
Amstenrade 181
Ancerville 244
Andaine 116
Andernach 300, 366, 390, *394*, 395, 396
  US Army POW holding camp (A7) *466*
Anderson, Maj. Gen. John *378*, *413*
Andlau 261
Andrae, Maj. *494*
Angelsdorf 371
Angers 58, *70*, 73, 84, 88, 91, 94, 114, 115, 119, 123
  Allied capture 121, *124*, 125
Anglemont 199, 202
Angoulême, transport bombed 45, 76, 127
Angweiler 253
Anhausen 475
Anholt 407, 422
Anizy-le-Château 122
Ankum 448
Annaburg 469
Annebault 137
Anneweiler 302, 409
Ansbach 447, 448, 463, 465
Anstel 384
Antwerp
  and Allied strategy 6, 167, *199*
  August, rail targets bombed 122
  September
    Allies occupy *161*, 163, 176
    sector 162, 179, 182, 185
  October
    Allied pressure to open port *219*
    sector *199*, 201–205, 207, 209, 213, 218, 220–221, 223, 225, 226
    V1 flying bomb attacks *260*
  November
    Express route (Antwerp-Brussels-Charleroi) *260*
    opening up of port 235, *241*
    V1 flying bomb attacks *260*
  December, as German counter-attack objective *281*, 298
  March, V2 rocket attacks *432*
Antwerp-Turnhout canal 186, 188, 189, 192, 198, 199
Apeldoorn 209, 239, 269, 331, 453, 454, 456, 458, 461
Apolda 450
Apollensdorf 486
Appenweier 344
Appingedam 472, 473
Arbergen 473
Arcis-sur-Aube 150
Ardennes
  and the Maginot Line *255*

Ardennes — *continued*
 September, Allied advance in 163, 164, 166, 167, 168, 171, 172
 November 237
 and Allied strategy 241, 242
 December/January, German offensive (Battle of the Bulge) 215, 280–323, 324, 328, 329, 331, 333, 337, 360, 374, 415, 515, 516
Arenberg, 10th Prince of 430
Arenberg, Duke Engelbert Marie von 430
Arenrath 389
Argentan
 June 45
 air reconnaissance flown 58
 Allied bombing 65, 66
 July, air attacks 70, 71, 72, 74, 85, 86, 87, 88, 106
 August
 air attacks 120, 125, 135
 Allied advance to 123, 124, 126, 128
 Allied capture 131–134, 136
 sector 142
Argonne forest 158
 Meuse-Argonne sector (WW1) 243
Arlon 296, 302, 303
Arloncourt 309
Armentières
 Allied capture 163
 railway yards bombed 56
Arnaville 164
Arnemuiden dyke 176
Arnetsried 473
Arnhem
 September, Operation 'Market-Garden' 6, 163, 176–177, 184–187, 188, 191, 198
 October
 Allied bombing 196, 202, 203, 213
 fighting in sector 200, 208, 209, 212
 November
 Allied bombing 243, 256
 fighting in sector 242
 December, Allied bombing 267
 January, Allied bombing 312, 331
 March, Allied bombing 411, 416, 418
 April 436, 442, 448, 453, 458, 464
 Allied bombing 430, 446, 450
 Allied capture 451, 454, 456
Arnoldsweiler 368
Arnsberg 391, 398, 399, 403, 437, 450
Arnstadt 450
Arras
 Allied air attacks 51, 105
 Allies liberate 156, 158, 159
 railway centre bombed 40, 96, 150
Arromanches, Mulberry harbour 47, 51
Arsdorf 298, 299
Artenay, railway yards bombed 62
Artzenheim 336, 343
Arvers peninsula 459
Arville, Allied bombing 66
Arzberg 470
Arzfeld 365
Arztenheim 343
Asbach 472
Asbeck 455
Asch, Czechoslovakia 470
Aschach 472
Aschaffenburg 252, 302, 309, 329, 369, 417–422, 426, 427, 429, 430, 434
 Allies capture 431, 433, 482
Ascoli, Lt H., RN 43
Asperden 360
Assault Beaches (Normandy)
 Gold 16, 20, 24, 30, 35, 47
 Juno 16, 17, 20, 22
 Omaha 16, 20, 24–29, 32, 34, 35, 45, 47, 51, 419
 Sword 16, 17, 20, 21
 Utah 16, 20, 24, 28–29, 34, 45, 107
 Liberty Highway 292
Assault Beaches (Riviera) (Operation 'Dragoon') 126–127
Assen 451, 465
Assenois 301, 302
Associated Press 516
Asten 183
Astheim 414
Athis 132
Atkins, Pte Thomas (British Army nickname) 223
Attendorn 420, 448, 450
Attnang-Puchheim 470
Aubut, Lt M. G. 196
Auchamps 163
Auenheim 326
Auersmacher 361, 362
Auerswalde 464

Augny 247
Augsburg
 January, Allied bombing 322
 March, Allied bombing 376
 April 472, 477, 479
 Allied bombing 470, 479
 Allied capture 480
Augustine, Sgt Bill (US Signal Corps) 58
Aulendorf 469
Aulnois-sur-Seille 240
Aulnoye 89
Aulock, Genmaj. Hubertus von 159
Aulock, Oberst Andreas von 129
Aumenau 419, 420
Aumontzey 244
Aunay, River 132
Aunay-sur-Odon 43, 44, 55, 111, 112, 113, 114, 115, 116
Auray 117, 121
Aurich 450
Auschwitz concentration camp 449
Aussen 270, 402
Aussig 462, 468
Authie, River 89
Authon 132
Autun 168, 169
Auvers-sur-Oise 129
Auw 344
Auxais 84
Avranches
 Allied aircraft seek targets 58
 Allied bombing 36, 59, 105
 Allies advance from 110, 111, 113
 Germans bomb 115
 US units reach 106
AVREs (Armoured Vehicles Royal Engineers) 251
Axel-Hulst canal 181
Ay, River 85, 87, 100, 102
Aywaille 171
Azerailles 233

Baal 204, 236, 250, 264, 280, 368
Baarle-Nassau 199, 200, 201
Babyloniënbroek 345
Baccarat 183, 186, 199, 202, 213, 222, 232, 234–238, 240, 244, 245, 246
Bachem 401
Bacon, Col Robert L. 268–269
Bad Bergzabern 410
Bad Berka 445
Bad Berleburg 430, 431
Bad Bertrich 399
Bad Bodendorf 389
Bad Brückenau 437
Bad Dürkheim 390, 402, 404, 405
Bad Godesberg 388, 390
 Hotel Dreesen 391
Bad Hersfeld 426
Bad Honnef 394, 395, 396, 398, 399
Bad Kissingen 443
Bad Kreuznach 216, 270, 306, 308, 322, 395, 396, 398, 402, 404,
 US Army POW holding camp (A15) 466
Bad Langensalza 439
Bad Lobenstein 457
Bad Mergentheim 429, 439
Bad Münster 204, 299, 308, 364, 395, 398
Bad Nauheim 420, 421, 422
Bad Oeynhausen 364, 398, 423, 432, 437
Bad Oldesloe 473
Bad Orb 430
Bad Rehburg 442
Bad Reichenhall 475
Bad Rodach 447
Bad Salzig 401
Bad Salzuflen 432
Bad Schwalbach 426
Bad Segeberg 491
Bad Tennstedt 446
Bad Wimpfen 430, 433
Badbergen 448
Badem 377
Baden Baden 450, 452, 454, 457
Baden-Württemberg 193
Badonviller 250
Baesweiler 203
Bagnoles-de-l'Orne 123
 Allied air attacks 56, 59
Bahren 457
Baker, Capt. C. A., USN 27, 47
Baker, Pfc Clifton 436
Baldersheim 348
Baldham, Munich 502
Balesfeld 384
Balgau 349
Ballenstedt 467, 469
Ballon d'Alsace 255
Balztenheim 343

Bamberg 434, 443, 445, 447, 449, 450, 452
 Allies clear 454
Bambesch, forts 255
Bambidersdroff fort 255
Bannholz wood 352
Bannstein 307
Bantzenheim 265, 354
Banz, Pte Samuel 482
Bar-sur-Seine 157
Barbery 123, 125
Barby 452, 456, 457, 459
 Elbe bridgehead 477
Bardenberg 207, 208, 209, 210
Bärenthal 310, 400
Barenton 114, 126, 135
Barkway, S/Sgt Geoffrey 19
Barlo 384
Barleben 454
Barmen 260, 396, 403
Barnes, Lt Col Hubert D. 45
Barnes, Lt-Cdr J. R., RN 33, 43
Barneveld 332, 461, 464, 469
Barneville-sur-Mer 50
Baron, Lt Richard 429
Barondorf 256
Baronweiler 245, 246
Barou 132
Barr, Robert (BBC) 327, 512
Barssel 455
Bartellot, Brig. Sir Walter 114
Baschleiden 301
Basel 249
Basil, Sgt Louis 169
Basle 473, 475, 477
Bassens 115
Bassum 442
Bastendorf 328, 329
Bastogne
 September 171, 172
 December, German counter-offensive 291–293, 294, 296–299, 300, 301, 302, 303
 January
 tide turns 306–320, 306, 312, 313, 315, 317, 319, 322, 324, 325, 326, 328, 329, 330, 332
 handing over ceremony 346
Basweiler 203
Bath dyke 176
Battenheim 348
Batterie Lindemann 196
Batterie Todt 196
Batzlow 459
Bauches du Désert 117
Baudrecourt 244
Baugnez crossroads massacre, Malmédy 289
Bauler 392
Baulny 158
Baumenheim 403
Baumholder 273
Baupte 44
Bavaria 193
Bavent 132
Bavigne 301, 302
Bay of Biscay 112
 Allies attack naval units 30, 119
Bayerlein, Genlt Fritz 271
Bayeux 33, 36, 40, 41, 52, 63, 72, 83, 206, 513
 Allied liberation of 30
Bayon 165
Bayreuth 438, 439, 440, 441, 443, 447, 449, 454, 461, 462, 468, 469
 Nazi cultural capital 457, 460
BBC 327, 511, 512, 514, 515, 516
 European Service 391
Beauchêne 118
Beaucourt 258
Beaufort 300
Beaugency
 bridge bombed 66
 German surrender 182
Beaulieu 115
Beaumesnil 113
Beaumont 161
Beaumont-sur-Sarthe 116
Beauraing 298, 300
Beautor 125
Beauvais 85, 133, 143, 150, 152
 Allied advance from 156, 158
 transportation bombed 59, 84, 114, 142
Bec d'Ambès 114
Béchy 243
Beckiem 420
Beckingen 402
Bedburg 357, 377
Bedheim 444, 445
Beeck 252, 254, 261, 264, 265
Beeden 319

Beek 248
Beerfelden 421
Beeringen 174
 Allied bridgehead 163, 164
Beethoven, Ludwig van, Fifth Symphony 391
Beffe 311
Bega, River 432
Beggendorf 201, 202, 203
Beho 331
Behren 317
Behringen 429
Beiderlinden, Brig. Gen. William 438
Beinheim 402
Bckond 392
Belfort
 July 87, 244, 245, 248
 August, Allied bombing 123
 September 175, 182, 188, 189, 192, 193
 October 196, 198, 199, 200, 202, 207, 209
 November 244, 245, 248, 249, 250, 255, 259, 260
 Allies clear 253, 256
Belfort Gap 6, 176, 177, 179, 244, 246, 247, 248, 249, 250, 251, 253, 254, 256, 257, 260
Belgium, frontier crossed 158–160
Bell, Ken 192
Belleville 116
Bellheim 216
Bellnhausen 420
Belmont 220
Belsen concentration camp 449
Beltheim 400
Bénaménil 185, 188
Bendorf 416
Benerville-sur-Mer 47, 136
Benfeld 318, 321, 342
Bengel 396
Bennwihr 298
Benonches 73
Benrath Chorbusch 385
Bensheim 419
Beratzhausen 473
Berchtesgaden 458, 475, 477, 493, 500–501
Berdorf 292, 300
Berg 237, 260, 264, 294, 308, 385
Berg-Gladbach 345, 348, 353, 389
Bergen, Germany 382, 399, 402, 456, 458
Bergen, Norway 318
Bergen op Zoom 200, 215, 218, 225, 228
Bergen-Belsen concentration camp 449
Bergerhausen 371
Bergheim 236, 376, 377
 Allied capture 426
Berghof: Hitler's mountain retreat 475, 500–501
Bergisch-Born 383
Bergisdorf 454
Berglern 486
Bergneustadt 420
Bergstein 264, 267, 269, 270, 271, 272, 273, 347, 348, 349
Bergues 167
Bergzabern 257, 330
Berigny 100
Beringe 251
Berkebile, Pte Paul 104
Berle 303, 316
Berlin
 and Allied strategy 176, 270, 426
 July, and attempted assassination of Hitler 93
 September, Operation 'Thunderclap' 212
 October, Allied bombing 202, 212
 November, Allied bombing 233, 246, 259
 December, Allied bombing 270, 273
 January
 airfields attacked 324
 Allied bombing 306, 308, 310, 311, 336, 337
 and Soviet drive towards 338
 February
 Allied bombing 343, 345, 347, 351, 356, 357, 361, 363–365, 367–371
 rail stations 370
 March
 Allied bombing 375–377, 383–387, 391, 393, 395, 396, 398, 399–403, 405, 407, 409, 411, 415, 417–420, 423
 Soviet advance 415, 427
 April
 Allied advance towards 456, 488

523

Berlin, April — *continued*
    Allied bombing 430, 431, 434, 441, 443, 445, 449, 450, 455, 458, 459, 463, 466, 468, 469, 473
    German Government and evacuation 458
    German retreat from Soviets 459
    Hitler's last days in Führerbunker 482–483
    Soviet objective 457
    Soviets reach 470, 483
  May
    German surrender 495, 508–509
    Hitler's remains disposed of 492
    post-war Zones/Sectors 193
Bernay 64, 84, 103, 136, 142
Bernburg 459
Bernières, Allied landings at 23
Bernkastel-Kues 377
Beroun 455, 462
Berrendorf 371
Berrwiller 346
Bersenbrück 448
Bertogne 318, 319, 320, 322
Berton, Yannick 58
Bertrichamps 238
Berus 260
Berville-sur-Mer, German military ferry bombed 39
Berzdorf 388
Besançon 166
Besenfeld 457
Besse 428
Bessenich 377
Best 180, 193, 225, 238
Besten 420
Bethancourt 156
Bethon 72
Béthouart, Gén. Emile 258
Béthune 160
Bettendorf 326, 327
Bettenfeld 392
Bettenhofen 342
Bettingen 270, 353, 370
Bettinghausen 439
Betts, Brig. Gen. Edward C. (G-2) 324
Betz, Capt. Alfred 144
Betzdorf 389, 395
Beuel 404, 407
Beuerbach 447
Beuren 402
Beurig 371
Beuzeville 142, 143
Beveland *see* South (Zuid) Beveland
Beveland Canal 226, 227
Bezange 191, 192, 220, 240
Bezarin, Col-Gen. Nikolai 508
Biarritz 242
Bibart 450
Biebelsheim, US Army POW holding camp (A14) 466
Biebrich 420
Bielefeld
  October, Allied bombing 196, 224
  January, Allied bombing 313, 335
  February, Allied bombing 353, 365, 368
  March 411
    viaduct bombed 387, 398, 403
  April 431
    Allies clear 436
Bienen 418
Biervliet 210, 212
Biesdorf 182, 354
Biesheim 343, 344, 346
Bieslautern 308
Bietigheim 415
Bièvre 164
Biezen 209
Biffontaine 222
Bigelbach 302, 303
Bigonville 296, 298
Bihain 317, 318
Billancourt, Renault factory 172
Billig 385
Billing, Oberfahnrich Günther 281
Bilzingsleben 448
Bingen 292, 302, 354, 385, 395, 402, 403, 407
Bingerbrück 403
Bining (Biningen) 270, 271
Binscheid 363, 364, 365
Binsfeld 332, 333, 335, 369, 386, 387
Birch, Stanley (Reuters) 512
Birgden 229, 260
Birgel 260, 280
Birgelen 333
Birgingen 256
Birkenhördt 409
Birkenfeld 274, 366, 368
Birstein 426
Bischofsgrün 468
Bischofsheim 319
Bischofteinitz 504
Bischoltz 332, 334
Bischwihr 339
Bischwiller 273
Bismark 454, 457
Bisping 253
Bitburg
  September 193
  December 298
  January 308, 320, 322, 332
  February 346, 359, 360, 366, 368, 370, 371
  March 375, 376, 383, 384, 385, 386, 387, 389, 390, 392, 397
Bitche (Bitsch)
  December 278, 282, 283, 284, 285, 287
  January 307–314, 317, 319, 322, 324–331, 334
  March 399, 400, 401
Bitschhoffen 399
Bitterfeld 459, 461, 467, 469, 470, 471
Bivels 363
Bizien, Sgt Marcel 143
Black Forest 448, 457, 459, 462, 465, 468, 469, 470, 471, 472
  battle for 473, 474, 477, 479, 480
Blainville, Allies bomb rail centre 64
Blâmont 244, 247, 248, 249, 250, 251, 252
Blanchelande 72
Blangy 142
Blankenberge 171, 192
Blankenburg 468, 470
Blankenheim 281, 330, 337, 343
Blankenrath 401
Blaskowitz, Generobst Johannes 503
Blatzheim 368, 370, 371
Blay, 21st Army Gp Tac HQ 40
Blaye, Bordeaux 115
Bleckede 471, 477, 486
Bleialf 181, 344, 345
Bleisransbach 369
Blerick, Venlo 267
Blies, River 277, 278, 279, 308, 309
Bliesbrucken 274, 278, 308, 310
Bliesransbach 368
Blitterswijck 257
Blodelsheim 351
Blois 80, 106, 116
Blomenberg 431
Blum, Léon 503
Blumenthal 278, 284
Bobbau-Steinfurth 467, 469, 470
Böblingen 427, 430
Bocholt
  December 279, 283
  January 330
  February 343, 353
  March 384, 398, 401, 402, 405, 407, 409, 422
Bochum 205, 236, 322, 398, 402
  Allied entry 448
Bocket 329
Bockholtz 334
Bodenbach 392
Bodenheim 404
Boehme, 1st Lt William 205
Boekhoute 229
Bogen 478
Böhlen 203, 356, 377, 401, 405
Böhr-Iggelheim, US Army POW holding camp (A17) 466
Boich 370
Bois d'Aulnois 241
Bois de Boulogne 144, 145, 148
Bois de Buron 113
Bois de Drusenheim 346
Bois de Faulx 186
Bois de la Fourasse 205
Bois de la Reserve 386
Bois de l'Hôpital 245
Bois de Meudon 148
Bois de Meulles 130
Bois de Nolaumont 315
Bois de Ronce 322
Bois de Tave 310
Bois de Wibrin 318
Bois du Homme 49
Bois du Hommet 84
Bois du Maister 309
Bois Givrycourt 256
Bois Halbout 125
Bois-le-Duc, *see* Zuid Willems Canal
Boizenburg 488
Boland, S/Sgt Oliver 19
Bolbec
  Allies liberate 158
  railways bombed 65
Böllenborn 409
Bollendorf 302, 353, 355, 357, 362
Bolling, Gen. Alexander R. 253
Bolsdorf 387
Bonacker 447
Bonn
  October, Allied bombing 217, 227, 234, 237, 289, 295, 300, 301, 302, 303, 312, 316, 337
  November
    Allied bombing 234, 237
    Allied strategy 241
  December, Allied bombing 289, 295, 300, 301, 302, 303
  January, Allied bombing 312, 316, 337
  February, Allied bombing 345, 346, 349, 354, 362, 369
  March
    Allied advance towards 386
    Allied bombing 383, 385, 391
    Allied capture 390, 391
    battle for 388
    fighting in sector 387, 388, 404, 407
Bonnal 300
Bonnbosq 137
Bonnerue 308, 309, 314, 315
Bönninghardt 387
Bönninghardt Forest 386
Bonnœil 126
Boofzheim 265, 315
Books
  American Forces in Action Series (US War Dept.) 271
  Dachau (Buechner) 481
  Warfare and Armed Conflicts (Clodfelter) 518
Boos 151, 388
Bopfingen 470, 471
Boppard 400, 401, 402, 408, 409, 416, 418, 420
Bor-Komorowski, Gen. Tadeusz 504
Bordeaux
  June, airfields bombed 45
  July, air attacks 80, 90
  August, Allied bombing 114, 115, 117, 122, 123, 125, 126, 127, 133
Borgentreich 430, 431, 439
Borken 260, 268, 274, 353, 396, 399, 402, 407, 415, 420, 422, 426
Bormann, Martin 475, 483
Born 329, 330, 333, 456
Borna 458, 459
Bornheim 387
Borr 377
Borschemich 371
Bortr, Lt Barthell 385
Boslar 264, 366
Bossei-la-Lande 86
Bothmer, Gen. Richard von 391
Bottrop 232, 264, 345, 415, 422
Botzdorf 387
Bougy 86
Boulaide 301
Boulogne
  Allied capture 192
  Allies by-pass 162
  Allies close in 163, 164, 166
  battle for 179, 181, 183, 184
  as 'fortress' 192
  installations bombed 59, 148, 166, 167, 173, 174, 176, 178, 197
  Le Portal captured 184
  Mont-Lambert captured 181
  naval vessels attacked 41, 46
  sector 182
Bourcy 309, 310, 325
Bourdenay 148
Bourg-Achard 148
Bourg-Leopold 164, 166
Bourges 86
Bourgtheroulde 146
Bourguébus 91, 93
Bourheim 254, 255, 256
Bourneville 146
Bourscheid 329, 330
Bourth 80, 85, 94
Bouvier-Muller, Mme 128
Bouzonville 256
Bovigny 322, 324, 325, 327, 328, 329, 330
Bowman, Pfc Raymond J. 467
Boxberg 397
Boxhorn 331
Boxmeer 189, 333
Boxtel 219, 221, 223
Brachelen 282, 334, 335
Bracht 336
Brackenheim 445
Bradley, Lt Gen. Omar N. 13
  advance into Germany 434, 438, 453, 458
  and Allied strategy 241, 242, 270, 342, 375, 453
  and Ardennes German counter-attack 280, 298, 301
  at Norfolk House 10
  at Siegfried Line 175
  in Bastogne 346
  break-out from Normandy 113, 157
Bradley, Omar — *continued*
  career 11
  confers with Allied commanders 35, 124, 153, 241, 453
  First Army HQ 40
  King George visits front 210–211
  and Montgomery 152
  Normandy strategy 131
  Operation 'Cobra' 94
  Operation 'Goodwood' 92
  'Overlord' strategy 62, 67
  Paris liberation 145
  and Patton 374
  and the press/media 515
  and Remagen bridge 388
  Rhine crossing 408, 410, 412, 413, 415, 417
  Rhine reached 258
  The True Glory (film) 419
  US forces regrouped 110
  visit to Ohrdruf concentration camp 448
Bradley, T/Sgt Robert 27
Braine-le-Comte 129
Brake 474
Brambauer 437
Bramsche 448
Brandenburg 193, 264, 265, 267, 268
Brandenberger, Gen. Erich 503
Brandenburg 427, 469
Brandscheid 176, 179, 343, 347, 348
Brandt, Bert (Press photographer) 215
Bras 91, 318
Braun, Eva 470, 483
Braunau 488, 490, 492–493
Braunlage 461
Braunschweig *see* Brunswick
Breberen 328
Brécey 102, 110, 111, 112
Brèche, River 156
Brecht 197
Breda 199, 219, 223, 225, 227, 228, 232, 234, 235, 238
  Allies free 236
Bredeweg 352
Bregenz 489, 490
Bréhal 105, 106
Breidfeld 333
Breisach 294, 343, 346, 348, 470
Breitenbach 419
Breitenstein 454
Breitscheid 410
Breker, Arno 502
Bremen
  September, Allied bombing 189
  October, Allied bombing 202, 209
  January, Allied bombing 334
  February, Allied bombing 368
  March, Allied bombing 394, 407, 409, 411, 423
  April 436, 440, 442, 444, 448, 473, 480, 481
    Allied advance 446, 467, 470
    Allied bombing 431, 434, 438, 449, 450, 458, 459, 469, 471, 472, 473
    Allied objective 453
    battle and Allied capture 474, 476, 478
  May 490, 494
Bremervörde 486, 490
Bremgarten 346
Bremm 358, 398
Bremscheid 400, 401
Brenig 387
Brenne valley 175
Brenner Pass 500
Brereton, Lt Gen. Lewis H. 176
Breskens 171, 175, 189, 207–210, 212, 213, 216–219, 221–222, 228, 229
  Allied capture 220
Bresle 156
Bresles 156
Brest 34, 145
  Allied advance to 112, 116, 117, 118, 157, 168
  Allied bombing 94, 143, 158, 160, 162, 163, 166, 167, 171, 178
  Allied capture 179–181
  German resistance 119, 121, 123, 125, 126, 128, 148, 150, 151, 167, 173, 174
  naval action off 74
  shipping bombed 117, 120, 127, 132, 142, 148, 150, 159
  submarine pens bombed 115, 125
Brest peninsula 43
Brette-Villette 86
Bretten 439
Bretteville-l'Orgueilleuse 36, 52
Bretteville-sur-Ay 84
Bretteville-sur-Laize 118, 125
Bretzenheim, US Army POW holding camp (A14) 466

524

Bréville 39
Brey 402
Bricquebec
  Allied air attacks 51
  Allied liberation 52
Briedel 401
Briel 462, 468
Briesach 259
Brilon 426
Brimingen 369
Briollay 115
Brionne 138, 139, 142
Briouze 133
Brisy 327
British Aluminium Company, Norfolk House 10
British Broadcasting Corporation see BBC
Brittany
  June, Allied bombing 35
  July, US advance 107
  August
    Allied bombing 147
    US advance 111–113, 115–121, 118, 123, 125, 126, 128, 131–134, 147–148, 150–151
  September, US advance 157, 167, 168, 173, 179–182, 206
  January 329
Britten 399
Broekheide 247
Broekhuizen 257, 264
Broglie 142
Brohl 390
Broich 270
Brooke, FM Sir Alan (CIGS)
  arrives in France 40
  Rhine crossing 412, 413, 417
  visit to Siegfried Line 377
Brooks, Maj. Gen. Edward H. 258, 503
Brotheridge, Lt Herbert 'Den' 19
Brotonne, bridge at 140
Brotonne Forest 146, 151
Brouvelieures 219, 220, 221
Brown, Capt. Bobbie, E., Medal of Honor 217
Browning, Lt-Gen. Frederick 178
Brownrigg, Capt. T. M., RN 20
Bru 228
Bruchhausen 394, 439
Bruchsal 339, 376, 430
Bruckberg 486
Bruckhausen 275, 418
Bruges, Allies advance towards 166, 167, 192
Brühl 236, 384, 387
Brünen 419
Brüngsberg 401, 402
Brünst 502
Brunswick (Braunschweig)
  October, Allied bombing 212, 220
  January, Allied bombing 321
  March, Allied bombing 383, 417, 421
  April 446, 448, 454, 467, 469, 470
    Allied bombing 427, 447, 449
    Allies clear 451, 455
Brussels
  July, air attacks in vicinity 80, 100
  August
    Allied air attacks 113, 151
    rail targets bombed 122
  September
    Allied liberation 160, 162, 163
    Allies advance from 163, 164
    Lille-Brussels highway 157
    Montgomery meets Eisenhower 163
  November
    Eisenhower outlines strategy 241
    Express route (Antwerp-Brussels-Charleroi) 260
  December, and German counter-attack 281
  January 308
  May 504
Brussels-Melsbroek 129
Brüx, Czechoslovakia 324
Bruyères 216, 218, 219, 225, 226, 232, 242, 243, 244, 245, 246
Bruz, Allied air attacks 59, 90
Bryant, Rear Adm. Carleton F., USN 27, 47
Bübingen 367, 368, 369, 383, 386
Buch 400
Buchen 417, 476
Büchenbeuren 401
Buchenwald concentration camp 447, 449
Buchet 346, 347
Buchholt 363
Buchholz 349, 377
Buchner, Col Wilhelm 503
Buchy 156

Bückeberg 439
Bucknall, Lt-Gen. Gerard 114
Bucy-lès-Pierrepont 148
Büderich 408, 409, 413
  road bridge 393
  US Army POW holding camp (A1) 466
Büdesheim 384
Buding 248
Büdingen 422
Buechner, 1st Lt Dr (later Col) Howard A., Dachau 481
Bueil 102
Buggenum 247
Bühl 454
Buir 280, 363, 370
Buisdorf 409
Bulge, Battle of see Ardennes
Bull, Maj. Gen. Harold R. (G-3) 324
Bullay 234, 307, 320, 324, 330, 396, 400
Bullen, Driver R. S. 53
Büllingen 282, 283, 298, 299, 332, 333, 337, 338, 342, 343, 344
Bully-Grenay 159
Bult 192
Bundenthal 284, 337
Burbach 260, 264, 385
Burden 329
Bure 313
Büren 264, 265, 426
Bures 132
Buret 329
Burg 390
Burggen 480
Burglengenfeld 473
Burgsinn 433
Burgsteinfurt 272, 343, 392, 393
Buriville 233
Buron 75
Burrough, Adm. Harold M. 505
Burscheid 450
Bürstadt 419
Burt, Capt. James M., Medal of Honor 217
Busbach 179, 181, 183, 185
Busch, FM Ernst 490, 495
Büschdorf 249
Büschel, SS-Unterscharf. Max 286
Büschhutten 445
Büsdorf 383
Busheyhead, 1st Lt Jack 481
Bütgenbach 287
Butzbach 391
Butzweiler 376
Buxtehude 471

Cabourg 133, 140
Cadzand 219, 226, 227
Caen
  June 30, 42, 46, 48
    Allied advance on 36, 39, 61
    bomb damage 71
    fighter aircraft combats 58
    German resistance 27, 33, 34, 35, 41, 43, 44, 49, 52, 54, 57, 59, 63, 64, 66
    German units bombed 31, 51
    industrial works bombed 56
    road systems/bridges bombed 27, 40
    stalemate 62
  July
    air attacks on German units 71, 79, 88
    battles in sector 70, 72, 73, 80, 85, 87, 88, 94, 96, 98, 99, 100, 101
    becomes Allied traffic and communications centre 107
    liberation 74–78, 90
    and Operation 'Goodwood' 89, 90, 91
    Winston and Churchill bridges 78
  August
    Allied bombing in area 110, 111, 113, 197
    fighting in sector 111, 116, 117, 118, 119, 125
Caen Canal 41
Caen Canal Bridge (later 'Pegasus Bridge') 18, 19
Cahagnes 106
Cahier 87
Caillouet 102
Cairo, 'Sextant' Conference 8, 12
Calais 171
  Allied bombing 182, 185, 186, 188
  Allied capture 192

Allies close in 163, 164, 166, 189, 191, 192
  as 'fortress' 192
  liberated 196, 197
  truce for civilians 193
  see also Pas de Calais
Calbe 441
Calcar
  February 355, 359, 360, 362, 363, 364, 365, 368, 370
  March 375, 413
Calonne, River 142
Calvörde 451
Cambrai 150
  communications bombed 40, 44, 73, 141
Cambremer 137
Camburg 450
Camp Gaillard 8
Campbell, Pfc Raleigh 359
Camprond 101
Canal de Derivation (Omleidings-kanaal) 247, 248, 249
Canal de Helena 251
Canisy 42, 100
Cantrell, Sgt David M. 361
Cap d'Antifer 95, 140
Cap de la Hague
  June
    Allies engage 64, 65, 66
    German deployments around 61
    naval forces engaged 43
  July, German resistance ends 70, 71
Cap de la Hève 85, 113, 134
Cap du Dramont 127
Cap Fréhel 77
Cap Gris Nez 89, 171, 189, 192–193
Cap Lévi 56
Capa, Robert (Life magazine)
  Cherbourg 58
  Omaha beach 26
  Zeppelin Bridge, Weisse Elster 467
Capelle 228, 232
Capellenhagen 442
Carden 394
Carentan
  June 30, 31, 33, 35, 36, 42, 43, 44, 45, 47, 57
  Allied bombing of bridges to north 30
  Allied capture 34, 40
  July, fighting around 74, 75, 76, 78, 79, 80, 83, 84, 86
Carhaix 116
Carolan, T/5 Wesley B. 292
Carpiquet 41, 71, 72, 73, 74
Carr, Maj. W. R. 512
Carrell, S/Sgt Voight 385
Carrouges 124
Carteret, Allied bombing 51
Casablanca Conference (1943), strategic directive 6
Caserta, Royal Palace: German surrender signed 480, 494
Casey, T/5 Ancel 320
Cassel 163
Cassino, and heavy bombing 197
Castrop 443
Castrop-Rauxel 243, 309, 387
Caudebec-en-Caux 40, 112, 140, 151, 156
  shipping attacked 64
Caumont 42, 45, 48, 49, 77, 93, 100, 101, 103, 105–106, 110, 113
  Operation 'Bluecoat' 102
Cauville 122
Celle 438, 443, 450, 451, 454, 518
Celles 299, 300
Cemeteries
  Becklingen War Cemetery, Soltau 518
  Breuna, Kassel 467
  Henri-Chapelle, Belgium: US War Cemetery 386
  La Cambe 117
  La Délivrande War Cemetery 19
  Le Rivier d'Allemont 245
  Lommel: German War Cemetery 323
  Margraten: Netherlands American Cemetery 467
  Normandy: First American Cemetery 27
  Normandy American Cemetery (Colleville-sur-Mer) 27, 29, 32, 97, 519
  Reichswald Forest 386
  Rochester, USA: Holy Sepulchre Cemetery 467
  Saint-Germain-en-Laye 308
  Uden War Cemetery 228
Cérences 74, 100, 105
Cerisy-la-Salle 101, 104
Cernay 279, 330, 332, 335, 337, 339, 342, 346

Cetturu 329
Chalaines 160
Chalampé 351, 354
Châlons-sur-Marne 86, 151, 152
Cham 486, 490
Chamberlain, Neville (British Prime Minister) 7
Chambois 131, 132, 133, 134, 135, 136, 137
Champ-du-Boult 115
Champagney 207
Champdray 244
Champeaux 133
Champigny 146, 148
Champlon 317, 318
Champs 307
Channel Islands 113
  see also Alderney; Guernsey; Jersey
Channel Tunnel 196
Chantilly 119
Chapelle-à-Wattines 160
Chapman, Sapper Frank 449
Charentonne, River 95
Charleroi 147, 160, 161, 162
  Express route (Antwerp-Brussels-Charleroi) 260
Charleville 150
Charmes 181, 182
Charny 140
Chartres
  June, Allied bombing 43, 45, 46, 49, 52, 53, 55, 57, 59, 60, 62, 65, 66
  July
    air reconnaissance 105
    Allies bomb area 70, 71, 74, 81, 83, 84, 88, 94, 103, 106
  August 153
    Allied bombing 111, 113, 115, 116, 127
    Allied liberation 132, 134, 144
Château d'Audrieu 43
Château de Tertu 80, 94
Château Matharel, Moselle 165
Château-Bréhain 244
Château-du-Loir, railway yards bombed 57
Château-Gontier 116
Château-Salins 182, 242, 243, 244
Château-Thierry 150, 151
Châteaubriand
  Allied advances 114
  Allied liberation 117
  Allies push beyond 124
  rail targets bombed 56
Châteaudun
  Allied bombing at 24, 85, 106
  Allied liberation 132
Châteauneuf 84, 117
Châtel-sur-Moselle 189
Châtellerault, fuel dump bombed 46, 120
Châtenois 175
Chaulnes 91
Chaumont 176, 296, 298, 299
Chaumont-en-Vexin 152
Chauny 55, 120
Cheb 443
Cheminot 241
Chemnitz 454, 457, 459, 461, 464, 468
  Allied bombing 348, 356, 357, 377, 383, 385, 430, 441, 449, 450, 458, 459
  Elbe bridgehead near 477
Chenicourt 204
Chenogne 303, 306, 307
Cherain 320, 322, 324, 325, 330
Cherbourg 33, 34, 37, 67
  Allied advance towards 37, 48, 52, 53, 54–55
  Allied encirclement and capture 48, 55, 56, 57–62, 63, 64, 65, 66, 173
  as Allied port 107
Cherbourg peninsula see Cotentin peninsula
Chérencé-le-Roussel 117
Chérisy, Allied bombing 55, 64, 81, 125
Cheshire, W/Cdr Leonard 31
Cheux, Allies enter 59, 61
Chiemsee 493
Chimay 158
Cholet 94
Choltitz, Gen. Dietrich von 142, 144
Christiansand 171
Christie, Sgt Jimmy (AFPU) 75
Churchill, Rhona (war correspondent) 413
Churchill, Winston S. 13
  and Allied strategy 270
  arrives in France 40
  and Gen. Eisenhower 12
  and Montgomery 152, 453
  and press/media 513
  Rhine crossing 412, 413

Churchill, Winston — continued
  and 'Sextant' Conference 8
  and Teheran Conference 8, *193*, *338*
  'V' for Victory sign *391*
  visits Siegfried Line *377*
  Yalta Conference *342*
Cielle 315
Cihotzki, SS-Sturmmann Rudi *130*
Cinq-Mars 83, 112
Cintheaux *117*, 118
Cirreux 329
Cité Graffenwald *332*
Clair-Tison 125
Clamecy *168*
Clark, Gen. Mark *501*
Clarke, Capt. C. P., RN 27
Clausthal-Zellerfeld 203, 450
Clerf, River 331, 332
Clermont 143, 158
Clervaux
  September 172
  December 289, *290*
  January 307, 317, 330, 331, 332, 333, 334, 335, 336, 338
  February 342, 349, 351, 352
Cleurie 202
Cleve 189, 203, 299, 349–360, *350*, *352*, *355*, 365
Cleve forest 359, 361
Clinchamps 136
Clingen 446, 448
Cloppenburg 427, 434, 446, 451, 454
Cloyes, Allied bombing 72
Cobbenrode 447
Coblenz
  September, Allied bombing 172
  October
    Allied bombing 205, 208, 210, 227
    V1 launch sites *260*
  November, Allied bombing 238, 257, 261
  December, Allied bombing 283, 292, 295, 299, 300, 301, 302
  January, Allied bombing 307, 308, 311, 312, 328, 337
  February
    Allied bombing 343, 349, 352, 354, 358, 361, 362, 363
    Allied plans for offensive *375*
  March 387, 388, 390, 391, *394*, 395, 396, 399, 400, 402, 410, 416, 418, *421*
    Allied bombing 383, 392, 395, 399, 403
    Allies clear city 401, 403, *404*
  April, US Army POW holding camp (A10) *466*
Cobreville 299
Cobru 322
Coburg 447, 448, 450, 452
Cochem 394, 395, 398
Codman, Col Charles R. *410*
Coesfeld 252, 279, 306, 343, 393, 395, 403, 407, 411
Coin-sur-Seille 184
Coincourt *191*, *192*, 209, 220
Col de la Slucht 267, 269
Cölbe 369, 375, 398, 415
Colditz 459
Colleville-sur-Mer *45*
  see also Cemeteries
Collins, 1st Lt Henry W. (USAAF 366th FG) *82*
Collins, Lt, RN 35
Collins, Maj. Gen. J. Lawton *211*, *298*, *385*
Collins, Sgt Max (AFPU) *173*
Colmar
  November 248, 251, 253
  December 270–274, 283–285, 287, 294, 297, 298, 300, 301–303
  January 306, 309, 310, 315, 316, 330, 331, 334, 335, 337, 339
  February 343, 344, 345, 346, 347, *348*, 351, 353, 357
  March 375
Colmar canal 335, 336, 339, 342, 343
Colmar forest 344
Colmar Pocket *274*, *279*, *328*, *329*, *332*, *333*, *336*, *347*
Cologne
  September 181
    Allied bombing 171, 191
  October 207
    Allied bombing 198, 201, 208, 212, 213, 216, 217, 226, 228, *232*
    V1 launch sites *260*
  November
    Allied bombing *232*, 233, 234, 236, 240, 242, 243, 247, 257, 259
    Kalk district 259
  December 267, 269, *286*

Cologne — continued
    Allied bombing 269, 271, 280, 283, 289, 297, 301
  January, Allied bombing 309, 311, 312, 313, 316, 321, 336, 337
  February 371
    Allied bombing 349, 351, 353, 354, 356, 358, 366, 368, 369, 371
    Allied plans for offensive *375*
  March *372*–373, *388*
    Allied bombing 376, 377, 383, 384, 389, 391, 396, 407
    Allied capture 386, 387
    Allied forces approach 375, *381*, 383
    battle for 385
    fighting in sector 377, 382, 384, 386, 417, 418, 421
  April, fighting in sector 426, 447, 450, 453
Colombelles 79, 80
Coltainville, Allied bombing 45, 46, 55
Colville, John (Churchill's private secretary) *413*
Colwell, Pfc Cyril F. (US Signal Corps) *247*
Combourg 90
Commanster 331
Commercy 158, 160
Commonwealth War Graves Commission *see* Imperial (later Commonwealth) War Graves Commission
Compiègne
  Allied advance near 156, 158
  Allied bombing 115, 150
Compogne 320, 322
Conches
  Allied bombing 55, 60
  Allied liberation 141
Condé 111, 125, 126, 128, 131
Condé-sur-Noireau *121*
  Allied bombing 45
Condé-sur-Seulles 34, *63*
Coningham, AM Sir Arthur *197*
Connantre 133
Connerré 114
Consdorf 287, 289, 296
Constance 479
Conthil 244
Corbeil 125, 141, 143, 146
Corbie 117, 156
Corlett, Maj. Gen. Charles E. *211*
Cormelles 90
Cornely, Frank *389*
Cornimont 210, 212, 217
Corny 244
Corrado, Carmen A. (US Signal Corps) *316*
Cossesseville 128
Cota, Maj. Gen. Norman D. *234*, *241*, *333*
Cotentin peninsula
  June 35, 39, 41, 43, 45, 47, *48*, 50–53
    Allied bombing 30, 39, 42, 44, 46, 49, 59
    and Allied strategy 6
    naval bombardment 38
    Utah assault beach *16*
  July
    Allied bombing 89
    Allied forces advance in 72, 73, 77
    US First Army bogged down 94
  August 152
  see also Cap de la Hague
Cottbus 358
Coudres, air attacks at 71
Coughlin, Maj. Robert *428*
Coullemelle 158
Coupesarte 134
Courtalain 116
Courtil 328
Courtrai, Belgium 93, 163
Coutances 48, *94*, *99*, *100*, 102–105
  Allied aircraft seek targets 58, 101
  Allied bombing 49, 72, 95
Couterne *123*
Coutures 197
Couville, Allies liberate 53
Coventry Cathedral *356*
Craig, Maj. Fred *478*
Crailsheim 434, 441, 443, 445, 447, 448, 462, 470, 471
Craon 83
Crawinkel 444
Creil 156
Crépon *52*
Crépy 156
Crerar, Gen. Henry *375*, *432*
Crest *151*
Creuilly 40
Creussen 457
Cristot *44*
Croisilles 122
Crombach *332*
Crozon peninsula *168*, *174*, *181*

Cruchten 358, 361
Cues 398
Culembourg 311
Culmont-Chalindrey 83
Currie, Maj. David V. (later VC) *134*
Cussy 75
Cuvergnon 150
Cuxhaven 453, 478
Czechoslovakia, Sudeten question *391*

Dachau concentration camp *472*, *481*, 504
Dachwig 446
Dahl *312*, 313, 314
Dahlen 345
Dahlquist, Maj. Gen. John E. *243*
Dahnen 351, 363
  Allied capture 364
Daily Mail 413
Daily Sketch 326, *335*, *363*
Daladier, Edouard *503*
Daldeiden 365
Dalfsen 451
Dalhain 244
Dallau 427
Dalrymple-Hamilton, Rear-Adm. F. H. G. 33
Dambach 307
Damblainville 132
Dannemarie 259
Danube, River 470, *471*, *472*, 473, 474, 475, 477, *478*, 479, *480*, 502
Daoulas peninsula 157
Darmschlag 502
Darmstadt 269, 332, 364, 376, 399, 407, 414, *418*, 419, 420, 421
  Allied capture 416, *417*
Darscheid 388
Dasbach 416
Dasburg *290*, 307, 319, 330, 349, 351, 363, 366
  Allies enter 364, 365
Daser, Gen. Wilhelm *235*
Datteln 391
Daun 270, 308, 361
Davis, Brig. Gen. Thomas J. *513*, *515*
Dawney, Col Christopher *495*
De Gaulle, Gén. Charles *505*
  and Alsace-Lorraine *337*
  in Bayeux *30*
  and German POWs *466*
  and Paris liberation *142*, *144*, *145*
De Koeckling 244
Dean, Maj. Gen. William F. *438*
Dean, Robert 7
Deauville, Allied capture 140
Dedenhausen 445
Deelen 456
Deggendorf 469, 478, 480, 486, 488
Dehlingen 269
Deidenberg *285*, *328*
Deiligenstadt 446
Delden 440
Delfzijl 474, 490
Delhoven 385
Delme 242
Delmenhorst 467, 469, 476
DeMarco Sgt (US Signal Corps) *159*
Dempsey, Lt-Gen. Sir Miles C. *91*
  advance to Elbe 446, 453
  commands British Second Army 13, *253*
  German peace overtures *494*, *495*
  meeting of commanders *375*
  Port-en-Bessin conference 35
Den Bosch *see* s'Hertogenbosch
Den Helder 173, 312, 453
Den Hout 235
Deneuvre 234
Dengoldsheim 325
Denkingen 466
Denmark
  and German surrender *495*, *496*
  Soviet advance to 488
Dennebouy, Loïc 46
Densborn 386
Derben 321
Derichsweiler 277, 278
Derikum 384
Derkum 384
Derval 114
Dessaint, André *298*
Dessau 324, 387, 454, 455, 457–459, 461, 467, 469–472
Destord 192
Destrich 245
Detmold 269, 432, 437
Deurne 186, *208*, 216, 217, 253
  Allied capture 188
Deurne canal 250
Deventer 213, 226, 261, 280, 336, 348, 438, 439, 440, 442, 450, 451
  Allied occupation 446

Devers, Lt Gen. Jacob L. *169*, *256*, *258*, *328*, *337*, *419*, *471*, *474*
Dexheim 407
Deycimont 199
Deyfosse 241
Dickerscheid 371
Dickweiler 292, 314
Dieblingen 268
Diedersdorf *459*
Diedingen 272
Diefenbach 260
Diekirch
  September 182, 183, 184
  December 296, 298, 299, 301, 303
  January 306, 326, 327, 328, 329, 331, 334, 335
  February 345, 349
Diemarden 444
Diemel, River 440
Dienstedt 450
Diepholz 436, 439
Dieppe 152, 156
  Allied bombing 142, 147, 157
  Allied train ferry *107*
  Allies liberate 158, *192*
  naval forces engaged 73
Dierfeld 394
Diesdorf 470
Dieteren 325
Dietersheim, US Army POW holding camp (A11) *466*
Dietfurt 477
Dietrich, SS-Oberstgruppenf. Josef *150*
Dietrichingen 401
Dietringen 480
Dieulouard *165*
Dieuze 218, 233, 244, 245, 250, 251, 253
Diez, US Army POW camp (A8) *466*
Dieze, River *221*
Dijon
  Allied advance to *168*, *169*, 175
  Allied bombing 74, 102, 119, 122, 131, 140
  Allied fighter-bombers operate 123
Dillenburg 389, 395, 419
Dillingen 203, 270, 272–274, 277–280, 282–285, 287, 289, 402, 472, 473, 475
Dilsen 189
Dimbleby, Richard (BBC reporter) *327*
Dinan 113, 115
Dinant 162, 164, *297*
Dinard *112*, 119, 121, 123, 125, 126, 128
  Allied occupation 131, 132
Dingden 419
Dingdorf 383
Dingelstädt 442, 446
Dinglingen 465, 469
Dinslaken 377, 414, 416, 418
Dinteloord 236, 237
Dinxperlo 422
Dirmingen 403
Disney, Col Paul A. *428*
Disternich 376
Distroff 240
Dives, River 132, 133, *135*
Dives-sur-Mer 133, 137
Dixmuide 166
Docelles 189
Dochamps *310*, *314*, 315
Dodewaard 207
Dohm 387
Dohr 396
Dol 74, 113, 114, 115
Dollbergen 307
Doller, River *256*, 260, 266, 273
Dolreuth 472
Domburg 234, 235, 237, 238, 239
Domfaing 220
Domfessel 268
Domfront 42, 46, 50, 87, 106, 126, 127, 128, 131, 132
Dommershausen 399
Dompaire *174*
Donaueschingen 346, 352, 369, 384, 393, 398, 399, 468, 470
Donauwörth 249, 449, 458, 475
Doncols 317, 318
Donges 95, 96
Dönitz, Grossadm. Karl, as Hitler's successor *486*, *490*, *494*, *496*, *504*, *516*
Donnay 125
Dordrecht 213, 219, 222, 232, 307, 321, 329, 331, 337
Dorf 394
Dorfen 489
Dormagen 385
Dormagen 445
Dornbirn 490
Dornot, Allies cross Moselle *164*
Dorsten 268, 306, 329, 391, 395, 399, 405, 407, 409, 415, 418–420
  Allied capture 422

526

Dortmund
   October, Allied bombing 202
   November, Allied bombing 246, 261
   December, Allied bombing 266
   January, Allied bombing 309, 336
   February, Allied bombing 345, 359, 363, 369, 370
   March, Allied bombing 375, 376, 377, 385, 387, 389, 391, 393, 395, 396, 401, 402, 415, 418
   April *433*, 437, 447
      Allied bombing 440, 448
      Allies clear 454
      Allies enter outskirts 443, 453
Dortmund-Ems Canal 307, *420*, 430, 432, 433, 436
Dorweiler 376
Dottesfeld 361
Douai
   Allied bombing 44, 99, 113, 123
   Allied capture 159
Doubs, River 245, 246, 247
Doullens 125, 150, *156*, 158
Douvres-la-Délivérande, radar installation 50
Dover, Adm. Ramsay as Flag Officer Commanding 11
Doveren 369
Downard, Lt Col 450
Downey, Senator Sheridan 516
Dozulé 133, 136, 137
Draaibrug 220
Drachselsried 478
Dransdorf 388
Dreiborn 345
Dreierwalde 436
Dreis 387
Dremmen 269, 334
Dresden
   January, Allied bombing in area 324
   February, Allied bombing *356*, 357, 358
   March, Allied bombing 377, 383
   April 468
      Allied bombing 430, 450, 455, 458, 459, 462, 469
      Allied objective *433*, *438*
   post-war: Frauenkirche as memorial 356
Dreumel 199
Dreux
   June, Allied bombing 36, 39, 41, 56, 58–60, 65, 66
   July, Allied bombing 70, 73, 74, 86, 91
   August
      Allied advance from 134, 140
      Allied bombing 111
      Allied liberation 132, 133, 136
Drielandenpunt/Dreiländereck *see* Vaalsberg, The: 'Three-Country Point'
Driesch 395
Drôme, River *84*
Drove 370
Drusenheim 313, 328, 346, 349, 352, 353, 354
Dubervill, Frank (AFPU) *42*
Ducey, dams near 110
Duclair 78, 150, 152
Duderstadt 446, 448
Dugny 122
Duisburg
   Allied bombing 212, *213*, 261, 264, 272, 330, 336, 349, 364, *420*
   Aussenhafen waterway *212*
   Hamborn *212*, 420, 422, *439*
   surrender to Allies 458
Duisdorf 388
Dülken 306
   Allies occupy 377
Dülmen 267, 269, 321, 343, 353, 354, 399, 403, 407, 409, 422
Dümmersee 442, 450
Düne, island of 465
Dunkirk
   1940 evacuation 11
   September (1944)
      Allied advance towards 167
      Allied bombing 157
      as 'fortress' *192*
   October, truce for civilians 200, 201
   November
      Allied air attacks 237, 239, 240, 241, 256, 260, 261
      sector 250
   December, Allied bombing 264, 265
   February, Allied bombing 345
   April, Allied bombing 468
Duppach 385
Düppenweiler 269
Dupuy, Col R. Ernest *144*, *153*, *511*, *512*
Dürboslar 251

Düren
   September 181
   October 202, 208, 210, 217, 227
   November 236, 238, 247, 248, 249, 250, 252, 256, 257, 259, 261, *366*
   December 265–269, 272, 274, 277, 278, 279, 280, 282, 285, 287, 298, 299
   January 307, 330, 337
   February 351, 363, 364, 366, *368*, *369*, 370, 371
   March 375, 376, 377, 383, 384
Durlach 316, 319
Dürnbach 502
Durrem 339
Durrenbucher Forest 480
Durstel 259
Dürwiss 253
Düsseldorf
   October, Allied bombing 212, 213, 216, 217, 220, 224
   November
      air battles over 252
      Allied bombing 234, 237, 240
      Allied strategy 241
   December, Allied bombing 269, 279
   January, Allied bombing 306, 321, 337
   February, Allied bombing 343, 348, 349, 356, 370
   March *382*, 387
      Allied bombing 376, 399, 422
      Düsseldorf-Oberkassel road bridge *382*
      Hamm (suburb) 353, *382*
   April, battle for 462

Earle, Peter *453*
East Germany *see* Germany (German Democratic Republic)
East Prussia *193*, *338*
Eauplet, Rouen *141*
Ebenhausen 469
Ebenshausen 423
Eberbach, Gen. Heinrich 150
Eberstadt 407
Ebrach 420, 427, 434
Ebsdorf 461
Echt 325, 326, 327, 328, 329, 330
Echtem 388
Echternach
   October 199, 203
   December 283, 287, 289, 292, 296, 298, 299, 300, 301, 302
   January 306, 314, 326
   February 349, 351, 354–362, 364, 369
   March 397
Echternacherbrück 356
Echtz 247, 274
Eckernförde 491, 494
Eckersberg 486
Écot 246
Écouché *131*, 134
Écouis 151
Écouviez 167
Écurcey 246
Eddy, Maj. Gen. Manton S. *94*
Ede 464
Edenkoben 311, 410
Edenland 486
Eder, River 426
Edersee dam 426
Ediger 396
Eede 215
Eem, River 470
Eferding 502
Eger, Czechoslovakia 447, 476, 478
Eggenfelden 473, 488
Ehingen 472
Ehlenz 376
Ehlers, S/Sgt Walter D., Medal of Honor *514*
Ehmen 321, 417
Ehr 400
Ehrang 183, 234, 295, 308, 387
Eich 395
Eichstätt 466, 477
Eidengesäss 429
Eifel region *394*
Eigelscheid 342, 343
Eilenburg 469, 472
Eilenstedt 448
Einbeck 446
Eindhoven
   21st Army Gp TAC HQ (Geldrop) *209*, *375*
   air attacks on 129
   and Operation 'Garden' *177*, 180, *183*, 186, 188, 189
   sector 208, 225
Eining 478
Einruhr 346
Eisborn 455

Eisenach 423, 429, 430, 432, 437, 439
Eisenhower, Gen. Dwight D.
   and Adm. Ramsay *308*
   Advanced CPs
      Gueux *189*
      Jullouville *189*
      Portsmouth: Sawyer's Wood ('Sharpener') *67*, *128*, *512*
      Tournières, Normandy ('Shellburst') *128*, *142*, *189*
   Allied bombing policy 97, 212
   Allied-Soviet link up 477
   American Forces in Action Series 271
   and Antwerp *161*, *199*, 219
   appointed to command European Theater (1942) *7*, *8*
   appointed to command SHAEF *8*, 12
   and Ardennes German counter-offensive 280, 289, 298, *301*, *323*, *337*
   at Norfolk House *10*
   at Siegfried Line *175*
   at Villa Montgomery, Granville *153*
   in Bastogne *346*
   break-out in Normandy *110*, *111*, 113, *124*, *135*
   broadcast (6 June 1944) *20*, *21*, *511*
   as C-in-C Mediterranean *8*
   career *8*
   Cherbourg captured *66*
   COSSAC *7*, *193*
   deployment of forces 274
   Directive to (1944) 9
   first D-Day landings 20
   forces commanded by *169*
   Geilenkirchen battle 248
   German unconditional surrender *496*, *504*, 507
   Holland offensive postponed 451
   King George VI visits *211*
   lands in Normandy 35, *128*, *142*
   and Leigh-Mallory's death *245*, *308*
   and 'Market-Garden' *163*, *176*, *199*
   and military occupation *397*
   Mons victory *159*
   and Montgomery *152*, *258*, *301*, *488*
   Operation 'Goodwood' *90*, *92*
   Paris liberation *142*, *144*
   and Patton's advance to Moselle *164*
   planning for 'Overlord' *12*–*13*, *13*, *62*, *67*
   and port of Dunkirk *192*
   Pte Slovik's execution *333*
   and public/press relations *512*, *513*, *514*, *515*, *516*
   and Remagen bridge *388*
   Rhine crossing *408*, *412*, *413*, *415*, *417*
   Rhine reached *258*
   and Ruhr pocket *428*
   SHAEF commanders *11*, *12*, *505*
   SHAEF Forward HQs 35, *67*, *152*, *153*, *163*, *189*, *360*
   and Stalin *324*
   strategy
      advance into Germany *433*
      advance to Elbe *453*, *458*
      and Berlin *457*, *488*
      'broad front' *163*, *176*, *241*, *242*
      disagreement *258*–*259*, *270*, *342*
      planning for March offensive *375*
      post-war *426*, *464*
      struggle for Caen *52*
   The True Glory (film) *419*
   and V1 flying bomb campaign *65*
   visits Aachen and Jülich *367*
   visits Greenham Common *18*
   visits Ohrdruf concentration camp *435*, *448*–*449*
   visits 'Eagle's Nest' *501*
Eisenschmitt 377, 388
Eitelsbach 386
Eitorf 418
El Alamein, Battle of *11*
Elbe, River *426*, *427*, *444*, 461, 470, 471, 481, 482, 486, 489, 490, *495*
   Allied advance towards *432*, *433*, *446*, *452*, *453*, *464*, *467*
   Allied forces reach 448, 454, 456–457, *456*, *458*, 459, 469
   link-up with Soviets *7*, *477*, *478*, *488*, 490
   and Soviet forces *457*, *487*
Elbe estuary *472*, *474*
Elbeuf 115, 136, 141, 142, 143, 150, *333*
   Allied bridgehead 148
Elbingerode 467
Eldingen 451
Elier 227
Elizabeth, Queen (later Queen Mother) 504
Elle, River 45
Ellen 369

Eller 294, 333, 336, 343, 377, 398
Ellern 400, 401
Ellewoutsdijk 175
Ellingen 416
Ellis, Cpl Edgar *169*
Ellis, Maj. L. F. *518*
Ellwangen 439, 471
Elmstein 330
Elphinstone, Capt. John Alexander 504
Elsass-Lothringen *see* Alsace-Lorraine
Elsdorf 260, 261, 370, 371, 470
Elsenborn 302, 331
Elsenborn ridge *282*
Elsenfeld 426
Elsenheim 331, 337
Elster, Genmaj. Botho *182*
Elster canal 464
Elsterwerda 468
Eltra 426
Elze 440
Embermenil 220
Embken 377
Emden *420*, 449, 450, 453, 459
Emelie 86
Émiéville *90*, 94
Emmendingen 297, 309, 316, 375, 407
Emmerich
   September 192
   October 203, 213
   November 239, 242
   February 344, 348, 357, 359, 365, 369
   March *375*, *394*, 403, 419, 420, 421
   March Allied capture *422*–*423*
   April
      Allied bombing in sector 426
      sector 430, *432*
Emonts family *241*
Ems, *see also* Dortmund-Ems Canal
Ems, River 432, 439, 440, 444, 446, 450, 451, 454, 464, 470, 481, 486
Ems-Weser canal 432
Ems estuary 468, 472, 473, 474, 476, 490
Enchenberg 271
Endingen 300
Engelsdorf 252
Engelskirchen 420
Engers 343, 414, 416
Enkenbach 407
Ennis, Brig. Gen. Riley F. *347*
Enns 504
Enns, River 502
Enschede 321, 418, 427, 429, 431
   Allied capture 430
Enschweiler 246
Ensdorf 404
Ensheim 399, 400
Ensival, Verviers, Château de Maison-Bois *210*
Entzheim 259
Enz, River 359, 447, 448
Enzen 339
Épaignes 143
Épernay 152
Épernon 81, 99, 114, 120, 122
Epfendorf 462
Epfenhofen 471
Épinal
   September *174*, 175, 184, 189, 192
      Allies occupy 188
   October, fighting in sector 196–200, 202, 203, 205, 207–210, 216, 218–220, 222–224, 226
Épône-Mézières 120, 122, 127
Eppeldorf 299, 302
Eppingen 430
Épron 76
Epte, River 152
Erbach 399
Erbendorf 470
Erchingen 280
Erezée *302*, *310*
Erfelden 414
Erft, River 209, 234, 273, 334, 371, 376, 377, 383, 384
   Allied bridgeheads across 375
Erfurt
   February 362, 369
   March
   April 426, 429, 431, *433*, 434, 439–441, 445–447, 450
      Allies clear 452
Ergoldsbach 486
Erkelenz 242, 260, 270, 274, 324, 325, 366, *369*, 371
Erlangen 461
Erle 420
Erndtebrück 393
Ernsbach 371
Ernzen 351, 355, 356, 357
Erp 186, 264, 377
Erpel 390
Erpeldange 326

Erskine, Maj.-Gen. George *114*

Erstein 261
Escaut canal 173, 174, 186
  see also Meuse-Escaut canal
Esch 301
  Allies clear of enemy 375
Eschdorf 299, 300, *312*
Eschede 451
Eschershausen 442
Eschringen 383
Eschweiler 181, 236, 247, 249, 250, 251, 252, 253, 331, 370, 371
Eselborn 332
Eslarn 474
Espins 122
Esquay 79, 86, *89*, 114
  German deployments at 70
Esschen 218, 219, 220, *225*
Essen
  October, Allied bombing 221, 223
  December, Allied bombing 277
  February, Allied bombing 366
  March, Allied bombing 389, 394, 399, 418
  April
    Allied bombing 433, *444*
    Allies clear 448
    Allies enter *444*, 445
    fighting in sector 447
Esslingen 371, 462, 470
Esson 123
Esterbrugge 472
Estrées-la-Campagne 120, 122
Estry 111, 120
Étampes
  Allies bomb railway centre 34, 42
  Allies liberate 140
Étaples
  Allied liberation 161
  rail targets bombed 77, 114, 115, 123
Etavaux 94
Éterville 78, 79, 94
Étrépagny 151
Ettelbrück 303, *312*
Ettingen 271
Ettlingen 401
Etzlingen 362
Eudenbach 405
Eupen 172, 179, *201*, 215
Eure, River 89, 132, 133, 140
Euren 383
Eusen, Victor *181*
Euskirchen
  September 193
  October 203, 204, 205, 210, 216, 227
  November 234, 240, 243
  December 266, 268, 269, 273, 274, 277, 278, 279, 280, 294, 297, 300
  January, Allied bombing 316, 328, 329, 331, 332, 333, 334
  February, Allied bombing 344, 345, 348, 352, 356, 368, 370
  March
    Allied bombing 375
    fighting in sector 383, 384, 385, 386, 387
Eutingen 363
Évrecy 44, 65, 70, 71, 72, 86, 87, 88, 114
Évreux
  June 45
    Allied bombing 38, 41, 55, 56, 65
    Allied fighter combats over 57
  July, Allied bombing 77
  August
    Allied air attacks 123, 127
    Allied liberation 141
Exloo 450

Faid 396
Falaise
  June
    air reconnaissance over 58
    Allied bombing 36, 43, 51, 58, 66
  July
    air attacks on German units 71, 74
    Allied advance 96
  August
    Allied advance towards 120, *121*, 122, 126, 128, *131*
    Allied bombing 123, 125, 126, 127, *135*
    Allies clear of enemy 132
    Canadian objective (Op. 'Totalize') *117*
    German retreat from 133, 134, 136
    Pocket eliminated 140, *142*
Falkenau 462
Falkenberg 251, 252, 253, 466, 468
Falkensee, Berlin 420
Farge 419, 423
Faubourg-de-Vaucelles 89, *90*, *91*
Faulquemont Fortified Sector 255
Fauville-en-Caux 158
Fayl-Billot 175

Faymonville 322, 324, 325, 326
Fecht, River *333*, 347
Felber, Gen. Hans *417*
Fell 392
Fellerich 365
Felsberg 265, *266*, 268
Felsner, Georg *323*
Fenberg, T/4 Bennett (US Signal Corps) *275*
Ferme de Mahenne *300*
Ferschweiler 351, 354, 355, 356
Fessenheim 349
Feuchtwangen 469
Fèves 246
Fiancey *151*
Fichtenberg 468
Fierlbrunn 481
Fiersbach 416
Film: *The True Glory* 22, *419*
Filsen 418
Finning 480
Finstingen 254, 255, 256, 257
Fischbach 334, 402
Fischenich 387
Fismes 123
Fitten 265
Flamersheimwald 387
Flamierge 313, 316
Flammersfeld 416
Fleck, Lt Egon *447*
Fleckenberg 441
Flensburg 476, 491
  Adm. Dönitz HQ (Mürwik suburb) *490*, *494*, *496*, *504*
Flers *121*, 131, 132
  Allied bombing 34, 43, 62, 64, 80
Fleury-sur-Andelle 152
Fleury-sur-Orne 90, *91*
Flieden 418
Fliessem 371
Fliesteden 383
Flin 183
Flockhart, Capt. Sandy *186*
Florennes 161
Florsbach 431
Flossdorf 264, 265, 266, 267
Flossenbürg concentration camp 472
Floverich 247
Floyd, Lt John E. *429*
Flushing (Vlissingen) 168, 175, 203, 208, 219, *227*, *233*, 234
  Allied capture *235*, 236
Flussbach 394
Foedrowitz, Michael *181*
Foertsch, Genlt Hermann 502
Föhren 390, 392
Folligny
  Allied bombing 46
  Allied strafing 48
Folpersviller 362
Folx-les-Caves 167
Fontaine-le-Pin 122
Fontainebleau 99, 119, 142, *148*
Fontenay-le-Pesnel 58, *59*, 60, 61, 63
Fontenoy 213
Forbach 360, 362–365, 367, 368, 370, 371, 383, 385, 386, 387, 389
Forchheim 457, 469, 479
Forêt d'Andaine 42, 50, 80, 131
Forêt d'Arques 152, 157
Forêt de Bride 244
Forêt de Brotonne *146*, 151
Forêt de Cerisy 38, 39, 41
Forêt de Champenoux 186
Forêt de Chantilly 129
Forêt de Château-Salins 243, 244
Forêt de Cinglais 95, 122, 123
Forêt de Compiègne 158, 159
Forêt de Conches, Allied air attacks 56, 59, 94, 95
Forêt de Grémecey 193, 197, 198, 241
Forêt de Grimbosq 40
Forêt de Guînes 162, 164
Forêt de la Crèche, Boulogne 183
Forêt de la Guerche 110
Forêt de la Londe *146*, 148
Forêt de Laigle 150
Forêt de Lyon 120
Forêt de Moncourt 224
Forêt de Mondon 186
Forêt de Mont-Castre 74, 80
Forêt de Montrichard 125
Forêt de Mormal 120
Forêt de Parroy 192, 199, 202, 207, 209, 210, 226
Forêt de Roumare 123
Forêt de Saint-Gâtien 142
Forêt de Saint-Germain 151
Forêt de Saint-Sever 114, 115, 116
Forêt de Samoussy 148
Forêt de Senonches 103
Forêt de Signy 158

Forêt d'Écouves, Allies bomb fuel dumps 60, 80
Forêt Domaniale de Champ 241, 243
Forêt L'Évêque 110
Forge à l'Aplé *310*
Forge-a-Cambro 122
Forges 106
Forges-les-Eaux 156
Formerie 156
Forrières 315
Forst, Aachen 205
Forstfeld 402
Fort Benning, Georgia 8, *11*
Fort de Plappeville, Metz 250, 271
Fort de Queleu, Metz 252
Fort d'Englos 120
Fort Dix, New Jersey 8
Fort Driant, Metz (Feste Kronprinz) 199, 200, 201, 202, 203, *204*, 272
Fort Eben-Emael 172
Fort Frederik Hendrik 209, 213, 218, 219, 220, 223
Fort Jeanne d'Arc, Metz 278
Fort Leavenworth 8
Fort Marival 257
Fort Montbarey *179*
Fort Saint Blaise 257
Fort Saint-Privat 264
Fort Saint-Quentin 271
Fort Schiesseck, Maginot Line 285, 287
Fort Simserhof, Maginot Line 285
Fort Sommy 257
Fortschwihr 339
Fosset 319
Fougères 114
  Allies bomb railway centre 32, 46
Fougerolles 179
Fouhren 331, 332
Fouillard, fuel dump bombed 46
Foulbec 132
Foulkes, Lt-Gen. Charles 503
Fouquerolles 156
Foy-Notre-Dame *297*, *300*, 319
Fraipertuis 227
Fraiture 313
Frameries 159
France
  Resistance in *142*, *172*, 513
  Vichy Government 474
Franco-Prussian War 266
Frank, Reichminister Hans 503, *506*
Frankenau 422
Frankenberg 395
Frankenstein 321, 404
Frankenthal *405*, 408, 409
Frankfurt-am-Main
  August, Allied bombing 128
  October, Allied bombing 205
  November 249
    Allied air attacks 247, 248, 252
    Allied strategy 241
  December
    Allied bombing 297, 302
    Allied strategy 270
  January
    Allied advance to 416
    Allied bombing 311, 314, 337
  February Allied bombing 360
  March
    Allied bombing 391, 396, 398, 399, 400, 402, 407, 411, 417
    Allied capture *418*, 420, 421
    fighting in suburbs 419
    sector of 421, 422
  April
    advance from bridgehead *428*
    fighting in sector 426, 429, 430
  post-war, SHAEF HQ *419*
Frasselt 352
Frauenberg 362, 384
Fraulautern 277, 302, 404
Frauwüllesheim 370, 371
Frechen 384
Freching 245
Freckenfeld 318
Fredeburg 445
Freeman, Lt Mark A. (US Signal Corps) *104*, *164*
Freialdenhoven 251
Freiburg
  November 259
  December 273, 283, 292, 297, 300, 303
  January 309, 322, 332
  February 348, 351, 353, 357, 364, 368, 370
  March 384, 407
  April 471
Freienohl 448
Freihaim 448
Freising 486
Freistett 316
Frelenberg *200*
Fremersdorf 254, 265
Fremifontaine 213

French, Lt Col Jules K. *182*
Frengkofen 477
Frénouville 91
Frenz 259, 261
Freren 440, 442
Freschweiler 358
Fresné-la-Mère 132
Fresnes-en-Saulnois 197, 240
Freudenberg 443
Freudenburg 363, 364
Freudenstadt 370, 459, 465
Frévent 127
Frick, Wilhelm *506*
Friedberg 395, 480
Friedeburg, Genadm. Hans-Georg von *490*, *494*, *495*, *496*, *497*, *504*, *508*
Friedel, Maj. Hans Jochen *490*, *494*, *495*, *496*, *497*
Friedrichsfeld 416
Friedrichshafen 369, 472, 477, 487
Friesenheim 313
Friesheim 377
Friesoythe 451, 454, 461
Frimmersdorf 382
Frisian islands 178, *463*, 472, 476, *494*, *496*
Fritzlar 237, 422
Frobach 384
Fromentel 132
Frommersbach 398
Fröndenberg 448
Frontigny 248
Frost, Lt-Col John *184*
Fuchshofen 270
Fuchsmühl 470
Fulda 300, 309, 403, 411, 417, 418, 426, 429, 430, 437, 439, 441
Fulda, River 430, 432
Fuller, 1st Lt Robert E. *444*
Furnes 168, 172
Fürstenau 440, 444, 448, 450
Fürstenfeldbruck 482
Fürstenhausen 271, 398
Furth 404, 478
Fürth, Nürnberg 438, 443, 465, 468
Füssen 480, 482, 489

Gaanderen *432*
Gacé 137, 140, *146*
Gaggenau, Daimler-Benz factory bombed 199
Gahlen 419
Gailenkirchen 439
Gaillon 142
Gale, Maj.-Gen. Richard, commands 6th Airborne Div. 18
Gambsheim 311, 312, 313, 315, 342, 343
Gamelin, Gén. Maurice 503
Gammersfeld 475
Gangelt 302
Garmisch-Partenkirchen 489
Garonne, River 120
Gartower Forest 470
Gathemo 118, 120, 121, 123, 125, 126
Gaumesnil *117*
Gause, Genlt. Alfred *150*
Gavin, Maj. Gen. James 178, *490*
Gavray 102, *105*, 106
Gavrus 86, *89*
Gdynia 284
Geertruidenberg 218, 236, 237, 313, 342
Geesthacht 488
Geffen *219*
Gegenbach 478
Gehan, forest of 207, 212
Geich 261
Geilchlingen 365
Geilenkirchen
  September 183–186
  October 199, *200*, 209, *215*
  November 238, 240, 247, 261
    battle for *248–249*, 250, *251*, *252–254*, 255–257, 260, *265*
  December 269, 302
  January *334*
    Operation 'Blackcock' 325
  February 359
Geinsheim 414, *417*
Geislautern 310, 398
Geislingen 438, 443, 449
Gélacourt 234
Geldern
  September 193
  October 213
  November 252
  December 268, 269
  February 352, 353, 354, 357, 364, 368
  March 375, 382, 384, 385
Geldrop see Eindhoven
Gelnhausen 426
Gelsenkirchen 238, 243, 254, 359, 366, 371, 375, 385, 389, 393, 403, 443
  Allied capture 448

Gemersheim 265
Gemünd 264, *290*, 344, 361, 384, 386
Gemünd forest 385
Gemünden 256, 418
Geneva Convention *442, 466*
Gengenbach 314
Gennep *355*, 356, 357
Gennevilliers 112
Genzler, Kriegsberichter *138*
George VI, King 504
  visits front *209–211*
Georgia, USA, National Guard unit *361*
Ger *118*, *122*, 126, 128, 131
Gera 438, 439, 443, 453, 454
Gérardmer 236, 238, 239, 240, *244*, 250, 252
Gerbercourt 243
Gerbéviller 181
Gerbroek 300, 319
Gereonsweiler 250, 251, 252, 253, 254
Gerhardt, Maj. Gen. Charles 88
Gerimont 308
German War Graves Commission *117*
Germany
  unconditional surrender *495–499, 502–506, 510, 515, 516*
  American Military Government Detachment *476*
  German Democratic Republic *338, 339, 356, 447*
  post-war de-Nazification *439*
  as post-war Federal Republic *266, 338*
  post-war Zones *193, 404, 426, 444, 447, 464, 488*
Germersheim 319, 331, 408, 409, 415
Germeter 210, 215, *236, 359*
Gernhart, Pfc Alfred *320*
Gernsbach 384
Gerolstein 183, 300, 308, 330, 387
Gerow, Maj. Gen. Leonard P. *211, 241*
Gersdorff, Oberst Rudolf-Christoph von *150*
Gersheim 282
Gerstheim 264
Geseke 395, 405, 411, 428
Gestorf 444
Gestungshausen 450
Gevenich 264, 366, 396
Gey 265, 274, 277, 278, 279
Geyen 383
Gheel 173, 180
Ghent
  advance from 171
  Allies enter *161*, 162, *163*, 168
  fuel depot bombed 133
  military targets bombed 100
  rail junction bombed 56
Giberville 90
Gibson, Lt William *430*
Giebelstadt 312, 409, 430
Gieboldehausen 446
Giesbeek 218
Gieschein 371
Giesel 426
Giesendorf 371
Giessen
  November 247, 257
  December 270
  February 360
  March 375, 376, 377, 383, 387, 389, 395, 398, 401, 402, 411, 418, 419, 422
  Allies reach 420, *421, 424*
Gilbert, Pfc Sam (US Signal Corps) *299, 306, 323*
Gilbert, SS-Unterscharf. Wilhelm *286*
Gillard, Frank (BBC reporter) *327*
Gillem, Gen. Alvan C. *253*
Gillenfeld 394
Gillespie, Pte Malvin A. *55*
Gilzem 371
Gindorf 386
Ginger, Sgt Bill. *147*
Ginsterhahn 395
Girbig, Werner *345*
Gironde, France 455, 458, 459, 465, 468, 469
Gironde, River 137
Gisors 91, 147
Gittermann, Oberlt Horst *191*
Gives 319
Givet 158, 162, 163, 166, 298
Givors, Allied bombing 123
Givors-Badin 99
Givroulle 320
Gladbach 375, 390
Gladbeck 411, 422
Gladdenstedt 454
Glauchau 457, 459
Glehn 385, 386
Gleidorf 441
Gleiwitz *339*
Glessen 371

Gleuel 385
Glimbach 264, 366
Glonville 213
Goch 191, 196, 240, 349–353, *350, 355*, 360, 361, 365, 366, 368, *370*, 375
  Allied capture *362*, 363, 364
  R. Niers railway bridge *239*
Goddelau 416
Godin, Pfc Bernard T. *113*
Goebbels, Joseph *511*
Goes *226*, *227*, 228
Goesdorf *312*
Göhrde Forest 471
Golkrath 370
Gollhofen 439
Golzheim 370
Gompertshausen 445
Gondenbrett 352
Gondorf 394
Gonfreville 85
Gonsenheim 407
Goodall, Cpl Doreen (ATS) *4*
'Gooseberry' breakwaters *47*
Göppingen 376
Gordon, Cpl James R. *296*
Gorges 85
Göring, Reichsmarschall Hermann *399*, *475*
Gorman, Sgt Edward M. *443*
Gornall, Capt. J. P., RN 37
Goslar 446
Gotha 427, 432, *435*, 439, 441, 442, 444, *448*
Göttingen 332, 430, 439, 441, 444, 446
  Allied capture 442
Gottmannsgrün 465
Gottstedt 447
Gouda, Allied bombing 238, 269
Gouesnou *167*
Gournay-en-Bray 133, 152
Gouvy 308, 330
Goville *514*
Grab 465
Grabow *490*, 491
Grafenau 488
Grafenhausen 416
Gräfenthal 452
Grafenwöhr 438, 443, 469
Grafwegen *353, 354*
Grainville-sur-Odon 63, 90
Gramastetten 500
Grand Slam bombs *398*
Grandcamp-le-Château 134, 136
Grandménil *296*, 298, 300, 301, 302, 303, 309, *310*, 314
Grandvillers 199
Granges-sur-Vologne 245
Granterath 370
Granville 106, *152*
  Allied bombing 46, 49, 52, 56, 59, 74, 86
  Allies clear 110
  SHAEF Forward HQ *152–153*, *163*, 189
Grave *178*
Gravelines
  Allied advances 164
  naval forces engaged 73
Gravelotte 191, 193
Gravendeel 269
Grebben 334
Grebenau *422*
Greenhalgh, L/Cpl Fred *19*
Gregory, Pfc William *203*
Greimerath 364, 377, 396
Greiveldange 189
Greiz 461
Grenoble *245, 308*
Grenzhausen 418
Greppen 470
Grevenbroich 209, 249, 256, 267, 280, 321, 334, 352, 366, 382
Grevenmacher 198, 199, 318, 364
Grezhausen 471
Griem, FM Ritter von *508*
Grier, Sgt Wayne *369*
Griesbach 486
Griesheim 416
Griethausen 356
Grimbosq 117
Grimlinghausen 385
Grimm, Arthur (PK photographer) *93*
Grissheim 346
Grobau 459
Groede 221, 223, 224, 225
Groep 299
Groesbeek *176*
Gronau 405
Grönebach 433
Groningen 332, 344, 438, 454, 456, 458, 461
Gröpelingen 480

Gros Rederchingen 274, 309, 310
Gross Blittersdorf 363
Gross-Umstadt 420
Grossaspach 434
Grosshau 256, 264, 272
Grosskampenberg *170*, 345, 348, 361
Grosslangenfeld 344
Grossrosseln 271
Grosssander 490
Grosstanchen 250
Grossweingarten 471
Grotewohl, Otto *447*
Grouven 371
Grow, Maj. Gen. Robert W. *107*
Grubbenvorst 256
Grüfflingen 336
Grun 494
Grünburg 400
Grune 317
Grunewald *363*
Grünstadt 356, 390
Gschwendt 477
Gudebrod, Morton 516
Guebling 246
Guebwiller 347
Guerches 87
Guernsey, Channel Islands 96
Gueux, Eisenhower's Advanced CP 189
Guingand, Maj.-Gen. Sir Francis de *497*
Guis 394
Gumbrechtshoffen 400
Gummersbach 448
Gundershoffen *401*
Gungolding 474, 475
Gungwiller 259
Gunningen 443
Günsche, Otto *483*
Güntersberge 457, 461
Günzburg 458, 475, 477
Gunzenhausen 459, 463, 466
Gürzenich *278*, 279, 280
Gusenburg 400
Güsten 250
Gustrow 441
Gutenbrunner Wald 257, 260
Gütersloh 353, 398, 409, 422, 432
Gutwasser 504
Gymnich 377

Haader 481
Haag 480
Haan 459
Haaren 204, *207*, 208, 209, 218
  Crucifix Hill 207
Habbelrath 377
Habiemont 289
Habkirchen 277, 278, 279, 280, 282, 284, 285, 308, 309, 399
Hablainville 233
Haboudange 243
Habscheid 337, 348, 355
Hachenburg 395
Hachiville 330
Häcklingen, Lüneburg *494*
Haffen 416
Hagen 266, 375, 399, 418, 420, 455, 458
Hagenest 457
Hagenow 490
Haguenau
  November 248, 260
  December 264, 265, 267, 269, 270, *274*, 275, 277, 278
  January 307, 331, 332, 333, 334
  February 343, 344, 345, 346, 349, 351, 352, 353, 354, 356, *357*, 358, 359
  March 396, 398, 399, 400, *401*, 402
Haguenau Forest 278, 315, 316, 318, 319, 400
Hahn, Pfc William *273*
Hähnlein 416
Haiger 398
Hainichen 453
Haislip, Maj. Gen. Wade H. 258, *415*, *461*
Halberstadt 448, 469
Halden 219
Halle 352, 371, 427, 434, 439, 441, 443, 449, 454, 457, 459, 469
  Allies clear 461, 467
Hallein 475
Hallenberg 421
Hallendorf 321
Haller 299
Hallschlag 324
Hallstadt 452
Halstroff 249
Haltern 268, 329, 335, 391, 395, 398, 399, 402, 407, *420*
Halvenboom 363
Halverde 442
Ham 150
Hambach forest 265, 369, 370

Hamburg
  October, Allied bombing 202, 212, 213, 223
  January, Allied bombing 306, 325
  February, Allied bombing *364*, 368
  March, Allied bombing 385, 387, 394, 405, 417, 423
  April 461, 471, 472, 473, 476, 481, 486
    Allied advance towards *446, 453*, 467
    Allied bombing 427, 431, 434, 438, 443, 445, 449, 458, 459, 469
  May 488
    surrender to Allies *491, 494, 496*
Hambye 104, 105
Hameln 431, *436*, 437, 439, 440
Hamich 250
Hamm, and Rhine crossing 408, 409
Hamm (Palatinate) 364, 405
Hamm (Ruhr)
  September, Allied bombing 189
  October 196, 198, 218, 220, 223
  November, Allied bombing 236
  December, Allied bombing 269
  January, Allied bombing 306, 311, 313, 337
  February, Allied bombing 359
  March, Allied bombing 418, 419
  April, battle for city 431, 433, 437, *439*
Hamm (suburb of Düsseldorf) see Düsseldorf
Hammelburg, US raid on POW camp *429*
Hammer 345
Hammerstein 403
Hamminkeln 418, 419
Hampont 242
Han-sur-Nied 244
Hanau 249, 272, 311, 312, 402, 418, 419, 420, 422, 426, 429
Handorf 201, 409
Hank 329
Hannoversch-Münden 439, 440, 442
Hannover
  October, Allied bombing 220, 222, 224
  January, Allied bombing 307, 311, 316, 330
  February, Allied bombing 349, 353, 368
  March, Allied bombing 383, 398, 399, 401, 403, *407*, 417, 420
  April
    Allied bombing 438, 440, 441, 443, 445, 449
    Allied objective *433*
    Allies clear 446, *454*
    sector 444, 450, 451
  see also Belsen
Hannoversch Münden 423
Hansen, Maj. Larry *153*
Haramont 156
Haraucourt 246
Harbouey 250
Harburg 202, 306, 325, 368, 385, 387, 469
Harcourt, air attacks at 71
Hard 475
Hardegsen 442
Hardehausen Forest 431, 437
Harderwijk 467
Hardt forest 348, 351
Hardt mountains 346, 349, 352, 356, 357, 395, 396, 399, 400, 402, 403, 404
Hardy, Bert (AFPU) *161*
Harff 256
Hargarten 395, 396
Hargreaves, WAC driver Pearlie *280*
Harrison, M/Sgt Gordon A. *271*
Harkebrügge 455
Harlange 303, 310, 311, 313, 316, 317
Harlingen 461
Harmon, Gen. Ernest N. *252*
Harper, Col Joseph H. *293*
Harperscheid 284, *344*, 345
Harpstedt 448
Harre 171
Harscheidt 351, 352
Harsefeld 472
Harspelt 355
Hart, Brig. Gen. Charles C. *210, 211*
Harth forest 264
Harton, Pte W. *354*
Harz Forest 452, 467
Harz mountains *438*, 459, 464, *468*
Harz pocket 461, 469, 470
Harzy 317
Hase canal 448
Hasede 440
Haselünne 427, 440, 442, 446, 450
Hasenfeld 352, 353
Haslach 363, 377, 491
Hasselburg 451

Hasselfelde 459
Hasselt 167
Hassfurt 450
Hassum 360
Hastenrath 250
Hatten 316, 317, 318, 319, 320, 322, 324, 325, 326, 327, 328, 402
Hattenhofen 482
Hattingen 402
Hatzenport 394
Hau 355
Hausach 317, 363
Hausen 251, 401
Hauserding 493
Haut-des-Forges 88
Haut-Fays 166
Haut-Mesnil 118
Haute-Bodeux *315*
Haute-Kontz 193
Havert 327
Havrenne 300
Hazebrouck, railway centre bombed 59
Hébécrevon 96, *98*
Hechtel 173, *177*
Hechtsheim, US Army POW holding camp (A13) *466*
Heckhalenfeld 343
Heckhuscheid 344
Heckling 249
Heddert 399
Hedomont 320
Heerenveen 456
Heerlen 182
Heesch 191
Heide, Schleswig-Holstein 321, 387
Heidelberg 326, 339, 369, 400, 409, 411, 417, 418, 419, 421, 427, 430
  Allied capture 422, *438*
Heiderscheid 296, 298, *303*
Heiderscheidergrund *312*
Heidesheim, US Army POW holding camp (A12) *466*
Heikant 353
Heilbach 366
Heilbronn
  January 328, 329, 339
  February 354, 371
  March 376
  April 427, 429, 430, 438, 448, 454, 457, 459, 462, 465, 468, 470
    battle for 431, 433, 434, 439, 441, 443, 445, 447, 450, 452
    US Army POW holding camp (A18) *466*
Heilder 327
Heilenbach 383
Heimbach 354, 377
Heimberger (US Signal Corps) *329*
Heimersheim 383
Heimerzheim 386
Heinerscheid 334
Heinsberg 247, 325, 330, 332, 333, 334, *335*, *366*, 445
Heistern 252, *254*, 255
Heiteren 349
Hekkens 355, *363*
Helden 249, 250, 251
Heldra 432
Helenaveen 251, 252
Helenenberg 375
Heligoland 465, 468, 494, *496*
Hellenthal 278, 284, 347, 348, 349, 357, 361
Hellevoetsluis 332
Hellimer 252
Helmarshausen 440
Helmern 431
Helmond 254
  Allied capture 188
Helsungen 430
Hemingway, Ernest *234*
Hemmingstedt 321, 405
Hemslingen 469
Hendrikx, Peter *467*
Hengelo 202, 203, 311, 325, 436, *452*
  Allies clear 432
Henke, Lt Hellmuth *293*
Hennebont 121
Hennecke, Konteradm. Walther 57, 61
Hennef 409, 410, 414
Hennethal 420
Hennigsdorf 402
Henningen 209
Henri-Chapelle *281*
  US War Cemetery *386*
Hensel, Capt. William E. *443*
Hentern 398
Henumont 320
Heppenbach 336
Heppendorf 371, *381*
Hepscheid 336
Herbach 200, 201, 202
Herbert, Lt Edward *269*

Herbertingen 459
Herbéviller 238
Herborn 419
Herbrechtingen 455
Herbsheim 317, 318
Herbstein 422
Herdorf 400
Herford 431
  Allied bombing 337, 364
  Germans surrender 436–437
Herforst 387
Hergarten 294
Herhahn 284
Héricourt *246*
Heringen 429
Hermeskeil 219, 400
Hermespand 352, 359, 360
Hermülheim 386
Herny 244
Herold, T/5 George W. (US Signal Corps) *180*
Hérouville 76
Herpelmont 205
Herresbach 337
Herrig 383
Herrlisheim 317, 324, 325, 326, 329, 345, 351
Herrnneuses 457
Herrsching 482
Hersberg 452
Hersbruck 458
Herschweiler 357
Herschwiesen 399, 400
Hersfeld 426, 429
Hertogenbosch see s'Hertogenbosch
Herve 171
Hervorst 360
Herzberg 429, 448, 459
Hesdin 161
Hesel 488
Hesse *193*
Hesseln 399
Hessling 363
Heusden 237
Heveadorp 448
Hewitt, Sgt Charles *160*
Hex 168
Heyking, Genmaj. Rudiger von *159*
Heymann, Anneliese *429*
Heymann, Lt Friedel *429*
Heyroth 392
Hiesfeld 418
Hilchenbach 445
Hilden 459
Hildesheim 398, 409, 440, 441, 442, 444
Hildfeld 433
Hill 112 79
Hill 229 123, 125
Hill 266 123
Hill 309 106
Hill 400 273
Hiller, T/5 Charles D. *193*
Hillesheim 298, 333, 344
Hilsprich 255
Hilvarenbeek 200, 201, 202
Hilversum 256, 269
Himes, Sgt Rodney *320*
Himmelsthür 442
Himmler, SS-Reichsführer Heinrich 504
Hindenburg, President Paul von *443*
Hinderhausen 330
Hinsingen 260
Hinterweiler 387
Hirnkirchen 480
Hirschbach 481
Hirschberg 445, 457, 474
Hirson *158*
Hirtzfelden 315
Hitler, Adolf
  and Albert Speer *502*
  and Allied Rhine crossing *415*
  annexes Alsace-Lorraine *337*
  and Ardennes counter-attack *280*, *281*
  and Bad Godesberg *391*
  Berghof mountain retreat *475*, *500–501*
  Braunau birthplace *492–493*
  building Reichsautobahns *403*, *418*
  Dönitz as successor *486*
  and destruction of towns *407*
  flying bomb campaign *65*
  July 1944 assassination attempt *92*, *93*
  and last stand in Berlin *458*, *470*, *482–483*, *492*
  Metz seized *204*
  Munich Putsch *482–483*
  and Nürnberg *460*, *461*, *463*
  orders Aachen to be held *205*
  orders counter-attack from Vosges mountains *174*
  orders counter-attack to Mortain *118*

Hitler, Adolf — continued
  removes von Kluge from command *137*
  and Saarlautern assault *269*
  Wagner and Nazi ideology *457*
  and the 'Westwall' *214*
  and Winter Olympics (1936) *489*
Hitzacker 417, 441
Hives 318
Hobart, Maj.-Gen. Percy *251*
Hobbs, Maj. Gen. S. Leyland *361*
Hochheim 420
Hochkirchen, Allied capture 375
Hochwald 371, 375, *413*
Hochwald Forest 376, 377, 382
Hockenheim 427
Hodges, Lt Gen. Courtney H. *128*, *205*, *210*, *211*, *241*, *242*, *408*, *415*, *438*, *515*
Hodister 316
Hoedekenskerke 227
Hoesdorf 345
Hoevelaken 469
Hof 447, 449, 450, 457, 459, 461, 465, 468
Höfen 179, 181, 292, 342, 344
Hoffeld 390
Hoffelt 329
Hofgeismar 439
Hoge, Brig. Gen. William M. *387*
Hohenstein 454
Höingen 447
Holdorf 450
Holin 465
Hollandsche Diep 237, 239, *240*
Hollange 299
Hollerath 346
Hollnich 349
Holsthum 362, 369
Holten 419
Holtz, Karl (Nazi gauleiter) *460*
Holtzwihr *333*
Hölzchen 366
Holzerath 398
Holzfeld 401
Holzheim 337, 338
Holzminden 429, 431, 440
Holzwickede 398, 411
Holzinger, Sgt Warner W. *170*
Holzlar 404
Homberg 223, 234, 240, 252, 330, 384, 385
Homburg
  November 237, 257
  December 279, 285, 295, 300, 303
  January 306, 307, 308
  February 351, 368
  March 393, 395, 398, 399, 407
Homme, River 316
Hommerdingen 361
Hommersum 358, 364
Hompesch 368
Hompré 301, 302
Hondzocht *160*
Honfleur 142, 143
Höngen 250, 326, 327, 328
Honnef 405
Hönningen 395, 396, 400, 401, 402
Honsfeld 283, *284*, 338
Honskirch 259
Hontem 330
Hontheim 179, 349
Honville 308
Hoogerheide 204
Hook of Holland 168, 173, 203
Hopfenohe 461
Hopsten 440
Horan, Congressman Walter *189*
Horb 465
Horkheim 452
Horn 248
Hornbach 401
Hornberg 351, 352
Horneburg 486, 488
Horrem 376
Horrocks, Lt-Gen. Sir Brian *174*, *248*, *253*, *416*, *446*, *470*, *476*
Hörsching 502
Horsford, Capt. Toby *496*
Horst 254, 334
Horstedt 480
Hoscheid 333
Hoscheiderdickt 334, 335
Hosingen 335
Höst *370*
Hosten 384
Hostenbach 271
Hotton 294, 296, 298, 299, 301, *309*
Hottot 52, 79, 80, 88, 90
  Allied capture *89*
Hottviller 282
Houffalize 300, 309, 311, 317, *319*, *320*, *322*, 327, 329, 330
  liberated *321*, 324

Houlgate
  Allied capture 140
  German battery at 51, 53, 136
Houmont 307
Houssay 116
Housseras 225
Hövel 400
Hoven 253, 254, 277
Howie, Maj. Tom *87–88*
Höxter 442
Hoya 446
Hubenstein 489
Hubermont 308
Hubert Folie 91
Huchem 269, 274, 366
Hüde 486
Huebner, Maj. Gen Clarence R. *415*
Huf 364
Huisberden 359
Hüls 401
Humain *300*, 301
Hummelo 432
Hundlingen 269
Huningue canal 349
Hunkirch 257
Hünningen 338
Hünshoven 249
Hünxe 418
Hupperdange 333
Hurless, Col Bernard F. *252*
Hürtgen
  September 191, 193
  October 198, 199, 203–205, 207–209, 212, 213, 231
  November 237–238, 240, 242, 243, 256, 257, 259, 260
    town surrenders *261*
  December, sector 265, 267, 268, 269, 270, 271, 274
  February 371
Hürtgen Forest 183, 203, 210, *215*, *234*, *236*, 237–241, 252–255, 261, *331*, *358*
Hüscheid 401
Husen 422
Hüttenrode 469
Hüttersdorf 402
Hüttingen 179
Huy
  and Allied advance 164, 166, 167
  Allied bombing of bridges 133
Hyenville 104

Ibbenbüren 430, 436, 439
Ichendorf 376
Ickern 433
Idenheim 375
Idstein 401, 421
Ifs 90
Igel 383
Igelsberg 459
Igersheim 433
Igoville 119
IJmuiden
  Allies bomb shipping 142, 280, 345, 351, 353, 398
  Allies bomb steel works 59
IJssel, River 226, *442*, 448, 450, *451*, 454, 458
IJsselmeer (Zuider Zee) 461
IJzendijke 216, 217
Île de Batz *34*
Île de Cézembre, Saint-Malo 125, *129*, 150, 152, 157, 158
Île d'Oléron 487, 489
Île d'Or (Golden Island) *127*
Île du Saulcy, Metz 252
Île Lacroix *140*
Île Napoléon 349
Îles Saint Marcouf 33
Ill, River 332, *333*, 343, 347, 348
Illange 246
Iller, River 489, 500
Iller canal 473, 475, 477, 479, 480, 482
Illertissen 475
Illiers-l'Évêque 41
Imgenbroich 342
Immendorf 247, *252*, 387
Immenstadt 489
Imperial (later Commonwealth) War Graves Commission *19*, *386*, *518*
Inde, River 264, 268, 279
Inden 260, 261, 264, 265, 266, 267, 274
Information, Ministry of *511*, *514*
Inglewood *163*
Ingolstadt 322, 376, 438, 448, 455, 466, 469, 470, 473, 475, 480
  entered and captured 477, 479
Ingweiler 260, 267, 332
Inn, River 488, *492*, 493, 500
Innsbruck 489, 490, 493, 500, *503*
Insenborn 300
Insmingen 255

Insviller 251, 252
Irl 477
Irlich 409
Irrel 359, 360, 371, 375
Irrhausen 365
Isar, River 486
Iserlohn 356, 377, 429, 458, 459
Isigny-sur-Mer 36, 47, 48
    Allied capture *33*, *34*
Ismay, Gen. Sir Hastings *377*
Issans *246*
Isselburg 407, 420
Issum 384
Italy
    Allied campaign in *11*
    German surrender in *480*, *494*
Ittenbach 401
Itzbach 265
Itzehoe 490

Jacobsen (PK photographer) *185*, *186*
Jagst, River *438*, *445*, *447*
Jakobwüllesheim 371
Jallaucourt 196, 197, 240
Jeandelaincourt 204
Jeanménil 228
Jebsheim *336*
Jena 403, 432, 445, 449, 450, 452, 454
Jenks, William *176*
Jersey, Channel Islands 35, 43, 56, 61, 120
Jesse, Kriegsberichter *149*
Jessnitz 469, 470, 471
Jeuxey 188
Jochsberg 465
Jodl, Genoberst Alfred *504*, *505*, *506*
Johannisbach valley *see* Bielefeld viaduct
Johanns-Rohrbach 254
Johnson, Pte William *519*
Johnston, Col (No. 32 Casualty Clearing Station) *449*
Joinville 158
Jones, Capt. E. H. Jones, USN 20, 45
Jones, Cdr B., RN 33
Jordan, Lt Col D. R. *188*, *264*, *435*, *511*, *520*
Jössnitz 459
Joubieval *318*
Joulines 39
Jousse, Pierre *113*
Jucken 366
Jugenheim 416
Juin, Gén. Alphonse *505*
Juliana Canal 329
Jülich
    October 204
    November 238, 242, 247–249, 253–257, 259, 260, 261, *366*
    December 265, 267, 268, 269, 270, 271, 272, 273, 274, 277, 278, 280
    February 369, 370
        Allied capture *366–367*, *368*, *377*
        Hexenturm (Witch's Tower) *366–367*
Jullouville, SHAEF Forward HQ *189*
Jüngersdorf 260, 261
Jünkerath 345
Junkersdorf 385
Juntersdorf 377
Juprelle 171
Jussarupt 226
Jussy, Allied bombing 57
Jüterbog 466
Juvigny-le-Tertre *120*, 131
Juvigny-sur-Seulles 89
Juvisy, Allied bombing (June) 30, 39

Kading, Pfc Kenneth *205*
Kaiserbaracke *285*, *286*
Kaiserberg 283
Kaiserlautern
    October 218
    November 237, 256
    December 272, 283, 295, 300, 301, 303
    January 306, 307, 308, 311, 319, 321, 322, 326, 330, 334, 336, 337
    February 352, 353, 356, 363, 364, 367, 370
    March 375, 376, 383, 385, 393, *395*, 398, 400, 402
        Allies enter *404*, 407
    post-war US base ('K-Town') *404*
Kalborn 336, 337
Kaldenkirchen 267
Kalenborn 398, 399, 400
Kall 269, 278, 300, 333, 337, 387
Kall, River *236*, 349
Kalmpthout 204, 218
Kaltenbrunner, Ernst *506*
Kaltennordheim 430
Kalverdijk 312

Kamberg 421
Kambs 308
Kamen 368, 369, 376, 383
Kamp 375
Kamp Lintfort, US XVI Corps HQ *412*, *413*
Kampe 455
Kampen 467
Kandel 285
Kanin, Garson (film director) *419*
Kapelle 226, 233
Kapellen 200, 356, 384
Kapellenhof 278
Kapelscheveer island 342
Kapfelberg 477
Kappel 426
Kappelkinger 255
Kapsweyer 283, 404
Kareth 474
Karlich 390
Karlingen 261, 264
Karlsbach 480
Karlsbad 462, 468
Karlshorst, Berlin, German surrender *508*
Karlsruhe
    September, Allied air offensive 172
    October, Allied air offensive 226
    December, Allied air offensive 265, 272, 277, 299, 301, 303
    January, Allied air offensive 309, 311, 316, 319, 332, 334, 339
    February, Allied bombing 344, 348, 356, 357, 362
    March
        Allied advance 415, 417
        Allied bombing 384, 402, 404, 405, 407, 418
    April
        Allied capture 434, 438, *471*
        sector 439, 441, 443, 445, 447, 448
Karlstadt 256
Kaschenbach 371
Kassel
    September, Allied bombing 191, 192
    October, Allied bombing 198, 203, 217, 222
    November, Allied bombing 237
    December
        Allied bombing 300, 303
        Allied strategy *270*
    January, Allied bombing 337
    February, Allied bombing 349
    March
        Allied advance to *417*, 422
        Allied bombing 375, 376, 377, 385, 391, 403, 405, 407
    April
        Allied bombing 441
        battle for 432, *434*, *435*
        fighting in sector 426, 428, 430, 431, *433*, *436*, 437, *438*, 439, 440, 442
Kastel 420
Kastellaun, Hundsrück Heights Road *399*
Kastl 472
Katernberg 443
Katzenbach 433
Kaufman, Sgt George A. *383*
Kaundorf 301
Kean, Maj. Gen. William B. *211*
Keeken 354
Keffenach 276
Kehl 457
Kehmen 298, 299
Keiberg 324
Keitel, FM Wilhelm (OKW commander) *92*, *93*, *508*
Keldenich 387
Kelhmath 474, 477
Kell 399
Kellenbach 402
Kelly, Sgt James F. *83*
Kembs 310
Kemnath 469
Kempen 216, 250, 269, 352, 353, 382
Kempten 450, 459, 479, 480
Kems 473
Kenn 386
Kennedy, Capt. Jimmy *214*
Kennedy, Edward *516*
Keppeln 370
Kerkrade 199
Kerling 240
Kermpt 167
Kerpen 227
Kersch 311
Kervenheim 376, 377
Kesfeld 361
Kessel 250, 358
Kesselring, FM Albert *502*
Kesternich 279, 280, 338
Kettwig 462

Keuchingen 298
Keula 440
Kevelaer 354, 356, 357, 365, 376, 377, 382
Key, Francis Scott, *The Star Spangled Banner* 383
Kiel *488*, *491*, *518*
    Allied bombing 394, 431, 434, 445, 453, 470, 475, 478, 490
Kielforde 494
Kienitz *339*
Kierberg 354
Kierdorf 268
Kilstett 331
Kinderbeuren 396
Kindweiler 351
Kinnard, Lt Col Harry *293*
Kinzel, Gen. Eberhard *490*, *494*, *495*, *497*
Kinzweiler 250
Kirchberg 260, 402
Kirchenlamitz 468
Kirchheim 387, 470
Kirchhellen 420
Kirchtimke 478, 480
Kirk, Rear Adm. Alan Goodrich, USN *16*, 20, 45
Kirkel 395
Kirn 311, 383, 403
Kirschheim 469
Kitzbühel *508*
Kitzingen 409, 420, 438
Kladde 236
Kladno 462
Klarenthal 398
Klatovy 469
Klattau 502, 504
Kleegarten 486
Klein Blitterdorf 363
Kleinengstingen 443, 445
Kleinhausen 419
Klenhau 261
Klettstedt 444
Kleve *see* Cleve
Kliding 396
Klimbach 280
Klingenmünster 410
Klötz 472
Klötze Forest 467, 469
Kluge, FM Hans-Günther von *92*–*93*, *137*
Klundert 236, 237
Knapsack 386
Knee, Capt. Derek *495*, *497*
Knight, Pte Norman *185*
Knocke 209, 228, 233, 234
Knöringen 475
Kobern 394
Koblenz *see* Coblenz
Kochendorf 371, 415, 445
Kocher, River 445, 447, 448, 450, 452
Koenich, Obergefr. Otto *385*
Koenig, Gén. Joseph-Pierre *142*, *145*
Kœnigsmacker 242, 244, 245, 250
Kogenheim 265
Kohlscheid 210, 212
Koll (PK photographer) *79*
Kölleda 448
Kollersberg 488
Kommerscheidt 236, 237, 349, 351
Konfeld 401
Koniev, Marshal Ivan *457*
Königshofen 429, 443
Königshoven 371
Königswinter 400, 401
Konz-Karthaus 227, 234, 296, 298, 299, 307
    Allied capture 377
Konzen 338
Köpfchen *215*
Kopp 385
Kopscheid, Allied capture 366
Korean War *511*
Korperich 363
Körrenzig 328
Korweiler 399
Koslar 253, 254, 255, 256, 259, 260, 261, 264
Kösslarn 488
Köthen 449, 457, 459
Kotzebue, 1st Lt Albert *478*
Kraft, Pte P. J. *192*
Kraiburg 448
Krancke, Adm. Theodor *92*
Kranenburg 352, *354*
Krautscheid 366
Krefeld 218, 267, 317, 337, 366, 377
    'Adolf Hitler' road bridge *382*, *383*
    Allies enter 377, 382, *383*
Kreinitz *478*
Krems, River 502
Krettnach-Obermennig 376
Krettnich 364, 402

Kretz 395
Kreuzau 280, 369
Kreuzburg 432
Kreuztal 385, 402
Kreuzweingarten 385
Kriestorf 488
Krinkelt *283*, 338, 343
Kronach 452
Krostitz 470
Kruchten 353
Krudenberg 419
Kruiningen 225
Krupp, Alfred *444*
Krupp of Essen *444*
Kückhoven 370
Kuckum 371
Kufferath 280, 282
Kuinre 467
Kulz 401
Kunheim 344
Kunkowitz 504
Kuntzig 245
Kunze, Hptm. *290*
Kursk, Battle of *193*
Kurth (PK photographer) *137*, *139*
Kurtscheid 414
Kürzell 459
Küsten canal 461, 464, 467, 470, 471
Küstrin *427*, *459*
Kuttingen 253
Kyll, River 375, 383, 384, 385, 386
Kyllburg 308, *397*
Kyritz 463, 478

La Barre-de-Semilly 83
La Bolle 244
La Bourgonce 234
La Bresse 213
La Carneille 132
La Chapelle 292
La Corbière, Jersey 120
La Coubre Forest 462
La Croix-Prie *103*
La Falize 313
La Ferrière-sur-Risle 132
La Ferté 85
La Ferté-Macé *123*, *124*, 128, 131, 132
La Ferté-sous-Jouarre 150
La Flèche 81
La Folletière 117
La Gleize *294*, *295*, 298, 299
La Haye-du-Puits 48, 58, 72–79, 84
    Allied capture *80*, *81*
La Haye-Pesnel 106
La Hougue 118
La Jourdainerie 85
La Londe 85
La Loupe, Allied bombing 49
La Mailleraye-sur-Seine 132
La Mancellière *84*
La Martinière *84*
La Nartelle *127*
La Pallice
    fuel depot bombed 123, 134
    U-Boat pens bombed 120, 122, 123, 125, 133
La Pernelle 39
La Plante *162*
La Possonnière 42
    Allies attack bridge *70*, 90
La Poterie 72
La Rive 22
La Rivière *24*
La Roche 292, 300, *311*, 313, *314*, 315, *316*, 317, 318, 319, 320, *321*
    Allied bombing 56, 110, 301, 307
La Roche-sur-Yon, air attacks on 62, 74
La Salle 238
La Samsonerie 88
La Thiboutière 141
La Tiboterie 86
La Traverserie 48
La-Haye-du-Theil *138*
Laacher See 395, 396
Labach 357
Labaroche 346
L'Abbaye 88
Labbeck 364, 376
Lachapelle 238
Lack, Col Norman *4*
Lacroix 247
Ladenburg 421
Laffeld 331
Laffenau 471
Lafley, 1st Lt Cedric *205*
Lage 364
Lagny 148
Lahn, River 343, 419, 420
Lahr 362
L'Aigle
    July, Allied bombing 70, 73, 77, 87, 99

L'Aigle — continued
    August
        Allied advance from *146*
        Allied advances 140
        Allied bombing 127
        Allied capture 140
Laing, Sgt Jock (AFPU)
    Caumont *102*
    Saint-Pierre-Tarentaine *114*
    Vassy *125*
Laize, River 123, 125, 126, 128
Laizon, River 126
Lake Constance 297, 371, 472, 477, 482, 487, 490
Lake Noir 289, 309
Lalanne, Dragon Emile *169*
Lam 481
Lambach 502
Lamberth, Maj. Emil *429*
Lambertsberg 376
Lambertsneukirchen 474
Lambrecht 321
Lamco Paper Sales Ltd *10*
Lammersdorf 183, 260, 261, 264, 280
    Siegfried Line at *331*
Lampertheim 419
Lancery, Adj. Emile *169*
Lancey, 1st Lt Lawrence De *213*
Landau
    October 213
    November 256, 261
    December 272, 277, 279, 282, 284, 285, 294, 303
    January 315, 316, 321
    February 348, 359, 363
    March 377, 393, 398, 400, 402, 403, 407, 409, 410
    April 473
    May 489
Landivy 114
Landkern 394
Landorf 246
Landsberg 473, 479, 480
Landscheid 329, 331, 390
Landshut 448, 486, 489
Lang, Capt. Steve *380*
Langen 418
Langenargen 297
Langenschwarz *429*
Langernsalze 440
Langerwehe 209, 210, 256, 257, 259, 260, 261, 267, 274
Langewiese 421, 430
Langgöns 421
Langlir *318*, 319, *322*
Langmeil 319
Langrune 16
Langstraat 382
Langsur 383
Langwaden 419
Lannion 133
Lanzerath 284
Laon 152, 158
    airfield bombed 48, 57, 63
    Allies enter 156
    rail centre bombed 56
    road transport bombed 150
Lapoutroie 292, 301
Lascelles, Lt The Viscount 504
Lascheid 376
Lathen 444
Latrop 437
Lattre de Tassigny, Gén. *see*
    Tassigny, Gén. Jean de Lattre de
Laubach 440
Laucha 440
Laudert 401
Laudesfeld 343
Lauenburg 467, *477*, 481, 486, 490
Laulne 84
Launstroff 250
Lauperath 366
Lauphcim 450
Laurenzberg 252
Lauter, River *521*
Lauterbach 421, 422, 426, 473
Lauterburg 279, 403, *521*
Lavacherie 319
Laval
    June
        Allied front *67*
        Allies bomb communications/railways 36, 43, 46, 61, 62
        bombing of German airfields 34
    July, Allied bombing 73, 84, 91
    August 116, *153*
    October, Allied capture 216
Laval, Pierre 474
Lavaselle 303
Lavelaye, Victor de *391*
Laveline 205

Laws, Sgt George (AFPU), first landings on D-Day *21*
Lawton Collins, Maj. Gen. J. *see*
    Collins
Le Bény-Bocage *102*, 110, *111*, 113, *114*, *115*
Le Bourget 151
Le Bray 45
Le Culot 129
Le Grand Bois 274, 327
Le Gras 301
Le Ham 41
Le Haut du Bosq *43*
Le Havre
    June
        Allied bombing 44, 45, 65
        and Allied strategy *6*, *67*
        naval bombardment 45, 47
    July
        Allied bombing 77, 85
        clash with E-Boats 85
    August
        Allied bombing of ships 110, 112
        naval skirmishes 113, 117, 120, 134, 136
    September
        Allied capture 172, *173*, *192*
        Allied naval bombardment 168
        Allies bomb 162, 163, 166, 171, *172*, *197*
        Allies close in 160
        battle for 168
    October, White Ball Express *260*
Le Hom 115
Le Hommet-d'Arthenay 84, 85, 86, 87
Le Lude 112, 117
Le Manoir, bridges bombed 110, 125
Le Mans
    June 66
        Allies bomb railways 36, 40, 46, 56
        bombing of German airfield 34, 44
    July, Allied bombing 72, 75, 85, 91, 96
    August
        Allied bombing 111, 116, 122
        Allied liberation 119, *124*
        Allied thrust from 126
Le Ménil 242
Le Merlerault, railway lines bombed 49
Le Mesnil-Adelée 112
Le Mesnil-Durand 84, 88
Le Mesnil-Gilbert 115
Le Mesnil-Herman 100
Le Mesnil-Patry *43*
Le Mesnil-Vigot 87
Le Neufbourg, Mortain *119*
Le Plessis-Grimoult *116*, 122
Le Repas *106*
Le Rivier d'Allemont *245*
Le Theil 55
Le Thillot 202–205, 207–210, 212, 213, 215, 216, 218
Le Tholy 225
Le Touquet, German E-Boats attacked off 43
Le Tourneur *114*
Le Tréport 158
    enemy shipping attacked 64
League of Nations *266*
Leake, 1st Lt Ernest *333*
Lebach 270, 273, 289, 322
Lébisey 75
Lech, River 479, 480, 489, 490, 493
Lechbruck 480
Lechenich 236, 383
Leckwitz: US-Soviet link-up *478*
Leclerc, Gén. Philippe 142, *144*, *419*
Leda, River 481
Leeheim 414
Leer 467, 474, 476, 480, 481, 486, 488, 490
Leese 440
Leeuwarden 332, 458
Legden 248
Leibowitz, Sgt Irwing *126*
Leiden 331
Leidenborn 362
Leiffart 267
Leigh-Mallory, ACM Sir Trafford (C-in-C AEF air forces) 13, *97*, *212*
    at Norfolk House *11*
    career *11*
    and Pegasus Bridge landings *19*
    death *245*, *258*, *308*
Leimersheim 408, 409, 415
Leimgardt, Dr *443*
Leine, River 444, *454*
Leintrey 244
Leiphcim 403

Leipzig
    Wagner's birthplace *457*
    January, Allied bombing 324
    February, Allied bombing *356*, 357, 371
    March, Allied bombing 377, 407
    April 452, 454, 455, 459, 470, 471, 477
        Allied bombing 427, 438, 439, 443, 445, 447, 450, 458, 459
        Allied objective *433*, *438*, 461
        Allies clear *467*, 469
        battle for *464*, *467*
Leitzkau 455
Lelbach 421
Lellingen 251
Lemberg 272, 315
Lemestroff 245
Lemgo 432
Lénault 122
Lengelern 335
Lengenfeld 465
Lengerich 396, 430, 442
Lengronne *100*, 104, 105
Lenkerbeck 384, 386
Lennep 393
Lens
    Allies occupy 159
    railway centre bombed 46, 123
Leonding 504
Leopold Canal 174, 182, 183, 202–205, 207–210, 212, 218, 224
Lépanges 199
Lépine 151
Les Authieux 142
Les Baraques 240
Les Champs-de-Losque 84
Les Foulons 127
Les Grandes-Loges 152
Les Granges 85
Les Loges 105
Les Mezières 85
Les Milleries 87
Les Moitresses 244
Les Pieux
    Allied bombing 49
    Allies liberate 53
Les Ponts-de-Cé 90, 110
Les Poulières 232
Les Sablons 44
Lessay 100
    Allied advance to *79*, 80, 83, 84, 85, 87, 88, 102
    Allied bombing 45, 72, 73, 74, 78
Létricourt 205, 208, 233
Leudersdorf 388
Leuna 457
Leutenheim 326
Leutesdorf 405, 407, 409
Leuth 352
Leutkirch 482
Leuze 160
Leverkusen, chemical works 224, 359
Levin, Mike (ONA) *385*
Lewis, Boyd Dewolf *521*
Lewis, Lt-Cdr P. B. N., RN 33
Leyherr, Oberstlt Maximilian 205, *219*
Leyr 186
Leyweiler 254
L'Hôpital 264
Liane, River 182
Liberty Highway *292*
Liblar 269, 285, 384
Libramont 298
Lich 420
Lichtenborn 365
Lichtenfels 450
Lichtenstein 500
Lidrezing 244
Liège *162*, 164, 166, 167, 168, 171, 172, *360*
Liéhon 244
Lieler 335
Lierneux *288*, 298, 300, 302, 312, *313*
Liessel 232, 233
Liessem 370
Life magazine *58*, *467*
Ligneuville *285*, 322, 327
Ligurian sea 480
Lille
    Allied bombing 39, 56, 120, 122, 147
    liberated 161, 163
Lille-Brussels highway *157*
Lillebonne 156
Lillers 160
Lilly 72
Limbourg 167, 172
Limburg 261, 351, 360, 400, 407, 418, 419, *421*
Limoges, Allied bombing 57, 58
Linda 459
Lindau 487

Lindern 261, 264, 265, 267, *359*
Linge, Heinz *483*
Linge canal 330
Lingen 348, 429, 436, 439, *440*, 442, 444
Lingèvres, battle for *53*
Link, Hptm. *494*
Linne 333, 334, 335
Linnich
    November 261
    December 264, *265*, 266, 269, 271, 272, 280, 284, 287
    January 328
    February 366, 368, 369, 370
Linz, Austria 475, 477, 488, 491, 500, 502, 504
Linz, Germany 394, 395, 396, 398
Lipp 349
Lippe canal 414, 418, 419, 420, 422
Lippe, River 430, 437
Lippe Seiten canal 431
Lippedorf 416
Lipperscheid 330
Lippstadt 201, 393, 396, *428*, 430
Lisieux
    Allied advance to 136, 137, 141
    Allied air attacks 51, 56, *71*, 84, 125, 127
    Allied air reconnaissance 64
    Allied front *67*, 140
    German resistance overcome 142
Lisle, railway bridge bombed 112
L'Isle-Adam 120, 129, 133
Lison 37
Lissendorf 218, 386
Livarchamps 301
Livarot 116, 117, 134, 136
Liverdun 168
Lixieres 205
Lizaine, River 246
Loccum 442
Lochem 183, 431
Lochrist 168
Loenhout 218
Löffingen 351, 371
Lohn 253, 254, 255
Löhne 398, 450
Löhnen 414
Lohr 433, 437
Loing, River 141
Loire, River
    June *31*, 45
    and Allied strategy *6*, *62*
    Allies bomb bridges over *32*, *38*, *42*, *52*, *70*
    July, Allied bombing 75, 76, 77, 83, 85, 87, 88, 90, 95, *96*, 106
    August
        Allied advance to *124*
        Allies bomb bridges 110, 111, 112
        Allies cross 123
    September *182*
Loire Estuary 57
Loire valley 119, 125
Lokeren 171
Lommersweiler 342
Lomré *318*
London
    Grosvenor Square (No. 28), ETOUSA Public Relations Office *10*
    Norfolk House AFHQ (St James's Square) *10*, *12*, *13*
    Senate House, University of London: Information Ministry *511*
    and SHAEF *513*–*516*
    V1 bomb attacks: Adastral House 65
    V2 rocket attacks *432*
Longchamps 151, 309, 310
Longeggoutte, forest of 207
Longen 394
Longerich 385
Longley-Cook, Capt. E. W. L., RN 37
Longsdorf 328
Longuich 394
Longvilly *291*, 324, 325
Löningen 450
Lonlay L'Abbaye *118*, *122*
Looker, Pte H. E. *192*
Loon op Zand 225, 227
Lorch 395
Lorient
    airfield bombed 30
    Allies close in 117, 118, 119, 121
    Germans hold out 123, 125, 126, 128, 182
    railways bombed 94
    submarine pens bombed 116
    surrender *197*
Lörrach 475
Lorraine 174, *191*, *271*
Lorry 248
Lorscheid 399, 402
Losheim 273, *284*, 345, 377, 400, 401
Loudéac 114

Louette-Saint-Pierre 164
Lougres 246
Louis XVI, King 280
Louisendorf 360
Louvain 161, 164
Louviers 141, 142, 150, 151
Louvigny 80, 90, 242
Lovell, Sgt Warden F. (US Signal Corps) 123
Lövenich 268, 369
Löwenstein 439, 458
Lower Saxony 193
Lozon, River, Allied bridgehead 87
Lübeck 488, 490, 491, 495
Luchem 247, 267, 268, 274
Lucherberg 261, 267, 268, 269, 274
Lucheux 119
Lucht, Gen. Walter 468
Lüdde-Neurath, Korvettenkapt. Walter 494
Lüdenscheid 433, 453, 455
Lüdermünd 429
Ludweiler 309, 310, 396
Ludwigsburg 429
Ludwigshafen
  September, Allied bombing 191
  October, Allied bombing 218
  December, Allied bombing 280
  January, Allied bombing 308, 311, 312
  February, Allied bombing 343
  March 410
    Allies enter 407, 409
  April 472
    US Army POW holding camp (A16) 466
Ludwigslust 490
  Allied bombing 364, 481
Ludwigswinkel 402
Lullange 329
Lullien, Jules 181
Lultzhausen 299
Lünebach 294, 375
Lüneburg 441, 464, 470
  Allied capture 467
Lüneburg Heath 461, 467
  Montgomery's 21st Army Gp Tac HQ and German surrender 486, 495–499
  Timeloberg ('Victory Hill') 486, 495–499, 518
Lünen 391, 418, 433
Lunéville
  July 86
  September 183–185, 188–189, 191
  October 202, 207, 209, 215, 216, 218, 220, 221, 222, 224, 227, 228
  November 233, 236, 238, 239, 241, 243, 244, 258
Lure 177, 184
Lutrebois 303, 306, 308, 309, 310
Lutz 399
Lützen 443
Lützendorf 203, 398
Lutzerath 395
Lützkampen 348, 363
Lützkendorf 352
Luxem 394
Luxembourg
  September 172, 173, 175, 182, 189, 192
    Luxembourg-German frontier 170, 171, 177, 179, 181, 185, 193
  October 197, 198, 199, 203, 242
  November 242, 256
  December, Battle of the Bulge 283, 284, 287, 290, 291, 298, 302, 303
  January, turning of the tide 306, 329
  February 351
    Germans driven from 365
Luxembourg (city) 168, 171, 226
  BBC broadcasts from 514, 515
  Gen. Bradley's HQ 408
  US Third Army HQ (Fondation Pescatore) 360
Luxeuil-les-Bains 243
Lykershausen 418
Lynch, Sgt Charles T. 121
Lyne, Maj.-Gen. Lewis 491
Lyon 99, 166
  Allied air operations 151, 172

Maas, River
  September 178
  October 197, 199, 219, 221, 227
  November 232, 233, 237, 239, 243, 247, 248, 250, 257, 260
  December 264, 267, 299, 300, 301, 303
  January 307, 311, 313, 314, 326, 329, 331, 333
  February 342, 349, 350, 355, 361
    Maaseik: Bristol Bridge 364
  March 375, 378, 382
  see also Meuse

Maas-Scheldt canal 177
Maasbracht 331
Maasbree 252, 253
Maaseik, Bristol Bridge (R. Maas) 364
Maashees 218
Maassluis 332, 345
Maastricht 179, 181
  Allied advance from 179
  Allied bombing of bridges 133
  Allied commanders meet 270
  Allied crossing near 173
  Allied liberation 175
  US Ninth Army HQ 248, 270, 377
MacArthur, Gen. Douglas, Eisenhower appointed to office of 8
McAuliffe, Brig. Gen. Anthony 292, 293
  awarded DSC 299
McBride, Maj. Gen. H. 493
MacDonald, Charles (historian) 261, 408, 471
McDowell, Cpl Jim 185
McHugh, Hugh (US Signal Corps) 121
McIvor, Pte H. 354
Mackenheim 331
Mackensen, Eberhard von (former German ambassador) 504
McKeogh, Sgt Mickey 280
Mackweiler 266
McLain, Maj. Gen. Raymond S. 367, 382
McLendon, Col Ernest L. 83
McNair, Lt Gen. Lesley J. 97
Macon, Maj. Gen. Robert C. 83
Mâcon (town) 166
Mactum 318
Madonne 174
Madru, Gaston (Paramount News) 143
Maeseyck 189, 300
Magdeburg
  September, Allied bombing 192
  October, Allied bombing 203
  January, Allied bombing 321, 324
  February, Allied bombing 345, 348, 349, 352, 356, 357, 358
  March, Allied bombing 377, 383, 391
  April
    Allied bombing 430, 431, 443, 455
    Allied capture 456
    Allied forces reach Elbe 448, 452, 456, 467
    Allied objective 454
    battle for 459, 461, 464
Mageret 291, 308, 312, 320, 322
Magerotte 302
Maginot, André 255
Maginot Line 255, 277, 278, 280, 283, 284, 285, 287, 318, 319, 320, 325, 326, 327, 328, 399, 402
Magnières 182
Mahlberg 348
Mahndorf 470
Maidenek, Poland: concentration camp 449
Maidières 165
Maiersgrün 504
Mailing 479
Mailly-sur-Seille 240
Main, River 416, 418–422, 426, 429, 430, 431, 433, 437, 443, 447, 450, 452
Mainberg 480
Maintenon 102, 113
Mainvilliers 112
Mainz
  September, Allied bombing 191
  October, Allied bombing 205, 218
  January, Allied bombing 319
  February, Allied bombing 343, 349, 371
  March
    Allied advance to 395, 404, 407
    Allied bombing 402, 404
    assault on the city 409
    fighting in sector 416, 418
    and Rhine crossing 408, 410, 414
  April, fighting in sector 426, 450
Maisborn 401
Maison Rouge 333
Maisoncelles-la-Jourdan 123, 125
Maisons-Laffitte, railway bridge bombed 59, 60
Maissin 166
Maizières-lès-Metz 199, 203–205, 207–208, 216, 218–221, 228, 242
Malaucourt 240
Malberg 385
Maldegem 174
Malderen 203
Maldingen 332
Malley, Capt. Charles 385
Malling 240

Malmédy
  September 172
  December 285, 287, 288, 292, 298, 299, 300
    Baugnez crossroads massacre 289
  January 319, 320, 322, 324, 327, 328, 338
Malmersdorf 481
Malta 342, 447
Maltot 78, 79, 84, 94, 95
Mamers 88
Mammendorf 482
Mande 308, 310, 311, 313, 315
Manderfeld 319, 345
Manderscheid 390, 392
Mangfall, River 489
Manhay 296, 299, 300, 301, 309, 314, 315
Mannheim
  October, Allied bombing 218, 269, 303, 319, 328
  December, Allied bombing 269, 303
  January, Allied bombing 319, 328, 329, 337
  February, Allied bombing 343, 352, 354, 361, 364, 370
  March 415, 422
    Allied bombing 376, 390, 400
    Allied capture 421
    fight for 420
  April, fighting in sector 427, 429, 438
Manonviller 236
Manstedten 383
Mantel 472
Mantes 32, 60
Mantes-Gassicourt
  Allied bombing 81, 84
  Allied bridgehead 148, 150, 151, 152
  Allies reach 134, 136, 146
  bridges bombed 40, 77, 78, 90, 110
  enemy forces engaged 148
Manteuffel, Gen. Hasso von 191, 290
Mapham, Sgt Jimmy (AFPU) 75
  at Tourville 89
  lands on Sword beach 21
Maquenoise 158
Marburg 385, 395, 402, 405, 428
Marche 168, 294, 296, 298, 299, 300, 301, 302, 310, 313, 315, 316, 319
Marchiennes 161
Marcourt 314, 315
Mardyck 250
Marguerin 102
Mariaweiler 277, 278, 279, 280, 282
Marie Antoinette 280
Marienau 384, 385
Marienbaum 371, 413, 416
Marienberg 395
Marienburg 442
Marigny 42, 86, 94, 98, 99, 100, 101, 102
Marilles 167
Maring 395
Mark, River 219, 232, 233, 235, 236, 238
Markolsheim 369
Markt 362, 450
Markt Dam 355
Marktbreit 430
Marly 247, 248
Marmagen 285
Marnach 290
Marne, River 148, 150, 151
  Allied bombing of bridges 111
Marne valley 152
Marne-Rhine canal 158, 201
Maromme 52
Marsal 189, 246
Marseille-en-Beauvaisis 152
Marshall, Gen. George C. 152, 417
  Allied strategy 259, 270, 342
  for 'Overlord' command 12
  lands in Normandy 35
  military occupation of Germany 397
  visits Montgomery 209
Marson 151
Martelange 296
Martinville 88
Marvelise 246
Marvie 298, 303
Maspelt 287, 337
Massenheim 421
Massinot, Henri 59
Massy 126
Massy-Palaiseau, railroad centres bombed (June) 30, 38
Masthorn 362
Mathes, Oberwachmeister Joseph 186
Mathieu, Seraphin 245
Mattox, Pte Paul 366
Matzen 371
Matzenheim 261
Maupertus 102
Mauron 114
Mauthausen concentration camp 473
Maxberg 480

Maxsain 418
Maxted, Stanley (BBC reporter) 327
Maxwell Taylor see Taylor, Maj. Gen. Maxwell D.
Maxwell-Hyslop, Capt. A. H., RN 45, 47
May-sur-Orne 96, 98, 116
Mayen
  October 210, 227
  November 234, 243
  December 269, 294
  January 307, 308, 317, 320, 329, 335, 336, 337
  February 348, 351, 358, 360, 368
  March 375, 388, 390, 392, 394, 395
Mayen-Kottenheim 269
Mayenne
  Allied advance from 123
  Allied bombing 32, 46, 84
  fighting in sector 119
  US capture 113, 116
Mayenne, River 116
Meador, Pte William 273
Méan, Château de Bassinnes 298
Meaux 76, 84, 150, 151
Mechelen 161
Mechernich 362
Mechtersheim 408, 409
Meckel 371
Meckenheim 377
Mecklenburg 193, 495
Medal of Honor
  Brown, Capt. Bobbie, E. 217
  Burt, Capt. James M. 217
  Ehlers, S/Sgt Walter D. 514
  Murphy, Lt Audie 333
  Pendleton, Sgt Jack J. 217
  Thompson, Sgt Max 217
Meddersheim 403
Medelsheim 284, 400
Medis 458
Medley, Cpl H. C. 133
Meeuwen 336
Mehr 416
Meiderich 272, 275
Meiggs, Lt William 429
Meijel 198, 225, 226, 227, 228, 234, 237, 247, 249, 250, 251
Meimbressen 437
Meine 448, 451
Meiningen 430, 439, 443, 447
Meinsdorf 454
Meisburg 386
Mcisenheim 403
Meisenthal 310
Melay 184
Mélisey 184
Melun 141, 142, 143, 146, 148
Meluskey, Capt. Victor J. 512
Memmingen 469, 479
Memorials
  Audrieu: to Royal Winnipeg Rifles 43
  Braunau: to Mauthausen concentration camp 493
  Buchenwald 447
  Dresden: Frauenkirche 356
  Grandménil 296
  Honsfeld: to US 99th Division 284
  Houffalize 321
  Karlshorst, Berlin: to Red Army 508
  Kienitz: to Soviet Army 339
  London, No. 20 Grosvenor Square: to Gen. Eisenhower 7
  Luxeuil-les-Bains 243
  Moselle: to US 5th Division 164
  Moulin de Renswiez: US First and Third Armies link-up 320
  Nehou, Saint-Sauveur-le-Vicomte: US Third Army command post 110
  Norfolk House, St James's Square 13
  Paris: Montparnasse and German surrender 144
  Renuamont: 'Voie de la Liberté' marker 292
  Saint-Lambert-sur-Dives 134
  Saint-Lô: to Maj. Howie 87, 88
  Sainteny 82
  Stolzembourg: Allied crossing into Germany 170
  Torgau: Soviet-Allied link-up 479
  Tournières, Bayeux: SHAEF Advance Command Post 'Shellburst' 128
  Val-Ygot V1 site 38
  Vernon bridge 49, 147
  Victory Hill: German surrender (later at Sandhurst) 499
  Washington DC: to US 2nd Division 4
  XXX Corps: Nienburg (later at Sandhurst) 446
  Zonhoven, Villa Magda: Montgomery's HQ 301

Ménarmont 222
Menditte, Chef d'Escadron Jacques de Bertereche de 347
Menning 479
Menton 184
Menzelen, railway bridge 393
Meppel 456
Meppen 268, 411, 434, 438, 439, 440, 442, 444
Merderet, River 36, 38
Merey 85, 122
Merken 260, 274, 277
Merkendorf 468
Merklingen 443
Merksplas 197
Merkstein 199
Merl 401
Merlscheid *284, 285*, 375
Mérode 261, 264, 274
Merrick, Lt Col Richard H. *514*
Mersch 171, 294, 366
Merseburg 192, 203, 242, 270, 459
 synthetic oil plant bombed 321, 434
Mersevey, Lt Col D. W. *476*
Merten 443
Mertesdorf 387
Mertzweiler 269
Merville 163
Merxheim 403
Merzenhausen 252, 260
Merzenich 181, 369
Merzig
 November 250, 251, 252, 256, 257
 December 264, 265, 266, 268, 272, 282
 January, Allied bombing 320
 March 400, 401, 402
Merzweiler 270, 271, 403
Meschede 443, 445, 447, 448
Meschenich 387
Meschers 458
Messei 94
Messerich 370
Meterik 254
Mettendorf 353, 364, 365, 369
Metz
 Allied advance *164*, 171, 181–186, 242, 243, 244, 245, *247*, 259
 Allied envelopment of 240, 249, 250, 251, 264
 and Allied strategy *241*
 Allies bomb 64, 122, 125, 150, 173, 204, 224
 battle for *204*, 252, 253
 possible site for SHAEF HQ *360*
 sector of 191, 193, 199, 203, 204, 205, 220, 234, 247, 248, 254, *255*, 256, 257, 271, 384
 Siegfried Line near 173
 surrender to Allies *250*, 269
 see also Fort de Plappeville; Fort Driant; Fort Jeanne d'Arc
Metz-en-Couture, château (German HQ) *150*
Metzervisse *240*, 247, 248
Meulan 151
Meurthe, River 183, 253
Meurthe valley 185, 186, 188, 189, 241, 242, 249
Meuse, River
 June, Allies bomb bridges *32*
 August, Allies bomb bridges *133*
 September 161, 175
  Allied advances 163, 164, 166, 167, 189
  Allies cross *158*, 160, *162*
 October, Allied bombing of bridges 210, 226
 November
  Allied advance 253
  Allied bombing of bridges 236
  Allied strategy *242*
 December, and Ardennes counter-attack *281, 297*
 see also Maas
Meuse-Argonne sector (WW1) *243*
Meuse-Escaut canal 175, 176, 185
Meyerode 334
Mézidon
 Allied air reconnaissance *64*
 Allies bomb 40, 42, 43, 49, 53, 56, 59, 60, 66, 126
 Allies occupy *132*
Michamps 308, 311, 324
Michelbach 386
Michelstadt 421
Middelaar 329, 354
Middelburg 218, *235*, 237, 238
Middleton, Capt. G. H., RN 47, 48
Middleton, Maj. Gen. Troy H. *181, 291, 292, 346*
Midgley, Sgt Norman (AFPU) *89*
 Beeringen *163*

Midgley, Sgt Norman — continued
 Gacé *146*
 Mont-Pinçon *116*
Mierchamps 318
Mignéville 240
Mihla 437
Miller, 2nd Lt William *500*
Miller, Cpl Harry (US Signal Corps) *273, 312*
Millingen 354, 390
Mills, Pte D. *354*
Milly-sur-Seine 148
Milne, Lt Gilbert (AFPU) *23*
Mimbach 401
Minden 359, 362, *436*, 439, 440
Minheim 398
Minquiers Rocks 43
Minsen 456
Mirecourt 175
Mirfeld 334
Mirville 95
Misburg 368, 398, 399
Mitlosheim 401
Mittelbau-Dora forced labour camp 468
Mittelrot 468
Mittelsdorf 430
Mittenwald 486
Mittersheim 253
Mittlach 347
Mittois, Caen *93*
Möckmühl 433
Modane 176
Model, FM Walter *137, 150*
 and Ardennes counter-attack *281*
Moder, River 260, 333, 334, 335, 343, 353, *357*, 358, 398, 399
Möderscheid 333
Mödrath 354
 Allies reach 375, 376, 377, 383
Moerdijk 218, 227, *238, 239, 240*, 241
Moergestel 223
Moers 384, 385
Möhn 376
Moinet 329
Moircy 302, 303, 307
Moisburg 306
Moissy ford *135*
Moivrons 204
Molbis 401
Möllen 414
Möllin 490
Molsheim 259, 260
Momexy 157
Mompach 193
Moncourt 221, 240
Mondrainville, German forces destroyed 64
Monheim 213, 269
Monnai 141, 142
Monneren 247
Monreal 387
Mons 162
 Allied victory *159*, 161
Monschau
 September 181
 October 201, 207, 208, 209, 224, 226
 November 237
 December 278, 279, 280
  Battle of the Bulge 282–285, 287, 289, 292, 294, 296, 298–300, 302
 January, turning of the tide 320, 338
 February 342, 343, 344, 345, 346, 347, 348, 349, 351, 352
Monsheim 277
Mont Cenis Pass 176
Mont-Lambert, Boulogne 181
Mont-Pinçon *116*, 117, 119, 120
Mont-Saint-Michel *153*
Montabard 134
Montabaur 398, 418
Montaigu 152
Montargis 84, 102, 141, 142, 143
Montbard *169*, 175
Montbéliard 248
Montcornet 158, 159
Montdidier 158
 Allied fighters strafe targets 55, 84
Montebourg 43, 44, *55*
 awarded Croix de Guerre 37
 liberated 52
Montélimar *151*
Montenach 243
Montenois 246
Montereau 142, 143, *148*
Montfort 329, 330, 331, 332, 333
Montfort-le-Gesnois, Allied bombing 72
Montfort-sur-Risle
 Allied advance to 143
 Allied air attacks 64, 78, 95, 114

Montgomery, Gen. (later FM) Sir Bernard L.
 21st Army Gp Tac HQs 35, 40, *453, 486, 495–499*, 518
 advance into Germany *433*, 453
 advance to Baltic *488*
 advance to Elbe *446*
 Ardennes counter-offensive *298, 301, 302, 309*
 arrives in Caen *78*
 at Norfolk House *10*
 and Berlin *457*
 career *11*
 ceases to command ground forces *152*
 Churchill visits HQ *377*
 confers with Gen. Horrocks *174*
 death of Adm. Ramsay *308*
 and Eisenhower *258, 342*
 Gen. Marshall visits *209*
 German peace overtures *490, 494*
 German surrender *495–499*
 King George VI visits front *209, 210*
 Lüneburg Heath Tac HQ *486, 495–499*, 518
 'Market-Garden' operation *176, 184*
 Normandy strategy *131*
 offensive in Holland *451*
 Operation 'Bluecoat' *102*
 Operation 'Goodwood' *91, 92*
 'Overlord' planning *12, 13, 62*
 and Paris liberation *145*
 and port of Antwerp *219*
 Rhine assault *350, 353, 390*
 Rhine crossing *408, 410, 411, 413, 416*
 Rhine/Ruhr offensive plans *242, 375, 394*
 single thrust strategy *163, 241, 270*
 Tac HQ Ostenwalde *453*
 Vernon bridge *147*
Montigny 244
 German units bombed 51
Montleban *318, 319, 320*
Montmédy 167
Montmirail 150
Montmorency 151
Montpinchon 104
Montreuil 112, 161
Montreuil-Bellay, Allied air attacks 50
Moon, Rear Adm. Don Pardee, USN 33
Moore, Lt Eugene J. (US Signal Corps) *92*
Moosburg, POW camp liberated 481, 486
Moran, T/4 Leo (US Signal Corps) *205, 322, 358*
Mörchingen 246
Moreuil 156
Morey 185
Morgan, Lt-Gen. Sir Frederick E.
 career *12*
 deputy Ch.-of-Staff SHAEF *12, 13, 505*
 invasion plans *47*
Morhet 294, 302
Morlaix 104
Morris, Sgt Bill *174*
Morsbach 346, 348, 443, 521
Mörsch 417
Morscheid 398
Mörsdorf 400
Morshausen 399
Mortain 113, 114, 117, *118–120, 121–126, 122, 124, 361, 419*
Mortange, River 221
Mortange (village) 222
Mortange forest 243
Morville-lès-Vic 241
Mosbach 411, 417
Moscow *508*
 Allied conference 324
Moselle, River
 September 168, 171, 186, 188
  Allied bridgeheads *164–165*, 172, 173, 174, 184, 188
  fighting to clear west bank 167
 October 196, 198, 199
 November 250
  Allied bridgeheads 240, 241, 244, 245, 247
  and Allied strategy *241*
 January 306, 333
  Allies clear west bank 318
 February 343, 348, 359, 363, 364, 365, 371
  Allied plans for offensive 375
 March 375, 376, 377, *380*, 383, 389, *394, 395*, 396, 398, 399, 401, 402, 403, 404, *407*
  Allied bridgeheads 399, 400

Moselle valley 175–177, 179, 181–182, 184, 188, 213, 216, 218, 221–222, 224, 226, 234, 235, 237
Moselotte, River 207, 208, 209, 210, 215, 218, 219, 234
Mostroff 298
Motte, Pte Louis *121*
Mouen 61
Mouffet 100
Moulin de Rensiwez *320*
Moulines 125
Moulins 102
Moyaux 142
Moyen 182
Moyland 361, 362, 364, 365, 366
 Schloss Moyland *355*
Moyland Wood *355*
Much 450
Mudau 422
Müddersheim 376
Müden 458
Mudersbach 433
Mudford, Capt. F. W., RN 33
Mueller, Merrill 'Red' (NBC) *512*
Mühl, River 500
Mühlbach 347
Mühlberg 458
Mühldorf 469, 493
Mühlhausen 333, 334, 427, 429, 432, 434, 437, 440, 442, 444, 448
Mühlheim 470
Mulberry harbours *47, 51*
Muldau 375
Mulde, River *426, 453*, 454, 457, 459, 469, 470, 471, 472, 477
Muldenau 375
Mulhouse
 Allied advances 252, 260, 264, 266, 273
 Allied bombing 123, 248, 269, 282, 316, 339
 Allies liberate 253, *256*
 fighting in sector 307, 315, 330, 331, *332*, 334, 348, 354
Müllendorf *284*, 285
Müller, Kriegsberichter Kurt *141, 149*
Müllheim 472
Mullingsen 440
Müncheberg *459*
Münchehof 446
München-Gladbach/Mönchengladbach
 November 248, 256
 December 269, 301
 January 334
 February 343, 366, 368, *369*
 March 375, 377
  Allied capture *376*
  US Ninth Army HQ *408*
Münchenbernsdorf 443
Munchhausen 351
Müngersdorf 385
Munich
 Hitler's Bürgerbraukeller (beerhall) Putsch *482–483*
 October, Allied bombing 224
 November, Allied bombing 249
 January, Allied bombing 313
 February, Allied bombing 360, 369
 March, Allied air operations 376
 April 479, 480, *481*
  Allied bombing 438, 445, 448, 449, 459, 468, 469, 470, 475, 477, 479
  Allied capture *482–483*
 May 486, 487, 489, 490, 493
Munshausen 336
Münster
 October, Allied bombing 196, 216, 220, 224, 227
 November, Allied bombing 249, 260
 December 289
  Allied bombing 268, 269
  fighting joined 283
  sector 282
 January
  Allied air attacks 310, 311, 319, 327, 328, 332, 337
  Allied air skirmishes 306, 310
 February, Allied bombing 354, 362
 March, Allied bombing 391, 401, 403, 407, 409, 411, 417, 422
 April
  Allies clear 431, 432
  battle for city *433*
Münster, Prince-Bishops of *430*
Münstereifel 270, 285, 298, 348, 353, 371
Münsterhausen 477
Muntzenheim 339
Munwiller *347*
Munzinger 362

Mûr-de-Bretagne, Allied air attack 72
Mürlenbach 386
Murphy, Col Michael *495*
Murphy, Lt Audie, Medal of Honor *333*
Murrange 338
Mürringen *282, 343, 344*
Museums
    Braunau (Hitler's birthplace): 'House of Responsibility' *493*
    Douvres-la-Délivrande: Le Musée Radar *50*
    Karlshorst, Berlin: to Red Army *508*
    La Roche: Musée de la Bataille des Ardennes *316*
    Oosterbeek: Hartenstein Hotel *185*
    Overloon *198, 264*
    Pegasus Bridge *19*
    Remagen *389*
    Schloss Moyland *355*
Musser, T/4 Arland B. (US Signal Corps) *481*
Mussolini, Benito *92*
Musweiler 392
Mutterhausen 314
Mützenich 344
Mutzig 259, 269

Nabburg 472
Nacken, Jakob *196*
Nagold 462
Nahbollenbach 383
Nahe, River 401, 403
Nambsheim 351
Namur
    August, Allied bombing of bridges 133
    September
        Allied advance from 163, 164, 166
        Allies reach *162*
Nancy
    August, Allied bombing 133
    September 167, 168, 174, 176, 177, 182, 185, 186, 188, 189, 192, 193
        Allied bombing *172*, 173
        Allied entry *175*
        Allied plan to capture *165*
        Allies reach vicinity 160
        casualties and Allied bombing *172*
        Siegfried Line near *173*
    October
        Allied bombing in area 219
        fighting in sector 196–205, 208, 209, 210, 218
    November *254*, 258
        and Allied strategy *241*
        fighting in sector 233, 240, 242, 243, 244
Nannhausen 401
Nantes
    June, Allied bombing 38, 49, 52, 56, 57, 62
    July, Allied bombing 73, 76, 77, 83, 84, 87, 90
    August
        Allied advance to 119, 123
        Allied bombing 110, 112, 116
        Allied capture 121
Napoléon Bonaparte, and Ulm *474*
Narbéfontaine 256
Narburg 411
Nassau 343
Nastatten 391
Nattenheim 371
Nauen 469
Naumburg 450, 471
Nay 85
NBC reporting *512*
Neckar, River 421, 422, 427, 430, 431, 438, 448, 452, 465, 468
Neckarelz 411
Neckargemünd 294, 409, 411
Neckarsteinach 419
Neckarsulm 376
Neder-Rijn (Lower Rhine) *176, 184*, 185, 191, 202, 208, 431, 432, 436
Nederweert-Eind 245
Neef 400
Neerpelt *177*
Neffe 308
Neffel, River 371, 376
Néhou, Saint-Sauveur-le-Vicomte, US Third Army command post *110*
Neisse, River *see* Oder-Neisse
Nemmerdorf *338*
Nennig 322, 325, 328, 329, 331, 334
Neroth 388
Nesselröden 429
Netphen 430, 431
Nette, River 234, 360
Netterden 422
Netzschkau 461
Neu Lussheim 419
Neu Ulm 249, 477

Neu-Breisach (Neuf-Breisach) 274, *333*, 344, 345, 346, 347, 348, 349
Neuberg 445, 480
Neubrandenburg 202
Neuburg 369, 403, 466, 480
Neudorf 475
Neuenburg 250, 351
Neuendorf 352, 353
Neuenhäusen 298
Neuenheerse 411
Neuenkirchen 273, 279, 285, 301, 308, 311, 356, 395, 398, 399, 400, 401, 404, 409
Neuenrade 453
Neuenstadt 445
Neuerberg 392
Neuerburg 294, 368
Neufchâteau 168, 175
Neufelden 491
Neufmesnil 73
Neuhaus 458
Neuheilenbach 385
Neuhof 344
Neukirchen 477, 480
Neulauterburg *521*
Neumarkt 449, 468, 469, 472
Neumünster 441, 453, 491
Neundorf 332
Neung-sur-Beuvron *182*
Neuötting 493
Neurath, Konstantin von (ex-Foreign Minister) 504
Neuruppin 469
Neuss 216, 218, 220, 236, 259, 330, 331, 356, *381, 384, 385*, 386
    Allies enter 377, *382*
    bridges at *382, 383*
Neustadt
    November 249
    December 283, 285
    January 306, 311, 315, 319, 330
    February 368
    March 375, 385, 402, 407, 409
    April 442, 444, 446, 447, 457
Neustädtel 453
Neuville-en-Condroz 166
Neuvy-sur-Loire 117
Neuwied 324, 352, 368, 409, 410
Neuwied-Irlich 356, 362
Nevers 86
Néville, Batterie Blankenese *64*
Newel 371
Newhouse, Cpl Billy (US Signal Corps) *80, 81*
Newman, Cpl Carl *169*
Nickenich 395
Nickols, Bruce *435*
Nideggen 270, 274, 296, 371, 376
Nied Français, River 244
Nieder Bolheim 371
Nieder Florstadt 420
Nieder Zerf 371
Nieder-Emmels *330*
Niederaussem 377
Niederbettingen 386
Niederbieber 410
Niederbreitbach 410
Niederbronn 401
Niederbronn-lès-Bains *275*
Niederdollendorf 402
Niederdrees 386
Niedergailbach 280
Niedergondershausen 399
Niederhau 368
Niederhausen 404, 421
Niederheide 249
Niederkrüchten 331
Niederlahnstein 337, 419
Niederlauch 383
Niedermarsberg 398
Niedermehlen 352, 353
Niedermerz 250
Niedernhall 448
Niedernstocken 444
Niederpleis 407
Niederrad, Frankfurt 419
Niederröblingen 450
Niederscheid 369, 375, 393, 398, 400
Niederschlettenbach 284, 403
Niedersgegen 362
Niederwampach 324
Niederweis 371
Niederwürzbach 401
Niedhausen 335
Niel 352
Nienburg 383, 409, *436, 446*
Nienhagen 192, 398, 443
Niers, River *239*, 356, 358, 359, 360
Niersbach 389
Nierstein 408, 409, *410*
Nieuport 168, *192*

Nieuport-Bains 173
Nieuw Vossemeer 236
Nieuwland 237
Nievenheim 385
Nijverdal 396
Nijkerk 243
Nijmegen
    September, Operation 'Market-Garden' *176, 178*, 180, 182, *183, 184*, 185, 186, 188, 189, 191–193
    October
        Allied air attacks 222
        fighting in sector 202, 203, 209, 212
        German resistance 196, 197
    November
        Allied air attacks 249, 256
        Allies advance from *242*
        road bridge *238*
    December, Allied air attacks 267, 269
    January
        Allied air attacks 330, 332, 336
        fighting in sector 326, 327, 328, 329, 333
    February
        Allied air attacks 351, 359
        Allies launch advance to Rhine from *350, 351, 352, 353*
        fighting in sector 354, 356
    March
        Allied advance from 414
        Allied air attacks 418
    April, fighting in sector 431, 432, 436
Nijverdal 446
Nims, River 370, 383, 384
Niort, Allied air attacks 55, 56, 76
Nirm 334
Nistelrode 191
Nittenau 473
Nivelles *162*
Nocher 313, 318, 326, 327
Noduwez 167
Nogent, Allied bombing 57
Nogent-le-Roi 76, 83, 117, 127
Nogent-le-Rotrou 40
Nogent-sur-Seine 122, 148
Nohfelden 204, 399
Nomeny 242
Nompatelize 238
Nonancourt, Allies liberate 140
Nonant 87
Nonnenbruch forest 330
Nonnweiler 300, 337
Noorder canal 236, 245, 247, 248
Norbie (US Signal Corps) *96*
Norbuth, T/5 Edward (US Signal Corps) *359*
Norddinker 439
Nordhausen 431, 432, 439, 445, 446, 447, 448, 450, 457
    forced labour camp *468–469*
Nordhorn 431, 432
Nördlingen 455, 462, 469
Norfolk House (St James's Square, London), as Allied Forces HQ (AFHQ) *10, 12, 13*
Norrey 62
Norrey-en-Auge 132
Norroy-le-Veneur 248
North Carolina, USA, National Guard *361*
North Rhine-Westphalia *193*
Northeim 439, 441, 446, 450
Norvenich, Allied capture 375
Nothum 303, 307
Nothweiler 298
Notre-Dame-de-Cenilly 102, 103
Notre-Dame-d'Elle 100
Notre-Dame-d'Estrées 133
Notscheid 398
Nottleben 444
Noville *291*, 320, 322, 324
Noyant 84
Noyen 112
Noyers 87, 88, 89, 106
Nuland 222
Nünschweiler 308
Nuremberg *see* Nürnberg
Nürnberg (Nuremberg)
    pre-war rise of Hitler in *460*
    Luitpoldhain *463*
    Zeppelinwiese stadium *462*
    October (1944), Allied bombing 199, 218
    November, Allied bombing 260
    January, Allied bombing 308
    February, Allied bombing 363, 364, 369, 370
    March, Allied air operations 376, 400
    April 450, 457, 471, 472, 473, 474, 479
        Allied bombing 427, 434, 438, 443, 445, 447, 449, 455, *460*, 477

Nürnberg (Nuremberg) — continued
    Allied entry and capture 459, *460–464*, 465, 468, 469, 470
    post-war: war criminal trials *443, 506*
Nusbaum 362
Nütterden *354*
Nuttlar 385

Obenheim 317
Ober Redwitz 469
Ober Reid 480
Oberammergau 482
Oberau 486
Oberauerbach 480
Oberdorla 432
Oberdrees 386
Oberembt 370
Oberemmel 376
Oberesch 257
Obergailbach 277, 308
Obergeckler 365, 366
Obergeich 274
Oberglaim 486
Obergondershausen 399
Oberhausen *202, 233, 264, 337, 410*
Oberhöcking 489
Oberhof 432
Oberhoffen *343, 344, 345, 346, 349, 351, 352, 353, 354, 355, 356, 357, 403*
Oberhomburg 260
Oberkappel 488
Oberkassel *382*, 403, 404
Oberkirch 352, 465
Oberkirchen 433
Oberlauch 383
Oberlimberg 265
Oberlungwitz 468
Obermaubach 298
Obermehlen 351
Obermorschwihr 346
Obermühlphal 316
Obernberg 493
Obernüst 429
Oberotterbach 283, 403
Oberpierscheid 368
Oberraden 369
Oberreifferscheid 376
Obersasbach *443*
Obersgegen 363
Obersinn 433
Oberstadtfeld 386
Oberstedem 371
Oberthal 273
Oberwampach 324, 325, 326, 328
Oberweis 370
Oberwesel 408, 409, *416*
Oberwürzbach, Siegfried Line at *400*
Oberzier 368
Obspringen 331
Ochsenfurt 433, 438, 445, 448, 450
Ockfen 366, 368
O'Daniel, Maj. Gen. John 'Iron Mike' *333, 462, 500*
Odeigne 312
Odenwald 420
Oder, River *338, 339, 415, 427*
Oder-Neisse post-war German border *338*
Odheim 441
Odon, River, Allied bridgehead 63–65, 70–72, 77, 78, 79
Oelsnitz 461
Oermingen 269
Oestereiden 431
Oetingen 316, 362
Ofden 204, 205, 215
Offenburg 265, 266, 272, 346, 348, 352, 358, 359, 457, 459
Offendorf 311, 345, 351
Offwiller 399
Ohlenberg 394
Ohmden 469
Ohnenheim 331
Ohrdruf 432, 442
    concentration camp *435*, 448–449
Ohsen *436*
Oidtweiler 204
Oirschot 223
Oise, River
    Allied bombing in area 57
    Allies bomb bridges *32*, 120, 129
Oissel, bridge bombed 116, 123, 125
Oldenburg 434, 455, 459, 463, 466, 467, 469, 470, 472–474, 476, 478, 486
    Allied capture 488, 491
Oldenzaal 243
Olef 284, 386
Olef, River 386
Olle, T/Sgt Stephen J. *29*
Olle Road (Utah) *29*
Olpe 420, 447
Olsberg 439
Olzheim 352

Ommen 399
Ommersheim 400
Ondefontaine 111, 114
Ondenval 324, 325, 326, 327
O'Neill, Chaplain (US Third Army) 273
Onsdorf 364
Oos 303
Oostburg 208, 209, 215, 218, 222, 224
Oosterbeek 184
  Hartenstein Hotel 185
  Onderlangs (now Golden Tulip Rijnhotel) 186
Oosterhout 228, 232, 235, 236
Operation
  'Alan' 221
  'Astonia' 173
  'Berlin' 457
  'Blackcock' 325, 335
  'Bluecoat' 102, 114
  'Bodenplatte' 307
  'Charnwood' 74
  'Clarion' 364
  'Cobra' 94, 102
  'Dragoon' 126–127, 169
  'Epsom' 56
  'Garden' 176–177
  'Goodwood' 78, 89–92, 94
  'Greif' 281
  'Grenade' 350, 366, 392
  'Hurricane' 212
  'Infatuate' 199
  'Lüttich' 118
  'Market-Garden' 176, 187, 199, 228
    see also Arnhem
  'Neptune' 16–17
  'Nordwind' 337
  'Overlord' see 'Overlord', Operation
  'Pheasant' 221
  'Plunder' 411
  'Stösser' 281
  'Thunderclap' 212, 356
  'Torch' see Sicily
  'Totalize' 117
  'Varsity' 411, 412
  'Veritable' 350, 355, 362, 392
  'Wacht am Rhein' 281, 297, 337
Opheusden 203
Opladen 386
Oppenhausen 399
Oppenheim 408, 409, 410, 415
  Allied advance to 395, 417
Öpping 488
Oranienburg 399, 447, 469
Orbec 134, 137, 139, 140, 141, 142
Orbec, River 140
Ordorf 385
Orléans
  June, Allied bombing 36, 41, 42, 56, 62, 64, 66
  July, Allied bombing 70, 72, 73, 77, 80, 86, 90, 106
  August
    Allied bombing 113, 115, 116
    liberation 132, 134, 136
  September, German surrender south of 182
Ornans 166
Orne, River 46, 48, 57, 66, 72, 73, 74, 79, 93, 94, 95, 98, 116, 126, 128, 132, 133
  Airborne Div. objective 18, 39
  Allied breakthrough 88
  Allied bridgehead 90, 117, 119, 120, 122, 123, 125
  German forces engaged 113, 115
  German withdrawal 130
  Winston Churchill Bridge 78
Orne valley 126
Ornitz, Arthur J. (US Signal Corps) 82
Ornitz, Pfc Donald R. (US Signal Corps) 299, 306
Orny 245
Orscholz 328, 363, 364
Orscholz-Riegel 215
Orsoy 385, 387, 408, 409
Ortho 319
Oschersleben 448
Oslo fjord 475
Osnabrück
  September, Allied bombing 189
  November, Allied bombing 234
  December, Allied bombing 269, 270, 275, 277
  January, Allied bombing 310, 321, 328, 329, 332, 334, 337
  February, Allied bombing 359, 362
  March, Allied bombing 391, 398, 403, 411, 417
  April
    Allied bombing 427, 430, 434
    Allied capture 436, 437
    Allies reach outskirts 431, 432
    sector of 439, 448, 451

Oss 189, 191, 197
Ossenberg 387, 390
Ost Onnen 440
Ostend
  Allies clear of enemy 168
  German E-Boat operations 37
Ostenwalde, 21st Army Gp Tac HQ 453
Osterfeld 275, 306, 365
Osterhagen 448
Osterode 439, 452
Ostheim 270
Osweiler 292
Otava, River 504
Othfresen 446
Otterberg 319
Otterlo 458
Ottersum 354
Ottweiler 351, 407
Oud-Gastel 228
Oudenaarde 161
Oudenbosch 232, 235, 236
Ouistreham 16, 51
Our, River
  September 170
  December 290, 297
  January 330, 336, 337, 338
  February 342, 343, 345, 349, 351, 352, 356, 361
Ourthe 332
Ourthe, River 168, 309, 314, 315, 316, 320, 321, 332
Overasselt 178
Overbroek 218
Overbruch 414
Overflakkee island 302, 391
Overloon 198, 199, 200, 201, 208, 209, 210, 212, 217
'Overlord', Operation
  airfield requirements 32
  Allied bombing campaign 172, 321, 356
  casualties 518
  commanders meet at Norfolk House 10
  Eisenhower appointed to command 8
  Eisenhower's Directive 9
  meeting with 'Dragoon' 169
  planning for 12–13, 13, 62, 67, 113, 193, 375
  and the press/media 511–512, 513
  The True Glory (film) 419
  see also Assault Beaches
Oxenius, Maj. Wilhelm 504

Pachtener Buchwald 271
Pacy 123
Pacy-sur-Armançon 133
Paderborn 201, 313, 325, 365, 393, 405, 409, 419, 421, 430, 431, 433
  Allies enter 422, 426, 428
Paimpol 133
Palzem 363
Panama Canal Zone 8
Panningen 249
Panzweiler 401
Papen, Franz von 443
Papenburg 467, 469, 470, 471
Parchim 486
Parennes, air attacks 61, 62
Parham, Capt. F. R., RN 33
Paris
  German occupation 30
  June 32, 41, 43, 49, 51, 55
    airfields bombed 45, 48
    Allied planning 62
    area & vicinity bombed 30, 37, 39, 45, 52, 55, 56, 57, 62, 65
    German reinforcements from 55, 57, 70
  July
    air attacks in vicinity 71, 73, 74, 75, 76, 77, 78, 80, 83, 86, 87, 89, 90, 95, 102, 103
    air reconnaissance 105
    attempt on Hitler's life 93, 137
  August 121, 123, 150, 151, 152
    Allied advance near 141, 146, 148
    Allied bombing in area 112, 113, 117, 122, 125, 127, 132, 133, 140
    Allied staff personnel in 153
    Allied strategy 113
    liberation 142–145, 419, 515
  September 182
    Allied advance from 156
  March (1945)
    Allied airfields 411
  Hotel Scribe (SHAEF Public Relations) 513, 514, 515, 516
  see also Saint-Germain-en-Laye
Parroy 209

Pas de Calais
  Allied advance in 453
  Allied bombing 37, 51, 52, 100, 114, 160
  enemy shipping attacked 150
  flying bomb sites attacked 53, 54, 56, 59
Pasing 468, 475
Passau 465, 488, 491, 493, 494, 500
Patch, Lt Gen. Alexander M. 169, 243, 256, 258, 274, 460, 461, 462
Paterson, Rear-Adm. W. R., commands Force 'D' 17
Pattern 255
Patton, Helen Ayer 110
Patton, Lt Gen. George S.
  and Allied strategy 241
  appointed to command US Third Army 128
  at Moselle 164
  in Bastogne 346
  Battle of the Bulge 299, 301, 302, 329
  as Bavaria Military Governor 481
  break-out in Normandy 110, 112, 131
  with Gen. Patch 169
  Hammelburg raid 429
  impatient for offensive 374
  Mauthausen concentration camp 473
  Ohrdruf concentration camp 435, 448
  ordered to slow advance 434
  and the press/media 515
  and R. Rhine 258, 394, 395, 399
  Rhine crossing 408, 410, 415, 416
  shortages in Third Army 268
  Sicily campaign 11
  visit of King George 211
  and the wet weather 273
Pauillac 114, 115
Paustenbach 331
Peckelsheim 430
Peffingen 353, 369
'Pegasus Bridge' see Caen Canal Bridge
Pegau 452
Peij 328
Peiper, SS-Obersturmbannf. Joachim 295
Pellingen 364, 375
Pelm 387
Pemsel, Genlt Max 480
Pendleton, Sgt Jack J., Medal of Honor 217
Penton, Derek (historian) 473
Percy 100, 102, 105, 106, 110, 111, 112, 115
Périers 74, 75, 78, 79, 80, 82, 86, 87, 88, 89, 93, 98, 99, 100, 101, 102
  Operation 'Cobra' 94–95
Perkam 480
Perleberg 478
Pernass, U/off. Manfred 281
Péronne 122, 125
Perseigne 116
Pétain, Marshal Philippe 474
Petershagen 436
Petit-Couronne 141
Petit-Spai 287
Petrony, Sgt Peter J. (US Signal Corps) 37
Pettoncourt 192
Pfaffenhofen 356, 480
Pfalzel 296, 384
Pforzheim 283, 339, 367, 369, 371, 415, 438, 447, 448, 465
  Allied capture 443, 471
Pfungstadt 416
Philbin, Lt Col Tobias R. 269
Philippine Islands 8
Philippsburg 309, 310
Phillips, Col Joseph B. 511
Piburn, Brig. Gen. Edwin W. 380
Pickliessem 385
Pier 261, 264, 274, 277
Pierlot, Hubert (Belgian Prime Minister) 160
Pierrefitte 133, 136
Pilgramsreuth 468
Pillingsdorf 457
Pilsen 455, 462, 465–466, 469, 470, 479, 482, 487, 489, 493, 502, 504
Pindorp 222, 223
Pingsdorf 386
Pingsheim 376
Pintsch 334
Pirmasens
  November 250
  December 266, 273
  January 306, 308, 311, 316, 337
  February 363
  March 384, 399, 401, 402, 403, 407, 409

Pirna 468
Pissot 85
Pithiviers, Allies liberate 140
Placy-Montaigu 104
Plaine river valley 247
Planet News 201
Plansee 489
Plattling 473, 481, 486
Plaue 447
Plauen 403, 407, 418, 438, 443, 450, 459
  Allied capture 461
Pleisse, River 454
Plön 488
  Dönitz HQ: Stadtheide barracks 486, 490
Plütscheid 377
Po, River 480
Pogue, Forrest C. 518
Pointblank directive 6
Pointe de Barfleur 33
Pointe de Grave 459, 462, 468
Pointe de la Coubre 459, 462
Pointe du Hoc 28
Poissy 148
Poitiers, Allied bombing 40, 78, 85
Poland
  German invasion of 339
  post-war boundaries 193, 338
  and Soviet offensive 338
Poldertje 223
Poleck, Oberst Fritz 497, 504
Pölitz 203, 319, 351
Pomerania 193
Pomigliano, Naples 245
Pommerieux 244
Pommern 394
Pompey 167
Poncet, Oberst von 464
Pont de la Roque 104
Pont-à-Mousson 164, 177, 181, 192, 240, 241, 244
  Saint-Martin's church 165
Pont-Arcy 151
Pont-Audemer 146, 148
Pont-de-l'Arche 146, 150
Pont-de-Roide 177, 179
Pont-Hébert 79, 80, 87
Pont-l'Abbé 39, 46, 47, 48
Pont-l'Évêque 140, 141, 142
Pont-sur-Seille 192
Pontaubault
  Allies bomb railway centre 32
  bridge 107
Pontivy 115
Pontoise 127, 151
Pontorson 83, 111, 112, 115, 153
Poppel 200, 201, 202
Pörndorf 488
Port-Boulet 42
Port-en-Bessin 16
  Allied commanders confer 35
  as Allied objective 24, 25
Portershaven 345
Portsmouth 65
  Eisenhower's Advanced CP 'Sharpener' (Sawyer's Wood) 67, 128, 512
  SHAEF Forward HQ 'Shipmate' (Millard's Wood) 35, 67, 152
  Southwick House (Admiralty HQ) 67
Postdorf 255
Poston, John 453
Poteau 286, 294, 327, 328
Potigny 85, 120
Potsdam 455
Potsdam Conference (1945) 338
Pötschke, SS-Sturmbannf. Werner 294
Pournoy 185
Poussy-la-Campagne 120
Pracht 398, 415
Prague 455, 462, 465, 468, 470, 473, 475, 477, 479, 487, 488
Preischeid 366
Presidential Citation, US 117th Infantry, 1st Bn 361
Pressath 470
Prether, River 371
Prezelle 470
Price, Charles (US Ambassador) 7
Priess, SS-Unterscharf. Josef 286
Pronsfeld 183, 375
Proussy 126
Provins 148
Prüm
  September 193
  October 196, 212
  December 283, 294
  January 307, 308, 312, 317, 319, 320, 330, 332, 334, 337
  February 343, 349, 351–362, 364, 366, 368, 371
  March 375, 376, 377, 383, 384, 385, 386, 387, 388, 390

Prüm, River 354, 355, 357, 358, 359, 360, 361, 362, 365, 369, 376
Prummern 250
Puffendorf 249
Pulheim 383
Pulversheim 345
Putanges 134
Putscheid 332, 333, 337
Putte 200, 201
Puttkamer, Konteradm. Karl-Jesko von 92
Püttlingen 268, 462
Pützlohn 254, 256

Quai d'Elbeuf, Rouen 140
Quakenbrück 442
Quaraille 246
Quebec Conference (1943) 12
Quedlinburg 467, 469
Quer-Dam 352
Quesada, Maj. Gen. Elwood R. 211
Quesnay 122
Quettehou, Allied bombing 49
Quévy-le-Grand 159
Quiberon 121
Quickborn 496
Quignon, Dragon Jean 169
Quilleboeuf 45, 78
Quincey, railways bombed 57
Quinéville 45
Quint 387

Raamsdonk 232
Raff, Col Edson D. 458
Raguhn 471
Rahm 443
Rahms 410, 414
Rainwater, Pte L. C. 296
Raids 93
Ralshoven 369
Ramage, Fred (Keystone) 314, 331
Rambervillers 193, 196, 225, 227, 228, 232, 233
Rambouillet 81
Ramcke, GenLt Hermann 181
Ramonchamp 204
Ramrath 384
Ramsay, Adm. Sir Bertram H.
  at Norfolk House 10
  C-in-C AEF naval forces 13
  career 11
  first D-Day landings 20
  Flag Offr. Commanding, Dover 11
  lands in Normandy 35
  death 308
Ramscheid 344
Rance estuary 112
Rânes 126, 128, 131, 132
Raon-l'Étape 243, 244, 247, 249
Rapilly 132
Rascheid 402
Rastatt
  November 258, 261
  December 265, 266, 299, 303
  January 313, 315, 316, 324
  February 348, 351, 352
  March 399
  April
    Allied capture 450, 452
    Siegfried Line at 441
Rastenburg FuHQ 92
Rath 369
Raudnitz 462
Rauray, Germans driven out 63
Rauville-la-Bigot
  Allied advance to 52
  Allies liberate 53
Rauxel 386, 399
Raymond, Col J. E. 380
Rayner, Lt-Cdr H. S., RCN 33
Réchicourt 250
Recht 326, 327
Recklinghausen 322, 384, 386, 398, 405, 411, 418, 426
Recogne 316
Recouvrance, Brest 181
Red Ball/White Ball Express 260
Red Cross 466
Redon 115, 116
Reed, Carol (film director) 419
Rees 359, 375, 408, 409, 411, 414, 416, 418, 419, 420
Regen, River 473
Regen 473, 474, 478, 480, 494, 502, 504
Regensburg 469, 473, 474, 477, 478, 480, 481
Regenstauf 474
Regne 314
Reherrey 235
Rehlingen 266
Reich 401
Reichelt, GenLt Paul 503
Reichenau 500

Reichshoffen 268
Reichswald Forest 186, 215, 240, 242, 350, 351–359, 353, 355, 362, 363, 368, 382
Reifert 401
Reifferscheid 390
Reil 395, 396
Reims 148, 156, 158, 292, 497
  Allies reach 152
  railway targets bombed 56
  SHAEF Forward HQ ('École Professionelle') 360, 388, 504, 508, 509, 516
Reinange 248
Reinhausen 444
Reiningen 255
Reinsfeld 400
Reipertswiller 308, 312, 324, 325, 326, 327, 328, 429
Reisdorf 306
Reisholz 213
Remagen 395
  and Allied bombing 336, 383, 398
  Allied bridgehead 392, 394, 396, 398, 399, 400, 402, 403, 404, 407, 409, 410, 414–419, 415
  and Allied strategy 7
  and Ludendorff railway bridge 387–389, 390, 399, 402, 408
  US Army POW holding camp (A4) 466
Remagne 302, 303, 307
Remels 490
Remich
  September 192, 193
  November 256
  January 320, 322, 325, 326, 327, 328, 329, 330, 331, 334, 335, 336
  February 348, 349, 354, 357, 358, 359, 362, 363
Remicourt 168
Rémilly 243
Remilly-sur-Lozon 87, 88, 90, 93
Remiremont 184, 239
Remoifosse 303
Remscheid 448
Rendel 421
Rendsburg 476
Rengsdorf 414
Rennes
  June
    Allied front 67
    Allies bomb airfield 34, 41, 51
    Allies bomb railway yards 32, 39, 41, 50
    Allies bomb road/rail links 62, 65
  July, air attacks 77, 87
  August
    Allied capture 112, 113, 114, 116
    Germans bomb 115
Renuamont 292
Rescheid 375
Resistance, French 142, 172, 513
Rethel 158
Rethem 450, 451, 454, 456
Rethorn 476
Retranchement 228
Rettigny 326, 327
Reusel 199
Reuth 384
Reutlingen 322, 376, 459
Revigny 89
Reyersweiler 315
Reynaud, Paul 503
Reynolds, Observer J. W. 245
Rhaunen 402
Rhea, Capt. P. M., USN 47
Rhede 368
Rheiderland peninsula 478
Rheinbach 224, 337, 348, 383, 387
Rheinberg 352, 368, 375, 375, 385, 386, 387, 408, 409
  US Army POW holding camp (A2) 466
Rheinböllen 400, 401
Rheinbreitbach 394
Rheindahlen 213, 242, 368, 371, 384
Rheine
  October, Allied bombing 201
  December
    Allied bombing 269, 300
    fighting joined 283
  January
    Allied air operations 306, 321
    Allied bombing 328, 336, 337
  February, Allied bombing 353, 359, 362
  March, Allied bombing 391, 392, 396, 407, 411
  April
    Allied bombing 427
    Allies reach 430
    sector 432, 436, 439, 440

Rheingönheim 410
Rheinzabern 216
Rhens 402, 408, 409, 416
Rheurdt 384
Rheydt 256, 257, 280, 300, 334, 352, 376, 384
Rhine Palatinate 193
Rhine, River
  September, Operation 'Market-Garden' 184, 186, 187
  October, Allied bombing in sector 206, 212, 219, 220, 224, 226
  November
    Allied bombing in sector 243, 259
    Allied plans to cross 258
    and Allied strategy 7, 241, 242
    Allies reach 244, 249, 250, 251, 256, 257, 258, 259
  December
    Allied fighting west of 277, 298
    Allied planning 270
    Colmar Pocket 279
    German destruction of bridges 266
    Germans cross 287, 297
  January
    Allied bombing of bridges 316, 321, 328, 336, 339
    fighting in sector 308, 310, 311, 312, 313, 325, 327, 328, 329, 333
  February
    Allied bombing of targets 343, 352, 357, 366, 368, 371
    Allied planning for 375
    Allied plans to clear west bank 342
    Allies reach 348
    fighting in sector 343, 344, 347, 349, 350, 354, 355, 356, 357, 358, 361, 369, 370
    German destruction of dykes 351
  March 381, 384, 385, 386, 390, 409
    Allied advance to 379, 394, 395, 401, 403, 404, 407
    Allied bombing of river traffic 375, 377, 391, 396
    Allies cross 383, 410–417, 429
    bridges over 382, 383, 387–389, 390, 392, 393, 399, 400, 401, 402
  April
    Allied crossings 427, 429, 473
    Rhine POW camps 466, 518
  see also Hollandsche Diep; Marne-Rhine canal; Neder-Rijn; Remagen; Rhône-Rhine canal
Rhine-Herne canal 443
Rhine valley 235, 282, 292, 302, 315, 316, 317, 332, 357, 359, 404
Rhineland
  September, Allied air attacks 193
  October, Allied air attacks 199, 208, 212, 213, 216, 218, 224, 226
  November, Allied air attacks 233, 250
  December, Allied air attacks 266, 269
  January, Allied bombing 324, 328
  February
    Allied bombing 367
    Operation 'Veritable' 350, 392
  March, 21st Army Gp operations 392
Rhöndorf 399, 400
Rhône valley
  and Allied strategy 6
Rhône-Rhine canal 259, 315, 339, 342, 348, 349
Ribbentrop, Joachim von 506
Ribécourt, Allied fighters strafe targets 55
Richards, Capt. F. G., USN 47
Richmond, 1st Lt Joe F. (USAAF 366th FG) 82
Ricklingen 444
Ridgway, Maj. Gen. Matthew B., commands 82nd Airborne 18, 298
Ried 500, 502
Riede 444
Riedseltz 279
Riedwihr 334
Riedwihr woods 333
Riegel 215, 316, 407
Rieneck 433
Riesa 459, 469
Rieth 445
Riggau 470
Rijssen 440, 446, 452
Rilland 223
Rimbeck 428
Rimlingen 274, 308, 314, 315, 360, 401
Ringel 299, 300, 302
Ringenberg 419
Ringhuscheid 368
Ringsheim 294

Rinnthal 315, 321, 337
Rinteln 437
Riol 395
Riorange 257
Risle, River 95, 131, 132, 142, 143, 146
Rittershoffen 317, 318, 319, 320, 326, 328, 402
Ritzing 249
Rivecourt 133
Rivenich 392
Riviera, southern France
  Allied advance from 166, 169
  Allied landings 126–127
  fighting around 184
Robert, Sgt Harold 385
Roberts, Cpl Bob 196
Roberts, Edward 'Ned' (United Press) 512
Roberts, Maj.-Gen. George 174
Robertson, 2nd Lt Bill 478
Robinson, Maj. (pilot) 153
Roblingen 401
Rochefort
  December 296, 297, 298, 300, 302, 303
  January 306, 309, 315
Rocherath 283, 338, 342, 343
  Military Government Detachment 333
Rochlitz, Elbe bridgehead 477
Rockenfeld 403
Rockenhausen 404
Roda 447
Roden 404
Rodenkirchen 388
Roder 337
Roding 473
Roer, River
  November 259
    dams 234
  December 265, 267, 268, 272, 273, 274, 277, 279, 280, 283, 287
  January 334, 335
  February 347, 353, 354, 364, 365, 368, 369, 370, 371
    Operation 'Grenade' 350, 366
  March 375, 376, 377, 381, 382
  see also Schwammenauel Dam
Roer valley 267, 271
Roerdorf 267
Roermond
  Allied advance towards 247, 248, 253, 377
  Allied bombing 210, 226, 227, 243, 279, 312, 332, 333
  Operation 'Blackcock' 325
  sector 307, 326, 331
Roetgen 175, 179, 181, 186, 189, 196, 215, 278, 282
  Pte Slovik's court-martial 333
  railway station 193
  see also Siegfried Line
Roetgenwald 176
Rogery 330
Roggendorf 385
Roggenhausen 351
Röhe 250
Röhl 375
Rohrbach 253, 360, 361
Rohrbach-lès-Bitche 271, 273, 520
Rohren 338
Röhrnbach 477
Rohrwiller 313, 345, 346
Roisdorf 388
Roitham 504
Rokycany 455
Rol, Col Henri 144
Rollesbroich 278, 282, 331
Rollingen 307
Romintener Heide 338
Rommel, Gen. Erwin, El Alamein to Tunisia defeat 11
Rommelfangen 363
Rommersheim 370
Romsée 166
Roncey 101
Ronchamp 198, 200
Ronchamps 317
Rondorf 387
Rongy 58
Ronneberg 459
Roosendaal 218, 221, 222, 224, 225, 227, 228
Roosevelt, President F. D. 13, 516
  and Allied strategy 270
  and Gén. de Gaulle 142
  and Gen. Eisenhower 8, 12, 259
  and 'Sextant' Conference 8
  and Stalin 324
  Teheran Conference 8, 193, 338
  Yalta Conference 342
  death 461
Root (US Signal Corps) 111

537

Rosbruck 521
Rosche 464
Rosenau *249*, 265
Rosenberg, Alfred *506*
Rosendorf 457
Rosenheim 465, 490, 493
Rosheim *328*
Rosiere 296, 298
Rositz 357, 377
Rosmalen *221, 222*
Rosport 301, 326
Rossbrücken 270
Rosser, Pte *450*
Rossfeld 317, 318
Rossschläg 482
Rostock *495*
Rotenburg 449, 469, 470, 471, 480, 481
Roth 346, 443
　Allied capture 364
Rothbach 346
Rothenbach 392
Rothenberg 459
Rothenberger, Warren J. (US Signal Corps) *240*
Rothenburg 439, 447, 450, 454, 457, 462, 468, 469, 470
Rots *42, 43*
Rott *175*, 176
　Allied HQ *241*
Rottbitze 399, *403*
Rottenburg 370
Rotterdam *238*, 489
　Allied bombing 166, 218, 302, 330, 354
Rottweil 346, 371, 399, 462, 469
Rouen *147*, 156
　Allied advance towards 151, 152
　Allied bombing *32*, 74, 89, 94, 95, 102, 105, 111, 113, 119, 136, 143, 148
　German withdrawal 140–141, *149*
　White Ball Express *260*
Rouffach 347
Rouges Eaux *244*
Roulers 164, 166
Roumont 319
Rouvre, River 132
Royan *182*, 455, 458, 459, 462
Rüdesheim 319
Rudolstadt 447, 452, 454
Rudolzhofen 448
Rügen island 386
Rugles 125
Ruhland 203, 324, 383, 401
Ruhlingen 269
Ruhr
　September
　　Allied bombing 188
　　and Allied strategy 7, *163*, *176*, *187*
　October
　　Allied bombing 196, 198, 205, *212*, 213, 217, 219
　　RAF Bomber Command's Second Battle of *202*
　November
　　Allied bombing 232, 233, 234, 235, 236, 239, 240, 241, 243, 250, 251, 252, 254, 261
　　Allied strategy *242, 270*
　December, Allied air attacks 268, 269, 277, 280, 297, 301, 302
　January, Allied bombing 309, 330, 331, 336
　February, Allied bombing 356, 362, 364, 365
　March *420*
　　Allied bombing 377, 383, 387, 389, 391, 393, 395, 396, 399, 401, 402, 403, 405, 407, 409, 418
　　and Bielefeld viaduct *398*
　April, reduction of pocket *428*, 430–433, *432*, 437, *439*, 440, 443, *444*, 445, 447, 448, 450, 454–455, *458*, 459, 462, 464
　post-war division of Germany *193*
Rührberg 346, 347
Rumbach 370, 409
Rumersheim 351
Rundstedt, FM Gerd von
　Allies capture 490
　Ardennes counter-attack *281*
　at Saint-Germain *280*
　and Westwall *277*
Rupertsbuch 475
Rurdorf 266
Rurich 260, 264, 366
Russelsheim 416
Rüthen 280, 431, 433, 445
Ruwer, River 386, 396
Ryan, Sgt James A. (US Signal Corps) *87, 88*

Saal 242
Saale, River 450, 452, 459
Saales Pass 255, 256, 257
Saalfeld 445, 450, 452, 454
Saalhausen 445
Saar
　and Franco-Prussian War *266*
　Allied strategy *163*
　　Allied air attacks 233, 248
　　and Allied strategy *241*
　and Allied strategy *374*
　as post-war Protectorate *266*
　see also Sarre
Saar, River
　October *215*
　November 257
　December 266, 267, 269, 277
　　Allied bridgeheads 255
　　Allied bridgeheads 272, 274, 279, 280, 282
　January 306, 309
　February 363, 364, 367–369, 371
　　Allied bridgeheads 365, 366
　March 375, 377, 383, 386, 387, 389, 396, 398, 399, 400, 401, 402, 404, *407*
　see also Sarre
Saar-Palatinate *215*, *394–408 passim*
Saar basin 258
Saar valley
　November 248, 257, 261
　December 264, 265, 267–273, *274*, 278, 280, 283, 285, 287, 289, 294, 302, 303
　January 308, 309, 310
　February 368
　March 403
Saarbrücken
　June, Allied bombing 63
　August, Allied bombing 123
　September, Allied bombing 171, 193
　October, Allied bombing 208, 212
　December, Allied bombing 265, 266, 269, 282, 301, 520, 521
　January
　　Allied bombing 319, 321, 324
　　fighting in sector 316, 317, 336, 339
　　German counter-attack repulsed 310
　February 365, 367, 368, 369
　　Allied bombing 357, 362, 363, 364
　March
　　Allied bombing 395, 399, 404
　　Allied capture 404, *407*
　　fighting in sector 375, 376, 384, 385, 390, 392, 394, 396, 398, 399, *400*, 401, 402, 403
Saarburg
　November 232, 252, 257, 259
　February 359, 362, 363, 364, 365, 366, 368, 369, 370, 371
　March 375, 376, 384, *395*, 396, 399, 401
Saareinsmingen 272, 274
Saargemünd *see* Sarreguemines
Saarhölzbach 400
Saarlautern *see* Saarlouis
Saarlouis (Saarlautern)
　November 260, 261
　December 264–274, *266, 268–269, 272*, 277, 279, 280, 282–285, 287, 294, 302
　January 306, 307, 308, 328, 329
　February 361, 363, 364
　March 375, *396*, 403, 404
Saarunion 261, 266, 267, 268, 269, 270
Saarwellingen 273
Sablé-sur-Sarthe 88, 91
Sachsenhagen 442
Sachsenhausen, Frankfurt 419
Sachsgrün 465
Sadler, Fred, RE *21*
Sadzot ('Sad Sack') *302*
Sainlez 301
Saint-Aignan 118
St Alban 404
Saint-Amarin 264, 328
Saint-Amé 200
Saint-André 127
Saint-André-de-Bohon 79, 83
Saint-André-de-l'Épine 80
Saint-André-de-l'Eure 140
Saint-André-sur-Orne 91, 93
St Arnaul forest 364
Saint-Avold *255*, 256, 257, 259, 260, 264
Saint-Barthélemy 117, 121, *361*
Saint-Benoît 232
Saint-Brieuc 117
Saint-Calais 132
Saint-Contest *75*, 76
Saint-Cyr 116
Saint-Denis-de-Méré 126

Saint-Denis-le-Gast *101*, 104, 105
Saint-Dié 240, 241, 242, 243, *244*, 247, 248, 249, 251, 256, 257, 258
　Allies enter 253
Saint-Dizier 157, 158
Saint-Étienne *172*
Saint-Florentin 84, 123
Saint-Georges-du-Vièvre 143
Saint-Germain 58
Saint-Germain-de-Tallevende 120
Saint-Germain-d'Ectot 90, 106
Saint-Germain-en-Laye, German HQ in West *93, 280*
Saint-Germain-sur-Ay 85
Saint-Gilles *94, 96*, 99
St Goar 401, 408, 409, *416*
Saint-Gorgon 193
Saint Helier, Jersey 120
Saint-Hilaire, viaduct bombed 65
Saint-Hilaire-du-Harcouët 87, 90
Saint-Hubert 167, 168, *297*, 300, 301, 302, 303, 307, 308, 309, 312, 314, 317
St Ingbert 395, 401, 407
Saint-Jean-de-Daye, Allied advance 66, 76, 77, 79
Saint-Jean-des-Essartiers 105
Saint-Jean-du-Marché 197
Saint-Jean-le-Thomas, Villa Montgomery 153
St Joost 329, 330, 331
Saint-Jores 72
St Jöris 250
Saint-Julien-le-Faucon 133
Saint-Lambert-sur-Dives *134, 135*
Saint-Lenaarts 198
Saint-Lô
　experience of heavy bombing *197*
　June *467*
　　advance to 50
　　Allied bombing 36, 45, 46, 59, *71*
　　and Allied strategy 6
　July 79, 80, 83, *84, 91*, 93, 98, *99*, 100, 102, 104, *206*
　　air attacks on 74, 78, 81, 85, 96, 98, 105, *203*
　　Allied capture *86–88*, 89
　　Operation 'Cobra' *94–95*
　August 152
　Place du Major Howie 87
Saint-Loup-sur-Semouse 177, 179
Saint-Lubin, railway track bombed 49
Saint-Lupien 148
Saint-Malo
　Allied bombing 77, 111, 115, 129
　Allied capture 132
　and Allied front 67
　battle for 115, 117, 118, 119
　Citadel 129
　German garrison holds out *112*, 121, 123, 125, 126, 128, 131
　German vessels attacked off 57, 72, 103
　Île de Cézembre 125, *129*, 150, 152, 157, 158
　Paramé suburb: US advance *129*
St Marie-aux-Mines *333*
Saint-Martin 42, 127
Saint-Martin-de-Fontenay 93
Saint-Martin-de-la-Lieue 137
Saint-Martin-de-Sallen 123
Saint-Martin-des-Besaces *84, 103*, 106, 110
Saint-Maurice 261
Saint-Maximin 123
St Michielsgestel *221, 223*
Saint-Mihiel 158, 160, 161
Saint-Nazaire
　Allied bombing 39, 62, 95, 96
　eventual surrender *197*
　Germans hold out *182*
Saint-Nicholas (Belgium) 171
Saint-Nicolas-de-Bliquetuit *140*
Saint-Nicolas-de-Pierrepont 73
St Odilienberg 335
Saint-Omer *162*, 163
Saint-Ouen 112, *152*
Saint-Pair 91
Saint-Patrice-de-Claids 85
Saint-Paul-de-Courtonne, Allied bombing 64
Saint-Philbert 132
St Philipsland 237
Saint-Pierre-d'Oléron 489
Saint-Pierre-des-Dives 132, 134
Saint-Pierre-du-Vauvray *147*
Saint-Pierre-Église, liberated 55
Saint-Pierre-la-Vieille 122, 123, 125
Saint-Pierre-Tarentaine *114*
Saint-Pois 111, 116
Saint-Pol 159
　railway centre bombed 40, 44
Saint-Quentin 91
　Allied bombing 56, 101, 158

Saint-Rémy 238
Saint-Rémy-des-Landes 72
Saint-Rémy-sur-Avre 116
Saint-Renan 157
Saint-Romain-de-Colbosc 156
Saint-Sauveur-le-Vicomte 49, 60, *61*
　Allies liberate 48
　see also Nehou (US Third Army command post)
Saint-Sever-Calvados 113
Saint-Sylvain 120, 122, 125
Saint-Symphorien 250
Saint-Trojan-les-Bains 487
Saint-Trond 129, 168
Saint-Vaast 56, 105
Saint-Valery-en-Caux 159
Saint-Vith
　September 174–176, 179
　October 225
　December, Battle of the Bulge *285*, 286, 287, 289, 292, 294, 298, 299
　January, turning of the tide 307–309, 311, 313, 314, 319, 320, 327–338, *330*
　February 342, 343, 344, 345, 346
Saint-Vivien l'Hôpital 459
Saint Wendel *172*, 300, 375, 399, 401, 402, 403
Sainte-Barbe 237
Sainte-Cécile 166
Sainte-Croix-Hague 55
Sainte-Honorine 79, 80
　Allies liberate 57
　German counter-attack near 60
Sainte-Honorine-du-Fay, railway bridge attacked 64
Sainte-Maxime *127*
Sainte-Menehould 157
Sainte-Mère-Église *29, 39*, *54*
　82nd Airborne capture *34*
Sainte-Opportune 85
Sainte-Pôle 246
Sainteny *75*, 77, 78, 80, 85, 86
　Allied capture *82–83*
Saintes, Allied bombing 57, 58, 76, 127
Saire, River 55
Salis, Pte John P. (US Signal Corps) *330*
Salle, River 450
Salm 388
Salm, River *288*, *309*, 314, *315*, 316, 319, 325, 390
Salmchateau 316
Salmrohr 392
Salvacourt 301
Salzbergen 359, 386
Salzburg 470, 475, 487, 493, 500, 502
Salzwedel 453, 457
Samoreau *148*
Samrée 316, 318
Sandhurst, Royal Military Academy 446
Sangatte 171
Sangerhausen 450, 452
Sanry-sur-Nied 243
Sapois 208, 250
Sarao, Pfc John T. *58*
Sardinia 12
Sarnoff, Col David 511
Sarre region (renamed Saar) *266*
　see also Saar
Sarre river/river valley 258, *268–269*
　see also Saar
Sarrebourg 201, *244*, 251, 258
Sarreguemines (Saargemünd)
　December 264, 266–274, *271*, *273*, 277–280, 282–285, 287, 292
　January 308, 309, 310, 314, 333
　February 349, 360, 361, 362
　March 395
Sarstedt 442
Sart 314
Sassnitz, Rügen 386
Satzvey 386
Sauckel, Fritz *506*
Sauer (Sûre), River
　December 300, 301, 302, 303
　January 306, *312*, 317, 327, 329, 330, 333
　February 349, 351, 353, 356, 359, 360, 361, 362
Saulgrub 482
Saumur
　June
　　Allied bombing 50, 56, 57, 58
　　railway tunnel bombed *31*
　July
　　bridge bombed 83
　　railways bombed 76, 81
Sausheim 348
Saverne 253, 337, 358, 365
Saverne Gap 252, 253, 254, 255, 264
Savojaards Plaat 212, 213

538

Saxony *193*
Saxony-Anhalt *193*
Schaefer, SS-Unterscharf. *286*
Schafberg *274*
Schaffhausen *398*
Schafstädt *443, 450*
Schaidt *285*
Schalbruch *327*
Schankweiler *360, 361, 362*
Schärding *493*
Scharnitz *489*
Schattawa *504*
Schatzhofen *481*
Schaufenberg *207, 209*
Scheck, Hans (PK photographer) *137*
Scheibenhard *282*
Scheid *172, 376*
Scheiden *399*
Scheldt, River *175, 181, 182, 192, 217, 225, 226, 227, 235*
  Allied defences *308*
  and port of Antwerp *219*
Scheldt estuary *175, 183, 192, 193, 199, 203–205, 207, 208, 209, 233*
  see also Walcheren Island
Scheldt pocket *216, 218, 220, 223, 228*
Scherpenseel *182*
Scheuern *369*
Scheuren *348*
Schifferstadt *390*
Schijndel *188, 192, 222, 223, 232*
Schilberg *327*
Schillersdorf *333, 334*
Schillingen *377, 399*
Schirnding *470*
Schirrheim *401*
Schirwindt *338*
Schlausenbach *348*
Schlegel *457*
Schleiden
  October *251*
  December *278, 285*
  January *320, 332*
  February *343, 347, 348, 349, 357, 371*
  March *375, 376, 384, 387*
Schleiz *443, 459*
Schleswig-Holstein *193, 321, 387, 488, 494, 496*
Schleswig-Holstein, Duke Albert of *430*
Schleswig-Holstein, Princess Valéria-Maria von *430*
Schleusingen *440*
Schlich *274*
Schlicherum *385*
Schlieben, Genlt Karl-Wilhelm von *61*
Schlierbach *342*
Schloss Nordkirchen *430*
Schlotheim *437*
Schmalkalden *437*
Schmallenberg *441, 445*
Schmarzmaar *385*
Schmerlecke *439*
Schmidt *234, 235–243, 236, 241, 348, 349, 351, 352, 358–359, 365*
Schmidt, Gefr. Wilhelm *281*
Schmidt, Paul (Hitler's interpreter) *92*
Schmidthachenbach *403*
Schmira *447*
Schnee Eifel *215*
Schnee Eifel forest *346, 347, 348*
Schneverdingen *461, 464*
Schoden *370*
Schoenberg *343*
Schöffelding *480*
Schöfweg *480*
Scholven *365*
Scholven-Buer oil plants bombed *202, 302*
Schönbach *367, 386, 387*
Schönecken *288, 383, 398*
Schöneseiffen *278*
Schönfeld *385*
Schongau *480*
Schönstein *426*
Schönthal *474*
Schoondijke *208, 209, 215, 217, 218, 220, 222, 223*
Schophoven *274, 278, 279, 280*
Schoppen *327, 328*
Schorbach *399*
Schorndorf *455*
Schotteheide *353*
Schouwen *302, 311, 321*
Schramberg *407*
Schrobenhausen *473, 479*
Schubert, Oberlt Walter *191*
Schulenberg *440*
Schuschnigg, Kurt *503*
Schwabach *455*
Schwäbisch Hall *430, 439, 459, 462*
Schwaigern *438*
Schwalb family *430*

Schwammenauel Dam, Roer river *234, 353, 354, 358, 383*
Schwand *465*
Schwandorf *473*
Schwanheim, Frankfurt *419*
Schwarzbach, River *407*
Schwarzburg *450*
Schwarzenbach *459, 465, 468*
Schwarzenborn *388*
Schwarzenfeld *472*
Schwarzwald *see* Black Forest
Schweigen *298*
Schweighausen *265*
Schweighofen *283*
Schweinfurt *395, 400, 432, 434, 445, 447*
  Allies enter *448, 450, 452*
Schweinheim *387, 429*
Schwelm *356, 383*
Schwenda *452*
Schwerdorff *249*
Schwerin *463, 481, 486, 488, 490*
Schwerin, Genlt Gerhard Graf von *219*
Schwerte *375, 393*
Schwirzheim *385*
Sechtem *384*
Secourt *242*
Sedan
  Allied advance *166, 168*
  Allied bombing *122*
Seddin *469*
Sée, River *107, 110*
Seehausen *457, 480*
Seelow Heights, battle for *459*
Seelze *398*
Sées *124*
Seffern *377*
Segendorf *410*
Seille, River *241, 250*
Seille valley *240*
Seine, River
  June *45*
  and Allied strategy *6, 62*
  Allies bomb bridges over *32, 38, 40, 59*
  Allies bomb river ferries *46*
  FFI destroy Vernon road bridge *49*
  July *95, 107*
  Allies bomb bridges *72, 89, 94, 95*
  E-Boats attacked *77, 85*
  August
    Allied bombing in area *122, 127, 131, 132, 133, 136, 149*
    Allied bridgeheads *146, 147, 148, 150, 151, 152*
    Allies advance to *111, 131, 134, 136, 142, 143, 145, 146*
    Allies bomb barges *112, 120, 134*
    Allies bomb bridges *110, 111, 114, 115, 125*
    German withdrawal to *137, 139, 140–141, 142, 147*
  September
    Allied crossings *156*
    Operation 'Astonia' *173*
Seiwerath *384*
Selb *469*
Sélestat *265, 266, 279, 280*
Selgersdorf *366*
Sellerich *349*
Selsingen *474*
Selsten *330*
Sélune, River *107*
Selz *277, 278*
Semussac *458*
Senheim *269*
Senlis *156*
Senonchamps *303, 308, 309*
Senonches, Allied bombing *49, 60, 99*
Sens *83, 112, 141*
  Allies liberate *140*
Sensfuss, Genlt Franz *419*
Sept-Vents *84*
Serqueux
  June, Allied bombing *24*
  August, Allies bomb railway targets *115, 129*
Serquigny *95*
Serrières *205*
Serrig *364, 365, 366, 368*
Sessenheim *325, 326, 327*
Setterich *250*
Setz *360*
Seulles, River *37, 104, 105*
Sevelen *379, 382*
Sevenig *355*
Sèves, River *85, 94, 95, 100*
Sèves (village) *94*
Sevez, Gén. François *505*
Sèvres bridge, R. Seine *143*
'Sextant' Conference, Cairo *8, 12*
Seyss-Inquart, Arthur *506*
'Shambles' area *135*

'Shellburst' SHAEF Advance Command Post (Tournières) *128, 142*
's-Hertogenbosch (Den Bosch)
  September *192, 193*
  October *204, 210, 219, 220, 221–222, 223, 224, 225*
  November *232*
  January *306*
Ships, British
  Argonaut 37
  Ashanti 33, 43
  Belfast 33, 45
  Broke (destroyer) *11*
  Diadem 51
  Emerald 25
  Erebus 136, 168, *233*
  Eskimo 33, 63
  Frobisher 33
  Glasgow 27
  Javelin 33
  Malaya 158
  Nelson 47
  Orion 37
  Ramillies 17, 47, 48, 51
  Roberts 233
  Rodney 17
  Scylla 20
  Tartar 33
  Wanderer 35
  Warspite 129, 168, *233*
Ships, Canadian
  Haida 33
  Huron 33, 63
Ships, French, *Le Normand* (coaster) *66*
Ships, German
  Tirpitz 227
  Z-24 (destroyer) *34*
  Z-32 (destroyer) *34*
  ZH-1 (destroyer) *34*
Ships, Polish
  Blyskawica 33
  Piorun 33, 43
Ships, United States
  Arkansas 47
  Augusta 20, 45
  Nevada 47
  Texas 27, 47
  US 513 (Landing Craft, Infantry) *127*
  US 1141 (Landing Craft, Tank) *127*
  US 1143 (Landing Craft, Tank) *127*
Sibret *301, 302*
Sicily
  and heavy bombing *197*
  Operation 'Torch' *8, 11, 12, 235*
Siedenburg *440*
Siedlinghausen *439*
Sieg, River *407, 418, 419, 422, 426, 431, 441*
Siegburg *386, 409, 437, 447, 448, 450*
Siegelbach *369*
Siegen
  December *282*
  January *337*
  February *343, 362*
  March *375, 385, 387, 389, 393, 395, 396, 402, 411, 418, 421, 422*
  April
    Allies enter *426*
    Allies mop up *429, 430, 431*
    fighting in sector *433, 437, 439, 441, 443, 445, 448, 450*
Siegfried Line ('Westwall')
  Aachen *175, 176, 203, 214–215, 234, 331*
  Allied advance to *283*
  Allied bombing *173, 279, 283, 311*
  and Allied strategy *6, 176*
  Allies breach *170, 174, 175, 203, 215, 344, 401, 403, 404, 409, 410*
  Brachelen *334*
  Churchill visits *377*
  defences of *255, 258, 325, 350, 351, 394, 402*
  Dillingen *272*
  Frezenberg *200*
  German resistance at *277, 280, 284, 445*
  Germans reinforce *162, 241*
  Goch *360*
  Grunewald *363*
  Lammersdorf *331*
  Oberwürzback *400*
  and Operation 'Market-Garden' *187*
  Palenberg-Übach sector: first set-piece attack *203*
  Rastatt *441*
  Roetgen *175, 215, 234*
  Saint-Vith *174*
  Scheid *172*
  Tettingen *329*
  Vaalserquartier *377*
  Zweibrücken *407*

Sienne, River *95, 103, 105*
Siersdorf *209*
Siershahn *395*
  US Army POW holding camp (A6) *466*
Sigmaringen *371, 471, 472, 474*
Sigolsheim *297, 302*
Silesia *193*
Sillegny *182*
Silverside, Sgt Johnny *355*
Simmer, River *317, 319*
Simmerath *278, 338*
Simmern *308, 311, 317, 319, 330, 377, 383, 401, 402*
  Allied entry *400*
Simpelveld *179*
Simpson, Lt Gen. William H. *167, 211, 242, 248, 270, 301, 367, 375, 377, 438*
  drive to Elbe *453*
  Rhine crossing *408, 411, 413*
Sinclair, Lt-Cdr E. N., RN *33*
Sindorf *371*
Singen *298*
Singling *271*
Sinnersdorf *377, 384*
Sinspelt *366*
Sinz *329, 336, 349, 352, 354, 357, 358, 359*
Sinzig *226, 243, 324, 330, 333, 336, 345, 352, 356, 358, 377*
  US Army POW holding camp (A5) *466*
Siptenfelde *457*
Sittard *181, 319, 324, 325, 326, 327, 328, 329, 330, 331*
Sivry *200, 201, 202, 205*
Skorzeny, SS-Obersturmbannf. Otto *281*
Sliedrecht *310*
Slovik, Pte Eddie *333*
Sluis *208, 209, 215, 228, 233*
Smith, Lt Col Thor (SHAEF public relations) *512*
Smith, Lt Gen. Walter Bedell
  and Allied strategy *342*
  at Norfolk House *10*
  career *11*
  Ch.-of-Staff SHAEF *11, 12, 153, 505*
  German surrender *506*
  and media relations *512, 513, 515*
  'Overlord' planning *13*
Smith, Lt 'Sandy' *19*
Smith, Trooper Fred *253*
Snagge, John *511*
Sneek *243*
Snyder, Pfc Tom *366*
Sobernheim *311, 356, 402, 403*
Soest *269, 375, 387, 393, 437, 439, 440, 445*
Sögel *446*
Soignolles *120, 122*
Soissons *151, 152, 159*
Solingen *236, 237, 359*
Soltau *449, 464, 486, 518*
Somain *123*
Sombernon *169*
Someren *183*
Somme, River *87, 88, 91, 150, 158, 159, 160, 161, 162*
  Allied bridgehead *156*
  and Allied strategy *6*
Somme canal *48*
Son, Wilhelmina Canal *178*
Sonderhausen *443*
Sonneberg *452*
Sonsbeck *354, 356, 364, 365, 371, 375, 376, 382, 386, 392*
Soonwald *400*
Sorpe dam *213*
Sorpetalsperre lake *450*
Sosterberg *129*
Sötenich *348, 387*
Soufflenheim *274*
Souleuvre, River *102, 110, 111*
Soumont-Saint-Quentin *85*
Sourdeval *117, 125*
Sours, T/5 Leon *380*
South Carolina, USA, National Guard *361*
South (Zuid) Beveland
  September *172, 173*
  October *199, 207, 210, 212, 216, 222, 223, 225–226, 227, 228*
  November *232, 233, 235*
Southampton *65*
Southwick House, Portsmouth (Admiralty HQ) *67*
Soviet Union
  advance to Elbe *453*
  and Baltic *488*
  battle for and capture of Berlin *457, 470*
  and Dresden bombing *356*

539

Soviet Union — continued
  Eastern Front battles *338–339*
  Nordhausen V-weapons *469*
  overruns concentration camps *449*
  and post-war division of Germany *193*, *338*, *426*, *444*, *447*, *464*, *488*
  Seelow Heights *459*
  Soviet link-up with Allies *7*, *477*, *478–479*, *486*, *487*, *488*, *490*, *516*
  and war strategy *324*
  see also Stalin, Marshal Josef
Sowa, SS-Oberscharf. Kurt *285*
Soy *294*
Spa *360*
Spaatz, Gen. Carl *212*, *505*, *508*
Spandau, Berlin *420*
Spang, Genlt Karl *119*
Spangle, Sgt William (US Signal Corps) *98*
Sparks, Brig. Gen. Felix L. *429*
Spatzenhausen *482*
Speer, Albert *502*
Speicher *289*
Speicherz *437*
Speldorf *416*
Spellen *414*
Sperrle, FM Hugo *92*, *490*
Spessart hills *437*
Speyer *270*, *283*, *408*, *409*, *410*, *417*, *427*, *438*
Spicheren *364*, *365*
Spier *450*
Spilker, Pte Jim *215*
Spirkelbach *410*
Sprang *232*
Sprendlingen *403*
Sprimont *319*
Stabroek *200*
Stade *469*, *488*
Stadl *480*
Stadlern *476*
Stadt Meckenheim *275*, *366*, *385*
Stadthagen *442*
Stadtkyll *332*, *333*, *344*
Stadtlohn *267*, *395*, *396*, *407*, *415*
  Allied capture *426*
Staffelfelden *346*
Stahle *440*
Stalin, Marshal Josef
  and Berlin *457*, *470*
  and Eisenhower's strategy *433*
  German surrender *508*
  Moscow conference *324*, *426*
  and Soviet war strategy *338*
  and Teheran Conference 8, 12, *193*, *338*
  Yalta Conference *342*
Stammeln *274*, *366*
Stars and Stripes 152, *169*, *302*, *517*
Stassfurt-Leopoldshall *447*
Stattmatten *325*
Staubing *469*
Staudinger, SS-Bdef. Walter *85*
Staudt *418*
Staufen *351*
Stauffenberg, Oberst Claus von *92*
Stavelot *286–287*, 289, 292, 296, 298, 299, 301, 311, 312, 319, 320, 322
Steckenborn *347*, 348
Steeg *218*
Steenbergen *228*, 236
Steenwijk *354*
Steffeshausen *338*, 342
Steig *346*
Stein *439*
Steinach *452*, 454
Steinbach *346*
Steinberg *401*
Steinbrück *319*
Steinfeld *283*, 410
Steinmehlen *354*
Steinstrass *369*
Steinwald forest *343*
Stembert, Hubert *315*
Stendal *431*, *433*, *443*, *444*, *452*, 454, 457, 494
Sterkrade *202*, *330*, 415
Sterpigny *326*
Stetternich *261*, *366*, 368
Stettin *319*
Stevensweert *328*, *329*, 331
Stewart, Maj. Hugh (photographer) *59*
Steyr *502*
Stieldorf *404*
Stiller, Maj. Alexander *410*
Stiring-Wendel *365*, *370*, 384, 385
Stocken *363*
Stockhausen *403*
Stockheim *264*, 274, 369, 459
Stöckigt *362*
Stod *489*, 493
Stolberg 181–185, 189, 191, 193, 209, 249, *250*, 252

Stolberg-Stolberg, Genmaj. Christoph von *161*
Stolzembourg *170*
Stolzenau *440*
Stommeln *382*, 384
Stotzheim *264*, 386
Stoumont *294*, *295*, 298
Straberg *385*
Straelen *267*, 377
Strasbourg
  August, Allied bombing 122, 123, 150
  September, Allied bombing 172
  November 250, 253, 254, 255, *258*, *259*, 261
    Allies occupy *249*, *256*, *257*, 258
  December 264, 265, 266, 267, 269, 272, 279, 297
  January, 311, 313–318, 321, 324, 327, 328, 329, 330, 331, *337*
  February 342, 343, 344, 347, 354, *357*, 358, 362
    Fort of Commerce 369
  March 376, 377, 384, 385, 390, 394, 396, 401, 408, 409
  April 439, 457, 459, 462, 465, 468, 470, *471*
Strass *274*
Strasswalchen *500*
Straubing *465*, *477*, 478, 481
Strauch *347*
Strehla: Allied-Soviet meeting *478*
Streicher, Julius *460*
Stribro *504*
Strobel, Lt Wallace C. (502nd Parachute Inf.) *18*
Strödt *401*
Ströhen *269*
Strong, Maj.-Gen. Kenneth *504*
Strotzbüsch *396*
Struth *440*, 442
Stuckange *247*
Stülpnagel, Gen. Carl-Heinrich von *92*, *93*
Stumpff, Genoberst Hans-Jürgen *508*
Sturmabteilung (SA), Hitler purges *391*
Sturzelbronn *402*
Stuttgart
  October, Allied bombing 218
  December, Allied bombing 268, 285, 300, 301
  January, Allied bombing 312, 328, 336, *337*, 339
  February, Allied bombing 355, 371
  March, Allied air operations 376, 395, 396, 409, 415, 418
  April
    Allied advance towards 454, 462, 468
    Allied bombing 427, 429, 430, 431, 434, 438, 439, 443, 445, 455, 458
    city captured *471*, 474
    city encircled 469, 470
    sector of 472, 473, 477, 479
Stützerbach *439*, 444
Stutzhaus *444*
Süchteln *264*
Suddinker *439*
Süggerath *249*
Suhl *432*, 437, 440, 442, 444
Sulingen *440*
Sülm *375*
Sulz *278*, 402
Sulzbach *500*
Sulzburg *474*
Sûre, River *see* Sauer
Surre *301*
Sürth *388*
Susloparoff, Maj. Gen. Ivan *505*, *508*
Susteren *325–326*
Swabian Pocket *475*
Sweeny, Maj. Charles *518*
Swinemünde *395*, 459
Swolgen *256*
Syke *442*
Sythen *395*, 405

Taben *298*, 363, 364, 365
Tachau *480*
Tadler *296*
'Tallboy' bombs *31*, *398*, *475*
Tambach *444*
Tandern *480*
Tangermünde *454*, *456*, *487*
Tarchamps *317*
Tassigny, Gén. Jean de Lattre de *256*, *258*, *274*, *279*, *337*, *471*, *474*, *508*
Tauber, River *433*, 450
Tauberbischofsheim *426*
Taus *491*
Taute, River *84*, 89
Tavigny *329*
Tawern *365*

Taylor, 1st Lt Bayard B. (USAAF 366th FG) *82*
Taylor, Maj. Gen. Maxwell D., commands 101st Airborne *18*, *176*, *299*, *346*
Tebbe, Maj. Gerhard *191*
Tedder, ACM Sir Arthur W. (Dep. C-in-C) *212*
  at Norfolk House *10*
  career *11*
  commanders meet *270*
  German unconditional surrender *507*, *508*
  Moscow conference *324*
  'Overlord' planning *13*
Tegel, Berlin *402*
Teheran Conference (1943) 8, 12, *193*, *338*
Temmels *364*
Tendon *189*
Tenenbaum, Lt Edward *447*
Tennessee, USA, National Guard unit *361*
Terborg *403*, *432*
Terheijden *219*, 228
Ternaard *456*
Terneuzen *183*
Tesser, Sgt Charles *314*
Tessy-sur-Vire *102*, 104, 105, 106, 110, 111
Téterchen *259*
Tetlow, Harold (*Daily Sketch*) *335*
Tettingen *256*, 320, 326, 327, *329*, 330, 335, 348
Teuge *451*
Teugn *480*
Teurthéville-Hague, Allies liberate *54*
Teutoburgerwald *432*, 437
Thailen *401*
Thale *469*
Thaleischweiler *308*
Thaler, SS-Oberscharf. Johann *118*
Thalmassing *480*
Thann *264*, 271, 272, 273, 274, 299
Thatcher, Rt. Hon. Margaret *7*
The Hague *489*
Thedingen *268*
Theobold, Kriegsberichter *118*
Theux *168*
Thiberville *142*
Thiel *166*
Thierfeld *465*
Thiersheim *469*
Thionville *171*, 237, *240*, 241, 242, 243, 244, 245, 246, 247, 248, 252, 253, 256
Thirimont *320*, 322, 325
Tholen *237*
Tholey *273*
Thomm *401*
Thompson, Cdr 'Tommy' *413*
Thompson, Sgt Max, Medal of Honor *217*
Thonbrunn *472*
Thorak, Josef (sculptor) *502*
Thorson, Brig. Gen. Truman C. *211*
Thouars, Panzer units based at *31*
Thumhausen *473*
Thür, River *266*, 346
Thür valley *267*, 272
Thuringia *193*
Thury-Harcourt *115*, 116, 123, 126
Tieffenbach *267*
Tierney, Pte *185*
Tietelsen *439*
Tilburg *200*, 201, *219*, *223–228*, *225*, 298, 299, 300, 303
Tillet *309*, 311, 312, 314, 315, 316, 317
Tilly, Seine crossing point *148*
Tilly-la-Campagne *96*, 98, 111
Tilly-sur-Seulles
  June, front at 36–40, *41*, 42–43, *44*, 45, 47–49, 51, *52–53*, 54–55, *56*, 58, 61–62, *63*, 64
  July
    fighting around 77, 78, 79, 80, 86, 87, 89
    German counter-attacks 71
Timeloberg ('Victory Hill') *see* Lüneburg Heath
Times, The *437*, *517*
Timmerman, Lt Karl *387*
Tinchebray *122*, 123, 125, 126, 128, 131
Tintange *299*
Tippelskirch, Gen. Kurt von *490*
Tirlemont *129*, 167
Tirschenreuth *472*
Titmaringhausen *421*
Tittling *477*
Todt, Dr Fritz *403*
Tondorf *281*, 285
Tongres *171*
Tonkogonov, General I. I. *493*
Tonneins *120*

Torcheville *252*
Torgau
  Allied bombing 468, 469
  Soviet-Allied link-up *478–479*, 516
Torigni-sur-Vire *93*, *104*, 106, 110, 111
Tosh, Pte (6th KOSB) *267*
Tôtes *156*
Touffreville *90*
Touques, River 127, *137*, 140, 141, *146*
Tournai *157*, *160*, 161
Tournedos-sur-Seine *141*
Tournières, Bayeux, Eisenhower's Advanced CP 'Shellburst' *128*, *142*, *189*
Tours
  June
    air reconnaissance 66
    bombing 38, 41, 45, 49, 56, 58
  July, Allied bombing 73, 77, 80, 81, 83, 84, 86, 96, 102, 106
  August, Allied bombing 110, 116, 120
Tours la Riche *76*, 90
Tourville *62*, 63, *89*
  German forces destroyed 64
Toury, railway yards bombed 62
Tragny *243*
'Transportation Plan' *32*
Trappes, Allied bombing 52
Trassem *363*
Traunstein *465*, 475
Travemünde *491*
Trendelburg *440*
Tréprel *128*
Treuchtlingen *449*
Treuen *465*
Treuenbrietzen *469*
Trévières, Allied capture *35*, *37*
Treysa *422*
Tribehou *84*
Trier
  September
    Allied advance towards 171
    Allied bombing 185
  October, Allied bombing 203
  November
    Allied bombing 234, 236, 243, 261
    V1 launch sites *260*
  December, Allied bombing 285, 289, 294, 296, 297, 300
  January, Allied bombing 307, 320, 324, 327, 328, 334, *337*
  February *369*, *371*, *374*
    Allied bombing 348, 352, 353, 356
  March
    Allied capture 377, *380*, 395, 396
    fighting in sector 375, 376, 383, 384, 386, 387, 389, 392, 394, *395*, 398, 399, 400, 401, 402
    Porta Negra Hotel *380*
Triptis *447*
Trittenheim *398*
Troarn *41*, 90, 91, 132
Troine *329*
Trois Frontières *see* Vaalserberg, The: 'Three-Country Point'
Trois Vierges *330*
Trois-Ponts *287*, 315
Troisdorf *302*
Tromso, *Tirpitz* at 227
Trou de Bra *309*
Trouville, Allies reach 140, 142
Troyes *143*, *146*, 148, 150, 157
Trun *131*, 132, 133
Tschernoschin *504*
Tübingen *430*, 463, 468
Tündern *439*
Tünsdorf *253*
Turckheim *315*, 346
Turnhout *191*, *193*, 196, 197, 198, 200
  see also Antwerp-Turnhout canal
Tüttlingen *393*, 399, 470
Twaddle, Maj. Gen. H. L. *268*
Twente canal *431*, 432, 439
Tyllburg *294*
Tyten *473*

Übach-Palenberg *199*, 200, 201, 202, *203*, 251
Ubagsberg *179*
Uckerath *416*
Udem
  February 356, 359, 364, 365, 366, 368, 369, 371
  March 375, 376
Uden *228*
Udenbreth *342*, 344, 345, 346, 361
Udenhausen *399*
Üdersdorf *387*
Uelzen *450*, 454, 456, 461, 464
  Allies clear *465*
Uerdingen *317*, 384
Uetterath *331*, 332
Uetze *407*

Uffenheim 448
Uffholtz 346
Ulm
  November 249
  December 283
  February 360, 369
  March 376, 384
  April 430, 438, 449, 450, 455, 458, 459, 466, 468, 469, 471, 472, 475, 477
  Allied capture 473, 474
Ulrichstein 421
Ultra decrypts, movements of 17. SS-Panzergrenadier-Div. 31
Underwood, Dick 153
United Nations, objectives 4
United States
  American Graves Registration Service 386
  Office of War Information 511
  and post-war division of Germany 193, 476
  US House of Representatives 189
  see also American Battle Monuments Commission
Units, Allied
  SHAEF (Supreme HQ Allied Expeditionary Force) 4, 10, 11
    communications 188
    and enemy POWs 466
    Forward HQs
      Granville 152–153, 163, 189
      Jullouville 152, 189
      Portsmouth ('Shipmate') 35, 67, 152
      Reims 360, 388, 504
      Versailles, Trianon Palace Hotel 189, 280, 360
    post-war Frankfurt HQ 419
    and the press/media 510–517
  1st Airborne Task Force 126
  First Allied Airborne Army 176, 518
  Allied Expeditionary Air Force (AEAF) 212
  Eastern Task Force 16–17, 20, 24
    Bombardment Force 'D' 17
    Force 'G' 16
    Force 'J' 16
    Force 'S' 16, 17
  Western Task Force 16, 20, 24
    Force 'O' 16
    Force 'U' 16
Units, British
  21st Army Group 11, 12, 13, 107, 131, 146, 169, 176, 206, 219, 350, 504
    advance into Germany 432, 433, 453
    Grave Registration Units 518
    No. 2 Operational Research Section 190
    reach Elbe 477
    Rhine crossing 408, 411, 422
    Rhineland operations 392
    Ruhr pocket 428
    Tac HQs 35, 40, 209, 375, 453, 486, 495–499
  Armies
    Second 13, 35, 41, 67, 89, 91, 102, 111, 114, 146, 156, 219, 248, 253, 375
      advance into Germany 432, 433, 453
      advance to Elbe 446, 477
      casualties 518
      inside Reich 277
      Operation 'Garden' 176
      Rhine crossing 408, 422
    Eighth 11, 41, 480
  Corps
    I Corps 12, 74, 146, 172
    I Airborne Corps 178
    II Corps 11
    V Corps 11
    VIII Corps 90, 91, 102, 111, 114, 125, 183, 446
    XII Corps 11, 89, 147, 161, 446
    XXX Corps 41, 102, 114, 146, 147, 150, 174, 199
      advance to Rhine 350
      at Bremen 470
      Battle of the Bulge 315
      break-out and advance 156
      Club Route 446
      Geilenkirchen battle 248, 253
      Operation 'Garden' 177, 184
      Rhine crossing 416
  Divisions
    1st Airborne 176, 184, 185, 186
    1st Armoured 12
    3rd Infantry 11, 20, 52, 75, 77, 198, 440, 446, 476
    6th Airborne 18, 31, 39, 41, 411, 488

Units, British, Divisions — continued
  7th Armoured 114, 161, 325, 491
  11th Armoured 59, 102, 111, 115, 125, 161, 174, 208, 219
  15th (Scottish) 89, 114, 147, 208, 219, 225, 408, 411, 422, 465, 477
  43rd (Wessex) 116, 146, 147, 248, 253, 446, 452, 476
  49th (West Riding) 43, 146, 173, 236, 240, 451
  50th 89
  51st (Highland) 41, 219, 222, 309, 316, 355, 408, 411, 446, 476
  52nd (Lowland) 335, 446, 470, 476
  53rd (Welsh) 219, 362
  79th Armoured 173, 226, 249, 251, 335
  Guards Armoured 103, 150, 156, 160, 174, 446
Brigades
  6th Guards Tank 225, 433
  8th 21
  8th Armoured 156, 335
  9th 77
  29th Armoured 59, 115
  33rd Armoured 75, 117
  34th Tank 173
  56th 77
  129th 116
  131st Infantry 325
  153rd 355
  155th Infantry 233
  158th 77
  Grenadier Guards 6th Guards Tank Bde, 4th Tank Bn 114
Regiments
  52nd Foot (Oxfordshire & Buckinghamshire Light Inf.) 19
  Black Watch 223, 355
    1st Bn 316
    5th Bn 222
  Cheshire Regt 414
  County of London Yeomanry, 3rd (Sharpshooters) 41
  Devonshire Regt
    2nd Bn 325
    12th Bn 39
  Dragoons
    4/7 53
    22nd 50
  Durham Light Infantry, 6th Bn 63
  East Lancashire Regt, 1st Bn 221–222
  East Riding Yeomanry 224
  East Yorkshire Regt
    2nd Bn 21
    5th Bn 24
  Fife and Forfar Yeomanry, 2nd Bn 59, 183, 437
  Glasgow Highlanders, 1st Bn 470
  Gloucestershire Regt, 2nd Bn 173
  Gordon Highlanders
    1st Bn 222
    5th/7th Bn 353
  Grenadier Guards 114, 160, 178, 183
    4th Bn 437
  Hampshire Regt 43, 452
  Hertfordshire Yeomanry 53
  Highland Light Infantry 354
  Household Cavalry 178
  Hussars, 11th 161, 496
  Hussars, 13th/18th 116
  Hussars, 23rd 115
  Irish Guards 177
  King's Own Scottish Borderers 225
    1st Bn 77
    4th Bn 233
    6th Bn 267
  King's Shropshire Light Infantry
    2nd Bn 77
    4th Bn 125, 183
  Lincolnshire Regt, 4th Bn 240
  Lothians and Border Yeomanry 249
  Middlesex Regt, 2nd Bn 21
  Monmouthshire Regt, 3rd Bn 264
  Northamptonshire Yeomanry
    1st Bn 117
    2nd Bn 125
  Parachute Regt
    1st Bn 184
    2nd Bn 184
    3rd Bn 184
    12th Bn 39, 437
  Royal Armoured Corps, 141st 179
  Royal Inniskilling Dragoon Guards, 5th Bn 161
  Royal Scots 267
  Royal Scots Fusiliers 114
  Royal Tank Regt, 7th 173
  Royal Ulster Rifles 198

British, Regiments — continued
  Royal Welch Fusiliers 221
  Royal Welsh Regt, 4th Bn 370
  Somerset Light Infantry, 4th Bn 147
  South Lancashire Regt, 1st Bn 21
  South Wales Borderers, 2nd Bn 173
  Welch Regt, 4th Bn 219
  Welsh Guards 160, 163
    1st Bn 156
  Wiltshire Regt, 5th Bn 147
Commandos
  1st Commando Bde 408, 411, 414
  No. 3 Commando 437
  No. 4 Army Commando 233
  No. 41 (RM) Commando 21, 50
  No. 45 (RM) Commando 437
  No. 47 (RM) Commando 24
  Special Air Service (SAS) 79
Royal Engineers (RE)
  26th Assault Sqn 50
  AVREs (Armoured Vehicles Royal Engineers) 251
  No. 3 Railway Construction and Maintenance Gp 238
  No. 84 Field Coy 21
  No. 607 Railway Construction Coy 239
  XXX Corps HQ RE 63
Medical, 8th Field Ambulance, RAMC 21
Misc. units, Army Film and Photographic Unit (AFPU) 21
Second Tactical Air Force 190, 197, 206, 245
RAF Commands
  Bomber Command 13, 202, 212, 232, 356, 420, 422, 444
  Fighter Command 11
RAF Groups
  No. 1 Group 475
  No. 5 Group 475
  No. 8 Group 475
  No. 12 Group 11
RAF Squadrons
  No. 83 Sqn 31
  No. 144 Sqn 34
  No. 404 Sqn 34
  No. 617 Sqn 31, 398, 475, 500
RAF Bombing Analysis Unit 135–136
Royal Observer Corps 245
Units, Canadian
  Armies, First Army 111, 117, 146, 156, 192, 199, 219, 350, 432, 453, 518
Corps
  I Corps 503
  II Corps 90, 91
Divisions
  2nd Infantry 192, 200, 225
  3rd Infantry 22, 41, 52, 192, 351, 422
  4th Armoured 117, 134, 192, 225, 440, 453
Brigades
  2nd Infantry 200
  9th Infantry 23
Regiments
  3rd Anti-Tank Regt 43
  6th Armoured Regt 44
  10th Armoured Regt (Fort Garry Horse) 42, 452
  Cameron Highlanders of Ottawa 43
  Essex Scottish Regt 200
  Fusiliers Mont Royal 488
  Lincoln and Welland Regt 453
  North Nova Scotia Highlanders 42
  North Shore Regt 22, 351
  Régiment de Maisonneuve 432
  Royal Hamilton Light Infantry 465
  Royal Regt of Canada 192
  Royal Winnipeg Rifles 42, 43
  South Saskatchewan Regt 91, 192
  Stormont, Dundas and Glengarry Highlanders 23
Companies, 6th Field Coy 43
Units, Dutch, Royal Netherlands Bde 'Princess Irene' 228
Units, French
  Armies, 1ère Armée 169, 243, 244, 249, 256, 258, 274, 279, 337, 408, 471, 474, 508, 518
Corps
  Ier Corps d'Armée 246, 258, 279, 328, 347
  IIème Corps d'Armée 279, 332
Divisions
  1ère Div. Blindée 249, 256, 279, 347

Units, French, Divisions — continued
  1ère Div. d'Inf. Marocaine 480
  2ème Div. Blindée 100, 131, 142–143, 169, 174, 257, 259, 500
  2ème Div. d'Inf. Marocaine 246
  5ème Div. Blindée 246, 336
  9ème Div. d'Inf. Coloniale 408
  11ème Div. Blindée 115
  French Forces of the Interior (FFI) 49, 142, 144, 182, 480
  Groupement Demetz 168
Regiments
  1er Régt de Fusiliers Marins 480
  2ème Régt de Cuirassiers 279
  2ème Régt de Dragons 168, 169
  3ème Régt de Tirailleurs Algériens 408
  4ème Régt de Tirailleurs Marocains 24
  5ème Régt de Chasseurs d'Afrique 332
  23ème Régt d'Inf. 408
  151ème Régt d'Inf. 408
Task Force Rouvillois 257
Escadrille Américaine (Sqn No. 124: later Lafayette Escadrille) 243
Units, German
  OKW 70, 92, 497, 504
  Armeegruppe H 428
  Armeegruppe (Heeresgruppe) G 182, 502, 503
  Heeresgruppe B 281, 428
  Panzergruppe West 85, 93
Armies
  1. Armee 258
  3. Panzerarmee 457, 495
  4. Panzerarmee 457
  5. Panzerarmee 150, 191, 281, 290
  6. Panzerarmee 281–282, 290, 294, 296
  7. Armee 79, 130, 137, 150, 156, 281, 290, 417
  9. Armee 457, 459, 494
  11. Armee 468
  12. Armee 494, 495
  15. Armee 281
  19. Armee 151, 503
  21. Armee 490, 495
  Armee Ligurien 480
Korps
  I. SS-Panzerkorps 70, 282
  II. SS-Panzerkorps 302
  LVI. Panzerkorps 459
  LXIV. Corps 471
  LXXXIV. Armeekorps 79
Divisions
  1. SS-Panzer 70, 118, 281, 286
  2. Panzer 290, 291, 297, 300
  2. SS-Panzer 83, 98, 101, 106, 118, 119, 296
  9. Panzer 300
  9. SS-Panzer 137
  9. Volksgrenadier 323
  11. Panzer 151, 329
  12. SS-Panzer 41, 42, 52, 70, 75, 85, 283
  12. Volksgrenadier 343
  17. SS-Panzergrenadier 31, 324
  21. Panzer 41, 52, 90
  25. Panzergrenadier 240
  47. Infanterie 159
  84. Infanterie 118
  116. Panzer 118, 219, 314
  246. Infanterie 205
  266. Infanterie 119
  275. Infanterie 98
  277. Volksgrenadier 343
  352. Infanterie 26, 84
  353. Infanterie 215
  712. Infanterie 222
  719. Infanterie 422–423
  Panzer-Lehr 41, 59, 96, 271, 290, 297, 300, 317, 459
Kampfgruppe(n)
  901 297
  Hansen 286
  Heintz 98
  Knittel 286
  Koblenz 404
  Müller 283
  Peiper 281, 282, 284, 287, 289, 294, 315
Brigades
  Führer-Grenadier-Bde 303
  Panzerbrigade 111 191
  Panzerbrigade 112 174
  Sturmgeschütz-Bde 280 186
Regiments
  Gebirgsjäger-Regt 136 336
  Grenadier-Regt 1215 247
  Panzer-Lehr-Regt 53, 56, 258
  Panzer-Regt 6 53

Units, German, Regiments — continued
   Panzergrenadier-Regt 10 *252*
   SS-Panzer-Regt 1 *70*
   SS-Panzer-Regt 2 *83, 118*
   SS-Panzer-Regt 10 *114*
   SS-Panzer-Regt 12 *36, 85*
   SS-Panzergrenadier-Regt 26 *42*
   SS-Panzergrenadier-Regt 38 *247*
  Battalions
   Panzer-Pionier-Bn 130 *290*
   Panzerjäger-Abt. 654 *139, 336*
   schwere Panzer-Abt. 503 *90, 116*
   SS-Panzer-Abt. 17 *31*
   SS-Panzer-Aufklärungs-Abt. 1 *286*
   SS-Panzer-Aufklärungs-Abt. 9 *184*
   SS-Panzer-Pionier-Bn 2 *98*
   SS-Sturmgeschütz-Abt. 2 *118*
  Companies, Propaganda-Komp. 698 *137*
  Hitlerjugend *59*
  Luftwaffe
   II. Fallschirm-Korps *84*
   3. Fallschirmjäger-Div. *84, 284*
   6. Fallschirmjäger-Div. *159*
   16. Feld-Div. (L) *76*
   91. Luftlande-Div. *48*
   Fallschirmjäger-Regt 20 *264*
  post-war Bundeswehr *435, 497*
Units, Polish
  Divisions, 1st Armoured *117, 236, 238*
  Brigades, 1st Parachute Bde *176*
Units, Soviet Union
  First Byelorussian Front *457, 508*
  First Ukrainian Front *339, 457, 478*
  Second Byelorussian Front *491*
  Third Byelorussian Front *338*
  Armies
   2nd Guards Tank *339*
   3rd Shock *457, 470*
   5th Shock *339, 470, 508*
   8th Guards *459*
Units, United States
  ETOUSA (US Army European Theater of Operations) *10*
  1st (later 12th) Army Group *11, 110, 169, 242, 258, 301, 410, 433, 438, 453*
  1st (notional) Army Gp *97*
  6th Army Group *169, 244, 256, 258–259, 328, 332, 337, 419, 471*
  Armies
   First
    June *11, 13, 40, 45, 514*
    July *80, 94, 103*
    August *111, 122, 128*
    September *156–157, 515*
    October *205, 206, 209, 210*
    November *241, 242, 248, 260*
    December
     Battle of the Bulge *298*
     inside Reich *277, 278*
    January
     link-up with Third Army *316, 320*
     turning of the tide *309, 313, 315, 319*
    February *358, 366, 371*
    March *408, 415, 417*
     advance on Cologne *381*
    April *428, 434, 438, 468*
    casualties *518*
   Third *8*
    August *110–111, 113, 118, 124, 128*
    September *156, 164–165, 168–169*
    October *204, 206*
    November *241, 242, 255, 258*
    December
     Battle of the Bulge *299, 302, 303, 360*
     inside Reich *277*
     shortages in *268*
     wet weather problems *273*
    January
     link-up with First Army *316, 320*
     turning of the tide *312, 315, 329*
    February *346, 369, 374*
    March *380, 394, 397, 404, 405, 408, 410, 415–418, 424, 429*
    April *447, 457*
     advance towards Soviets *434*
     War Crime Investigation Team *472*
    May, advance into Austria *492*
    casualties *518*
   Fifth *500, 501*

Units, United States, Armies — cont.
   Seventh *157, 166, 167, 169, 243, 244, 256, 337, 349, 404, 405, 431, 438, 441, 450*
    advance to Austria *471*
    assault on Nürnberg *460*
    casualties *518*
    Dachau *481*
    drive to Rhine *258–259, 274–275, 277, 396*
    Garmisch *489*
    Rhine crossing *408, 415, 429*
    Siegfried Line *400, 407*
   Ninth *167–168, 182, 206, 241, 242, 248, 252, 260, 265, 270, 334, 366, 369, 375, 385*
    advance into Germany *420, 430, 432, 433, 434, 436, 438, 453, 454, 456*
    Battle of the Bulge *298, 301*
    casualties *518*
    inside Reich *277, 376, 378, 381, 384*
    Nordhausen *469*
    Rhine assault *350, 395*
    Rhine crossing *408, 411, 413, 422*
    Ruhr pocket *428*
   Fifteenth *518*
  Corps
   II Corps *11*
   III Corps *303, 317*
   V Corps *103, 104, 121–122, 170, 415*
   VI Corps *247, 258, 259, 503*
   VII Corps *62, 82, 83, 94, 123, 124, 159, 162, 205, 298, 311, 315, 316, 318, 381, 428*
   VIII Corps *80, 94, 106, 107, 179, 181, 242, 291, 292, 303, 306, 395*
   IX Corps *8*
   XII Corps *164–165, 312, 395*
   XIII Corps *253, 366*
   XV Corps *113, 123, 124, 131, 148, 174, 258, 415, 502*
   XVI Corps *378, 412, 413, 428*
   XVIII Airborne Corps *315, 488*
   XIX Corps *87, 104, 158, 200, 242, 253, 301, 366, 367, 382, 428*
   XX Corps *124, 148, 164, 395*
   XXI Corps *347, 396*
  Divisions
   1st Infantry *94, 120, 123, 159, 162, 205, 215, 217, 391, 438*
    at Omaha *26–27*
   2nd Armored *94, 101, 122, 158, 203, 252, 253, 309, 314, 383, 420, 428, 430, 436, 456*
   2nd Infantry *37, 122, 167, 180, 282, 344, 464, 467, 477*
    Washington Memorial *4*
   3rd Armored *94, 99, 105, 123, 124, 157, 159, 162, 175, 215, 309, 315, 318, 381, 385, 428, 469*
   3rd Infantry *8, 333, 348, 408, 460, 462, 482, 500*
   4th Armored *100, 106, 107, 112, 271, 298, 299, 306, 395, 406, 415, 417, 429, 435, 447*
   4th Infantry *94, 95, 142–143, 395*
   5th Armored *124, 170, 215, 469*
   5th Infantry *103, 148, 164, 204, 250, 371, 395, 399, 406, 408, 410, 415, 417, 418*
   6th Armored *105, 106, 107, 168, 317, 418, 424, 434, 447, 477*
   7th Armored *148, 208, 288, 296*
   8th Armored *386, 443, 468*
   8th Infantry *37, 81, 167, 242, 358*
   9th *58, 64, 94, 175, 234*
   9th Armored *291, 387*
   10th Armored *291, 328, 380, 395, 438, 474*
    Team Cherry *291*
    Team Desobry *291*
    Team O'Hara *291*
   11th Armored *319, 320, 395, 457, 473, 490*
   12th Armored *347, 395, 450*
   14th Armored *357*
   17th Airborne *316, 411, 433, 444*
   20th Armored *482*
   24th *8*
   26th Infantry *306, 312, 395*
   28th Infantry *11, 145, 170, 234, 236, 241, 328, 333*
   29th *27, 33, 87, 88, 122, 167, 179, 180, 229, 291, 366*
   30th Infantry *94, 96, 200, 203, 288, 361, 408, 411, 436, 455, 456, 460*
   35th Infantry *254, 378–379*
   36th 'Infantry' *127, 243, 277, 357*

Units, United States, Divisions — cont.
   42nd Infantry *431, 450, 481, 482*
   44th Infantry *244, 438, 474*
   45th Infantry *127, 275, 408, 429, 460, 481*
   63rd Infantry *336, 400*
   65th Infantry *395*
   69th Infantry *464, 477*
   70th Infantry *407*
   75th *311*
   76th Infantry *369, 380, 395, 477*
   78th Infantry *331, 358*
   79th Infantry *60–61, 80, 81, 408, 411, 444, 521*
   80th Infantry *131, 132–133, 165, 255, 273, 312, 349, 395, 397, 404, 408, 434, 463, 492–493*
   82nd Airborne
    advance to Saint-Sauveur *48*
    Battle of the Bulge *295, 315*
    crosses Elbe *477*
    drive to Rhine *347, 358*
    German surrender *490*
    Operation 'Market' *176, 178*
    'Overlord' objectives *18*
    Pont-l'Abbé *46*
    Sainte-Mère-Église *34, 39*
   82nd (as infantry) *11*
   83rd Infantry *82, 83, 129, 182, 309, 322, 381, 382, 383, 420, 456, 477*
   84th Infantry *248, 253, 297, 309, 310, 314, 316, 320, 359, 454, 456*
   87th Infantry *395, 408, 477*
   89th Infantry *395, 408, 416, 435, 477*
   90th Infantry *113, 131, 134, 240, 277, 317, 329, 395, 472*
   94th Infantry ('Patton's Nugget') *329, 395*
   95th *247, 250, 266, 268, 272*
   99th Infantry *282, 284*
   100th 'Century' *247*
   101st Airborne *34*
    at Berchtesgaden *500*
    Battle of the Bulge *292, 293, 299, 315, 346*
    Operation 'Market' *176, 225*
    'Overlord' objectives *18*
   102nd Infantry *253, 265, 334, 487*
   103rd Infantry *299, 401, 489*
   106th Infantry *516*
  Regiments
   2nd Infantry *103–104*
   7th Infantry *500*
   8th Infantry *95*
   10th Infantry *164*
   11th Infantry *164, 204, 399, 408, 410*
   12th Infantry *142*
   13th Infantry *112, 385*
   15th Infantry *8, 333, 348*
   16th Infantry *162, 215*
   16th Regt Combat Team (RCT) *26*
    3rd Bn *25*
   18th Infantry *514*
   19th Infantry *8*
   23rd Infantry *467*
   26th Infantry *217*
   28th Infantry *333*
   32nd Armored *105, 428*
   38th Infantry *37*
   39th Infantry *58, 175, 234*
   41st Armored Infantry *122*
   47th Infantry *58*
   53rd Infantry *271*
   67th Armored *428*
   83rd Infantry *313, 318*
   104th Infantry *306*
   109th Infantry *333*
   110th Infantry *291*
   112th Infantry *234*
   116th Infantry *87*
   117th Infantry *203, 408, 455*
    1st Bn (Presidential Citation) *361*
   119th Infantry *408*
   120th Infantry *96, 119, 120, 288, 408*
   141st Infantry *127*
   142nd Infantry *357*
   157th Infantry *275, 429, 481, 482*
   175th Infantry *33, 366*
   254th Infantry *336*
   255th Infantry *400*
   273rd Infantry *478*
   290th Infantry *311*
   309th Infantry *358*
   310th Infantry *331*
   313th Infantry *60–61, 408*
   314th Infantry *61*
   315th Infantry *408, 521*
   317th Infantry *165, 312, 408, 493*

Units, United States, Regiments — cont.
   318th Infantry *132, 165, 434*
   319th Infantry *312, 404*
   320th Infantry *378*
   324th Infantry *474*
   327th Glider Infantry *293*
   329th Infantry *322*
   330th Infantry *83, 382*
   331st Infantry *82, 129*
   333rd Infantry *310*
   334th Infantry *249*
   335th Infantry *253, 297*
   345th Infantry *408*
   347th Infantry *408*
   353rd Infantry *408*
   354th Infantry *408, 416, 435*
   358th Infantry *39, 240, 329*
   359th Infantry *317*
   376th Infantry *329*
   377th Infantry *247*
   378th Infantry *247, 250*
   379th Infantry *268–269*
   385th Infantry *369*
   395th Infantry *472*
   398th Infantry *247*
   405th Infantry *253, 487*
   406th Infantry *252*
   501st Parachute Infantry *178*
   502nd Parachute Infantry *18*
   504th Parachute Infantry *183*
   505th Parachute Infantry *37, 176, 183*
   506th Parachute Infantry *292*
   507th Parachute Infantry *316, 458*
   508th Parachute Infantry *315*
   517th Parachute Infantry *347*
   531st Engineer Shore *29*
  Battalions
   9th Armored Infantry *447*
   10th Armored Infantry *299*
   15th Engineer Combat *58*
   23rd Armored Infantry *164*
   27th Armored Infantry *408*
   31st Tank *164*
   37th Tank *271*
   38th Tank *271*
   42nd Tank *319*
   68th Tank *106*
   82nd Engineer Combat *121*
   146th Engineer Combat *234*
   166th Engineer Combat *312*
   291st Engineer Combat *288*
   298th Engineer Combat *55*
   320th Antiaircraft Balloon *45*
   320th Engineer Combat *269*
   372nd Field Artillery *282*
   461st Antiaircraft Artillery *237*
   490th Port *45*
   526th Armored Infantry *288*
   612th Tank Destroyer *284*
   634th Tank Destroyer *205*
   643rd Tank Destroyer *382*
   644th Tank Destroyer *283*
   702nd Tank *303*
   703rd Tank Destroyer *318*
   705th Tank Destroyer *179*
   736th Tank *382*
   741st Tank *464*
   745th Tank *455*
   747th Tank *88*
   749th Tank *60*
   756th Tank *244*
   761st Tank *45*
   771st Tank *433*
   771st Tank Destroyer *252*
   801st Tank Destroyer *37, 284*
   803rd Tank Destroyer *88*
   834th Aviation Engineer *32*
   893rd Tank Destroyer *236*
   969th Field Artillery *45*
  Companies
   165th Signal Corps Photographic Coy *322, 359, 385*
   166th Signal Corps Photographic Coy *299*
   167th Signal Corps Photographic Coy *310*
   306th Railhead Coy *519*
   327th Quartermaster Service Coy *45*
   385th Quartermaster Truck Coy *45*
   464th Ordnance Evacuation Coy *252*
   582nd Engineer Dump Truck Coy *45*
  Rangers, 2nd Bn *28*
  4th Cavalry Sqn *314*
  14th Cavalry Group *284, 286*
  24th Cavalry Recon Sqn *316*
  25th Cavalry Reconnaissance Sqn *100, 106*

Units, United States, Companies — cont.
  85th Cavalry Reconnaissance Sqn *170*
  86th Cavalry Recon Sqn *169*
  113th Cavalry Group *158*
  116th Cavalry Reconnaissance Sqn *396*
  Counter Intelligence Corps *397*
  Graves Registration Service *254*
  National Guard *361*
  Task Force Baum *429*
  Task Force Butler *151*
  Task Force Kane *381*
  Task Force Lovelady *157, 175, 318*
  Task Force Mayes (14th Cavalry Gp) *286*
  Task Force X (2nd Armored Div.) *252*
  USAAF
    Eighth Air Force 13, *71, 97, 117, 172, 202, 212–213, 345, 356, 364, 395*
    Ninth Air Force 20, *28, 32, 71, 97, 206, 288, 323*, 515
    Fifteenth Air Force *172*
  USAAF Commands
    VIII Bomber Command *212*
    IX Tactical Air Command *101, 205, 206*
    IX Troop Carrier Command *293*
    XIX Tactical Air Command *206, 463*
    XXIX Tactical Air Command *206*
    IX Engineer Command *206*
  USAAF Division: 9th Bomb *450*
  USAAF Groups
    91st BG *444*
    366th FG *82*
    394th BG *206*
    398th BG *213*
    401st BG *364*
    458th BG *288*
  USAAF Squadrons, 454th BS, Distinguished Unit Citation *307*
Unkel *394*
Unna 359, *375, 385*, 411, 448
Unterensingen *470*
Unterneubrunn *447*
Unteröwisheim *430*
Uphusen *472*
Upper Silesia *339*
Urbès *264*
Urfahr *502*
Urftstausee (Urft lake) *346, 348, 383*
Urftsperre Dam (Urft river dam) *346, 347, 353*
Urmitz, US Army POW holding camp (A9) *466*
Urquhart, Maj.-Gen. Robert E. *185*
Urschmitt *396*
Urspelt *333*
Ursulinen Nunnery *443*
Ürzig *395*
Ushant *33*
Utrecht
  October, Allied bombing *210*
  November, Allied bombing 236, *238, 240, 243, 252, 256*
  January, Allied bombing *306, 307, 311, 312, 321, 324, 325, 328, 331, 336*
  March, Allied bombing *402*
  April, Allied bombing *448, 450*
Utscheid *369*
Üttfeld *362*
Utweiler *292, 399*
Üxheim *268*

V-weapons
  forced labour camps *468–469*
  tonnage dropped *172*
V1 flying bomb *65, 260*
  sites bombed (June) *38*
V2 launch sites, Allied objective *432*
Vaals *377*
Vaalserberg, The: 'Three-Country Point' *365*
Vaalserquartier, Siegfried Line at *377*
Vacognes *114*
Vacqueville *238*
Vahl-Ebersing *260*
Vaihingen *429*
Vaires 76, *89*
Val-Ygot V1 site bombed *38*
Valenciennes 161
  Allied bombing 46, *120*
Valenton *133*
Valkenswaard *177*
Vallendar *416*
Vallières *250*
Vallo *475*
Valognes *33, 52, 54*
  Allied bombing 46, *51, 55*
  Allies liberate *53*

Vandenburg, Gen. Hoyt *153*
Vannes 94, 116
Varennes *158*
Varlosen *442*
Varssefeld *268*
Vassy *125, 135*
Vaucelles *88*
Vaudreville *250*
Vaumoise *156*
Vaxy *244*
Vechta *451*
Veckerhagen *440*
Veen *387, 388, 390*
Veere *208, 238*
Vegesack *419*
Veghel *178, 186, 222*
Veldrom *437*
Vendôme *99, 105, 133*
Vengeons *123, 125*
Venlo
  October *210, 216, 226, 227*
  November *236, 247, 250–257, 260*
  December *266, 267, 298, 300*
  January *306*
  February *368*
  March *379, 380, 384*
    Allied capture *377, 378*
Vennemann, Wolfgang (PK photographer) *84*
Venray *198, 209, 215, 216, 217*, 218
Ver *16*
Verberie *133*
Verden *436, 464, 470*
Verdon *465*
Verdun 159, *360*
  Allied liberation *158*
Verlautenheide *204, 205, 209, 215*
Verleumont *314*
Verneuil
  Allied advances *140*
  Allied bombing 56, *115*
  Allied liberation *141*
Verney *244*
Vernon
  Allies bomb railway bridge *32*
  'David' and 'Goliath' bridges *147*
  FFI destroy road bridge *49*
  Seine bridgeheads *146, 147*, 148, *150*, 151
Verrières *93*, 98, 100
Versailles *145, 308*
  railway centres bombed 30, 36
  SHAEF Forward HQ (Trianon Palace Hotel) *189, 280, 342, 360*
Versailles, Treaty of (1920) *266*
Verson, Allied capture *72*
Vervezelle *220*
Verviers, Château de Maison-Bois, Ensival *210*
Vervins *157*
Vesle, River *152*
Vesly *84*
Vesoul *175, 176*
Vesqueville *309, 317*
Vessem *184*
Vettelschoss *400, 401*
Vettweiss *264, 277, 371, 375*
Vezins, dams near *110*
Vian, Rear-Adm. Sir Philip, commands Eastern Task Force *16*, 20
Vianden
  September *170*
  December *283, 289, 290, 298*
  January *331–333, 336, 337*
  February *355, 356, 361, 363, 364, 365, 366, 369*
Vianen *311, 312*
Vichy Government of France *474*
Victoria Cross, Currie, Maj. David V. *134*
Victoria, Queen *430*
'Victory Hill' see Lüneburg Heath
Vidouville *103*
Vie, River *136*
  Allied bridgeheads over *133, 134*, 140
Viehoven *279*
Vielsalm *288, 314, 322, 325, 326, 327*
Vierlingsbeek *213*
Viersen *237, 250, 352, 368*
  Allies occupy *377*
Vierzon, Allied bombing *64, 70, 75, 94*
Vieux Breisach *347, 348*
Vigny *242*
Vilaine, River *116*
Villebaudon *101*, 104
Villedieu 72, *74*, 110, 111, 113
Villeneuve-Saint-Georges 73, *85, 143*
Villennes-sur-Seine *148*
Villereux *322*
Villerot *161*

Villers-Bocage
  experience of heavy bombing *197*
  June 62
    Allied air attacks 66
    British armour reach *41*, 61
  July
    Allied advance 87
    German armour attacked 70
  August, fighting around 112, 113
Villers-Bretonneux *156*
Villers-la-Bonne-Eau *302, 307, 309, 316*
Villers-sur-Mer, Allied capture *140*
Villers-Tournelle *158*
Villingen *363, 371*
Vimont 80, *122*, 123
Vimoutiers *130, 137*, 140
  Allied bombing 43, *135*
Vimy Ridge *159*
Vincey *157*
Vipiteno, Italy *500*
Vire, River 38, 45, 59, 75, 76, 78, *84*, 85, 88, 89, 91, 104, 114, *125*
  Utah assault beach *16*
Vire (town)
  June *41*
    Allied bombing 24, 43, 46, *71*
  July
    Allied bombing *72, 74*
    Allied bridgehead 78, 79
    US capture *102*
  August 117, 118, 120, *121*, 123, 126
    Allied advance from 111, 115, 116
Vire et Taute Canal 48
Vishnevsky, General S. V. *493*
Visselhövede *467, 469*
Vissoule *329*
Vitré *115*
Vitry, railway bombed 65
Vitry-le-François *151*
Vittel, US 6th Army Gp HQ (Heritage Hotel) *258*
Viviers *241*
Vlatten *368*
Vleuten *324*
Vlissingen see Flushing
Vlotho *364, 398, 415*
Vöcklabruck *502*
Voegtlinshoffen *346*
Vogelbach *279*
Vogelsheim *347*
Vohenstrauss *473*
Vöhringen *475*
Vohwinkel *306, 307*
Volkel *129*
Völkingen *309, 404, 521*
Voorthuizen *461*
Vorde *414*
Vörden *448*
Vorwerk *480*
Vosges mountains
  September *193*
    Hitler orders counter-attack *174*
  October *202–205, 208–210, 213, 215–218, 221–223, 225–227*
  November *234, 236, 238, 242, 243, 258, 259, 260, 261*
    fighting in *244, 246, 250, 252, 254–257*
  December *265–267, 269, 270, 272, 273, 274, 278, 280, 282, 284, 285, 287, 289, 292, 294, 299*
  January *308–311, 314–316, 318–320, 328, 333, 336, 337*
  February *342, 347, 349*
Vossenack *209, 234, 235, 236*, 238, 239, 240, 241
Vreden *219, 405, 407*
Vrouwenpolder *240*
Vseruby *486*
Vyshinsky, Andrei *508*

Waal, River *184*, 185, 199, 202, 207, *351, 352*, 431
Waalwijk *232*
Wachtum *450*
Wadern *401*
Wagenberg *236*
Wagenborgen *472*
Wageningen *330, 464, 503*
Wagner, Konteradm. Gerhard *490, 494, 495, 497*
Wagner, Richard *457*
Wahle, Genmaj. Carl *159*
Wahlhausen *336*
Wahlrod *419*
Waimes *286*
Waizenkirchen *500*
Walbach *347, 421*

Walbourg *274*
Walcheren Island 176, *199*, 203, 208, 216, 221, *227*, 228, 232, *233*, 234, 237, 239
  Allied bombing 173, 178, 185, 221, 226, 241
  Allied capture *235*
  see also Westkapelle
Waldbach *395*
Waldbilling *299*
Waldbreitbach *410*
Waldbrunn *426*
Waldenrath 203, 331
Waldesch *400*
Waldfeucht *329, 330, 331*
Waldkirch *471*
Waldkonigen *390*
Waldneukirchen *504*
Waldniel *371*
Walker, Pte C. D. *196*
Wallach *408*
Walldorf *427*
Wallendorf *215, 317, 349, 351, 352, 354, 356*
Wallerfangen *268*
Wallern *491*
Wallhausen *398*
Wallwork, S/Sgt Jim *19*
Walsdorf *331*
Walsheim *283, 284, 285*
Walsrode *458*
Walsum *408, 409, 414*
Walsumermark *419*
Waltrop *433*
Wangen *487*
Wangerooge Island *469, 474, 494*
Wanne-Eickel *209, 249, 324, 344, 384*
Wanssum *264, 267, 314*
Warbeyen *358*
Warburg *420, 421, 430, 437, 439*
  Allies reach *426, 428, 431*
Warchenne, River *288*
Warden *361*
Wardin *291, 307, 308, 311, 314, 317, 318, 322*
Wardt *385*
Warnach *298*
Warren, Lt-Col Trumbull *495, 496*
Warsaw *338*
  uprising *504*
Warstein *443*
Wartberg *502*
Wascheid *349*
Washington Times Herald 152
Waspik *232*
Wassenburg *330*
Wasserbillig *193, 333, 359, 371, 375*
Wasserburg *493*
Waters, Lt Col John *429*
Watervliet *212*, 213
Wattermal *333*
Watzerath *355*
Wavre *164*
Waxweiler *294, 368, 375*
Weerd *253*
Weerdinge *450*
Weert *235, 245, 246*
Weeze *240, 242, 356, 359, 364, 365, 368, 369, 375–377, 384*
Wegberg *242, 325, 331, 369*
Wegscheid *486*
Wehldorf *474*
Wehrden *270, 398, 438*
Weichs, FM Maximilian Reichsfreiherr von *490*
Weida *459*
Weiden *472, 473*
Weidenberg *457*
Weidenthal *402*
Weidingen *369*
Weiher *417*
Weik, Tech/Sgt James R. *331*
Weilburg *401, 419, 420*
Weiler *335, 336, 396*
Weilerswist *274, 383, 384*
Weimar *352, 438, 441, 447, 450*
  Nazi Party rallies in *460*
Weingarten *463, 469, 473*
Weinsfeld *354*
Weinsheim *383*
Weiskirchen *399, 400*
Weissbach *457*
Weisse Elster, Zeppelin Bridge *467*
Weissenburg *472*
Weissenfels *452*
Weissenhorn *445*
Weissenstadt *459, 465, 468*
Weisten *331, 332*
Weiswampach *334, 336, 342, 355*
Weisweiler *254, 255, 256, 257, 259, 273*
Weiten *363*
Weiterstadt *416*

543

Welchenhausen 338, 342
Welferdingen 270
Wellesley, Col Arthur (later Duke of Wellington) 223
Wellingen 250
Wellington, Duke of *see* Wellesley, Col Arthur
Welsfeld *397*
Welz 250, 265
Wenau 251
Wendisch-Evern, Lüneburg Heath *486*
Wengerohr 298, 336, 352, 394
Wenzenbach 474
Wenzendorf 306
Werbeln 308
Werben 454
Werbomont *315*
Werdau 461
Werl *443*, 445
Werlte *453*
Wernigerode 461
Wernitz, Baroness Berta von *430*
Werra *430*
Werra, River *430*, 431
Wertingen 475
Wesel
  October 213, 226
  February 343, 352, 353, 357, 359, 361, 362, 365
  March 375, 376, 377, 382, 386, 387, *390*, *392*, 394, 395, 401, 408, 409, *411*, 413, 415, 416, 418, 419
  Allied capture *414*
  April, advance from bridgehead *428*
Wesenau 504
Weser, *see also* Ems-Weser canal
Weser, River 383, 407, 411, 419, 432, *436*, 437, *438*, 439, 440, *446*, 469, *472*, 474, *476*, 480
Weser estuary 472
Wesseling 228
Wessem 189, 247
Wessem canal 245
West Germany *see* Germany (Federal Republic)
Westen 449
Westerburg 385, 391, 395, 405
Westerhausen *456*
Westheim 465
Westervoort 451
Westkapelle *199*, 216, *233*, 234, 235
Westönnen *443*
'Westwall' *see* Siegfried Line
Wetter 458
Wettlingen 369
Wetzlar 385, 395, 402, 419
Weyerbusch 395
Weygand, Gén. Maxime 503
Wezep 407
Whinney, Lt-Cdr R. F., RN 35
White, S/Sgt Dewey J. *521*
Whitehead, Don (war correspondent) *26*
Wiblingen 475
Wibrin 322
Wickenrodt 402
Wickrathberg 269
  US Army POW holding camp (A3) *466*
Widdersdorf 384
Wied, River 400, 402
Wiehagen 445
Wierden 274
Wiesbach 273
Wiesbaden
  August, Allied bombing *128*
  October, Allied bombing 218
  February, Allied bombing 344, 362

Wiesbaden — *continued*
  March
    Allied advance to 419, 420
    Allied bombing 377, 383, 391, 399
    Allies clear 421, 422
  April, Allies clear area *426*
Wiesbaum *388*
Wiesenfeld 437
Wihr-en-Plaine 339
Wilck, Oberst Gerhard *219*
Wildenfels 465
Wildenrath 329
Wildermuth, Oberst Eberhard *173*
Wildeshausen 448
Wildetaube 459
Wildstein 453
Wiley, Sgt Arthur P. *288*
Wilhelmina, Queen *225*
Wilhelmina Canal *178*, *225*, *238*
Wilhelmsbronn 267
Wilhelmshaven *420*
  Allied bombing *201*, *205*, 213, 423, *478*
Wilkes, Sgt Bert (AFPU) *173*
Willemstad 238, 239, *240*
Williams, T/5 William E. (US Signal Corps) *310*
Willingen 260
Willprechtszell *480*
Willwerath 353, 376
Wilmot, Chester (BBC reporter) *327*
Wilson, Capt. R. *380*
Wilson, Cpl S. J. R. *192*
Wilson, Gen. Sir Henry *126*
Wiltz
  November *242*
  December 289, 292, 302, 303
  January 306, 307, 312, 313, 314, 316, 318, 320, *323*, 326, 327, 329, 330, 331, 332, 333
Wiltz, River 329
Wilwerdange 332, 333, 334
Wilwerwiltz 331
Winant, Lt John G., Jr. 504
Wincheringen 363
Winden 261, 298, 299, 332, 410
Windensolen 339
Windhagen 402, 403
Wingeshausen 441
Wingen 267, 311, 312, 313, 402
Winkhausen 437, 439
Winnekendonk 371, 375
Winnigen 394
Winringen 377
Winschoten 454, 456
Winsen 469
Wintelre 183
Winterberg 430, 433, 437, 439
  Allied capture 431, *504*
Winterscheid 343
Winterspelt *170*, *171*
Winterswijk 384, 407
Winzenheim 345
Wipperfürth 417, 420, 453
Wirtzfeld *282*, *338*
Wismar 453, 478, *488*, 490, 491, *495*
Wissant 171
Wissembourg
  December *274*, *276–277*, 279, 280, *282*–*285*, 289, 294, 298–303, *521*
  January 313, 318, 332
  March *393*, 403, 404, 410
Wissen 395
Wissersheim 376, 377
Withof *219*
Witt, Fregattenkapt. Hermann *57*
Wittelsheim *332*, 339, 342

Witten 277, 402
Wittenberg 486
Wittenberge *433*, 459, 467, 470, 478, 490
Wittenburg 459, 469
Wittenheim 313, 339
Wittenwiller 316
Wittingen 454, 457
Wittlich 261, 337, 343, 345, 348, 356, 392, 394, 395, 396, 399
Wittmann, SS-Obersturmf. (later SS-Hauptsturmf.) Michael *41*, *117*
Wittringen 272
Wittstock 463
Witzenhausen 440, 444
Wixhausen 418
Wochern *329*
Woensdrecht 212, 213, 215, 221, 222, 223, *226*
Woerden 243
Wohlsbach 447
Woippy *247*
Wolf, Cdr H. G. de, RCN *33*
Wolfen 469, 470
Wolfenbüttel 448
Wolfgantzen 346
Wolflingen 273
Wolfratshausen 445
Wolfsberg 452
Wolfsheim 403
Wolfskehlen *417*
Wolfskirchen 259, 260
Wollseifen 346
Wöllstein 403
Wolmirstedt 454
Wolsfeld 370
Wolz, Genmaj. Alwin *491*, *494*
Wood, Lt David *19*
Wood, Maj. Gen. John S. *112*
Worblingen 471
Wormeldange 203
Worms 277, *319*, 376, 402, 409, 410, 414, *415*, 416, 418
  Allied advance to 395
  Allied bombing 364, *406*
  Allied capture 404, *406*, 419
  Ernst Ludwig Bridge *406*
  POW cage at *441*
Worringen 385
Wülfen 391, 395
Wulferstedt 448
Wülfrath 389
Wüllenrath 371
Wunsiedel 469
Wuppertal 458
Würm 252, 284, 285
Würm, River 198, 334
Würmsee Lake 489
Würrich 401
Würselen 207, 209, 210, 212, 213, 215, 220, 249
Würzburg
  January 312
  February 348, 352, 370
  March 383, 400, 402, 418
  April 426–427, 429, 430, 434, 443, 450
  battle for *431*, 433, 437, 439
Wurzen 459
Wüschheim 401
Wustermark 469
Wustweiler 269
Wuustwezel 219, 220
Wyler 353

Xanten
  December 268
  February 353, 356, 357, 364, 369, 370

Xanten — *continued*
  March 375, 376, 382, 384, 385, *386*, 387, 408, 409, *411*, *413*, *416*
  Allied capture *390*, *392*
  battle for *388*

Yalta Conference (1945) *338*, *342*, *447*
Yonne, River 87, 140
Young, Pfc Edward De *482*
Youngblood, Capt. George L. *383*
Ypres 164
Yvetot 158
Yvrandes 128

Zabern 250
Zeebrugge 172
  Allied capture *192*, 234
Zeitz 324, 418, 427, 452, 453, 454
Zelderheide 354
Zell 314, 331, 377, 401
Zella Mehlis 437
Zera, Capt. Max *215*
Zerbst 453, 459, 467
Zerf 383, 384
Zetten 327, 328, 330
Zeven 469, 470, 473, 474, 478, 480, 481, 486
Zevenaar 432
Zevenbergen 236
Zewen 383
Zhukov, Marshal Georgi 457, 459, *492*, *508*
Ziegelheim 457
Ziereis, Franz (Mauthausen commandant) *473*
Zimmingen 257
Zinsel, River *193*, 400
Zinswiller 400
Zinzingen 363
Zonhoven, Villa Magda: Montgomery's HQ *301*
Zons 386, 387
Zossen 399
Zuid Beveland *see* South Beveland
Zuid Willems Canal *178*, *183*, 184, 185, 186, *221*, 235
Zuider Zee 427, 459, 464, 467, 468
Zuidzande 226, 227
Zülpich 268, 273, 278, 294, 296, 307, 345, 366, 368, 377, 383
Zundert 225
Zutphen 212, 218, 238, 243, 274, 312, 337, 436, 439, 445, 450, 458
  Allied capture *432*, *442*
Zutzendorf 260
Zweibrücken
  December 264, 267, 273, 277
  January 316
  February 353, 356, 364
  March 375, 385, 393, 395, 398, 399, 400, 401, 403
  Allied capture 404, *407*, 409
Zwettl 500
Zwickau 203, 403, 440, 449, 465
Zwiesel 469, 474
Zwirner (PK photographer) *130*
Zwolle
  October 218, 227
  November 239, 243, 252, 256, 260, 261
  December 271, 280, 299
  January 337
  February 345, 354
  March 399, 407
  April 438, 440, 448, 450
  Allies reach 454, 456
Zyfflich 352

H. de Weerd
Middellaan 34
NL-7314 GC
Holland (+31-55-355.2181)